ENCYCLOPEDIA OF THE
HARLEM RENAISSANCE

ENCYCLOPEDIA OF THE
HARLEM RENAISSANCE

VOLUME 2
K-Y
INDEX

CARY D. WINTZ
PAUL FINKELMAN
EDITORS

ROUTLEDGE
NEW YORK · LONDON

Published in 2004 by

Routledge
An Imprint of the Taylor and Francis Group
270 Madison Avenue
New York, NY 10016
www.routledge-ny.com

Published in Great Britain by
Routledge
An Imprint of the Taylor and Francis Group
2 Park Square
Milton Park, Abingdon
Oxon OX14 4RN
www.routledge.co.uk

10   9   8   7   6   5   4   3   2   1

Printed on acid-free, 250-year-life paper
Manufactured in the United States of America

Library of Congress Cataloging-in-Publication Data

Encyclopedia of the Harlem Renaissance/edited by Cary D. Wintz and Paul Finkelman
        p. cm.
Includes bibliographical references and index.
ISBN 1-57958-389-X
1. African American arts—New York (State)—New York—History—20th century—Encyclopedias.
2. Harlem Renaissance—Encyclopedias. I. Wintz, Cary D., 1943– II. Finkelman, Paul, 1949–
NX512.3.A35E53 2004
700′.89′9607307471—dc22   2004016353

DEDICATION

We dedicate this work to John Wright, agent par excellence. He was a part of this endeavor from the beginning and guided the project through difficult times.

CONTENTS

Alphabetical List of Entries

Alphabetical List of Entries

MAP

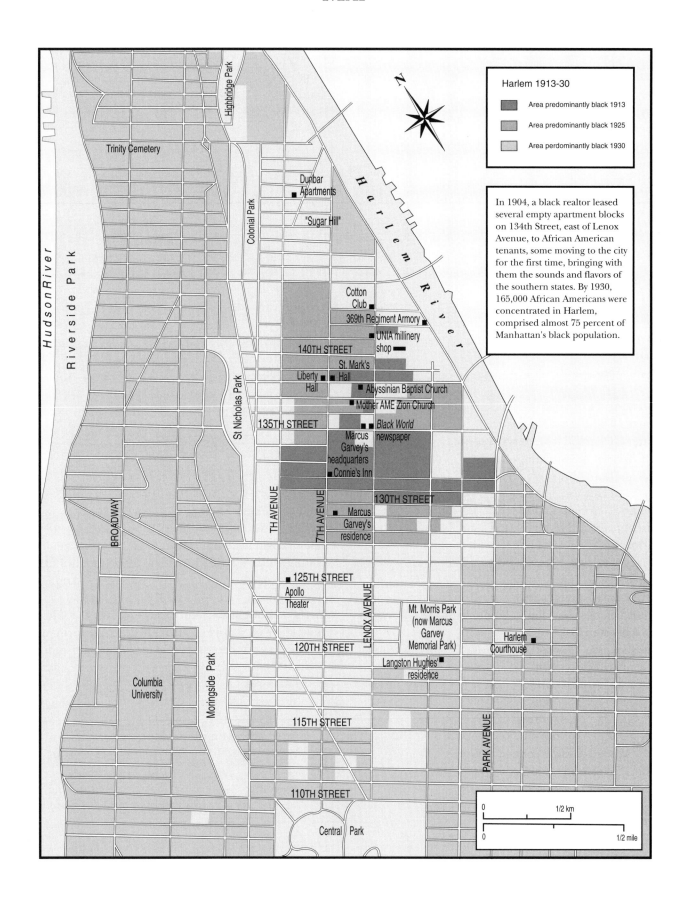

Harlem 1913-30

- Area predominantly black 1913
- Area predominantly black 1925
- Area perdominantly black 1930

In 1904, a black realtor leased several empty apartment blocks on 134th Street, east of Lenox Avenue, to African American tenants, some moving to the city for the first time, bringing with them the sounds and flavors of the southern states. By 1930, 165,000 African Americans were concentrated in Harlem, comprised almost 75 percent of Manhattan's black population.

Trinity Cemetery

Highbridge Park

Harlem River

Hudson River

Riverside Park

Colonial Park

Dunbar Apartments

"Sugar Hill"

Cotton Club

369th Regiment Armory

UNIA millinery shop

140TH STREET

St Nicholas Park

St. Mark's Hall

Liberty Hall

Abyssinian Baptist Church

Mother AME Zion Church

135TH STREET

Black World newspaper

Marcus Garvey's headquarters

Connie's Inn

BROADWAY

TH AVENUE

7TH AVENUE

130TH STREET

Marcus Garvey's residence

125TH STREET

Apollo Theater

LENOX AVENUE

Mt. Morris Park (now Marcus Garvey Memorial Park)

Harlem Courthouse

120TH STREET

Columbia University

Moringside Park

Langston Hughes' residence

115TH STREET

PARK AVENUE

110TH STREET

Central Park

0   1/2 km

0   1/2 mile

K

Karamu House

Karamu House—a settlement house, neighborhood center, and complex for the fine arts and performing arts in Cleveland, Ohio—has served the city and helped launch the careers of numerous African American artists since the era of World War I. It was organized as the Playhouse Settlement in 1915 and later renamed Karamu, Swahili for "place of joyful gathering." The center was an outgrowth of committee work done in 1914 by members of the Men's Club of the Second Presbyterian Church, who had sensed that the cultural and social needs of the neighborhood—the Central Avenue District, at that time a community of "Jewish, Colored, and Italian peoples"—were being neglected. The committee discovered that "the better class of colored people" there were also interested in establishing a racially integrated social settlement. Early supporters of the idea included the African American author Charles Waddell Chesnutt and the Cleveland Association of Colored Men.

There was almost unanimous concern among local leaders about problems facing and related to the growing population of poor African American migrants from the South. After completing its own preliminary investigation, the committee hired a white couple, Russell and Rowena Jelliffe, who were graduates of Oberlin College and the Chicago School of Civics, to conduct a more extensive survey of the Central Avenue District. The Jelliffes found that the residents "were being denied any hope of or exposure to decent schooling, housing, jobs, recreational facilities and cultural advantages." In 1915, at the request of the Men's Club, the Jelliffes moved to Cleveland to head the Playhouse Settlement and to develop programs that would address some of the needs identified in their study. Having worked at Chicago's Hull House Settlement, they came with some practical experience in social work, but they often described their early activities in Cleveland as "learn as you go." In a small frame house that was both their own home and the settlement center, game rooms, reading rooms, and classes in sewing, cooking, and crafts "were offered and eagerly received." The Cleveland Board of Education also made space and equipment available in the Longwood School, including the gymnasium, printing presses, domestic science rooms, and paid teachers "to conduct classes and clubs there." In 1919, the settlement agency was formally incorporated as the Neighborhood Association. The Karamu Theater was founded in 1927, in a building adjacent to the original complex. With encouragement from the celebrated African American actor Charles Gilpin, a resident troupe called the Gilpin Players raised funds to furnish their performance space, support other settlement activities, and endow scholarships for promising students in the performing and visual arts.

During and after the Great Depression, the Jelliffes, Chesnutt (who was now a member of the settlement's board), and others worked with the schools and other agencies to foster creativity and interracial cooperation in social settings. These Clevelanders were pioneers in what became part of a national movement. By bringing new works to the stage and casting actors of all nationalities and racial backgrounds, the Jelliffes provided an alternative to the stereotypical plots and roles popular in mainstream American theater.

Langston Hughes was an alumnus of Karamu House. As a student at Cleveland Central High, he had been more interested in the graphic arts than in literature and had taught art to some of the younger students; he later taught graphics at the settlement. The Karamu Theater also produced six of Hughes's plays, which helped to establish it as a "focal point for both Negro and white dramatists writing for the Negro theater." When the Jelliffes retired from Karamu, Hughes expressed his gratitude in the poem "For Russell and Rowena Jelliffe."

REGENNIA N. WILLIAMS

See also Chesnutt, Charles Waddell; Gilpin, Charles; Harlem Renaissance in the United States: 4—Cleveland; Hughes, Langston

Further Reading

Blood, Melanie N. "Theatre in Settlement Houses: Hull House Players, Neighborhood Playhouse, and Karamu Theatre." *Theatre History Studies*, 16, 1996, pp. 5–69.

Hughes, Langston. *The Big Sea*. New York: Thunder's Mouth, 1986. (Reprint.)

Looman, Glen. "Karamu House: The Establishment and Evolution of a Settlement House for Cleveland's African American Community, 1914–1923." Ph.D. dissertation, Cleveland State University, 1997.

Rampersad, Arnold. *The Life of Langston Hughes*, Vol. 1, *1902–1941, I, Too, Sing America*. New York: Oxford University Press, 1986.

Rampersad, Arnold, and David Roessel, eds. *The Collected Poems of Langston Hughes*. New York: Knopf, 1995.

Silver, Reuben. "A History of the Karamu Theatre of Karamu House, 1915–1960." Ph.D. dissertation, Ohio State University, 1961.

Kellogg, Paul U.

Paul U. Kellogg attended the Civic Club Dinner of 21 March 1924—an event that was held in honor of Jessie Redmon Fauset's first novel and that James Weldon Johnson used to announce the emerging Harlem Renaissance to the white literary establishment. Kellogg was so impressed that he devoted the March 1925 issue of *Survey Graphic*, the social work magazine he edited, to black literature and art. For the six previous years, *Survey Graphic* had featured nationalist cultural movements such as the "new Ireland" and the "new Russia" and had drawn attention to the emerging cultural pluralism in the United States. For Kellogg, the issue on black art would be an extension of this larger project.

Kellogg wanted to promote acceptance of African Americans and was looking for an approach that would be a departure from both the economic-educational method of Hampton and Tuskegee institutes and the political ideology of those fighting for legal rights in the face of discrimination and lynchings. Accordingly, he turned to the affirmation that could be found in works of art. Kellogg was predisposed toward the views of James Weldon Johnson and Alain Locke rather than those of Fauset, *The Crisis*, and particularly W. E. B. Du Bois, with whom he had had a falling-out a decade earlier.

Kellogg called on Locke to be a guest editor of the "Harlem issue," which featured the work of James Weldon Johnson, Charles S. Johnson, Rudolph Fisher, Du Bois, Countee Cullen, Anne Spencer, Angelina Grimké, Claude McKay, Jean Toomer, Langston Hughes, W. A. Domingo, Arthur Schomberg, and Walter White, among others. Importantly, Locke later expanded his work on this issue into an anthology, *The New Negro* (1925).

The March 1925 issue of *Survey Graphic* was reviewed favorably by H. L. Mencken, Waldo Frank, and Marcus Garvey, among others, and sold extremely well: 42,000 copies. In fact, this was the best-selling issue of *Survey Graphic* before World War II. However, some writers of the Harlem Renaissance criticized the issue. One point of contention was that Winold Reiss, who had illustrated other issues of the magazine, also worked on the "Harlem issue"; Fauset complained about the artwork because it was not what she considered appropriately "representative." Others said that there were limits to Kellogg's acceptance of African Americans. Kellogg was deeply involved in and committed to the support of black art and the Harlem Renaissance; however, as Hutchinson notes, his viewpoint still seemed to keep African American art in a subordinate position (1995 429). Kellogg's essay "The Negro Pioneers," for example, argued that African Americans were becoming Americanized by entering into the experiences of immigration and pioneering. He was countered on this point by others, among them Du Bois, who argued that the African American experience carried a cultural authority all its own. These debates raised by the "Harlem issue" of Kellogg's magazine were continued with the publication of Locke's book.

Kellogg made a vital contribution to the Harlem Renaissance through the "Harlem issue" of *Survey Graphic*, but the nature of that contribution also highlighted some of the ideological fissures in the movement, that would later divide it.

Biography

Paul Underwood Kellogg was born 20 September 1879, in Kalamazoo, Michigan. His parents were Frank Israel Kellogg, a businessman; and Mary Foster Underwood. He entered Columbia University in 1901. Kellogg wrote for the Kalamazoo *Daily Telegraph* after high school; joined *Charities Magazine* with his brother Arthur in 1902, and through his work there completed a study of life in Pittsburgh that would be published as the *Pittsburgh Survey* (1910–1914) and would serve as a model of research methods used for social reform; became editor of *Charities Magazine* (retitled *Survey Magazine* and later *Survey Graphic*) in 1912 and promoted it as a social work journal; served as editor of *Survey Graphic* until the magazine folded in 1952; and crusaded for social reform throughout his life. Kellogg died in 1958.

AMANDA M. LAWRENCE

See also Civic Club Dinner, 1924; Frank, Waldo; Locke, Alain; Mencken, H. L.; New Negro, The; Reiss, Winold; Survey Graphic; *specific writers*

Further Reading

Chambers, Clarke A. "Paul Underwood Kellogg." In *American National Biography*, ed. John A. Garraty and Mark C. Carnes. New York: Oxford University Press, 1999, Vol.12, pp. 504–505.

Hutchinson, George. *The Harlem Renaissance in Black and White*. Cambridge, Mass.: Belknap Press of Harvard University Press, 1995.

Wintz, Cary D. *Black Culture and the Harlem Renaissance*. Houston, Tex.: Rice University Press, 1988.

Kerlin, Robert

Robert Kerlin, a white socialist academic who taught at colleges throughout the American South during a long career, edited three collections of work by black writers. In response to a wave of race riots that occurred in several northern cities just after World War I, the black press presented a variety of news articles and opinion columns. Kerlin gathered material from leading African American newspapers and published a well-regarded anthology, *The Voice of the Negro* (1919). In his introduction, Kerlin described the extent and influence of these newspapers and urged that whites who wished to understand African Americans should read the black press. In 1921, *The Nation* published a letter Kerlin had written protesting the treatment of blacks in Arkansas; Kerlin was immediately fired from his teaching post at the Virginia Military Institute, where he had served for more than a decade.

Kerlin also edited two early anthologies of African American poetry: *Contemporary Poetry of the Negro* (1921) and *Negro Poets and Their Poems* (1923). *Negro Poets and Their Poems*, the more widely read of the two, includes selections from and commentary about more than sixty poets including Phillis Wheatley, Angelina Weld Grimké, Georgia Johnson, Anne Spencer, Langston Hughes, Claude McKay, Walter Everette Hawkins, and Joseph S. Cotter Jr. Kerlin explained that, in selecting poems for his anthology, he looked primarily for "passion." His biographical notes and critical commentary are effusive, and thirty-six of his profiles contain photographs or portrait sketches. Chapter 1 of *Negro Poets and Their Poems* is a historical overview of folk song and pre-twentieth-century poets. Later chapters treat contemporary poets in groups, labeled "The Present Renaissance of the Negro," "The Heart of Negro Womanhood," "Dialect Verse," "The Poetry of Protest," and so on. Kerlin acknowledged earlier work by James Weldon Johnson and Arthur Schomberg as his guide in selecting poets for inclusion. *Negro Poets and Their Poems* received little serious critical attention, but it was reviewed briefly in some of the major magazines of the day.

In 1924, Kerlin wrote the lyrics for Samuel Barber's score "My Fairyland." By the 1930s, his political attention had shifted to the labor movement.

Biography

Robert Kerlin was born in Newcastle, Missouri, on 22 March 1866. He studied at Central College in Fayette, Missouri (A.M., 1890); at Johns Hopkins University, the University of Chicago, and Harvard (without completing a degree); and at Yale (Ph.D., 1906). He worked as a professor of English, Missouri Valley College,

1890–1894, 1901–1902; Southwestern University, 1902–1903; State Normal College, Warrensburg, Missouri, 1903–1906; Yale, 1906–1907; State Normal School, Farmville, Virginia, 1908–1910; Virginia Military Institute, 1910–1921; State Normal School, West Chester, Pennsylvania, 1922–1927; Potomac State College, Keyser, West Virginia, 1927–1933; and Western Maryland College, 1933–1940. He was active in the ministry of the Methodist Episcopal Church, 1895–1898; and was chaplain for the Third Missouri Volunteers during the Spanish-American War, 1898. Kerlin died in Cumberland, Maryland, on 21 February 1950.

CYNTHIA BILY

See also Cotter, Joseph Seamon; Grimké, Angelina Weld; Hughes, Langston; Johnson, Georgia Douglas; Johnson, James Weldon; McKay, Claude; Nation, The; Schomburg, Arthur A.; Spencer, Anne

Publications

Mainly for Myself. 1897. (Original poems.)
The Voice of the Negro. 1919.
Contemporary Poetry of the Negro. 1921.
Negro Poets and Their Poems. 1923.

Further Reading

Knight, Lucian Lamar, ed. *Biographical Dictionary of Southern Authors*. Detroit, Mich: Gale, 1910, 1978.
Potter, Vilma R. "Race and Poetry: Two Anthologies of the Twenties." *College Language Association Journal*, 29 (March 1986).
Who Was Who in America, Vol. 3, *1951–1960*. Marquis Who's Who, 1966.

King, Billy

William (Billy) King, born in Whistler, Alabama, in 1875, was a living link between the Harlem Renaissance and nineteenth-century black minstrelsy. He left home at an early age and found a niche in black minstrel shows as part of the famous Georgia Minstrels in the late 1890s.

In 1898 he teamed with Clarence Bush to form King and Bush Wide Mouth Minstrels. They toured successfully until 1902, when the troupe became stranded in Texas. King rejoined the Georgia Minstrels, in which the great Billy Kersands was the main attraction, and established himself along with Kersands as one of the four leading comedians of the troupe; he was noted for his stylish dressing.

In 1911 King went into vaudeville. He formed his own stock company in 1912, the same year he married Hattie McIntosh, widow of a famous minstrel. He wrote prolifically for shows performed at the various theaters where his company was based, including the Central in Atlanta (1912), the Lyric in Kansas City (1913), and the Star in Savannah (1914).

In 1915, he established a permanent base for his company at the white-owned Grand Theater in Chicago. From 1916 until 1923, he wrote, staged, and performed in a remarkable series of musical comedies and sketches, often changing shows every week. At least forty-four shows can be identified, mostly complete presentations although some were supporting sketches for white vaudeville. Many of them toured the black vaudeville circuits for which King was a booking agent, including Harlem's Lafayette Theater. He was also involved in operating theaters in Louisville, Chattanooga, Atlanta, Savannah, Birmingham, Jacksonville, Mobile, and elsewhere.

King's stock company employed a large roster of performers, many of whom went on to greater things. An early protégée was Gertrude Saunders, later famous in *Shuffle Along*. Other notable names included the comedian Billy Higgins, the female impersonator Andrew Tribble, the dancer Ida Forsyne, Lottie Gee (also of *Shuffle Along*), and Maude Russell. King also claimed to have helped promote the early career of Florence Mills.

His innovations included the clowning and chorus girl routine that later made Josephine Baker famous. He did not balk at including social and political satire on the race question, causing Lester Walton to describe one show as being like a protest meeting held under the auspices of the National Association for the Advancement of Colored People (NAACP). When King's long run at the Grand Theater finally ended, he went back to vaudeville, taking the Billy King Road Show on tour from 1923 until it disbanded in Oklahoma City in 1925. The band stayed together as Walter Page's Blue Devils, the original nucleus of the Count Basie Orchestra.

King continued in show business, but after 1925 his career is obscure. He played in Earl Dancer and Ethel Waters' show *Vanities* in 1926 but later sought an injunction to prevent them from using his material. In 1937 he was elected president of the Colored Actors'

Billy King, c. 1907. (Library of Congress.)

Protective Society, which was based in New York. In 1967 Langston Hughes and Milton Melzer listed him in their "golden dozen" of all-time best black comedians. The date of King's death is unrecorded.

Biography

William (Billy) King was born in Whistler, Alabama, in 1875. He was a cofounder of King and Bush Wide Mouth (later Colored) Minstrels, 1898–1902; a member of the Georgia Minstrels, 1902–1911; and founder and owner of the Billy King Stock Company, 1912–1923. He was elected president of the Colored Actors' Protective Society, New York, 1937. The date of King's death is unknown but was probably sometime in the 1960s.

BILL EGAN

See also Baker, Josephine; Blackface Performance; Forsyne, Ida; Lafayette Theater; Mills, Florence; Minstrelsy; Muse, Clarence; Musical Theater; Shuffle Along; Theater Owners' Booking Association; Vaudeville; Waters, Ethel

Theatrical Productions and Performances

1912: *Two Bills from Alaska.*
1914: *Two Bills from Alaska* (second edition).
1914: *Carnation.*
1914: *Out in the Street.*
1914: *The Runaway's Return.*
1916: *The Rivals.*
1916: *The Undertaker's Daughter.*
1916: *Preparedness.*
1916: *The Other Fellow.*
1917: *Exploits in Africa.*
1917: *The Face at the Window.*
1917: *The Final Rehearsal.*
1917: *Hotel Nobody.*
1917: *The Kidnapper.*
1917: *Lady for a Day.*
1917: *The Lonesome Mile.*
1917: *A Mother-in-law's Disposition.*
1917: *Neighbours.*
1917: *Raiding a Cabaret.*
1917: *The Senator.*
1918: *The Board of Education.*
1918: *Catching the Burglar.*
1918: *Chief Outlanchette.*
1918: *The Con Man.*
1918: *The Heart Breakers.*
1918: *My Rich Uncle.*
1918: *At The Beach.*
1918: *Goodby Everybody.*
1918: *In the Draft.*
1918: *Mr Jazz from Dixie.*
1918: *The Night Raid.*
1918: *Now I'm a Mason.*
1918: *The Rich Uncle.*
1919: *Exploits in Africa.*
1919: *Over the Top.*
1919: *They're Off.*
1920: *China Town.*
1920: *Hello Dixieland.*
1920: *The New Americans.*
1920: *Lime Kiln Club.*
1921: *Trip Around the World.*
1922: *Moonshine.*
1922: *Darktown Jubilee.*
1922: *Hello Sue.*
1922: *Hits and Bits.*
1922: *Moonshine.*
1922: *Whirl of Joy.*
1923: *Burgleton Green versus Spark Plug.*
1923: *Whirl of Pleasure.*

1924: *Hits and Bits*. (1924 edition.)
1923–1925: *Billy King Road Show*.
1926: *Vanities*. (With Earl Dancer and Ethel Waters.)

Further Reading

"Billy King's Unpublished Memoirs." *Leigh Whipper Papers*. Moorland-Spingarn Collection, Howard University, Washington, D.C.

Fletcher, Tom. *The Tom Fletcher Story: 100 Years of the Negro in Show Business*. New York: Burdge, 1954, p. 196.

"Hughes, Langston" and "Melzer, Milton." In *Black Magic: A Pictorial History of the Negro in the Performing Arts*. New York: Crown, 1968, p. 336.

Kellner, Bruce, ed. *The Harlem Renaissance: A Historical Dictionary for the Era*. New York: Methuen, 1984, p. 210.

Page, Walter. "About My Life in Music, as Told to Frank Driggs." *Jazz Review*, November 1958, pp. 12–15.

Pearson, Nathan W. *Goin' to Kansas City*. Urbana and Chicago: University of Illinois Press, 1994.

Peterson, Bernard L., Jr. *The African American Theatre Directory, 1816–1960*. Westport, Conn.: Greenwood, 1993a, p. 112.

———. *A Century of Musicals in Black and White*. Westport, Conn.: Greenwood, 1993b.

———. *Profiles of African American Stage Performers and Theatre People, 1816–1960*. Westport, Conn.: Greenwood, 2001, p. 158.

Sampson, Henry T. *Blacks in Blackface: A Source Book on Early Black Musical Shows*. Metuchen, N.J., and London: Scarecrow Press, 1980, pp. 94–96.

———. *The Ghost Walks*. Metuchen, N.J.: Scarecrow, 1988.

Walton, Lester. "Review of *Over the Top* at Lafayette Theater." *New York Age*, July 26, 1919.

Kirkpatrick, Sidney

The baritone Sidney Kirkpatrick acted and entertained in minstrel shows, vaudeville, musicals, and dramas during the period of the Harlem Renaissance. His first professional engagement was with Billy Kersands's Minstrels in 1902–1903. He was hired as a singer with Richards and Pringle's Minstrels in 1909. Later, he went into vaudeville with his wife, Laura Bowman; they toured the United States and Europe together for nearly ten years with the Dark Town Entertainers, a group Kirkpatrick had founded. The repertoire of this group was unique in theatrical circles. The members sang and danced, with Bowman, the highlight of the evening, performing varied characterizations in costume. One of her favorites was "Salome," from the opera of that name.

In 1914, Kirkpatrick played the title role in *Captain Rufus*, a military comedy that had first been produced by the Pekin Theater in Chicago in 1907. In 1917, he appeared in the second production of the Frederick Douglass Film Company, *The Scapegoat*, which had its premiere on 15 May, at the Simplex Theater in New York City. The impressive cast also included Abbie Mitchell, Walker Thompson, Maude Jones, and Leon Williams. This film—an adaptation of a story by Paul Laurence Dunbar—was widely reviewed by critics of the time and was so successful that it was booked by white as well as black motion picture houses.

Bowman and Kirkpatrick separated in 1918, but they continued to perform together with the legendary Lafayette Players in Harlem in such shows as *His Honor, the Mayor* (1918); *Shades of Hades* (1922), in which Kirkpatrick played Satan; and *That Gets It* (1928). They also performed together in 1923 in the landmark productions of the Ethiopian Art Players, a group formed by Raymond O'Neil and the wife of Sherwood Anderson. These presentations included *Salome*, in which Kirkpatrick was praised for his portrayal of King Herod; *The Chip Woman's Fortune*, in which he played the role of Silas Green; and *A Comedy of Errors*, in which he played the merchant Aegeon. Kirkpatrick made his final appearance on Broadway in 1928, as Enos Green in *Meek Mose*, written by Frank Wilson and produced by Lester Walton. He died two years later.

As his career developed during first two decades of the twentieth century, Kirkpatrick had come to be one of the favorites among many talented performers in Harlem. In addition, his professional affiliations with major production groups and other influential artists of this era contributed to his own success in the performing arts as well as the continuing development of other black Americans in this field.

Biography

The date of Sidney Kirkpatrick's birth is uncertain. Kirkpatrick performed with Billy Kersands's Minstrels, 1909; and played the title role in *Captain Rufus*, 1914. He also performed in *The Scapegoat*, 1917; *His Honor, the Mayor*, 1918; *Shades of Hades*, 1922; *Salome*, 1923; *The Chip Woman's Fortune*, 1923; *A Comedy of Errors*, 1923;

That Gets It, 1928; and *Meek Mose*, 1928. He founded the Dark Town Entertainers. Kirkpatrick died in New York City in 1930.

CARMEN PHELPS

See also Ethiopian Art Players; Lafayette Players; Minstrelsy; Mitchell, Abbie; Walton, Lester; Wilson, Frank

Further Reading

Johnson, James Weldon. *Black Manhattan*. New York: Da Capo, 1930.

Mapp, Edward. *Directory of Blacks in the Performing Arts*. Metuchen, N.J.: Scarecrow, 1978.

Peterson, Bernard. *The African-American Theatre Directory, 1816–1960*. Westport, Conn.: Greenwood, 1997.

———. *Profiles of African American Stage Performers and Theatre People, 1816–1960*. Westport, Conn.: Greenwood, 2001.

Sampson, Henry T. *Blacks in Black and White: A Source Book on Black Films*. Lanham, Md.: Scarecrow, 1995.

Spradling, Mary Mace, ed. *In Black and White: A Guide to Magazine Articles, Newspaper Articles, and Books Concerning More Than 15,000 Black Individuals and Groups*, 3rd ed., 2 vols. and Supplement. Detroit, Mich.: Gale Research, 1980, 1985.

Knopf, Alfred A.

Alfred A. Knopf founded the publishing house Alfred A. Knopf, Inc., in New York in 1915 and then served as chairman of this highly respected firm until 1972. Knopf was interested in poetry, European literature in translation, and literature that touched on issues of the day; and he shepherded the house through a tremendously productive period in the 1920s. During this time, the firm emerged as both the leading venue for writers of the Harlem Renaissance—publishing works by Langston Hughes, James Weldon Johnson, Nella Larsen, Carl Van Vechten, and Walter White, among others—and a dominant force in the American literary marketplace at large. The Knopf imprint (which later became a subsidiary of Random House) is still recognized through its "Borzoi" icon, an image of a Russian hound.

Alfred Knopf was born in New York City, the son of Samuel Knopf and Ida Japhe Knopf, Jewish immigrants from Europe. Alfred's mother died when he was four years old. Samuel Knopf became successful in advertising, and in 1906 the family moved from Manhattan to Long Island. Knopf was educated first at public schools, then at the MacKenzie School in Westchester, New York, before receiving a bachelor of arts degree from Columbia University in 1912. At Columbia, he studied literature with Brander Matthews; Bernard Boyeson, who was an early American advocate of Russian writers; and Joel Spingarn, who would later become a prominent publisher and an activist with the National Association for the Advancement of Colored People (NAACP). Knopf also wrote for, and became advertising manager of, the *Columbia Monthly*. After graduation, Knopf traveled in Europe and Britain, where he met and stayed with the writer John Galsworthy. On returning to the United States, Knopf cast aside his plans to attend Harvard Law School and, with some difficulty and using his father's connections, found a position in the accounting department of the publishing firm Doubleday, Page, and Company. During the period around 1915, the publishing industry was not generally open to Jews; and it was still in the process of becoming an industry located almost exclusively in New York. The opening up of the publishing business, along with its newly centralized location in New York, helped fuel those aspects of the Harlem Renaissance that relied on receptive mainstream white publishers and a consolidation of cultural outlets in New York.

In 1915, after a brief stint with the firm of Mitchell Kennerley, Knopf launched his own business with the financial assistance of his father and the enthusiastic editorial assistance of the woman he would marry in 1916, Blanche Wolf. In 1916, Knopf's new house published a number of Russian, German, and French works in translation and a book of music criticism by Carl Van Vechten, *Music and Bad Manners* (1916). Van Vechten, a white critic and man about town, would come to play a significant role in the Knopfs' support of African American writers and subjects. Van Vechten's first novel, *Peter Whiffle* (1922), was a best-seller for the company and on that basis Van Vechten was able to build his influence. Knopf demonstrated his interest in the burgeoning genre of African American literature by publishing Walter White's controversial novel about the riots in Atlanta, *The Fire in the Flint*, in 1924. The following year, after meeting White through Alfred Knopf's introduction, Van Vechten began to exert his influence in support of Langston Hughes and then other African American writers.

When Van Vechten and Hughes first became friends, in 1925, Hughes had just won a prize for his poem "The Weary Blues." Van Vechten insisted on reading a collection of Hughes's poems, made suggestions, and—most important—brought the poems to Knopf for consideration. Hughes's first book, *The Weary Blues* (1926), began what would become a long and complex relationship among Hughes, Van Vechten, Alfred Knopf, and Blanche Knopf. Emily Bernard's collection of letters between Van Vechten and Hughes (2001) suggests both the helpful and the manipulative aspects of the relationship between the older established white writer and the younger, unknown, but promising African American. Ultimately, Bernard finds much of value in the assistance Van Vechten gave to Hughes, indicated perhaps best by the longevity of their friendship but also by the efficacy of that first gesture: "Van Vechten's one lunch date with Alfred Knopf meant that Hughes could quit his tedious day job doing research" (Bernard 2001, p. xxi).

Van Vechten soon became the most notable—and in some quarters the most notorious—white popularizer of the Harlem Renaissance, with the publication by Knopf of his best-selling novel *Nigger Heaven* (1926). The novel was condemned by many critics even as it opened market-driven publishing opportunities for ever more African American writers. The Knopf publishing house went on to bring out such landmarks as James Weldon Johnson's *Autobiography of an Ex-Colored Man*, which it reissued in 1927 to great acclaim—and to a much wider audience than Johnson had achieved when the work was originally issued by a lesser-known publisher in 1912. Knopf also published Nella Larsen's pair of novels, *Quicksand* (1928) and *Passing* (1929).

Alfred Knopf's personal style, at least by his own account, seems to have played a role in the success and high reputation of his firm. In his unpublished memoirs, probably written in the 1960s, Knopf remembers the early days of the firm fondly: "1920 completed our first five years and we marked this anniversary with the publication of *The Borzoi, 1920*, a small volume which I think is unique in publishing. It shows our authors to have been a happy family in the early days, for many of them wrote pieces for it, about other authors on the list" (Moore and Lewis 1992). The sense of a "family" was underscored by the social relations that developed between the Knopfs and their authors. Knopf writes warmly of the period from 1924 to 1928, when the couple lived at 1148 Fifth Avenue and entertained guests such as George Gershwin, who played the piano; Paul Robeson, who sang; and James

Alfred A. Knopf, photographed by Carl Van Vechten, 1935. (Library of Congress.)

Weldon Johnson, who recited his poems. At the same time, however, Knopf was not a gentleman publisher; he was running a business and he needed to make money. According to the critic Clifton Fadiman, in his introduction to another promotional retrospective collection put out by the Knopf publishing house in 1965 to celebrate its fiftieth anniversary, the company "was started not as a playboy's exercise but as a business. It has remained one, with attention methodically paid to the superior attractions of black ink over red" (1965, ix).

In addition to its role in the Harlem Renaissance, Alfred A. Knopf, Inc., emerged as a major publisher of nationally and internationally renowned authors. During the period of the Harlem Renaissance, Knopf's list included Wallace Stevens, Ezra Pound, Willa Cather, T. S. Eliot, Edmund Wilson, H. L. Mencken, Dashiell Hammett, E. M. Forster, and Thomas Mann.

Biography

Alfred Abraham Knopf was born 12 September 1892 in New York City. He studied at public schools in New

York; MacKenzie School, Westchester, New York; and Columbia University (A.B., 1912). He worked in the accounting department of Doubleday, Page, and Company, 1912–1914; founded the publishing house Alfred A. Knopf, Inc., 1915; and became chairman emeritus in 1972. He was publisher of *American Mercury*, 1924–1934. Knopf was chairman of the Advisory Board on National Parks, Historic Sites, Buildings, and Monuments of the National Park Service; a member of the American Historical Association and the New York State Historical Society; a trustee of the American Scenic Historic Preservation Society; and a member of the Overseers' Visiting Committee of the English Department of Harvard University. He died in Purchase, New York, 11 August 1984.

JOSHUA BOAZ KOTZIN

See also American Mercury; Autobiography of an Ex-Colored Man; Fire in the Flint, The; Gershwin, George; Hughes, Langston; Johnson, James Weldon; Knopf, Alfred A., Inc.; Knopf, Blanche; Larsen, Nella; Mencken, H. L.; Nigger Heaven; Passing: Novel; Publishers and Publishing Houses; Quicksand; Robeson, Paul; Spingarn, Joel; Van Vechten, Carl; White, Walter

Further Reading

Bernard, Emily, ed. *Remember Me to Harlem: The Letters of Langston Hughes and Carl Van Vechten, 1925–1964.* New York: Knopf, 2001.

Fadiman, Clifton, ed. *Fifty Years.* New York: Knopf, 1965.

Flora, Peter. "Carl Van Vechten, Blanche Knopf, and the Harlem Renaissance." *Library Chronicle of the University of Texas*, 22(4), 1992.

Knopf, Alfred A., ed. *The Borzoi 1920: Being a Sort of Record of Five Years' Publishing.* New York: Knopf, 1920.

Lewis, Randolph. "Langston Hughes and Alfred A. Knopf, Inc., 1925–1935." *Library Chronicle of the University of Texas*, 22(4), 1992.

Moore, Heather, and Randolph Lewis, eds. "The Education of a Publisher: Selections from the Memoirs of Alfred A. Knopf." *Library Chronicle of the University of Texas*, 22(4), 1992.

Knopf, Alfred A., Inc.

The publishing house Alfred A. Knopf, Inc., was founded by Alfred Knopf in New York in 1915. With the financial assistance of his father, Samuel Knopf,

and the editorial guidance of his wife, Blanche Wolfe Knopf, Alfred guided the house through a tremendously productive period in the 1920s as it emerged as both the leading venue for writers of the Harlem Renaissance—publishing works by Langston Hughes, James Weldon Johnson, Nella Larsen, Carl Van Vechten, and Walter White, among others—and as a dominant force in the American literary marketplace at large. The Knopf imprint (which became a subsidiary of Random House) still uses its logo of a borzoi, a Russian hound.

The advent of Alfred A. Knopf, Inc., was an important development in the Harlem Renaissance both because of the particular works it published and because of the larger trends of which it was an exemplary part. During the period around 1915, the publishing industry was still an elite Anglo-American business, and it was still in the process of becoming an industry located mostly in New York. Opening up the publishing business to Jews such as the Knopfs, along with the industry's newly centralized location in New York, helped fuel those aspects of the Harlem Renaissance that relied on receptive mainstream publishers and a consolidation of cultural outlets in New York. Alfred Knopf's interest in European literature—described by Randolph Lewis as "a wider definition of what was publishable"—was combined with Blanche Knopf's "fluency in French and fondness for French culture," which "made her a perfect envoy to Parisian literary circles." Lewis adds: "This multicultural attitude made the house of Knopf atypical among the literary publishers of New York, ideal for alternative American voices from outside the literary establishment—such as those of African American writers" (1992, 53).

In 1916, the new house published a number of Russian, German, and French works in translation and a book of music criticism by Carl Van Vechten, *Music and Bad Manners* (1916). Van Vechten, a white critic and man about town, would play an important part in the Knopfs' support of African American writers and subjects. Van Vechten's first novel, *Peter Whiffle* (1922), was a best-seller for the company, and on that basis Van Vechten was able to build his influence. Knopf demonstrated his own interest in the burgeoning genre of African American literature by publishing Walter White's controversial novel about riots in Atlanta, *The Fire in the Flint*, in 1924; the following year, after meeting Walter White through Alfred Knopf's introduction, Van Vechten began to exert his influence in support of, first, Langston Hughes and then other African American writers.

When Van Vechten and Hughes first became friends in 1925, Hughes had just won a prize for his poem "The Weary Blues." Van Vechten insisted on reading a collection of Hughes's poems, made suggestions, and—most important—brought the poems to Knopf for consideration. Hughes's first book, *The Weary Blues* (1926), began what would become a long and complex relationship among Hughes, Van Vechten, Alfred Knopf, and Blanche Knopf. Emily Bernard's collection of letters between Van Vechten and Hughes (2001) suggests both the helpful and the manipulative aspects of their relationship. Ultimately, Bernard seems to find much of value in the assistance Van Vechten gave Hughes, which was perhaps indicated best by the longevity of their friendship.

Van Vechten had considerable muscle to flex at Knopf when he decided to help Hughes. Hughes had impressed the black literati with his early poems, but none of his mentors in Harlem had the power to get his work published. "Van Vechten's one lunch date with Alfred Knopf meant that Hughes could quit his tedious day job doing research" (Bernard, xxi).

Van Vechten soon became the most noted—and was considered by some the most notorious—white popularizer of the Harlem Renaissance, with the publication by Knopf of his best-selling novel *Nigger Heaven* (1926). The novel was condemned by many critics even as it opened up a market, and thus publishing opportunities, for increasingly more African American writers. The Knopf publishing house, partially through Van Vechten's influence, went on to bring out such landmarks as its reissue in 1927 of James Weldon Johnson's *Autobiography of an Ex-Colored Man*; this had first been published in 1912, when it had only a small press run, but now it found a much wider audience. Knopf also published Nella Larsen's novels *Quicksand* (1928) and *Passing* (1929).

The relationship between the Knopfs and Langston Hughes illustrates how financial considerations, always a source of concern, could produce tension over questions of creative and political autonomy. When money became more of an issue, the Knopfs put more pressure on Hughes to produce marketable work: "The financial pressures of the early 1930s forced the shortcomings of the Knopfs' treatment of Hughes to the surface; with fewer people buying books, the Knopfs became less tolerant publishers" (Lewis 1992, 56). Also, as Hughes, in the early 1930s, became more politically engaged with causes that were not exclusively African American, economic and ideological fissures began to appear: "The Knopfs,

with Van Vechten's support, as many letters indicate, implicitly and explicitly urged Hughes to focus his writing on racial subjects. Political themes were only acceptable if they stuck to primarily racial issues" (Lewis 1992, 57). Despite these problems, Hughes seems to have appreciated his long-standing relationship with the Knopfs. He wrote to them in 1941: "Dear Alfred and Blanche, This June marks for me twenty years of publication—largely thanks to you as my publishers. With my continued gratitude and affection . . . Langston Hughes" (Lewis 1992, 62).

Lewis concludes:

> Financial pressures in the early years of the Depression took a toll on the Knopf-Harlem relationship, as did age. The Knopfs were no longer the "new breed" of publisher; younger, more daring publishers assumed this role. With the Knopfs reaching middle age and their firm growing in reputation, they gradually entered into the fold of the publishing establishment, letting someone else save the world from commercial publishing of the narrow-minded variety. (63)

At the same time as it was participating in the triumphs and conflicts of the Harlem Renaissance, Alfred A. Knopf, Inc., emerged as a major publisher of nationally and internationally regarded authors. During the period of the Harlem Renaissance, Knopf's list included Wallace Stevens, Ezra Pound, Willa Cather, T. S. Eliot, Edmund Wilson, H. L. Mencken, Dashiell Hammett, E. M. Forster, and Thomas Mann—the "publishing establishment" indeed.

JOSHUA BOAZ KOTZIN

See also Autobiography of an Ex-Colored Man; Fire in the Flint, The; Hughes, Langston; Johnson, James Weldon; Knopf, Alfred A.; Knopf, Blanche; Larsen, Nella; Mencken, H. L.; Nigger Heaven; Passing: Novel; Publishers and Publishing Houses; Quicksand; Van Vechten, Carl; White, Walter

Further Reading

Bernard, Emily, ed. *Remember Me to Harlem: The Letters of Langston Hughes and Carl Van Vechten, 1925–1964.* New York: Knopf, 2001.

Fadiman, Clifton, ed. *Fifty Years.* New York: Knopf, 1965.

Flora, Peter. "Carl Van Vechten, Blanche Knopf, and the Harlem Renaissance." *Library Chronicle of the University of Texas*, 22(4), 1992.

Knopf, Alfred A., ed. *The Borzoi 1920: Being a Sort of Record of Five Years' Publishing.* New York: Knopf, 1920.

Lewis, Randolph. "Langston Hughes and Alfred A. Knopf, Inc., 1925–1935." *Library Chronicle of the University of Texas*, 22(4), 1992.

Moore, Heather, and Randolph Lewis, eds. "The Education of a Publisher: Selections from the Memoirs of Alfred A. Knopf." *Library Chronicle of the University of Texas*, 22(4), 1992.

Knopf, Blanche

As a director of Alfred A. Knopf, Inc., Publishers, from its founding in 1915 until her death in 1966, Blanche Knopf helped many authors of the Harlem Renaissance gain a wider audience by the seemingly simple means of recognizing their talent and accepting and publishing their work. Under her guidance, the new firm quickly developed a reputation as a publisher of high-quality literary books. While Blanche Knopf is best known as the publisher who introduced English translations of important European writers, including Sigmund Freud, Albert Camus, and Thomas Mann, to the United States, she was also responsible for the fact that Alfred A. Knopf, Inc., became one of the most significant publishers of the writers of the Harlem Renaissance.

When Blanche Wolf and her future husband, Alfred (they married in 1916), established the publishing firm of Alfred A. Knopf, Inc., in 1915, there were no models for a woman who wished to do serious work as a book editor and publisher. In this period there was no question that the firm would bear Alfred's name alone, or that his title would be (and would remain) a bit more impressive than Blanche's, although the two were equal in their responsibilities, their talent, and their accomplishments. As the firm grew, Alfred made full use of the contacts he made through male-only organizations such as the Publishers' Lunch Club, while Blanche became adept at using her social connections to cultivate writers. Her work with writers was personal and individual; writers with whom she worked received invitations to lunch and personal letters from her regularly.

For the first several years of her work with the firm, the multilingual Knopf focused on learning about the technical aspects of book publishing and on acquiring the works of French writers. But the firm also took on an angry novel about riots in Atlanta,

Walter White's *The Fire in the Flint* (1924). Like most of the company's books, *The Fire in the Flint* sold respectably, but it was by no means a best-seller. Two years later, the company published White's second novel, *Flight* (1926), about Atlanta's black middle class and African Americans who "passed" in the North. As a black writer whose work was being issued by a major publisher of the 1920s, White was in small group. Most black writers at the time published and sold their own work, or they found their work accepted by a very few small presses in New York that turned out good books but could not reach a national audience. With Knopf, White found himself in a community of recognized writers with a supportive editor. A letter that White wrote to Knopf in 1928, as he was working on *Rope and Faggot* (1929)—a book about lynching in the United States, which Knopf published—includes greetings to Carl Van Vechten and to other writers of the Harlem Renaissance who were also published by Knopf.

It was through her friendship with Carl Van Vechten, the controversial white author of the novel *Nigger Heaven* (1926), that Knopf was encouraged to take on the works of more black American writers. Van Vechten was fascinated by the culture of Harlem, and he had asked the Knopfs for an introduction to Walter White. With White as his guide, he became acquainted with many of the important writers and musicians of Harlem in the 1920s, and he wrote reviews and criticism of their work. He suggested to Blanche that Knopf, Inc., turn its attention to "the Negro question," and she agreed to consider manuscripts Van Vechten sent her way.

In 1925, Van Vechten brought Blanche a manuscript of a collection by an unknown poet, Langston Hughes. At Van Vechten's urging, Blanche agreed to publish *The Weary Blues* (1926), making Hughes the first African American poet to be published by a major firm in the United States. Knopf took Hughes under her wing, guiding his manuscript through the production and marketing process, and also helping him with personal and professional advice and encouragement. Knopf acted in some ways as Hughes's agent, negotiating royalties and speaker's fees that he was too timid to ask for himself. Hughes's second collection of poetry, *Fine Clothes to the Jew* (1927), was, in Knopf's view, too political and not as marketable as his first book. Although Knopf and Hughes disagreed about the direction of his work, and their professional relationship grew strained as Hughes's work became more political and less profitable, Knopf, Inc., continued to publish Hughes's work, including the novel *Not without Laughter* (1930).

Knopf took on the work of several other writers of the Harlem Renaissance, in many cases acting on Van Vechten's advice. Important Knopf publications include James Weldon Johnson's *Autobiography of an Ex-Colored Man* (1927) and *Black Manhattan* (1930); Nella Larsen's two novels, *Quicksand* (1928) and *Passing* (1929); and Rudolph Fisher's *Walls of Jericho* (1930). A pattern emerged with these books: Van Vechten identified the work; Knopf edited and published it; and, frequently, Van Vechten wrote the introduction. Knopf also published the work of Van Vechten, including the sensational *Nigger Heaven*. The title of that novel was intended to be offensive and eye-catching, and it was both. The book was intended as a sympathetic portrayal of urban African American life, but many readers found it condescending.

Alfred A. Knopf, Inc., was a business, and Blanche Knopf accepted manuscripts that she expected would turn a profit for the company. But she considered manuscripts that most publishing houses at the time would not consider, she nurtured new talents, and she made it possible—and profitable—for African American writers of the 1920s to reach a national audience.

Blanche Knopf. (Library of Congress.)

Biography

Blanche Wolf Knopf was born 30 July 1894 in New York City. She was educated by private governesses and at the Gardner School. With Alfred A. Knopf, her future husband, she founded the publishing company Alfred A. Knopf, Inc., in New York City (1915), and the Borzoi colophon and imprint (1916). She was the firm's office manager, 1916–1921; its director and vice president, 1921–1957; and its director and president, 1957–1966. Her awards included the following: French Legion of Honor, Chevalier (1949) and Officer (1960); Brazilian Order of the Southern Cross, Cavaliero (1952) and Oficial (1964); honorary degrees from Franklin and Marshall College (1962), Western College for Women (1966), and Adelphi University (1966); and the Women's National Book Association Skinner Award (1966). She died 4 June 1966 in New York City.

CYNTHIA BILY

See also Autobiography of an Ex-Colored Man; Black Manhattan; Fine Clothes to the Jew; Fire in the Flint, The; Fisher, Rudolph; Hughes, Langston; Johnson, James Weldon; Knopf, Alfred A.; Knopf, Alfred A., Inc.; Larsen, Nella; Nigger Heaven; Not without Laughter; Passing: Novel; Quicksand; Van Vechten, Carl; Walls of Jericho, The; Weary Blues, The; White, Walter

Further Reading

Flora, Peter. "Carl Van Vechten, Blanche Knopf, and the Harlem Renaissance." *Library Chronicle of the University of Texas*, 22(4), 1992.

Henderson, Cathy, comp. *The Company They Kept: Alfred A. and Blanche W. Knopf, Publishers: An Exhibition Catalog*, ed. Dave Oliphant. Austin: University of Texas at Austin, 1995.

Knopf, Alfred A. "Blanche W. Knopf, July 30, 1894–June 4, 1966." *Borzoi Quarterly*, 15(3), 1966.

Rampersad, Arnold. *The Life of Langston Hughes*, 2 vols. New York and Oxford: Oxford University Press, 1986.

Krigwa Players

The Krigwa Players Little Theater Group was founded in 1925 by *Crisis* magazine at the urging of W. E. B. Du Bois. By all accounts, the Krigwa Players were dedicated to the production of theater by, for, about, and near black Americans, with a special emphasis on the production of plays with a racially conscious message. The name Krigwa (originally Crigwa) is an acronym representing the initial sounds and letters of the legendary Crisis Guild of Writers and Artists. Famous members of the Krigwa Players included the artist Aaron Douglas (who painted the scenery for the group) and the playwrights Mary T. Burrill (who wrote *Aftermath* and *They That Sit in Darkness*), Willis Richardson (who wrote *The Chip Woman's Fortune* and *Bootblack Lover*), May Miller (who wrote *Riding the Goat* and *Harriet Tubman*), and Georgia Douglas Johnson (who wrote *Blue Blood* and *Sunday Morning in the South*). The contributions of Krigwa to the development of black theater are vast: the group awarded prizes to encourage blacks to write drama, used *Crisis* as an outlet for establishing guidelines for budding dramatists, provided space for the workshopping of dramas in progress, and served as a training ground for black actors and actresses.

Success stories attributable to Krigwa are abundant. For example, when the administration of Howard University refused to grant the Howard Players permission to perform some of Willis Richardson's works (because the administrators considered them propaganda), Richardson was encouraged by Du Bois to submit his plays to black theater houses and to *Crisis*. Richardson's first-place award in the first annual Krigwa drama contest helped bring national attention to his work. Another example of Krigwa's successful promotion of black theater practitioners is May Miller, whose plays had previously been staged primarily in educational environments with little financial support for her work. Miller was able to advance her theater career by winning prizes in Krigwa's playwriting contests and by joining the Baltimore Krigwa group as director, performer, and actor. Additionally, two of Krigwa's performers—Richard Hughly and Doralyn Spence—joined professional casts in downtown theaters after the successes of the Krigwa group in the Belasco tournament.

Theophilus Lewis, the black drama critic for the *Messenger*, praised Krigwa and other "little theater" groups operating in black communities for staging serious and potentially educational plays by blacks. Du Bois described the Krigwa Players as a group dedicated to presenting black community theater, with special attention to noncommercial theater with a political message: even more specifically, they supported developing propaganda plays that could be used to politically uplift and to educate African Americans. Occasionally, the Krigwa Players would include interpretive dancing on their programs, but Krigwa's promotion of political

theater was especially important because, without the help of a communal group, this type of theater was not likely to gain an audience. It rarely appealed to wealthy theatergoers, theater owners, or any other group without a strong allegiance to the black community.

The Krigwa "little theater" movement quickly found support not only in New York but also in other areas of the country. The original Krigwa Players operated under the direction of Charles Burroughs and met in the basement of the New York Public Library on 135th Street—a space offered by the librarian, Earnestine Rose. Material support for the group came from a variety of sources. Amy Spingarn provided the money for the prizes that the group awarded. The New York Public Library provided stage space, dressing rooms, and lighting equipment. The players wrote their own plays, acted the parts, furnished audiences, and attended to any other necessary aspects of production. The Krigwa Players soon had extensions in Cleveland, Ohio; New Haven, Connecticut; Baltimore, Maryland; Washington, D.C.; and Denver, Colorado.

The Krigwa Players' first major production took place on 25 October 1926, as they enlivened the *Crisis* awards dinner with performances of Willis Richardson's *Compromise* and Eulalie Spence's *Fool's Errand*. In addition, they regularly offered local weekend performances and participated in small competitions for one-act plays. In May 1927, the New York group entered a national "little theater" tournament and again presented *Fool's Errand*, in a performance that was praised in the *New York Times* as a close second to the top performance of the tournament. In June 1927, Spence's *The Hunch* was performed by the Krigwa Players of Washington, D.C. In 1928, *The Crisis* reported that the group was not meeting as regularly as before but that it had performed Mary Burrill's *Aftermath* in the Belasco tournament, with the encouragement of the tournament's promoters.

By 1930, there is no record of the group's activities, and their practice and performance space was given to the Harlem Experimental Theater. Various explanations for the demise of Krigwa have been offered. Du Bois said that after the group won the national "little theater" contest, its activities slowed because its best members were lured away by downtown theaters, which could give performers more money and greater exposure; however, the fatal blow, according to Du Bois, was the onset of the Depression. This second reason seems somewhat unlikely, though, since other black acting troupes, such as the Harlem Experimental Theater, survived.

Another explanation was given by some group members, who said they left because of Du Bois's increasingly heavy-handed promotion of the propaganda play, without respect for their individual artistic concerns: while they understood the need for political theater, they did not want to limit their art to political themes. For instance, Eulalie Spence—one of the first writers to have her work produced by Krigwa—grew increasingly frustrated because Du Bois was insisting that she write about issues which were not engaging for her. Still another explanation had to do with money: the New York group was said to have dissolved over a disagreement about the money that had been won in the tournament of 1927; when Du Bois claimed the total amount for expenses, without sharing any of the prize with the group members, some of them became embittered and left the troupe. In any case, after the group in New York broke up, Krigwa groups across the country soon did the same.

Though the life of Krigwa was short and its concerns were often controversial, it had a significant role in the developments of black theater at the time and significant effects on the black theater that followed.

ETHEL A. YOUNG-MINOR

See also Community Theater; Crisis, The; Douglas, Aaron; Du Bois, W. E. B.; Fool's Errand; Johnson, Georgia Douglas; Lewis, Theophilus; Little Theater Tournament; Messenger, The; 135th Street Library; Richardon, Williss

Further Reading

Archer, Leonard. *Black Images in the American Theatre: NAACP Protest Campaigns.* Brooklyn, N.Y.: Pageant-Poseidon, 1973.

Hutchinson, George. *The Harlem Renaissance in Black and White.* Cambridge, Mass.: Harvard University Press, 1995.

Kellner, Bruce. *The Harlem Renaissance: A Historical Dictionary for the Era.* Westport, Conn.: Greenwood, 1984.

Lester, Julius, ed. *The Seventh Son: The Thoughts and Writings of W. E. B. Du Bois.* New York: Random House, 1971.

Lewis, David Levering. *When Harlem Was in Vogue.* New York: Oxford University Press, 1982.

Mitchell, Loften. *Black Drama.* New York: Hawthorn, 1967.

Labor

The Harlem Renaissance has sometimes been interpreted largely in terms of race. Analyses, however, are incomplete without an understanding of the important fact that the vast majority of black Americans, including Harlemites, were working people. Indeed, the lives of working black Americans provided much of the subject matter for the authors, poets, painters, and photographers of the Harlem Renaissance. It was this focus as much as anything that distinguished early authors of the renaissance, such as Claude McKay, Langston Hughes, and Jean Toomer, from their black predecessors. Particularly significant for their art was the great movement of blacks from the South to the North that was happening during the time of the Harlem Renaissance. Much of what the authors observed and wrote about concerned the difficult transition of rural agricultural folk into an urban working class.

In the early twentieth century, black Americans were so constrained by systematic racial oppression and discrimination that the structure of black America was radically different from that of white America. In Harlem during the 1920s, 90 percent of black Americans were blue-collar workers. Not only were black Americans excluded from skilled, supervisory, and managerial positions (except in black businesses); they were also excluded from entire industries, segregated into positions requiring strength and endurance, and often given the dirtiest and most dangerous tasks. In 1930, for example, the following occupations in America were most heavily occupied by blacks: laborers in fertilizer factories (84.1 percent), laborers in turpentine farms and distilleries (82 percent), launderers and laundresses not in a laundry (75.1 percent), porters other than those in stores (73.5 percent), cooks other than those in hotels and boardinghouses (68.5 percent), operatives in fertilizer factories (67.6 percent), laborers in cigar and tobacco factories (59.5 percent), operatives in turpentine farms and distilleries (53.1 percent), bootblacks (50.6 percent), and midwives (50.1 percent; "The Negro in Industry" 1936, 976).

Because opportunities for work for black men were infrequent, and because black men's work was insecure, the proportion of black women in the paid labor force was greater than that of women in almost any other group—although opportunities were even more restricted for black women than for black men. In 1934, for instance, about 25 percent of all women over the age of fifteen were in the paid workforce, but the figure for black women was about 50 percent. In 1925, 45 percent of married black women worked, whereas the rate for all married women was about 15 percent. Of all child workers, 36 percent were black. Six times more black girls under age sixteen worked than white girls. Four times more black women over age sixty-five worked than white women.

Not only were employers reluctant to hire black men; labor unions and white workers were generally also hostile. Studies of New York City by George S. Schuyler, published in 1927, revealed that no blacks worked as salesclerks in major department stores. Macy's hired blacks as elevator operators, cafeteria workers, and escalator men; but Gimbels refused all black labor, claiming that white workers and shoppers would object. Of the large employers in New York, not one hired blacks as semiskilled or skilled workers. In the transit systems, no drivers were black; the systems that did hire blacks used them as porters or messengers.

World War I was a watershed for African Americans. It marked the first time that black Americans in large numbers were able to break the "agricultural ceiling." Half a million blacks left the South for northern and western cities between 1916 and 1920. While the war lasted, despite residential segregation and differential wage rates, black workers had opportunities in mass-production industries at much better rates of pay than they were used to. Following peace and the economic collapse of 1921–1922, there was a recovery; during the rest of the 1920s 800,000 more blacks left the South. The proportion of all blacks living in cities rose from 27 percent in 1916 to about 35 percent in 1920, then to 43 percent in the late 1920s, and then to nearly 50 percent by 1940. In Harlem, the number of blacks rose from 73,000 in 1920 to 164,000 in 1930 (25 percent were foreign born).

However, pervasive racism and other factors contributed to low occupational levels among black migrants. In New York City, the economy revolved around skilled and white-collar jobs and small manufacturing firms. Few opportunities existed for unskilled and unschooled labor such as those offered elsewhere. A majority of the migrants from the South had not completed grade school, and few had any vocational training. Opportunities for adult education in Harlem were minimal. During the 1920s, blacks made little headway in improving their occupational opportunities.

Harlem was, if nothing else, poor. The poorest 50 percent of blacks in New York City lived on the equivalent of 46 percent of the income of the poorest 50 percent of whites. In addition to low wages and frequent periods of unemployment, black Harlemites paid more in rent (up to 40 percent of their income) to live in more crowded conditions than existed anywhere else in the nation, and they were in worse health.

The relationship between black Americans and the organized labor movement was troubled, to say the least. In 1890, the American Federation of Labor (AFL) had banned the color bar and refused to grant a charter of affiliation to the National Association of Machinists, which maintained such a bar; in 1891 the AFL had hired George L. Norton to organize black workers. By the end of the decade, however, the AFL had changed: it accepted the autonomy of member unions, and the nation witnessed an aggressive exclusion of skilled black workers from their trades. In 1900,

the AFL convention gave official sanction to Jim Crow in organizing. By 1910, twelve union affiliates in good standing had constitutional or ritual bans on black members, and a range of less formal exclusionary mechanisms were in place. High initiation fees, tacit agreements, discriminatory technical exams, special licenses, and a ban on blacks as apprentices all worked against black union membership. Even when national unions were not unsympathetic to black workers, individual locals often were. Blacks in search of work were sometimes able to find it only by replacing striking white workers. New York City's black longshoremen, for example, gained a foothold in the late 1890s when the exclusionary white union struck their employers.

The black community thus became not only suspicious of organized labor unions but in many cases hostile to them. The outstanding leader of his generation, Booker T. Washington, promoted individual self-help and opposed unions. After Washington's death in 1915, Marcus Garvey was the most influential black leader to oppose unions. As early as 1902, on the other hand, the group around W. E. B. Du Bois recommended that blacks support the labor movement even while denouncing its racist practices. By 1915, attempts to organize national, as opposed to just local, unions of black workers began to bear fruit. In that year, Robert L. Mays organized the Railwaymen's International Industrial Benevolent Association, which would peak in 1920 with 15,000 members. Rienzi B. Lemus founded the Brotherhood of Dining Car Porters in 1920. Most important, the activities of A. Philip Randolph and Chandler Owen in Harlem led to attempts to organize elevator operators in 1918 and shipyard workers in the National Brotherhood Workers of America the following year, and to an invitation to Randolph in 1925 to head the newly founded Brotherhood of Sleeping Car Porters. In Harlem, the other great promoter and organizer of black labor was the socialist Frank R. Crosswaith.

As the Harlem ghetto developed, the problems of employment stirred both the Urban League and the National Association for the Advancement of Colored People (NAACP). During World War I, the New York Urban League involved itself in labor matters when it started the Committee for Improving the Industrial Conditions of Negroes and held conferences with the AFL in what turned out to be a long and fruitless effort to get the federation to stop discriminatory practices. Pressure from NAACP led, in 1918, to the establishment of the United States Division of Negro

Economics under the Department of Labor (the division was scrapped in 1921). NAACP tried again in 1924 when it proposed an Interracial Labor Commission to try to improve relations with the AFL and end discrimination. None of these efforts succeeded.

In 1925, several developments marked a turning point in black labor history. The National Urban League formed its Department of Industrial Relations to lobby and agitate continually for better opportunities for black workers. The American Communist Party established the American Negro Labor Congress. Frank Crosswaith, A. Philip Randolph, and the Urban League formed the Trade Union Committee for Organizing Negro Workers; and the Pullman porters began their long fight for recognition. Harlem was crucial in all these efforts. Even by 1928, however, only 4 percent of the members of the AFL in New York City were black—though the foundation for improvement had nevertheless been laid.

Throughout what is generally known as a prosperous decade, black workers experienced little affluence. Declines occurred in industries where they were most heavily concentrated—agriculture, coal, lumber, iron, and steel. The construction industry was also uneven. Earlier than in many areas of the country, the economy in New York City slowed down and unemployment rose. Floyd J. Calvin reported in *Opportunity* in May 1929 (a few months before the stock market crashed in October) that over the previous year, because of an economic slowdown, blacks had been replaced by whites in such normally "black" jobs as laying pavement and collecting garbage.

Blacks were hit earliest and hardest by the Depression. The Urban League surveyed twenty-five cities in 1930 and found a decrease of 34.5 percent in the number of available jobs for blacks and an increase of 40 percent in demand. In New York City at the end of 1930, only 42.5 percent of black workers were in full-time employment, compared with 64.2 percent of native-born whites. Similarly, only 31.9 percent of black women workers were employed full time, compared with 74.7 percent of native-born white women. Blacks became unemployed sooner and stayed unemployed longer than whites.

Despite some exceptions, relief programs and their implementation almost universally discriminated against blacks, either through exclusion of job categories containing the largest numbers of blacks, such as domestic service workers and agricultural workers, or through differential payments. In Harlem by 1933, almost 50 percent of all families received unemployment relief but only 9 percent of work relief jobs went to blacks. The whole community in Harlem took action to increase the representation of blacks in employment and to improve opportunities. In 1933, the Reverend John H. Johnson spearheaded the Citizens League for Fair Play (CLFP). Ira Kemp and Arthur Reid formed the Harlem Labor Union (HLU) to gain employment in Harlem for black workers. Sufi Abdul Hamid founded the Harlem Industrial Clerical Alliance. Crosswaith and Randolph started the Harlem Labor Council (HLC). While CLFP worked on boycotts to force companies to hire blacks—"Don't buy where you can't work"—Hamid's organization was denounced as little better than racketeering, forcing firms to employ blacks by offering "protection" to those that did. HLU made an impact, but the most solid achievements came from HLC, which was involved in organizing black workers all over the city. Through the efforts of HLC, 4,000 black workers joined the Building Service Employees Union. HLC also worked with the International Ladies Garment Workers Union to organize black women. By 1938 it claimed to have organized more than 50 percent of all Harlemites in unions. The successes of the Brotherhood of Sleeping Car Porters (BSCP), long delayed, resulted in acceptance into the AFL in 1935 and a contract with the staunchly antiunion Pullman Company in 1937. The BSCP, together with the emerging CIO, formed the backdrop to the phenomenal increase of Harlem's black trade unionists. In addition, the Harlem riot of 1935 revealed the powder keg created by prolonged discrimination and jolted city government and employers into opening up employment to blacks. The transformation was startling. When the Federal Writers' Project published its *New York Panorama* in 1938, the authors could say: "Perhaps the strongest of Negro organizations in Harlem are the trade unions. . . . Since the depression and the inception of the Congress of Industrial Organizations, there is hardly a trade or profession in Harlem that is not organized." Harlem had become the heart not only of black America but also of black labor in segregated America.

STEPHEN BURWOOD

See also Brotherhood of Sleeping Car Porters; Communist Party; Du Bois, W. E. B.; Federal Writers' Project; Garvey, Marcus; Great Migration; Hamid, Sufi Abdul; Harlem: 2—Economics; National Association for the Advancement of Colored People; National Urban League; Owen, Chandler; Randolph, A. Philip; Riots:

4—Harlem Riot, 1935; Schuyler, George S.; Washington, Booker T.

Further Reading

Anderson, Jervis. *This Was Harlem, 1900–1950.* New York: Farrar, Straus, Giroux, 1982.

Foner, Philip S., and Ronald L. Lewis, eds. *The Black Worker: A Documentary History from Colonial Times to the Present,* Vol. 6, *The Era of Post-War Prosperity and the Great Depression, 1920–1936.* Philadelphia, Pa.: Temple University Press, 1981.

Greenberg, Cheryl Lynn. *Or Does It Explode? Black Harlem in the Great Depression.* New York and Oxford: Oxford University Press, 1991.

Harris, William H., *The Harder We Run: Black Workers Since the Civil War.* New York and Oxford: Oxford University Press, 1982.

Johnson, James Weldon. *Black Manhattan.* New York: Arno and New York Times, 1968. (Originally published 1930.)

Meier, August, and Elliott Rudwick. "Communist Unions and the Black Community: The Case of the Transport Workers Union, 1934–1944." *Labor History* (Spring 1982). (Reprinted in Melvyn Dubofsky and Stephen Burwood, eds. *The Great Depression and the New Deal,* Vol. 6, *Women and Minorities during the Great Depression;* New York and London: Garland, 1990.)

"The Negro in Industry." *Monthly Labor Review,* 42, April 1936, p. 976.

Osofsky, Gilbert. *Harlem: The Making of a Ghetto—Negro New York, 1890–1930.* New York: Harper and Row, 1966.

Ottley, Roi. *New World-A-Coming.* New York: Arno and New York Times, 1968. (Originally published 1943.)

Trotter, Joe W., and Earl Lewis, eds. *African Americans in the Industrial Age: A Documentary History, 1915–1945.* Boston, Mass.: Northeastern University Press, 1996.

Wintz, Cary D. *Black Culture and the Harlem Renaissance.* Houston, Tex.: Rice University Press, 1988.

Lafayette Players

The Lafayette Players Stock Company, commonly known as the Lafayette Players, was New York's first African American stock company to concentrate on legitimate theater. From 1915 to 1923, the company resided at the Lafayette Theater, one of the major playhouses in Harlem. The company presented more than 250 productions that included original works by African American playwrights as well as revivals of popular comedies and the classics. The stated goals of the Lafayette Players were to raise the standards of African American acting and dramatic productions, demonstrate that black actors could excel in dramatic roles as well as in song and dance, and provide the black community of Harlem with an alternative to vaudeville and minstrel shows, which often ridiculed African Americans. The actor Charles Gilpin, who became famous in the title role in Eugene O'Neill's *The Emperor Jones* (1920), was among the founding members of the company. Other well-recognized members included Ida Anderson, Andrew Bishop, Laura Bowman, Inez Clough, Evelyn Ellis, Clarence Muse, Evelyn Preer, and Arthur "Dooley" Wilson.

The Lafayette Players were founded in 1915 by the actress and former dancer Anita Bush, as the Anita Bush Stock Company. The company made its first stage appearance at the Lincoln Theater in Harlem on 15 November 1915, with a production of Billie Burke's *The Girl at the Fort.* The players had been gathered only two weeks earlier, when Eugene Elmore, the manager of the Lincoln, had given Bush permission to perform there with a troupe of her own. Shortly after their opening at the Lincoln, the players followed Elmore to the nearby Lafayette Theater, where their first production, *Across the Footlights,* opened on 27 December 1915. In 1916, because of financial difficulties, Anita Bush sold the managing rights of her company to the comanager of the Lafayette, Lester Walton. She remained with the players until 1920, however, and it was she who chose most of their repertoire. In March 1916, the troupe was renamed the Lafayette Players Stock Company. In the same year, Walton sold the management rights of the Lafayette Players to the Elite Amusement Corporation, which hired Elmore to manage the troupe. In 1917 the Lafayette Players were taken over by the Quality Amusement Company, and in 1919 Walton was reinstalled as the company's manager.

As their productions became famous, the Lafayette Players organized road companies; in 1916–1917 two of these offspring toured on different circuits, appearing in Chicago, Philadelphia, Washington, Baltimore, Richmond, Norfolk, and other large cities on the East Coast. When the Lafayette Theater was turned into a vaudeville house in 1923, the Lafayette Players disbanded as a residential troupe and concentrated on their traveling companies. They reunited as a stock company in 1928, when Robert Levy, who now headed the Quality Amusement Corporation, invited them to move to Los Angeles. The Lafayette Players performed at the newly built Lincoln Theater in Los Angeles, until the economic hardships of the Great Depression finally forced them to dissolve in 1932.

The Lafayette Players had an almost exclusively African American audience. They presented a repertoire that changed weekly, staging abridged versions of popular Broadway plays. Many of these plays were being performed by black actors, and for black spectators, for the first time. The players obtained stock-company rights to numerous Broadway hits, particularly comedies, melodramas, and classics; but their repertoire occasionally also included original plays, operas, and musical revues. Among the most successful productions of the Lafayette Players were the Broadway melodramas *Within the Law* (1915–1916) and *Madame X* (1916–1917); Jerome Kern's musical *Very Good Eddie* (1917–1918); and adaptations of *The Count of Monte Cristo* (1916–1917), *Dr. Jekyll and Mr. Hyde* (1916–1917), and Goethe's *Faust* (1917–1918).

In Los Angeles, the Lafayette Players performed before racially mixed audiences. This turned out to be a challenge for the company, because black and white patrons often had conflicting expectations about how African Americans should be portrayed onstage. Nevertheless, the players continued to present—successfully—their usual offering of popular works from the white stage, which now included Eugene O'Neill's *Desire under the Elms* as well as DuBose Heyward's *Porgy*.

The Lafayette Players generally received favorable reviews, which were regularly published nationwide in the black press. However, progressive theater critics and intellectuals, including Theophilus Lewis, Lester Walton, and James Weldon Johnson, attacked the company for being too "white" with regard to the scope and style of its productions. The Lafayette Players favored light-skinned actors and actresses; in fact, dark-complexioned performers such as Clarence Muse sometimes whitened their faces. Moreover, not only was the repertoire taken almost exclusively from Broadway; the performances also followed the conventions of the white stage.

Considering their need to survive financially, the Lafayette Players operated within a rather narrow framework of opportunities. Their popularity depended on the range of their repertoire, and also on their low ticket prices. Well into the 1920s, they were the least expensive legitimate theater company in New York and on the road. Furthermore, the concept of a black legitimate theater that would present original works and develop its own dramatic conventions was only just emerging during the time when the Lafayette Players were active. Nevertheless, to meet audiences' demand for authentic portrayals of blacks onstage, and to compensate for a general lack of plays written by and for African Americans, the company did occasionally commission works from within its own ranks. Andrew Bishop's *It Happened in Harlem* (1917–1918) and *An Automobile Honeymoon* (1917–1918) are probably the best-known examples.

As the first and major African American legitimate theater company in Harlem during the Harlem Renaissance, the Lafayette Players helped pave the way for the development of modern African American theater in the United States. In taking productions from the white repertoire and having black actors present them to black audiences, the company overcame racial barriers in casting and broke away from the traditional portrayals of African Americans onstage. Perhaps the company's most significant achievement was training African American actors in a variety of dramatic roles, many of which had never before been given to black performers. The Lafayette Players not only fostered the theatrical careers of a whole generation of African American actors but also helped raise the general standards of black theatrical entertainment.

ASTRID HAAS

See also Anita Bush Theater Company; Bush, Anita; Clough, Inez; Ellis, Evelyn; Gilpin, Charles; Johnson, James Weldon; Lafayette Theater; Lewis, Theophilus; Lincoln Theater; Madame X; Muse, Clarence; Porgy: Play; Preer, Evelyn; Walton, Lester; Wilson, Arthur "Dooley"

Further Reading

Anderson, Jervis. *This Was Harlem: A Cultural Portrait, 1900–1950*, 2nd ed. New York: Farrar, Straus, and Giroux, 1982.

Isaacs, Edith J. R. *The Negro in the American Theatre*. College Park, Md.: McGrath, 1968.

Kellner, Bruce, ed. *The Harlem Renaissance: A Historical Dictionary for the Era*. New York: Methuen; London: Routledge and Kegan Paul, 1987.

Kornweibel, Theodore, Jr. "Theophilus Lewis and the Theater of the Harlem Renaissance." In *The Harlem Renaissance Remembered*, ed. Arna Bontemps. New York: Dodd, Mead, 1972.

Mitchell, Loften. *Black Drama: The Story of the American Negro in the Theatre.* New York: Hawthorn, 1967.

Patterson, Lindsay, ed. *Anthology of the American Negro in the Theatre: A Critical Approach.* International Library of Negro Life and History, New York, Washington, and London: Publishers Company, 1968. (2nd printing.)

Thompson, Sister M. Francesca, O.S.F. "The Lafayette Players, 1917–1932." In *The Theater of Black Americans,* Vol. 2, *The Presenters: Companies of Players; The Participators: Audience and Critics—A Collection of Critical Essays,* ed. Erroll Hill. Englewood Cliffs, N.J.: Prentice Hall, 1980.

Vorder Brugge, Andrew. "Lafayette Players." In *American Theatre Companies, 1888–1930,* ed. Weldon B. Durham. Westport, Conn.: Greenwood, 1987.

Lafayette Theater

The Lafayette Theater at 132nd Street and Seventh Avenue was built in 1912 by John Mulonski; during the 1910s and 1920s it became one of the most important theaters in Harlem catering to the African American community. The Lafayette, which at one time was called "House Beautiful," was the largest theater in Harlem; it was also the first major playhouse there to desegregate: as early as 1912, African American theatergoers were allowed to sit in the orchestra. From 1915 to 1923, the Lafayette was home to an important theatrical troupe, the Lafayette Players. The theater became known as a "cradle of stars" (Anderson 1982, 236); among the many prominent actors, singers, and musicians who appeared on its stage were Charles Gilpin, Duke Ellington, Fletcher Henderson, Florence Mills, Bessie Smith, Mamie Smith, Ethel Waters, and Arthur "Dooley" Wilson. Because of the variety and the high artistic standards of its productions, the Lafayette was both a popular and a critical success. Its presentations were reviewed nationwide in black newspapers, and critics acknowledged its significance in the development of African American theater and acting during the Harlem Renaissance.

Like most other theaters of the time, the Lafayette was originally owned and managed by whites. This began to change in 1914, however, when Lester Walton, a black journalist, leased the Lafayette—which had been a vaudeville and movie theater—and took over the duties of comanager. Walton broadened the Lafayette's range of productions and in 1915 persuaded Anita Bush to transfer her theatrical company to the Lafayette from a rival theater, the Lincoln. Less than a year later, the Anita Bush Stock Company changed its name to the Lafayette Players Stock Company; the troupe soon became known simply as the Lafayette Players. Walton also pushed for a blacks-only employment policy at the Lafayette. Owing to disagreements within the management, Walton left the Lafayette Theater in 1916, but he continued to support it in his journalistic writing. Management rights of the theater and its stock company were sold to the Elite Amusement Corporation, a theatrical syndicate controlling African American playhouses; and then were sold to another syndicate, the Quality Amusement Corporation.

In 1919 the Lafayette became a completely African American enterprise, when two black Philadelphians—the bankers E. C. Brown and Andrew F. Stevens—bought controlling ownership of Quality Amusement. They also brought Lester Walton back to the management staff. Walton left the Lafayette again in 1923, when Frank Schiffman and Leo Brechler bought the theater in order to turn it into a vaudeville house.

The economic downturn of the Great Depression forced Schiffman and Brechler to close the Lafayette in 1934. During the New Deal era, however, it was revived as a legitimate theater for the Federal Theater Project (FTP) of the Works Progress Administration; from 1935 to 1939 it served as the headquarters of FTP's New York Negro Unit. During this period the Lafayette became famous as the theater where Orson Welles's production of a "voodoo" *Macbeth* (1936) was staged. This was an adaptation of Shakespeare's play set in Haiti in the 1820s and included elements of African American and Afro-Caribbean culture. In 1939 the Lafayette was turned into a movie theater; eventually, it was turned into a church. A black theater impresario, Robert Macbeth, revived the Lafayette's dramatic tradition in 1966, when he leased a wing of the building and founded the New Lafayette Theater.

The Lafayette Theater seated 2,000 patrons, and its audiences were almost exclusively African American. Productions offered there followed the typical stock repertoire schedule, with a bill that changed weekly and with daily matinee and evening performances on Monday through Saturday. On Fridays an additional midnight show lasted until four o'clock in the morning. Wallace Thurman vividly recalled the lively atmosphere of these shows, which usually attracted a noisy crowd, turning the auditorium itself into a stage.

The Lafayette offered a wide range of productions. The Lafayette Players regularly presented abridged versions of Broadway comedies and melodramas as well as classics, such as *Within the Law* (1915–1916), *Madame X* (1916–1917), and *Dr. Jekyll and Mr. Hyde* (1916–1917). In 1916 the Lafayette Theater participated in the tercentenary celebrations of Shakespeare's death with a production of *Othello*, and in 1923 the theater was host to productions of *The Comedy of Errors* and *The Taming of the Shrew* performed by the Ethiopian Players, a company based in Chicago. The Lafayette's fame, however, rested mainly on its productions of musical revues, such as Porter Grainger and Fredie Johnson's *Aces and Queens* (1925), and *Mississippi Days* (1928), starring Bessie Smith. Many of the shows presented at the Lafayette were simply replicas of recent Broadway hits. A popular success could also inspire new versions; Lew Leslie's *Plantation Revue* (1922), for instance, was immediately modified and revived as *Club Alabam* during the same season.

Although reviews of the productions at the Lafayette were generally favorable, progressive theater critics, writers, and intellectuals, such as Theophilus Lewis, Lester Walton, Wallace Thurman, and Harold Cruse, complained that the Lafayette was too "white" in the content and style of its presentations. In those days, however, legitimate drama that dealt seriously with black life and race relations was rare. Thus, not only criticism of its policies but also time was needed before the Lafayette began to produce works by African American playwrights, such as Andrew Bishop's *It Happened in Harlem* (1918) and Frank Wilson's *Pa Williams's Gal* (1923). Critics also objected to the Lafayette's practice of casting mostly light-skinned performers who might pass for white. There were no dark-complexioned chorus girls at the Lafayette, and dark-skinned actors occasionally whitened their faces for performances.

Although the Lafayette Theater never resolved the tension between the taste of its mass audience and the aesthetic or political demands of some of its critics, it did have a prominent place in the cultural life of Harlem during the 1910s and 1920s, and it was widely acclaimed by patrons and reviewers alike. As a completely black-operated house offering employment and theatrical training to a generation of African American actors, the Lafayette came to represent a "focal point of ethnic pride" (Vorder Brugge 1987, 254) for Harlem's black community.

ASTRID HAAS

See also Anita Bush Theater Company; Bush, Anita; Ethiopian Art Players; Lafayette Players; Lewis, Theophilus; Pa Williams's Gal; Thurman, Wallace; Walton, Lester; *specific performers*

Further Reading

Anderson, Jervis. *This Was Harlem: A Cultural Portrait, 1900–1950*, 2nd ed. New York: Farrar, Straus, and Giroux, 1982.

Harlem 1900–1940: An African American Community—An Exhibition Portfolio from the Schomburg Center for Research in Black Culture, New York Public Library. (Web site.) Kellner, Bruce, ed. *The Harlem Renaissance: A Historical Dictionary for the Era.* New York: Methuen; London: Routledge and Kegan Paul, 1987.

Kornweibel, Theodore, Jr. "Theophilius Lewis and the Theater of the Harlem Renaissance." In *The Harlem Renaissance Remembered*, ed. Arna Bontemps. New York: Dodd, Mead, 1972.

Mitchell, Loften. *Black Drama: The Story of the American Negro in the Theatre.* New York: Hawthorn, 1967.

Thompson, Sister M. Francesca, O.S.F. "The Lafayette Players, 1917–1932." In *The Theater of Black Americans*, Vol. 2, *The Presenters: Companies of Players; The Participators: Audience and Critics—A Collection of Critical Essays*, ed. Erroll Hill. Englewood Cliffs, N.J.: Prentice Hall, 1980.

Thurman, Wallace. *The Blacker the Berry.* New York: Macaulay, 1928.

Vorder Brugge, Andrew. "Lafayette Players." In *American Theatre Companies, 1888–1930*, ed. Weldon B. Durham. Westport, Conn.: Greenwood, 1987.

Larsen, Nella

Nella Larsen, one of the most important novelists of the Harlem Renaissance, is also the most mysterious. Published biographies have been rife with error, and accurate information is difficult to come by. Larsen's original name was Nellie Walker. She was born in Chicago in 1891 to a Danish immigrant whose maiden name was Mary Hansen and a "colored" cook from the Danish West Indies (later the U. S. Virgin Islands) whose name was Peter Walker. Within a year Walker died, or perhaps abandoned the family. Mary then married a white Dane, Peter Larsen, and gave birth to a second daughter, Anna Elizabeth. Throughout Nella's childhood, her working-class family suffered from intense animosity directed toward a white woman with a "mulatto" daughter, while racial tension escalated around them in the rapidly segregating near South side of Chicago.

Sometime between 1895 and 1897, Mary Larsen took her daughters to Denmark, possibly fleeing persecution. They returned in 1898, and the girls attended, briefly, a private school for German and Scandinavian children in the "white" neighborhood to which Peter Larsen had moved. Within months, the family moved back to a "mixed" race district, and Nella entered the public school system. She did well academically, but her neighborhood was rapidly turning into a racial battleground. In the fall of 1907, the family sent her to the normal school at Fisk University, in hopes that she could find a place in the black middle class. After her first year, however, she was told not to return. She next went to live in Denmark with relatives of her mother, but by 1912 Larsen returned to the United States and entered the Lincoln Hospital and Home Training School for Nurses in the Bronx, New York.

Larsen excelled at Lincoln and was then accepted for the position of head nurse at Tuskegee Institute's hospital in Alabama. She was quickly disillusioned, working fourteen hours a day under insulting conditions, and finding the philosophy of the school as well as its treatment of pupil nurses insupportable. At the end of a year, she resigned and returned to Lincoln Hospital. Then, in 1918, she took a position with the Bureau of Preventable Diseases in the Bronx, a group that was on the cutting edge of the new field of public health.

Soon Larsen met and married Dr. Elmer S. Imes, a graduate of Fisk University who had recently received a Ph.D. in physics from the University of Michigan and who shared Larsen's love of books and was well connected to the African American elite. Nella Larsen Imes, as she now signed her name, had finally achieved a foothold in the higher echelons of black society. In 1919 she published two articles on Danish children's games, riddles, and rhymes for *The Brownies' Book*, the first African American children's magazine. Larsen's love of reading and her new connections in black Harlem led her to take an interest in library work. In the fall of 1922, having resigned from her nursing position and having worked for several months in the library, she entered the library school of the New York Public Library, the first black woman to be admitted for formal training in the profession. After graduation, she worked for a year in the Children's Room of the Seward Park Library and then took over the children's division at the 135th Street branch library, the nerve center of the Harlem Renaissance.

As interest in African American subjects and writers grew, Larsen began writing fiction. In 1926 two of her stories—"Freedom," and "The Wrong Man"—appeared under the pen name Allen Semi in *Young's Magazine*, a "pulp" periodical aimed at working-class readers. Resigning from the library in 1926 to concentrate on writing, Larsen entered the interracial world of high bohemian intellectuals, growing particularly close to Carl Van Vechten, author of the controversial novel *Nigger Heaven*. At Van Vechten's urging, she submitted her first novel, *Quicksand*, to Alfred A. Knopf, who published it in 1928 under her maiden name. The next year, Larsen was awarded the Harmon Foundation's bronze medal for literary achievement among Negroes. Soon afterward, her second novel, *Passing*, was published by Knopf with considerable fanfare.

Larsen was now considered one of the most important black novelists of the day. In the January 1930 issue of the prestigious magazine *Forum*, she published the story "Sanctuary," about an old black woman in the American South who harbors a fugitive fleeing a white sheriff after killing the woman's own son. The story marked a significant departure from her earlier fiction, but readers quickly noticed detailed parallels between "Sanctuary" and the story "Mrs. Adis" by the British author Sheila Kaye-Smith. Confronted with accusations of plagiarism, Larsen claimed that she had based the story on one told years earlier by a patient in the nursing home at Lincoln Hospital. The editors accepted her explanation, but among some circles in Harlem her reputation was badly damaged.

At about this time Larsen won a Guggenheim Fellowship to write a novel concerning the effect on African Americans of differences in intellectual and physical freedom between America and Europe. From September 1930 until January 1932, Larsen lived in Majorca, Paris, and Málaga, working partly on this project but mostly on another, called "Mirage," that she described as her "white novel." The latter was rejected by her publisher; of the former, no record remains.

Elmer Imes started work as a professor of physics at Fisk University while Larsen was abroad. He was, she knew, in love with a popular white administrator at the school. Having put off any decision about how to respond, on her return to the United States in January 1932 Larsen took an apartment in New York and postponed joining Imes in Nashville; eventually she agreed to try living on campus. She found herself in an excruciating position, and her behavior grew erratic as she hung on to force the most favorable terms for a divorce, which finally came in August 1933.

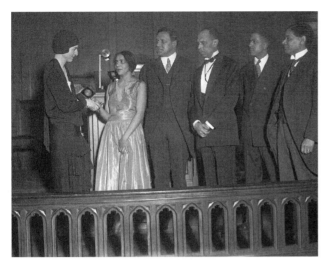

Winners of Harmon Award, at Zion Church. Left to right: Miss Harmon (daughter of the founder) congratulates the winners, Nella Larsen Imes; Channing H. Tobins; James Weldon Johnson; a proxy of Claude McKay; and Dr. George Haynes, secretary of a committee on race relations. (© Bettmann/Corbis, n.d.)

Larsen moved back to New York, took an apartment on Second Avenue near Stuyvesant Park, and maintained herself financially with her alimony, but the divorce was psychologically devastating. Other romantic disappointments ensued as she sank into alcoholism and depression. Between 1934 and 1937, still failing to place any of her fiction and fearing abandonment by friends, she gradually withdrew into herself. From 1938 to 1944, she practically disappeared, cutting off her friends, moving to a new apartment, and falling into a spiral of addiction.

Elmer Imes's death of cancer in 1941 eventually forced Larsen to earn a living. From 1944 until 1961, she worked as a staff nurse and then nurse supervisor at Gouverneur Hospital on the lower east side, and from 1961 to 1963 she worked at Metropolitan Hospital, serving east Harlem. Highly respected on the job, she quickly leapfrogged over her colleagues into higher-paid supervisory positions; but she was not entirely free of alcohol and drugs. She was forced to retire in June 1963 when the hospital realized that she had passed her seventieth birthday. (She was actually seventy-two.) She died of a heart attack in her apartment eight months later. For several days, no one missed her; finally the police answered a call from the building supervisor and found her body. The first person they contacted to claim it—probably a relative of Imes's—refused. One of Larsen's friends, the nurse Alice Carper, saw to the funeral arrangements and buried Larsen in her own family plot, with more than fifty nursing colleagues present. Larsen's sister Anna

inherited her estate, exclaiming with surprise when informed of the death, "Why, I didn't know I had a sister"—which, of course, was a lie. Larsen is buried in Cypress Hills Cemetery off the Triborough Expressway in New York, under the name Nella Imes.

Biography

Nella Larsen (née Nellie Walker) was born in Chicago on 13 April 1891. In 1892 her father, Peter Walker, died; her mother remarried a white Dane, Peter Larsen, and gave birth to Nella Larsen's half sister, Anna Elizabeth. From about 1895 to 1898 Nella Larsen lived in Denmark with her mother and half sister; from 1898 to 1907 she lived with her family on the near South side of Chicago. In 1907–1908 she studied at Fisk University's Normal School. In 1908–1909 she again lived in Denmark. In 1912–1915 she attended Lincoln Hospital and Home Training School for Nurses in the Bronx, New York. In 1915–1916 she was head nurse at the John A. Andrew Memorial Hospital, Tuskegee Institute; in 1916–1918 she was assistant superintendent of nurses and an instructor at Lincoln Hospital and Home; in 1918–1921 she was a public health nurse at the Bureau of Preventable Diseases in New York. She married Elmer S. Imes, a research physicist, on 3 May 1919. Her "Three Scandinavian Games" and "Danish Fun" were published in the *Brownies' Book* in June–July 1919. In 1922–1926 she attended the Library School of the New York Public Library and worked as a children's librarian at the Seward Park and Harlem branches. (Larsen was the first black woman to graduate from a library school.) "The Wrong Man" and "Freedom" were published in *Young's Realistic Stories Magazine* in January and April 1926, under the pen name Allen Semi. In 1928 *Quicksand* was published. In 1929 Larsen won the Harmon Foundation Bronze medal for Literary Achievement among Negroes; also in 1929 *Passing* was published. During 1930–1932 "Sanctuary" was published in *Forum* (January 1930); Larsen was accused of plagiarism; she won a Guggenheim Fellowship; she lived in Majorca, Paris, and Málaga; and she wrote a novel called *Mirage* (unpublished). During 1932–1933 she moved to Fisk University. She divorced Elmer Imes on 30 August 1933 and returned to New York. In 1938, suffering from alcoholism, depression, and possibly drug addiction, she cut off all friendships, moved to a new apartment, and "disappeared." In 1944 she began working as a staff nurse at Gouverneur Hospital; she was quickly promoted to supervisor of nurses for the night shift. In 1961 Gouverneur Hospital closed; Larsen transferred to Metropolitan Hospital as night supervisor in the psychiatric ward. In March of 1964 Larsen died alone in her apartment. Larson was rediscovered in the twenty-first century, and her novels were reissued.

GEORGE HUTCHINSON

See also Brownies' Book, The; Harmon Foundation; Knopf, Alfred A.; 135th Street Library; Passing: Novel; Quicksand; Van Vechten, Carl

Selected Works

"Three Scandinavian Games." *The Brownies' Book*, June 1919.
"Danish Fun." *The Brownies' Book*, July 1919.
"The Wrong Man." *Young's Realistic Stories Magazine*, January 1926. (Published under the name Allen Semi.)
"Freedom." *Young's Realistic Stories Magazine*, April 1926. (Published under the name Allen Semi.)
Quicksand. New York: Knopf, 1928. New edition: 2002.
Passing. New York: Knopf, 1929. New edition: 2003.
"Sanctuary." *Forum*, January 1930.

Further Reading

Davis, Thadious M. *Nella Larsen, Novelist of the Harlem Renaissance*. Baton Rouge: Louisiana State University Press, 1994.
Hutchinson, George. "Nella Larsen and the Veil of Race." *American Literary History*, Summer 1997, pp. 329–349.
Larson, Charles R. *Invisible Darkness: Jean Toomer and Nella Larsen*. Iowa City: University of Iowa Press, 1993.

Lawrence, Jacob

Jacob Lawrence is arguably one of the most important American artists of the twentieth century. Although he was not active during the Harlem Renaissance, his work directly reflects the importance of Harlem both as a place and as an artistic community.

Lawrence was born in 1917 in Atlantic City, New Jersey, the eldest child of Jacob and Rosa Lee Lawrence. His father worked as a railroad cook but in 1919 moved the family to Easton, Pennsylvania, in order to seek work as a coal miner. Lawrence's parents separated when he was seven, and in 1924 his mother moved the children to Philadelphia, where, because of the types of jobs she held—primarily live-in domestic work—they spent time in and out of foster homes. They moved to Harlem when Lawrence was twelve years old. In Harlem, he spent many hours listening to relatives and neighbors describe their lives in the South and their journey northward, themes that would later appear in his art.

Shortly after his arrival in Harlem—because his mother wanted to keep him out of trouble—Lawrence enrolled at the Utopia Children's Center, a settlement house that provided an after-school program in arts and crafts. The center was operated by the painter Charles Alston, who recognized Lawrence's talent and encouraged him. After graduating from grade school, Lawrence attended the High School of Commerce and continued to paint on his own. As the Great Depression deepened, his mother lost her job, the family had to go on relief, and Lawrence dropped out of high school before his junior year to help by working at odd jobs. In 1936 he joined the Civilian Conservation Corps (CCC) and was sent to upstate New York, where he planted trees and built dams. When he returned to Harlem, he became actively involved with another New Deal program, the Harlem Community Art Center, directed by the sculptor Augusta Savage. There he began painting his earliest scenes of Harlem. As a teenager, Lawrence hung out at the Harlem branch of the YMCA, where he became friendly with "Professor" Seifert, a self-taught expert on African and African American culture. Lawrence was profoundly influenced by Seifert, who, he explained, "wanted to get black artists interested in art . . . to select as our content black history." Seifert encouraged Lawrence to visit the public library as well as local museums to learn more about the African and African American past. Seifert also gave Lawrence access to his personal collection.

As the Depression continued, hard times persisted for Lawrence and his family. Yet he maintained that, in Harlem, the Depression "was actually a wonderful period. . . . There was a real vitality in the community." In part this vitality was due to the Works Progress Administration (WPA), which established jobs for blacks in a variety of fields. Most significant for Lawrence were the WPA's art projects, in particular the Federal Arts Project (FPA). With the help of Augusta Savage, Lawrence was assigned to the FPA's easel project. The FPA paid artists, black and white, a living wage—$23.60 a week—and, according to Lawrence, that was a lot of money at the time.

While working with the FPA, Lawrence became interested in the life of the black revolutionary Toussaint-Louverture, founder of the republic of Haiti. Lawrence felt that no single painting could capture Toussaint's numerous achievements and that he would therefore need to paint the entire story. Series of paintings would become one of Lawrence's signature traits. A year after completing the Toussaint-Louverture series, Lawrence began work on a forty-panel series depicting the life of the abolitionist Frederick Douglass; in 1939 he did a thirty-painting series, *The Life of Harriet Tubman*; and in 1940–1941 he painted the famous *Migration Series*, with a grant (his first of three) from the Rosenwald Foundation. All these series reflected his strong interest in African American history.

With regard to the *Migration Series*, Lawrence said:

By the time I was in Harlem, I decided to paint this series—I wasn't thinking of sales or of a gallery. I liked storytelling. I went to the Schomburg Library and selected events from the North and the South. I think that the series alternates from South to North. I just got into it. I didn't separate it—I wasn't looking at it from the inside out or the outside in. This was such a part of my life. . . . I was doing research at the time. I guess it was both emotional and intellectual. . . . We are absolutely a people telling stories. It seems like we were born talking and telling people about it. The series came out of that—people talking about people coming up from the South. This tradition continues. . . . Another family arrives.

When Lawrence created a series, he would work on all the panels at once, one color at a time, going from dark to light. A striking characteristic of his work is his use of bright colors, a trait that he attributed to his experience of living in Harlem:

We lived in a deep depression. Not only my mother, but the poor people in general. In order to add something to their lives, they decorated their tenements and their homes in all of these colors. I've been asked, Is anybody in my family artistically inclined? I've always felt ashamed of my response and I always said no, not realizing that my artistic sensibility came from this ambience. I did have this influence, but I didn't realize it was taking place. It's only in retrospect that I realized that I was surrounded by art. You'd walk Seventh Avenue and look in the windows and you'd see all these colors in the depth of the depression. All these colors. You'd walk though

Harlem and go to the Apollo theater, and the jokes that were being told! The pathos! People would laugh, but it was a comedy on a very profound, deep, philosophical level. But you can only see this, you can only realize this., in retrospect.

Essentially, then, Lawrence's sense of color was communal, coming directly from the streets of Harlem.

In general, Lawrence's pictures tell a story not only visually but also verbally. The *Migration Series*, for instance, has a caption for each image, such as the following text for the sixth panel: "The trains were packed continually with migrants." In this regard, it is worth noting that for Lawrence the railroad was an important symbol of the great migration:

I didn't realize that there were so many symbols of railroad stations, bus stations, people travelling! But that's what migration is. You think in terms of people on the move, people moving from one situation to another. Crossroads, bus stations, and train stations— moments of transition—it certainly was a moment of transition in the history of America and for the race. It's one of the big movements in our country. And I want to say this, too: I don't think the blacks in making a movement just contributed to their own development. It contributed to American development. Look at your structure of the cities—the passion, the energy, the vitality. Not always positive— some of it quite negative—but it's there and I think we have added to, and not taken from, our growth. When I say our, I'm using that in a larger context. And I think that we have made a contribution in making this move. Many people tried to keep us out. You had your riots. But we made a tremendous contribution to the American growth, to the American development of America.

The *Migration Series* met with immediate acclaim and with praise from critics, and it secured Lawrence's reputation. Shortly after it was completed, Alain Locke brought Lawrence to the attention of Edith Halbert, the head of the respected Downtown Gallery. She in turn exhibited the entire series and arranged for *Fortune* magazine to run a story on Lawrence and to reproduce twenty-six of the paintings. Half of the sixty panels in the series were sold to the Museum of Modern Art in New York and the other half to the Phillips Collection in Washington, D.C.

Lawrence followed the *Migration Series* with *The Life of John Brown* (twenty-two panels), *Harlem* (thirty-two

Jacob Lawrence. (Library of Congress.)

panels), *War* (fourteen panels), *The South* (ten panels), *Hospital* (eleven panels), and *History of the American People* (thirty panels). *Hospital* was painted during and after his own nine-month stay at Hillside Psychiatric Hospital, where he had gone voluntarily for treatment, citing the stresses of fame. Lawrence also completed a number of individual paintings and drawings inspired by African American history and by his own life experiences.

As his fame grew, Lawrence was in demand as a teacher. He taught at the Black Mountain School in North Carolina; the Pratt Institute and the New School for Social Research in New York; the Five Towns Music and Art Foundation in Cedarhurst, Long Island; and elsewhere. In 1970, he became a full professor at the University of Washington in Seattle, where he lived until his death in 2000.

Lawrence's work has been represented in numerous individual and group shows, and he received many awards, commendations, and honorary doctorates. His lifework may perhaps be summed up in his own assertion that "the Negro experience is the American experience."

Biography

Jacob Armstead Lawrence was born in Atlantic City, New Jersey, on 7 September 1917 and moved at the age of twelve to Harlem, where he attended public schools. He won a scholarship to the American Artists School (organized by the John Reed Club, a communist group) at 131 West Fourteenth Street in 1937. He worked for six months in the Civilian Conservation

Corps (CCC) near Middletown, New York, in 1936 and made drawings of life in the CCC. He married Gwendolyn Knight in 1941. Also in 1941, *Fortune* published a color portfolio of twenty-six panels of his series *The Migration of the Negro*, with text; and the Downtown Gallery showed the series in its main gallery. Lawrence served in the armed forces during World War II, at one point on the USS *Sea Cloud*, a weather patrol boat that was the navy's first racially integrated ship. In 1949 he voluntarily entered Hillside Hospital in Queens, New York, for treatment of depression; the *New York Times Magazine* had an article on this episode: "An Artist Reports on the Troubled Mind," and an exhibition of his hospital paintings opened at the Downtown Gallery in October 1950. In 1951 he received an award from the Committee for the Negro in the Arts. Lawrence taught at Black Mountain College in Asheville, North Carolina (summer session, 1946); at Five Towns Music and Art Foundation in Cedarhurst, Long Island (1955–1962, 1966–1968); at the Pratt Institute in New York (1958–1970); at the New School for Social Research in New York (1966–1969); at the Art Students League in New York (1967–1969); at the Skowhegan School of Painting and Sculpture in Maine (summer 1968); and at the University of Washington, as a full professor (beginning in 1970). He served as president of the New York chapter of the National Institute of Arts and Letters (1957); as president of the artists' committee of the Student Non-Violent Coordinating Committee (SNCC, 1963); as a member of the advisory board for the founding of the Museum of African Art in Washington, D.C.; as a member of the coordinating committee for an exhibition of contemporary African art sponsored by the American Society of African Culture (AMSAC); and as a member of the National Screening Committee for the Fulbright-Hays scholarship program (1965–1967). Lawrence exhibited in Nigeria in 1964. He was an artist in residence at Brandeis University in Waltham, Massachusetts, in February–May 1965; a visiting artist at California State College in Hayward (September 1969–March 1970); and a visiting artist at the University of Washington in Seattle (March–June 1970). Lawrence was appointed commissioner of the National Council of Arts by President Jimmy Carter in 1979; was elected to the American Academy of Arts and Letters in 1983; and was inducted into the American Academy of Arts and Sciences in 1995. He received the Artist Award from the College Art Association, the NAACP Third Annual Great Black Artists Award, and the Images Award for Outstanding Achievement in Art from the

University of Pittsburgh (1988); the National Medal of Arts from President George H. W. Bush (1990); the Medal of Honor from the National Arts Club, New York (1993); the Charles White Lifetime Achievement Award in Los Angeles and the Edwin T. Pratt Award from the Urban League of Metropolitan Seattle (1994); an award from the American Civil Liberties Union and the Washington State Medal of Merit (1998); a Lifetime Achievement Award from the Americans for the Arts and Seattle's Golden Umbrella Award and Mayor's Master Artist Award (1999); and numerous honorary doctorates. He established the Jacob and Gwendolyn Lawrence Foundation to promote the creation, exhibition, and study of American art (1999). Lawrence died in Seattle on 9 June 2000, at age eighty-two.

JOAN SAAB

See also Alston, Charles; Artists; Federal Programs; Great Migration; Locke, Alain; Savage, Augusta; Second Harlem Renaissance; Works Progress Administration

Selected Solo Exhibitions

1936: In studio of Addison Bates, a cabinetmaker.

1938: Harlem YMCA, exhibition sponsored by James Weldon Johnson Literary Guild.

1942: "The Migration of the Negro." Museum of Modern Art, New York (even-numbered panels); Phillips Memorial Gallery; Washington, D.C. (odd-numbered panels).

1943: Harlem paintings. Downtown Gallery; New York.

1944: "Paintings by Jacob Lawrence: Migration of the Negro and Works Made in U.S. Coast Guard." Museum of Modern Art, New York.

1953: "Performance: A Series of New Paintings in Tempera by Jacob Lawrence." Downtown Gallery, New York.

1960: Retrospective. Brooklyn Museum, New York. (National tour.)

1962: Exhibition in Lagos and Ibadan, Nigeria. Organized by AMSAC and the Mbari Artists' and Writers' Club Cultural Center.

1963: Paintings pertaining to the civil rights movement. Terry Dintenfass, New York.

1964: Brandeis University. (Traveled to Morgan State College.)

1968: "The Life of Toussaint L'Ouverture." (Fisk University.)

1976: "Graphics by Jacob Lawrence." Francine Seders Gallery, Seattle.

1977: "The Life of John Brown." Detroit Institute of Arts.

1977: "Jacob Lawrence: Paintings and Graphics from 1936 to 1978." Chrysler Museum of Art; Norfolk, Virginia.

1982: "Jacob Lawrence: The Builder." Mississippi Museum of Art, Jackson.

1984: "Jacob Lawrence: Fifty Years of His Work." Jamaica Arts Center; New York.

1985: Colored-pencil drawings. Francine Seders Gallery, Seattle.

1989: "Jacob Lawrence: Paintings and Drawings"; "Jacob Lawrence: Drawings and Prints." (Tour, Caribbean and Africa, sponsored by United States Information Agency.)

1989: "Jacob Lawrence: The Washington Years." Tacoma (Washington) Art Museum.

1989: "Jacob Lawrence: A Continuing Presence." Syracuse (New York) University.

1992: Whatcom Museum of History and Art, Bellingham, Washington.

1992: "Jacob Lawrence: An American Master." East Carolina University, Greenville.

1992: "Jacob Lawrence: The Early Decades, 1935–1950." Katonah (New York) Museum of Art.

1993: "Jacob Lawrence: An Exhibition Presented by the Black Alumni of Pratt Institute." Pratt Institute, Brooklyn, New York.

1993: "Jacob Lawrence: Paintings, Drawings, and Prints." Midtown Payson Galleries, New York.

1994: "Jacob Lawrence: Works on Paper." University of Pennsylvania, Philadelphia.

1994: "Jacob Lawrence: Prints and Drawings." Shasta College, Redding, California.

1997: "Jacob Lawrence: An American Vision—Paintings and Prints 1942–1996." Museum of Northwest Art, La Conner, Washington.

1998: Savannah (Georgia) College of Art and Design.

1998: "Jacob Lawrence as Muralist." Francine Seders Gallery, Seattle, Washington.

2000: "Games." Francine Seders Gallery, Seattle, Washington.

Further Reading

Bearden, Romare, and Harry Henderson. *A History of African-American Artists from 1792 to the Present.* New York: Pantheon, 1993.

Driskell, David, et al. *Harlem Renaissance Art of Black America.* New York: Studio Museum in Harlem, 1987.

Patton, Sharon. *African American Art.* New York and London: Oxford University Press, 1998.

Powell, Richard. *Rhapsodies in Black: Art of the Harlem Renaissance*. Berkeley: University of California Press, 1997.

Wheat, Ellen Harkens. *Jacob Lawrence, American Painter*. Seattle: University of Washington Press, 1986.

Lee, Canada

Canada Lee (Leonard Lionel Cornelius Canegate) was an actor on Broadway and in films who played classical roles and, as his career continued, roles that portrayed blacks in a less stereotypical way than was usual in the 1920s and 1930s. He was a violinist and a jockey during his youth; he changed his name to Canada Lee when he became a prizefighter as a young man. After World War II, black characters in films and onstage became more multidimensional, and Lee took advantage of the opportunity to perform in a variety of roles.

Lee's role as Bigger Thomas in the stage version of Richard Wright's *Native Son* (1940 and 1941) is memorable. His portrayal of Joe in Alfred Hitchcock's movie *Lifeboat* (1944) is one of his best performances. Also noteworthy is his performance as Stephen Kumalo in the movie version of Alan Paton's *Cry, the Beloved Country* (1952). Sidney Poitier costarred in that movie, his first.

In the early 1930s, Canada Lee acted onstage in Orson Welles's *Voodoo Macbeth* (1936), and in many productions of the Works Projects Administration's Federal Theater Project, which helped black actors hone their skills as they worked with talented directors and attended workshops. Lee also appeared in *The Tempest* (1945), and he put on whiteface makeup as a character in *The Duchess of Malfi* (1946).

In the 1940s, Lee's connections with progressive causes, including his efforts to change racial images onstage and in films, became a liability. He participated in rallies, took petitions to Congress, was seen with controversial people, and allied himself with the National Association for the Advancement of Colored People (NAACP) and Walter White. During these years he also decided to become a producer in order to avoid menial roles. *On Whitman Avenue* (1946), a work he produced with Mark Marvin, attracted the attention of the House Un-American Activities Committee (HUAC) in 1947 because of its portrayal of liberal groups. Because Lee would not appear before HUAC, his name was never officially cleared, despite his public statements denying that he had communist affiliations. He was harassed by HUAC and the Federal Bureau of Investigation; was blacklisted from films, radio, and television; and became destitute. *Cry, the Beloved Country* (1952) was his last film.

Lee is seldom mentioned today, partly because he was a casualty of the communist scare; however, his pioneering work as a classical actor, his portrayal of nonstereotypical blacks onscreen, and his credits as a director helped to broaden job opportunities for blacks in Hollywood. He opened doors of opportunity for blacks to perform in a wider range of dramatic roles. For example, his son, Carl Lee, also became an actor and performed in *The Connection* (1962), *Super Fly* (1972), and *Gordon's War* (1973). The younger Lee also cowrote *The Cool World* (1964) with Shirley Clarke.

Biography

Canada Lee (Leonard Lionel Cornelius Canegate) was born 3 March 1907 in New York City. He had public schooling in Harlem and was a violinist and a jockey as a young adult. He changed his name to Canada Lee when he became a boxer; an eye injury ended his boxing career in 1933. His stage credits include *Voodoo Macbeth* (1936), *Native Son* (1940 and 1941), and *The Tempest* (1945). His movies include *Lifeboat* (1944), *Body and Soul* (1947), and *Cry, the Beloved Country* (1952). Lee was falsely labeled a communist in the 1940s and was blacklisted from films, radio, and television. He died 10 May 1952.

LOU-ANN CROUTHER

See also Federal Programs; Second Harlem Renaissance; White, Walter; Works Progress Administration; Wright, Richard

Selected Work: Stage

Voodoo Macbeth. 1936.
One-Act Plays of the Sea. 1937.
Haiti. 1938.
Mamba's Daughters. 1939.
Big White Fog. 1940.
Native Son. 1940, 1941.
The Tempest. 1945.
The Duchess of Malfi. 1946.
On Whitman Avenue. 1946.
Set My People Free. 1948.

Selected Work: Films

Keep Punching. 1939.
Farmer Henry Browne. 1942.
Lifeboat. 1944.
Body and Soul. 1947.
Lost Boundaries. 1949.
Cry, the Beloved Country. 1952.

Further Reading

Bogle, Donald. *Toms, Coons, Mulattoes, Mammies, and Bucks: An Interpretive History of Blacks in American Films*. New York: Continuum, 1973. (See also 3rd ed., 1994.)

———. *Blacks in American Films and Television: An Encyclopedia*. New York: Garland, 1988.

Cripps, Thomas. *Making Movies Black: The Hollywood Message Movie from World War II to the Civil Rights Era*. New York: Oxford University Press, 1993.

Gill, Glenda E. "Canada Lee: Black Actor in Non-Traditional Roles." *Journal of Popular Culture*, 25(3), 1991.

Leab, Daniel. *From Sambo to Superspade: The Black Experience in Motion Pictures*. Boston, Mass.: Houghton Mifflin, 1975.

Mapp, Edward. *Blacks in American Films: Today and Yesterday*. Metuchen, N.J.: Scarecrow, 1972.

Null, Gary. *Black Hollywood: The Negro in Motion Pictures*. Secaucus, N.J.: Citadel, 1975.

Patterson, Lindsay, ed. *Black Films and Film-Makers: A Comprehensive Anthology from Stereotype to Superhero*. New York: Dodd, Mead, 1975.

Sampson, Henry T. *Blacks in Black and White: A Source Book on Black Films*. Metuchen, N.J.: Scarecrow, 1977. (See also 2nd ed., 1995.)

Lee, George

George W. Lee's literary work serves as a southern "countervoice" to the Harlem Renaissance. Lee is best-known for his hagiography of Beale Street in Memphis, Tennessee; he also is credited as the author of a realistic anti-sharecropping novel that offered rural black southerners a voice. His work has a strongly pro-business bent that constitutes a critique but also an extension of the artistic and philosophical concerns of the Harlem Renaissance.

Lee was born in Mississippi in 1894 and spent several years of his childhood as a sharecropper. He attended high school and college at Alcorn Agricultural and Mechanical College, graduating in 1917. He enlisted in the U.S. Army and fought in World War I as a second lieutenant. In Memphis, he had a productive career in insurance, eventually serving as vice president for two of the nation's most successful black-owned insurance companies. Lee became an important force in state and national Republican politics, placing African Americans in political and municipal positions, corresponding with three presidents, and serving as a delegate to several national conventions. In the early 1960s the party's white members unseated Lee and other African Americans from positions of leadership. However, he continued to be politically active, speaking nationwide on issues of education and desegregation through the Improved Benevolent and Protective Order of Elks of the World. Lee died in an automobile accident in Memphis in 1976.

James Weldon Johnson encouraged Lee to finish his first work, *Beale Street: Where the Blues Began* (1934), an account of the colorful figures in a legendary area in Memphis. It became a commercial and critical success and was a selection of the Book of the Month Club. By choosing Beale Street as his subject, Lee established Memphis and the South as a setting for African American contributions to artistic and economic enterprises. His catalog of Beale Street's businessmen and companies emphasizes his belief in the centrality of economics to racial uplift.

Lee's *River George* (1937) traces the downfall of Aaron George, the son of a sharecropper who hoped that his college education could help him free his race from economic and social bondage. According to Lee, he wrote this book to prove himself to the literati of the Harlem Renaissance, who had attributed the success of his first work simply to its subject, not to the talents of its author. *River George* follows George (a character from *Beale Street: Where the Blues Began*) from the Mississippi delta to Memphis and New York City—a gesture toward the "great migration" of African Americans from the farm to the city and from the South to the North. Lee questions the usefulness and productivity of the Harlem Renaissance, favoring instead talented African Americans across the nation, coupled (troublingly) with white paternalism. The novel searches for effective ways to protest against white racist society but admits defeat, symbolized by the lynching that ends it. The reaction of the critics of the day to *River George* was disappointing.

Lee's last work, *Beale Street Sundown* (1942), is a collection of short stories, some of which had originally appeared in *Negro Digest*, *World's Digest*, and *Southern Literary Messenger*. Like *Beale Street: Where the Blues Began*, it focuses on the people of Beale Street.

Biography

George Lee was born 4 January 1894 near Indianola, Mississippi. He attended public school in Indianola and completed high school and college coursework at Alcorn Agricultural and Mechanical College, Lorman, Mississippi (1917). He worked as a bellhop during summers at Gayoso Hotel in Memphis, Tennessee (1910–1917). He was a second lieutenant in the U.S. Army, Ninety-Second Division, 268th Regiment, Company C (1917–1919). He was an insurance salesman at Mississippi Life in Memphis (1919), then a manager, then a vice president (1920–1924); later he was a manager (1924–1939) and a vice president (1939–1976) at Atlanta Life in Memphis. Lee was a member of the Improved Benevolent and Protective Order of Elks of the World (1926–1976) and was Elks' Best Orator (1926). He was national director, Veterans for Hoover (1928); was on the Tennessee Republican Executive Committee (1942–1962); and was grand commissioner of education in the Elks (1951–1976). Lee was named one of ten "Most Useful Men" by the *Chicago Defender* in 1951, for his voter registration efforts in Memphis. He was the first African American for whom a post office was named (in Memphis, 1956). He received a Certificate of Honor from the Lincoln League of Memphis in 1962. He was appointed colonel aide-de-camp, Gov. Buford Ellington (1967) and Gov. Winfield Dunn (1973); and he was honorary sergeant-at-arms, Tennessee House of Representatives (1973). His portrait was hung in the Tennessee state capitol in 1973. Also in 1973, he received the American Legion Post 27 R.Q. Venson Appreciation Award. Lee died in Memphis on 1 August 1976.

SCOTT HICKS

See also Johnson, James Weldon

Selected Works

Beale Street: Where the Blues Began. 1934.
River George. 1937, 1975.
Beale Street: Sundown. 1942.

Further Reading

Brown, Sterling A. "The American Race Problem as Reflected in American Literature." *Journal of Negro Education*, 8(3), 1939.

Clark, Edward D. "George Washington Lee." In *Dictionary of Literary Biography*, Vol. 51, *Afro-American Writers from the Harlem Renaissance to 1940*, ed. Trudier Harris. Detroit, Mich.: Gale Research, 1987.

Clark, Mary B., processor. "George W. Lee Collection." Housed in Memphis and Shelby County Room, Memphis-Shelby County Public Library and Information Center, 1986.

Gloster, Hugh M. *Negro Voices in American Fiction*. Chapel Hill: University of North Carolina Press, 1948.

Houston, Helen R. "Lee, George Washington." In *The Oxford Companion to African American Literature*, ed. William L. Andrews, Frances Smith Foster, and Trudier Harris. New York: Oxford University Press, 1997.

Tucker, David M. *Lieutenant Lee of Beale Street*. Nashville, Tenn.: Vanderbilt University Press, 1971.

——— *Memphis since Crump: Bossism, Blacks, and Civic Reformers, 1948–1968*. Knoxville: University of Tennessee Press, 1980.

Leslie, Lew

Lew Leslie was white, a fact many people have been surprised to discover, so closely was he associated with black entertainment during the Harlem Renaissance era. After an undistinguished early career in vaudeville Leslie gravitated to promotion, organizing revues for Broadway. An early protégée of his was the vaudeville star Belle Baker. He coached and partnered her, then married her in 1909. Though they were divorced by 1919, they remained close friends ever afterward.

The first sign of Leslie's interest in black entertainment came in 1921, when he presented the white actress Tess Gardella in blackface as Aunt Jemima in George White's *Scandals*. However, the definitive moment of his life came when he saw Florence Mills in *Shuffle Along*; from then on, Leslie was driven by a consuming vision—to glorify the black American showgirl as Ziegfeld had glorified white showgirls. From 1922 to 1927, Leslie starred Florence Mills in a succession of elaborate, fast-paced revues (*Plantation Revue*, *Dover Street to Dixie*, *Dixie to Broadway*) that made her the toast of Broadway and ultimately a superstar in London and Paris. Later versions of his revues were called the *Blackbirds* series, after her theme song, "I'm a Little Blackbird Looking for a Bluebird."

When Mills died tragically in 1927, Leslie continued his *Blackbirds* series. *Blackbirds of 1928* was the most successful, bringing international fame to the dancer Bill "Bojangles" Robinson and the singer Adelaide Hall. During the Great Depression—which also undermined the Harlem Renaissance—later versions of *Blackbirds* (1930–1936) had only mixed success at home and overseas. However, these shows helped the careers of many black performers such as the Nicholas Brothers, Eubie Blake, and Valaida Snow and gave them international exposure; the shows also included notable hit songs such as Blake's "Memories of You." The last of the series, *Blackbirds of 1939*, was a flop but gave valuable exposure to a young Lena Horne.

Whitebirds (1927), as its name implies, had a white cast; it was an attempt to cash in on the success of *Blackbirds* in London, but it was a financial disaster. Apart from the *Blackbirds* shows, Leslie mounted two notable productions during the 1930s: the ambitious all-white *International Revue* (1930), which was panned as a pretentious attempt to use an ill-assorted set of international stars; and *Rhapsody in Black* (1931), starring Ethel Waters and Valaida Snow, which was praised for abandoning stereotypes of blacks.

Leslie was a paradoxical figure. He created huge employment opportunities for black performers, but leaders of the Harlem Renaissance such as Theophilus Lewis and W. E. B. Du Bois objected to his use of stereotyped material. Despite his faith in black performers, he entrusted most of the music and writing to whites. An amiable, generous man in private, he was ruthless in business, saving money by playing stars off against each other. Though he was solicitous for the welfare of his performers, he was a perfectionist who drove them relentlessly in rehearsal.

After 1939 Leslie's career as a producer languished, and he worked as a talent scout for a theatrical agency. When he died in 1963, many of the black stars he had worked with attended his funeral to express their respect and affection. Despite the justified accusations of stereotyping, he influenced the style of black shows for a generation, abandoning the libretto-based approach for a modernized, fast presentation that allowed the performers to strut their stuff. By featuring a female superstar, Florence Mills, he also broke with

the convention that black shows were usually built around two male comedians.

Biography

Lew Leslie (Lev Lessinsky) was born 15 January 1890 in New York City. His theatrical productions included *Plantation Revue* (Plantation Club, New York, 1922–1924, various editions); *Dover Street to Dixie* (Pavilion Theater, London, 1923); *Dixie to Broadway* (Broadhurst Theater, New York, 1924); *Blackbirds of 1926* and *Blackbirds of 1927* (Pavilion Theater, London); *Whitebirds* (Majestic Theater, London, 1927); *Blackbirds of 1928* (Liberty Theater, New York); *Lew Leslie's Blackbirds* (Royale Theater, New York, 1930); *International Revue* (Majestic Theater, New York, 1930); *Rhapsody in Black* (Sam H. Harris Theater, New York, 1931); *Blackbirds of 1933* (Apollo Theater, New York); *Blackbirds of 1934* (Coliseum Theater, London); *Blackbirds of 1936* (Gaiety Theater, London); *Lew Leslie's Blackbirds of 1939* (Hudson Theater, New York). There were also some *Blackbirds* shows in Europe, mainly in Paris. Leslie was the inaugural producer of the floor show at the Cotton Club in Harlem (1923). He died in Orangeburg, New York, 10 March 1963.

BILL EGAN

See also Blackbirds; Blake, Eubie; Cotton Club; Hall, Adelaide; Lewis, Theophilus; Mills, Florence; Musical Theater; Robinson, Bill "Bojangles"; Shuffle Along; Ward, Aida; Waters, Ethel

Further Reading

Bordman, Gerald. *American Musical Theatre: A Chronicle.* New York, Oxford University Press, 1978.
"Lew Leslie." *New York Times*, 13 March 1963. (Obituary.)
Moore, James Ross. "Lew Leslie." In *The American National Biography*, Vol. 15, ed. John A. Garraty and Mark C. Carnes. New York: Oxford University Press, 1999.
Reed, Bill. *Hot from Harlem: Profiles in Classic African-American Entertainment.* Los Angeles, Calif.: Cellar Door, 1998. (See ch. 4, "Valaida Snow.")
Stearns, Marshall, and Jean Stearns. *Jazz Dancing: The Story of American Vernacular Dance.* New York: Macmillan, 1968.
Woll, Allen. *Dictionary of the Black Theatre: Broadway, Off-Broadway, and Selected Harlem Theatre.* Westport, Conn.: Greenwood, 1983.

———. *Black Musical Theatre: From Coontown to Dreamgirls*. New York: Da Capo Press, 1991. (See especially ch. 7.)

Lewis, Sinclair

During the 1920s no American writer was more successful than Sinclair Lewis, and in 1930 he became the first American to receive the Nobel Prize for literature. His prestige and his frequent residence in New York City would qualify him as being of some note in a study of the Harlem Renaissance. Lewis also had some direct connection with the renaissance, primarily through his friendship with Walter White. However, it is appropriate to point out that his biographer Mark Schorer (1961) does not mention any connection with the Harlem Renaissance whatsoever but merely has an index entry, "Negroes, HSL's [Lewis's] interest in"—seemingly, this interest was first awakened in 1940 with his initial research for his novel *Kingsblood Royal* (1947).

During the Harlem Renaissance, Lewis was widely considered the foremost critic of American hypocrisy, yet his renowned novels of the decade largely ignore racial issues. Regarding Lewis's first seven books, Charles Cooney (1975) observes that "the few Negro characters who meander through Lewis's novels range from innocuous to mildly derogatory." Yet Lewis's satirical style and overt social concerns did have an impact on many writers of the Harlem Renaissance.

Lewis left his childhood home in Minnesota to attend Yale University and after graduation embarked on a career as a writer. He traveled and managed to support himself as a journalist and a writer of short stories and novels until 1920, when his book *Main Street* made him one of the most recognized literary figures in America. *Main Street* is about the romantic Carole Kennicott and her discovery of the petty, mean-spirited attitudes beneath the veneer of small-town American life. Lewis followed *Main Street* with *Babbitt*, for which he invented the city of Zenith—the setting for several of his future novels as well. George F. Babbitt, like Carole Kennicott, seeks to escape his successful but ultimately stultifying life: in his case, selling real estate. The book's power lies in the contrast between Babbitt's conformist behavior and his rebellious thoughts. He takes advantage of everyone he encounters, yet never fully recognizes that he is morally compromised. The book struck such a chord that the word "Babbittry," to describe a sort of unthinking commercialism, entered the language. In the 1920s, Lewis also published his three other most renowned novels: *Arrowsmith*, *Elmer Gantry*, and *Dodsworth*. In each, Lewis examines how success in America can become a perpetual round of self-congratulatory activities, which eventually threaten any true social improvement.

Lewis won the Pulitzer Prize in 1925 for *Arrowsmith* but declined the award. Many commentators have assumed he refused the prize largely because he was bitter about not receiving it for *Main Street* (despite the committee's original vote for that work) or for *Babbitt*. In his strongly worded refusal, he implored other writers not to accept such awards, because acceptance leads to admitting the authority of awarding institutions, and he asked rhetorically "whether any prize is worth that subservience" (Schorer). Ironically, though, when in 1930 he became the first American to be awarded the Nobel Prize for literature he accepted that award almost without reservation. These awards and Lewis's response to them did much to make him a public figure. He pointedly criticized the literary establishment, and his attacks—like the characterizations in his novels—were so cruel that they alienated many other writers. For this reason, and because there was a general dismissal of his particular brand of "social realism," Lewis has disappeared from most of the major anthologies of American literature.

Interestingly, Lewis's struggle to have his naturalism accepted as great literature parallels the struggles of many writers of the Harlem Renaissance, who often found their own artistic vision being denounced and demeaned as "primitivist." Stylistic and thematic debts to Sinclair Lewis can be seen in such varied writers as Wallace Thurman, whose novel *The Blacker the Berry* has a narrative tone reminiscent of Lewis's best works; and Jessie Fauset, whose repeated criticism of the hypocrisy of the middle class echoes some of Lewis's observations. Also, later realist writers such as Richard Wright were able find a more receptive public in part because Lewis's best-sellers had altered the literary marketplace.

Lewis did, moreover, offer direct encouragement to some writers of the Harlem Renaissance, most notably Walter White and Claude McKay. Lewis supplied a very favorable quotation for the dust jacket of White's first novel (ranking it with *A Passage to India* as one of the two most important novels of the year). This led to a decades-long friendship between the two men; and Lewis not only gave White a thorough

Sinclair Lewis, c. 1900–1940. (Library of Congress.)

Ebony magazine for promoting interracial understanding, but most of the reviewers found it an "oversimplified 'sociological tract' and a total failure as a work of art" (Schorer).

Schorer concludes that Lewis "is one of the worst writers in modern American literature, but without his writing one cannot imagine modern American literature." Similarly, one could assert that Lewis was a figure very tangential to the Harlem Renaissance, but that without his writing and influence the fiction of the Harlem Renaissance would undoubtedly have looked much different.

Biography

Sinclair Lewis was born 7 February 1885 in Sauk Center, Minnesota. He studied at Yale University (A.B., 1908). His awards included a Pulitzer Prize for *Arrowsmith* in 1925 (refused); the Nobel Prize for literature (1930); election to the National Institute of Arts and Letters (1935); and election to the American Academy of Arts and Letters (1938). Lewis died in Rome, Italy, 10 January 1951.

NEIL BROOKS

See also Fauset, Jessie Redmon; Fire in the Flint, The; McKay, Claude; Randolph, A. Philip; Thurman, Wallace; White, Walter; Wright, Richard

Selected Works

Free Air. 1919.
Main Street. 1920.
Babbitt. 1922.
Arrowsmith. 1925.
Mantrap. 1926.
Elmer Gantry. 1927.
The Man Who Knew Coolidge. 1928.
Dodsworth. 1929.
Ann Vickers. 1933.
It Can't Happen Here. 1935.
Kingsblood Royal. 1947.

Further Reading

Cooney, Charles F. "Walter White and Sinclair Lewis: The History of a Literary Friendship." *Prospects*, 1, 1975, pp. 63–79.

analysis of *The Fire in the Flint* but also helped him with his second novel, *Flight*. In addition, Lewis wrote a very strong recommendation that helped White secure a Guggenheim fellowship. On White's suggestion, Lewis visited Claude McKay in Paris; and McKay later said, "Lewis gave me a few cardinal and practical points about the writing of a book or novel" (Cooney). Lewis further demonstrated that he no longer condemned all literary prizes when, in 1935, he agreed to serve on the Spingarn Medal Committee of the National Association for the Advancement of Colored People (NAACP). In his first year on the committee, Lewis recommended that McKay be given the award, and in his second year he voted for A. Philip Randolph; he resigned from the committee before completing his three-year term, however.

Toward the end of his career, Lewis published *Kingsblood Royal* (1947), a novel in which the protagonist, Neil Kingsblood, discovers that he has black ancestry and thus by state law is black. This book was rather poorly received. It was given a citation by

Hutchisson, James M. *The Rise of Sinclair Lewis, 1920–1930*. University Park: Pennsylvania State University Press, 1996.

Hutchisson, James M., ed. *Sinclair Lewis: New Essays in Criticism*. Troy, N.Y.: Whitston, 1997, pp. 94–109.

Schorer, Mark. *Sinclair Lewis: An American Life*. Toronto: Heinemann, 1961.

Lewis, Theophilus

Theophilus Lewis was the leading theater critic during the Harlem Renaissance. From 1923 to 1927 he wrote primarily for A. Philip Randolph and Chandler Owens's magazine *The Messenger*, where he was also the coauthor of a column, "Shafts and Darts: A Page of Calumny and Satire," with the *Messenger*'s editor George S. Schuyler. Lewis was an iconoclastic and sharply biting writer who repeatedly called for significant improvements in the composition and direction of African American theater, particularly dramatic productions. He proposed the establishment of a national African American theater that would eschew stereotypes and "colorism" in favor of realistic roles and casting without regard to skin color.

Lewis was born in Baltimore in 1891. Although he had very little formal education, he was a devotee of the theater from his teens onward. Not long before World War I began, Lewis traveled to New York City and made the acquaintance of Randolph and Owen. After serving in the army during the war, Lewis moved to Detroit for three years and then, in 1922, obtained employment as a postal clerk in New York.

After showing a theater review to Randolph, Lewis was commissioned to write regular reviews for the *Messenger*, albeit with no remuneration except the price of his tickets. According to Kornweibel (1972), Lewis's columns were the only ones from Harlem that offered a discriminating perspective on theater. Lewis was fairly consistent throughout his career in urging African Americans to create a theatrical tradition distinct from that of white Americans, and especially from any vestiges of the minstrel tradition. Lewis had a low opinion of African American comedies and musical revues, primarily because they abounded with racial stereotypes. Most African American musicals, Lewis wrote, were "compounded of sheer imbecility sugar-coated with music and dancing" and, because they so often relied on low humor and nudity, degraded such fine actors and singers as Charles Gilpin

and Florence Mills. In addition, Lewis decried the overwhelming tendency for directors to cast only light-skinned African Americans in their productions. His opposition stemmed from a black cultural nationalism that was at odds with the ideas of many of the *Messenger*'s other columnists, who frequently condemned separate cultural institutions and argued against cultural differences.

Nonetheless, Lewis was apparently the first black theater critic to address the dearth of aesthetically, morally, or culturally sound plays and roles for African Americans. Lewis argued that theater productions which appealed to the intelligence of African American audiences would help foster the careers of black playwrights. Actually, there were very few African American playwrights in the 1920s, and far fewer who had access to Broadway or even to off-Broadway—and those who did catered to the lowest common denominator among their black audiences, making development of high-quality theater highly improbable. Lewis believed that black theater should be based on serious study of African American folk experiences, rather than on the aspirations of the black bourgeoisie. Accordingly, he encouraged young playwrights such as Eubie Blake and Noble Sissle, and his friends Wallace Thurman and William Jourdan Rapp; he also encouraged emerging "little theater" groups such as the Aldridge Players, the Krigwa Players, the National Ethiopian Art Theater, and the Tri-Arts Club. Lewis hoped that these groups would form the foundation of a national black theater.

In addition, Lewis's satirical "Shafts and Darts" columns, which he wrote with Schuyler from April 1924 through August 1925, allowed him to discuss a number of cultural and political issues, including the rise and fall of Marcus Garvey and the Universal Negro Improvement Association (UNIA), the National Association for the Advancement of Colored People (NAACP), African American literature, and, again, the lack of high-quality dramatic productions. Lewis also reviewed new books for the *Messenger*; he was among the first to react positively to Langston Hughes's *Weary Blues* and the controversial *Fine Clothes to the Jew*.

After the Harlem Renaissance began to decline, Lewis seldom wrote for African American publications. He converted to Catholicism in the 1930s and then wrote primarily for Catholic magazines and journals until the early 1970s; however, in most of his columns he still continued his campaign for high-quality African American drama. Today he is one of the lesser-known African American dramatic critics, but unquestionably one of the most important.

Biography

Theophilus Lewis was born 4 March 1891 in Baltimore, Maryland, and studied at public schools there. He served in the U.S. Army in 1917–1918 and was a clerk in the U.S. Post Office in 1922–c. 1955. He was a member of the Commission on Human Rights, New York City (1950s); the Epworth League, Salem Missionary Church, New York City (beginning in 1911); Friends of Negro Freedom (1920–c. 1928); and the Independent Political Council, New York City (1913). Lewis wrote for *America, Catholic World, Commonweal, Harlem, Interracial Review, Messenger, Opportunity*, and the Pittsburgh *Courier*. He died in 1974.

DARRYL DICKSON-CARR

See also Blake, Eubie; Krigwa Players; Messenger, The; National Ethiopian Art Theater; Schuyler, George S.; Sissle; Noble; Theater; Thurman, Wallace; Tri-Arts Club

Selected Works

"Same Old Blues." *Messenger*, 7, January 1925, pp. 14–15, 62.
"Survey of the Negro Theater—Ill." *Messenger*, 8, October 1926, pp. 301–302.
"Reflections of an Alleged Dramatic Critic." *Messenger*, 9, June 1927, pp. 193, 200.
"If This Be Puritanism." *Opportunity*, 7(4), April 1929, p. 132.
"The Frustrations of Negro Art." *Catholic World*, 155, April 1942, pp. 51–57.
"Reflections on the Subscription Theatre." *America*, 123, 11 July 1970, pp. 26–27.

Further Reading

Anderson, Jervis. *A. Philip Randolph: A Biographical Portrait*. Berkeley: University of California Press, 1986. (Reprint.)
Grimes-Williams, Johanna L. "Theophilus Lewis." In *The Oxford Companion to African American Literature*, ed. William L. Andrews, Frances Smith Foster, and Trudier Harris. New York: Oxford University Press, 1997, p. 437.
Hutchinson, George. "Mediating 'Race' and 'Nation': The Cultural Politics of *The Messenger*." *African American Review*, 28(4), Winter 1994, pp. 531–548.
———. *The Harlem Renaissance in Black and White*. Cambridge, Mass., and London: Belknap Press of Harvard University Press, 1995.
Kornweibel, Theodore. "Theophilus Lewis and the Theater of the Harlem Renaissance." In *The Harlem Renaissance Remembered*, ed. Arna Bontemps. New York: Dodd, Mead, 1972, pp. 171–189.
———. *No Crystal Stair: Black Life and the Messenger, 1917–1928*. Westport, Conn.: Greenwood, 1975.
Schuyler, George S. *Black and Conservative: The Autobiography of George S. Schuyler*. New Rochelle, N.Y.: Arlington House, 1966.
———. "The Reminiscences of George S. Schuyler." In *The Oral History Collection of Columbia University*, ed. Elizabeth B. Mason and Louis M. Starr. New York: Oral History Research Office, 1979. (Originally published 1972.)

Liberator

The *Liberator* was an avant-garde publication founded, owned, and edited in its first years by the socialist writer Max Eastman. It covered economic and political news and views, as well as art, poetry, fiction, and criticism. Eastman began the magazine in 1918 as a successor to *The Masses*, a radical periodical he had edited from 1913 to 1917, which had been banned by the government. Eastman was intolerant of "dogma and rigidity of mind," and in the *Liberator* he welcomed a wide range of leftist views and took a stand against censorship. In 1921, he asked the poet Claude McKay to become an associate editor of the *Liberator*; shortly thereafter he handed the reins to McKay and the writer Michael Gold as coeditors.

Under the direction of McKay and Gold, the circulation of the *Liberator* rose from 50,000 to 60,000; its format became more elegant; and illustrations by socially minded artists like William Gropper and Stuart Davis made a sharp impact. Contributors included talented people such as Art Young, Boardman Robinson, Robert Minor, Maurice Becker, Helen Keller, and Cornelia Barns; McKay also published several poems by e.e. cummings. Initially, McKay decided not to publish a short story submitted by Jean Toomer; later, when he noticed that Toomer's work was appearing elsewhere, however, the *Liberator* did publish one of Toomer's poems in 1922.

Seven of McKay's own poems—overtly political works about lynchings of African Americans—were published in the *Liberator* in 1919. His sonnet "If We Must Die," which expressed militant politics within a traditional poetic form, was unprecedented; in fact, one publisher later it considered too incendiary to be included in a collection of McKay's poetry, and Alain Locke considered it too radical to be included in *The New Negro*. Langston Hughes, who subscribed to the *Liberator*, got his first taste of African American revolutionary concepts from McKay's militant poems.

Gold and other left-wing associates eventually took the magazine in a clearly Marxist direction; although McKay tried to reserve a certain amount of space in each issue for racial topics, he lost the battle. Eastman warned McKay that if they "published too much material about the Negroes, our white readers would dismiss the magazine, not the material. They would stop buying and reading it." Disappointed over the magazine's policies and wanting to see the Bolshevik Revolution up close, McKay left for Russia in late 1922.

After McKay returned from abroad, having immersed himself in the ideas of Marx and Lenin, he invited various socialists, Marxists, and black nationalists to strategy sessions at the *Liberator*. This caused Eastman to worry about surveillance by the Justice Department; McKay, for his part, used one of his last articles in the *Liberator* to criticize Eastman.

Undercapitalization, a weak distribution network, and a lack of broad appeal shortened the life of many magazines like the *Liberator*. The *Liberator* continued to veer toward the communist line; eventually it merged with some other communist periodicals, and in 1924 it became the *Workers' Monthly*, a journal of Marxist thought owned by the Communist Party.

KATHLEEN COLLINS

See also Communist Party; Eastman, Max; McKay, Claude

Further Reading

Kellner, Bruce, ed. *The Harlem Renaissance, A Historical Dictionary for the Era*. New York: Methuen, 1984.
Lewis, David Levering. *When Harlem Was in Vogue*. New York: Penguin, 1987.
Watson, Steven. *The Harlem Renaissance, Hub of African-American Culture, 1920–1930*. New York: Pantheon, 1995.

Lincoln Motion Picture Company

The Lincoln Motion Picture Company was founded in Los Angeles in 1916 by the actor Noble M. Johnson, who had already achieved considerable recognition and now starred in the new company's productions. In 1918 Noble Johnson brought in his brother George P. Johnson, who established an impressive distribution network that drew on the patronage of the black middle class in major cities, including Chicago, New York, Pittsburgh, and Los Angeles. George Johnson also devised a method of distribution to small-town establishments that could not afford to rent prints, and he advertised the company's films in newspapers such as the Chicago *Defender* and the *Amsterdam News*.

Lincoln's films were intended to present images of black people as normal human beings with talent and intelligence, and to avoid the negative stereotyping that was prevalent during this period: its productions offered the first blacks in film who did not conform to the usual roles of mammies, spear-wielding natives, or slapstick and burlesque comedians. In keeping with the ideology of uplift generally espoused by black leaders, these films emphasized decidedly middle-class values and achievements. Moreover, except for the cameraman Harry Grant, who was also a stockholder, the production company itself was all black.

Lincoln produced five narrative films—*Realization of a Negro's Ambition* (1916), *Trooper of Company K* (1916), *Law of Nature* (1917), *Man's Duty* (1919), and *By Right of Birth* (1921)—and two newsreels: *Lincoln Pictorial* (1918) and *A Day with the Tenth Cavalry at Fort Huachauca* (1922). In addition to Noble Johnson, its regular actors included Clarence Brooks, Beulah Hall, and A. Collins.

Lincoln's first "photoplay" (the term used for film productions), *Realization of a Negro's Ambition*, was a testament to the virtues of hard work and earnestness. The hero, a graduate of the Tuskegee Institute, leaves home to seek his fortune in the oil fields of California; rescues the daughter of the owner of an oil company; and returns home, where he finds oil on the family farm. The film opened in white-owned theaters catering to blacks, as well as in public-gathering places such as churches and schools; it was also shown at the Tuskegee Institute. Two of the four prints that were made were copyrighted by white-owned film companies: Carver Film and Supply and Queen Feature Service.

The next film, *Trooper of Company K*, was about the "Carrizal incident," an episode during the Mexican War in which all-black troops were virtually wiped out. It too starred Noble Johnson and Beulah Hall. *Trooper of Company K* played to both black and white audiences; it was shown in two white theaters in New Orleans and drew large crowds throughout the Midwest and the South.

Law of Nature, released in 1917, was the last movie in which Noble Johnson starred; he resigned from Lincoln soon afterward, possibly at the insistence of Universal, a studio with which he was also under contract. (Johnson was such a strong attraction that Lincoln's films were evidently drawing moviegoers away from Universal's.) Ultimately, Lincoln could not survive the loss of its star.

A Man's Duty and *By Right of Birth* were Lincoln's final films. *A Man's Duty*, with its traveling road show of actors and dancers, was shown in all of the then forty-eight states of the nation. *Heart of a Negro* was announced as the next release, but it was never produced. The Lincoln Motion Picture Company ceased operations in 1923.

AUDREY THOMAS MCCLUSKEY

See also Brooks, Clarence; Film; Film: Black Filmmakers; Johnson, Noble

Further Reading

Birchard, Robert S. "Lincoln Motion Picture Company (1916–1921)." In *Silents Majority*. c. 1997. (Web site.)

Cripps, Thomas. *Making Movies Black: The Hollywood Message Movie from World War II to The Civil Rights Era*. New York: Oxford University Press, 1993.

George P. Johnson Negro Film Collection: Collection 1042. Los Angeles: University of California Los Angeles Library, Photographic Department., 1974. (See also microfiche: Indiana University, University of California Berkeley, and Florida State University–Tallahassee.)

Sampson, Henry T. *Blacks in Black and White: A Source Book on Black Films*, 2nd ed. Metuchen, N.J.: Scarecrow, 1995.

Lincoln Theater

The Lincoln Theater opened in 1909 at 56–58 West 135th Street, between Fifth and Lenox avenues, to serve Harlem's burgeoning African American population. The new owner, Maria C. Downs, converted what had been a nickelodeon into a 300-seat theater, and its success allowed her to build a new 850-seat theater on the same site in 1915. Along with the Lafayette Theater (which desegregated in 1914), the Lincoln was Harlem's most important venue for bringing entertainment to black audiences during the 1910s and 1920s.

The defection to the white *Ziegfeld Follies* of the great black comedian Bert Williams in 1910 signaled the end of black Broadway's first great age, one that would not be revived until the phenomenal success of *Shuffle Along* in 1921. The virtual banishment of African Americans from downtown stages, however, encouraged the development of a vital theater within Harlem itself, financed, performed, and attended by members of the community. In 1914, the actress and dancer Anita Bush, who had been born in Brooklyn and who had performed with Williams in around 1904, organized a Colored Dramatic Stock Company at the Lincoln in order to offer black audiences serious drama—that is, to break away from the all-singing, all-dancing format which usually constrained black performers. By 1915, the organization was called the Anita Bush Stock Company, and by 1916 it had moved to the Lafayette. Samuel Hay (1994, 173–174) suggests this move might better be described as a "hostile takeover" on the part of Maria Downs and the Lafayette Players.

The Lincoln continued to present drama, but by the 1920s it was better known as a raucous movie and vaudeville house popular with recent migrants from the South: "the kind of people," the *Messenger*'s drama critic Theophilus Lewis wrote with bourgeois dismay

Lincoln Theater, c. 1915. (Brown Brothers.)

and fascinated pride, "who kick the varnish off the furniture, plaster chewing gum on the seats and throw peanut shells in the aisles" (quoted in Fraden 1994, 73). In *The Big Sea* (1940), Langston Hughes fondly recalled one summer night in 1927 when Jules Bledsoe stopped a performance of Eugene O'Neill's *The Emperor Jones* to deliver a lecture on theater manners to an audience that had "howled with laughter" at the spectacle of Bledsoe running naked through a stage forest pursued by his fears. Hughes added that "their manners had been all right at all the other shows at the Lincoln, where they took part in the performance at will" (1940, 258–259).

As a stop on the Theater Owners' Booking Association circuit, the Lincoln was the New York showcase for national black jazz and vaudeville acts like Williams, Butterbeans and Susie, Ethel Waters, and the blues singers Bessie Smith, Ma Rainey, Mamie Smith, and Alberta Hunter. In 1919, the Lincoln hired the young Fats Waller at $23 a week to play its new $10,000 Wurlitzer organ for silent films and vaudeville acts.

In 1929, the Lincoln was sold to Frank Schiffman and Leo Brecher, businessmen who were busy consolidating Harlem's entertainment industry. The Lincoln was designated to show movies while live entertainment (including Waller) was moved to the Lafayette.

RYAN JERVING

See also Anita Bush Stock Company; Bledsoe, Jules; Bush, Anita; Community Theater; Emperor Jones, The; Hughes, Langston; Hunter, Alberta; Lafayette Players; Lafayette Theater; Lewis, Theophilus; Messenger, The; O'Neill, Eugene; Rainey, Gertrude "Ma"; Shuffle Along; Smith, Bessie; Smith, Mamie; Theater Owners' Booking Association; Waller, Thomas "Fats"; Waters, Ethel; Williams, Egbert Austin "Bert"

Further Reading

Fraden, Rena. *Blueprints for a Black Federal Theatre, 1935–1939*. Cambridge and New York: Cambridge University Press, 1994.

Hay, Samuel A. *African American Theatre: An Historical and Critical Analysis*. Cambridge and New York: Cambridge University Press, 1994.

Hughes, Langston. *The Big Sea*. London and New York: Knopf, 1940. (Reissue, New York: Hill and Wang, 1993.)

Newman, Richard. "The Lincoln Theatre." *American Visions*, 6(4), August 1991.

Singer, Barry. *Black and Blue: The Life and Lyrics of Andy Razaf*. London and New York: Schirmer–Simon and Schuster Macmillan, 1992.

Waller, Maurice, and Anthony Calabrese. *Fats Waller*. New York: Schirmer, 1977.

Lindsay, Vachel

Of his birthplace—Springfield, Illinois—Vachel Lindsay wrote, "Everything begins and ends there for me." In a profound way this is true of his life. Lindsay drew on the people and landscape of Illinois as the material for his art and also as the yardstick for judging that art. For Lindsay, poetry was necessarily popular and democratic. He strove to create art that would appeal to the common people, in Springfield and beyond.

Lindsay's first book was a prose memoir recalling his journeys across America as a tramp, exchanging his goodwill and poetic recitations for money and lodging. From this start, Lindsay rose quickly to become a central figure in the popularization of free verse in America. His poem "William Booth Enters Heaven" (1914) brought him wide acclaim and took him to the top of the American avant-garde. In 1914 the Irish poet William Butler Yeats, visiting America, said that Lindsay's poetry had a "strange beauty," legitimizing the new avant-garde in the eyes of the conservative press. By the end of that year, with the publication of Lindsay's poem "The Congo" in the magazine *Poetry* and his volume *The Congo* shortly thereafter, Lindsay's dramatic reading style and his verse—which was influenced by vaudeville—became wildly popular, and he embarked on a rigorous schedule of readings and lectures nationwide which he would keep up for years.

Lindsay, along with Carl Sandburg and Edgar Lee Masters, defined modernism for the Harlem Renaissance. His chanted verse and dramatic cadences anticipated the use of jazz and ragtime in poetry, but it was Lindsay's populism that made him so influential a figure in the renaissance. Lindsay was first and foremost concerned about how to create poetry that would sing to the masses. Famously, he claimed to have discovered Langston Hughes while appearing at a hotel where Hughes was working as a busboy. Hughes dropped a packet of poems on Lindsay's table; Lindsay read them that night, and then he surprised his audience by announcing that he had discovered a black poet working right there in the hotel. However, Lindsay did not realize that Hughes had already been discovered: Alfred Knopf had a contract to publish Hughes's *Weary Blues.*

Lindsay's most famous poem, "The Congo," is subtitled "A Study of the Negro Race." The poem draws on the concept of African Americans as barely concealed primitives and portrays black people's coming into civilization as a source of a vital new poetry. Although "The Congo" now reads as stereotyped, condescending, and even offensive, Lindsay claimed that it had been inspired when he discussed the plight of the Negro with a black lawyer in Springfield, Charles Gibson.

Lindsay's interest in helping black America was sincere, if sometimes misguided. In 1926 he was a judge for *Opportunity*'s annual literary contest; that same year he was also one of the respondents in a symposium in *The Crisis*: "The Negro in Art—How Shall He Be Portrayed?" Lindsay was also involved in civil rights causes; for example, he wrote letters of protest to newspapers after two black men were lynched in Springfield in 1908, and he made a point of including black colleges on his reading tours.

By the 1920s, Lindsay's career was in decline. He himself came to hate reading "The Congo," although his audiences kept on demanding to hear it. In 1931, faced with the critical failure of his later work, and battling exhaustion and illness, Lindsay committed suicide (by drinking Lysol) in the home in Springfield where he had been born.

Biography

Nicholas Vachel Lindsay was born in Springfield, Illinois, 10 November 1879. He attended Hiram College in Ohio (1897–1900); the Chicago Art Institute and the New York School of Art (1900–1905). He was a pen-and-ink designer (1900–1910) and a lecturer on art history (1905–1910). His honors included Phi Beta Kappa (Harvard, 1922); a Litt.D. from Baylor University, and a Litt.D. from Hiram College (1930). Lindsay died in Springfield 5 December 1931.

STEVEN NARDI

See also Crisis, The: The Negro in Art—How Shall He Be Portrayed? A Symposium; Hughes, Langston; Knopf, Alfred A.; Opportunity Literary Contests; Weary Blues, The

Selected Works

General William Booth Enters Heaven and Other Poems. 1913.
Adventures While Preaching the Gospel of Beauty. 1914.
The Congo and Other Poems. 1914.
The Art of the Moving Picture. 1915. (Rev. ed., 1922.)
The Golden Whales of California and Other Rhymes in the American Language. 1920.
Collected Poems. 1925.

Further Reading

Masters, Edgar Lee. *Vachel Lindsay: A Poet in America.* New York: Scribner, 1935.
Flanagan, John T., ed. *Profile of Vachel Lindsay.* Columbus, Ohio: Merrill, 1970.
Harris, Mark. *City of Discontent.* Indianapolis, Ind.: Bobbs-Merrill, 1952.
Wolfe, Glenn Joseph. *Vachel Lindsay: The Poet as Film Theorist.* New York: Arno, 1973.

Lippincott, J. B., Publisher

J. B. Lippincott, one of America's oldest publishing houses, was started by Joseph Ballinger Lippincott in 1836. He established his own firm by buying the business of a bookseller in Philadelphia named Clarke and later acquiring Jacob Johnson and Company, a publisher—also in Philadelphia—that had been in existence since 1792. In its early years, Lippincott was known for publishing bibles, prayer books, and literature. The company's list diversified through the 1850s, and Lippincott became the largest publishing, distributing, and manufacturing office in the world, establishing its reputation as a seller of medical books, religious books, and textbooks.

Lippincott's Magazine was launched in 1868 to boost the firm's literary publishing list. It became an important venue for Rudyard Kipling, Oscar Wilde, Jack London, and Arthur Conan Doyle, all of whom published complete novels or novelettes in the magazine; it was one of the leading magazines of its type until it merged with *Scribner's* in 1916.

Although a poem by Alice Dunbar Nelson appeared in *Lippincott's Magazine* in 1902 and William Stanley Braithwaite's *A Tale of a Walled Town and Other Verses* was published by the firm in 1921, Lippincott's list during the heyday of the Harlem Renaissance showed no significant investment in works by black writers. Rather, Lippincott's principal contribution to the Harlem Renaissance was its publication of Zora Neale Hurston's major works in the 1930s and 1940s.

Bertram Lippincott took over as editor during this time and brought a new perspective to the conservative firm. Lippincott discovered Hurston's work when he read "The Gilded Six-Bits" in *Story Magazine* in 1933, and he wrote to her asking if she had a novel. Although she had not yet begun writing the text that would become her first novel, *Jonah's Gourd Vine*, Hurston convinced Lippincott that she was already working on it, and he offered her an advance. Lippincott was interested in Hurston's blending of fiction and folklore, and published *Jonah's Gourd Vine* in 1934. He eagerly published Hurston's next four books—*Mules and Men* (1935), *Their Eyes Were Watching God* (1937), *Tell My Horse* (1938) and *Moses, Man of the Mountain* (1939)—although the last two did not sell well.

When Lippincott urged Hurston to write an autobiography as her next project, she initially disagreed; he prevailed, however, and *Dust Tracks on a Road* was published in 1942. This book is marked by inconsistencies that are very likely a result of Hurston's and Lippincott's contrary expectations for its content. When, in 1945, Lippincott rejected Hurston's proposal for a novel about the upper strata of African American life, she called him a "timid soul" and stated that he thought America was not yet ready for this kind of text. Her later essay "What White Publishers Won't Print" may have been related to Lippincott's rejection of her idea.

Aside from its promotion of Zora Neale Hurston's works, J. B. Lippincott contributed little to the Harlem Renaissance. Still, the role this publishing house played in establishing Hurston as a major figure of the 1930s is notable indeed.

AMANDA M. LAWRENCE

See also Hurston, Zora Neale; Publishers and Publishing Houses; Their Eyes Were Watching God

Further Reading

Dzwonkoski, Peter. "J. B. Lippincott Company." *Dictionary of Literary Biography*, Vol. 49, *American Literary Publishing Houses, 1638–1899*. Detroit, Mich.: Gale Research, 1986, pp. 261–266.

Hemenway, Robert. *Zora Neale Hurston: A Literary Biography*. Urbana: University of Illinois Press, 1977.

Stern, Edith M. "J. B. Lippincott Co.: 'An Eye to the Book Chance.'" *Saturday Review of Literature*, 14 June 1941, pp. 11–12.

Tebbel, John. *Between Covers: The Rise and Transformation of Book Publishing in America*. New York: Oxford University Press, 1987.

Literary and Artistic Prizes

During the Harlem Renaissance, several sponsors had contests for outstanding literary, artistic, and scientific achievement. These sponsors included The National Association for the Advancement of Colored People (NAACP), through its magazine *The Crisis*; the National Urban League, through its magazine *Opportunity*; private foundations; and individual patrons whose purpose was to encourage young writers and artists and to have the best of their work published. Such contests went on throughout the 1920s and early 1930s. Most were eventually discontinued for various reasons—financial constraints, a lack of worthy entries, and a desire to forgo white patronage—but they left an important legacy. Among the eminent literary figures who achieved recognition, and whose work was promoted, through these contests were Arna Bontemps, Countee Cullen, Langston Hughes, Zora Neale Hurston, and Nella Larsen.

As early as 1922, the blues singer Trixie Smith won the first concert competition of the 369th Infantry Regimental Band, sponsored by Black Swan Records. But the literary and artistic prizes of the Harlem Renaissance officially got under way in the summer of 1924, when W. E. B. Du Bois, the editor of *The Crisis*, received $300 to sponsor an annual literary competition. The donors were Amy E. Spingarn, daughter of a wealthy mill owner in New Jersey; and her husband, Joel Spingarn, who was a literary editor at the publishing firm Harcourt Brace and a member of the board of NAACP. In September 1924, Charles S. Johnson, the editor of *Opportunity*, announced a creative writing contest of his own, both to encourage literary achievement and to promote African American social and political causes.

From their inception, the contests raised concerns having to do with the content, goals, and patronage of the sponsoring magazines. Regarding content and goals, in early 1926 the poet Claude McKay responded to the proliferation of awards with an essay (unpublished) called "Negro Life and Negro Art," in which he argued that the contests were, ill-advisedly, channeling artistic expression toward racial propaganda. With regard to patronage, although the Urban League and the NAACP supported the arts during the 1920s, this situation began to change as the decade wore on: increasing numbers of prizes and fellowships were sponsored by white businesses, foundations, and entrepreneurs. White patronage was at first considered an encouraging development in interracial relations, but eventually it came to be seen as inimical to African American uplift—and, as noted earlier, this was one reason why the magazines finally ended the awards. Du Bois, for one, had misgivings about certain white publishers that he believed were perpetuating sensationalist images of Harlem and African Americans. Nevertheless, for quite a few years the contests and award ceremonies provided a prominent venue in which emerging writers and artists could meet each other and publicize their work.

The Crisis

The Crisis, which had been founded by Du Bois in 1910, was a high-quality journal that urged the eradication of racism in America and emphasized African American sources of the nation's cultural landscape. Before undertaking its literary contests, it had published work by little-known poets and writers such as Georgia Johnson, Mary Effie Lee, and Lucian Watkins; had offered the Spingarn medal for African American achievement in several categories; and, in December 1922, had run a short-story competition. *The Crisis* formally announced its first literary contest in October 1924. The rules were few, calling for plays, poems, fiction, and essays dealing with some aspect of Negro life; the categories also included illustration and song. The first awards dinner was held in November 1925 at the Renaissance Casino in Harlem. The prestigious panel of judges, selected by Du Bois and Jessie Fauset (the literary editor of *The Crisis*), included Sinclair Lewis, Charles Chestnutt, Eugene O'Neill, H. G. Wells, and the African American anthologist and literary critic William Stanley Braithwaite.

The following year, the award money was increased. Langston Hughes won a prize in the contest of 1926; and Du Bois announced the Krigwa prizes (originally Crigwa, an acronym standing for Crisis Guild of Writers and Artists), sponsored by white and black patrons. Du Bois, who was a firm believer in the power of art to promote racial uplift, established the Krigwa workshop to encourage young playwrights,

writers, and artists. In 1927 he formed the Krigwa Academy, comprising everyone who had received two prizes (first or second) in the contests run by *The Crisis*. Du Bois also believed firmly that African American life should be presented in positive terms; nevertheless the Krigwa competition invited submissions on all facets of black life.

Du Bois's ambivalence about the goals set by *The Crisis* became manifest in the announcement of the prizes for 1927. Substantial prize money came from African American businesses and the Empire State Federation of Women's Clubs rather than from whites. Prizes were to be awarded not only for artistic achievements but also for achievements in African American economic activities. *The Crisis* continued to acknowledge creative works with the Amy Spingarn awards and with a cash award from Charles Chestnutt, but the rules for the contest became more restrictive, urging submissions that promoted black business and social causes over those of an artistic nature. Although Mae Virginia Cowdery of Philadelphia won first prize for poetry, the general feeling at *The Crisis* was that the quality of the entries and the stature of the judges had declined. Du Bois decided to eliminate the annual prizes and banquets in favor of modest monthly Spingarn awards for poetry and fiction. Toward the end of 1928, *The Crisis* had abandoned its arts and literature categories altogether, maintaining only the Charles Chestnutt honoraria and the economic prizes, with its own editors acting as judges.

The Crisis revived its contests in 1931 with a Du Bois Literary Prize of $1,000, established by Mrs. E. R. Mathews. First prize went to James Weldon Johnson for *Black Manhattan*. There was no winner in 1932, and enthusiasm for the contests continued to fade: prizes were postponed, submissions decreased, and there was a lack of qualified judges. Interest in *The Crisis* itself also declined as Du Bois struggled with the direction the magazine should take and dampened the enthusiasm of artists with his exacting demands and restrictions.

Opportunity

Founded in 1923, *Opportunity: A Journal of Negro Life* was committed to promoting talented African American artists, writers, and poets whose work was often neglected by other periodicals. Its editor, Charles S. Johnson, furthered this goal by inaugurating *Opportunity*'s literary contest in September 1924; entries depicting varied aspects of African American life were requested.

Johnson had raised awareness of black literature earlier that year as the host of a party at the Civic Club on 21 March 1924; the guests had included many literary luminaries, such as Alain Locke, who served as master of ceremonies. The ensuing enthusiasm for African American writing led to a gift of $500 from Mrs. Henry G. Leach to sponsor a creative-writing contest run by *Opportunity*.

To Johnson's delight, *Opportunity* received numerous submissions in fiction, poetry, and drama, and the winners were announced at a banquet in New York City on 1 May 1925. An integrated panel of twenty-four judges included Robert C. Benchley of *Life* magazine, Alexander Woollcott of the New York *Sun*, Henry G. Leach of *Forum*, and James Weldon Johnson. First prize for fiction went to John Matheus for "Fog"; second prize to Zora Neale Hurston for "Spunk" and Dorothy West (then age nineteen) for "The Typewriter"; and third prize to Eric Walrond for "The Voodoo's Revenge." Langston Hughes won first prize for poetry for "Weary Blues"; Hurston's play *Color Struck* shared second prize for drama with Warren A. MacDonald's *Humble Instrument*; and E. Franklin Frazier, Sterling Brown, and Laura D. Wheatley won prizes for essays.

The first *Opportunity* awards also established important relationships in New York's literary milieu. Among the guests at the banquet were the publisher Alfred Knopf, the essayist and novelist Fannie Hurst, and several members of the Van Doren family. It was at this banquet that Langston Hughes and Zora Neale Hurston met for the first time, and Hurston first became acquainted with Fannie Hurst, who soon thereafter hired Hurston as her companion and personal secretary. Distinguished magazines such as the *Nation*, *Vanity Fair*, and *Harper's* solicited further work from several prizewinners, including Countee Cullen; the black West Indian merchant Caspar Holstein gave Johnson the funds to sponsor a second contest.

The following year, *Opportunity* received 1,276 entries for its contest, which had been extended to include journalism, musical composition, and the Alexander Pushkin Poetry Prize. The second awards ceremony was held in April 1926; the judges this time included Robert Frost, Vachel Lindsay, Jean Toomer, James Weldon Johnson, Alain Locke, Carl Van Doren, and William Stanley Braithwaite. Zora Neale Hurston received second prize for her short story "Muttsy," and Arna Bontemps received the Pushkin prize for "Golgotha Is a Mountain." Arthur Fauset (Jessie Fauset's half brother), Joseph Cotter Seamon, Dorothy West, and John Matheus also won prizes. Many award-winning works appeared in the June issue—the "Contest Number"—of *Opportunity*.

The *Opportunity* awards of 1927 were successful but also controversial. Winners included Sterling Brown (who was awarded the first prize in poetry for "When De Saints Go Ma'ching Home"), Helene Johnson (who won second prize in poetry for "Summer Matures"), and Nellie R. Bright (who won third prize for poetry). Arna Bontemps won his second Pushkin prize for "The Return," and Georgia Douglas Johnson won first prize for her play *Plumes*. Nevertheless, four months later the Urban League suspended the contests. One judge resigned from the panel; Charles Johnson and others deplored the inferior critical standards applied to many submissions; and the writer Wallace Thurman lamented that the prizes seemed to be based on racial rather than literary merit. Financial troubles set in as well, when a five-year grant from the Carnegie Corporation ended in 1927 and *Opportunity* sold just 11,000 copies a month during 1928; also, Johnson left *Opportunity* in 1928 for a professorship in sociology at Fisk University.

Like *The Crisis*, *Opportunity* later resumed its contests. It held a banquet on 5 May 1933 honoring Arna Bontemps with first prize for "A Summer Tragedy" and Marieta Bonner and Henry B. Jones with honorable mentions. Pearl S. Buck was the guest of honor, and the judges included Sterling Brown, Fannie Hurst, and John Day (the president of John Day Publishing Company). By the following year, however, the contests were permanently discontinued.

Other Prizes

Additional prizes included the NAACP's Spingarn Medal for exemplary work by an African American, awarded to William Stanley Braithwaite in 1918; and various Amy Spingarn awards. In 1925, Rudolph Fisher won a first prize for a story in the Spingarn contest in literature and art; Willis Richardson won the Amy Spingarn prize for his play *The Broken Banjo*. Funding for prizes in 1926 included the Boni and Liveright prize of $1,000 for an outstanding novel by an African American writer (although this was never awarded, for lack of a worthy recipient); $600 from Amy Spingarn for the forthcoming *Crisis* contest; $1,000 from Casper Holstein; and a cash award from Carl Van Vechten for *Opportunity*.

In 1921, Marcus Garvey's weekly newspaper, *Negro World*, ran a Christmas literary competition with dozens of cash prizes for essays, poems, and short stories combining creative talent with race-consciousness. One notable entrant was Eric Walrond, who won first prize in the category "Africa Redeemed" for his short story "A Senator's Memoirs."

The William E. Harmon Foundation sponsored annual prizes in science, education, literature, music, fine arts, industry, and race relations. Seven prizes were designated for African American contestants, and an eighth for an eligible contestant of any ethnicity. At the Harmon Foundation's awards ceremony on 12 February 1928, James Weldon Johnson accepted the gold medal and $400 for Claude McKay, and Nella Larsen received the bronze medal and $100 for her novel *Quicksand*.

Other prizes included those of the Garland Fund, and the Louis Rodman Wanamaker awards for musical composition.

Conclusion

The literary and artistic contests of the Harlem Renaissance were invaluable in promoting and publishing the work of talented black Americans. Yet the momentum of these contests slowed for several reasons. First, editors at both *The Crisis* and *Opportunity* believed that the submissions during the late 1920s lacked the vibrancy and spontaneity of earlier entries. Second, noting decreasing circulation at both magazines, many sponsors sensed a waning public enthusiasm for the arts and diverted their funds elsewhere, despite major publications of black prose and poetry at the time, including Alain Locke's *The New Negro*. *The Crisis*, for its part, seemed to have lost much of its aplomb, publishing literature haphazardly and engendering controversy over poorly run contests in 1928 and 1929. Third, there were varying and increasingly complex opinions as to the means of racial uplift. Whereas the announcements of the early contests had encouraged diverse literary representations of black life, Du Bois, for one, later believed in only one acceptable portrayal of the African American experience. Fourth, Du Bois's exertion of rigid control over the contests run by *The Crisis* alienated a new generation of artists and writers. Fifth, Charles Johnson at *Opportunity* faced financial difficulties and the question of whether the magazine and its literature were still effective vehicles for the Urban League.

As a result of all these factors, the prizes of the Harlem Renaissance—although they connoted dazzling literary success—ultimately succumbed to financial distress, artistic disputes, and ongoing racial tension.

KRISTIN E. CZARNECKI

See also Black Manhattan; Boni and Liveright Prize; Bontemps, Arna; Braithwaite, William Stanley; Brown, Sterling; Chesnutt, Charles Waddell; Civic Club Dinner, 1924; Cowdery, Mae Virginia; Crisis, The: Literary Prizes; Cullen, Countee; Du Bois, W. E. B.; Fauset, Jessie Redmon; Frazier, E. Franklin; Garland Fund; Harmon Foundation; Holstein, Casper; Hughes, Langston; Hurst, Fannie; Hurston, Zora Neale; Johnson, Charles Spurgeon; Johnson, Georgia Douglas; Johnson, James Weldon; Larsen, Nella; Locke, Alain; Matheus, John Frederick; Negro World; Opportunity Literary Contests; Smith, Trixie; Spingarn, Joel; Walrond, Eric; Wanamaker Award; West, Dorothy; *other specific writers and artists*

Further Reading

Bontemps, Arna, ed. *The Harlem Renaissance Remembered.* New York: Dodd, Mead, 1972.

Dettmar, Kevin J. H., and Stephen Watt, eds. *Marketing Modernisms: Self-Promotion, Canonization, and Rereading.* Ann Arbor: University of Michigan Press, 1996.

Hutchinson, George. *The Harlem Renaissance in Black and White.* London and Cambridge, Mass.: Belknap Press of Harvard University Press, 1995.

Ikonne, Chidi. *From Du Bois to Van Vechten: The Early New Negro Literature, 1903–1926.* Westport, Conn.: Greenwood, 1981.

Lewis, David Levering. *When Harlem Was in Vogue.* Oxford and New York: Oxford University Press, 1981.

Marks, Carole, and Diana Edkins. *The Power of Pride: Stylemakers and Rulebreakers of the Harlem Renaissance.* New York: Crown, 1999.

Martin, Tony. *Literary Garveyism: Garvey, Black Arts, and the Harlem Renaissance.* Dover, Mass.: Majority, 1983.

Singh, Amritjit, William S. Shiver, and Stanley Brodwin, eds. *The Harlem Renaissance: Revaluations.* London and New York: Garland, 1989.

Literary Criticism and the Harlem Renaissance

Much literary criticism was written during the Harlem Renaissance, although it took slightly different forms from the literary criticism written today. Analyses and interpretations of fiction, poetry, and drama in the 1920s appeared as review essays, rather than the extended academic essays that we currently associate with literary criticism. During the Harlem Renaissance, some literary criticism appeared in books and anthologies, but its more common venues were the popular magazines of the time: *The Crisis* and *Opportunity* in particular, but also *The Messenger* and some white journals like *Vanity Fair*.

Some white writers, such as Carl Van Doren and H. L. Mencken, reviewed literature by African Americans, but work by and about African Americans received its most frequent and extensive attention from other African Americans. The writers of reviews and essays included many of the most prominent African American participants in the Harlem Renaissance: W. E. B. Du Bois and Jessie Fauset, whose essays appeared mostly in *The Crisis*; Alain Locke and James Weldon Johnson, who contributed reviews to *The Crisis*, *Opportunity*, and other magazines; and Charles S. Johnson, who wrote about literature primarily for *Opportunity*. Literary critics for the *Messenger* included George Schuyler, whose reviews also were published in other publications; Theophilus Lewis, who wrote about drama; and Wallace Thurman, whose barbed critiques also appeared in white magazines and in *Fire!!* A number of anthologies published during the 1920s also included important critical essays: Among these are James Weldon Johnson's *The Book of American Negro Poetry* (1922; revised 1931); Alain Locke's *The New Negro* (1925); Countee Cullen's *Caroling Dusk* (1927), and Charles Johnson's *Ebony and Topaz* (1927). Benjamin Brawley, William S. Braithwaite, and Sterling Brown also deserve note as literary critics: All three published books and essays about African American literature, although much of Brown's work appeared in the years after the Harlem Renaissance.

These critics used a range of criteria to assess literature. Some of the critical essays of the time merely debated those criteria, without reference to specific texts. But most essays analyzed an individual book or play and described its strengths and weaknesses. In the early years of the renaissance, many of the writers of literary criticism measured texts by the degree to which they offered portrayals of African Americans that challenged racist stereotypes and assumptions. This criterion was applied most often to works of fiction or drama. For example, in 1923 Montgomery Gregory argued that the realistic portraits of African Americans in Jean Toomer's *Cane* were important

complements to the caricatures so often present in literature by white writers. Similarly, Gregory heralded Fauset's *There Is Confusion* in 1924, asserting that it presented "the better elements of our life to those who know us only as domestic servants, 'uncles,' or criminals" (181). Such arguments were common in the literary criticism of the Harlem Renaissance; the reviewers' belief in the importance of new images of African Americans is clear in the laudatory reviews of work like Fauset's that presented well-educated, property-holding, "respectable" African American characters.

This hope that literature might help undermine racism also led to condemnations of books that were seen as presenting "negative" images of African Americans. These included blatantly racist novels by white southern writers such as Thomas Dixon, whose novel *The Clansman* (1905) was the basis for the movie *The Birth of a Nation* (1915). Writers in the major African American magazines warned their readers about these depictions, as well as those in more subtly demeaning texts that seemed perhaps more well-intentioned but still advanced racist stereotypes. Also viciously denounced were texts by African Americans that, in reviewers' minds, were counterproductive to the goal of presenting positive images of African Americans. For example, Claude McKay's *Home to Harlem* (1928) received outraged criticism from Du Bois, who declared that he felt like taking a bath after he read it. Perhaps the one book that was most criticized along these lines was Carl Van Vechten's *Nigger Heaven* (1926). Again, Du Bois led the charge, writing that the book was "a blow to the face" and "an affront to the hospitality of black folk" (81), particularly because it was written by a white writer who had been assumed to be a "friend" of African Americans. Du Bois found the title misleading and objectionable, but he also was offended by what he saw as the book's focus on cabaret scenes, its reveling in the details of a "wildly, barbaric drunken orgy" (81), and its caricatures of African Americans. Other reviewers, however, were much more positive about the novel, and their responses to it hint at a shift away from the expectation that literature should work as propaganda.

One place where the various positions in this debate were articulated was "The Negro in Art: How Shall He Be Portrayed?," a symposium launched in *The Crisis* in early 1926. Implying that too much literature presented African Americans "at their worst," the opening questionnaire asked whether writers had a duty to present more positive images of African Americans. Du Bois made clear his own answer to this question in "Criteria of Negro Art," which he included in the October 1926 issue of *Crisis*. In this essay, a transcription of a speech he had delivered to a meeting of the National Association for the Advancement of Colored People (NAACP), Du Bois issued his famous proclamation that he did not "care a damn for any art that is not used for propaganda"; he also insisted that black writers had a "bounden duty" to focus on beauty, truth, and goodness (296). Ironically, Du Bois had declared in an editorial, "Negro Art," in 1921 that expecting art to work as propaganda was wrong and would be harmful. Many of the other contributors to the symposium of 1926 agreed with his earlier argument. Langston Hughes, for example, insisted, as he would insist in his famous essay "The Negro Artist and the Racial Mountain," that artists needed to be free to create work according to their own experiences and desires. Others agreed with Hughes, and many declared themselves to be more concerned with the demands of art than the need for propaganda.

The critique of the idea that literature should present positive images of African Americans became more pronounced in the mid- to late 1920s. Wallace Thurman was one of the most vocal writers to articulate this opposition; in fact, he pointedly attacked the expectation that literature and the arts should work as propaganda. For example, in an essay in *Fire!!* he wrote that racist readers probably wouldn't believe that characters like Fauset's were realistic; if they assumed that the less-respectable characters in a book like *Nigger Heaven* were typical African Americans, they probably already believed "such poppy-cock, . . . without any additional aid from Mr. Van Vechten" (1926, 47). In other words, Thurman challenged the validity of the hope that literature could serve the social purpose of undermining racism. Furthermore, here and elsewhere, he insisted that expecting literature to work as propaganda was counterproductive, that it limited what writers thought they could create and, by oppressing their creative tendencies, weakened the artistic merit of the work produced. He insisted that the criterion by which literature should be measured was quality, not content. This position—art for art's sake—was articulated, for example, in the opening statement of *Fire!!*, which defined the magazine as "interested only in the arts" (2). Thurman's essays and reviews were perhaps among the most sharply worded of the arguments along these lines, but many other literary critics of the Harlem Renaissance agreed with Thurman on these points.

Still another set of reviewers focused on the importance of the quality rather than the content of literature by African Americans because they believed that the work's quality could serve as an argument against racism. This criterion was applied to literature in all genres. In his preface to the first edition of *The Book of American Negro Poetry*, for example, James Weldon Johnson asserted that "the amount and standard of literature and art" produced by a group of people was critical to judgments about that group (1922, 9). This assumption underlay many of the reviews of texts by African American writers. Significantly, many reviews were published with photographs of the authors; these made visible the race of their creators, as if to ensure that their work "counted" as a credit to the race. This idea that well-written literature was an important demonstration of the skills of African Americans also seems to have fit into the sense of purpose for the literary contests run by *The Crisis* and *Opportunity* from 1925 to 1927, the Civic Club dinner held by Charles Johnson in 1924, and other events designed to draw reviewers' attention to high-quality work by African American writers.

The question of what made a text notable for its quality was, of course, also subject to debate. Critical discussions ensued about what formal aspects made a text worthy of note. One of the most debated issues was the question of language—in particular, whether writers should use dialect in their work. Poetry was most often the focus of this debate. James Weldon Johnson, for example, argued in the preface to the first edition of *The Book of American Negro Poetry* that the use of traditional dialect was outdated and problematic; he declared that there was a need for black writers to use the vernacular in new and innovative ways, but he also argued that traditional dialect had too many demeaning connotations to be useful to poets in the Harlem Renaissance. Young poets like Hughes and Sterling Brown did use the speech of "ordinary" black people in their poetry, however, and their innovative use of language was heralded by literary critics—including Johnson in his preface to the second edition of his book—who saw their work as marked by important literary innovations.

Another set of critics debated ideas about culture that had implications for literary criticism. Participants in the Harlem Renaissance voiced a range of opinions about whether African American writers should reflect distinctive elements of African American culture in their work—and even whether distinctive elements of African American culture existed. George

Schuyler's essay "Negro Art Hokum," published in *The Nation* in June 1926, was a particularly strong piece on this topic. Arguing that black and white people in America were subject to the same cultural and social forces, Schuyler insisted that black culture did not exist as a separate, distinct entity; that nationality rather than race had the most significant impact on creative work. By extension, Schuyler asserted, African American writers and artists should not be expected to create work that differed significantly from work created by white American writers and artists. Langston Hughes's response, published a week later in the same magazine, was "The Negro Artist and the Racial Mountain." Opening with a critique of poets who wanted their work to be judged without regard to their race, Hughes attacked what he called an "urge within the race toward whiteness," a desire to be "as little Negro and as much American as possible" (1926, 91). In contrast to Schuyler, Hughes called for the black artist to maintain "his racial individuality" and to create "a racial art" (93). Hughes offered folk music and jazz as examples of specifically racial art forms, and he mentioned his own poetry, particularly his "jazz poems," as demonstrating the possibility of literature that was formally linked to black culture. Diametrically opposed to Hughes's poetry, in terms of their formal elements, were McKay's Elizabethan sonnets. To critics who believed that black culture was distinct from white culture, literature like McKay's poems was seen as missing the opportunity to add something unique to American literature.

A related issue that was debated in the literary criticism of the Harlem Renaissance was whether African American writers should focus on the African American folk, rather than the elite. Poets like Hughes and Brown often portrayed the "low-down folks, the so-called common element," as Hughes referred to them in "The Negro Artist and the Racial Mountain" (92). Zora Neale Hurston's plays and fiction also were full of such characters, as were stories written by Wallace Thurman and others. Such work did not fit the demands of reviewers who believed that it was depictions of the talented tenth—or at least of middle-class African Americans—that would do the most to improve perceptions of African Americans. But texts that focused on the black folk also had many supporters. Charles Johnson, for example, repeatedly called for fiction that focused on the "lower classes," as did white writers like Carl Van Vechten, who encouraged African American writers to mine the black folk for fresh, innovative material. They and others either saw such work as complementing propaganda literature by ensuring that the folk as well as the elite were depicted, or they saw it as complementing literature by white Americans in adding realistic and sympathetic depictions of the black folk to the national literary tradition.

Whatever their own positions in these arguments about literary criteria, many reviewers also recognized the influence of audiences' demands on writers' work. In some cases, critics pointed to African Americans' expectations as part of the problem. For example, Theophilus Lewis, in his reviews in the *Messenger* of plays by and about African Americans, often called for more "serious" black drama but bemoaned the lack of support from black audiences for such work. Too many African Americans, he argued, were too fond of dancing and comedies to sufficiently support the development of theater in a way that would nurture an understanding and appreciation for black culture. More often, though, the demands of white audiences were the focus of discussion. One of the assumptions behind the symposium in *The Crisis* on "Negro in Art," for example, was that white publishers were interested only in literature that conformed to certain stereotypes of African Americans—an assumption with which many of the respondents to the survey disagreed. If it were true, though, the demands of those publishers might persuade writers to create work that fit those expectations. On the other hand, the idea that literature should serve as propaganda also primarily assumed that white readers were the intended audience, and it potentially pushed writers to produce more propaganda literature. In fact, as the Harlem Renaissance wound down, literary critics often used this concern over the effect of literature on white readers to attack the movement. Richard Wright, for example, in his devastating critique of the literature of the Harlem Renaissance, argued that the movement's participants had been too focused on white readers; in his essay "Blueprint for Negro Writing" (1937), he characterized the writers of the Harlem Renaissance as "prim and decorous ambassadors who went a-begging to white America" (194). Ironically, then, as a new generation of literary critics rose to prominence in aftermath of the Harlem Renaissance, the literature of the movement was dismissed on the basis of the very criteria for which it had been praised two decades earlier.

The fact that so much of the literary criticism published during the Harlem Renaissance appeared in periodicals has made its study time consuming and challenging, for it requires archival research on magazines like *The Crisis*, *Opportunity*, and the *Messenger*. However, relatively recent critical work on the literary criticism of the movement demonstrates the insights to be gained from such study. For example, George Hutchinson (1995) offers an overview of the main concerns of literary critics who wrote for *The Crisis*, *Opportunity*, and the *Messenger*, focusing particularly on the work of their drama critics. Furthermore, a number of collections of primary materials from the movement have been published since the 1990s, including Sondra Kathryn Wilson's three readers (1999a; 1999b; 2000) and the first two volumes of Cary Wintz's six-volume series on the Harlem Renaissance. These make at least some of the movement's literary criticism more easily accessible, thus opening the door for continued analysis of this important body of work.

ANNE CARROLL

See also Cane; Crisis, The; Crisis, The: The Negro in Art—How Shall He Be Portrayed? A Symposium; Ebony and Topaz; Fire!!; Home to Harlem; Messenger, The; New Negro, The; Nigger Heaven; Opportunity; There Is Confusion; Vanity Fair; *specific individuals*

Further Reading

Du Bois, W. E. B. "Negro Art." *The Crisis*, June 1921.

———. "Criteria of Negro Art." *The Crisis*, October 1926a.

———. "Review of *Nigger Heaven*, by Carl Van Vechten." *The Crisis*, December 1926b.

Gregory, Montgomery. "Review of *Cane*, by Jean Toomer." *Opportunity*, December 1923.

———. "The Spirit of Phillis Wheatley." *Opportunity*, June 1924. (Review of *There Is Confusion*, by Jessie Fauset.)

Hughes, Langston. "The Negro Artist and the Racial Mountain." *The Nation* (June 23, 1926). (Reprinted in *The Portable Harlem Renaissance Reader*, ed. David Levering Lewis. New York and London: Penguin, 1994.)

Hutchinson, George. *The Harlem Renaissance in Black and White*. Cambridge, Mass.: Belknap Press of Harvard University Press, 1995.

Johnson, James Weldon. *The Book of American Negro Poetry*. New York: Harcourt Brace, 1922. (See also rev. ed., 1931.)

Lewis, David Levering. *When Harlem Was in Vogue*. New York and Oxford: Oxford University Press, 1981.

"The Negro in Art: How Shall He Be Portrayed? A Symposium." *The Crisis*, February–October 1926.

Schuyler, George. "Negro Art Hokum." *Nation*, 16 June 1926. (Reprinted in *The Portable Harlem Renaissance Reader*, ed. David Levering Lewis. New York and London: Penguin, 1994.)

Thurman, Wallace, "Fire Burns: A Department of Comment." *Fire!!* 1926.

Wilson, Sondra Kathryn, ed. *The Crisis Reader*. New York: Modern Library—Random House, 1999a.

———. *The Opportunity Reader*. New York: Modern Library—Random House, 1999b.

———. *The Messenger Reader*. New York: Modern Library—Random House, 2000.

Wintz, Cary, ed. *Black Writers Interpret the Harlem Renaissance*. New York and London: Garland, 1996a.

———, ed. *The Emergence of the Harlem Renaissance*. New York: Garland, 1996b.

———, ed. *The Politics and Aesthetics of "New Negro" Literature*. New York: Garland, 1996c.

Wright, Richard, "Blueprint for Negro Writing." *New Challenge*, 2, Fall 1937. (Reprinted in *The Portable Harlem Renaissance Reader*, ed. David Levering Lewis. New York and London: Penguin, 1994.)

Literature: 1—Overview

The literature of the Harlem Renaissance, or the New Negro movement, not only was an affirmation of the artistic sensibility and the intellectual potential of the African Americans gathered in Harlem in the years 1910–1930, but it also connected black culture to the avant-garde aesthetics being developed on both sides of the Atlantic. The literary Harlem Renaissance can be seen as beginning with the opening of the musical *Shuffle Along* in 1921 and with the publication of Claude McKay's *Harlem Shadows* (1922), Jean Toomer's *Cane* (1923), and Jessie Redmon Fauset's *There Is Confusion* (1924). *Cane* in particular—a sophisticated collage of modernism and folk materials, poetry and prose, advanced urban milieus and mythic rural Georgia—reflected characteristic themes concerning unresolved conflicts between the psychological and the political, the personal and the social, the North and the South, and white modernist formalized elitism and black social advancement.

The renaissance of African American literature was influenced by the "great migration" of the early twentieth century, in which African Americans moved from the rural South to major cities in the North. The resulting concentration of creative artists in urban settings—poets, dramatists, essayists, fiction writers, dancers, painters, singers, and musicians—encouraged interchange and productivity. Often, these artists had a common goal: to develop new forms of artistic expression for the African American experience. Over the span of a few decades, Harlem became the black capital of the world; it was seen as a new mecca where the "niggerati" (as they called themselves, ironically) could undertake a formal exploration of popular culture—leading to new kinds of poetry and music and attracting unprecedented national and international attention. Although earlier writers such as Paul Laurence Dunbar and Charles W. Chesnutt had received national recognition, it was during the Harlem Renaissance that far more mainstream publishers and critics came to take African American literature seriously.

The riots that erupted during the "red summer" of 1919, whatever their ill effects, were also a source of energy for intellectuals and artists. In July 1919, Claude McKay's "If We Must Die" appeared in the *Liberator*, a white left-leaning publication; this poem, which contained an impassioned protest against racial violence, became an anthem for the whole movement. W. E. B. Du Bois, Alain Locke, James Weldon Johnson, and Jessie Fauset, who were among the foremost instigators and oracles of the Harlem Renaissance, argued that the inferior status of African Americans could be countered by affirming their intellectual quality, and equality, through art and literature. James Weldon Johnson wrote, in his preface to *The Book of American Negro Poetry*, "The world does not know that a people is great until the people produces great literature and art."

Du Bois, in *The Souls of Black Folk* (1903), had anticipated the new sensibility that would be celebrated during the Harlem Renaissance: he affirmed the dignity and cultural potential of African Americans and indicted the history of prejudice, on the part of white America, that had imposed a "double-consciousness" on blacks, obliging them to measure themselves "by the tape of a world that looks on in amused contempt and pity." Du Bois's argument was significant for literature, implying the existence of a new psychic territory, a connection between knowledge and power, and an interdependence between power and the awareness of one's own talent. Moreover, his theory of the "talented tenth" suggested that the achievements of black intellectuals would be a beacon for the black multitudes. Du Bois influenced the concept of the New Negro that Locke defined in 1925 in a special

issue of *Survey Graphic* illustrated by Winold Reiss. The New Negro was a revolutionary affirmation of black self-reliance, which at the time overlapped with the notion of modernism. It is worth noting that the special issue of *Survey Graphic* in which this idea was propounded had resulted from a grand dinner given by Charles S. Johnson, the editor of *Opportunity*, in order to introduce young African American writers to the white literary establishment of New York.

Du Bois was also the founder of the National Association for the Advancement of Colored People (NAACP), an organization that had a role in the birth of the New Negro movement and lent its support to literary production. In November 1910, the NAACP founded its official magazine, *The Crisis*, edited by Du Bois, which became a literary and artistic outlet for many black intellectuals and helped to undermine stereotypes of blacks in literature and art. Jessie Fauset was its literary editor from 1919 to 1926, and in that capacity was the first to publish the most distinguished African American poets. Moreover, William S. Braithwaite commented appreciatively on the writers Georgia Douglas Johnson, James Weldon Johnson, and Claude McKay in *The Crisis* as early as the issue of April 1918.

Other periodicals—such as *Opportunity*, edited by Charles S. Johnson—gave writers many occasions for publication. *Harlem* (1928) and the short-lived *Fire!!* (1926), both edited by Wallace Thurman, were highly influential, as was *Negro World*; the latter was a periodical of the extravagant Jamaican nationalist Marcus Garvey, through which he expanded the reach of his Universal Negro Improvement Association and publicized his "back to Africa" ideology.

The Harlem Renaissance was part of an international artistic climate of formal experimentation. On the other side of the Atlantic, some artistic trends focused on the beauty and sophistication of African art and showed a new interest in and a new emphasis of the black body. Similar trends occurred in literature: for example, the most influential poem of the 1920s, T. S. Eliot's *The Waste Land* (1922), borrowed its syncopations, which expressed the pace of modern life, from jazz rhythms. It is true that some people would come to regard this "exoticism" as only another form of exploitation by whites; nevertheless, the new interest in Africa and African America did make black culture an acknowledged source of artistic inspiration. Many white creative artists of the 1920s, including writers such as Sherwood Anderson, Fannie Hurst, Eugene O'Neill, Waldo Frank, and DuBose Heyward, incorporated black characters and idioms into their works.

"Primitivism"—which is sometimes dismissed as a morbid bent toward the workings of the supposedly "savage" mind—was also a tremendously progressive force. Claude McKay maintained that Negro primitivism should be considered a revolutionary future rather than a past to escape from; and Locke insisted that the modernist treatment of African art might help African Americans to perceive their spiritual heritage in ways that would enable them to understand and to shape their own distinctive experiences in the new world. The poet Countee Cullen, for one, used African and European images to explore his African roots. Furthermore, the African presence in European art encouraged other black writers in the United States to reevaluate their African heritage and to include it in their literary works. Langston Hughes, Zora Neale Hurston, Nella Larsen, Claude McKay, Richard Bruce Nugent, Jean Toomer, and Wallace Thurman all pondered how their heritage could be considered an inspiration rather than a hindrance. Mixing folk tradition, highly refined modernist techniques, free verse in the style of Walt Whitman, and syncopated prose, they overturned all the conventions about African American writing. Among the poets, Hughes fervently affirmed the elements that were common to black life, whether rural or urban; he wanted to avoid the modernists' cryptic, elitist tone and adopt a voice that would be both personal and communal. He was acclaimed for *The Weary Blues* (1926); in *Fine Clothes to the Jew* (1927) he explored the terse, double-edged language of blues and the new linguistic possibilities of dense jazz rhythms, providing an alternative to dialect poetry and (as the white critic Howard Mumford Jones said) "a really new verse form to the English language." In fiction, Zora Neale Hurston provided a connection to the black folk heritage that Locke, her mentor, considered the essence of "New Negro" literature. In drama, playwrights such as Georgia Douglas Johnson drew from a black folk reservoir. The first drama by an African American—Willis Richardson's *The Chip Woman's Fortune*—was staged in 1923.

White creative artists as well as African Americans represented black life; financial support from white patrons—the "salon Negrotarians" such as Charlotte Mason, Waldo Frank, Carl Van Vechten, and Nancy Cunard—also proved significant, albeit controversial, for the growth of the movement. Van Vechten's best-seller *Nigger Heaven* (1926) was a depiction of nightlife in Harlem, conveying seediness through glittering prose. It had a mixed reception: most African Americans dismissed Van Vechten an exploiter of fashionable black themes, but some, like Claude McKay, Wallace Thurman, Nella Larsen, and Charles S. Johnson, supported the book. Langston Hughes, in his autobiography, *The Big Sea*, praised Van Vechten, noting that Van Vechten's generous promotion of black culture had been instrumental in establishing connections between African American writers like Hughes himself, Nella Larsen, and Rudolph Fisher and the publisher Alfred Knopf. (In 1927 Knopf would also reissue James Weldon Johnson's novel of 1912, *The Autobiography of an Ex-Colored Man*.)

The New Negro movement was not monolithic but was characterized by internal differences and tension. The publication of Claude McKay's *Home to Harlem* (1928) and Wallace Thurman's *Infants of the Spring* (1932) caused considerable controversy. Thurman, especially, was a leader of the new literary bohemians, but both novels offered a firsthand, vibrant account of Harlem's street life, with its pimps and prostitutes, derelicts, loan sharks, racketeers, and hustlers—an atmosphere that had little to do with the "theology" of the talented tenth. Thurman's first novel, *The Blacker the Berry* (1929), and Nella Larsen's *Passing* (1929) examined the complexities of skin color as a central theme in black life and concluded that, despite the optimism of the New Negroes, a color hierarchy—related to a class hierarchy—still existed within the black community. (Du Bois, for example, scorned the uneducated Marcus Garvey; and Richard Bruce Nugent revealed a certain "color chauvinism" when he met the dark-skinned Thurman—confirming the persistence of these thorny intraracial issues.)

Perhaps predictably, the movement did not transcend discrimination against women. Women writers attested to the persistence of sexist attitudes among the New Negroes. Jessie Fauset and Marieta Bonner, for instance, had to find covert forms of artistic expression so as not to openly defy the roles or the literary conventions imposed on women. Zora Neale Hurston did have the temerity to confront the narrow-mindedness of blacks and whites; in her essays and novels, she challenged the sexism and class snobbery of the Harlem Renaissance. She received some criticism for supposedly pandering to white readers, but her innovative aesthetics combined a mastery of folk materials with advanced writing techniques (such as a mixture of direct and indirect narration); her work, together with Jean Toomer's, stands out as perhaps the highest literary achievement of the renaissance.

The thematic concerns of the renaissance writers, like their experiments with literary form, were promising and far-reaching. These writers dealt innovatively with vital issues such as identity, interracial and intraracial prejudice, gender roles, sexual exploitation, passing, and black artistic independence and white patronage—exposing the realities and ironies of black life.

After 1929, however, the glamour of the Harlem Renaissance, "not so gay and sparkling beneath the surface as it looked," faded. Literary figures such as McKay and Hurston, as well as many others, left Harlem and in some cases disappeared into obscurity. Still, the movement would have an impact on American arts and letters for decades to come.

PAOLA BOI

See also Braithwaite, William Stanley; Crisis, The; Cunard, Nancy; Du Bois, W. E. B.; Fauset, Jessie Redmon; Fire!!; Frank, Waldo; Great Migration; Harlem: A Forum of Negro Life; Johnson, Charles Spurgeon; Liberator; Mason, Charlotte Osgood; Negro World; New Negro; Opportunity; Primitivism; Riots: 2—Red Summer of 1919; Shuffle Along; Survey Graphic; Talented Tenth; Van Vechten, Carl; White Patronage; *specific writers*; *specific works*

Further Reading

Anderson, Jervis. *This Was Harlem: A Cultural Portrait, 1900–1950*. New York: Farrar, Strauss, and Giroux, 1981.

Baker, Houston A. *Modernism and the Harlem Renaissance*. Chicago, Ill.: University of Chicago Press, 1987.

Bell, Bernard W. *The Afro-American Novel and Its Tradition*. Amherst, Mass.: University of Massachusetts Press, 1987.

Bontemps, Arna. *Black Thunder*. New York: MacMillan, 1936.

———, ed. *American Negro Poetry*. New York: Hill and Wang, 1963.

Bontemps, Arna. *The Harlem Renaissance Remembered*. New York: Dodd, Mead, 1972.

De Jong, James. *Vicious Modernism: Black Harlem and the Literary Imagination*. Cambridge and New York: Cambridge University Press, 1990.

Du Bois, W. E. B. *The Quest of the Silver Fleece*. Chicago, Ill.: McClurg, 1911.

Fabi, M. Giulia. *Passing and the Rise of the African American Novel*. Urbana and Chicago: University of Illinois Press, 2002.

Fisher. Rudolph. *The Walls of Jerico*. New York: Knopf, 1928.

Gates, Henry Louis, Jr., ed. *The Prize Plays and Other Acts, Zora Neale Hurston, Eulalie Spence, Marieta Bonner, and Other African American Women Writers 1910–1940*. New York: G. K. Hall, 1996.

Horton, James Oliver, and Lois E. Horton. *Hard Road to Freedom: The History of African America*. New Brunswick, N.J.: Rutgers University Press, 2001.

Huggins, Nathan Irving. *Harlem Renaissance*. New York and Oxford: Oxford University Press, 1971.

Huggins Nathan Irving, ed. *Voices from the Harlem Renaissance*. New York and Oxford: Oxford University Press, 1996. (Originally published 1976.)

Hughes, Langston. *The Big Sea*. London: Pluto, 1986. (Originally published 1940.)

———. *The Collected Poems*, ed. Arnold Rampersad. New York: Vintage, 1994.

Hughes Langston, and Zora Neale Hurston. *Mule Bone: A Comedy of Negro Life*. New York: HarperPerennial, 1991. (Originally published 1931.)

Hurston, Zora Neale. *Dust Tracks on the Road*. New York: Lippincott, 1942.

Hutchinson, George. *The Harlem Renaissance in Black and White*. New York and Oxford: Oxford University Press, 1996.

Johnson, Charles S. *The Negro in American Civilization: A Study of Negro Life and Race Relations in the Light of Social Research*. New York: Holt, 1930.

Johnson, James Weldon, ed. *The Book of American Negro Poetry*. San Diego, Calif.: Harcourt Brace Jovanovich, 1983. (Originally published 1922.)

Johnson, James Weldon. *Along This Way: The Autobiography of James Weldon Johnson*. New York: Viking, 1968. (Originally published 1931.)

———. *The Autobiography of an Ex-Colored Man*. New York: Random House, 1989. (Originally published 1912.)

Kirschke, Amy Helene. *Aaron Douglas: Art, Race, The Harlem Renaissance*. Jackson: University Press of Mississippi, 1995.

Lewis, David Levering. *When Harlem Was in Vogue*. New York: Knopf, 1981.

Locke, Alain. *The Negro and His Music*. Washington, D.C.: Associates in Negro Folk Education, 1936. (Reprint, New York: Arno and New York Times, 1969.)

———. *The New Negro: Voices of the Harlem Renaissance*. New York: Atheneum, 1992. (Originally published 1925.)

McKay, Claude. *Home to Harlem*. Boston, Mass.: Northeastern University Press, 1987. (Originally published 1928.)

Powell, Richard J. *The Blues Aesthetics: Black Culture and Modernism*. Washington, D.C.: Washington Project for the Arts, 1989.

———. *Black Art and Culture in the Twentieth Century*. London: Thames and Hudson, 1997.

Redding, Saunders J. *To Make a Poet Black*. Ithaca, N.Y.: Cornell University Press, 1988. (Originally published 1939.)

Schoener, Allon, ed. *Harlem on My Mind: Cultural Capital of the World, 1900–1968*. New York: Random House, 1995. (Originally published 1968.)

Simawe, Saadi A. *Black Orpheus: Music in African American Fiction from the Harlem Renaissance to Toni Morrison*. New York: Garland, 2000.

Thurman, Wallace. *The Blacker the Berry*. New York: Scribner, 1996. (Originally published 1929.)

———. *Infants of the Spring*. New York: Modern Library, 1999. (Originally published 1932.)

Wall, Cheryl A. *Women of the Harlem Renaissance*. Bloomington and Indianapolis: Indiana University Press, 1995.

Watson, Steven. *The Harlem Renaissance, Hub of African American Culture, 1920–1930*. New York: Pantheon, 1995.

Wilson, Sondra Katryn, ed. *The Crisis Reader: Stories, Poetry, and Essays from the NAACP's Crisis Magazine*. New York: Modern Library, 1999.

Literature: 2—Children's

Children's literature flourished during the Harlem Renaissance. In plays and pageants, in the children's magazine *The Brownies' Book*, and in texts by major authors like Langston Hughes, Arna Bontemps, and Countee Cullen, writers discussed and debated black childhood, the future of black children, and the potential for art to change black communities. Importantly, for children's writers of the Harlem Renaissance, the "New Negro" would arise from the young Negro. By cultivating the racial self-image and political awareness of young black readers, writers attempted to transform race relations in America. As an aspect of emerging cultural nationalism, children's literature directed attention to the black child as an icon of progress and revolutionary possibilities. This turn toward children's literature as a means of nation building was not limited to Harlem or to the 1920s. In other urban centers of the North and Midwest and in rural communities in the South throughout the 1920s, 1930s, and 1940s, writers advanced progressive images of black childhood. Additionally, books for black children during the renaissance inaugurated a tradition of African American children's literature emphasizing black history and heroism.

Periodicals

As editor of *The Crisis*, W. E. B. Du Bois issued a "Children's Number" in October of nearly every year from 1912 to 1934. These issues included children's poetry, short stories, and nonfiction narratives; discussions of parenting and education; photographs of "perfect babies"; and coverage of baby beauty contests held by the National Association for the Advancement of Colored People (NAACP).

The popularity of the "Children's Numbers" inspired Du Bois to found one of the earliest literary magazines for black children, *The Brownies' Book* (1920–1921). Under the expert eye of Jessie Redmon Fauset, the magazine issued Langston Hughes's first published poems and short stories, as well as works by Nella Larsen, Willis Richardson, James Weldon Johnson, and others. Although its subscriptions numbered only 4,000, *The Brownies' Book* reached children nationwide. It included various genres and viewpoints—such as pan-Africanism, black fairy tales; dialect stories of the South, descriptions of black industrialists—but the writers had in common the goal of preparing young people to contend with racism and oppression.

When *The Brownies' Book* ceased publication in 1921, *Crisis* continued its commitment to black children's literature, albeit on a smaller scale. It published the poet Effie Lee Newsome's "Little Page" nearly every month from March 1925 to November 1930. Offering "Things That Children Will Love and Learn" (January 1926), Newsome cultivated children's positive self-image by comparing their blackness to beautiful features of the natural world; she also offered descriptions of her own childhood and her experiences in the South and in Ohio.

Other periodicals included Carter G. Woodson's *Negro History Bulletin*, founded in 1937, which offered biographies and historical narratives for school-age children.

Drama

Staged in schools, community centers, and churches nationwide, dramas for children allowed communities to address local concerns as well as the larger topics of black nationhood and cultural identity. Many of the plays were not published, however, and exist only in archives and private collections.

Much of children's drama of the renaissance adhered to Du Bois's proclamation in "Criteria of Negro Art" (1926), "I do not care a damn for any art that is not used for propaganda." For example, Mary Church Terrell's "Historical Pageant-Play Based on the Life of Phyllis Wheatley" (1932) aimed to increase children's self-respect through reflection on the accomplishments of African ancestors. Washington, D.C., where Terrell's pageant was staged, was an important site for the development of children's drama, since playwrights drew on Howard University's theater program and Carter G. Woodson's Association for the Study of Negro Life and History.

Black history was central to much children's drama. Playwrights like May Miller, Willis Richardson, Alice Dunbar-Nelson, and Louise Lovett depicted historical figures so as to shape contemporary black identity; as actors and audience members, children were able to walk in the shoes of Harriet Tubman, Frederick Douglass, Sojourner Truth, and others. Some playwrights, though, like Langston Hughes in "The Gold Piece" (*Brownies' Book*, 1921), were more concerned with the domestic sphere and its influence on black children's ethics. And Willis Richardson—who published a body of children's plays and was an editor of *Plays and Pageants from the Life of the Negro* (1930) and *The King's Dilemma and Other Plays for Children* (1956), a collection of his early dramas—used fantasy to explore the ability of the imagination to transform black children's social conditions.

Black Presses

Perhaps the most important black press for children's literature was Carter G. Woodson's Associated Publishers, which issued more than a dozen picture books, poetry collections, and histories aimed at children. These texts were often written by female schoolteachers and became an important means of revitalizing black education. Black teachers throughout the nation sent Woodson lesson plans, manuscripts, and poems on black history, many of which he published in the *Negro History Bulletin* and as individual volumes through Associated Publishers. Effie Lee Newsome issued her book of poetry, *Gladiola Garden* (1940), through Woodson's house, which also published many lesser-known writers, like Gertrude

Parthenia McBrown, Jane Dabney Shackelford, and Helen Adele Whiting. The painter Lois Mailou Jones (who also did illustrations for *Negro History Bulletin*) illustrated nine of Associated Publishers' books during the 1930s and 1940s. Black representatives sold Woodson's children's texts successfully throughout the South and Midwest, even during the Great Depression. Today, these texts might seem conservative and conciliatory, but in the context of Jim Crow their approach can be understood as strategic rather than defeatist.

Major Figures

Major writers who turned to children's literature toward the end of the 1920s did so for economic as well as ideological reasons. Langston Hughes, who had published in *The Brownies' Book* at age nineteen, collaborated with the novelist and poet Arna Bontemps on *Popo and Fifina: Children of Haiti* (1932), *The Pasteboard Bandit* (written in 1935, published in 1997), "Bon-Bon Buddy" (unpublished, 1935), and "The Boy of the Border" (unpublished, 1939). Both Hughes and Bontemps found themselves increasingly interested in children as a means to reach a mass audience. Bontemps himself published a dozen children's books from 1932 to 1955, including historical narratives like *Chariot in the Sky* (1951), illustrated folktales like *The Fast Sooner Hound* (with Jack Conroy, 1942), and nonfiction like the acclaimed *Story of the Negro* (1948). Bontemps's *Lonesome Boy* (1955) is generally considered the capstone of early black children's literature. Hughes published a book of poetry, *The Dream Keeper* (1932); many texts in the Watts "First Book" series, including *First Book of Negroes* (1952) and *First Book of Jazz* (1955); and *Famous Negro Athletes* (1954) and *Famous Negro Music Makers* (1955) in Dodd, Mead's "Famous American" series.

Countee Cullen wrote almost exclusively for children after 1930. In *The Lost Zoo* (1940) and *My Lives and How I Lost Them* (1942), envisioning an urbane child reader, he manipulated and parodied adult literary conventions such as footnotes, prologues, and epilogues. Ellen Tarry—who is best known for her account of the renaissance in *The Third Door: Autobiography of an American Negro Woman* (1955)—was perhaps the earliest writer of picture books for black children. Her *Janie Belle* (1940), *Hezikiah Horton* (1942), *My Dog Rinty* (1946), and *The Runaway Elephant* (1950) set the stage for later writers' interest in interracial dynamics and the urban experience.

Unlike other "New Negro" children's writers of the period, Bontemps, Hughes, Cullen, and Tarry were published by mainstream houses, and they reached a more integrated audience. Their association with mainstream publishers entailed some compromises (as Hughes and Bontemps report in their extensive correspondence), but all four writers were gratified to see black children's books take their place in the national literary world.

KATHARINE CAPSHAW SMITH

See also Association for the Study of Negro Life and History and Journal of Negro History; Bontemps, Arna; Brownies Book; Crisis, The; Cullen, Countee; Howard University; Hughes, Langston; Jones, Lois Mailou; Richardson, Willis; Woodson, Carter G.; *other specific writers and editors*

Further Reading

Alvarez, Joseph A. "The Lonesome Boy Theme as Emblem for Arna Bontemps's Children's Literature." *African American Review*, 32(1), 1998.

Gray, Christine Rauchfuss. *Willis Richardson: Forgotten Pioneer of African-American Drama.* Westport, Conn.: Greenwood, 1999.

Harris, Violet J. "Race Consciousness, Refinement, and Radicalism: Socialization in *The Brownies' Book.*" *Children's Literature Association Quarterly*, 14(4), Winter 1989.

Johnson, Dianne. *Telling Tales: The Pedagogy and Promise of African American Literature for Youth.* Westport, Conn.: Greenwood, 1990.

Nichols, Charles H., ed. *Arna Bontemps—Langston Hughes Letters, 1925–1967.* New York, Dodd, Mead, 1980.

Smith, Katharine Capshaw. "Constructing a Shared History: Black Pageantry for Children during the Harlem Renaissance." *Children's Literature*, 27, 1999.

Literature: 3—Drama

The evolution of black drama in America was quite slow. In fact, compared with other literary genres, drama could be regarded as a new field for African American writers; the Harlem Renaissance, so rich in poetry and fiction, was relatively poor in drama. Historically, slavery and its aftermath, as well as prejudice, are obvious explanations; however, the comparative lack of black dramatists—in contrast to black poets and novelists—in the first half of the twentieth century can also be explained by the fact that drama is a totally public genre. A play needs to be staged; staging costs money; investors are therefore needed; and investors expect to make a profit. At the time of the Harlem Renaissance, professional theaters, which were owned and run mostly by whites, were reluctant to produce black drama because there was no guarantee of a satisfactory box office. On the other hand, black playwrights were active in amateur theaters, and many black playwrights, men and women, were seriously involved in establishing genuine black drama.

White Playwrights and Black Drama

One factor motivating black dramatists, even if they were effectively excluded from commercial American theater, was the way blacks were being portrayed onstage. Some theatrical roles did exist for black performers, especially in musicals, but these roles were almost invariably stereotyped. In the early 1820s, white entertainers had begun to imitate African American songs, dances, dialects, and manners; minstrel shows developed in the 1840s. Minstrelsy became extremely popular, and its sentimental, melodramatic, and mocking images dominated the American stage until the 1920s. Consequently, black characters—as presented to white theater audiences by white playwrights—were fixed types such as the buffoon, the tragic mulatto, the primitive, the Christian slave, and the black beast. At around the end of World War I, a few white playwrights set out to create a more realistic picture of blacks and black life and to give black characters more verisimilitude. They were seeking new materials for drama; the folk tradition, which was to be a hallmark of black drama during the Harlem Renaissance and later, appealed to them. Eugene O'Neill, Paul Green, Marc Connelly, Dorothy and DuBose Heyward, and Ridgely Torrence did initiate a new folk drama; but despite their seriousness and their integrity, and although many blacks were in sympathy with their efforts, these white dramatists could not have firsthand knowledge of the black experience. Arguably, then, black dramatists were needed to find genuine material for drama and to mold it truthfully.

O'Neill's plays about African Americans, most notably *The Emperor Jones* (1920) and *All God's Chillun Got Wings* (1924), are a case in point. The black characters are presented as emancipated but at the same time as "chained" because they are, in one way or another, psychologically subjugated: they exist in a state of fear and resentment. Thus these characters, who seem fated to fail in the white world, confirm white people's stereotypes of blacks. O'Neill's depiction of blacks has been problematic for black critics, who feel that, whatever he intended, he did little to improve the image of African Americans onstage.

A second example is Paul Green, who was the most prolific white dramatist to write about black people and their issues but who seems to have envisaged failure as their ultimate fate. His play *In Abraham's Bosom: The Tragedy of a Southern Negro* (1926)—which attracted a great deal of attention on Broadway and won a Pulitzer prize—focuses on Abraham McCranie, a black man who dreams of leading his people out of the bondage of poverty and ignorance through education. *In Abraham's Bosom* powerfully illustrates the workings of racism in the minds of blacks as well as whites, and it is a moving drama; in the end, though, the protagonist cannot realize his dream.

A third example is Marc Connelly's *Green Pastures* (1930), his only play about blacks and his only play on a religious subject; it too won a Pulitzer prize. This biblical drama, presented in southern American Negro dialect, had an all-Negro cast that included a Negro actor playing the role of God; it was extremely popular and tremendously successful on Broadway—but it too seems to end in failure, as human sympathy is extended to a suffering God.

DuBose Heyward's novella *Porgy* (1925), set in a Negro quarter in Charleston, South Carolina, at the turn of the twentieth century, is a fourth example. It was widely considered one of the two most successful fictional works of the Harlem Renaissance (the other being Jean Toomer's *Cane*); Dorothy and DuBose Heyward turned it into a play (1927), also called *Porgy*, on which the libretto of George Gershwin's opera *Porgy and Bess* was based. The protagonist, Porgy, is a crippled street vendor who falls in love with Bess, the mistress of a black "bad man," and is eventually defeated. The play proceeds from life, love, and hope toward murder, resignation, and loneliness.

By contrast, Ridgely Torrence's earlier *Three Plays for a Negro Theatre*, staged between 1914 and 1917, marked a turning point in black drama because they broke away from stereotypes of black characters, presenting Negroes as human beings with dignity and the potential for tragedy. *Granny Maumee* (1914), hailed as a serious and truthful play about Negroes from the Negro point of view, is the story of a proud, vengeful black matriarch whose sense of her duty as a

Christian eventually prevails as she confronts her son's white murderer, who happens also to be the rapist of her daughter and the father of her grandson. The other two of the *Three Plays* were *The Rider of Dreams* (1917) and *Simon the Cyrenian* (1917).

Black Theories and Black Theater

All these white dramatists, then, served as a motivation for black dramatists and thus heralded a new dawn for black drama. In addition, two figures who worked diligently for the development of African American drama were W. E. B. Du Bois and Alain Locke. Although Du Bois and Locke disagreed about several aspects of black drama, they agreed that it needed to be promoted, and they both emphasized the importance of black culture as its proper source.

African American drama by African Americans emerged in Harlem and elsewhere during the early 1920s and was accepted as giving a more authentic view of blacks than works by white playwrights could offer. This black drama could be divided into two distinct categories: race plays and folk plays. Race plays dealt with pertinent racial issues such as prejudice, oppression, and miscegenation and often constituted propaganda directed toward social change. Folk plays were intended mainly to educate and entertain without offending the audience. The basic differences between race and folk drama regarding purpose and subject matter reflected Du Bois and Locke's opposite attitudes.

Du Bois believed strongly that African American drama had to serve a purpose, which was clearly propagandistic. He advanced this theory in *The Crisis*, the magazine of the National Association for the Advancement of Colored People (NAACP), of which he was the editor; and he applied it in his own pageant *The Star of Ethiopia* (1915). At this time NAACP organized a drama committee to encourage black playwrights to address the black experience; later, in 1925, Du Bois and Charles S. Johnson, the editor of the National Urban League's magazine *Opportunity*, launched contests for the best one-act plays of the year, which they would publish in *The Crisis* and *Opportunity* respectively, thus providing exposure for new playwrights. In 1926, to contribute further to the development of black drama, Du Bois organized the Crigwa Players (an acronym for Crisis Guild of Writers and Artists; the name was later changed to Krigwa). In his article "Krigwa Players Little Negro Theatre: The Story of a Little Theatre Movement," which was published in *The Crisis*, Du Bois laid down four fundamental principles for the new drama: "the plays of a real Negro theatre must be about us . . . by us . . . for us . . . and near us." These criteria imply race drama.

Du Bois's conviction that black drama should be propaganda for the race clashed with Alain Locke's concept of black drama as an art, not a vehicle for messages. Locke's alternative to race drama was folk drama or art drama. Locke and Montgomery T. Gregory promoted folk plays at Howard University, where Gregory organized the department of dramatic arts as a step toward a national Negro theater. This was the first institution to provide professional training in theater for aspiring black playwrights and performers. The Howard dramatic arts department had an advisory board consisting mostly of successful white theater practitioners and academics; it included Ridgely Torrence and Eugene O'Neill, the drama critic Robert Benchley, Professor George Baker of the renowned "Harvard 47" workshop, and the presidents of Harvard University and Smith College. Gregory believed that to survive and be accepted in the United States, black drama would have to reach not only blacks but all of American society—and that this could best be done by art plays rather than race plays. He and Locke both considered the stage to be a means of entertaining an audience and of preserving African American folk culture. In "Steps toward the Negro Theatre," published in *The Crisis* in 1922, Locke heralded the concept of Negro theater as distinct from race drama.

In a sense, the Harlem Renaissance was a battleground for Du Bois's and Locke's conflicting visions of theater; much of the literature produced by black literati—poets, essayists, and novelists as well as dramatists—reflected this crucial conflict. Eventually, though, the principles of Gregory, Locke, and Howard University's dramatic arts department seemed to win out: African American drama found its voice in the folk tradition; the folk element became a defining feature of most drama, professional and amateur, of the Harlem Renaissance.

This folk element was derived from slavery, the rural culture of the South, and the migration to the industrial North—and from racial oppression and prejudice as crucial factors (if not the most crucial factor) in black history. It should be noted, however, that folk drama did not take the form of "problem plays"; unlike race drama, it did not deal with issues like miscegenation, lynching, and passing. Instead, it dealt with issues such as poverty and with black history, and it explored the lives of black people. Borrowing almost nothing from white culture, folk drama initiated a new black

aesthetics, as well as a form of black nationalism. These plays were unlike most of the plays about black life written by white dramatists; the black stereotypes popular with white producers and their white audiences were replaced with more genuine portrayals. As was mentioned earlier, this kind of drama tended to cut off black playwrights from professional theaters, but many of their works were performed in small community theaters, churches, and college auditoriums.

Black Drama on Broadway

The first black hit on Broadway was actually a sensational musical comedy, *Shuffle Along* (1921), written by four black artists: Flournoy Miller, Aubrey Lyles, Noble Sissle, and Eubie Blake. *Shuffle Along* differed from earlier revues in its tightly structured plot and how it blended the story with the music in an organic whole.

Willis Richardson was the first black playwright to have a serious drama produced on Broadway. This was *The Chip Woman's Fortune* (1923), a one-act folk drama that had been prepared for Broadway under the patronage of Eugene O'Neill and was a great success. Richardson, a prolific dramatist, differed from most of his contemporaries in that he avoided themes having to do with tension between blacks and whites, focusing instead on the ordinary problems faced by ordinary black people. He wrote about poverty, gossip, jealousy, extravagance, greed, and family problems. Richardson's main influence on the Harlem Renaissance was this shift away from the usual emphasis on racial strife, along with the absence of white characters in his plays. He avoided depictions of blacks as victimized by whites, and his stage was not dominated by white culture. Richardson was a pioneer in dramatizing black Americans and their lives and in attempting to correct distorted stereotypes of blacks.

Garland Anderson's *Appearances* (1925) was the second black play and the first full-length black play to reach Broadway. It espoused a philosophy of self-sufficiency traceable to Booker T. Washington, emphasizing the work ethic and individual initiative as the path to success in capitalist America. Frank Wilson's *Meek Mose* was the next black play on Broadway, in 1928.

The poet, novelist, and editor Wallace Thurman collaborated with William Rapp on a play, *Harlem*, that was staged on Broadway in 1929 and was one of the first black plays to become a box-office success there. *Harlem* was a controversial play; it received quite negative reviews from black critics, who objected to its picture of Harlem as a wild, exotic playground, a corrupt place where gambling, prostitution, sexual promiscuity, and murder were everyday experiences. In underlining the primitive and sensational elements in black life, Thurman seemed to be appealing to white tastes and perpetuating stereotypes; his intention, though, was to give a genuine portrait of urban blacks, in particular by using vernacular and idiomatic expressions—which he explained in a glossary that accompanied the playbill.

Of the plays by African American dramatists, Langston Hughes's *Mulatto* (1935) had the longest run on Broadway. Hughes was seriously interested in black drama but believed that, although an honest American Negro literature had been achieved, Negro theater still remained to be developed. For his own dramatic works, he took various themes from his poetry: the legacy of slavery, the African heritage, black rural and urban folk culture, and racial oppression. Hughes created both race plays and folk plays.

Mulatto is in the tragic mode of black folk drama. Here Hughes changes the familiar stereotype of the tragic mulatto, making this figure militant rather than meek and gentle. The mulatto character, who desires above all else to be recognized as his white father's son, ultimately kills first his father and then himself. Hughes saw tragedy as intertwined with historical, social, and political injustice, and his tragic figures in *Mulatto*, *Emperor of Haiti* (1934), and *Front Porch* (1938) are all involved in broad social issues and conflicts.

Mule Bone, which Hughes wrote with Zora Neale Hurston (in the 1930s, although it was not staged until 1991 because of a disagreement between them), is in the comic folk mode. *Little Ham* (1936), *When the Jack Hollers* (1936), and *Joy to My Soul* (1936) are also in the comic folk mode. *Little Ham*, a comedy of urban life that blends satire with social issues, is a romantic play with a large cast of more than forty characters; it is about the black world of Harlem and is written for that world alone—Hughes uses a vernacular that few whites would know.

Hughes also tried his hand at poetic drama in the experimental play *Don't You Want to Be Free* (1939), which chronicled the experience of slavery through music and dance.

In the 1930s, Hughes's ideology shifted to the left; in plays like *Blood on the Fields* (1934), *Angelo Herndon Jones* (1936), and *The Organizer* (1938) he used leftist ideology to interpret social injustice. These were his problem plays, or race plays.

Taken as a whole, Hughes's drama of the 1930s grew out of the black drama of the previous decade, was in various dramatic modes, and offered a panoramic view of black life. It is extremely inclusive: it embraces a keen race-consciousness, racial tension, comic and tragic folk elements, rural and urban motifs, poverty, the experience of slavery, family conflicts, and social and economic inequities. Underlying his tragic and comic folk drama and his race drama is a constant emphasis on social rectification.

Race Drama

Willis Richardson, Garland Anderson, Frank Wilson, Wallace Thurman, and Langston Hughes were prominent black dramatists whose work was staged on Broadway during the Harlem Renaissance. Anderson, Wilson, and Thurman had plays on Broadway before the stock market crash in 1929. After the crash, it became nearly impossible for a black dramatist to find a commercial producer; however, as noted previously, works by black playwrights were produced in churches, lodges, and community halls; were published in periodicals such as *The Crisis*, *Opportunity*, *Carolina*, and *Birth Control Review*; and were entered in contests sponsored by *The Crisis* and *Opportunity*. In addition, some black theater groups, such as the Harlem Suitcase Theater, Negro People's Theater, and Rose McClendon Players, were formed during the Harlem Renaissance. The Federal Theater Project, particularly the Negro Unit at the Lafayette Theater in Harlem, also provided opportunities for black actors and dramatists. It is true that many black dramatists, by staying within the black community, did not achieve the popularity they might have had on Broadway. However, the few black plays that were produced on Broadway at the time were neither race plays that might challenge a white audience nor folk plays that might present the black heritage to whites; the considerable black theater that took place in communities, even if it did not reach a large public at the time, did contribute to the development of African American drama.

A notable early example of black race drama was Angelina Weld Grimké's *Rachel* (1916), commissioned by NAACP to counter D. W. Griffith's *Birth of a Nation* (1915). *Rachel* was presented by the drama committee of the District of Columbia branch of the NAACP at the Myrtilla Miner Normal School, and the playbill stated that it was "the first attempt to use the stage for race propaganda in order to enlighten the American people relative to the lamentable condition of ten million of colored citizens in this free Republic." *Rachel* addresses the psychological impact of racism on black women;

the protagonist is so deeply affected by racism that she decides never to marry and never to have a child. The play became controversial and aroused considerable unease in the black community—particularly among members of the NAACP, its sponsor—because of its overtly political, propagandistic nature. For example, Gregory and Locke (who espoused folk or art drama rather than race drama) dissented from the ideological platform of the NAACP's drama committee.

Still, *Rachel* was an influential play, one of the first of a succession of serious protest and propaganda dramas, many of which were written by women. Dominant themes in these plays were lynching, poverty, miscegenation, and passing; like *Rachel*, the plays tended to be grim, ending with the death of the main character or with his or her complete disillusionment. Alice Dunbar Nelson's *Mine Eyes Have Seen* (1918) considers the question of a black man's loyalty during wartime to a country that has offered him only prejudice and oppression. In Mary Burrill's *Aftermath* (1919), a young black hero returns from the war to find that his father has been lynched and decides to take the law into his own hands. Another play by Burrill, *They That Sit in Darkness* (1919), is a tract for birth control: It is about an impoverished woman who dies after bearing too many children. Ottie Graham's *Holiday* (1923) exemplifies the theme of the tragic mulatto. In this play, a mulatto mother leaves her brown-skinned daughter to be raised by friends and then, years later, precipitates a tragedy when she decides to reveal her identity to the daughter. The daughter, unable to accept the truth, commits suicide; and the mother, unable to live with her guilt, does the same. In Myrtle Livingston Smith's *For Unborn Children* (1926), a mulatto man—not wanting to have children who would undergo what he has experienced—leaves his white fiancée and finally offers himself to a lynch mob. In Georgia Johnson's *A Sunday Morning in the South* (1925), an innocent young black man, suspected of flirting with a white woman, is taken from his family on a Sunday morning and hanged. Marieta Bonner, in *The Purple Flower* (1928), a surrealistic play, condemns "white devils." In May Miller's *Stragglers in the Dust* (1930), a black charwoman is convinced that the body in the tomb of the unknown soldier in Washington, D.C., is that of her son, who was killed in action during World War I.

Folk plays, which were written by men and women, often focused on the lighter side of the black experience. Religion, class-consciousness, morality, and love were favorite themes of folk drama. The folk dramatist Eulalie Spence, for instance, intentionally avoided racial themes in favor of universal themes. In her article "A Criticism of the Negro Drama" (published in *Opportunity* in 1928), she stressed entertainment as the most important element of drama, arguing that black people go to the theater to laugh, not to "have old fires and hates rekindled"; she herself was basically a writer of comedies—such as *The Hunch* (1927), which centers on a love triangle in Harlem. However, Spence's play *Her* (1927) is a mystery that juxtaposes religion and superstition, and her *Undertow* (1929)—about a woman who returns from the South after many years to take back the man she loves from his wife—is more of a melodrama.

Many folk plays were set in the South, and these tended to be less lighthearted than other folk drama: they often portray whites as antagonists and end with death. In G. D. Lipscomb's *Frances* (1925), a young black woman's father forces her into a sexual liaison with a white foreman. In Randolph Edmonds's *Breeders* (1930), a young black woman's white master tries to force her into a sexual relationship with a black man in order to bear strong slave children, but she commits suicide. In John Mathews's *Ti Yette* (1930), a black man murders his sister rather than let her marry her white lover. Such folk drama often presented whites as cruel and cunning, who lured and cheated innocent, unsuspecting blacks. In Joseph Mitchell's *Help Wanted* (1929), a black couple move to Chicago in hope of a better life, only to be cheated out of receiving credit for their money-saving invention. And even folk plays set in the North frequently presented the African American as being like a caged bird: emancipation, in such plays, has led to a new form of slavery—black people are enslaved not only by the oppressiveness and prejudice of white society but also by their own lack of education, lack of confidence, lack of experience, and lack of the material resources needed for survival in a free land.

To address this new, post-Emancipation slavery, some dramatists set out to educate black people. Willis Richardson and May Miller, for instance, compiled an anthology of dramas of the 1920s and early 1930s, *Negro History in Thirteen Plays* (1935), that was intended for black schools. Carter G. Woodson, who wrote the preface, said that this anthology was a "step of the Negro toward the emancipation of his mind from the slavery of the inferiority complex." The plays chosen by Richardson and Miller interpreted history through myth, legend, and fiction and offered impressive alternatives to the stereotypes of blacks that were usual in American theater. Helen Webb Harris's *Genifrede* (1922) and *Frederick Douglass* (1923), Willis Richardson's *Flight of the Natives* (1927), and May Miller's *Graven Images*

715

(1929) were all plays that tried to liberate the black audience from its past in slavery and reconstruct a history that would convey hope, pride, and glory.

Although Zora Neale Hurston is known mainly as a novelist (*Their Eyes Were Watching God*, 1937) and an anthropologist (*Mules and Men*, 1935), she also wrote plays such as *Color Struck* (1925), *The First One* (1927), and (with Langston Hughes, as mentioned earlier) *Mule Bone* (1931). In *Color Struck*, a black girl is damaged by illogical standards of beauty. *The First One* is a history play that reinterprets the relationship between the biblical Noah and his darker son, Ham; it parodies a version of the biblical story which was circulated during the antebellum period to convince blacks that slavery was part of God's design. Hurston, in her typical playful style, presents a whole family of Hams— artists who do not believe that being black is a curse, whatever Noah might have intended. *Mule Bone: A Comedy of Negro Life* combines amusing anecdotes from Hurston's folklore collection *Mules and Men* with Langston Hughes' bluesy humor.

The Legacy of Black Drama

Black drama written during the Harlem Renaissance encompassed a great variety of themes, styles, and approaches. What has survived from that era, however, is quite a small body of works. A few black playwrights— perhaps five—had their work performed on Broadway; some playwrights received productions from amateur groups in schools, lodges, churches, and so on, reaching a limited audience; and plays that won the drama contests sponsored by *Opportunity* and *The Crisis* were published, as were plays by the important figures of the renaissance, such as Langston Hughes and Zora Neale Hurston. The rest of the dramatists and their works were, for a long time, doomed to obscurity. Not until the 1990s were many of these plays brought to light in anthologies and collections. The "lost plays" of the Harlem Renaissance that have been found relatively recently testify to the extensive dramatic activity of the renaissance period, despite the adverse circumstances facing black dramatists. Freeing themselves from the influence of stereotypes and turning to a black audiences, however small that audience may have been, these playwrights strove to develop a true African American drama.

ASLI TEKINAY

See also Authors: 4—Playwrights; Blacks in Theater; Carolina Magazine; Community Theater; Crisis, The: Literary Prizes; Du Bois, W. E. B.; Federal Programs; Johnson, Charles Spurgeon; Krigwa Players; Locke, Alain; Opportunity Literary Contests; Theater; Woodson, Carter G.; *specific playwrights and works*

Further Reading

Du Bois, W. E. B. "The Drama among Black Folk." *The Crisis*, 1916.

———. "Criteria of Negro Art. *The Crisis*, 1926a.

———. "Krigwa Players Little Negro Theatre." *The Crisis*, 1926b.

Gray, Christine Rauchfuss. *Willis Richardson: Forgotten Pioneer of African American Drama*. Westport, Conn.: Greenwood, 1999.

Gregory, Thomas Montgomery. "The Drama of Negro Life." In *The New Negro*, ed. Alain Locke. New York: Atheneum, 1970. (Originally published 1925.)

Gregory, T. Montgomery, and Alain Locke, eds. *Plays of Negro Life*. New York: Harper and Row, 1927.

Hatch, James V., and Lee Hamalian, eds. *Lost Plays of the Harlem Renaissance: 1920–1940*. Detroit, Mich.: Wayne State University Press, 1996.

Hatch, James V., and Ted Shine, eds. *Black Theatre U.S.A.: Plays by African Americans—The Early Period (1847–1938)*. New York: Free Press, 1996.

Hughes, Langston. "The Negro Artist and the Racial Mountain." In *The New Negro Renaissance*, ed. Arthur P. Davis and Michael W. Peplow. New York: Holt, Rinehart, and Winston. (Originally published 1926.)

Locke, Alain. "Steps toward the Negro Theatre." *The Crisis*, 1922.

———. "The Negro and the American Stage." *Theatre Arts Monthly*, 10, 1926.

Locke, Alain, ed. *The New Negro*. New York, 1925.

Patterson, Lindsay, ed. *Black Theatre: A Twentieth-Century Collection of the Work of Its Best Playwrights*. New York: Dodd, Mead, 1971.

Spence, Eulalie. "A Criticism of the Negro Drama." *Opportunity*, 28 June 1928.

Turner, Darwin T., ed. *Black Drama in America: An Anthology*, 2nd ed. Washington, D.C.: Howard University Press, 1994.

Literature: 4—Fiction

Fiction produced during the Harlem Renaissance reflects the social, historic, and political influences present in the immediate aftermath of World War I. Participation by blacks in the war that was to make the world safe for democracy, along with their keen awareness of continued racial oppression in postwar America, resulted in awakened pride, race-consciousness, militancy, and assertiveness—traits that were evident among writers of fiction and in their works. This boldness manifested itself in a rejection of stifling western literary aesthetics and a search for original narrative forms and techniques. By no means is the fiction monolithic, however. Rather, there are diverse political concerns, strategies, and subjects. For instance, writing reflecting the "talented tenth"—such as the works of Jessie Redmon Fauset and Nella Larsen—is vastly different from the bohemian emphasis of the Jamaican-born Claude McKay. George Schuyler's satiric works, or those of Rudolph Fisher, contrast sharply with the impressionism of Jean Toomer's masterpiece *Cane*. Among all writers of fiction, though, there is a narrative concern with the attempt of blacks to explore the complex bicultural self. This discussion will focus on just a few representative novels.

The Color Line

A number of novelists turned their attention to the talented tenth, the elite segment of the race that was to offer leadership to the masses (Du Bois, 1903). Foremost among the issues confronting this group was color. Because quite a few of the talented tenth were light enough to pass for white and thus cross the color line, questions regarding the nature, scope, and consequences of passing assumed paramount importance. Nella Larsen's *Quicksand* (1928) is a compelling rendering of a young woman's efforts to find a place within a society polarized along lines of race, gender, and class. The heroine, twenty-three-year-old Helga Crane, is the daughter of a West Indian father and a Danish mother. Refined, well educated, and strikingly beautiful, Helga exemplifies the ideals of the talented tenth. But she is unable to find genuine satisfaction in either bourgeois white society or the black world. The narrative unfolds against a backdrop involving Helga's search for herself—one that takes her from the rural South, where at the opening she is a schoolteacher, to Chicago, New York, Denmark, back to New York, and finally to a small town in Alabama. When she returns to the South she becomes the wife of a dull, overbearing country preacher. Helga abandons her aspirations for the finer things in life: exquisite clothes, fine food, and elaborate furnishings. Instead, she is mired in domesticity, subject to her husband's authoritarian rule. As the novel closes, Helga, worn

down by a life of endless childbearing, is pregnant with her fifth child.

Much of the significance of *Quicksand* has to do with Larsen's rather sympathetic portrayal of a heroine facing a crisis. Helga is not simply a stereotypical tragic mulatto poised between the black and white worlds and unable to find genuine acceptance in either society; she is a psychologically complex woman. Larsen is careful to offer a representation of Helga's inner life. The young woman is far too refined for the small-town southern community where she teaches, and she is clearly out of place among the people who are disdainful of her because of her manner, bearing, and taste. A painful rejection by her white uncle in Chicago prompts her meeting with Mrs. Hayes-Rore, an independently wealthy widow who rescues the destitute Helga, takes her to New York, and finds her a place to stay and a job. But Hayes-Rore's pompous manner and pretentious speeches about race are unappealing to Helga. Anne Grey, a socialite widow in Harlem, is well connected but overly consumed by the issue of race. She too befriends Helga, who, however, is either unable or unwilling to establish a lasting bond with Grey.

Helga's crisis is not only a matter of race; she also struggles with her nascent sexuality, which she both revels in and denies. The confusion surrounding her sexuality prompts her to end her engagement to James Vayle, a well-connected teacher. She also refuses a proposal from Axel Olsen, a Swedish painter who, like the other Europeans, sees Helga not as an individual but as something exotic. The character who has by far the strongest impact on Helga's sexual self is James Anderson, principal of the school where she teaches. In New York, Anderson kisses Helga passionately, and she believes that he loves her. When she learns of his engagement to Anne Grey, Helga is devastated. In a rush of emotions, Helga finds herself in a storefront church in Harlem, where she surrenders to God and to the minister's seductive powers.

Larsen uses quicksand skillfully as a metaphor, interweaving this motif throughout the narrative. The image suggests the various influences—both internal and external—conspiring to bring about the heroine's tragic fall. The harder Helga tries to extricate herself from the quagmire of race, class, and gender, the more those forces entrap her. Perhaps this is Larsen's own pronouncement on the limited options of a mixed-race woman. Even so, one cannot ignore the role that Helga's poor judgment plays in determining her fate: her painful dilemma is intensified by what she herself does or refuses to do. In any case, the novel is a forceful treatment of passing and its consequences; and although the portrait of Harlem is superficial, Larsen presents a memorable account of the challenges often faced by the black middle class.

Jessie Fauset's *Plum Bun* (1929) is perhaps less convincing than *Quicksand* but is still compelling in its treatment of the bourgeoisie. *Plum Bun* deals with passing largely through the experiences of Angela Murray, an attractive, ambitious art student; and her younger sister Virginia, a music teacher. Angela, like her mother, is fair skinned and can pass for white; but Virginia is dark skinned like her father. The sisters have been reared in an all-black working-class neighborhood in Philadelphia; they are left alone after both parents die within a relatively short time. Angela then studies art in New York and is established in Greenwich Village; there, as in Philadelphia, she decides that refraining from announcing her race will allow her freedom and mobility. She is attracted to a rich young white man, Roger Fielding, who is interested only in seducing her. When Virginia arrives, Angela is torn between her desire to pass in the white world and her sisterly bond. Rather than risk exposure, Angela chooses to estrange herself from Virginia.

Although Fauset appears to avoid dealing directly with racial issues in her treatment of the black middle class, the resolution of the novel emphasizes the importance of race. What sets the stage for this affirmation is the relationship between Angela and Rachel Powell, a young black woman pursuing a career in art. The climax of the novel occurs when Rachel is denied passage to Europe on an art scholarship because she is black. Angela is outraged and realizes that her own scholarship was a matter of color, not talent or merit. But it is mainly Virginia's example that makes Angela realize she is mistaken in denying her racial identity. Virginia enters the world of black artists and intellectuals in Harlem and is comfortable. Through her sister's example, then, Angela comes to see how superficial her own life has been.

Angela's conflict with Virginia symbolizes a war between the black and the white self; *Plum Bun*, like other novels of the Harlem Renaissance, touches not only on the racial prejudice of white America but also on "colorism" among blacks, an attitude that leads some of them to deny their cultural heritage. In exploring this theme, Fauset includes a number of highly improbable situations. That the two sisters should become romantically involved with the same man, who also passes for white, is unlikely. Anthony, who thinks Angela is white, is unaware of her relationship to Virginia. Once Angela announces her heritage publicly, she and Anthony are reunited. Virginia then returns to her first love, Martin, and to Philadelphia. In the end, individual characters learn that happiness cannot be achieved through a rejection of one's true identity.

Wallace Thurman's *The Blacker the Berry: A Novel of Negro Life* (1929) focuses on Emma Lou Morgan's struggle to be accepted by light-skinned blacks. Because she is dark, Emma Lou is mistreated by her fair-skinned family. Emma Lou's mother was light-skinned and expected her daughter to be even lighter. The mother's most serious flaw is her belief that "white is right," an ideal which she upholds at every turn; she makes her daughter's life miserable by repeatedly and unfavorably comparing Emma Lou's color with that of others. Unfortunately, Emma Lou comes to accept her mother's pronouncements, internalizing western standards of beauty.

In an effort to escape the rejection she experiences at home, Emma Lou goes to a university in California. There, through a series of humiliating experiences, she learns that her fair-skinned classmates ostracize her as readily as her family does. She uses various skin whiteners and bleaching creams, but to no avail; in fact, some of these products accentuate her blackness. To make matters worse, she prefers light-skinned boyfriends who take advantage of her emotionally and sexually. But finally, as a result of a painful encounter with one of her lovers, she comes to accept herself as she is.

Thurman deals head-on with the color-consciousness that was prevalent during the Harlem Renaissance. Emma Lou represents the black Americans who failed to embrace Marcus Garvey's slogan "Black is beautiful." *The Blacker the Berry* lacks subtlety in its portrayal of Emma Lou and her pervasive self-hatred, however, and the issue of color prejudice is much more complex than Thurman indicates. Because he fails to address the intricacies of intraracial prejudice, he oversimplifies a very complicated psychosocial issue. Nevertheless, in her divided allegiance and her preoccupation with white standards and ideals, Emma Lou personifies the "double consciousness" that W. E. B. Du Bois considered central to black life in a nation polarized by race.

Literary Primitivism

Whereas some novelists chose to depict the tragedies and triumphs of the middle class, others, like Claude McKay, focused on the experiences of the working class. McKay's *Home to Harlem* (1928) is an exposé of the seamier side of Harlem—the jook joints, speakeasies, and cabarets frequented by the displaced urban masses. Here, outside the social mainstream, people have a certain joie de vivre that is reflected in their carefree lifestyle and attitudes. Jake Brown, the protagonist, takes unofficial leave from the army during World War I after being assigned noncombatant duties in Europe. He returns to New York as a stoker and finds that Harlem is a safe haven. After an affair with a prostitute, Felice, who declines to keep his money, he continues to search for her. His search takes him through the underworld of Harlem, where he comes into contact with a wide range of characters. Congo Rose, for example, is an entertainer who takes Jake as a lover when he is broke. Agatha, an assistant in a beauty parlor, is a paragon: sincere, warm, and congenial. Zeddy Plummer is a gambler who reports Jake to the authorities as a deserter. Susy is a prostitute who supports Zeddy. Billy Biasse is Jake's friend who operates a longshoremen's gambling apartment.

McKay, unlike Larsen or Fauset, focuses on the proletariat, the working class, rather than on the talented tenth with their painfully proper ways. As a result, he was strongly criticized by Du Bois, who felt that literature should be political and should serve the purpose of racial uplift. Du Bois, along with a number of others, reasoned that when blacks write about themselves they should put their best foot forward, and that McKay had therefore let down the race. However, McKay does introduce a character, Jake's comrade Ray, who is bookish and serves as a foil to Jake. Through Ray, McKay establishes tension between the intellectual and the primitive. Ray is a Haitian who has attended Howard University, and he no doubt represents McKay, a Jamaican who had studied at Tuskegee Institute. Ray is a voice for McKay's social and philosophical views, believing that blacks should regain their self-confidence by understanding the past glories of black civilization. But Ray is also pessimistic, decrying his education at Howard, unable to accept marriage to Agatha, and unable to accept the challenges of life in Harlem; eventually he leaves America for Europe.

Jake, who lacks formal education, is McKay's ideal black American. Free from materialism, spirited, and streetwise, he is the classic picaresque hero. He represents the unlettered masses. Jake's one goal is to find Felice again so that they can enjoy life together. One of his most significant traits is resilience. He is able to endure the vicissitudes and misfortunes of life and yet remain positive. Thus the message McKay conveys is that the primitive black can cope with the uncertainties of life whereas the intellectual cannot.

Home to Harlem offers a vivid and realistic portrait of Harlem's underworld and its denizens. Scenes in nightclubs and cabarets give the reader insights into life among the struggling masses. The novel is, as well, a vehicle for McKay's political views, especially his views on class and race. He explores social issues of everyday urban life, such as overcrowding, unemployment, and discrimination.

The Satiric Novel

Through the lens of satire, novelists are able to maintain artistic distance between themselves and their sometimes very serious subject matter, holding all of society—black and white—up for scrutiny. George Schuyler's *Black No More* (1931) offers an examination of color prejudice. The novel opens when a black doctor named Crookman discovers an electric process that can make black people white. This discovery makes the doctor rich but causes an upheaval in America: black leaders lose their followers; white supremacist organizations are at a loss because race can no longer be easily discerned; alarming numbers of white women give birth to black babies. At the end of the novel, "Nordicized" blacks are found to be actually whiter than born Nordics. A black beautician then invents a skin stain to turn white skin light brown, and everyone starts trying to darken up.

Schuyler aims his attack at race leaders who exploit the color line for personal gain, and he is as unrelenting toward the talented tenth as toward the unlettered masses. In the world of *Black No More*, brown, not black, is beautiful. The novel suggests that the root of the color problem is capitalism and the free enterprise system, because those who are most vehemently opposed to Crookman's process are businessmen. Schuyler rejects both capitalism and racism and offers socialism as the solution for national ills. Yet the novel ends on an ambivalent note, suggesting uncertainty about the materialist American dream and those who pursue it.

Rudolph Fisher, in *The Walls of Jericho* (1928), satirizes the social extremes of Harlem: not only the pretensions of the "dickties"—the middle-class elite—but also the earthiness of the low-down folk. He also pokes fun at the whites who patronize haunts in Harlem. Merrit, a fair-skinned black lawyer who can pass for white, buys a home in one of the last white neighborhoods in Harlem. Shine, one of the black movers who bring in Merrit's furniture, falls in love with Linda, Merrit's maid. Whites, presumably, set fire to Merrit's house, and the author shows how class tension between Jinx and Bubber, the other movers, and Merrit is relaxed in the face of a racial struggle. As it turns out, though, Merrit's house was burned not by whites but by one of his black enemies.

A major contribution that this novel made to the fiction of the Harlem Renaissance is its use of the vernacular, especially street talk between Jinx and Bubber. The humor of this pair of characters is expressed largely in the slang of the times. The novel abounds with signifying, playing the dozens (talking about someone's ancestors, especially the mother), and terms for describing an opponent's worthlessness. Fisher's chief purpose, however, was to examine the complexities, and particularly the foibles, of Harlemites. He attempted to debunk what he saw as myths about Harlem; at the same time as he depicted middle-class attitudes of the day, he was also able to look at all of black life objectively. By making the villain in *The Walls of Jericho* black rather than white, he suggested that the white man is not always the black man's problem.

Folklore and Fiction

During the Harlem Renaissance, a number of novelists found material in black expressive culture: symbolic acts of religion, speech, and music. A coalescence of oral and written forms resulted in texts with a rich, complex substructure harking back to the vernacular tradition. Zora Neale Hurston's *Their Eyes Were Watching God* (1937) follows the life of Janie Crawford as she comes of age and finds her identity both as an African American and as a woman. The action is set in rural Florida—mostly in Eatonville, Hurston's own birthplace. Janie is the product of an illicit relationship between her mother, Leafy, and a schoolteacher. After seeing sixteen-year-old Janie kissing a young man, Nanny, Janie's grandmother (a former slave), arranges a marriage to Logan Killicks, an older, propertied farmer. The marriage is unhappy; Logan intends to break Janie's spirit by making her submissive and forcing her to work alongside him in the fields. Janie leaves him in order to marry Joe Starks, a citified, smooth-talking, ambitious older man who offers her the "front porch" existence Nanny values. But Joe turns out to be no different from Logan. He wants Janie to remain subservient in a socially prescribed place and refuses to let her associate with the folk.

Joe's early death (he dies of kidney failure) allows Janie to begin the process of self-discovery. She enters a third marriage with Virgible Tea Cake Woods, an itinerant blues man and gambler who is her ideal. Although he is fourteen years her junior and unemployed, he allows her space to be herself. With Tea Cake, Janie travels to South Florida, where she works on the muck, the rich soil in which vegetables flourish. Here, among migrant workers, she steps down from the pedestal on which southern women were expected to remain and comes into her own. No longer does Janie try to live as her well-meaning grandmother would like; instead, she lives according to her own plans. Her happiness is brief, however; Tea Cake is bitten by a rabid dog during a flood, and Janie is forced to shoot him. After being acquitted of murder, she returns to Eatonville, where she tells her life story to her best friend, Phoeby.

Their Eyes Were Watching God reveals Hurston's skill not only as a writer of fiction but also as a folklorist: she captures brilliantly the customs and language of everyday people. Janie's account of her life, spoken in black dialect, is a literary device that allows the heroine to tell her own story. The text is notable for its authenticity and its fidelity to black folk speech. Some passages read much like poetry, as Hurston blurs the boundary between oral and written forms. Storytelling is an aspect of the folk tradition, allowing the transmission of values from one generation to the next; Janie's growth is suggested by her connection, or reconnection, with the vernacular tradition. With Tea Cake, particularly, Janie reaffirms the historic black past, and her voice signifies her empowerment within a white, patriarchal society.

Hurston's work is a classic within the African American novelistic tradition. Hurston tells the story of Janie in richly poetic language, and that story becomes a saga of the historic black quest for the self. Although Richard Wright (1937) criticized *Their Eyes Were Watching God* for Hurston's avoidance of overt social protest and argued that she had perpetuated racial stereotypes, more recent critics have given a more balanced assessment of its contribution to black letters. Moreover, a number of women novelists today—such as Alice Walker—consider Hurston their literary "foremother."

Langston Hughes's *Not Without Laughter* (1930)—his first novel—is about the coming of age of Sandy, a young, impressionable boy growing up in Stanton, a small midwestern town; the novel describes how Sandy must choose his path in life. His family is presided over by Aunt Hagar, who is a former slave and a community mainstay. She and his mother, Anjee, are domestics, as are all the women in the family. His aunt Harriet, who is restless and rebellious, tires of small-town life and turns to prostitution. Jim Boy, Sandy's absent father, is an itinerant railroad worker who plays blues and is constantly at odds with the churchgoing Hagar. When Hagar dies, Sandy goes to live with his prim, proper Aunt Tempy. Tempy tries to impose her conservative lifestyle on him, but he comes to reject her way of life and eventually joins his mother and Harriet in Chicago, where he works as an elevator boy.

Not without Laughter takes up various ideologies of America in the period after World War I. Hughes creates a broad range of unique characters whose response to racial oppression typifies that of other blacks struggling to make sense of their changing world. In the tradition of Booker T. Washington, the pious Aunt Hagar is conciliatory toward southern whites, believing that accommodation is the only way to achieve racial harmony, and she wants her grandson to follow in Washington's footsteps. Tempy, an elitist who joins the Episcopal church, espouses values similar to those of W. E. B. Du Bois. Free-spirited and worldly, Harriet and Jim Boy embrace the lifestyle of the working-class poor. The reader assumes that Sandy will reject Hagar's strict religiosity, Tempy's elitism, and even the blues lifestyle of his father and aunt to chart his own course in life.

The setting of this novel—Stanton's Bottom, an all-black neighborhood where individuals are free to abandon social restraints—is far removed from urbanized Harlem. Its contribution to the fiction of the Harlem Renaissance has to do with Hughes's deft rendering of secular and sacred folk forms that have allowed blacks to endure oppression. Spirituals deriving from the church are a central part of the life he depicts, especially for older people like Aunt Hagar; and blues expresses the sorrows and successes of the younger generation. Spirituals and blues, and also the story-telling of the men at the barbershop and pool hall, indicate the ability to the folk to survive and also indicate their sensibility, "laughing to keep from crying." The novel's central message is that no matter how difficult life might be, it is not without laughter.

Jean Toomer's *Cane* (1923), frequently regarded as the greatest literary achievement of the Harlem Renaissance, is an experimental work that also relies heavily on aspects of black folklore. *Cane* defies classification: it is a rather loose combination of poetry, prose sketches, and an unfinished drama that resulted from a visit by Toomer (who was born in the North) to Sparta, Georgia. The author tries to capture the essence of the South and its inhabitants, paying tribute to their culture and customs during a time when large numbers of African Americans were migrating to the urban North. It has a three-part structure corresponding to black people's epic search for their beginnings. Part One is set in the rural South and offers a portrait of the region and the people living there—especially the women, who remain psychologically intact despite externally imposed limitations. Part Two, focusing on the North, deals with life in a fast-paced, materialistic urban environment. Part Three returns to the South, developing the experiences of Kabnis (no doubt representing Toomer), who attempts but fails to establish meaningful cultural, social, and psychological ties with the region. Unity is achieved through recurring patterns, symbols, and images such as pine, cane, dusk, African vestiges, and ascent.

Cane is a hauntingly lyrical work of fiction but is also highly autobiographical. Its theme centers on the importance of the land in the lives of African Americans. Those who remain close to the rural past, in all its beauty and terror, remain psychologically whole; those who seek to deny or suppress the past are fragmented. Not surprisingly, then, the characters in Part Two seem superficial, lacking the depth and complexity of their southern counterparts. Thus the text is critical of the migration to the North and the subsequent pursuit of materialist values—values that are clearly at odds with the spirituality of the rural past. By moving up the socioeconomic ladder, individuals have distanced themselves geographically and psychologically from their own vibrant history.

More than any other figure, the biracial Kabnis epitomizes the racial ambivalence of blacks. Kabnis, a schoolteacher, is erudite, refined, and cultured but obviously neurotic and paranoid. He spends much of his time carousing with prostitutes and fretting over racial issues rather than pursuing his teaching career. The emphasis in Part Three is on possible responses to oppression, as well as on the religion that was vital to community life. However, Toomer focuses not so much on the physical violence that blacks often faced as on the psychological assaults to which black men such as Kabnis were subjected. In the end, Kabnis is in a cellar, symbolically outside the social mainstream, unable to take charge of his life. Although the work closes with a promise of new beginnings, represented by a sunrise, neither Kabnis's personal problems nor the searing racial problems have been resolved.

Cane does not present a conventional world of exotics or primitives. Rather, it is a montage of seemingly disparate pieces that in fact make up a tightly structured, unified whole. In this work Toomer explores his thesis—that America has given birth to a new race, which has subsumed all the old identities—and chronicles the black experience in the early twentieth century. *Cane* signaled a new era for black artistic expression.

Conclusion

The fiction of the Harlem Renaissance, in sum, is a varied genre representing a major aspect of the movement. The many themes the authors explored reflect numerous concerns of African Americans during the renaissance period. The authors of this fiction speak in uniquely individual voices as they tell and retell the story of a journey from bondage to freedom in an American promised land; they take up key issues that later authors would also treat.

MAXINE LAVON MONTGOMERY

See also Authors: 2—Fiction; Passing; Primitivism; Talented Tenth; *specific writers and works*

Further Reading

Bell, Bernard. *The Afro-American Novel and Its Tradition.* Amherst: University of Massachusetts Press, 1989.

Bone, Robert. *The Negro Novel in America*, rev. ed. New Haven, Conn.: Yale University Press, 1965.

Brown, Sterling. *The Negro in American Fiction.* New York: Atheneum, 1969. (Originally published 1937.)

Davis, Arthur P. *From the Dark Tower: Afro-American Writers 1900 to 1960.* Washington, D.C.: Howard University Press, 1981.

Du Bois, W. E. B. *The Souls of Black Folk: Essays and Sketches.* Greenwich, Conn.: Crest, 1965. (Originally published 1903.)

Gayle, Addison, Jr. *The Way of the New World: The Black Novel in America.* Garden City, N.Y.: Doubleday Anchor, 1975.

Hughes, Langston. "The Negro Artist and the Racial Mountain." *The Nation*, 23 June 1926, pp. 692–694.

Locke, Alain, ed. *The New Negro.* New York: Atheneum, 1968. (Originally published 1925.)

Turner, Darwin T. *In a Minor Chord: Three Afro-American Writers and Their Search for Identity.* Carbondale: Southern Illinois University Press, 1971.

Wright, Richard. "Between Laughter and Tears." *New Masses*, 5 October 1937.

Literature: 5—Humor and Satire

Before the Harlem Renaissance, the most popular public presentations of African American humor were generally limited to depictions by whites, in such forms as Joel Chandler Harris's "Uncle Remus" stories or minstrels performing material such as Ernest Hogan's infamous song "All Coons Look Alike to Me." The comedy that emerged during and after the Harlem Renaissance reflected the diverse political, religious, and economic interests of its creators, as well as their various views of race itself. Of course, this diversity is not news to anyone who has had access to the private folklore of African Americans: in feigned reverence and mockery of their white "superiors" and other inside jokes, and in their basic everyday interactions with each other, one could easily see that there was more to African Americans than their previous representations had suggested. And because much of African Americans' previous experience had been marked by various forms of oppression, it should not be surprising that the humor and satire of the Harlem Renaissance added depth, rage, and even tragedy to the earlier formula of black buffoonery.

Works such as J. A. Rogers's *From "Superman" to Man* (1917), Walter White's *Flight* (1926), Rudolph Fisher's *Walls of Jericho* (1928), Claude McKay's *Banjo* (1929), and Countee Cullen's *One Way to Heaven* (1932) satirized white society; works such as Wallace Thurman's *The Blacker the Berry* (1929) and *Infants of the Spring* (1932, a book in which Thurman memorably used the term "niggerati") targeted blacks; and novels such as George Schuyler's *Black No More* (1931) targeted not only blacks and whites, but also race itself. Of course, with this variety of comic approaches came varying views on how race should be depicted comedically. Two examples are George S. Schuyler and Zora Neale Hurston.

Perhaps the most prominent satirist of the Harlem Renaissance was George S. Schuyler, a conservative socialist and iconoclast whose wit was directed at both blacks and whites. Writing a column for the *Pittsburgh Courier*, as well as articles for widely respected periodicals such as the *Messenger* and *American Mercury*, Schuyler frequently satirized race as a cultural concept, considering such a concept illegitimate; this focus may account for the lack of black folk humor in his work. Encouraged by H. L. Mencken, Schuyler often mocked whites' self-deception, as well as "black art," black nationalism, and apologists for the race, in such pieces as "Our White Folks," "Blessed Are the Sons of Ham," "Our Greatest Gift to America," and "Negro Art Hokum"; this last piece was an article in which he claimed that there can be no such thing as black art because there are no cultural differences between blacks and whites. In 1931, Schuyler published two novels, *Slaves Today* and the aforementioned *Black No More*. The latter is a science fiction novel about the aftermath of blacks' crossing the color line after surgically becoming white; in it Schuyler lampoons W. E. B. Du Bois, James Weldon Johnson, Walter White, Marcus Garvey, the National Association for the Advancement of Colored People (NAACP), the Universal Negro Improvement Association (UNIA), and the Ku Klux Klan.

In contrast to Schuyler, whose view seems to preclude folk humor, Zora Neale Hurston put black folk humor at the center of her work—much of which is set in Eatonville, Florida, the all-black town where she spent much of her youth. Some scholars are reluctant to refer to Hurston as a writer of the Harlem Renaissance, because she did not publish her first novel until 1934; however, she had published a handful of stories during the latter half of the 1920s, and these place her among an elite group of renaissance writers. Before publishing her four novels between 1934 and 1948 (the most famous of these is *Their Eyes Were Watching God*, 1937), Hurston studied anthropology with the paternalistic Franz Boas, and she later produced two studies of folk life—*Tell My Horse* (1938), a study of Haiti and Jamaica, and *Mules and Men* (1935), a study of Negro "lies" (folk humor)—in addition to a number of articles, short stories, and plays. Many of the same characters and episodes reappear in more than one of Hurston's various works, acquiring different meanings in different contexts. Hurston made a noteworthy contribution by bringing black private humor into the public domain via anthropology and literature. Some critics have found the recurrent material simplistic or uninteresting, however; and some (such as Richard Wright) saw her humor as pandering to white audiences by putting blacks on display, an argument that has been made against anthropology in general. In addition to writing novels and stories,

Hurston also aspired to fame in the performing arts, and in 1927 she collaborated with Langston Hughes on *Mule Bone*, an adaptation of her short story "The Bone of Contention" for which she was to provide the dramatic structure. A feud cut short their collaboration and their friendship, however, and the play was not performed until 1991, at Lincoln Center.

In addition to comic literature, black performance comedy of the time had tremendous and lasting mass appeal. Plays such as Flournoy Miller and Aubrey Lyles's *Shuffle Along* (1921) and *Runnin' Wild* (1923) introduced popular dances like the time steps, the buck-and-wing, the soft-shoe, rapid-fire tap dancing, and the Charleston to white audiences. Other examples of popular black comedy and musical performances include *Chocolate Dandies* (1924), which featured Josephine Baker; *Dixie to Broadway* (1924); *Africana* (1927); *Weather Clear—Track Fast* (1927); and Fats Waller's *Hot Chocolates* (1929).

Also at this time, some black performers started achieving success and popularity in the film industry, although usually in regressive roles. For example, in *Hearts in Dixie* (1929), Stepin Fetchit (Lincoln Perry) played a clownish, baffled character; he went on to appear in twenty-six films from 1929 to 1935 and created a type that would pave the way for such stars as Bill "Bojangles" Robinson. Simply dismissing such performances as stereotypes would be an oversimplification, ignoring the fact that these performers gained a degree of fame and wealth which had eluded many other African Americans, and created a new type of African American lifestyle.

MICHAEL MIKLOS

See also American Mercury; Boas, Franz; Cullen, Countee; Fisher, Rudolph; Hughes, Langston; Hurston, Zora Neale; Infants of the Spring; McKay, Claude; Mencken, H. L.; Messenger, The; Niggerati; Pittsburgh Courier; Rogers, Joel Augustus; Schuyler, George S.; Thurman, Wallace; Walls of Jericho, The; White, Walter; *specific individuals and works in theater and film*

Further Reading

Fauset, Jessie. "The Gift of Laughter." In *The New Negro: Voices of the Harlem Renaissance*, ed. Alain Locke. New York: Atheneum, 1992. (Originally published 1925.)

Favor, J. Martin. "Color, Culture, and the Nature of Race: George S. Schuyler's *Black No More*." In *Authentic*

Blackness: The Folk in the New Negro Renaissance. Durham, N.C.: Duke University Press, 1999.

Foxx, Redd, and Norma Miller. *The Redd Foxx Encyclopedia of Black Humor.* Pasadena, Calif.: Ward Ritchie, 1977.

Hutchinson, George. "'Superior Intellectual Vaudeville': American Mercury." In *The Harlem Renaissance in Black and White.* Cambridge, Mass.: Belknap Press of Harvard University Press, 1995.

Jackson, Blyden. "The Harlem Renaissance." In *The Comic Imagination in American Literature*, ed. Louis D. Rubin Jr. New Brunswick, N.J.: Rutgers University Press, 1973.

Kuenz, Jane. *"Black No More:* George Schuyler and the Politics of 'Racial Culture.'" In *Harlem Renaissance Re-Examined*, ed. Victor A. Kramer and Robert A. Russ. Troy, N.Y.: Whitston, 1997.

Lowe, John. "Hurston, Humor, and the Harlem Renaissance." In *Harlem Renaissance Re-Examined*, ed. Victor A. Kramer and Robert A. Russ. Troy, N.Y.: Whitston, 1997.

Marks, Carole, and Diana Edkins. *The Power of Pride: Stylemakers and Rulebreakers of the Harlem Renaissance.* New York: Crown, 1999.

Scruggs, Charles. "The Age of Satire: The Teacher and His Pupils." In *The Sage in Harlem: H. L. Mencken and the Black Writers of the 1920s.* Baltimore, Md.: Johns Hopkins University Press, 1984.

Watkins, Mel. *On the Real Side: A History of African American Comedy from Slavery to Chris Rock.* Chicago, Ill.: Lawrence Hill, 1999.

Literature: 6—Nonfiction

The nonfiction of the Harlem Renaissance—essays, editorials, literary criticism, histories, and so on—performed several important tasks. First, it defined the mind-set of young black intellectuals and creative artists and differentiated them from the older, genteel African American men and women of letters. Second, it heightened black people's racial consciousness and class consciousness—frequently, in particular, seeking an identification with the working classes. Third, it sought to discover and convey what was authentic and deserving of preservation in African life and thought. Fourth, it sought to demolish stereotypes of blacks and replace them with an authentic picture of black people's strengths and weaknesses. The following discussion will briefly consider just a few of the many aspects of nonfiction.

A primary goal of African American and European-American writers—both men and women—who published nonfiction during the Harlem Renaissance was to reawaken black peoples' dormant racial consciousness and racial pride. As a consequence, they made a deliberate attempt, as Alain Locke put it, to rehabilitate "the race in world esteem."

Ironically, the quest for a strong self-image for black people had begun during what has been generally considered a period of racial accommodation, as exemplified by Booker T. Washington. Nevertheless, this period saw a proliferation of racially conscious, historical achievements in literature, by writers such as W. E. B. Du Bois, Kelly Miller, John E. Bruce, and W. H. Councill; and it also saw the emergence of institutions—founded by Arthur A. Schomburg and Carter G. Woodson—that disseminated historical writings intended to foster an enhanced racial image for African Americans. During this same period, Du Bois and later Charles S. Johnson wrote sociological treaties that examined the impact of a racist society on the lives of most African Americans. Furthermore, Locke's philosophical lectures on the nature of both interracial and intraracial relations provided an intellectual basis for the "New Negro" movement. The nonfiction literature of the time of Booker T. Washington provided historical, sociological, and philosophical foundations for the young creative artists who would attempt to re-create an essential racial culture in the 1920s and early 1930s.

Before the self-image of black people could be enhanced, the culture makers felt they needed to destroy a subservient attitude that was supposedly a salient characteristic of the older generation of "plantation Negroes." Accordingly, between 1917 and 1923, leftist, centrist, and conservative periodicals all bombarded the reading public with a new image. This concept of a "New Negro" contrasted starkly with an earlier image which had originated in antebellum abolitionist literature and that S. P. Fullin, a writer in the late 1960s, described as "Christlike."

The socialist image of this New Negro was offered by W. A. Domingo in A. Philip Randolph and Chandler Owens's periodical, the *Messenger.* Domingo's New Negro met "violence with violence," resisted the exploitation of his labor, and, unlike accommodationists such as Booker T. Washington and W. H. Councill, demanded "social equality." Finally, Domingo's New Negro sought to identify his interests with those of the white working class.

W. E. B. Du Bois's position at this time was represented in the organ of the National Association for the Advancement of Colored People (NAACP), *Crisis*. Du Bois was impressed by the Bolshevik Revolution in the emergent Soviet Union (which he visited in 1926), and he stressed the importance of the laboring classes. He concurred, then, with Domingo's assertion that the working classes were the key constituency in fostering radical political and economic change in the United States after World War I.

A position that was more conservative than either Domingo's or Du Bois's was offered in *Opportunity*, the monthly magazine of the National Urban League. Charles S. Johnson, a distinguished sociologist who had been trained at the University of Chicago and who served as a patron for young, aspiring African American graphic artists and writers of fiction and nonfiction, became the editor of *Opportunity* in 1923. The magazine's stated intention was to examine and analyze "Negro life as it is with no exaggerations." In consequence, this publication tried to appeal to the educated layperson, especially with its economic and sociological studies.

Some European Americans—perhaps especially leftists—also contributed to the image of the New Negro and the concept of a "Negro arts movement." For example, Max Eastman, owner of the magazine *Liberator*, appointed the West Indian darling of the European-American left, Claude McKay, as an associate editor and then a coeditor, in order to give better and deeper coverage of working classes' articulation of their struggle for liberation.

Much of the nonfiction that came out of Harlem and other black communities in the United States proffered a color-blind universalistic worldview and argued that the militant New Negro could play an essential role in the radical transformation of American life and society. Nevertheless, the "Negrotarians"—a term coined by the writer, folklorist, and anthropologist Zora Neal Hurston to describe the moderate and conservative elements of the civil rights establishment, which attempted to harness the content and direction of the "New Negro" movement—gained prominence between 1923 and 1927. When Locke brought out his anthology *The New Negro* in 1925, to an enthusiastic reception, the generational clash between African Americans was well under way. Young creative artists, Locke pointed out in his foreword, were revolting against a genteel tradition that focused on the victimization of African Americans. Black and white writers who believed that moral suasion was useless preached a brand of cultural and economic nationalism which emphasized self-reliance, self-respect, and racial pride; they expected their nationalism to replace appeals to the conscience of European Americans regarding racial oppression and exploitation.

Locke's anthology included one article—"Durham: Capital of the Black Middle Class," by E. Franklin Frazier—that extolled the virtues of capitalism and thus deviated from the party line of the American leftist radicals and socialists who had emerged after World War I. Frazier stated that a strong black economic base was essential for the revitalization of African American culture. In essence, he thought that his fellow writers were overly dependent on white capitalists and therefore could not serve the cultural and nationalist functions that the literary critics and creative artists had intended. Frazier's emphasis on self-determination reflected an attempt by African Americans of the past to transform the economic as well as the social structure so as to create an order in which blacks would become socially independent.

These varying viewpoints also led to different approaches to culture. For instance, Charles S. Johnson used *Opportunity* to examine and analyze critically the cultural production of the Harlem Renaissance. He was devoted to building the self-esteem and racial pride of black migrants who were traumatized by their transitional status in both northern and southern urban-industrial areas. Johnson argued time and again in the pages of *Opportunity* that the solution to the problems causing anomie among blacks was a revitalization of the rural folk culture which had traditionally unified and sustained blacks in their quest for full integration into mainstream American society. In his nonfiction writing, Johnson argued that art was utilitarian, that it was a means toward an end—integration.

Du Bois also argued that it was a necessity for the works of African American creative artists to have a utilitarian function. Accordingly, when he reviewed Locke's anthology *The New Negro*—in a controversial article published in *Crisis* in January 1926—he was critical of Locke's philosophy of art for art's sake. Du Bois believed that such a concept of art would result in works that were dangerously introspective, formalistic, and too far removed from reality to have any "tangible" use. He therefore attempted to formulate criteria of utility that could guide the writing of the "Negro Renaissance." These criteria evidently influenced his reaction to Claude McKay's slice-of-life novel *Home to Harlem* (1928); he found it so repugnant that he commented, "After the dirtier parts of its filth . . . I feel distinctly like taking a bath." Du Bois opened the pages of *Crisis* to social scientists who, he believed (sometimes mistakenly), could provide a significant part of his arsenal as he made his case for art as propaganda. Du Bois admired the work of Melville Herskovits, a Jewish immigrant who was Franz Boas's student and who at this juncture was emphasizing the assimilability of African Americans into the United States. (Later, Herskovits would provide empirical evidence for Du Bois's hypothesis about African retentions in the Americas.)

Langston Hughes summed up his own response and that of young writers such as Zora Neale Hurston, Nella Larsen, Wallace Thurman, and Countee Cullen in an article published in 1926 in *The Nation*: "The Negro Artist and the Racial Mountain." This was a declaration of the young writers' independence from the staid confines of Du Boisian propaganda. Drawing on the resources of black culture—including folklore and blues—they celebrated an essential blackness that was part of their cultural identity and heritage.

VERNON J. WILLIAMS JR.

See also Authors: 3—Nonfiction; Black History and Historiography; Boas, Franz; Bruce, John Edward; Crisis, The; Domingo, Wilfred Adolphus; Du Bois, W. E. B.; Frazier, E. Franklin; Herskovits, Melville; Johnson, Charles Spurgeon; Literary Criticism and the Harlem Renaissance; Locke, Alain; Messenger, The; Miller, Kelly; New Negro; Opportunity; Schomburg, Arthur A.; Woodson, Carter G.

Further Reading

Baker, Houston A. *Modernism and the Harlem Renaissance.* Chicago, Ill.: University of Chicago Press, 1987.

Fabre, Genviève, and Michael Ferth. *Temples for Tomorrow: Looking Back at the Renaissance.* Bloomington: Indiana University Press, 2001.

Huggins, Nathan Irwin. *Harlem Renaissance.* New York: Oxford University Press, 1971.

———. *Voices of the Harlem Renaissance.* New York: Oxford University Press, 1995.

Hutchinson, George. *The Harlem Renaissance in Black and White.* Cambridge, Mass.: Belknap Press of Harvard University Press, 1995.

Lewis, David Levering. *When Harlem Was in Vogue,* New York: Random House, 1979.

Lewis, David Levering, ed. *The Portable Renaissance Reader.* New York: Penguin, 1994.

Locke, Alain, ed. *The New Negro.* New York: Albert and Charles Boni, 1925.

Wintz, Cary D. *Black Culture and the Harlem Renaissance.* Houston, Tex.: Rice University Press, 1988.

Literature: 7—Poetry

Regarding poetry, it is convenient to mark the beginning of the Harlem Renaissance with the publication of Claude McKay's forcible sonnet "If We Must Die" in 1919 and to see it as ending around 1932, a year after James Weldon Johnson issued the expanded edition of his *Book of American Negro Poetry*. During that thirteen-year span, some of the most distinguished voices in American poetry emerged, including Johnson, McKay, Angelina Weld Grimké, Anne Spencer, Jean Toomer, Langston Hughes, and Countee Cullen. They were joined by Alice Dunbar Nelson, William Stanley Braithwaite, Jessie Redmon Fauset,

Countee Cullen. (Brown Brothers.)

Georgia Douglas Johnson, Frank Horne, Sterling Brown, Gwendolyn Bennett, Arna Bontemps, Richard Bruce Nugent, Waring Cuney, Helene Johnson, and Mae Cowdery—poets whose reputation after the renaissance waned slightly, but whose contributions to the explosion of poetic art in the 1920s were nevertheless valuable and vast. Together, these writers produced a body of poetry that was unprecedented in its volume, variety, and achievement. The work of this period is notable particularly for its innovation and for expanding the repertoire of themes commonly treated in verse. The poets of the Harlem Renaissance took older, established forms, such as the sonnet, and made them new by reflecting on contemporary conditions and by addressing questions of race. They also created novel poetic forms, arranging the rhythm and structure of some of their poems after the musical models of jazz, bebop, and blues. And in representing the real lives and the real speech of black Americans of the time, the renaissance poets confirmed that everyday experience—especially everyday black experience—deserves and rewards serious poetic consideration.

Writing "Brown Poems" in the 1920s

Although Alain Locke's *The New Negro* (1925) is routinely identified as being the first anthology to document a pioneering aesthetic among black artists, it rather belatedly recognized the achievement of a new poetry that had already been flourishing for several years. Between 1922 and 1925, three major, original anthologies of contemporary black verse were published (a fourth would appear in 1927). Also, in 1922, McKay published his *Harlem Shadows*, which confirmed the emergence of a new sensibility that would animate the work of poets associated with the Harlem Renaissance. *Harlem Shadows* was followed by several individual volumes of poetry that proved to be equally modern in their conception and formidable in their achievement, including Toomer's *Cane* (1923); Hughes's *The Weary Blues* (1926), *Fine Clothes to the Jew* (1927), and *The Dream Keeper* (1932); Cullen's *Color* (1925), *Copper Sun* (1927), and *The Black Christ and Other Poems* (1929); and James Weldon Johnson's *God's Trombones: Seven Negro Sermons in Verse* (1927). Dozens of books and hundreds of poems were published by these and other black poets during the 1920s. The interest and influence of white patrons helped make the publication and recognition of much of the renaissance verse possible, but even more

significant were the contributions of talented black editors, publishers, and reviewers of poetry, such as James Weldon Johnson, Braithwaite, Fauset, Locke, and Cullen. They were all poets of some stature, but, with the exception of Johnson and Cullen, were and are best known as promoters of poetry.

The poems composed by black writers around the 1920s are so varied in form, tone, style, and theme that it is difficult to generalize about them. Nevertheless, all the poets of the Harlem Renaissance struggled with the question of whether, and how, to "Write poems—/brown poems/Of dark words." These lines, from Gwendolyn Bennett's poem "Advice," suggest how a poet's artistic choices are affected when that poet is black. For all the renaissance poets, race inevitably informed the way they thought about what subjects and what language to choose.

Still, different poets dealt differently with what Langston Hughes called the "racial mountain." For instance, though Braithwaite, Horne, Cuney, and Georgia Johnson sometimes identified black figures or themes in their poems, there is little indication that race as a sociopolitical concern is central to their artistic thinking. They usually preferred to write about abstract concepts—especially love, death, beauty, and God—though often from a very personal perspective.

Georgia Johnson, for instance, composed many capable and quite popular verses about women's experience with love and longing. The pathos of her poetry is well represented by the last lines of "The Heart of a Woman": "The heart of a woman falls back with the night,/And enters some alien cage in its plight,/And tries to forget it has dreamed of the stars,/While it breaks, breaks, breaks on the sheltering bars."

Like Johnson, Horne traded in a certain sentimentality, which is especially in evidence in his series "Letters Found Near a Suicide." Even so, there and in his best poems, Horne, again like Johnson, usually avoids the maudlin; both showed themselves attentive to the craft of writing poetry. Braithwaite, too, conscientiously composed his pieces, in which he was inclined to reflect on such topics as time and fate, beauty and joy, memory and mortality.

These were not the only poets of the Harlem Renaissance disposed to comment on abstractions and on the human condition generally. However, in the work of the majority of poets of that period, much more common situations predominate, and the subject of race is more explicitly—if variously—treated. Gwendolyn Bennett declares her affection for other black women in "To A Dark Girl," when she attests, "I love you for your brownness." Similarly, Helene Johnson praises the splendor of a young black man in her "Sonnet to a Negro in Harlem": "You are disdainful and magnificent—/... You are too splendid for the city street." Mixed with Johnson's sensual admiration for this young man is a nonsexualized racial pride that is commonly expressed in renaissance poetry. She makes no apologies for the man's self-confidence; indeed, she suggests that not enough of his peers are following his lead.

In "The Shroud of Color," Countee Cullen is somewhat more conflicted about the impact of race on one's will and power, admitting, "'Lord, being dark' I said, 'I cannot bear/The further touch of earth, the scented air.'" By contrast, Claude McKay is certain of his ability to live nobly and ably, and of his capacity to respond to racial injustices: "I possess the courage and the grace/To bear my anger proudly and unbent."

Sometimes, racial themes seemed to be too ponderous to be accommodated by poetic lines, as Hughes implies in one piece: "In the Johannesburg mines/There are 240,000/Native Africans working./What kind of poem/Would you/Make out of that?/. . ." But his skepticism is enabling; the response to his question is contained in the fact of the poem itself. He suggests that no subject is too great for poetry, so long as we are willing to expand our idea of what poetry is.

For many poets of the Harlem Renaissance, the question of how best to write "brown poems," or poems that were uniquely their own, entailed not only considering what topics to address but what type of language to use. Most preferred to compose in the vernacular, using everyday language and syntax to express their ideas, paving the way for a practice that would become almost universal in American poetry written in the second half of the twentieth century. However, Cullen, for one, usually favored a formal, literary mode and sometimes even archaic language—one of his poems is entitled "The Wind Bloweth Where It Listeth." He disparaged the use of dialect in poetry and wishfully announced that "the day of dialect as far as Negro poets are concerned is in the decline."

Cullen's prediction was not borne out by the verse compositions of his day, however, as James Weldon Johnson, Sterling Brown, and Hughes, among others, became well known for their folk poems and their work written in dialect. The challenge for them was to write authentic folk poetry without relying on the kind of dialect verse that Paul Laurence Dunbar wrote. Though Dunbar was revered by most renaissance poets, his work was seen as possessing a certain quaintness and modesty that the poets of this new age did not wish to replicate in their own work. One way to modernize dialect was to combine folk language with new musical forms, as Hughes did in "Bound No'th Blues," which begins, "Goin' down the road, Lawd,/Goin' down the road./Down the road, Lawd,/Way, way down the road./Got to find somebody/To help me carry this load." Here Hughes inserts an unexaggerated dialect into a blues pattern of stating a problem, reiterating that problem, and then projecting a solution. However, the solution, such as it is, is not discovered at the end of the poem but inheres in its process—reflecting the function of blues itself—and the poet refuses to offer the kind of moral the reader might expect from a poem by Dunbar or others like him.

Another way for renaissance poets to refresh dialect is revealed in Brown's "Strong Men," which blends standard language and dialect, playing one off the other in a pattern of call and response typical of some forms of jazz: "They put hammers in your hands/And said—Drive so much before sundown./*You sang:/Ain't no hammah/In dis lan',/Strikes lak mine, bebby . . .*" Here the standard language contextualizes and leavens the nonstandard lines so that the latter do not become "humorous or pathetic," as James Weldon Johnson warned was the fate of most dialect verse.

The "language" of jazz was in fact another method that renaissance poets used for updating dialect. Toomer's "Portrait in Georgia," for instance, has jazz-like syncopation: "Hair—braided chestnut,/coiled like a lyncher's rope,/Eyes—fagots,/Lips—old scars, or the first red blisters/Breath—the last sweet scent of cane."

The staggered rhythms and irregular tempo of jazz became hallmarks of Harlem Renaissance poetry, and they are one manifestation of some poets' urge to devise forms appropriate to their experience. In order to create new forms, the poets had first to know old ones and understand the past; thus, to think about writing "brown poems" also meant considering one's place as a black poet in the older tradition. Some felt a considerable—if also productive—conflict about being black and yet taking up an art form whose most famous serious practitioners have been white. Cullen's memorable lines articulate this conflict: "Yet do I marvel at this curious thing:/To make a poet black, and bid him sing!" Many, like James Weldon Johnson, partly resolved this conflict by looking back to Dunbar and to the traditions of "Black and unknown bards of long ago" whose "lips [were able] to touch the sacred fire" of poetic inspiration. Others, such as Langston Hughes, were convinced that they could create a new tradition which would be more authentically "American" than the predominantly white tradition which most students of poetry knew at the time. Hughes may well have been speaking of American poetry when he wrote, "O, yes,/I say it plain,/America never was America to me,/And yet I swear this oath—/America will be!"

Still, although Hughes focused on the future, several renaissance poets stayed trained on the past. Cullen addressed a lyric poem "To John Keats, Poets, at Spring Time," and Anne Spencer also invoked the nineteenth-century poets whom she had read and studied, inserting herself as well as other black poets into the largely white tradition that preceded them. In the short poem "Dunbar," she laments, "Ah, how poets sing and die!/Make one song and Heaven takes it;/Have one heart and Beauty breaks it;/Chatterton, Shelley, Keats, and I—/Ah, how poets sing and die!" Her grief for the passing of great poets is mitigated by her faith in the feeling that links poets across generations.

But even as Spencer identifies with these men, she acknowledges that the question of poetic traditions is even more complicated for women writers. In her poem "Letter to My Sister," she contends that "It is dangerous for a woman to defy the gods," referring to male figures of authority—in poetry and elsewhere—from the past as well as in the present. And if defiant acts by women were threatening, how much more so were the acts of black women, as Spencer once proclaimed: "I proudly love being a Negro woman—it's so involved and interesting. *We* are the PROBLEM— the great national game of TABOO."

While black women may have presented a "problem," they participated significantly and influentially in the creative activity of the Harlem Renaissance— more so than in society in general. Black women published alongside men in leading journals during the 1920s, and their poems were included in contemporary anthologies. Jessie Fauset served as literary editor of *The Crisis* from 1919 to 1926, during which time she discovered the work of Langston Hughes and others. Georgia Johnson held salons at her home in Washington, D.C., which attracted male and female intellectuals and encouraged and inspired many young artists.

Yet, despite the contributions of women writers, and despite recent scholarship which has raised their status, the poets of the Harlem Renaissance whose legacy has persisted are almost exclusively men. The reason may be that the most accomplished women poets of the period wrote comparatively few poems and had relatively short careers as poets. Hughes spoke for himself as well as for many contemporary scholars of the renaissance when he speculated that, "On Anne Spencer's table/There lies an unsharpened pencil—/As though she has left unwritten/Many things she knows to write." But the poems that she, Grimké, and others have left behind are worthy of study, are reasonably well-preserved, and are integral to understanding what we now recognize as the tradition of the Harlem Renaissance.

Two Landmark Anthologies: *The Book of American Negro Poetry and Caroling Dusk*

A fair number of the best-known poems written by the women of the Harlem Renaissance are, like those written by the men, most accessible to us today in two anthologies published in the 1920s: James Weldon Johnson's *The Book of American Negro Poetry* and Cullen's *Caroling Dusk: An Anthology of Verse by Negro Poets*. Both texts are remarkably valuable resources for understanding the range and accomplishments of the renaissance poets.

Johnson's collection was first published in 1922, then published in a second, enlarged edition in 1931. It was the first book-length compilation of the work of modern black poets. Perhaps more famous now than the anthology itself is Johnson's preface, "Essay on the Negro's Creative Genius." This influential and continually illuminating essay reveals Johnson's belief— which he shared with many of the figures of the renaissance—that artistic achievement can be tied to social and political advancements:

> The final measure of the greatness of all peoples is the amount and standard of the literature and art they have produced. The world does not know that a people is great until that people produces great literature and art. No people that has produced great literature and art has ever been looked upon by the world as distinctly inferior.

Published in 1927, *Caroling Dusk* contained some of the most recently produced poems of its day and, uniquely, included brief biographies that in almost every case were written by the poets themselves. In his foreword, Cullen (like Johnson) emphasizes the variety of the work by black poets: "The conservatives, the middlers, and the arch heretics will be found among them as among the white poets." Cullen goes on to deny that there is any organic unity among the poems written by blacks during the 1920s, and to downplay the idea that novelty is their most worthy characteristic: "to say that the pulse beat of their verse shows generally such a fever, or the symptoms of such an ague, will prove on closer examination merely the moment's exaggeration of a physician anxious to establish a new literary ailment." Cullen was suspicious of efforts to identify an aesthetic of the "New Negro," fearing that such identifications would keep the work of black poets on the margins of American literature. Even more than Johnson, Cullen hoped that the renaissance poets would participate fully in a "national literature" and would be recognized simply as poets, without the qualification "Negro."

In addition to Johnson's and Cullen's anthologies, two other major poetry collections and a few smaller volumes of verse appeared during the 1920s to showcase black writers. Robert Kerlin published *Negro Poets and Their Poems* in 1923 and issued a revised version in 1935. Newman White and Walter Jackson, two self-identified "southern white men," brought out *An Anthology of Verse by American Negroes* in 1924. White (a professor at Trinity College, which would later become Duke University) and Jackson (a professor at the North Carolina College for Women, now the University of North Carolina at Greensboro) had the specific purpose of providing a text for college students. Their editorial note is rather dated, and some of their comments suggest a custodial attitude, yet their effort to incorporate the work of black poets into the college curriculum seems to have been motivated by a genuine interest in expanding the canon of American literature and not, as was the case with some other white critics and teachers, by a prurient interest in the "exoticism" of the contemporary Negro.

Whatever White's and Jackson's motivations were, James Weldon Johnson and Sterling Brown had a similar idea. Published in conjunction with the second edition of Johnson's anthology was an "Outline of Study," prepared by Brown "for the use," according to Johnson, "of teachers and students." Like White and Jackson's anthology, Brown's "Outline" and Johnson's preface indicate their hope not only of making the poetry of the Harlem Renaissance available to appreciative readers but also of making it an object of critical appraisal and study.

The fact that four separate collections dedicated to black poetry appeared within the span of five years attests to the importance, vitality, and continuous renewal of the poetry of the Harlem Renaissance. In addition, Alain Locke's anthology *The New Negro* contained some poems; and pamphlets such as Kerlin's *Contemporary Poetry of the Negro* (1921) and Locke's *Four Negro Poets* (1927)—both put out by mainstream publishing houses—further documented the fecundity of the renaissance imagination and the willingness of publishers to make it known to readers.

Black Journals, the Little Magazines, and Modernism

The publishing of poetry during the Harlem Renaissance was perhaps most vibrant in periodicals. Almost all the major and minor poets of the renaissance first found an audience by presenting their work in journals dedicated to black life, such as *The Crisis*, the official publication of the National Association for the Advancement of Colored People (NAACP); and *Opportunity*, published by the National Urban League. These journals sponsored literary contests, granting recognition as well as much-needed financial rewards to many fledgling poets. Yet some of the younger artists considered these magazines too conservative, and several of the principal figures of the Harlem Renaissance came together in 1926 to found *Fire!!* It was intended to be a quarterly publication that would, as Hughes explained, "burn up a lot of the old, dead conventional Negro-white ideas of the past, *épater les bourgeois* into a realization of the younger Negro writers and artists, and provide us with an outlet for publication not available in the limited pages of the small Negro magazines then existing." Only one issue of *Fire!!* was ever published, however, and these artists had to return to other venues.

Before and especially after the demise of *Fire!!* renaissance poets published widely in the prestigious "little magazines": *Poetry: A Magazine of Verse, Dial, Messenger, Broom, Others, Little Review, Liberator,* and its successor *New Masses.* These journals promoted avant-garde literature (and often left-wing politics), and appealed to a primarily white highbrow readership. It was largely through these little magazines that the Harlem Renaissance and modernism intermingled. "Modernist" is a term used to describe certain trends in art and literature during the period from about 1914 to 1945. Briefly, modernist art was experimental, and many modernists valued fragmentation over unity and implication over direct communication or description; they aimed to reproduce the workings of the mind rather than transcribe some supposedly objective reality.

Modernists were producing strikingly original verse in the 1920s, when the Harlem Renaissance was flourishing. During that decade, white American poets (modernists and others) such as Wallace Stevens, William Carlos Williams, Ezra Pound, H. D., Marianne Moore, John Crowe Ransom, T. S. Eliot, Edna St. Vincent Millay, e. e. cummings, Hart Crane, Allen Tate, and Robert Penn Warren all published significant volumes of poetry. All the white modernist poets were familiar with the poetry of the Harlem Renaissance, and Pound, H. D., Crane, and Williams were personally acquainted with several renaissance figures. Jean Toomer had a close association with Hart Crane and other literary people such as Waldo Frank and Van Wyck Brooks; as a result, he occupies a unique place at the intersection of modernism and the Harlem Renaissance, and his eclectic *Cane* is considered a masterpiece of modernism. It is a pastiche of verse and prose, written in many voices, most of which are rural and southern. On the surface, the poetry does not appear difficult, yet many of Toomer's lines resist easy explication, such as the enigmatic ending of the prose poem "Harvest Song": "O my brothers, I beat my palms, still soft, against the stubble of my harvesting. (You beat your soft palms, too.) My pain is sweet. Sweeter than the oats or wheat or corn. It will not bring me knowledge of my hunger."

Like Toomer, Richard Bruce Nugent, Hughes, and other renaissance poets shared with their modernist counterparts an interest in experimenting with form, genre, and perspective. Nevertheless, while the Harlem Renaissance and modernism were not wholly independent movements, they influenced each other largely indirectly. Many poets of the Harlem Renaissance—but only a very few white poets—were committed to traditional forms, particularly the sonnet. Only a few leading white writers displayed much political consciousness, and most of them were disinclined to describe social conditions concretely. Furthermore, many modernists preserved a distinction between high and low culture, and they valued erudition and at times seemed to revel in abstruseness. By contrast, even if most of the poets of the Harlem Renaissance were middle class and educated—unlike the vast majority of black Americans of their era—they showed more interest in what Johnson called the "lower strata" of society and they almost uniformly aimed to create a poetry that was accessible (in theory if not in practice) to most of the literate public.

Racial Identity and Poetic Identity: The Implications of Genre

To some extent, poets of the Harlem Renaissance were torn between their populist impulses and their higher literary aspirations. This was one manifestation of W. E. B. Du Bois's concept of "two-ness," a split consciousness that many black Americans felt and still feel. Cullen invokes this "two-ness" when he speaks of the "double obligation of being both Negro and American." This condition, he says, "is not so unified as we are often led to believe." For the Harlem Renaissance poets, this double obligation often presented itself when they had to choose a form in which to express their ideas. Cullen, whose prosody was conservative, advocated in his foreword to *Caroling Dusk* the power of traditional literary elements: "As heretical as it may sound, there is the probability that Negro poets, dependent as they are on the English language, may have more to gain from the rich background of English and American poetry than from any nebulous atavistic yearnings toward an African inheritance."

Claude McKay, whom few would characterize as "conservative," nevertheless embraced predominantly white English and American literary history, though only to a point, skillfully combining traditional forms and political protest in his sonnets "To the White Fiends," "Africa," "The Harlem Dancer," "America," "Enslaved," "The White House," "Outcast," and, most famously, "If We Must Die." McKay took an old and very rigid poetic genre and made it new and relevant to his own project by examining within its bounds unconventional, contemporary subjects. He is particularly affecting in his final couplets, as in "If We Must Die": "Like men we'll face the murderous, cowardly pack,/Pressed to the wall, dying, but fighting back!" and in "The White House": "Oh, I must keep my heart inviolate/Against the potent poison of your hate."

Although he also composed Petrarchan sonnets (in which an octave is followed by a sestet), McKay preferred the Shakespearean form (which contains three quatrains and a couplet). Among his best efforts at the Shakespearean sonnet is "America," which opens: "Although she feeds me bread of bitterness,/And sinks into my throat her tiger's tooth,/Stealing my breath of life, I will confess/I love this cultured hell that tests my youth!" As a Jamaican immigrant, McKay perhaps initially idealized the United States and its promise of success to all who exerted sufficient effort, but his enthusiasm for and belief in meritocracy was tempered by his understanding of America's entrenched racism. McKay closes another sonnet, "The Lynching," with the ominous observation, "And little lads, lynchers that were to be,/Danced round the dreadful thing in fiendish glee." Still, despite the despair in some of his poems, McKay ultimately wants to affirm that if he successfully bears the burdens of today, he will live to see the promise of the future. In "Harlem Dancer," one of his most frequently anthologized pieces, McKay might well be describing himself when he says of the title figure, "To me she seemed a proudly-swaying palm/Grown lovelier for passing through a storm."

Langston Hughes found it more difficult to articulate his vision within traditional poetic forms, as he suggests in "Aesthete in Harlem": "Strange,/That in this nigger place,/I should meet Life face to face/When for years I had been seeking/Life in places gentler speaking/Until I came to this near street/And found Life—stepping on my feet!" The rhymes suggest conventional models, but the anomalous opening line and the irregular meter throughout the poem indicate that Hughes's hand is quite free. His play is deliberate, as is indicated by the poem's last word, a pun on poetic feet. (In standard meter, syllables are grouped in particular ways to create what is called a "foot.") The "life" that he discovers in Harlem does not conform to predetermined poetic models, but this conflict is liberating and exhilarating.

Hughes's discomfort with traditional forms hardly constituted a limitation for him. He was an extremely prolific writer of poetry, prose, and drama; very early in his career he had the skill and the confidence to create a new poetry when he found old forms inadequate, while at the same time insinuating himself into the most venerable poetic traditions. In "I, Too," Hughes lays claim to the assertiveness and expansiveness of the nineteenth-century American poet Walt Whitman, who wrote: "I am large. . . . I contain multitudes." Hughes responds: "I, too, sing America," claiming his rightful place as an American citizen and an American poet.

Although Hughes invokes Whitman's audacity, his claims are understated and he hopes for ordinary achievements. For instance, Hughes envisions a day when he won't be sent "to eat in the kitchen/When company comes" and says of the guests, "They'll see

how beautiful I am/And be ashamed." This reference to his own physical beauty recalls his poem "My People": "The night is beautiful,/So the faces of my people." But in "I, Too" beauty may also indicate a quality of his poem: "they" will see the value in his poetry and be ashamed for having held a narrow concept of what constitutes good poetry. By extension, Hughes' pronouncement suggests that social justice may derive from white society's recognition of black poets' equal power to create verse. In the final line, Hughes announces, "I, too, am America." The repetition of "too" emphasizes his desire to be part of the national identity but also emphasizes the divide between black and white. Hughes's voice is legitimately American but is not raceless.

Hughes devised a great range of poetic personae: an escaped slave, a historian of American and African life, a poor single mother, a soldier, a member of the Ku Klux Klan, a new Ph.D., an American prophet, and so on. But he also enjoyed recording the "voice" of Harlem as a whole. "Air Raid Over Harlem," subtitled "Scenario for a Little Black Movie," begins with this exchange: "Who you gonna put in it?/*Me.*/Who the hell are you?/*Harlem.*/Alright, then."

Hughes not only put Harlem into many of his poems but, along with his fellow poets of the 1920s, put poetry into Harlem. If it was true before the Harlem Renaissance that "Harlem/Knows a song/Without a tune—/The rhythm's there:/But the melody's/Bare," as Hughes once asserted, this was not the case by the end of the renaissance. Hughes and others bestowed on Harlem the melody it needed and deserved, and in so doing helped set a new course in American literature.

The Legacy of the Harlem Renaissance

Many of the poets of the period continued to write after the end of the Harlem Renaissance, and several of them turned to fiction, drama, and criticism. Hughes wrote in other forms, but he also continued to compose poetry for decades. His verse, along with that of the other central poets of the 1920s, helped shape the work of Melvin Tolson, Robert Hayden, Margaret Walker, and Gwendolyn Brooks, all of whom began their careers as writers in the 1930s and are sometimes identified as belonging to the tail end of the renaissance.

Among the more recent poets who inherited the legacy of the Harlem Renaissance are Derek Walcott, Audre Lorde, Sonia Sanchez, Amiri Baraka, Jay

Wright, Lucille Clifton, June Jordan, Clarence Major, Michael S. Harper, Nikki Giovanni, Alice Walker, Yusef Komunyakaa, Ai, Ntozake Shange, Rita Dove, Thylias Moss, Patricia Smith, Essex Hemphill, Carl Phillips, and Elizabeth Alexander. Thanks in part to the efforts of their predecessors of the renaissance, these poets continue to find poetry pliable enough to accommodate their multiple voices and to pursue their wide-ranging visions.

JEANNINE JOHNSON

See also Authors: 5—Poets; Bennett, Gwendolyn; Bontemps, Arna; Braithwaite, William Stanley; Brooks, Gwendolyn; Brown, Sterling; Cane; Color; Cowdery, Mae Virginia; Crisis, The: Literary Prizes; Cullen, Countee; Cuney, Waring; Dunbar, Paul Laurence; Fauset, Jessie Redmon; Fine Clothes to the Jew; Fire!!; God's Trombones; Grimké, Angelina Weld; Harlem Shadows; Hayden, Robert; Horne, Frank; Hughes, Langston; Johnson, Georgia Douglas; Johnson, Helene; Johnson, James Weldon; Kerlin, Robert; Literary and Artistic Prizes; Locke, Alain; McKay, Claude; Modernism; Nelson, Alice Dunbar; Nugent, Richard Bruce; Opportunity Literary Contests; Poetry: Dialect Poetry; Spencer, Anne; Tolson, Melvin; Toomer, Jean; Walker, Margaret; Weary Blues, The

Further Reading

Bloom, Harold, ed. *Black American Poets and Dramatists of the Harlem Renaissance*. New York: Chelsea House, 1995.

Cullen, Countee, ed. *Caroling Dusk: An Anthology of Verse by Negro Poets*. New York: Harper, 1927. (See also *Caroling Dusk: An Anthology of Verse by Black Poets of the Twenties*. New York: Carol, 1993.)

Honey, Maureen, ed. *Shadowed Dreams: Women's Poetry of the Harlem Renaissance*. New Brunswick, N.J.: Rutgers University Press, 1989.

Hughes, Langston. "Harlem Literati in the Twenties." In *Remembering the Harlem Renaissance*, ed. Cary D. Wintz. New York: Garland, 1996.

Hull, Gloria. *Color, Sex, and Poetry: Three Women Writers of the Harlem Renaissance*. Bloomington: Indiana University Press, 1987.

Hutchinson, George B. "The Whitman Legacy and the Harlem Renaissance." In *Walt Whitman: The Centennial Essays*, ed. Ed Folsom. Iowa City: Iowa University Press, 1994.

Johnson, James Weldon, ed. *The Book of American Negro Poetry*. New York: Harcourt Brace, 1922. (See also rev. ed., 1931; reprinted, 1958, 1969.)

North, Michael. *The Dialect of Modernism: Race, Language, and Twentieth-Century Literature*. New York: Oxford University Press, 1994.

Primeau, Ronald. "Frank Horne and the Second Echelon Poets of the Harlem Renaissance." In *The Harlem Renaissance Remembered*, ed. Arna Bontemps. New York: Dodd, Mead, 1972.

Rampersad, Arnold. "Langston Hughes and Approaches to Modernism in the Harlem Renaissance." In *The Harlem Renaissance: Revaluations*, ed. Amritjit Singh et al. New York: Garland, 1989.

———. "The Poetry of the Harlem Renaissance." In *The Columbia History of American Poetry*, ed. Jay Parini. New York: Columbia University Press, 1993.

Roses, Lorraine Elena, and Ruth Elizabeth Randolph, eds. *Harlem's Glory: Black Women Writing, 1900–1950*. Cambridge, Mass.: Harvard University Press, 1996.

Smith, Gary. "The Black Protest Sonnet." *American Poetry*, 2, Fall 1984, pp. 2–12.

Woods, Gregory. "Gay Re-Readings of the Harlem Renaissance Poets." In *Critical Essays: Gay and Lesbian Writers of Color*, ed. Emmanuel S. Nelson. New York: Haworth, 1993.

Little Theater Tournament

The National Little Theater Tournament, held in New York from 1923 to 1931, was an influential competition for amateur theater groups. The contest was an outlet of recognition and support for "little theater" organizations, providing national exposure in a Broadway setting. Several black little theater groups of the Harlem Renaissance competed in the tournament with white groups and earned prizes as well as critical praise.

The National Little Theater Tournament was the brainchild of Walter Hartwig, executive secretary of the New York Drama League, which supported little theater groups in the city. The tournament grew from an unofficial competition that Hartwig organized, in 1921, between the Nyack Club Players and the Forest Hills Garden Players, two little theater companies in the New York area. This pairing led to other informal competitions, until 1923, when Hartwig invited groups within 100 miles of New York City to participate in a formal contest.

The date of the first National Little Tournament was 7 May 1923. It featured twenty groups in a week-long competition at the Bayes Theater on Broadway. Four plays were performed from Monday through Friday, with four finalists chosen to compete for a silver trophy cup on Saturday. David Belasco, the prolific Broadway producer and director, contributed the silver trophy and his name to the prize for the winner of the finalists' competition. The tournament was therefore sometimes referred to as the Belasco Little Theater Tournament or the Belasco Cup Match. The East West Players of Manhattan won the trophy in the 1923 competition for their performance of George Calderon's *The Little Stone House*.

Belasco's sponsorship of the silver trophy cup was an attempt to appease little theater artists. He was critical of the little theater movement and its departure from the popular melodrama that was a staple of his own Broadway productions. Belasco's involvement with the tournament was minimal, however, other than his contribution of the prize and his participation in judging the finals of the competition in 1924.

Other prizes in the contest included $200 to each of the four finalists. The drama publisher Samuel French sponsored two additional prizes of $200 for the first- and second-best presentations of original unpublished plays from the four competition finalists. Winning the Samuel French prize meant publication of the play by French's company and rights controlled by Samuel French Publishers as the playwright's agent. Playwrights who won the Samuel French Prize received royalties from the publication of their works.

The National Little Theater Tournament reflected and enhanced the growth of amateur theater groups in the United States. The increased artistic output of the Harlem Renaissance coincided with this burgeoning little theater movement. These amateur groups were known for producing plays that strayed from the melodrama that was popular in Broadway theaters at the time. Randolph Edmonds—a dramatist, college professor, and father of black educational theater—described the little theater movement as the best chance for developing authentic black theater (1949). Blacks had control of the productions from start to finish, without pressure from white backers to perpetuate racial stereotypes or otherwise compromise the presentation of the plays.

In 1927, the Krigwa Players (originally Crigwa, an acronym for Crisis Guild of Writers and Artists), a black little theater group sponsored by W. E. B. Du Bois and *The Crisis* magazine, performed a work by the black female playwright Eulalie Spence—*The Fool's Errand*—and won first prize in addition to a $200 Samuel French Prize for one of the best unpublished plays. Friction developed between Du Bois and Spence when he kept the prize money to cover his expenses. The Krigwa Players also performed Mary P. Burrill's *Aftermath* during the tournament of 1928. Randolph Edmond's Morgan Players, representing the drama club at Morgan State University in Baltimore, Maryland, performed in the National Little Theater Tournament in 1929. Although the Morgan Players did not win a prize, their performance of Paul Green's *The Man Who Died at Twelve O'Clock* was ranked fourth out of the twenty groups performing that year.

Following the inaugural National Little Theater Tournament in 1923, the competition broadened to include national and international (primarily English) amateur theater groups. Regional tournaments imitated the competition held in New York, and by 1928 fifty little theater tournaments had been held nationwide. The organizer, Walter Hartwig, financed the tournament in New York by requiring entrance fees from groups in the contest. The groups could sell tickets to their performances to recoup entrance fees and earn additional money. Many regional theater competitions copied this financing plan.

One-act plays were the standard for most of these tournaments, and the National Little Theater Tournament groups performed thirty 50-minute plays in the contest through 1930. In 1930, Hartwig expanded the competition to include original, unpublished long plays, which were performed during the week after the one-act competition. Samuel French offered a $1,000 prize for the winner of the long-play contest, and the magazine *Theater Arts Monthly* awarded a silver cup. The Morningside Players of Columbia University won with their performance of *The New Freedom* by Marjorie Paradis.

In 1931, one-act plays were dropped from the National Little Theater Tournament, since the Depression was putting a financial strain on little theater groups. Only ten groups could afford to pay the entrance fee for the contest. The long-play competition in 1931 was the last of the National Little Theater Tournament contests. Although Hartwig announced his intention to continue the tournament, he could not find competitors, and the contest was never revived.

HEATHER MARTIN

See also Community Theater; Fool's Errand; Green, Paul; Krigwa Players

Further Reading

Dart, Peter A. "The National Little Theatre Tournament 1923–1931." *Educational Theatre Journal*, 16, 1964.

Dean, Alexander. *Little Theatre Organization and Management for Community, University, and School: Including a History of the Amateur in Drama.* New York: Appleton, 1926.

Edmonds, Randolph. "The Negro Little Theatre Movement." *Negro History Bulletin*, 12(4), 1949.

Hill, Errol G., and James V. Hatch. *A History of African American Theatre.* Cambridge and New York: Cambridge University Press, 2003.

Perry, Clarence Arthur. *The Work of the Little Theatres: The Groups They Include, the Plays They Produce, Their Tournaments, and the Handbooks They Use.* New York: Russell Sage Foundation, 1933.

"The Torchbearers Arrive: Whys and Wherefores of the Little Theatre Tourney, Which Again Impends." *New York Times*, 6 May 1928, sec. 9.

Williams, Allen. "S. Randolph Edmonds." In *Dictionary of Literary Biography*, Vol. 51, *Afro-American Writers from the Harlem Renaissance to 1940*, ed. Trudier Harris. Detroit, Mich.: Gale Research, 1987.

Liveright, Horace

If any one event signaled the arrival of the Harlem Renaissance as a literary phenomenon, it would be the Civic Club dinner given by Charles S. Johnson of the National Urban League on 21 March 1924. The guests included Alain Locke, James Weldon Johnson, and W. E. B. Du Bois; supportive white writers and critics such as Eugene O'Neill, H. L. Mencken, and Carl Van Vechten; and aspiring young black authors. The purpose of the dinner (or at least its ostensible purpose) was to celebrate the publication by Boni and Liveright of Jessie Redmon Fauset's novel *There Is Confusion.* Standing to toast Fauset—and Jean Toomer, whose *Cane* had been published by Boni and Liveright the previous year—Horace Liveright noted the difficulties involved in marketing books of merit and urged the writers in his audience to present a rounded rather than sanitized view of Negro life.

Liveright's comments reveal the aesthetic judgment that enabled him, as a publisher, to connect the writers of the Harlem Renaissance to the bohemian and avant-garde left of Greenwich Village. As a major publisher of the 1920s, Liveright was important in defining and identifying modernist artists and pro-gressive intellectuals. Throughout the 1920s, his firm would take risks and fight censorship in order to publish many of the books that came to define American modernism: Ezra Pound's *Poems 1909–1921*, T. S. Eliot's *The Wasteland*, all of Eugene O'Neill's work, Ernest Hemingway's *In Our Time*, Theodore Dreiser's *An American Tragedy*, Stephen Crane's *The Bridge*, and William Faulkner's *Soldier's Pay*. In addition, Boni and Liveright published Sigmund Freud, Bertrand Russell, Havelock Ellis, Upton Sinclair, Leon Trotsky, and Jack Reed—writers who shaped progressive thought during this era. Therefore, Boni and Liveright provided an important venue for its black authors: Jean Toomer, Jessie Fauset, and Eric Walrond.

Horace Brisbin Liveright was born in 1886 and raised in Philadelphia. He had written a comic opera, worked on Wall Street, and failed at a number of marketing ventures when, in 1916, he met Albert Boni, who was a bookseller in Greenwich Village and, like Liveright, was looking for an investment partner. Boni's idea was to publish reprints of modern classics and sell them in a series of inexpensive editions. Liveright was enthusiastic, and in May 1917 the firm of Boni and Liveright opened for business at 105 West Forty-Eighth Street, offering the first twelve titles in the Modern Library series. Modern Library reissued hard-to-find and out-of-print works—attractively bound in limp leatherette and inexpensively priced at sixty cents each—by such authors as Friedrich Nietzsche, Oscar Wilde, Maxim Gorki, August Strindberg, and Fyodor Dostoyevsky. The venture was an immediate success and an important event in American publishing; it was also to prove important in shaping the literary canon. In the decades to follow, new generations of writers would find themselves published in Modern Library along with the classics of the past.

With income from Modern Library and a growing reputation for publishing contemporary literature, Liveright was able to have a rather brilliant private life. He had an image as a jazz age entrepreneur, and his lavish parties, attended by blacks and whites, never lacked for liquor or stimulating conversation. Professionally, Liveright would risk publishing innovative and radical authors when mainstream commercial publishers would not take a chance. Who, then, but Horace Liveright would give serious consideration to *Cane*, a highly experimental book dealing with racial themes and written by an unknown Negro author?

Jean Toomer first met Liveright in 1922 through Waldo Frank, an avant-garde writer in Greenwich

Village whose work Boni and Liveright published without much financial return. At that time, Frank was one of Toomer's closest friends. The two had corresponded throughout 1921–1922, critiquing each other's work and enthusiastically pursuing a new modernist aesthetic. Toomer introduced Frank to the American South and black culture during a week they spent together in Spartanburg, South Carolina; Toomer was in turn introduced by Frank to the literary scene in Greenwich Village, meeting Georgia O'Keefe, Alfred Stieglitz, and Hart Crane as well as Horace Liveright.

Liveright published Toomer's masterpiece, *Cane*, in 1923, with an introduction by Waldo Frank. Although critics, both black and white, gave the book favorable reviews, it was not a financial success, selling only 500 copies. Nevertheless, Liveright offered Toomer a contract for a second, unspecified book (which was never actually completed). By the time of the Civic Club dinner in 1924, however, Toomer had begun to distance himself from both literary production and identification as a black man. When Boni and Liveright's publicity for *Cane* emphasized that Toomer was a new, talented Negro writer, he objected to the mention of race—an attitude which Liveright found difficult to understand.

Liveright's decision to publish a second work of fiction by a black author, Jessie Fauset's *There Is Confusion*, suggests his openness to a "rounded" view of Negro life. Although his publishing career reflected his support of progressive causes and sexual freedom, *There Is Confusion* is a novel of the Negro upper class and is almost Victorian in its depiction of sexual matters. Advertisements for this book featured the gathering of the Negro elite at the Civic Club dinner and compared Fauset's treatment of the upper class to Edith Wharton's.

The West Indian short-story writer Eric Walrond was the third significant author of the Harlem Renaissance whose work was published by Boni and Liveright. Walrond was raised in Barbados and Panama, was educated in Spanish and English, studied literature at Columbia University, wrote for Marcus Garvey's *Negro World*, and was an important link between aspiring black writers and white publishers. He had been the business manager of *Opportunity* since 1925 when Liveright advanced him money for a trip to Panama. The result was the short-story collection *Tropic Death*, published by Boni and Liveright in 1926. Walrond's experimental and expressionistic prose, like Toomer's, was modernist and exotic, rich in dialect

and allegory; it was highly praised by Du Bois and others. Walrond went abroad with Guggenheim funding in 1926, again under contract to Boni and Liveright; as with Toomer, however, Liveright's investment failed to yield a second book. Walrond died in England in 1956, without publishing again.

By 1928 the heyday of Boni and Liveright was over. In 1925 Liveright sold the firm's most reliable source of profit, the Modern Library, to pay for a series of poor theatrical and stock investments. Although the firm continued to publish important books, its financial situation weakened. Liveright had invested heavily in the stock market, and he never recovered from the crash of 1929. In the early 1930s, he lost the business and moved to Hollywood to work for Paramount, where he tried, unsuccessfully, to produce Dreiser's *An American Tragedy* with the filmmaker Sergei Eisenstein of the Soviet Union. Still looking for new publishing ventures, Liveright died broke and alone in New York in 1933. Upton Sinclair gave the eulogy at his funeral.

Biography

Horace Brisbin Liveright was born 10 December 1884 in Oceola Mills, Pennsylvania. He attended public schools in Philadelphia. He was a bond salesman and an investment manager (1904–1916); a cofounder with Albert Boni of the publishing house Boni and Liveright (1917); publisher, Boni and Liveright (1917–1928); publisher, Horace Liveright (1928–1933); and an adviser at Paramount Studios (1931). Liveright died in New York on 25 September 1933.

MICHAEL ZEITLER

See also Boni and Liveright; Civic Club Dinner, 1924; Fauset, Jessie Redmon; Frank, Waldo; Johnson, Charles S.; Modernism; Publishers and Publishing Houses; There Is Confusion; Toomer, Jean; Walrond, Eric

Further Reading

Darden, Tom. *Firebrand: The Life of Horace Liveright*. New York: Random House, 1995.

Gilmer, Walker. *Horace Liveright: Publisher of the Twenties*. New York: Lewis, 1970.

Hutchinson, George. *The Harlem Renaissance in Black and White*. Cambridge, Mass.: Belknap Press of Harvard University Press, 1995.

Lewis, David Levering. *When Harlem Was in Vogue*. New York: Knopf, 1981.

Tebbel, John. *A History of Book Publishing in the United States*, Vol. 3. New York and London: Bowker, 1978.

Wintz, Cary. *Black Culture and the Harlem Renaissance*. Houston, Tex.: Rice University Press, 1988.

Liza

Liza—a musical comedy with book by Irvin C. Miller, score (words and music) by Maceo Pinkard, and "special lyrics" by Nat Vincent—was produced by Al Davis and had its premiere on 27 November 1922 at Daly's Sixty-Third Street Theater. Its cast included Irvin Miller, the team of R. Eddie Greenlee and Thaddeus Drayton, and Emmett ("Gang") Anthony, comedians; Gertrude Saunders (the "falsetto comedienne") and Margaret Simms, singers; and Maude Russell and Johnny Nitt, dancers.

Liza was originally titled *Bon Bon Buddy, Jr.*, and had a trial run at the Lafayette Theater in Harlem during August and September 1922. It was one of at least five black shows to open during that year attempting to duplicate the immense success of *Shuffle Along* (1921) and was the only one to succeed, running for more than two years in various configurations.

The story of *Liza* concerned a woman—the daughter of a small-town mayor—who has fallen in love with a schoolteacher. The young man is unjustly accused of embezzling public funds. In the end the truth comes to light, the young man is exonerated, and the happy couple are able to wed. The songs in the show included "Tag Day," "Pleasure," "I'm the Sheriff," "Liza," "Memories," "Just a Barber Shop Chord," "That Brown-Skin Flapper," "On the Moonlit Swanee," "Essence," "Forget Your Troubles," "My Old Man," "Runnin' Wild Blues," "The Charleston Dance," "Dandy," "My Creole Girl," "Planning," "The Ghost Dance," "Love Me," "Jimtown Speedster," and "Don't Be Blue," as well as several untitled numbers.

Liza was scored for a modified theater orchestra, consisting—according to composer Darius Milhaud, who saw the show—of flute, clarinet, saxophone, two trumpets, trombone, percussion, two violins, viola, cello, and string bass. (Presumably there was also a piano.)

The show was widely reviewed in the mainstream press by major critics of the day, including Alexander Woollcott and Heywood Broun. The reviewers particularly praised the dancing in *Liza*, as well as the general liveliness and fast pace. The loose story line and script were accounted trite and weak, although some critics found some of the comedy pleasing. The score was received favorably, but without excitement; although Pinkard wrote some immortal songs, including "Sweet Georgia Brown" and other hits, none of his best work appeared in *Liza*.

Liza is of lasting historical importance for two reasons that were not readily apparent at the time. It was a major influence on Milhaud, as a source for his famous *ballet nègre* of 1923, *La création du monde*. *Liza* also heralded a major change in American dance. It was in this show that Maude Russell (the "slim princess,"1897–2001) and a chorus line, the Dancing Honey Girls, performed a number called "The Charleston Dance." This was the first appearance of the Charleston on a New York stage. It would become the ubiquitous dance of the jazz age, although it did not rise to its full popularity until the mid-1920s, following its success in the show *Runnin' Wild*.

ELLIOTT S. HURWITT

See also Lafayette Theater; Miller, Irvin; Musical Theater; Runnin' Wild; Shuffle Along

Further Reading

Broun, Heywood. Article in *New York World*, 28 November 1922.

Liza clippings file, Billy Rose Theater Collection, Performing Arts Library, New York Public Library.

Milhaud, Darius Milhaud. "L'évolution du jazz-band et la musique des nègres d'Amériques du nord." *Courrier Musical*, 25(9), May 1923.

Peterson, Bernard. *A Century of Musicals in Black and White*. Westport, Conn.: Greenwood, 1993.

Woollcott, Alexander. Article in *New York Herald*, 28 November 1922.

Locke, Alain

In the pantheon of African American intellectuals who helped to spur on the artistic, social, and political flowering of the Harlem Renaissance, few names occupy as prominent a place as that of Alain Locke. Locke was formally trained and vastly accomplished as a philosopher, but his life and work far transcend the role traditionally ascribed to that profession. As a result of his more than forty years as a prominent member of the faculty at Howard University and his exemplary record of publication on a variety of subjects, Locke exerted a broad influence on African American arts, sociology, and education, among other areas. Locke's status as a cultural authority during the height of the Harlem Renaissance was perhaps rivaled only by that of W. E. B. Du Bois, James Weldon Johnson, Charles S. Johnson, and a select group of others. Although he was not a creative artist himself, Locke's intellectual work not only shaped the Harlem Renaissance but also significantly altered the development of modern American thought in general. His status as a prominent, albeit somewhat closeted, gay figure has also been more fully acknowledged only in recent years. On the whole, Locke's life is marked throughout by a genteel brand of cerebral struggle against the numerous problems he perceived in American society.

Locke was born into a well-to-do African American family in Philadelphia in 1885 and benefited most from this privileged situation in terms of his education. After a distinguished high school career, Locke spent two years training to become a teacher in Philadelphia before matriculating at Harvard, where he earned a bachelor's degree in philosophy and graduated magna cum laude in 1907. That same year, Locke was awarded a Rhodes scholarship as a representative of his home state, Pennsylvania. When he departed for Oxford in the fall of 1907, he officially became the first African American Rhodes scholar in the history of that prestigious program. He continued his post-baccalaureate studies in philosophy for another five years, the first four of which (1907–1910) were completed at Oxford. He subsequently spent a year (1910–1911) at the University of Berlin, where Du Bois had also studied for three years in the early 1890s. Locke distinguished himself at both institutions, excelling at his scholastic work even as he bore the significant burden of being considered a pacesetter for his entire race (a task he actually welcomed, however). He wrote an article called "Oxford Contrasts" in 1909 for *The Independent*, a British periodical, on the triumphs and tribulations associated with his experience as an African American student at Oxford. This piece was reprinted in *Colored American Magazine* that same year, marking Locke's first written contribution to the project of racial uplift associated with the so-called talented tenth. Du Bois had coined this phrase in an essay of 1903 to denote the black intellectual elite

that he believed would lead the entire race to a better position in American society. This group was composed mostly of educated, prosperous, urban African American men from the spheres of business, education, art, medicine, religion, and law. In Du Bois's conception, they were morally obliged to elevate the status of their comparatively powerless lower-class brethren. Locke's later articulation of the characteristics of the "New Negro" borrowed heavily from Du Bois's writings on the talented tenth.

After he returned to the United States, Locke embarked on a six-month tour of the American South. During this tour, the prejudice and intolerance he himself witnessed drove home the necessity of positively demonstrating the capabilities of African Americans. Once he had returned from his travels, Locke moved to Washington, D.C., and quickly accepted a position as an assistant professor at Howard University. He remained at Howard for four years in this role; among his important contributions during this time was the cofounding of the Stylus Society there in 1916. This society, which would last for more than seventy years, published *Stylus*, a literary magazine that included contributions from students (Zora Neale Hurston contributed a piece as an undergraduate in 1921) and faculty members.

In 1916, after four eventful years at Howard, Locke was made a full professor in the philosophy department. Having attained this goal, he decided again to follow Du Bois's example and pursue a doctoral degree at Harvard. Following two years of diligent research and teaching, Locke earned his doctorate in 1918 and returned to Howard to resume his professorial post. He published a wide variety of articles during this period, ranging from occasional philosophical discourses and pedagogical polemics to literary and artistic criticism. He began to contribute regular pieces to *Opportunity*, the monthly journal of the National Urban League, after Charles S. Johnson founded that publication in 1923. *Opportunity* quickly became one of the most prominent African American literary magazines of the day. Claude McKay, Countee Cullen, Langston Hughes, and Zora Neale Hurston were frequent contributors or subjects of reviews in the early years of the journal, and Locke began to mingle freely among the members of the talented tenth because of his association with it. Locke wrote dozens of reviews and other short pieces for *Opportunity* throughout his life and served as a judge in a number of the literary contests that the publication sponsored.

The New Negro: An Interpretation (1925), the work that would become perhaps the most lasting achievement of Locke's career (and one of the masterpieces of the Harlem Renaissance), arose directly from his collaboration with Johnson in the publication of *Opportunity*. Johnson put together the dinner that became known as the Civic Club dinner of March 1924. The purpose, or presumed purpose, of this dinner was to celebrate the publication of Jessie Redmon Fauset's first novel, *There Is Confusion* (1924). However, Johnson also saw it as an occasion to bring together a large number of the most gifted African American artists and writers—many of whom had already been published in *Opportunity*—with prominent sympathetic white figures in the publishing industry in New York. Fauset was literary editor of *The Crisis* at the time, a position that put her in contact with most of the rising young African American talents in literature. Johnson added to the attractiveness of the event by proposing that Locke serve as the toastmaster. Locke's acceptance of this offer provided the dinner with a marquee name to advertise as its master of ceremonies.

The dinner, although a fairly modest event by the standards of New York's literary world, was a great success and brought Locke and Johnson into contact with Paul U. Kellogg, the editor of *Survey Graphic*, a popular magazine dealing with issues related to social work. The magazine was set to publish a "Mexico number" in May 1924, and Locke proposed a similar African American issue to Kellogg. This "Harlem number" would feature the work of many of the artists represented at the dinner, as well as a number of specially commissioned pieces and commentaries. Locke also nominated himself for the role of editor, a move that gave him a chance to put his own theories of elite-centered racial uplift into practice. Kellogg agreed, and the March 1925 issue of *Survey Graphic* came out with poems by Cullen, Hughes, McKay, Angelina Grimké, Jean Toomer, and Anne Spencer, as well as essays and stories by Du Bois, Rudolph Fisher, James Weldon Johnson, Albert Barnes, and others.

During the production of this issue of *Survey Graphic*, Locke and some of the other principals began to consider producing a book-length volume that would include much of the same material but with a wider scope. Albert Boni, who had recently started a publishing company along with his brother Charles, approached Kellogg in January 1925 and made preliminary inquiries about the possibility of republishing a large portion of the "Harlem number" in a book, of which Locke would again be the editor. Boni wished to produce a work that would expand the focus outward from Harlem to include more of the general cultural revitalization within African American society. Kellogg agreed to allow the Boni brothers and Locke to use much of the material from the "Harlem number"; Locke's work on *The New Negro* began almost as soon as he had finished the work for *Survey Graphic*.

The title of the anthology came from a phrase that had been in use to varying degrees since before the turn of the century. Booker T. Washington, Fannie Barrier Williams, and N. B. Wood had put together the collection *A New Negro for a New Century* in 1900 as a call for a general revision of the role of African Americans in the twentieth century. The "New Negro" movement predated the anthology that bore its name by at least ten years, and its membership took on a distinctly urban, middle-class, educated character. The racial pride that was associated with this group fell somewhere between the assimilationism of Washington and the outright separatism supported by more radical figures. Much like the talented tenth before it, the New Negro movement was represented by the poets, painters, politicians, businessmen, scholars, and musicians who made up the African American cultural elite. This movement intended to demonstrate the ways in which the rest of the race could find its own identity without being assimilated into the dominant white culture. The inherent pluralism of the New Negroes meshed well with Locke's personal philosophy about the nature of race, as well as his somewhat elitist ideas about the means by which African Americans could find a place for themselves.

As Locke transformed the *Survey Graphic* number into *The New Negro*, he reduced the three-part structure of the original into two sections: "The Negro Renaissance" and "The New Negro in a New World." This new division is illustrative of Locke's desire for his contributors to create art not *for* African Americans but *as* African Americans. Locke's essay "The New Negro" led off the first section, stating the manifesto of the New Negro movement in no uncertain terms:

> The younger generation is vibrant with a new psychology; the new spirit is awake in the masses, and under the very eyes of the professional observers is transforming what has been a perennial problem into the progressive phases of contemporary Negro life. (47)

Two additional essays on African American art and literature follow Locke's introduction and provide a historical context for the creative material collected in the first part of the anthology, situating the Harlem Renaissance at the leading edge of a long line of creative art by blacks in America. The New Negroes involved in the artistic flourishing of the 1920s are thus rightly not seen as a spontaneous outburst of creativity but as the most recent high point in long, upward-moving cultural curve.

The anthology contains original fiction and poetry by many of the most celebrated artists of the Harlem Renaissance. Toomer contributed (albeit apparently without his consent) two of the short stories that made up his masterpiece *Cane* (1923): "Carma" and "Fern." Also included are short stories by Fisher ("Vestiges: Harlem Sketches" and "The City of Refuge"), John Matheus ("Fog," winner of *Opportunity*'s literary prize in 1925), Fauset ("The Gift of Laughter"), Hurston ("Spunk"), Bruce Nugent ("Sahdji"), and Eric Walrond ("The Palm Porch"), as well as a one-act folk play by Willis Richardson called "Compromise." The poetry section features contributions (many of which appeared in the "Harlem number" as well) from Cullen, Toomer, James Weldon Johnson, Hughes, McKay, Georgia Douglas Johnson, Spencer, Grimké, and Lewis Alexander.

Locke contributed several essays to the anthology, including a piece on the development of traditional African American religious songs ("The Negro Spirituals"). Other prominent contributors of nonfiction included Montgomery Gregory ("The Drama of Negro Life"), Charles S. Johnson ("The New Frontage on American Life"), James Weldon Johnson ("Harlem: The Cultural Capital"), Kelly Miller ("Howard: The National Negro University"), E. Franklin Frazier ("Hampton-Tuskegee: Missioners of the Mass" and "Durham: Capital of the Black Middle Class") and Elise Johnson McDougald ("The Task of Negro Womanhood"). The anthology closes with a strikingly revolutionary piece by Du Bois called "The Negro Mind Reaches Out." Like Locke, Du Bois places racial issues before class issues, but he asserts that there is an important connection between the two, as befits his more socialistic political perspective. In sum, *The New Negro* showcased a broad range of African American artistic and intellectual achievement and proved to be an instant success and source of pride, not only for its contributors but for its readers as well.

Locke's editing of *The New Negro* was not without controversy, however. His opinions about the unquestioned leadership role of the cultural elite were not universally accepted in the African American artistic community. Furthermore, his insistence on the pragmatic purpose of African American art and literature as a means of building racial consciousness ran contrary to the goals of writers like Cullen or Toomer who were seeking to break away from the limitations inherent in being labeled "black" writers. Criticism of Locke's judgment in his editorial decisions has been expressed by those who claimed that Locke was actually furthering the goals of assimilation and by those who claimed that he was advancing a black nationalist position in his selection of material for the book. Hutchinson (1995) attempts to negotiate a solution to this seeming contradiction by outlining the various different forces with which Locke had to contend in putting the volume together, such as including both black and white audiences, considering questions of marketability and profitability, and—perhaps most difficult of all—finding a way to blend the many different ideologies of African American thought into a coherent whole. This last point is the one for which Locke is most frequently attacked, either for over-accentuating writers who agreed with his own racial philosophy or for excluding dissenting voices. Locke had significant and largely permanent fallings-out with Cullen, McKay, and Hurston in the decade following the publication of *The New Negro*.

Countee Cullen resented Locke's insistence on writing predominantly for the purpose of culture building. Although Cullen deals with African themes and images in his poems, their form is derived more from the romanticism of English writers like Keats and Shelley than from the traditional folkloric forebears that Locke would have preferred. Cullen did make some attempts to follow Locke's advice and experimented with primitive elements as much as (if not more than) any of the other major poets of the 1920s. However, to Cullen's Anglophile poetic sensibility, this was simply too narrow a stricture for his artistic expression. Following a squabble about compensation for his poetic contributions to the "Harlem number," Cullen largely broke away from Locke's influence, although he still allowed Locke to use his work on occasion.

Claude McKay, on the other hand, was already politically and aesthetically at odds with Locke before 1925. He became enraged when Locke used his poetry without permission (or with unauthorized alterations) on several occasions, including in *The New Negro*. This led McKay to refuse categorically to allow Locke any further use of his poems in anthologies. When Locke charged that McKay was hurting the New Negro movement by this refusal, McKay angrily

Portrait of Alain LeRoy Locke, 1943–1944, by Betsy Graves Reyneau (1888–1964); oil on canvas. (© National Portrait Gallery, Smithsonian Institution/Art Resource, N.Y.)

replied by letter that Locke was being tyrannical in his desire for aesthetic control over African American arts. Locke made a public reply of sorts in 1937, in an article for *New Challenge* entitled "Spiritual Truancy," in which he accused McKay of being selfish in writing solely according to his personal tastes. The great schism between individual expression and communal responsibility that cleaved the Harlem Renaissance apart is clearly present in this exchange.

Locke had greatly assisted Zora Neale Hurston in the beginning of her career, both by including her work in *The New Negro* and by publicly extolling the virtues of some of her later writings. However, their relationship soured quickly after Locke's negative review (oddly negative, given the work's subject matter and somewhat folkloric tone) of her novel *Their Eyes Were Watching God* (1937). She subsequently referred to Locke, in a letter to James Weldon Johnson, as a

"malicious, spiteful little snot" and an intellectual hypocrite. She eventually almost entirely disavowed Locke's positive influence on her career, claiming that it was Charles S. Johnson who was responsible for her inclusion in *The New Negro*.

Although the ultimate cause of the disagreements between Locke and his onetime protégés is still open to question, Locke's aestheticism was certainly at odds with the values of many members of this younger generation of African American writers. This conflict was felt very keenly by the younger generation of the Harlem Renaissance, many of whom pointedly departed from the classical scholasticism of Locke and experimented with more radical forms of literary and social endeavor in the decades to come.

One key figure in African American letters with whom Locke maintained a close (albeit occasionally antagonistic) relationship was Du Bois, even though the latter's political stance was increasingly distant from that of Locke. Du Bois had criticized Locke's belief in the power of art to effect political change. However, when Locke, by then chair of the philosophy department, was peremptorily fired from Howard in 1925, it was chiefly Du Bois who came to his defense. Du Bois petitioned Jesse Edward Moorland, one of the trustees of the university, on Locke's behalf. His argument was predicated not on his friendship with Locke (which was lukewarm) but rather on an insistence that Locke, as one of the finest scholars in America, belonged at the best African American university in America. Locke was somewhat grudgingly reinstated two years later and remained at Howard until 1953.

Despite the growing antagonism toward Locke among some of the literati of Harlem, *The New Negro* received considerable acclaim and remains a seminal text of the period. It also led Locke to produce a number of other works that continued to aim at an expression of the New Negro aesthetic. Two years after *The New Negro* was published, he produced two separate collections of African American literature—*Four Negro Poets* (1927) and *Plays of Negro Life: A Sourcebook of Native American Drama* (1927)—which he coedited with Montgomery Gregory. *Four Negro Poets*, a thirty-two-page chapbook, includes poems by Cullen, Hughes, Toomer, and McKay, and an introductory essay by Locke entitled "The Poetry of Negro Life." *Plays of Negro Life* is a collection of twenty "plays for the Negro theatre" by both black and white writers. While neither work breaks much new ground, both provide elaboration on means of expressing the artistic ideals associated with *The New Negro*.

As a bibliographic companion to these two pieces, Locke published *A Decade of Negro Self-Expression* (1928). This work, produced while he was a visiting professor at Fisk University in Nashville, consists mainly of an annotated list of books written by African Americans from the outbreak of World War I through the mid-1920s. Locke also began writing what would become a twenty-four-year series of annual publications in which he reviewed the preceding year's books by and about African Americans. From 1929 through 1943, these reviews appeared in *Opportunity*; thereafter, until 1952, they were published in *Phylon*, a leading African American scholarly journal founded by Du Bois in 1940. These pieces represent Locke's greatest contribution to scholarship following the height of the Harlem Renaissance, bringing together his insightful and often opinionated annotations and a comprehensive catalog of information that greatly facilitated the study of African American history and culture.

Biography

Alain LeRoy Locke was born in Philadelphia, Pennsylvania, 13 September 1885. He studied at Ethical Culture and at Central High School in Philadelphia; Philadelphia School of Pedagogy, 1902–1904; Harvard University (A.B., 1907; Ph.D., 1918); Oxford University, 1907–1910; and the University of Berlin, 1910–1911. He was an assistant professor of philosophy and English at Howard University, in Washington, D.C., 1912–1916; a professor, 1916–1953; and chair of the philosophy department, 1921–1953. He founded the literary magazine *Stylus* and the Stylus Society at Howard, 1916. Locke was a visiting professor, Fisk University, Nashville, 1927–1928; cofounder of Associates for Negro Folk Education, 1935; Inter-American Exchange professor, Université de Port-au-Prince, Haiti, 1943–1944; visiting professor, University of Wisconsin–Madison, 1945–1946; president of the American Association for Adult Education, 1946–1947; visiting professor, New School for Social Research, New York, 1947; visiting professor, City College of New York, 1948. His awards included a Rhodes scholarship, 1907; and an honorary doctorate from Howard University, 1953. Locke died in New York City on 10 June 1954.

DEREK MAUS

See also Civic Club Dinner, 1924; Du Bois, W. E. B.; Howard University; New Negro; New Negro Movement; New Negro, The; Opportunity; Stylus; Survey Graphic; Talented Tenth; *specific individuals*

Selected Works

"Oxford Contrasts." *Independent*. (Reprint, "A Negro Student at Oxford." *Colored American Magazine*, 1909.)

Race Contacts and Inter-Racial Relations: A Study in the Theory and Practice of Race. 1916. (Reprint, *Race Contacts and Interracial Relations: Lectures on the Theory and Practice of Race*, ed. and intro. Jeffrey C. Stewart. 1992.)

The New Negro: An Interpretation. 1925. (As editor; reprints, 1968, 1970, 1992.)

Four Negro Poets. c. 1927. (As editor.)

Plays of Negro Life: A Source-Book of Native American Drama. 1927. (As compiler and editor, with Montgomery Gregory; reprint, 1970.)

A Decade of Negro Self-Expression. 1928. (As editor.)

The Negro in America. 1933.

The Negro and his Music. 1936. (Reprint, 1969.)

Negro Art: Past and Present. 1936.

"Spiritual Truancy." *New Challenge*, 1937.

The Negro in Art: A Pictorial Record of the Negro Artist and of the Negro Theme in Art. 1940. (As editor and annotator; reprints, 1969, 1971.)

When Peoples Meet: A Study in Race and Culture Contacts. 1942. (As editor, with Bernhard J. Stern; rev. ed., 1946.)

World View on Race and Democracy: A Study Guide in Human Group Relations. 1943. (As compiler and annotator.)

The Negro in American Culture, ed. Margaret Just Butcher. 1957. (Based on materials left by Locke.)

The Critical Temper of Alain Locke: A Selection of His Essays on Art and Culture, ed. Jeffrey C. Stewart. 1983.

The Philosophy of Alain Locke: Harlem Renaissance and Beyond, ed. Leonard Harris. 1989.

Further Reading

Baker, Houston A., Jr. *Modernism and the Harlem Renaissance*. Chicago: University of Chicago Press, 1987.

Bontemps, Arna. *The Harlem Renaissance Remembered*. New York: Dodd, Mead, 1972.

Hutchinson, George. *The Harlem Renaissance in Black and White*. Cambridge, Mass.: Belknap Press of Harvard University Press, 1995.

Linnemann, Russell J., ed. *Alain Locke: Reflections on a Modern Renaissance Man*. Baton Rouge: Louisiana State University Press, 1982.

Loughery, John. *The Other Side of Silence: Men's Lives and Gay Identities—A Twentieth-Century History*. New York: Holt, 1998.

Posnock, Ross. *Color and Culture: Black Writers and the Making of the Modern Intellectual*. Cambridge, Mass.: Harvard University Press, 1998.

Singh, Amritjit. *The Novels of the Harlem Renaissance: Twelve Black Writers, 1923–1933*. University Park: Pennsylvania State University Press, 1975.

Tidwell, John Edgar, and John Wright. "Alain Locke: A Comprehensive Bibliography of His Published Writings." *Callaloo*, 4, February–October 1981.

Washington, Johnny. *Alain Locke and Philosophy: A Quest for Cultural Pluralism*. Westport, Conn.: Greenwood, 1986.

Wintz, Cary D. *Black Culture and the Harlem Renaissance*. College Station: Texas A&M University Press, 1996.

Loggins, Vernon

For his doctoral work at Columbia University, Loggins studied African American literature written before the twentieth century, producing the first serious scholarly analysis of this literature. In 1931, Columbia University Press published the dissertation as a book, *The Negro Author: His Development in America to 1900*. The book was and is significant because it presented the literature as worthy of serious study, and because Loggins included virtually all the major and minor African American authors known at the time. In his research, he relied heavily on the Arthur A. Schomburg collection of the New York Public Library, and on suggestions made by Charles S. Johnson, James Weldon Johnson, and others. Loggins's analysis is frequently marked with the racial stereotyping common to the period, as when he praises the "African temperament," the "mystic Negro mind," or the "primitive mind" of various writers. Examining Phillis Wheatley, he finds her poems unmoving and uninteresting but is amazed by the fact that a slave had composed poetry at all.

Works produced during the late nineteenth century by W. E. B. Du Bois and Charles W. Chesnutt, two important figures in the Harlem Renaissance, are analyzed in *The Negro Author*. Additionally, Loggins uses a quotation from Countee Cullen to support his claim that "it is unfair criticism to expect too much" of black poets like Paul Laurence Dunbar, because of the disadvantages they faced.

In 1937, Loggins published another critical work, *I Hear America . . . : Literature in the United States since 1900*. In this volume, Loggins writes approvingly of Julia Peterkin and Paul Green, two white southern writers who created sympathetic black characters, but he does not include any African Americans who were among the important writers of the first third of the twentieth century. Later in his career, Loggins published other books of literary criticism, including studies of the works of Nathaniel Hawthorne and William Shakespeare.

Biography

Vernon Loggins was born on 10 January 1893, in Hempstead, Texas. He studied at the University of Texas (A.M., 1917), University of Chicago (A.M., 1917), and Columbia University (Ph.D., 1931), and additionally at New York University, the University of Montpellier, and the Sorbonne. He taught at the University of Minnesota, Minneapolis (1917–1918); Alabama Polytechnic Institute, Auburn (1919–1920); New York University, New York City (1920–1925); and Columbia University (1925–1960). Loggins was a scholar of American literature and the author of books, short stories, reviews, essays, and poems (1924–1968). He was a member of the Poetry Society of America and the International Institute of Arts and Letters. Loggins died on 3 October 1968 in New York City.

Cynthia Bily

See also Chesnutt, Charles Waddell; Cullen, Countee; Du Bois, W. E. B.; Dunbar, Paul Laurence; Green, Paul; Johnson, Charles Spurgeon; Johnson, James Weldon; Peterkin, Julia Mood

Selected Works

The Negro Author: His Development in America to 1900. 1931.

I Hear America . . . : Literature in the United States since 1900. 1937.

Further Reading

Baker, Houston A., Jr. *The Journey Back: Issues in Black Literature and Criticism*. Chicago, Ill.: University of Chicago Press, 1980.

Burke, William Jeremiah. *American Authors and Books,
1640 to the Present Day.* New York: Crown, 1972.

Ethridge, James M., et al., eds. *Contemporary Authors,* 1st
rev., Vols. 5–8. Detroit, Mich.: Gale, 1963.

Jackson, Blyden. *The Waiting Years: Essays on American
Negro Literature.* Baton Rouge: Louisiana State University Press, 1976.

*Who Was Who among English and European Authors,
1931–1949.* Detroit, Mich.: Gale, 1978.

Who Was Who among North American Authors, 1921–1939.
Detroit, Mich.: Gale, 1976.

Lovinggood, Penman

Penman Lovinggood Sr.—an author, tenor, and
composer—was born in Texas in 1895. During the
first decades of the twentieth century he was active in
New York City as a church soloist, concert tenor,
music columnist, and music teacher.

In 1921, in Brooklyn, he published a slender
volume, *Famous Modern Negro Musicians*: brief essays on
nineteen contemporary figures. His criteria for selection were that "these here included are famous, and
likewise Modern Musicians." Eileen Southern, in her
introduction to a reprint edition (1978), notes that this
was "the first survey of black music since the epochal
publication in 1878 of James Monroe Trotter's *Music
and Some Highly Musical People,* and there was not to
be another study until 1934, the publication date of
Maude Cuney-Hare's *Negro Musicians and Their
Music.*" Lovinggood's work is also noteworthy because
his approach is in accordance with the ideas of W. E. B.
Du Bois and Alain Locke regarding the New Negro
and the advancement of the race—ideas that encouraged "classical" performance and composition rather
than the blues and jazz genres of Harlem.

Lovinggood tended to omit biographical information but assessed the musicians in terms of their contribution to the race. Following are some examples.
Samuel Coleridge Taylor: "He burned his vital energy
up in successive musical creations. He stands with the
Masters, and is the greatest Negro Musician." Henry
T. Burleigh: "America's greatest Art-Song writer, and
the American Negro's foremost composer. His work
with the Negro Spiritual has been a devoted and
masterful achievement . . . [conveying] the full beauty
of the music of his own people." R. Nathaniel Dett: the
"most characteristically racial composer." J. Rosamond
Johnson: "His moving style is always graceful and his

insight into the weaving of harmonies . . . is indeed
illuminating." (Johnson was Lovinggood's vocal
teacher, and later Lovinggood was a member of Johnson's vocal quartet.) Will Marian Cook (as a violinist):
"One forgets the structure, form and style of the piece
and is conscious only of the delight in the pure, unal-
loyed movement." Carl R. Diton: "Creative effort
reveals more and more the pure gold of the native musical mine, and well-spring." Roland W. Hayes: "Hailed
as the race's greatest singer." Marian Anderson: "Miss
Anderson possesses the most perfect vocal organ in
itself in the race." Clarence Cameron White (as a violinist): "Mr. White is recognized by the musical people
of both races, as one of the race's greatest musicians."

In November 1925 Lovinggood made his own
musical debut at Town Hall; in October 1927 he appeared at Steinway Hall. A reviewer in the *New York
Times* (23 October 1927) said of the latter performance
that Lovinggood had "revealed a smooth, velvety
tone, which was well produced and of fair range and
volume. His performance was especially enjoyable in
the spirituals, which he imbued with true expressiveness and simplicity." During the 1930s Lovinggood
performed with J. Rosamond Johnson's quartet and
also with W. C. Handy's orchestra.

In 1936 Lovinggood's opera *Menlelek* was performed by the American Negro Opera Association;
the cast included Carl Diton. In 1942 Lovinggood
organized the Drum and Bugle Corps in Englewood,
New Jersey.

Biography

Penman Lovinggood Sr. was born 25 December 1895
in Austin Texas. He studied at Samuel Houston
College in Austin (which his father had founded), and
later with William Happich in Philadelphia and with
J. Rosamond Johnson in New York City. Lovinggood
was active in New York during the first decades of the
twentieth century as a church soloist, concert tenor,
music columnist, and music teacher. He published
Famous Modern Negro Musicians in 1921. He made his
debut at Town Hall in November 1925; in October
1927 he gave a well-received performance at Steinway
Hall. In 1936 his opera *Menlelek* was performed by the
American Negro Opera Association. Lovinggood received the Wanamaker prize for composition and the
Griffith Music Foundation's silver-bronze medal. In
1945 he settled in Compton, California, and established
a publishing firm, Lovingood Company (1947–1963).

At this time he changed the spelling of his name and added the designation "Sr." Lovinggood died in Compton on 4 August 1993.

JOHN GALM

See also Burleigh, Harry Thacker; Cook, Will Marion; Dett, Robert Nathaniel; Handy, W. C.; Hayes, Roland; Johnson, John Rosamond; White, Clarence Cameron

Selected Works

Evangeline and Gabriel. (Opera.)
Famous Modern Negro Musicians. Press Forum, 1921. (See also New York: Da Capo, 1978, with foreword by Eileen Southern.)
"I Am Sure, My Love." (For voice with piano accompaniment; words by Zella.)
Menlelek. 1936. (Opera.)

Further Reading

Anderson, E. Ruth. *Contemporary American Composers: A Biographical Dictionary.* 1976.
Carter, Madison. *An Annotated Catalogue of Composers of African Ancestry.* 1986.
Floyd, Samuel A., and Martha Reisser. *Black Music in the United States: An Annotated Bibliography.* 1983.
Kellner, Bruce, ed. *The Harlem Renaissance: A Historical Dictionary for the Era.* 1984.
Southern, Eileen. *Biographical Dictionary of Afro-American and African Musicians.* 1982.

Lowe, James

James B. Lowe's acting career included three Hollywood productions during the 1920s, but he is best known for having played the leading role in Universal Studios' 1927 film adaptation of *Uncle Tom's Cabin*, directed by Harry Pollard. Other than Paul Robeson, Lowe was the only African American actor to play the lead in a Hollywood film with white actors in the lesser roles. Lowe was also the first black actor to be ballyhooed by his studio. Despite these credits, though, he is mainly associated with the racist stereotype of the "Tom." The Tom had originated earlier than the movies—in popular entertainments of the nineteenth century—but it took on startling staying power on film.

Bogle (1998) describes the Tom as a docile male character with a nearly religious faith in the whites who abuse him; and Noble observes that "the term 'Uncle Tom' has in a hundred years come to mean all that is considered most contemptible in Negro mentality" (1948, 32). As portrayed by Lowe, Uncle Tom is doggedly devoted to Little Eva, his white master's daughter, and thus is a conventional character, but Lowe's own charisma added a new dimension to the role.

An effusive press release about *Uncle Tom's Cabin* read as follows:

> James B. Lowe has made history. A history that reflects only credit to the Negro race, not only because he has given the "Uncle Tom" character a new slant, but because of his exemplary conduct with the Universal company. They look upon Lowe at the Universal Studio as a living black god. . . . Of the directors, critics, artists, and actors who have seen James Lowe work in the studio there are none who will not say he is the most suited of all men for the part of "Tom." Those who are religious say that a heavenly power brought him to Universal and all predict a most marvelous future and worldwide reputation for James B. Lowe. (quoted in Bogle)

Bogle argues, however, that "Tom still came off as a genial darky, furnished with new color but no new sentiments." He adds, though, "Yet to Lowe's credit, he did his tomming with such an arresting effectiveness that he was sent to England on a promotional tour" (6). Such a tour was an entirely novel practice on the studio's part.

Lowe made no further films, but his collaboration with Universal and Pollard remains the best remembered of half a dozen film versions of *Uncle Tom's Cabin*. (In one of these, made twelve years before, Harry Pollard himself had played the role of Tom in blackface.)

Biography

James B. Lowe was born 12 October 1879 in Georgia. His performances include Tom in *Uncle Tom's Cabin* (1927), Rastus in *Blue Blazes* (1926), and Cook in *The Demon Rider* (1925). Lowe died on 19 March 1963 in Los Angeles, California.

TERRI FRANCIS

See also Film: Actors; Film: Blacks as Portrayed by White Filmmakers

Further Reading

Bogle, Donald. *Toms, Coons, Mulattoes, Mammies, and Bucks: An Interpretive History of Blacks in American Films*, 3rd ed. New York: Continuum, 1998, pp. 4–7.

Bowser, Pearl, et al., eds. *Oscar Micheaux and His Circle: African-American Filmmaking and Race Cinema of the Silent Era*. Bloomington and Indianapolis: Indiana University Press, 2001.

Diawara, Manthia, ed. *Black American Cinema*. New York: Routledge, 1993.

Ellison, Ralph. *Shadow and Act*. New York: Random House, 1964.

Elsaesser, Thomas, ed. *Early Cinema: Space/Frame/Narrative*. London: British Film Institute, 1990.

Everett, Anna. *Returning the Gaze: A Genealogy of Black Film Criticism, 1909–1949*. Durham, N.C.: Duke University Press, 2001.

Kellner, Bruce, ed. *The Harlem Renaissance: A Historical Dictionary for the Era*. New York: Methuen, 1984.

Noble, Peter. *The Negro in Silent Films*. London: Knapp, Drewett, 1948.

Null, Gary. *Black Hollywood: The Negro in Motion Pictures*. Secaucus, N.J.: Citadel, 1975.

Stewart, Jacqueline. "Migrating to the Movies: The Emergence of Black Urban Film Culture." Dissertation, University of Chicago, 2000. (See also Ann Arbor, Mich.: UMI, 2000.)

Lulu Belle

Lulu Belle (1926) is a play by Charles MacArthur (1895–1956) and Edward Sheldon (1886–1946). MacArthur was a highly successful newspaper columnist before becoming a playwright; in later life, he edited the magazine *Theatre Arts*. His best-known plays were *The Front Page* (1928) and *Twentieth Century* (1932), both written in collaboration with Ben Hecht. *Lulu Belle* was MacArthur's first play; he completed it with the assistance of Edward Sheldon, an established and influential dramatist. Sheldon was the author of *The Nigger* (1909), a dramatic portrait of a white southern politician who rises to the governorship of his state and then faces a crisis when he learns that he is one-eighth black.

Lulu Belle is about a character who has much in common with Carmen in Bizet's opera. The first of the play's four acts is set in San Juan Hill, near Fifty-ninth Street in Manhattan; this was the major black community before the development of Harlem. Lulu Belle is a blues singer, dancer, and vamp who seduces George Randall, an honest barber, and takes him away from his wife and children. Throughout the play Lulu Belle has premonitions of death, but she refuses to change the course she has set for herself. In the second act, set in a furnished room in Harlem that she now shares with George, she drugs and robs a male victim and forces George to help her conceal the crime. By the third act, bored with George's jealousy, Lulu Belle jilts him in a Harlem nightclub. In rapid succession, George finds out that his son is dead; George refuses to leave Lulu Belle even though she no longer wants him; Lulu Belle has George beaten by another of her boyfriends, a boxer; George stabs the boxer; Lulu Belle turns George over to the police; and Lulu Belle leaves both George and the boxer for a French vicomte who has been slumming in the club. The last act is set in Paris, five years later. George, who has been released from prison, finds Lulu Belle and, in a jealous rage, kills her. As the curtain falls, he cradles her in his arms.

Lulu Belle opened on 9 February 1926; it was produced and directed, with spectacularly realistic scenery, by the legendary David Belasco at the theater that bore his name. The play had more than fifty speaking parts, and the cast consisted of 100 African American and fifteen white actors. This use of an integrated cast was viewed as a progressive step, but the leading roles were filled by two white performers in blackface: Lenore Ulric playing Lulu Belle and Henry Hull playing George. Evelyn Preer, a veteran of the Lafayette Players, had the role of Ruby Lee, Lulu Belle's best friend.

Brooks Atkinson, the critic for the *New York Times*, was most impressed by the acting, dancing, and scenery: "*Lulu Belle* is splendid showmanship; but it retains few of the elements of drama" (10 February 1926, 20). James Weldon Johnson also admired the acting, considering Hull's makeup and dialect "beyond detection" (1977, 205). Though he considered the play no more than "sensational melodrama," he thought that it was significant because of the realistically staged scenes of black life in New York and the mixed cast. *Lulu Belle* was a major success in its time, running for 461 performances.

FREDA SCOTT GILES

See also Johnson, James Weldon; Lafayette Players; Preer, Evelyn; San Juan Hill

Further Reading

Archer, Leonard C. *Black Images in the American Theatre.* Brooklyn, N.Y.: Pageant-Poseidon, 1973.

Bond, Frederick W. *The Negro and the Drama.* Washington, D.C.: Associated Publishers, 1940.

Dorlag, Arthur, and John Irvine, eds. *The Stage Works of Charles MacArthur.* Tallahassee: Florida State University Foundation, 1974.

Hecht, Ben. *Charlie: The Improbable Life and Times of Charles MacArthur.* New York: Harper, 1957.

Isaacs, Edith J. R. *The Negro in the American Theatre.* New York: Theatre Arts, 1947.

Johnson, James Weldon. *Black Manhattan.* New York: Atheneum, 1977. (Originally published 1930.)

Kellner, Bruce, ed. *The Harlem Renaissance: A Historical Dictionary for the Era.* New York: Methuen, 1984.

Mantle, Burns. *The Best Plays of 1926–1927.* New York: Dodd, Mead, 1928.

Lyles, Aubrey

Through his partnership with Flournoy Miller, Aubrey Lyles was a significant influence in black comedy. Lyles was born in Jackson, Tennessee, in 1883. He attended Fisk University as a medical student in the early 1900s. When tiny Lyles faced tall Flournoy Miller in a boxing bout, they hammed it up to the delight of their fellow students. This led to their theatrical partnership. In 1906 Lyles and Miller became resident playwrights and performers for the innovative Pekin Stock Company in Chicago.

They wrote a succession of light entertainments for the Pekin, including *The Mayor of Dixie* (1906), *The Husband* (1907), *Doctor Knight* (1908), and *The Colored Aristocrats* (1909)—their first starring vehicle. Their characters Steve Jenkins (Miller) and Sam Peck (Lyles) became their stage personae thereafter. Lyles and Miller's comedy style broke from the tradition of Bert Williams and George Walker, which featured a comedian and a straight man with singing and dancing. Miller and Lyles, by contrast, were equal partners in straight comedy.

Following their successes at the Pekin, they toured on vaudeville circuits in the midwest. Their appearances in New York earned them a tour of the east coast on the prestigious Keith circuit. The conventions of the time decreed that they perform in blackface, but their style was far from the stereotypes of minstrelsy. In addition to their famous slapstick boxing, they intro-

duced several much-imitated routines. These included "mutilatin' the language" ("You gotta be repaired for that") and "indefinite talk," in which they anticipated the completion of each other's sentences.

In 1915 they played successfully in the well-known *Charlot's Revue* in England. On their return they starred in *Darkydom*, which had an impressive black cast including Abbie Mitchell. After more years in vaudeville, they collaborated (in 1921) with the composer-lyricists Noble Sissle and Eubie Blake on a musical about a mayoral contest in the mythical town of Jimtown (based on the earlier *Mayor of Dixie*). The result was *Shuffle Along*, which many believe launched the Harlem Renaissance.

Shuffle Along brought fame and fortune, but Lyles was shy (in contrast to his boastful stage persona). He compensated by using his wealth to give lavish parties. He kept a menagerie of exotic animals and owned a Rolls Royce whose luxurious appointments were legendary in Harlem. After *Shuffle Along* closed in 1923, Miller and Lyles created another great black show of the 1920s, *Runnin' Wild*, and other similar shows (*Rang Tang, Keep Shufflin'*) but never managed to re-create the magic of *Shuffle Along*. Between 1922 and 1925, Miller and Lyles also made about a dozen 78-rpm recordings on the OKEH label.

Lyles was angered by the producers of the radio series *Amos 'n' Andy*, who, he believed, had plagiarized his material; and by Carl Van Vechten, who had accused him of stereotyping. *Time* magazine reported Lyles's angry outburst against Van Vechten at a welcome-home gathering for Florence Mills in 1927.

In 1929 Lyles split from Miller. Influenced by Marcus Garvey's ideas, he spent a year in Africa. On his return, his solo production *Runnin' de Town* flopped. He then teamed with Miller again. They made two short talkies for RKO and a brief unsuccessful radio series on CBS. Their unconventional musical drama *Sugar Hill* received mixed reviews.

While working on a revival, *Shuffle Along of 1933*, Lyles underwent surgery for gastric ulcers. During his convalescence in New York, he died of preexisting pulmonary tuberculosis on 28 July 1932.

Biography

Aubrey Lyles was born in Jackson, Tennessee, in 1883. He studied at Fisk University. He was a resident playwright at the Pekin Theater Stock Company (1906–1909), with his partner, Flournoy Miller. Lyles and Miller then toured in vaudeville, performed in revues and musicals, and in 1921 collaborated on *Shuffle Along*. In 1929 Lyles split from Miller; they later collaborated again, though not as successfully as before. Lyles died in New York on 28 July 1932.

BILL EGAN

See also Blake, Eubie; Miller, Flournoy; Mills, Florence; Mitchell, Abbie; Musical Theater; Runnin' Wild; Shuffle Along; Sissle, Noble; Van Vechten, Carl; Vaudeville

Theatrical Productions and Performances

1906: *The Man from 'Bam.*
1907: *The Mayor of Dixie; The Oyster Man; The Husband.*
1908: *Doctor Knight; The Colored Aristocrats.*
1912: *The Charity Girl.*
1913: *The Cabaret.*
1915: *Charlot's Revue* (London); *Darkydom.*
1918: *Who's Stealin'.*
1919: *Upstairs and Down Below.*
1920: *Tunes and Funnies of 1920.*
1921: *Shuffle Along.*
1922: *Step On It; The Flat Below.*
1923: *Runnin' Wild.*
1924: *Going White; Honey; Negro Nuances; Struttin' Along Liza; Struttin' Time; Backbiters.*
1927: *Rang Tang.*
1928: *Keep Shufflin'.*
1930: *Runnin' de Town.*
1931: *Lazy Rhythm; Sugar Hill.*

Films

1929: *Harlem Knights; Harlem Mania.*

Further Reading

"Death of Aubrey Lyles Shatters Hope of 'Shuffle Along' Revival." *Afro-American*, 6, August 1932, p. 16.
Peterson, Bernard L., Jr. *The African American Theatre Directory, 1816–1960*. Westport, Conn.: Greenwood, 1993a, p. 162.
———. *A Century of Musicals in Black and White*. Westport, Conn.: Greenwood, 1993.
———. *Profiles of African American Stage Performers and Theatre People, 1816–1960*. Westport, Conn.: Greenwood, 2001, p. 184.

Sampson, Henry T. *Blacks in Blackface: A Source Book on Early Black Musical Shows*. Metuchen, N.J., and London: Scarecrow Press, 1980, pp. 111–114, 115–117.
Slide, Anthony. *The Encyclopaedia of Vaudeville*. Westport, Conn.: Greenwood, 1994, p. 345.
Watkins, Mel. *On the Real Side: Laughing, Lying, and Signifying*. New York: Touchstone–Simon and Schuster, 1995.
Woll, Allen. *Black Musical Theatre: From Coontown to Dreamgirls*. New York: Da Capo, 1991.

Lynching

Lynching is a means of social control in which a mob serves as prosecutor, jury, judge, and executioner. The phrase "lynch law" derives from the unofficial court of Charles Lynch, a planter in Virginia who tried Tory loyalists during the Revolutionary War. Owing to a lack of a standardized judicial system, lynch law was a common practice in the rapidly expanding United States. After the Civil War, the lynching of African Americans in particular served as a crucial means of maintaining white supremacy. Because justifications for lynching and the lynching ritual itself constituted a particularly sexualized attack on black bodies, lynching during the Harlem Renaissance is perhaps most usefully approached in both psychosexual and socioeconomic terms.

History

The lynching of African Americans peaked after radical Reconstruction, as southern whites worked

Two men are lynched in Marion, Indiana, 9 August 1930.
(© Bettmann/Corbis.)

to prevent blacks from participating in the economy and in politics. The withdrawal of northern troops in 1877 paved the way for the systematic economic, social, and political disenfranchisement of the newly emancipated slaves. Lynching functioned as the extralegal counterpart to Jim Crow and to the "separate but equal" legal system. Though the rate of lynching had decreased significantly by the 1920s, 477 African Americans were lynched between 1919 and 1930, according to statistics compiled by the Tuskegee Institute.

In this era, lynching typically occurred in a rural or semirural community in a southern or border state. The mob, composed largely of working-class whites, usually assembled through word of mouth. Sometimes, however, a lynching was advertised in advance in a newspaper or broadside. Legal authorities generally overlooked the lynching. The victim was first physically brutalized—shot, castrated, or otherwise dismembered—then often set on fire and hanged in public view. Before or after death, the victim might be dragged through the white and black sections of town. Afterward, participants salvaged "souvenirs" such as body parts, bone, hair, and scraps of clothing. For some whites, a lynching was a spectacle that served as a ritualized celebration of racial supremacy; and many black communities were terrorized by the constant threat of lynching. In this way, lynching maintained the institutionalized racial and economic hierarchies of Jim Crow.

Explanations

There is no single explanation for lynching. At the time a lynching took place, the reason—that is, the accusation involved—might range from a criminal act to a petty infraction of the social code. Relatively recent scholarship has offered economic and psychosexual explanations. Tolney and Beck (1995) correlate lynching in the South with vacillations in the cotton market. Although their conclusions cannot be applied universally, because the lynching rate decreased as terrorized laborers fled north, their findings support theories linking the "great migration" to the threat of lynching. The threefold rise in lynching that occurred after the stock market crash of 1929 also suggests a link between this form of violence and economic crises.

A very common reason, or pretext, for lynching was an accusation of rape. Although Raper (1933) and Franklin (1967) found that only one-third of all male

victims of lynching had been accused of sexual assault, the influence of this rationale indicates a link between psychosexual forces and socioeconomic explanations. The pervasive stereotype of the sexually uncontrollable black man (as opposed to the "civilized" white gentleman) was offered to justify the disenfranchisement and oppression of blacks. The presumed object of the black male's sexual desire, the chaste white woman, symbolized wealth and privilege. An accusation of interracial rape, then, was a call for white men to assert their "natural" rights of social, economic, and political domination over blacks and over white women. Smith (1990) argues that a "homosocial triangle" defined the mythology of rape and lynching and obscured the rape of black women. Just as white and black men were opposed with regard to violence and sexuality, so were white and black women. If black women, like black men, were thought naturally promiscuous, the rape of a black woman could not be considered a crime. The mythology of interracial rape and lynching, then, served an ideological function in terms of the economic and social competition between the races. The Scottsboro case of 1931 seems to illustrate this complex of forces.

Representations

In the creative art of the Harlem Renaissance, scenes of lynchings expressed tension regarding differences of gender, class, geography, and race. For instance, in Jean Toomer's *Cane* (1923) the threat of lynching emasculates and silences the black male artist who is attempting to voice racial pride—one quality that, according to Alain Locke, characterizes the New Negro (1925, 11). Toomer dramatizes this situation through Kabnis's hysterical fear of whites, the lynching of Mame Lamkins and her unborn child, the poem "Portrait in Georgia," and the story "Blood-Burning Moon."

Similarly, in James Weldon Johnson's *Autobiography of an Ex-Colored Man* (1912), a lynching causes the protagonist to abandon the South and to vow "to voice the joys and sorrows, the hopes and ambitions, of the American Negro" (147–148). For the ex-colored man, the lynching both reinforces and dissolves the color line, as fear propels him to flee northward and pass as a white man. Southern male characters in Richard Wright's *Uncle Tom's Children* (1938) are also impelled northward by the threat of lynching. In these stories, Wright explores how lynching furthers class exploitation, revealing how stereotypes of black masculinity and white femininity frustrate the possibility of interracial labor solidarity. Wright's influential *Native Son* (1940) also powerfully indicts this system.

The visual artists Jacob Lawrence and Aaron Douglas produced notable representations of lynching. In panel 15 of Lawrence's series *Migration of the Negro*, a figure is shown grieving under an empty noose. The caption, "It was found that where there had been a lynching, the people who were reluctant to leave at first left immediately after this," links the great migration to lynching. Lawrence does not show either the victim's body or the lynch mob; this seems to suggest his condemnation of the mob and the crowd of spectators, since he refuses to validate their point of view. Aaron Douglas contrasts a lynching with working and dancing figures in panel 3 of his famous mural *Aspects of Negro Life*. The juxtaposition of life and death in this panel, which has the title *The Idyll of the Deep South*, suggests the strength and resilience of African Americans.

Unlike Lawrence, other artists made a point of representing the brutal spectacle itself. Billie Holiday's song "Strange Fruit" (a setting of a poem by Lewis Allen), and Claude McKay's sonnet "The Lynching," use vivid representations to incite protest. Two works concerned with visual convention are Langston Hughes's "Christ in Alabama" (about the Scottsboro boys) and Countee Cullen's "Black Christ"; both use the image of crucifixion to point out Christians' racism.

Dramas about lynching offer another perspective. These plays arose from a convergence of the "little theater" movement and the Harlem Renaissance; they include works by Georgia Douglas Johnson, Alice Dunbar Nelson, and Angelina Weld Grimké (among others) and suggest one kind of tension characterizing Locke's aesthetics of the New Negro. Using aspects of the folk tradition such as call and response, the plays emphasize Negroes' "difference" in the context of demands for equal treatment under American law. In the literature of the Harlem Renaissance—and in fact Harris (1984) argues that this is true of African American literature in general—representations of lynching serve as symbols of shared experience testifying to black people's protest, resistance, and survival.

SONDRA GUTTMAN

See also Antilynching Crusade; Autobiography of an Ex-Colored Man; Cane; Civil Rights and Law; Cullen, Countee; Douglas, Aaron; Grimké, Angelina Weld; Holiday, Billie; Hughes, Langston; Jim Crow; Johnson, Georgia Douglas; Johnson, James Weldon; Lawrence, Jacob; Lynching: Silent Protest Parade; McKay, Claude; National Association for the Advancement of Colored People; Nelson, Alice Dunbar; Racial Violence: Riots and Lynching; Scottsboro; Toomer, Jean; Wright, Richard

Further Reading

Allen, James, et al. *Without Sanctuary: Lynching Photography in America*. Santa Fe, N.M.: Twin Palms, 2000.

Best, Stephen Michael. "'Stand by Your Man': Richard Wright, Lynch Pedagogy, and Rethinking Black Male Agency." In *Representing Black Men*, ed. Marcellus Blount and George Cunningham. New York: Routledge, 1995.

Franklin, John Hope. *From Slavery to Freedom: A History of Negro Americans*. New York: Knopf, 1967. (See also 8th ed., 2000.)

Harris, Trudier. *Exorcising Blackness: Historical and Literary Lynching and Burning Rituals*. Bloomington: Indiana University Press, 1984.

Locke, Alain. "The New Negro." In *The New Negro: An Interpretation*, ed. Alain Locke. New York: Albert and Charles Boni, 1925. (See also New York: Scribner, 1997.)

Moses, Norton H., comp. *Lynching and Vigilantism in the United States: An Annotated Bibliography*. Westport, Conn.: Greenwood, 1997.

National Association for the Advancement of Colored People (NAACP) Staff. *Thirty Years of Lynching in the United States, 1889–1918*. New York: NAACP, 1919. (See also New York: Arno, 1969.)

Perkins, Kathy A., and Judith L. Stephens, eds. *Strange Fruit: Plays on Lynching by American Women*. Bloomington: Indiana University Press, 1998.

Raper, Arthur. *The Tragedy of Lynching*. Chapel Hill: University of North Carolina Press, 1933.

Smith, Valerie. "Split Affinities: The Case of Interracial Rape." In *Conflicts in Feminism*, ed. Marianne Hirsch and Evelyn Fox Keller. New York: Routledge, 1990.

Stephens, Judith L. "Racial Violence and Representation: Performance Strategies in Lynching Plays of the 1920s." *African American Review*, 33(4), 1999.

Tolney, Stewert E., and E. M. Beck. *A Festival of Violence: An Analysis of Southern Lynchings, 1882–1930*. Carbondale and Edwardsville: University of Illinois Press, 1995.

Toomer, Jean. *Cane*. New York: Liveright, 1923. (Reprint, 1993.)

White, Walter. *Rope and Faggot: A Biography of Judge Lynch*. Ayer, 1978. (Originally published 1929.)

Wright, Richard. *Native Son*. New York: Harper and Row, 1940. (See also New York: HarperPerennial, 1993a.)

———. *Uncle Tom's Children*. New York: World, 1938. (See also New York: HarperPerennial, 1993b.)

Lynching: Silent Protest Parade

The first massive African American protest in American history took place when some 8,000 to 10,000 African Americans marched down Fifth Avenue in New York City on 28 July 1917 in a "parade of silent protest against acts of discrimination and oppression" ("Negroes in Protest March" 1917, 12). The silent protest parade—which had been organized by the National Association for the Advancement of Colored People (NAACP), church officials, and civic leaders shortly after riots broke out in East St. Louis—was a dramatic appeal to President Wilson to address lynching, disenfranchisement, Jim Crow, and mob violence. Because the march "turned protest into something like organized and conspicuous theater" Douglas contends that the silent protest parade marks the true beginning of the Harlem Renaissance (1995, 328).

The paraders assembled at Fifty-ninth Street and Fifth Avenue and marched thirty-six blocks downtown to Madison Square Park. They were led by about 800 children, some no older than six, dressed entirely in white. Following the children were white-clad women, then rows of men dressed in black. The marchers walked wordlessly to the sound of muffled drumbeats. Despite their silence, their concerns were articulated on neatly stenciled banners and signs.

According to news reports, the march drew attention, respect, and support from whites and blacks alike. The mayor of New York City, John Purroy Mitchel, had diverted traffic and established a protective police presence; an estimated 20,000 spectators, some in tears, were as silent as the marchers. One newspaper reported that "the parade in all respects was one of the most quiet and orderly demonstrations ever witnessed on Fifth Avenue" ("Negroes in Protest March," 12).

Although the police ordered the removal of one banner, which depicted a black woman kneeling before President Wilson and begging him to secure democracy in America before taking it abroad, they had no objection to the other banners and placards, some of which read:

"Thou shalt not kill."

"America has lynched without trial 2,867 Negroes in thirty-one years and not a single murderer has suffered."

"We have fought for the liberty of white Americans in six wars; our reward is East St. Louis."

"Memphis and Waco—Centers of American Culture?"

"Taxation without representation is tyranny."

"We are maligned as lazy and murdered where we work."

"Your hands are full of blood."

"Mother, do lynchers go to heaven?"

During the parade, black Boy Scouts handed out leaflets which posed the question, "Why Do We March?" and answered: "We march because we deem it a crime to be silent in the face of such barbaric acts. . . . We march in memory of our butchered dead, the massacre of honest toilers who were removing the reproach of the laziness and thriftlessness hurled at the entire race" (Du Bois 1917, 241).

The riots in East St. Louis, to which some of these statements were referring, had taken place in May and July and had destroyed at least $400,000 worth of property, driven 6,000 African Americans out of their homes, and resulted in the death of at least forty African Americans. In an extensively researched article for *The Crisis*, W. E. B. Du Bois and a white social worker, Martha Gruening (1917), attributed the riots to the hostility of white union workers toward black strikebreakers. The strike involved had ended in May, but white laborers in the packing industry, troubled by the mass migration of African Americans from the South, had remained wary. Tension was exacerbated by union leaders who continued to call for "drastic action" against the "influx of undesirable negroes" (phrasing that appeared in a letter from Edward F. Mason, reprinted as a facsimile in *The Crisis*, 1917, 221). On 2 July 1917 drastic action was taken. Rioting ensued when a group of white policemen, who may have been mistaken for gun-wielding joy-riders, drove into a black neighborhood and were fired on by the residents. The next morning, the city erupted. Eyewitnesses likened the mob to a manhunt, describing how rioters sought out blacks to beat, mutilate, stab, shoot, hang, and burn.

Stunned by the events in East St. Louis, leaders of the Harlem branch of the NAACP met to discuss a method of protest. The field secretary James Weldon Johnson, recalling an idea developed years before by Oswald Garrison Villard, suggested a silent protest parade. In order to reach all African American citizens of New York, Johnson formed a parade committee that included pastors from several leading churches and influential members of the black community.

Johnson also hoped that the march would draw attention to the NAACP's antilynching crusade. The crusade was spurred on by an article that appeared in *The Crisis* in 1916, about a mob that had attacked a mentally retarded adolescent in a courtroom in Waco; Johnson himself investigated the lynching of an accused ax-murderer who was burned alive in Memphis. In April 1917, *The Crisis* featured a letter from the NAACP to Woodrow Wilson requesting that in his inaugural address he "say something against the barbaric system of lynching which prevails in various parts of this country" ("A Letter to the President," 284). By 1919, in *Thirty Years of Lynching in the United States 1889–1918*, the NAACP would report that, nationwide, 3,224 lynchings had claimed the lives of 702 whites and 2,522 blacks.

Yet despite the direct appeal to the president, and despite the national publicity surrounding the violence, black leaders had been turned away from the White House, and Samuel L. Gompers of the American Federation of Labor (AFL) had publicly excused the white workers of East St. Louis. Thus a new kind of "drastic action" seemed to be in order. Joining in Johnson's strategy of "firm but friendly pressure" were the parade's organizers: the grand marshal, Captain W. H. Jackson; the parade president, Reverend Dr. H. C. Bishop; the vice president, Reverend F. A. Cullen; the secretary, Reverend Dr. Charles Martin; and the first deputy marshal, J. Rosamond Johnson. The parade committee also included Allen Wood, A. B. Cosey, C. H. Payne, Reverend E. W. Daniels, and John Nail. Marching with these leaders was W. E. B. Du Bois, who had just returned from his research in East St. Louis.

In the years following the march, James Weldon Johnson lobbied strenuously for the Dyer antilynching bill. That bill ultimately failed, but the silent protest parade heralded the rise of a new militancy among blacks. Without uttering a word, African Americans

had expressed their unity, and in so doing had developed a powerful new voice.

REBECCA MEACHAM

See also Antilynching Crusade; Crisis, The; Cullen, Frederick Asbury; Johnson, James Weldon; Johnson, John Rosamond; Lynching; Nail, John E.; National Association for the Advancement of Colored People; Riots 1: Overview, 1917–1921; Villard, Oswald Garrison

Further Reading

Douglas, Ann. *Terrible Honesty: Mongrel Manhattan in the 1920s*. New York: Farrar, Straus, Giroux, 1995.

Du Bois, W. E. B. "The Negro Silent Parade." *The Crisis*, 14(5), 1917.

Du Bois, W. E. B., and Martha Gruening. "The Massacre of East St. Louis." *The Crisis*, 14(5), 1917.

Johnson, James Weldon. *Black Manhattan*. New York: Knopf, 1930. (See also New York: Arno and New York Times, 1968.)

———. *Along This Way: The Autobiography of James Weldon Johnson*. New York: Viking, 1933. (See also New York: Da Capo, 2000.)

Kellogg, Charles Flint. *NAACP: A History of the National Association for the Advancement of Colored People*, Vol. 1, *1909–1920*. Baltimore, Md.: Johns Hopkins University Press, 1967.

"A Letter to the President." *The Crisis*, 13(6), 1917.

Lewis, David Levering. *W. E. B. Du Bois: Biography of a Race, 1868–1919*. New York: Holt, 1993.

"Negroes in Protest March on Fifth Avenue." *New York Times*, 29 July 1917, p.12.

Thirty Years of Lynching in the United States, 1889–1918. New York: National Association for the Advancement of Colored People, 1919. (Reprint, New York: Negro Universities Press–Greenwood, 1969.)

Ottley, Roi, and William J. Weatherby. *The Negro in New York: An Informal Social History, 1626–1940*. New York: Praeger, 1967, 1969.

St. James, Warren D. *NAACP: Triumphs of a Pressure Group, 1909–1980*. Smithtown, N.Y.: Exposition, 1958. (See also 2nd ed., 1980.)

Lyrical Left

When Floyd Dell, a bohemian extraordinaire (although he had been raised in Iowa), declared 1912 the "lyric year," he praised Edna St. Vincent Millay's seamless sonnets about free love. But he also extolled the rise of a new American progressivism that was reconciling clashing styles of rebellion and that promised to revolutionize both private life and the nation's public business. For Dell and his comrades in the bohemian stronghold of Greenwich Village, New York, at its height in the 1910s and 1920s, the expressive energy and integrative logic of lyric verse suggested a model for politics as much as a postromantic literary ideal. Now that the traditionally isolated lyric poet was learning to emerge from his or her quiet solitude, they assumed, the most sensitive young American rebels could learn to break down the doors between contemplation and action, sexual and economic liberation, the studio and the barricades. *The Masses*, the exemplary magazine of bohemia in the Village, preached the gospel of synthesis through eight worthy passions: "fun, truth, beauty, realism, freedom, peace, feminism, revolution." As leftist positions hardened during the Great Depression, Dell and his associates' hope for an inclusive lyric socialism, with headquarters in the cafés and walk-up apartments of downtown Manhattan, began to seem self-indulgent, naïvely utopian, even decadent. A more flattering revisionist view was prompted by the renewal of "personal politics" in the late 1960s—politics willing to discover a usable past in the thought and manners of Randolph Bourne, Van Wyck Brooks, Mabel Dodge, Crystal and Max Eastman, John Reed, and other artist-rebels in the Village. Since the 1970s, historians have been unembarrassed to declare that the "lyrical left" created by these rebels was the first, the heartiest, and perhaps the most indigenous American left of the twentieth century.

In its early years, the native habits of the lyrical left included indifference to the emergence of Harlem as a black intellectual capital. Although this left had an unprecedented openness to American Jews, southern and eastern European immigrants, and products of the white working class—Dell himself was the son of a butcher—few Harlemite thinkers other than the feminist Grace Nail Johnson and the socialist Hubert Harrison regularly participated in Village circles before World War I. Recent scholarship has nevertheless emphasized that the lyrical left was a force shaping the self-conscious Harlem "renaissancism" of the late 1910s. Lewis (1994), for example, argues that the Village bohemia was in fact the major incubator of the renaissance during its primary stage. From 1917 to 1923, he contends, Harlem's rebirth was piloted from

Washington Square more frequently than from any uptown address.

Lewis's notion of a first-phase "bohemian renaissance" is supported by the fact that Claude McKay and Jean Toomer—perhaps the foremost pioneers of, respectively, the poetry and prose of the Harlem Renaissance—both had links to, or even entanglements in, the Village. McKay was born in Jamaica, and his initial travels along the track of the great Afro-Caribbean migration were followed by a similarly crowded bohemian itinerary once he arrived in the United States. Like thousands of others who made the escape from the provinces to downtown New York "the defining cultural journey of most of the century" (Stansell 2000), McKay concluded that Manhattan, Kansas, was too small for great achievements. In 1914, before he knew the ins and outs of Harlem, he was patronizing the larger Manhattan's Greenwich Village, where what he conceived as his atheistic socialism and peasant "pagan" temperament harmonized with its post-Christian era. McKay's frequent publications in organs of the lyrical left such as *The Masses* and *Seven Arts* led to an editorship at the *Liberator*, then the world's only Marxist journal to pattern its content and working method on Village conversation. By the time that *Harlem Shadows*, the first poetry collection of the Harlem Renaissance, appeared in 1922, McKay was one of the most visible and influential people in the bohemia of the lyrical left—a referee at its signature magazine, an epitome of its innovative left-literary synthesis, and an intimate friend of its famous figures.

Jean Toomer's affiliation with the lyrical left was more fitful and less conspicuous. Unlike McKay, who chose some of the first ingredients of *Cane* (1923) for the *Liberator*, Toomer never assumed a formal position within the literary institutions of bohemian Manhattan. Nevertheless Toomer's literary identity took shape on contact with the lyrical left. In the aftermath of a brief trip to the Village in 1920, the aristocratic wanderer and serial college dropout known as Nathan Pinchback Toomer read Romain Rolland's *Jean Christophe* (1904), reconceived his artistic fate, and rechristened himself Jean Toomer. The new Toomer's intensely lyrical prose, freshly dedicated to African American voices, was received as grist for the mill by many journals of the lyrical left—not just the *Liberator*. *Broom*, *Dial*, *Double-Dealer*, and *S4N* ran pieces by Toomer which inspired people like Sherwood Anderson who were searching high and low for a way to "get inside the niggers and write about them with some intelligence" (Lewis 1994, xxi). Toomer took from the

Village nearly as much as he gave. White critics down-town were "receptive of what the English, the Irish, the Teuton, the Latin, the Slav, the Chinese, the Japanese, the Jew, the Negro, have to give," he said. Their tran-scendence of "the narrow implications of the entire Anglo-Saxon ideal"—if not the entire vocabulary of antiblack racism—had much to teach "we who have Negro blood in our veins, who are culturally and emotionally the most removed from the Puritan tra-dition," but who "are its most tenacious supporters" (Hutchinson 1995, 131). In particular, one white critic with connections to the Village, Waldo Frank, author of the influential anti–Anglo-Saxon medita-tion *Our America* (1919), went with Toomer on a southern expedition that partly inspired the setting of *Cane*—Georgia. Significant traces of the styles, values, and prejudices of the lyrical left can be found in *Cane* as well as in *Harlem Shadows*, both classics of the literature of the Harlem Renaissance.

The impact of the lyrical left on the movement in Harlem did not end in 1923 with the appearance of Toomer's novel and the official closing of the bo-hemian renaissance. As Hutchinson notes, the con-cept of cultural pluralism, crucial to Alain Locke's thinking in and beyond the anthology *The New Negro* (1925), owed a good deal to theorists of the lyrical left such as the "transnationalist" Randolph Bourne; Locke's dialogue with Horace Kallen—who was his classmate at Harvard and a fellow Rhodes scholar— was not the sole inspiration for his abandonment of "Anglo-conformity." Locke's controversial proposal that African Americans could pursue political libera-tion through artistic means was similarly informed by a fundamental presumption of the lyrical left: that the arts could rewire the American mind and thus remake the American social order. The core strategy of the Harlem Renaissance, which Lewis (1994) calls "civil rights by copyright," appears much less fantastic when viewed in relation to the insistence of the lyrical left on the indissolubility of art and life.

Ideas of sexual liberation that characterized the lyrical left played a comparably long-lasting role in attacks by members of the Harlem Renaissance on black Victorianism. In the free-love poetry and prose of such New Negroes as McKay, Toomer, Langston Hughes, and Helene Johnson, there are plentiful and sometimes queer linkages between rebellious black bodies; these echo Village bohemians' interweaving of the bonds of love, practical morality, and radical politics. In general, the positive influence of the lyrical left on Harlem's erotic literature has been

underexamined. No less underexamined, however, is the critical response of Harlem's authors to the si-lence of the Village on the ties among race, free-love bohemia, and everyday wage labor. Consider, to take just one example, McKay's sixteen-line lyric "Alfonso, Dressing to Wait at Table," a poem prominently fea-tured in *Harlem Shadows*. Although he must prepare himself to serve, the figure who lends the poem its name lives far from the uninspired work the title pre-dicts. In the eyes of McKay's approving speaker, Alfonso removes any self-ridicule from the waiter's required parody of aristocratic dress; in his case, the man makes the clothes, and his beauty outstrips fashion in everything but its capriciousness: "His moods are storms that frighten and make glad,/His eyes were made to capture women's hearts." Praise is not confined to Alfonso's sexual charisma; the poem's desired object is also flattered as a self-conscious free lover, a winning propagandist of "wine and clinking glasses/And riotous rakes . . . ," and an artist of literally moving talent: "Alfonso's voice of mellow music thrills/Our swaying forms and steals our hearts with joy." To indulge in a contradiction in terms, Alfonso is thus revealed to be a natural bohemian, by rights a prince of the Village, readier than most to muddle the distinction between passion and art, not to mention the distinction between male feminism and womanizing. The last stanza of Alfonso's unveiling, however, brings bohemian can-onization to a sudden, apostrophizing halt: "O Alfonso! wherefore do you sing/. . . Soon we shall be beset by clamouring/Of hungry and importunate palefaces." The nearly ridiculous formality of rhyme and diction underscores the disproportion between the waiter's job and the waiter's capacity. The bohemian idyll of enlivening, cross-class conversation over food and wine is drowned out by unreasonable, racially loaded orders.

In *Harlem Shadows*, "Alfonso" is followed by a suite of three analogous poems sketching harassed workers, all of which take aim at the poet-celebrity who made Village bohemia sensible to a national au-dience. The intimate addressee of McKay's lyrics "Dawn in New York," "The Tired Worker," and "When Dawn Comes to the City" is Edna St. Vincent Millay; their intertextual task is to remember skepti-cally her poem "Recuerdo" (1920), the bohemian rhapsody that begins with the hypnotic lines "We were very tired, we were very merry—/We had gone back and forth all night on the ferry." As Miller (1998) observes, "Recuerdo" testifies that its "we" are merry precisely because they are tired, not in spite of it; they meet a lazy dawn with a code "of bohemian antiproductivity and a dynamic of pure circulation," having preempted the morning commute with an evening whirl, a floating purposefulness without a purpose. The would-be bohemians in McKay's poems, by contrast, are trapped in a circular desire for antiproductivity. Their spirit also thrills to dawn in New York, but for them the protective shadows wane; the bohemian love connection to the city ends at eight in the morning. The culprit, typically revealed in a puncturing final couplet, is the need to "go darkly-rebel to . . . work" ("Dawn in New York").

What McKay dramatizes in these poems of New York's dawn is something close to Marcuse's notion of the "temporal dismemberment of pleasure," the shattering distribution of happiness into "small separated doses" through the regimentation of the working day (1974). American "Freudo-Marxism" began in Greenwich Village, after all, with its premonition that eros could flower within civilization if socialism repealed both surplus value and surplus repression. Given the poems' signifying take on Millay, however, it would be mistaken to ignore McKay's less neighborly additions to Village conversation. The dark and rebellious speakers of *Harlem Shadows* enter the cross-talk of middle- and working-class bohemians straight from workplaces difficult to libidinalize—a pantry rather than a garret office, say. They bring with them more skepticism about the pairing of wage work and equality than did many Village feminists, who audaciously invested such work with redemptive force adequate to emancipate "new women" from Victorian motherhood. Above all, however, McKay's speakers infiltrate the bohemian public sphere to caution that unfree labor could break bohemia's faith in a smooth transit between private and public liberty, free love and civic good. By the conclusion of *Harlem Shadows*, these speakers have thus created a genre of bohemian lyric *interruptus* with morals of its own—McKay's would-be bohemians not only confess that the lyrical left is part of the lineage of the Harlem Renaissance but advise Villagers against great expectations for "no more separate spheres."

WILLIAM J. MAXWELL

See also Broom; Cane; Eastman, Crystal; Eastman, Max; Frank, Waldo; Harlem Shadows; Harrison, Hubert; Hughes, Langston; Johnson, Helene; Liberator; McKay, Claude; Seven Arts; Toomer, Jean

Further Reading

Diggins, John Patrick. *The Rise and Fall of the American Left*. New York: Norton, 1992.

Hutchinson, George. *The Harlem Renaissance in Black and White*. Cambridge, Mass.: Belknap–Press of Harvard University Press, 1995.

Lewis, David Levering, ed., *The Portable Harlem Renaissance Reader*. New York: Penguin, 1994.

Marcuse, Herbert. *Eros and Civilization: A Philosophical Inquiry into Freud*. Boston, Mass.: Beacon, 1974. (Originally published 1955.)

Miller, Nina. *Making Love Modern: The Intimate Public Worlds of New York's Literary Women*. New York: Oxford University Press, 1998.

Stansell, Christine. *American Moderns: Bohemian New York and the Creation of a New Century*. New York: Metropolitan–Holt, 2000.

M

Mabley, Jackie "Moms"

The vaudevillian, stand-up comic, and star of stage and screen Jackie "Moms" Mabley (1897–1975) had a long, productive career that spanned the years from the Harlem Renaissance through the black arts movement. Her original name was Loretta Mary Aiken; she claimed that she acquired her stage name by "taking it" from a Canadian-born boyfriend—they had only a brief relationship but she decided to keep his name because she liked it. Her ability to find humor in unlikely situations such as this one was something she attributed to her determination to overcome the many adversities she encountered in her daily life.

Following a difficult and short childhood, during which she had experienced the death of her father when she was eleven and had been raped by two local men, Mabley left home just before her fourteenth birthday to join a minstrel show. She changed the date of her birth from 1897 to 1894 and entered the adult world of African American performers on the Theater Owners' Booking Association (TOBA) circuit, during the days of segregation and Jim Crow. The husband-and-wife dance team Butterbeans and Susie were among the first well-known professional acts with whom she performed, very early in her career.

By the 1920s, Mabley began performing in Harlem, in venues such as the Cotton Club, Connie's Inn, and the Savoy Ballroom, where she shared billings with Duke Ellington, Louis Armstrong, and Cab Calloway, among others, and perfected her stand-up comedy routines. Her credits as a performer in musical theater included *Bowman's Cotton Blossoms* in 1919, and *Look Who's Here* and *Miss Bandana* in 1927. In the following decade she was cast in *The Joy Boat*, *Sidewalks of Harlem*, *Red Pastures*, *Blackberries*, *Swingin' the Dream*, and the Broadway production *Fast and Furious*, in which she performed with the writer and folklorist Zora Neale Hurston. During this period, Mabley also began to develop the character "Moms" that would make her famous.

Mabley made her film debut in 1933 in *The Emperor Jones*, which starred Paul Robeson. In the 1940s she performed in the films *Killer Diller* and *Boarding House Blues*. Even during her difficult days on the road, Mabley was able to help provide for three generations of family members, and she bought a house in Washington, D.C., where Mabley's mother lived until her death in 1946.

Mabley's career received a huge boost when she appeared on television in the 1960s and 1970s, in the shows of the Smothers brothers, Bill Cosby, Merv Griffin, Mike Douglas, Ed Sullivan, Garry Moore, and Flip Wilson. Her growing popularity led to performances at Carnegie Hall, the Kennedy Center, and the White House, and on college campuses across the country.

Mabley's classic comedy routines are preserved on more than twenty-five recordings, including *Moms Mabley: The Funniest Woman in the World* (on the Chess label), which sold one million copies. For many people, the crowning achievement of her career was the making of *Amazing Grace*, her first full-length motion picture, in 1974, just before her death in 1975. Mabley was a multitalented artist, but she is best remembered as "Moms," a granny who wore a floppy hat, seemed to be toothless, loved children, and was a churchgoer—but for whom few topics other than religion were off limits. Mabley's humor included comments about racism, homosexuality, and her own flings with younger men. "Moms" was eulogized as someone who had enjoyed a good laugh whenever or wherever she could find or create one.

Biography

Jackie "Moms" Mabley (Loretta Mary Aiken) was born in 1897 in Brevard, North Carolina, where she attended public schools. Her parents were James P. and Mary Aiken. She left school and home at the age of thirteen to join a minstrel show. Mabley performed on the Theater Owners' Booking Association circuit in comedy and musical theater; appeared in several films during the 1930s and 1940s; appeared on stage, on television, and in films in the 1960s and 1970s; and made numerous audio recordings in the 1960s and 1970s. She died 23 May 1975.

REGENNIA N. WILLIAMS

See also Armstrong, Louis; Calloway, Cabell "Cab"; Cotton Club; Ellington, Duke; Emperor Jones, The; Hurston, Zora Neale; Savoy Ballroom; Theater Owners' Booking Association

Selected Films

The Emperor Jones. 1933.
Boarding House Blues. 1948.
Killer Diller. 1948.
Amazing Grace. 1974.

Discography

Moms Mabley at the Playboy Club. 1961.
Young Men, Si, Old Men, No! 1962.
Live at Sing Sing. 1970.
Stars of the Apollo Theater. 1973.

Further Reading

Bogle, Donald. *Brown Sugar: Eighty Years of America's Black Female Superstars.* New York: Harmony, 1980.
Dance, Daryl Cumber, ed. *Honey, Hush!—An Anthology of African American Women's Humor.* New York: Norton 1998.
"Moms Mabley: She Finally Makes the Movies." *Ebony,* April 1974.
"Moms Mabley, 77, Comedienne of TV, Stage and Radio, Dead." *New York Times,* 24 May 1975, p. 26.
Sampson, Henry J. *Blacks in Black and White: A Source Book on Early Black Musical Shows, 1865–1910.* Metuchen, N.J.: Scarecrow, 1988.
Watkins, Mell, ed. *African American Humor: The Best Black Comedy from Slavery to Today.* Chicago, Ill.: Lawrence Hill, 2002.
Williams, Elsie A. *The Humor of Jackie Moms Mabley: An African American Comedic Tradition.* New York: Garland, 1995.

Macaulay

Macaulay was a publishing company based in New York City, which was probably founded around 1909. The earliest documentation of its existence is from 1909: an advertisement for Hornor Cotes's novel of the Civil War, *The Counterpart.* Macaulay specialized in histories, poetry, criticism, literary translations, and inexpensive popular literature. It also published nonfiction under the imprint Gold Label Books, which was launched in 1931. The most noteworthy of Macaulay's publications came out between 1927 and 1933 and include the following: Macaulay's anthology *American Caravan: A Yearbook of American Literature* (1927), Malcolm Cowley's translations of Henri Barbusse's *Jesus* (1927), William Carlos Williams's *A Voyage to Pagany* (1928), Matthew Josephson's *Zola and His Time* (1928), John Dos Passos's *Airways, Inc.* (1928), Maurice Barrés's *The Sacred Hill* (1929), Robert M. Coates's *The Eater of Darkness* (1929), Wallace Thurman's *The Blacker the Berry* (1929) and *Infants of the Spring* (1932), George S. Schuyler's *Black No More* (1931), Wallace Thurman and A. L. Furman's *Interne* (1932), and Robert M. Coates's *Yesterday's Burdens* (1933). The company also published works by Michael Gold.

In addition to publishing work by George Schuyler and Wallace Thurman, Macaulay's main connection to the Harlem Renaissance came through V. F. Calverton (George Goetz), who founded the magazine *Modern Quarterly* (1923–1940) and compiled *An Anthology of American Negro Literature* in 1929. Calverton was a new editor for Macaulay in 1929 and tried to lure Langston Hughes away from Alfred A. Knopf, Inc. He did not succeed with Hughes, but Calverton did encourage George Schuyler to write *Black No More* and was influential in getting the book published by Macaulay in 1931. Calverton was most likely also responsible for the firm's hiring of Wallace Thurman for an editorial position in 1932. Thurman's position was advertised in *Crisis* in September 1932; according to Hughes, Thurman "was the only black to hold such a prominent position with a major publishing firm during the Renaissance" (Wintz 1988, 89). Thurman seems to have been mainly concerned with the publication of popular fiction, and he left the company early in 1934.

In June 1934, more than half of the Macaulay's employees participated in the first strike to take place in a publishing house. This strike, along with a second strike in September 1934, led to changes in the relationship between the National Labor Relations Board and publishing houses. The last work of fiction published by Macaulay was *The Strange Death of Adolf Hitler* (1939), by an anonymous author. The firm declared bankruptcy in 1941. The printers J. J. Little and Ives obtained the company, and Citadel Press bought its publications.

APRIL CONLEY KILINSKI

See also Calverton, V. F.; Hughes, Langston; Infants of the Spring; Publishers and Publishing Housese; Schuyler, George S.; Thurman, Wallace

Further Reading

Hutchinson, George. *The Harlem Renaissance in Black and White.* Cambridge, Mass.: Belknap Press of Harvard University Press, 1995.

Notten, Eleonore van. *Wallace Thurman's Harlem Renaissance.* Atlanta, Ga.: Rodopi, 1994.

Stauffer, Alison Tanner. "Macaulay Company." *American Literary Publishing Houses*, 2 vols., ed. Peter Dzwonkoski. Detroit, Mich.: Gale Research, 1986, pp. 214–216.

Tebbel, John. *A History of Book Publishing in the United States*, Vol. 3, *The Golden Age between Two Wars, 1920–1940.* New York: Bowker, 1978.

Wintz, Cary D. *Black Culture and the Harlem Renaissance.* Houston, Tex.: Rice University Press, 1988.

Mack, Cecil

Cecil Mack was an enterprising figure in the New York music world during the early twentieth century. He was involved in the biggest dance craze of the period and, more significantly, played an integral role in

the first African American–owned music publishing company. Today, however, he is little remembered, and few details are known about his life.

Mack, whose birth name was Richard Cecil McPherson, was born in Norfolk, Virginia, in 1883. He took private music lessons and soon headed for New York, where he worked steadily under the professional name Cecil Mack. His first published song was "Never Let the Same Bee Sting You Twice" (1900), written with the composer Chris Smith. The vaudeville team of Bert Williams and George Walker recorded Mack's "Good Morning, Carrie" (music by J. Tim Brymn) for the Victor Company in 1901. Soon thereafter, Mack scored his first big hit with "Teasing."

In 1905 Mack organized the Gotham Music Publishing Company. The actual ownership is unknown, and the company lasted only four months before merging with another firm in New York, Attucks Music (named after Crispus Attucks, the first black soldier killed in the Revolutionary War). Both firms had published mostly songs written by African Americans. Gotham-Attucks, also known as the "House of Melody," released work by Will Marion Cook, Mack, and others, as well as tunes from Williams and Walker's Broadway shows, *In Abyssinia* and *Bandanna Land*. The cover art of Gotham-Attucks's output notably broke with the tradition of racist stereotypes, and the material itself avoided the denigrating excesses of the "coon songs" popular at the time. Along with Cook, Mack was very likely the firm's guiding force (R. C. McPherson is listed as "secretary and treasurer and general business director").

In 1910 Gotham-Attucks published "That's Why They Call Me Shine" (later known as simply "Shine"), which Mack had probably written about a real man who had been badly beaten by the New York City police in a race riot. James Weldon Johnson probably drew from the same source for his character Shine in *Autobiography of an Ex-Colored Man* (1912). Other songs by Mack—mostly written for various musicals—include "Please Go Away and Let Me Sleep," "You're in the Right Church but the Wrong Pew," and "The Little Gypsy Maid."

With James P. Johnson, Mack wrote the songs for the musical *Runnin' Wild* (1923). By far the most popular was "Charleston," a tune Johnson had written ten years earlier, for which Mack provided lyrics. The song, which Elisabeth Welch performed in the show, took on a fevered life beyond Mack's now forgotten verses. The Charleston became the signature dance of the jazz age, easily eclipsing the bunny hug, the turkey trot, and even the shimmy. In 1925 the *New York Times* reported that the dance had become so popular that black domestic workers often needed to demonstrate knowledge of it so they could teach the steps to their prospective white employers. At the peak of the craze, fifty people died in the Pickwick Club in Boston when the dance hall collapsed because of overvigorous "Charlestonning."

Mack's career continued at its same busy pace. In 1925, he became a member of ASCAP (such membership was extremely rare then for African Americans); later that year he formed Cecil Mack's Southland Singers. He also led the Cecil Mack Choir, which was prominently featured in Lew Leslie's production of *Rhapsody in Black* (1931). Mack contributed lyrics for this show and provided arrangements for its folk songs and spirituals. He died in 1944.

Biography

Cecil Mack (Richard Cecil McPherson) was born in Norfolk, Virginia, 6 November 1883. He was educated at Norfolk Mission College and Lincoln (Pennsylvania) University; spent one semester at the University of Pennsylvania Medical School; and studied music with Melvin Charlton. Mack was associated with the vaudeville team Williams and Walker. He organized the Gotham Music Publishing Company, 1905; and was codirector, secretary, and treasurer of the Gotham-Attucks Music Publishing Company, 1905–1911. He joined ASCAP in 1925. Mack died in New York City on 1 August 1944.

GREGORY MILLER

See also Autobiography of an Ex-Colored Man; Cook, Will Marion; Johnson, James P.; Leslie, Lew; Runnin' Wild; Williams, Egbert Austin "Bert"

Selected Works

"Never Let the Same Bee Sting You Twice." 1900.
"Good Morning, Carrie." 1901.
"Good Night Lucinda." 1902.
"The Little Gypsy Maid." 1904.
"Teasing." 1904.
"Zona, My Congo Queen." 1904.
"He's a Cousin of Mine." 1906.
"I'm Miss Hanna from Savannah." 1908.
"That's Why They Call Me Shine." 1910.

"Charleston." 1923.
"Mistah Jim." 1925.
"You for Me, Me for You." 1925.
"Ain't We Got Love." 1937.
"Huggin' and Muggin'." 1937.

Further Reading

Hatch, James V. *Black Image on the American Stage: A Bibliography of Plays and Musicals, 1770–1970.* New York: DBS, 1970.

Peterson, Bernard L., Jr. *A Century of Musicals in Black and White: An Encyclopedia of Musical Stage Works by, about, or Involving African Americans.* Westport, Conn.: Greenwood, 1993.

Roach, Hildred. *Black American Music: Past and Present.* Boston, Mass.: Crescendo, 1973. (Rev. ed., 1976. Malabar, Fla.: Krieger, 1985; 2nd ed., 1992.)

Sampson, Henry T. *The Ghost Walks: A Chronological History of Blacks in Show Business, 1865–1910.* Metuchen, N.J.: Scarecrow, 1988.

Madame Sul-Te-Wan

Madame Sul-Te-Wan (Nellie Conley, 1873–1959) was born in Louisville, Kentucky, and introduced to show business at an early age by her mother, a laundress for burlesque performers. She began her career under the tutelage of and with the encouragement of two burlesquers, Mary Anderson and Fanny Davenport. Sul-Te-Wan's first performance was in a tap-dancing contest in which she won the first prize, a granite dishpan and spoon. Later, she worked in Cincinnati, Ohio, at the Dime Museum with a vaudeville company called the Three Black Cloaks. She then formed her own troupes, the Black Four Hundred and the Rare Black Minstrels. Her father, Silas Crawford Wan, reportedly either a Hawaiian or a Hindu priest, supposedly called her Sul-Te, which became her stage name.

Although she already had a budding career in traveling circuses and Negro vaudeville by design, her career in Hollywood movies was purely accidental, stemming largely from an introduction to the director-producer D. W. Griffith, who was a fellow Kentuckian. Madame Sul-Te-Wan's motion picture career coincided with a watershed in cinema history—Griffith's *Birth of a Nation* (1915). Working as a domestic on the set, Sul-Te-Wan aligned herself closely with

Griffith, who upgraded her position and cast her in what was her own first role in motion pictures and also the first for an African American woman. This was a departure from Griffith's usual policy: he had previously refused to hire African American actors, especially males who would have direct contact with white actresses, and instead had used white actors in blackface to portray all the African American characters. Sul-Te-Wan was the only exception. She played a maid, a role that posed little threat to the sanctity of white womanhood; her character did have the dubious distinction of taunting another character, Dr. Cameron, and spitting on him, however. The spitting scene became her most memorable. The Majestic Motion Picture Company fired Sul-Te-Wan soon after filming ended, accusing her of stealing a book from the set and inciting African Americans to protest against the film on its release.

Throughout the 1920s, Madame Sul-Te-Wan acted in a series of Negro comedies produced by L-KO studios. In the major Hollywood studio pictures in which she appeared, however, she almost always played one-dimensional domestics and supernatural savages. Many of her performances went uncredited or were simply given descriptions such as "harmonica player" and "woman at slave auction." Even when she played the pivotal role of Tituba, an accused witch, in *The Maid of Salem* (1937), she received only fifteenth billing. Nevertheless, she was perhaps the first African American actress to work consistently in Hollywood, and she appeared in a number of notable films, such as *Uncle Tom's Cabin* (1927) and *Ladies They Talk About*, with Barbara Stanwyck (1933).

Madame Sul-Te-Wan's legacy included the careers of her daughter, Ruby Dandridge, who appeared in several comedies as a domestic; and her granddaughter, Dorothy Dandridge. Of the three women, Dorothy Dandridge was the most popular and received the most acclaim from critics; she also was nominated for an Academy Award as best actress (the first such nomination for an African American actress), for her performance in *Carmen Jones* (1954); Madame Sul-Te-Wan also had a small part in that film. Madame Sul-Te-Wan died in 1959 at the Motion Picture Country Home in Woodland Hills, California.

Biography

Madame Sul-Te-Wan (Nellie Conley) was born 7 March 1873 in Louisville, Kentucky. She performed in circuses and Negro vaudeville and was the first African American actress in motion pictures, appearing in D. W. Griffith's *Birth of a Nation* (1915). She was the grandmother of actress Dorothy Dandridge. Madame Sul-Te-Wan died in Woodland Hills, California, 1 February 1959.

CANDICE LOVE

See also Birth of a Nation, The

Selected Filmography

The Birth of a Nation. 1915.
Hoodoo Ann. 1916.
Intolerance. 1916.
The Children Pay. 1916.
Stage Struck. 1917.
Manslaughter. 1922.
The Lightening Rider. 1925.
The Narrow Street. 1925.
Uncle Tom's Cabin. 1927.
Queen Kelly. 1929.
Sarah and Son. 1930.
The Thoroughbred. 1930.
Pagan Lady. 1931.
Heaven on Earth. 1931.
King Kong. 1933.
Ladies They Talk About. 1933.
A Modern Hero. 1934.
Imitation of Life. 1934.
Black Moon. 1934.
Maid of Salem. 1937.
In Old Chicago. 1937.
The Toy Wife. 1938.
Kentucky. 1938.

Madame Sul-Te-Wan in *Maid of Salem*, 1937. (Photofest.)

Tell No Tales. 1939.
Torchy Plays with Dynamite. 1939.
Safari. 1940.
Maryland. 1940.
King of the Zombies. 1941.
Sullivan's Travels. 1942.
Revenge of the Zombies. 1943.
Carmen Jones. 1952.
Something of Value. 1957.
The Buccaneer. 1958.
Tarzan and the Trappers. 1959.

Further Reading

Bolden, Tonya. *The Book of African American Women*. Holbrook, Mass.: Adams Media, 1996.

Cripps, Thomas. *Slow Fade to Black: The Negro in American Film, 1900–1942*. New York: Oxford University Press, 1977.

Madame X

Madame X was originally a three-act French courtroom drama, *La femme X* (1908), by Alexandre Bisson (1848–1912). It was translated into English by John Raphael and was adapted for both the British and the American theater, made into six American motion pictures, and made once into a television drama. The dates of some of the American versions coincided with the Harlem Renaissance, and *Madame X* was one of the productions of the Lafayette Players.

The basic story has been modified in various ways, depending on the resources that were available to stage and film directors. Despite the different settings and the different identities created for the characters, however, it remains a conventional cautionary tale. A woman's love affair is exposed by her husband, and the woman—impelled either by him or by her own guilty conscience—leaves their baby son with him and sets out to live alone. Without the protection of her respectable family, the woman sinks lower and lower, eventually becoming directly or indirectly involved with prostitution, blackmailing, trafficking, and other criminal offenses. After many years, she becomes embroiled in a murder case and is put on trial. Too poor to pay for her defense, she is assigned a young lawyer who happens to be her grown-up son. She becomes aware of this during the course of the trial, but to protect his reputation and her husband's,

she herself simply remains Madame X, even when facing the threat of being convicted. Different versions of the story have different endings. In some, she dies during the course of the trial; in others, her son exonerates her, though still without knowing who she is.

Madame X had its British premier at the Globe Theater on 1 September 1909, with a cast that included Lena Ashwell, Winifred Harris, Sydney Valentine, O. P. Heggie, and Edmund Gwenn. It had its American premiere in 1910, evidently on 7 February (though according to some records the date was 1 February or 2 January), at the New Amsterdam Theater in New York. A total of 125 performances were recorded. Madame X was played by Dorothy Donnelly, who would repeat the role in the first (silent) film adaptation of the play in 1916. In 1927 the play was presented at the Earl Carroll Theater, for twenty-two performances.

Silent film versions of *Madame X* were directed by George F. Marion (in 1916) and Frank Lloyd (in 1920). The first talking film of the story was a celebrated adaptation in 1929, directed by Lionel Barrymore and starring Ruth Chatterton; a version in 1937 was directed by Sam Wood and starred Gladys George; the first color version was a famous production of 1966 starring Lana Turner; and a film version was made for television in 1981. Attempts to update the characters and the events have in general been discouraging.

AMY LEE

See also Lafayette Players

Further Reading

Halliwell, Leslie. *Halliwell's Film Guide*, 7th ed. London: Grafton, 1989.

Hanson, Patricia King, and Alan Gevinson. *The American Film Institute Catalog of Motion Pictures Produced in the United States: Feature Films, 1931–1940*. Berkeley: University of California Press, 1993. (Film entries, M–Z.)

Internet Broadway Database. (Web site.)

Loney, Glenn. *Twentieth-Century Theatre*, Vol. 1. New York: Facts on File, 1983.

Madden, Owen Vincent "Owney"

Owen Vincent (Owney) Madden was born in Liverpool, England, of Irish stock in June 1892. He came to America in 1903, at age eleven, and was soon engaged in street gang activities in New York, in a notorious neighborhood called Hell's Kitchen. In 1910, he became the leader of the Gopher Gang, which engaged in petty crime and street violence. In 1912, he was shot at least six times by members of a rival gang; he survived, but his injuries would cause him problems in later years. By 1914 he had been arrested forty-four times but never convicted, until a rival for the leadership of the Gophers was slain. Protesting his innocence, Madden was sentenced to ten to twenty years and entered Sing Sing in 1915.

Madden was a model prisoner, earning the warden's trust and keeping a low profile, and he was paroled in 1923. He had recognized the potential offered by the arrival of Prohibition in 1919. Behind a veneer of respectability, avoiding the ostentation that characterized other mobsters such as Legs Diamond and Dutch Schultz, he became the elder statesman of New York's underworld. With a large network of trusted partners and lieutenants, he operated rackets in brewing, bootlegging, illegal gambling, laundries, protection, speakeasies, and boxing. In spite of his reputation for ruthlessness, Madden was considered a man of integrity and loyalty by his associates.

As a front for his rackets Madden operated nightclubs, including the Silver Slipper, Hollywood Paradise, Kit Kat Club, Connie's Inn, and most famously Harlem's Cotton Club, which was started in 1923 and was run by his lieutenant Frenchy De Mange. Lew Leslie originally developed the entertainment side, assisted by the songwriter Jimmy McHugh. All the performers were black; all the other staff members were white; and only white patrons were admitted. Performers and musicians found that the gangsters treated them well, even generously. They helped maintain the gangster's legitimate front. For many white tourists, the strictly segregated Cotton Club epitomized the Harlem Renaissance.

Typical of Madden's style was an episode in 1930 when rival mobsters threatened to compete with him in Harlem by starting up the fancy Plantation Club. Cab Calloway, who had been newly contracted, turned up on opening night to find that the club had been wrecked. It never opened. Shortly afterward, Madden offered Calloway an engagement at the Cotton Club, forcing Calloway's agent to relinquish a tight contractual arrangement.

Madden, still on parole, carefully avoided publicity, but he could not completely avoid the attention of the police. He had been linked to a stolen liquor truck in 1924, and in 1925 the Cotton Club had been charged with violations of Prohibition. Madden stayed out of prison despite many such incidents, but eventually, in 1932, he went back to Sing Sing for parole violations. Again a model prisoner, he was released for reasons of health in 1933.

In 1935, after his first marriage ended in divorce, he married the daughter of a postmaster in Hot Springs, Arkansas—a town that was then notorious as a gangsters' playground and a center of illicit gambling. Madden lived there quietly for thirty years, contributing generously to charities. He died of chronic emphysema in 1965.

Biography

Owen Vincent "Owney" Madden was born in Liverpool, England, in June 1892. He arrived in America in 1903. He became the leader of the New York Gopher Gang (1910), was convicted of manslaughter (1914), and was imprisoned in Sing Sing (1915–1923). He established the Cotton Club in 1923. He was imprisoned in Sing Sing again in 1932 and was paroled 1933. Madden died in Hot Springs, Arkansas, 24 April 1965.

BILL EGAN

See also Calloway, Cabell "Cab"; Cotton Club; Ellington, Duke; Leslie, Lew; Nightclubs; Nightlife; Numbers Racket; Organized Crime

Further Reading

Asbury, Herbert. *Gangs of New York*. New York: Avon, 1950.

Calloway, Cab, and Bryant Rollins. *Of Minnie the Moocher and Me*. New York: Crowell, 1976.

Haskins, Jim. *The Cotton Club*. London: Robson, 1985.

Nown, Graham. *The English Godfather: Owney Madden*. London: Ward Lock, 1987.

"Owney Madden, 73, Ex-Gangster, Dead." *New York Times*, 24 April 1965. (Obituary.)

Variety, 28 April 1965. (Obituary.)

Walker, Stanley. *The Night Club Era*. New York: Frederick A. Stokes, 1933. (See also paperback edition, Baltimore, Md.: Johns Hopkins University Press, 1999.)

Magazines and Journals

The magazines and journals of the Harlem Renaissance indicate much of the range of expression in African American thought and art during the 1920s and 1930s.

No single magazine, however, adequately captures the character of the artists, critics, and thinkers who appeared in various publications. This is due to the often differing ideologies and visions of the magazines and the individuals and organizations behind them, the economic trends of the time, and the diverse contributors and works. The most significant contribution of these magazines and journals is the plethora of voices that emerged from their pages to further explore and define an African American literature.

Crisis, the monthly magazine of the National Association for the Advancement of Colored People (NAACP), was founded by W. E. B. Du Bois and began publication in 1910. It received a higher degree of support than had been achieved by any previous African American magazine (Johnson and Johnson 1979, 31; subsequent page citations are to this source). Its full title was *The Crisis: A Record for the Darker Races*, after a popular poem by James Russell Lowell, "The Present Crisis." Du Bois edited the magazine; its objective, as stated by him, was to "set forth those facts and arguments which show the danger of race prejudice, particularly as manifested today toward colored people" (33). From the beginning, Du Bois issued a call for a renaissance of African American art, essays, and literature, and *Crisis* went on to publish established authors as well as new voices; these included Gwendolyn Bennett, W. S. Braithwaite, Charles Chessnut, Countee Cullen, Paul Lawrence Dunbar, Jessie Redmon Fauset, Rudolph Fisher, Langston Hughes, Georgia Johnson, James Weldon Johnson, Alain Locke, Claude McKay, and Jean Toomer. Jessie Fauset, literary editor of *Crisis* from 1919 to 1926, worked with Du Bois to publish works of many of the most esteemed African American writers of the time. These artists enjoyed increasingly widespread attention that was due in large part to their exposure in *Crisis*. From 1925 to 1928, the magazine sponsored an annual contest with money prizes for stories, plays, poems, essays, and illustrations. The pages of *The Crisis* were also dedicated in part to reviews of literature for children. An issue dedicated entirely to children appeared once a year, and Du Bois and Fauset edited a children's magazine called *The Brownies' Book* in 1919 and 1920. During his reign at *Crisis*, Du Bois also called for a greater production of drama by and about African Americans (42). The circulation of the magazine peaked in 1919 at nearly 100,000 copies. According to Ray Wilkins, *Crisis* was so widely read because it contained news about African Americans not available anywhere else (35). Du Bois attributed a large part of the magazine's success to the fact that it was very much, in his words, "a personal organ and the expression of myself" (34). The magazine promoted Du Bois's politics, notably pan-Africanism. Du Bois used his editorials to espouse his ideological interests and offer his own commentary. His colleagues and the NAACP's board of directors often fought with him about the personal direction the magazine took in its editorials and overall vision but *The Crisis* attained such popularity that the arguments ceased for a number of years, resuming again only when circulation decreased. A number of factors contributed to this downturn: the Depression, competing periodicals, reactions to the effects of Du Bois's own shifting ideals, and a lack of big-money advertisers. Du Bois became involved in the debate over art versus propaganda during the 1920s, initially supporting art—and the open, honest portrayal of African American life—rather than propaganda. On reading Alain Locke's *The New Negro*, however, Du Bois came out in strong opposition to the idea of art for art's sake and openly criticized writers who exposed the seedier elements of African American life. He felt that writers should focus on and tell the stories of educated African Americans, not, as he put it, those of "beggars, scoundrels, and prostitutes" (quoted, 46). This new stance, along with Du Bois's outspokenness regarding particular writers of the time, caused a notable decline in support for him and undermined the magazine's position as the leading African American literary voice. As *The Crisis* lost much of its readership, the board of directors informed Du Bois that he would no longer have complete control over the magazine. He resigned his editorship in 1934 and was replaced by the more moderate Ray Wilkins. *Crisis* is still in publication as a bimonthly magazine, although it is no longer owned by the NAACP.

The Messenger (1917–1928), established by A. Philip Randolph and Chandler Owen, is considered one of the first radical African American journals. It was created to espouse socialist ideals but eventually shifted its focus to union politics, becoming "a platform for the Brotherhood of Sleeping Car Porters," a group headed by Randolph (31, 57). *The Messenger* had a succession of subtitles. In the beginning, it was alternately subtitled *Journal of Scientific Radicalism* and the *Only Radical Negro Magazine in America*. In 1923, when the magazine became more literary in focus, the subtitles were *New Opinion of the New Negro* and *World's Greatest Negro Monthly*. In its initial stage, the journal criticized Du Bois and other African American leaders of the time and eschewed apolitical or moderately political art and literature. During its second stage, in 1923–1925, George Schuyler and Theophilus Lewis achieved primary editorial control. Together they shifted the literature that was published in it away from socialist verse and toward more creative work by poets and short-story writers such as Josephine Cogdell, Countee Cullen, Langston Hughes, Thomas M. Henry, Georgia Douglas Johnson, and Eric Walrond. Lewis and Schuyler also reviewed artistic and cultural events and news. Schuyler created a column in which he often promoted his views on integration, race, and culture (59). Lewis contributed a column dedicated to discussing African American drama. The third phase of the magazine came in about 1926, when Wallace Thurman took over briefly as editor. Thurman put a call out for submissions of literature by and about African Americans, stating that the magazine would "pay liberally" for those it published (60). This policy proved successful: *The Messenger* published works by Arna Bontemps, Anita Scott Coleman, Zora Neale Hurston, Langston Hughes, Helene Johnson, Richard Bruce Nugent, and Dorothy West, among others. After Thurman left *The Messenger*, other contributing editors followed, but the ultimate leadership of the magazine still rested with Randolph and Owens. *Messenger* stopped publishing in 1928 when Randolph decided to concentrate his efforts and money on the Brotherhood of Sleeping Car Porters. During its years of publication, the magazine's circulation never exceeded 5,000 copies a month (62).

Opportunity (1923–1949) was the journal of the National Urban League (NUL, an organization founded in 1911 to meet the housing and occupational needs of southern black migrants). Charles S. Johnson, a member of NUL, edited its first periodical, the *Urban League Bulletin*, during 1921 and 1922. The bulletin, a bimonthly publication, included information about the local leagues and national body and had space for editorials and topics of current interest (48). In October 1922 the organization successfully pushed to expand beyond the bulletin to a magazine that would be "an official organ," with "advertisements and second-class mailing privileges (48). In January 1923, *Opportunity: Journal of Negro Life* became that magazine. Although *Opportunity* had an active readership, its circulation eventually peaked at 11,000, never reaching the magnitude of *Crisis*. Also, unlike *Crisis*, *Opportunity* was never self-supporting and therefore had to depend on an outside annual grant. Its contributors were never paid for their work (48). *Opportunity*

started without "poems or stories, but there were articles on such topics as black labor, housing, and child placement"; later issues of the magazine, however, included more and more creative work, such as art, fiction, and poetry, along with articles and news of local current events (49). Writers whose work appeared in the magazine include Gwendolyn Bennett, Countee Cullen, Langston Hughes, Georgia Douglas Johnson, and Claude McKay. *Opportunity* sponsored literature and art contests and published the work of the winners, between 1925 and 1927, in a yearly issue dedicated to the contests. Charles Johnson took a different approach from Du Bois, avoiding personal editorials; in fact, Johnson clearly expressed his dislike for Du Bois' style of editorship and thus helped to create a definite philosophical difference between the two magazines (50). This division became more clear cut when Johnson took up the argument against Du Bois's position in the debate over art versus propaganda. Johnson reacted to Du Bois's conservatism by encouraging writers to express themselves openly and freely (51). Johnson had great success at the helm of *Opportunity* but resigned in 1928 when he accepted the chairmanship of the department of social sciences at Fisk University. Also in 1928, *Opportunity* lost its yearly grant. The editorship was taken up by Elmer A. Carter, who largely shifted the magazine's focus away from the arts and toward sociology and economics (57). In the 1930s, *Opportunity* did not have a definitive identity, as the editor and the board argued over its purpose and direction; it vacillated between the literary and the political. Publication ceased with the winter issue of 1949.

Fire!! was a single-issue magazine, appearing in November 1926, that was initially conceived by Langston Hughes and Richard Bruce Nugent and then edited by Wallace Thurman with an editorial board consisting of Hughes, Nugent, Zora Neale Hurston, Gwendolyn Bennett, John P. Davis, and Aaron Douglas. *Fire!!*, subtitled *Devoted to Younger Negro Artists*, was the first African American magazine that was "both independent and essentially literary" (77). Hughes wrote that the magazine's creators wanted "to express [themselves] freely and independently— without interference from old heads, white or Negro" and "to provide . . . an outlet for publishing not existing in the hospitable but limited pages of *The Crisis* and *Opportunity*" (quoted, 78). The title *Fire!!* is significant: the magazine was intended to ignite the consciousness of its readers, and its writers boldly challenged conservative elements of the African American literati. The one issue had commentary promoting a full spectrum of African American stories and representations, as well as short stories, Nugent's drawing depicting a naked African woman, and potentially controversial selections of poetry and fiction. *Fire!!* received general support from *Opportunity*, from writers such as Countee Cullen, from smaller African American magazines, and—unexpectedly, months after its release—from Du Bois. It was also greeted with some negative reviews, notably from Alain Locke; poor distribution and insufficient financing, however, contributed most to its demise. The board members initially agreed to share expenses for the publication, as the magazine had no outside funding. However, Wallace Thurman, the only member with a steady income, had to shoulder most of the financial burden of publishing it. The first issue cost so much to produce that there was no money for further issues—in fact, Thurman would spend the next few years paying off debts to the printer. Most of the copies of that first issue were later burned in a fire that broke out in the building where they were being stored (78, 79).

After the demise of *Fire!!*, Zora Neale Hurston unsuccessfully attempted to obtain support to start another magazine while Wallace Thurman created and edited *Harlem: A Forum of Negro Life*, a journal that he intended be a more moderate version of *Fire!!* (84). *Harlem*, like *Fire!!*, lasted for only one issue, which was published in November 1928. It included essays by Theophilus Lewis, Alain Locke, Richard Bruce Nugent, and Walter White; poems by Helene Johnson, Georgia Douglas Johnson, Alice Dunbar Nelson, and Effie Newsom; stories by Roy de Coverly and George Little; and illustrations. Thurman abandoned his moderate stance in the later pages of the issue, where he criticized Du Bois and promoted the unwholesome side of life in Harlem (87). Further issues of *Harlem* had been planned, but readers did not respond favorably to Thurman's initial effort.

Fire!! and *Harlem* were the first of what would be called African American "little magazines" of Harlem. Such magazines were not limited to Harlem, however. *Black Opals* (1927–1928) was a magazine from Philadelphia created by Jessie Redmon Fauset's brother, Arthur Huff Fauset (89), and intended for the work of young Philadelphians. The first issue was published in spring of 1927 and was followed at the end of that year by a Christmas issue edited by Gwendolyn Bennett. The third and final issue appeared in June 1928 under the direction of an editorial board (90). Along with the work of young Philadelphians, *Black Opals* had pieces by Alain Locke and Langston

Hughes. The Boston Quill Club, an African American literary group, published *Saturday Evening Quill* (1928–1930), an annual magazine with works mostly by Bostonian poets, dramatists, essayists, and illustrators. Other contributors included Waring Cuney, Helene Johnson, and Dorothy West. *Stylus*, named after a literary group at Howard University, first appeared in 1916 under the leadership of Alain Locke. Its initial issue contained mostly student submissions and special contributions from better-known writers (68). *Stylus* did not publish its next issue until May 1921; and the third issue did not appear until 1929. While Zora Neale Hurston was a student at Howard and a member of the Stylus literary group, two of her short stories were published in this magazine. In the mid-1930s, near the end of the Harlem Renaissance, the little magazine *Challenge*, edited by Dorothy West, was produced in Chicago. Its first issue included an editorial by James Weldon Johnson calling for conservatism in African American literature; West herself, though, eventually called for more social realism (she went through shifts of political ideology and focus during her editorship). *Challenge* included works by Arna Bontemps, Countee Cullen, Langston Hughes, Zora Neale Hurston, Helene Johnson, and Claude McKay, as well as works by unknown and younger writers. It lasted until 1937 and was quickly followed by what would be the sole issue of *New Challenge*, a politically leftist magazine edited jointly by Dorothy West, Marion Minus, and Richard Wright (116).

At the end of the 1920s and into the years of the Depression, African American popular magazines published apolitical entertainment fiction along with their regular columns and features. Two of the most successful of these magazines were *Abbott's Monthly* (1930–1933) and *Bronzeman* (1929–1933). *Abbott's Monthly* was introduced one month after the stock market crash, yet it sold as many as 100,000 copies (110). Along with light fiction, both magazines published works by J. Max Barber, Chester Himes, Langston Hughes, and Richard Wright. *Metropolitan* (1935), also a popular magazine, published work by Jessie Redmon Fauset, Rudolph Fisher, and Countee Cullen. Other popular magazines of the 1930s, such as *Dawn*, *Mirror*, and *Brown American*, were read mostly by local or regional audiences (110).

During the second half of the 1920s, single issues of magazines managed by whites began to appear. In March 1925, *Survey Graphic* published a "Harlem number" edited by Alain Locke. The issue included essays, stories, and drawings that focused on life in

Harlem. Its cover described Harlem as a mecca; and in an editorial and an article, Locke extolled Harlem as a cultural promised land and predicted that the people of Harlem would be responsible for a birth of a "vital folk literature" (70). Also in this issue, Locke defined his use of the term "New Negro." Locke chose for the "Harlem number" works by Countee Cullen, W. E. B. Du Bois, the cultural anthropologist Melville Herskovitz, Langston Hughes, Charles S. Johnson, Claude McKay, Arthur Schomburg, Jean Tooomer, and Walter White. In October 1926, the poetry journal *Palms* published an issue focusing on African American poetry; this issue was edited by Countee Cullen and included work by Lewis Alexander, Gwendolyn Bennett, Arna Bontemps, William Braithwaite, Countee Cullen, W. E. B. Du Bois, Jessie Redmon Fauset, Langston Hughes, Helene Johnson, and Richard Bruce Nugent. *Carolina Magazine*, a literary journal of the University of North Carolina, published a "Negro number" in May 1927, a "Negro poetry number" in May 1928, and a "Negro play number" in April 1929 (74).

RACHEL DAVIS

See also Black Opals; Brownies' Book, The; Carolina Magazine; Challenge; Crisis, The; Du Bois, W. E. B.; Fauset, Arthur Huff; Fauset, Jessie Redmon; Fire!!; Harlem: A Forum of Negro Life; Johnson, Charles Spurgeon; Lewis, Theophilus; Locke, Alain; Messenger, The; New Challenge; Opportunity; Owen, Chandler; Palms; Randolph, A. Philip; Saturday Evening Quill; Schuyler, George S.; Stylus; Survey Graphic; Thurman, Wallace; West, Dorothy; Wright, Richard; *specific writers*

Further Reading

Andrews, William L., Frances Smith Foster, and Trudier Harris, eds. *The Oxford Companion to African American Literature.* New York: Oxford University Press, 1997.
Crisis. (Web site.)
Johnson, Abby Arthur, and Ronald Maberry Johnson. *Propaganda and Aesthetics.* Amherst: University of Massachusetts Press, 1979.

Manhattan Casino

The Manhattan Casino (later the Rockland Palace) was an elaborate hall at 280 West 155th Street and Eighth Avenue, established in about 1910. It had a ca-

pacity of 6,000 and was used for balls and dances; benefits; sports; and religious, civic, and promotional events. During the Harlem Renaissance, a number of famous figures appeared there.

For example, the composer and conductor James Reese Europe engaged the Manhattan Casino on 27 May 1910 for the debut of the new Clef Club Orchestra, which had more than 100 players and performed ragtime, blues, and jazz. The Clef Club was a fraternal organization and union for black musicians; Europe was one of its organizers, and its president. He was also associated with Vernon and Irene Castle, a famous white dance team who popularized ballroom dancing and performed many popular steps that came from black culture. On 22 April 1915, the Castles supervised a dance competition at the Manhattan Casino, the "Castle Cup Contest," for which Europe's Society Orchestra supplied the music.

During the 1920s, Fletcher Henderson and his band—considered the foremost early big jazz ensemble—played at the Manhattan Casino. At various times his group included famous musicians such as Louis Armstrong (trumpet), Coleman Hawkins (tenor saxophone), and Don Redman (alto saxophone).

The popular blues singer Lucille Hegamin appeared at the Manhattan Casino on 30 April 1920, 25 September 1920, and 22 April 1921. Hegamin was among the earliest black women to make recordings; she also performed in the second company of the black musical *Shuffle Along*. Noble Sissle, who wrote the lyrics for *Shuffle Along* (1921), later organized his own orchestra (1928). It made its first appearance in New York City at the Manhattan Casino—which by then had been renamed the Rockland Palace—in the late 1930s. Sissle's orchestra included Sidney Bechet, a jazz pioneer from New Orleans.

The Frogs (1908–mid-1920s), a fraternal organization of black theater professionals (and later of other professionals as well), held one of the largest social events in Harlem at the Manhattan Casino: the "Frolic of the Frogs," a fund-raiser for indigent performers, presented annually in August. Famous Frogs included Bob Cole, James Reese Europe, J. Rosamund Johnson, George Walker, and Bert Williams; the "Frolic," which lasted all night, featured a dance and vaudeville revue and prizes for the costumes.

During this period as well, Marcus Garvey invited the journalist and activist Ida B. Wells Barnett to address a crowd of almost 3,000 at a meeting of his Universal Negro Improvement Association held in the Manhattan Casino. And the National Association for the Advancement of Colored People (NAACP) gave its annual whist tournament and dance there.

On 7 December 1924 the National Ethiopian Art Theater, a black "little theater" group (1924–1925), presented a program of one-act plays at the Manhattan Casino.

A famous event held at the Manhattan Casino in the 1920s and early 1930s was the annual drag costume ball given by Hamilton Lodge No. 710 of the Grand Order of Odd Fellows. Hamilton Lodge was a black social club, but its drag ball, which attracted some 2,000 men and women, was nonsegregated. Whites attended it, and sometimes whites such as Carl Van Vechten and the playwright Avery Hopwood served as judges.

The lindy, or lindy hop, a popular dance, was born at the Manhattan Casino—in 1928, at the Harlem Dance Derby marathon. One of the remaining contestants, the dazzling Harlemite dancer "Shorty George" Snowden, broke away from his partner and began executing some steps alone. When asked what he was doing, Snowden, thinking of Charles Lindbergh's famous solo flight across the Atlantic, answered, "The lindy."

As of the present writing, the site of the Manhattan Casino is a parking lot.

MARVIE BROOKS

See also Armstrong, Louis; Barnett, Ida B. Wells; Bechet, Sidney; Clef Club; Cole, Bob; Europe, James Reese; Garvey, Marcus; Hegamin, Lucille; Henderson, Fletcher; Homosexuality; Johnson, John Rosamond; National Ethiopian Art Theater; Shuffle Along; Sissle, Noble; Van Vechten, Carl; Williams, Egbert Austin "Bert"

Further Reading

Badger, H. Reid. "James Reese Europe." In *Encyclopedia of African-American Culture and History*, ed. Jack Saltzman, David Lionel Smith, and Cornel West. New York: Macmillan, 1996, Vol. 2, pp. 917–918.

Brooks, Tilford. *America's Black Musical Heritage*. Englewood Cliffs, N.J.: Prentice Hall, 1984, pp. 102–103.

Judge, Mark Gauvreau. *If It Ain't Got That Swing*. Dallas, Tex.: Spence, 2000.

Malone, Jacqui. *Steppin' on the Blues: The Visible Rhythms of African American Dance*. Urbana, University of Illinois Press, 1996, pp. 142–144.

Neihart, Ben. *Rough Amusements: The True Story of A'Lelia Walker, Patroness of the Harlem Renaissance's Down-Low Culture*. New York: Bloomsbury, 2003.

Peterson, Bernard L. *The African-American Theatre Directory, 1816–1960*. Westport, Conn.: Greenwood, 1997.

Schoener, Allon, ed. *Harlem on My Mind*. New York: Random House, 1969, p. 47.

Southern, Eileen. *Biographical Dictionary of Afro-American and African Musicians*. Westport, Conn.: Greenwood, 1982.

Stearns, Marshall Winslow, and Jean Stearns. *Jazz Dance*. New York: Macmillan, 1968, pp. 96–98, 315.

Thorpe, Edward. *Black Dance*. Woodstock, N.Y.: Overlook, 1990, pp. 88–89.

Thurman, Wallace. *Negro Life in New York's Harlem: A Lively Picture of a Popular and Interesting Section*. Little Blue Book 494. Girard, Kan.: Haldeman-Julius, c. 1927.

Maran, René

In the 1920s, René Maran was a literary star: his novel *Batouala* (1921) had received the prestigious Prix Goncourt in France; in the United States, in September 1922, a headline in *The Crisis* proclaimed, "The Whole World is Reading It!" Black magazines were filled with pictures and discussions of Maran. Critics discerned Maran's influence in works such as Claude McKay's *Banjo* (1929) and Carl Van Vechten's *Nigger Heaven* (1926) and acclaimed Maran as the precursor of the bourgeoning New Negro movement. Along with such hyperbole, there was also anxiety and dissension over the novel's primitivism and its episodic structure. The story is about a "grossly sensuous" tribe under the subjection of a cruel chief—Batouala—in the Oubangui-Chari region of French Equatorial Africa; some critics feared that it would reinforce racist stereotypes (Martin 1983, 96). Nevertheless, Maran continued to be celebrated, and the brisk sales of the first English translation of *Batouala* in the United States indicated that the Harlem Renaissance had a diasporic aspect.

Maran's stellar debut actually stymied his literary career. He spent much of the 1920s and 1930s perfecting each page of *Batouala* for a "definitive edition," which was published in 1938. His other novels, including *Djouma* (1927), were less celebrated and were never translated into English, despite the best efforts of Alain Locke, who became a lifelong friend. Although Maran was disappointed, he promoted the writing of the Harlem Renaissance in Paris. He wrote the first French-language article praising Jessie Fauset, Countee Cullen, Langston Hughes, and Walter White in December 1925. In 1924, Maran helped edit the short-lived *Les Continents*, the first black newspaper in Paris; its edition of September 1924 featured poetry by Cullen, Hughes, McKay, and Jean Toomer. Locke wrote a preface in French, his first published description of the new spirit of young "Africo-Américaine" poets that he would praise in *The New Negro* (1925).

Locke singled out Cullen's poem, "The Dance of Love (after Reading René Maran's *Batouala*)" as an illustration of a "new intellectual commerce between the continents" sparked by Maran's international acclaim (quoted in Edwards 2003, 113; subsequent page citations are to this source). Cullen alluded to the controversial chapter "Ga'nza" in *Batouala* and suggested the interest that black writers "in the life" had in the "glorious dance [during which] all things are permitted, even perversions and sins against custom" (85). That dance features Batouala's wife Yassigui'ndja acting "as the male" with "an enormous painted wooden phallus" tied about her waist, and another woman who "had never known a man" (86). After little resistance, Yassigui'ndja's woman "melted to the ardor of the phallus as a fog melts in the rising sun" (86). So does Yassigui'ndja, when her partner "stirred the desire in the male figure by delaying his satisfaction" (86). The two end in "a breathless convulsion of short shivering movements, . . . immobile, happy, enraptured" (87). This orgasmic gender play offers Cullen a mitigating metaphor "to voice his own sensuality mingled with an American puritan ethic" and indicates another legacy influenced by Maran (Dixon 1977, 756). If *Batouala* "did more to encourage the return of the Harlem Renaissance to the sources of blackness," same-sex desire was evidently a factor in that homecoming (Fabre 1975, 342).

Biography

René Maran was born in Martinique on 15 November 1887. His family moved to Gabon (west Africa) in 1890, but he was educated in France, graduating in 1909. His novel *Batouala* appeared in 1922 and won the Goncourt prize. Maran then worked in the French colonial service but resigned (1923), returned to Paris, and became a pan-African activist. He worked as an editor at *Les Continents* (1924) and later (1930) at a literary journal, *Revue du Monde Noir*. Maran died on 9 May 1960.

SETH CLARK SILBERMAN

See also Batouala; Francophone Africa and the Harlem Renaissance; Locke, Alain; McKay, Claude; New Negro, The; Nigger Heaven; Van Vechten, Carl

Further Reading

Dixon, Melvin. "Toward a World Black Literature and Community." *Massachusetts Review*, 18(4), Winter 1977, pp. 750–769.

Edwards, Brent Hayes. *The Practice of Diaspora: Literature, Translation, and the Rise of Black Internationalism.* Cambridge, Mass.: Harvard University Press, 2003.

Fabre, Michel. "René Maran, the New Negro, and Negritude." *Phylon*, 36(3), 1975, pp. 340–351.

Ikonné Chidi. "René Maran and the New Negro." *Colby Library Quarterly*, 15(4), December 1979, pp. 224–239.

Maran, René. "Le mouvement Negro-litteraire aux états-Unis." *Vient de Paraître*, December 1925, p. 645.

———. *Batouala: A True Black Novel—The Definitive Edition*, trans. Barbara Beck and Alexandre Mboukou. Washington, D.C.: Black Orpheus, 1972. (Originally published 1938.)

Martin, Tony. *Literary Garveyism: Garvey, Black Arts, and the Harlem Renaissance.* Dover, Mass.: Majority, 1983.

Nwezeh, E. C. "René Maran: Myth and Reality" *Odu: A Journal of West African Studies*, 18, July 1978, pp. 91–105.

Mason, Charlotte Osgood

Charlotte Osgood Mason has become one of the best-known white patrons of the Harlem Renaissance—somewhat ironically, because she required that the artists she supported refer to her as "Godmother" and not reveal her identity. In turn she referred to her protégés as "godchildren."

Mason came from a wealthy family and became still wealthier when, in 1886, she married Rufus Osgood Mason, a physician. On her husband's death in 1905, Mason used some of her money to finance anthropological studies of American Indians, especially those from the Southwest; she herself participated in some of the fieldwork. In addition to her interest in American Indians, Mason found psychology and studies of the psychic world intriguing; she wrote *The Passing of the Prophet*, which was published in 1907 in *North American Review*.

During the 1920s, Mason's interest in "primitive" art forms and the people she associated with primitivism—such as American Indians and African Americans—increased. Consequently, Mason used some of her wealth to finance the artistic production of some of the most talented black artists associated with the Harlem Renaissance. She invested thousands of dollars to pay for research, travel, and living expenses for black artists such as Aaron Douglas, Arthur Huff Fauset, Langston Hughes, Zora Neale Hurston, Hall Johnson, Alain Locke, Claude McKay, and Louise Patterson Thompson, to name a few.

Mason's interest in black art began with her fascination with Alain Locke, whom she referred to as her "precious brown boy." Locke introduced Mason to some of the most talented visual artists, singers, and musicians of the Harlem Renaissance. Mason used Locke as a liaison between herself and black artists; in fact, Locke arranged and took responsibility for persuading various black artists to accept financial support from Mason. In addition to individual artists, Mason provided financial support for the Negro Art Institute, which Locke founded in 1924. One purpose of this institute was to help support black writers so that they could produce works challenging the stereotype of blacks as intellectually and socially inferior. Mason's support of the institute came with strings attached: she insisted that the literature of writers associated with the institute must maintain the "primitive purity" she associated with African American people and culture. In short, Mason insisted on art which reinforced her belief that African Americans had a special affinity with the primitive and the world of the spirit.

Mason's own stereotypical notions about what constituted black art and her desire to claim ownership of the art being produced by her protégés caused serious conflict between herself and the artists she supported. A number of the artists associated with the Harlem Renaissance used their art as a vehicle not only for artistic expression but also for other purposes: to protest against American racism, violence, and the overall discrimination African Americans experienced; and to counter the prevailing stereotype of blacks as exotic primitives. As a result, although several writers benefited from Mason's financial generosity, many of the relationships she developed with black artists during this period were short lived. In addition to the conflicts over the content and ownership of the art, there were other problems: many of Mason's protégés thought that she herself was racist and described her as, at times, cruel.

Mason's relationship with Hurston and Hughes was the most controversial and seems to reveal the racism and cruelty which many of her protégés complained about, and which led them to sever their ties with her. Both Hughes and Hurston were impressed by Mason's wealth and admired her for her philanthropy and for the learned company with which she surrounded herself. At the same time, these two talented young black writers became troubled because Mason wanted them to produce work that would reinforce and perpetuate current racial stereotypes.

Mason met Hughes during one of his weekend visits to New York in early 1927. Initially, he was struck not only by her material wealth but by her apparent kindness and her intellectual acumen. Their meeting ended with her giving him $50, because he had fascinated her with his discussion of his poetry. One week later, Hughes sent Mason a thank-you card, and she invited him back to her apartment in New York to discuss his goals as an artist. During this second meeting, in April of 1927, Hughes revealed to Mason that his main goal was to write a novel. She encouraged him to pursue this dream and offered to provide monetary support for the summer so that he could focus on his novel (Hughes 1940). Helped by Mason's financial support, Hughes wrote a draft of *Not without Laughter*. He revised it during his senior year at Lincoln University, and on his graduation Mason decided to give him a monthly allowance so that he could focus on his art. She also read the first and revised drafts of Hughes's novel and offered him feedback as an unofficial editor.

Early in their relationship, Hughes had given Mason unwavering admiration. But as time went on and he began to write pieces that were more overtly critical of the status quo, he became repelled by Mason's ostentation—her apartment on Park Avenue, her servants, and so on. He wrote a number of political and satirical works that exposed the disparity between upper-class and lower-class Americans; and he became preoccupied with exploring race and class as social and political themes—a preoccupation that is illustrated in his poems "Advertisement for the Waldorf-Astoria" and "Park Bench," among others. The publication of these two poems, in particular, marked a turning point in his relationship with Mason (Wintz 1996). She found his political poetry disturbing and tried to persuade him to move away from such overtly political work. During this period, Hughes and Hurston were in the process of writing their play *Mule Bone*, and Louise Patterson Thompson, an educator and labor organizer, was working as a secretary for them, at Mason's request. Mason's paternalistic, controlling personality caused Thompson to end her own relationship with her patron; Thompson then worked diligently to influence Hughes as he grappled with the problem of when and how to break his dependance on "Godmother." As it happened, when Hughes refused to abandon his political writing, his relationship with Mason was irreparably damaged; in addition, he continued to resist Mason's attempts to force him to reproduce stereotypes of the "primitive" in his work. Eventually, he asked Mason to stop providing him with financial support. Hughes (1940) notes Mason's belief that African Americans were "America's great link with the primitive, and they had something very precious to give the Western world" and adds that he himself did not "feel the rhythms of the primitive surging through me, and so I could not live and write as though I did."

Mason became Hurston's patron in December 1927, providing money—$200 a month—so that Hurston could do research on African American folklore. This money was paid on the condition that Mason would maintain ownership of the folklore Hurston collected; once again, the relationship became strained because of a conflict between the desires of the artist and desires of the patron. In this case, the relationship was complicated by additional factors. First, some of Hurston's contemporaries accused her of playing a stereotypical "darky" role in order to win Mason's favor. Second, Hurston's apparent admiration for Mason led some of these contemporaries to question Hurston's allegiance to other African Americans. Third, many historians and literary scholars suggest that a degree of adoration existed between Hurston and Mason. A close reading of Hurston's commentary on Mason suggests, rather, that Hurston, in the tradition of the trickster, was shrewdly manipulating the relationship in order to maintain a privileged position among the artists Mason supported; in any case, Hurston came to have misgivings about Mason. After having been, or having played the role of, an appreciative, dutiful protégé, at various stages she began to question her patron's desire to impose control over her artistic creativity. The monetary support Mason provided did allow Hurston to produce a number of literary works; however, Hurston did not reach her full artistic potential until she broke with Mason and published *Their Eyes Were Watching God* in 1937.

The relationship Mason had with Hughes, Hurston, Locke, Thompson, and a number of others exemplifies the complex dynamics that existed between white patrons and African American artists during the Harlem Renaissance, and it also suggests an underlying racial conflict. Eventually, many of the artists Mason supported created satirical pieces criticizing their patron for her paternalism and racism. For instance, Hughes, in his collection of short stories *The Ways of White Folks* (1933), satirized Mason and other supposedly liberal supporters of African Americans and especially of African American artists: Mason's desire to control her protégés and their art is illustrated by his characters Dora Ellsworth (in "The Blues I'm Playing") and Anne and Michael Carraway (in "Slave on the Block"). Similarly, Rudolph Fisher satirized Mason through his character Agatha Camp in *The Walls of Jericho* (1928). Hurston offered a critique when she ironically described Mason as a "benevolent" benefactress in *Dust Tracks on a Road* (1942).

By insisting on primitivism, Mason stifled, or was in effect attempting to stifle, some of the most prominent artists of the period. Ultimately, though, the constraints Mason placed on her "godchildren" became too much for at least some of them. As the Harlem Renaissance came to a close, many of Mason's "godchildren" ended their relationship with her. Mason then shifted her emphasis from African American culture to other cultures, and eventually she died in obscurity.

Biography

Charlotte Osgood Mason (Charlotte Vandervere Quick) was born 18 May 1854. She married Rufus Osgood Mason in 1886 and was widowed in 1905. She then turned her attention to anthropological studies of southwestern American Indians. She published *The Passing of the Prophet* in 1907. Beginning in the 1920s she became a patron of African American arts and provided financial support to African Americans including Aaron Douglas, Langston Hughes, Zora Neale Hurston, Alain Locke, and Claude McKay. Mason died in New York 15 April 1946.

DEIRDRE J. RAYNOR

See also Douglas, Aaron; Fauset, Arthur Huff; Fisher, Rudolph; Hughes, Langston; Hurston, Zora Neale; Johnson, Hall; Locke, Alain; McKay, Claude; Negro Art Institute; Not without Laughter; Patterson, Louise Thompson; White Patronage

Further Reading

Bernard, Emily. *Remember Me to Harlem: The Letters of Langston Hughes and Carl Van Vechten, 1925–1964.* New York: Knopf, 2001.

Hughes, Langston. *The Big Sea*. New York: Knopf, 1940.

Hurston, Zora Neale. *Dust Tracks on a Road*. New York: HarperPerennial, 1991. (With a new foreword by Maya Angelou.)

Kellner, Bruce, ed. *The Harlem Renaissance: A Historical Dictionary for the Era*. New York: Methuen, 1987.

Lewis, David Levering. *When Harlem Was in Vogue*. New York: Oxford University Press, 1979.

Walker, Alice, ed. *I Love Myself When I Am Laughing: A Zora Neale Hurston Reader*. New York: Feminist Press at City University of New York, 1979.

Wintz, Cary D. *Black Culture and the Harlem Renaissance*. Austin: Texas A&M University Press, 1996.

Matheus, John Frederick

Despite his relatively small reputation as a writer of the Harlem Renaissance, John Frederick Matheus was a pioneer in the movement as a creative artist and an instructor. Besides being a prolific author, he was fluent in seven languages, traveled extensively, and was a respected professor at several universities in the United States and in Haiti.

Matheus was born in West Virginia in 1887. His main vocation was teaching: he taught for more than thirty years at West Virginia State College, and after his retirement in 1953 he was a sought-after visiting professor, teaching for another twenty years at several colleges and universities. However, his writing never abated. His literary work can be divided into two periods, dominated by different interests that led to shifts in form and style.

In the first period, 1925 to 1934, Matheus wrote almost entirely fiction. In 1925, his story "Fog"—probably his best-known work—won an award in *Opportunity*'s literary contest, appeared in Alain Locke's *The New Negro*, and was included in the honors list in Edward J. O'Brien's *Best Short Stories of 1925*. "Fog" explores the racial attitudes of passengers on a train during a fateful ride in a coal-mining region in West Virginia. In 1926, Matheus's sketch "Sand" took first place in the "personal experience" category in *Opportunity*'s contest; his one-act drama "Cruiter" also won a first prize from *Opportunity*; and his short story "Swamp Moccasin" won a first prize in the Krigwa (originally Crigwa; an acronym of the Crisis Guild of Writers and Artists) contest for *The Crisis*. "Cruiter" tells of the separation of a rural southern grandmother and her grandson when a northern recruiter encourages the young man to take a factory job in Detroit.

Matheus also wrote poetry, which appeared in *The Crisis*, *Opportunity*, and *The Chronicle*. His poem "Requiem" was included in Countee Cullen's anthology *Caroling Dusk* (1927). "Ti Yette," a play published in *Plays and Pageants from the Life of the Negro* in 1930, focuses on conflict between two siblings, one light-skinned, the other dark-skinned, in New Orleans. Matheus's early fiction often explored the lives of rural southern African Americans.

During the second period of Matheus's writing, roughly 1934–1970, his work consisted largely of articles—journalistic essays, educational statistics, translations, and book reviews. Many of his reviews appeared in *CLA Journal*, *Modern Language Journal*, *Negro History Bulletin*, and *Quarterly Review of Higher Education among Negroes*. In 1936, he won an award for best reviews of the year from *Journal of Negro History*. Several of Matheus's essays explored the role of foreign languages in African American life.

Matheus continued to write fiction occasionally during this period, though infrequently. He published two short stories in 1937: "Sallicoco" in *Opportunity* (a story inspired by his trip to Liberia), and "What Kind of Man" in *Arts Quarterly*. As a result of a trip to Haiti in 1927 (the first of two; the other was in 1945) with the composer Clarence Cameron White, he wrote *Ouanga* ("charm for evil" in Creole), a drama and operatic libretto with music by White; it had its premiere in 1949. Matheus and White also collaborated on an uncompleted opera, "Cocomacaque: a Musical Drama of Haiti."

Matheus was engaged in international activities as well. In 1930, for example, he spent six months in Liberia as secretary to Dr. Charles S. Johnson, who was the American member of a commission investigating charges of forced labor there; in 1945–1946, he was director of the teaching of English in the national schools of Haiti. He was also involved in many professional organizations, including the College Language Association (he was its treasurer from 1938 to 1975); the Modern Language Association; and Alpha Iota Lambda Chapter of Alpha Phi Alpha.

At the time of his death in 1983, Matheus may have been the last surviving writer of the Harlem Renaissance.

Biography

John Frederick Matheus was born 10 September 1887 in Keyser, West Virginia. At age twelve he published poems in two newspapers in Steubenville, Ohio, where his family had moved when he was nine; at fourteen he won a prize in an essay contest sponsored by a local women's club. He studied at Steubenville (Ohio) High School (1905); Western Reserve (A.B., 1910); Columbia University (M.A., with a Teachers College diploma as teacher of French, 1921); the Sorbonne in Paris (1925); and the University of Chicago (graduate work, 1927). He taught at Florida A&M College in Tallahassee (1911–1913); was an auditor at Florida A&M (1911–1913); and was head of romance languages at West Virginia State College (1922–1953). He was a foundation director in 1945–1946 and was then at Maryland State College (1953–1954), Dillard University (1954–1957), Morris Brown College (1958–1959), Texas Southern University (1959–1961), Hampton Institute (1961–1962), and Kentucky State University (1962). He wrote stories, plays, poems, and articles for *Opportunity*, *The Crisis*, and other journals and was included in several anthologies, such as Alain Locke's *The New Negro* (1925). He wrote the libretto for *Ouanga* (1949), with music by Clarence Cameron White. His awards included prizes in the literary contests run by *Opportunity*, Krigwa, and *The Crisis*. He was married to Maude Roberts and later to Helen Taylor. Matheus died in Tallahassee, Florida, on 21 February 1983.

STEVEN G. FULLWOOD

See also Crisis, The: Literary Prizes; Cullen, Countee; Krigwa Players; Locke, Alain; Opportunity Literary Contests; White, Clarence Cameron

Selected Works

"Fog." *Opportunity*, May 1925. (Also in *The New Negro: An Interpretation*, ed. Alain Locke. New York: Albert and Charles Boni, 1925.)

"Sand." *Opportunity*, July 1925.

"Swamp Moccasin." *The Crisis*, December 1926.

"Cruiter." In *Plays of Negro Life: A Source-Book of Native America Drama*, ed. Alain Locke and Montgomery Gregory. New York and London, Harper, 1927.

"Requiem." In *Caroling Dusk, An Anthology of Negro Poetry*, ed. Countee Cullen. New York: Harper, 1927.

"Haiti Is a Riot of Color." *Crisis*, November 1929.

"Ti Yette." In *Plays and Pageants from the Life of the Negro*. Washington, D.C.: Associated Publishers, 1930.

"African Footprints in Hispanic-American Literature." *Journal of Negro History*, 23, July 1938.

"A Negro State College Looks at Foreign Language." *Journal of Negro Education*, April 1938.

"What Good Are Foreign Languages to American Negroes?" *Quarterly Review of Higher Education among Negroes*, October 1942.

"Cruiter." *Black Theatre USA: Plays by African Americans 1847 to Today*, ed. James V. Hatch and Ted Shine. New York: Free Press, 1996.

Further Reading

Andrews, William L., Frances Smith Foster, and Trudier Harris, eds. *The Oxford Companion to African American Literature*. New York: Oxford University Press, 1997.

Brawley, Benjamin. *The Negro Genius: A New Appraisal of the Achievement of the American Negro in Literature and the Fine Arts*. New York: Biblo and Tannen, 1972.

Hatch, James V., and Leo Hamalian, eds. *Lost Plays of the Harlem Renaissance*. Detroit, Mich.: Wayne State University Press, 1996.

Kellner, Bruce, ed. *The Harlem Renaissance: A Historical Dictionary for the Era*. Westport, Conn.: Greenwood, 1984.

Rush, Teresa Gunnels, Carol Fairbanks Myers, and Ester Spring Arata, eds. *Black American Writers Past and Present: A Biographical and Bibliographical Dictionary*. Metuchen, N.J.: Scarecrow, 1975.

Matthews, Ralph

Ralph Matthews had a long career as one of the most widely read black journalists in the United States. He began in 1924 as a reporter with the Baltimore *Afro-American*, which became the largest-selling black newspaper on the eastern seaboard, reaching its highest circulation in the late 1930s. Its staff developed a reputation for excellent national and international coverage of news; its motto was "Independent in all things—neutral in none." At the *Afro-American*, Matthews worked alongside respected journalists such as Lula Jones Carrett, Arthur Carter, Jimmy Hicks, Max Johnson, Cliff Mackay, Herb Mangrum, Bob Maynard, Bettye Moss, I. Henry Phillips, Al Sweeney, and Vincent Tubbs, on a floor of the building known as the "Ivory Castle" because of the inhabitants' lofty talent. Like other *Afro-American* editors, Matthews held high standards for political, social, and economic equality.

After eleven years in Baltimore, Matthews was named editor of the *Afro-American* in Washington, D.C., where he stayed until 1947. He continued working in a series of editorial posts at *Afro-American* papers: Newark, New Jersey (1947–1951); Washington, D.C. (1951–1954), Philadelphia (1959–1964), and back to Washington from 1964 until his retirement in 1968. He left the *Afro-American* chain, where he had developed a role as a troubleshooter, for a five-year stint as editor of the Cleveland *Call and Post* from 1954 to 1959. Over the course of his career, he covered some of the leading stories of his time, including civil rights, the coronation of George VI of Great Britain in 1936, and the Korean War. For sixteen years he ran "New Faces Guild," a variety show sponsored by the *Afro-American* for the benefit of a children's hospital and other charities.

Matthews received the Wendell L. Wilkie public leadership award for national political reporting; in 1977, he was cited by the National Newspaper Publishers Association for his writing and for his "ability to establish great newspapers and watch them make their mark in history as fighters for the black cause." Matthews died in 1978.

Biography

Ralph Matthews was born in about 1904 in Harford County, Maryland; he grew up in Baltimore and attended Morgan State College and the Columbia University School of Journalism in New York. He became a reporter with the Baltimore *Afro-American* in 1924; eleven years later he became editor of the *Afro-American* in Washington, D.C., where he stayed until 1947. He then worked at the *Afro-American* papers in Newark, New Jersey (1947–1951); Washington again (1951–1954); Philadelphia (1959–1964); and Washington once more (1964–1968.) During 1954–1959 he left the *Afro-American* chain to work at the Cleveland *Call and Post*. Matthews retired in 1968 and died in 1978.

KATHLEEN COLLINS

See also Baltimore Afro-American; Journalists

Further Reading

Kellner, Bruce, ed. *The Harlem Renaissance: A Historical Dictionary for the Era*. New York: Methuen, 1984.

Vincent, Theodore G. *Voices of a Black Nation: Political Journalism in the Harlem Renaissance*. San Francisco, Calif.: Ramparts, 1973.

McClendon, Rose

The distinguished actress Rose McClendon (Rosalie Virginia Scott) was born in Greenville, South Carolina, in 1884; her parents moved the family to Harlem in 1890. She began singing at Saint Mark's African Methodist Episcopal Church and developed her love of theater while sponsoring, directing, and performing in plays there. Her professional career was launched in 1919, when she had a small part in the Bramhall Players' production of *Justice*; she also appeared in another Broadway production, *White Mule*, and performed on radio in the series *John Henry*.

McClendon was one of the strongest actresses of the Harlem Renaissance; although she was short and slight, she had an impressive command of the stage, and she was capable of affecting the emotions of the audience with a simple gesture or just a change of expression. She was acknowledged as the "first lady of Negro drama," and critics called her the "Negro Duse," after the famous Eleonora Duse (1858–1924). Like Duse, McClendon had an acting style that enabled her to portray human suffering and to convey powerful emotions realistically but with extraordinary economy of means. Playwrights called on Rose McClendon when they wanted the crème de la crème.

In 1924, McClendon starred opposite Charles Gilpin and later Paul Robeson in *Roseanne*. She gained prominence in 1926 as an aging mulatto madam in Clement Wood's *Deep River*, an opera with jazz staged and produced on Broadway by Arthur Hopkins. As the legend goes, Ethel Barrymore came to see *Deep River*, having been advised not to leave before the end so that she would be sure to see McClendon's performance. The critic Alexander Woollcott of *New York World* reported that Barrymore did stay till the end and then sought out Hopkins to say that Rose McClendon could teach all actresses distinction. Also in 1924, McClendon played the role of Goldie McAllister opposite Jules Bledsoe and Abbie Mitchell in Paul Green's folk tragedy *In Abraham's Bosom*; the play won a Pulitzer Prize, and McClendon won an acting award from the *Morning Telegraph*. In the late 1920s, McClendon toured in Dorothy and DuBose Heyward's play *Porgy*, as Serena, the wife of Crown's victim. Despite some opposition by blacks to the production, McClendon and the Theatre Guild cast achieved a hit in New York and London from 1927 to 1929.

In the 1930s McClendon was supposed to appear in John Houseman's production of *Medea*, with a cast including mulatto children and black choruswomen but otherwise white; however, this daring plan had to be put aside when McClendon fell ill. In 1931, McClendon collaborated with Richard Bruce Nugent to write the one-act play "Taxi Fare"; that year she also starred in Paul Green's *House of Connelly*. In 1932, along with Langston Hughes and others, McClendon was appointed to the "Sponsoring Committee for Production of a Soviet Film on Negro Life." Also in 1932, she appeared in James Knox Millen's *Never No More*; Brooks Atkinson, the drama critic of the *New York Times*, described her performance as both majestic and humble: "She acts from the inside out . . . . and confirms the high esteem in which she has long been held." McClendon became familiar to theatergoers in *Black Souls*, *Brain Sweat*, *Roll Sweet Chariot*, *Panic*, and—especially—*Mulatto* (1935), in which she played the slave Cora, the mother of the colonel's mulatto child. *Mulatto*, which was written by Langston Hughes, ran for 375 performances, the second-longest run for a work by a Negro playwright. Hughes was delighted that McClendon had set Broadway afire, but the producer, Martin Jones, was evidently not; Jones refused to give McClendon her full salary as a star, considering it too much for a Negro. Moreover, Jones refused to provide her transportation to the theater (she had to take the subway back and forth from her home in Harlem), and neither she nor Hughes was welcome to attend Jones's whites-only postproduction party. During the run of *Mulatto*, McClendon became ill and had to leave the cast; Cora was her last "mammy" role.

To fight stereotyped roles such as mammies, McClendon was one of the organizers of the Negro People's Theater (1935). She wanted black performers, especially women, to have parts in legitimate theater productions that would portray black America in a more positive light and thereby empower African Americans. She and John Houseman also headed the sixteen "Negro Units" established by this Federal Theater Project (FTP). McClendon was the spokeswoman for the Negro Units and, interestingly, blocked an attempt by Hallie Flanagan, the director of FTP, to give the directorship of the Harlem unit to a black person. McClendon argued that it would be advantageous for blacks to have an apprenticeship under a white leader. McClendon was on the advisory board of Actors Equity Association (the actors' union); directed plays at the Harlem Experimental Theater; and gave a great deal of her time to advising amateurs. In her last days, she recorded her hope for a "Negro theater that would develop not an isolated Paul Robeson, an occasional Bledsoe or Gilpin, but a long line of first-rate actors."

The Rose McClendon Players (1938–1941)—a semiprofessional group founded after her death in 1936—continued her legacy.

Biography

Rose McClendon (Rosalie Virginia Scott) was born 27 August 1884, in Greenville, South Carolina; her parents, Sandy Scott and Tina Jenkins, moved to Harlem in 1890, when she was six years old. McClendon attended Edina Public School—P.S. 40 and Sergeant Dramatic School in New York City; she won a scholarship to the American Academy of Dramatic Art in 1916. On 27 October 1904 she married Henry Pruden McClendon, who was a chiropractor and a porter on the Pennsylvania Railroad. Her Broadway credits included *Justice* (1919), *White Mule* and *Roseanne* (1924), *Deep River* (1926), *In Abraham's Bosom* (1926), *Porgy* (1927–1929), *The House of Connelly* (1931), *Never No More* (1932), and *Mulatto* (1935); her regional credits include *The Cat and the Canary*, *Brain Sweat*, *Black Souls*, *Roll Sweet Chariot*, and *Panic*. She also performed on radio. McClendon was a cofounder of the Negro People's Theater; a codirector of sixteen Negro Units of the Federal Theater Project (Works Progress Administration); and a coauthor of "Taxi Fare." McClendon died at her home in Harlem on 12 July 1936; she is buried in Mount Hope Cemetery in Westchester County, New York.

SHIRLEY BASFIELD DUNLAP

See also Black and White; Bledsoe, Jules; Gilpin, Charles; Green, Paul; Hughes, Langston; Mitchell, Abbie; Mulatto; Nugent, Richard Bruce; Porgy: Play; Robeson, Paul; Saint Mark's Methodist Episcopal Church

Further Reading

Andrews, William L., Frances Smith Foster, and Trudier Harris, eds. *The Oxford Companion to African American Literature*. New York: Oxford University Press, 1997.
Bogle, Donald. *Brown Sugar*. New York: Da Capo, 1980.

Gill, Glenda E. "Rose McClendon: The Black Eleonora Duse." Paper presented at the annual convention of American Society for Theater Research, Ohio State University, 12 November 1988.

Haskins, James. *Black Theater in America*. New York: Crowell, 1982.

Hatch, James V. *Black Image on the American Stage*. New York: Drama Book Specialists, 1970.

Isaacs, Edith J. R. *The Negro in the American Theatre*. College Park, Md.: McGrath, 1968 (originally published in 1947).

Mitchell, Loften. *Black Drama: The Story of the American Negro in the Theatre*. New York: Hawthorn, 1967.

———. *Voices of the Black Theatre*. Clifton, N.J.: James T. White and Co., 1975.

Rampersad, Arnold. *The Life of Langston Hughes*. New York: Oxford University Press, 1986.

Tanner, Jo A. *Dusky Maidens: The Odyssey of the Early Black Dramatic Actress*. Westport, Conn.: Greenwood, 1992.

McGuire, George Alexander

Bishop George Alexander McGuire (1866–1934) is best-known for his prominence in Marcus Garvey's Universal Negro Improvement Association (UNIA). He was also an important theological figure in his own right. McGuire, a naturalized American, was born in Antigua. He immigrated to the United States in 1894 and became an ordained minister in the Protestant Episcopal Church. By 1901 he had risen sufficiently to be appointed rector of Saint Thomas's Episcopal church in Philadelphia. Saint Thomas's served the African American elite of Philadelphia and was one of the most prestigious congregations in African America, having been started in 1794 by Absalom Jones, one of the founders—together with Richard Allen of the African Methodist Episcopal Church—of organized African American Christianity.

In 1905 McGuire was made the Protestant Episcopal church's archdeacon for Colored Work in the Diocese of Arkansas, thus becoming the church's highest-ranking African American and the first to achieve the rank of archdeacon. His next major appointment was to the parish of St. Bartholomew's in Cambridge, Massachusetts. During this period, he also studied medicine at Jefferson Medical College. In 1913 McGuire returned home to Antigua, where he practiced medicine and served as a minister in the Church of England, the English counterpart of the Episcopalians.

McGuire returned to the United States in 1919, just as Garvey's UNIA was gathering momentum. Like thousands of other race-conscious intellectuals who joined UNIA, McGuire eagerly embraced the organizational framework Garvey provided to combat racism and to articulate an independent philosophy of racial uplift. Long before UNIA, McGuire had fought his own battles against racism in the Protestant Episcopal church.

McGuire was elected first chaplain-general of UNIA at its inaugural international convention in New York in August 1920. In this position, he wrote two important documents of UNIA: *Universal Negro Ritual* and *Universal Negro Catechism*. The latter had both religious and historical sections, reflecting his interest in religion and race history. (At Saint Thomas's, he had been an early member of African America's first historical association, the American Negro Historical Society.) In September 1921, McGuire founded the African Orthodox Church (AOC), envisaged as a home for blacks of the Protestant Episcopal persuasion who wanted ecclesiastical independence.

McGuire would have liked to have seen AOC designated as the official church of UNIA, but Garvey was unwilling to grant such an exclusive privilege to any denomination. McGuire accordingly resigned from his position at UNIA on the formation of AOC. He ensured official "orthodox" status for his new church by arranging apostolic succession for himself. He had himself reordained bishop in the American Catholic church; he was then ordained first bishop of the new AOC by a representative of the Russian Orthodox church.

McGuire seems to have briefly joined some of Garvey's adversaries in late 1921, but by 1925 he wrote a moving preface to Volume 2 of *The Philosophy and Opinions of Marcus Garvey*, edited by Garvey's wife Amy Jacques Garvey shortly after her husband's imprisonment in Atlanta. In 1924, the newly organized conclave of AOC unanimously elected McGuire archbishop of the church. During the remaining decade of his life McGuire built AOC into a thriving international church. Branches were eventually established in Canada, Barbados, Cuba, South Africa, Uganda, Kenya, Miami, Chicago, Harlem, Boston, Cambridge (Massachusetts), and elsewhere. The official organ of AOC, *The Negro Churchman*, became an effective link for the far-flung organization. Wherever it existed, AOC remained a sort of ecclesiastical reflection of Garvey's ideas of racial independence and uplift.

Biography

George Alexander McGuire was born in Antigua, in the then British West Indies, 26 March 1866. He was educated at Mico College and Nisky Theological Seminary in the Danish (later U.S.) Virgin Islands; immigrated to the United States in 1894; was ordained in the Protestant Episcopal church; became rector of Saint Thomas's Episcopal Church in Philadelphia in 1901; became the Protestant Episcopal church's archdeacon for Colored Work in the Diocese of Arkansas in 1905; was appointed to Saint Bartholomew's parish in Cambridge, Massachusetts; studied medicine at Jefferson Medical College; returned to Antigua in 1913, practicing medicine and serving as a minister; returned to the United States in 1919; joined the Universal Negro Improvement Association and was elected its chaplain-general (1920); and founded the African Orthodox Church in 1921 and resigned from UNIA. McGuire died 10 November 1934.

TONY MARTIN

See also Garvey, Marcus; Universal Negro Improvement Association

Further Reading

Ball, Wendy, and Tony Martin. *Rare Afro-Americana: A Reconstruction of the Adger Library.* Boston, Mass.: G. K. Hall, 1981.

Burkett, Randall K. *Black Redemption: Churchmen Speak for the Garvey Movement.* Philadelphia, Pa.: Temple University Press, 1978.

Martin, Tony. *Race First: The Ideological and Organizational Struggles of Marcus Garvey and the Universal Negro Improvement Association.* Dover, Mass,: Majority, 1986. (Originally published 1976.)

The Negro Churchman. Millwood, N.Y.: Kraus Reprint, 1977.

McKay, Claude

The poet, novelist, essayist, and political activist Claude McKay was one of the most versatile and talented intellectuals of the Harlem Renaissance. Although his standing among twentieth-century intellectuals has never been in doubt, McKay has always been surrounded by controversy. It is easy to see why: he was politically radical; he was not only a freethinker but also a militant rationalist and vociferously anti-Christian; he was, as he put it himself, "suicidally frank," and what he was frank about was seldom flattering. Though he taught the virtues of group life, he was an individualist, a freelance, and a loner; he hated bourgeois civilization and its pretensions and consistently identified himself with the black working class against all comers; as a proud black man, he despised the "superstitions"—his word—of racism as well as colorism; he saw his role as a writer and intellectual as that of truth teller, however embarrassing and discomforting the truth might turn out to be; he was decidedly anti-capitalist and anti-imperialist and never refrained from saying so; he was a man of peace but advocated the virtues of retaliatory violence; he loved passionately and hated passionately—he was especially known for his hatred. Given such a complex character, it is little wonder that McKay remains the most misunderstood figure of the Harlem Renaissance.

McKay's relationship to the Harlem Renaissance is in many ways quite peculiar. He looked at the artistic dimension of the movement, if movement it was, with great interest but a jaundiced eye—and from afar. As he makes clear in *A Long Way from Home* (1937), McKay never thought much of those who claimed to lead the renaissance. Alain Locke, regarded by some as the "dean" of the movement, was in McKay's eyes a cowardly "pussy-footing professor," especially after Locke, on political grounds, censored McKay's militant submissions to *The New Negro* (1925), the influential anthology Locke edited. Two of the other leading figures of the Harlem Renaissance, W. E. B. Du Bois and Walter White, McKay thought, subordinated artistic integrity to shortsighted, reformist racial goals. McKay said that White was a "propaganda angel" who, like Du Bois, believed that the Negro should always be made to put his best foot forward in depictions by black artists: no washing of dirty linen in public—it hurts the race. James Weldon Johnson was the only other major figure of the older generation of renaissance writers for whom McKay had genuine affection and respect, as an artist, as a critic, and as a man. The feeling was mutual, and when McKay published *Harlem: Negro Metropolis* (1940), he dedicated it to the memory of Johnson, who had died two years earlier.

Despite his formidable literary presence, McKay was physically absent from not only Harlem but the United States for almost the entire period of the renaissance. In the autumn of 1919, soon after writing his militant sonnet "If We Must Die," McKay left the United States to spend more than a year in London.

He returned to New York in January 1921 but was off again by September 1922, this time to bolshevik Russia. After eight months in Russia, he moved to Berlin, thence to Paris, the South of France (mainly Marseilles), Barcelona, and finally Tangiers, where he lived for six years before returning to the United States in 1934, by which time the Harlem Renaissance was over.

Despite his misgivings and his absence, however, McKay's work constitutes a major contribution to the Harlem Renaissance and today is a crucial part of its literary canon. "If We Must Die," which Richard Wright called a "new and strange cry," is often considered the opening salvo of the renaissance. It was published during the "red summer" when African Americans across the nation defended themselves against racist violence, and it urged them not to be hunted, penned, and slaughtered like hogs but to fight back, even while dying:

> O kinsmen! we must meet the common foe!
>
> Though far outnumbered let us still be brave,
>
> And for their thousand blows deal one deathblow!
>
> What though before us lies the open grave?
>
> Like men we'll face the murderous, cowardly pack,
>
> Pressed to the wall, dying, but fighting back!

As Joel Augustus Rogers later noted, this poem became the "Negro Marseillaise." And McKay became, according to the poet Melvin Tolson, "the symbol of the New Negro and the Harlem Renaissance." In praising McKay, the black socialists—congregated around A. Philip Randolph and the *Messenger* magazine—and the black nationalist Garveyites for once sang from the same hymnal. Black preachers recited "If We Must Die" from their pulpits, black schoolchildren learned it by heart, and black newspapers across the country reprinted it, beginning the process of making it the most widely anthologized work written by a black poet. A similarly rapturous reception awaited *Harlem Shadows* when it appeared in 1922; *Negro World*, for instance, ran not one but two rave reviews of the volume.

By the end of the year, however, McKay was once again gone. As early as 1919, despite the persecution of radicals during the "red scare," he had openly come out in favor of the Bolshevik revolution. "Every Negro who lays claim to leadership," he wrote in *Negro World*, "should make a study of Bolshevism and explain its meaning to the colored masses. It is the greatest and most scientific idea afloat in the world today," which if put into practice "might make these United States safe for the Negro." He was now off to Lenin's Russia and would not return until more than a decade had passed. Although he continued to write poetry, he now increasingly turned his hand and time to prose. The first major public fruit of this endeavor was *Home to Harlem*, a picaresque novel revolving around the adventures of Jake, an African American deserter from World War I, and his return to Harlem. The novel also features Ray, McKay's alter ego, a Haitian intellectual driven into exile by the American occupiers of Haiti. Drawing substantially on McKay's experience as a Pullman waiter and its attendant black proletarian life, the novel is resolutely set in the African American working class, eschewing those whom McKay derisively called "nice Negroes," the Afro-American elite. Indelicate and uncompromising, but in many ways tender, in its depiction of Harlem's working class at work and play, *Home to Harlem* was the first novel by a black person to head the list of best-sellers in the *New York Times*. Not surprisingly, however, it was trounced in the black press. Garvey, in a front-page editorial review of the book, called McKay a "literary prostitute" to the white racist public, a traitor to his race; he said that *Home to Harlem* was "a damnable libel against the Negro." Du Bois, who rarely agreed with Garvey, concurred. Du Bois said that the book, though "not wholly bad," catered to the "prurient demand" of a decadent white readership, and that he himself, after reading certain passages— "the dirtier parts of its filth"—had felt "distinctly like taking a bath." McKay did not take this lying down. From Barcelona he wrote to Du Bois, saying that he did not care about Du Bois's opinion of *Home to Harlem*, since Du Bois's own writings never revealed "any comprehension of esthetics" and Du Bois was therefore "not competent or qualified to pass judgment upon any work of art." As for Garvey, McKay contemptuously dismissed him as "a West Indian charlatan" (before he died, however, McKay would revise his appraisal of Garvey in a radically more favorable direction). But despite his bravado, McKay was hurt by his black critics. Similar objections arose after *Banjo* came out the following year. James Weldon Johnson was the only member of the older generation to publicly write favorable comments about McKay's fiction. Even McKay's old friend Arturo (Arthur A.) Schomburg wrote an unfavorable review of *Home to Harlem* and questioned McKay's motives for writing it.

The clash between McKay and his critics was more a matter of philosophy than a question of venal motives. McKay, through circumstances and to a lesser extent by choice, had worked and lived among the African American proletariat. (He consistently referred to himself in his post-Jamaican exile as "not only a Negro, but a worker.") This was the world he knew best, and this was the world he depicted in both *Home to Harlem* and *Banjo*. As McKay points out in his riposte, "A Negro Writer to His Critics" (1932), as an artist he cannot go along with the "nice Negroes" who believe that "Negroes in literature and art should be decorous and decorative." Like Langston Hughes ("The Negro Artist and the Racial Mountain," 1926), he sees no crime in depicting black proletarian life as he found it. "I want to see Negro artists express themselves to the limit," McKay wrote to a friend in 1927. "They should exclude nothing, limit themselves to nothing. They should make their voices as strong, sweet, broad, strange, sad, happy and varied as all Negro life itself is." He expressed sympathy for his critics' position, but as an artist he could not help them by censoring himself in the way they desired; it was shortsighted and inimical to the artistic enterprise. "We must leave the real appreciation of what we are doing to the emancipated Negro intelligentsia of the future," he told James Weldon Johnson, adding sarcastically, "while we are sardonically aware now that only the intelligentsia of the 'superior race' is developed enough to afford artistic truth." It is noteworthy that none of McKay's critics claimed that the world he depicted did not exist, or that his depiction was inaccurate; the criticism instead focused on the very depiction of that world for public gaze.

Despite the reaction of black critics, McKay had his defenders among the people who really counted in the forward movement of the artistic side of the Harlem Renaissance: the young writers. Langston Hughes, the most gifted of the lot, adored McKay—from his first encounter with McKay's poetry as a schoolboy in Cleveland right up to his death. It was McKay, he said, who had set him on the road to becoming an artist. He loved *Home to Harlem* and declared McKay "the best." Gwendolyn Bennett expressed a similar love for McKay. As late as 1928, Wallace Thurman, despite misgivings about McKay's attachment to the sonnet as a literary form, acknowledged McKay's mental depth. More than the rest of the black poets, Thurman observed, McKay "has really had something to say"; moreover, "he is the only Negro poet who ever wrote revolutionary or protest poetry." Eric Walrond, Arna Bontemps, Zora Neale Hurston, Dorothy West, and even Countee Cullen, the

most straitlaced and conservative of the group before the 1930s, expressed deep admiration for McKay and his work, both privately and publicly. McKay became close friends with many of them after he returned to the United States in 1934.

During the 1920s, McKay served as the chief conduit for the work of renaissance writers in Europe. Through a close friendship with sisters Paulette and Jeanne Nardal in particular, he put African Americans in contact with African and Caribbean intellectuals in Paris. It was McKay who first introduced Locke to the Nardal sisters, who were Martinican writers and editors of an influential and pioneering journal, *La Revue du Monde Noire*. McKay's poetry was translated and published in France; all his novels, including *Home to Harlem* and *Banjo*, set in Marseilles, were quickly translated into French. *Banjo*, in particular, exercised an enormous influence on the *négritude* movement that developed in the 1930s, led by Aimé Césaire, Léopold Sedar Senghor, and Léon Gontran Damas.

Despite his focus on fiction during the 1920s, McKay continued to write poetry. Many of his poems remain unpublished, but a substantial number appeared in American journals such as *The Crisis* and *Opportunity*. He also wrote essays; the most remarkable is "Soviet Russia and the Negro," published in two parts in *The Crisis* (December 1923 and January 1924), about his "magic pilgrimage" to bolshevik Russia, a powerful apologia extolling the merits of bolshevism for oppressed blacks.

Through the waning days of the Harlem Renaissance, McKay published *Gingertown* (1932), a collection of short stories set in Harlem and the Caribbean, and then his best novel, *Banana Bottom* (1933), set in his native Jamaica at the turn of the century. These works hardly sold; the Depression had annihilated the market for black novels. McKay returned from Tangiers in 1934 to a Harlem in such a desperate situation that it was hardly recognizable. He soon found work with the Federal Writers' Project (FWP) and tried to form an all-black Negro Writers' Guild among the black writers of FWP; due to vociferous opposition from black members of the Communist Party, however, the Negro Writers' Guild was destroyed. By 1938, McKay was out of work, largely, he plausibly claimed, because of the machinations of his communist enemies in FWP. He had offended both the Communist Party and the establishment in the National Association for the Advancement of Colored People (NAACP) by his critical and "suicidally frank" travelogue, *A Long Way from Home*, published the previous year. After *Harlem: Negro Metropolis* appeared in 1940, matters got worse: McKay was more isolated than ever, and he suffered severe hardship and ill health, including several strokes, in the 1940s. McKay's black nationalist tendencies became even more pronounced during the Depression years. He powerfully propounded them in newspaper articles, including his column in the *Amsterdam News*; most forcefully in the final chapter of *A Long Way from Home*; and in his blistering attack in *Harlem: Negro Metropolis* on the hypocrisy and shenanigans of the Communist Party regarding the "Negro question."

Through the efforts of Ellen Tarry, a black Catholic member of FWP, McKay received needed help from the Catholic church. In 1944 he moved to Chicago, where he did work with progressive Catholics. To the consternation of his closest friends, who had admired his forthright atheism, McKay converted to Catholicism toward the end of 1944. He died on 22 May 1948 and was buried in New York. He was fifty-six years old.

The final, so-called Catholic, phase of McKay's life is the most misunderstood and therefore deserves the mention of a few basic facts. McKay worked for Bishop Bernard Sheil and the Catholic Youth Organization; both the man and the organization were among the most progressive forces in Chicago during the Depression. Sheil delivered stirring May Day speeches to workers, and he was highly respected in Chicago's African American community. The pacifist-socialist Catholic Worker Movement, led by Dorothy Day, was the other organization with which McKay established the closest ties. He contributed some important later poems to its newspaper, the *Catholic Worker*. As he wrote to a friend in 1946, there is "a formidable left wing" in the Catholic church, to which he belonged. He denounced American imperialism and sided with the Soviet Union against Britain and the United States in the early days of the cold war. In an angry letter to Max Eastman, his former Trotskyist friend who had become a vehement "cold warrior," he wrote:

> I try to see things from the standpoint of right and wrong and when Soviet Russia is wrong I will say so. When the U.S. and Great Britain are wrong I will say so too, and the two latter in my mind are more often wrong than the Soviet nation. I am certainly never going to carry the torch for British colonialism or American imperialism abroad.

McKay—a longtime admirer of the vanquished Leon Trotsky, whom he met during his sojourn in Russia—

now developed a grudging admiration for the cunning and "genius of His Satanic Majesty," Joseph Stalin, and for Stalin's chess game with the western powers in Europe. Writing in February 1945, he confessed, however, that he was awaiting the denouement "in fear and trembling."

He denounced America and Britain as hypocrites and fascists and spoke of the "fascist-oppressed Negroes" in the United States and the British empire at a time when both the United States and Britain claimed to be fighting a war against fascism. He published "Look Within" in the *Catholic Worker* in January 1945:

> Lord, let me not be silent while we fight
>
> In Europe Germans, Asia Japanese
>
> For setting up a Fascist way of might
>
> While fifteen million Negroes on their knees
>
> Pray for salvation from the Fascist yoke
>
> Of these United States.

The following year, again in the *Catholic Worker*, he published "Tiger," describing the white man as a tiger at his throat drinking his blood as his life ebbs away, "And muttering that his terrible striped coat/Is Freedom's and portends the Light of Day."

> Europe and Africa and Asia wait
>
> The touted New Deal of the New World's hand!
>
> New systems will be built on race and hate,
>
> The Eagle and the Dollar will command.
>
> O Lord! My body, and my heart too, break—
>
> The tiger in his strength his thirst must slake!

In the "Cycle Manuscript"—his last major work, his testament—McKay sang in sonnet form in praise of Garvey, declaring at the end "nothing the professors do can sever / You from the people to whom you belong forever."

McKay's so-called anticommunism was largely aimed at white communists in the United States whom he saw as opportunistic and untrustworthy with regard to the struggles of African Americans. Despite his bitter disagreements with the Communist Party, however, McKay never cooperated with the agents of the Federal Bureau of Investigation who came to him for information. When an emissary from the Dies Committee (an anticommunist congressional outfit) came to see him in September 1939, McKay said, "I'm sure that the real America would not think

I was contributing anything to good citizenship by being a son-a-bitch." An agent came again the year before McKay died, and the answer was the same. The agent's notes of the meeting read: "McKay was somewhat reluctant to discuss his past activities and stated that he had no desire to discuss individual Communists as he did not care to get anyone in trouble."

As McKay repeatedly said, he was always pro-union and pro-working class, and in many ways he remained a socialist, stating in one of his last pieces of writing: "I can see nothing wrong about a planned economy. . . . If the richest country in the world had planned beforehand, it might have avoided a ten-year depression and a second world war." He repeatedly expressed his admiration for Henry Wallace, who ran for president on the American Labor Party ticket in 1948. The fact that Wallace was the candidate supported by the Communist Party did not deter McKay. He especially liked Wallace's anti-racist and anti-imperialist positions.

Claude McKay, photographed by Carl Van Vechten, c. 1920–1940. (Library of Congress.)

McKay's abiding loyalty was to the black working class, the kind of people with whom he worked on the Pullman trains and in other menial jobs. Those were his people. As he put it in "The Negro's Tragedy," another of the sonnets from the "Cycle Manuscript," which was also published in the *Catholic Worker*:

> It is the Negro's tragedy I feel
> Which binds me like a heavy iron chain,
> It is the Negro's wounds I want to heal
> Because I know the keenness of his pain.

Grappling with the Negro's tragedy was a constant in McKay's turbulent life, including the period after his unexpected turn to Catholicism. And despite his failing health, powers, and resources, after his conversion he remained—as he told Max Eastman at the time— "no less a fighter."

Biography

Claude McKay (Festus Claudius McKay) was born 15 September 1889 in James Hill, Clarendon, Jamaica. He was the youngest of eleven children, eight of whom lived to maturity, born to Hannah Ann Elizabeth Edwards McKay and Thomas McKay, prosperous peasant proprietors. In 1897, he went to live with his eldest brother, Uriah Theodore McKay, a schoolmaster in Saint James, western Jamaica, who educated him. He went to Kingston to train as a tradesman, but left soon afterward as a consequence of an earthquake in 1907. He met the English aristocrat and folklorist Walter Jekyll in 1909. McKay went to Kingston and worked in a match factory before joining the Jamaican constabulary in 1910; he left the constabulary in October 1911, having served for seventeen months. He published his first volume of verse, *Songs of Jamaica* (1912), quickly followed by *Constab Ballads* in the same year. In July 1912 he left Jamaica, a freethinker and a Fabian socialist, for study at Tuskegee Institute in the United States; he left Tuskegee the same year for Kansas State College in Manhattan, Kansas. He abandoned college in 1914 and went to New York; with a friend, he opened a restaurant in Brooklyn that soon failed. In 1914 he married his childhood sweetheart, but the marriage effectively ended within six months when his wife returned to Jamaica pregnant. McKay then led an itinerant proletarian life, at one point working as a Pullman waiter. In 1916, he published his first poem since leaving Jamaica, in *Seven Arts* under the name Eli Edwards. In 1918, an autobiographical sketch was published in *Pearson's Magazine*, edited by Frank Harris; McKay established close friendships with Harris and with Max and Crystal Eastman, editors of the *Liberator*. McKay joined Industrial Workers of the World in 1919 and in the same year published "If We Must Die" in the *Liberator* to both notoriety and wide acclaim. He left for London and the Netherlands in the autumn of 1919. He joined Sylvia Pankhurst's Workers' Socialist Federation and worked with her on the *Workers' Dreadnought*, in which he published many articles and some of his most radical poems. In 1920 he published *Spring in New Hampshire and Other Poems*, his first collection since leaving Jamaica. He returned to New York in January 1921 and was soon made associate editor of the *Liberator*. He joined the African Blood Brotherhood—a black revolutionary socialist organization—and became a member of its supreme council. He published *Harlem Shadows* in 1922 and soon thereafter left for Russia, where he stayed for more than eight months, leaving for Berlin in June 1923. He wrote "Soviet Russia and the Negro," published in two parts in *Crisis* (1923–1924). He left Berlin for Paris, then settled in Marseilles. In 1926 he finished a novel, "Color Scheme," which he destroyed after failing to find an American publisher. In 1928, *Home to Harlem* was published to acclaim and derision; *Banjo* was published a year later, followed by *Gingertown* (1932) and *Banana Bottom* (1933). In the late 1920s McKay moved between Marseilles and Barcelona; in 1928 he finally settled in Tangiers, where he remained until his return to the United States in 1934. He worked in the Federal Writers' Project up to 1938, when he was dismissed (ostensibly because he was not a citizen); he wrote a column for the *Amsterdam News* and articles in various journals including the *Nation*, *New Leader*, and *Jewish Frontier* in the 1930s. He published a travelogue, *A Long Way from Home* (1937). McKay was attacked by members of polite Negro society (such as Alain Locke) as well as the Communist Party. (Zora Neale Hurston spoke up in his defense.) In 1940 he published *Harlem: Negro Metropolis*, which offended the Communist Party and fellow travelers. He wrote a novel, *Harlem Glory*, but failed to find a publisher. In 1942 McKay became ill and was unemployed and almost destitute. He was cared for by Catholics, in particular the black writer Ellen Tarry, and became associated with a Catholic organization, Friendship House in Harlem. He got work in a shipyard in Newark in 1943 but suffered a severe stroke;

he began writing "Cycle Manuscript" while recovering in Connecticut. In April 1944 he moved to Chicago to work for the Catholic Youth Organization led by Bishop Bernard J. Sheil, a progressive force in the Catholic Church. McKay reestablished contact with Dorothy Day of the socialist-pacifist Catholic Worker movement, whom he had known from his days at the *Liberator*. On 11 October 1944 he was baptized and received into the Catholic church. He finished "My Green Hills of Jamaica" in 1946. McKay died in Chicago on 22 May 1948, age fifty-six.

WINSTON JAMES

See also African Blood Brotherhood; Amsterdam News; Bennett, Gwendolyn; Du Bois, W. E. B.; Eastman, Max; Federal Programs; Garvey, Marcus; Harlem: Negro Metropolis; Harlem Shadows; Home to Harlem; Hughes, Langston; Johnson, James Weldon; Liberator, The; Locke, Alain; Negritude; New Negro, The; Riots: 2—Red Summer of 1919; Rogers, Joel Augustus; Schomburg, Arthur A.; Thurman, Wallace; Workers' Dreadnought; Wright, Richard; *specific writers*

Selected Works

A Long Way from Home: An Autobiography. New York: Harcourt Brace and World, 1970. (Originally published 1937.)

Harlem: Negro Metropolis. New York: Dutton and Company, 1940.

The Passion of Claude McKay: Selected Poetry and Prose, 1912–1948, ed. Wayne Cooper. New York: Schocken, 1973.

Further Reading

Cooper, Wayne F. *Claude McKay: Rebel Sojourner in the Harlem Renaissance*. Baton Rouge: Louisiana State University Press, 1987.

James, Winston. *Holding Aloft the Banner of Ethiopia: Caribbean Radicalism in Early Twentieth Century America*. New York: Verso, 1999.

———. *Fierce Hatred of Injustice: Claude McKay's Jamaica and His Poetry of Rebellion*. New York: Verso, 2000.

———. "A Race Outcast from an Outcast Class: Claude McKay's Experience and Analysis of Britain." In *West Indian Intellectuals in Britain*, ed. Bill Schwartz. Manchester, UK: Manchester University Press, 2003.

McLeod, Alan L. *Claude McKay: Centennial Studies.* New Delhi, India: Sterling, 1992.

Tillery, Tyrone. *Claude McKay: A Black Poet's Struggle for Identity.* Amherst: University of Massachusetts Press, 1992.

Mckinney, Nina Mae

The actress, singer, and dancer Nina Mae McKinney was the first black woman to play a significant role in a Hollywood film: *Hallelujah* (1929), in which she initiated the character of the sultry black temptress. This film also marked the beginning of an irksome stereotype; for years to come, lighter-skinned black women would be cast as exotic sexual objects.

McKinney was born in South Carolina in 1912 and lived with an aunt, Carrie Sanders, who was a maid for a rich white couple. As a girl, McKinney was talented and eager to woo an audience. She performed stunts on her bicycle while riding to the post office to pick up mail for her aunt's employer, and she acted in plays at a local industrial school for black children. At age thirteen, she joined her mother, Georgia Crawford McKinney, in New York City. Soon she was performing in nightclubs in Harlem; in 1928 she was given a role in Lew Leslie's Broadway musical *Blackbirds*; while still in her teens, she went to Hollywood during its brief period of interest in producing all-black films. After starring as the seductive Chick in *Hallelujah*, she was called "the screen's first black love goddess." In this film, a "bad girl"—Chick—lures a country preacher (played by Daniel Haynes) away from his congregation and into a life of sin; her death frees him to reclaim his virtue. *Hallelujah* was hugely successful, but some black critics considered it trite and stereotypical. According to some black film historians, it suggests that blacks have a natural bent toward violence and immorality, and its ending has disturbing social implications: the immoral racially mixed black woman serves as an object lesson against miscegenation and represents a threat to racial harmony.

McKinney received glowing reviews for her performance in *Hallelujah*, obtained a five-year contract with MGM, and appeared in two other films while she was under contract—*Safe in Hell* (1931) and *Reckless* (1935). She was not able to repeat her success, however; like many other African American artists of the period she went to Europe, where she found acceptance. She sang in cafés in Paris and London and was billed as the "black Garbo"; she also toured in Dublin and Budapest. In 1930, having returned from Europe, she appeared on Broadway in *Congo Road*; however, she still found Hollywood indifferent to her when she returned there in 1932.

Later, she met Paul Robeson abroad and starred with him in a stylized British production, *Sanders of the Rivers* (1935). McKinney played an African princess, with a southern accent, glitzy costumes, and makeup. Most of her film work during the late 1930s and 1940s consisted of roles in all-black independent productions such as *Gang Smashers* (1938), *The Devil's Daughter* (1939), *Straight to Heaven* (1939), *Mantan Messes Up* (1946), and *Night Train to Memphis* (1946). She starred as a discontented mulatto in *Pinky* (1949); some critics consider this her most notable role.

During the 1930s and 1940s, McKinney toured the United States with her own band. (When she returned to South Carolina with the band for a benefit performance in Columbia, the seating in the auditorium was segregated.) In the 1950s and 1960s, she lived in Athens, Greece, where she was called the "queen of nightlife." She returned to New York shortly before she died. In her honor, her likeness was placed on a brick wall near the courthouse in her hometown, Lancaster, along with pictures of other famous natives, including President Andrew Jackson.

Biography

Nina Mae (Nannie Mayme) McKinney was born 12 June 1912 in Lancaster, South Carolina. She attended public schools in Lancaster and New York City. She began her professional career as a dancer in nightclubs in Harlem. Her first film, *Hallelujah* (1928), established her as the archetypal tragic mulatto. She performed in several other films from the 1930s through the 1940s, including *Pinky* (1949), which is considered her strongest role. She launched a singing career in Europe and led a band in United States; her credits also include *Congo Road* on Broadway and several black independent films. She was married to the jazz musician Jimmy Monroe. McKinney died in New York City on 3 May 1967, at age fifty-four.

AUDREY THOMAS McCLUSKEY

See also Blackbirds; Hallelujah; Robeson, Paul

Filmography

Hallelujah. 1929.
They Learned about Women. 1930.
Safe in Hell. 1931.
Pie, Pie, Blackbird. 1932.
Kentucky Minstrels. 1934.
Sanders of the River. 1935.
Reckless. 1935.
The Black Network. 1936.
On Velvet. 1938.
Gang Smashers. 1938.
Straight to Heaven. 1939.
The Devil's Daughter. 1939.
Swanee Showboat. 1940.
Together Again. 1944.
Dark Waters. 1944.
The Power of the Whistler. 1945.
Night Train to Memphis. 1946.
Mantan Messes Up. 1946.
Danger Street. 1947.
Pinky. 1949.
Rain. 1951.

Further Reading

Bogle, Donald. *Blacks in American Films and Television: An Illustrated Encyclopedia*. New York: Garland, 1988.
———. *Toms, Coons, Mulattoes, Mammies, and Bucks: An Interpretative History of Blacks in American Films*. New York: Continuum, 1999.
Johnson, Helen A. *Black America Onstage*. New York: Graduate Center of the University of the State of New York, 1978.
Mapp, Edward. *Blacks in American Films: Today and Yesterday*. Lanham, Md.: Scarecrow, 1972.
Null, Gary. *Black Hollywood: The Negro in Motion Pictures*. Secaucus, N.J.: Citadel, 1975.
Sampson, Henry T. *Blacks in Black and White: A Source Book on Black Films*, 2nd ed. Metuchen, N.J.: Scarecrow, 1995.

Mencken, H. L.

In the 1920s, Henry Lewis (H. L.) Mencken was one of the most publicly recognized intellectuals of the day. A journalist, editor, prolific author, and social and literary critic, Mencken turned his satiric wit on the cultural landscape of the United States, in particular battling the "genteel tradition" and the vestiges of Puritanism that he saw as stifling America's artists and thinkers.

Many luminaries of the Harlem Renaissance expressed admiration for Mencken at one time or another. In his autobiography, James Weldon Johnson wrote that in the 1910s, "Mencken had made a sharper impression on my mind than any other American then writing." In 1918, Johnson called Mencken "the cleverest writer in America today," and went on express his admiration for the controversial stands that Mencken often took, saying that "the best part of Mencken is truth." Nella Larsen, W. E. B. Du Bois, Countee Cullen, Zora Neale Hurston, and the editor of the influential black newspaper the *Pittsburgh Courier* all read Mencken with interest and often praised him. Mencken earned their respect, in part, by using his own editorial position to challenge prevailing views of race, attacking the Ku Klux Klan and other such groups and drawing attention to African American cultural contributions through his reviews and essays.

Mencken was also an advocate for black writers, encouraging their work and helping to get it into print. Walter White, for example, said that Mencken encouraged him to write his first novel, *The Fire in the Flint*. When the manuscript was rejected by one publisher, Mencken persuaded his own publisher, Alfred A. Knopf, to take it. As the editor of the magazines *Smart Set* and *American Mercury*, Mencken often opened their pages to black writers, including White, Cullen, Du Bois, and Eric Waldrond, providing them with a national forum at a time when they were usually restricted to black-oriented periodicals. Mencken

H. L. Mencken, photographed by Carl Van Vechten, 1932.
(Library of Congress.)

favored no writer of the Harlem Renaissance more than George Schuyler, whose satiric bent was similar to Mencken's, and who appeared in *American Mercury* more than any writer other than Mencken himself during Mencken's tenure there.

Like most whites associated with the Harlem Renaissance, Mencken has not escaped controversy. Some commentators have accused him of harboring racist (and anti-Semitic) views. Often these charges are based on Mencken's frequent use of derogatory terms for African Americans. His essays on African Americans are filled with terms such as "coon," "darky," and "niggero," although in most cases his intention was obviously satiric. The appearance of such terms in his posthumously published diary is more difficult to dismiss, however.

Biography

Henry Louis Mencken was born 12 September 1880 in Baltimore, Maryland. He graduated from the Baltimore Polytechnic Institute as valedictorian (1896). He was a reporter at the *Baltimore Herald* (1899–1901); editor, *Baltimore Sunday Herald* (1901–1903); city editor, *Baltimore Morning Herald* (1903–1904); city editor, *Baltimore Evening Herald* (1904–1905); editor in chief, *Baltimore Herald* (1906); news editor, *Baltimore Evening News* (1906); editor, *Baltimore Sunday Sun* (1906–1910); editor, *Baltimore Evening Sun* (1910–1916); coeditor, *Smart Set* (1914–1923); coeditor, *Parisienne* (1915–1916); coeditor, *Saucy Stories* (1916); coeditor, *Black Mask* (1920–1921); contributing editor, *Nation* (1921–1932); editor, *American Mercury* (1924–1933); and columnist and political correspondent, *Baltimore Sunpapers* (1919–1941). He married Sara Powell Haardt on 27 August 1930. In 1948 he had a stroke that ended his career. Mencken died on 29 January 1956 in Baltimore.

ERIK BLEDSOE

See also American Mercury; Cullen, Countee; Du Bois, W. E. B.; Fire in the Flint, The; Hurston, Zora Neale; Johnson, James Weldon; Larsen, Nella; Pittsburgh Courier; Schuyler, George S.; Walrond, Eric; White, Walter

Selected Works

The American Language: A Preliminary Inquiry into the Development of English in the United States. 1919. (Plus later revisions and supplements.)

Prejudices: First Series. 1919. (First of several in subsequent years.)
The American Credo: A Contribution toward the Interpretation of the National Mind. 1920. (With George Jean Nathan.)
Notes on Democracy. 1926.
James Branch Cabell. 1927. (Rev. ed., 1928.)
Treatise on the Gods. 1930. (Rev. ed., 1946.)
Making a President: A Footnote to the Saga of Democracy. 1932.
Treatise on Right and Wrong. 1934.
The Vintage Mencken, ed. Alistair Cooke. 1955.
Prejudices: A Selection, ed. James T. Farrell. 1958.
The Diary of H. L. Mencken, ed. Charles A. Fecher. 1989.

Further Reading

Douglas, Ann. *Terrible Honesty: Mongrel Manhattan in the 1920s.* New York: Farrar, Straus, and Giroux, 1995.
Hobson, Fred. *Mencken: A Life.* New York: Random House, 1994.
Hutchinson, George. *The Harlem Renaissance on Black in White.* Cambridge, Mass.: Harvard University Press, 1995.
Johnson, James Weldon. *Along This Way.* New York: Viking, 1943.
Scruggs, Charles. *The Sage in Harlem: H. L. Mencken and the Black Writers of the 1920s.* Baltimore, Md.: Johns Hopkins University Press, 1984.
———. "H. L. Mencken and James Weldon Johnson: Two Men Who Helped Shape a Renaissance." In *Critical Essays on H. L. Mencken*, ed. Douglas C. Stenerson. Boston, Mass.: G. K. Hall, 1987.

Messenger, The

Founded in 1917 by coeditors A. Philip Randolph and Chandler Owen, *The Messenger* was published erratically until 1919 and thereafter monthly until 1928. As a result of its opposition to World War I and its advocacy of radical labor unionism (the Industrial Workers of the World), the editors were indicted and charged with offenses under the Espionage Act, although they were not convicted. After the war, its support for the Bolshevik revolution and for socialism at home led the federal government to describe it as "the most dangerous of all the Negro publications." The editors muted its militancy in the early 1920s while leading a campaign against Marcus Garvey. In 1925, *The Messenger* became the official publication of the Brotherhood of Sleeping Car Porters, which Randolph undertook to organize. When the fortunes of the fledgling union plummeted in 1928, however, the magazine folded for lack of finances.

The Messenger, *The Crisis* (the magazine of the National Association for the Advancement of Colored People, NAACP), and *Opportunity* (the magazine of the National Urban League) were perhaps the only nationally circulated black periodicals to actively promote the Harlem Renaissance. *The Messenger*'s political-economic orientation, however, dictated the view that cultural nationalism was secondary to more activist "New Negro" strategies for the progress of the race. Nevertheless, *The Messenger* opened its pages to poems and short stories by new and unknown writers as well as writers with already established reputations, and it gave additional space to cultural criticism—although without developing a unifying philosophy for the renaissance. Four individuals were primarily responsible for the magazine's literary emphasis: Randolph, who had a prior interest in amateur theater; the theater critic Theophilus Lewis; George S. Schuyler, managing editor in the mid-1920s; and Wallace Thurman, who, although he was on the staff only a short time, used his literary contacts to solicit contributions from, among others, Langston Hughes and Arna Bontemps.

One of *The Messenger*'s two greatest contributions to the Harlem Renaissance was opening its pages to aspiring writers. Although its motive was to radicalize the black proletariat rather than to promote literature, *The Messenger* printed Claude McKay's "If We Must Die" in 1919 when *The Crisis* feared to do so. Other poems followed, but it was not until 1923 that the magazine began to print works for their literary rather than their political merit. In sum, in 101 issues *The Messenger* published more than 250 poems by about ninety individuals, most of whom did not establish a literary reputation but did consider themselves participants in the renaissance.

In addition to unsolicited poetry by unknown writers, work by most of the significant poets of the Harlem Renaissance was printed in *The Messenger*. Langston Hughes was recognized as a literary "hot property"; sixteen of his poems appeared in the magazine, along with eight by a fellow student at Lincoln University, Edward L. Silvera. Others of the Harlem group besides Hughes and McKay who had poems published in *The Messenger* were Bontemps, Countee

Cullen, Wesley Curtwright, and Johnathan Henderson Brooks. Georgia Douglas Johnson, the doyenne of a literary circle in Washington, D.C., published sixteen poems; other poets from that group who appeared in the magazine were Lewis Alexander, Angelina Grimké, and Walter Everett Hawkins. Members of Boston's Saturday Evening Quill Club who published in *The Messenger* included Helene Johnson (poems), Eugene Gordon (a monthly feature on the best editorials in the black press), and Dorothy West (a short story). The magazine also printed thirty-five short stories, including some by Zora Neale Hurston, Eric Walrond, and Thurman, and three autobiographical stories by Hughes which were later incorporated into *The Big Sea* (1940). Finally, Schuyler published a Menckenesque monthly column, "Shafts and Darts," using wit and satire to skewer the likes of Marcus Garvey.

The second major contribution of *The Messenger* was its thoughtful and consistent commentary on black theater during the Harlem Renaissance. This was the work of the drama critic Theophilus Lewis, whose honest but sympathetic monthly columns from 1923 to 1927 sought to develop an ideology for a national black theater. He applauded popular musical revues for their irreverence and their accessibility to the masses, although he believed that only serious drama, based on black values and rooted in a black consciousness, could produce a genuinely racial theater. Despite this view, he applauded works by white playwrights that offered meaningful roles to black actors, like Eugene O'Neill's *All God's Chillun Got Wings*. Lewis believed that a greater number of such meaty roles would eventually emerge from black "little theater" groups, and he invariably found something positive in reviewing even the most pedestrian plays. Such efforts, he hoped, would lay the foundation for a future national black theater.

Regarding music, however, *The Messenger* took a conservative stance. Jazz and blues were not art, but merely raw materials from which a higher culture might be built. The magazine instead sought to encourage interest in classical music through articles on the composers Samuel Coleridge-Taylor and Robert Nathaniel Dett, the pianist Helen E. Hagen, and the tenor Roland Hayes. The magazine longed for productions of black opera to replace the "musical pablum" of blues.

Despite *The Messenger*'s unwillingness to appreciate black popular musical culture, it made a number of important contributions to the Harlem Renaissance. Theophilus Lewis was, in the opinion of writers like Bontemps, simply the best theater critic of the era. The magazine published as many poems and short stories as did *The Crisis* and *Opportunity*, although major figures like Cullen, Hughes, and McKay published much less in *The Messenger* than in the other two magazines, regarding it as a distinctly third choice. On balance, *The Messenger* was a major proponent and encourager of the Harlem Renaissance, although it suffers somewhat in comparison with the other two monthlies because its circulation was less than theirs and because it never had someone who functioned exclusively as a literary editor. The renaissance would have been much poorer without any of these magazines: their ultimate significance lies in their encouragement of aspiring artists by publishing these artists' works.

THEODORE KORNWEIBEL

See also Bontemps, Arna; Brotherhood of Sleeping Car Porters; Crisis, The; Dett, Robert Nathanie; Garvey, Marcus; Grimké, Angelina Weld; Hayes, Roland; Hughes, Langston; Hurston, Zora Neale; Johnson, Georgia Douglas; Johnson, Helene; Lewis, Theophilus; McKay, Claude; Opportunity; Owen, Chandler; Randolph, A. Philip; Schuyler, George S., Thurman, Wallace; Walrond, Eric; West, Dorothy

Further Reading

Anderson, Jervis. *A. Philip Randolph: A Biographical Portrait.* New York: Harcourt Brace Jovanovich, 1973.

Kornweibel, Theodore. "Theophilus Lewis and the Theater of the Harlem Renaissance." In *The Harlem Renaissance Remembered*, ed. Arna Bontemps. New York: Dodd, Mead, 1972.

———. *No Crystal Stair: Black Life and the Messenger, 1917–1928.* Westport, Conn.: Greenwood, 1975.

———. *"Seeing Red": Federal Campaigns against Black Militancy, 1919–1925.* Bloomington: Indiana University Press, 1998.

———. *"Investigate Everything": Federal Efforts to Compel Black Loyalty during World War I.* Bloomington: Indiana University Press, 2001.

Pfeffer, Paula F. *A. Philip Randolph, Pioneer of the Civil Rights Movement.* Baton Rouge: Louisiana State University Press, 1990.

Meyer, Annie Nathan

Annie Florance Nathan Meyer was born 19 February 1867 in New York City to Annie Florence Nathan and Robert Weeks Nathan. The Nathan family is of a notable U.S. Sephardic Jewish lineage and can be traced to Gershom Mendes Seixas, who served as minister of Congregation Sherith Israel in New York during the Revolutionary War. Meyer spent most of her life in New York except for a brief time in Green Bay, Wisconsin, where the family moved following her father's financial losses on the stock market in 1875. The family fell apart after this financial setback; her mother turned to drugs and died in 1878. Following their mother's death, Annie and her three siblings returned to New York to live with their grandparents.

The Nathan children attended public schools, but when her older sister Maud married, Annie Nathan quit school to manage the family's household. Through outside tutoring, she prepared for college and enrolled in the Collegiate Course for Women at Columbia University in 1885. To her disappointment, she learned that the women's curriculum was not the same as that for men at Columbia. After marrying a prominent physician, Alfred Meyer, on 15 February 1887, she left Columbia and studied independently, developing her literary skills. Her experience at Columbia University sent her on a quest to establish a college for women. On 28 January 1888, in an article in *The Nation*, Meyer began her campaign for the creation of New York's first women's college. Barnard College, named for a former president of Columbia University who supported higher education for women, formally opened on 7 October 1889 with seven students. Meyer maintained close ties with the college throughout her life and served on the board of trustees from 1893 through 1942. In 1915, her daughter Margaret was among the graduating class. On Meyer's seventieth birthday, the Annie Nathan Meyer Drama Library was established by Barnard College.

Meyer, a liberal, was active in numerous causes, some of which were controversial, such as the anti-suffrage movement. She also participated in numerous organizations, including the Daughters of the American Revolution (DAR), the League of Women Voters, and the National Council of Women. Her liberal ideas facilitated her willingness to work with the National Association for the Advancement of Colored People (NAACP); to sponsor Zora Neale Hurston as Barnard's first black student; and to donate books on black history and culture to Hunter College. In 1932, the Provincetown Players produced her play *Black Souls*, which dealt with racial problems. Meyer was a prolific writer, having written twenty-six plays, three of which were produced on Broadway; eleven books;

numerous short stories, essays, and addresses; and hundreds of letters to newspapers. Her last book, *It's Been Fun*, was scheduled for publication at the time of her death. Following her death in 1951, an editorial in the *New York Times* described her as "a lively and constructive force for good in this city," possessing a "sense of humor that was one of her useful weapons in winning an argument."

Biography

Annie Florance Nathan Meyer was born 19 February 1867 in New York City, where she would spend most of her life. Her parents were Annie Florence Nathan and Robert Weeks Nathan. She enrolled at Columbia University in 1885; married Alfred Meyer, a physician, on 15 February 1887; left Columbia to study independently; was instrumental in the founding of Barnard College in 1889; and served on Barnard's board of trustees from 1893 to 1942. She was an activist in many causes; a participant in many organizations; and an author of books, plays, and essays. Meyer died of a heart attack on 23 September 1951.

KAREN COTTON MCDANIEL

See also Hurston, Zora Neale; Provincetown Players

Further Reading

"Annie Nathan Meyer." *New York Times*, 25 September 1951, p. 28.

Brody, Seymour. "Annie Nathan Meyer." In *Jewish Heroes and Heroines of America: 150 True Stories of American Jewish Heroism*. Hollywood, Fla.: Lifetime, 1996.

Gordon, Lynn D. "Annie Nathan Meyer and Barnard College: Mission and Identity in Women's Higher Education, 1889–1950." *History of Education Quarterly*, 26(4), 1986, 503–522.

"An Inventory of the Annie Nathan Meyer Papers." (Web site.)

"Mrs. Meyer Dead; Barnard Trustee." *New York Times*, 24 September 1951, p. 27.

Micheaux, Oscar

Few African American artists have had a career spanning such a breadth of time and genres, or have achieved such a high degree of popularity, as Oscar Micheaux. Following his first novel, which was published just before World War I, Micheaux would go on to write half a dozen full-length works of fiction over the next four decades. Yet it was in the new twentieth-century medium of film that he gained his greatest success as a storyteller, directing and producing more than forty movies between 1919 and 1948. Micheax's movies—part of the genre called "race films"—addressed multiple aspects of the African American experience and were aimed specifically at black audiences. Still, his work remained on the periphery of the intellectual and cultural movement known as the Harlem Renaissance. The elite of the movement often regarded film itself as "low-grade" entertainment, and Micheaux's frequent use of negative stereotypes and his emphasis on conservative values earned him much criticism from black leaders.

Micheaux's early life shaped many of the values that he would inject into his novels and films. He was born in 1884 near Murphysboro, Illinois, the fifth of thirteen children. At age seventeen, he joined his older brother in Chicago, the destination of thousands of African Americans during the "great migration." Although Chicago's booming economy allowed for steady employment that helped sustain a growing black community, Micheaux found urban life too hectic and oppressive. Within a year, he took a job as a Pullman porter, which allowed him to travel, save money, and, especially, perfect the kinds of social skills in dealing with whites that would aid him as a young entrepreneur. In 1905, he used his savings to acquire a homestead in southern South Dakota, where he spent several years living in a sod house and raising crops. Black pioneers were a rarity in rural South Dakota, but apparently he gained the trust and respect of his white neighbors. Having removed himself from the urban centers of African American culture in the east, Micheaux often expressed disgust with blacks who huddled in overgrown cities rather than pursue opportunities for land ownership and self-employment in the American west, as he had done.

This was the theme of his first published book, *The Conquest* (1913), an autobiographical account of his experiences as a farmer on the great plains. The hero, Oscar Devereaux (a name very close to Micheaux's own), is a hardworking, enterprising young black man who becomes a western pioneer and rises above his poor, unambitious relatives. Much of *The Conquest* provides a sociological study of agricultural and community life of the area around the Rosebud reservation; later in the novel there is an explanation of Devereaux's failed marriage to the daughter of a demagogic black preacher, whose interference causes the couple to divorce—a story based directly on Micheaux's experience with his first wife, Orlean McCracken. Indeed, Micheaux's book seemed an attempt both to express his personal bitterness over the divorce and to condemn the values of his former in-laws. Micheaux dedicated *The Conquest* to Booker T. Washington, the black educator whose advocacy of self-help and economic advancement collided with the growing "Niagara movement," popular among black professionals, which encouraged racial solidarity and attainment of social and legal rights. Although the Niagara movement gradually gained strength in subsequent decades, Micheaux would remain steadfastly loyal to Washington's ideas, portraying himself and his fictional heroes as self-made men who won the respect of whites through hard work rather than through confrontations with racism.

Micheaux's ideal self-made man was no mere facade. Having had his previous short stories rejected by publishers, he paid for the costs of printing *The Conquest* (anonymously) out of his own pocket, and even set up his own distribution system for marketing the book, first among his neighbors in South Dakota and then by traveling personally to the homes of black people across the South. His experience as an African American author and bookseller formed the basis for his second novel, *The Forged Note*, in 1915. By this time, Micheaux's homesteading operations had failed—most of his land had been lost to bank foreclosures—and writing appeared the most likely way to make a living. The profits generated by *The Conquest*, although meager, financed the establishment of his new firm, the Western Book and Supply Company. In 1917, the company published his third and longest novel, *The Homesteader*, which amounted to a reworking of *The Conquest* albeit with more melodrama and complexity. Like Oscar Devereaux, the protagonist of The *Homesteader*, Jean Baptiste, is a black pioneer who leaves city life for the openness of the west—and he too searches fruitlessly for romance, first with Agnes, the white daughter of a local farmer; and then with Orlean McCarthy, the daughter of a mean-spirited black minister in Chicago. *The Homesteader* was a success with the reading public and critics alike, though many readers found its ending contrived (Agnes is revealed to be part black and therefore a suitable partner for Baptiste, so that they can marry and live happily ever after).

The Homesteader also served as Micheaux's vehicle into the medium of film. In 1918, he was approached by two young black filmmakers, George and Noble Johnson, about adapting the novel into a movie. The parties signed a contract and began filming in Los Angeles. Micheaux, with his characteristic aplomb, however, insisted on directing the film himself, and so the deal was canceled. Undeterred, he renamed Western Book and Supply the Micheaux Book and Film Company and began selling stock to white farmers in the plains states in hopes of producing the screen version of *The Homesteader* himself. With a budget of $15,000, he hired a cast of actors and shot the eight-reel production in a leased studio in Chicago. *The Homesteader*—the longest African American film to that date—opened in 1919 just as black veterans were returning from the war in Europe. Thanks to Micheaux's genius in promoting it, the film played in New York, Chicago, and important midwestern cities; was applauded by black newspapers like the *Chicago Defender*; and earned Micheaux a sizable profit.

Little is known about Micheaux's personal life in the 1920s, although judging from the sheer volume of films that his company produced, these were certainly his most prolific years as a storyteller. At the same time as the burst of creative energy in the arts and literature during that decade, African American filmmakers produced silent "race movies" that blacks could see in churches, private homes, armories, and segregated theaters. In films produced by whites at that time, black characters were often depicted as stereotypical clowns and toadies; in race films, by contrast, many black characters were proud, dignified role models. Moreover, the plots of race films often addressed subjects considered taboo in mainstream films, such as lynching, interracial romance, and prejudice. In the aftermath of a series of race riots that erupted in the summer of 1919, such topics could be seen as inflammatory; consequently, Micheaux and other African American directors often had to answer to local boards of reviewers and censors and cut footage that white authorities considered too controversial.

Micheaux did not shrink from controversy and in fact even used it as an opportunity for advertising. *Within Our Gates* (1920) depicted the lynching of a black sharecropper who was accused of murdering his vicious landlord. When southern censors and theaters rejected the film because of at least one very graphic scene, Micheaux ran ads in black metropolitan newspapers promising to deliver the uncut version that "tells it all." In another film, *The Brute*, also released in 1920, Micheaux presented the story of a black prizefighter and dealt with the complicated subject of domestic abuse in African American families. In *The Symbol of the Unconquered*, he returned to a western theme: a gallant black frontiersman helping a young woman to defend her land. The ending is reminiscent of *The Homesteader*: the protagonist learns that the heroine has been passing for white, and so she becomes his love. Several of Micheaux's other films also have this theme: a black hero and a white woman are kept apart by society's fear of miscegenation until the revelation of "a drop of black blood" makes their union possible. Some critics have faulted Micheaux for apparently condoning the "one-drop rule," but others have seen in his stories an attempt to mock white America's insistence on rigid racial boundaries.

Despite the popularity of his work, the financial pressures of independent filmmaking gave Micheaux little time to enjoy his success. As his company expanded, he insisted on personally supervising all its functions, from writing scenes to directing and even to handling routine accounting. Michaeux often financed his productions by selling theater owners first rights to a new release, sometimes accompanied by actors who would perform a scene for the benefit of a prospective investor.

By the late 1920s, race films—unable to compete with the high-quality films produced by the major studios—were suffering a decline. As a consequence, the Micheaux Book and Film Company declared bankruptcy in 1928. A year later, Micheaux married the actress Alice Russell, whose financial and emotional support revived his career. In 1931, with the backing of white theater owners in Harlem, he released his first sound picture, a full-length feature film called *The Exile*, yet another romanticized account of his experiences in the west.

While *The Exile* did reasonably well and enjoyed a long run, Micheaux's "talkies" never attained the same level of success as his silent pictures. His films in the 1930s were basic reworkings of themes he had established earlier: for example, *Veiled Aristocrats* (1932) was an attack on African American elites and *God's Stepchildren* (1938) was about a railroad porter who saves money to buy a farm. Although social commentary remained important in all his works, the Great Depression also caused Micheaux to be more mindful of market demands. Increasingly, he augmented his plots with singing, dancing, or comedy acts, some of which were popular numbers known to patrons of the Cotton Club in Harlem and other nightspots. By the

late 1930s, reviewers were regularly lambasting his films as predictable and amateurish.

Micheaux returned to writing novels during the years of World War II, an endeavor he had abandoned after his initial successes as a filmmaker. Struggling with arthritis and often confined to a wheelchair, he relied more on his wife, Alice, who sometimes appeared in his films, to edit his manuscripts and assist with their sale and distribution. *The Case of Mrs. Wingate* (1945) deals with an interracial romance between a white woman in Georgia and her black chauffer, with an added melodramatic plot involving fascist spies and an attempt to assassinate Eleanor Roosevelt. International spies also appeared in his detective tale, *The Story of Dorothy Stanfield* (1946). By this time, Micheaux had such a loyal following for both his books and his films that these works sold quite well. However, critics faulted him for telling unrealistic stories in which African Americans appeared in roles and situations improbable for the time; these critics also objected to Micheaux's habit—which bordered on libel—of retaliating against actual persons who had offended him by depicting them as thinly disguised villains. After an eight-year hiatus, Micheaux returned to film with *The Betrayal* (1948), an adaptation of his last pioneer novel, *The Wind from Nowhere*. Once again, black audiences appeared to enjoy the movie whereas black and white critics alike described

Oscar Micheaux. (Photofest.)

it in terms such as "ridiculous" and "a preposterous, inept bore." *The Betrayal* proved to be Micheaux's last major project; his health continued to suffer, and he died of a heart attack while on a trip to Charlotte, North Carolina, in 1951.

Micheaux's personal and professional lives were truly inseparable. Not only did his own experiences provide the plots for many of his works, but the marginalization—both geographic and ideological—that he felt, relative to the leaders of African American society, became the standard conflict of his stories. Micheaux's contributions to black culture rest in the enormous popularity of his books and films with ordinary African Americans, in his insistence that film could do more than entertain but could address social issues relevant to race relations, and in the shaping of his own persona as a role model for independent black filmmaking. That tradition would be revived following the civil rights movement, some twenty years after his death.

Biography

Oscar Micheaux was born 2 January 1884 near Murphysboro, Illinois. He moved to Chicago to work as shoeshine boy and Pullman porter in 1901; bought a homestead and became a farmer near Gregory, South Dakota, in 1905; and in 1913 wrote and published his first novel, *The Conquest*, which was followed by two additional novels, *The Forged Note: A Romance of the Darker Races* (1915) and *The Homesteader* (1917). He founded the Micheaux Book and Film Company in 1918 and produced a film version of *The Homesteader* in 1919. Micheaux released numerous films through the 1920s: *Within our Gates*, *The Brute*, and *The Symbol of the Unconquered* (1920); *The Gunsaulus Mystery* (1921); *The Dungeon* (1922); *The House behind the Cedars* (1923); *Body and Soul* and *Son of Satan* (1924); *The Conjure Woman* (1926); and *The Wages of Sin* (1928). The book and film company went bankrupt in 1928. Micheaux married the actress Alice Russell in 1929. The first all-black feature-length film, *The Exile*, was produced in 1931; *The House behind the Cedars* was remade as *Veiled Aristocrats*, a sound version, in 1932. *Swing* and *God's Stepchildren* were released in 1938; *Lying Lips* was released in 1939. Micheaux returned to writing fiction with the publication of *The Wind from Nowhere* (1944), *The Case of Mrs. Wingate* (1945), *The Story of Dorothy Stanfield* (1946), and his last novel, *The Masquerade* (1947). His last film, *The Betrayal*, was released in 1948. Micheaux died in Charlotte, North Carolina, on 26 March 1951.

JAMES N. LEIKER

See also Film; Film: Black Filmmakers; Johnson, Noble; Niagara Movement; Race Films

Further Reading

Bowser, Pearl, and Louise Spence. *Writing Himself into History: Oscar Micheaux, His Silent Films, and His Audiences*. New Brunswick, N.J.: Rutgers University Press, 2000.

Cripps, Thomas. *Slow Fade to Black: The Negro in American Film, 1900–1942*. New York: Oxford University Press, 1993.

Dorsey, Learthen. "Introduction." In *The Conquest: The Story of a Negro Pioneer*. Lincoln: University of Nebraska Press, 1994a. (Bison Book edition.)

———. "Introduction." In *The Homesteader: A Novel*. Lincoln: University of Nebraska Press, 1994b. (Bison Book edition.)

Elder, Arlene. "Oscar Micheaux: The Melting Pot on the Plains." *Old Northwest*, 2(3), 1976, pp. 299–307.

Fontenot, Chester J., Jr. "Oscar Micheaux, Black Novelist and Film Maker." In *Vision and Refuge: Essays on the Literature of the Great Plains*, ed. Virginia Faulkner with Frederick C. Luebke. Lincoln: University of Nebraska Press, 1982.

Gaines, Jane. "Fire and Desire: Race, Melodrama, and Oscar Micheaux." In *Black Cinema: History, Theory, Criticism*, ed. Manthia Diawara. New York: Routledge and Chapman, Hall/American Film Institute, 1993.

Green, J. Ronald. "The Micheaux Style." *Black Film Review*, 7(4), 1992, pp. 32–34.

———. "Micheaux versus Griffith." *Griffithiana*, 60–61, 1997, pp. 32–49.

Hebert, Janice. "Oscar Micheaux: A Black Pioneer." *South Dakota Review*, 11(4), Winter 1973–1974, pp. 62–69.

hooks, bell. "Micheaux: Celebrating Blackness." In *Black Looks: Race and Representation*. Boston, Mass.: South End, 1992.

Regester, Charlene. "Black Films, White Censors: Oscar Micheaux Confronts Censorship in New York, Virginia, and Chicago." In *Movie Censorship and American Culture*, ed. Francis G. Couvares. Washington, D.C.: Smithsonian Institution Press, 1996.

Reid, Mark. *Redefining Black Film*. Berkeley: University of California Press, 1993.

Van Epps-Taylor, Betti Carol. *Oscar Micheaux: A Biography*. Rapid City, S.D.: Dakota West, 1999.

Young, Joseph A. *Black Novelist as White Racist: The Myth of Black Inferiority in the Novels of Oscar Micheaux*. Westport, Conn.: Greenwood, 1989.

Miller, Flournoy

Flournoy E. Miller was born in Columbia, Tennessee, in 1887, the son of a black newspaper editor and the second of three brothers, all significant in black entertainment (the other two were Irvin and Quintard). While studying at Fisk University, he and Aubrey Lyles formed a comedy act, writing their own material.

In 1906 Miller and Lyles joined the innovative Pekin Stock Company in Chicago as performers and resident playwrights. Working at the Pekin gave them contact with major figures like Will Marion Cook, Jesse Shipp, Joe Jordan, and Will Vodery. They contributed material to Ernest Hogan's last production, *The Oyster Man*, and wrote original shows. One show, *The Colored Aristocrats*, introduced the comic Jimtown personae, Steve Jenkins (Miller) and Sam Peck (Lyles), that would be associated with them evermore, significantly influencing the history of black—and blackface—entertainment. Another show, *The Husband*, helped launch Charles Gilpin's career.

In 1909 Miller and Lyles embarked on a vaudeville career that took them to New York. The conventions of the time dictated that black comedians perform in blackface, but Miller and Lyles's witty verbal humor and clever slapstick were far removed from the inanities of minstrelsy. They perfected several comedy devices that were imitated by comedians, black and white, for many years. These included a famous prizefighting routine; "indefinite talk," in which they anticipated the completion of each other's sentences; and "mutilatin'" the language ("I's regusted.")

After several successful years in vaudeville, including an English season in 1915 (*Charlot's Revue*), they achieved even greater fame in 1921, collaborating with the musical duo Noble Sissle and Eubie Blake on the sensational *Shuffle Along*. This set the style for black shows for more than a decade, inspiring many imitations, including use of the Jimtown pair, Jenkins and Peck, in shows written by others.

After *Shuffle Along*, Miller and Lyles continued writing, producing, and performing in musicals and dramas, with mixed success. Their biggest successes were *Runnin' Wild* (1923) and *Rang Tang* (1927). Numerous attempts to re-create the magic of *Shuffle Along*, such as *Keep Shufflin'* (1928), fell flat, though they provided opportunities for black entertainers. In 1928 the pair split. Miller continued writing and performing—for instance, in *Blackbirds of 1930*, a reunion with Eubie Blake. Miller and Lyles themselves reunited in 1930, collaborating on shows and short films.

By 1930 the radio show *Amos 'n' Andy*, by Correll and Gosden, white performers similar in style to Miller and Lyles, had become highly successful. Miller and Lyles's own radio show failed, though, and in 1932 they threatened to sue Correll and Gosden for plagiarism. Lyles died shortly afterward.

During the 1930s, Miller's career moved increasingly toward film. Teamed with the comedian Mantan Moreland, he performed in, and wrote for, many black movies from 1933 to 1956, including westerns like *Harlem Rides the Range* (1939). He moved to Hollywood but was occasionally still involved in theater, as in the final unsuccessful *Shuffle Along of 1952*. By 1940 he had made peace with the producers of *Amos 'n' Andy*, becoming a scriptwriting consultant for the show and later recommending Tim Moore for the role of Kingfish in the television version.

Flournoy Miller died in Hollywood on 6 June 1971. His association with *Shuffle Along* ensures that his memory will endure. He was an innovator who advanced black comedy and entertainment significantly, although his achievements are partly overshadowed today by association with the stereotypes of the blackface era.

Biography

Flournoy E. Miller was born in Columbia, Tennessee, on 14 April 1887. He studied at Fisk University. He was a resident playwright at the Pekin Theater Stock Company, 1906–1909; and founder of the Bijou Stock Company in Jacksonville, Florida, 1908. Between 1922 and 1925 he and Aubrey Lyles made about a dozen 78 rpm recordings on the OKEH label. Miller died in Hollywood on 6 June 1971.

BILL EGAN

See also Amos 'n' Andy; Blackbirds; Blackface Performance; Blake, Eubie; Cook, Will Marion; Gilpin, Charles; Jordan, Joe; Lyles, Aubrey; Miller, Irving; Miller, Quintard; Moore, Tim; Moreland, Mantan;

Musical Theater; Runnin' Wild; Shipp, Jesse A.; Shuffle Along; Sissle, Noble

Theater Productions and Performances

1906: *The Man from 'Bam.* (Pekin Stock Company.)

1907: *The Mayor of Dixie; The Oyster Man; The Husband.* (Pekin Stock Company.)

1908: *Doctor Knight* and *The Colored Aristocrats.* (Pekin Stock Company.)

1908: *Ephraham Johnson from Norfolk.* (Bijou Stock Company, Jacksonville, Florida.)

1912: *The Charity Girl.*

1913: *The Cabaret.*

1915: *Darkydom.*

1915: *Charlot's Revue.* (London.)

1918: *Who's Stealin.*

1919: *Upstairs and Down Below.*

1920: *Tunes and Funnies of 1920.*

1921: *Shuffle Along.*

1922: *Step On It.*

1922: *The Flat Below.* (Dama, Lafayette Theater.)

1923: *Runnin' Wild.*

1924: *Going White; Honey; Negro Nuances; Struttin' Along Liza; Struttin' Time; Backbiters.*

1927: *Rang Tang.*

1928: *Keep Shufflin'.*

1929: *Great Day; A Great Day in N'Orleans.*

1930: *Blackbirds of 1930.*

1931: *Lazy Rhythm; Sugar Hill.*

1933: *Shuffle Along of 1933.*

1934: *Get Lucky.*

1935: *Cotton Club Parade.*

1938: *Dixie Goes High Hat.*

1939: *Hollywood Revue.*

1942: *Harlem Cavalcade.*

1947: *Kitchen Opera.*

1949: *Sugar Hill.* (Revival, California; also known as *Meet Miss Jones.*)

1952: *Shuffle Along of 1952.*

Films

1929: *Harlem Knights; Harlem Mania.*

1933: *That's the Spirit.*

1938: *Mystery in Swing; The Bronze Buckaroo; Harlem Rides the Range.*

1939: *Harlem on the Prairie; Double Deal.*

1940: *Mr. Washington Goes to Town.*

1941: *Professor Creeps; Lucky Ghost.*

1943: *Stormy Weather.*

1946: *Mantan Runs for Mayor.*

1948: *She's Too Mean for Me; Come On, Cowboy; The Return of Mandy's Husband.*

1951: *Yes Sir, Mr. Bones.*

1956: *Rockin' the Blues; Untamed Mistress.*

Further Reading

Peterson, Bernard L., Jr. *The African American Theatre Directory, 1816–1960.* Westport, Conn.: Greenwood, 1993a, p. 162.

——. *A Century of Musicals in Black and White.* Westport, Conn.: Greenwood, 1993b.

——. *Profiles of African American Stage Performers and Theatre People, 1816–1960.* Westport, Conn.: Greenwood, 2001, p. 184.

Sampson, Henry T. *Blacks in Blackface: A Source Book on Early Black Musical Shows.* Metuchen, N.J.: Scarecrow, 1980, pp. 111–114, 115–117.

Slide, Anthony. *The Encyclopaedia of Vaudeville.* Westport, Conn.: Greenwood, 1994, p. 345.

Watkins, Mel. *On the Real Side: Laughing, Lying, and Signifying.* New York: Touchstone–Simon and Schuster, 1995.

Woll, Allen. *Black Musical Theatre: From Coontown to Dreamgirls.* New York: Da Capo, 1991.

Miller, Irvin

Irvin C. Miller was a producer, comedian, and playwright, active from 1908 to the 1950s. He was one of three brothers in show business, the most famous being the actor-impresario Flournoy Miller and the youngest being the producer Quintard Miller.

Irvin Miller was educated at Fisk University. He performed at Chicago's Pekin Theater in 1908, in shows produced by Flournoy. He was with Scott's Black American Troubadours in 1910 and wrote his first show, *Happy Sam from 'Bam*, while with this company. He wrote and produced *Mr. Ragtime* in 1914, while he was with Kid Brown's company, and he costarred with Brown. For fifteen years Miller performed as a duo act with different partners: in 1913–1918 with the singer Esther Bigeou, his wife at the time; in about 1918–1919 with Henry "Gang" Jines; and in around 1920–1928 with Emmett "Gang"

Anthony. He and Anthony became quite prominent in black show business.

Miller specialized in revues featuring beautiful showgirls, snappy dancing, and comedy. Several of his shows appeared repeatedly in new editions from year to year, in the manner of the Ziegfeld Follies. *Broadway Rastus* was mounted in 1915, 1919, 1920, 1921, 1923, 1924, 1925, and 1928; *Brown Skin Models* annually from 1924 to 1954; and *Brown Skin Revue* in 1925. Miller was still sending companies out to tour the hinterlands with shows of this type after World War II.

Miller reached the height of his creativity and success in the early 1920s. He had two successful shows in 1921: *Alabama Bound* (based on a version of *Broadway Rastus*), and *Put and Take*. His greatest success came in 1922 with his script for *Liza* (original title, *Bon Bon Buddy, Jr.*), produced by Al Davis.

Miller's other shows included *Georgia, Runnin' Wild, Sugar*, and *Desires of 1927* (all in 1927); *Carolina Nights, That's My Baby, Blue Baby, Desires of 1928, Bad Habits of 1928*, and the "oriental" show *Tokio* (all in 1928); *Circus Showman* (1929); *Red Pastures* (1930); *Club Hollywood Revue* (1931); *Harlem Scandals* (1934); *Harlem Broadcast* (1936); and *Harlem Express* (1945). Particularly in the late 1920s, these shows were of variable quality; in some cases, Miller's involvement with them went no farther than allowing his name to be used and collecting some of the box office receipts. In the season of 1927–1928 alone he mounted ten productions at the behest of the Theater Owners' Booking Association alone, in addition to other shows in the same years. Not all his shows were aimed exclusively at the African American market; he sent his "Mikado Entertainers" (apparently an early version of *Tokio*) out on the Pantages vaudeville circuit.

Miller was adept at getting publicity. In 1927 he announced his intention to build a home in New Jersey for unwed chorus girls and the offspring of their liaisons. By this time, he was also involved in the career of a boxer, Joe Boykins. In 1941 Miller was instrumental in the capture of the murderer of a theater owner in Helena, Arkansas. Miller remained active into the mid-1950s, hiring small companies of young chorus girls, comedians, and musicians to tour the remnants of the black vaudeville circuit in late editions of his *Brown Skin Models*. He died in 1967.

Miller's shows were noted for the beauty of their showgirls; several also involved talented figures of the Harlem Renaissance. *Broadway Rastus* of 1919 featured songs from the Pace and Handy catalog, including Handy's hit "Beale Street Blues"; Maceo Pinkard ("Sweet Georgia Brown") wrote music for the 1925 edition, as well as for *Liza*, which featured some fine dancers and comedians; and Shelton Brooks ("Some of These Days," "The Darktown Strutters' Ball") appeared in the *Brown Skin Models* of 1927.

Biography

Irvin C. Miller was born in 1884 in Columbia, Tennessee; he was one of three brothers in show business (the others were Flournoy and Quintard). Irvin Miller was educated at Fisk University; he performed at the Pekin Theater in Chicago in 1908 and with Scott's Black American Troubadours in 1910; wrote his first show, *Happy Sam from 'Bam* while with Scott's company; wrote, produced, and costarred in *Mr. Ragtime* in 1914, while with Kid Brown's company; worked for fifteen years as a duo with various partners; and produced or otherwise contributed to numerous revues. Miller died in 1967.

ELLIOTT S. HURWITT

See also Brooks, Shelton; Handy, W. C.; Liza; Miller, Flournoy; Miller, Quintard; Theater Owners' Booking Association

Further Reading

Baltimore Afro-American, 2 July 1927.
New York Amsterdam News, 3 January 1923; 5 October 1927; 11 October 1941.
Peterson, Bernard. *Profiles of African American Stage Performers and Theatre People, 1816–1960*. Westport, Conn.: Greenwood, 2001.
Pittsburgh Courier, 8 October 1927; 5 November 1927; 7 January 1928; 18 February 1928.

Miller, Kelly

Kelly Miller's life and work place him squarely among the savants of his time. He was a major contributor to the thought, institution building, and consciousness raising among African Americans between 1880 and 1915 that were a necessary precondition for the birth of the "New Negro" of the 1920s and the Harlem Renaissance. He was "a leader whose instincts favored moderation, reasonableness, harmony, and whose preferred terrain was the common ground between extreme positions" (Wright 1978, 180). Miller served with distinction as an inspiring teacher and administrator at Howard University for most of his academic career, but his national importance derived from his intellectual leadership both as an advocate for his race and as a mediator between supporters and opponents of Booker T. Washington. According to Meier (1966, 267), Miller "voiced the aspiration toward a cultural nationalism not only in his call for the study of Negro history, but also in his belief in a Negro genius in music literature and the arts." Miller is usually overlooked as a contributor to the Harlem Renaissance, but his philosophical outlook put him in the ranks of thinkers such as Alain Locke and W. E. B. Du Bois.

Long before the Harlem Renaissance, Miller embraced the notion of stimulating African American cultural development, serving as a cofounder and president of the American Negro Academy. The academy was limited to forty members, and its mission included promoting literature, science, and the arts; fostering higher education; publishing scholarly work; defending African Americans against vicious attacks; and stressing the importance of a "talented tenth" to lead the masses. "Upon the enlightened Negro has been imposed unusual responsibility and opportunity for service," he wrote in 1908. "He becomes the inevitable leader and exemplar of his people. They look to him as their guide, philosopher, and friend."

Miller was a noteworthy scholar. In *Educational Review, Dial, Journal of Social Science*, and other leading journals, he argued that African Americans needed wise leadership and that only higher education could provide such leaders. His monograph-length chapter "The Education of the Negro" in a report of the Bureau of Education in 1900–1901 not only displayed a careful marshaling of facts and figures from raw local and state data, but also offered a penetrating analysis of the socialization of African American children through the manipulation of the formal educational process by southern whites and the stratagems of African American teachers to counteract the process and promote race consciousness among these children. Miller's essay "The Harvest of Race Prejudice" appeared in March 1925 in the landmark "Harlem number" of the magazine *Survey Graphic*, which was republished in expanded book form as *The New Negro* (1925).

Miller was one of the first African American scholars to write regularly for the black press, with a syndicated column that appeared weekly for nearly twenty years in more than 100 newspapers. At the height of his fame, Miller estimated that his column was read by some half a million newspaper subscribers. He was an extremely forceful and prolific essayist, pamphleteer, and public speaker, whose frank analysis of race relations was directed at friend and foe alike, ranging from the segregationist Thomas Dixon Jr., to Oswald Garrison Villard of the National Association for the Advancement of Colored People (NAACP). To those who objected to his pessimism about race relations, he replied, "I want the younger generation to open its eyes. I want to inspire them with courage. Not a blind impotent inane optimism which exults in vain conceit and empty boasting. . . . History discounts and discredits such fatal optimism" (Eisenberg 1960, 185).

In his lectures, books, and essays Miller sought to delineate the basic issues of race relations. Though devoid of elaborate statistical tables, Miller's publications were nonetheless marked by prescient observations derived from his careful study of the raw data. In "Enumeration Errors in Negro Population," Miller explained how the U. S. Census Bureau had compounded some relatively minor initial errors into a serious undercount in the census of 1920.

The emergence of Marcus Garvey and his movement following World War I created a leadership crisis among African Americans. In response to Garvey's challenge and competing visions of group progress among middle-class African American leaders, Miller proposed that the warring factions meet in a great council or "Sanhedrin" to formulate a common program of action for African American progress and achieve a unity of effort. Held in Chicago during February 1924, the Sanhedrin was attended by more than fifty organizations represented by approximately 500 delegates, including James Weldon Johnson of the NAACP, George Edmund Haynes of the Federal Council of Churches of Christ in America, Channing H. Tobias of the African American branch of the YMCA, and a future president of Howard University, Mordecai Johnson. Delegates presented recommendations on a number of issues, including health care, the participation of women in civic affairs, financial assistance to farmers and students, and conditions of urban life for African Americans. Critics of the conference such as Du Bois, however, noted the meeting's weak stand on lynching, segregation, and racial discrimination in industry, as well as its failure to say much of value about housing, intermarriage, union labor, or the resurgence of the Ku Klux Klan. In the end, the conference accomplished virtually nothing. A second attempt to hold a unity conference under the auspices of the communist-controlled National Negro Congress in 1936 also failed. Sadly, old jealousies, poor planning, and Miller's inability to institutionalize the idea of the Sanhedrin led to the eventual collapse of the drive for unity.

By the 1930s Miller's leadership of the race had come to an end. In an era dominated by the competing ideologies of Marxism and capitalism, his pragmatism and lack of a definite philosophy made him a leader of the "old crowd." He would continue to write his weekly newspaper column, but the younger and more militant generation of African Americans thought that his views on important issues were out of step with the realities of the modern age. Ironically, that newer generation owed its existence, in large part, to Miller's tireless efforts as a teacher and advocate for the race.

Biography

Kelly Miller was born 23 July 1863 in Winnsboro, South Carolina. His parents were Elizabeth Roberts and Kelly Miller Sr.; he was the sixth of ten children. He received his primary education at Fairfield Institute in Winnsboro, South Carolina; attended the preparatory department, Howard University, 1880–1882; attended Howard University, 1882–1886 (bachelor of science, 1886); served as a clerk in the U. S. Pension Office, 1882–1886; studied advanced mathematics with Captain Edgar Frisby at the United States Naval Observatory, 1886–1887; was the first African American admitted to the graduate school of John Hopkins University in mathematics, philosophy, and astronomy, 1887–1889; and was awarded a master of arts degree in mathematics (1901) and a doctor of laws degree (1903) from Howard. Miller was a teacher at M Street High School in Washington, D. C. (1889–1890) and was appointed a professor of mathematics at Howard University in 1890. He married Annie May Butler in 1894; they had five children: Newton, Paul, Irene, May, and Kelly Jr. He was a co-founder of the American Negro Academy in 1897. In 1907 he was appointed dean of the college of arts and sciences at Howard, a post he held for twelve years. He founded Howard's sociology department in 1895 and was a professor of sociology at Howard from 1895 to 1934 and its chairman of sociology from 1915 to 1925.

Miller organized Howard's Moorland Foundation in 1914; it was reorganized as the Moorland-Spingarn Research Center in 1973. He was a board member of the National Association for the Advancement of Colored People as well as the National Urban League. Miller was the author of *Radicals and Conservatives* (1908), *Race Adjustment* (1908), *Out of the House of Bondage* (1910), *The Disgrace of Democracy—An Open Letter to President Wilson* (1917), *History of the Negro in the World War for Human Rights* (1920), and *The Everlasting Stain* (1924). He organized the Negro Sanhedrin in Chicago, Illinois, 1924. Miller died in Washington, D. C., 29 December 1939.

MONROE H. LITTLE JR.

See also Garvey, Marcus; Haynes, George Edmund; Howard University; Johnson, James Weldon; New Negro, The; Survey Graphic; Talented Tenth; Villard, Oswald Garrison

Further Reading

Eisenberg, Bernard. "Kelly Miller: The Negro Leader as a Marginal Man." *Journal of Negro History*, 45(3), July 1960, pp.182–197.

Holmes, D. O. W. "Phylon Profile: Kelly Miller." *Phylon*, 6(2), 1945, pp. 121–125.

Jones, Butler Blackwell. "The Tradition of Sociology Teaching in Black Colleges: The Unheralded Professionals." In *Black Sociologists: Historical and Contemporary Perspectives*, ed. James Blackwell and Morris Janowitz. Heritage of Sociology Series. Chicago, Ill.: University of Chicago Press, 1974, pp. 121–163.

Meier, August. "The Racial and Educational Philosophy of Kelly Miller, 1895–1915." *Journal of Negro Education*, 29(2), Spring 1960, pp. 121–127.

———. *Negro Thought in America, 1880–1915*. Ann Arbor: University of Michigan Press, 1966.

Roberts, Samuel K. "Kelly Miller and Thomas Dixon, Jr., on Blacks in American Civilization." *Phylon*, 41(2), 1980, pp. 202–209.

Wright, W. D. "The Thought and Leadership of Kelly Miller." *Phylon*, 39(2), 1978, pp. 180–192.

Miller, Quintard

Quintard Miller was born in Columbia, Tennessee, in 1895. His father was the editor of a black newspaper, the *Nashville Globe*. He was the youngest of three brothers, all prominent in black musical theater. His early career is obscure. There is a suggestion that he may have spent some time with the Pekin Stock Company, perhaps in association with his elder brothers. He also spent some time with the Sandy Burns Stock Company, where he met his future stage partner, Marcus Slayter.

Miller emerged in 1920 as a full-blown producer, as well as a comedian-actor, with the show *Broadway Gossips*, and from then until the late 1930s he was a prolific producer and performer. He occasionally collaborated with his more famous brothers, Irvin C. and Flournoy Miller, but he mostly operated independently of them. From 1920 to 1922, he wrote and produced nine shows on his own, as well as performing in his brother Irvin's productions *Bon Bon Buddy Jr.* and *Liza*.

In 1923 he teamed up with the comedian-actor Marcus Slayter, who was also a dancer and choreographer. Slayter had also worked with Sandy Burns, as well as stock companies run by Billy King and Eddie Hunter. Known as Miller and Slayter, the pair produced and performed in twelve shows from 1923 to 1926, including a production of *Shuffle Along* in Kansas City. Their show *Dixie Brevities* ran in an annual form from 1926 to 1928. Miller also performed during this period in several more of his brother Irvin's productions.

None of Quintard Miller's shows had an impact comparable to Flournoy Miller's *Shuffle Along* and *Runnin' Wild*, or even to Irvin Miller's *Put and Take* and *Liza*. Quintard Miller's productions had no original music of significance; they relied on a speedy revue format. The book was typically a rehash of familiar themes, even including Flournoy Miller and Aubrey Lyles's "Jimtown" characters, Jenkins and Peck. Nevertheless, these shows were a significant feature of black Broadway during the 1920s and created employment for a regular troupe of capable performers including the character actor George Wiltshire, as well as occasional opportunities for big names like Bessie Smith, Johnny Hudgins, Greenlee and Drayton, Butterbeans and Susie, and Willie Covan.

These were mostly touring shows, and their travels included the circuit of the black-owned Quality Amusement Company. In the early 1920s Quality Amusement controlled eight theaters in major cities, including the Lafayette in New York; the Howard in Washington, D.C.; and the Dunbar in Philadelphia.

This gave black audiences in regional centers some idea of what the new black Broadway phenomenon was about.

With the onset of the 1930s and the Depression, the frenetic pace of Quintard's productions slackened off; only four shows are recorded from 1930 to 1936. His final show as a performer, along with his partner Slayter, was in his brother Flournoy's *Dixie Goes High Hat* (1938). He retired from the theater in the 1940s and died in 1979.

Biography

Quintard Miller was born in Columbia, Tennessee, 9 May 1895. He was the younger brother of Flournoy Miller and Irvin Miller, who were also prominent in theater. He emerged as a producer and comedian-actor in 1920 with the show *Broadway Gossips* and was a performer and producer from then through the 1930s. In 1923 he and Marcus Slater became stage partners; they produced and performed in twelve shows. Miller retired from theater in the 1940s and is reported to have run a catering business in Los Angeles. He died in Los Angeles in March 1979.

Bill Egan

See also Hunter, Eddie; King, Billy; Lafayette Theater; Liza; Musical Theater; Miller, Flournoy; Miller, Irvin; Shuffle Along; Smith, Bessie

Theater Productions and Performances

1920: *Broadway Gossips*.
1921: *Darktown Scandals of 1921*; *Folly Town*; *Some Baby*; *Tunes and Topics*; *Why Worry?*
1922: *Bon Bon Buddy Jr.*; *The Devil*; *Liza*; *This Way Out*; *Hearts of Men*.
1923: *The Mayor of Jimtown*; *Broadway Rastus of 1923*; *Sheik of Harlem*; *Tunes and Topics*.
1924: *Annie Oakley*; *Step Along*; *The Flat Above*; *Take It Easy*.
1926: *Broadway Brevities*; *Charleston Fricassee*; *Dixie Brevities*; *Harlem Butterflies*; *Miss Dinah of 1926*; *Shuffle Along* (Kansas City edition).
1927: *Bare Facts*; *Dixie Brevities of 1927*.
1928: *Dixie Brevities of 1928*.
1930: *Cabaret Prince*.
1934 and 1935: *Get Lucky*.
1936: *Harlem on Parade*.
1938: *Dixie Goes High Hat*.

Further Reading

Kellner, Bruce, ed. *The Harlem Renaissance: A Historical Dictionary for the Era.* New York: Methuen, 1984, p. 245.

Peterson, Bernard L., Jr. *A Century of Musicals in Black and White.* Westport, Conn.: Greenwood, 1993.

———. *Profiles of African American Stage Performers and Theatre People, 1816–1960.* Westport, Conn.: Greenwood, 2001, pp. 183, 227.

Sampson, Henry T. *Blacks in Blackface: A Source Book on Early Black Musical Shows.* Metuchen, N.J.: Scarecrow, 1980, p. 117.

Mills, Florence

Florence Mills was a celebrated entertainer and the first black female star to win international acclaim at the beginning of the twentieth century. During the Harlem Renaissance and the jazz age of the 1920s, Mills enthralled audiences around the world with her talent for comedy, her phenomenal ability as a dancer, and her flutelike singing voice. She was known as "Harlem's dainty singer" and the "queen of happiness"; James Weldon Johnson described her voice as "full of bubbling, bell-like, birdlike tones." When she performed her signature song, "I'm a Little Blackbird Looking for a Bluebird," Johnson said, "she did it with such exquisite poignancy as always to raise a lump in your throat." Mills excelled in a number of forms of jazz and tap dancing, distinguishing herself from other dancers with her legendary acrobatic movements.

Mills was born in 1895 in Washington, D.C. She displayed her exceptional musical talents early in life, performing in local amateur hours and dance contests; she won her first dance contest, a buck-and-wing competition, at the age of three. Mills was already becoming popular locally and was invited to perform for diplomats and dignitaries. Billing herself as "Baby Florence," she made her professional debut in 1903 in the road company of Bert Williams and George Walker's show *Sons of Ham.* This brought her under the tutelage of a renowned black entertainer, the ragtime singer and cakewalker Aida Overton Walker, who had performed in the original company of *Sons of Ham* and had made the song "Miss Hannah from Savannah" a hit. Walker became a mentor and role model to Baby Florence and taught her the song, which Mills then sang in the show. As a result of her success in *Sons of Ham*, Mills—at age eight—joined the touring company of the white vaudeville team Bonita and Hearn as a dancing "pick," or pickaninny. The role of the pick was to dance and sing onstage with the white performers to enhance their routines. Mills's tenure as a pick ended when she was arrested for being under age. Her family then moved to Harlem, and Mills began attending school.

In 1910, Mills, then age fourteen, returned to show business. She and her sisters, Olivia and Maude, formed the Mills Sisters, a song-and-dance team that performed in theaters in Harlem, including the famous Lincoln Theater, and in black vaudeville houses along the East Coast. The Mills Sisters specialized in ballads and popular songs. Eventually, Mills grew tired of the vaudevillian's demanding lifestyle—constant traveling, the uncertain living conditions that black entertainers faced while on the road, low pay, and long hard hours—and left to try her hand as a cabaret entertainer. In 1916, Mills moved to Chicago and became a member of the Panama Trio with Ada "Bricktop" Smith and Cora Green. The trio performed in the black-and-tan Panama Café, a notorious honky-tonk on State Street on Chicago's South Side. At the Panama Café, Mills worked with the jazz legends Alberta Hunter, Glover Compton, and Mezz Mezzrow and became acquainted with the renowned Bill "Bojangles" Robinson, who began giving her tap-dancing lessons. After a shooting scandal resulted in the closing of the Panama Café, the Panama Trio disbanded. Mills returned to vaudeville, joining the Tennessee Ten, a successful black traveling show. The dance director of the Ten, Ulysses "Slow Kid" Thompson—who was himself an acrobatic tap and "rubberlegs" dancer—eventually became Mills's husband, and her extraordinary dancing style was greatly influenced by the combination of Thompson's acrobatics and Robinson's tap technique.

Mills's big break came in 1921 when she replaced Gertrude Saunders, star of the hit black musical *Shuffle Along*, when Saunders left the show. Opening off-Broadway, *Shuffle Along* took theatergoers by storm with its high-stepping dancing and lively jazz. Mills, now age twenty-six, was a sensation and became an overnight star. Her success in *Shuffle Along* prompted the white promoter Lew Leslie to hire her and Kid Thompson to perform nightly at his Plantation Restaurant on Broadway. Leslie's all-black floor show was built around Mills (although the show also had notable visiting performers such as Paul Robeson); and it was so successful that he turned it into a Broadway production, the *Plantation Review*, which opened on 22 July 1922 at the Forty-Eighth

Street Theater. This was a milestone in Mill's career: her work would be seen by New York critics and she was expanding the racial boundaries of show business. Mill's debut on Broadway was a tremendous success; the magazine *Billboard* noted that her name appeared in lights, "an even one hundred of them."

Mill then had a series of triumphs and "firsts," even though at times her successes were tarnished by racism. In 1923, famous British impresario C. B. Cochran brought the *Plantation* show to the London Pavilion, renaming it *From Dover to Dixie*. In London, Mills faced opposition from white performers, and newspaper headlines announced that the "Negro problem" was being brought to London; she was a huge success, however, and each night received an ovation from the packed house the moment she walked onto the stage. When she returned to New York, she was invited to be a guest star in the *Greenwich Village Follies* at the Winter Garden Theater. White cast members threatened to walk out in protest against a black performer's receiving a higher billing than theirs, but they backed down and the show went on. In 1924, Mills opened in a new show, *Dixie to Broadway*, in which she introduced her theme song, "I'm a Little Blackbird Looking for a Bluebird" (considered a thinly veiled protest against racial injustice). In June 1924, she became the first black headliner in vaudeville at the famous Palace Theater. This honor was followed in 1925 by her show *Blackbirds*, in which she also performed in France and England.

Mills always saw herself as representing her race. She was known for her charitable activities and for speaking out on racial issues and promoting the National Association for the Advancement of Colored People (NAACP). She sought not only personal recognition but recognition for African Americans, "believing that every white person pleased by her performance was a friend won for the race." Mills died of appendicitis in 1927.

Biography

Florence Mills was born 25 January 1895 in Washington, D.C. She was the youngest daughter of John and Nellie Winfrey, two former slaves. Her professional debut was in Williams and Walker's show *The Sons of Ham*, 1903. Her professional performances included *Bonita and Hearn Vaudeville Show*, 1904; Mills Sisters, 1910; Panama Trio, Chicago, Illinois, 1916; Tennessee Ten, 1917; Panama Trio (re-formed), tour of Canada and the West,

1918; Tennessee Ten, 1919; Lincoln Theater, Harlem, 1920; *Shuffle Along*, Broadway, 1921; *Plantation Review*, Broadway, 1922; *Dover to Dixie*, London, 1923; *Greenwich Village Follies*, New York, 1923; *Dixie to Broadway*, Broadway, 1924; Palace Theater, New York, 1925; *Blackbirds*, New York, France, and England, 1925 and 1926; Aeolian Hall, New York, 1925. Mills was the first to star in a review built exclusively around black female singing and dancing, *Dixie to Broadway*; created the first major show made up solely of black American music, *Blackbirds*; was the first black woman to be offered a part in a major white show, *Greenwich Village Follies*; and was the first black woman headliner at the Palace Theater. She died in New York City, 1 November 1927, at age thirty-one.

JANICE TUCK LIVELY

See also Black and Tan Clubs; Blackbirds; Hunter, Alberta; Johnson, James Weldon; Leslie, Lew; Lincoln Theater; Robinson, Bill "Bojangles"; Shuffle Along; Smith, Ada; Willams, Egbert Austin "Bert"

Further Reading

Hine, Darlene Clark, Elsa Barkly Brown, and Rosalyn Tenborg-Penn, eds. *Black Women in America: An Historical Encyclopedia*. Bloomington: Indiana University Press, 1994.

James, Edward T., Janet Wilson, and Paul S. Boyer, eds. *Notable American Women, 1607–1950: A Biographical Dictionary*. Cambridge, Mass: Belknap Press of Harvard University Press, 1971.

Lewis, David Levering. *When Harlem Was in Vogue*. New York: Penguin, 1997.

Logan, Rayford W., and Michael R. Winston, eds. *Dictionary of American Negro Biography*. New York: Norton, 1982.

Marks, Carole, and Diana Edkins. *The Power of Pride: Stylemakers and Rulebreakers of the Harlem Renaissance*. New York: Crown, 1999.

Newman, Richard. *Words Like Freedom: Essays on African-American Culture and History*. West Cornwall, Conn.: Locust Hill, 1996.

Stearns, Marshall, and Jean Stearns. *Jazz Dance: The Story of American Vernacular Dance*. New York: Schirmer, 1994.

Minstrelsy

The minstrel show, which originated in America in the 1840s, was a highly popular form of entertainment during the nineteenth century. Its phenomenal success in the United States, as well as in Europe and the far east, demonstrates its appeal to audiences of many social classes. The minstrel show became the training ground for many performers; it also provided a foundation for other popular theatrical entertainments. It was in decline during the first two decades of the twentieth century, but audiences were able to see acts that were similar to minstrelsy in many venues, including vaudeville, the variety show, burlesque, and Broadway musicals—and as late as 1910, more than ten minstrel troupes were still touring the United States.

A number of African American troupes that featured songwriters such as Sam Lucas (1848–1916), James Bland (1854–1911), and Gussie Davis (1863–1899) toured North America, Europe, east Asia, and Australia during the latter part of the nineteenth century, but by the turn of the twentieth century, the only well known black minstrel who was still performing regularly in minstrelsy was Billy Kersands (1842–1915). Kersands's long career had begun in the 1870s when he was as part of Callender's Georgia Minstrels. He appeared with many other companies, and at his death he was the lead comedian of the Dixie Minstrel troupe.

African American minstrel troupes appeared soon after the conclusion of the Civil War. The troupes followed the accepted practice of "blacking up" when they appeared onstage. Even after they left minstrelsy for variety, vaudeville, and musical theater, some comedians continued to "blacken up." In their appearances in genres other than minstrel shows, African American comedians perpetuated the burnt-cork characters familiar to audiences who attended popular entertainments. Several other traditions also migrated to the other popular entertainments, including the use of stock minstrel characters with descriptive names, the use of dialect for some roles, the use of plots derived from farce, and the use of African American dance steps as the basis of the choreography.

The most prominent of the blackface performers who continued minstrel traditions after the turn of the twentieth century was Bert Williams (1876–1922). As one of the most popular acts on Broadway, Williams, with his partner, George Walker (1872–1911), portrayed stock characters known to audiences from the afterpiece farces that concluded each minstrel show. Walker portrayed a fast-talking dandy who was always eager to inflict his shady schemes on everyone who met him; Williams's stage persona was a slow-witted, slow-speaking, gullible but wily and canny survivor who usually had the last laugh. Their characters were based, in part, on the antebellum minstrel characters Zip Coon and Jim Crow, respectively. Williams and Walker's important shows include *The Sons of Ham* (1900), *In Dahomey* (1902), and *Abyssinia* (1905). In all these full-length musicals, the names of the characters recall those used in nineteenth-century minstrel shows, such as Shylock Homestead; Dr. Straight, a fakir; George Reeder, an intelligence officer; Henry Stampfield, a letter carrier; Leather, a bootblack; Hustling Charlie, promoter of the Get the Coin Syndicate; and Miss Primly. The extant scripts confirm that a number of brief humorous skits were joined together to make a full-length evening. Many were built around a song or dance that featured one of the stars. In *Sons of Ham*, for example, Williams, in disguise, is introduced by Walker as a doctor whose specialty is phrenology. After attracting a crowd by imitating a barker at a medicine show, Williams sings one of the earliest hits, "The Phrenologist Coon"; in this song, he parodies the pseudoscience of phrenology by telling the crowd that as long as they put some coins in his hand, he can tell them anything they want to hear.

After Walker's death in 1911, Williams continued playing similar roles as he starred in various editions of the *Ziegfeld Follies*. In one of his most famous performances, Williams portrayed a railroad porter who helped an English tourist, played by Leon Errol, to navigate his way out of the recently rebuilt Grand Central Terminal. The skit takes place during the reconstruction; Williams and his customer make their exit through the terminal on narrow girders and beams. While they are balancing on girders and lurching through the construction site, the two comedians discuss politics and social issues of the day. But mishaps continue to occur. After saving Errol several times from falling off girders, Williams receives a five-cent tip for his services. He grumbles at the stinginess of his customer. At that point, when Errol slips once again, Williams lets him fall into the excavation and throws his suitcase after him. Though long suffering, he has had the last laugh again. Bert Williams was revered as one of the greatest comedians of his time. He composed more than sixty songs, and he was a recording star for Victor and Columbia. He made several silent films; *A Natural-Born Gambler* (1916) preserves his famous pantomime poker game, which was seen in *Follies of 1914*. His character Jim Crow served as the prototype for stereotypical African American characters of the 1920s, 1930s, and 1940s, including those played by Flournoy Miller and Stepin Fetchit, as well as the character Andy in *Amos 'n' Andy*.

During the 1910s, black musical theater continued to show that it had roots in minstrelsy. Although the plots of these musicals were somewhat more substantial, they replicated the types of plots that audiences knew from the previous decade; minstrel caricatures, old jokes, and descriptive names still appeared in almost every show. Several new teams toured the country, including that of Flournoy Miller and Aubrey Lyles and the team of J. Homer Tutt and Salem Tutt Whitney. In Tutt and Whitney's *How Newtown Prepared*, for example, audiences saw the "grand old veterans," Private Arsenal, Sergeant Duposal, Major Bragg, and Colonel Hullabaloo, as well as Eagle Eye (an Indian chief) and Said Pasha (a Turkish prince). The use of double entendre and descriptive names was one of the major characteristics of minstrelsy from its earliest days. Their continuing use through the nineteenth century and the first three decades of the twentieth demonstrates the long-lasting influence of the minstrel show.

The presence of dialect roles in African American musicals is another characteristic associated with minstrelsy. The character types who speak in dialect are generally represented as ignorant and lower class, but streetwise. They are prone to mispronouncing polysyllabic words (as in the stump speeches that were heard in the minstrel show), and to mangling the niceties of grammar. Characters who spoke in dialect were seen in virtually every African American theater during the Harlem Renaissance.

Most of the scripts for African American book musicals during the renaissance still had only a thread of a plot; the narrative was regularly suspended at various points in the show to allow performers to present their specialties. Book musicals in the 1920s, like those earlier in the century, were, in effect, a collection of brief skits that were strung together. Their plots, which usually featured up-to-date post—World War I topical references and unsubtle references to famous people in the news, continued in the tradition of nineteenth-century low-comedy farces and were familiar to contemporary audiences not only through minstrelsy but from early black musicals and the African American vaudeville circuit. Plots were usually centered on an illegal or crooked scheme. In *Shuffle Along* (1921), two friends who own a grocery store in Jimtown and who want to be mayor of the town try to outwit each other in fixing the election; at the end, neither of them succeeds. In *The Chocolate Dandies* (1924),

the scheme is to "fix" a horse race. Some of the horses in the musical were named after recent African American shows: *Runnin' Wild*, *Shuffle Along*, and *Liza*. The plot opens with a race between horses that have been "doped" by one of the jockeys; the race is held and is won by Dumb Luck. The odds on Dumb Luck were 100 to 1, so the horse's owner, Mose Washington, collects $10,000 on his $100 bet. Washington then becomes president of the town's bank, and the former owners rob the bank and send him a letter informing him that he will go to jail for ten to thirty years because he has not protected the bank from robbers. As he is absorbing the bad news, there is a run on the bank—the depositors storm it to withdraw their money—but he escapes. In *Rang Tang*, two barbers steal an airplane from Jimtown's airport and land in Africa. Their comic adventures are the basis for most of the musical, which compares and contrasts the customs of American and African society.

African American revues, which gained in popularity during the Harlem Renaissance, were similarly influenced. The revue did not have to maintain the logic of a story line for the entire evening, since, by definition, it is a collection of separate scenes and acts. In *Dixie to Broadway* (1924), the opening "Evolution of the Colored Race," is followed by a plantation scene in which a song and dance, "Put Your Old Bandanna On," celebrates antebellum life in the South. Florence Mills (1896–1927) then appeared to sing "Dixie Dream," which also refers nostalgically to the plantation, with its "fields of white"; she dreams that she is back "once more in my Dixie home." In the subsequent scenes of Act 1, the audience saw a haunted-house skit in which the comedian Hamtree Harrington pantomimed fright at seeing a ghost; a double-entendre song, "He Only Comes to See Me Once in a While," sung by Cora Green; another number by Florence Mills, "Jungle Nights in Dixieland"; a tap dance by several of the men; a cross-dressing skit, "Mandy, Make Up Your Mind," in which Florence Mills played the groom; and a closing number, "Jazz Time Came from the South," performed by the entire company. In *Blackbirds of 1928*, the opening prologue, "Way Down South," again celebrated life on the old plantation; it was followed by Aunt Jemima's stroll and a scene in Jungleland, which featured eccentric dances while Adelaide Hall sang Dorothy Fields and Jimmy McHugh's "Diga, Diga, Do." Other scenes included a boxing sequence, a card game in a gin mill in Harlem, and a marriage ceremony in a minister's apartment on 135th Street in the middle of Harlem. In all these scenes, the traditions of the minstrel show is apparent: a nostalgic look at the old way of life, as exemplified by the plantation; a caricature of African American superstition, in a haunted house or graveyard; a parody of African dances; the cross-dressing that was an important part of nineteenth-century minstrelsy; and the double-entendre low humor of the farce. Dialect performers; specialty acts; blackface comedians; and skits all reflected comically, in the minstrel tradition, on African American life.

Although professional minstrel shows were rapidly disappearing from theaters, they were still popular with audiences. Many were produced by amateur groups, who used the published manuals, with jokes for the end men in the opening semicircle, brief skits, music, and suggestions for staging and costumes. Amateur minstrel shows continued to be performed in many communities across the country at least through the 1950s.

JOHN GRAZIANO

See also Amos 'n' Andy; Blackbirds; Blackface Performance; Chocolate Dandies; Fetchit, Stepin; Fields, Dorothy; Hall, Adelaide; Harrington, James Carl "Hamtree"; Liza; Lyles, Aubrey; Miller, Flournoy; Mills, Florence; Runnin' Wild; Shuffle Along; Williams, Egbert Austin "Bert"

Further Reading

Bean, Annemarie, James V. Hatch, and Brooks McNamara. *Inside the Minstrel Mask: Readings in Nineteenth Century Blackface Minstrelsy.* Middletown, Conn.: Wesleyan University Press, 1996.

Graziano, John. "Sentimental Songs, Rags, and Transformations: The Emergence of the Black Musical, 1895–1910." In *Musical Theatre in America*, ed. Glenn Loney. Westport, Conn.: Greenwood, 1984.

———. "Black Musical Theater and the Harlem Renaissance Movement." In *Black Music in the Harlem Renaissance*, ed. Samuel A. Floyd Jr. Westport, Conn.: Greenwood, 1990.

Mahar, William J. *Behind the Burnt Cork Mask.* Urbana: University of Illinois Press, 1999.

Riis, Thomas L. *Black Musical Theater in New York, 1890 to 1915.* Washington, D.C.: Smithsonian Institution Press, 1989.

Sampson, Henry T. *Blacks in Blackface: A Source Book on Early Black Musical Shows.* Metuchen, N.J.: Scarecrow, 1980.

Smith, Eric Ledell. *Bert Williams: A Biography of the Pioneer Black Comedian.* Jefferson, N.C.: McFarland, 1992.

Southern, Eileen. *The Music of Black Americans: A History*, 3rd ed. New York: Norton, 1997.

Woll, Allen. *Black Musical Theatre: From Coontown to Dreamgirls.* Baton Rouge: Louisiana State University Press, 1989.

Mitchell, Abbie

Abbie Mitchell was a child prodigy who, in her early teens, took voice lessons from Harry T. Burleigh; Burleigh had studied with Antonín Dvořák at the National Conservatory of Music. In 1887, when she was not yet fourteen years old, she auditioned for Paul Laurence Dunbar and Will Marion Cook's one-act musical *Clorindy, or the Origin of the Cake Walk.* Dunbar and Cook recognized her talent, and during the summer of 1898 she appeared in *Clorindy* with Ernest Hogan at the Casino Roof Garden. The following year she married Cook and starred in his *Jes' Lak White Fo'ks*, another one-act musical presented at the Roof Garden. In 1902, she played the ingénue in Bert Williams and George Walker's *In Dahomey*, which was one of the first African American musicals on Broadway and was also a huge hit in London.

On her return to New York, Mitchell was seen in *The Southerners* (1904), another musical by Cook. In 1905, she joined the Memphis Students, a singing and dancing group. Their act at Proctor's Twenty-Third Street Theatre was so successful that they were booked in Hammerstein's Victoria Theater, where they gave more than 150 performances. A tour of Europe included performances at the Olympia Theater in Paris, the Palace Theater in London, and the Schumann Circus in Berlin. Mitchell toured briefly with the Black Patti Troubadours and in early 1908 starred in Williams and Walker's *Bandanna Land.* As her marriage to Cook was ending, Mitchell joined a tour of the Nashville Students. In 1909, she starred as Minnehaha in Cole and Johnson's *The Red Moon*, which toured Europe after its New York run.

In 1912, because of a throat ailment, Mitchell turned to acting. In 1915, as a member of the original Lafayette Players of Harlem, she was seen in many dramas, including *Dr. Jekyll and Mr. Hyde*, *The Count of Monte Cristo*, *Charley's Aunt*, and *Othello*. After World War I, Mitchell joined Cook and his Southern Syncopated Orchestra on a tour of Europe; she decided to remain in Paris to study voice with Jean de Reszke and his teacher Giovanni Sbriglia. During the 1920s, she performed in concerts throughout Europe, singing French *mélodies*, German *lieder*, and African American spirituals. On her return to the United States in 1927, Mitchell appeared with Jules Bledsoe in Paul Green's *In Abraham's Bosom* at the Provincetown Playhouse. She was also seen in *The House of Shadows*, and with Helen Hayes in George Abbott's *Coquette* (1928), and she sang on the radio station WNBC.

Mitchell joined the faculty of Tuskegee Institute as head of the voice department in 1931. She also continued to perform, giving an "all-Negro" song recital in New York's Town Hall in 1931; in addition, she appeared as Santuzza in Mascagni's *Cavalleria Rusticana* in 1934, as Clara in Gershwin's *Porgy and Bess*, in Langston Hughes' *Mulatto* in 1935, and as Addie in Lillian Hellman's *The Little Foxes* in 1939. Although she had studied the title role in Verdi's *Aida*, and she hoped to sing in opera regularly, her dream never materialized. Mitchell served as executive secretary of the Negro Actors' Guild. In 1959, she was asked to appear in Lorraine Hansberry's *A Raisin in the Sun*, but her deteriorating eyesight prevented her from joining the cast.

Mitchell was sometimes described as a mezzosoprano, though she sang the soprano aria "Ritorna vincitor!" from *Aida*. Photographs show that she had an elegant bearing, and it was noted that her voice was natural, pure, and mellifluous.

Biography

Abbie Mitchell was born 25 September 1884 on the lower east side of Manhattan, to an African American mother and German-Jewish father. She was raised by a maternal aunt in Baltimore, where she was enrolled in a convent school and was soon recognized as a child prodigy. In her early teens, she returned to New York, where she studied with Harry T. Burleigh. In 1898 she appeared in Paul Laurence Dunbar and Will Marion Cook's *Clorindy, or the Origin of the Cakewalk*; in 1899 she married Cook and starred in his musical *Jes' Lak White Fo'ks*. She appeared in Bert Williams and George Walker's *In Dahomey* (1902) and Cook's *The Southerners* (1904); joined the Memphis Students, a singing and dancing group (1905); toured with the Black Patti Troubadours; starred in Williams and Walker's *Bandanna Land* (1908); joined the Nashville Students; starred in Cole and Johnson's *The Red Moon*

(1909); became an actress (1912) and performed with the Lafayette Players (1915); studied voice again in Paris after World War I; performed in concerts around Europe (1920s); returned to the United States and appeared in plays such as Paul Green's *In Abraham's Bosom* (1927); joined the faculty of Tuskegee Institute (1931) but continued to perform; appeared in Mascagni's *Cavalleria Rusticana* (1934), George Gershwin's *Porgy and Bess* (1935), Langston Hughes's *Mulatto* (1935), and Lillian Hellman's *The Little Foxes* (1939); and was executive secretary of the Negro Actors' Guild. Mitchell died 16 March 1960.

JOHN GRAZIANO

See also Bledsoe, Jules; Burleigh, Harry Thacker; Cook, Will Marion; Dunbar, Paul Laurence; Green, Paul; Lafayette Players; Mulatto; Porgy and Bess; Singers; Williams, Egbert Austin "Bert"

Further Reading

Commire, Anne, ed. *Women in World History: A Biographical Encyclopedia.* Detroit, Mich.: Gale Group, 1999.

Hine, Darlene Clark. *Women in America: An Historical Encyclopedia.* Brooklyn, N.Y.: Carlson, 1993.

Logan, Rayford W., and Michael R. Winston. *Dictionary of American Negro Biography.* New York: Norton, 1982.

Smith, Jessie Carney, ed. *Notable Black American Women.* Detroit, Mich.: Gale Research, 1992.

Southern, Eileen. *Biographical Dictionary of Afro-American and African Musicians.* Westport, Conn.: Greenwood, 1982.

Modern Quarterly

In March 1923, in the inaugural issue of the *Modern Quarterly*, the opening editorial declared that it was a "socialist magazine." It was published in Baltimore, Maryland, by the editor V. F. Calverton (a pseudonym for George Goetz) and his associates, and it reflected their leftist views. It included socialist commentary, literary criticism, book reviews, poetry, fiction, and articles on sociology and science., It differed from other radical journals of the time (e.g., *Seven Arts*, *Masses*, and *Liberator*), however, by publishing opposing viewpoints together in the same issues. In addition to editing the magazine, Calverton contributed to it regularly as a writer. The content of *Modern Quarterly* was closely tied to Calverton's views, and he was the driving force behind the publication. Over the years, it featured more social, literary, political, and economic criticism and less creative work. The magazine ran from 1923 to 1940.

Modern Quarterly had developed from gatherings Calverton held in his home in Baltimore. He spearheaded fund raising for the publication, raising money from annual dinners and from lecturing. The magazine was intended for an intellectual audience and had subscribers in the United States and abroad. In 1933, Calverton's magazine changed to a monthly publication schedule, and its name was changed to The Modern Monthly.

Calverton frequently featured black writers in Modern Quarterly. W. E. B. Du Bois, Langston Hughes, Charles S. Johnson, Alain Locke, George Schuyler, Melvin B. Tolson, and other writers of the Harlem Renaissance were published in the magazine. Its open commentary on race and its promotion of desegregation reflected Calverton's views. He held social intellectual gatherings with blacks and whites and lectured at black institutions. Modern Quarterly also carried advertisement for black publications such as Opportunity and Crisis. Calverton was a contributor to Opportunity and other black periodicals.

Modern Quarterly offered black intellectuals a rare opportunity to present their views in a white publication. Hubert Harrison, who had been born in the Caribbean, put forth an alternative view of America's racial problems in the issue of September—December 1926, in his article "The Real Negro Problem." Alain Locke discussed the past and future of blacks in American literature in "American Literary Tradition and the Negro" (May—July 1926). Charles S. Johnson reviewed Locke's anthology The New Negro in the pages of Modern Quarterly. Other writing by blacks included Du Bois's essay "The Social Origins of American Negro Art" (October—December 1925) and Hughes's poem "Listen Here Blues" (May—July 1926).

As an anti-Stalinist, Calverton was frequently at odds with the Communist Party; he was also critical of the party's segregationist policies. He also differed from moderate conservative black leaders such as Du Bois by advocating class struggle within the black community. However, the openness of Modern Quarterly to writers of differing viewpoints made it a popular publication among intellectuals. This popularity subsided when many intellectuals became loyal to the Communist Party and to the fight of the Soviet Union against fascism. Calverton's stance against World War II—which was thus the stance of Modern Quarterly—also caused a dwindling of readership and of financial support. Modern Quarterly ceased publication with Calverton's death in 1940.

HEATHER MARTIN

See also Calverton, V. F.; Communist Party; Crisis, The; Du Bois, W. E. B.; Harrison, Hubert; Hughes, Langston; Johnson, Charles S.; Liberator, The; Locke, Alain; Opportunity; Seven Arts; Schuyler, George S.; Tolson, Melvin

Further Reading

Abbott, Philip. Leftward Ho!—V.F. Calverton and American Radicalism. Westport, Conn.: Greenwood, 1993.

Genizi, Haim. "V.F. Calverton, a Radical Magazinist for Black Intellectuals, 1920–1940." Journal of Negro History, 57(3), 1972.

———. "The Modern Quarterly, 1923–1940: An Independent Radical Magazine." Labor History, 15(2), 1974.

Hook, Sidney. "Modern Quarterly, a Chapter in American Radical History: V. F. Calverton and His Periodicals." Labor History, 10(2), 1969.

Nash, Michael. "Schism on the Left: The Anti-Communism of V. F. Calverton and His Modern Quarterly." Science and Society, 45(4), 1981–1982.

Wilcox, Leonard. V. F. Calverton: Radical in the American Grain. Philadelphia, Pa.: Temple University Press, 1992.

Modernism

The Armory Show of 1913 in New York City introduced Americans to European modernism. The term "modernism" encompassed a broad range of avant-garde artistic expression that broke with the forms, images, and ideas of nineteenth-century western art. At the time of World War I, art critics applied the term to such nonrepresentational painting as cubism, fauvism, post-impressionism, futurism, and dada but also used it to describe avant-garde movements in all the arts. Modernists often disdained naturalistic representation and conventional narratives and rejected the values and sensibilities of the western genteel classes, including middle-class attitudes toward sexuality, class, gender, and race. Before World War I, most American modernists lived and worked in New York's Greenwich Village, not Harlem. Nonetheless, the modernist assault on everything bourgeois led New York's modernists to Harlem and many Harlemite artists to modernism.

Several things beckoned modernists to Harlem. Because it was a virtually all-black neighborhood, many modernists, themselves bound by racial and class stereotypes, imagined its residents to be unsullied by debilitating bourgeois traits; in their minds, Africans and African Americans were thus more authentic. Moreover, the police of New York City failed to enforce many municipal ordinances in Harlem, especially laws that involved petty crime and vice. Unpoliced and morally unregulated, individuals in Harlem could freely pursue almost any activity, including the consumption of illegal alcohol and drugs and the gratification of a wide variety of sexual passions and whims. For many, this meant the freedom to be modern. Finally, during World War I Harlem became the showcase of a revolutionary new music. Following the war, jazz transformed American music and brought African American musicians and composers to center stage. By 1920 Harlem had become a major center of jazz, a music that many considered synonymous with "modern."

The African American musicians of Harlem altered the rhythm and sound of New York, giving the city's modernists an explicitly American and modern music. In nightclubs in Harlem, New York's modernist avant-garde discovered jazz. With the jazz revolution, the modern art of New York acquired an American voice, not just in sound and rhythm but also in its very spirit. Owing to its west African influences, jazz gave New York's modernists, black and white, a means to express their modernity in less narrowly western modes. During the jazz age, Harlem's African American artists redefined what it meant to be modern and American. They created a new, more encompassing notion of the modern—free of the racism implicit in European-based modernism—as they challenged the limits and frustrations dictated by western racism.

In the winter of 1924, Paul Whiteman's "First American Jazz Concert" introduced white New Yorkers to jazz. Downtown, far from Harlem, in the comfortable confines of the Aeolian concert hall, Whiteman offered a watered-down version of Harlem's jazz. The concert received a positive if condescending reaction. Olin Downes, the music critic for the *New York Times*, wrote sympathetically that *Livery Stable Blues* "is a glorious piece of impudence, much better in its unbuttoned jocosity and Rabelaisian laughter than other and

more polite compositions that came later" (13 February 1934). American avant-garde composers, however, understood from the start that jazz was far more than light entertainment. The modernist composer Aaron Copland recounted, "When I finished with my studies in Europe, I returned home with a strong desire to write recognizably American music. Jazz seemed to supply the basic source material for such music" (quoted in Thompson 1941, 46). Writing in 1924, the art critic Gilbert Seldes of New York pronounced: "Jazz is . . . the symbol, or the byword, for a great many elements in the spirit of the times—that as far as America is concerned it is actually our characteristic American expression" (1924, 83). American moderns saw in jazz an indigenous source for an American music, rich in new themes, interesting rhythms, and novel sounds, an expression of a "primitive" people, uninhibited by bourgeois culture.

Such attitudes both pleased and concerned Harlem's intellectuals. The year after white New York discovered jazz, these Harlemites launched an offensive against western intellectual racism. In 1925 Alain Locke (who was the first African American Rhodes scholar) inaugurated the Harlem Renaissance—or propelled it forward—with his anthology *The New Negro*, published by Albert and Charles Boni's modernist press in Greenwich Village. In this remarkable document, Locke offered an expansive collection of modern poetry, fiction, and essays that set the agenda for Harlem's cultural flowering. *The New Negro* brought to public attention the work of several unknown writers, outlining the enormous possibilities for black creativity. Locke's belief in Harlem's nascent renaissance was warranted. In the interwar decades, Harlem offered black artists and writers resources and an appreciative audience for their work. For example, during the 1920s the periodicals *Crisis* and *Opportunity*, which were based in Harlem, published many works of literature, and in turn Harlem's writers and artists produced an impressive number of modern works, some of exceptional quality—especially Claude McKay's novels; Zora Neale Hurston's fiction inspired by folklore; and Langston Hughes's poetry inspired by blues.

Locke, however, was disquieted by the infatuation that many modernists had with primitivism and their association of primitivism with Africa and African Americans. He cautioned:

Liberal minds today cannot be asked to peer with sympathetic curiosity into the darkened Ghetto of a segregated race life. . . . Nor must they expect to find a mind and soul bizarre and alien as the mind of a savage, or even as naive and refreshing as the mind of the peasant or the child. . . . No more Uncle Remuses, Aunt Chloe's or Jemimas or pickaninnies. (1936, 48)

Locke asked Harlem's artists to transcend the narrow conventions of western art, creating a genuinely modern and human art: "Negro art does not restrict the Negro artist to a ghetto province, but only urges him to sustain his share in its interpretation, with no obligation but the universal one of a duty to express himself with originality and unhampered sincerity" (61).

Art, however, required patronage, and African American art found few patrons. In 1926, the William E. Harmon Foundation established an annual competition and exhibition for African American artists, awarding a gold medal and $400 in eight fields of artistic expression. Although modest, the Harmon prizes granted black artists formal recognition for their work, and the annual Harmon exhibitions brought to public attention scores of previously unknown black artists. The artists and prizewinners included the sculptors Augusta Savage and Richmond Barthé and the painters William Henry Johnson, Palmer Hayden, and Archibald Motley. The Harmon Foundation ended its awards and exhibitions in 1934.

For painting and sculpture, the Harlem Renaissance proved a time of planting and nurturing. In the 1920s, however, perhaps only one artist in Harlem, Aaron Douglas, had a significant impact. Douglas had grown up and received his professional training in Kansas. In 1925 he came to Harlem. Responding to Locke's artistic imperative for the "New Negro," Douglas adopted a cubist-precisionist manner and committed himself almost exclusively to African American themes. Douglas illustrated several publications of the Harlem Renaissance, including *Crisis*, Locke's *New Negro*, and James Weldon Johnson's *God's Trombones*. In *God's Trombones*, Douglas combined stylized African imagery with cubist shapes and flattened perspectives.

Before the Harlem Renaissance, African American artists had generally failed to achieve recognition in painting and sculpture. In music, however, African American spirituals, ragtime, blues, and jazz came to define American popular music and dance. In the 1920s, several black singers fulfilled Locke's hopes for an African American music, including Roland Hayes, Marian Anderson, and Paul Robeson, all of whom received national recognition in the 1920s and all of whom sang music inspired by African Americans. William Grant Still, however, was the pride of the Harlem Renaissance. Still had been educated at Wilberforce University and Oberlin College in Ohio and during World War I had composed for W. C. Handy. In the 1920s, Still focused almost exclusively on African American themes. His modern compositions included *Darker America*, *From the Black Belt*, *La Guiablesse*, and his masterpiece, *Afro-American Symphony*, performed in 1931 by the Rochester Philharmonic Symphony, the first major orchestra to play a symphony composed by an African American (Floyd 1990; Southern 1983, 395–456).

In Harlem, modern art often expressed itself commercially. In 1921 Eubie Blake and Noble Sissle produced the runaway hit *Shuffle Along*, featuring Josephine Baker and Florence Mills, the first Broadway musical produced and performed by blacks in more than a decade. In the 1920s, Mills, Charles Gilpin, Paul Robeson, and Bill "Bojangles" Robinson consistently received top billing on Broadway; Fletcher Henderson, at the Roseland Ballroom, just off Times Square, directed the first important jazz orchestra, opening the way for the big swing bands of the 1930s and 1940s. Harlem's entertainers affirmed the same racial pride championed by the Harlem Renaissance. Like its painters and writers, Harlem's musicians realized that their art contributed much to American life. Finally, it seemed, their day had come.

After World War I, despite persistent and pervasive racism, modern American culture became suffused with African American culture. In the great migration to northern cities, southern blacks carried with them far more than their meager material possessions. Leaving the rural South, they brought to America's cities a rich, complex, evocative culture. Drawing on their west African and southern folk roots, African American blues singers, dancers, artists, and jazz musicians provided modernist American artists with an alternative, nonwestern mode of expression. African American colors, patterns, rhythms, and values became a part of American culture. Such art challenged the boundaries between art and entertainment, western and nonwestern, male and female, white and black. Duke Ellington, Langston Hughes, Aaron Douglas, and other participants in the Harlem Renaissance bridged the racial chasm that had fragmented modern life. In the 1920s and 1930s, however, Harlem and most of its residents remained apart, distant from the rest of the city. Despite the pervasive presence of jazz and other modern arts, racism continued to separate New York's modern artists.

PETER M. RUTKOFF
WILLIAM B. SCOTT

See also Anderson, Marian; Barthé, Richmond; Black Bohemia; Blake, Eubie; Crisis, The; Douglas, Aaron; God's Trombones; Harmon Foundation; Hayden, Palmer C.; Hayes, Roland; Henderson, Fletcher; Jazz; Johnson, William H.; Locke, Alain; Motley, Archibald J., Jr.; New Negro, The; Primitivism; Robeson, Paul; Roseland Ballroom; Savage, Augusta; Shuffle Along; Sissle, Noble; Still, William Grant

Further Reading

Bearden, Romare, and Harry Henderson. *A History of African American-Artists*. New York, 1993.

Floyd, Samuel A., Jr., ed. *Black Music in the Harlem Renaissance*. Westport, Conn., 1990.

Gendron, Bernard. "Jamming at Le Boeuf: Jazz and the Paris Avant-Garde, 1917–1923." *Discourse*, Fall-Winter 1989–1990.

Lewis, David Leverings. *When Harlem Was in Vogue*. New York, 1981.

Locke, Alain. *Negro Art: Past and Present*. New York, 1936.

Ogren, Kathy J. *The Jazz Revolution*. New York, 1989.

Rubin, William, ed. *Primitivism in Twentieth-Century Art*. New York, 1984.

Scott, William B., and Peter M. Rutkoff. *New York Modern: The Arts and the City*. Baltimore, Md., 2001.

Seldes, Gilbert. *The Seven Lively Arts*. New York, l924.

Singal, Daniel Joseph, ed. *Modernism Culture in America*. Belmont, Calf., 1991.

Southern, Eileen. *The Music of Black Americans*. New York, 1983.

Spencer, Jon Michael. *The New Negroes and Their Music*. Knoxville, Tenn., 1997.

Thompson, Oscar. *Great Modern Composers*. New York, l941.

Moore, Frederick Randolph

The newspaper publisher Frederick Randolph Moore (1857–1943) was a lifelong and active member of the Republican Party; was personally acquainted with every president from Ulysses Grant to Herbert Hoover; was present at the assassination of President James Garfield in 1881; and attended every Republican National Convention from 1908 to 1920. Unlike many black leaders, Moore never shifted allegiance to the Democrats, but he did not hesitate to criticize the Republican Party when it disappointed African Americans' hopes. He bitterly attacked President William Taft for giving in to the "lily-white" faction within the party in the South. Nevertheless, Taft appointed him minister to Liberia in 1912, although the appointment was merely symbolic; Woodrow Wilson had already won that year's presidential election, and Moore served only one month, during which he remained in New York.

From age eighteen on, Moore was a messenger to seven successive secretaries of the Treasury; he accompanied Secretary Daniel Manning on overseas business and was named a temporary assistant secretary of the Treasury. After leaving the Treasury Department, Moore took a position with the Western National Bank in New York. In 1905 he resigned to become publisher of *Colored American Magazine*. Moore had been an ally of Booker T. Washington in the 1890s and to some degree was his spokesman at *Colored American Magazine* and later at *New York Age*. Moore was also connected with Washington's other lieutenants in black politics and business, such as T. Thomas Fortune and Emmett Scott. In association with these men, Moore became active in the Negro Protective League (a business organization), its successor the Afro American League, and, most important, the Afro-American Building and Loan Association.

In 1907 Moore purchased *New York Age*, a leading black paper that had formerly been published by *Fortune*. Moore had written for the paper for decades. He moved *New York Age* from its original offices in Chatham Square (today's Chinatown) to West Forty-Sixth Street in 1910, and to West 135th Street in Harlem in 1919. He built his own printing plant for *New York Age*, at a time when few black papers owned one. Moore continued to publish the paper until his death in 1943.

Despite his moderate politics, Moore was a fierce and outspoken opponent of lynching and Jim Crow laws in the south. In this respect, he broke firmly with the gradualism of Booker T. Washington's group. He also joined progressive campaigns in the North, particularly a movement of the 1930s whose slogan was "Don't buy where you can't work." However, he never abandoned Washington's conservative emphasis on an economic rather than an educational model for racial success.

Moore was elected an alderman of New York City twice, in 1927 and 1929. During this period he worked tirelessly for the Colored Merchants Association (CMA), but, particularly with the onset of the Great Depression, it became virtually impossible to persuade black consumers to buy according to racial loyalty rather than price. In 1933, Moore turned against CMA, which folded the following year. In his later years he was particularly active with the National Urban League and in numerous local organizations in Harlem.

Biography

Frederick Randolph Moore was born 16 June 1857, the son of a slave woman and a white father; he was raised in Washington, D.C. He worked as a newsboy and then (from age eighteen) as a messenger to seven secretaries of the Treasury, as well as accompanying one, Secretary Daniel Manning, on overseas business. He later worked for the Western National Bank in New York; he resigned in 1905 and became publisher of the *Colored American Magazine*; in 1907 he bought *New York Age*, which he continued to run until he died. He was a lifelong active member of the Republican party and was elected an alderman of New York City in 1927 and 1929. He was also active in business associations and, later in life, in the National Urban League. Moore married Ida Lawrence in 1879. They had eighteen children, of whom six survived to adulthood. Moore died 1 March 1943 in New York City.

ELLIOTT S. HURWITT

See also Fortune, Timothy Thomas; National Urban League; New York Age; Scott, Emmett Jay; Washington, Booker T.

Further Reading

Afro-American Investment and Building Company Collection, Schomburg Center for Research in Black Culture, New York Public Library.

Baltimore Afro-American, 6 March 1943. (Obituary.)

Booker T. Washington Papers, Library of Congress.

Ingham, John N., and Lynne B. Feldman, "Frederick Randolph Moore." In *African-American Business Leaders: A Biographical Dictionary*. Westport, Conn.: Greenwood, 1994.

New York Age, 6 March 1943. (Obituary.)

New York Times, 3 March 1943. (Obituary.)

Werner, Ludlow W. "The New York Age: Lusty Veteran." *Crisis*, 45(3), March 1934.

Wiseman, John B. "Frederick Randolph Moore." In *Dictionary of American Negro Biography*, ed. Rayford W. Logan and Michael R. Winston. New York: Norton, 1982.

Moore, Richard B.

Richard Benjamin Moore was an Afro-Caribbean intellectual and radical activist who contributed to the development of black Marxism, organized labor, and cultural nationalism in the United States. He immigrated from Barbados to New York City in 1901, settled in Harlem, and became involved in grassroots politics. He was a founding member of the Harlem branch of the Socialist Party in 1918 but grew disheartened by its failure to attack racism and abandoned it in 1921. He then joined the Workers Party, the local branch of the Communist Party of the United States (CPUSA) in Harlem. With Cyril Briggs, Grace Campbell, and others, Moore established the African Blood Brotherhood (ABB), a secret organization for people of African descent that emphasized armed self-defense against white supremacists. Though ABB was short lived, it marked an attempt by the Communist Party to merge racial concerns with labor politics. Moore also served on the executive board and council of directors of the American Negro Labor Congress (ANLC) in 1925 and became a contributing editor of its organ, *Negro Champion*. In 1931 Moore was elected vice president of International Labor Defense (ILD), which had a crucial role in the Scottsboro case. Moore was instrumental in pushing ILD and the Communist Party to demonstrate a commitment against racism. By the 1940s, however, Moore moved away from Marxism and toward pan-Africanism as a means of black liberation. He was charged with racial chauvinism and expelled from CPUSA in 1942.

Moore also contributed to the Harlem Renaissance by promoting literary and intellectual developments rooted in the black experience. He became a wholehearted pan-Africanist intellectual and studied informally throughout the 1930s with figures such as anthropologist Louis Leakey and historian William Leo Hansberry. In the 1940s, he lectured on the history and political affairs of the African diaspora, in accordance with his heightened race-consciousness.

In 1940 Moore formed a partnership with Angelo Herndon and started Pathway Press, specializing in racially conscious texts such as a commemorative edition of *The Life and Times of Frederick Douglass*. Also in 1940, Moore founded the Frederick Douglass Historical and Cultural League as a public forum for the local Harlem community. In 1942, he established the Frederick Douglass Book Center, which specialized in the African diaspora; it remained a cultural and intellectual hub in Harlem until it burned down in 1968. Moore acquired some 15,000 books on the experience of black people around the world (the collection is now housed in Barbados), and he was directly involved with developing a curriculum to promote greater racial sensitivity in the educational system of New York City.

Moore also focused on decolonization. His earliest foray into this movement was his effort to organize mass demonstrations and relief during the Italian-Ethiopian crisis of 1935. Two years later he became involved with endorsing Caribbean independence and help found the American-West Indian Defense Committee. He participated more intensely in Caribbean advocacy organizations during the 1940s and 1950s, hoping to establish a federation of West Indian nations. In 1953, he delivered a speech in Harlem, to British representatives and many supportive Harlemites, about this proposed federation. Although the federation movement faltered in the 1950s, many Caribbean islands did gain political independence from European powers a decade later; in 1966, Moore was invited to return to Barbados for a celebration of its independence.

Throughout his life, Moore devoted himself to ending white supremacy. His most profound contribution to that struggle was *The Name "Negro"—Its Origin and Evil Use* (1960), in which he argued that the word "Negro" was unacceptable because of its "slave origin" and detrimental connotations; he proposed "Afro-American" as a more positive alternative.

Biography

Richard Benjamin Moore was born on 9 August 1893 in Hasting, Christ Church, Barbados. His family immigrated to New York City in 1901 and settled in Harlem. He was a founding member of the African Blood Brotherhood, 1919–1924; was a member of the executive board and council of directors of the American Negro Labor Congress (ANLC), 1925; was a contributing editor to *Negro Champion*; was elected vice president of International Labor Defense, 1931; was a cofounder of Pathway Press, 1940; and established the Frederick Douglass Book Center, 1942–1968. Moore died on 18 August 1978 in New York.

J. M. FLOYD-THOMAS

See also African Blood Brotherhood; American Negro Labor Congress; Briggs, Cyril; Communist Party; Pan-Africanism; Scottsboro

Further Reading

James, Winston A. *Holding Aloft the Banner of Ethiopia: Caribbean Radicalism in America, 1900–1932*. New York: Verso, 1997.

Kornweibel, Theodore, Jr. *Seeing Red: Federal Campaigns against Black Militancy, 1919–1925*. Bloomington: Indiana University Press, 1998.

Moore, Richard B. *Caribs, "Cannibals," and Human Relations: A Revealing Exposure of Smears and Stereotypes*. Patchogue, N.Y.: Pathway, 1972.

———. *The Name "Negro": Its Origin and Evil Use*, ed. and intro. W. Burghardt Turner and Joyce Moore Turner. Baltimore, Md.: Black Classic, 1992. (Originally published 1960.)

Turner, W. Burghardt, and Joyce Moore Turner, eds. *Richard B. Moore, Caribbean Militant in Harlem: Collected Writings, 1920–1972*, intro. Franklin W. Knight. Bloomington: Indiana University Press, 1992.

Watkins-Owens, Irma. *Blood Relations: Caribbean Immigrants and the Harlem Community, 1900–1930*. Bloomington: Indiana University Press, 1996.

Moore, Tim

Harry Roscoe "Tim" Moore is best known today for his role as George "Kingfish" Stevens in the television version of *Amos 'n' Andy* during the 1950s. However, this came at the tail end of a long career in black entertainment.

While dancing for pennies on the streets of Rock Island, Illinois, around 1900, Moore was recruited to join a vaudeville act, Cora Miskel and Her Gold Dust Twins, as one of the twins. He toured England with this act. On his return in around 1901–1902 he joined Dr. Mick's Traveling Medicine Show. He left show business to be a jockey briefly, before taking up a successful career as a professional boxer (he claimed to have won 84 of 104 fights).

He returned to the stage in 1908 with a notable one-man show of *Uncle Tom's Cabin* in which he presented a profile in blackface or whiteface depending on which character he was playing. With his first wife, Hester, he formed a vaudeville troupe, the Georgia Sunflowers, which lasted several years. They toured in Asia, Australia, and the Pacific. In 1916, with his second wife, Gertie, he created *Tim Moore's Chicago Follies*. They regularly toured the Theater Owners' Booking Association (TOBA) circuits until 1925, building up a strong following among black audiences.

As well as his own touring productions, Moore played in numerous other shows as a featured comedian in the 1920s, and also in an early black silent film, *His Great Chance* (1923). Though he worked in the blackface tradition, he had established a reputation as a clever stand-up comedian writing and performing his own material. He had perfected a con-man routine developed in his early vaudeville years and also sometimes portrayed a blackface Scotsman, complete with kilt. His success brought him to the attention of Lew Leslie, who gave him the leading comic role in the highly successful *Blackbirds of 1928*. Moore continued to be featured in most of Leslie's later *Blackbirds* shows, including the European-based versions in 1934 and 1936, as well as the final version in 1939, which also featured Lena Horne.

Moore appeared in several other black revues throughout the 1930s, such as *Fast and Furious* (1931), which included Jackie "Moms" Mabley. He was a regularly featured comedian at Harlem's Apollo Theater and the Alhambra. In 1931 he had a role in Oscar Micheaux's movie *Darktown Revue*. Moore continued playing nightclub and cabaret engagements into the 1940s. His last theater engagement was Ed Sullivan's *Harlem Cavalcade* in 1942. His final film role was as a transvestite in *Boy! What a Girl!* (1947).

While he was living quietly in retirement at home in Rock Island in 1950, he was recommended by his old friend Flournoy Miller for the part of "Kingfish" in the planned television version of *Amos 'n' Andy* (which had begun as a radio series). Despite the show's controversial racial image, Moore's reworking of his con-man routine created a memorable portrayal that is still recalled with affection by many people, both black and white. The show ended in 1953. Moore died in Los Angeles in 1958.

Biography

Harry Roscoe "Tim" Moore was born in Rock Island, Illinois, 9 December 1887. He joined a vaudeville act in around 1900; joined Dr. Mick's Traveling Medicine Show in about 1901–1902; was a jockey (briefly) and then a professional boxer; had a one-man show of *Uncle Tom's Cabin* in 1908; formed a vaudeville troupe, the Georgia Sunflowers; produced *Tim Moore's Follies*, 1916–1925; performed in numerous shows as a comedian in the 1920s and 1930s; he also performed in nightclubs, cabarets, films, and—memorably—in the television series *Amos 'n' Andy* in the early 1950s. Moore died in Los Angeles 13 December 1958.

BILL EGAN

See also Alhambra Theater; Amos 'n' Andy; Apollo Theater; Blackbirds; Blackface Performance; Leslie, Lew; Mabley, Jackie "Moms"; Micheaux, Oscar; Miller, Flournoy; Theater Owners' Booking Association

Theater Productions and Performances

1908: *Uncle Tom's Cabin.* (One-man show.)
1909: *Georgia Sunflowers.*
1916–1925: *Chicago Follies/Tim Moore's Follies.*
1919: *A Wedding in Jazz.*
1923: *Rosie's Wedding Day.*
1924: *Aces and Queens.*
1925–1926: *Rarin' to Go.*
1925: *Lucky Sambo.* (*Aces and Queens* renamed.)
1927: *Southland Revue; Take the Air.*
1928–1929: *Blackbirds of 1928.*
1931: *Fast and Furious.*
1932: *Harlem Scandals of 1932; Blackberries of 1932.*
1934: *Blackbirds of 1934.*
1936: *Blackbirds of 1936.*
1939: *Blackbirds of 1939.*
1942: Ed Sullivan's *Harlem Cavalcade.*

Films and Television

1923: *His Great Chance.*
1931: *Darktown Revue.*
1946: *Boy, What a Girl.*
1951–1953: *Amos 'n' Andy.*

Further Reading

Peterson, Bernard L., Jr. *The African American Theatre Directory, 1816–1960.* Westport, Conn.: Greenwood, 1993a.

———. *A Century of Musicals in Black and White*. Westport, Conn.: Greenwood, 1993b.

———. *Profiles of African American Stage Performers and Theatre People, 1816–1960*. Westport, Conn.: Greenwood, 2001.

Sampson, Henry T. *Blacks in Blackface: A Source Book on Early Black Musical Shows*. Metuchen, N.J.: Scarecrow, 1980.

Watkins, Mel. *On the Real Side: Laughing, Lying, and Signifying*. New York: Touchstone–Simon and Schuster, 1995.

Woll, Allen. *Dictionary of the Black Theatre*. Westport, Conn.: Greenwood, 1983.

Morand, Paul

Paul Morand, a French modernist author, published more than sixty books of fiction, travel, criticism, and autobiography during a career that lasted some sixty years. By the end of the twentieth century, his fame had dimmed in France and he was little known in the English-speaking world, but two of his early books were widely read in translation and discussed during the Harlem Renaissance.

Magie noire (1928; issued in the United States as *Black Magic*, 1929) is a collection of eight short stories, inspired by Morand's travels through Africa as part of his diplomatic duties for the French government. The stories show black Africans in Europe and the United States struggling to deal with the changing world, and generally finding themselves incapable of keeping pace with whites. In "Syracuse, or the Panther Man," for example, a wealthy and educated African American becomes a screaming naked savage when he sees an African mask for the first time in a museum in Brussels; in "Good-Bye, New York," a light-skinned black woman from New York takes a cruise around the world and is driven mad by prejudice. It seems that Morand was attempting to treat those of African descent sympathetically, but his black characters are mere stereotypes; most of them long to return to Africa or revert to a supposed ancestral black essence, and they are unable to find peace and success in modernized societies like those found in Harlem, New Orleans, or Liberia. The stories are sprinkled with specific details of life in these locations, and several critics commented that Morand had a better feel for skyscrapers, music, and costume than he did for people. The book is illustrated with drawings by Aaron Douglas, an important artist of the Harlem Renaissance. The drawings, incorporating both western and African elements, were among Douglas's most influential works.

For one of his nonfiction travel books of the period, *New York* (1929, translated 1930), Morand drew on official visits he had made to the United States in 1925 and 1927. The book reveals a writer who finds New York fascinating and amusing. He celebrates museums and hockey and shopping, and he demonstrates his fascination with Harlem's nightlife and with the opportunities New York offered for members of different races to interact. His passages describing Harlem are lively and detailed, presenting an interesting outsider's point of view.

Both books were controversial in the 1930s, as intellectuals of the Harlem Renaissance debated the extent to which Morand's portrayals were insightful or patronizing.

Biography

Paul Morand was born in Paris, France, on 13 March 1888. He was educated at the Institution Sainte-Marie; Lycée Carnot, 1899–1903 (degree not completed); was tutored privately by Jean Giraudoux, 1905; and studied at the Écoles des Sciences Politiques, 1909–1912. He was an attaché, diplomat, and ambassador for the French government, 1913–1927, 1932–1944, 1953–1955; an editorial board member at the newspaper *Figaro*, 1933–1939; and a writer and translator, 1919–1976. He was elected to the Académie Française in 1968. Morand died in Paris on 23 July 1976.

CYNTHIA BILY

See also Douglas, Aaron

Selected Works

Magie noire. 1928. (*Black Magic*. 1930.)
New York. 1929. (Translated 1930.)

Further Reading

Burrus, Manuel. *Paul Morand, voyageur du vingtième siècle*. Paris: Séguier, 1986.

Lemaître, Georges. *Four French Novelists: André Gide, Marcel Proust, Jean Giraudoux, Paul Morand*. London: Oxford University Press, 1938.

Place, Georges G. *Paul Morand*. Paris: Éditions de la Chroniques des Lettres Françaises, 1975.

Thibault, Bruno. "Paul Morand." *Dictionary of Literary Biography*, Vol. 65, *French Novelists, 1900–1930*, ed. Catharine Savage Brosman. Detroit, Mich.: Gale, 1988.

Van Noort, Kimberly Philpot. *Paul Morand: The Politics and Practice of Writing in Postwar France.* Atlanta, Ga.: Rodopi, 2001.

Moreland, Mantan

Most scholars would agree that, with regard to his career, Mantan Moreland is about as far removed from the goals and ideas of the Harlem Renaissance as an artist can get. A highly successful comic, Moreland appeared in more than 300 films during the 1930s and 1940s, playing nervous black characters who fled at every sign of danger. The diminutive Moreland delighted white and black audiences alike with his rolling eyes and exaggerated facial expressions, but his humor seemed totally at odds with the efforts of the renaissance to produce works that portrayed African Americans as dignified role models rather than as offensive caricatures. Whatever the attitude toward his legacy, Moreland left a mark as a comedian that is difficult to ignore.

Moreland was born in 1901; his penchant for entertaining emerged during his childhood years in Monroe, Louisiana, where his friends nicknamed him "Google Eyes." At around age fourteen (some accounts say he was as young as twelve), Moreland ran away at least twice, once to become a dancer with a carnival, and later to join a traveling medicine show; in both cases, he was forcibly returned to his home by the juvenile authorities. In the 1920s, Moreland toured briefly with a minstrel troupe before playing on the "chitlin circuit," the colloquial term for all-black vaudeville shows. There, he perfected his craft as a comedian by playing backup for famous comics such as Flournoy Miller, Benny Carter, and most notably Tim Moore, a former prizefighter who later played the role of Kingfish on the television program *Amos 'n' Andy*.

The slapstick-burlesque road shows in which Moreland developed his style evolved from nineteenth-century minstrel troupes and the crude "coon humor" that was popular around the United States. Middle-class professionals, particularly those of the Harlem Renaissance, derided such comedy as racist and demeaning, an opinion shared by contemporary historians. Yet, as some cultural theorists have pointed out, vaudeville shows required more skill than minstrelsy, and overall they marked an shift toward a more respectable image for black comedians. "Mutilatin' the language" (as in "you gotta be repaired for that") became a staple of Flournoy Miller's act, whereas Moreland's own "indefinite talk" routine, which he regularly performed live and unrehearsed with his partner Ben Carter, required ample skills in delivery and timing:

A. How come you can't pay me now?

B. Horse races

A. What track you play at?

B. I play over there at . . .

A. That track's crooked. Why don't you play over here around . . .

B. That's where I lost my money! . . . I bet on a horse and that rascal didn't come in until . . .

A. Was he that far behind?

B. Yeah!

A. Who was the jockey ridin' him?

B. A jockey by the name of . . .

A. He can't ride! I thought he went out there to ride for . . .

B. He did! But they fired him. He came on back . . .

Moreland and Carter could continue such patter indefinitely, each finishing the sentences of the other without allowing the conversation to reach a stopping point. Despite the stereotypical content, the grammar and dialect of such exchanges was probably a more accurate reflection of the speech patterns of average, uneducated African Americans in the 1920s than the literary accomplishments of the black elite.

Moreland's background in live comedy provided much of the style that later defined him as a movie actor. A typical stage buffoon, he used physical mannerisms and gestures that held the audience's attention: delivering his lines at a staccato pace, punctuating a joke by rolling or popping his eyes, or affecting a facial expression with his elastic features to convey a range of emotions from surprise to terror to lechery. His popularity earned him offers to perform in *Connie's Inn Frolics of 1927* and *Blackbirds of 1928, 1930*, and *1932*. Though he received mostly secondary roles with little dialogue, Moreland's antics were such that observers found it difficult to watch anyone else with whom he was sharing the stage.

Hollywood studios had a need for black men with such talent. Lazy black characters like Rastus or "coon servant" types like Stepin Fetchit drew the laughter of white audiences even while confirming their prejudices. Moreland's film debut came with *That's the Spirit* in 1932; it was followed five years later by a supporting role in *The Spirit of Youth*, which was about the life of a professional boxer and had an all-black cast including Joe Louis. As in his stage work, Moreland would be typecast in minor, insignificant roles where he provided his formulaic routines and gestures. His films were mostly low-budget independent productions, although he worked with some great comedy teams like Laurel and Hardy, and also with figures such as Redd Foxx and Lucille Ball who later became famous in the transition to television. Through the late 1930s and 1940s, Moreland was almost ubiquitous in American films, making cameo appearances in literally hundreds of grade-B productions.

Moreland found his niche playing the sidekick in comic mystery tales such as *Cosmo Jones, Crime Smasher* (1943) and in horror films like *King of the Zombies* (1943). The inane writing and plots were partly redeemed by Moreland's humor, as in his use of signature lines like "Feets, do your duty." His most recurrent role was Birmingham Brown, the black chauffeur of the Chinese detective Charlie Chan. The Chan films capitalized on a dual set of ethnic images by contrasting the calculating Asian sleuth and his sons, who spoke broken English and were given to philosophical musings, with Brown's perpetually frightened demeanor and hilarious avoidance of danger. American audiences identified with Brown because of the way that Moreland imbued the character with a commonsense instinct of self-preservation, juxtaposed against the cold rationality of the Asians:

Number 1 son: Confucius remind us, Birmingham, that he who fights and runs away . . .

Brown: I know . . . will live to run another day!

Number 1 son: If you're scared, Birmingham, just keep saying to yourself, "I'm not afraid . . . I'm not afraid."

Brown: I'm not afraid. *I'm* not afraid. I'm *not* afraid.

Number 1 son: How do you feel now?

Brown: I feel like a liar!

In other mystery films, Moreland's characters could be seen commenting on the action from the sidelines or occasionally even rescuing the protagonist from danger, though always with extreme reluctance.

Although the National Association for the Advancement of Colored People (NAACP) regularly denounced Moreland's work as perpetuating ignorance and stereotypes, his films undeniably did well with African American moviegoers. At theaters in Harlem, he had top billing in advertisements for the Chan films. In the late 1940s, Toddy Studios commissioned him to star in a series of cheap but raucously funny movies produced for all-black cinemas. Moreland occasionally did have roles in grade-A pictures as well as in numerous radio programs, and apparently he was even considered as a replacement for Shemp Howard in the Three Stooges comedy team. Through the decade of World War II, his trademark role of the "fainthearted Negro" would be endlessly repeated by imitators, but Moreland's expert use of physical expressions and body language somehow conveyed the individuality of each character, despite the banal dialogue given to him by unimaginative screenwriters.

The black civil rights movement of the 1950s brought a downturn in Moreland's popularity. As African Americans defied a century of discrimination and segregation laws, the image of a clownish, scared black man no longer held much power to entertain. No longer in demand in movies, Moreland tried to revive his stage career by turning to the nightclub circuit. His finances suffered, and by the early 1960s, when a severe stroke left him incapacitated, he was nearly bankrupt. After 1964, however, Moreland's health and reputation experienced an amazing recovery. He appeared in 1964 in the horror picture *Spider Baby* with Lon Chaney Jr., and he went on to play cameos in two prominent films directed by Carl Reiner later in the decade. As the television and motion picture industries became more open to African Americans, experienced black actors like Moreland enjoyed a resurgence. He worked on a few situation comedies such as the *Bill Cosby Show*, and even revived his "indefinite talk" routine for television commercials. His last roles included a part in Melvin Van Peebles's satire *The Watermelon Man* (1970) and in *The Young Nurses* in 1973. Moreland died of a heart attack in Hollywood that same year, at age seventy-two.

Film critics of the post–civil rights era have not been kind in their analyses of Mantan Moreland and other black actors who portrayed tricksters, lethargic servants, and lovable cowards in the early decades of moviemaking. Yet Moreland carved a place for himself in the film industry during a time of intense racial oppression and when the doors of major studios were almost universally closed to people of color. Evidencing what W. E. B. Du Bois called "double consciousness," Moreland developed a physical repertoire that allowed him to produce ambiguous images that whites perceived as clownish and unthreatening, but that fellow blacks could interpret as sly and clever. At the very least, his work testifies to the expertise of an entertainer who could assess the mood of his audiences and use self-parody to keep them laughing.

Biography

Mantan Moreland was born 4 September 1901 in Monroe, Louisiana. He left home at age fourteen, in 1915, to join a traveling circus; toured with a minstrel troupe and became a well-known vaudeville circuit actor in the 1920s; appeared in *Connie's Inn Follies of 1927* and *Blackbirds of 1928, 1930,* and *1932;* and moved to Hollywood and began appearing in low-budget independent films in the late 1930s. His most famous role was "Birmingham Brown," assistant to the detective Charlie Chan in a series of fifteen films from 1944 to 1948. Moreland was considered as a replacement for Shemp Howard in the comedy team the Three Stooges in 1955. He began appearing in nightclub acts in the late 1950s. He suffered a severe stroke in the early 1960s but made numerous cameo appearances in films and television sitcoms in the late 1960s. He appeared in his last major film, *The Watermelon Man,* in 1970. Moreland died of a heart attack in Hollywood, California, 28 September 1973.

JAMES N. LEIKER

See also Miller, Flournoy; Moore, Tim

Selected Filmography

That's the Spirit (1932); *The Spirit of Youth* (1937); *Shall We Dance* (1937); *Next Time I Marry* (1938); *There's That Woman Again* (1938); *Harlem on the Prairie* (1938); *Two-Gun Man from Harlem* (1938); *Irish Luck* (1939); *One Dark Night* (1939); *Riders of the Frontier* (1939); *Tell No Tales* (1939); *Frontier Scout* (1939); *Laughing at Danger* (1940); *Millionaire Playboy* (1940); *On the Spot* (1940); *Star Dust* (1940); *Chasing Trouble* (1940); *Drums of the Desert* (1940); *Up in the Air* (1940); *Hi'Ya, Sailor* (1941); *Let's Go Collegiate* (1941); *Mr. Washington Goes to Town* (1941); *You're Out of Luck* (1941); *Cracked Nuts* (1941);

Dressed to Kill (1941); *Ellery Queen's Penthouse Mystery* (1941); *Sign of the Wolf* (1941); *Four Jacks and a Jill* (1941); *The Gang's All Here* (1941); *Hello Sucker* (1941); *Cabin in the Sky* (1942); *Footlight Serenade* (1942); *Law of the Jungle* (1942); *Mexican Spitfire Sees a Ghost* (1942); *The Palm Beach Story* (1942); *Phantom Killer* (1942); *Andy Hardy's Double Life* (1942); *Eyes in the Night* (1942); *The Strange Case of Dr. Rx* (1942); *Tarzan's New York Adventure* (1942); *Footlight Serenade* (1942); *Freckles Comes Home* (1942); *Girl Trouble* (1942); *Phantom Killer* (1942); *A-Haunting We Will Go* (1942); *Cosmo Jones, Crime Smasher* (1943); *King of the Zombies* (1943); *Hit the Ice* (1943); *Melody Parade* (1943); *You're a Lucky Fellow. Mr. Smith* (1943); *Revenge of the Zombies* (1943); *Sarong Girl* (1943); *She's For Me* (1943); *Slightly Dangerous* (1943); *Swing Fever* (1943); *We've Never Been Licked* (1943); *Mystery of the Riverboat* (1944); *Bowery to Broadway* (1944); *Charlie Chan in the Secret Service* (1944); *Moon over Las Vegas* (1944); *Pin Up Girl* (1944); *Charlie Chan in Black Magic* (1944); *The Chinese Cat* (1944); *Chip off the Old Block* (1944); *See Here, Private Hargrove* (1944); *South of Dixie* (1944); *This is the Life* (1944); *Meeting at Midnight* (1944); *The Scarlet Clue* (1945); *The Jade Mask* (1945); *Captain Tugboat Annie* (1945); *The Shanghai Cobra* (1945); *The Spider* (1945); *She Wouldn't Say Yes* (1945); *Dark Alibi* (1946); *Riverboat Rhythm* (1946); *Shadows over Chinatown* (1946); *Tall, Tan and Terrific* (1946); *The Chinese Ring* (1947); *The Trap* (1947); *Juke Joint* (1947); *Sky Dragons* (1948); *The Mystery of the Golden Eye* (1948); *Docks of New Orleans* (1948); *The Feathered Serpent* (1948); *The Shanghai Chest* (1948); *The Chinese Ring* (1948); *Spider Baby* (1964); *The Patsy* (1964); *Enter Laughing* (1967); *The Comic* (1969); *The Watermelon Man* (1970); *The Young Nurses* (1973).

Further Reading

Berlin, Howard M. *The Charlie Chan Film Encyclopedia.* Jefferson, N.C.: McFarland, 2000.

Bogle, Donald. *Toms, Coons, Mulattoes, Mammies, and Bucks: An Interpretive History of Blacks in American Films,* 3rd ed. New York: Continuum, 1994.

Boskin, Joseph. *Sambo: The Rise and Demise of an American Jester.* New York: Oxford University Press, 1986.

Cripps, Thomas. *Slow Fade to Black: The Negro in American Film. 1900–1942.* New York: Oxford University Press, 1977.

———. *Black Film as Genre.* Bloomington: Indiana University Press, 1978.

Patterson, Lindsay. *Black Films and Film-Makers: A Comprehensive Anthology from Stereotype to Superhero.* New York: Dodd, Mead, 1975.

Reid, Mark A. *Redefining Black Film.* Berkeley: University of California Press, 1993.

Sampson, Henry T. *Blacks in Blackface: A Sourcebook on Early Black Musical Shows.* Metuchen, N.J.: Scarecrow, 1980.

Schechter, William. *The History of Negro Humor in America.* New York: Fleet, 1970.

Watkins, Mel. *On the Real Side: Laughing, Lying, and Signifying—The Underground Tradition of African-American Humor That Transformed American Culture, from Slavery to Richard Pryor.* New York: Simon and Schuster, 1994.

———, ed. *African American Humor: The Best Black Comedy from Slavery to Today.* Chicago, Ill.: Lawrence Hill, 2002.

Morrison, Frederick Ernest

As a baby, Frederick Ernest Morrison (c. 1912–1989) was thrust into films by his father, a cook based in New Orleans whose own ambitions for a film career had led him to Hollywood, where he eventually found himself working for a movie producer. Thanks to his father's connections in Hollywood and to his infectious beaming smile, little Ernie Morrison came to the attention of the father of the child star Baby Marie Osborne, who was looking for a black youngster to appear alongside his daughter in one of her films. Morrison made his film debut with Baby Marie Osborne in 1917 at the age of five.

In 1919, Morrison came to the attention of the white comedy producer Hal Roach, who wanted to sign Morrison to appear under the sobriquet "Sunshine Sammy" in a series of short films starring the popular white comedians Snub Pollard and Harold Lloyd. Roach's films were a far cry from the early motion pictures called "race films" produced by independent black filmmakers such as Oscar Micheaux. Roach understood that stereotypes of blacks were what sold at the box office. In these shorts, Morrison played the role of a tiresome pest who constantly interfered with everyone else's affairs. His performances were so impressive that Roach decided to showcase his talents and make him a member of a new comedy series called *Our Gang*, about the adventures of a group of white and black children from a working-class background. The series was innovative in that it featured the white and black children on equal terms rather than as foils against one another. As far as children were concerned, audiences had no problem with this arrangement. As a child actor, however, Morrison had little choice in the roles he played. Whether they were children or adults, white audiences were comfortable with seeing African Americans portray stereotyped comic or clown characters who were nonthreatening—and what better example could there be than a smiling black youngster? From 1922 to 1924, Morrison, now referred to exclusively as "Sunshine Sammy," appeared in twenty-eight *Our Gang* shorts and became the highest-paid black performer in the movies.

Sometime in 1924, at the ripe age of twelve, Morrison was persuaded by his frustrated father-manager to leave cinema for the vaudeville circuit as a tap dancer, singer, and comedian with his own band called "Sunshine Sammy and His Hollywood Syncopators." He continued on this path for the next fifteen years, learning a great deal about entertaining along the way. In 1940, Morrison returned sporadically to films and played the character Scruno in Monogram's *East Side Kids*. He was also periodically cast in a few Twentieth-Century-Fox musicals as a member of the dancing Step Brothers.

During World War II, Morrison found time to entertain troops with the USO. After the war, he gave up show business and took a job as a quality-control inspector at an aerospace firm based in Los Angeles. He retired in the early 1970s, but he emerged briefly to appear in guest spots on such television series as *Good Times* and *The Jeffersons*. In 1987, Ernie "Sunshine Sammy" Morrison was inducted into the Black Filmmakers Hall of Fame.

Biography

Frederick Ernest Morrison was born in about 1912. He made his film debut with Baby Marie Osborne in 1917 at the age of five. In 1919, he was signed by the white comedy producer Hal Roach to appear as "Sunshine Sammy" in a series of short films starring Snub Pollard and Harold Lloyd. From 1922 to 1924, Morrison appeared in twenty-eight *Our Gang* shorts. In 1924, he went on the vaudeville circuit as a tap dancer, singer, and comedian with his own band; in 1940 he returned to films. Morrison retired in the early 1970s and died in 1989.

JAMES SMALLS

See also Film: Blacks as Portrayed by White Filmmakers; Micheaux, Oscar; Race Films

Further Reading

Bogle, Donald. *Tom, Coons, Mulattoes, Mammies, and Bucks: An Interpretive History of Blacks in American Films.* New York: Viking, 1973.

Cripps, Thomas. *Slow Fade to Black: The Negro in American Film, 1900–1942.* New York: Oxford University Press, 1977.

Null, Gary. *Black Hollywood: The Negro in Motion Pictures.* Secaucus, N.J.: Citadel, 1975.

Morton, Ferdinand Q.

The politician and attorney Ferdinand Quentin Morton was born in Mississippi in 1881 and grew up there and in Washington, D.C. He studied for three years at Harvard, where he was a star of the debating team, and then studied law at Boston University. He received his bachelor of laws degree in 1909, moved to New York City, passed the bar exam, entered the firm of Wheaton and Curtis, and allied himself with the Tammany Hall Democratic Party under the sponsorship of Charles F. Murphy. In 1916, Morton was elected leader of the United Colored Democratic Association (United Colored Democracy) and was appointed assistant attorney general. In 1922, he was named to the Civil Service Commission by Mayor John F. Hylan; Morton would serve on this commission for twenty-six years, surviving four investigations that resulted in the resignations of several colleagues (he was chairman of the commission for several years in the 1940s). In 1924, Morton declined the offer of a judgeship. During the 1920s, he had a close friendship with Mayor Jimmy Walker and was also connected with Governor Al Smith. When Smith ran for the presidency in 1928, Morton initially refused to campaign for him after discovering that the campaign headquarters was segregated; he then relented and did work for Smith, but refused reimbursement of expenses on the grounds that the funds were tainted by racism. In 1932, Morton initially opposed Franklin D. Roosevelt's nomination for the presidency because Roosevelt, as governor of New York, had quarreled with Tammany Hall. In 1935, Morton ran for the state assembly but lost the seat for

Harlem to a white candidate and openly decried the election as having been corrupt and rigged.

Throughout his long career in politics, Morton worked for the people of Harlem, particularly in matters involving government jobs. He was instrumental in the appointment of several black judges. A staunch opponent of racial separatism, he quarreled over this matter with W. E. B. Du Bois in the pages of *Crisis*. On both tactical and psychological grounds, Morton took positions that in retrospect seem prescient as well as sensible:

> You advocate withdrawal behind the barriers because members of the majority group . . . "refuse to treat me like a man." That psychological reaction is precisely the thing that must be discouraged in our youth. . . . We will not build separate institutions . . . when our country's institutions are our birthright. There is not one which we have not helped to establish.

A stoic by nature, and a tough and persistent political brawler, Morton received the following unusual accolade in the magazine section of the Baltimore *Afro-American* in 1935: "astute politician . . . never cries when hit." And the *Tattler* noted, in 1930: "Morton . . . taught the Negroes of New York that politics is a business that calls for hard selfish thinking instead of idealistic sentiment." Morton had his critics, however, one of whom, the columnist "Capitan" in the *Louisiana Weekly*, wrote some incisive and telling attacks.

Morton never married, and he claimed to live entirely for his work. An enthusiastic baseball fan, he served a term as commissioner of Negro Baseball. His last years were marred by Parkinson's disease, and he retired from the Civil Service Commission at the beginning of 1948. He entered a sanatorium in Washington, D.C. and died in 1949.

Biography

Ferdinand Quentin Morton was born 9 September 1881, in Macon, Mississippi, and was raised there and, from age nine, in Washington, D.C. His father was a schoolteacher in Macon and later a clerk in the Treasury Department. Morton attended public schools in Washington; Phillips-Exeter Academy, graduating in 1902; Harvard (for three years); and Boston University (bachelor of laws, 1909). He joined the law firm Wheaton and Curtis in New York City; allied himself with Tammany Hall; was elected leader of United Colored Democracy (1915); was appointed assistant attorney general (1916); and was named to the Civil Service Commission (1922), on which he served for twenty-six years (including several years as its chairman in the 1940s). He also served a term as commissioner of Negro Baseball. He developed Parkinson's disease, retired from the Civil Service Commission in 1948, and entered a sanatorium in Washington, D.C. He died in a hospital there in November 1949, following injuries suffered when he fell asleep while smoking.

ELLIOTT HURWITT

See also Baltimore Afro-American; Du Bois, W. E. B.; Inter-State Tattler; Party Politics; Politics and Politicians; United Colored Democracy

Further Reading

Baltimore Afro-American, 12 November 1949. (Obituary.)

Brisbane, Robert H. The Black Vanguard. Valley Forge, Pa.: Judson, 1970.

"Capitan." "Harlem, Morton, and United Colored Democracy." Louisiana Weekly, 16 January 1932.

Ferdinand Q. Morton clippings file, Schomburg Center for Research in Black Culture, New York Public Library.

Morton, Ferdinand Q. "Segregation." Crisis, August 1934.

Murphy, George B., Jr. "Commissioner Ferdinand Morton Tells Why He Is a Bachelor." Baltimore Afro-American, 19 September 1931.

New York Age, 12 November 1949. (Obituary.)

"The Statesmanship of Ferdinand Q. Morton." Tattler, 22 August 1930.

Titus, E. K. "Morton Muses Over Loss of Hard Fight in Harlem." New York World-Telegram, 18 September 1935.

Morton, Jelly Roll

Jelly Roll Morton (Ferdinand Joseph La Menthe)—a pianist, composer, arranger, and bandleader in classic jazz—is among the most colorful and controversial figures in the history of this music. During the 1920s, Morton brought jazz to new heights with a series of recordings that demonstrated the greatness of early New Orleans ensemble playing and also influenced the future big band style by showing that swinging jazz could result from combining solo improvisation with complex written arrangements. However, Morton's adventurous life and his constant self-aggrandizement, sometimes at the expense of others, often overshadowed his importance as a pioneering genius in jazz composing, arranging, and piano playing.

Morton was born in New Orleans, probably in 1885 or 1890, and as a child was drawn to the music of his surroundings: ragtime, spirituals, opera, blues, marches, vocal quartets, and Spanish guitar music. These experiences would lead to his love of the piano, and they would influence the development of his highly original concepts of jazz improvisation and form. Morton's brief period of formal piano instruction was supplemented by learning from blues pianists and the ragtime piano "professors" of New Orleans' Storyville red-light district, where he soon worked as a soloist.

After being ejected from home for working in brothels, Morton began an errant lifestyle that took him throughout the South, trying his hand at gambling, pimping, and pool hustling. He also became a traveling vaudevillian and adopted the name Jelly Roll (and Morton, based on his stepfather's last name, Mouton). He traveled about the country, challenging and defeating lesser pianists with his style of ragtime, blues, jazz, and even classical pieces. By 1914 Morton began to write out the original compositions that he had made up and refined over the years. He published his "Jelly Roll Blues" (the first published jazz score) in 1915. From 1914 to 1917, Morton was active in Chicago's Southside night life as a bandleader, using his handwritten musical arrangements for the first time.

Morton moved to Los Angeles in 1917 and for the next five years wrote new compositions, led bands, and performed up and down the West Coast. In 1923, seizing new opportunities presented by the publishing and recording industries, he moved back to Chicago, where he had his greatest period of productivity, renown, and artistic success. He wrote, published, and recorded songs at a rate that surpassed anyone else in jazz at the time. Among his earliest sessions were band recordings and piano solos, including some of his best works, like "King Porter Stomp" and "New Orleans Joys." Morton's piano style was his own unique creation: a blend of the forms and techniques of ragtime and the feeling of the blues with his own laid-back sense of swing. In his early solo piano style, Morton often conveyed the sounds of other instruments with lines, melodies, riffs, and effects that appear later in versions recorded by full bands.

During this time, he began a collaboration with the Melrose brothers' publishing company and record store, which served as his base of operations for putting out new material, rehearsing bands for recordings, and gaining exposure in the music community. He continued to record band numbers and produced two duets with Joseph "King" Oliver. National exposure came when compositions like his "Wolverine Blues" were recorded and played by bands all over the country.

On the heels of Louis Armstrong's recordings with the Hot Five and Hot Seven—which helped to shift attention toward improvised solo playing in jazz—Morton recorded his greatest body of work, which focused on collective ensemble playing. Morton's sessions with the Red Hot Peppers in 1926 and 1927 are among the most significant body of jazz recordings. Here his extended concept of New Orleans—style jazz is beautifully displayed with a series of colorful melodies, shifting moods, solo breaks, arranged harmony parts, improvised solos, surprising effects, and driving rhythms. Morton was a true artist who experimented with instrumentation, tone colors, rhythms, and form. His band orchestrations were extensions of his solo piano style and were thus tinted with blues inflections, Afro-Caribbean rhythms, subtle dynamics, dissonance, and counterpoint, all of which he saw as crucial to jazz. Morton's work of the mid-1920s also introduced new elements in jazz recording, such as trios, arranged clarinet "choirs," and improvisation based on a single chord.

When activities on Chicago's Southside slowed down, Morton toured for a year and then moved to New York in 1928. Despite his best efforts, he was never a big success in New York. The man who had been at the top of Chicago's jazz world now experienced a downward spiral in his career and his life, from which he never recovered. During his five years in New York, Morton constantly had problems finding competent musicians and work. His insistence on regular rehearsals and on strict adherence to sometimes difficult written scores—and his preference for musicians from New Orleans—made it hard for him to assemble and keep a good band.

In the late 1920s, jazz was growing in many directions—all of them away from Morton's New Orleans concept of an ensemble. In the mind of the public and of forward-thinking jazz musicians, Morton was no longer in fashion. The flashy hot improvised solos of Louis Armstrong and the emerging big bands that depended more on arrangements were now in vogue. Morton's laid-back, bluesy piano style seemed tame compared with the trendy faster, fuller, more aggressive, technically complex Harlem stride piano, the style of James P. Johnson, Willie "the Lion" Smith, and Fats Waller. Some musicians saw Morton as a second-rate has-been. To make matters worse, Morton became a target of scorn and ridicule as a result of his own continual bragging about being the world's greatest pianist and the inventor of jazz and about the superiority of New Orleans musicians, and as a result of his complaint that New York musicians were thieves who could not play jazz or swing. However, Morton also had a reputation for being able to back up his claims, and on occasion he proved that he could at least hold his own with the stride players.

In 1928 and 1929, Morton recorded several piano solos and a new version of the Red Hot Peppers, who had been working with him at a dance hall in Harlem called Rose Danceland. Although he was able to find work over the years playing at ballrooms and college dances in the area, Morton's engagements became fewer and fewer. Due to poor record sales and the economic effects of the Depression, he was dropped by the Victor recording label in 1930. He now spent much of his time standing outside the Rhythm Club in Harlem, arguing with and preaching to musicians about organizing, protecting their rights, the shortcomings of other musicians, and of course his own greatness.

The main targets of Morton's verbal assaults were organizations like ASCAP, Melrose Publishing, MCA booking agency, and the musicians' union, which he felt were either stealing from him or preventing him from collecting the royalties that were rightfully due to him as a composer and a recording artist. He believed that a concerted effort by these agencies and a voodoo curse placed on him were the causes of his declining career and his other misfortunes. Some of Morton's beliefs were not completely without merit. The Melrose brothers had been cheating him out of royalties for years; he had also been denied membership in ASCAP for several years because of its racist practices, so that had had received no payment for other people's performances of his songs. Although his own piano and band style was considered old fashioned, several of his compositions, such as "Wolverine Blues," "Milenburg Joys," and especially "King Porter Stomp" (in versions for big bands) had become hits for Benny Goodman, Fletcher Henderson, and others, and they were constantly being recorded and played on radio across America.

Much has been made of the fact that, although Morton and Duke Ellington (as the first and second great jazz composers) had some similar artistic and conceptual ideas, there was a long-standing and sometimes viciously outspoken bitterness between them. In interviews, Ellington belittled Morton as a pianist and composer. Morton, for his part, called Ellington a fake and a thief whose acclaimed "jungle style" had been stolen from Morton's earlier recordings. Actually, Ellington's style of the late 1920s and early 1930s showed considerable influence from New Orleans jazz, and it is unimaginable that he would have been unaffected by the greatest composer in that tradition, Morton. Morton's "Jungle Blues" (1927)–which has the same title as a different tune written by Ellington in 1929—does have the dark "primitive" minor mood, bluesy effects, and general feeling of Ellington's later work. And several of Ellington's recordings of the period have melodic devices, breaks, and attention to sound, mood, and form that were introduced by Morton. Ellington's recording of "Dicty Glide" (1929) has very similar elements as those in Morton's classic version of "The Pearls" (1927): a steady staccato bass line, melodic and rhythmic saxophone solo quotations, and Ellington's brief phrase in Morton's style that opens his piano solo.

Feeling jinxed and overpowered, unable to succeed in New York, and fed up with the music business, Morton moved to Washington, D.C., in 1935. He ended up serving as entertainment, bartender, bouncer, and barrel opener in a small dive called the Jungle Inn. Though his customary fancy clothes, big car, and front tooth diamond helped to keep up appearances, the proud Morton was broke and slipping deeper into obscurity. With the help of a friend and business associate, Roy Carew, Morton started a publishing company and began a vigorous campaign to reestablish his career and collect royalties from the Melrose brothers and ASCAP. He sent letters seeking justice everywhere, even to the U.S. Supreme Court and the White House.

In 1938 Morton created a stir in the jazz world when *Down Beat* magazine published a letter he wrote in which he affirmed his claim to having invented jazz and also called the respected "father of the blues," W. C. Handy, a fraud and an imposter. He may have done this to get attention, but, if so, the plan backfired: he was now being perceived by some people as laughable or even crazy, a jealous egomaniac who blamed others for his own failure. Morton's attempt to be heard did have one positive result, however: Alan

Lomax taped a series of interviews with him for the Library of Congress that same year. The many hours of Morton talking, playing, and singing make up one of the most detailed and important oral histories in American music.

These sessions eventually led to the publication of Morton's biography, *Mr. Jelly Roll* (1949). Morton provides descriptions, names, dates, places, and musical examples as they relate to the early history of jazz in New Orleans. He demonstrates examples of influential musical genres and shows how he transformed them into his own personal style of jazz. He becomes the first major early jazz figure to give insight into the unwritten rules and principles of melody, harmony, rhythm, effects, instrumentation, and color, as they relate to different styles.

After recording several piano solos for small labels, Morton moved back to New York in 1939 with high expectations of reviving his career. He recorded several fresh-sounding piano solos and band sides for the Bluebird label. The band recordings are of standard New Orleans material, done in a much looser and less arranged form than the material of the Red Hot Peppers. These sessions feature several prominent New Orleans musicians, including Sidney Bechet and Albert Nicholas. In 1940 Morton made his last recordings, introducing his popular ballad "Sweet Substitute." He spent his last months in New York playing in clubs and trying to sue his former publishers for not paying his royalties. When ASCAP finally granted Morton membership, it was in the lowest category, which yielded insultingly low payments. His last national exposure came when he performed two songs in a show on NBC radio.

In the winter of 1940, the broke and ailing Morton drove across the country to Los Angeles to handle family business and to try to restart his career there. As he grew weaker (from heart failure), Morton rehearsed a big band in music that he had written shortly before leaving New York. Morton's last compositions included several revolutionary pieces containing advanced harmonic ideas. He had hoped that his new music and band would rival the leading swing orchestras of the day, like Count Basie's and Duke Ellington's. Jelly Roll Morton died in July 1941 without having a chance to perform or record his new material.

Given the range and scope of Morton's recordings (nearly 200 songs), compositions (more than 100 songs), and arrangements, he was one of the greatest creative forces in jazz. He invented his own virtuoso solo piano style. He was among the first to conceive of jazz compositions in terms of written arrangements, and he published written music long before jazz recording began. Morton was also among the first to announce the new New Orleans sound and spread it across America. Through his experimentation with melodic and rhythmic variation, nuance, sound textures, effects, color, and moods, he expanded and inspired new possibilities in jazz composition and arranging.

Nearly fifty years after Morton's death, his music began to be revived and his life began to be reexamined. Both the music and the life were presented in numerous ways: in theater, documentaries, tribute concerts, books, radio shows, and endless record reissues. While much of the attention has focused on his contribution to jazz, some of it has had to do with the more sensational aspects of his life: in particular, there has been a popular but distorted analysis of Morton, a light-skinned Creole, as a self-loathing man who despised his own race. This distortion may have developed because outsiders can rarely understand the eccentric character terms, views, and humor of the black Creole culture of New Orleans. In Morton's case, his actions spoke louder than his words. He spent his entire life working in the context of a black folk tradition, surrounded by black musicians whom he considered the

greatest performers of jazz. He spoke out against injustices to blacks (including himself) that came from a racist entertainment industry. Moreover, Morton did not pass himself off as being of another race (although his appearance would have allowed this) even when he was living in California, where it was a common practice for insecure New Orleans Creoles to "become Hispanic." Musicians who were close to Morton have said that he did not harbor any deep-seated hatred for other blacks; he merely expressed a "Crescent City version" of black signifying and self-humor that was, and remains, a common cultural characteristic.

Late in his life, Jelly Roll Morton predicted that he would gain his due recognition and make an impressive return, and eventually he proved to be right.

Biography

The exact birth date of Jelly Roll Morton (Ferdinand Joseph La Menthe, or Lamothe) remains unclear; it is often cited as either 20 September 1885 or 20 October 1890. He came from a Creole family in New Orleans, Louisiana. He briefly had formal piano instruction; also learned from blues pianists and ragtime piano "professors" in Storyville, the red-light district in New Orleans; and was soon performing as a soloist there. He then became a traveling vaudevillian and pianist and adopted the name Jelly Roll; began writing down his compositions c. 1914; was a bandleader in Chicago, 1914–1917; moved to Los Angeles in 1917 and back to Chicago in 1923; composed, performed, and made recordings in Chicago; moved to New York in 1928 but had difficulties there; moved to Washington, D.C., in 1935; made taped interviews for the Library of Congress in 1938; moved back to New York in 1939; made his last recordings in 1940 and moved back to Los Angeles. Morton died 10 July 1941 in Los Angeles, California.

MICHAEL WHITE

See also Armstrong, Louis; Bechet, Sidney; Blues; Ellington, Duke; Handy, W. C.; Jazz; Johnson, James P.; Music; Oliver, Joseph "King"; Smith, Willie "the Lion"; Waller, Thomas "Fats"

Selected Compositions

"Black Bottom Stomp"
"The Crave"
"Dead Man Blues"

Jelly Roll Morton. (Brown Brothers.)

"Fingerbreaker"
"Freakish"
"Frog-I-More Rag"
"Georgia Swing"
"Jelly Roll Blues"
"Jungle Blues"
"King Porter Stomp"
"Milenburg Joys"
"Mr. Jelly Lord"
"New Orleans Blues"
"The Pearls"
"Shreveport Stomp"
"Sidewalk Blues"
"Sweet Substitute"
"Tom Cat Blues"
"Wild Man Blues"
"Winin' Boy Blues"
"Wolverine Blues"

Recordings

Ferd "Jelly Roll" Morton. Retrieval 79002. (Piano solos, 1923–1926.)

Jelly Roll Morton Centennial: His Complete Victor Recordings, 1926–1939. Bluebird 2361.

Jelly Roll Morton: Last Sessions, 1939–1940. GRP/Commodore 403.

Jelly Roll Morton's Library of Congress Recordings of 1938. Rounder 1091, 1092, 1093 and 1094. (4 CDs, various titles.)

Further Reading

Balliet, Whitney. *Jelly Roll, Jabbo, and Fats.* New York: Oxford University Press, 1984.

Depogny, James, ed. *Ferdinand "Jelly Roll" Morton: The Collected Piano Music.* Washington, D.C.: Smithsonian Institution Press, 1982. (Sheet music for solo piano.)

Jasen, David A., and Gene Jones. *Black Bottom Stomp: Eight Masters of Ragtime and Early Jazz.* New York: Routledge, 2002.

Kennedy, Rick. *Jelly Roll, Bix, and Hoagy.* Bloomington: Indiana University Press, 1994.

Levin, Floyd. *Classic Jazz.* Berkeley: University of California Press, 2000.

Lomax, Alan. *Mr. Jelly Roll.* Berkeley: University of California Press, 2001. (Originally published 1949.)

Pastras, Phil. *Dead Man Blues: Jelly Roll Morton Way Out West.* Berkeley: University of California Press, 2001.

Reich, Howard, and William Gaines. *Jelly's Blues.* New York: Oxford University Press, 1968.

Russell, William. *Oh, Mister Jelly: A Jelly Roll Morton Scrapbook.* Copenhagen: JazzMedia APS, 1999.

Williams, Martin. *Jelly Roll Morton.* New York: Barnes, 1963.

———. *Jazz Masters of New Orleans.* New York: Da Capo, 1979.

Wright, Laurie. *Mr. Jelly Lord.* Chigwell, Essex, UK: Storyville, 1980.

Motley, Archibald J. Jr.

The painter Archibald J. Motley Jr. of Chicago consciously dedicated himself to depicting African Americans. Through his portraiture and genre scenes, Motley created a visual legacy that extended the issue of representation beyond the boundaries of New York's Harlem. Optimistically, he believed that art could end racial prejudice by dispelling negative stereotypes, a sentiment espoused by both W. E. B. Du Bois and Alain Locke. Motley's striking paintings of stylish urban African Americans correspond to the image and concept of the "New Negro." During his academic training at the School of the Art Institute of Chicago from 1914 to 1918, Motley synthesized a variety of approaches to the composition, color, and meaning of art. He believed that each element of a painting should be carefully considered for both its significance and its aesthetic contribution to the overall composition.

After graduation, Motley began to exhibit works in Chicago, winning prestigious prizes and critical acclaim. In 1919 the *Chicago Defender* published his article "The Negro in Art," in which he urged other black artists to paint African American subjects and to uphold academic principles, avoiding modernist expressionism. His own *Mending Socks* (1924), a portrait of his paternal grandmother Emily, shows his skill at rendering the texture of objects realistically, as well as his ability to capture a sitter's likeness. Each object that the artist included in this work was selected for its aesthetic and iconographic meaning. For example, the portrait of Emily Motley's former mistress, shown on the wall in the upper left of the painting, adds visual balance to the composition yet is also an unsettling reminder of slavery. This painting was voted the most popular work when it was exhibited at the Newark Museum in 1927; its sentimentality reflects the artist's commitment to portraying both the appearance and the character of his subjects.

Motley's success led to his first solo exhibition at the New Gallery in New York City in 1928. Because of the commercial success of works that exoticized black culture, the dealer of the New Gallery requested that the artist expand his repertoire to include depictions of "voodoo" and African cultures. After doing research on his assigned subject in sources such as *National Geographic* and *Asia: The Magazine of the Orient*, Motley created a series of five paintings reflecting the biases and misunderstandings that were perpetuated in these magazines. Although Alain Locke had urged African American artists to reestablish a connection with African cultures by adopting the geometric forms of African sculpture, Motley maintained a critical distance by depicting Africa as mirage from the past, complete with demons, dinosaurs, and giant apes. Reviewing Motley's exhibition, a critic for the *New York Times Magazine* (Jewell 1928)—who was evidently racially prejudiced—rhapsodized over the "jungle works," largely ignoring the portraits and urban scenes and claiming that Motley's creative urge was linked to superstitions and mysteries rather than to ambition and skill. Some other critics reacted similarly, conflating the artist's imagery and his racial identity. For example, a reviewer for the *Chicago Daily News* (Williams 1928) concluded that although the African images were derived from the artist's research, "there was something innate" in his "makeup that made him sense and express the mystery that hovers over such themes." Not all the reviewers acclaimed the series; one of them (Mannes 1928) described the paintings as "the cheapest most blatant ten-twent-thirt illustrations." Another (M.P. 1928) described such works as the "imaginings of boy's Voodooland," but praised the portraits that compared favorably "with the best output of the Academy." Nearly every painting in the exhibition was sold, including a portrait sold to John E. Nail, a real estate magnate in Harlem.

Also in 1928, Motley won a gold medal for the fine arts from the Harmon Foundation for his portrait *Octoroon Girl* (1925). As the antiquated title indicates, this work depicts a woman of mixed race: an octoroon was supposedly one-eighth African American and seven-eighths Caucasian. During Motley's time, the validity of determining racial identity through biological characteristics was hotly debated, as anthropologists such as Franz Boas argued that race was in fact a social construction. The artist's position on this issue remains ambiguous. Through what he referred to as "scientific studies," he painted various "Negro types" such as the "octoroon," the "quadroon," the "mulatress," and "pure" African Americans, apparently equating external appearance with internal character. Yet he also called into question the reliability of such methods of classification and the social consequences. Motley stated that their different skin tones and facial features made African American subjects far more attractive and interesting to paint than European-Americans. Through his interest in documenting these differences in portraiture, he refuted the concept of a uniform blackness and provided a "visual rebuttal" to the negative stereotype of African American that was common in popular culture during this period (Patton 1998, 123). But although Motley was aware of the pressure to produce "positive images," he rejected the demand for art as propaganda, repeatedly stating that he intended to depict African Americans "honestly," including the humor and pathos of black life. In genre scenes of the street life of Chicago's "Bronzeville," with its cabarets and pool halls, he frequently exaggerated spatial perspective, color, and the posture and physiognomy of his figures. Because visual art has a strong and enduring impact, and because it could presumably have a harmful effect on people's perception of African Americans, race leaders such as Locke criticized Motley's works as "lurid" and "grotesque" (1936, 69). Other viewers disagreed, though, appreciating the provocative, satirical nature of these scenes.

Despite his criticism, Locke supported Motley's successful application for a Guggenheim fellowship. This fellowship allowed Motley to travel to Paris in 1929. During his year abroad, Motley studied the works of old masters in the Louvre and painted several portraits, street scenes, and cabarets. His most famous work from this period is *Blues* (1929), a close-up view of dancers and musicians in a Parisian club that seems to suggest the syncopation of jazz through the artist's use of alternating forms.

Returning to Chicago in 1930, Motley continued to paint and exhibit his works both locally and nationally. In 1935 he was invited to be a visiting artist at Howard University, where he taught art classes. He also won a commission from the United States Treasury Relief Project for a mural at the post office in Wood River, Illinois. From 1935 to 1940, Motley joined other artists in Chicago who were employed by the Illinois Art Project, a division of the Federal Arts Project of the Works Progress Administration (WPA), which provided employment for artists during the

Archibald J. Motley Jr. (1891–1981), *The Jazz Singers*, c. 1934; oil on canvas, 32 1/8 by 42 1/4 inches. (Provenance: WPA, 1934. Permanent collection, Western Illinois University Art Gallery, Macomb, Illinois. Courtesy Western Illinois University Art Gallery.)

Depression. He created murals and easel paintings, adapting his style to the didactic narratives favored by the WPA. Motley's commitment to promoting social and racial equality is especially apparent in his paintings from this period, such as *Playground (Recess)* of c.1940, which shows a diverse group of children playing together. After the WPA was disbanded, Motley and many other artists had to find employment elsewhere. Resourcefully, Motley joined the graphic design crew of Styletone, a manufacturer of hand-painted shower curtains in Chicago. He also continued his artistic work, broadening his subject matter by traveling to Mexico in 1953. For several years afterward, Motley painted images inspired by the landscape and people of Guanajuato and Cuernevaca. During the 1960s and 1970s, he returned to depictions of African American life. Although his productivity slowed, he continued to paint until his death in 1981.

Motley's contribution to the Harlem Renaissance continues to be appreciated and investigated. Recent scholarship has focused on his concept of racial identity. His determination to expand the canon of American art to include images of African Americans by African Americans remains a relevant concern.

Biography

Archibald John Motley Jr. was born 7 October 1891 in New Orleans, Louisiana. In 1893 his family moved to Chicago, where he attended public schools in the Englewood district. He began studies at the School of the Art Institute of Chicago in 1914 and graduated in 1918. He worked at various odd jobs while submitting paintings to group exhibitions. His first solo exhibition was at the New Gallery in New York City. Motley studied in Paris while on a Guggenheim fellowship in 1929–1930; was a visiting instructor at Howard University in Washington, D.C., in 1935–1936; was employed by the Works Progress Administration Illinois Art Project intermittently from 1935 to 1940; was commissioned by the Treasury Department to paint a mural for the Wood River, Illinois, post office in 1937; taught art at South Side Community Art Center in Chicago in 1941; and painted for industrial design firms in Chicago (Styletone from 1948 to 1956 and Artistic during 1957). His awards included the School of the Art Institute of Chicago Joseph N. Eisendrath and Frank G. Logan prizes, 1925; Harmon Foundation Gold Medal, 1928; John Simon Guggenheim Fellowship, 1929–1930; recognition by President Jimmy Carter for his contribution to American art; and an honorary doctorate from the School of the Art Institute of Chicago, 1980. Motley died in Chicago on 16 January 1981.

AMY MOONEY

See also Artists; Chicago Defender; Federal Programs; Harmon Foundation; Locke, Alain; Nail, John E.; Works Progress Administration

Individual Exhibitions

1928: New Gallery, New York.
1933: Chicago (Illinois) Women's Club.
1957: Chicago Public Library.
1991: Chicago Historical Society.

Selected Group Exhibitions

1917: "Paintings by Negro Artists." Arts and Letters Society, Chicago.
1921: "Twenty-Fifth Annual Exhibition by Artists of Chicago and Vicinity." Art Institute of Chicago.
1927: "Painting and Watercolors by Living American Artists." Newark (New Jersey) Museum of Art.
1929: "Exhibit of the Fine Arts by American Negro Artists." Harmon Foundation and Commission on the Church and Race Relations, Federal Council of Churches. International House, New York.
1929: "Exhibition of Paintings and Sculpture by American Negro Artists." National Gallery of Art, Smithsonian Institution, Washington, D.C.

1930: "Udstilling af Amerikansk Kunst." American-Scandinavian Foundation, American Federation of Arts, and American Institute of Architects, Copenhagen, Denmark.

1988: "Three Masters: Eldzier Cortor, Hughie Lee-Smith, Archibald J. Motley, Jr." Kenkeleba Gallery, New York.

1989: "The Blues Aesthetic: Black Culture and Modernism." Washington (D.C.) Project for the Arts.

1990: "Against the Odds: African American Artists and the Harmon Foundation 1923–1943." Newark (New Jersey) Museum of Art.

2000: "Rhapsodies in Black: Art of the Harlem Renaissance." Hayward Gallery, London, England.

Further Reading

Bearden, Romare, and Harry Henderson. *A History of African American Artists from 1792 to the Present.* New York: Pantheon, 1993.

Bernard, Catherine. *Afro-American Artists in Paris: 1919–1939.* New York: Hunter College, 1989.

Greenhouse, Wendy. "An Early Portrait by Archibald J. Motley, Jr.," *American Art Journal,* 1 and 2, 1998.

Greenhouse, Wendy, and Jontyle Theresa Robinson. *The Art of Archibald J. Motley, Jr.* Chicago, Ill.: Chicago Historical Society, 1991.

Jacobson, Jacob Z., ed. *Art of Today: Chicago 1933.* Chicago, Ill.: L. Stein, 1933.

Jewell, Edward Alden. "A Negro Artist Plumbs the Negro Soul." *New York Times,* 25 March 1928.

Locke, Alain. *Negro Art: Past and Present.* Washington, D.C.: Associates in Negro Folk Education, 1936.

Mannes, Myra. "Gallery Notes." *Creative Art,* 2(4), April 1928.

Mooney, Amy M. "Representing Race: Disjunctures in the Work of Archibald J. Motley, Jr." *Museum Studies,* 24(2), 1999.

M.P. "The Art Galleries." *New Yorker,* 10 March 1928.

Patton, Sharon. *African American Art.* New York: Oxford University Press, 1998.

Powell, Richard. *The Blues Aesthetic: Black Culture and Modernism.* Washington, D.C.: Washington Project for the Arts, 1989.

———. *Black Art and Culture in the Twentieth Century.* London: Thames and Hudson, 1997.

Reynolds, Gary A., and Beryl J. Wright. *Against the Odds: African-American Artists and the Harmon Foundation, 1923–1943.* Newark, N.J.: Newark Museum of Art, 1990.

Robinson, Jontyle Theresa. "The Art of Archibald John Motley, Jr.: A Notable Anniversary for a Pioneer." In *Three Masters: Eldzier Cortor, Hughie Lee-Smith, Archibald John Motley, Jr.* New York: Kenkeleba Gallery, 1988.

Williams, Marguerite B. "Putting a Race in Pictures: Archibald Motley's Story." *Chicago Daily News,* 31 July 1929.

Woodall, Elaine. "Looking Backward: Archibald J. Motley and the Art Institute of Chicago." *Chicago History,* 8, Spring 1979.

Moton, Robert Russa

Robert Russa Moton, a child of slaves, was a distinguished American educator, an adviser to every president from Woodrow Wilson through Franklin D. Roosevelt, and a consistent advocate of interracial goodwill. His achievements are now largely unknown, however, because Moton, unlike some of the more vocal figures of the era, preferred to induce social, economic, and political change quietly.

Moton's education inspired him to help fellow African Americans. Following early tutoring from his mother, Moton attended a free school for blacks. In 1885 he enrolled in Hampton Institute, a school famous for its industrial offerings. At Hampton, Moton imbibed heavy doses of the "Hampton spirit," a call to lead and serve others. As a result, he abandoned plans to become a tradesman, preferring instead to pursue a teaching career. Once again, however, Moton's plans changed when he became Hampton's assistant commandant of cadets in 1890. In the following year, Moton assumed the post of commandant, which made him the highest-ranking African American administrator at Hampton. Moton's position also entailed a number of speaking and fund-raising engagements. Moton was often accompanied by Booker T. Washington, the founder of Tuskegee Institute and Hampton's most illustrious graduate; thus, Moton could observe Washington's poise and character firsthand. Besides helping Moton polish his skill at public relations, the tours enabled him to assess the nation's race relations and the plight of rural blacks.

In 1915, following Washington's death, Moton accepted the presidency of Tuskegee Institute, an African American institution modeled on Hampton's plan. Moton assumed this responsibility with a determination to transform Tuskegee into a world-class educational institution. When the nation prepared for war, Moton assisted the mobilization effort by transforming Tuskegee into a technical training school for 1,200 students. He also successfully lobbied for Emmett J. Scott's appointment as an assistant to Newton Baker, the secretary of war. After much wrangling, Moton also secured a training camp for African American officers at Fort Des Moines, Iowa. In addition, he traveled to France to oversee the treatment of African American troops. Moton's investigation and subsequent report silenced the "whispering gallery" by disproving charges that black troops were incompetent and unruly.

When the 1920s began, Moton became involved in the struggle for racial equality. In *Finding a Way Out* (1921), in *What the Negro Thinks* (1929), in newspaper articles, and in his public appearances, Moton regularly addressed the topic of deteriorating race relations in the United States. His comments were always frank and sincere. When a rash of violent race riots erupted just after the end of World War I, Moton helped organize the Council on Interracial Cooperation. He also implored Presidents Wilson and Harding to denounce lynching, mob action, and all other forms of racial injustice. To halt lynchings, Moton authorized Tuskegee's Department of Records and Research to issue annual reports on lynchings in the United States. The findings, combined with widespread editorial condemnation of the practice and the efforts of Ida B. Wells Barnett, substantially reduced the number of lynchings.

W. E. B. Du Bois, William Monroe Trotter (the fiery editor of the *Boston Guardian*), and James Weldon Johnson criticized Moton's strategy of compromise. They resented Moton's apparent willingness to placate rather than antagonize wealthy southerners. Some activists believed that Moton should have been more militant and aggressive in protesting racial injustice, especially in the South. Black intellectuals also feared that Moton's promotion of industrial and vocational training at the expense of academic studies threatened to confine African Americans to positions of perpetual servitude.

Although stung by the harsh criticism, Moton, a man of peace who believed in reason and the power of righteousness, remained committed to his strategy of strengthening black institutions at the local, state, and national levels. Although critical of segregation, Moton believed that African American institutions could enhance black people's participation in the civic life of their communities. He also felt that, as blacks gained enhanced strength through their institutions, they would be better prepared to secure the rights and privileges that other Americans enjoyed. Moton's support was especially evident in the business arena.

In 1924, he played a key role in establishing the National Negro Finance Corporation in Durham, North Carolina. Moton was also the director of the Dunbar National Bank following its establishment in Harlem in 1928, and he served as president of the National Negro Business League throughout the 1920s.

Moton's showdown with the Alabama Ku Klux Klan, however, demonstrated that he would, when necessary, challenge white authorities and confront any attempts to subordinate blacks. In 1923 Moton learned that government officials had selected Tuskegee as the site for a new hospital for black veterans. To his dismay, however, he was informed that, despite previous assurances from President Warren G. Harding to the contrary, the medical facility would be staffed by white physicians and nurses. Refusing to accept the decision, Moton lobbied state and federal officials to allow qualified black professionals to fill positions designed to care for African American veterans. Even death threats failed to dissuade him. At one point during the crisis, Moton informed a hostile crowd that he had always believed in interracial cooperation. If he was mistaken, he said, then perhaps it was best if they followed through with their threats and killed him. Moton's defiance eventually forced military leaders to examine the matter. The controversy subsided when General Frank T. Hines, director of the Veterans Bureau, recommended hiring qualified black nurses and physicians to staff the new veterans' hospital.

Moton, the recipient of the Harmon Award in 1930 and the Spingarn Medal in 1932, never wavered in his belief that people of goodwill, regardless of color, could secure justice and equal opportunity for all Americans. Although he was criticized during the Harlem Renaissance for being a "Washingtonian," Moton was not a timid devotee of gradualism. Throughout his life, he consistently condemned discrimination and the hatred it bred. He also believed that mutual understanding and cooperation would eventually solve the nation's racial, economic, civic, and political problems. Moreover, his efforts to disseminate Mahatma Gandhi's message of nonviolent protest had a powerful influence on future generations of African American activists.

Biography

Robert Russa Moton was born 26 August 1867 in Amelia County, Virginia. He studied at a public school in Prince Edward County, Virginia, and at Hampton

(Virginia) Normal and Agricultural Institute (teachers' course, 1890; postgraduate course, 1895). He was an assistant commandant of cadets at Hampton Institute in 1890–1891 and commandant of cadets from 1891 to 1915; and president of Tuskegee Institute in Alabama from 1916 to 1935. He was a trustee for several educational institutions, including the People's Village School, Mount Meigs, Alabama; Industrial Home School for Colored Girls, Peake, Virginia; Negro Reform School for Boys, Hanover, Pennsylvania; and Fisk University, Nashville, Tennessee. Moton was also a member of the Executive Committee on Interracial Cooperation, 1918; director of the American Bible Society, 1921; chair of the Colored Advisory Commission for disaster relief after the Mississippi flood in 1927; and a member of President Herbert Hoover's National Advisory Commission on Education, 1930. He received honorary degrees from Virginia Union University, Wilberforce University, Oberlin College, Lincoln University, Williams College, Harvard University, and Howard University. His awards included the Harmon Award in Race Relations, 1930; and the Spingarn Medal, 1932. Moton died in Capahosic, Virginia, on 31 May 1940.

JON L. BRUDVIG

See also Antilynching Crusade; Barnett, Ida B. Wells; Du Bois, W. E. B.; National Negro Business League; Scott, Emmett Jay; Spingarn Medal; Trotter, William Monroe; Washington, Booker T.

Selected Works

"A Negro's Uphill Climb." 1907.
Racial Goodwill. 1916.
Finding a Way Out. 1921. (Reprint, 1969.)
The Negro of Today: Remarkable Growth of Fifty Years. 1921.
"The Status of the Negro in America." 1922.
"The Negro in the South." 1924.
What the Negro Thinks. 1929.

Further Reading

Anderson, Eric A., and Alfred A. Moss. *Dangerous Donations: Northern Philanthropy and Southern Black Education, 1902–1930.* Columbia: University of Missouri Press, 1999.

Anderson, James D. *The Education of Blacks in the South, 1860–1935.* Chapel Hill: University of North Carolina Press, 1988.

Daniel, Pete. "Black Power in the 1920s: The Case of Tuskegee Veterans Hospital." *Journal of Southern History,* 36, August 1970.

Eisenstadt, Peter, ed. *Black Conservatism: Essays in Intellectual and Political History.* New York: Garland, 1999.

Engs, Robert F. *Educating the Disenfranchised and Disinherited: Samuel Chapman Armstrong and Hampton Institute: 1839–1893.* Knoxville: University of Tennessee Press, 1999.

Hughes, William Hardin, and Frederick D. Patterson, eds. *Robert Russa Moton of Hampton and Tuskegee.* Chapel Hill: University of North Carolina Press, 1956.

Myrdal, Gunnar. *An American Dilemma: The Negro Problem and Modern Democracy,* 2 vols. New York: Harper and Row, 1944. (See also Twentieth Anniversary ed., New York: Harper and Row, 1962.)

Mulatto

Langston Hughes's play *Mulatto* opened at the Vanderbilt Theater in New York on 24 October 1935. The production ran for 373 consecutive performances, becoming the longest-running Broadway play by a black writer until Lorraine Hansberry's *A Raisin in the Sun* broke that record in 1959. *Mulatto,* which is based on Hughes' short story "Father and Son," was written in 1930 and was later made into an opera—*The Barrier* (1950)—by the composer Jan Meyerowitz. *Mulatto*'s commercial success on Broadway and during its subsequent tour is notable, for it exposed to a racially mixed audience the issues surrounding miscegenation, a recurrent theme in the literature of the Harlem Renaissance.

Set on a plantation in Georgia, *Mulatto,* like Hughes's poem "Cross" (1931), presented the plight of a young man in conflict with his biracial identity. Eighteen-year-old Robert "Bert" Lewis is the son of Colonel Thomas Norwood, a white plantation owner, and Norwood's black housekeeper and mistress, Cora. Bert returns home after being away at school and is no longer willing to stay in his place (walk through the back door, speak politely to whites, or labor in the fields) as determined by the racial and social codes of conduct in the South. Bert feels entitled to equal treatment and the same privileges as whites. When Norwood tells Bert to leave the state before the townspeople come after him for his public impudence, Bert strangles his father. At the end of the play, Cora wants to hide her son from the lynch mob, but Bert commits suicide before the townsmen can reach him.

Mulatto, scene from the stage production with J. Kirkwood and M. Gilbert. (Billy Rose Theatre Collection, New York Public Library, New York City. © The New York Public Library/Art Resource, N.Y. Photo: White Studio, anonymous.)

The significance of *Mulatto* to the Harlem Renaissance derived from its subject matter and its performance history. It was a very early—if not the first—Broadway drama in which the classic conflict between father and son had a racial dimension. Moreover, Cora, a character that Hughes had created particularly for the actress Rose McClendon, gained more depth as the play progressed; at its conclusion, she scorns her relationship with Norwood and withstands a slap across the face from the overseer. Thus, depending on one's interpretation, Hughes presented two black characters, Bert and Cora, who challenged social codes in order to control their own lives. Martin Jones, the producer of the Broadway production in 1935, however, changed certain passages of the script and added a rape scene without Hughes's knowledge or consent. The changes may have increased box-office sales, but they may have also perpetuated a stereotype of blacks as violent and sexually promiscuous—an image that the playwrights of the Harlem Renaissance sought to dispel.

Mulatto received mixed reviews; the reaction of critics and audience members ranged from disgust to enthusiasm, and the sensationalism of the altered script caused some people to disregard its political implications. Hughes wrote mostly comedies and musicals for the stage, but this serious drama set off considerable controversy in its attempt to critique the racial caste system of the South. *Mulatto* brought Hughes recognition as a playwright and brought issues of race and class to the forefront of the American stage during a period when Broadway did not usually produce plays by blacks or hire blacks as actors.

MELINDA D. WILSON

See also Hughes, Langston; McClendon, Rose

Further Reading

Barksdale, Richard K. "Miscegenation on Broadway: Hughes's *Mulatto* and Edward Sheldon's *The Nigger*." In *Critical Essays on Langston Hughes*, ed. Edward J. Mullen. Boston, Mass.: G. K. Hall, 1986.

Bienvenu, Germain. "Intracaste Prejudice in Langston Hughes's *Mulatto*." *African American Review*, 26(2), 1992, pp. 341–353.

Hatch, James V., and Ted Shine, eds. *Black Theatre U.S.A.: Plays by African Americans, 1847 to Today*, rev. and expanded ed. New York: Free Press, 1996. (Originally published 1974.)

Plum, Jay. "Accounting for the Audience in Historical Reconstruction: Martin Jones's Production of Langston Hughes's *Mulatto*." *Theatre Survey*, 36, 1995, pp. 5–19.

Sanders, Leslie Catherine, ed. *The Plays to 1942: Mulatto to the Sun Do Move*. Vol. 5 of *The Collected Works of Langston Hughes*. Columbia: University of Missouri Press, 2002.

Turner, Darwin. "Langston Hughes as Playwright." In *The Theatre of Black Americans: A Collection of Critical Essays*, ed. Errol Hill. New York: Applause, 1987, pp. 136–147. (Originally published 1980.)

Murphy, Carl J.

One of the most important figures in African American history was Carl J. Murphy (1889–1967), the gifted and charismatic publisher-editor of the Baltimore *Afro-American* from 1922 to 1967. He was one of the nine children of John H. Murphy, the owner of the *Afro-American*. Carl Murphy was a newsboy for the paper but then went to college rather than work his way up through its ranks. He attended Howard University, where he majored in German; he then received a fellowship to Harvard University. Such a fellowship was an honor rarely bestowed on blacks in the early 1900s; in fact, Murphy was one of only two blacks in Harvard's graduate school. He graduated from Harvard in 1913 with an M.A. in German. In 1914 he studied at Jena University in Germany. He was caught in Germany by the outbreak of World War I but returned home in October 1914.

Murphy next became an instructor in German at Howard University. During World War I, he volunteered for the Colored Officers' Training Camp at Fort Des Moines, Iowa, but was determined to be too short (at 5 feet 1 inch) and was rejected. In 1918 Murphy gave up his position at Howard to become the editor of the *Afro-American*. Carl Murphy impressed his family with his editorial and managerial skills, and his brothers chose him to publish the newspaper after their father's death in 1922.

Murphy's academic and scholarly background manifested itself in the extremely high quality of editorials—mostly written by him—that ran in the *Afro-American*, and in the depth and breadth of its columnists and reporters. As a result, the *Afro-American* became one of the most highly regarded newspapers on the east coast. Among the renowned figures whom Murphy hired to write for the *Afro-American* were Countee Cullen, Charles H. Houston, Langston Hughes, James Weldon Johnson, Claude McKay, Kelly Miller, J. Saunders Redding, Walter White, William Worthy, and the legendary sportswriter Sam Lacy, who, as the paper's sports editor in the 1940s and 1950s, was instrumental in the desegregation of professional athletics.

Throughout the 1920s, 1930s, and 1940s, Murphy encouraged the *Afro-American* crusade for racial justice and advancement locally, statewide, and nationally. Among the causes Murphy led were equal pay for black teachers in Baltimore, an increase in black membership on the Baltimore city council, and black representation on the local school board and in the police department. Nationwide, the *Afro-American* supported antilynching legislation; it also supported increased federal patronage for black Republicans. With regard to national politics, however, the newspaper was a maverick. Murphy was very progressive for his time and was attracted to leftist views and politicians. Unlike his peers in the black press, he went out on a limb politically. For example, in 1924 he endorsed the

third-party candidate, Robert La Follette, for the presidency. In 1928 he had the *Afro-American* support the Democratic Party's candidate, Alfred E. Smith. Then in the 1930s the newspaper gave covert endorsements to candidates of the Communist and Socialist parties for local, state, and national offices.

Unlike many of its competitors among the black press, the *Afro-American* expanded and prospered during the Great Depression. It established branch offices and editions in Washington, Philadelphia, Richmond, and Newark; by 1940, Murphy presided over a newspaper chain that stretched all along the East Coast. The *Afro-American* sent six reporters overseas to cover World War II, more than any other black newspaper and more than quite a few white newspapers. Consequently, the circulation, income, and influence of the *Afro-American* reached unprecedented highs during these years. The *Afro-American* became a million-dollar company in 1945 and remained at that level for many years afterward.

Murphy was a not only a great journalist but also a great civic leader. In the 1930s, he encouraged and helped finance a case, *Murray v. Maryland*, that opened the University of Maryland Law School to blacks. Murphy was a member of the national board of directors of the National Association for the Advancement of Colored People (NAACP), and in 1935 he was midwife at the rebirth of its moribund Baltimore branch. In the process he launched the career of Lillie B. Jackson, perhaps the most important civil rights leader in Baltimore and one of the most influential in the nation.

Murphy played a vital role in the creation of Morgan State College (later Morgan State University). When Maryland bought this institution from the Methodist Church in 1939, Murphy became a member of its board of regents and then chairman. In that capacity, Murphy used the *Afro-American* and his own influence to ensure that Morgan received an equitable share of state funding. His interest in Morgan was rewarded, as the school's physical plant, faculty, and student services were greatly upgraded. To honor Murphy, Morgan's fine arts center is named for him.

In the 1950s, Carl Murphy's influence extended nationwide as the *Afro-American* supported NAACP's efforts to desegregate public education. For this, Murphy received the NAACP's Spingarn Medal in 1955. Under his still-vigorous leadership, the *Afro-American* crusaded locally and nationally for civil rights in the 1960s.

Little went on in black Baltimore and the nation that escaped Carl Murphy's editorial notice. A man of extremely high intellectual, moral, ethical, and spiritual standards, Murphy refused to tolerate racism anywhere he found it. Nor would he tolerate failure, or even mediocrity, in any endeavor undertaken by black folk. The *Afro-American* never hesitated to blast individuals, black and white, who did not act in the highest interests of black and white communities. Murphy's unwavering commitment to excellence is shown by the exponential growth of the *Afro-American* in the years he ran the newspaper, his promoting the rebirth and growth of the Baltimore NAACP, and his shepherding Morgan State College to prosperity and growth in the 1940s, 1950s, and 1960s.

Carl Murphy died in 1967, full of years, honors, and success. He left a prosperous and powerful newspaper that is still a meaningful voice for African Americans in Baltimore, in Washington, and elsewhere on the East Coast. Carl Murphy's passing left a void in Baltimore and the nation that has yet to be filled.

Biography

Carl J. Murphy was born in 1889, one of the nine children of John H. Murphy, owner of the Baltimore *Afro-American*. Carl Murphy was educated at Howard University, earned a graduate degree in German from Harvard University, and became a professor of German at Howard. He joined the *Afro-American* in 1918 and was chosen by his family to take it over in 1922 after his father's death. He established branch offices and editions, and by 1940 presided a chain of newspapers that extended throughout the East Coast. Murphy died in 1967.

HAYWARD "WOODY" FARRAR

See also Baltimore Afro-American; Black Press; Civil Rights and Law; Cullen, Countee; Hughes, Langston; Johnson, James Weldon; Journalists; McKay, Claude; Miller, Kelly; Redding, Jay Saunders; White, Walter

Further Reading

Detweiler, Frederick G. *The Negro Press in the United States.* Chicago, Ill.: University of Chicago Press, 1922.

Farrar, Hayward. *The Baltimore Afro-American 1892–1950.* Westport, Conn.: Greenwood, 1998.

Ford, Nick A. *Best Short Stories by* [the Baltimore] *Afro-American Writers.* Baltimore, Md.: Afro-American, 1950.

Huggins, Nathan Irvin. *Harlem Renaissance.* New York: Oxford University Press, 1971.

Pride, Armistead. *A History of the Black Press.* Washington, D.C.: Howard University Press, 1997.

Suggs, H. Lewis, ed. *The Black Press in the South, 1865–1979.* Westport, Conn.: Greenwood, 1983.

Vincent, Theodore G. *Voices of a Black Nation: Political Journalism in the Harlem Renaissance.* Trenton, N.J.: Africa World, 1973.

Wolseley, Roland E. *The Black Press U.S.A.* Ames: Iowa State University Press, 1971.

Muse, Clarence

Clarence Muse acted for more than sixty years and appeared in more than fifty movies. During the early years of the Harlem Renaissance, he acted on the stage in the South and in the East. In the 1920s, he lived in New York City and was a member of the Lincoln Players. He was also a founder and member of New York's Lafayette Players. Muse moved to Chicago for a while, and then moved to Hollywood after performing in *Hearts in Dixie* (1929), the first all-black movie. For the next fifty years, he worked regularly in minor and major film roles.

Perhaps there will always be controversy about Muse's legacy, because we are still dealing with the issues he wrote about in his pamphlet "The Dilemma of the Negro Actor" (1932). Many early black actors were offered roles that required them to be dutiful servants, thankful menial laborers, buffoons, and happy darkies. If black actors wanted to work, they had, initially, no option other than these types of roles. Muse was a contemporary of Stepin Fetchit but was a different kind of actor, even though his early roles were similar in type to those Fetchit made famous. Many critics have indicated that Muse's talents, range, and capability were, unfortunately, hardly tapped.

Even though Muse was featured in some roles that some blacks found and still find degrading, many have noted that he did not play some of those roles with much enthusiasm, and he was not as involved in the stereotypical roles as he was in the roles that required more of his talent. One of his finer roles was Nigger Jim in *Huckleberry Finn* (1931). Not surprisingly, the roles he wrote for himself were usually better than the roles others assigned him. For example, his acting in *Broken Strings* (1940) is some of his best;

829

and it has been suggested that Muse's help with the script is the reason for his memorable performance.

When the National Association for the Advancement of Colored People (NAACP) and other groups complained about roles for black actors in the early 1940s, Muse at first wanted these groups to be quiet so that black actors could work, regardless of the roles. His point of view changed, however, when he was asked to work on the script of *Song of the South* (1946), but quit after his attempts to upgrade the roles of blacks were disregarded. Muse disliked the images of blacks in this movie, and spoke out against it.

The issues Muse discussed in his pamphlet about the dilemma of the Negro actor proved to be persistent. Is any representation better than none? Does it matter how black actors are portrayed on the screen? Robert Townsend's movie *Hollywood Shuffle* (1987) analyzed essentially the same questions that Muse had tackled more that fifty years earlier. In retrospect, it may be easy to call actors like Clarence Muse, Stepin Fetchit, and Hattie McDaniel Uncle Toms, mammies, minstrels, and coons, but they opened doors so that later black actors, like Canada Lee, could have roles that were more dramatic and multidimensional.

Biography

Clarence Muse was born 7 October 1889 in Baltimore, Maryland. He studied at Dickinson College, Carlisle, Pennsylvania (international law degree, 1911). He had a career in music and acting in the South; he was acting in New York City by the 1920s with the Lincoln Players and Lafayette Players; and he wrote the screenplay for *The Sport of Gods* (1921). Muse's first major film role was in *Hearts in Dixie* (1929), which had the first all-black screen cast. Muse worked in Hollywood for fifty years; he sang the title role in DuBose Heyward's *Porgy* (1929). He published a pamphlet, "The Dilemma of the Negro Actor" (1932); wrote the song "When It's Sleepy Time Down South," which was performed by Louis Armstrong; composed a black symphony, *Harlem Heab'n*; co-wrote a screenplay with Langston Hughes, *Way Down South* (1939); co-wrote, produced, and acted in *Broken Strings* (1940); was an executive member of the Hollywood Victory Committee during World War II; and was a member of Hollywood Writers Mobilization. He received an

honorary doctor of humanities degree from Bishop College, Dallas, Texas, in 1972. Muse died in Perris Valley, California, 13 October 1979.

Lou-Ann Crouther

See also Fetchit, Stepin; Film: Actors; Hearts in Dixie; Lafayette Players; Lee, Canada

Selected Works

Hearts in Dixie (1929), *Hallelujah* (1929), *A Royal Romance* (1930), *Rain or Shine* (1930), *Huckleberry Finn* (1931), *Dirigible* (1931), *Last Parade* (1931), *Secret Witness* (1931), *Woman from Monte Carlo* (1932), *Cabin in the Cotton* (1932), *Winner Take All* (1933), *Washington Merry-Go-Round* (1933), *From Hell to Heaven* (1933), *Broadway Bill* (1934), *The Count of Monte Cristo* (1934), *So Red the Rose* (1935), *Show Boat* (1936), *Follow Your Heart* (1936), *Spirit of Youth* (1937), *Way Down South* (1939), *Broken Strings* (1940), *Maryland* (1940), *Zanzibar* (1940), *Tales of Manhattan* (1934), *Shadow of a Doubt* (1943), *Heaven Can Wait* (1943), *Watch on the Rhine* (1943), *Two Smart People* (1946), *Joe Palooka in the Knockout* (1947), *An Act of Murder* (1948), *Riding High* (1950), *Porgy and Bess* (1959), *Buck and the Preacher* (1972), *Car Wash* (1976).

Further Reading

Bogle, Donald. *Blacks in American Films and Television: An Encyclopedia*. New York: Garland, 1988.

———. *Toms, Coons, Mulattoes, Mammies, and Bucks: An Interpretive History of Blacks in American Films*. New York: Continuum, 1973. (See also 3rd ed., 1994.)

Cripps, Thomas. *Slow Fade to Black: The Negro in American Film, 1900–1942*. New York: Oxford University Press, 1977.

———. *Making Movies Black: The Hollywood Message Movie from World War II to the Civil Rights Era*. New York: Oxford University Press, 1993.

Huggins, Nathan Irvin. *Harlem Renaissance*. New York: Oxford University Press, 1971.

Leab, Daniel. *From Sambo to Superspade: The Black Experience in Motion Pictures*. Boston, Mass.: Houghton Mifflin, 1975.

Mapp, Edward. *Blacks in American Films: Today and Yesterday*. Metuchen, N.J.: Scarecrow, 1972.

Null, Gary. *Black Hollywood: The Negro in Motion Pictures*. Secaucus, N.J.: Citadel, 1975.

Patterson, Lindsay, ed. *Black Films and Film-Makers: A Comprehensive Anthology from Stereotype to Superhero.* New York: Dodd, Mead, 1975.

Sampson, Henry T. *Blacks in Black and White: A Source Book on Black Films.* Metuchen, N.J.: Scarecrow, 1977. (See also 2nd ed., 1995.)

Music

The following discussion focuses on the people who were influential creators and performers of music. All achieved distinction and stretched the boundaries of their art, and most of them flourished during the 1920s. Each epitomized the "New Negro" as described by the leaders of the Harlem Renaissance and interpreted by later writers: the idea that African Americans would project a new image and a new sense of worth as a result of outstanding accomplishments.

These "new musicians" excelled as composers and performers of either ragtime, musical theater, jazz, and other popular styles, or of music in European classical forms and styles. Significantly, many of the European-oriented musicians incorporated in their work either quotations or suggestions of traditional songs, such as spirituals and blues, documenting and celebrating, rather than rejecting, their African American heritage.

Although not all the leaders of the Harlem Renaissance shared the same views as to the direction of black culture, they did usually agree that literature and the arts were to be used as a means of securing economic and cultural equality with the white population by bringing honor and glory to the Negro race. Equality would result from outstanding achievements in the arts. Most leaders of the Harlem Renaissance agreed that black Americans should honor their heritage while striving for higher cultural and artistic achievements. For example, a symphonic work by an African American would incorporate some aspect of black culture—perhaps a theme based on a Negro spiritual or a characteristic melody, rhythm, or cultural reference. Also, a vocal recital would include artistic arrangements of spirituals, in addition to western European art songs.

As this new music evolved, western European notation could not adequately reproduce the slides, tone bending, and other fluctuations of pitch and rhythm characteristic of traditional black music. Thus, some degree of melodic embellishment and improvisation and a strong rhythmic impulse became central to the performance of much new black music.

Black folk music is a product of the rural culture of the South, but the large number of black Americans who moved to northern cities during the early part of the twentieth century responded well to a merging of these rural folk traditions and urban, composed music. The minstrel song was a product of these merging traditions. Typically, it was lively, syncopated, and often humorous. But these songs were originally written by white Americans for white Americans, were sung by white Americans in blackface, and were a caricature of the Negro way of life, often portraying black Americans as comical and illiterate. Although this portrayal had little to do with the realities of black culture, the songs became an important part of American popular music.

Popular Music and Jazz

Jazz—like American society—is also a product of many influences. In some ways, it represents a merging of cultures and musical styles, yet in other ways it retains distinct ethnic characteristics. In the late nineteenth century and the early twentieth, Americans—both black and white—sang and danced to syncopated, "jazzy" music. Some roots of jazz were thus in the existing popular music of Americans of the North and the South and could be found in the melodies and rhythms of the songs and dance music of Tin Pan Alley, minstrel shows, vaudeville, blues and gospel traditions, syncopated orchestras, brass bands of New Orleans, and ragtime.

By the 1920s, the nation's flourishing economy benefited many places of entertainment. Harlem had become the center for nightclubs, floorshows, and other venues for hearing this new black music. Many white people wanted to go out at night to hear it and would go to "whites-only" clubs in Harlem, sometimes after attending classical concerts or theater in downtown or midtown Manhattan. This was the new syncopated music—created and performed by black Americans and listened to, danced to, and enjoyed throughout the 1920s, the jazz age. The following sections highlight major African American artists who contributed significantly to the advancement of American popular music and jazz during this decade.

Blues Songs

Blues songs originally were part of the folk tradition of African Americans, especially in the Deep South.

831

Antecedents of blues included work songs, field hollers, and sorrow songs—although blues songs existed long before they were called "blues" and long before they were put into twelve-bar choruses with identifiable, predictable chord progressions. Likewise, blues songs existed long before blues poetry was created in aab form. As folk music, it was sung by individuals who usually created the words, often as they were singing—sharing themes and experiences (such as problems concerning work or a relationship) with any listeners who might be near by.

In the early years of the twentieth century, blues songs were collected as folk songs; by the 1920s, however, blues poetry was being newly created and blues songs were being newly composed. They were arranged for singers with instruments—perhaps a single guitar, or perhaps a more elaborate instrumental ensemble. These songs were published, recorded, and disseminated, and many became popular parts of vaudeville and minstrel shows, nightclub floor shows, and musical theater productions. The careers of "blues singers" became firmly established.

W. C. (William Christopher) Handy (1873–1958) was the acknowledged "father of the blues." He was a composer, bandleader, music publisher, and the first person to popularize blues. In 1908, he and his partner, Harry Pace, established the Pace and Handy Music Company in Memphis, Tennessee. Handy came to Harlem from Memphis in 1918 and became part of the emerging Negro movement—the Harlem Renaissance. Like others, he saw it as an opportunity for personal success. He and Pace moved the music company to New York, but it was dissolved in 1921. Pace then established the Black Swan Phonograph Company, and Handy established—with his brothers—the Handy Brothers Music Company. Handy became active in publishing music by black songwriters and composers, and he organized concerts of black music, including one in Carnegie Hall in 1928. Through these efforts, he brought the music of many black songwriters and performers to the public's attention. The Handy family, as of this writing, still owns and operates the Handy Brothers Music Company in New York City.

Handy's first compositions—"Memphis Blues" (1912) and "Saint Louis Blues" (1914)—achieved widespread popularity. His style was to incorporate blues idioms in his songwriting, rather than quoting from preexisting folk-blues songs or spirituals. His autobiography, *Father of the Blues*, was published in 1941.

William Christopher Handy, photographed by Carl Van Vechten, 1941. (Library of Congress.)

The most popular of early-twentieth-century blues singers was Bessie Smith (1894–1937), the "empress of the blues." Smith was a successful vaudevillian, blues and jazz singer, and recording artist during the 1920s and early 1930s. The "classic" blues style that she brought into the jazz repertoire was intense, expressive, and very personal. Smith began touring professionally in 1912, and she made some 200 recordings from 1923 to 1933. She recorded regularly with such greats as Louis Armstrong, James P. Johnson, and members of Fletcher Henderson's band. She was the featured performer in the film *Saint Louis Blues* (1929). (For a detailed analysis of Bessie Smith's singing style, see Schuller 1968, 226–241.)

Other famous classic blues singers of the 1920s included Ma Rainey, Clara Smith, Mamie Smith, and Alberta Hunter.

Ragtime, Stride, and Musical Theater

Other composers and arrangers, such as Will Marion Cook and James Reese Europe, had introduced rag rhythms and bold harmonies in vaudeville and musical theater. By the 1920s, these innovations had become commonplace. Likewise, the blues style was becoming a significant part of mainstream popular music. Syncopated ragtime music and blues songs were increasingly incorporated into much of the popular music of Tin Pan Alley.

By the 1920s, American popular music was already heavily influenced by ragtime and stride—both solo piano styles. Two significant contributors to ragtime were Scott Joplin (who also contributed significantly to opera) and Eubie Blake (who also contributed significantly to musical theater).

Scott Joplin (1868–1917) died before the "official" start of the Harlem Renaissance, yet his contributions are compatible with its philosophy. Joplin grew up in Texarkana, became an itinerant musician, and by 1896 had settled in Sedalia, Missouri. By 1899, he had composed his first piano rag: "Maple Leaf Rag," ultimately one of his most popular compositions.

Joplin's rags are full of energy and vitality, highly syncopated, and immediately appealing. To the extent possible, Joplin insisted that they be played according to the written notes and not too fast. He considered his rags a serious art form—at a higher artistic level than rags played in vaudeville, in minstrel shows, on the streets of New Orleans, or on the showboats on the Mississippi River. He sought to bring care and skill to his compositions. He not only helped shape the "classic ragtime" style but also elevated the composing and performing of piano rags to the functional equivalent of piano miniatures by European classical composers of the nineteenth century.

John Stark, in Sedalia, became the primary publisher of Joplin's rags and dubbed Joplin the "king of ragtime writers." Joplin wanted to do more than compose and perform rags, however. He wanted to compose for theater as well, and in 1899 he produced *The Ragtime Dance*, a tableau for dancers and singer-narrator. His Scott Joplin Opera Company presented his ragtime opera, *A Guest of Honor*, in 1903. Both productions were notably unsuccessful.

By 1907, Joplin had moved to New York City, where he spent the final ten years of his life. In 1911, he published his first opera score, *Treemonisha*, but failed to get backers for a staged production. In 1915, he financed his own production at the Lincoln Theater in Harlem—a single performance without scenery, costumes, or orchestra. He did not live to see a full production of *Treemonisha*. In 1972, during the ragtime revival of the 1960s and 1970s, however, *Treemonisha* was given a full-scale production in Atlanta. Robert

Shaw was the conductor, Katherine Dunham was the choreographer, and T. J. Anderson prepared the orchestration. In 1975, the Houston Grand Opera also produced *Treemonisha*. Gunther Schuller prepared the orchestration—for Dixieland band with added winds and strings—and also conducted the orchestra.

Perhaps as a result of the ragtime revival and the renewed interest in his music, Scott Joplin was publicly recognized with a posthumous Pulitzer Prize in 1976 and a commemorative postage stamp in 1983. Compact discs of the Houston Grand Opera production of *Treemonisha* are readily available as of this writing—as are many of Joplin's rags that have been remastered from piano rolls. His complete works have been collected by Vera Brodsky Lawrence and published by the New York Public Library (1972, 1981).

Eubie Blake (1883–1983) achieved success as a ragtime pianist and composer, as a vaudeville performer, and especially as the composer of two musicals: *Shuffle Along* (1921), which ran on Broadway for 504 performances, and *The Chocolate Dandies* (1924). His collaborator on each was his vaudeville partner, Noble Sissle. Blake and Sissle incorporated into their musicals all the styles that were then extant in black folk and popular music: ragtime, minstrel songs, vaudeville, cakewalks and other dance music, and spirituals.

Blake's pianistic abilities also influenced the style of "Harlem stride piano," a term describing principally the piano styles of James P. Johnson and Fats Waller. Stride piano evolved from ragtime and ultimately changed the course of jazz piano style. Pianists such as Johnson and Waller often were hired to play at Harlem cabarets in Harlem, at house-rent parties, and at sophisticated events of the white social set. Listeners responded enthusiastically to the energy of stride piano, its improvisation, and what must have been perceived as highly technical piano wizardry. Stride was designed to entertain, even impress, the revelers; and the pianists accommodated the tastes of their patrons.

Clubs and Floor Shows: The Entertainers

Minstrel songs and shows were popular by the middle of the nineteenth century. By the beginning of the twentieth century, vaudeville became increasingly popular. But by the 1920s, the former patrons of vaudeville were switching their allegiance to movies and to floor shows in nightclubs and huge ballrooms, although some preferred the more seductive cabarets and intimate nightclubs and bars that had emerged in

Harlem. Many restaurant owners introduced dancing and floor shows. These new venues were more respectable—and safer—than the cellar clubs and "below the street" bars. Jazz, the new black music, became one of the ideal forms of music for these new "entertainment centers."

One of the most noted of the new venues was the Cotton Club. Like many of the clubs, it was "whites-only," although the patrons were served and entertained by blacks. This "safe" environment made it easier to attract white patrons to Harlem, people who generally lived in downtown or midtown New York. As noted earlier, they would often go to the opera or theater in midtown and afterward go uptown to Harlem to enjoy the black music and the black entertainers.

The careers of black musicians and dancers were often created or stimulated by their participation in these lavish floor shows. For example, Duke Ellington played at the Cotton Club from 1927 to 1932, and this engagement provided him with a large audience (including radio listeners) and an effective showcase for his big band arrangements and compositions. He and his music became well known.

Performers' careers were also enhanced by appearances in black musical theater on Broadway and elsewhere. Josephine Baker (1906–1979)—a singer, dancer, and entertainer—began her career as a thirteen-year-old in a touring black vaudeville troupe. In the early 1920s she joined the chorus line of Sissle and Blake's *Shuffle Along*, and she was featured in its sequel, *Chocolate Dandies*. After a stint in a New York nightclub revue, she became a comic dancer in the chorus line of *La Revue Nègre* in Paris. But the show was revised to take advantage of Baker's beautiful and exotic appearance. Her dancing was featured, but her feather costume was perhaps more memorable. This run lasted three months. After a twenty-five-country world tour in 1928–1929, Baker shifted from novelty dancing to singing love ballads and also became a leading actress in films. She learned the French language and starred in French films, including a remake of Offenbach's operetta *La Créole* (1934). She became a French citizen and remained professionally active (and politically active) nearly until her death.

Ethel Waters (1896–1977) was a singer of blues, jazz, and popular music and was prominent in the nightclub scene in Harlem during the 1920s and into the 1930s. Her style and technique anticipated and in fact influenced future jazz singers. Waters began recording in 1921, but she was not content just to record songs. She used her recordings to entice people to come to her live performances, where she used her theatrical flair to draw the audience to her. She was a blues singer—perhaps more of a song stylist—who sang blues in a more refined style than the original, folksy blues singers. Her performances and her recordings were aimed mostly at black audiences; later, though, she became a star on Broadway and in films. Waters began touring with the Billy Graham Crusades in 1960 and continued to do so until 1975; this was a considerable contrast to her previous career.

Syncopated Orchestras and Jazz Bands

The good jazz musicians in the first decades of the twentieth century were mobile, willing to go where the best employment was and, perhaps more important, where the best jazz musicians were. One example of this mobility was the response to a "call" from Charles S. Johnson and Alain Locke to come to Harlem and participate in what was to be the Harlem Renaissance. W. C. Handy came from Memphis; Eubie Blake from Baltimore; Duke Ellington from Washington, D.C.; and Fletcher Henderson from Atlanta. Musicians were also brought by the "lure [of] potential success in an exciting environment" (Floyd 1990, 2).

Most scholars assign the beginnings of jazz to New Orleans—a cosmopolitan city populated by white and black Americans and Creoles. One section of New Orleans, Storyville, was a district where black musicians could find employment—primarily in its clubs, bars, and brothels. In 1917, Storyville was closed down, drying up employment for jazz musicians. The musically able ones went to Chicago, New York, Los Angeles, Kansas City, St. Louis, or San Francisco; they included Jelly Roll Morton, Kid Ory, King Oliver, and Louis Armstrong.

Jazz is a merging of cultures and styles: ragtime, blues, syncopated dance music, and popular songs from minstrels and vaudeville. Essentially it evolved from the performance practices of African Americans: the moods and melodic fluctuations of their blues songs, the syncopated rhythms of their dance music, and the freedoms they took in the creative process—that is, their freedom to improvise. These are some of the characteristics that musicians brought from New Orleans to Harlem, to other parts of New York, and to other cities.

James Reese Europe (1881–1919) was born in Mobile, Alabama, to a musical family. The family moved to Washington, D.C., when Europe was ten. In 1903, at age twenty-two, he moved to New York and began playing piano in Harlem nightclubs. In 1910, Europe founded the Clef Club, an organization that was part social club and part booking agency. It provided musicians to entertain at society parties and dances but also organized performing groups within the club. One group was the Clef Club Orchestra, which had 125 members and included the usual instruments of the string family as well as mandolins and banjos. The orchestra played music by black composers. It first appeared in Carnegie Hall in 1912 and then again in 1913 and 1914. These performances gave the orchestra greater respectability in white society, which in turn resulted in more bookings for elite society functions.

At the start of World War I, Europe enlisted in the army, and his commander asked him to form a military band. This all-Negro band entertained troops and citizens everywhere it visited, and it was always received with great enthusiasm. It was not the typical military band. Members were highly creative in the way they played their instruments and the way they moved. The military band had, in fact, become to a large extent a jazz band.

Louis Armstrong (Satchmo, 1898–1971) became one of the most successful and popular jazz musicians in history. He honed his skills in New Orleans, then moved to Chicago in 1922 to play with King Oliver. In 1924, Armstrong moved to New York to join the Fletcher Henderson Orchestra; he then returned to Chicago, where he made perhaps his most important recordings during the late 1920s with his groups the Hot Five and the Hot Seven. Armstrong had a very successful and illustrious career as a popular entertainer, recording artist, and movie actor.

Armstrong's innovations were formed in New Orleans. They included creative embellishments and improvisations; a swing rhythm; a unique singing quality and style, including scat singing (singing in the manner of instrumental improvisation); and his own personality as a performer. This type of new "hot jazz," in New Orleans and later in Chicago, was typically performed with a small instrumental ensemble, perhaps three melody instruments (cornet or trumpet, clarinet, and trombone) and a rhythm section of string bass or tuba, piano and guitar or banjo, and drums.

Armstrong's impact altered the course of both popular music and jazz, contributing significantly to the development of African American musical styles as a dominant force in twentieth-century music.

Fletcher Henderson (1897–1952) began his professional career in New York as a song demonstrator

Louis Armstrong in *Every Day's a Holiday*, 1937. (AP/Wide World Photos.)

with the Pace-Handy Music Company. When Harry Pace founded his recording company and the Black Swan label, Henderson began putting together instrumental groups to back up the Pace singers. From this experience, he became a bandleader, organizing various groups for clubs and dances. He performed in Club Alabam and then the Roseland Ballroom, where he remained for a decade. These bands were dance bands, not jazz bands, and were little influenced by the new "hot jazz" coming out of New Orleans. But although most bands in northern urban areas were dance bands, meeting a widespread craving for social dancing, the new jazz was becoming popular.

In 1924, Henderson brought in Louis Armstrong from Chicago as the band's jazz specialist. Armstrong's hot swing and melodic invention influenced the musicians in Henderson's band and other musicians in New York, who began to copy Armstrong's solo style. Armstrong left Henderson within a year, but the seed had been sown. By 1926, Henderson's band played excellent jazz. Additionally, Henderson's arrangements—mostly of the work of Don Redman—became the basic pattern of big band arrangements for decades: reed, brass, and rhythm sections with each section alternately taking the lead and providing supportive riffs, always swinging.

Henderson eventually fell into financial difficulties and sold his best arrangements to Benny Goodman, thus initiating the popular swing bands of the 1930s.

Edward Kennedy (Duke) Ellington (1899–1974) was a jazz bandleader, pianist, arranger, and composer, and a leading figure in big band jazz from the 1920s until his death. As previously noted, he and his band played at the Cotton Club in Harlem from 1927 to 1932. His work earned him honorary doctorates, the Presidential Medal of Honor, and membership in the National Institutes of Arts and Letters. Numerous biographies, discographies, essays, and musical analyses fully document the contributions of this distinguished musician.

Classical Music

Most of the African American classical musicians were highly educated, having studied at the best music schools or privately with outstanding white European-trained musicians. African Americans who wanted to create music in classical forms and styles had to determine individually to what extent and in what ways they would adhere to "higher," cultivated classical forms and yet retain that which was basic to their black cultural heritage.

One point of view among leaders of the Harlem Renaissance was to keep folk and popular idioms out of classical concert music. However, most writers and musicians valued the concept of black nationalism, which implied incorporating traditional black melodic idioms and dance rhythms into classical music. Spirituals, for instance, were arranged in the style of art songs and were included as thematic material in symphonies, concertos, and symphonic poems. A composer might incorporate a spiritual without modifying it, but most composers would vary a spiritual to suit their own compositional style.

Composers

Harry T. Burleigh (1866–1949) was the first black American to achieve distinction as a classical composer and arranger; he was best-known for his arrangements of Negro spirituals. Burleigh studied at the National Conservatory of Music in New York, most notably with its director, Antonín Dvořák. Burleigh also became a choir member at Saint George's Episcopal Church, which had a prominent, wealthy, white congregation; he remained there for fifty-two years. In addition, he became a soloist at Temple Emanu-El, an affluent synagogue in New York, and remained there for twenty-five years. He was also a music editor for Ricordi Publishing for thirty-six years.

Burleigh composed or arranged 265 vocal works—mostly for solo voice and piano accompaniment—and 187 choral arrangements of black spiritual melodies. He died in 1949. At his funeral, his pallbearers included Eubie Blake, Noble Sissle, and W. C. Handy.

William Levi Dawson (1899–1990) was a composer, arranger, and choral conductor. He graduated from Tuskegee Institute and later returned there to direct the Tuskegee Choir for twenty-five years. In his symphonic music, he used folk song idioms. His best-known work, *Negro Folk Symphony*, is a four-movement composition based (as its title indicates) on Negro folk music but having the same symphonic form used by European composers who drew on the folk melodies and idioms of their own cultures. *Negro Folk Symphony* was given its world premiere in 1934 with Leopold Stokowski conducting the Philadelphia Orchestra.

Nathaniel Dett (1882–1943) was a composer, pianist, and conductor. His formal education included a bachelor of music degree from Oberlin Conservatory in 1908 (he was the first black American to receive this degree at Oberlin), and a master of music degree from the Eastman School of Music in 1932. In 1929, he studied with Nadia Boulanger in France. Dett was director of music at Hampton Institute from 1913 to 1931 and was also director of its choir.

Dett is now best known for his numerous arrangements of spirituals, although he also composed three extended works for chorus and orchestra; a widely performed choral piece, "Listen to the Lambs"; and eight suites for piano, of which *In the Bottoms* and *Magnolia Suite* are perhaps best known.

Florence Price (1888–1953) was the first black woman to achieve widespread recognition as a symphonic composer; she was also a teacher. Price graduated from the New England Conservatory of Music in 1906 with diplomas in organ and piano. Her prizewinning *Symphony in E Minor* was performed in 1933 by the Chicago Symphony Orchestra; this exposure led to further performances of her works in the United States and in Europe. Price achieved even more recognition when Marian Anderson sang her arrangement "My Soul's Been Anchored in de Lord" and her composition "Songs to the Dark Virgin." The latter was a setting of a text by Langston Hughes.

Price's compositional style would be considered conservative; she did not use the twentieth-century compositional techniques that were in vogue during the 1920s and the 1930s. Using western European forms, she did incorporate elements of her Negro heritage, however, though she did not quote actual Negro folk or spiritual melodies.

William Grant Still (1895–1978) is undoubtedly the best-known African American composer of classical music in the western European style. Among his most familiar works is Symphony No. 1, the *Afro-American Symphony*. Its was premiered in 1931 by the Rochester Philharmonic Orchestra, becoming the first symphony composed by a black American to be performed by a major symphony orchestra.

Still worked for Pace and Handy's music publishing company in Memphis and then in New York City. In 1921, he played oboe in the orchestra of Eubie Blake's *Shuffle Along* on Broadway and on tour. In 1923, he studied at the New England Conservatory in Boston and in New York City with Edgard Varèse. In the late 1920s, Still received grants and awards and created jazz arrangements for Artie Shaw. The première of his opera *A Bayou Legend* was broadcast on PBS in 1981.

Still's best-known works used Negro and other American folk idioms. Still, Burleigh, and Dett can probably be said to represent a culmination of at least one ideal of the Harlem Renaissance—to incorporate Negro folk materials into "higher" forms of western European art.

Performers

This ideal was also pursued by solo recitalists. Marian Anderson, Roland Hayes, and Paul Robeson were among the best singers to incorporate black music, particularly spirituals, into their recitals.

Marian Anderson (1897–1993) was a contralto who performed concerts worldwide, winning critical acclaim for her presentation of art songs, arias from operas and oratorios, and spirituals—usually in the same recitals. In 1925, Anderson won first prize in a competition sponsored by the New York Philharmonic, which enabled her to be featured as a soloist with that orchestra. She made her Carnegie Hall debut in 1928. By 1935, with the help of Sol Hurok (her manager for thirty years), Anderson became a world-class artist, touring across the United States and throughout Europe. She would return to Carnegie Hall more than 150 times. Later in her career, she became the first black singer to join the roster of the Metropolitan Opera, paving the way for many to follow.

Anderson received numerous honorary doctorates and awards, including the Presidential Medal of Freedom (1963), the United Nations Peace Prize (1977), a Congressional Gold Medal (1978), the first Eleanor Roosevelt Human Rights Award (1984), and a concert tribute at Carnegie Hall celebrating her seventy-fifth birthday. In 1991, she received a Grammy Award for Lifetime Achievement.

Roland Hayes (1887–1977), a tenor, attended Fisk University and then continued vocal studies in Boston, where he made his debut recital in 1917. He then toured throughout the United States. In 1920, he continued his studies in Europe, gave recitals, and appeared with major orchestras in London, Paris, Amsterdam, Berlin, and Vienna. He returned to the United States, making his Carnegie Hall debut in 1923.

Like Marian Anderson, Hayes shaped a career by presenting recitals of European classics and Negro spirituals—a career that, in his case, lasted for fifty years. At first he was not able to get professional management, so he scheduled his own concerts and tours, becoming well known in African American communities. He financed his own recitals in the major concert halls of Boston, then went to Europe for a series of concerts that included a performance for King George V and Queen Mary of Great Britain. Thereafter, when he returned to America, he now was able to get professional management: the manager of the Boston Symphony, William Brennan, who signed Hayes up for thirty concerts.

Paul Robeson (1898–1976) was a bass-baritone, a movie actor, and a political activist. He received a bachelor of arts degree from Rutgers University and a law degree (LLB) from Columbia University. He became well known for his singing of black spirituals and made his first national tour in 1926. This was followed by stage productions in England (*Show Boat* and *Othello*). His best-known films made in the mid-1930s were *The Emperor Jones* and *Show Boat*.

Robeson's activism was centered in his recognition of the cultural importance of the common people; accordingly, he learned the languages and folk songs of other cultures. He then took on working-class concerns and became a communist. As his political and cultural rhetoric intensified, his popularity as a singer decreased. He became depressed at the loss of contact with audiences and friends and was virtually isolated in the 1960s and 1970s; before then, however, he had received any number of honors and accolades.

DAVID WILLOUGHBY

Cotton Club; Harlem: 3—Entertainment; House-Rent Parties; Jazz; Minstrelsy; Music: Bands and Orchestras; Musical Theater; Musicians; Nightclubs; Roseland Ballroom; Saint Louis Blues; Shuffle Along; Singers; Spirituals; *specific individuals*

Recordings

Anderson, Marian. *Marian Anderson*. RCA 7911, 1990; BMG Classics, 1989. (1 CD. Music by Bach, Handel, Schubert, and Brahms; three spirituals.)

Armstrong, Louis. *The Hot Fives and Hot Sevens*. JSP Records. JSPCDLOUISBOX1 (JSPUSA.com/Products), 1999. (4 CDs.)

At the Jazz Band Ball: Early Hot Jazz, Song, and Dance, 1925–1933. Yazoo, 1993. (Videocassette. Performed by Louis Armstrong, Duke Ellington, Bessie Smith, and many others).

Burns, Ken. *Ken Burns Jazz Collection: Fletcher Henderson*. Legacy 061447, 2000. (1 CD.)

Dett, R. Nathaniel. *Magnolia Suite, In the Bottoms, and Eight Bible Vignettes*. New World Records 80367, 1992. (1 CD. Denver Oldham, piano.)

Joplin, Scott. *Elite Syncopations*. Sony, 2003; Biograph, 1987; Musical Heritage Society, 1989. (1 CD. Original recordings remastered.)

Price, Florence B. *Symphony No. 3*; *Mississippi River Suite*; and *The Oak*. Koch International Classics 7518, 2001. (1 CD.)

Price, Still, and Bonds. *Black Diamonds*. Cambria Records 1097, 1993. (1 CD. Althea Waites, piano.)

Rhapsodies in Black: Music and Words from the Harlem Renaissance. Rhino, 2000. (4 CDs and a 100-page booklet. Songs performed by Ma Rainey, Alberta Hunter, Bessie Smith, Ethel Waters, and Paul Robeson. Bands include Louis Armstrong, Fletcher Henderson, and Duke Ellington. Writers include Langston Hughes, Zora Neale Hurston, Claude McKay, Sterling Brown, W. E. B. Du Bois, and Arna Bontemps. Readers include modern actors and entertainers such as Quincy Jones, Lou Rawls, Gregory Hines, Ice-T, and LeVar Burton.)

Smith, Bessie. *The Essential Bessie Smith*. Sony Music Entertainment, 1997. (2 CDs.)

Smithsonian Collection of Classic Jazz, Vol. 1. New York: CBS Special Products, 1987. (1 CD of five. From rags of Scott Joplin to the blues of Bessie Smith to the shouts of James P. Johnson. Also includes performances by Jelly Roll Morton, Fats Waller, and Louis Armstrong.)

Still, William Grant. Symphony No. 1 (*Afro-American*)./ Duke Ellington. Suite from *The River*. Chandos 9154, 1993. (1 CD.)

Still, William Grant. Symphony No. 2 (*Song of a New Race*)./William Levi Dawson. *Negro Folk Symphony*./ Duke Ellington. *Harlem*. Chandos CHN 9226. (1 CD.)

Further Reading

Anderson, Paul Allen. *Deep River: Music and Memory in Harlem Renaissance Thought*. Durham, N.C.: Duke University Press, 2001.

Fabre, Geneviève, and Michael Feith, eds. *Temples for Tomorrow: Looking Back at the Harlem Renaissance*. Bloomington: Indiana University Press, 2001.

Floyd, Samuel A. *Black Music in the Harlem Renaissance: A Collection of Essays*. Knoxville: University of Tennessee Press, 1990.

Kramer, Victor A., and Robert A. Russ, eds. *Harlem Renaissance Re-Examined*. Troy, N.Y.: Whitston, 1997.

Krasner, David. *A Beautiful Pageant: African American Theatre, Drama, and Performance in the Harlem Renaissance, 1910–1927*. New York: Palgrave Macmillan, 2002.

Locke, Alain. *The Negro and His Music*. New York: Arno Press and New York Times. 1969. (Originally published 1936.)

Ogren, Kathy J. *The Jazz Revolution: Twenties America and the Meaning of Jazz*. New York: Oxford University Press, 1989.

Schuller, Gunther. *Early Jazz: Its Roots and Musical Development*. New York: Oxford University Press, 1968.

Southern, Eileen: *The Music of Black Americans: A History*, 3rd ed. New York: Norton, 1997.

Spencer, Jon Michael. *New Negroes and Their Music: The Success of the Harlem Renaissance*. Knoxville: University of Tennessee Press, 1997.

Tirro, Frank. *Jazz: A History*. New York: Norton, 1977.

Wall, Cheryl A. *Women of the Harlem Renaissance*. Bloomington. Indiana University Press, 1995.

Music: Bands and Orchestras

During the Harlem Renaissance, the very definition of bands and orchestras was altered. Previously, a band was considered an ensemble of wind and percussion instruments playing music for military functions, outdoor funerals, and park concerts; this term now also included small ensembles called "jazz bands." An orchestra had been defined as an ensemble of bowed string instruments and fewer wind and percussion instruments. The orchestra was intended to play the music of the western European composers in a concert setting and also to perform at social events for wealthy, aristocratic patrons. In New York City and particularly Harlem in the 1920s, the term "jazz orchestra" began to be used to designate an ensemble of eight to ten players of trumpets, trombones, saxophones-clarinets; and a rhythm section consisting of piano, banjo, string bass, tuba, and drums. Sometimes, in the "sweet orchestras," two or three violins would be used.

Another important innovation in Harlem and elsewhere in New York City was the establishment of specifically named ensembles, such as the Fletcher Henderson Orchestra and the Cotton Club Orchestra, in which the musicians might change nightly, depending on who was available. This practice was possible because in New York many talented musicians could play in many styles this practice differed significantly from that of traditional ensembles such as the King Oliver Band playing in Chicago, which would have the same musicians every night.

To understand this change in established bands and orchestras, it is useful to look at the social and economic situation of Harlem in the 1920s. During this period, black migration from the southeastern United States to New York—as well as discriminatory real estate policies—caused overcrowding and a housing shortage, and many blacks were forced to live in Harlem. Thus black musicians who worked in the Broadway theaters, society orchestras, or recording studios in downtown or midtown New York typically had to travel to work and return home to Harlem.

Band in a Box

One result of the overcrowding was an economic crisis: limited incomes and limited housing. A popular solution was the "rent party," a well-advertised event featuring food, alcohol, dancing, and music. The party would begin on a weekend afternoon and end the following morning. Music was provided by a "band in a box," the piano player. The three famous players most in demand were James P. Johnson, composer of "Carolina Stomp," the "cutting piece" used for stride piano contests; Thomas "Fats" Waller, called the "summation of the Harlem piano style"; and Willie "the Lion" Smith.

James Reese Europe and the Clef Club Orchestra

The first African American band signed to a recording contract was that of James Reese Europe, which was contracted in 1914 by Victor Records. By this time, Europe had established a booking agency called the Clef Club, which had more than 180 musicians listed who could play at many types of functions and venues. In the Clef Club orchestra, Reese created a unique sound by having the first violins accompanied by the second violin parts played by mandolins and banjos. This strumming effect was enhanced by ten pianos, two clarinets (no oboe), two baritone horns (no French horns), trombone (no bassoons), and saxophones; the musicians also sang as well as played their instruments.

James Reese Europe led the band of the 369th Regimental Military Unit (known as the "Harlem Hell Fighters") during World War I while serving on active duty as a machine gunner. The band performed many concerts in Paris and gained an international reputation. When the 369th was excluded from the victory parade in Washington, D.C., it held its own parade in New York City on 17 February 1919, starting in lower Manhattan and ending on Lenox Avenue in Harlem playing "Here Comes My Daddy Now."

James Reese Europe was also important as the musical director for the dancers Vernon and Irene Castle in their ballroom at "Castle House," where the fox-trot was introduced to America. With all these musical activities, Europe set the stage for the versatility and variety of Harlem's bands and orchestras.

After Europe's death in 1919, Will Marion Cook took over the Clef Club orchestra, which presented concerts with Paul Robeson. Cook later established the New York Syncopated Orchestra, also known as the Southern Syncopated Orchestra or the American Syncopated Orchestra, and gave concerts in many parts of the United States. A concert program might include waltzes by Brahms, Cook's own composition "Rain Song," Nathaniel Dett's "Listen to the Lambs," W. C. Handy's "Memphis Blues," and Negro spirituals sung a cappella.

"Sweet" Dance Music Orchestras

As the new dances such as the fox-trot, Castle walk, Charleston, black bottom, shimmy, turkey trot, and lindy hop became popular, public ballrooms were established; one example was the Roseland Ballroom in downtown New York City. The first important band to play for this "sweet" dancing was Fletcher Henderson's. Henderson and his orchestra played at the Roseland Ballroom from 1924 to 1926. This orchestra, as recorded playing "Copenhagen" in 1924, consisted of eleven pieces: three trumpets, trombone, three saxes-clarinets, banjo, tuba, drums, and piano. (On this recording, a new trumpet player had joined the band as soloist—Louis Armstrong.) Henderson was experimenting with a concept later known as the "big band," in which the musicians played arrangements contrasting the different sections and timbres of the ensemble instead of relying on soloistic improvisation.

Another important sweet dance orchestra was that of Paul Whiteman, known as the "king of jazz." In his recording of "Charleston" in 1925, the orchestra consisted of three violins, two trumpets, two trombones, four saxes-clarinets, banjo, tuba, and drums. Whiteman's orchestra presented important concerts such as "Experiment in Modern Music" (1924), which featured the premier of George Gershwin's *Rhapsody in Blue* as well as "Livery Stable Blues."

Several society orchestras in Harlem consisted of women, such as the Negro Women's Orchestra and Civic Association; the Famous Ladies Orchestra, led by Marie Lucas; and the Ladies Orchestra, conducted by the bass player Hallie Anderson.

Benny Carter was typical of the Harlemite orchestra musician who had to read music, improvise, know the popular styles, and play alternately in two or three different ensembles. Carter, a young player in the 1920s, began a career with Fletcher Henderson as a sax and trumpet player and an arranger. Carter played in Harlem's nightclubs, in ballroom orchestras, and in Broadway theater orchestras; later he worked on musical scores for Hollywood films. He had "absolute expertise, musical knowledge, and a brilliant style of arranging. He took advantage of unique sonorities afforded by the jazz big band" (Lowe 2000).

"Hot" Dance Music Orchestras

In 1929 a radio broadcast from the Cotton Club in Harlem began with an A-flat dominant seventh chord from the band. Then the announcer, Irving Mills, manager of the Duke Ellington Orchestra, said: "Welcome to our famous Cotton Club. Introducing the greatest living master of 'Jungle Music'—that rip-roaring harmony hound, none other than Duke Ellington. Take your bow, Dukie. The first number is the 'Cotton Club Stomp.'"

With this introduction, Mills presented Ellington's unique orchestra to the radio audience. In 1927, when Ellington had been invited to lead a house band at the Cotton Club, he needed to enlarge his ensemble from eight players to eleven to accommodate the large production numbers of the singers and dancers. The new orchestra had two trumpets, trombone, three saxophones-clarinets, guitar-banjo, bass-tuba, drums, and piano. Later Ellington added another trumpet, two trombones, and a fourth saxophone-clarinet. Unlike many other orchestra leaders, Ellington was able to keep the same musicians working with him. This enabled him to compose for specific instruments and for the unique qualities of each musician. Thus he wrote "Concerto for Cootie"—that is, Cootie Williams—rather than just a concerto for trumpet.

Miguel Covarrubias (1904–1957), *Rhapsody in Blue*, c.1925; oil on canvas. (CH96189, Christie's Images, private collection/Bridgeman Art Library.)

Duke Ellington and his band in the early 1930s. (Brown Brothers.)

Ellington's orchestra and other hot dance orchestras featured many soloists, unlike the sweet orchestras that relied on written arrangements.

New Orleans jazz bands were also popular as "hot" ensembles. Wilbur Sweatman's Original Jazz Band, for instance, consisted of the typical instrumentation of clarinet, trumpet, trombone, piano, and drums. Another hot jazz band was that of William "Chick" Webb, who opened the famous Savoy Ballroom in 1926. (In 1934, Webb would introduce the young Ella Fitzgerald to the jazz world.) The Savoy, which was advertised as the "house of happy feet," was open to whites and blacks, unlike the "whites-only" Cotton Club.

As Duke Ellington began to tour nationally and internationally, Cab Calloway and his musicians became the house band at the Cotton Club in 1931. Calloway had started his ensemble a few years before at Connie's Inn, which was a similar venue. His orchestra remained the same size as Ellington's.

It is worth noting that when Louis Armstrong came to Harlem in 1924, he was able to transcend the New Orleans format and play with big bands, blues bands, and jazz bands. Everybody wanted him.

Broadway Theater Orchestras

Shuffle Along, by Noble Sissle and Eubie Blake, was the first successful Broadway musical written, produced, and performed by African Americans. After its opening in 1921 it ran for some 500 performances and spawned three national touring companies. Noble Sissle had worked with James Reese Europe and led a jazz orchestra; Blake was a vaudeville performer and ragtime pianist. Their thirteen-piece orchestra for *Shuffle Along* consisted of violin, viola, cello, bass, flute, clarinet, oboe, alto saxophone, two trumpets, trombone, piano, and drums. The members of the orchestra included William Grant Still, oboe (later musical director of Black Swan Records and composer of the *Afro-American Symphony*), and Hall Johnson, violist with the Negro String Quartet and leader of the Hall Johnson Singers.

Theater ensembles sometimes had musicians onstage as well as in the orchestra pit. These musicians were experienced and versatile, playing not only in the theater but also in recording studios, nightclubs, and jazz sessions, sometimes all in the same day.

Recording Bands and Orchestras

Recording orchestras were developing at the same time as jazz and dance orchestras. Jazz was in fact the

first music to be recorded from its beginnings, or nearly so. However, the recording techniques and equipment imposed many restrictions on the music, such as the three-minute length of a recording, the single microphone, and the limited dynamic range, which excluded certain instruments. Consequently, the early recordings give an incomplete and distorted representation of the actual performance practices of the period. Perhaps innovations such as longer performances, extended compositions, subtler timbres, and an expanded dynamic range could have begun earlier if the recording industry had been more advanced.

Whereas the big bands ruled the ballrooms and variety clubs, blues singers ruled the recordings. The popularity of these singers stimulated a new industry called "race records." In 1921 Okeh Record Company recorded Mamie Smith and the Jazz Hounds playing "Crazy Blues." The recording sold more than a million copies the first year, at seventy-five cents a copy, indicating that there was a market for selling music to African Americans. The other recording companies started to record blues singers, and race records began. The typical blues band consisted of piano, cornet, and rhythm instruments such as guitar, banjo, and drums, but Gertrude "Ma" Rainey recorded Thomas Dorsey's "Chain Gang Blues" in 1925 in New York with a larger blues band: cornet, trombone, clarinet, bass sax (played by Coleman Hawkins), banjo, and Fletcher Henderson on piano.

Although Rainey recorded mostly in Chicago, she had an enormous influence on many blues singers such as Bessie Smith and others who recorded in New York. From 1923 to 1928, Rainey recorded ninety-two songs for Paramount Records. Her story and her recording practices are presented in August Wilson's play *Ma Rainey's Black Bottom* (1984).

In 1923 the young Bessie Smith recorded "Gulf Coast Blues" and "Down Hearted Blues" with Clarence Williams on piano. That recording sold 750,000 copies in a year, rivaling Mamie Smith's "Crazy Blues." Bessie Smith recorded many songs with Henderson's Hot Six, an ensemble that included Fletcher Henderson on piano, with clarinet, banjo, cornet, and trombone. Bessie Smith's recording of W. C. Handy's "Saint Louis Blues" with Louis Armstrong (1925) is considered a classic of this era.

Clarence Williams recorded a great deal of instrumental blues with his band, Clarence Williams's Blue Five. This band featured Sidney Bechet on soprano saxophone and included Williams playing piano, with clarinet, trombone, and banjo. In 1925, Williams recorded "Cake Walking Babies from Home" featuring Louis Armstrong on trumpet.

The first recording company owned by African Americans was started by Henry Pace, who recorded Ethel Walters in 1921. The recording, "Down Home Blues," sold 500,000 copies in six months and made the company a success. With Fletcher Henderson as recording director and William Grant Still as music director, the company, later to be known as Black Swan Records, became very well known. Black Swan arranged a national tour with Fletcher Henderson and the Black Swan Troubadours to capitalize on its success.

Music of the "Talented Tenth"

Some people, impressed by the philosophy of "advancing the Negro race" as espoused by W. E. B. Du Bois, Alain Locke, and James Weldon Johnson, felt that jazz and entertainment music were to be shunned, and that nobler music should be developed. This was the reason for Penman Lovinggood's book *Famous Modern Negro Musicians* (1921). Lovinggood offered a series of short essays on nineteen composers; classically trained singers, conductors, and instrumentalists; and concert promoters. His subjects included Roland Hayes, James Reese Europe, Paul Robeson, and Marian Anderson. Lovinggood was expressing ideas related to the concept of the "talented tenth," a term used by Du Bois to refer to the upper 10 percent or so—the leadership—of the African American population.

William Christopher (W. C.) Handy had come to New York to open a publishing house with Henry Pace in 1918. He conducted an orchestra and chorus at Carnegie Hall in 1928 in a program of black music of the nineteenth and twentieth centuries. Edward Gilbert Anderson established the Harlem Symphony Orchestra and the Renaissance Theater Orchestra in the 1920s. The Negro String Quartet gave many concerts in Harlem and New York City. In 1925, this quartet accompanied the famous tenor Roland Hayes in his Carnegie Hall debut. The members of the quartet were Felix Weir, first violin; Arthur Boyd, second violin; Hall Johnson, viola; and Marion Cumbe, cello. Hall Johnson became the leader of the Hall Johnson Singers, who had their debut in 1928 at the Pythian Temple and Town Hall in New York City. They later recorded for RCA Victor Company.

Another important vocal ensemble was led by Eva Jessye. The *Major Bowes Family Radio Hour* and the *General Motors Hour* both featured the Eva Jessye Choir. At a later date—from 1930 to 1942—the Monarch

Symphonic Band performed in Harlem, led by Fred Simpson. Floyd (1990) notes that in 1917 the Jenkins Orphanage Band played in a production of DuBose Heyward's *Porgy*—the work on which George Gershwin's opera *Porgy and Bess* was based.

John K. Galm

See also Clef Club; Cotton Club; House-Rent Parties; Jazz; Music; Musical Theater; Nightclubs; Roseland Ballroom; Savoy Ballroom; Shuffle Along; Talented Tenth; *specific individuals*

Further Reading

Abdul, Raoul. *Blacks in Classical Music: A Personal History*. New York: Dodd, Mead, 1977.

Badger, Reid. *A Life in Ragtime: A Biography of James Reese Europe*. New York: Oxford University Press, 1995.

Cuney-Hare, Maud. *Negro Musicians and Their Music*. Washington, D.C.: The Associated Publishers, 1936.

Dance, Stanley. Liner notes. *The Complete Fletcher Henderson*. Bluebird, 1976.

Ellington, Edward Kennedy. *Music Is My Mistress*. New York: Doubleday, 1973.

Floyd, Samuel A., Jr., ed. *Black Music of the Harlem Renaissance: A Collection of Essays*. New York: Greenwood, 1990.

Lowe, Allen. "Foot Stompers, Cross Dressers, and Swingers: The Big Bands, Singers, and Musicians of the Harlem Renaissance." In *Rhapsodies in Black: Music and Words from the Harlem Renaissance*. Rhino, 2000.

Morgan, Thomas, and William Barlow. *From Cakewalks to Concert Halls: An Illustrated History of African American Popular Music from 1895 to 1930*. Washington, D.C.: Eliott & Clark, 1992.

Southern, Eileen. *The Music of Black Americans*, 3rd ed. 1997.

Ward, Geoffery C. *Jazz: A History of America's Music, Based on a Documentary Film by Ken Burns*. New York: Knopf, 2000.

Musical Theater

Young Langston Hughes once claimed that he attended Columbia University so he could see *Shuffle Along*, a Broadway musical of 1921 written and performed by African American artists. He credited the show with giving a "scintillating send-off to that Negro Vogue in Manhattan" known as the Harlem Renaissance: "For nearly two years it was always packed. It gave the proper push—a pre-Charleston kick—to the vogue that spread to books, African sculpture, music, and dancing." While most studies have concentrated on these aspects of the Harlem Renaissance, they have tended to ignore the role of African American musical theater during this period. African American musicals as a form moved into the mainstream of American culture during the 1920s, bringing black performers, writers, directors, and composers into the mainstream as well. Their innovations spread among their white counterparts as the giants of musical theater history such as George Gershwin, Irving Berlin, and Jerome Kern became inspired by the music, performers, and themes of African American musical theater.

Shuffle Along was not the first musical written, performed, and produced by African American talent. This honor belongs to both Will Marion Cook's *Clorindy, the Origin of the Cakewalk* and Bob Cole's *A Trip to Coontown*, which appeared briefly on Broadway in 1898. Yet in the twenty-three year interim, African American musical productions were few and far between. Some of the original innovators had died early, some were hired away by white producers (Florenz Ziegfeld hired the talented Bert Williams to appear in

Shuffle Along, scene with two actors in blackface. (© Billy Rose Theatre Collection, New York Public Library for the Performing Arts, Astor, Lenox, and Tilden Foundations. Photographer: White Studio.)

his *Ziegfeld Follies*), and others shifted to other forms of cultural production, such as classical music or poetry. As a result, there was no continuing tradition within African American musical theater in the first two decades of the twentieth century.

Shuffle Along premiered in May 1921 with few expectations of success; but it soon became a surprise hit, and its 504-performance run was surpassed only by Jerome Kern's *Sally*, which opened the same season. The composer Eubie Blake and the lyricist Noble Sissle created a score that delighted critics and audiences with its modern tempi. The cast of unknowns was catapulted to stardom. The leads Flournoy Miller and Aubrey Lyles (who also wrote the libretto for the show) appeared on Broadway every season throughout the 1920s. Even members of the replacement cast (Florence Mills) and the chorus (Josephine Baker, Paul Robeson, and Adelaide Hall) found *Shuffle Along* the first step to international stardom. *Shuffle Along* legitimized the African American musical. It proved to producers that audiences would support African American talent on Broadway, not always an obvious conclusion in earlier years. As a result, *Shuffle Along* spawned a series of imitators, turning the African American musical into a staple of entertainment during the 1920s. At the same time, it influenced white creators of the genre to acknowledge the talent, the music, and even the themes in their own creations.

The creators of *Shuffle Along* were talented but generally unknown. Flournoy Miller and Aubrey Lyles were the creators of the show's libretto. They had met while students at Fisk University and had entered the world of entertainment as comedians in the black vaudeville circuit. Their comedy skits burlesqued southern life and combined a healthy dose of malapropisms with acrobatic dancing. One of their skits, "The Mayor of Dixie," became the foundation for the plot of *Shuffle Along*. Although they did have their fans in the years before *Shuffle Along*, they had remained generally unknown. Within a year after the show's premiere, they were billed as "America's Foremost Colored Comedians." They remained Broadway stars throughout the 1920s.

The composer (James Hubert "Eubie" Blake) and lyricist (Noble Sissle) of *Shuffle Along* met at a party in Baltimore in 1915 and began a long musical collaboration. Blake, a talented ragtime pianist, joined with Sissle to compose "It's All Your Fault," which was sung by Sophie Tucker. World War I interrupted their partnership, but soon after the armistice they rejoined each other as a performing team, the Dixie Duo, on the vaudeville circuit. Miller and Lyles later approached them with the proposition of creating a musical comedy for Broadway—a somewhat outlandish notion, since black musicals had been absent from Broadway for several years.

Sissle and Blake wrote the score for the new show and performed in it as well. While most Broadway musical scores of this period still relied on European models of musical production, Blake introduced jazz and blues rhythms to the Broadway stage, featuring such songs as "I'm Just Wild about Harry" (later Harry Truman's campaign song), "Love Will Find a Way," and "I'm Craving for that Kind of Love." As a result, *Shuffle Along* echoed contemporary popular music in ways that other shows did not.

As white audiences flocked to the show, the crew of *Shuffle Along* also encouraged African Americans to attend. When the show first opened, African Americans were relegated to the balconies of most New York theaters. The *Shuffle Along* company tried to break down these barriers, both by staging performances at times when African Americans might be more likely to attend—midnight performances proved quite popular—and by loosening the informal segregation process that reigned in most New York theaters. As a result, *Shuffle Along* paved the way for the end of theatrical segregation in New York City. James Weldon Johnson noted in 1930, "At the present time the sight of colored people in the orchestras of Broadway theatres is not considered a cause for immediate action or utter astonishment."

As the audiences became integrated, so too did the Broadway musical theater. *Shuffle Along* was a novelty at the time it opened, but it ultimately legitimized black musical comedy on Broadway. In just three years, New Yorkers saw nine musicals written by and starring African Americans: *Put and Take* (1921); *Strut Miss Lizzie, Plantation Revue, Oh Joy,* and *Liza* (1922); *How Come?* and *Runnin' Wild* (1923); and *The Chocolate Dandies* and *Dixie to Broadway* (1924). African American composers also wrote melodies for three shows with white casts in 1923: C. Luckeyeth Roberts's *Go-Go* and *Sharlee,* and Sissle and Blake's *Elsie.* By 1922, a song from the *Ziegfeld Follies* noted the new trend, as the star Gilda Gray sang "It's Getting Dark on Old Broadway."

Runnin' Wild was the most successful of the succeeding shows. Not surprisingly, it featured two veterans of *Shuffle Along*—Miller and Lyles—in leading roles. It also continued the tradition of using contemporary African American music and themes in the score. While "Old Fashioned Love" became the immediate

hit of the show, another song from the score swiftly attracted greater attention. The composer James P. Johnson and Cecil Mack included a song and dance number, "The Charleston," for the new show. Although the Charleston as a dance was not new, the new song ultimately became the symbol of the roaring twenties. Johnson said he composed various "Charlestons" over the years, but the version used in *Runnin' Wild* became the most popular of the genre. Both the contemporary tone of the music and the farcical libretto continued to draw audiences to the new African American musical.

Although the early African American musicals remained the product of African American performers and writers, as the 1920s progressed more white producers became interested in the profitable genre and reshaped it in a variety of ways. Many of these shows were streamlined into revues—collections of songs, dances, and skits, without the libretto and extensive scenery. These revues, produced by the likes of Lew Leslie and George White, were extremely profitable, efficient, and inexpensive to produce. Shows such as *Dixie to Broadway* (1924) and *Blackbirds of 1928* achieved long runs despite their abbreviated format. During this period, much of the creative control shifted to white producers and writers who used elements and themes from the earlier shows created by African Americans. *Blackbirds of 1928* had a vibrant score, but it was created by a white songwriting team, Jimmy McHugh and Dorothy Fields. As a result, African Americans became recognized as the performers in these hit musical shows, but creative control was slowly draining away.

Although white audiences continued to flock to productions performed by African Americans—on Broadway and in Harlem as well—African American critics found little to praise in them. The musicals of the late 1920s seemed to be borrowing stereotypical elements from the earlier works, and to be pushing African American creative talents to the sidelines. Many of the African American critics of the Harlem Renaissance lost their enthusiasm for this unique genre and criticized the turn to white control. Others, such as Alain Locke and Charles S. Johnson, criticized the form for its escapist tendencies (this was often a complaint about musical comedy in general), arguing that musical comedy ignored the critical social and economic issues of the age.

The African American musical weathered the early days of the Great Depression with some difficulty. On the one hand, African American musicals continued to be produced during these dismal times. One reason for the genre's survival was its inexpensive production costs. The shows produced during the Depression had minimal scenery (*Rhapsody in Black* in 1931 maintained only a dark curtain), and smaller and smaller casts. Producers continually cut wages during this period; considering the lack of alternatives, African American actors often accepted the cuts. On the other hand, by the early 1930s the genre was recognized to be in decline, as performers as well as the creative talents behind the African American musicals sought other avenues to success and indeed work.

Although the boom in African American musical theater during the 1920s rivaled the successes of the literary lights of the Harlem Renaissance, prominent authors and critics often tended to ignore the remarkable success that the creators of these entertainments had in bringing their work into the American mainstream. The stars of these shows appealed to both white and African American audiences, and the melodies from the shows had a similar appeal. White authors of the musical theater had often ignored African American performers and their culture before the 1920s. After the explosion of talent during the Harlem Renaissance, this became an impossibility. Jerome Kern and Oscar Hammerstein II, for example, chose African American performers and musical themes for *Show Boat* (1927), their adaptation of Edna Ferber's novel of the same name. The hit of the show, the enduring "Ol' Man River," was sung first in New York by Jules Bledsoe, and later in London by Paul Robeson. Irving Berlin chose Ethel Waters for his revue *As Thousands Cheer* in 1933, after seeing her perform at the Cotton Club. She sang several numbers in the show, including "I've Got Harlem on My Mind," but the song that stopped the show each evening was her rendition of "Supper Time," a solo about her husband's lynching. This was certainly a serious turn for what is often called an "escapist entertainment." Waters became the highest-paid female performer on Broadway during the show's run. George and Ira Gershwin followed suit a few years later with *Porgy and Bess* (1935), their ambitious African American opera for the Broadway stage. Many of the performers featured in *Porgy and Bess* had earned their stripes in the African American musicals of the 1920s.

As the most prominent composers, lyricists, and librettists looked to African American musical comedy for inspiration during and after the Harlem Renaissance, changes were also occurring in the structure of the audience. African American musicals brought African American audiences into Broadway theaters and slowly helped to break down

the remaining walls of segregation in New York City's theaters. Similarly, talented African Americans, whether onstage or behind the scenes, were no longer a rarity, as individuals moved to the forefront in the various theatrical crafts. Although the harsh days of the Depression slowed the continued integration within the world of legitimate theater, Broadway theater was an integrated force by the late 1930s. This, too, would have a downside: musicals and dramas created by African Americans would tend to diminish as both creators and performers found themselves welcome in the formerly white world of the Broadway theater. Whenever this window of opportunity started to narrow, both African American musicals and drama would find a new place on the Broadway stage.

ALLEN WOLL

See also Baker, Josephine; Blackbirds; Blake, Eubie; Bledsoe, Jules; Chocolate Dandies; Fields, Dorothy; Hall, Adelaide; Johnson, Charles S.; Johnson, James P.; Leslie, Lew; Locke, Alain; Lyles, Aubrey; Mack, Cecil; Miller, Flournoy; Mills, Florence; Music; Porgy and Bess; Robeson, Paul; Runnin' Wid; Shuffle Along; Sissle, Noble; Waters, Ethel

Further Reading

Dictionary of the Black Theatre: Broadway, Off-Broadway, and Selected Harlem Theatre. Westport, Conn.: Greenwood, 1983.

Kimball, Robert, and William Bolcom. *Reminiscing with Sissle and Blake.* New York: Viking, 1973.

Woll, Allen. *Black Musical Theatre: From Coontown to Dreamgirls.* Baton Rouge: Louisiana State University Press, 1989.

Musicians

The Harlem Renaissance began in one musical era and ended in another. It was born during the age of the marching band, aptly symbolized by the parade of James Reese Europe and his 369th Regiment "Harlem Hell Fighters" Band up Fifth Avenue, from midtown to Harlem, in the spring of 1919. By the time the Harlem Renaissance ended, with the onset of the Great Depression a decade later, the jazz age was in full cry, blues had been a craze for more than a decade, and brass bands (such as James Europe's) and the ragtime style that had characterized their most up-to-date repertoire were going into a decline.

Music Publishing

In the early twentieth century, mechanical music reproduction was in its infancy. Musical amateurs were legion, many owned pianos, and the sheet music business was an enormous industry. Leading music publishers of the Harlem Renaissance were located, not in Harlem itself, but in midtown Manhattan, home of Tin Pan Alley. The most important was the Pace and Handy Music Publishing Company, which moved to New York in 1918. In 1921, when Harry Pace left the partnership to found Black Swan Records, the company was reconstituted as Handy Brothers Music Company, under the leadership of its primary songwriter, W. C. Handy (1873–1958), and his brother Charles (1889–1980). This company formed the nucleus around which other publishers clustered. Most important were the Clarence Williams Music Publishing Company, which arrived in New York in 1921, and the Perry Bradford Music Publishing Company. Williams published some major hits, and Bradford was involved in securing the first recordings by an African American blues singer. These entrepreneurs rented offices in the Gaiety Theater Building at Broadway and Forty-fifth Street. They were joined there by lesser companies, run by the songwriters Spencer Williams, Porter Grainger, Henry Troy, and Bud Allen. Some of these enterprises were honest independent efforts; others were "fronts" for white publishers cashing in on the popularity of black music by setting up an office with a couple of black employees as a facade. A few small music publishers were located in Harlem itself, such as the Arrow Music Publishing Company, Q. Roscoe Snowden, and Payton-Brown. Most were short lived, though, and published little music. In Brooklyn, the entertainer Alex Rogers and the ragtime pianist Luckey Roberts ran a small firm from about 1920 to 1924, initially to supply material to Bert Williams, the nonpareil comedian of the era.

Of all the music publishing houses, by far the longest lived has been Handy Brothers Music Company, still run by the Handy Family on Broadway as of this writing. Beginning in Memphis in 1913 as a conduit for hit songs written by Handy himself, it later published successful songs by others, including "A Good Man Is Hard to Find" (1918) by the vaudevillian Eddie Green (1896–1950), and "Sugar" (1926) by Maceo Pinkard (1897–1962). As an incubator for young talent during the Harlem Renaissance, the company had few peers. The composer William Grant Still and the bandleader Fletcher Henderson both entered New York's musical life as employees of Pace Handy. So did Daniel Haynes, who went on to fame on the stage, then starred in the first big-budget, all-black Hollywood feature film, *Hallelujah*, in 1929. That same year, Handy was involved in the production of the only film Bessie Smith ever made, *Saint Louis Blues*, named for his greatest song hit. Smith was one of Handy's illustrious friends in show business who made his office in Times Square a meeting place and a refuge. Others included George Gershwin, J. Rosamond Johnson, and Eubie Blake. In later years it was a hangout for jazz musicians, who sometimes cut "demo" recordings there. Handy was also close to writers and intellectuals of the Harlem Renaissance, including Langston Hughes and Carl Van Vechten. He published some songs with lyrics by Hughes, including one, "Golden Brown Blues" (1926), for which Handy himself wrote the music. Finally, Handy's book *Blues: An Anthology* (1926) was of great importance in the dissemination of African American culture.

Music Promotion

African Americans were also in the business of booking musical talent during the Harlem Renaissance. The Clef Club, in addition to its crucial role in concert production and general musical uplift, served as a musical clearinghouse and booking agency. Long after it fell from the limelight, it continued to function commercially under the leadership of Fred "Deacon" Johnson. The composer and music arranger Will Vodery (1885–1951) was an active booking talent from Times Square as early as 1916. As late as the 1950s, musicians from Harlem such as the songwriter Maceo Pinkard continued to run services providing entertainment for parties. There was also an active promotional network in the press. Some journalists, such as Salem Tutt Whitney of the Indianapolis *Freeman*, promoted mainly their own productions and those mounted by their friends. More independent writers also operated in mainstream publications, such as "Billboard" Jackson, who derived his nickname from the magazine he wrote for and was a leader in the entertainment field. The journalist, diplomat, and entrepreneur Lester A. Walton worked on behalf of the race, including entertainers, while writing for the *New York World* in the 1920s.

Recordings

African Americans were heard on records virtually from the beginning of the recording industry, performing minstrel and comic pieces, spirituals, and other music. The biggest African American recording star was the legendary comedian Bert Williams, whose records for Columbia were immensely popular. Many small record companies still existed in the early 1920s, and several recorded black blues and jazz musicians, mostly in New York. These companies included Okeh, Emerson, Brunswick, Perfect, and Harmony. The dominant record company of the period, Victor (later RCA Victor), made many of its recordings in a converted church building it owned in Camden, New Jersey. In addition, one company, owned and operated by blacks, was of enormous importance for the Harlem Renaissance—Black Swan Phonograph Company.

The Pace Phonograph Corporation, producer of Black Swan Records, was founded at the beginning of 1921 and began issuing recordings the following spring. Unlike the leading music publishers, it was located in Harlem, first at 2289 Seventh Avenue, then at 257 West 138th Street. While this was not actually the first black-owned record company (the short-lived Broom Records has that distinction), Black Swan was the first such company to issue hit records, advertise widely, and become an important presence in American culture. Black Swan reflected the tastes of its proprietor, Harry H. Pace (1884–1943), a highly educated and ambitious businessman and a disciple of W. E. B. Du Bois. Like Du Bois, the real estate magnate John Nail, and most of the Black Swan's other investors, Pace had little use for blues and jazz, preferring classical music and spirituals. He allowed his young employees, such as Fletcher Henderson, to guide him in the recording of pop music, however, and this practice paid off handsomely in a series of hit recordings by Ethel Waters. Nevertheless, much of Black Swan's catalog was taken up with recordings of opera arias and other short classical selections. While these are of lesser interest to music fans today, they are of inestimable worth as historical documents. From the Black Swan records of Florence Cole-Talbert, Revella Hughes, and Ivan H. Browning we can reconstruct the sound of the black concert singers of approximately 1920.

Classical Musicians

In the early decades of the twentieth century, African Americans were not heard in white symphony orchestras or opera houses. Classically trained musicians such as Will Marion Cook (1869–1944) and R. Nathaniel Dett (1882–1943) had to find other avenues for the expression of their considerable talent. Cook made his greatest mark in musical theater, with such scores as *Clorindy, or the Origin of the Cakewalk* (1898) and *In Dahomey* (1902–1903), two of the finest shows in the history of American theater. Dett also wrote music of very high quality, such as the piano suite *In the Bottoms* (1913), but he made his career as a teacher at such black schools as the Hampton Institute. Teaching would prove the primary musical outlet for black classical musicians during this period. A few solo pianists attempted concert careers, among them Hazel Harrison and Helen Hagan, both of whom gave recitals in New York in the early 1920s. It was rare to see a black soloist with a white orchestra; nevertheless, Raymond Lawson played concertos with the Hartford Symphony on more than one occasion beginning in 1911. In classical music, as in so many areas of American life, African Americans created their own institutions to support performance and education. Some white musicians and philanthropists showed an interest in providing music instruction to African Americans. In New York, one remarkable example was the Music School Settlement for Colored People, founded by the violinist David Mannes, who was active between 1911 and 1919.

One African American who broke through numerous barriers in the music world was Harry T. Burleigh (1866–1949). He is best remembered today for his arrangements of spirituals, such as "Deep River," but he also wrote classical songs of distinction. As a staff arranger with the New York office of the Italian music publisher Ricordi, Burleigh was in a central position in New York's classical music world. He was the first African American to become an officer of the American Society of Composers and Publishers, was a prestigious private music instructor, and was a popular recital artist for several decades. Most prominently, he had a remarkable career as a baritone soloist at Saint George's Episcopal Church on Stuyvesant Square from 1894 to 1946, and at Temple Emanu-El from 1900 to 1925. By the late 1930s, his singing during the services had become so popular that music lovers were being turned away at Saint George's doors at Easter. Nor was Burleigh the only African American musician in New York to achieve this degree of success in both Christian and Jewish sacred music. His friend Melville Charlton (1880–1973) was the organist at the Union Theological Seminary for nearly thirty years, and at the Temple of the Covenant from 1914 to 1924.

African Americans were not particularly active in the performance of chamber music during the Harlem Renaissance. However, the Negro String Quartet—consisting of Arthur Boyd and Felix Weir, violins; Hall Johnson, viola; and Marion Cumbo, cello—concertized in the 1920s. Another important cellist of the era was Leonard Jeter, an active freelance musician and teacher. Allie Ross, a capable violinist and conductor, had a notable career in the 1920s. In 1927 he conducted *Jazz Symphony*, a complex and difficult work by the avant-garde composer George Antheil, in a concert at Carnegie Hall. W. C. Handy hired the orchestra for this engagement, and A'Lelia Walker provided a rehearsal space and ample funds to ensure adequate rehearsal time. For classical musicians of the Harlem Renaissance, there was often crossover work to be had in pop, whether in musical theater bands or in recording studios. Marion Cumbo made records with both Clara Smith and Eva Taylor, and Leonard Jeter recorded with Ethel Waters (and also played in the pit band for the show *Shuffle Along*). The presence of a cello on 1920s blues records may seem surprising today, but it reflects common musical practices of the period. The standardized jazz-band format that we now take for granted did not take shape until the dawn of the swing era. Many of the early blues and jazz bands—including New Orleans bands and other hot bands—featured a violin as a melody instrument.

The most remarkable example of a crossover musician in the Harlem Renaissance was William Grant Still (1895–1978), a thoroughly trained musician who studied with the avant-garde composer Edgard Varèse. Still was proficient on both the oboe and the cello, two very difficult and dissimilar instruments. He played cello with W. C. Handy's Memphis Blues Band in the summer of 1916, and also wrote some arrangements for Handy during those months. He rejoined Handy in 1919, now in New York, where he wrote many arrangements for publication by the Pace and Handy Music Company. He also played cello in a large concert band under Handy's direction during this period. In early 1921, he joined Harry Pace in the new enterprise of Black Swan records, where he was soon active as arranger and studio conductor. Later in 1921, he joined the pit band of the Broadway hit *Shuffle Along*, playing oboe. This band also included the choral conductor Hall Johnson (1888–1970) on viola, led by the show's composer Eubie Blake at the piano. In the 1920s and 1930s, Still made a name for himself as a composer of classical music, while writing sophisticated arrangements for such pop music figures as Don Voorhees, Willard Robison, and Artie Shaw.

Popular, Dance Band, and Theater Musicians

A broad middle category between the classical and popular categories was occupied by musicians who played light classics, music for dancing, and theater tunes. Many, like Still, were active in several musical genres, the boundaries of which were somewhat more fluid than they are today. Around 1900, the leading bandleader in this area was Professor Walter F. Craig (1854–1920s); his orchestra was popular with African Americans in New York for more than three decades, playing for picnics and other occasions. The career of the bandleader and composer Ford Dabney (1883–1958) encompassed several styles and formats, including a stint leading a brass band, with which he made recordings around 1920. The high point of his performing career was leading the band for Ziegfeld's *Midnight Frolic*, a highly popular late-night entertainment that featured such star entertainers as Bert Williams. For these engagements in 1916–1917, Dabney's Syncopated Orchestra consisted of eleven pieces: flute, clarinet, trumpet (the early jazz star "Cricket" Smith), trombone, piano (Dabney), drums, mandolin, two violins, cello, and double bass. This instrumentation suggests a sound between that of a "palm court" orchestra and a theater pit band; many published "stock" arrangements issued by music publishers had a similar layout of parts.

The most prominent director of popular music in New York at the beginning of the Renaissance was James Reese Europe (1880–1919). Early in his career he was involved in musical theater in New York. With the establishment of the Clef Club in 1910, he became a leader in African American musical uplift, directing a large, unique orchestra made up largely of plucked string instruments. With this massive ensemble, Europe led the first concert of African American music at Carnegie Hall in 1912. Curiously, many of the musicians who played the banjo, bandoneon, and harp-guitar in Europe's Clef Club Orchestra read little if any music. This is not to contradict the reputation Europe and his men had for highly disciplined performances, a renown that was richly deserved. The majority of his men played by ear, however, clustering, in rehearsals, around a few reading colleagues, who learned the parts first. The others then "caught the tune" from them, playing the parts with varying degrees of detail, giving the overall texture of the sound an extraordinary layered richness.

In 1914, having left the Clef Club, Europe became music director for the popular dance team of Vernon and Irene Castle, playing ragtime to accompany the new social dances such as the fox-trot. In the final phase of his career, he led a brass band of African American and Puerto Rican musicians during World War I. The version of brass band ragtime played by this "Harlem Hell Fighters" unit was immensely popular in France, and the musicians made several exemplary records on their return to America. Some of the musicians associated with Europe, such as the trumpeter Cricket Smith, the trombonists Ward "Dope" Andrews and Herb Flemming, and the drummer Buddy Gilmore, were important in the transition to jazz, the new music of the 1920s. The band's vocalist, Lieutenant Noble Sissle, went on to a highly successful partnership in vaudeville and songwriting with the pianist Eubie Blake. Their musical *Shuffle Along* (1921) would set the standard for work of its kind.

Musical theater in the Harlem Renaissance was a blend of old and new elements, including holdovers from minstrelsy, particularly in comic routines and in the use of blackface. Newer elements included syncopated forms of black music, first ragtime and then early jazz and blues. Dance was enormously important, and pretty light-skinned chorus girls were as important in the theater as they were in such cabarets and nightspots as the Cotton Club. Some, such as Fredi Washington and Josephine Baker, would become stars in their own right. Musical comedy singers, such as Florence Mills and Gertrude Saunders, were also crucial to a show's success. Mills was the biggest star of black entertainment between the death of Bert Williams in 1922 and her own sudden, premature death in 1927. The line between singers, dancers, and actors was extremely thin and porous during this period, and a number of recordings were made by performers who were not primarily singers, and not jazz or blues singers by any means. They sang in a style that is extinct today, and their few surviving recordings sound strange to our ears: a shrill, high-pitched warbling, with an overabundance of vibrato and a coy theatricality. A recording made in 1921 of Saunders singing "I'm Craving for That Kind of Love," a hit by Sissle and Blake from *Shuffle Along*, is a revealing artifact of this culture. Eight decades later, the style is unmistakably archaic.

Ragtime Musicians

Although ragtime was primarily a solo piano genre originating in the midwest, a good deal of ragtime was played and composed in New York. Some of the most important practitioners of the music were there, and much New York ragtime was for instrumental ensemble or was vocal. The brass band of James Reese Europe, previously discussed, was a first-rate ragtime band, and there were others in New York, including those led by Ford Dabney and J. Tim Brymn (1881–1946). Like Europe, Brymn was an army bandleader in France during World War I. As for solo pianists, the ragtime musicians who are best remembered today, New York was host to Scott Joplin, the greatest composer of the genre, for the last decade of his life, 1907–1917. By the time of his death, New York had quite a few fine ragtime pianists in residence. Some were locals, such as Fats Waller (1904–1943); some came from near the city, such as Willie "the Lion" Smith (1897–1973) from New York State and James P. Johnson (1891–1955) from New Jersey. Still others were from the eastern seaboard: Eubie Blake (1883–1983) from Baltimore and Charles Luckyeth ("Luckey") Roberts (1887–1968) from Philadelphia. All but Smith were also composers of importance. Some, such as Luckey Roberts, were very successful entertainers in the decades around World War I, supplying music to the same high-society families that danced to the music of James Reese Europe's band during his time with Vernon and Irene Castle.

Eventually, New York ragtime would evolve into a more virtuosic musical style known as "stride," which was in full flower by the end of the 1920s. The pianists who were able to master this very difficult art, which required an extremely active and agile left hand, tended to be New York ragtime masters such as Johnson and Waller. Johnson later branched out into the composition of longer symphonic forms. Waller wrote popular song standards with the brilliant lyricist Andy Razaf (1895–1973).

Blues Musicians

Country blues, as performed by male vocalists to the accompaniment of their own guitar, played almost no part in the Harlem Renaissance. Although some folk blues pioneers and "songsters" traveled to New York in the late 1920s to make records, such musicians did not stay in the city long. In "commercial," "city," or "vaudeville" blues, however, the situation was quite different. This was a prevalent new style on the black vaudeville circuit throughout much of the United States, beginning in the southeast and in such cities as Chicago and Memphis. The style had established a foothold in New York by the end of World War I. It is impossible to ascertain when blues was first heard in New York, but in 1918 W. C. Handy, later known as the "father of the blues," arrived in the city to open a new office for his music publishing business. He had already published his greatest songs in Memphis, among them "Saint Louis Blues," "Yellow Dog Blues," "Joe Turner Blues," and "Beale Street Blues." (His first song hit, "Memphis Blues," actually more of a ragtime song, was no longer his property.) Handy's arrival in New York coincides roughly with the rise of the blues craze nationwide. Blues in sheet music already sold extremely well, and there were a great many false blues (blues in name only) on the market. By 1920, there was enough interest in the music for the record companies to begin releasing blues records by African American women. The vaudevillian and music publisher Perry Bradford (1893–1970) was the first to successfully push for this innovation, and in 1920 Fred Hager of Okeh Records permitted him to record Mamie Smith. The first records were successful, and within the next three years most of the best blues "shouters" were immortalized on disk: Ma Rainey, Lucille Hegamin, Albert Hunter, Clara Smith, Edith Wilson, Ethel Waters, Eva Taylor, and the greatest of them all, Bessie Smith.

Jazz Musicians

Early jazz, from approximately 1915 until about 1930, fell into two broad camps according to performance practice. The one generally given the most attention, purely improvised music by small groups, was actually a minority practice. Small combos numbering approximately five players would work up tunes in rehearsal, weaving their lines around one another's in a crude polyphony that at its best was quite viscerally exciting. This earliest jazz style originated in New Orleans around 1915. In that year, the Creole Band, led by the trumpeter Freddie Keppard, played New York on a vaudeville tour. The best-known early Dixieland ensemble, and the first to record, was the Original Dixieland Jazz Band (white); some of its members were musical illiterates. Their "routining" (playing of memorized riffs) relates to vaudeville and novelty music, and several leading early jazz performers were in fact more comedians than musicians. Ted Lewis

(white) incorporated a good deal of corny verbiage into his act. Jimmy Durante, a fine early jazz pianist, eventually relegated music to a sideline in his comedy career. Wilbur Sweatman (1882–1961), an African American veteran of minstrel bands, developed an act in which he played three clarinets at once.

The earliest black jazz musicians actually living in Harlem emerged from the older musical genres such as ragtime and from bands such as James Europe's, or from the minstrel and vaudeville circuit. The first jazz recordings all featured white musicians, and African American players recorded first as accompanists to blues singers. Most of the musicians featured on these records had little sense of what we would consider jazz style, and their performances now sound somewhat stiff and wooden. Nonetheless, such musicians as the trumpeter Joe Smith, the clarinetist Ernest "Sticky" Elliott, and the violinist Leroy Parker reflect the prevailing style of the day. Some of their contemporaries were fine musicians. They were often remarkably versatile: Garvin Bushell (1902–1986) played clarinet, several sizes of saxophone, oboe, and bassoon. Musicians of this caliber never stopped studying and improving themselves; in old age, Bushell viewed his recordings of the 1920s with a certain embarrassment and disdain.

Many musicians on early blues and jazz records were reading from either published or handwritten parts. This was apparently true, for example, of the sessions recorded by the singer Lucille Hegamin for Arto Records in 1921, as surviving parts (now in private hands) attest. As Mark Tucker's oral history with Bushell (1988) revealed, the boundary between note reading and "cutting loose" (improvising) was forever shifting. The notion that early blues and jazz records were made by illiterate performers who played entirely "from the heart" is a misunderstanding fueled by wishful thinking, a "noble savage" myth that may be romantic but is in any case condescending.

As new musicians arrived in town to take advantage of the boom in recordings and club work during the 1920s, the competition for those already on the scene stiffened. Soloists like Johnny Dunn, a trumpeter from Memphis who reigned as the king on his instrument in the early 1920s, were unable to withstand the arrival of superior practitioners from elsewhere, such as Louis Armstrong, Cladys "Jabbo" Smith, James "Bubber" Miley, and Rex Stewart. There were trombonists like Charlie Green, Jimmy Harrison, and Benny Morton; clarinetists like Buster Bailey and Barney Bigard; saxophonists like Coleman Hawkins,

Gene Sedric, and Don Redman; and a host of others. Exempt from this law of the jungle were Harlem's piano players; New York already had the best in the business. Even a jazz master like Jelly Roll Morton stood no chance of unseating titans like James P. Johnson, Luckey Roberts, Willie "the Lion" Smith, and Fats Waller. In late-night "cutting contests," these virtuosos showed off their tricks and tested one another's mettle.

The busiest recording artists of the 1920s were Fletcher Henderson and Clarence Williams, two pianists with widely diverging backgrounds and careers. Henderson (1897–1952), scion of a middle-class educated family in Georgia, originally came to New York to study chemistry at Columbia University but took a summer job with the Pace and Handy Music Company and soon gave up science for music. He moved with Harry Pace to Black Swan Records the following winter and became the house pianist and recordings manager. Throughout the 1920s, Henderson was in great demand as an accompanist to blues singers. By the mid-1920s he was also the leader of the first important black jazz orchestra. Clarence Williams (1893–1966) came from a rural background near New Orleans. He entered show business early, appearing in traveling shows at the age of twelve. By 1916, he was a bandleader and songwriter, and he soon founded a music publishing company with his duo performing partner, the violinist Armand Piron. The partnership dissolved after the company moved to Chicago in 1918, and Williams arrived on Tin Pan Alley in 1921, a prolific and successful tunesmith and publisher. Less active than Henderson as an accompanist, he formed several bands and made many fine recordings with them. Williams's records featured such jazz greats as the trumpeter Joseph "King" Oliver, the clarinetist Buster Bailey, and the pianist James P. Johnson.

The larger jazz orchestras consisted entirely of reading musicians, many with a good deal of classical training. They played a repertoire that ranged from light classics to the more polite, "sweet" dance music that was also known as jazz in this period. The most famous were well-drilled units led by such white bandleaders as Paul Whiteman and Vincent Lopez. Black bands also played this sort of material, which was popular with both races. The first great African American jazz orchestra, led by Fletcher Henderson, played largely from written arrangements, including doctored versions of "stock arrangements" purchased from publishers. In the mid-1920s, two major developments brought orchestras such as Henderson's

firmly into the jazz age. The first was the arrival in his band of "hot" soloists, such as Louis Armstrong, Buster Bailey, and Coleman Hawkins, who used their solo choruses to enrich the expressive range of the orchestral jazz medium. Equally important was the rise of the jazz arranger. Bandleaders such as Henderson and his brother Horace did some arranging of their own, but they also cultivated talented arrangers within their ensembles. The two greatest figures in this development both worked with Henderson: Don Redman (1902–1964) in the late 1920s, and Benny Carter (1907–2003) in the early 1930s. Both were multi-instrumentalists whose primary instruments were the woodwinds, and both later became important bandleaders. Redman, from West Virginia, played clarinet and alto saxophone. Carter, a native of New York's San Juan Hill (the West Sixties), made hit recordings as a trumpet soloist as well as being one of the greatest alto saxophonists, and in his seventy-five-year career composed a great deal of original music.

Much of the music played by "jazz" bands in the 1920s sounds corny to listeners today; the style of such once-popular bandleaders as "Fess" Williams will probably never experience a revival. The "hotter" variety of jazz came to the fore only gradually. The great hot bands in New York tended to have long residencies at particular jazz clubs, often in Harlem, where they attracted considerable patronage, usually exclusively white. Most famous was the Cotton Club, where the orchestras of Andy Preer, Duke Ellington, and Cab Calloway held sway in succession. The numerous venues ranged from large ballrooms—the Manhattan Casino and the Alhambra Ballroom—to small clubs like the Nest and the Lenox Club. Small's Paradise, a club owned and operated by blacks, catered to African American patrons. Its excellent orchestra, led by Charlie Johnson, though little remembered today, was among the finest in New York in 1927–1928, as surviving recordings confirm. Sidney De Paris and "Jabbo" Smith were featured on trumpet, and Benny Carter and Benny Waters in the reed section; the latter two also wrote arrangements for the band, including the Carter's first. Stylistically, their work, as heard on such records as De Paris's feature "The Boy in the Boat," pointed toward the future: deeply expressive music with a bluesy groove. Other bands of the 1920s playing in this funkier style included Thomas Morris and his Past Jazz Masters and the Gulf Coast Seven, led by June Clark on trumpet.

This was the musical environment in which Duke Ellington (1899–1974) rose to fame at the Cotton Club;

his first trademark was called "jungle music." With the trumpeter "Bubber" Miley soloing on such features as "East Saint Louis Toodle-Oo," the Ellington band accompanied the famous Cotton Club chorus lines. Ellington, originally from Washington, D.C., arrived in New York in 1923 and worked as a sideman with the veteran vaudevillian Wilbur Sweatman. Ellington's next job was with a group known as the Washingtonians, led by the banjo player Elmer Snowden. Early in 1924, Ellington took over this band, which played various club dates, gradually taking shape as the Duke Ellington Orchestra that would become world famous. Among Ellington's band mates in the early years were musicians who would help to define his sound: Miley; the trombonist Joe "Tricky Sam" Nanton; the bassist Wellman Braud; and the drummer Sonny Greer. They began to make a series of classic recordings for Vocalion in 1926; the following year, on the death of Andy Preer, they became the resident band at the Cotton Club. Over the next four decades, Ellington would outstrip all his rivals as a composer and bandleader, evolving new styles of orchestral jazz.

As the Harlem Renaissance waned, the sound of the jazz band itself was changing. The popularity of the violin diminished; the guitar began to assert itself against the banjo, and the double bass against the tuba. As the swing era dawned, a new, streamlined sound, dominated by synchronized saxophone, trumpet, and trombone sections, would characterize urban dance music in America. Composers such as Ellington, singers such as Cab Calloway and Ethel Waters, and bands led by Louis Armstrong, Count Basie, Claude Hopkins, Jimmy Lunceford, and Lucky Millinder ushered in a new era. Arranger-bandleaders like Don Redman and Benny Carter were crucial in defining this new sound, which would be prevalent until the mid-1940s. By the early 1930s, they were creating works of great sophistication. Redman's "Chant of the Weed," recorded by Harlan Lattimore and his Connie's Inn Orchestra in 1932, is still impressive for its harmonic daring, sinuous section work, and aura of mystery. Musically ambitious as well as entertaining, it was a harbinger of things to come.

ELLIOTT S. HURWITT

See also Black Swan Phonograph Company; Blues; Blues: An Anthology; Blues: Women Performers; Clef Club; Cotton Club; Jazz; Music; Musical Theater; Pace Phonographic Company; Saint Louis Blues; Singers; Small's Paradise; *specific individuals*

Recordings

The Best of Early Ellington. Decca CD, 1996. (Dating from 1926–1931.)

Black Manhattan. Paragon Ragtime Orchestra, dir. Rick Benjamin. New World Records, 2003.

The Chronological Clarence Williams, 12 vols. Classics Records, c. 1994–1996.

Fletcher Henderson: Developing an American Orchestra, 1923–1937. Smithsonian Collection/Columbia Special Products, 1977.

Jabbo Smith and His Rhythm Aces. Jazz Archives, 1993. (2 CDs.)

James Reese Europe's Harlem Hell Fighters Band. Memphis Archives, 1996.

Jazz Odyssey, Vol. 3, *The Sound of Harlem*. Columbia Records, 1964. (3 LPs.)

Jazz the World Forgot. Yazoo Records, 1996. (2 CD vols.)

Smithsonian Collection of Classic Jazz, rev. ed. 1994.

Souvenirs of Hot Chocolates. Smithsonian Collection, 1978.

Further Reading

Allen, Walter. *Hendersonia, the Music of Fletcher Henderson and His Musicians: A Bio-Discography*. Highland Park, N.J.: Allen, 1973.

Badger, Reid. *A Life in Ragtime: A Biography of James Reese Europe*. New York: Oxford University Press, 1995.

Bradford, Perry. *Born with the Blues*. New York: Oak, 1965.

Bushell, Garvin, as told to Mark Tucker. *Jazz from the Beginning*. Ann Arbor: University of Michigan Press, 1988.

Charters, Samuel B., and Leonard Kunstadt. *Jazz: A History of the New York Scene*. New York: Da Capo, 1981. (Originally published 1962.)

Chevan, David. "Written Music in Early Jazz." Ph.D. dissertation, CUNY Graduate Center, 1997.

Cuney-Hare, Maude. *Negro Musicians and Their Music*. Washington, D.C.: Associated Publishing, 1936.

Handy, W. C. *Father of the Blues*. New York: Boni and Boni, 1926. (Introduction and notes by Abbe Niles.)

Harker, Brian. " 'Telling a Story': Louis Armstrong and Coherence in Early Jazz." *Current Musicology*, 63, 1999, pp. 46–83.

Hurwitt, Elliott S. "W. C. Handy as Music Publisher: Career and Reputation." Ph.D. dissertation, CUNY Graduate Center, 2000.

Kimball, Robert, and William Bolcom. *Reminiscing with Sissle and Blake*. New York: Viking, 1973.

Lord, Thomas. *Clarence Williams*. Chigwell, Essex, UK: Storyville, 1976.

Morgan, Thomas L., and William Barlow. *From Cakewalks to Concert Halls*. Washington, D.C.: Elliott and Clark, 1992.

Rust, Brian. *Jazz Records, 1897–1942*, 4th ed. New Rochelle, N.Y.: Arlington House, 1978.

Schuller, Gunther. *Early Jazz: Its Roots and Musical Development*. New York: Oxford University Press, 1968.

Southern, Eileen. *Biographical Dictionary of Afro-American and African Musicians*. Westport, Conn.: Greenwood, 1982.

———. *The Music of Black Americans: A History*, 2nd ed. New York: Norton, 1983.

Stewart, Rex. *Jazz Masters of the 1930s*. New York: Macmillan, 1972.

Thygesen, Helge, Mark Berresford, and Russ Shor. *Black Swan: The Record Label of the Harlem Renaissance*. Nottingham, UK: VJM, 1996.

Tucker, Mark. *Ellington: The Early Years*. Urbana: University of Illinois Press, 1991.

Walton, Lester A. "Dabney's Orchestra Is Making History." *New York Age*, 21 December 1916.

Waters, Ethel. *His Eye Is on the Sparrow*. New York: Da Capo, 1992. (Originally published 1950.)

Nail, John E.

John E. Nail was born in 1883. In 1904, he was persuaded by Philip A. Payton to join the Afro-American Realty Company, which was based in Harlem. Nail immediately took advantage of a recession that was lowering real estate prices in Manhattan. Withheld loans and foreclosed mortgages caused landlords to drop rents and accept more diverse tenants as building owners tried to recover their investments. Nail united black renters and white landlords while simultaneously eroding an unwritten "covenant" whereby certain blocks in Harlem blocks were supposed to remain white. Nail and his associates found new black tenants who were willing to pay higher rates for better-quality housing in Harlem, and Afro-American Realty helped thousands move into homes and apartments between Fifth and Seventh avenues despite vocal opposition from the white Property Owners Protective Association of Harlem. Afro-American Realty protected its market by acquiring five-year leases on properties owned by whites and rented them at 10 percent above deflated market prices.

Migration to Harlem increased when displaced families left Manhattan's Tenderloin district during the construction of Pennsylvania Station between 1906 and 1910. Nail and Henry C. Parker left Payton to open their own firm, Nail and Parker, in 1907. Nail served as president, and Parker was the corporate secretary-treasurer. The company expanded into full-service real estate operations by providing mortgages and by purchasing, selling, managing, and appraising properties. Nail argued that black ownership in Harlem would permanently undermine discriminatory real estate practices. He urged blacks to invest in property in Harlem to secure the future of the black community in the area, a practice that also benefited his business.

Nail was considered one of Harlem's primary "deal makers." His firm acted as agent for Saint Philip's Protestant Episcopal Church when the church bought aggregate properties in Harlem for $1,070,000. Nail and Parker also sold $200,000 worth of property to Madame C. J. Walker, who had amassed a fortune developing hair-care products. The company also brokered the move of the black YMCA and the Equitable Life Assurance Properties, which included the sophisticated town houses on Strivers' Row. In 1929, Nail and Parker was granted the management contract for the largest apartment building in Harlem, then owned by the Metropolitan Life Insurance Company.

Nail vigorously supported cultural activities and commercial ventures in Harlem. He provided financial support to the Colored Merchants' Association, which had been created to advance racial solidarity and economic stability, and he briefly served as vice president of the New York Urban League. He was chair of the finance committee of the 135th Street branch of the YMCA, and he donated money to programs sponsored by the National Association for the Advancement of Colored People (NAACP). Nail often raised money for independent artists and causes he respected. He and Eugene Kinckle Jones gathered funds for the artist Augusta Savage, who later founded Savage Studio of Arts and Crafts in New York and served as an assistant supervisor at the Works Progress Administration. Nail also joined W. E. B Du Bois as a director on the board of Black Swan Records.

Nail's detractors said that he was intractable and insensitive to progressive causes. Some tenants claimed that Nail was an exploitative landlord who overcharged his tenants. Nail's philosophy reflected that of Booker T. Washington, who emphasized the importance of establishing an economic foundation on which blacks could build a stronger and more stable community; this philosophy clashed with the visions of Marcus Garvey, the founder of the Universal Negro Improvement Association (UNIA). Garvey's black nationalism and "back to Africa" program repelled Nail, who was interested in supporting African American economic development rather than establishing unity among African migrants across the world.

Nail joined Robert Abbott, the publisher of the *Chicago Defender*, the entrepreneur Harry Pace, NAACP's field secretary William Pickens, and four additional outspoken African American leaders seeking to discredit Garvey. Nail and this "committee of eight" were convinced that Garvey was undermining their efforts to balance race relations. The group drafted a letter to Harry M. Daugherty, United States attorney general during the Harding administration, in which they said: "The movement known as the Universal Negro Improvement Association has done much to stimulate the violent temper of this dangerous element [a reference to Garvey's coalition of immigrants and frustrated black citizens]. . . . Its president and moving spirit is one Marcus Garvey, an unscrupulous demagogue, who has ceaselessly and assiduously sought to spread among Negroes distrust and hatred of all white people." Garvey responded by calling the committee "Uncle Tom Negroes." This episode reflected a split between elite black business representatives and community leaders on the one hand and, on the other, lower-income and middle-class blacks who supported Garvey's celebration of African culture.

Although Nail and Parker temporarily weathered the Depression, the firm collapsed in 1933. Nail eventually formed the John E. Nail Company and continued to solidify his strong reputation among business and real estate leaders. He was the first black member of the Real Estate Board of New York, and he became the only sitting black member of the Housing Committee of New York. Nail also served President Herbert Hoover as a consultant for his Committee on Housing during the Depression. Nail's connections to Harlem's cultural beacons remained strong. James Weldon Johnson married Nail's sister, Grace Nail Johnson, who preserved voluminous writings and letters by Harlemite authors and artists.

Nail died in 1947; obituaries appeared in the *New York Times* and the *New York Herald-Tribune* on 6 March and in *New York Age* on 15 March.

A John E. Nail *Scrapbook* is held at Yale University's Beinecke Rare Book and Manuscript Library. The *Scrapbook* is one element of the James Weldon Johnson Collection, which was founded in 1941 by Carl Van Vechten. Grace Nail Johnson contributed her husband's papers to it. The Schomburg Center for Research in Black Culture has the personal papers of William Pickens, which include letters from Nail.

Biography

John E. (Jack) Nail was born 22 August 1883 in New London, Connecticut. He was raised in New York City, where his father, John Bennett Nail (d. 1942), managed a profitable restaurant, hotel, and billiard parlor on Sixth Avenue and owned several properties in Manhattan; the elder Nail was the first African American to receive a credit rating from Dun and Bradstreet and was a silent partner in his son's business interests. John E. Nail worked briefly for his father after graduating from high school, then opened his own real estate office in the Bronx. In 1904, Philip A. Payton persuaded him to leave this business and join the Afro-American Realty Company, based in Harlem. Nail and Henry C. Parker left Payton to open their own firm, Nail and Parker, in 1907, with Nail as president and Parker as corporate secretary-treasurer. Nail married Grace Fairfax in 1910; they had no children. Nail and Parker's firm collapsed in 1933; Nail later formed the John E. Nail Company. Nail's sister married James Weldon Johnson. Nail died in New York City 6 March 1947.

R. JAKE SUDDERTH

See also Abbott, Robert Sengstacke; Afro-American Realty Company; Black Swan Phonograph Company; Garvey, Marcus; Johnson, James Weldon; Jones, Eugene Kinckle; Pace, Harry H.; Payton, Philip A.; Pickens, William; Saint Philip's Protestant Episcopal Church; Savage, Augusta; Tenderloin; Walker, Madame C. J.; Washington, Booker T.

Further Reading

Boris, Joseph J., ed. *Who's Who in Colored America: A Biographical Dictionary of Notable Living Persons of African*

Descent in America. New York: Who's Who in Colored America, 1929.

Crisis, March 1925. (Contains a profile of Nail.)

Draper, Theodore. *The Rediscovery of Black Nationalism*. New York: Viking, 1970.

Garvey, Amy Jacques, ed. *Philosophy and Opinions of Marcus Garvey*. Dover, Mass.: Majority, 1986.

Ingham, John N., and Lynne B. Feldman. *African-American Business Leaders: A Biographical Dictionary*. Westport, Conn.: Greenwood, 1994.

Johnson, James Weldon. *Black Manhattan*. New York: Da Capo, 1991.

Kranz, Rachel C., ed. "James Weldon Johnson." In *The Biographical Dictionary of Black Americans*. New York: Facts on File News Services, 1992.

Nail, John. E. "$20,000,000 in Negro Holdings." *New York Evening Mail*, 26 January 1918.

Osofsky, Gilbert. *Harlem: The Making of a Ghetto—Negro New York, 1890–1930*. New York: Harper and Row, 1966.

Nance, Ethel Ray

Through her secretarial and administrative work with W. E. B. Du Bois and Charles S. Johnson, Ethel Ray Nance made significant contributions to the Harlem Renaissance and became instrumental in its reconstruction in later years. Nance's relationship with Du Bois began in 1921, when she was twenty-two, and lasted until his death in Ghana in 1963. Nance, the daughter of the president of the Duluth, Minnesota, chapter of the National Association for the Advancement of Colored People (NAACP), first met Du Bois at the St. Paul NAACP. Her relationship with Johnson started in 1923: As the director of research for the Urban League, he attended its national conference in Kansas City, Missouri, where the impressive Nance was employed as an executive secretary for the local chapter. Nance moved to New York in 1924 to become Johnson's executive secretary; she assisted him in his sociological research and at *Opportunity* magazine (of which he was the founder and editor) through the winter of 1925. Years later, in 1953, Nance once again joined Johnson's staff, running his office for a short time during his tenure as Fisk University's first black president. At the time of Nance's retirement in 1977, there was a renewed interest in the Harlem Renaissance and her participation in it.

Du Bois and Johnson were only two of the African American executives who wanted Nance to work for them; she was an enormously gifted young woman who had received national attention in the black press in 1923 for breaking the secretarial color bar in the Minnesota State Legislature. After graduating from high school in 1919, her father had taken her on long trips, by train, during which he had introduced her to black leaders—and also to the racist conditions under which their southern relatives were still living. In 1921, three black men were lynched near her own home in Duluth; this incident left her with a lifelong dedication to the black cause.

When Nance joined Johnson's staff in 1924, in addition to running his office she carried on independent research and functioned as managing editor of *Opportunity*. She wrote news items, screened manuscript submissions, and read proofs. A short sketch by Nance appeared in *Opportunity* in 1924, but she did not envision a writing career for herself; she focused on supporting the work of others, with confidence in her own artistic taste. She knew Aaron Douglas's Afrocentric art from her days in Kansas City, where he taught high school, and she recommended his work for inclusion in Alain Locke's anthology *The New Negro* in 1925. Countee Cullen respected her literary judgment and sought her opinion on some of his poems.

Nance served as Johnson's talent scout and his link to the younger generation; she reviewed new books and literary publications from historically black colleges and universities and brought promising writers to his attention. She waged a campaign to get Douglas to New York and persuaded Du Bois to hire him at *The Crisis*; she also offered Douglas (as she offered Zora Neale Hurston at another time) temporary use of the sofa in "Dream Haven," the apartment she shared with Regina Anderson and Louella Tucker at 580 Saint Nicholas Avenue in Harlem. Nance was the model for a character in Carl Van Vechten's novel *Nigger Heaven*—Olive Hamilton, the "responsible secretary-stenographer"—but she herself deplored the book.

Nance made the first cuts on submissions in *Opportunity*'s literary contest of 1925, handled negotiations with the panel of judges, gave Johnson many ideas for the awards dinner, and was in charge of the seating arrangements at the Fifth Avenue Restaurant. At the dinner, she shared a table with two of the winners: Countee Cullen and Langston Hughes, who were both visitors to "Dream Haven."

Although Nance was not actually employed by Du Bois until years later, she spent a lot of time with him while she was working at *Opportunity*, consulting him, sharing ideas about art and politics, and—as she did for Johnson—putting him in contact with the younger generation. Du Bois respected her organizational skills, which had first come to his attention in 1922 when she sent him petitions she gathered in Minnesota for the Dyer antilynching bill. Nance, unlike many others, was at ease with the formidable Du Bois and brought out his playful side, which was rarely visible. As her meager salary from *Opportunity* dwindled toward the end of each month, she felt free to call Du Bois and get dinner invitations for herself and her roommates. She credited Du Bois with awakening her to intellectual life.

Nance remained in Harlem for less than two years. In late 1925 she took a month's leave from *Opportunity* to care for her ailing mother in Duluth and then decided to stay there as caretaker (a decision she still regretted many years later). However, she retained the spirit of uplift and racial pride of the Harlem Renaissance. She organized book clubs, did volunteer work with civil rights groups, and founded and participated in historical societies devoted to documenting and celebrating the achievements of black America. She became the first black policewoman in Minnesota (1928) and the first black woman ship inspector in Seattle, Washington (1943). In 1945, Du Bois, who was a consultant at the founding meeting of the United Nations, brought her to San Francisco as his secretary, a position she considered the peak of her career. Following a brief period in New York to conduct research for Du Bois, she returned to San Francisco, serving as administrative assistant in the NAACP's new West Coast Regional Office. She had a series of pioneering secretarial and administrative positions, ending with seven years at the San Francisco African American Historical and Cultural Society, which she had helped found decades earlier. She retired in 1977.

During the 1960s, renewed interest in the Harlem Renaissance prompted Nance to publish an article on *Opportunity*'s dinner of 1925; it also made her the subject of several valuable interviews for oral histories. She contributed to volumes on the renaissance published by Arna Bontemps, Nathan Huggins, and David Levering Lewis. In 1978, at age seventy-nine, Nance was awarded a B.A. from the University of San Francisco and was honored as the university's oldest graduate. She remained intensely engaged in civic activities and in documenting the black presence in California and also worked on a memoir of Du Bois (which was unpublished as of this writing). When Nance died in

1992, the San Francisco Board of Supervisors adjourned out of respect for her memory.

Biography

Ethel Ray Nance was born 13 April 1899 in Duluth, Minnesota; she was the daughter of a Swedish immigrant mother and a race-conscious black father who had migrated to Minnesota from North Carolina. Nance studied at public schools in Duluth and at the University of San Francisco (B.A., 1978). She was a secretary for the Minnesota State Relief Commission, Moose Lake, Minnesota, 1919–1922; Minnesota House of Representatives, 1923; Urban League, Kansas City, Missouri, 1923–1924; and New York Urban League, 1924–1925. She was associate head resident, Phillis Wheatley Settlement House, Minneapolis, 1926–1928; a policewoman in Minneapolis, 1928–1932; secretary to the commissioner of education, St. Paul, Minnesota, 1937–1940; secretary at the Hampton Institute, 1940–1943; secretary at the Federal Public Housing Authority, Seattle, Washington, 1944–1945; secretary–research assistant to W. E. B. Du Bois, San Francisco, 1945; and administrative assistant, West Coast Regional Office, NAACP, San Francisco, California, 1945–1953. Nance also worked for Fisk University, Nashville, Tennessee, 1953–1954; Veterans Administration, San Francisco, 1954–1956; San Francisco Unified School District, 1956–1964; United States Post Office, San Francisco, 1964–1969; and San Francisco Historical and Cultural Society, 1970–1977. Her awards included a certificate of recognition from the San Francisco Unified School District, 1964; a certificate of merit from the San Francisco Negro Historical and Cultural Society, 1965; a scholarship to the University of California, 1968; and the Sojourner Truth Award, San Francisco, 1981. She was a member of the Association for the United Nations, Sickle Cell Anemia Research Federation, San Francisco Historical and Cultural Society, National Council of Negro Women, and National Association for the Advancement of Colored People (NAACP). Nance was married twice and had two sons. She retired in 1977 and died in San Francisco on 11 July 1992.

ONITA ESTES-HICKS

See also Anderson, Regina M.; Cullen, Countee; Du Bois, W. E. B.; 580 Saint Nicholas Avenue; Hughes, Langston; Hurston, Zora Neale; Johnson, Charles Spurgeon;

Nigger Heaven; Opportunity; Opportunity Awards Dinner; Opportunity Literary Contests; Survey Graphic; Van Vechten, Carl

Selected Works

"And Along Came Ben." *Opportunity*, January 1924, p. 24.

"The New York Arts Renaissance: 1924–1926." *Negro History Bulletin*, April 1968, pp. 15–19.

Further Reading

Bontemps, Arna. *The Harlem Renaissance Remembered*. New York: Dodd Mead, 1972.

Huggins, Nathan Irvin. *Harlem Renaissance*. New York: Oxford University Press, 1971.

Hull, Gloria. *Color, Sex, and Poetry: Three Women Writers of the Harlem Renaissance*. Bloomington: Indiana University Press, 1987.

Kirschke, Amy Helene. *Aaron Douglas: Art, Race, and the Harlem Renaissance*. Jackson: University Press of Mississippi, 1995.

Lewis, David Levering. *When Harlem Was in Vogue*. New York: Knopf, 1981. (See also Penguin ed., 1997.)

———. *W. E. B. Du Bois: The Fight for Equality and the American Century, 1919–1963*. New York: Holt, 2000.

Shockley, Ann Allen. Interview with Ethel Ray Nance, 18 November 1970.

Smith, Jessie Carney. "Ethel Nance." In *Notable Black American Women*. Detroit, Mich.: Gale Research, 1992, pp. 789–792.

Taylor, David Vassar. Transcript of an interview with Ethel Nance, 15 May 1974.

Ulansky, Gene. "A Quiet Storm," *Excel*, Fall 1989, pp. 40–42.

Van Vechten, Carl. *Nigger Heaven*. Urbana: University of Illinois Press, 2000.

Watson, Steven. *The Harlem Renaissance, Hub of American Culture, 1920–1930*. New York: Pantheon, 1995.

Wintz, Cary D. *Black Culture and the Harlem Renaissance*. Houston, Tex.: Rice University Press, 1988.

Nation, The

The Nation, a weekly journal devoted to politics and the arts, was founded in 1865. Under the leadership of its first editor, E. L. Godkin, *The Nation* supported the Fourteenth Amendment's extension of the franchise to black men, but the magazine then failed to support radical Reconstruction and adopted an antiunion and culturally conservative perspective. During the 1920s, under the editorship of Oswald Garrison Villard, it was one of a few white publications to take a major interest in the Harlem Renaissance. Villard served as the magazine's editor from 1918 until 1932 and guided its strong support for trade unions, pacifism, anti-imperialism, women's rights, and racial justice. For most of its history from that time to this, *The Nation* has been one of the foremost left-liberal magazines in the United States.

Throughout the 1920s and into the 1930s, *The Nation* published poems, essays, and book reviews by or about many of the leaders of the Harlem Renaissance, including Countee Cullen, W. E. B. Du Bois, E. Franklin Frazier, Langston Hughes, Alain Locke, Claude McKay, George Schuyler, and Walter White. It covered the activities of the National Association for the Advancement of Colored People (NAACP) and the National Urban League. *The Nation* also reported on and editorialized about a number of topics of interest to participants in the Harlem Renaissance: antiracism movements, the southern "oligarchy," the Ku Klux Klan, segregation, the antilynching movement, prejudice, the achievements of African Americans, race riots, Jim Crow, voting rights, and justice for Haiti and other parts of the Caribbean. There were, however, limitations on the magazine's racially progressive stance, including its relative inattention to black female leaders of the renaissance and its dismissal of Marcus Garvey and black nationalism.

The most famous contribution of *The Nation* to the Harlem Renaissance was the publication, in 1926, of an exchange between George S. Schuyler and Langston Hughes concerning the nature of Negro art in America. In "The Negro-Art Hokum," Schuyler claimed that such art was nonexistent in that there were no racial or cultural differences between blacks and whites in the United States. In "The Negro Artist and the Racial Mountain," Hughes argued that standing in the way of the realization of Negro art was the very attitude of men like Schuyler, which shaped a "racial mountain": the desire of many blacks to be just like whites. In contrast, Hughes argued that the black masses provided the source for an art, best exemplified by jazz, that was based in racial themes.

Perhaps the final essay on the Harlem Renaissance to be published by *The Nation* was Claude McKay's "Harlem Runs Wild." In this essay, McKay argued that the riot in Harlem in 1935, which has been said to mark the end of the renaissance, was not a race riot but a gesture of despair resulting from extreme poverty and resentment at the refusal of white merchants in Harlem to hire black workers. The progressive racial politics of the magazine continued after the 1930s, but the Harlem Renaissance faded from *The Nation* as it did from the nation.

MICHAEL BENNETT

See also Hughes, Langston; McKay, Claude; Riots: 4—Harlem Riot, 1935; Schuyler, George S.; Villard, Oswald Garrison

Further Reading

Hughes, Langston. "The Negro Artist and the Racial Mountain." *Nation*, 23 June 1926.

Hutchinson, George. *The Harlem Renaissance in Black and White*. Cambridge, Mass.: Belknap Press of Harvard University Press, 1995.

Lewis, David Levering, ed. *The Portable Harlem Renaissance Reader*. New York: Viking, 1994.

McKay, Claude. "Harlem Runs Wild." *Nation*, 3 April 1935.

Schuyler, George S. "The Negro-Art Hokum." *The Nation*, 16 June 1926.

National Association for the Advancement of Colored People

The National Association for the Advancement of Colored People (NAACP) is the oldest and most celebrated civil rights organization in the United States. Since its formation in 1909, the group has been at the forefront of numerous struggles for equality in America, calling on the nation as a whole to abide by the Fourteenth and Fifteenth amendments to the Constitution, and to end all racial violence and discrimination—social, political, and economic. The group's activities during the 1920s and the era of the "New Negro" movement are central to its history, for during this period the NAACP matured into the civil rights organization that has been a beacon of light for many African Americans for much of its existence.

Before the creation of the NAACP, other groups had constructed platforms on which it would build. For example, the Afro-American League—later the Afro-American Council—was assembled in 1890 and created

Twentieth annual session of the NAACP, 1929. (Library of Congress.)

a strategy to confront discrimination in America that was similar to that of the NAACP. Around the turn of the twentieth century, a group of radicals, led by W. E. B. Du Bois and William Monroe Trotter, began to challenge what they perceived as the Afro-American Council's conservative leadership and the influence of Booker T. Washington within the organization. By 1905, Du Bois and Trotter created their own group, the Niagara movement, which was dedicated to persistent agitation for civil rights, equal education, and general human rights. Both the Afro-American Council and the Niagara movement would continue their struggles up to the development of the NAACP.

The creation of the NAACP was precipitated by an article by William English Walling, in which he graphically described two days of racial violence that took place in Springfield, Illinois, in August 1908 and lamented that there was no "large and powerful body of citizens" prepared to respond and come to the aid of the black population. Mary White Ovington wrote to Walling, asking him to meet her and a few others in New York to discuss the "Negro problem." During January 1909, Ovington, Walling, Dr. Henry Moskowitz, Oswald Garrison Villard, Charles E. Russell, Bishop Alexander Walters, and Rev. William Henry Brooks met, discussed the race question, and decided to call a larger conference to address the issue. In February, the group presented a call written by Villard and signed by sixty prominent black and white Americans, including W. E. B. Du Bois, Ida B. Wells Barnett, Mary Church Terrell, and Jane Addams. The call reflected the platforms of the Afro-American Council and the Niagara movement, emphasizing the protection of black people's rights guaranteed by the Fourteenth and Fifteenth amendments.

In response to the call, the National Negro Conference, held 30 May–1 June 1909, created the Committee of Forty, whose mission was to develop plans for the creation of an effective organization tentatively called the "Committee for the Advancement of the Negro Race." The committee's plans were implemented the following year at a second annual conference, during which the organization's permanent name was adopted and its first officers were selected. They included Moorfield Storey as president, William E. Walling as executive committee chairman, John E. Milholland as treasurer, Oswald Garrison Villard as disbursing treasurer, Frances Blascoer as executive secretary, and W. E. B. Du Bois, the only black officer, as director of publicity and research.

Once the organization was created, it immediately began what has been nearly a century of militant protest and litigation against the denial of African Americans' constitutional rights. Within the first year, the group began agitating for better job opportunities for blacks and greater protection from racial violence in the South. The group also established its first local branch in Chicago and, under the guidance of Du Bois, launched *The Crisis*, a magazine that quickly became the leading voice in the black struggle. Du Bois published political articles and literary works aimed at educating the readership, white and black, about black culture, black history, and American racism. He hoped to instill pride in the African American community and stir readers of both races to action. *The Crisis* grew from its initial publication of 1,000 copies in 1910 to a circulation of 16,000 the following year, and to almost 104,000 by 1919.

By the end of the association's fifth year, it had twenty-four branches and had initiated numerous crusades against discrimination. Among other things, the group had begun campaigning against the exclusion of black lawyers from the American Bar Association, laid the groundwork for a legal attack on residential segregation, protested against a number of anti-intermarriage bills, and objected to President Woodrow Wilson's policy of segregating African American government employees. During the next few years, the group continued to battle against racism and racial injustice, campaigning, for example, against the film *The Birth of a Nation*. The organization also called for the African American population to "close the ranks" in support of the war effort; the association's president would argue a case, involving residential segregation in Louisville, before the U.S. Supreme Court.

During and just after World War I, a series of race riots in numerous cities took place throughout the nation, the worst occurring in East St. Louis in 1917 and in Chicago in 1919. The NAACP responded in 1917 by conducting a silent parade of 15,000 people in Harlem.

In 1919, the group called for the creation of a Legal Defense Fund to employ lawyers to increase the association's attempts to end such lynching and mob violence and to bring the culprits to justice. Also in 1919, the organization published its famous study *Thirty Years of Lynching in the United States, 1889–1918*.

Although the migration of African Americans to the North during the 1910s created real as well as imagined competition for jobs, housing, and recreational space and precipitated much of the racial violence during the period, it also aided the development and growth of the NAACP. During this period of turmoil, many northern and southern African Americans joined the organization. In fact, the number of black members grew so quickly that by 1920 their membership fees were supplying most of the association's income. More important, during this period African Americans began to play a role in the organization's leadership. In 1916, James Weldon Johnson was hired as field secretary, and in 1918, Walter White became assistant executive secretary.

During the next decade, the organization entered "young adulthood," maturing and increasingly taking actions that laid the foundation for full adulthood. In the 1920s, in addition to its continued propaganda campaign against lynching and other forms of racial violence, the NAACP stepped up its use of the courts to challenge racial injustices. The organization applied two criteria when deciding on a case: first, whether it involved injustice or discrimination related to race, and second, whether it would establish a precedent for protecting black people's rights as a whole. (These criteria were applied on the national level; local branches continued to accept nearly any case involving injustice.)

In the wake of the racial violence that closed the 1910s, the NAACP lobbied the Republican Party to introduce legislation in Congress making lynching a federal crime. Nothing came of its efforts in the election year (1920); in 1922, however, as a result of lobbying by James Weldon Johnson, who was now the association's executive secretary (1920–1930), the NAACP was successful in getting the House of Representatives to pass an antilynching bill introduced by Congressman L. C. Dyer of Missouri. However, a filibuster in the Senate, led by a coalition of northern Republicans and southern Democrats, later killed the bill. Ironically, on the same day that the Senate crushed the Dyer bill, a mob in Kirby, Texas, burned three African Americans alive, making it obvious that federal legislation was needed.

In the face of such blatant disregard for the rights and welfare of black Americans, the NAACP pressed forward. Regardless of its failure to gain the passage of federal legislation and its frustration with the lack of commitment by national political parties to issues that were critical to the African American community, many in the association did see some positive aspects of their battles on Capital Hill. As James Weldon Johnson commented, "The Dyer Anti-Lynching Bill did not become law, but it made of the floors of Congress a forum in which the facts were discussed and brought home to the American people as they had never been before."

The NAACP's antilynching campaign was central to this growing public awareness. Along with the group's lobbying activity, there were the propaganda campaign in *The Crisis* and the investigative activities of Walter White. After a mob brutally attacked the association's executive secretary, John Shillady, while he was in Texas investigating a lynching, White, an African American from Atlanta who had fair complexion, blond hair, and blue eyes, became the organization's chief investigator of lynching and mob violence.

White, often posing as a northern white journalist, penetrated white communities where racist crimes had occurred. One such incident followed events in Phillips County, Arkansas. In late 1919, African American sharecroppers' attempts to form a union precipitated a violent confrontation with armed whites that ended with a massacre of black farmers. In a hasty trial, twelve blacks were sentenced to death. The NAACP, led by a local black attorney, Scipio A. Jones, set out to reverse the convictions. The organization took the case to the Supreme Court, where Moorfield Storey argued it. The Supreme Court reversed the convictions and remanded the cases to the lower courts. On the district level, Jones retook control of the cases and secured either discharges, commutation of sentences, or short prison terms for the twelve defendants.

This victory—which came in 1923, a year after the Senate had killed the Dyer bill—demonstrated that the NAACP's legal and investigative strategy could strike a decisive blow against Jim Crow. During this period, the organization also chipped away at America's system of segregation, achieving minor successes against white Democratic primaries in the South. This long struggle began in July 1924, when Dr. Lawrence A. Nixon attempted to cast his ballot in a primary election in East El Paso, Texas. Three years later the Supreme Court ruled in a 5–4 decision that states could not lodge discriminatory practices in the party executive committees, although it failed to determine whether conventions could bar African American members. With this modest victory, the NAACP pressed forward, continuing to strike at the all-white primaries. The fight would require three more decisions by the Supreme Court over the next three decades.

The NAACP also forged ahead, though with less success, in its legal struggle against restrictive covenants that encouraged the segregation of a growing northern urban black population into overcrowded city neighborhoods. Since its inception, the NAACP had waged a war against residential segregation, most often initiating legal action after some sort of provable intimidation or lawlessness. During the first two decades of its existence, the association initiated investigations of housing segregation in cities such as Kansas City, Baltimore, Philadelphia, Cleveland, and Minneapolis. The organization also gained favorable decisions from the Supreme Court in cases originating in Louisville, Kentucky (*Buchanan v. Warely*, 1917), and Richmond, Virginia (*City of Richmond v. Deans*, 1930).

The most celebrated case involving residential segregation, however, grew out of an incident in Detroit. On 8 September 1925, Dr. Ossian Sweet, a middle-class African American surgeon, moved his family into a hostile white neighborhood in Detroit's East Side. Some people immediately protested his presence, and on the following day the objections became much more aggressive: An angry mob surrounded the property and pounded the house with stones and gunfire. Sweet, along with his two brothers, Otis and Henry, and a few friends who had joined them in anticipation of trouble, fired on the mob and killed one of the whites in the street. Once the bullets began to come from the house, the police, who had been idly standing by, moved in and arrested Sweet and the rest of the occupants. The NAACP took on their defense; after a hung jury in the first trial, in 1927 it gained an acquittal of Sweet's brother Henry and a dismissal of all the other cases.

At the end of the 1920s, the NAACP gained a legal or lobbying victory that demonstrated its strength and influence. After the death of Justice Edward Terry Sanford of the Supreme Court, President Herbert Hoover chose Judge John J. Parker of the Fourth Circuit Court to succeed him. Parker, a North Carolinian who as a gubernatorial candidate had supported the disenfranchisement of African Americans, immediately drew objections from the NAACP. With the support of labor unions, which had their own qualms about Parker, the NAACP set into motion coalitions against him and lobbied the Senate not to confirm his nomination. Within two months the Senate did reject the nominee—an action that at the time had rarely been seen in Washington.

Because the vote in the Senate had been close (41–39), the association moved against the recalcitrant senators. In the general elections after the confirmation hearing, the NAACP waged campaigns against incumbent senators who represented regions of the country where African American voters could unseat them. Senator Henry Allen of Kansas was one of the first to feel the effect at the polls; over the next four years, senators from California, Missouri, Indiana, Ohio, Pennsylvania, West Virginia, New Jersey, Connecticut, and Rhode Island also lost their seats. Such political action demonstrated the strength the organization had gained during the 1920s. Earlier, in 1922, the NAACP had not possessed the muscle nor the political capital to wage such campaigns against senators who voted against the Dyer antilynching bill.

The NAACP also played a central role in the evolution of the cultural movement of the decade variously known as the Harlem Renaissance or the New Negro movement. *The Crisis* had become the voice of postwar African America, and it gave space in its pages to young black writers and encouraged them to hone their craft and create work that would dismantle the negative stereotypes of African Americans appearing in much of American literature and art.

During the 1920s *The Crisis* published literary works by Gwendolyn Bennett, Anita Scott Coleman, Countee Cullen, Langston Hughes, Fenton Johnson, Georgia Douglas Johnson, Claude McKay, and Jean Toomer, among numerous illustrious authors; it also published literary criticism by William Stanley Braithwaite and others. Furthermore, in 1924, *The Crisis*, in conjunction with the NAACP and Amy Spingarn, established annual prizes in literature and art, which became an important showcase for new talent. The review board for the prizes included Sinclair Lewis, Edward Bok, Charles W. Chesnutt, Robert Morse Lovett, Witter Bynner, Van Wyck Brooks, Carl Van Doren, Zona Gales, James Weldon Johnson, Eugene O'Neill, H. G. Wells, and Amy Spingarn. The recipients of the awards included Arna Bontemps, Frank Horne, Countee Cullen, and Langston Hughes for poetry; Rudolph Fisher and Anita Scott Coleman for short stories; Hughes for essays; and Willis Richardson for drama. In addition, in 1926, *The Crisis* published a symposium—"The Negro in Art: How Shall He Be Portrayed?"—on the rising cultural movement. Contributors to the roundtable included Sherwood Anderson, W. E. B. Du Bois, Sinclair Lewis, and Vachel Lindsay.

Although *The Crisis* had published literary works since its inception, its ability to do so was greatly enhanced during Jessie Redmon Fauset's tenure as its literary editor (1919–1926). Fauset herself wrote poetry, short stories, and novels. In early 1924, Boni and Liveright published her first novel, *There Is Confusion*; and over the next decade she would write three more novels: *Plum Bun* (1929), *The Chinaberry Tree* (1931), and *Comedy: American Style* (1933). Fauset's numerous poems, essays, and short stories appeared in a number of periodicals, including *The Crisis* and the NAACP's *Brownies' Book*—a magazine for children that Du Bois started in 1920 and that was edited by Fauset and Augustus Granville Dill.

In addition to being a central contributor to the Harlem Renaissance, Fauset was an important talent scout and mentor of the burgeoning movement. Together with Du Bois, the chief editor of *The Crisis*, Fauset set out to create a forum for young writers to publish their work and to convey a new image of African America to the community as well as to the nation as a whole. According to Langston Hughes, one of the emerging artists of the period, Fauset, along with a few others, "midwifed the so-called New Negro literature into being. Kind and critical—but not too critical for the young—they nursed us along until our books were born." As literary editor, Fauset introduced writers such as Hughes, Gwendolyn Bennett, Countee Cullen, Fenton Johnson, Georgia Douglas Johnson, Claude McKay, and Jean Toomer to a national audience.

During the same year that Fauset's *There Is Confusion* was published, another active member of the NAACP became a working participant in the mushrooming literary activity of the African American community. In 1923, Walter White, the association's assistant secretary and chief investigator of lynching, tried his hand at artistic expression. He produced the manuscript of his first novel, about an African American doctor who has been trained in the North and then returns to his native small town in Georgia. After some revisions and wrangles with publishers, White's novel, *The Fire and the Flint*, appeared under the Knopf imprint, about five months after *There Is Confusion*. White received praise for his artistic vision and his realistic portrayal of southern life. Two years later, he published a second novel, *Flight* (1926); this in turn was followed a few years later by a study of the social, economic, and sexual influences of lynching, *Rope and Faggot: The Biography of Judge Lynch* (1929).

White was also an important mentor to many young writers, and he became a link between the growing black artistic community and the white world of money, publicity, and publishers. Once *Fire in the Flint* had achieved modest success, White used his new literary weight to connect with people in high places. He soon impressed many cultured benefactors and publishing heavyweights like Alfred A. Knopf, Horace Liveright, Sinclair Lewis, and Carl Van Vechten. He used his new contacts to help publish the work of young writers, such as Countee Cullen's first collection of poetry, *Color* (1924). White also commented on the growing literary and cultural movement in a number of essays published in various newspapers and journals during 1925 and 1926, including a series of literary columns in the *Pittsburgh Courier* called "The Spotlight."

The poet, novelist, essayist, and lyricist James Weldon Johnson, the NAACP's executive secretary, also contributed his share to the New Negro movement. As the poet and professor Sterling Brown remarked, by his "interpretations of Negro poetry and music, by his occasional essays on the problems of Negro writers, and by his own creative work James Weldon Johnson succeeded more than any predecessor in furthering the cause of Negro artists." Even before the Harlem Renaissance, Johnson had been one of the few African Americans to publish a novel, although anonymously. This was *The Autobiography of an Ex-Colored Man* (1912). The novel attracted renewed interest in 1927, when Johnson announced that he was its author. During the same year he published a collection of lyrical verse, *God's Trombones: Seven Negro Sermons in Verse* (1927), in which he captured the imagery, style, and fervor of traditional black preachers and the African American church. On the eve of the renaissance, he had edited a large anthology, *The Book of American Negro Poetry* (1922); during the renaissance, he collaborated with his brother, the composer and singer John Rosamond Johnson, in publishing two collections of spirituals: *The Book of American Negro Spirituals* (1925) and *The Second Book of American Negro Spirituals* (1926).

Like Johnson, W. E. B. Du Bois, the association's director of research and editor of *The Crisis* (1910–1934), was an elder statesman of the renaissance. Before the era of the New Negro, Du Bois had already established himself as an intellectual and was widely acclaimed as an author and international scholar. By 1920 he had published numerous articles in a wide range of journals, including *The Crisis, Atlantic Monthly*, and *The Nation*. He had been a professor at Atlanta University and had also published many books, including a sociological study, *The Philadelphia Negro* (1898); a famous collection of essays, *The Souls of Black Folk* (1903); his first novel, *The Quest of the Silver Fleece* (1911); a biography, *John Brown* (1909); and a second collection of essays and verse, *Darkwater: Voices from within the Veil* (1920).

Du Bois had been urging a reawakening of black art for a number of years. Since the late nineteenth century, Du Bois had been seeking the most effective means of establishing Africa's descendants among the world's recognized peoples. According to Du Bois, one way to gain such universal recognition was through the arts—in *The Souls of Black Folk* he gave precedence to music, the "sorrow songs"—and the New Negro renaissance offered encouragement that black poets, novelists, painters, and playwrights might win this larger recognition. Du Bois argued in the early 1920s that African Americans would be regarded "as human" when their art "compels recognition." James Weldon Johnson was in agreement with this idea; he noted in the preface to *The Book of American Negro Poetry* that "the final measure of the greatness of all peoples is in the amount and standard of the literature and art they have produced." Du Bois, as the editor of *The Crisis*, played a central role in developing and encouraging young writers and promoting the movement. He also continued his high level of scholarly and literary production with the publication of numerous essays in journals and two more books, *The Gifts of Black Folk* (1924) and the novel *Dark Princess* (1928).

Despite Du Bois's initial hope that the artistic production of young black artists would bring worldwide recognition to African Americans, within a few years of the beginning of the renaissance he had become disillusioned with the movement and many of its artists. His frustration was occasioned by a continued outpouring of so-called realistic renderings of Harlem's street life and the lives of the lower classes. Two extreme examples of such writing are *Nigger Heaven* (1926), by the white author Carl Van Vechten, and Claude McKay's *Home to Harlem* (1928). In the symposium "The Negro in Art" that *The Crisis* held in 1926, Du Bois accused many of the younger writers of failing to recognize their political and social responsibilities. "All art is propaganda," he asserted, "and ever must be, despite the wailing of the purist." Two years later, Du Bois published his second novel, *Dark Princess*, to illustrate his point. The story centers on a black man who falls in love with a beautiful Indian princess, and on a plot among representatives of the darker nations of the world to rid themselves forever of white domination.

As the 1920s came to a close, the NAACP lost some of its interest in the new literary movement; as the Depression set in, the renaissance itself waned. During the next decade, the association focused its energy on its major objective—the dismantling of the Jim Crow system. During the 1930s, the NAACP would experience some setbacks with the resignations of James Weldon Johnson in 1930 and Du Bois in 1934, but the organization still pushed forward with its agenda, an agenda greatly aided in the early 1930s by the formation of its legal committee. Before this time, the association had worked with numerous—mainly white—lawyers who worked pro bono or for a nominal fee. By mid-1935, after deciding to develop its own legal staff, the group hired Charles H. Houston, dean of Howard Law School, as its full-time special counsel. Houston put together a legal team that had a considerable black presence and that included his former student Thurgood Marshall.

The NAACP's new legal staff developed a two-pronged strategy to fight discrimination in education in the South. It directly attacked the exclusion of blacks from professional and graduate programs at southern state schools, and indirectly contested segregation and discrimination at the primary and secondary levels with regard to salaries, facilities, and length of school terms. The group sought to force the South either to strengthen African American institutions or to desegregate on the basis that it was too costly to keep separate institutions open. The first step in the new legal strategy was to win victories on the local and state levels in order to create a precedent that the association could build on to dismantle the Supreme Court's decision in *Plessy v. Ferguson*. On this premise the NAACP, now under the leadership of Walter White, started along the road to *Brown v. Board of Education*. Or, to change the metaphor, using the foundation that it had laid during the 1920s, the association helped construct the modern civil rights movement.

SHAWN LEIGH ALEXANDER

See also Antilynching Crusade; Brownies' Book, The; Civil Rights and Law; Crisis, The; Crisis, The: Literary Prizes; Crisis, The: The Negro in Art—How Shall He Be Portrayed? A Symposium; Du Bois, W. E. B.; Fauset, Jessie Redmon; Johnson, James Weldon; Niagara Movement; White, Walter; *other specific individuals*

Further Reading

Factor, Robert L. *The Black Response to America: Men, Ideals, and Organization, from Frederick Douglass to the NAACP.* Reading, Mass.: Addison-Wesley, 1970.

Goings, Kenneth W. *The NAACP Comes of Age: The Defeat of Judge John J. Parker.* Bloomington: Indiana University Press, 1990.

Hine, Darlene Clark. *Black Victory: The Rise and Fall of the White Primary in Texas.* Millwood, N.Y.: KTO, 1979.

Huggins, Nathan Irvin. *Harlem Renaissance.* New York: Oxford University Press, 1971.

Hughes, Langston. *Fight for Freedom: The Story of the NAACP.* New York: Norton, 1962.

Janken, Kenneth Robert. *White: The Biography of Walter White, Mr. NAACP.* New York: New Press, 2003.

Johnson, James Weldon. *Along This Way: The Autobiography of James Weldon Johnson.* New York: Da Capo, 2000. (Originally published 1933.)

Kellogg, Charles Flint. *NAACP: A History of the National Association for the Advancement of Colored People*, Vol. 1, *1909–1920.* Baltimore, Md.: Johns Hopkins University Press, 1967.

Levy, Eugene. *James Weldon Johnson: Black Leader, Black Voice.* Chicago, Ill.: University of Chicago Press, 1973.

Lewis, David Levering. *When Harlem Was in Vogue.* New York: Oxford University Press, 1979.

———. *W. E. B. Du Bois: Biography of a Race, 1896–1919.* New York: Holt, 1993.

———. *W. E. B. Du Bois: The Fight for Equality and the American Century, 1919–1963.* New York: Holt, 2000.

Meier, August. *Negro Thought in America, 1880–1915: Racial Ideologies in the Age of Booker T. Washington.* Ann Arbor: University of Michigan Press, 1963.

Meier, August, and John H. Bracey. "The NAACP as a Reform Movement, 1909–1965: To Reach the Conscience of America." *Journal of Southern History*, 59(1), February 1993, pp. 3–30.

Meier, August, and Elliott M. Rudwick. "Attorney's Black and White: A Case Study of Race Relations within the NAACP." *Journal of American History* 62(4), 1976, pp. 913–946.

Ross, B. Joyce. *J. E. Spingarn and the Rise of the NAACP.* New York: Atheneum, 1972.

Rudwick, Elliott, and August Meier. "The Rise of the Black Secretariat in the NAACP, 1909–1935." *Crisis*, 84(2), 1977, pp. 58–69.

Schneider, Mark R. *"We Return Fighting": The Civil Rights Movement in the Jazz Age.* Boston, Mass.: Northeastern University Press, 2002.

Scruggs, Charles W. "Alain Locke and Walter White: Their Struggle for Control of the Harlem Renaissance." *Black American Literature Forum*, 14, Autumn 1980, pp. 91–99.

Tushnet, Mark V. *The NAACP's Legal Strategy against Segregated Education, 1925–1950.* Chapel Hill: University of North Carolina Press, 1987.

Vose, Clement E. *Caucasians Only: The Supreme Court, the NAACP, and the Restrictive Covenant Cases*. Berkeley: University of California Press, 1959.

Wedin, Carolyn. *Inheritors of the Spirit: Mary White Ovington and the Founding of the NAACP*. New York: Wiley, 1998.

White, Walter. *A Man Called White: The Autobiography of Walter White*. Athens: University of Georgia, 1995. (Originally published 1948.)

Wilson, Sondra Kathryn, ed. *The Crisis Reader*. New York: Modern Library, 1999a.

———, ed. *In Search of Democracy: The NAACP Writings of James Weldon Johnson, Walter White, and Roy Wilkins (1920–1977)*. New York: Oxford University Press, 1999b.

Zangrando, Robert L. *The NAACP Crusade against Lynching, 1909–1950*. Philadelphia, Pa.: Temple University Press, 1980.

National Association of Negro Musicians

The National Association of Negro Musicians (NAMN) is an organization dedicated to the advancement of African Americans in the field of classical music. The violinist and composer Clarence Cameron White of Boston issued the first call for such an organization by letter in March 1916; his suggestion was reiterated by the composer Robert Nathaniel Dett, then a professor at the Hampton Institute, in October 1918. In the following spring, Nora Holt invited leading musicians to her home in Chicago to honor White. Holt (1885–1974) was a composer and journalist based in Chicago; she served at two times as the music critic of the *Defender* and, after further study in Europe, moved to New York, where she wrote for the *Amsterdam News* in the 1940s. She and Henry L. Grant became the cofounders of NAMN, and for many years she was a leading figure in the association. Grant—a composer, pianist, and choir conductor—was director of the Washington Conservatory of Music, taught at the elite Paul Laurence Dunbar High School in Washington, D.C., and counted a young Duke Ellington among his students. In May 1919, Holt and Grant held an informal conference in connection with the annual festival given by the music department of Dunbar High School. Thirty-three musicians attended.

The National Association of Negro Musicians was formally founded in the wake of this meeting, under the leadership of Holt and Grant. Its first annual convention was scheduled to be held in Chicago that July. The convention was held but was small: It coincided with a race riot in Chicago, and several delegates who learned of the bloodshed as they were arriving turned around at the Chicago train depot. Nevertheless, the organization was successfully launched. The original officers and members of the board of directors included Holt, White, the violinist Kemper Harreld, and the composer and educator Carl Rossini Diton.

The organization soon established branches throughout the United States. Branch 1, in Chicago, quickly came to the forefront of the national organization. Some branches were closely affiliated with other local and regional music organizations, such as the Chicago Music Association and the Indianapolis Music Promoters. As NANM gained in prestige, other musical luminaries served on the board or gave financial support, W. C. Handy and Harry T. Burleigh among them.

Before World War II, presidents of NANM served two- or three-year terms. The first president was Henry Grant (1919–1922); he was followed by Clarence Cameron White (1922–1924), Robert Nathaniel Dett (1924–1926), Carl Diton (1926–1928), J. Wesley Jones (1928–1930), Lillian LeMon (1930–1933), Maude Roberts George (1933–1935), Camille L. Nickerson (1935–1938), and Kemper Harreld (1938–1940). The rotating presidency allowed musicians with regional affiliations (Diton of New York, LeMon of Indianapolis, Harreld of Atlanta) to take the lead in turn.

NANM's activities centered on its national conventions, held most often in Chicago (those held in Chicago included the first one in 1919 and the convention of 1923). In alternating years the convention rotated to other cities, including New York in 1920, Nashville in 1921, Columbus in 1922, Cleveland in 1924, Indianapolis in 1925, Philadelphia in 1926, St. Louis in 1927, Detroit in 1928, and Dallas in 1929.

The promotion of African Americans in concert music, particularly opera and classical song, has been the primary focus of the organization from the outset; NANM was helpful to many singers, starting with the great contralto Marian Anderson, who won the first annual scholarship. Among the illustrious singers who benefited from NANM's sponsorship since then have been Roland Hayes, Shirley Verrett, Grace Bumbry, William Warfield, Adele Addison, Robert McFerrin, and George Shirley. Composers and arrangers assisted by NANM have included Harry T. Burleigh, William Grant Still, Florence Price, John Wesley Work, and Margaret Bonds. NANM has also sponsored work by educators and scholars such as Maud Cuney-Hare,

Alain Locke, Carl Diton, Eileen Southern, and Doris McGinty. NANM has remained focused on concert or "art" music traditions; for many years, it made no attempt to extend its mandate to the more commercially viable popular music. More recently, gospel music and jazz have gained in acceptance, and NANM has honored some gospel musicians, including stars such as James Cleveland.

In New York, the leading member of NANM for many years was George Washington Glover (1888–1993), who was a founding member in 1919 and remained active until late in his very long life. For eighteen years he was chairman of the Department of National Exhibits and Archives for the organization, and for many years he functioned as its unofficial historian. Initially ,there was only one New York branch, which was named in honor of educator David I. Martin (c. 1880–1923). Closely affiliated with this, by way of Glover and his friend Blanche K. Thomas, was the Thomas Music Study Club. Other branches of NANM in New York City included those named for Carl Diton (for a time there were two of these), Lillian Dunn Perry, and Rev. A. Merrill Willis in Manhattan; Mu-Te-Or (Brooklyn); and the B Branch (Jamaica, Queens). Additional branches were established in Mount Vernon and upstate New York.

In its early decades, NANM followed an explicit policy of promoting "art" song and opera, specifically deemphasizing what its charter described as more "negroid" styles. It also went to some lengths to promote performances of selections from a particular work by one of its leading members, the opera *Ouanga* by Clarence Cameron White. More recently, its mission has included promotion of "love and appreciation of traditional and contemporary Negro music," "use of Negro folk themes as a basis for compositions," the promotion of higher professional standards, and resistance of the "desecration of Negro spirituals."

ELLIOTT S. HURWITT

See also Anderson, Marian; Burleigh, Harry Thacker; Cuney-Hare, Maud; Dett, Robert Nathaniel; Handy, W. C.; Hayes, Roland; Holt, Nora; Locke, Alain; Still, William Grant; White, Clarence Cameron

Further Reading

Diton, Carl. "The National Association of Negro Musicians." *The Crisis*, May 1923, pp. 21–22.

George Washington Glover Papers, Schomburg Center for Research in Black Culture, New York Public Library.

Glover, George W. "A Brief History of the Organization." In *National Association of Negro Musicians Presents Second Annual Scholarship Concert*. New York Philharmonic, 1965. (Program booklet.)

Holt, Nora. "The Chronological History of the NANM." *Music and Poetry*, July 1921. (Reprinted in *Black Perspective in Music*, 2, Spring 1974, pp. 234–235.)

Hutchison, Clara E. "The National Association of Negro Musicians, Inc., 1919–1930." 1930. (NANM pamphlet.)

Southern, Eileen, and Doris McGinty, eds. *National Association of Negro Musicians: A Documentary History*. Chicago, Ill.: Center for Black Music Research, 2004.

National Colored Players

The National Colored Players were a short-lived "little theater" group, active in the autumn of 1929. The group presented three productions at the West End Theater on Saint Nicholas Avenue near 125th Street. The first of these productions, *Seventh Heaven*, began a one-week run on 7 October with Ida Anderson, Vere E. Johns, and George Randol in the leading roles. It was followed by *Crime*, a drama about an underworld heist; and finally by *The Gorilla*, the lightest of the three plays. All three works were by white authors and had all been successfully produced on Broadway before their run in Harlem. *Seventh Heaven* (by Austin Strong) had run for 704 performances in 1922 (the fifth-longest Broadway run up to that time), and it was made into a successful silent film in 1927. *The Gorilla* (by Harold Lloyd's screenwriter, Harold Spence) had run for 257 performances in 1925; a critic for *Variety* wrote at the time that it was "the shootingest, shoutingest melange of chills and thrills and yells ever concocted." *Crime* (by Samuel Shipman and John Hymer) had run for 186 performances beginning in February 1927.

The National Colored Players should be seen primarily as a showcase for revivals in Harlem of past Broadway hits, and it was in this light that a columnist for the *Inter-State Tattler* described the company in October 1929. In addition to Anderson and her costars, the ensemble included J. Homer Tutt, one of the most prominent theater men of the Harlem Renaissance.

ELLIOTT S. HURWITT

See also Inter-State Tattler

Further Reading

Inter-State Tattler, 11 October 1929.

Kellner, Bruce, ed. *The Harlem Renaissance: A Historical Dictionary for the Era*. Westport, Conn.: Greenwood, 1984.

National Ethiopian Art Theater

The National Ethiopian Art Theater (NEAT) in New York was a short-lived "little theater" group and school that promoted playwriting and dramatic performance by blacks. Organizers and teachers of NEAT included Anne Wolter and Henry Creamer.

Theophilus Lewis, an ardent supporter of black theater who was the foremost drama critic during the Harlem Renaissance, noted the first public performance (19 June 1924) of students from NEAT's school in his theater column for *The Messenger*. The program featured dance numbers as well as choral singing. According to Lewis, NEAT's ultimate goal was to build a school and a theater in the Broadway district. Although Lewis supported the goal of creating an organization to feature black dramatic talent, he encouraged the group to locate its theater in Harlem, where it could benefit from the support of blacks in the community in addition to focusing on developing black dramatists and actors.

Lewis commented favorably on NEAT's attempt to bring drama to the stage during a time when musicals were the most popular form of stage entertainment. The lack of black playwrights who focused on dramatic works (instead of musicals and comedies), however, meant that NEAT and other black little theater groups frequently performed dramas written by whites. The public's taste for low comedy and imitations of white tastes in drama often dictated the types of works presented by black theater groups. Lewis also noted NEAT's practice of using brown-skinned women in dance performances when the norm for most shows was light-skinned women in dance choruses.

Critics noted other performances by NEAT, including a presentation of three one-act plays at the Lafayette Theater in Harlem on 15 October 1924. The author and critic George Schuyler (1924) praised "Cooped Up" by Eloise Bibb Thompson as a "play written by one who knows life and the ingredients of real drama." The evening's performances also included "Being Forty" by Eulalie Spence and "Bills," which

Schuyler dismissed as an unfunny comedy. Both Eloise Bibb Thompson and Eulalie Spence were students at the NEAT school.

The National Ethiopian Art Theater School disbanded in 1925. Other black little theater groups of the 1920s and 1930s included the Tri-Arts Club, the Inter-Collegiate Association, the Sekondi Players, the Krigwa Players, and the Aldridge Players.

HEATHER MARTIN

See also Krigwa Players; Lafayette Theater; Lewis, Theophilus; Schuyler, George S.; Tri-Arts Club

Further Reading

Kornweibel, Theodore, Jr. "Theophilus Lewis and the Theater of the Harlem Renaissance." In *The Harlem Renaissance Remembered*, ed. Arna Bontemps. New York: Dodd, Mead, 1972.

Lewis, Theophilus. "Theatre." *Messenger*, 6(8), August 1924.

———. "The Theater: The Souls of Black Folks." *Messenger*, 7(7), July 1925.

Peterson, Bernard L., Jr. *The African American Theatre Directory, 1816–1960: A Comprehensive Guide to Early Black Theatre Organizations, Companies, Theatres, and Performing Groups*. Westport, Conn.: Greenwood, 1997.

Schuyler, George S. "Theatre." *Messenger*, 6(11), November 1924.

National Negro Business League

On 23 August 1900, Booker T. Washington and his close business associates founded the National Negro Business League (NNBL) in Boston, Massachusetts. T. Thomas Fortune, editor and publisher of *New York Age*, was appointed chairman of the NNBL's executive committee, and Andrew Carnegie provided capital for the fledgling group. The NNBL was committed to black people's economic independence, and it promoted the "commercial, agricultural, educational, and industrial advancement" of African Americans. Washington served as president until his death in 1915.

Detractors of the NNBL said that it was simply the centerpiece of the "Tuskegee machine"; these critics took exception to Washington's anointment by the press as the spokesman for black Americans across the nation. As head of the Tuskegee Normal and Industrial Institute in Tuskegee, Alabama, since 1881, Washington had a history of enticing members of the black entrepreneurial class in northern cities to join organizations he personally sponsored. Under his direction, Tuskegee became one of the leading African American educational institutions in the nation. Its programs emphasized industrial training, self-discipline, and trade-specific instruction as a means to economic independence. Washington attributed his interest in the NNBL to work and travel related to the institute.

The records of the NNBL suggest that it was more than simply an operation of Tuskegee and Washington. Numerous elite black businessmen (and women) from across the United States participated. Its ranks also included large numbers of the rising black middle class. Broad activism and aggressive recruitment defined the NNBL. The association's leaders argued that black businesses could not thrive unless their prosperity was spread throughout the community and supported by other local businesses. The annual conference proceedings for 1900–1919 show that cooperation and community linkages were championed, as were communication links among African American business owners. Black executives, publishers, scholars, and a wide range of professionals across the United States were constantly recruited. NNBL officials also produced important demographic and statistical data, including one of the most comprehensive surveys of the growth and location of black businesses in the history of the United States.

Local leagues expanded the organization and met regularly in stores and offices to plan regional activities. Presentations about the growth of black business were prevalent, as were events designed to raise money. Barbecues were popular, often well advertised, and well attended. In addition, to encouraging the growth of businesses owned by blacks, local leaders called for trade with member suppliers and mandated rules and procedures. According to August Meier (1966), the Kansas City league even established a special oversight committee to identify those members who failed to patronize black enterprises. Chapter leaders of local U.S. Chamber of Commerce offices, who followed the successes of the NNBL closely, were effective partners in these efforts. They offered their cities as possible sites for league conventions, provided the league with the names of African American businessmen, and recommended ongoing cooperative efforts and events.

While local networks inspired growth in numbers, connections with large business entities led to investment. In addition to Carnegie, the retail magnate John Wanamaker and Julius Rosenwald of Sears, Roebuck advocated the NNBL's mission. Wanamaker

was the advertised speaker at one of the NNBL's annual meetings, and Rosenwald was a member of the board of trustees of the Tuskegee Institute. Officers of the NNBL also worked with other established promoters of business development, such as the Association of National Advertisers and the J. Walter Thompson advertising agency in New York. The NNBL also maintained an informal connection with the prestigious Associated Advertising Clubs of the World, using the manager Carl Hunt as a valuable contact. The NNBL complemented other black associations formed during this period, and members developed the confidence necessary to launch similar programs. While the National Association for the Advancement of Colored People (NAACP) emphasized social and legal objectives, the NNBL invigorated business initiatives and black economic advancement. The NNBL's secretary, Albon L. Holsey, founded the Colored Merchants' Association (CMA) in 1930, and Richard Wright established the National Negro Bankers Association and played a vital role in financing several small enterprises, notably grocery, bakery, and cleaning firms.

Although it is difficult to credit the NNBL with the explosive growth of black business ownership in early twentieth-century America, statistics suggest that the group was a key participant during a stimulating period of African American capitalism. Between 1888 and 1934, 134 black banks were established; the number of black businesses increased from 4,000 in 1867 to 50,000 in 1917. More than 200 black newspapers were published as the twentieth century began; by 1920, almost 75,000 businesses were owned by African Americans in the United States. The majority of these firms tended to be funeral parlors, hotels, barbershops, hair product manufacturers, grocery and drug stores, restaurants, and shoe repair shops. A survey by the NNBL in 1928 showed a general lack of surplus for many of these firms. Of 1,534 black businesses in thirty-three cities, 43.4 percent recorded profits of below $5,000, and only 8.9 percent recorded profits of more than $25,000. Economic conditions during the Depression created further hardship. Of the aforementioned 134 African American banks established between 1888 and 1934, only 12 remained in operation in 1938.

The NNBL grew to 40,000 members at its high point, and it supported 400 delegates representing thirty-four states at annual conventions until operations ceased in 1933. The organization's legacy has continued to shape economic fulfillment agencies. The National Student Business League (NSBL), founded in 1900 with the help of Booker T. Washington, has flourished for years and provides training for African American business students. The National Business League (NBL) credits its founding to the NNBL. The association's literature states, "Yet, it was not until 1900 that an organized federation of merchants and tradesmen was established to promote and protect the financial and commercial interests of Black entrepreneurs. Under the leadership and guidance of Dr. Booker T. Washington, a former slave who became one of the most influential leaders of his day, a few hundred men and women launched the organization that is now the National Business League." The NBL has headquarters in Washington, D.C.

R. JAKE SUDDERTH

See also Fortune, Timothy Thomas; Washington, Booker T.; Wright, Richard

Further Reading

"Booker T. Washington and the National Negro Business League." In *Seven on Black: Reflections of the Negro Experience in America*, ed. William G. Shade and Roy C. Herrenkohl. Philadelphia, Pa.: Lippincott, 1969. (Interview with Louis Harlan.)

Burrows, John Howard. "The Necessity of Myth: A History of the National Negro Business League, 1900–1945." Ph.D. dissertation, Auburn University, 1977.

Hamilton, Kenneth, consulting ed. "Records of the National Negro Business League." Department of History, Southern Methodist University.

Lee, J. R. E. "Highlights on Early History of the National Negro Business League." *Quarterly Journal*, 9, October 1940, pp. 9–13.

Meier, August. *Negro Thought in America, 1880–1915*. Ann Arbor: University of Michigan Press, 1966.

Washington, Booker T. "The National Negro Business League." *World's Work*, 4(2), October 1902, pp. 2671–2675.

The Peabody Microfilm Collection at Hampton University has made available the published proceedings of the Annual Conventions of the National Negro Business League.

National Urban League

New York City became the logical setting for an organization designed to ease the burden of urban life for African Americans. During the late nineteenth and the early twentieth centuries, thousands of southern rural blacks sought employment in northern industries. A need existed to ease the transition from farm to factory for men and women alike. Black people formed organizations designed to promote advancement for their race by overcoming segregation and racial discrimination. Among white people, however, the reasons for helping Negro migrants varied. Some believed that African Americans should be integrated into the larger society in order to enable white people to live more comfortably among blacks. Others contended that as long as discrimination against Negroes continued, true democracy in the United States could never be realized. And still others had pragmatic reasons for instituting reforms that could help black migrants. These progressives feared class and racial conflict, industrial unrest, and unsavory housing conditions that could result in disease epidemics—all of which would prove inimical to the urban lifestyle of the privileged elite. None had a better grasp of the problem than wealthy progressive reformers residing in New York City. These influential white men and women established chapters like the Armstrong Association and the Association for the Protection of Negro Women to handle the influx of black migrants.

At the turn of the twentieth century, several social service organizations evolved that worked to ameliorate the conditions of the black masses. By 1905, sixty-four agencies operated in New York City and Philadelphia to administer to the needs of disadvantaged blacks. Included among the service agencies were the Committee on Urban Conditions (CUC), the Committee for Improving the Industrial Condition of the Negroes in New York City (CIICN), the National League for the Protection of Colored Women (NLPCW), and eventually the National League on Urban Conditions Among Negroes (NLUCAN). Although the agencies were scattered and uncoordinated and had different objectives, all were devoted to sustaining and improving the condition of African Americans.

Migrants required immediate assistance, and some relief occurred in the churches and social service missions in the Bronx, Brooklyn, and Harlem. Unfortunately, short-term solutions for dependent migrants failed to resolve constant problems attributed to the evil influences of urban malaise, ranging from shysters who shortchanged women and ran prostitution rings to industrial and housing discrimination that reduced black men and women to a subhuman existence. Equally important, migrants needed someone to act as an employment broker—an individual or organization responsible for finding jobs and providing training necessary for gainful employment in an urban, industrial milieu.

Several men and women, black and white, endeavored to solve the burgeoning problems related to the great black migration. Included among the beneficent white people were Frances A. Kellor, general director of the Inter-Municipal Committee on House Research, and Ruth S. Baldwin, the wealthy socialite wife of the railroad tycoon William H. Baldwin Jr. Blacks possessing a similar interest in ameliorative work were Dr. Eugene P. Roberts, a physician who had graduated from Lincoln University (Pennsylvania) and New York Medical College; and William L. Bulkley, a graduate of Claflin University in South Carolina, Wesleyan, and Syracuse University, where he earned a Ph.D. in ancient and foreign literature. Later, prominent white men like L. Hollingsworth Wood, Edwin R. A. Seligman, and Oswald Garrison Villard, and blacks like Rev. Reverdy Ransom and the shoe manufacturer Samuel R. Scottron added luster to the migrant reform movement.

Despite the interest and talent of those who volunteered to mitigate the problems that migrants faced, the need to coordinate the various programs and create a full-time professional staff became increasingly evident. George E. Haynes—a graduate of Fisk University and Yale Divinity School, with a Ph.D. from Columbia—embarked on a research project and became the individual responsible for proving that the black migrant community remained underserved. Haynes's work led to the creation of another organization, the Committee on Urban Conditions Among Negroes in New York (CUCANNY). This organization enabled the participants to realize the need to coordinate all social service and philanthropic work in New York City and other industrial cities.

Therefore, on 16 October 1911, the most prominent service organizations—CUCANNY, NLPCW, and CIICN—merged, and, invoking the motto "Not alms but opportunity," the National League on Urban Conditions Among Negroes (NLUCAN) came into being. It would be officially renamed the National Urban League (NUL) on 4 February 1920. Haynes became the first chief executive officer and accepted responsibility for training black professional social workers to administer to the needs of migrants. To carry out his mission, he established a training center at Fisk and divided his time between training social workers there and carrying out his administrative responsibilities in New York. During Haynes's tenure, the league eschewed paternalism and embarked on a mission to create prospects for black employment. Although its headquarters were in New York City, the NUL evolved to become the most prominent black social service organization in the United States.

When the board members of the league realized that Haynes's training responsibilities at Fisk prevented him from providing adequate oversight of day-to-day operations, Haynes was ousted from the directorship in favor of Eugene Kinckle Jones. Jones established organizational priorities and used the resources at his disposal to carry out his mission. Jones had been born into a highly educated family in Richmond, Virginia, and seemed destined to lead. His mother, Rosa, had graduated from Howard University and the New England Conservatory of Music and taught music at Hartshorn College in Richmond; his father, Joseph E. Jones, acquired a baccalaureate degree from Colgate University and served on the faculty at Richmond Theological Seminary (Virginia Union University) as a professor of homiletics and church history. With this background, Eugene Jones had little recourse but to further his education and thereby serve his people. After graduating from Virginia Union and earning a master's degree from Cornell in sociology, Jones eventually moved to New York City in 1911 to become the first full-time secretary of the Committee on Urban Conditions.

By 1916 Jones' star qualities enabled him to become the league's director. Under Jones's direction, the league evolved from an organization established to train black urban leaders to one that provided direct services and assistance to the black urban poor. Moreover, Jones displayed the thinking of a visionary who recognized that the league had a national responsibility to look after the social welfare of all African Americans. He promoted the separation between the national office, housed in New York City, and the New York Urban League—the latter headed by James H. Hubert. The change proved beneficial for disadvantaged blacks nationally. The national office now directed itself to upgrading the condition of Negroes in a coordinated way and on a national scale.

Jones proved himself to be the right man at the right time to lead the NUL. Of quiet demeanor, extremely industrious, and fact oriented, Jones unobtrusively but forcefully brought recognition to NUL. Indeed, Jones's temperament was ideal for the work at hand. Unlike the National Association for the Advancement of Colored People (NAACP), which generated funds through membership dues, the NUL depended exclusively on grants and donations from corporations and wealthy benefactors. Jones' soft-spoken, results-orientated approach made him the ideal leader for the league. Hence, under Jones's direction the league became extremely attentive to concerns and dictates of benefactors like the Rockefeller Foundation, Carnegie interests, and the Julius Rosenwald Fund.

Directly or indirectly, Jones's middle-class demeanor permeated the entire national association. Cleanliness, thrift, punctuality, proper morals, and other lessons were dispersed by NUL affiliates throughout the United States. It was the intention of Jones and other officials of the league to refute the prejudicial thinking of white employers who believed in the inferiority, indolence, and limited intelligence of the Negro.

In addition to finding employment for urban black workers, one of the primary goals Jones had in mind was the extension of the Urban League's services. During the 1920s, the national office brought seventeen new affiliates into the organization from as far South as Tampa and Atlanta and as far west as Los Angeles, and a scattering of chapters existed in cities like Baltimore, Louisville, Omaha, and Minneapolis–St. Paul. In addition to seeking employment for migrants, the centers established day nurseries, kindergartens, and clinics. The league also expanded its fellowship program to train social workers, many of whom studied at the New York School of Social Work. Jones also augmented the number of affiliates in cities including Atlanta, Baltimore, Kansas City, Los Angeles, Louisville, Minneapolis–St. Paul, Omaha, and Tampa. For children, Jones and his associates created a range of activities, organizing ball games, picnics, and stage plays and sponsoring pageants and lectures. Seeking "softer" methods to acquire access for blacks into mainstream America, Jones left it to the NAACP to agitate for equality; he himself avoided controversy and solicited the support of whites for the NUL's social service programs.

Another key to the success of the National Urban League may be observed through the calculated approach the organization took in acquiring information about the needs of African Americans. In 1920, Jones presented a proposal to the Carnegie Corporation to underwrite a research and investigations department to provide affiliate chapters with data on the "Negro question" locally and nationally. Reformers and potential benefactors alike could receive accurate information about African Americans so that proper solicitations could be made and decisions rendered to improve their condition. If the department proceeded as Jones expected, the NUL would be the most accurate repository of information about contemporary blacks in the nation. The Carnegie Corporation underwrote the department, awarding the sum of $8,000 annually over a three-year period. The National Urban League had taken a step toward greatness.

In order to continue making steps to help African Americans, Jones and the national board realized the necessity for collecting accurate data on the condition of the Negro. The NUL therefore needed an erudite, effective person to head the research department. One of the best decisions Jones made as executive secretary was his choice of Charles Spurgeon Johnson to head the NUL's new research arm. Johnson had been a student of the esteemed professor Robert E. Park of the University of Chicago, who had served as director of the Chicago Urban League; he profoundly believed that information could prove essential in helping African Americans acquire opportunities for advancement. With Johnson at the helm between 1922 and 1928, the research department enabled Jones to target corporations and other entities that could offer gainful employment to black urbanites. Jones used the information—facts and figures—to spearhead a "jobs for hire" program and to obtain money for other programs deemed essential to find work for African Americans. The Urban League's research department would allow New York to become the established center for information about the nuances of change in the lives of African Americans.

In addition to collecting data, the national office recognized a need to disseminate immediate information to subordinate leagues, interested parties, benefactors, and the general public. As the newly appointed head of the research department, Johnson was given an additional task. By December 1921, he would edit and produce the first edition of the "Urban League Bulletin," directed toward the larger society. Despite the early successes of the bulletin, however, a broader, more comprehensive publication had been envisioned by members within the NUL. Therefore, under Johnson's direction, on 19 January 1923, the magazine *Opportunity: Journal of Negro Life* made its initial appearance. Its name was derived from the NUL's slogan, "Not alms but opportunity," and it did far more than publicize facts and statistics germane to employment and living conditions. Indeed, *Opportunity* not only provided information on black aspirations and needs but, perhaps even more important, served as an outlet for the flowering of Negro culture and contributed significantly to publicizing the talent of the new black cognoscenti and intellectuals who made up the Harlem Renaissance. By 1924 *Opportunity* had won such acclaim that the league felt obliged to create a literary contest in which awards were offered for poetry, short stories, essays, plays, and personal sketches on life. Later contests incorporated awards for musical composition and constructive journalism. Winners of the various prizes included writers like Countee Cullen, E. Franklin Frazier, Zora Neale Houston, Langston Hughes, and Eric Waldron.

The national office also interceded on behalf of Arthur Schomburg to secure a repository for his vast collection of memorabilia—pamphlets, artifacts, letters, newspapers, manuscripts, and books—that chronicled the black diaspora. When the collection was offered to the NUL in 1926, Eugene Kinckle Jones, Charles S. Johnson, and a prominent white man, Hollingsworth Wood, encouraged the Carnegie Corporation to purchase the collection for $10,000. Although the donation proved far less than the value of Schomburg's collection, permanent housing was established, so that the material would be accessible to the general public, in a Harlem branch of the New York Public Library; the branch was eventually named for Schomburg.

Almost simultaneously with Jones's vision for establishing a means for disseminating information about the league through the "Bulletin," the national director recognized that the procurement of jobs for blacks required the creation of an industrial department. By November 1923 Jones had presented a proposal to the Rockefeller Foundation and received $4,500 in matching funds to create a department of industrial relations. By 1925 the national office acquired the additional funds from Julius Rosenwald so that the department could distribute black workers to sites and cities in need of labor. Furthermore, this new department would coordinate local employment agencies with potential employees, work directly with corporations to prepare opportunities for black workers, encourage black employees to perform their duties efficiently and effectively, and endeavor to gain admission of blacks into trade unions.

After Jones acquired funding, he had the task of finding a suitable industrial secretary. As it happened, T. Arnold Hill, executive director of the Chicago Urban League, became available to head the new department. Hill proved ideal for the job. His experience in Chicago had enabled him to acquire fund-raising skills, acumen as a leader, and a profound understanding of what was needed to be a successful director of the Department of Industrial Relations. Hill knew that he must gain insight about the needs of corporate America, understand the industrial training given to black workers, and function as a liaison between corporations and potential Negro employees. Additionally, to be effective, Hill realized the need to place good workers in jobs commensurate with their talent. This would prove the best way to ensure promotion for individual employees and to protect future hiring possibilities for the entire race. Hill had also prepared to work closely with labor unions to enhance blacks' prospects for work with the trade union movement. Therefore, when Hill arrived in New York on 8 April 1925 to carry out his outlined mandate, he was prepared for the task at hand.

Jones endeavored to encourage white employers to hire black help by publicizing black people's aptitudes for work. Simultaneously, the NUL made overtures to labor with the intention of lowering racial barriers that precluded African Americans from entering unions and finding work as artisans. If the Department of Industrial Relations was to succeed, the league had to be respected by both the business elite and the forces of labor and work aggressively to achieve cooperation between industrialists and union leaders.

Fortunately, the location of the NUL in New York City, and the existence of Harlem and the populace that gravitated there seeking employment, proved advantageous to African American workers. For more than a decade, members of the league's board successfully solicited corporate America to acquire financial support for the organization and place blacks in jobs. The rapport established in the nation's business center enabled Hill and the NUL to support black workers' involvement in unions with relative impunity. While black newspaper editors, ministers, and the nationally renowned Black Elks supported the Pullman Company against striking black unionists, only NUL leaders like Jones and Hill, with tacit support from the NAACP, supported A. Philip Randolph in his struggle to organize and defend the Brotherhood of Sleeping Car Porters. By 1927, Hill had generated sufficient enthusiasm among African Americans to forge a bond with unions that he sponsored and helped organize a "Negro in Industry Week." The purpose of this "week" was to instill within black institutions—such as fraternal organizations, churches, lodges, the YMCA and YWCA, and the National Negro Business League—an acceptance of unionization. Only the early advent of the Great Depression, which initially affected African Americans, prevented the NUL's union movement from being extremely successful.

The leaders of the NUL realized that to bring African Americans into trade unions required effective, highly trained social workers. In 1919, Jones hired Alexander L. Jackson, who had graduated from Harvard with honors, to serve as the league's educational secretary. In keeping with Booker T. Washington's philosophy of advancement of the Negro through industrial education, the need for trained social workers who could act as instructors became urgent. Furthermore, since the NUL no longer used the services of its previous educational director, George Haynes at Fisk, something had to be done. Jackson used his Ivy League training to solicit blacks attending prestigious colleges and recruited them to pursue careers in social work. The league's fellowship program, which had begun earlier in the century, received enormous stimulation and experienced great success under Jackson's direction. Scores of African Americans attending prestigious colleges and universities applied for and received grants from the league.

Although many organizations in Harlem flourished during the 1920s, the National Urban League, to some extent, found itself in difficulties. Although the NUL dedicated itself to finding work for blacks and to elevating the standard of living for those who were indigent, Jones and members of the NUL's hierarchy received criticism for the league's inability to acquire support from African Americans. Critics specifically pointed to the example of Marcus Garvey, who had raised hundreds of thousands of dollars for the Universal Negro Improvement Association from enthusiastic black followers. Jones, according to Parris and Brooks (1971), raised only $68,000 from wealthy white donors, corporations, and African Americans combined. Confidence in Jones's leadership eroded further when the Commission on Interracial Cooperation (CIC), led by Dr. Will Alexander, acquired a significant following in the South and gained acclaim, through its Atlanta headquarters, by servicing regions beyond the purview of the NUL. Further difficulties arose when George Haynes's Department of Race Relations of the Federal Council of Churches of Christ in America achieved national visibility and recognition. Both of these agencies recognized that the NUL was weakest in the South, the region where most blacks lived. Therefore, the CIC and the disgruntled Haynes acquired influence at the expense of the league's national office in New York. By 1925, a special conference held in Cincinnati with the theme "Toward Interracial Cooperation" operated without Eugene Kinckle Jones's influence, input, or subsequent appreciation and recognition. Only the direct involvement of Charles S. Johnson with the conference of 1928 in Washington,

D.C., righted the ship and brought recognition and respect to the NUL and Jones.

Proud and taciturn, Jones refused to sacrifice his dignity to curry favor with white benefactors. For example, the league encouraged Standard Oil and the Metropolitan Life Insurance Company to broaden employment opportunities for African Americans, but these companies remained intransigent; neither of them agreed to present information about hiring practices to Jones and the board. Jones' sense of integrity and independence prevented him from pleading with the companies to provide blacks with respectable blue- and white-collar jobs and perhaps limited the NUL's ability to conduct large-scale programs during the 1920s. Nevertheless, the organization remained strong and proved capable of withstanding challenges encountered during the Great Depression.

H. VISCOUNT NELSON

See also Brotherhood of Sleeping Car Porters; Haynes, George Edmund; Johnson, Charles Spurgeon; Jones, Eugene Kinckle; Labor; 135th Street Library; Opportunity; Opportunity Literary Contests; Schomburg, Arthur A.; Villard, Oswald Garrison

Further Reading

Moore, Jess Thomas, Jr. *A Search for Equality: The National Urban League, 1910–1961.* University Park: Pennsylvania State University Press, 1981.

Nelson, H. Viscount "Berky." *The Rise and Fall of Modern Black Leadership: Chronicle of a Twentieth Century Tragedy.* New York: University Press of America, 2003.

Parris, Guichard, and Lester Brooks. *Blacks in the City: A History of the National Urban League.* Boston, Mass.: Little, Brown, 1971.

Weiss, Nancy J. *The National Urban League, 1910–1940.* New York: Oxford University Press, 1974.

Negritude

Négritude—in English, negritude—is the literary and cultural movement associated with francophone writers of African descent principally during the 1930s and 1940s, most notably Léon Damas, Aimé Césaire, and Léopold Senghor. Although there have been many definitions and descriptions of the term *négritude*, the three elements that characterized the works of these authors were valuing black and African cultures, rejecting the French policy of cultural assimilation, and promoting black and African agency.

France, like many other European states, imported large numbers of African slaves to work on sugar plantations throughout the Caribbean basin and consequently held Africans and peoples of African descent to be inferior to Europeans. Although the French First Republic abolished slavery during the French Revolution, people of African descent in these French territories did not receive citizenship until 1848, as did residents of the four communes of Senegal (Dakar, Saint Louis, Gorée, and Rufisque). The French government classified the rest of the inhabitants of Senegal and its other colonies as *indigènes*, or natives, and considered them subjects without the rights and privileges of citizens. The policy of assimilation assumed the superiority of French culture to all others. Accordingly, subjects had no political rights or rights of representation in the French national assembly. An *indigène*, however, by adopting and practicing the French language and French culture (and paying a significant fee), could be classified as *évolué*, or evolved, and could receive the rights of citizenship. Only a very small minority of Africans in French colonies achieved *évolué* status, however; the assimilated elite tended to collaborate with French rulers, while, for the vast majority of the people living under France's colonial occupation, the spirit of liberty, fraternity, and equality was little more than rhetoric. Furthermore, by the 1930s the ideas of scientific racism, which proclaimed the biological inferiority of African peoples (particularly as espoused by Gobineau), dominated French intellectual circles and broader French society as well.

Négritude, therefore, can be defined as taking pride in or promoting a positive image of African heritage individually and collectively. Given the political and cultural climate in Paris in the 1930s (the zenith of European colonialism), the assertions of black pride made by Damas, Senghor, and Césaire were very radical.

Several scholars have traced the beginnings of *négritude* to a short-lived journal, *Légitime Défense*, which was published by a group of Martinican students in Paris in 1932. Led by Etienne Léro, the group called for an end to racial discrimination against people of African descent (particularly from French territories in the Caribbean), an abolition of bourgeois hierarchical values, and a recognition of black and African racial difference as positive rather than as a deficiency. Heavily influenced by French surrealist and Marxist

ideologies, *Légitime Défense* was banned by French authorities after only one issue. Other scholars have argued that *négritude* began with the publication of *La Revue du Monde Noir*, under the leadership of the Martinican sisters Andrée, Jane, and Paulette Nardal, in 1931–1932. Both publications significantly influenced the founders of *négritude*: Léro's group raised the theme of black alienation resulting from capitalist exploitation and racial discrimination, and they called for a new form of literary expression free from French canons; the Nardal sisters held weekly salons in which young African and Afro-Caribbean students came together to discuss a variety of issues and read their poetry. It was also in these salons that the francophone writers met Harlemite literati, including Langston Hughes and Claude McKay.

Another significant influence on the incipient movement were developments in ethnology, or cultural anthropology, most notably works by Leo Frobenius and Maurice Delafosse that argued for the historicity and positive contributions of West African cultures and states, contrary to the racist ideology of Gobineau. Similarly, René Maran's historical novel, *Batouala*, which exposed French exploitation of the people in its African colonies, had an effect on the young poets' critique of French colonial society. In 1934, Damas, Senghor, and Césaire published another short-lived journal, *L'Étudiant Noir* (*The Black Student*), which built on the themes found in *Légitime Défense* and *La Revue du Monde Noir*. One of the principal themes of *négritude* that the authors of *L'Étudiant Noir* apparently stated (the journal is no longer extant) was the commonality of experiences of French colonialism on the part of Caribbean blacks and Africans. According to Césaire, the objective of the publication was "to reunite Black people who are considered French by law and nationality to their own history, traditions, and languages, to the culture which truly expresses their soul."

In 1937, Damas published the first collection of his poetry, *Pigments*. Several of the poems contain significant critiques of French assimilationist policies. "Hoquet" ("Hiccups"), for example, provides a scathing view of the rules associated with the proper conduct observed by black elite families in the Caribbean (Damas was born and raised in French Guiana and attended secondary school in Martinique, where he met Césaire). In 1939, French authorities banned the book in their African colonies because Baoulé-speakers in the Ivory Coast recited the last poem in the collection, "Et Cetera"—in which Damas exhorted Senegalese soldiers in the French army to leave the Germans in peace and liberate Senegal instead—while resisting the military draft. Damas published a collection of essays, *Retour de Guyane* (*Return from Guiana*), in 1938, and edited the first anthology of poets from the French colonies, *Poètes d'expression française d'outre mer* (*Poets of Overseas France*) in 1947. Damas served one term as Guiana's representative to the French national assembly following World War II, and he taught in the United States at the University of the District of Columbia and Howard University. He died in 1978.

Aimé Césaire wrote his monumental poem *Cahier d'un retour au pays natal* (*Notebook of a return to the native land*) in 1938. Although the journal *Volontés* published significant portions of the work in 1939, it did not receive critical acclaim until it was published in its entirety with an introduction by surrealist philosopher André Breton in 1947. It was in *Cahier* that Césaire coined and first used the term *négritude*. Surrealist in its structure, syntax, and imagery, *Cahier* is as much a psychological journey toward the young Césaire's interior self-realization as a poet and a person of African descent as a critique of French exploitation and testament to African agency in the Caribbean and on the continent. Kennedy (1975) described *Cahier* as "the only possible introduction to Césaire's work." Similarly, Kesteloot (1991) proclaimed it "the national anthem of blacks the world over." During World War II, Césaire returned to Martinique to teach and, with his wife, Suzanne, edited the surrealist journal *Tropiques*. After the war, he served as Martinique's representative in the French assembly and as mayor of Fort-de-France. At the time of this writing, he continued to serve as mayor. Césaire's most important later works include his famous essay *Discourse on Colonialism* and the plays *La tempête* (*The Tempest*, based on Shakespeare's play), *La tragédie du roi Christophe* (about a king in early nineteenth-century Haiti), and *Une saison au Congo* (about the life and death of Patrice Lumumba).

Of the three founders of *négritude*, Léopold Senghor has been regarded as the champion of African contributions to the twentieth-century world, and this can be seen clearly in his essay "Ce que l'homme noir apporte" ("That Which the Black Man Carries," 1939). Senghor wrote the poems in the first two collections of his work, *Chants d'ombre* (*Songs of Darkness*) and *Hostes Noires* (*Black Hosts, Black Victims*), between 1936 and 1945. They were published in 1945 and 1948, respectively. Also in 1948, Senghor edited and published the second anthology of francophone

African poetry, *Anthologie de la nouvelle poésie nègre et malgache* (*Anthology of the New Black and Malagasy Poetry*), which included a controversial introductory essay by Jean-Paul Sartre, "Orphée Noir" ("Black Orpheus"). In addition to helping Damas and Césaire discover or rediscover African cultures, Senghor had a significant impact on a fellow Senegalese, Alioune Diop, the founder of the enormously influential journal *Présence Africaine* and the Société Africaine de Culture (African Society of Culture). Like Damas and Césaire, Senghor also served as a deputy from Senegal in the French national assembly. In 1960, he became president of an independent Senegal, an office he held until his resignation in 1980. He left Senegal and lived in France until his death in 2001.

Much of the criticism that *négritude* received as a movement stems from various definitions of the concept, particularly Senghor's and Sartre's. Césaire defined *négritude* as "the awareness of being black, the simple acknowledgment of a fact that implies the acceptance of it, a taking charge of one's destiny as a black man, of one's history and culture," whereas for Senghor it was "the cultural patrimony, the values and above all the spirit of Negro African civilization." Building on the implicit essentialist and universalist ideas in Senghor's definition, Sartre defined *négritude* as the "being-in-the-world of blacks," but further as

> the upbeat of a dialectical progression; the theoretical and practical assertion of white supremacy is the thesis; the position of negritude, as an antithetical value, is the moment of negativity. But this negative moment is not sufficient in itself, and the blacks who make use of it are aware of this. They know its aim is to prepare a synthesis or realization of the human in a society without races. Thus negritude exists in order to be destroyed. It is a transition, not a result, a means and not a final ending.

In effect, Sartre made the essentialism implicit in Senghor explicit. Furthermore, to the extent that Senghor's understanding of culture as it related to a universal "spirit of Negro African civilization" is essentialist, it is understandable given that he no doubt developed his understanding of culture from the early ethnologists who reified concepts such as culture as a matter of course. Nigel Gibson characterized *négritude* as defined by Césaire as "subjective negritude," and as defined by Sartre following Senghor as "objective negritude." The revolutionary theorist (and Martinican) Frantz Fanon was more accepting of "subjective negritude" and critical of "objective negritude" because of "the historical specificity of racism and colonialism": that is, they were not universals; rather, they were contingent on specific historical contexts. In short, Fanon was far more critical of Sartre than any of the *négritude* poets. Furthermore, Kesteloot argued that *négritude* literati were more interested in the realization of human society without racism than in its realization without race. The criticisms of anglophone African writers, such as the Nigerian Wole Soyinka and the South African Ezekiel Mphalele, argued for the existence of and preferred separate black and African "national" literatures versus a universal black literature and spirit. Curiously, Langston Hughes noted that, had the term *négritude* been used in the 1920s, he and the Harlem literati "might have been called poets of *négritude*."

The poet-politicians of *négritude* intended their literary works to have a political impact. They saw political involvement as an extension of their ideology: All three served in the French national assembly, Senghor was president of Senegal, and Césaire was the mayor of Fort-de-France. Radicals criticized both Senghor and Césaire: Senghor voted for union with France in the referendum of 1958; Césaire received André Malraux, France's minister of information, who denied that the French army used torture during the Algerian war. Yet the success and significance of *négritude* can be measured by its impact on the generations of black and African intellectuals and nationalists who led movements against Western colonialism.

While scholars have chronicled the relationship between *négritude* and the Harlem Renaissance, its interaction with other contemporary literary movements is less well known. Manuel Ferreira wrote about the influence of *négritude* on *claridade*, a literary movement of the 1930s in Cape Verde. Damas dedicated "Il est des nuits" to the Afro-Cuban poet Alejo Carpentier. Senghor noted that the Haitian Jean Price-Mars's *Ainsi parla l'oncle* influenced his thought. Thus, *négritude* was one of several literary movements among black and African people in the Atlantic world in the early twentieth century. These movements were the intellectual forebears of later black and African movements for political and social liberation from western colonialism.

NICHOLAS M. CREARY

See also Batouala; Césaire, Aimé; Damas, Léon; Francophone Africa and the Harlem Renaissance; Francophone Caribbean and the Harlem Renaissance;

Hughes, Langston; Maran, René; McKay, Claude; Senghor, Léopold

Further Reading

Césaire, Aimé. *Discourse on Colonialism*. New York: Monthly Review, 2000.
———. *Notebook of a Return to the Native Land*. Middletown, Conn.: Wesleyan University Press, 2001.
Damas, Léon Gontran. *Pigments*. Paris: Présence Africaine, 1962.
Kennedy, Ellen Conroy. *The Negritude Poets: An Anthology of Translations from the French*. New York: Viking, 1975.
Kesteloot, Lilyan. *Black Writers in French: A Literary History of Negritude*. Washington, D.C.: Howard University Press, 1991.
Senghor, Léopold Sédar. *Négritude et humanisme (Liberté I)*. Paris: Éditions du Seuil, 1964.

Negro: An Anthology

Negro: An Anthology, collected and edited by Nancy Cunard, was the largest and the most radical of the anthologies to come out of the Harlem Renaissance. It was published in 1934, nine years after Alain Locke had issued *The New Negro*, and it can be read as an updated version of Locke's anthology. Like *The New Negro*, *Negro* includes literature, essays, sociological studies, and photographs. *Negro* is much broader in focus than Locke's anthology, however, and, at 855 pages, more thorough: *Negro* includes 250 contributions by 150 writers, and it firmly sets the history and achievements of African Americans in a global context, with sections on the history, culture, and social development of the West Indies and South America, Europe, and Africa. *Negro* is also more militant than its predecessor: It includes coverage of racism and violence against African Americans, with essays on lynching, the Ku Klux Klan, and the Scottsboro trial. It also includes a number of essays attacking imperialism and capitalism and lauding the potential of communism and socialism to help fight racism and injustice.

Whereas *The New Negro* is understood as the defining volume of the Harlem Renaissance and is well known to scholars of the movement, *Negro* has never received much attention. In the 1930s, only a very few periodicals reviewed it. More recently, Chisholm (1979) and Ford (1970) have offered accounts of Cunard's creation of the anthology, and a few essays have been devoted to it, but scholarship on *Negro* remains scant.

The obscurity of *Negro* is at least partly a result of its limited availability. The first edition was published by Wishart in London in 1934 at Cunard's expense, and she was unable to find an American publisher. Wishart printed only 1,000 copies of the volume, and the bombing of London during World War II destroyed several hundred copies that had not yet been sold. After the war, according to Chisholm, copies were "virtually unattainable," available only at very high prices on the rare book market (1979, 222). The version that Ford edited in 1970 is more widely available; however, he abridged the contents to 464 pages.

Still, the anthology offers an insightful coda to the Harlem Renaissance, particularly in its original form. First, it is an important source of work by some of the significant writers of the period. *Negro* includes, for example, poetry by Arna Bontemps, Sterling Brown, Countee Cullen, and Langston Hughes, as well as essays by Locke, W. E. B. Du Bois, Arthur Schomburg, and Walter White. A number of essays by Zora Neale Hurston, including "Characteristics of Negro Expression," were originally published in *Negro*. The anthology also includes contributions by notable white literary figures, including Theodore Dreiser, Ezra Pound, and William Carlos Williams; Samuel Beckett translated a number of essays from French writers.

Second, *Negro* demonstrates the importance of musicians and performers of the period; it includes a selection of photographs of and essays about young African American musicians, actors, and performers active during the 1920s and 1930s, including Louis Armstrong, Cab Calloway, Duke Ellington, Ethel Waters, and Bill "Bojangles" Robinson. *Negro* is a reminder that the work and the influence of these writers and artists did not end with the close of the 1920s, nor did the interest in black culture.

Negro also demonstrates that the concerns of the 1920s extended into the 1930s. Cunard's goal for the volume, as she describes it in her foreword, was to record "the struggles and achievements, the persecutions and the revolts against them, of the Negro peoples" (iii). A sense of frustration with the continuing racism against African Americans permeates the volume; it matches the frustration often found, for example, in Du Bois's editorials in *The Crisis*, the journal he edited for the National Association for the Advancement of Colored People (NAACP). The essays on black culture, in contrast, are laudatory in tone; they praise the literature, art, music, and performances by black people in the United States, the Caribbean, and Africa, implicitly offering such work as evidence that disproves the often assumed inferiority of black people. *Negro* shares with so many works of the previous decade, then, the optimistic feeling that the arts could serve the political purpose of undermining racism.

A number of aspects of *Negro* set it apart from other work of the Harlem Renaissance and made it controversial, however. The espousal of communism in the volume is probably its most distinctive and divisive element. The arguments about the benefits of communism are heavy handed; Cunard, for example, states in her foreword, "The Communist world-order is the solution of the race problem for the Negro" (iii). Moreover, she had little patience or understanding for anyone who did not share this belief, and she was quite outspoken in her criticism of people with whom she disagreed about politics or strategies, even if they were contributors. For instance, although she included contributions from a number of members of the NAACP, including Du Bois, White, and William Pickens, she also included an essay in which she attacked Du Bois, *The Crisis*, and the NAACP as reactionary—and even placed her critique immediately ahead of Du Bois's essay.

Another controversial aspect of the anthology is the fact that its editor, Cunard, was a white British woman born into a high-class, well-off family who was not afraid of controversy in her own life. She dedicated *Negro* to Henry Crowder, an African American musician whom she had met in Italy in 1928 and with whom she had a long affair. Cunard's interest in and relationships with Crowder and other black men caused quite a scandal and received a good deal of press; as McSpadden (1997) points out, Cunard's reputation for "sexual adventurousness" and her interest "in all things African"—particularly men—made her credibility as the editor of this anthology questionable (60).

Cunard's editorial policies and organization also are debatable. North (1994), for example, argues that the anthology is indiscriminate and lacks organization, although McSpadden describes the benefits of its complexities. And, certainly, some of the texts are problematic, such as William Carlos Williams' sexist and racist essay, "The Colored Girls of Passenack." In spite of—or perhaps because of—these controversies, however, *Negro* calls for much more scholarly attention.

Anne Carroll

See also Cunard, Nancy; Du Bois, W. E. B.; Locke, Alain; New Negro, The; Scottsboro; White, Walter; *other specific individuals*

Further Reading

Chisholm, Anne. *Nancy Cunard: A Biography*. New York: Knopf, 1979.

Ford, Hugh. "Introduction." In *Negro: An Anthology*, comp. and ed. Nancy Cunard. London: Wishart, 1934. (See also: *Negro: An Anthology*, ed. and abridged Hugh Ford. New York: Frederick Ungar, 1970.)

Friedman, Alan Warren, ed. *Beckett in Black and Red: The Translations for Nancy Cunard's Negro (1934)*. Lexington: University Press of Kentucky, 2000.

Marcus, Jane. "Bonding and Bondage: Nancy Cunard and the Making of the Negro Anthology." In *Borders, Boundaries, and Frames: Essays of Cultural Criticism and Cultural Studies*, ed. May Henderson. New York: Routledge, 1995.

McSpadden, Holly Ann. "Transgressive Reading: Nancy Cunard and the Negro." In *Essays on Transgressive Readings: Reading over the Lines*, ed. Georgia Johnston. Lewiston, N.Y.: Mellen, 1997.

North, Michael. "'Characteristics of Negro Expression': Zora Neale Hurston and the Negro Anthology." In *The Dialect of Modernism: Race, Language, and Twentieth-Century Literature*. New York: Oxford University Press, 1994.

Negro Art Institute

The Negro Art Institute—known formally as the American (National) Institute of Negro Letters, Music, and Art—was the first of three major attempts by the civil rights leader Walter White (1893–1955) to obtain broad-based support for artists of the Harlem Renaissance. Patterned after the American Negro Academy (ANA), which was founded in 1897, the Negro Art Institute was conceived in 1923 to train and cultivate black writers, musicians, and visual artists. It immediately found advocates in the philosopher Alain Locke (1885–1954), who was a member of the ANA, and the activist James Weldon Johnson (1871–1938), who served with White as an officer of the National Association for the Advancement of Colored People (NAACP). According to the NAACP's records, plans for the incorporation of the Negro Art Institute and the configuration of its board were outlined in a memorandum dated 13 April 1923. Although unsigned, the document was probably written by Locke, who made suggestions as to additional supporters beyond the members of the board, and who recommended New York or Chicago as a possible location for the institute, because both cities had an abundance of cultural and financial resources.

White, who worked tirelessly for the NAACP for nearly forty years, was not only a staunch civil rights activist but also an award-winning author. As such, he championed the NAACP's support of black artists, particularly writers, and used the NAACP's publications to highlight their works, inform the public about the state and nature of black art, and foster relationships between artists and critics. The Negro Art Institute was an outgrowth of this interest, and it was hoped that the institute would function not merely as an academy but also as a vehicle through which to raise global awareness about black genius and creativity.

An application for financial support of the institute was submitted, unsuccessfully, to the Garland Fund. Following this rejection, Locke invited the wealthy widow Charlotte Osgood Mason (1854–1946) to underwrite the project. Mason, who supported a number of African American literary and visual artists throughout the 1920s and 1930s, initially agreed but later withdrew her support. Although it is unclear why Mason abandoned the project, she seems, in any case, to have been an improbable sponsor for an institution intended to cultivate scholarly pursuits, intellectual engagement, and the notion of black erudition: Mason was a "primitivist" who coerced her beneficiaries into creating works that emphasized the visceral and childlike nature of black people as she understood them.

Unable to obtain financial backing, White and his colleagues appear to have relinquished their plans for the institute. By 1924, White's correspondence no longer refers to the project, nor is it mentioned in his biography. A second, similar endeavor, the Negro Foreign Fellowship Fund, was attempted in 1924, again by White, Locke, and Johnson, in order to finance travel and study abroad for black artists and scholars. An application for a subsidy was submitted to the American Fund for Public Service but was rejected because the proposal fell outside the scope of the fund's objectives. A third and final venture to support black art was conceived by White in 1927, when he wrote to a former director of the Harmon Foundation (which had independently begun to offer awards to black artists) for assistance, but his request was again rejected. Despite these disappointments, White continued to aid black artists on an individual basis and through his advocacy of the NAACP's literary awards.

LISA FARRINGTON

See also Garland Fund; Harmon Foundation; Johnson, James Weldon; Locke, Alain; Mason, Charlotte Osgood; White, Walter

Further Reading

Lewis, David Levering. *When Harlem Was in Vogue.* New York: Knopf, 1981.

Waldron, Edward E. *Walter White and the Harlem Renaissance.* Port Washington, N.Y.: Kennikat, 1978.

Negro Art Theater

The Negro Art Theater was a "little theater" group founded in the Abyssinian Baptist Church. The troupe's efforts were spearheaded by Adam Clayton Powell Jr., son of the pastor of Abyssinian, who would take over his father's pulpit and later was elected to Congress. Only one production is known to have been mounted by the Negro Art Theater: *Wade in the Water*, in June 1929. It starred Laura Bowman (1878–1957), a prominent stage actress during the Harlem Renaissance.

ELLIOTT S. HURWITT

See also Abyssinian Baptist Church

Further Reading

Mitchell, Loften. *Black Drama: The Story of the American Negro in the Theatre.* New York: Hawthorn, 1967.

Kellner, Bruce, ed. *The Harlem Renaissance: A Historical Dictionary for the Era.* Westport, Conn.: Greenwood, 1984.

Negro Experimental Theater

The Negro Experimental Theater, a "little theater" company, was active from 1929 to 1931. It used the names Negro Experimental Theater and Harlem Experimental Theater more or less interchangeably. It was founded at the Harlem branch of the New York Public Library, at 135th Street, in February 1929 by the librarian Regina Anderson Andrews (who would function as its executive secretary for much of its existence) and the teacher Dorothy Peterson. Others who led this venture included the critic Theophilus Lewis, the playwright Jessie Redmon Fauset, and the teacher Harold Jackman. The troupe was made up largely of actors from the Lincoln Theater Company, which was already prominent in Harlem.

On 24 June 1929, the Negro Experimental Theater presented Georgia Douglas Johnson's one-act play "Plumes," directed by Jackman; his departure for Europe shortly thereafter apparently coincided with a period of relative inactivity for the group.

In February 1931, the Negro Experimental Theater moved its activities to the parish house of Saint Philip's Episcopal Church. There it mounted an ambitious season that included *Little Stone House* by George Calderon, *The Rider of Dreams* by Ridgely Torrence, and *Climbing Jacob's Ladder* by Regina Andrews (writing under the pseudonym Ursula Trelling, and apparently the only black writer among the company's playwrights). *The Rider of Dreams* had originally appeared in 1917 as one of Torrence's *Three Plays for a Negro Theater*, presented by a pioneering company known simply as the Colored Players. On 24 April 1931, the "Harlem Experimental Theatre" produced a triple bill consisting of *A Sunny Morning* by Joaquin and Serafin Quintero (with Regina Andrews in the cast), *The Rider of Dreams*, and *Climbing Jacob's Ladder*. Rose McClendon, a leading actress of the Harlem Renaissance, directed *The Rider of Dreams* on this occasion; the other two plays were directed by Robert Dunmore. Aaron Douglas, a leading artist of the renaissance, designed the striking cover image for the program, a copy of which is in the Schomburg Center.

ELLIOTT S. HURWITT

See also Anderson, Regina M.; Douglas, Aaron; Fauset, Jessie Redmon; Jackman, Harold; Johnson, Georgia Douglas; Lewis, Theophilus; Lincoln Theater; McClendon, Rose; 135th Street Library; Peterson, Dorothy Randolph; Saint Philip's Protestant Episcopal Church; Three Plays for a Negro Theater

Further Reading

Inter-State Tattler, 5 July 1929.

Mitchell, Loften. *Black Drama: The Story of the American Negro in the Theatre.* New York: Hawthorn, 1967.

Kellner, Bruce, ed. *The Harlem Renaissance: A Historical Dictionary for the Era.* Westport, Conn.: Greenwood, 1984.

Negro World

Published in Harlem, *Negro World* was the weekly newspaper of Marcus Garvey's Universal Negro Improvement Association (UNIA). Two prominent editors of *Negro World* were William H. Ferris and W. A. Domingo, although Domingo eventually broke with Garvey.

Negro World was founded in 1919 and flourished in the 1920s, with its messages of black nationalism and racial pride. Striving to appeal to a broad audience of blacks from various backgrounds and geographical areas, Marcus Garvey made a point of including Spanish and French sections in his newspaper. This enhanced the ability of *Negro World* to reach far beyond Harlem. In fact, the wide dissemination of the newspaper disturbed authorities in some places. In particular, the British authorities considered the paper's anticolonial message so potentially subversive that they banned *Negro World* in the West Indies.

Although *Negro World* preached black capitalism and was therefore distinct from socialist papers, it nevertheless was part of a vibrant black radical press. Other contemporary periodicals that also emphasized black culture and black nationalism included *The Messenger*, *Voice*, *Crusader*, and *Emancipator*.

Indeed, all these newspapers played a critical role in spreading the Harlem Renaissance. For example, *Negro World*, like the black press as a whole, frequently sponsored poetry contests, publishing the work of previously unknown writers. Often, poems were chosen not primarily on the basis of their literary merit but on the basis of their message. By exposing the public to art with a message, *Negro World* conveyed the idea that the literary could be the political.

The political message of *Negro World* was, of course, more overt in its editorials than in the poetry it featured. Like the UNIA itself, the editorials in *Negro World* urged blacks to go back to Africa, since American society was hopelessly racist. If blacks chose to stay in the United States, they should at least develop separate social and economic institutions of their own. Many blacks heeded the call for separation within the United States and helped organize the UNIA's black businesses, such as Universal Laundries and Universal Restaurants.

In addition, *Negro World* served the purpose of fund raising. For instance, it helped raise money for Garvey's ill-fated Black Star Line. This shipping venture was intended, in part, to bring blacks from the United States to Liberia to establish an independent colony there, but the Black Star Line fell victim to mismanagement and corruption.

Negro World eventually also collapsed when Marcus Garvey was jailed and later deported. During its tumultuous lifetime, however, the newspaper served an important function in igniting a widespread interest in black art and culture.

JANICE TRAFLET

See also Black Star Line; Domingo, Wilfred Adolphus; Emancipator; Ferris, William H.; Garvey, Marcus; Messenger, The; Universal Negro Improvement Association

Further Reading

Jordan, William. *Black Newspapers and America's War for Democracy, 1914–1920.* Chapel Hill: University of North Carolina Press, 2001.
Martin, Tony. *Literary Garveyism: Garvey, Black Arts, and the Harlem Renaissance.* Dover, Mass.: Majority, 1983.

Negrotarians

The writers, artists, and intellectuals of the Harlem Renaissance were highly dependent on the financial assistance and social leverage of white patrons such as Carl Van Vechten (1880–1964), Joel Spingarn (1875–1939), Charlotte Osgood Mason (1854–1946), and Fannie Hurst (1889–1968), who were first nicknamed "Negrotarians" by Zora Neale Hurston. Whether motivated by what is now known as political correctness, voyeurism, vanity, or genuine compassion, the Negrotarians played a crucial role in expanding the market for the culture of black Harlem. In addition, they often developed friendships and creative partnerships with Harlemites that long outlasted the most fashionable period of the renaissance.

Many forms of white patronage existed, some more benignly intended than others. Segregated nightclubs like the Cotton Club and the Savoy catered to a white middle-class clientele that had a taste for the exotic.

Parties were thrown in Harlem and downtown Manhattan by wealthy socialites; at these parties, ambitious, talented blacks could mingle with prominent writers, book publishers, and celebrities, including Theodore Dreiser, Salvador Dalí, Paul Robeson, and Ethel Barrymore. Annual prizes for achievements by blacks in the arts and other professional fields were funded by Spingarn, Van Vechten, and the William E. Harmon Foundation. Jobs, schooling, and money for personal expenditures were provided for those individuals who showed the most promise, like Hurston and Langston Hughes.

Van Vechten was by far the most active and enthusiastic of all the Negrotarians, as his friend James Weldon Johnson and others have testified. Van Vechten was born in Iowa to a liberal middle-class family, and he took an early interest in black ragtime musicians and vaudeville performers while he was a student at the University of Chicago. He came to New York as a journalist and began writing cultural reviews for the *New York Times*. After reading Walter White's protest novel *The Fire in the Flint* (1924), Van Vechten asked the publisher Alfred A. Knopf to introduce him to the author. Through White, Van Vechten met many of Harlem's luminaries, including Johnson, Hughes, and Countee Cullen. From then on, Van Vechten was deeply involved in the social life and cultural production of black Harlem. He and his wife, the actress Fania Marinoff, became renowned for giving lavish integrated parties at their home on West Fifty-fifth Street.

Van Vechten's promotional activities on behalf of Hughes, Johnson, Hurston, and many others coincided with his own reputable career as a writer and photographer (a large collection of his photographic portraits is stored at the Library of Congress.) His novel *Nigger Heaven* (1926) caused quite a stir over its provocative title, which derives from a slang term for the upper gallery of a theater, where blacks were permitted to sit. Writing in *The Crisis*, W. E. B. Du Bois called the book a "cheap melodrama," and objected to its subtext of primitivism. Others condemned the book without reading it, although the ensuing controversy ensured its popular success. While its racial politics have certainly dated, *Nigger Heaven* is actually much less incendiary than its title would suggest, and it remains interesting for its local-color descriptions of middle-class bohemian life at the height of the Harlem Renaissance. Hughes writes about the controversy over *Nigger Heaven* in the first volume of his autobiography, *The Big Sea* (1940), taking the novel's critics to task and praising Van Vechten for writing "sympathetically

and amusingly and well about a whole rainbow of life above 110th Street that had never before been put into the color of words."

Aside from Van Vechten, the main benefactor of Hughes and Hurston was Charlotte Osgood Mason, whom they addressed as "Godmother" to her evident delight. A wealthy heiress, Mason indulged in several eccentric pastimes, including anthropology and the occult. She was especially fascinated with Native American and African American folk cultures, finding them somewhat more appealing than the decadent ways of modern society. Hurston's biographer, Robert Hemenway (1977), estimates that Mason "contributed between fifty and seventy-five thousand dollars to New Negro writers and artists," and notes that she insisted on the confidentiality of her donations.

Soon after meeting Mason in 1927, Hurston signed a contract of employment with her to fund a series of trips through the South for the purpose of collecting folklore, under the supervision of the renowned anthropologist Franz Boas at Columbia University. These trips ultimately provided Hurston with the material that appeared in her classic anthology and travel narrative *Mules and Men* (1935). For the next several years, Hurston kept Mason enticed with trickster and hoodoo tales and flattered her with ingratiating letters, all in an effort to sustain her urgently needed support. She even played on Mason's latent racism by signing her letters "your little pickaninny."

Hurston had reason to be anxious, for Mason expected her protégés to surrender control of their work in exchange for her financial backing. In a letter to Hughes, Hurston complained that Mason "ought not to exert herself to supervise every little detail [of the trips]. It destroys my self-respect and utterly demoralizes me for weeks." This was no exaggeration, for Mason demanded an itemized list of purchases and complained whenever she felt that Hurston was being "extravagant." Even more discouraging was Mason's insistence that Hurston not use her collected folklore materials for any commercial purpose, which delayed the publication of *Mules and Men* for many years. Hughes was less tolerant of Mason's intrusive demands than Hurston and ended his dealings with Mason in 1930, motivated in part by a dispute over his emerging radicalism.

Nevertheless, both Hughes and Hurston expressed their gratitude to Mason for her generosity. On the whole, Harlem embraced the Negrotarians. The painter and caricaturist Miguel Covarrubias, a beneficiary of both Mason and Van Vechten, once drew a humorous portrait of the latter as a Negro minstrel, which he titled "Carl Van Vechten—A Prediction." Spingarn, a Jewish literary critic at Columbia University who was one of the founders of the National Association for the Advancement of Colored People (NAACP) and served on its board, and his philanthropist wife, Amy, are remembered fondly in Hughes's *The Big Sea*. The best-selling author Fannie Hurst, also Jewish, is celebrated in Hurston's autobiography *Dust Tracks on a Road* (1942) as one of her dearest friends. When Hurston was tried on false charges of molesting a ten-year-old boy in 1948, Hurst, her former employer, became a close confidante.

A more cynical view of the Negrotarians can be found in Wallace Thurman's roman à clef, *Infants of the Spring* (1932). Thurman's white characters, clearly modeled on Van Vechten and other real-life acquaintances, regard Harlem either as an exotic, sexually enticing spectacle or as a cause for their own political martyrdom. Most critics today respond to the contribution of the Negrotarians to the Harlem Renaissance with considerable ambivalence. At the very least, however, these patrons should be given credit for their willingness to extend substantive gestures of goodwill across the color line, at a time when very few whites had the courage to do so.

DARYN GLASSBROOK

See also Covarrubias, Miguel; Cullen, Countee; Dreiser, Theodore; Harmon Foundation; Hurst, Fannie; Hurston, Zora Neale; Infants of the Spring; Johnson, James Weldon; Mason, Charlotte Osgood; Robeson, Paul; Spingarn, Joel; Thurman, Wallace; Van Vechten, Carl; White Patronage

Further Reading

Bernard, Emily, ed. *Remember Me to Harlem: The Letters of Langston Hughes and Carl Van Vechten*. New York: Vintage, 2002.

Hemenway, Robert E. *Zora Neale Hurston: A Literary Biography*. Urbana: University of Illinois Press, 1977.

Hughes, Langston. *The Big Sea: An Autobiography*. New York: Hill and Wang, 1993. (Originally published 1940.)

Hurston, Zora Neale. *Dust Tracks on a Road*. Library of America. New York: HarperPerennial, 1996. (Originally published 1942.)

Kaplan, Carla, ed. *Zora: A Life in Letters*. New York: Doubleday, 2002.

Kellner, Bruce. *Carl Van Vechten and the Irreverent Decades*. Norman: University of Oklahoma Press, 1968.

Thurman, Wallace. *Infants of the Spring*. New York: Modern Library, 1999. (Originally published 1932.)

Van Vechten, Carl. *Nigger Heaven*. Urbana, Ill.: University of Chicago Press, 2000. (Originally published 1926.)

Wintz, Cary D. *Black Culture and the Harlem Renaissance*. Houston, Tex.: Rice University Press, 1988.

Nelson, Alice Dunbar

Alice Dunbar Nelson (or Dunbar-Nelson, 1875–1935) had a long and varied career as a teacher, writer, and leader in the black women's social movement and the early civil rights movement. On completing her secondary education, she studied English literature, psychology, art, and music at Cornell, Columbia, and the University of Pennsylvania. Her academic interest in English literature culminated in a thesis focused on the influence of writing by Milton and Wordsworth. She would herself become one of the most prominent African American women poets of the Harlem Renaissance.

Nelson's exemplary writing provided her with many opportunities to become involved in the social activism that most interested her, and her skill as a writer also affected her personal life. In 1897, she began a relationship with prominent black poet Paul Laurence Dunbar. Dunbar had read some of her poetry and had become intrigued by a photograph he saw of her in a journal published in Boston. The two began a courtship by exchanging letters in 1897, and they were married on 8 March 1898.

Accounts of the relationship suggest that the two admired each other as artists but had little in common aside from their interest in the arts. Some of the problems between them resulted from Nelson's ambivalence about her position as a wife and woman within the constraints of the Victorian age at a time when the "new woman" of the modern era was emerging. The marriage was also strained by Nelson's family, by the demands of Dunbar's career, and by his alcoholism; in 1902, Nelson left Dunbar permanently (Hull 1987).

After the split with Dunbar, Nelson left Washington, D.C., and moved to Wilmington, Delaware, where she taught high school from 1902 to 1920. In 1916, she married Robert J. Nelson. By all accounts, their relationship was not as tempestuous as her marriage with Dunbar had been but was more of a partnership that developed from a shared interest in journalism as well as social and political activism. Nelson and her new husband worked together to publish the Wilmington *Advocate*, and they also published *Masterpieces of Negro Eloquence* (1914).

During her second marriage, Nelson developed more of a sense of herself as an African American woman. This new sense of racial identity, coupled with her interest in women's rights, becomes clear in some of her essays and articles, including "Negro Women in War Work" (1919), "Politics in Delaware" (1924), "Hysteria," and "Is It Time for Negro Colleges in the South to Be Put in the Hands of Negro Teachers?" In essays such as these, she explored the role of black women in the workforce, education, and the anti-lynching movement. Nelson's journalistic writing reflects her social activism: She was a participant in the Women's Committee of the Council of National Defense, National Federation of Colored Women's Clubs, National Association of Colored Women, League of Independent Political Action, Delta Sigma Theta Sorority, Middle Atlantic Women's Suffrage Campaign, and League of Colored Republican Women (Hull 1984).

Nelson's writing also reflects her belief that African Americans needed to have equal access to jobs, education, and other benefits associated with being American; her belief in the equality of men and women; and her opposition to social and political practices that condoned and perpetuated the oppression of women and African Americans. She also expressed her concern about racial categorization and the ambivalence she felt as a person of mixed race (she was of Creole heritage).

Racial ambivalence plagued Nelson throughout her life, and it had affected her marriage to Dunbar. Nelson's own family was part of a socially elite group of African Americans living in New Orleans in the period after slavery ended. The family's sense of elitism was rooted in a belief, on the part of some of its members, that African Americans of "mixed race" were somehow superior to "pure" African Americans. Consequently, the family never really accepted Dunbar, who had physical characteristics they associated with "pure" African descent.

Nelson had begun her literary career at the age of twenty with the publication of *Violets and Other Tales* (1895). Although she is best known for her poetry, this first publication included short stories, sketches, reviews, and essays as well as poems. One recurring theme in *Violets and Other Tales*, as well as in Nelson's

later works, is the plight of women. Nelson examines the status of women in a male-dominated society and the effects of societal constraints, based on gender, on those who try to live up to the Victorian ideal of womanhood. Welter (1976) argues that the lives of upper-class white women in the nineteenth century were governed by four tenets: piety, purity, submissiveness, and domesticity. Nelson developed her skills as a writer at a time when women were in a precarious position, making a transition from such Victorian propriety to a new concept; this "new woman" was appearing in a number of literary works written by American women at the turn of the twentieth century and well into the early years of the new century. To illustrate this transitional situation and the constraints that still persisted, Nelson focused on both African American and white women at various socioeconomic levels.

Nelson herself experienced discrimination based on gender throughout her life, in her interactions with men in her life and in her career. For instance, before marrying Dunbar, she had started to develop a career as an educator, but she was divided between her desire to marry and her desire to work. When she first became involved with Dunbar, she was working in a school in Brooklyn where women teachers could not be married; thus, when she and Dunbar did marry, she had to hide the fact for a while.

Nelson also addressed racial themes in her writing. She expanded her analysis of the "woman question" to explore intersections of race, ethnicity, class, and gender in pieces such as "Violets," "The Woman," "At Eventide," "Tony's Wife," "Elizabeth," and "Ellen Fenton." As previously mentioned, she herself was ambivalent in matters of race because she was of mixed race (she could have passed as white if she had chosen to do so). In *The Goodness of St. Rocque and Other Stories* (1899), Nelson focused specifically on Creole culture. As she matured as a writer, she confronted racial prejudice and American racism in a more direct way in stories such as "Natalie," "The Pearl in the Oyster," "The Stones of the Village," and "Brass Ankles Speaks."

In addition to providing a study of race and gender in connection with identity formation, Nelson explores other markers of identity, such as ethnicity, religion, and class, in some of her short fiction. Hull (1988) notes that Nelson was "inclined to write about difference—for example, Catholic versus Protestant, Anglo versus Creole." In writing about difference, Nelson forces the reader to call into question societal norms that put the white race, men, and certain religions in a privileged position.

During the Harlem Renaissance, Nelson concentrated more on developing her craft as a poet, and she also served as a role model and mentor for some younger creative artists. The poetry she had written before the renaissance was characterized by an emphasis on love and on lyrical verse about nature. But at the time of the renaissance—although she continued to develop themes of love and nature—her poems also reflected her heightened interest in politics and in using art, at least to a certain degree, to influence social change. Most of the poetry she produced during this period was published in the journals *The Crisis* and *Opportunity* between 1917 and 1928. James Weldon Johnson also included some of her poems in his *Book of American Negro Poetry* (1931). Two of her most famous protest poems are "I Sit and Sew" (1927) and "The Proletariat Speaks" (1929).

Poetry also gave Nelson a form in which to express her sexuality. Her diary includes some previously unpublished poetry that, according to Hull (1984), reveals her lesbianism. Actually, Nelson's sexual orientation remains somewhat of a mystery; in any event, she was a passionate writer in this regard as well as when she was concerned with the social and political advancement of African Americans and women.

Nelson died of heart disease in 1935. She had lived a full and intriguing life, despite the difficulties she faced as a woman in a new era and as a social activist taking up the cause of racial equality. Current scholars consider her talented and worthy of study in her own right, not just as the wife of Paul Laurence Dunbar. She is likely to be remembered for what her fiction, essays, and poetry have added to the African American literary tradition and to the American literary canon.

Biography

Alice Dunbar Nelson (Alice Ruth More) was born 19 July 1875 in New Orleans, Louisiana. She studied English, education, and psychology at Straight College, New Orleans; Cornell; Columbia; the Pennsylvania School of Industrial Art; and the University of Pennsylvania. She worked as a teacher in New Orleans from 1892 to 1896; published *Violets and Other Tales* in 1895; married Paul Laurence Dunbar 8 March 1898; published *The Goodness of St. Rocque and Other Stories* in 1899; left Dunbar in 1902 and moved to Wilmington, Delaware; worked at Howard High School from 1902 to 1920; worked as a writer and editor for *AME Church Review* in 1913–1914; published *Masterpieces of Negro Eloquence* in 1914; married the journalist Robert J. Nelson 20 April 1916; and published her work in a number of African American periodicals and books (including *The Crisis, Opportunity, Ebony, Negro Poets and Their Poems,* and *Caroling Dusk: The Book of American Negro Poetry*) between 1917 and 1931. She started writing her diary in 1921. She was a leader in the antilynching crusade in 1922. Nelson died 18 September 1935.

DEIRDRE J. RAYNOR

See also Antilynching Crusade; Crisis, The; Dunbar, Paul Laurence; Opportunity

Further Reading

Andrews, William, ed. *The Oxford Companion to African American Literature.* New York: Oxford University Press, 1997.

Gates, Henry Louis, et al. *The Norton Anthology of African American Literature.* New York: Norton, 1997.

Honey, Maureen. *Shadowed Dreams: Women's Poetry of the Harlem Renaissance.* New Brunswick, N.J.: Rutgers University Press, 1989.

Hull, Gloria T., ed. *Give Us Each Day: The Diary of Alice Dunbar-Nelson.* New York: Norton, 1984.

———. *Color, Sex, and Poetry: Three Women Writers of the Harlem Renaissance.* Bloomington: Indiana University Press, 1987.

———, ed. *The Works of Alice Dunbar-Nelson.* New York: Oxford University Press, 1988.

Wall, Cheryl. *Women of the Harlem Renaissance.* Bloomington: Indiana University Press, 1995.

Welter, Barbara. *Dimity Convictions: The American Woman in the Nineteenth Century.* Columbus: University of Ohio Press, 1976.

New Challenge

New Challenge was intended as a literary quarterly that would be a continuation of *Challenge,* an earlier magazine that had been founded by Dorothy West and edited by her from March 1934 until April 1937. The editors of *New Challenge* stated in their first editorial that their purpose was to represent change and reorganization, "not only with the idea of a change in policy, but also in terms of the best way to fulfill plans for relating it to communities beyond New York City . . . as the organ of regional groups composed of writers opposed to fascism, war, and general reactionary policies."

New Challenge appeared in a single issue, Fall 1937. The divisional content of the new quarterly remained similar in headings and format to that of its predecessor, except that it included sociopolitical articles, an expanded book review section, and letters to the editor. These three additions and the inclusion of more submissions in the sections devoted to stories, poetry, and articles made *New Challenge* larger than *Challenge*. The editors expected an increase in the audience for *New Challenge* and in the number of contributors: Progressive writers from across the country, both Negro and non-Negro, who could place their writings in the proper perspective with regard to the life of the Negro masses, were invited to make submissions; the editors asked, however, that the "bigot and potential fascist keep away from our door."

The editorial appearing in *New Challenge* was jointly written by West, Marian Minus, and Richard Wright. The editors outlined the goal of *New Challenge*, which was the perfection of social consciousness among the Negroes nationwide. It aimed to "point social directives and provide a basis for the clear recognition of and solution to the problems which face the contemporary writer in the realistic portrayal of Negro life." Wright's "Blueprint for Negro Writing" further emphasized the new quarterly's artistic goals.

Under Wright's and Minus's influence, *New Challenge* was temporarily an organ through which the new social protest literary movement of the 1930s found a voice. West did not fully agree with Wright's literary manifesto and his new mission to further reorganize *New Challenge*; however, she endured the infighting and ideological differences that surfaced in the editorial backroom, until after the first and only issue of *New Challenge* was published in 1937, thereby exhibiting the early literary promise of notable writers such as Ralph Ellison, Robert Hayden, and Frank Yerby.

PEARLIE PETERS

See also Challenge; West, Dorothy; Wright, Richard

Further Reading

Daniel, Walter C. "Challenge Magazine: An Experiment That Failed." *CLA Journal*, 19, June 1976, pp. 494–503.
Ferguson, Sally. "Dorothy West." In *Dictionary of Literary Biography*, 76. Detroit, Mich.: Gale Research, 1988.
Guinier, Genii. *Black Women Oral History Project: Interview with Dorothy West, 6 May 1978*. Cambridge, Mass.: Schlesinger Library of Radcliffe College, 1981, pp. 1–75.
Peters, Pearlie. "The Resurgence of Dorothy West as Short-Story Writer." *Abafazi: Simmons College Review of Women of African Descent*, 8(1), Fall–Winter 1997, pp. 16–22.

New Deal

The New Deal (1933–1938) was the most radical response to a peacetime emergency in American history. The Great Depression (1929–1941) was the deepest and most extended economic downturn ever to strike the United States. Black Americans were among the worst affected.

In March 1933, a new government headed by Franklin Delano Roosevelt assumed office. At that point, 24.7 percent of the nation's workforce was unemployed. Many more worked part time or worked for substantially reduced wages. In speeches and through the new medium of radio, President Roosevelt drew the direct analogy that, to overcome the nation's problems, there needed to be a mobilization of the nation's resources for a war on economic collapse.

The New Deal was an exercise in crisis management, an experiment to see what would work. As identified by the president, the task was threefold: to provide relief, recovery, and reform (so that nothing like this would happen again). Most immediately, the banking system needed resuscitation. Next, the unemployed needed relief (private, local, and state coffers simply could not cope with the demand). Finally, industry and agriculture needed urgent efforts to avoid cutthroat competition and low prices.

New Deal Agencies

In 1933, relief was offered to Americans through the Federal Emergency Relief Administration (FERA); the Civilian Conservation Corps (CCC), aimed at providing work-relief for young men; the Civil Works Administration (CWA), which provided work-relief jobs in construction projects to get people through the winter; and the Public Works Administration (PWA), which used unemployed Americans to build dams, schools, lighthouses, sewer systems, bridges, and tunnels. In 1935, after the U.S. Supreme Court found much of the first New Deal to be unconstitutional, a huge new agency, the Works Progress Administration (WPA), was created to provide work relief.

To provide succor to ailing industries, the National Recovery Administration was established in 1933. Mutually acceptable codes of conduct were set up to eliminate harmful business practices industry by industry. Most of the 541 codes followed guidelines that abolished child labor, established a norm of a forty-hour workweek, and set a minimum wage. In agriculture, the Agricultural Adjustment Act (AAA) established an agency committed to raising farm prices. To do this, farmers were paid not to grow crops. A smaller supply would lead to higher prices and thus increase farm income. On a regional level, the Tennessee Valley Authority (TVA) provided development in the form of dams, rural electrification, and jobs to one of the poorer sections of the nation.

In 1935, new legislation, the Wagner or National Labor Relations Act, established the right of workers to organize into labor unions of their choosing, to define and regulate "unfair practices" on the part of employers in trying to avoid unionization. In addition, the Resettlement Administration (RA), then the Farm Security Administration (FSA), tried to resettle poor rural folk on better land and to make sure sharecroppers and tenants received a fairer share of agricultural relief. Of great importance to Americans in 1935 was the passage of the Social Security Act. This provided, for the first time, a national system of accident insurance and old age benefits, as well as a system of unemployment insurance and Aid to Dependent Children. Finally, 1935 saw the establishment of the National Youth Administration (NYA) to provide work relief for young people who had left school, and work for students remaining in school to enable them to complete their education. After this burst of reform, the New Deal faded. The only other significant piece of legislation enacted under Roosevelt was the Fair Labor Standards Act in 1938. This legislation, much amended, provided for a minimum wage.

The New Deal did not end the Depression, but it did contribute mightily to economic recovery by 1937. In that year, a recession undid much progress, and not until war-related orders came rolling in, particularly throughout 1940, would the worst of the Depression, with its stubbornly high unemployment levels, come to an end.

African Americans and New Deal Agencies

African Americans were hit earliest and hardest by the Depression. A survey of twenty-five cities conducted by the Urban League in 1930 found a 34.5 percent decrease in the number of available jobs for blacks and an increase of 40 percent in demand. Similarly, only 31.9 percent of black women workers were employed full time compared with 74.7 percent of native-born white women. In 1931, the U.S. Bureau of the Census held a Special Unemployment Census. It found that in manufacturing, unemployment was 31.7 percent for native-born whites, 29.9 percent for foreign-born whites, and 52 percent for blacks. Among service and domestic workers, unemployment was 17.7 percent for native-born whites, 12.4 percent for foreign-born whites, and 30.7 percent for blacks. Blacks were unemployed sooner and longer than whites. They were added twice as frequently to the relief rolls because of loss of private employment than whites and left the rolls by finding private employment at only half the rate of whites.

Black workers were subjected to discrimination in employment, segregation into the least desirable jobs, exclusion from opportunities to gain skills or promotion, and hostility from white coworkers and employers. For black Americans, the promise of the New Deal at its inception was not that it would wipe away all the oppression, but that it would offer some hope to alleviate the worst of their suffering. Many observers of the New Deal and black America have noted that it failed to end discrimination and that its legislation even institutionalized some of the worst practices. Most also point out, though, that the Roosevelt administration gave more attention to African Americans than any previous administration since Reconstruction. A survey of the major legislation and New Deal agencies will provide a better picture.

CCC offered work relief for young men, country living, good food, and fresh air. It was the single program that blacks most lauded. Between 1933 and 1942, 200,000 black youths went through the program. As in so many of the New Deal programs, however, selection of enrollees was left to local committees or the staff. Some excluded blacks completely, and others admitted only a few. Of the first 250,000 men in the program, less than 3 percent were black. CCC camps were run by the army, and army regulations included segregation. Improvements were made after 1936, owing mainly to effective lobbying of the federal government by the National Urban League and the National Association for the Advancement of Colored People (NAACP), but this meant the establishment of all-black camps in areas where no blacks had previously been admitted and integrated camps in areas with no tradition of segregation. In addition, there were racial quotas that limited African Americans to their numbers in the overall population. With a disproportionate need compared with numbers, this was a decided hardship.

FERA provided jobs with a specified wage rate, benefits were given on the basis of need rather than a racial quota, jobs were created for black professionals, self-help projects were funded, and federal regulations were enacted to raise relief standards in states and to discourage discrimination. As with so many New Deal programs, there was also a downside for African Americans. Nondiscrimination could not be enforced, because no mechanism was provided; eligibility for FERA programs was decided locally; and project development was also locally controlled, leading to prejudiced policies. The result was that it was easier for black Americans to get relief under FERA than to get jobs; because of the strength of local control, lobbying did little to improve matters. Nevertheless, FERA did provide some concrete help to black Americans. Around 30 percent of the appropriation for low-cost housing projects was devoted to blacks. In 1935, thanks to FERA, 20 percent of students at the all-black West Virginia State College received jobs to help them stay in school, and FERA gave $281,000 in scholarships to black schools and colleges. As a result of other programs, in 1934, 6,000 sharecropper families in Alabama received eight months' relief in a lump sum and a four-room house for less than $300 per farmer. The following year, FERA did the same for another 14,000.

PWA tended to help black Americans more than some New Deal programs. The reason was the chief administrator, Harold Ickes, the former head of the Chicago NAACP. Ickes was one of a handful of New Dealers supportive of equal rights for blacks. Like the others, however, during the early New Deal he was often reluctant to push his beliefs. A major problem in PWA, as in CWA and WPA later, was that projects were contracted out to local companies that negotiated with labor unions. Most of the construction trades unions excluded blacks either formally or informally. Only in the low-cost housing division did Ickes insist that, if the total amount paid to skilled workers per month did not show a set percentage paid to blacks (the proportion of blacks in the local population), this would count as prima facie evidence of discrimination by the contractor.

NYA was one of the brightest spots for African Americans under the New Deal. Again, it was administered by a sympathetic head—Aubrey Williams—and was heavily influenced by Mary McLeod Bethune,

whom he appointed to head the Division of Negro Affairs. Black administrators were appointed at every level of the organization, and by 1940 20 percent of NYA appropriations went to black young people. The program was relatively small and poorly administered, however.

In the largest New Deal programs—NRA, AAA, and WPA—the situation for African Americans was just as mixed. WPA gave jobs to 3.5 million Americans in the first year of its creation. It focused on labor-intensive, relatively inexpensive programs. Under its administrator, Harry Hopkins, discrimination was banned, there were no racial quotas to restrict African Americans, and aid went to the most needy. WPA was established as the economy was showing signs of recovery, however, and wages for WPA projects were set deliberately lower than wages in the private sector. In some areas of the South, black WPA workers were released at harvest time and therefore forced to work for planters at even lower wages. In addition, funds were not sufficient for everyone who needed the work, and responsibility for relief payments was returned to the states, which meant lower levels than under federal programs. As with its predecessors, projects were developed and administered locally; this arrangement allowed discriminatory practices to continue. Similarly, wages were set according to geographical calculations. Because a majority of the black population lived in the southeast region, and it set the lowest wages, blacks were disproportionally disadvantaged. By 1939, as general economic recovery continued, a rule was instituted that no one could be on WPA projects for more than eighteen months. As the last hired, blacks were most severely affected. Also by 1939, though, WPA provided basic earnings for one-seventh of all black families in America.

The National Recovery Administration (NRA) also got off to a rocky start as far as African Americans were concerned. Initially, only one black adviser was hired by the institution, and she was quickly excluded, ignored, and then fired. Throughout 1934, there was not even a black clerk in NRA's bureaucracy. Reflecting prevailing conditions and the lack of political influence from the black community, NRA's industry codes, while not acceding to requests by businesses for differential wages for black workers, discriminated against black workers by accepting complex occupational and geographical differentials that effectively gave most African Americans lower wages than whites. In industries covered under the codes that did not discriminate, employers often fired blacks in order to hire whites, precisely so that they did not have to pay equal minimum wages. In addition, industry codes were usually drawn up by the larger firms. Minimum wages sometimes forced smaller, more marginal, particularly southern manufacturing businesses to close. Disproportionate numbers of African Americans were affected because their jobs had depended on acceptance of lower wages than those prevailing in the industry.

The segregated nature of much of black work in America was reflected by the absence of industry codes (and therefore minimum-wage requirements) in heavily black industries. In industries covered by NRA codes, if companies dealt with labor unions, blacks often suffered because of union bans on black members, discriminatory initiation practices, or local hostility to black workers. Worse, the codes allowed industries to raise prices in order to aid economic recovery, so black Americans found themselves pushed out of jobs and at the same time faced a higher cost of living. Somewhat mitigating the harmful effects of the NRA codes for blacks was the fact that the codes were widely evaded; as a result, some black workers obtained jobs under the minimum wages stipulated.

AAA was less murky in its effects on African Americans. It did not help at all, and in fact it led to the displacement of many black sharecroppers and tenants, a process accelerated by the introduction of mechanization of crop production even in cotton during the 1930s. First, the federal government payments to farmers not to grow crops were made to landowners in the South, not to tenants or sharecroppers. Whereas for most crops federal payments were split evenly between landowners and tenants, under the cotton code 90 percent went to landowners; there were no mechanisms to ensure payment by landowners of the remaining 10 percent to their tenants. All disputes under the AAA codes were adjudicated by local committees. Owing to the prevailing racial code of the region, the result was that not a single black farmer was on any AAA committee in the South. The rejection of the NAACP's attempts to get blacks hired as part of the AAA apparatus led, in 1934, to its conclusion that black Americans could find no remedy to their troubles under AAA. Successor organizations to AAA after 1935 attempted to address the problem of discrimination in agriculture against tenants and sharecroppers, but with mixed results. In 1937, the FSA declared that tenants could obtain loans to purchase land, but only 3,400 blacks were able to do so. On the other hand, new funds were provided for rural rehabilitation, relief, and resettlement. Despite the principle of local

administration of programs, 23 percent of the benefits in the South were received by blacks.

Beyond relief programs, other major New Deal legislation affected black Americans. The Wagner Act did not contain any ban on racial discrimination in labor unions. Although the NAACP lobbied hard for one, resistance was stiff from both labor unions and employers. The result was that contracts between employers and unions that provided for the closed shop tended to reinforce socially exclusive norms and thus worked to the detriment of black workers. With the rise of the Congress of Industrial Organizations (CIO) after 1937, certain industries experienced less discrimination; union leaders had realized that in those industries with significant numbers of black workers—such as automobiles, steel, packinghouses, and rubber—it would be impossible to organize effectively along industrial (as opposed to craft) lines without being all-inclusive. This did not mean that there was a cessation of discrimination against black workers, even in these more "progressive" new unions. Union leaders occasionally took severe action against racist locals; more often, however, as with the Transport Workers Union in New York and Philadelphia, they talked equality while playing a political balancing act so as not to alienate their white members.

Beyond industrial policy reforms, there was also the widely hailed effort to forge a true welfare state. Most significant was the Social Security Act of 1935. Initially, it did not positively affect many black Americans. Exemptions from coverage under the act included all household domestics and farm laborers, categories that covered two-thirds of black employment. As with much other New Deal legislation, no specific provisions in the act banned discrimination. Similarly, much of the administration of the new act was placed in the hands of state and local officials with the ability to adjust payments and eligibility standards in line with local standards. Efforts by the NAACP and the National Urban League (NUL) to have all workers covered and for the act to be administered nationally failed on the reefs of racial insensitivity and the anxiety of liberals to get at least some legislation passed in this area.

The New Deal, Harlem, and the Harlem Renaissance

Most accounts of the Harlem Renaissance end with the close of the 1920s. Indeed, the economic collapse represented by the crash on Wall Street did profoundly affect the environment within which Harlem's artists and writers could work, although it was not the only factor in explanations for the decline of this remarkable phenomenon. Nevertheless, the blossoming of black cultural production did not end in 1929 but continued throughout the decade of the Depression, aided to some extent by New Deal programs. Its thrust did change. By February 1930, there was five times more unemployment in Harlem than in other parts of New York City. In the city as a whole, by the end of that year only 42.5 percent of black workers were in full-time employment, compared with 64.2 percent of native-born whites. By 1931, between ten and twenty families were evicted each day. More than 10,000 people lived in cellars and basements. During the summer of 1934, more than 19,000 families in Harlem were still dependent on relief. A continued influx into Harlem led to rapid deterioration. Society itself was politicized, and this had an impact on how cultural expressions were framed. While the black population of New York increased by only 1 percent during the 1930s, the number voting in presidential elections shot up by 50 percent. And whereas 60 percent of the black electorate voted Republican in 1932, by 1936, 75 percent voted Democratic (for the New Deal). Large numbers of Harlemites became even more radical as a result of the challenges of the Depression. Political protest and even revolt were manifested through the Harlem boycott of 1934 and the Harlem riot of 1935. Civil rights became a major issue both in Harlem, through the activity of black Americans, and at the national level for the first time since Reconstruction with the creation by Attorney General Frank Murphy of the Civil Liberties (subsequently Civil Rights) section of the Justice Department.

New Deal programs also gave support to black artists and writers. In Harlem, in contrast to the situation in the 1920s, thirty-four adult education centers were set up under WPA. Art classes were offered through the Federal Arts Project. The artist Aaron Douglas and the sculptor Augusta Savage were both active during the Harlem Renaissance and the New Deal years. Savage was particularly successful in getting jobs for promising black artists with the Federal Arts Project (FAP). Perhaps most notably, she was a mentor to Jacob Lawrence. A Negro Unit of the Federal Theater Project employed 700 blacks nationally by mid-1936. In Harlem, the first full-scale black Shakespearean production, known popularly as "Voodoo Macbeth," became a citywide sensation, running for ten weeks in Harlem and eight weeks in downtown Manhattan; it then toured the country under a program sponsored by WPA. More than 200 black authors were employed by the Federal Writers' Project (FWP). Under the auspices of FWP, Ralph Ellison and Richard Wright were first published. Publications in the history and sociology of black America also owed their research funding to FWP.

Conclusion

The New Deal did not end America's recent history of institutionalized and social racial discrimination. It did not significantly move African Americans to a situation of greater equality in America. Nor did it single-handedly save the Harlem Renaissance. Its significance for black America in general and Harlem in particular was that it provided a safety net below which people could not drop. Through relief payments and work relief, the New Deal aided black Americans in ways the federal government had never before attempted and helped them survive a Depression to which they might otherwise have succumbed. For artists and writers, the New Deal sometimes meant the difference between being able to develop their art and starving. Symbolically, the New Deal gave new hope that oppression could be lifted and that there were at least some possibilities for exerting pressure for change. Despite his refusal to push for antilynching legislation, for example, President Roosevelt spoke out at least once publicly on the issue, desegregated the federal government (with the notable exception of the Federal Bureau of Investigation), graciously received foreign black diplomats at the White House, appointed the first black federal judges since Reconstruction, consulted regularly with the "black brain trust," approved of black advisers in many of the various New Deal agencies, increased the number of black federal employees from fewer than 50,000 in 1932 to more than 150,000 by 1941, and generally promoted the belief that, for the first time, government cared for all Americans. His wife, Eleanor Roosevelt, was particularly important in bringing the concerns of black Americans to the president and in pushing hard on her own account for black advancement. Though substantive change was still distant, the New Deal offered black Americans a glimpse of improvement, one that they embraced and used to its utmost. For African Americans' cultural production, the New Deal offered at least some opportunities to continue and develop new talents and initiatives.

STEPHEN BURWOOD

See also Bethune, Mary McLeod; Douglas, Aaron; Ellison, Ralph; Federal Programs; Federal Writers' Project; Lawrence, Jacob; Riots: 4—Harlem Riot, 1935; Savage, Augusta; Works Progress Administration; Wright, Richard

Further Reading

Anderson, Jervis. *This Was Harlem*. New York: Farrar, Straus and Giroux, 1982.

Bernstein, David E. *Only One Place of Redress: African Americans, Labor Regulations, and the Courts from Reconstruction to the New Deal*. Durham, N.C.: Duke University Press, 2001.

Greenberg, Cheryl Lynn. *Or Does It Explode? Black Harlem in the Great Depression*. New York: Oxford University Press, 1991.

Hamilton, Dona Cooper. "The National Urban League and the New Deal." *Social Service Review*, 58, March 1984.

Sears, James M. "Black Americans and the New Deal." *History Teacher*, 10, Spring 1976.

Sitkoff, Harvard. *A New Deal for Blacks: The Emergence of Civil Rights as an Issue: The Depression Decade*. New York: Oxford University Press, 1978.

Valocchi, Steve. "The Racial Basis of Capitalism and the State, and the Impact of the New Deal on African Americans." *Social Problems*, 41, August 1994.

Wolters, Raymond. *Negroes and the Great Depression: The Problem of Recovery*. Westport, Conn.: Greenwood, 1970.

———. "The New Deal and the Negro." In *The New Deal: The National Level*, ed. John Braeman, Robert H. Bremner, and David Brody. Columbus: Ohio State University Press, 1975.

New Masses

The New Masses (1926–1948) was one of several Marxist literary and political magazines of the 1920s, 1930s, and 1940s that exposed a culturally diverse working-class and radical audience to contemporary African American culture and politics. Developing in part out of two earlier left-wing periodicals, *The Masses* (1911–1917) and *The Liberator* (1918–1924), *New Masses* appeared monthly between May 1926 and September 1933 and weekly between January 1934 and January 1948.

In the issue of June 1926, the white novelist John Dos Passos, then a member of the magazine's executive board, expressed his hope that *New Masses* would be a forum for distinctly American ideas. Eschewing "phrases, badges, opinions, banners imported from Russia or anywhere else," he called for a magazine that, like "a highly flexible receiving station," would "find out what's in the air in the country anyhow" (20). Although *New Masses* became increasingly affiliated with international communism throughout the late 1920s and early 1930s, the magazine maintained a keen interest in the literature, music, and political struggles of black America. In addition to publishing work by black writers, reviews of their work, and reviews of books about black history and culture, *New Masses* regularly featured articles on such varied subjects as black literary aesthetics, black "protest songs," lynching, the Scottsboro case, and the conditions of black sharecroppers.

At various times during the late 1920s and early 1930s, the magazine's long roster of contributing editors included Langston Hughes, Claude McKay, Jean Toomer, Eric Walrond, and Walter White. Hughes, McKay, and White, as well as Alain Locke and George S. Schuyler, were among the black intellectuals who published in *New Masses* during this period. Later, the magazine printed the work of Gwendolyn Bennett, Sterling Brown, Countee Cullen, Ralph Ellison, Louise Thompson Patterson, Richard Wright, and others. On 5 October 1937, for example, *New Masses* featured Wright's contentious review of Zora Neale Hurston's *Their Eyes Were Watching God*.

Among the writers conventionally associated with the Harlem Renaissance, Hughes was the figure most closely identified with *New Masses*. In its pages, he published the poem "Advertisement for the Waldorf-Astoria," the play *Scottsboro Limited*, and many other poems, plays, short stories, translations, and essays. Beginning in the early 1930s, the magazine's literary critics often portrayed Hughes as the brightest hope for a new, class-conscious black literature. According to these critics, Hughes challenged the conviction of the "talented tenth" that literary and artistic expression, not political struggle, was the surest foundation for blacks' social progress. A list of recommended books published in the issue of 2 October 1934 praised the short stories in Hughes's *The Ways of White Folks* (1934) for shattering "the illusion that through 'culture' Negro intellectuals . . . can solve their race problem" (28). Notwithstanding such attacks on the dominant ideology of the Harlem Renaissance, however, *New Masses* served as an important venue for Hughes as well as other black writers. Also, unlike many mainstream and left-wing periodicals of this period, *New Masses* consistently acknowledged black Americans' cultural and political presence on the national scene.

MATTHEW CALIHMAN

See also Bennett, Gwendolyn; Brown, Sterling; Cullen, Countee; Eastman, Max; Ellison, Ralph; Hughes, Langston; Liberator; Locke, Alain; Lynching; McKay, Claude; Messenger, The; Modern Quarterly; Patterson, Louise Thompson; Schuyler, George S.; Scottsboro; Toomer, Jean; Walrond, Eric; White, Walter; Wright, Richard

Further Reading

Cruse, Harold, *The Crisis of the Negro Intellectual*. New York: Quill, 1967.

Hutchinson, George. *The Harlem Renaissance in Black and White*. Cambridge, Mass.: Belknap Press of Harvard University Press, 1995

Klein, Marcus. *Foreigners: The Making of American Literature, 1900–1940*. Chicago, Ill.: University of Chicago Press, 1981.

Naison, Mark. *Communists in Harlem during the Depression*. Urbana: University of Illinois Press, 1983.

North, Joseph, ed. *New Masses: An Anthology of the Rebel Thirties*. New York: International, 1969.

Smethurst, James Edward. *The New Red Negro: The Literary Left and African American Poetry, 1930–1946*. New York: Oxford University Press, 1999.

New Negro

The phrase "New Negro" was in use long before the Harlem Renaissance. It has been used in African American discourses at least since 1895; the concept or concepts associated with it evolved over the years to become critical to the African American scene during the first three decades of the twentieth century, receiving the most attention during what were perhaps the peak years of the Harlem Renaissance, 1917–1928. The term has a broad relevance to the period in American history known as post-Reconstruction, whose beginnings were marked symbolically by the notorious Compromise of 1877 and whose impact on black Americans culminated in 1896 with the U.S. Supreme Court's decision in *Plessey v. Ferguson*, which practically obliterated the gains African Americans had made through the Fourteenth and Fifteenth amendments to the Constitution. Gates (1988), who has provided a comprehensive treatment of this evolution from 1895 to 1925, notes the profound irony marking post-Reconstruction, when, in conjunction with their reenslavement, "blacks regained a public voice, louder and more strident than it had been even during slavery." In this context, it is also interesting to consider the syzygy, or lineup, of African American leaders and their personalities and styles in 1895. That year, W. E. B. Du Bois, with a Ph.D. from Harvard in hand, embarked on his long career in scholarship and civil rights; Booker T. Washington delivered his "Atlanta compromise" speech; and Frederick Douglass died. For three years previously, Douglass—having been persuaded back into the public domain by Ida Wells Barnett after a long time of silence and retreat—had been making some of the most bitter and most despairing speeches on "race." Despite their rhetorical and ideological differences, these three leaders were speaking up during the 1890s, a decade that was described by the black historian Rayford Logan as the "nadir" of African American history and was marked by nearly 2,000 documented lynchings.

In various writings—such as an editorial in the *Cleveland Gazette* in 1895; commentaries in other black newspapers; the book *A New Negro for a New Century* (1900), edited by Booker T. Washington, Fannie Barrier Williams, and N. B. Wood; and *The New Negro: His Political, Civil, and Mental Status and Related Essays* (1916), a compilation by William Pickens—the New Negroes were seen as men and women (mostly men) of middle-class orientation who often demanded their legal rights as citizens and almost always wanted to craft new images that would subvert and challenge old stereotypes. In the anthology *The New Negro: An Interpretation* (1925)—which had grown out of a special issue of *Survey Graphic* on Harlem—the editor, Alain Locke, contrasted the "old Negro" with the "New Negro," stressing black Americans' assertiveness and self-confidence during the years following World War I and the great migration. Racial pride had been part of African Americans' literary and political self-expression in the nineteenth century and had been reflected in the writings of Martin Delany, Bishop Henry Turner, Frances E. W. Harper, Frederick Douglass, and Pauline Hopkins; but it now found a new purpose and definition in the journalism, fiction, poetry, music, sculpture, and paintings of numerous figures associated with the Harlem Renaissance, which is also known as the New Negro movement.

During the Harlem Renaissance, the term "New Negro" inspired a wide variety of responses from the participants and promoters. According to a militant Negro editor writing in 1920, this "new line of thought, a new method of approach" included the possibility that "the intrinsic standard of Beauty and aesthetics does not rest in the white race" and that "a new racial love, respect, and consciousness may be created." It was felt that African Americans were poised to assert their own agency in culture and politics instead of just remaining a "problem" or "formula" for others to debate about. The New Negroes of the 1920s, the "talented tenth," included poets, novelists, and blues singers creating their art out of Negro folk heritage and history; black political leaders fighting against corruption and for expanded opportunities for African Americans; businessmen working toward the possibility of a "black metropolis"; and Garveyites dreaming of a homeland in Africa. All of them shared a desire to shed the image of servility and inferiority of the shuffling "old Negro" and achieve a new image of pride and dignity.

No one has articulated the hopes and possibilities associated with the idea and ideal of the New Negro more thoroughly than Alain Locke, who would later describe himself as the "midwife" to aspiring young black writers of the 1920s. *The New Negro*, whose publication by Albert and Charles Boni in December 1925 was the culmination of the first stage of the New Negro renaissance in literature, was put together, in Locke's words, "to document the New Negro culturally and socially—to register the transformations of the inner and outer life of the Negro in America that have so significantly taken place in the last few years." This anthology, as previously noted, was based on a special "Harlem issue" of *Survey Graphic* that appeared in March 1925 and sold 42,000 copies (a record that *Survey Graphic* would not surpass until World War II). Locke emphasized the national and international scope of the New Negro movement, comparing it to the "nascent movements of folk expression and self-determination . . . in India, in China, in Egypt, Ireland, Russia, Bohemia, Palestine, and Mexico." Locke's philosophy of cultural pluralism is analogous to the thinking of many of his white contemporaries, especially Waldo Frank, V. F. Calverton, Randolph Bourne, and Van Wyck Brooks. According to Locke, who shared the optimism of other progressive reformers, "the conditions that are molding a New Negro are [also] molding a new American attitude." He defined the creed of his own generation as "the efficacy of collective effort, in race

co-operation." Like some black political leaders of the period, Locke seems to have believed that the American system would ultimately work for African Americans, but he refused to recognize a disagreeable aspect of the system—the need for political leverage. Such an approach implied excessive dependence on the good intentions of influential white men. In terms of art and literature, Locke saw no conflict between being "American" and being "Negro," but rather an opportunity for enrichment through cultural reciprocity. In a way, Locke was reinterpreting Du Bois's concept of "double consciousness" and applying it to aesthetics and culture; there seems to have been enough room in Locke's view for many different kinds of talents to exist and thrive together. With regard to African art, Locke believed that the most important lesson the black artist could derive from it was "not cultural inspiration or technical innovations, but the lesson of a classic background, the lesson of discipline, of style, of technical control."

Responses to Locke's anthology and his concept of the New Negro varied. W. E. B. Du Bois, for instance, thought that, at one level, the concept implied a rejection of the accommodationist politics and ideology represented by Booker T. Washington and his followers around the turn of the twentieth century. (Despite Washington's access to the White House and to mainstream politicians, violence against African Americans had continued unabated, and little progress had been made in civil rights or economic opportunities.) There were also expressions of doubt and skepticism, however, such as those from Eric Walrond and Wallace Thurman.

Eric Walrond, the young West Indian author of *Tropic Death* (1926), considered all contemporary black leaders inadequate or ineffective in dealing with the cultural and political aspirations of the black masses. In 1923, in his essay "The New Negro Faces America," Walrond declared the New Negro to be "race conscious":

> He does not want . . . to be like the white man. He is coming to realize the great possibilities within himself. . . . The New Negro, who does not want to go back to Africa, is fondly cherishing an ideal—and that is, that the time will come when America will look upon the Negro not as a savage with an inferior mentality, but as a civilized man. . . . The rank and file of Negroes are opposed to Garveyism; dissatisfied with the personal vituperation and morbid satire of Mr. Du Bois, and prone to discount Major [Robert] Moton's Tuskegee as a monument of respectable reaction.

By 1929, Wallace Thurman—a bohemian leader of young writers associated with "Niggeratti Manor" and with journals such as *Fire!!* and *Harlem*—was talking about the New Negro as a fad of white Americans that had already come and gone. In several pieces of journalism and literary essays, Thurman castigated the white and black middle-class readers whose interest in the work of younger black writers made it harder for those writers to think and create independently. In one such essay, "The Negro Literary Renaissance," Thurman says:

> Everyone was having a grand time. The millennium was about to dawn. The second emancipation seemed inevitable. Then the excitement began to die down and Negroes as well as whites began to take stock of that in which they had reveled. The whites shrugged their shoulders and began seeking for some new fad. Negroes stood by, a little subdued, a little surprised, torn between being proud that certain of their group had achieved distinction, and being angry because a few of the arrived ones had ceased to be what the group considered "constructive," having, in the interim, produced works that went against the grain, in that they did not wholly qualify to the adjective "respectable."

In 1929, Thurman had begun his second novel, *Infants of the Spring* (1932), a satire in which he took himself and his peers to task as decadent and undisciplined, declaring that all his contemporaries except Jean Toomer were mere journeymen. Although Thurman admired Alain Locke for his sympathy with and support of young Negro writers, the salon scene in Chapter 21 of his novel suggests Locke's failure to organize these highly individualistic young writers into a cohesive movement.

There was, then, no consensus on the significance of the term "New Negro" during the Harlem Renaissance. Moreover, many later commentators, such as Cruse (1967), would consider Locke's view of the New Negro politically naïve or overly optimistic, and they would particularly take exception to his belief that, in a pluralistic American society, political and economic benefits for all African Americans might result from a wider recognition of the literary and cultural expression of the artists of the Harlem Renaissance. As late as 1938, Locke was defending his views against charges by John P. Davis and others that his emphasis was primarily on the "psychology of the masses" and not on offering any one solution to the "Negro problem." Osofsky

(1965) argued that the New Negroes of the 1920s had actually helped to reinforce new white stereotypes of black life that were different from but no more valid or accurate than the old stereotypes. Gates (1988) dismissed the construction of the New Negro as a dubious venture in renaming, merely a "bold and audacious act of language."

For African Americans, World War I highlighted the widening gap between the nation's rhetoric regarding "the war to make the world safe for democracy" and the reality of disenfranchised and exploited black farmers in the South or the poor and alienated residents of northern slums. In France during the war, black soldiers experienced the kind of freedom they had never known in the United States; meanwhile, at home, southern blacks were swelling the population of existing black ghettoes or creating new ones. The frustrations and disappointments of the war years—dramatized in the riots of the "red summer" of 1919—led to a new spirit of militancy that found expression, for example, in Claude McKay's sonnets "If We Must Die" and "America." In the 1920s, the rich and diverse contributions made by journals such as *The Crisis*, *Opportunity*, and *The Messenger* helped to interpret for their growing readership the powerful impact that World War I and the great migration had made on the African American masses.

The concept of "New Negro" has thus had a checkered history since it was first introduced in the nineteenth century, and there are varied interpretations of its long-term significance. There is no doubt that, despite the difficult issues of race and class in the 1920s, a new spirit of hope and pride marked black activity and expression in all areas. All the participants in the Harlem Renaissance, regardless of their age, ideology, aesthetics, or politics, shared this sense of possibility at least on some level. The middle-class leaders of the National Association for the Advancement of Colored People (NAACP) and the Urban League were deeply suspicious of the flamboyant, demagogic Marcus Garvey, who in turn saw Du Bois and others as dark-skinned whites. Yet virtually all of them subscribed to some form of pan-Africanism. Locke and Charles Spurgeon Johnson, moreover, rejected cultural separatism and endorsed a hybridism derived from the black experience and Euro-American aesthetic forms.

Perhaps what is most important for latter-day culture and literature is the insistence of the New Negro on self-definition, self-expression, and self-determination in many spheres—a striving after what Locke called "spiritual emancipation." The debates during the Harlem

Renaissance regarding art and propaganda, representation and identity, assimilation versus militancy, and parochialism versus globalism broadened the perspectives on art, culture, politics, and ideology that have developed among African Americans since the 1930s—especially the perspectives offered by Richard Wright, Ralph Ellison, and Toni Morrison.

AMRITJIT SINGH

See also Calverton; V. F.; Ellison, Ralph; Fire!!; Frank, Waldo; Infants of the Spring; Johnson, Charles Spurgeon; Locke, Alain; McKay, Claude; New Negro Movement; New Negro, The; Pickens, William; Riots: 2—Red Summer of 1919; Survey Graphic; Talented Tenth; Thurman, Wallace; Walrond, Eric; Washington, Booker T.; Wright, Richard

Further Reading

Cruse, Harold. *The Crisis of the Negro Intellectual.* 1967.

Gates, Henry Louis, Jr. "The Trope of a New Negro and the Reconstruction of the Image of the Black." *Representations*, Fall 1988.

Huggins, Nathan. *Harlem Renaissance.* 1971.

Lewis, David Levering. *When Harlem Was in Vogue.* 1981.

Locke, Alain, ed., *The New Negro.* 1992. (New intro. Arnold Rampersad.)

Osofsky, Gilbert. *Harlem: The Making of a Ghetto.* 1965.

Parascandola, Louis, ed. *"Winds Can Wake Up the Dead": An Eric Walrond Reader.* 1998.

Singh, Amritjit. *The Novels of the Harlem Renaissance.* 1976, ch. 1.

Singh, Amritjit, and Daniel M. Scott, III, eds. *The Collected Writings of Wallace Thurman: A Harlem Renaissance Reader.* 2003. (See Introduction, Parts 4 and 5.)

New Negro Art Theater

The New Negro Art Theater, a "little theater" group, was active, primarily as a dance company, in 1929–1931. The troupe was founded by Hemsley Winfield (1906–1934), a native of Yonkers who did much to invent Negro concert dance in America. He first won fame in 1929 in the role of Salome (in Oscar Wilde's play of that name), which he performed in drag at the Cherry Lane Theater in Greenwich Village after the company's female lead took ill. The New Negro Art Theater Dance Company came into its own when it staged a program of "serious," or classical, black dance at the Theater in the Clouds in the Chanin Building on 29 April 1931. The modern dance pioneer Ruth St. Denis was among the sponsors for this event, which drew an overflow crowd. The program included dances inspired by African themes and spirituals, a dance based on the Cambodian temples at Angkor Wat, and a set of specialty numbers danced by Winfield. The company performed *Salome* again in August 1931, earning Winfield a mixture of praise and ridicule in the press. The leading female dancers in his eighteen-person troupe included Ollie Burgoyne and Edna Guy.

Over the next two years, the New Negro Art Theater Dance Company performed widely in New York, at the Nicholas Roerich Museum, International House of Columbia University, the Westchester County Center in White Plains, the Roxy Theater, and other venues. Winfield went on to dance the role of the Witch Doctor in the world premiere of Louis Gruenberg's version of *The Emperor Jones* at the Metropolitan Opera in January 1933. Members of the New Negro Art Theater made up his ensemble for this event, billed as the Hemsley Winfield Ballet. Winfield was very much the leading spirit of the New Negro Art Theater's dance company, and it did not survive his early death in January 1934.

ELLIOTT S. HURWITT

See also Emperor Jones, The; Gruenberg, Louis

Further Reading

Hemsley Winfield clippings file. Schomburg Center for Research in Black Culture, New York Public Library.

Hughes, Langston, and Milton Meltzer. *Black Magic: A Pictorial History of Black Entertainers in America.* New York: Bonanza, 1971.

Kellner, Bruce, ed. *The Harlem Renaissance: A Historical Dictionary for the Era.* Westport, Conn.: Greenwood, 1984.

New Negro Movement

"New Negro movement" is often used interchangeably with "Harlem Renaissance," "Negro renaissance," "New Negro renaissance," or "first Negro renaissance" (in contrast to a "second black renaissance" of the 1960s and 1970s). These terms refer generally to the artistic and sociocultural awakening among African Americans in the 1920s and early 1930s. "New Negro movement" is sometimes used to suggest African Americans' broad response to the political and economic implications of the great migration and Word War I, with "Harlem Renaissance" or "Negro renaissance" reserved for the concomitant cultural and artistic activity. As is abundantly evident in the extensive writings from the period, however, as well as in the growing commentary since the 1970s, the social and political impulses of these years were intertwined with cultural and artistic expression.

More blacks participated in the arts than ever before, and this florescence of creativity included music, poetry, theater, drama, fiction, painting, and sculpture. The needs of the new self-expression in literature were served by many black journals, such as *The Crisis*, *Opportunity*, and *The Messenger*, as well as by other leading journals such as *American Mercury*, *Bookman*, *Independent*, *Modern Quarterly*, *The Nation*, *New Republic*, *Saturday Review*, and *Survey Graphic*. By 1924, many people had become conscious of this literary upsurge and tried to direct and influence it. Alain Locke, who described himself later as a "midwife" to the younger generation of Negro writers, propounded the concept of a Negro renaissance and tried to shape it into an artistic movement. In 1925, Locke edited *The New Negro*, an anthology of poems, stories, essays, and paintings about all strata of black life, initiating a historically significant debate on black writing. The term "New Negro," though not original with Locke, caught on in black circles even more than his concept of cultural pluralism. New Negro societies sprang up in several large cities, and it became fashionable to declare oneself a member of the New Negro coterie.

As regards time, "Harlem Renaissance" frequently refers to a brief period: for some, only the peak six or seven years, 1923–1929; for others, about twenty to thirty years, from 1909–1910 (when the National Association for the Advancement of Colored People and *The Crisis* were founded), or 1914 (when World War I began), or 1917 (the year McKay published his poem "Harlem Dancer") until 1937 (when Zora Neale Hurston published *Their Eyes Were Watching God*). One might argue that the New Negro movement was longer, possibly extending from the late nineteenth century to, say, 1948 (when President Harry Truman integrated the armed forces); some literary scholars and historians, including Brown (1955) and Franklin (1967), see the New Negro movement as a continuing phenomenon. As Hull (1987), Stepto (1989), and Wall (1995) note, the timing of the Harlem Renaissance or

the New Negro movement depends on several factors, especially genres, artists' gender or regional background, and scholars' own ideological biases. In any case, the Harlem Riot of 1935 drew attention to rising crime and unemployment in Harlem and signaled the end of whites' honeymoon period with this presumed artistic and cultural paradise; literary historians generally agree that Richard Wright's *Native Son*, published in 1940, heralded a new phase of harsh realism in African American writing, definitively marking the end of the Harlem Renaissance in literature and the arts.

As regards terminology, "New Negro" was used long before the Harlem Renaissance. Its first use may have been in 1895 in the *Cleveland Gazette*, where it referred to a group of blacks who had just secured a civil rights law in New York. It also appeared in books like *A New Negro for a New Century* (1900), edited by Booker T. Washington, Fannie Barrier Williams, and N. B. Wood; and William Pickens's *The New Negro* (1916). The New Negroes were seen as middle class, as demanding their legal rights, and as wanting to develop new images that would challenge old stereotypes. Alain Locke's contribution in the 1920s was to link the sociopolitical import of "New Negro" to the artistic and cultural expression of the period. In several essays included in his anthology *The New Negro* (1925)—which grew out of a special "Harlem issue" of *Survey Graphic*—Locke contrasted the New Negro with the "old Negro," stressing black Americans' assertiveness and self-confidence during the years following World War I and the great migration. Racial pride had been part of African Americans' literary and political self-expression in the nineteenth century and was reflected in the writings of Martin Delany, Frederick Douglass, Frances E. W. Harper, Pauline Hopkins, and Bishop Henry Turner; but it had a new purpose and definition in the journalism, fiction, poetry, music, sculpture, and painting of the Harlem Renaissance.

Brown (1955) has questioned the use of the term "renaissance" to describe the creative activity of blacks in the 1920s. This term seems justified by the intense interest of African American writers in coming to terms with the peculiar racial situation in the United States, however, and in exploring their emotional and historical links with Africa and the American South. Their interest was prefigured in the work of many nineteenth-century black writers, and in the 1890s in the poetry, fiction, and essays of Paul Laurence Dunbar, James Weldon Johnson, Charles W. Chesnutt, Sutton E. Griggs, and W. E. B. Du Bois. The most significant link between the 1890s and the 1920s was Du Bois, who held that "the problem of the twentieth century" was "the problem of the color line" and crystallized his concept of "double consciousness" in *The Souls of Black Folk* (1903)—which was read by most young black writers and of which Claude McKay said, "The book shook me like an earthquake."

As regards place, Brown stressed that the New Negro phenomenon extended beyond Harlem in space as well as time:

> The New Negro is not to me a group of writers centered in Harlem during the second half of the twenties. Most of the writers were not Harlemites; much of the best writing was not about Harlem, which was the show-window, the cashier's till but no more Negro America than New York is America. The New Negro has temporal roots in the past and spatial roots elsewhere in America, and the term has validity, it seems to me, only when considered to be a continuing tradition.

For this reason, too, "New Negro renaissance"—which would include literary and artistic activity in African American communities throughout the United States—is arguably a better descriptive label than "Harlem Renaissance." For instance, before he arrived in Harlem on Labor Day in 1925, Thurman had been trying to create a community of young black artists in Los Angeles that included Arna Bontemps and Fay Jackson. He published his own work and that of others in *The Outlet*, a literary journal he edited from September 1924 to March 1925; he also wrote a literary column, "Inklings," in the black newspaper *Pacific Defender*. In Boston, the cousins Helene Johnson and Dorothy West, and many others, established a literary group and published in *The Quill*, a magazine edited by Eugene Gordon from 1928 to 1930. West edited *Challenge: A Literary Quarterly*—later *New Challenge*, whose first and only issue in 1937 included "Blueprint for Negro Writing" by its associate editor, Richard Wright. Others associated with Boston were the anthologist William Stanley Braithwaite and the poet Waring Cuney. Philadelphia contributed three distinguished "New Negroes"—Alain Locke, Jessie Redmon Fauset, and Ethel Waters—and a group in Philadelphia published *Black Opals*. Communities of writers, dramatists, and artists were located in Chicago and Indianapolis, and "little theater" groups existed in New Haven, Connecticut, and Cleveland. Literary figures gathered for food and conversation in Anne Spencer's garden in Lynchburg, Virginia, during the first three decades of the twentieth century. And Rubin (1971) emphasizes the importance of Washington, D.C., "for the production of both significant art and contributing artists." New Negroes associated with Washington, D.C., included Lewis Alexander, Gwendolyn Bennett, Sterling Brown, E. Franklin Frazier, Montgomery Gregory, Alain Locke, Kelly Miller, May Miller, Richard Bruce Nugent, Willis Richardson, Jean Toomer, and Carter G. Woodson. Many of these writers met regularly at the home of Georgia Douglas Johnson, joined there frequently by her friend Angelina Weld Grimké.

Still, whatever the merits of "New Negro renaissance," the term "Harlem Renaissance" has become firmly established for the emergence of arts not just in Harlem but also among African Americans all over the United States in the 1920s and the 1930s. For various reasons, since at least 1971 (when Huggins's *Harlem Renaissance*, the first major study of this period, appeared), the strong presence of Harlem has shaped our evolving awareness of the New Negro movement. Many socioeconomic and cultural factors made Harlem particularly significant among the black communities that developed in northern cities as a result of the great migration. While it is important to acknowledge the other urban centers, the term "Harlem Renaissance" reflects the sociocultural complexity of the New Negro movement and gives Harlem credit for its contributions.

Harlem has indeed become a metaphor for all the factors that shaped the lives of African Americans in the urban North. World War I and the great migration were new elements in African Americans' self-awareness relative to American democratic ideals. During the war, the experiences of black troops, especially those serving abroad, revealed discrepancies between the promise of freedom and the caste status of African Americans and raised expectations that democracy would also be won at home. Just after the war, during the "red summer" of 1919, race riots erupted in twenty-six cities across the nation; it was in reaction to these riots that Claude McKay wrote his poem "If We Must Die," published in *Liberator*. Drawn by the promise of industrial jobs in the North in the years following the gradual cessation of immigration from Europe and Asia, southern blacks had been pouring into northern cities; perhaps 500,000 blacks migrated North between 1910 and 1920, and 800,000 in the 1920s. In addition, there were migrants from the Midwest, the West, and the West Indies. As Rudolph Fisher indicates in his story "The City of Refuge" and Wallace Thurman indicates in his play *Harlem*, despite

897

the poverty and overcrowding in the urban North, the migrants saw it as an escape from the violence and bigotry of the South, and they developed a new self-respect and racial consciousness. Moreover, segregation stimulated the growth of a black middle class whose main function was to provide services (such as barber shops, funeral parlors, beauty shops, and grocery stores) that did not interest white businesses.

Although Harlem symbolized the new spirit of blacks throughout the North, however, it was in some ways distinct from other black neighborhoods of the time. First, it developed from a white, upper-middle-class suburb, and not from the continued decline of a poor white area, as was usually the case. Second, it was large: The community grew from 14,000 blacks in 1914 to 175,000 by 1925 and more than 200,000 by the beginning of the Depression. Third, it was diverse. The interaction of blacks from all parts of the United States, the West Indies, and even Africa contributed to a highly sophisticated and race-conscious community—something unprecedented in American history. Because of its diversity, Harlem became a testing ground for clashing racial and political viewpoints and for artistic innovation and experimentation. In 1925, in an essay written for Locke's anthology *The New Negro*, James Weldon Johnson described Harlem as "a city within a city, the greatest Negro city in the world. . . . It has its own churches, social and civic centers, shops, theaters and other places of amusement. And it contains more Negroes to the square mile than any other spot on earth." And Locke wrote: "In Harlem, Negro life is seizing upon its first chances for group expression and self-determination."

The "Harlem Negro" had a new militancy that was expressed through civil rights organizations such as the National Association for the Advancement of Colored People (NAACP), the National Urban League, and the all-black Brotherhood of Sleeping Car Porters organized by A. Philip Randolph; and in the "back to Africa" movement of the charismatic Marcus Garvey, who came to Harlem from Jamaica in 1916. The essence of Garvey's message was that black was superior to white and that the destiny of the Negro race lay in Africa, not America; his Universal Negro Improvement Association (UNIA) provided a much-needed outlet for racial pride and self-assertion. Still, most of Garvey's followers had no desire to exchange their present lot for an unknown future in Africa; most middle-class African American leaders, including Du Bois, Randolph, James Weldon Johnson, and Walter White, considered Garvey a threat to their own influence with both blacks and whites, and to the cause of civil rights in the United States. Whereas Garvey seemed to make a mystique of blackness, these other leaders thought of racial pride mainly as a useful tool in the fight to obtain greater opportunities for African Americans.

In many ways, the New Negro movement was a response by educated, middle-class blacks to the same changes that drew the masses to Garveyism; the Harlem Renaissance was a logical extension of the New Negroes' racial, cultural, and political thinking into art, music, theater, and literature. For example, freed from the timid conformity of earlier generations, black American painters and sculptors experimented in a variety of styles and attempted a more objective and effective self-portrayal. Among the younger artists who offered striking depictions of black life and black people were Richmond Barthé, Aaron Douglas, Palmer Hayden, Malvin Gray Johnson, Lois Mailou Jones, Archibald J. Motley Jr., James Amos Porter, Augusta Savage, and Hale Woodruff. In literature, the first stage of the renaissance culminated in Locke's anthology *The New Negro*, which was compiled, in his words, "to document the New Negro culturally and socially—to register the transformations of the inner and outer life of the Negro in America that have so significantly taken place in the last few years." By the end of the twentieth century, scholars were finding links between the race-centered "low modernism" of Harlem Renaissance writers such as Langston Hughes, Claude McKay, and Jean Toomer and the despairing "high modernism" of white writers such as T. S. Eliot, James Joyce, W. B. Yeats, Gertrude Stein, and Ezra Pound.

With regard to literature, it is significant that younger writers of the period received support from many mentors, white and black, including V. F. Calverton, Du Bois, James Weldon Johnson, Carl Van Vechten, Walter White, and Jessie Redmon Fauset. In particular, Fauset, as the literary editor of *The Crisis*, modulated and broadened Du Bois's genteel and propagandistic goals for literature. But if anyone matched the enthusiasm and vigor of Alain Locke in promoting the concept of a renaissance in the 1920s, it was sociologist Charles Spurgeon Johnson, who was the first editor of *Opportunity* and who later became the first black president of Fisk University. Under the influence of Robert E. Park, a sociologist associated with the renaissance in Chicago, Johnson saw the African American as a marginal person, who, although torn between two cultures, could stand apart and view each objectively. For Johnson, the transition of blacks from folk culture to industrial culture was an inevitable and painful process. He stressed the need for African Americans to understand and absorb this change from the rural South to the urban North, and he intended *Opportunity* "to stimulate and encourage creative literary effort among Negroes . . . to encourage the reading of literature both by Negro authors and about Negro life . . . to bring these writers into contact with the general world of letters . . . to stimulate and foster a type of writing by Negroes which shakes itself free of deliberate propaganda and protest." In 1927, Johnson edited *Ebony and Topaz*, which in many ways was a companion volume to Locke's *The New Negro* and reflected black writers' increasing maturity and independence in portraying black life.

The long-standing "invisibility" of African American life and culture probably explains some of weaknesses of the Harlem Renaissance, which in turn would explain its failure to make its full impact on the literature and art of the day. One such weakness was primitivism. In this regard, Huggins (1971) argues that "the black-white relationship has been symbiotic. . . . Blacks have been essential to white identity (and whites to blacks)." As a result, blacks have often served the purpose of upholding stereotypes. The "Negro fad" of the 1920s—which Wallace Thurman castigated in *Infants of the Spring* as well as in his essays and book reviews—encompassed European Americans' interest in jazz, in African art, and perhaps in returning to the values of preindustrial society. In the popular version of this fad, however, blacks were simply uninhibited primitives. White American writers such as Gertrude Stein, Eugene O'Neill, Paul Green, Vachel Lindsay, Sherwood Anderson, and e. e. cummings portrayed blacks as instinctively simple and abandoned, in contrast to fretful, mechanized whites. Carl Van Vechten's *Nigger Heaven* (1926) was the most influential novel by a white writer in establishing the image of the Negro as primitive: It appealed to a widespread interest in the Negro, and it sold more than 100,000 copies in several editions—clearly indicating the commercial value of such books. Some black writers, especially Claude McKay, had different and broader uses for primitivism; but many writers of the New Negro renaissance jumped onto Van Vechten's bandwagon. Primitivism as a fad cannot be blamed entirely on Van Vechten or on other whites who wrote about the Negro during the 1920s, but it is likely that the publication of *Nigger Heaven* made many black writers keenly aware of the commercial possibilities of the primitivistic formula, and it made it more difficult for

many of them to develop their artistic potential individually or as a group with significant shared goals.

AMRITJIT SINGH

See also American Mercury; Black Opals; Brotherhood of Sleeping Car Porters; Challenge; Crisis, The; Ebony and Topaz; Garveyism; Great Migration; Great Migration and the Harlem Renaissance; Harlem Renaissance in the United States: 1–9; Hurston, Zora Neale; Infants of the Spring; Locke, Alain; McKay, Claude; Messenger, The; Modern Quarterly; National Association for the Advancement of Colored People; National Urban League; New Negro; Nigger Heaven; Opportunity; Primitivism; Riots: 2—Red Summer of 1919; Riots: 4—Harlem Riot, 1935; Saturday Evening Quill; Survey Graphic; Wright, Richard; *other specific individuals*

Further Reading

Baker, Houston. *Modernism and the Harlem Renaissance.* 1987.

Bontemps, Arna, ed. *The Harlem Renaissance Remembered.* 1972.

Brown, Sterling. "The New Negro in Literature, 1922–1955." In *The New Negro Thirty Years Afterward*, ed. Rayford Logan. 1955.

Franklin, John Hope. *From Slavery to Freedom*, 3rd ed. 1967.

Helbling, Mark. *The Harlem Renaissance: The One and the Many.* 1999.

Huggins, Nathan. *Harlem Renaissance.* 1971.

Hughes, Langston. *The Big Sea.* 1940.

Hull, Gloria. *Color, Sex and Poetry: Three Women Writers of the Harlem Renaissance.* 1987.

Hutchinson, George. *The Harlem Renaissance in Black and White.* 1996.

Lewis, David Levering. *When Harlem Was in Vogue.* 1987.

Perry, Margaret. *The Harlem Renaissance: An Annotated Bibliography and Commentary.* 1982.

Rampersad, Arnold. "Langston Hughes and Approaches to Modernism in the Harlem Renaissance." In *The Harlem Renaissance: Revaluations*, ed. A. Singh, W. Shiver, and S. Brodwin. 1989.

Rubin, Lawrence. "Washington and the Negro Renaissance." *Crisis*, 88, April–May 1971, pp. 79–82.

Singh, Amritjit. *The Novels of the Harlem Renaissance.* 1976.

Singh, Amritjit, and Daniel M. Scott, III, eds. *The Collected Writings of Wallace Thurman: A Harlem Renaissance Reader.* 2003.

Stepto, Robert S. "Sterling A. Brown: Outsider in the Harlem Renaissance?" In *The Harlem Renaissance:*

Revaluations, ed. A. Singh, W. Shiver, and S. Brodwin. 1989.

Thurman, Wallace. *Infants of the Spring*. 1932. (Reprint, 1992.)

Wall, Cheryl A. *Women of the Harlem Renaissance*. 1995.

New Negro, The

The New Negro is widely recognized as the defining volume of the New Negro movement. Edited by Alain Locke and published in late 1925, this anthology of more than 450 pages includes essays defining the New Negro and explaining the movement; a section of creative literature by African Americans containing short stories, poems, a play, and transcriptions of folklore; arguments about the importance of literature, music, and art by African Americans; sociological studies of African Americans' employment opportunities and migration to northern cities; and descriptions of African American communities around the United States. The final pieces are an essay by W. E. B. Du Bois on the global implications of the New Negro movement and an extensive bibliography of additional reading. The book also includes black-and-white graphic designs and drawings by Aaron Douglas and Winold Reiss and a series of portraits by Reiss. It offers, then, a complex, multimedia portrait of the New Negro.

The New Negro began as a special issue of the magazine *Survey Graphic* on "Harlem: Mecca of the New Negro." This issue was also edited by Locke, and its contents became the core of his book, although many of the essays from *Survey Graphic* were expanded or edited significantly for the book. There also are significant differences in the overall emphases of the two works: The scope of *The New Negro* is national and even international rather than local, it devotes far more attention to the creative arts than *Survey Graphic* did, and the portraits of "Harlem Types" from *Survey Graphic* are replaced in the book with portraits of the leaders of the movement.

Some of these changes hint at significant thematic concerns of the Harlem Renaissance. One of Locke's first steps in the opening essay of the book is to define the New Negro in contrast to the "old Negro." Locke sets up this definition of the New Negro as a rejection of African Americans not as they had been in the past but as they had been represented; in other words, he identifies the New Negro as stunningly different from the historical fiction—the myth—of the "old Negro."

In fact, a number of essays in the book emphasize the importance of the past to the assessment of African Americans in the 1920s. At the same time, though, the book looks toward the future, emphasizing that "Negro youth" demonstrate the potential of the race.

The book also is an important assertion of race consciousness. Locke emphasizes in his foreword that a "renewed race-spirit" was growing among African Americans, and the book nurtures this positive sense of collective identity. Baker (1987) argues that the book's graphic designs establish an Africanist context for the entire volume; the connection between African Americans and Africa is also asserted in an illustrated essay on African art and in Du Bois's essay. The book, then, is an articulation of a race consciousness that unites blacks from across the United States and from throughout the African diaspora. Significantly, though, the book also clearly emphasizes African Americans' identity as American and their contributions to American culture. In his foreword, for example, Locke identifies African American culture as an integral part of American culture, an argument that is repeated by a number of the other contributors to the volume.

The book also raises questions about the significance of images of African Americans created by African Americans, rather than by nonblack artists or writers. Locke emphasizes in his foreword the importance of self-portraiture, the need for self-expression rather than portrayal by others, but the book includes contributions from black and white writers and artists. In fact, Douglas was the only African American visual artist to have his work included in the book, and his black-and-white drawings are overshadowed by the full-color portraits by Reiss, a white Bavarian artist known by the mid-1920s for his portraits of German peasants, Native Americans, and Mexicans. This ironic aspect of the original volume is hidden by the fact that Reiss's portraits have been omitted from the Macmillan edition of *The New Negro* and are reproduced in black-and-white in a few earlier reprints.

The subject of these portraits also raises the question of class as a dimension of Locke's definition of the New Negro. The portraits in *Survey Graphic* were grouped in two series, "Harlem Types" and "Four Negro Women." The people depicted were anonymous members of the folk, with the single exception of Elise Johnson McDougald, a teacher, school principal, and writer. In *The New Negro*, however, Locke replaced most of these portraits with portraits of the elite, including intellectual leaders like himself and Du Bois as well as writers like Jean Toomer and Countee

Cullen. The portraits in the book thus use the elite rather than the folk to define the New Negro. The written texts in the book do draw attention to the folk, however, from the characters portrayed in the fiction and poetry to Locke's argument in the essay "The New Negro" that the masses are in fact leading the transformation of the race, even if they are not quite articulate yet. Although some critics of the book have argued that it presents an elitist depiction of the New Negro, then, it does include both the folk and the elite in its definition.

Critics also have drawn attention to certain aspects of African Americans' lives and experiences that are left out of or deemphasized in *The New Negro*. Blues, for example, receives little attention, and the question of sexuality is never addressed. Nor is Marcus Garvey's movement, nor the radical socialism of the period. Furthermore, the New Negro is almost exclusively male, and the importance of African American women in the movement is given only minimal attention. But Locke seems to have strived for inclusiveness, to the extent that *The New Negro* includes texts with strikingly different or even contradictory assessments of the New Negro. Despite its omissions, *The New Negro* is a complicated and diverse portrait of the New Negro, one that is an important and collaborative act of self-definition and self-representation by participants in the Harlem Renaissance.

ANNE CARROLL

See also Cullen, Countee; Du Bois, W. E. B.; Douglas, Aaron; Locke, Alain; New Negro; New Negro Movement; Reiss, Winold; Survey Graphic; Toomer, Jean

Further Reading

Baker, Houston A., Jr. *Modernism and the Harlem Renaissance*. Chicago, Ill.: University of Chicago Press, 1987.

Hutchinson, George. "Producing *The New Negro*." In *The Harlem Renaissance in Black and White*. Cambridge, Mass.: Belknap Press of Harvard University Press, 1995.

Lewis, David Levering. *When Harlem Was in Vogue*. New York: Oxford University Press, 1979.

Long, Richard. "The Genesis of Locke's *The New Negro*." *Black World*, 25(4), 1976.

Rampersad, Arnold. "Introduction." In *The New Negro*, ed. Alain Locke. New York: Atheneum, 1992.

Stewart, Jeffrey C. *To Color America: Portraits by Winold Reiss*. Washington, D.C.: Smithsonian Institution Press for National Portrait Gallery, 1989.

Wintz, Cary D. *Black Culture in the Harlem Renaissance*. Houston, Tex.: Rice University Press, 1988.

New York Age

New York Age was one of the most influential black newspapers of its time. Its first incarnation was as the *Globe* (founded in 1880). The *Globe* became the *Freeman* in 1884 and *New York Age* in 1887. The driving force behind *New York Age* and its previous incarnations was the editor Timothy Thomas Fortune, a journalist and activist.

Fortune used *New York Age* to promote his ideas for the uplift of black Americans. Unlike most other black leaders and newspapermen of the day, who were loyal to the Republican Party, he criticized the Republicans for failing to protect the rights of black citizens in the South and across the United States. Booker T. Washington was a friend, mentor, and financial backer of Fortune and of *New York Age*. Fortune's politically independent spirit often put the two at odds, however.

Fortune employed Ida B. Wells at *New York Age* after her own newspaper offices in Memphis, Tennessee, were destroyed in 1891. Wells wrote articles on lynching for Fortune and gave national exposure to the problem. Fortune also helped Wells secure lecture engagements to further her antilynching message.

In addition to emphasizing the need for blacks to express their political power, Fortune advocated the development of creativity and racial pride. *New York Age* included serialized articles about important people and events in black history.

New York Age was incorporated in 1907 with Booker T. Washington as a principal (but secret) stockholder. The plan was to extend the newspaper's distribution and influence on the national level. The New York Age Publishing Company had Fortune as its president and Jerome Peterson as the secretary-treasurer. Although the newspaper expanded, Fortune found it difficult to share responsibilities for running the enterprise. His own problems with drinking and depression intensified the pressure on him. Eventually his decline prompted him to sell his shares in *New York Age* (in 1907) and step down as editor.

Thereafter Fred R. Moore ran *New York Age*, but his tenure as editor signaled the decline of the newspaper both in appearance and in content. Booker T. Washington controlled the editorial content through

901

his influence on Moore and his funding of the paper: Washington had financed Moore's buyout of Fortune. Under Moore's leadership, *New York Age* became more sensational and less an arbiter of political opinion among African Americans. The paper no longer had a strong editorial view. Although Washington financed the paper, Moore often strayed from Washington's and the Republican Party's political views. Although Fortune returned to *New York Age* as associate editor in charge of the editorial page from September 1911 to September 1914, the newspaper never regained its earlier influence.

James Weldon Johnson, one of the most significant authors during the Harlem Renaissance, wrote for *New York Age* during World War I. Johnson's editorials—which included a byline, unlike editorials in other black newspapers of the time—focused on racism, especially in the South. Johnson advocated self-help and nonviolent protest among African Americans. *New York Age* urged blacks to demonstrate their loyalty to the United States, while still speaking out against the suppression of blacks' civil rights. The paper also supported the silent protest parade in New York City in 1917; this march was a mass statement against the practice of lynching in the United States.

New York Age folded in 1953. After Fortune's tenure, its circulation and influence never reached a level to compete with more popular black newspapers such as the *Chicago Defender, Baltimore Afro-American, Pittsburgh Courier,* and *Norfolk Journal and Guide.*

HEATHER MARTIN

See also Antilynching Crusade; Barnett, Ida B. Wells; Fortune, Timothy Thomas; Johnson, James Weldon; Journalists; Lynching: Silent Protest Parade; Moore, Frederick Randolph; Washington, Booker T.

Further Reading

Drake, Donald E. "Militancy in Fortune's New York Age." *Journal of Negro History*, 55(4), 1970.

Jordan, William G. *Black Newspapers and America's War for Democracy, 1914–1920.* Chapel Hill: University of North Carolina Press, 2001.

Pride, Armistead S., and Clint C. Wilson II. *A History of the Black Press.* Washington, D.C.: Howard University Press, 1997

Seraile, William. "Fortune, Timothy Thomas." In *American National Biography*, ed. John A. Garraty and Mark C. Carnes. New York: Oxford University Press, 1999.

Thornbrough, Emma Lou. "American Negro Newspapers, 1880–1914." *Business History Review*, 40(4), 1966.

———. *T. Thomas Fortune: Militant Journalist.* Chicago, Ill.: University of Chicago Press, 1972.

Niagara Movement

The Niagara movement was an African American political and social movement founded in 1905 by leading intellectuals, such as W. E. B. Du Bois, William Monroe Trotter, and John Hope. Those who joined the Niagara movement were generally second-generation intellectuals who represented the radical wing of the African American civil rights movement. They offered an alternative to Booker T. Washington's plan for African American social, economic, and political advancement, which emphasized thrift, cleanliness, property ownership, industrial education, manual labor, and postponement of political and civil rights. At the time, Du Bois and Trotter were two of the most vociferous critics of Washington and his program of racial accommodation. They felt that Washington, the founder and president of Tuskegee Institute, was using his power over the African American press to control the opinions and attitudes of whites regarding African Americans; in other words, he was masterfully silencing his critics so that most people would believe black Americans unreservedly supported his program of racial uplift through accommodation and patience.

Du Bois opened his public attack on Washington's program in 1903 with *The Souls of Black Folk*, which forcefully deconstructed Washington's program as an unrealistic plan for racial progress. In a brilliantly written essay entitled "Of Mr. Washington and Others," Du Bois criticized Washington's "Atlanta compromise" speech of 1895 and argued the folly of attempting to gain economic rights while abandoning the struggle for social and political rights. Du Bois argued that African Americans had to fight for all of their constitutionally guaranteed rights as the only way of ensuring their economic progress. He believed that the struggle for civil rights must be waged on a number of fronts. Du Bois's assault on Washington's program was also a response to Washington's actions after the so-called Boston riot of 1903, an incident in which William Monroe Trotter and others had heckled Washington as he attempted to deliver a speech at an African Methodist church in Boston. Trotter had established himself as one of Washington's most bitter critics when he opened his newspaper the *Boston Guardian* in 1902 to challenge Washington's leadership. In a series of brutal editorials, Trotter said that Washington's program was a surrender to white racism and an abandonment of the fight for social equality.

The attacks by Du Bois and Trotter symbolized a changing of the guard and can been seen as ushering in the "New Negro" movement, which in turn can be seen as a precursor of the Harlem Renaissance. The "Boston riot" and the publication of *The Souls of Black Folk*—both in 1903—precipitated the movement to formulate a program that would rival Washington's. Trotter and Du Bois met in 1905 to discuss organizing a concerted approach to countering Washington's perceived monopoly over the mainstream press. Du Bois then sent letters to sixty known critics of Washington, inviting them to meet in Niagara Falls, New York. (Actually, the group received accommodations on the Canadian side of the border, since it was difficult for them to find a hotel on the American side.)

The Niagara movement began in June 1905 when Dubois, Trotter, John Hope, and twenty-seven others held a secret meeting in Buffalo, New York (near Niagara Falls), at the home of Mary Talbert, who was a prominent member of the Michigan Street Baptist Church in Buffalo. The group outlined an aggressive platform called the "declaration of principles," which called for freedom of speech and criticism, manhood suffrage, the abolition of all distinctions based on race, the recognition of the basic principles of human brotherhood, educational equality, and respect for the working man. In opposition to Washington's program, the group advocated direct action to protest against racial discrimination and demanded immediate, full, and equal rights. Even though the organizational charter never mentioned Washington, it was obvious that the group disapproved of his leadership and questioned his program. The Niagara plan offered an aggressive radical alternative to Washington's gradualist approach of racial uplift from the bottom up. Niagara also represented an effort by the "talented tenth" to regain control of the African American agenda and redirect the civil rights agenda.

Washington used at least two strategies against the Niagara movement: His spies infiltrated it, and he coordinated a vitriolic attack on it in the black press. The Niagara movement weathered the storm, however, and survived to meet the next year at Harpers Ferry, West Virginia, where Du Bois issued a manifesto demanding full and equal rights for all citizens of the United States. In subsequent years, the movement met in Boston and in Oberlin, Ohio. The leaders of the Niagara movement clearly wanted to recapture the fervor of the abolitionists and make the racial issue an ethical one, and they succeeded in assembling some of the most prominent African Americans of the period.

The Niagara movement spread slowly but strategically. In its heyday, there were more than 150 members representing perhaps thirty-four states. The movement was hampered by internal and external conflicts, however. Du Bois and Trotter, for instance, feuded over notions of equality and the place of women, and they disagreed on the goals and timetables for the organization. Trotter also found himself feuding with other members of the organization, further weakening the movement. The organization was chronically short of funds and never had a designated headquarters. In 1907, Trotter resigned from his leadership position. In 1908, Du Bois and Trotter both failed to attend the national convention. In 1908, also, Trotter formed a new organization called the Negro American Political League, which better fit his radical agenda. Du Bois also had begun to move away from the organization. In 1909, he encouraged the remaining members to join the newly formed National Association for the Advancement of Colored People (NAACP). That year, the NAACP swallowed up the Niagara movement, incorporating some of its ideas.

The Niagara movement was important to African American racial progress because it was one of the first attempts by African American intellectuals to raise the banner of full equality—to move beyond the reactionary stage of the post-Reconstruction era to an organized, aggressive answer to racial oppression. The movement also emphasized the ability of African Americans to apply intellectual solutions to practical problems. One of its tenets was its emphasis on a liberal arts education, and so it also generated renewed interest in the academic training of black leaders.

ABEL A. BARTLEY

See also Du Bois, W. E. B.; National Association for the Advancement of Colored People; New Negro Movement; Talented Tenth; Trotter, William Monroe

Further Reading

Fox, Stephen R. *The Guardian of Boston: William Monroe Trotter*. New York: Atheneum, 1970.

Lewis, David Levering. *W. E. B. Dubois: Biography of a Race, 1868–1919*. New York: Holt, 1993.

Nigger

A number of works have been written with the title *Nigger*. The 1922 novel by Clement Wood (1888–1950), a white writer from Alabama, is a serious work of fiction in which Wood presents an unsentimental view of the South and African Americans. Wood's novel is realistic in tone, tracking a family from slavery to the early 1920s. W. E. B. Du Bois approved of Wood's later writing on Alabama, and Wood was highly regarded during the Harlem Renaissance: He won awards in literary competitions run by Du Bois's journal *The Crisis* and by *Opportunity* and himself served as a judge for such contests, in various categories.

Still, *Nigger* received mixed reviews when it appeared in 1922. Black reviewers had a number of reservations. They admitted that Wood's characters were a decided improvement over the typical works of most white southern authors, such as Thomas Nelson Page, Thomas Dixon, and Octavus Roy Cohen. Wood had humanized his characters and presented dignified portrayals of African Americans. However, Benjamin Brawley, James Weldon Johnson, and other black literati of the Harlem Renaissance held that these characters were just sanitized images of old stereotypes. In spite of Wood's sympathetic views of African Americans, the novel contained too many one-dimensional figures, patronizing views, and perpetuations of old myths. The critic for the *New York Times* gave a generally favorable review but noted that the characters were mainly types, with each one representing a particular kind of Negro. For instance, Jake, who had grown up in slavery, was symbolic of the "old southern Negro." Two of his sons were well educated and were well suited to "office work," but the only jobs they could get were in Birmingham's mills. A third son was an example of the "overdressed vicious Negro" who is destined to wind up on a chain gang. One of Jake's daughters is so light skinned that she attempts to pass as white; another daughter becomes a street prostitute. Other characters also represent similar types of African Americans and even periods of history.

Some readers, on the other hand, loved the book. Most reviewers noted that Wood knew his Alabama—his scenes there generally rang true—and that he was on the correct side of the racial issue, sparing no pity for vicious white racists. The reviewer for the *Boston Transcript* described the book as "the epic of emancipation"; the reviewer for *Dial* said that it was almost great; the reviewer for the *Greensboro* (North Carolina) *Daily News* said that it had brilliance and power. Unlike others, however, this last reviewer was unimpressed by Wood's grasp of Alabama, remarking that Wood had seemed to fill in his background by throwing "India ink" at it.

The *Springfield Republican*, perhaps, had the most perceptive review. After praising Wood for his knowledge of Alabama and his sympathetic approach to racial justice, the reviewer found fault with the book for being "sketchy" and—most tellingly—suggested that, despite the sympathetic content, the title would repel black readers.

In fact, the title was evidently so offensive that this novel is never mentioned in *Twentieth Century Authors* (Kunitz and Haycroft 1942) or in its first supplement (1955)—despite an otherwise positive account of Clement Wood's work as a novelist, poet, music lyricist, educational leader, and lawyer. African American publications of the day do mention Wood's novel, though, generally in a favorable light as a sympathetic portrayal of the difficult fight for emancipation and equal rights.

FRANK SALAMONE

See also Brawley, Benjamin; Cohen, Octavus Roy; Crisis, The: Literary Prizes; Johnson, James Weldon; Opportunity Literary Contests

Further Reading

Bookman, 56, December 1922, p. 497. (Review.)

Boston Transcript, 22 November 1922, p. 8. (Review.)

Dial, 73, December 1922, p. 680. (Review.)

Fikes, Robert. "Adventures in Exoticism: The 'Black Life' Novels of White Writers." *Western Journal of Black Studies*, 26(1), 2002, p. 6. (Web site.)

Kunitz, Stanley, and Howard Haycroft.. *Twentieth Century Authors: Biographical Dictionary of Modern Literature*. New York: Wilson, 1942. (See also 1st supplement, 1955.)

Lowney, John. "Haiti and Black Transnationalism: Remapping the Migrant Geography of Home to Harlem." *African American Review*, 34(3), 2000, p. 413. (Web site.)

Mumford, Kevin J. "Lost Manhood Found: Male Sexual Impotence and Victorian Culture in the United States." *Journal of the History of Sexuality*, 3(1), 1992, pp. 33–57.

New York Times, November 1922. (Review.)

Nyren, Dorothy, ed. *A Library of Literary Criticism: Modern American Literature*, 3rd ed. New York: Ungar, 1960.

Springfield Republican, 4 February 1922, p. 2. (Review.)

Nigger Heaven

Carl Van Vechten's novel *Nigger Heaven* (1926) initially drew attention by its inflammatory title and the flamboyant reputation of its white author. The novel's significance goes far beyond those factors, however. The controversy caused by Van Vechten's book brought unprecedented attention to Harlem's social and artistic culture and helped create a market for African American literature. Whether readers viewed *Nigger Heaven* as art or exploitation, they bought, read, and discussed it widely.

The novel is peopled with a range of characters whose interactions reflect Harlem's energy. Mary Love, a prim, intellectual, race-conscious librarian, tries to shun the advances of Randolph Pettijohn, the "bolito king," who believes that marrying her will make him respectable. Instead, Mary loves and plans to marry Byron Kasson, a frustrated aspiring writer who struggles unsuccessfully to overcome deep ambivalence about his racial identity. Byron—highly educated and with coloring "the shade of coffee diluted with rich cream"—grows increasingly bitter and sensitive to racism, both real and imagined. In his pain, Byron turns to the beautiful, self-indulgent, and fabulously wealthy Lasca Sartoris, a femme fatale of the first order. This love conflict unfolds within a variety of settings: Members of the upper-class elite discuss art in well-appointed drawing rooms; rowdy and lascivious drunks spend long nights in jazz clubs and speakeasies; politically conscientious young intellectuals debate the "race problem." Virtually every character was an identifiable caricature of some noteworthy Harlemite, and many readers took special delight in trying to assign the proper identities.

Numerous conversations in the novel refer explicitly to Carl Van Vechten's own literary contemporaries (Gertrude Stein in particular is lauded here), as well as the popular musical and theatrical performers of the day. *Nigger Heaven* also embraces other fictional worlds of the Harlem Renaissance, borrowing as a character Mimi Daquin, the heroine of Walter White's novel *Flight* (1926). Gareth Johns, a fictional character who appeared in other novels by Van Vechten, also appears

Carl Van Vechten, 1925. (Library of Congress.)

here. A particularly amusing and curious feature of the novel is a series of footnotes claiming to interpret black culture for the white reader; the very first footnote points readers to "a glossary of the unusual Negro words and phrases employed in this novel." The promised explanation proves elusive, however, a joke best illustrated in the twinned entries "*boody*: see hootchie-pap" and "*hootchie-pap*: see boody." The novel generously cites the lyrics and poetry of the Harlem Renaissance, with an opening epigraph from Countee Cullen's poem "Heritage" and numerous borrowings from jazz and blues songs. An unresolved copyright dispute required Van Vechten to replace lyrics that appeared in the first six printings. He collaborated with his friend the poet Langston Hughes, who devised lyrics specifically for *Nigger Heaven* that appeared in the seventh printing and thereafter.

Nigger Heaven achieved an immediate sellout of 16,000 copies; it had nine printings in the first four months it appeared on the market. It was initially banned in Boston, and readers in Harlem had passionate responses to it. James Weldon Johnson admired and promoted the novel, arguing that Van Vechten was "the first well-known American novelist to include in a story a cultured Negro class without making it burlesque or without implying reservations and apologies." W. E. B. Du Bois, however, despised and condemned *Nigger Heaven*, charging that it "is a blow in the face," and "an affront to the hospitality of black folk" (quoted in Lewis 1994). Many of Van Vechten's black friends privately supported his endeavor and saw it as an attempt to educate white readers about black culture. The black actress Edna Thomas wrote to Van Vechten, "Fool the public if you must, darling; but you and I know that you've gotten a lot of propaganda off your chest, don't we?" Alain Locke concurred, writing, "It's art—but at the same time subcutaneous propaganda" (quoted in Pfeiffer 2000). Public support was not always so strong, however.

Even in the 1980s and 1990s, when the novel was out of print, energetic critical reaction to it continued unabated. Many critics persisted in challenging Van Vechten's right to write such a book in the first place, and many contemporary responses to the novel continue to reflect outrage at his presumption in doing so. Arguing that Van Vechten was motivated by "a mixture of commercialism and patronizing sympathy," Lewis (1981) charges that from "the point of view of racial uplift, *Nigger Heaven* was a colossal fraud in which the depiction of the Talented Tenth in high baroque barely muffled the throb of the tom-tom." Although many critics acknowledge Van Vechten's efforts to promote developing black writers, they maintain a response to the novel that is at best skeptical and at worst downright hostile. Cooley (1989), for instance, says that Van Vechten "brought writers of both races together, striving to overcome prejudice and misunderstanding" but simultaneously insists that *Nigger Heaven* "was perfectly packaged for that insatiable white appetite in the 1920s for anything black and primitive." O'Meally (1989) goes further, charging that Van Vechten's writings "make clear that he never gave up the cliché image of blacks as a naturally arty and primitive people whose 'savage' qualities and spontaneity, zest for life, moon-times tardiness, free sex and instinctive good humor were their great gift." The vituperative tone to which Van Vechten's novel continues to drives such critics demonstrates its continued political resonance.

Van Vechten insisted that the title was meant to be ironic, and the novel extends this assertion with its references to the segregated balconies in theaters. Van Vechten's biographer, Kellner (1968), has long argued that the novel must be understood in the context of its author's ongoing involvement in black culture, noting, for instance, that in the process of revising his manuscript, "Passages were cut that might adversely reflect on the Negro in the eyes of white readers; for example 'We're most of us lazy, and indirect, and careless, and if we get anywhere it's usually luck.'" Thus *Nigger Heaven* raises a number of compelling questions about the role of the novel in society. Even as it parodies romantically simplistic depictions of artistic development, it celebrates the Harlem Renaissance through its energetic and amusing portraits.

KATHLEEN PFEIFFER

See also Cullen, Countee; Du Bois, W. E. B.; Hughes, Langston; Johnson, James Weldon; Locke, Alain; Van Vechten, Carl; White, Walter

Further Reading

Bernard, Emily. "What He Did for the Race: Carl Van Vechten and the Harlem Renaissance." *Soundings: An Interdisciplinary Journal*, 80(4), 1997.

Cooley, John. "White Writers and the Harlem Renaissance." In *The Harlem Renaissance: Revaluations*, ed. A. Singh, W. S. Shiver, and S. Brodwin. New York: Garland, 1989.

Kellner, Bruce. *Carl Van Vechten and the Irreverent Decades.* Norman: University of Oklahoma Press, 1968.

———. "Carl Van Vechten's Black Renaissance." In *The Harlem Renaissance: Revaluations*, ed. A. Singh, W. S. Shiver, and S. Brodwin. New York: Garland, 1989.

Lewis, David Levering. *When Harlem Was in Vogue.* New York: Oxford University Press, 1981.

———. *Harlem Renaissance Reader.* New York: Viking, 1994.

O'Meally, Robert G. "Harlem Renaissance Man." *Times Literary Supplement*, 30 September 1989.

Perkins, Margo V. "The Achievement and Failure of *Nigger Heaven:* Carl Van Vechten and the Harlem Renaissance." *CLA Journal*, 42(1), 1998.

Pfeiffer, Kathleen. "Introduction." In *Nigger Heaven*, by Carl Van Vechten. Urbana: University of Illinois Press, 2000.

Worth, Robert. "*Nigger Heaven* and the Harlem Renaissance." *African American Review*, 29(3), 1995.

Niggerati

"Niggerati" is a term said to have been coined by Zora Neale Hurston—from "nigger" and "literati"—during the black artistic revival known as the Harlem Renaissance. With an unprecedented circulation of music, painting, poetry, and prose, the black experience became a highly salable commodity. Hurston was all too aware of the way black writers were unduly influenced and often exploited by the white establishment that made publication possible. Her term suggests the public's persistent view of blacks as uncomplicated stereotypes and the depictions in popular culture of educated blacks as a mere facade for a lurking primitiveness. The increase in publishing opportunities for blacks during the Harlem Renaissance was coupled with significant restrictions on their creativity, and success was often linked to censoring the political and sensationalizing the primitive. The commodification of black writers and black subjects by white patrons and white publishers who were entertained by their cultural production yet continued to deny their humanity was a persistent problem that added a new dimension to the idea of art as propaganda. Hurston's own patron, Charlotte Osgood Mason, limited her creative choices, frequently attributed childlike qualities to her, and controlled her productivity and mobility through strict spending guidelines reinforced by requests for detailed records of Hurston's expenditures.

"Niggerati" simultaneously referred to and mocked members of the black literary intelligentsia like Langston Hughes, Wallace Thurman, Alain Locke, and Hurston herself. Within the black expressive culture, where verbal agility was highly valued, Hurston had a reputation for being controversial and was known for her quick wit and her ability to capitalize on key linguistic moments. She satirized her social and intellectual peers without failing to turn the lens inward as the self-proclaimed "queen of the niggerati." In this time of unprecedented cultural production, multiple different interpretations of black life competed in the literary marketplace, and Hurston was critical of black writers who assimilated to establishment culture or valued "high" or "white" art at the expense of the folk or the "Negro farthest down." Hurston, Hughes, and Thurman chose an aesthetic response to this political conflict in 1926 with the creation of a controversial magazine called *Fire!!* that they paid for, edited, and published. Because of their limited financial resources, they were able to produce only one issue of *Fire!!*—but it stands as a compelling reaction against the institutional appropriation of art and what Hurston characterized as "the intellectual lynching we perpetuate upon ourselves."

The end of World War I was an impetus for dramatic change, and the Harlem Renaissance was a time when the Negro was in vogue. For African Americans, it reflected an unequaled period of optimism, but also a certain naïveté about the role and power of the artist in American culture. The cultural recognition that fueled the artistic renaissance proved unsustainable and short lived. Like many artists of the time, Hurston struggled to support herself and her writing without patronage. "Niggerati" acknowledged and in some ways anticipated the limits of cultural production that was unable to move blacks beyond the status of "nigger." African American literati struggled in a society that continued to systematically repress them, and Hurston's term remains an ironic comment on the dashed hope that literary achievement would translate into social and political racial uplift.

Toni Irving

See also Fire!!; Hughes, Langston; Hurston, Zora Neale; Infants of the Spring; Locke, Alain; Mason, Charlotte Osgood; Thurman, Wallace

Further Reading

Bontemps, Arna, ed. *The Harlem Renaissance Remembered*. New York: Dodd, Mead, 1972.

Hemenway, Robert. *Zora Neale Hurston: A Literary Biography*. Chicago: University of Illinois Press, 1977.

Hurston, Zora Neale. "What White Publishers Won't Print." In *I Love Myself When I Am Laughing . . . and Then Again When I Am Looking Mean and Impressive: A Zora Hurston Reader*, ed. Alice Walker. New York: Feminist, 1979, pp. 169–173.

Johnson, Barbara. "Thresholds of Difference: Structures of Address in Zora Neale Hurston." In *Zora Neale Hurston: Critical Perspectives Past and Present*, ed. Henry Louis Gates Jr. New York: Amistad, 1993, pp. 130–140.

Lewis, David Levering. *When Harlem Was in Vogue*. New York: Oxford University Press, 1979.

Locke, Alain. *The New Negro*. New York: Arno, 1968. (Originally published 1925.)

Thurman, Wallace, ed. *Fire!!* Westport, Conn.: Negro Universities Press, 1970. (Originally published 1926.)

Wall, Cheryl A. "Zora Neale Hurston: Changing Her Own Words." In *Zora Neale Hurston: Critical Perspectives Past and Present*, ed. Henry Louis Gates Jr. New York: Amistad, 1993, pp. 76–97.

Nightclubs

Harlem's nightclubs, also known as cabarets, were public centers of black sociability and entertainment. The rise of urban nightlife, encouraged by a postwar economic boom, made nightclubs a primary recreational destination for New Yorkers in the 1920s. Nightclubs, and the music and performances they fostered, occupy a key place in debates about the value of "high" and "low" cultural forms with regard to the Harlem Renaissance. Because patrons sometimes indulged in, or at least tolerated, illicit drugs and alcohol, gambling, public dancing, sexual pursuit, homosexuality, and prostitution, nightclubs earned an exaggerated reputation for sexual excess, criminality, and exoticism. Many Harlemite intellectuals who advocated "lifting up" the race by translating Negro folk art into western aesthetic forms viewed nightclubs as "low" culture and approached them with ambivalence, embarrassment, or disapprobation. Other black intellectuals and artists, however, eschewed such middle-class pretensions and celebrated the community and music of nightclubs as an important expression of the black masses.

These debates helped shape the philosophy and aesthetics of the Harlem Renaissance. Many authors used nightclubs and cabarets as the setting and inspiration of their works, to much controversy. The reception of Carl Van Vechten's novel *Nigger Heaven* (1926) and Claude McKay's novel *Home to Harlem* (1928) illustrates the dispute over nightclubs and the proper subject matter for renaissance literature. Van Vechten's novel celebrates Harlem's nightclubs while portraying the black middle class as sexually and socially repressed. The white author's sensational, primitivist account helped bring Harlem's nightlife to the attention of white Manhattan; with some significant exceptions, however, the novel was censured by most of Harlem. *Home to Harlem* takes the viewpoint of the working-class and criminal inhabitants, providing a tour through cabarets and vice districts. McKay's novel was denounced by much of the renaissance elite, who accused him of pandering to the basest tastes of a white readership hungry for an authentic account to follow up *Nigger Heaven*. W. E. B. Du Bois wrote of *Home to Harlem* in a review: "After the dirtier parts of its filth I feel distinctly like taking a bath." Others, such as James Weldon Johnson and Wallace Thurman, defended the book. These debates about nightclub culture reflect a deeper conflict over concepts of sexuality, gender, criminality, class, and race.

Description

Nightclubs were a unique social space combining dining, drinking, and performances. The musical acts and other performances took place not on a stage but on the floor among the patrons seated at tables, allowing for an untraditionally informal relationship between performer and spectator. Performers had to compete with sometimes raucous audience members more interested in their own party than the show. Nightclubs also served as a public place for patrons to dance, providing a spectacle for the rest of the club. The proximity of the patrons, the informal style of the performances, and amply flowing alcohol created public intimacy through physical and psychic contact. As a late-night venue, many cabarets would not be crowded until well after midnight. "Cabaret-hopping" was common, with people moving from one club to the next through the course of the night. Most nightclubs had a life span of no more than a few years—often considerably less—as establishments either changed hands, were renamed and reimagined, or went out of business.

History

The history of black nightclubs in New York begins in the 1860s, when a black tavern owner, Ike Hines, opened a basement saloon in Greenwich Village. Anybody who could sing, dance, or play an instrument was invited to perform for a crowd of spectators who gathered night after night to socialize and relax. Imitators proliferated, and over the next several decades, as black neighborhoods were pushed increasingly northward in Manhattan by white expansion and ever-higher real estate costs, these clubs remained centers of black social life and entertainment. From the 1890s through the 1910s, the Tenderloin district of the West Twenties to the West Sixties was known as "black Bohemia," and its nightclubs and cabarets became popular destinations for New Yorkers seeking entertainment, camaraderie, and vice. Many of the nightclubs that later became institutions in Harlem in the 1920s and 1930s originated in the Tenderloin.

Nightclubs achieved wild popularity in the 1910s and 1920s, and white entrepreneurs began a campaign to make them more "respectable" for the middle and upper classes. The adoption of the French word *cabaret* was intended to capitalize on the reputation, if not the substance, of Parisian establishments. The designation "nightclub" developed in the 1910s when some cabarets tried to get around the city's curfew, which did not apply to private social clubs, by drawing up bylaws and collecting dues so members could drink and socialize as late as they liked. More commonly, however, cabarets simply closed their doors when the curfew arrived at two o'clock in the morning and declared the remaining customers members of a "club." Nightclubs that cultivated an interracial clientele were known as "black and tans" and were widely viewed as disreputable by the middle class of both races, although they also had progressive defenders. In an article in *The Messenger* in 1925, Chandler Owen called the black and tans "America's most democratic institution."

When alcohol was banned under Prohibition, most cabarets became "speakeasies," the name given to any illegal establishment that served bootleg liquor. Speakeasies were often temporary business ventures and operated very discreetly, earning a reputation by word of mouth, and sometimes requiring a secret knock, a password, or the company of a recognized patron. Some historians, such as Erenberg (1981), argue that Prohibition-era nightclub culture was a lesser derivative of the earlier "true" cabarets; others see it as simply a different phase of development.

Harlem's Nightclubs

Harlem's nightclubs ranged from large establishments seating several hundred to intimate cellars. Opened in 1925, Small's Paradise at 135th Street and Seventh Avenue was one of the largest. Patrons were seated by reservation only, and it was famous for its big bands, lavish floor shows, and waiters who served drinks while dancing the Charleston. It had a high cover charge and exorbitantly priced drinks, but the owner, Ed Smalls, welcomed blacks along with the white clientele. Wallace Thurman details an evening at Small's Paradise in his novel *The Blacker the Berry* (1929) from the viewpoint of his protagonist, Emma Lou, who is conscious of being one of the only black patrons, and the darkest. Edmond's Cellar (at 132nd Street and Fifth Avenue), the nightclub where the blues singer Ethel Waters rose to fame, was a typical small basement cabaret. It seated between 150 and 200 patrons at small tables wedged around what Waters (1950) described as a "handkerchief-size dance floor" and a three-piece band. Its low ceiling and lack of ventilation forced it to close for the summer. The Sugar Cane Club (135th Street and Fifth Avenue) was an underworld haunt entered through a narrow underground passage. Like most cabarets, the Sugar Cane would pack in twice the number of people who could reasonably fit in the small space.

Other nightclubs included Happy Rhone's (143rd Street and Lenox Avenue); Banks' Club (133rd Street between Lenox and Fifth Avenues); Jerry's Place (on 135th Street), known to have good dancing; the Alhambra (126th Street and Seventh Avenue), a cabaret

within the Alhambra Theater; the Garden of Joy (139th Street and Seventh Avenue), the blues singer Mamie Smith's open-air cabaret, torn down in the mid-1920s to build the Abyssinian Baptist Church; the Capitol Palace (139th Street and Lenox Avenue), a basement club with a small, always crowded dance floor; the Lenox Club (143rd Street and Lenox Avenue), notorious for its risqué revues; Harry Pyle's place (138th Street and Fifth Avenue); Connor's (135th Street between Lenox and Fifth avenues); and the Bamboo Inn (on Seventh Avenue), which attracted Harlem's rich and stylish.

The block of 133rd Street between Lenox and Seventh avenues was so lined with nightclubs that it was called "Jungle Alley." Cabaret goers could eat good southern fare all night while listening to the torch singer Elmira at Tillie's Chicken Shack. Or they could stop in at Harry Hansberry's Clam House, which featured Gladys Bentley wearing a tuxedo and singing her own risqué lyrics to popular songs. The Clam House often drew the "pansy trade"—gays, lesbians, and bisexuals. The Catagonia Club, known informally as Pod's and Jerry's, featured the jazz pianist and composer Willie "the Lion" Smith (who also had a financial stake in the club) in the early 1920s and Billie Holiday in the 1930s. Harlemites could mingle with Broadway and Hollywood stars at this crowded basement speakeasy, and the piano would be buried under mink coats by the end of the night. Many musicians would end up at Mexico's or the Rhythm Club after their own sets at other nightclubs. If patrons at these clubs were lucky, they might witness a "cutting contest" among instrumentalists to see who could outplay the other. These clubs would typically stay open well past dawn.

While lesbians and gay men were welcomed at many cabarets, several clubs developed a predominantly homosexual clientele. Female impersonators were popular at many cabarets, such as Lulu Belle's (Lenox Avenue). The Hot Cha (132nd Street and Seventh Avenue) was another club that welcomed black gay men. Harlem's queer culture was important for black as well as white homosexuals, who created a social network at nightclubs, drag balls, and rent parties.

Segregated Nightclubs

By the end of the 1920s, there were almost a dozen exclusively white, segregated cabarets in Harlem. Fisher (1927) describes returning to Harlem after being away for five years: "The best of Harlem's black cabarets have changed their names and turned white"; he finds his favorite nightclubs overrun by downtown New Yorkers who want to experience the culture of the Negro. The popularization of anthropology and psychoanalytic theories of the unconscious made the "primitive" an important fantasy in the modern European American imagination—someone free of the strictures, responsibilities, and sexual repression of modern "civilized" society. White urban sophisticates, drawing on colonialist constructions of Africa, attached this notion to black urban Americans, turning to Harlem and especially its cabarets to experience temporary unrestraint.

The novelist, patron, and socialite Carl Van Vechten probably did most to alert white Manhattan to the exoticism of Harlem. His articles in *Vanity Fair* on blues and black theater, and especially his novel *Nigger Heaven*, painted a seductive picture; many white New Yorkers ventured to Harlem as a bohemian "transgression" of their class values and mores—a practice known as slumming. While Van Vechten had a sincere interest in promoting the artists of Harlem and contributed materially to the Harlem Renaissance, most white cabaret goers in Harlem were less earnest. Although only a small percentage of Harlemites regularly patronized nightclubs, in the imagination of white Manhattan Harlem existed only as its nightlife. Whites who were slumming in Harlem were not interested in any actual material conditions that conflicted with their notion of dancing, fun-loving Negroes. By the 1920s, white nightclub owners in Harlem had carefully constructed segregated cabarets that played to white racist fantasies of the primitive, sexual Negro. Harlem's largest and most extravagant nightclubs were whites-only establishments where, except for light-skinned patrons who could pass as white, blacks were welcomed only as employees: waiters, busboys, cooks, and, above all, entertainers.

Barron Wilkins's Exclusive Club (134th Street and Seventh Avenue) moved to Harlem from the Tenderloin in the early 1900s. Duke Ellington and the Washingtonians played there in the early 1920s. It billed itself as a colored club but catered exclusively to white and very light-skinned patrons. Rudolph Fisher, who was turned away because he was too dark, wrote that Barron's "wasn't a Negro cabaret; it was a cabaret run by Negroes for whites." Ethel Waters maintained that "the ordinary working colored people weren't wanted there and knew better than to try and get in." Barron Wilkins had political clout and kept up good relations with the police so that his club would not be closed for serving alcohol during Prohibition. He was murdered in 1924 not far from his club by a gangster and gambler known as Yellow Charleston, who was rumored to be supplying Wilkins with bootleg whiskey.

Perhaps the most famous and elegant of all nightclubs was the Cotton Club (142nd Street and Lenox Avenue). Originally opened as Club Deluxe by the black former heavyweight boxing champion Jack Johnson, it was bought in 1923 by a white gangster, Owen Vincent "Owney" Madden, and reopened as the Cotton Club. Madden increased the seating capacity and redecorated the space with an antebellum theme, complete with bales of cotton and a plantation shack. Politicians, financiers, movie stars, and socialites flocked to the Cotton Club; by the mid-1920s, more than 700 people would crowd inside on weekends to dine, dance, mingle, be seen, and catch the renowned performances. The Cotton Club produced two Broadway-style revues a year. These lavish floor shows resembling the productions of Florenz Ziegfeld featured glamorous light-skinned chorus girls befeathered in revealing costumes. Duke Ellington rose to national fame when he began playing there in 1927. He and his Jungle Band (as it was dubbed shortly after debuting at the Cotton Club) supplied the music for the revues and played incidental music when the patrons themselves were dancing. When CBS radio began coast-to-coast broadcasts of Ellington's sets, the Cotton Club became a national phenomenon. Ellington left in 1930, but the Cotton Club continued to thrive throughout the decade, finally closing its doors on 10 June 1940.

George and Connie Immerman's club, Connie's Inn (131st Street and Seventh Avenue), was known for its musical revues such as *Keep Shufflin'* (1928) and *Hot Chocolates* (1929). The Plantation Club (126th Street and Lenox Avenue) opened in 1929 as a competitor to the Cotton Club. The Plantation managed to lure away one of the Cotton Club's premier acts: Cab Calloway and his orchestra. Owney Madden retaliated by having some of his men ransack the Plantation.

Among the many segregated nightclubs, Leroy's (135th Street and Fifth Avenue), run by Barron Wilkins's brother, Leroy Wilkins, was perhaps the only black cabaret that barred white customers.

Performances

Harlem's clubs were an important venue for black singers and musicians, and jazz and blues predominated. Small nightclubs could accommodate a modest band and perhaps a solo vocalist who would circulate around the room throughout the evening. The relationship between performer and spectator was more informal and relaxed in these intimate settings than in a theater or at a concert. Patrons could dance, drink, and socialize during the shows, and the performers themselves would often have a drink at the bar between sets. Bandleaders like Duke Ellington and Cab Calloway played jazz for the white audiences at the Cotton Club, and afterward they might keep playing at black cabarets until the early morning. James P. Johnson, Willie "the Lion" Smith, and Luckey Roberts were celebrated for stride piano, a style of improvisation refined in Harlem clubs that involves usingthe left and right hand in unison or counter rhythms.

In the 1910s and 1920s, nightclubs were a site for the emergent urban blues, typically performed by women vocalists such as Mamie Smith, Bessie Smith, and Ethel Waters. Carby (1992) and Davis (1998) note that nightclubs provided a place for the articulation of working-class black women's experience. Blues lyrics—often about extramarital affairs, domestic disillusionment, bisexuality and lesbianism, and women's social oppression—and the female performers' obvious sexuality and self-determination contributed to a notion that cabarets perpetuated moral deterioration. A number of musicians and performers included descriptions of nightclubs in their autobiographies, and Langston Hughes drew on blues and the cabaret in his poetry. *The Weary Blues* (1926), his first collection, was inspired by the cadence of Harlem's nightlife. Poems such as "Cabaret," "Jazzonia," "The Cat and the Saxophone (2 A.M.)," and "Harlem Night Club" capture the intensity, intoxication, and depth of the nightclub. His second collection, *Fine Clothes to the Jew* (1927), also depicted cabarets, performers, and cabaret goers.

Many larger cabarets featured extensive musical revues—short, fast-paced spectacles, with lively musical performances, energetic dance numbers, and scarcely any plot. On a raucous night, the dancers might "show their laundry"—lift their skirts and reveal their undergarments—to the whoops and hollers of the crowd. Successful cabaret revues frequently moved to the Broadway stage; for example, *Keep Shufflin'* (1928) and *Hot Chocolates* (1929) first appeared at Connie's Inn. Also, patrons could take to the dance floor themselves, and whites and blacks came to nightclubs to show off or watch others practice the popular dances of the time, such as the Charleston, black bottom, and shimmy.

Policing and Regulations

Prohibition—imposed by the Eighteenth Amendment to the Constitution and enforced by the Volstead Act

(1919)—made it a federal offense to produce or sell intoxicating beverages. New Yorkers, like most urbanites nationwide, considered Prohibition provincial, unsophisticated, and irrelevant to their lifestyle. This attitude was exemplified by the fashionable mayor of New York, Jimmy Walker, who appeared constantly at cabarets around town, often with a different showgirl on his arm each night.

Prohibition had the paradoxical effect of multiplying the number of nightclubs. Although cabarets were routinely raided and alcohol was seized, New York City developed a thriving nightlife. The demand for alcohol under Prohibition facilitated the illegal production and distribution of bootleg liquor. Nightclubs often fell into the hands of organized criminals and gangsters, who made huge profits by selling alcohol.

The possibility of police raids led to a newer type of nightclub: smaller, less extravagant, and more easily transportable. One way cabaret operators sought to circumvent Prohibition was by providing "setups": Nightclubs would serve ginger ale or other mixers in iced glasses into which patrons could pour their own gin or whiskey from a flask. Many clubs owners, however, loath to forgo serving profitable bootleg liquor, provided full service but claimed to investigators that they offered only setups. Even more typically, nightclub owners shared some of their profits with police investigators, who then looked the other way. In 1924, New York City voted to suspend local enforcement of Prohibition, leaving the investigation of the city's more than 100,000 speakeasies and nightclubs to just a few federal inspectors. Raids of cabarets continued until the Twenty-first Amendment repealed Prohibition in 1933, however.

In 1926, Mayor Walker tightened the city's regulation by requiring cabarets to be licensed. Until this time, cabarets had fallen through the cracks of city ordinances, being neither restaurants nor theaters, but now the city defined a cabaret as any space that served food or drink in combination with music or dancing. The legislation and regulation of establishments that were functionally illegal under federal law was a tacit acknowledgment of the failure to enforce Prohibition. Chevigny (1991) argues that the city ordinance "must have been largely directed at the black music and dance that was performed at the Harlem clubs, as well as the social mixing of the races."

In 1931, the oversight of cabarets was transferred from the Department of Licenses to the police department, which began to use the ordinance to monitor not just establishments but performers and employees. By 1940 the police department had expanded the requirements for a cabaret license to include "identity cards" for all cabaret performers. These cards, issued only after a fingerprint check, could be denied to anyone whom the police felt was not "of good character," and was refused to any musician with a criminal record. The identity cards were not abolished until 1967.

The city's nightclubs were also under the surveillance of vice commissions and progressive reform groups, some involving religious evangelism, that wanted to combat what they perceived as a moral decline. For instance, the New York Society for the Suppression of Vice opposed the new sexual freedom claimed by women in the 1910s and 1920s; and the Committee of Fourteen (1905–1932) was an antiprostitution organization. Such groups saw New York as a modern-day Sodom and Gomorrah, and nightclubs as places for loose women and interracial mixing where girls in particular could be tempted or exploited. According to Carby, protecting the virtue of girls was ultimately a rationale for policing the sexuality of urban black women. Despite ideological differences, these vice commissions and reform organizations had similar goals and aided in the arrests of thousands of New Yorkers.

Another source of policing was the weekly *New York Age*, under the editorship of Fred R. Moore, who took it on himself to lead an assault against Harlem's cabarets and speakeasies ("hootch joints"). Moore gave front-page coverage to the illegal operations, applied public pressure to the city police and federal Prohibition agents to crack down on law-breaking establishments, and even published the addresses of known speakeasies and cabarets, inviting the police to shut them down. Moore often went to court to testify against nightclubs and try to prevent them from reopening. He and his paper were awarded a special citation of appreciation from the city.

SHANE VOGEL

See also Black and Tan Clubs; Blues; Cotton Club; Fine Clothes to the Jew; Harlem: 3—Entertainment; Home to Harlem; Hot Chocolates; Jazz; Johnson, John Arthur; Jungle Alley; Madden, Owen Vincent "Owney"; New York Age; Nigger Heaven; Nightlife; Primitivism; Small's Paradise; Vanity Fair; Weary Blues, The; *specific writers, musicians, and entertainers*

Further Reading

Anderson, Jervis. *This Was Harlem: A Cultural Portrait 1900–1950*. New York: Farrar, Strauss and Giroux; Toronto: McGraw-Hill Ryerson, 1982.

Bradford, Perry. *Born with the Blues*. New York: Oak, 1965.

Carby, Hazel V. "Policing the Black Woman's Body in an Urban Context." *Critical Inquiry*, 18, 1992.

Chevigny, Paul. *Gigs: Jazz and the Cabaret Laws in New York City*. New York: Routledge, 1991.

Davis, Angela Y. *Blues Legacies and Black Feminism: Gertrude "Ma" Rainey, Bessie Smith, and Billie Holiday*. New York: Vintage, 1998.

Erenberg, Lewis. *Steppin' Out: New York Nightlife and the Transformation of American Culture*. Chicago, Ill.: University of Chicago Press, 1981.

Fisher, Rudolph. "The Caucasian Storms Harlem." *American Mercury*, 1927.

Garber, Eric. "A Spectacle in Color: The Lesbian and Gay Subculture of Jazz Age Harlem." In *Hidden from History: Reclaiming the Gay and Lesbian Past*, ed. Martin Duberman, Martha Vicinus, and George Chauncey Jr. New York: Penguin, 1989.

Haskins, James. *The Cotton Club*. New York: Random House, 1977.

Mumford, Kevin. *Interzones: Black/White Sex Districts in Chicago and New York in the Early Twentieth Century*. New York: Columbia University Press, 1997.

Smith, Willie "the Lion," with George Hoefer. *Music on My Mind: The Memoirs of an American Pianist*. Garden City, N.Y.: Doubleday, 1964.

Waters, Ethel, with Charles Samuels. *His Eye Is on the Sparrow*. New York: Doubleday, 1950.

Nightlife

The Harlem Renaissance offered black and white Americans a unique experience. The expression of black culture during the 1920s and 1930s exposed white Americans to the intellectual and artistic ability of blacks. This transference of culture was evident in several ways, but none so obvious as the physical interaction that occurred in the nightclubs, salons, and parties on any given evening in Harlem. Nightlife there was more than illegal liquor served in smoky bars and crowded dance clubs. It was an opportunity for African Americans to interact in a relatively safe environment, and it also gave whites and blacks a chance to mingle socially. Harlem's nightlife brought blacks and whites together unlike any other venue in the United States.

Life in this black neighborhood was overcrowded, overpriced, and overwhelming. Black migrants from around the country and from every socioeconomic class squeezed into any available living space. Some were educated; some were illiterate. Some were pious; some were not. Black southerners fleeing the "new South" sought better economic, political, and social opportunities; for many, northern cities became a popular destination. Harlem attracted black migrants not only from the South but also from the West, Midwest, and West Indies who were interested in the neighborhood's growing reputation as a mecca for "New Negroes."

Manhattan, the artistic center for white Americans, became the same for blacks. Between 1890 and 1930, the number of African American actors, artists, authors, and musicians in the United States nearly tripled. Many ventured to New York City hoping to join an evolving cultural movement: the Harlem Renaissance. Along with Harlem's development as the center of African American culture, its nightlife became legendary, attracting not only blacks but also whites as participants and onlookers. Some whites wished to absorb black culture, while others were content to be spectators. James Weldon Johnson pointed out in *Black Manhattan* (1930) that most Harlemites did not partake of the nighttime festivities; rather, they were hardworking, law-abiding citizens who were trying to make ends meet and had neither the money nor the inclination to venture into nightclubs. However, some Harlemites and numerous black and white visitors basked in the neon lights of the world-renowned neighborhood.

The area between 125th and 135th streets and Seventh and Lenox avenues in upper Manhattan was the center of Harlem's nightlife, with cabarets, bars, lounges, ballrooms, taverns, grills, rib joints, and theaters for residents and visitors. Initially, white "slummers" came to Harlem for illegal liquor. Although the Eighteenth Amendment prohibited the manufacture, distribution, and sale of alcohol, illegal liquor was available at numerous establishments throughout New York City. Nightclubs were operated by both blacks and whites; some were businessmen, and some were gangsters. The developing organization of white crime families ensured the availability of liquor.

Harlem's Nightlife

Liquor was the primary draw for black and white visitors to Harlem in the early 1920s. The Eighteenth Amendment provided a market for entrepreneurial bootleggers, small-time criminals, and ethnic gangs. In speakeasies, clubs, saloons, and ballrooms, alcohol was available or at least tolerated. A growing interest in African American culture also prompted owners and managers to provide entertainment for their customers.

Nightlife, chronicled in novels such as Carl Van Vechten's *Nigger Heaven* and Claude McKay's *Home to Harlem*, attracted many people who were interested in experiencing the vogue of Harlem. Huggins (1971) and some other historians believe that Harlem served as a spectator sport for many whites; for others, it satisfied vices. Besides liquor there were narcotics, gambling, and sex. Harlem's nighttime establishments included upscale cabarets, dance halls, and theaters as well as seedy bars and cathouses. While the masses danced and drank bootleg booze at clubs, socialites and intellectuals sipped cocktails at salons and private soirees, and truck drivers, domestics, and laborers had less expensive drinks at rent parties. Those interested in games of chance, drugs, and prostitution also met their needs.

Although Harlem was a thriving black neighborhood by day, at night many of its establishments were segregated. At most places, only blacks employed as dancers, musicians, bouncers, and waiters could gain entry. It is estimated that these clubs employed more than 2,000 African Americans in the 1920s. Black customers were often excluded, however, except for famous personalities like Bill "Bojangles" Robinson. The management wanted to appeal to white patrons' perception of black culture without offending them. Dancers, servers, and musicians were often required to wear costumes that accentuated what whites believed to be the "primitiveness" of African Americans.

Many of the nightspots, like Barron Wilkins's Exclusive Club and the Cotton Club, did everything possible to project contemporary racial stereotypes and prevent intermingling. Although managed by African Americans, Barron's did not allow black customers. The white gangster Owen Madden designed the interior of the Cotton Club to suggest a jungle complete with palm trees and vines, and the entertainment had the same theme, with leopard-print costumes and "jungle" dancing and music, all meant to convey eroticism. The Cotton Club's revues had names such as "Hot Chocolate," "The Blackberries," and "Brown Sugar." Advertisements for the shows were racy, depicting partially clothed black men and women in risqué poses.

Like liquor, jazz drew not only thrill seekers but also white music enthusiasts to Harlem. Jazz was crucial to the growing interest in African American culture during the Harlem Renaissance. It was uniquely American and had evolved from the black community. White musicians and aficionados helped to acculturate jazz and make it part of mainstream America. Privately, musicians played together, passing along techniques. Publicly, bandstands remained segregated until Benny Goodman invited Teddy Wilson and Lionel Hampton to join his band in 1934.

One of the most recognized jazz artists and popular attractions in Harlem was Duke Ellington. Ellington played at the Lafayette Theater, Barron Wilkins's Exclusive Club, and Connie's Inn before becoming the headliner at the Cotton Club in 1927. He composed the "Cotton Club Stomp" as its anthem. On Monday evenings, the Cotton Club broadcast Ellington and the Washingtonians nationally, enhancing the popularity of jazz and the legend of Harlem. Ellington was popular among people of all races. And although he found the Cotton Club's atmosphere degrading at times, he liked its upscale clientele. Some of his peers criticized him for playing "whites-only" music. His sound differed from the New Orleans style, and his song titles—such as "Black Beauty" and "Jungle Night in Harlem"— also drew criticism. To his credit, Ellington was aware of the restrictions placed on African Americans after dark in Harlem, and in 1928 he persuaded the management of the Cotton Club to integrate.

The few nightspots that did not discriminate were very popular with black Harlemites. The Apollo, Lincoln, and Lafayette were among their favorites, as was the Alhambra after it integrated in the mid-1920s. Both the Lybia and Edmond's provided opportunities for new talent while serving as Harlem's most fashionable meeting places. At the Oriental, only whites who were accompanied by black patrons were welcomed. These nightspots were not overrun with white slummers, but rather they served as an escape for Harlemites from the Caucasian invasion. They provided first-rate entertainment.

One very popular integrated establishment was the Savoy, an immense ballroom covering an entire city block on Lenox Avenue. Some African American patrons there carried business cards and offered dance lessons to whites. Often the black dancers performed elaborate routines for the entertainment of the white patrons. The Savoy—one of the largest clubs in Harlem—was decorated with marble staircases and thick carpeting; it had a soda fountain and two stages that allowed the

Broadside advertising appearances at the Apollo Theater by Ruth Brown, the Miles Davis Trio, Thelonious Monk, and Johnny Richards and Band, 1936. (Schomburg Center for Research in Black Culture, New York Public Library.)

club to host two bands at once. Some of the biggest names of the period were headliners at the Savoy: Louis Armstrong, Duke Ellington, Ella Fitzgerald, and Fletcher Henderson. Edgar Sampson led the club's house band and composed its anthem, "Stompin' at the Savoy."

Another popular form of entertainment in Harlem was concerts, known as "battles," showcasing more than one band. On Wednesday 12 December 1928, the Savoy held a "battle of jazz." Six of the most popular jazz bands in New York played in front of 2,000 spectators for an admission price of eighty-five cents. It was estimated that another 2,000 people were turned away. The participants included Duke Ellington, Ike Dixon, Lockwood Lewis, Charlie Johnson, Arthur Gibbs, and Lloyd Scott. Actually, the occasion was less a battle than a festival. Such engagements were not really competitions but rather an opportunity to bring together top names to play for the excitement and entertainment of the audience—which showed appreciation by dancing, stomping, and cheering. In later years, other venues, like the Rockland Palace, hosted similar events.

Nightclubs, bars, and cafés were not the only meeting places for Harlemites. Private parties were another source of entertainment. Cocktail parties were popular among socialites and intellectuals, and rent parties tended to draw from the working class, although guests at either type of gathering were not limited by economic or social class. Underground institutions catered to more illicit interests in drugs and sex.

Private soirees for the social set often featured cocktails, poetry readings, and discourse on current events. These gatherings included Harlem's elite but were not exclusive to Harlem; they might be held at the homes of black and white luminaries living in other parts of the city. Young poets, writers, artists, and entertainers were invited to the homes of members of the African American avant-garde such as W. E. B. Du Bois; Jessie Redmon Fauset, the literary editor of *The Crisis*; and the activist Walter White of the National Association for the Advancement of Colored People (NAACP). These parties were covered in the social columns of various black newspapers. They provided opportunities for young, struggling artists to mingle with their peers, elders, and potential white patrons.

In 1927, A'Lelia Walker, the heiress to her mother's cosmetics empire, established a salon for these purposes at her town house on 136th Street. It was called the "Dark Tower" after a poem by Countee Cullen and was for a time fashionable among black literati and white socialites. Walker's town house was also used for poetry readings and art exhibits, and she gave lavish parties there. Walker was a very generous hostess, and invitations to her soirees—overflowing with people, liquor, and food—were greatly sought after.

Rent parties in Harlem, held mostly by the working class, offered Harlemites an alternative to crowded dance halls and bars and an escape from white curiosity seekers. These parties, which originated in the South, were used to raise money for living expenses. The host or hostess provided food, drink, and entertainment in exchange for a small fee. Posters hung around the neighborhood announced the date, time, location, and admittance charge—usually twenty-five cents. The liquor was either bought from bootleggers or homemade. The food was popular soul food: fried fish, chitterlings, and greens. Bessie Smith, the "empress of the blues," paid homage to the parties in her song "Give Me a Beer and Another Pig's Foot." The lindy, a popular dance, is sometimes said to have started at a rent party before being immortalized at the Savoy. Few white visitors attended rent parties except as the guests of blacks; in fact, most whites who went slumming were not even aware of these local neighborhood events.

Some residences also served as fronts for illegal activities. A "buffet flat," or after-hours club, was a private home that also provided access to gambling, narcotics, and prostitution. The hosts and hostesses were pimps, madams, and drug dealers. Most of the guests were not Harlemites but out-of-towners—salesmen, truck drivers, and railroad workers passing through and looking for a good time. The entertainment

might center on erotic acts that were said to satisfy any taste. In their songs, both Count Basie and Fats Waller referred to the "Daisy Chain," also known as "101 Ranch," which was infamous for its "sex circus." The local police were usually bribed not to interfere; privately hired bouncers tried to keep the peace.

Harlem's nightlife did not discriminate by sexual orientation. Garber (1990) believes that the Harlem Renaissance marked an important period in gay history. The migration of African Americans into northern neighborhoods and the subsequent attraction of whites to black urban culture helped to delineate gay communities and create a shared consciousness. Gay Harlemites interacted with the larger community at work and church but also maintained their own institutions.

Private parties and cabarets were open to people of all sexual orientations. A'Lelia Walker always invited her gay friends to her soirees. Popular nightspots included the upscale Hot Cha and the Hansberry Clam House. The headliner at the Hot Cha was a female singer in men's clothing. Drag balls were also very popular throughout Harlem, drawing as many as 6,000 people, some of whom were straights who came to gawk. On at least one occasion, the white socialite Carl Van Vechten served as a judge of a drag contest.

Harlem's Nightlife in Literature and Art

Like nightclubs, many theaters in Manhattan remained segregated, and black playwrights had a difficult time having their work taken seriously. During the 1920s, the theme of African American life and culture appeared in only nineteen plays performed in New York City, and only four of these were by black playwrights. Black stage actors compensated by creating their own venues, "little theaters." The actress Rose McClendon also provided opportunities for African Americans. To assist struggling playwrights, she cofounded the Negro People's Theater in Harlem and appeared at the Harlem Suitcase Theater in Langston Hughes's play *Mulatto*.

Several figures of the Harlem Renaissance dealt with Harlem's nightlife in their creative works. Both Langston Hughes and Claude McKay made numerous references to the neighborhood's evening festivities in their poetry. In "Railroad Avenue," Hughes called attention to the "fish joints and pool rooms." In "Harlem Shadows," McKay wrote of women "wandering street to street."

McKay also dealt with Harlem's culture in his controversial novel *Home to Harlem* (1928). The main character, Jake, returns to Harlem after World War I in search of work, fun, and love, not necessarily in that order. At Uncle Doc's he drinks and shoots pool with his old buddies. Later, Jake stops at Aunt Hattie's basement restaurant for home-cooked food like pork chops and coconut pie. He mentions that Barron's still caters to whites, as does Madame Suarez's buffet flat. Some of the "talented tenth" harshly criticized McKay's portrayal of Harlem's nightlife. They felt that his work exaggerated the uncouth aspects of Harlem and undermined their own attempts to uplift the race.

An earlier novel by Carl Van Vechten—his best seller *Nigger Heaven* (1926)—was similarly criticized. It was both controversial and educational, scandalizing some readers and fascinating others. The protagonist is an aspiring novelist frustrated by the increasing number of whites invading Harlem. His friends bemoan their inability to patronize segregated clubs and theaters. They are incensed by the lack of opportunities for African Americans who are denied jobs by employers more interested in hiring lighter-skinned blacks. Out of sheer frustration, one character decides to pass as white. Van Vechten sought to expose white Americans to Harlem by depicting the various types of people living, working, and partying there. In the novel, he ridiculed white slummers and black loafers while highlighting the frustration of black professionals and working-class people who suffered the consequences of Harlem's popularity.

As with *Home to Harlem*, many of the talented tenth reacted negatively to *Nigger Heaven*. W. E. B. Du Bois and others believed that Van Vechten was making a mockery of Harlem and insulting its residents. Critics cringed at the title itself and Van Vechten's description of the unseemly side of Harlem. Narcotics, gambling, bootleg liquor, and prostitution were all aspects of the neighborhood that many in the talented tenth preferred to ignore. Their hope was to establish African Americans as educated, talented, and sophisticated, and Van Vechten's portrayal did not help their cause.

Like Van Vechten and McKay, Wallace Thurman also immortalized Harlem's nightlife in his novels. In Thurman's *Infants of the Spring* (1932), most of the characters live in a rooming house on 136th Street called "Niggeratti Manor," based on the actual living arrangements of Thurman, Langston Hughes, and other black literati. The residents are modeled on actual people from the generation of the Harlem Renaissance, and the novel parodies their lifestyle. This motley crew consists of would-be artists, musicians, and writers.

Few have any talent, and most are not serious about their art. They spend their days trying to figure out the source and time of their next drink and meal. The rent parties at "Niggeratti Manor" were renowned, and Thurman depicts them in their most basic form—guests are asked to bring groceries. This "donation party" yields canned goods, packages of sugar, and bags of potatoes in return for gin. The guests represent all classes and races: black and white schoolteachers, college boys, lawyers, medical professionals, and socialites. Because many of Harlem's elite also attended rent parties, they too were included in Thurman's satire. Thurman explains that, following an evening of interracial dancing, drinking, and cuddling, guests awoke with a painful racial hangover. In *The Blacker the Berry* (1929), Thurman depicts one party where characters based on himself, Langston Hughes, Zora Neale Hurston, and other black literati discuss race relations with a white friend—to the mortification of the novel's black protagonist, who is astounded by the wild, drunken behavior of the partygoers in front of their white guest.

Harlem's nightlife was also shown in visual art: for example, by Archibald Motley, who painted everyday life in the neighborhood. His *Black Belt* (1934) and *Saturday Night* (1935) depict couples enjoying an evening on the town. In *Black Belt*, couples dressed in evening wear move along the street, a policeman directs traffic, and a man buys a newspaper from a boy as a driver waits in a taxi. In *Saturday Night*, patrons of a nightclub enjoy the music, dance, and smoke cigarettes. Motley's *The Liar* (1936) is set in a pool hall where men gather to hear each other's exploits. Motley was interested in the reality of black life in the city, including its nighttime forays.

Whether in life, fiction, or art, Harlem was an extraordinary place. It was the "Negro mecca" because of its attraction for people from different regions, classes, occupations, and races. It provided Harlemites with economic, social, and cultural opportunities. For visitors, it was entertaining and hip. It came to epitomize the jazz age with its cabarets, speakeasies, and clubs. In Harlem, there was something for everyone.

AMY CARREIRO

See also Cotton Club; Harlem: 3—Entertainment; Home to Harlem; Homosexuality; House-Rent Parties; Infants of the Spring; Jazz; McClendon, Rose; Motley, Archibald J. Jr.; Nigger Heaven; Nightclubs; Organized Crime; Savoy Ballroom; Talented Tenth; Walker, A'Lelia; *specific writers, musicians, and entertainers*

Further Reading

Bascom, Lionel C., ed. *A Renaissance in Harlem: Lost Voices of an American Community*. New York: Oxford University Press, 1995.

Charters, Samuel, and Leonard Kundstadt. *Jazz: A History of the New York Scene*. New York: Doubleday, 1962.

Garber, Eric. "A Spectacle in Color: The Lesbian and Gay Sub-Culture of Jazz Age Harlem." In *Hidden From History: Reclaiming the Gay and Lesbian Past*, ed. Martin B. Duberman et al. New York: Penguin, 1990.

Haskins, Jim. *The Cotton Club*. New York: Hippocrene, 1994.

Huggins, Nathan I. *Harlem Renaissance*. New York: Oxford University Press, 1971.

Hughes, Langston. *The Big Sea: An Autobiography*. New York: Knopf, 1940.

Johnson, James Weldon. *Black Manhattan*. New York: Knopf, 1930.

Lewis, David Levering. *When Harlem Was in Vogue*. New York: Knopf, 1981.

McKay, Claude. *Harlem: Negro Metropolis*. New York: Dutton, 1940.

Ward, Geoffrey C. *Jazz: A History of America's Music*. New York: Knopf, 2000.

Wintz, Cary D. *Black Culture and the Harlem Renaissance*. Houston, Tex.: Rice University Press, 1988.

Not without Laughter

Langston Hughes's novel *Not without Laughter* (1930) uses a deceptively simple coming-of-age narrative to dramatize the intellectual concerns of the Harlem Renaissance, while it also celebrates the vitality of ordinary African American life.

Set in Kansas between 1912 and 1919, the novel traces the maturation of James "Sandy" Williams from adolescence into young adulthood amid changes in black American political and cultural life. Sandy—the only child of Anjee, a domestic worker, and Jimboy, an itinerant laborer and blues singer—grows up in a matriarchal, multigenerational household, raised predominantly by his mother, his young aunt Harriett, and his grandmother Hager, while his father pursues work in other cities. The book is episodic in structure, presenting Sandy's development through a series of events that include his movement from an all-black to an integrated classroom, his sudden understanding of Jim Crow's insidious effects after not being allowed

into a carnival, and his initiation into working life when he takes his first job. As these episodes progress, Sandy becomes aware of the vicissitudes and inequities of American racial politics and the various approaches African Americans take to redress them. Throughout, Hughes dramatizes the tension between "New Negro" assertiveness and "traditional" black American strategies of accommodation, most clearly through conflict between the free-spirited and self-possessed Harriett, who resists convention to pursue a career as a blues singer, and the novel's redoubtable matriarch, Hager, who has unwavering faith in God and a commitment to Christian morality.

As Hughes himself acknowledged, Sandy is an autobiographical character. But the supporting cast and the milieu differ from Hughes's own family life and immediate experience. As Hughes recalled in *The Big Sea* (1940), he wished to create characters removed from his own storied genealogy (which included the abolitionist Charles Langston and the black congressman John Mercer Langston) and instead base his fictional family on more "typical" families he had known as a boy in the Midwest. The novel's cultural fabric, though, with its detailed representations of African American folk expression and community, was influenced by Hughes's travels through the South in the summer of 1927. Hughes had been invited to read his poems at Fisk University in June, and he decided to tour the southern states afterward. Encouraged by Zora Neale Hurston, he used this trip to explore the wealth of southern black folk material. Hurston, who was collecting material for the folklorist Franz Boas, accompanied Hughes for part of the journey as he educated himself in folk blues, backwoods church services, and the practice of "conjure." Rampersad (1986) notes that Hughes expressed amazement at the joy evinced by the presumably subjugated black southerners he encountered. Through his exposure to the "living culture" of southern blacks, Hughes was convinced of its potential for social cohesion and political reparation, both of which were to figure significantly in *Not without Laughter*.

Indeed, in its reverential attention to African American communal expressivity—men signifying in a barber shop; teenagers moving to a ragtime band at a community dance; neighbors improvising blues between their yards on a summer night—*Not without Laughter* anticipates later black American novels that celebrate community, such as Hurston's *Their Eyes Were Watching God* (1937) and Albert Murray's *Train*

Whistle Guitar (1974). Hughes's attention to blues in *Not without Laughter*, specifically through Jimboy (who improvises folk verses on his guitar) and Harriett (who becomes a successful blues singer rather like Bessie Smith), complements his use of the blues form in his early poetry collections *The Weary Blues* (1926) and *Fine Clothes to the Jew* (1927). For the characters in *Not without Laughter*, blues can be an outlet for social commentary. This is the expressive mode that Jimboy and Harriett use; for Harriett, who becomes a successful blues singer, there are material rewards as well.

Although the novel criticizes the injustices that result from Jim Crow and presents strategies for black resistance, it also examines class hierarchies within the African American community. Another African American novelist, George S. Schuyler, reviewing *Not without Laughter* for the Pittsburgh *Courier*, said: "More than a novel, it is a social document, an epic on the sable lowly that white American and bourgeois black American look down upon" (quoted in Dace 1997). Hughes dramatizes intraracial class tension through the character of Tempy, with whom Sandy lives for a time near the novel's conclusion. Tempy, Hager's eldest daughter, is a superior woman who has married into middle-class privilege and treats her family with veiled disdain. Tempy actively supports racial advancement through education and cultural refinement, but she is an ambiguous figure because of her contempt for the "too Negro" folk forms—blues, spirituals, ragtime—that Hughes champions. Tempy's scorn suggests Hughes's critique of the black bourgeoisie, which he considered myopic with regard to folk expression. Graham (1993) remarks that *Not without Laughter* reveals Hughes's twofold commitment to class awareness and aesthetic concerns. In dramatizing reactions to black folk culture, he is able both to support that culture and to condemn the ideology that cannot appreciate it.

Not without Laughter is also significant for having led to the formalization of Hughes's three-year relationship with his patron, Charlotte Osgood Mason. Determined to see Hughes complete a novel, Mason offered to pay him $150 a month so that he could work on a project of that length. The offer promised security for Hughes, who had been supporting himself somewhat haphazardly at Lincoln University through royalties from his poetry collections *The Weary Blues* and *Fine Clothes to the Jew*. However, although the arrangement did relieve Hughes of some financial anxieties, it also seems to have impeded his creative vision at times. Shields (1994) has argued that Mason influenced Hughes's revisions considerably as *Not without Laughter* made its

way from manuscript to published text. Reconstructing the novelist's intentions from the manuscript and from unpublished letters, Shields suggests that Mason's benevolence entailed undue censorship, aimed at suppressing Hughes's "increasingly strong left-wing political notions in the novel." Even if the published version does not approach the socialist document that the writer seems to have planned, however, *Not without Laughter* does stand as one of the most politically intriguing novels of the Harlem Renaissance.

Michael Borshuk

See also Boas, Franz; Fine Clothes to the Jew; Hughes, Langston; Hurston, Zora Neale; Mason, Charlotte Osgood; Pittsburgh Courier; Schuyler, George S.; Weary Blues, The

Further Reading

Bell, Bernard. *The Afro-American Novel and Its Tradition.* Amherst: University of Massachusetts Press, 1987.

Dace, Tish, ed. *Langston Hughes: The Contemporary Reviews.* Cambridge, UK: Cambridge University Press, 1997.

Graham, Maryemma. "The Practice of a Social Art." In *Langston Hughes: Critical Perspectives Past and Present.* New York: Amistad, 1993, pp. 213–235.

Hughes, Langston. *The Big Sea*, intro. Arnold Rampersad. New York: Hill and Wang, 1993. (First published 1940.)

Rampersad, Arnold. *The Life of Langston Hughes*, Vol. 1, *1902–1941: I, Too, Sing America.* New York: Oxford University Press, 1986.

Shields, John P. "'Never Cross the Divide': Reconstructing Langston Hughes's Not without Laughter." *African American Review*, 28(4), 1994, pp. 601–613.

Wall, Cheryl A. "Whose Sweet Angel Child? Blues Women, Langston Hughes, and Writing during the Harlem Renaissance." In *Langston Hughes: The Man, His Art, and His Continuing Influence.* New York: Garland, 1995, pp. 37–50.

Nugent, Richard Bruce

Richard Bruce Nugent is a valuable source of information about the Harlem Renaissance and also played a significant role in the movement as a writer and artist. Nugent first arrived in New York in the early 1920s, when he and his younger brother joined their widowed mother. At that point, the Harlem Renaissance was already under way, but Nugent—who was working as a delivery boy and bellhop and entering an art apprenticeship—did not yet discover it. He did, though, explore avant-garde circles in Greenwich Village, both sexually and artistically.

In New York in 1924, at age nineteen, Nugent decided to become an artist. This decision prompted his mother to send him home to Washington, where he immediately entered other artistic circles that were indirectly connected to the Harlem Renaissance. Nugent started attending the literary salons of the African American poet Georgia Douglas Johnson; at these salons he made contact with Washington's intellectual elite. It was in Washington that Nugent first met Alain Locke, a leading figure in the Harlem Renaissance who taught at Howard University, and also one of the young stars of the renaissance, Langston Hughes. His friendship with Hughes paved Nugent's way to the core of the movement; his initiation, in 1925, was at the Krigwa Awards ceremony, where he became acquainted with other the central figures of the renaissance, including W. E. B. Du Bois and Carl Van Vechten.

Whereas most other young artists involved in the movement aimed at a career, Nugent chose a bohemian existence. He was one of the few artists of the Harlem Renaissance who established close contact with the white avant-garde, crossing Harlem's boundaries and regularly visiting Greenwich Village. He also stood out as perhaps the only figure of the renaissance who openly displayed his homosexuality. Nugent was familiar with sexologists' works on homosexuality and seems to have embraced what could be described as a positively defined queer identity. In retrospect, he accepted the term "gay" to describe his sexual orientation. Nugent was also well known for his striking dress and mannerisms—Van Vechten once described Nugent arriving at a party "with his usual open chest and uncovered ankles. I suppose soon he will be going without trousers" (1987, 96). Nugent was almost always without any financial means, and at the height of the Harlem Renaissance he lived with another enfant terrible of the movement, Wallace Thurman, whose home at 267 West 136th Street was known for wild parties and a general state of drunken chaos. Nugent's own creative process fit in with this environment. He recalled writing on paper bags and toilet paper. Characteristically, Hughes once had to retrieve Nugent's poem "Shadow" (later published in *Opportunity* in 1925) from a wastebasket where it had been discarded because it looked like trash. Nugent proceeded the same way with his art, even though he apparently favored drawing over writing: He lost or destroyed many of his artworks or simply gave them away.

Nevertheless, Nugent managed to get his work into the major publications of the Harlem Renaissance: His short story "Sahdji" was featured in Locke's anthology *The New Negro* (1925); his poems and drawings were published in *Opportunity* and also in *Ebony and Topaz* (1927); and he famously contributed the piece "Smoke, Lilies, and Jade," the first openly homoerotic story published by an African American, to the controversial magazine *Fire!!* (1926). His work was outstanding in style and content. Whereas other writers of the renaissance frequently focused on matters of race, Nugent concentrated on beauty and aesthetics, playing with color contrasts. He often adopted a decadent style, and he also challenged his readers with formal devices such as the elliptical stream of consciousness in "Smoke, Lilies, and Jade." Nugent's drawings testify to an aesthetic heritage harking back to Aubrey Beardsley and Erté, yet with African motifs blended in. With regard to theme and content, the works he created during the renaissance include a wide variety of topics that range from the African themes in "Sahdji" to his collection of Bible stories in the late 1920s. His large body of work also includes the novel "Geisha Man" (which has a Japanese theme) and his autobiographical account of the Harlem Renaissance years, "Gentleman Jigger," appended to Wallace Thurman's *Infants of the Spring* (1932). Homosexuality is a frequent theme in Nugent's work and was a significant factor in his overall comparatively poor publishing record; it was also the reason why Nugent almost never gave his full name in his publications. His mother accepted his sexual orientation but stipulated that he was not to publicly "disgrace" the family name.

More than any other artist of the Harlem Renaissance, Nugent was active in almost all cultural areas—writing, drawing, and even acting during the period of the renaissance and afterward. He was, for instance, in the cast of the successful play *Porgy*, which had a Broadway run and traveled to England in early 1929. Much later, Nugent experienced his own renaissance: In the early 1970s he was discovered as a resource on the Harlem Renaissance, and in the early 1980s he was used as a source of information on gay history. In 1981, Thomas H. Wirth, a collector of African American literature, met and befriended Nugent—a significant event, as they not only arranged and compiled various interviews but also established a Nugent collection. (The Richard Bruce Nugent Papers are in the private collection of Wirth in Elizabeth, New Jersey.)

Biography

Richard Bruce Nugent (Richard Bruce) was born in 1906 in Washington, D.C. He attended Dunbar High School. In the early 1920s he came to New York, where he worked as a delivery boy for Youmans Hats and as a bellhop at the Martha Washington Hotel; was an apprentice at the catalog house of Stone, Van Dresser; and took art classes at the New York Evening School of Industrial Arts and at Traphagen School of Fashion. He was an actor in *Porgy*, 1927–1930; worked for the WPA Writers' Project, late 1930s; was involved in the Negro Ballet Company, late 1940s; married Grace Marr, December 1952; and was a cofounder of the Harlem Cultural Council, late 1960s. Nugent's wife died in 1969. Nugent died of congestive heart failure, 27 May 1987.

A. B. Christs Schwartz

See also Ebony and Topaz; Fire!!; Harlem Renaissance in the United States: 9—Washington, D.C.; Homosexuality; Hughes, Langston; Infants of the Spring; Johnson, Georgia Douglas; Locke, Alain; New Negro, The; Opportunity; Porgy: Play; Thurman, Wallace; Van Vechten, Carl

Selected Works

"Sahdji." In *The New Negro*, ed. Alain Locke. 1925.

"Shadow." *Opportunity*, October 1925.

"Smoke, Lilies, and Jade." *Fire!!*, 1, 1926.

Cover illustration. *Opportunity*, March 1926. (Male head.)

In *Caroling Dusk: An Anthology of Verse by Negro Poets*, ed. Countee Cullen. New York: Harper, 1927.

"Narcissus." *Trend*, 1, 1933.

"Beyond Where the Star Stood Still." *Crisis*, December 1970.

"Lighting Fire!!" Metuchen, N.J.: Fire!!, 1981. (Insert, originally published 1926.)

Gay Rebel of the Harlem Renaissance: Selections from the Work of Richard Bruce Nugent, ed. and intro. Thomas H. Wirth. Durham, N.C.: Duke University Press, 2002.

Further Reading

Garber, Eric. "Richard Bruce Nugent." *Afro-American Writers from the Harlem Renaissance to 1940*. Detroit, Mich.: Gale, 1987.

Hatch, James V., "An Interview with Bruce Nugent—Actor, Artist, Writer, Dancer." *Artists and Influences*, 1, 1982.

Helbling, Mark, and Bruce Kellner. "Nugent, Richard Bruce." In *The Harlem Renaissance: A Historical Dictionary for the Era*. New York: Methuen; London: Routledge, 1987.

Johnson, Charles S., ed. *Ebony and Topaz: A Collecteana*. New York: Opportunity, 1927.

Schwarz, A. B. Christa. *Gay Voices of the Harlem Renaissance*. Bloomington: Indiana University Press, 2003.

Silberman, Seth Clark. "Lighting the Harlem Renaissance A-Fire!! Embodying Richard Bruce Nugent's Bohemian Politic." In *The Greatest Taboo: Homosexuality in Black Communities*, ed. Delroy Constantine-Simms. Los Angeles, Calif.: Alyson, 2001.

———. "Looking for Richard Bruce Nugent and Wallace Henry Thurman: Reclaiming Black Male Same-Sexualities in the New Negro Movement." *In Process*, 1, 1996.

Smith, Charles Michael. "Bruce Nugent: Bohemian of the Harlem Renaissance." In *In the Life: A Black Gay Anthology*, ed. Joseph Beam. Boston, Mass.: Alyson, 1986.

Thurman, Wallace. *Infants of the Spring*. New York: Macaulay, 1932.

Van Vechten, Carl. *Letters of Carl Van Vechten*, ed. Bruce Kellner. New Haven, Conn.: Yale University Press, 1987.

Wirth, Thomas H. "Fire!! in Retrospect." Metuchen, N.J.: Fire!!, 1981. (Insert to *Fire!!*, 1926.)

———. "Richard Bruce Nugent." *Black American Literature Forum*, 19, 1985.

Numbers Racket

The numbers racket is a system of "policy" gambling in which people wager on a three-digit number, with the winning number each day corresponding to a particular stock report—such as the volume of shares traded on the New York Stock Exchange—printed in a newspaper. "Policy," which refers to all games in which numbers are used to determine the winners, was a socially accepted form of gambling that united many sectors of African American and Latino communities in urban areas, particularly at the height of its popularity during the 1920s and 1930s. Numbers specifically generated a livelihood for both players and operators in areas that did not have access to legitimate commercial institutions such as banks, credit associations, and loans and realty enterprises that typically excluded minorities. Although the average player never struck it rich in the numbers, many black policy bankers became rich enough to contribute to philanthropic enterprises that helped better the community at large, thereby sustaining the goal of self-determination that was popular during the "New Negro" movement.

Numbers (in Spanish, *la bolita*) as we know it today originated among Afro-Caribbean immigrants and took hold in Harlem, Chicago, Detroit, Philadelphia, and other urban locales with a high concentration of African Americans. Players could place bets at any number of local establishments, including pool halls, barber shops, beauty parlors, convenience stores, newsstands, and dry cleaning stores. Neighborhood "runners" (bet collectors) would gather the bets and then turn over the number slips and money to a controller, who kept the accounts tabulated and who generally oversaw a dozen or so runners. Finally, the controller reported to a banker who paid off the winners.

This form of gambling served a number of economic and cultural purposes, especially in African American communities. Players often had long-term plans for any winnings they earned; thus, for them, policy was a form of savings and investment, albeit a somewhat illusory one. Most people bet daily with small amounts of money (as little as a penny) that they would not or could not deposit in traditional bank accounts because of institutionalized racism and lack of access to banks. Although a significant portion of a family's income typically went into betting—usually with little or no return on the investment—numbers gambling was often the only viable economic institution for urbanites who were black, poor, or both.

In minority communities, no social stigma was attached to playing numbers; moreover, numbers was not seen as a vice of poor or immoral individuals, but was tacitly and publicly sanctioned throughout the community. Numbers and other forms of policy were managed by individuals, many of them not career criminals but middle-class professionals who owned other, legitimate businesses. Numbers was such a communal pastime that it infiltrated peoples' dreams (literally and figuratively), had an impact on small businesses, and even overlapped with other popular activities such as sports. In order to determine lucky numbers, some players referred to dream books that listed a three-digit number for every symbol found in a dream. These books could be purchased in small shops in black neighborhoods or in *botanicas* in Spanish-speaking neighborhoods. A day's event that was significant to minorities (e.g., a baseball star's batting average), however, could determine the most popular number played.

Although policy was (and remains) illegal, it was played openly throughout the 1920s, especially in Harlem, and few operators feared arrest or violent repercussions. Initially, white gangsters dismissed the numbers racket as a penny game for the poor and referred to it as a "nigger pool." Consequently, operators and bankers—who were mainly black and Latino—developed the institution freely and with no scrutiny by whites. Casper Holstein, a West Indian, is often credited with originating numbers policy in Harlem and was considered the foremost "policy king" of his day. In fact, Carl Van Vechten based a fictional character in his popular novel *Nigger Heaven* (1926) on Holstein: Randolph Pettijohn, the "bolita king." From his earnings, Holstein provided funds to build Harlem's first Elks Lodge. He also financially supported the literary contests in the Urban League's *Opportunity* magazine and donated thousands of dollars to charity. In Pittsburgh, Pennsylvania, Sonnyman Johnson, a numbers man, helped fund the Homestead Grays, an all-black baseball team, and Gus Greenlee purchased Greenlee Field, the first black-owned field, with the money he made from the numbers. Other successful bankers include Madame Stephanie St. Clair, a West Indian migrant known as the "policy queen" of Harlem; Jose Enrique Miro, a Puerto Rican; and Joseph Mathias Ison, another West Indian.

At the end of Prohibition, many whites who were former bootleggers directed their attention to the numbers racket and successfully pushed out the mostly black operators, frequently using violence. Dutch Schultz, a prominent Jewish gangster of Harlem, is perhaps the most prominent example. During the 1920s, the racket in Harlem was divided into smaller syndicates and lacked big bankers who could handle a large "hit" (win). Schultz capitalized on this fracturing and forcefully attempted to control the numbers market. His tactics temporarily sent Madame St. Clair into hiding, but most bankers succumbed to Schultz, who eventually consolidated the fragmented syndicates and made the industry even more profitable. Most black policy controllers lacked the political clout and police contacts necessary to protect their interests in the racket, and by 1935 the highest echelon of African American bankers had been driven out. Blacks in Chicago, who were better organized politically, maintained their hold until the early 1950s.

State-sanctioned lottery games have since replaced numbers gambling; however, numbers runners figure prominently in African American literature and film, such as Julian Mayfield's *The Hit* (1957), Robert Deane

Pharr's *The Book of Numbers* (1969), Louise Meriwether's *Daddy Was a Numbers Runner* (1971), and in the collected works of Chester Himes and the playwright August Wilson. Generally speaking, these texts illuminate the communal nature of the racket, but they also indict the racist economic forces that allowed such gambling to persist. These literary representations testify to the ongoing cultural resonance of the numbers racket.

LA TONYA MILES

See also Holstein, Casper; Nigger Heaven; Opportunity Literary Contests; Organized Crime; Van Vechten, Carl

Further Reading

Ianni, Francis A. *Black Mafia*. New York: Pocket Books–Simon and Schuster, 1975.

Light, Ivan. "Numbers Gambling among Blacks." *American Sociological Review*, December 1977.

McKay, Claude. *Harlem: Negro Metropolis*. New York: Dutton, 1940.

Mayfield, Julian. *The Hit and the Long Night*. Boston, Mass.: Northeastern University Press, 1989. (Originally published 1957, 1958.)

Meriwether, Louise. *Daddy Was a Numbers Runner*. New York: Feminist Press at City University of New York, 1986. (Originally published 1970.)

Pharr, Robert Deane. *The Book of Numbers*. Charlottesville: University of Virginia Press, 2001. (Originally published 1969.)

Redding, J. Saunders. "Playing the Numbers." *North American Review* (6), December 1934.

Schatzberg, Rufus, and Robert J. Kelly. *African American Organized Crime*. New Brunswick, N.J.: Rutgers University Press, 1997.

Van Vechten, Carl. *Nigger Heaven*. New York: Knopf, 1926.

Oliver, Joseph "King"

Joseph "King" Oliver was a pioneer of the New Orleans jazz style. After leaving New Orleans for Chicago around 1918, he was the generating force and initiator of the important King Oliver Creole Jazz Band, to which Louis Armstrong was a major contributor.

According to Allen and Rust (1987), Oliver's musical life can be divided into several periods. The first period, 1908–1918, was in New Orleans. The most important group Oliver played with during this time was the Kid Ory Band, and it was Ory who nicknamed Oliver "King." The second period, 1918–1921, was in Chicago. The third period, called the California period, was in 1921–1922. This was a brief venture with Ory, but Oliver did have the good fortune to play with the Jelly Roll Morton Band in California. (Incidentally, in 1921, Kid Ory's band made the first recording by African American jazz artists.) The fourth period, again in Chicago, was 1922–1924. Fifth was a touring period from 1924 to about 1927. Oliver's sixth period, 1927–1931, was in New York. His seventh and final period, 1931–1938, is called the touring years; this was a troublesome time with only a few bright spots.

Oliver's heyday extended from the time of Buddy Bolden, a cornetist turned trumpeter who was legendary in New Orleans, through the time of Freddie Keppard and finally the master, Louis Armstrong. Oliver stood out as the best cornetist-trumpeter of his day and was Armstrong's idol. When Freddie Keppard left Oliver's band in 1922, Oliver immediately sent a telegram to Armstrong, offering him a job. At that time Oliver was in Chicago, and Armstrong later said that he would not have left New Orleans for anyone else but Oliver. Armstrong considered Oliver his mentor, had great respect for him, and called him "Papa Joe."

This strategic move by Oliver may be considered to have begun the flowering of the Creole Jazz Band. The ensemble became the focal point of jazz in Chicago, as a number of excellent recordings attest; it was the envy of the jazz world. Perhaps especially because of its two masterful cornetists, the group attracted many members of the jazz community of Chicago, among them Bix Beiderbecke and Paul Whiteman, who would come to hear the Creole Jazz Band night after night, following their own gigs, and try to figure out exactly what made it unique. They were particularly impressed by the improvised cornet breaks and by the idea of double improvisation between Oliver and Armstrong, who improvised without interrupting the flow of the music or disrupting the rest of the ensemble; many listeners thought that there must have been some kind of secret agreement between the two cornetists and the group. At this time, in addition to Oliver and Armstrong on cornets, the Creole Jazz Band included Johnny Dodds on clarinet and his brother Baby Dodds on drums; Honore Dutrey on trombone; and Lil Hardin, piano (and in 1923, Bill Johnson on bass). All the musicians in the ensemble knew exactly what they were expected to do; they were also able to anticipate what would happen throughout a piece, so that they could keep the perfect balance for which they were noted. Baby Dodds later said of Oliver's band: "That outfit had more harmony and feeling of brotherly love than any I ever worked with. . . . We worked to make music, and we played music to make people like it" (Gara 1992). The ensemble had a marvelous spirit of freedom and spontaneity but also maintained responsible, balanced control of the musical texture. It was also one of the first named groups to record the New Orleans jazz style, in a series of milestone recordings in 1923. The most memorable side was probably "Dippermouth Blues" (with King Oliver and Louis Armstrong on cornets, Johnny Dodds on clarinet, Honore Dutrey on trombone, Lil Hardin on piano, Bud Scott on banjo and vocal break, and Baby Dodds on drums). These recordings are considered an important part of the jazz tradition and legacy.

In 1924, Oliver wanted to tour with his band, but the Dodds brothers and Dutrey did not want to tour, and only Armstrong and Hardin decided to go. This split was evidently due to certain financial improprieties on Oliver's part. Baby Dodds notes that he instigated the breakup, mainly because he and the others felt that Oliver was handling income and payments unfairly and that there was no proper accountability—in other words, that they were not getting their fair share of the profits. Immediately after the breakup, Oliver restructured the group and named it the Dixie Syncopators. This new ensemble (sometimes also called the Dixielanders) toured first in the Midwest and later throughout the United States. Also around 1924, Armstrong left Oliver to join Fletcher Henderson's band. (And in February 1924, Armstrong and Hardin were married.) At this time, a movement was under way from collective improvisation (music making) to the premier art of solo playing, and Armstrong was emerging as the leading solo artist.

For Oliver's group, touring proved to be laborious and stressful. Moreover, touring led to continual changes of personnel, and as a result the ensemble became less distinctive and therefore less influential. Although Oliver still had high standards and still chose talented players, bookings became fewer and fewer. The band did have an engagement at the famous Savoy Ballroom in New York in 1927, however. During this period, Oliver was asked to lead a band at the new Cotton Club, but he refused the position, which then went to Duke Ellington. (Turning this job down was poor judgment on Oliver's part, since the Cotton Club, of course, went on to become famous.)

In 1928, although his health had been failing for some time and his day as a musical powerhouse was past, Oliver was able to get an excellent recording contract with Victor Records. But he was still hampered by mismanagement, by poor musical decisions, by his own reluctance to extend his musical growth into the jazz revival movement, and by his worsening health, which made it difficult for him to blow into his instrument and caused him great distress. At one point Louis Armstrong—on tour in Savannah, Georgia—encountered Oliver by chance on the street; seeing the condition of his former mentor, Armstrong bought Oliver clothes and gave him money. Oliver was then a janitor in a pool hall, just barely existing. He died in Savannah, penniless and obscure, in 1938. Oliver's sister, Victoria Davis, who had been like a mother to him when he was a youngster, used her rent money to bring his body to New York for burial. She also gave up her own plot in Woodlawn Cemetery for him.

Biography

Joseph "King" Oliver was born in New Orleans, Louisiana, in 1885. During his period in New Orleans he played with Kid Ory. Oliver worked in Chicago in 1918–1921, in California in 1921–1922, and again in Chicago in 1922–1924; during this time, the King Oliver Creole Jazz Band became the envy of the jazz world and was the first named jazz group to make historic recordings (1923–1924). Oliver toured from 1924 to about 1927, then worked in the New York area in 1927–1931 but lost a chance to play at the new Cotton Club. His final touring period was 1931–1938. Oliver, who is considered the first major solo cornetist, died in Savannah, Georgia, 10 April 1938.

MALCOLM BREDA

See also Armstrong, Louis; Jazz; Morton, Jelly Roll; Music; Musicians; Ory, Edward "Kid"; Savoy Ballroom

Further Readings

Allen, Walter C., and Brian A. L. Rust. *King Oliver.* Chigwell, UK: Storyville, 1987. (Rev. Laurie Wright.)
Gara, Larry. *The Baby Dodds Story*, rev. ed. Baton Rouge: Louisiana State University Press, 1992. ("As told by.")
Morgenstern, Dan. *Jazz People.* New York: Abrams, 1976.
Ramsey, Frederic, Jr., and Charles Edward Smith, eds. *Jazzmen.* New York: Harvest–Harcourt Brace Jovanovich, 1967.
Williams, Martin J. *Jazz Heritage.* New York: Oxford University Press, 1985.
———. *Jazz in Its Time.* New York: Oxford University Press, 1989.

———. *Jazz Masters of New Orleans*. New York: Da Capo, 1978.

———. *King Oliver*. Kings of Jazz Series. New York: Barnes-Perpetua, 1961.

On Trial

On Trial (1914), by the white playwright Elmer Rice (Elmer Leopold Reizenstein), is a courtroom melodrama incorporating flashbacks. This was Rice's first successful production; it opened at the Candler Theater in New York on 14 August 1914; was an immediate hit with audiences and critics; was hailed as the first American play to use the flashback technique; ran for 365 performances at the Candler; and, along with subsequent productions, proved a financial windfall for Rice.

On Trial opens in a courtroom as the final juror in the murder trial of Robert Strickland is being chosen. Strickland has been accused of killing a prosperous businessman, his associate Gerald Trask, and attempting to steal $10,000 from the victim. Through flashbacks during the testimony, the jurors, others in the courtroom, and the audience attending the play learn the real circumstances behind Trask's murder. Strickland planned to move with his wife, May, and daughter, Doris, to Cleveland, in an effort to begin anew after failed business deals in New York. He settled a debt of $10,000 with Trask but later discovered that Trask, a married philanderer, had taken advantage of May when she was a girl. Strickland shoots and kills Trask after interrupting an attempt by Stanley Glover (Trask's secretary) to steal the $10,000 from the safe in the library at Trask's home. All this information emerges from testimony by Glover, Joan Trask (Gerald Trask's wife), Doris, and May, which is enacted onstage in flashback scenes.

Although the flashback was common in movies of the time, *On Trial* was the first recorded American stage production to use it. Rice had first read about the flashback technique in an article in the magazine *Bookman* by Clayton Hamilton, who was a drama critic and a lecturer on theater at Columbia University. Intrigued by the concept of moving a play backward in time, Rice decided that a trial would be the perfect setting for achieving flashbacks in a believable manner. He developed the story involving the specific characters in *On Trial* after concentrating on ways to do this. A "jackknife" stage—two platforms that pivoted like knife blades—allowed the quick shifts from the courtroom to the flashbacks. Arthur Hopkins, the producer of *On Trial*, had remembered the jackknife stage from plays he had seen in Europe and worked with Rice to use it in *On Trial*.

Rice was a radical and a socialist. However, *On Trial*, as a melodrama, exemplifies the popular fare that he would continue to write and produce in order to make money. The Lafayette Players, an African American theater group in Harlem, staged a production of *On Trial*, one of a number of successful plays by white authors that the group produced from 1916 to 1923.

Elmer Rice's best-known and most critically acclaimed plays were an expressionistic work, *The Adding Machine* (1923), and a naturalist work, *Street Scene* (1929). Rice won a Pulitzer Prize for *Street Scene*, which he adapted in the 1940s into a musical with lyrics by Langston Hughes and a score by Kurt Weill.

HEATHER MARTIN

See also Hughes, Langston; Lafayette Players

Further Readings

Behringer, Fred. "Elmer Rice." In *Dictionary of Literary Biography*, Vol. 7, *Twentieth-Century American Dramatists*, ed. John MacNicholas. Detroit, Mich.: Gale Research, 1981.

Durham, Frank. *Elmer Rice*. New York: Twayne, 1970.

Hogan, Robert. *The Independence of Elmer Rice*. Carbondale: Southern Illinois University Press, 1965.

Palmieri, Anthony F. R. *Elmer Rice: A Playwright's Vision of America*. Rutherford, N.J.: Fairleigh Dickinson University Press, 1980.

Rice, Elmer. *Minority Report: An Autobiography*. New York: Simon and Schuster, 1963.

Vanden Heuvel, Michael. *Elmer Rice: A Research and Production Sourcebook*. Westport, Conn.: Greenwood, 1996.

135th Street Library

During the Harlem Renaissance, the 135th Street Branch of the New York Public Library, at 103 West 135th Street, was a site of intense artistic, educational, and cultural activity and a gathering place for artists, historians, intellectuals, and writers. The library also purchased Arthur Schomburg's collection of materials on black culture in 1926 and greatly augmented it over the years.

The 135th Street Library—a three-story neoclassical limestone building—was designed by the architect Charles F. McKim of McKim, Mead, and White; opened on 14 January 1905; and was designated a landmark in 1981. It was one of the early branches in the New York Public Library system, and it was a typical example—with the adult circulation area on the first floor, a children's room on the second floor, and an adult reading room on the third floor.

By the 1920s, the demographics in Harlem had changed dramatically, so that 50 percent of the population consisted of people of African descent from the United States, the Caribbean, and Africa. Accordingly, Ernestine Rose, a white librarian from Bridgehampton, Long Island, was appointed head librarian at the 135th Street Library and was asked to adapt it to the new needs of the community. Rose recognized the importance of developing a collection of black literature and history, and of sponsoring art exhibitions and literary discussions. She also believed in having an integrated staff, and she hired the first black librarian in the New York Public Library system, Christine Allen Latimer, and the first Puerto Rican library assistant, Pura Belpré White (who was also black), to serve the Spanish-speaking population.

The 135th Street Library also had a group of other librarians and volunteers, including Regina M. Anderson, Roberta Bosely, Gwendolyn Bennett, Jessie Redmon Fauset, and Ethel Ray Nance, who helped organize readings of poetry and drama and discussions of books. Countee Cullen regularly gave readings of his poetry at this library; Nella Larsen was employed there; and a work area was set aside where Langston Hughes, Claude McKay, Eric Walrond, and others could do research and writing. Weekly lectures on black history at the library were organized by Hubert Harrison, who also encouraged the public to borrow books on relevant topics.

The children's floor was considered very advanced, with the best resources and with librarians and assistants whose activities included dramatic storytelling and the organization of reading clubs to introduce children to black literature. Areas of this floor were reserved for art and literature programs, in which the artists Romare Bearden and Jacob Lawrence and the writers Langston Hughes and James Baldwin were involved.

The 135th Street Library held its first large exhibition of works by black artists from 1 August to 30 September 1921. This exhibition, organized by Augustus Granville Dill, included some 200 paintings and sculptures and was the start of a series of annual exhibitions. (W. E. B. Du Bois, James Weldon Johnson, and Arthur Schomburg were on the planning committees.) Over the years, artists such as Laura Wheeler Waring, Louise Latimer, William Ernest Braxton, and Albert Smith participated in these exhibits; and Hale Woodruff and Aaron Douglas had solo shows. Exhibitions of African sculpture were organized by Alain Locke, and Schomburg assisted with exhibits of books, prints, and manuscripts.

In 1924, a citizens' committee—whose elected officers were Schomburg, Johnson, Harrison, and John Nail—decided to remove the rarest materials from circulation and create a special "Negro" reference library. To add to this collection, donations and loans of books, journals, and prints were solicited from the private libraries of individuals such as John Bruce, Louise Latimer, Harrison, George Young, Charles D. Martin, and Schomburg. From this initial effort, a Division of Negro Literature, History, and Prints was developed; it opened on 8 May 1925. In 1926, a $10,000 grant from Andrew Carnegie allowed the New York Public Library to augment the existing material by purchasing Schomburg's personal collection, which consisted of more than 10,000 volumes, manuscripts, pamphlets, etchings, and other items by and about black people, in many languages. The enlarged collection opened with considerable fanfare on 14 January 1927; it was said to be the largest collection of its kind made available to the public, and it received notices in *Amsterdam News*, *Opportunity*, and the *New York Times*.

By now the 135th Street Library had become the cultural center of Harlem. Moreover, it was in close proximity to major institutions such as Harlem General Hospital, the YMCA and YWCA, a large elementary school, and two of the largest churches in Harlem. Schomburg continued to add to its collection, worked as an unpaid consultant and buyer, participated in staff meetings, taught young scholars, and in general lent his expertise. He also served as an adviser to performing groups that met in the library, such as the Krigwa Players and the Negro Little Theater—precursors of the American Negro Theater, which would be founded in the library's basement in 1940.

During the Great Depression, the 135th Street Library faced declining budgets and the deterioration of the building, and it had to curtail its services; it continued its role as a literary and cultural center, however. In 1932, funding from the Carnegie Corporation, Andrew Carnegie, and the American Association for Adult

Education allowed the formation of a program called the Harlem Experiment in Community Adult Education and permitted the library to hire Schomburg as curator of the collection of the Division of Negro Literature, History, and Prints, a position he held until his death in 1938. The Harlem Workshop, with assistance from the 135th Street Library through the Harlem Adult Education Committee, was formed in 1933 to teach art to the public under the directorship of James Lesesne Wells, a graphic artist and art teacher from Howard University. In 1934, the library, with sponsorship from the Public Works Administration, commissioned Aaron Douglas to create four works for its walls; these murals are called *Aspects of Negro Life*. The library also encouraged additional exhibitions and public presentations.

After Schomburg's death, Lawrence Dunbar Reddick took over his curatorship. A memorial service for Schomburg was held at the library on 8 June 1939; the following year, Reddick recommended that the Division of Negro History, Literature, and Prints be renamed the Schomburg Collection of Negro History and Literature. Although continually plagued by insufficient budgets, inadequate staffing, and poor physical facilities, the Schomburg Collection continued to grow in the 1940s through donations and purchases. Finally, it outgrew its space in the library; in 1980, a large new building on Lenox Avenue between 135th and 136th streets was constructed and named the Schomburg Center for Research in Black Culture. This structure would eventually be connected to the original landmark building. The Schomburg Center is now one of the research libraries of the New York Public Library, devoted to "collecting, preserving, and providing access to resources documenting the experiences of peoples of African descent throughout the world, with emphasis on blacks in the Western Hemisphere."

CLAUDIA HILL

See also Anderson, Regina M.; Bearden, Romare; Bennett, Gwendolyn; Cullen, Countee; Douglas, Aaron; Fauset, Jessie Redmon; Harrison, Hubert; Hughes, Langston; Krigwa Players; Larsen, Nella; Lawrence, Jacob; McKay, Claude; Nance, Ethel Ray; Schomburg, Arthur A.; Walrond, Eric; Waring, Laura Wheeler; Woodruff, Hale; *other specific individuals*

Further Readings

Carley, Rachel. *Schomburg Collection for Research in Black Culture (originally the West 135th Street Branch Library,* *New York Public Library), 103 West 135th Street, Borough of Manhattan: Built 1904–10–05, Architect Charles F. McKim, of McKim, Mead, and White*. New York: Landmarks Preservation Commission, 1981. (Report.)

Dain, Phyllis. *The New York Public Library: A History of Its Founding and Early Years*. New York: New York Public Library, Astor, Lenox, and Tilden Foundations, 1972.

New York Public Library. *Schomburg Center for Research in Black Culture*. New York: New York Public Library, Research Libraries, c. 2002. (Web site.)

Reminiscences of Pura Belpré White. 1976. (In the Oral History Collection of Columbia University.)

Schomburg Center for Research in Black Culture. *The Legacy of Arthur A. Schomburg: A Celebration of the Past, a Vision for the Future—An Exhibition at the Schomburg Center for Research in Black Culture, 23 October 1986–28 March 1987*. New York: New York Public Library, Astor, Lenox, and Tilden Foundations, 1986.

Sinnette, Elinor Des Verney. *Arthur Alfonso Schomburg, Black Bibliophile and Collector*. Detroit, Mich.: New York Public Library and Wayne State University Press, 1989.

Tibbets, Celeste. *Ernestine Rose and the Origins of the Schomburg Center*. Schomburg Center Occasional Paper Series, 2. New York: Schomburg Center for Research in Black Culture, New York Public Library, 1989.

O'Neill, Eugene

Eugene O'Neill, considered one of America's great modern playwrights, played an important though controversial role in the development of African American theater by introducing black actors and new black themes to American theater during the Harlem Renaissance. O'Neill, by casting black actors in serious roles, was the first white author to break through the racial barrier in New York's theaters. Before O'Neill, black actors had appeared on Broadway mainly if not only as stock minstrel figures; the occasional serious roles for black characters were performed by white actors in blackface. Although O'Neill used an all-black cast as early as 1918, in *The Dreamy Kid*, it was *The Emperor Jones* (1920) and *All God's Chillun Got Wings* (1923) that catapulted O'Neill and his leading black actors—Charles Gilpin and Paul Robeson—into national attention.

The Emperor Jones tells the tale of Brutus Jones, a black American Pullman porter with a criminal past, who rises to power on a West Indian island by exercising the predatory will to overpower white capitalists and by playing on the islanders' superstition. The islanders rebel, however, and when Jones hides in the jungle he encounters spectral visions not only of his own past, but of the slave auction block, the middle passage, and Africa. Over the course of the evening, Jones sheds all signs of civilization and becomes what one reviewer called a "hysterical and crouching savage" before he is killed by the islanders.

White reviewers responded almost entirely favorably, in no small part because of Gilpin's extraordinary performance. The reaction from black reviewers was mixed; many were angry at Gilpin for his willingness to participate in what they considered the play's racist theme—that all blacks are essentially primitive, despite a veneer of "white" culture. The reviewer for the militant Garveyite publication *Negro World* wrote: "To be sure it is pronounced a great play by the critics, but they are white, and will pronounce anything good that has white supremacy as its theme. . . . We imagine that if Mr. Gilpin is an intelligent and loyal Negro his heart must ache and rebel within him as he is forced to belie his race" (17 May 1921, quoted in Krasner 1995). Langston Hughes recalled in his autobiography, *The Big Sea* (1940), that when the play was staged in Harlem, the black audience "naturally . . . howled with laughter. . . . They shouted at Jones to 'come on out o' that jungle—back to Harlem where you belong'" (quoted in Cooley 1989, 16). Many prominent black intellectuals approved of the play, though, mainly because, in its attempt to deal with the "black psyche," it seemed to promise new horizons for black themes and actors. The drama critic Montgomery Gregory expressed a sentiment shared by many: "*The Emperor Jones*, written by O'Neill, interpreted by Gilpin, and produced by the Provincetown players, will tower as a beacon-light of inspiration" (quoted in Krasner).

All God's Chillun Got Wings violated a taboo: It describes an interracial marriage that is devastated by the implacable forces of racism. Jim Harris—a hardworking and studious black man who repeatedly fails the bar exam—marries Ella, a poor white woman from the slums whom he has known since childhood. Ella is emotionally unstable, and in her weaker moments her deep-seated racism surfaces in vicious attacks, emotional and physical, against her husband. The play ends with the couple sharing a hallucinatory regression to childhood, a time when they seemed innocent of racism's destructive power. The play caused a considerable scandal even before it opened. In one scene, the white actress playing Ella—Mary Blair—was supposed to kiss the hand of Paul Robeson, the actor who played her husband. When this was reported, there were numerous threats of violence from the Ku Klux Klan and others against O'Neill, his family, and the actors. The Society for the Suppression of Vice and the mayor of New York City attempted to have the play closed; they were unsuccessful, but the city did manage, by invoking child labor laws, to ban the child actors from performing in the first scene.

Some black leaders objected to what they considered racism in *All God's Chillun Got Wings* (for example, at one point Jim expresses his desire to be Ella's "black slave") and also thought it would have an ill effect on race relations. Adam Clayton Powell Sr., for example, said that the play seemed to corroborate the white supremacists' fantasy that access to education and money would encourage black men to marry white women (Black 1999, 301). However, W. E. B. Du Bois considered this work a model for black playwrights who, in his opinion, refused to depict African Americans realistically for fear of contributing to antiblack propaganda:

Happy is the artist that breaks through any of these shells, for his is the king[dom] of eternal beauty. He will come through scarred, and perhaps a little embittered—certainly astonished at the almost universal misinterpretation of his motives and aims. Eugene O'Neill is bursting through. He has my sympathy, for his soul must be lame with the blows rained upon him. But it is work that must be done. (quoted in Musser 1998, 86–87)

Alain Locke concurred with Du Bois, declaring that "the fine collaboration of white American artists. . . has helped in the bringing of the materials of Negro life out of the shambles of conventional polemics, cheap romance and journalism into the domain of pure and unbiased art" (1925, 14).

O'Neill's plays were frequently produced by many of the best black dramatic groups, and magazines such as *The Crisis* asked O'Neill to be a judge for their literary contests (Hutchinson 1995, 160). In a letter to A. Philip Randolph that was published in *The Messenger*, O'Neill encouraged black writers to "Be yourselves! Don't reach out for *our* stuff which *we* call good! Make *your stuff* and *your good*! You have within your race an opportunity—and a shining goal!—for new forms, new significance. . . . There ought to be a Negro play written by a Negro that no

Eugene O'Neill, photographed c. 1920–1940. (Library of Congress.)

University (1914–1915). He was married first to Kathleen Jenkins (later Pitt-Smith), 1909–1912; they had one son, Eugene O'Neill Jr. His second marriage was to Agnes Boulton (later Kaufman), 1918–1929; their children were Shane Rudraighe O'Neill and Oona O'Neill Chaplin. His third marriage was to Carlotta Monterey, 1929–1953. O'Neill wrote or drafted more than sixty plays, many of which were staged by the Provincetown Players. His awards included the Nobel prize for literature in 1936, and four Pulitzer prizes (one posthumously) for *Beyond the Horizon* (1920), *Anna Christie* (1922), *Strange Interlude* (1928), and *Long Day's Journey into Night* (1957). O'Neill died in Boston on 27 November 1953, of a degenerative brain disease.

JOHN CHARLES

See also Du Bois, W. E. B.; Emperor Jones, The; Gilpin, Charles; Hughes, Langston; Locke, Alain; Messenger, The; Negro World; Powell, Adam Clayton Sr.; Provincetown Players; Randolph, A. Philip; Robeson, Paul

Selected Works

Beyond the Horizon. 1918.
The Moon of the Caribbees. 1918.
The Dreamy Kid. 1918.
Anna Christie. 1920.
The Emperor Jones. 1920.
The Hairy Ape. 1922.
All God's Chillun Got Wings. 1923.
Desire under the Elms. 1924.
The Great God Brown. 1925.
Strange Interlude. 1927.
Mourning Becomes Electra. 1931.
The Iceman Cometh. 1939.
A Moon for the Misbegotten. 1943.
Long Day's Journey into Night. 1941.

Further Readings

Black, Stephen A. *Eugene O'Neill: Beyond Mourning and Tragedy.* New Haven, Conn.: Yale University Press, 1999, p. 301.
Cooley, John. "White Writers and the Harlem Renaissance." In *The Harlem Renaissance: Revaluations*, ed. Amritjit Singh, William S. Shiver, and Stanley Brodwin. New York: Garland, 1989.

white could ever have conceived or executed" (quoted in Hutchinson, 17).

Although O'Neill was a pioneer, his work, like many other modernist treatments of black people, was handicapped by prevailing racial stereotypes. Cooley maintains that O'Neill "approached his black portraits with insensitivity and maladroitness, perpetuating pejorative images of black life" (15)—an assertion that may be supported by the fact that *The Emperor Jones* and *All God's Chillun Got Wings* are seldom performed today.

Biography

Eugene Gladstone O'Neill was born 16 October 1888 in New York City, the youngest son of Ella (Quinlan) O'Neill and James O'Neill Sr., an actor. He was educated at a Roman Catholic boarding school, the Academy of Mount Saint Vincent, in Riverdale, New York; De La Salle Academy, New York City; Betts Academy, Stamford, Connecticut; Princeton University (1906–1907); and Harvard

Hutchinson, George. *The Harlem Renaissance in Black and White*. Cambridge, Mass.: Belknap Press of Harvard University Press, 1995, pp. 17, 158–166, 189–197.

Krasner, David. "Whose Role Is It Anyway? Charles Gilpin and the Harlem Renaissance." *African American Review*, 29(3), 1995, pp. 483–496.

Locke, Alain. "Youth Speaks." *Survey Graphic*, 53(11), 1 March 1925. (Reprinted in *The Critical Temper of Alain Locke*, ed. Jeffrey C. Stewart. New York: Garland, 1983, p. 14.)

Musser, Charles. "Troubled Relations: Paul Robeson, Eugene O'Neill, and Oscar Micheaux." In *Paul Robeson, Artist and Citizen*, ed. Jeffrey C. Stewart. New Brunswick, N.J.: Rutgers University Press, 1998, pp. 81–102.

O'Neill, Eugene. "Comments on the Negro Actor." *Messenger*, 7, 1925, p. 17.

Opportunity

Opportunity: A Journal of Negro Life is generally recognized as one of the most important periodicals of the Harlem Renaissance. Like *The Crisis* and *The Messenger*, it served as a source for news and information about African Americans and as an outlet for the work of African American writers and artists. But there are significant differences among the three journals in terms of their attention to literature and art. Charles Spurgeon Johnson, the editor of *Opportunity* from 1923 to 1928, placed more emphasis on African American culture than did the editors of the other two journals. Scholars generally distinguish *Opportunity* from *The Crisis* and *The Messenger* because of its focus on African American culture.

There also are differences in tone and content among the three journals. Hutchinson (1995) points out that the tenor of each of the journals reflects the ideology of its parent organization and editors. *The Crisis*, published by the National Association for the Advancement of Colored People (NAACP) and edited by W. E. B. Du Bois, focused primarily on political issues, emphasized protest and propaganda, and tended to be polemical. A. Philip Randolph and Chandler Owen launched *The Messenger* as a socialist journal; its primary concerns were labor and economic issues, although it also included literature and art after 1922, and it often included biting editorials from iconoclasts like George Schuyler. *Opportunity*, on the other hand, was published by the National Urban League (NUL), an organization that was founded with the goal of improving race relations, and the journal mirrored the NUL's emphasis on diplomacy and gradualism in its approach to tension between black and white Americans.

The attention to the arts in *Opportunity*, however, went well beyond the original intentions of the NUL. The organization was founded in 1911 with the mission of improving race relations, encouraging interracial cooperation, and promoting understanding between black and white Americans. Members believed that the best way to achieve these goals was through studies of employment, housing opportunities, and social services available to African Americans in northern cities; such studies, they felt, could be used by social institutions to improve social and economic conditions for African Americans. In December 1921, the NUL began publishing the results of these studies in the *Urban League Bulletin*, but in 1922, the board of directors decided to expand the bulletin into a larger format, with more popular appeal. *Opportunity* was the result.

Johnson had worked with the Urban League since 1917, and his background as a sociologist made him a logical choice for editor. Johnson had attended graduate school at the University of Chicago under Robert Park, who was a noted sociologist and the first president of the Chicago Urban League. Johnson worked as the head of the Department of Research and Investigations for the branch. In the aftermath of the riots in Chicago in 1919, he served as the associate executive secretary of the Chicago Commission on Race Relations, a group of six white and six black civic leaders, businessmen, and politicians who had been appointed by Governor Frank Lowden of Illinois to study the violence. The commission published the results of its survey as a 672-page book, *The Negro in Chicago* (1922). In part, the commission concluded that the tension between black and white residents of the city had been exacerbated by the militant rhetoric used in both black and white newspapers, and it emphasized how dangerous biased and distorted reporting could be. Those conclusions seem to have shaped Johnson's work as the editor of *Opportunity*, for the journal rarely included the kind of fiery editorials often found in *The Crisis*, especially in the 1910s. Instead, the stated goal of *Opportunity* was to spread facts about African Americans.

It is not surprising, then, that the most frequent features of the journal, particularly in its early issues, were sociological studies. These studies present a wealth of information about African Americans' lives in the 1920s. They report on housing, employment, recreational, and educational opportunities available to African Americans. They also document the continuing discrimination African Americans faced in both the North and the South. Although *Opportunity* claimed to be objective, such reports often presented implicit—and sometimes explicit—arguments about African Americans. For example, in an essay written by Johnson and published in the issue of September 1923 about the causes of the migration of African Americans from the rural South to northern cities, Johnson argues that better opportunities in the North, rather than intimidation by the Ku Klux Klan, motivated many African Americans to migrate. He uses that information to insist that these migrants would be ambitious, industrious workers. A report on the lack of affordable housing for African Americans published in the May 1923 issue emphasizes that other ethnic minorities faced similar problems, thus defining housing difficulties as a widespread problem and preventing readers from blaming African Americans. *Opportunity* also included numerous refutations of pseudoscientific racism, exposing the flaws inherent in the many studies of the period that purported to prove African Americans' inferiority. In such cases, the apparently objective studies in *Opportunity* promote particular understandings of African Americans or dispute assumptions made about African Americans.

From its first issues, *Opportunity* complemented these studies with other texts that drew readers' attention to African Americans' achievements. These included articles about the establishment and accomplishments of African American institutions, such as a series of reports on "Our Negro Colleges," accounts of meetings of social or professional organizations, and occasional articles about the founding and activities of branches of the YMCA that were meant for African Americans. Monthly columns such as "Pot Pourri," "Bulletin Board," and "Social Progress" compiled accounts of significant accomplishments of African American business owners, employees, politicians, students, athletes, entertainers, and so on. These features usually were illustrated by photographs of the people involved; *Opportunity* thus became a source of both information about and visual images of successful African Americans.

Even in the very first issues, there also are hints that the arts would become an important focus of the journal. The inaugural issue included a review of two exhibits of work by African American painters, and the second issue included an editorial announcing that the contributors to *Opportunity* would write about and

illustrate drama, music, art, and literature by African Americans. Later issues included long and frequent reviews of novels, poetry, and plays written by or about African Americans, often illustrated by portraits of writers and performers; and discussions of African and African American art, with photographs of the artists or the works. The poets Gwendolyn Bennett and Countee Cullen each contributed regular columns during the late 1920s. Most issues also included creative work: short stories, poems, and plays, as well as visual art on the cover and inside the magazine.

Johnson believed that the arts could play an important role in improving interracial relations, and he saw the publication of work by African American writers and artists as an important aspect of *Opportunity*. He believed that many white publishers assumed that creative and scholarly work by African Americans was substandard, and he felt that they tended to dismiss it rather than considering it seriously. *Opportunity*, then, became a forum in which to prove such assumptions wrong. Johnson also promoted creative work by African Americans through the Civic Club dinner, which he hosted in March 1924. He invited a number of white editors and publishers as well as many of the most promising black writers. He hoped that the evening's events would bring the quality of the writers' work to the attention of the editors and publishers and result in increased publishing opportunities for the writers. It worked: The dinner was the catalyst for a special issue of the magazine *Survey Graphic* on Harlem and the New Negro that was published in March 1925; its contents would become the core of Alain Locke's anthology *The New Negro* (1925).

Johnson also encouraged the recognition of African American writers through *Opportunity*'s annual contests for literature, the first of which he announced six months after the Civic Club dinner. The contest of 1925 was followed by contests in 1926 and 1927, and many of the prizewinning entries were published in special issues of *Opportunity*. The contests were meant, as an announcement of the first one explained, to encourage the literary efforts of African Americans, to identify talented African American writers, to promote the development of a body of literature about African Americans, and to create a market for such literature. *Opportunity*'s criteria were relatively nonprescriptive: most categories were open in terms of content, stipulating only that the entries should focus on African Americans. Although *Opportunity* clearly had social goals for art by African Americans—one announcement emphasized that African American writers could use their work to replace "outworn representations" and "make themselves better understood"—the journal also discouraged propaganda and protest in literature and art. For *Opportunity*, however, that did not require the "best foot forward" approach advocated by literary critics like Du Bois who encouraged writers to focus on the more progressive aspects of the race; *Opportunity* welcomed a thorough exploration of all aspects of African Americans' lives.

The hope that sociological essays, news stories about African Americans' accomplishments, and creative texts would increase understanding seems to indicate that white readers were the target audience for *Opportunity*. In fact, it is estimated that as many as 33 to 40 percent of the magazine's readers were white (Robbins 1996). But Johnson also believed that these texts were important for African American readers. He was one of the first sociologists to emphasize the toll that discrimination and segregation took on African Americans (Pearson 1977), and he believed that African Americans needed to be convinced of the accomplishments of blacks as much as white readers did. In 1928, he wrote that he had hoped *Opportunity* would enable African Americans to see interest and beauty in their own lives, and that the journal would, in this way, help build their self-esteem.

Both creative and expository texts in *Opportunity*, finally, presented complex arguments about African Americans' identity in relation to America and to Africa. On the one hand, the journal nurtured the growth of African Americans' communal consciousness and pride. As Hutchinson emphasizes, however, the goal in this project was not separatism but, in fact, the development of an integrated America. Johnson was a cultural pluralist who believed that respect and opportunities for African Americans should not depend on their assimilation into white America; he conceived of American national culture as uniting diverse elements. Accordingly, contributors to *Opportunity* frequently argued, particularly in essays about folk music and poetry, that African Americans were making important and distinctive contributions to American culture. *Opportunity* also frequently turned its attention to African culture, using its coverage of African art, for example, to nurture African Americans' pride in their African heritage. By emphasizing both the American and the African aspects of African Americans' identity, experiences, and culture, *Opportunity* asserted the complexity of this identity and insisted that integration into American culture and

society could and should allow for the preservation of distinct aspects of African American culture.

Unlike *The Crisis*, *Opportunity* was never self-supporting. At its peak, in 1927, it had a circulation of only 11,000 readers (Johnson and Johnson 1979). The NUL received a grant in the mid-1920s that helped finance the journal, but the grant was not renewed in 1927. Perhaps the cancellation of the yearly contest in 1927 was also a sign that things were going downhill. In any case, in 1928, Johnson left New York City and the NUL for Fisk University, where he established the Department of Social Sciences and the Race Relations Institute. He became the university's first black president in 1947. In the meantime, the NUL changed the focus of *Opportunity* to rest more squarely on the sociological and economic aspects of African Americans' lives. The journal struggled during the Depression, became a quarterly in 1943, and ceased publication with the issue of winter 1949 (Gilpin 1972). It was revived in 1996 by the NUL, but as a general-interest magazine with little focus on the arts.

ANNE CARROLL

See also Bennett, Gwendolyn; Civic Club Dinner, 1924; Crisis, The; Cullen, Countee; Du Bois, W. E. B.; Johnson, Charles Spurgeon; Messenger, The; National Association for the Advancement of Colored People; National Urban League; Opportunity Awards Dinner; Opportunity Literary Contests; Owen, Chandler; Randolph, A. Philip; Schuyler, George S.; Survey Graphic

Further Readings

Carroll, Anne. "'Sufficient in Intensity': Mixed Media and Public Opinion in *Opportunity*." *Soundings*, 80(4), 1997.

Gilpin, Patrick. "Charles S. Johnson: Entrepreneur of the Harlem Renaissance." In *The Harlem Renaissance Remembered*, ed. Arna Bontemps. New York: Dodd, Mead, 1972.

Hutchinson, George. "Toward a New Negro Aesthetic." In *The Harlem Renaissance in Black and White*. Cambridge, Mass.: Belknap Press of Harvard University Press, 1995.

Johnson, Abby Arthur, and Ronald Maberry Johnson. "Toward the Renaissance: *Crisis, Opportunity*, and *Messenger*, 1910–1928." In *Propaganda and Aesthetics: The Literary Politics of Afro-American Magazines in the Twentieth Century*. Amherst: University of Massachusetts Press, 1979.

Lewis, David Levering. *When Harlem Was in Vogue*. New York: Oxford University Press, 1979.

Mott, Christopher M. "The Art of Self-Promotion; or, Which Self to Sell? The Proliferation and Disintegration of the Harlem Renaissance." In *Marketing Modernisms: Self-Promotion, Canonization, Rereading*, ed. Kevin J. H. Dettmar and Stephen Watt. Ann Arbor: University of Michigan Press, 1996.

Pearson, Ralph L. "Combating Racism with Art: Charles S. Johnson and the Harlem Renaissance." *American Studies*, 18(1), 1977.

Robbins, Richard. "Research, Renewal, Renaissance." In *Sidelines Activist: Charles S. Johnson and the Struggle for Civil Rights*. Jackson: University Press of Mississippi, 1996.

Wilson, Sondra Kathryn, ed. *The "Opportunity" Reader: Stories, Poetry, and Essays from the Urban League's "Opportunity" Magazine*. New York: Random House, 1999.

Wintz, Cary. *Black Culture and the Harlem Renaissance*. Houston, Tex.: Rice University Press, 1988.

Opportunity Awards Dinner

The *Opportunity* awards dinner was the official forum through which the winners of the literary contests held by the magazine *Opportunity* were publicly announced and honored. The first dinner was held in the spring of 1925; however, its format and mood were perhaps set one year earlier, on 21 March 1924, when approximately 100 writers, publishers, editors, and critics gathered at the Civic Club in New York for a dinner hosted by Charles Spurgeon Johnson, the editor of *Opportunity*. The Civic Club dinner had initially been conceived on a smaller scale to celebrate the publication of Jessie Redmon Fauset's first novel, *There Is Confusion*, but had developed into a major literary and social event at which prominent figures (black and white) were introduced to emerging young black writers and their works. Johnson, as the host, offered opening remarks and then turned control of the the the program over to Alain Locke, the appointed master of ceremonies, who presided and also offered his interpretation of the "New Negro."

The Dinner of 1925

The first *Opportunity* awards dinner was held on 1 May 1925 in New York at the Fifth Avenue Restaurant, at the corner of Twenty-fourth Street, to announce the first, second, and third prizes in the five divisions of the contest. The 316 guests included young hopefuls and influential figures in the world of letters, such as the master of ceremonies, John Erskine, professor of English at Columbia University and president of the Poetry Society of America; and judges, patrons, and writers: Clement Wood, Blanche Colton Williams, Montgomery Gregory, Henry Goddard Leach, L. Hollingsworth Wood, Eugene Kinckle Jones, Fannie Hurst, Paul and Arthur Kellogg, Arthur Schomburg, Paul Robeson, Rudolph Fisher, Jessie Redmon Fauset, Carl Van Vechten, Alain Locke, James Weldon Johnson, Carl Van Doren, Jean Toomer, and others. This elaborate event was, of course, covered extensively in *Opportunity*, and the account included sketches supplied by Francis Holbrook. In addition, the *New York Herald-Tribune* carried a complimentary review—under the headline "A Negro Renaissance"—in which the dinner was described as a "novel sight" with "white critics, whom 'everybody' knows, Negro writers, whom 'nobody' knew—meeting on common ground" (*Opportunity* 1925, 187).

As a result of this mingling of intellectuals, relationships and publishing opportunities that might not otherwise have materialized were developed. Perhaps the most noteworthy example was the relationship formed between Carl Van Vechten and Langston Hughes. Van Vechten was so taken with Hughes's "The Weary Blues" that he immediately began making arrangements to publish it. Less than three weeks after the awards dinner, Hughes had received a contract from Alfred A. Knopf for his first collection of poetry.

The Dinner of 1926

The second awards dinner was held on 1 May 1926, again at the Fifth Avenue Restaurant. This time, the guest list had increased to approximately 400—probably as a result of the success of the first contest. The number of entries had nearly doubled since the first competition, and public interest seems to have grown as well.

John Macy, author of *The Spirit of American Literature* and *The Story of The World's Literature*, was the chairman of this second dinner. In his opening remarks, he emphasized the universality of art, encouraging the guests to "rejoice because *good work* has been done, not that good work has been done by *Negroes*." However, he added that consideration must also be given to oneself and one's race: "All artists in the world must express intensely their race, nation, time, family, personality. . . . Every man to his own racial and individual nature and belief and mother tongue" (1926, 185). Macy then turned control of the program over to the chairmen of the contest divisions, who announced the winners in their respective categories.

Entertainment was also provided; the Bordentown Chorus, under the direction of Frederick Work, sang Negro spirituals. Charles Johnson would later comment that the performance "served well to enliven the evening and to join, pleasantly, the maturer contributions of Negro music to the beginnings of a new contribution in letters" (1926, 186).

The Dinner of 1927

The third awards dinner—once more at the Fifth Avenue Restaurant—was held on 7 May 1927, with Professor John Dewey presiding. The guest list, as before, included an array of influential literary figures, and the program was similar in format to the two previous dinners. However, *Opportunity*'s coverage of this third dinner was not as extensive. Furthermore, whereas its earlier reports had focused more on the literary and intellectual aspects of the events, the account of the third dinner consisted of a detailed description the social atmosphere through the eyes of Eugene Gordon (1927), who had won the contests twice in the short-story category.

In a whimsical essay, Gordon detailed everything from the "expansive white and gold and mirrored dining room," to the main course of "broiled spring chicken, peas, and mashed potato." He depicted individuals, such as "Mrs. Charles S. Johnson, petite, serious-faced and luminous-eyed," and described the attempts of newcomers as well as veterans to match important names with the right faces. Gordon said that he had obtained the signatures of the guests at his table and had even taken a "chunk of bread" as a souvenir. Perhaps, consciously or unconsciously, he sensed an ending; if so, he was right. Within a matter of months, it was learned that the literary contest would not be continued; this, then, had been the last *Opportunity* awards dinner. In the three years of its existence, the dinner had done much to achieve the initial purpose of the literary contests: It fostered "a market for Negro writers and for literature about Negroes," and it also brought "these writers into contact with the general world of letters" (Johnson 1924, 258).

VERONICA ADAMS YON

See also Civic Club Dinner, 1924; Hughes, Langston; Johnson, Charles Spurgeon; Opportunity; Opportunity Literary Contests; Van Vechten, Carl; Weary Blues, The; *specific individuals*

Further Readings

Austin, Addell P. "The Opportunity and Crisis Literary Contests, 1924–1927." *College Language Association Journal*, 32(2), 1988.

Gilpin, Patrick J. "Charles S. Johnson: Entrepreneur of the Harlem Renaissance." In *The Harlem Renaissance Remembered*, ed. Cary D. Wintz. New York: Garland, 1996.

Gordon, Eugene. "The *Opportunity* Dinner: An Impression." *Opportunity*, 5(7), July 1927.

Johnson, Charles S. "An Opportunity for Negro Writers." *Opportunity*, 2(21), September 1924.

———. "The Contest." *Opportunity*, 3(29), May 1925.

———. "The *Opportunity* Dinner." *Opportunity*, 3(30), June 1925.

———. "The Awards Dinner." *Opportunity*, 4(42), June 1926.

Macy, John. "The Kingdom of Art." *Opportunity*, 4(42), June 1926.

"A Negro Renaissance." *Opportunity*, 3(30), June 1925. (Reprinted from *New York Herald-Tribune*.)

Watson, Steven. *The Harlem Renaissance: Hub of African-American Culture, 1920–1930*. New York: Pantheon, 1995.

Wintz, Cary D. *Black Culture and the Harlem Renaissance*. Houston, Tex.: Rice University Press, 1988.

———. *The Emergence of the Harlem Renaissance*. New York: Garland, 1996.

Opportunity Literary Contests

The *Opportunity* literary contests were established by *Opportunity: A Journal of Negro Life*, a monthly publication of the National Urban League. The first contest was officially announced in the issue of August 1924 by Charles S. Johnson, the editor of *Opportunity* and also the organizer of the contests. The September 1924 issue gave more details, including Johnson's explanation of the purpose of the competition:

> It hopes to stimulate and encourage creative literary effort among Negroes; to locate and orient Negro writers of ability; to stimulate and encourage interest in the serious development of a body of literature

about Negro life, drawing deeply upon these tremendously rich sources; to encourage the reading of literature both by Negro authors and about Negro life, not merely because they are Negro authors but because what they write is literature and because the literature is interesting; to foster a market for Negro writers and for literature by and about Negroes; to bring these writers into contact with the general world of letters to which they have been for the most part timid and inarticulate strangers; to stimulate and foster a type of writing by Negroes which shakes itself free of deliberate propaganda and protest. (1924, 258)

Johnson had called for submissions relating to "some phase of Negro life, either directly or indirectly," initiating a series of three major literary competitions that would prove effective in promoting the work of participants in the Harlem Renaissance.

The Contest of 1925

The first contest was open for entries from September to 31 December 1924, and it generated a total of 732 submissions from black writers across the country. The twenty-four judges, eighteen of whom were white, included influential figures such as Fannie Hurst, Zona Gale, Alain Locke, James Weldon Johnson, and John Macy. The prize money, $500, was donated by Mrs. Henry G. Leach, who was a board member for the Urban League and, in Johnson's words, a "long, thorough sympathizer with the struggles of Negroes for social as well as artistic status" (January 1925, 3).

The winners of the first, second, and third prizes and honorable mentions in each of the five divisions of the contest were announced in New York on 1 May 1925 at a special dinner, and also in *Opportunity*'s issue of May 1925. First prize went to John Matheus (short story), Langston Hughes (poetry), E. Franklin Frazier (essay), G. D. Lipscomb (play), and G. A. Steward (personal-experience sketch). Zora Neale Hurston received the most awards (four): both second prize and honorable mention in each of two divisions (short story and play). Sterling Brown and Countee Cullen also received awards.

This first contest was noted in an editorial in the *New York Herald-Tribune,* which introduced to the general public many Negro writers who were already known in black literary circles. Pleased with the success of the contest, Johnson advised participants

who were interested in "this whole developing movement to *stand by*" (May 1925, 131).

The Contest of 1926

The second annual contest was eagerly awaited. Johnson had whetted the public's literary appetite by publishing several award-winning works from the first competition in *Opportunity* and by emphasizing the outside publishing opportunities that were being made available to the winners. Langston Hughes's first collection of poems, *The Weary Blues*, had been contracted by Alfred A. Knopf, and John Matheus's "Fog" had been selected for inclusion in Alain Locke's anthology *The New Negro.*

Interest in the second contest was also heightened by the addition of a new division—musical compositions—and two special prizes: the Alexander Pushkin poetry prize and the Federation of Colored Women's Clubs (FCWC) prizes for constructive journalism. This expansion of the competition was due in large part to a donation of $1,000 by Casper Holstein, a West Indian entrepreneur who hoped to inspire gifted blacks "to scale the empyrean heights of art and literature" (1925, 308).

Johnson noted in the March issue of *Opportunity* that the number of entries had notably increased (to more than 1,200), and that the poetry and short-story categories were yielding a "higher level of craftsmanship." Awards were announced on 1 May 1926 at a special dinner, and then published in a special edition of *Opportunity* in June. The recipients of prizes included some previous winners, such as John Matheus, Countee Cullen, Zora Neale Hurston, and Sterling Brown. New winners included Gwendolyn Bennett, Dorothy West, and Arna Bontemps, recipient of the Pushkin poetry prize.

The Contest of 1927

The third literary contest followed the format of the earlier competitions, and Holstein again donated $1,000 in prize money. Nevertheless, a few differences were apparent, the first being the focus of the contest.

Pointing out that many previous manuscripts "failed to attain recognition," Johnson announced that more emphasis would be placed on guiding "these prodigal energies to the most promising sources of power" and stimulating "a product that can in larger degree and volume stand without the need of apology;

that need not at any point rely upon sheer eroticism for its acceptance" (1926, 304).

In addition to this shift in focus, another new category—pictorial awards—was added; the first prize in this category went to Aaron Douglas. Also, five special Buckner awards were offered for "entries that showed conspicuous promise." The donor was George W. Buckner of St. Louis, Missouri, and the prize winners were Blanche Taylor Dickinson, Dorothy West, Emily May Harper, Frank Horne, and Sterling Brown. Other winners of note were Georgia Douglas Johnson, who received first prize for her play *Plumes*, and Arna Bontemps, who again received the Pushkin poetry prize.

Four months after these awards were presented, Charles Johnson announced that the contest would be suspended for a year in order to provide additional time for writers to fine-tune their works and to experiment with multiple manuscripts "in search of the most effective channels of expression" (1927, 254). In 1928, though, the contest was not reopened. The magazine did eventually sponsor some additional competitions, however, and the contests of 1925, 1926, and 1927 had proved instrumental in supplying a venue for up-and-coming black writers, introducing Negro writers to the general public, facilitating outside publishing opportunities for some of the contestants, and launching the careers of many figures of the Harlem Renaissance.

VERONICA ADAMS YON

See also Bennett, Gwendolyn; Bontemps, Arna; Brown, Sterling; Cullen, Countee; Douglas, Aaron; Frazier, E. Franklin; Holstein, Casper; Horne, Frank; Hughes, Langston; Hurst, Fannie; Hurston, Zora Neale; Johnson, Charles Spurgeon; Johnson, Georgia Douglas; Johnson, James Weldon; Locke, Alain; Matheus, John Frederick; National Urban League; New Negro, The; Opportunity; Opportunity Awards Dinner; Weary Blues, The; West, Dorothy

Further Reading

Austin, Addell P, "The Opportunity and Crisis Literary Contests, 1924–1927." *College Language Association Journal*, 32(2), 1988.

Gilpin, Patrick J. "Charles S. Johnson: Entrepreneur of the Harlem Renaissance." In *The Harlem Renaissance Remembered*, ed. Cary D. Wintz. New York: Garland, 1996.

Holstein, Casper. "The Holstein Prizes." *Opportunity*, 3(34), October 1925.

Johnson, Charles S. "An Opportunity for Negro Writers." *Opportunity*, 2(21), September 1924.

———. "The Donor of the Contest Prizes." *Opportunity*, 3(25), January 1925.

———. "The Contest." *Opportunity*, 3(29), May 1925.

———. "The Third *Opportunity* Contest." *Opportunity*, 4(46), October 1926.

———. "The *Opportunity* Contest." *Opportunity*, 5(9), September 1927.

Watson, Steven. *The Harlem Renaissance: Hub of African-American Culture, 1920–1930*. New York: Pantheon, 1995.

Wintz, Cary D. *Black Culture and the Harlem Renaissance*. Houston, Tex.: Rice University Press, 1988.

———. *The Emergence of the Harlem Renaissance*. New York: Garland, 1996.

Organized Crime

The migration of African Americans to northern cities in the early 1900s brought some of them into contact with organized crime. While many first- and second-generation Americans, mainly Italians and Irish, dominated this underworld, black Americans also participated and gained money and prestige in their neighborhoods. Although African American criminals never achieved the syndication of ethnic gangs, they contributed to the development of organized crime as an American institution. In the period after World War I, black neighborhoods like Harlem became valuable markets for illegal liquor and gambling.

Organization of criminal operations in America began during Prohibition, when the Eighteenth Amendment (1918) illegalized the manufacturing, sale, and transportation of alcohol. Unintentionally, Prohibition created economic opportunities for people regardless of race or ethnicity. Enterprising criminals, recognizing the demand for illegal alcohol, supplied urban establishments with liquor. Prohibition did not eliminate the market for alcohol; rather, it contributed to the development of organized crime, as urban gangs constructed local, state, and national syndicates.

The illegal liquor industry, or bootlegging, involved a large network of breweries, ships, trucks, storage facilities, bars, restaurants, and nightclubs. Intimidation, violence, and bribery were crucial to its success, and police and politicians received compensation for ignoring these illegal activities. Drinking establishments, or speakeasies—some independently owned and some owned by gangsters—met the demand of thirsty Americans undeterred by the federal law. Harlem, like the South Side of Chicago and other black urban neighborhoods, became a boomtown for bootleggers.

In the early years of the twentieth century, Harlem's population increased, as did the number of its drinking establishments. Such establishments also existed in other parts of New York City, but many bars opened particularly in Harlem, hoping to capitalize on the population explosion there. Usually, these were small establishments that sometimes offered live music. In the period after World War I, the popularity of jazz drew more white and black visitors into Harlem, creating a need for even larger venues.

In many cities, white gangsters recognized the potential for profits and began supplying alcohol to illegal drinking establishments in black neighborhoods. Harlem was no exception. The white gangster Owen Madden took over Harlem's Club Deluxe from the boxer Jack Johnson in 1923 and renamed it the Cotton Club. Madden's gang had acquired the club while he was serving time in prison at Sing Sing for murdering a rival gangster.

Generally, speakeasies were supplied directly by white gangsters, such as Madden, who owned breweries; alternatively, the liquor was shipped into the city and distributed to local clubs. Gangsters easily controlled local police and politicians with bribes; however, state and national law enforcement agents and political reformers proved more troublesome. Even Madden was not immune. In 1923, he was arrested outside the city, in Westchester County, while traveling with a shipment of stolen liquor. That time, he was released after claiming that he had only caught a ride on the truck and had not been aware of the its contents. In 1925, however, Madden did not get off as easily. A federal judge closed the Cotton Club when its management was accused of violating the Eighteenth Amendment. Madden was able to plead guilty to a lesser charge and reopened the club after paying a fine.

White gangsters were not above using violence and intimidation to maintain their monopoly on bootlegging in Harlem. Barron Wilkins, the owner of a popular nightclub there, may have been the victim of gangsters in 1926; he was murdered outside his club after complaining about an order of bootleg liquor he had received. Likewise, Madden and his associates were not to be trifled with. In 1930, the Plantation

Club, a popular rival nightspot, hired Cab Calloway and his band. Calloway had filled in at the Cotton Club while its house band was out of town, and Madden's crew reportedly destroyed the Plantation Club in retaliation for hiring Calloway and siphoning off patrons from the Cotton Club. Madden's gang was also said to be responsible for murdering the owner of the Plantation Club.

Madden's dealings with Duke Ellington and the Washingtonians exemplified the pros and cons of working for gangsters. In November 1927, Ellington and his band made their first appearance at the Cotton Club. The following week, under contract, they traveled to Philadelphia to perform at the Standard Theater. Their engagement was cut short when the management of the Standard advised them to return to New York. Madden wanted the band to appear exclusively at the Cotton Club, and he had suggested that it was in the Standard's best interest to oblige. While headlining at the Cotton Club through 1930, Ellington and his band were allowed to play other venues. They were expected to keep their standing date at the Cotton Club, however, even if that meant playing a day show at Princeton University or a breakfast dance in the Bronx before taking the stage at Madden's club in the late evening. Despite these restrictions, Ellington enjoyed the "elegance" of the club and its sophisticated clientele and commented that his relationship with Madden was friendly.

In addition to supporting establishments that provided access to illegal alcohol, Harlem was the birthplace of the modern numbers game—a gambling game based on the daily closing results of the New York Stock Exchange. No one is certain of its origins. Some people speculate that it was a variation of a betting game in New England. Others give credit to Hispanic immigrants who played a similar type of lottery; still others credit Casper Holstein, a West Indian resident of Harlem. According to one popular theory, Holstein devised the idea while working as a janitor; he suggested that people place bets on the likelihood of the closing value at the New York Stock Exchange. Earlier forms of number games were based on lotteries; numbers were drawn, information was disseminated to bookies, payouts and collections were made. Under Holstein's rules, the numbers were reported daily in the newspaper, so the game could not be fixed. The winning numbers were determined by the last two digits of the "exchange's total," and a third digit was decided by the last number of the "balances' total." The winning three digits paid off at 600 to 1. In a variation called "bolita," bets were made on two of the three numbers, and the odds were 80 to 1. The numbers soon became immensely popular and profitable; thousands of dollars were made daily. By the early 1920s, Harlem had more than thirty independent numbers houses, or "banks," employing as many as twenty people each.

The people who worked in Harlem's numbers racket were loosely organized. Some acted as runners, keeping track of the bets, or as policy bankers who oversaw the money, payouts, and collections. Although Harlem's underworld followed the ethnic model, employing family and friends, it was not as structured as a traditional syndicate. In Harlem, unlike in other parts of the city, there were no dons (bosses), capos (lieutenants), or soldiers (enforcers). The Harlem underworld would not achieve that degree of organization until after World War II, when street gangs became involved in drug trafficking.

Although many criminal organizations during the 1920s and 1930s were multiethnic, those in Harlem were equal-opportunity employers. Blacks and women were involved in the day-to-day operations. The policy houses allowed African Americans to participate in a type of financial investment scheme not available through more typical channels. Players were often working-class men and women as well as people from the middle and upper classes. They might be janitors, cooks, and washerwomen or teachers, lawyers, and physicians. The numbers game was more than gambling; it was a respectable social event. Bets were made in bars, grocery stores, beauty parlors, and barber shops. The policy banks also created employment opportunities; establishments opened to fill other needs associated with this type of gambling. Because African Americans did not have access to traditional sources of investment, capital, savings, and loans, Harlemites created lending houses.

The system was lucrative for those involved. Racketeers drove expensive cars, wore fashionable clothes, invested in local property, and supported cultural improvements. Stephanie St. Claire, "Madame Queen of policy," claimed to have earned millions. Within a year of devising the game, Holstein had secured several income properties, a nightclub called the Turf Club located on 136th Street, and a farm in Virginia. It was estimated that he was worth more than $500,000. He was chauffeured in a new Lincoln sedan and liked to attend horse races. Holstein also used his earnings to support cultural and educational endeavors. For example, he sponsored a literary award for the aspiring literati of the Harlem Renaissance, and he built homes and provided educational assistance for blacks living in the South. Holstein was a popular figure and appears in Carl VanVechten's novel *Nigger Heaven* (1926) as a character called Randolph Pettijohn, "the bolita king."

At the outset, the numbers racket in Harlem was neither violent nor well organized. In other northern cities, African Americans gained influence with local white politicians and police who in turn protected the interests of black racketeers. Most of this influence came from bribes. The uncoordinated efforts of black racketeers in Harlem ultimately caused their downfall, because they never established political clout. Additionally, their lack of muscle and influence left them vulnerable to more aggressive and vicious white criminals from other parts of the city. Initially, white gangsters ignored the Harlem numbers racket and saw the enterprise as a "nigger's pool" based on penny bets. They erroneously believed that Harlemites were too poor to make the game profitable.

Eventually, though, because Harlem's numbers operation was profitable, it attracted the attention of crime operatives in other boroughs of New York City. The first white gangster who tried to take over operations in Harlem was Hyman Kassell, a bootlegger and policy banker who operated several speakeasies in the neighborhood. In the mid-1920s, he attempted to organize the rackets by controlling legal establishments, such as restaurants and retail stores, and used them as a base of operations. Ultimately, Kassell failed to create a monopoly, but other white gangsters were not deterred.

Holstein became a victim of white gangsters in 1928 when five white men kidnapped him. He was unable to identify his captors but did tell the police that he had been bound and gagged for two days. Holstein reported that his kidnappers approached him in police uniforms and brandished pistols. After informing Holstein that they were taking him to a police station for questioning, the men forced him into an automobile and pistol-whipped him, beat him, and robbed him of his cash and jewelry, totaling more than $2,000. An earlier demand for a ransom of $50,000 helped the police identify Holstein's abductors. Five men from the Bronx with ties to white organized crime were subsequently arrested.

Holstein's kidnapping was not the only high-profile abduction in Harlem. In 1930, problems arose between Dutch Schultz (Charles Harman)—a white bootlegger from the Bronx—and one of his gang members, Vincent "the Mick" Coll. The disagreement resulted in bloodshed, including the murder of a black child who was caught in the cross-fire on a street in Harlem. Coll, on the run and in need of money, kidnapped two men associated with Owen Madden's gang and Connie's Inn, a nightclub in Harlem. Coll demanded a ransom, which Madden paid, and the men were released. Coll was later murdered by Schultz's men.

By 1931, organized crime in New York was syndicated under several crime families. Dutch Schultz, recently promoted to the position of don, became aware of the potential wealth associated with Harlem's numbers game. Using his influence with politicians and police, as well as violence and intimidation, Schultz was able to close down the independents and take over Harlem's racket. Only bankers willing to pay for his protection were allowed to remain in business. Not all the racketeers in Harlem accepted Schultz's hostile takeover. Stephanie St. Claire resisted, and she was brash enough to make their feud public. She testified before a government hearing that corrupt politicians and police had forced her to lose income by unjustly targeting her business for police harassment. St. Claire attributed this to gender discrimination and the local government's relationship with Schultz. The government's retribution was eight months in jail on what she declared were trumped-up charges.

Investigations into the numbers racket by aggressive reformers in the 1930s challenged the position of white gangsters in Harlem. Likewise, the repeal of Prohibition in 1933 prompted white gangsters to explore other options to earn illegal profits. The Seabury investigations into New York City's organized crime families in the mid-1930s reduced the number of policy houses in Harlem. Schultz continued his extortion racket by focusing on restaurants and club owners, but in 1935, he was murdered by other New York crime families after brazenly threatening to kill the crime fighter Thomas Dewey.

With the passing of Schultz, the Genovese family assumed control of Harlem's numbers racket for the next fifty years. However, pressure from reformers reduced the number of operators in Harlem. Many African American policy bankers were either jailed or put out of business by Dewey's aggressive reforms. Holstein also retired from the numbers racket because of government investigations; he was arrested in 1935, was convicted of racketeering, and spent a year in prison. Some policy bankers in Harlem were

indicted for tax fraud by the Internal Revenue Service. For example, Wilfred Adolfus Blunder (who had earned more than $1.7 million) and Enrique Miro (who had accumulated more than $1.2 million) had never bothered to pay federal income tax. Reformers also targeted bootleggers. In 1932, Owen Madden returned to jail for parole violations and escaped an impending investigation for tax evasion. He was released the following year, retired, and left New York. Prohibition was over.

Organized crime had a lasting and significant effect on Harlem. As the Harlem Renaissance ended, the nature of organized crime changed. In the late 1930s, the presence of organized crime in Harlem continued, and blacks remained involved in minor roles. Harlemites ran policy banks; white gangsters maintained control of the numbers and narcotics rackets. Socially and economically, organized crime contributed to the demise of Harlem in the post-renaissance period. It undermined social institutions, glorified criminals, and justified violence. As African Americans became empowered by the civil rights movement in the late 1960s, so did black gangsters. Street gangs began to fill the void left by the deteriorating ethnic syndicates and gained control of operations in their own neighborhood. As white gangsters lost power, black gangsters came to control Harlem.

AMY CARREIRO

See also Calloway, Cabell "Cab"; Cotton Club; Ellington, Duke; Holstein, Casper; Johnson, John Arthur; Madden, Owen Vincent; Nigger Heaven; Nightclubs; Nightlife; Numbers Racket

Further Reading

Haskins, Jim. *The Cotton Club*. New York: Hippocrene, 1994.

Johnson, James Weldon. *Black Manhattan*. New York: Knopf, 1930.

McKay, Claude. *Harlem: Negro Metropolis*. New York: Dutton, 1940.

Redding, J. Saunders. "Playing the Numbers." *North American Review*, 6, December 1934, pp. 533–542.

Schatzberg, Rufus, and Robert J. Kelly. *African-American Organized Crime: A Social History*. New York: Garland, 1996.

Ward, Geoffrey C. *Jazz: A History of America's Music*. New York: Knopf, 2000.

Woodwiss, Michael. *Crime, Crusades, and Corruption: Prohibitions in the United States, 1900–1987*. Totowa, N.J.: Barnes and Noble, 1988.

———. *Organized Crime and American Power: A History.* Toronto: University of Toronto Press, 2001.

Ory, Edward "Kid"

Edward "Kid" Ory made a significant contribution to the music of the Harlem Renaissance although he spent virtually no time in New York.

Ory began his professional career in 1894, at age eight; with neighborhood friends, he built homemade instruments, formed a band, and (charging admission) held fish fries in an empty house, where his band played ragtime. With the profits, Ory bought his first trombone. He played many instruments throughout his career—bass, banjo, clarinet, trumpet, saxophone, piano, guitar, and drums—but he excelled on the trombone. Ory became the most famous practitioner of the "tailgate" style of playing, in which the trombone is used for rhythmic effects, fills, and glissandi; in this manner, the trombone works with the bass to establish a solid foundation under the trumpet and clarinet. Ory was known as a forceful soloist, especially effective at slow blues.

Ory moved to New Orleans in 1911. After studying with private teachers and occasionally sitting in with Buddy Bolden's band, Ory joined a combo led by Lewis Mathews. Ory took over its leadership in 1917, and it became perhaps the premier band in the region. The band's trumpet chair was filled first by Mutt Carey, later by King Oliver, and still later by the young Louis Armstrong. The band's clarinetists included, at various times, Jimmy Dodds, Sidney Bechet, Jimmie Noone, and George Lewis.

Tired of the crime in New Orleans, and having been advised by his doctor to move to a drier climate, Ory went to California in 1919 and established the first all-black New Orleans–style jazz group on the West Coast. In 1921, Ory's Sunshine Orchestra recorded at least seven songs, including "Society Blues," "Ory's Creole Trombone," and "When You're Alone Blues," for Sunshine records, a black enterprise. (Nordskog also claimed the sessions, and on its labels the band is called Spike's Seven Pods of Pepper.) These records, the first to feature an all-black jazz band, predate recordings by King Oliver's important Creole Jazz Band, by Jelly Roll Morton

(solo piano), and by Armstrong's Hot Five and Hot Seven.

From 1924 to 1929, Ory worked at various venues in Chicago and recorded widely there with Oliver, Morton, Lil Armstrong, Tiny Parham, Ma Rainey, Williams's Stompers, and Luis Russell. Ory was an original member of Louis Armstrong's Hot Five (under Armstrong's leadership, the Hot Five and the Hot Seven produced the most important records of early jazz). The group recorded Ory's famous composition "Muskrat Ramble" on 26 February 1926. (Actually, Ory may simply have written down this song rather than composing it; some people, including Sidney Bechet, have identified it as a tune that Buddy Bolden used to play, "The Old Cow Died and the Old Man Cried.")

In the midst of the Depression, and no doubt adversely affected by the increasing predominance of swing, Ory moved back to California and ran a chicken farm with his brother from 1930 to 1939. He returned to music via groups led by Barney Bigard (1942) and Bunk Johnson (1943), and in 1944, he became a regular on Orson Welles's popular radio show. This show helped renew an interest in Dixieland jazz. In the 1940s and 1950s, Ory played regularly in Los Angeles (where he opened his own club, On the Levee, in 1954) and Europe, and recorded with Henry "Red" Allen, Papa Celestin, Leadbelly, and others. Ory also had small roles in the films *New Orleans* with Louis Armstrong (1947), *Crossfire* (1947), *Mahogany Magic* (1950), and *The Benny Goodman Story* (1956). He died in Hawaii in 1973.

Biography

Edward "Kid" Ory was born in La Place, Louisiana, on 25 December 1886. He had a public school education and also studied music privately. He sat in with Buddy Bolden's band; led own band in New Orleans, 1917; then led Ory's Creole Jazz Band in Los Angeles, 1919–1924; and made the first jazz records by an all-black group. Ory then worked with several bands: King Oliver's, 1925–1927; Dave Peyton's, 1927; Clarence Black's, 1927–1928; the Chicago Vagabonds, 1928–1929, Leon Rene's "Lucky Day" orchestra, 1929; and bands in Los Angeles, 1929–1930. He was a co-owner of a chicken ranch, 1930–1939; re-formed his own band, 1941; worked with Barney Bigard's group in 1942 and with Bunk Johnson in 1943; performed regularly on Orson Welles's radio show for Standard Oil, 1944; joined ASCAP, 1952; led his own group at the

Newport Jazz Festival of 1957 and at the Berlin Festival of 1959; owned a nightclub in Los Angeles, On the Levee, 1958–1961; and played at the New Orleans Jazz Festival, 1971. Ory won the *Record Changer* all-time, all-star poll in 1951. He died in Honolulu, Hawaii, on 23 January 1973.

GREGORY MILLER

See also Armstrong, Louis; Bechet, Sidney; Jazz; Music; Oliver, Joseph "King"; Rainey, Gertrude "Ma"

Selected Works

"Muskrat Ramble." 1926.
"Ory's Creole Trombone." 1927.
"Savoy Blues." 1927.
Ory's Creole Trombone: 1922–1944. (ASV AJA 5148.)
Kid Ory: 1922–1945. (Jazz Classics 1069.)

Further Reading

Bergreen, Laurence. *Louis Armstrong: An Extravagant Life.* New York: Broadway, 1997.

Kenney, William Howland. *Chicago Jazz: A Cultural History, 1904–1930.* New York: Oxford University Press, 1993.

Levin, Floyd. *Classic Jazz: A Personal View of the Music and the Musicians.* Berkeley: University of California Press, 2000.

Mills, Jesse. "Creole Trombone: Kid Ory and Early Recorded Jazz in Los Angeles." Ph.D. diss., University of California, Los Angeles, 1999.

Peretti, Burton W. *The Creation of Jazz: Music, Race, and Culture in Urban America.* Urbana: University of Illinois Press, 1992.

Schuller, Gunther. *Early Jazz: Its Roots and Musical Development.* New York: Oxford University Press, 1968.

Southern, Eileen. *The Music of Black Americans: A History.* New York: Norton, 1971. (See also 3rd ed., 1997.)

Wright, Laurie. *Walter C. Allen and Brian A. L. Rust's "King" Oliver.* Chigwell, UK: Storyville, 1987.

Ovington, Mary White

Mary White Ovington was born in Brooklyn, New York, on 11 April 1865, just two days after General Robert E. Lee surrendered to General Ulysses S. Grant, ending the Civil War. The daughter of a prominent abolitionist family, Ovington followed in the footsteps of many elite young women of her generation by dedicating herself to reform efforts. After spending two years at Radcliffe College, in 1895 Ovington helped to found the Greenpoint Settlement in Brooklyn as a model tenement for white working-class families. In her memoirs, *Black and White Sat Down Together: The Reminiscences of an NAACP Founder*, Ovington admits that she gave no thought at this early stage of her career to the plight of black people living in the North. But in 1903, when she was thirty-eight, she heard Booker T. Washington speak in Manhattan. "To my amazement," she later recalled, "I learned that there was a Negro problem in my city." Ovington's encounter with Washington proved to be a decisive moment; she dedicated the remainder of her life to the fight for racial justice.

Ovington left Greenpoint later that year and quickly embarked on a study of employment and housing conditions in black Manhattan. As a fellow in social work at Mary Kingsbury Simkhovitch's Greenwich House, Ovington pursued her research for five years. In 1908, she moved into the Tuskegee Apartments on Sixty-third Street near Eleventh Avenue, in New York's San Juan Hill district. This was the first model tenement opened for black residents, and Ovington had been instrumental in its construction. She had approached Henry Phipps, a philanthropist committed to providing decent, affordable housing to the city's working poor, and had convinced him of the desperate need within the black community for low-cost housing; Phipps then built the Tuskegee. Ovington was the only white tenant in the building. Living in one of the most congested regions of the city, Ovington finally had an insider's look into black life in Manhattan.

She published the results of her study in 1911, exposing the hardships faced by the city's black population. The book, *Half a Man: The Status of the Negro in New York*, was sharply critical of race relations in the North. Ovington blamed racial prejudice for undermining black men's ability to find any but the most menial jobs. The low wages and frequent bouts of unemployment that these men experienced, she noted, obligated many black women to remain in the workforce until late in life, inverting traditional patterns of gender behavior. Overall, she argued in her study, black people in New York City experienced discrimination in housing, education, and the workplace. Under these conditions, Ovington stressed, they had to struggle to survive and raise their families.

Confronted with her own findings, Ovington immersed herself in efforts to improve the condition of the city's black population. Her critique of the economic situation faced by the city's poorest group led her to develop sympathy for socialism. She joined the Socialist Party in 1905, but she criticized the party for its failure to support women's rights; instead, she focused her efforts on two recently formed organizations in New York: the National League for the Protection of Colored Women, and the Committee for Improving the Industrial Condition of Negroes in New York. These groups, among the few to address the problems facing the city's blacks, merged in 1911 to become the National Urban League (NUL).

In the meantime, Ovington participated in the National Conference on the Negro in 1909. At the second National Negro Conference in 1910, the group, which included W. E. B. Du Bois and Ovington, adopted an organizational structure and a name: the National Association for the Advancement of Colored People (NAACP). The NUL and the NAACP served parallel purposes: to improve the economic and social conditions of black people in cities nationwide and to promote blacks' rights as citizens.

Ovington served briefly as acting executive secretary of the NAACP in 1910–1911. During her tenure in that position, the NAACP began to develop its antilynching campaign. Ovington, along with two other workers in the organization, wrote antilynching pamphlets, attended meetings, and raised money. This was, however, a bleak time for the nation's black population. "Just when one thought that the public was becoming educated," Ovington wrote, "some frightful lynching would occur or some especially heinous example of legal justice would come to the NAACP office."

During World War I, with so many volunteers away at war, Ovington served as acting chairman of the NAACP's board of directors. Her appointment became permanent in 1919, when the board formally elected her to the position. She remained in that role until 1932, when she became the NAACP's treasurer. Ovington worked for the NAACP in this capacity until 1947, when she ceased her activity in the organization altogether.

In addition to her organizational activities, Ovington was a prolific writer. Among her works were two children's books, *Hazel* and *Zeke*; *Portraits in Color*, biographical sketches of prominent African Americans; a play about Phillis Wheatley; and the

Mary White Ovington, c. 1930–1940. (Library of Congress.)

story of her own involvement in the NAACP, *The Walls Came Tumbling Down*. Much of her writing focused on social critique. After the lynching of Leo Frank, a Jewish factory worker who had been convicted of murdering a girl named Mary Phagan, in 1915 Ovington published "Mary Phagan Speaks" in the *New Republic*. The story, told in the voice of the dead girl, condemned the men of Marietta, Georgia, who were passionately aroused by her death but had cared so little for her in life. Also in 1915, Ovington published "The White Brute," a story condemning the rape of black women by white men.

Ovington died in 1951, having dedicated her life to ameliorating the discrimination faced by blacks in all aspects of American society: raising money, demanding civil equality, and fighting for racial justice. Walter White, the NAACP's executive secretary, called her a "fighting saint"; and the NAACP itself declared her the "mother of the new emancipation." Nevertheless, Ovington died before she could see the realization of her long-held dream: voting rights for black Americans throughout the United States.

Biography

Mary White Ovington was born 11 April 1865 in Brooklyn, New York. She studied at Packer Collegiate Institute (graduating in 1890) and Radcliffe College (1891–1893). She was a registrar at Pratt Institute in Brooklyn; head worker at Greenpoint Settlement in Brooklyn, 1895–1903; a fellow in social work at Greenwich House in Manhattan, 1904–1905; a founding member of the National Association for the Advancement of Colored People (NAACP), 1909; executive secretary of the NAACP, 1910–1911; chairman of the board of directors of the NAACP, 1917–1932; and treasurer of the NAACP, 1932–1947. Ovington was also a member of the National League for the Protection of Colored Women, the Committee for Improving the Industrial Condition of Negroes, the Urban League, and the Socialist Party. She was the author of several works, and a contributor to *Charities and the Commons, Annals of the American Academy of Political and Social Sciences, The Masses, New Republic, Evening Post, Southern Workman,* and *the Crisis.* Ovington died in Auburndale, Massachusetts, in 1951 at the age of eighty-six.

MARCY SACKS

See also Antilynching Crusade; National Association for the Advancement of Colored People; National Urban League; San Juan Hill; Washington, Booker T.

Selected Works

Half a Man: The Status of the Negro in New York. New York, 1911.

Hazel. 1913.

Portraits in Color. 1927.

Zeke. 1931.

Phyllis Wheatley. 1932.

The Walls Came Tumbling Down. New York, 1947.

Black and White Sat Down Together: The Reminiscences of an NAACP Founder, ed. Ralph E. Luker. New York, 1995. (From "Reminiscences." *Baltimore Afro-American,* 1932–1933.)

Further Reading

Osofsky, Gilbert. *Harlem: The Making of a Ghetto—Negro New York, 1890–1930.* New York, 1963.

Scheiner, Seth M. *Negro Mecca: A History of the Negro in New York City, 1865–1920.* New York, 1965.

Wedin, Carolyn. *Inheritors of the Spirit: Mary White Ovington and the Founding of the NAACP.* New York, 1997.

Owen, Chandler

Little is known of the early life of Chandler Owen. He was born North Carolina, studied at Virginia Union University in Richmond, and around 1913 moved to New York City, where he undertook graduate study in social work with funding from the National Urban League. Owen met A. Philip Randolph in New York in 1915; the two would be closely allied during the years of the Harlem Renaissance and would remain lifelong friends. Through Randolph's influence—and his own study of radical social thought—Owen decided to quit the moderate Urban League for the Socialist Party in 1916. A year later, he campaigned for the socialist Morris Hillquit, who was running for mayor of New York City. Owen and Randolph operated an employment agency for black workers during World War I; in conjunction, they also edited *Hotel Messenger,* a newsletter for a local hotel workers' union. After they published an editorial that was critical of the union itself, they were fired, but they immediately reestablished the paper as *The Messenger,* which they edited from November 1917 to 1928.

The Messenger was the most prominent black socialist publication of the Harlem Renaissance, and pitched itself as "the only radical Negro magazine in America." It found its voice in World War I, when the Socialist Party of America was the only major political organization to speak out against the war, and when African Americans were deeply divided over participation in the war effort. In *The Messenger,* Owen and Randolph espoused a standard socialist critique of the war, but they also challenged the assumption of white radicals that racism would simply disappear following a socialist revolution. They endorsed African American labor union organizing, the radical interracial unionism of the Industrial Workers of the World, woman's suffrage, and socialist revolution in Russia. They were unsparing in their criticisms, taking on African American ministers and conservative black Republican disciples of the late Booker T. Washington, as well as racial liberals such as W. E. B. Du Bois. Owen coined the phrase "new crowd Negro" to distinguish black socialism from the accommodationism that he saw in Du Bois's support for the war. *The Messenger* was suppressed after publishing an article critical of the war in the July 1918 issue, and Owen and Randolph were indicted for treason; the charges were later dismissed. During the war years, the magazine was published only sporadically (partly owing to surveillance and censorship by federal authorities); it became a monthly in 1919 and reached a peak circulation of approximately 20,000 readers in 1920.

Owen continued his socialist organizing in the immediate postwar years. In 1919, he and Randolph founded the National Association for the Promotion of Labor Unionism Among Negroes in New York, a cooperative venture of white and black socialists. The group disbanded in the early 1920s. Owen ran for the New York state assembly on the Socialist Party ticket in 1920. He also emerged as an outspoken critic of Marcus Garvey and the Universal Negro Improvement Association, arguing that African Americans must pursue political and economic gains within the American system. In May 1920, in Washington, Owen and Randolph founded the Friends of Negro Freedom, which pushed the "Garvey must go" movement. In January 1923, the group published an open letter to U.S. Attorney General Harry M. Daugherty urging him to deport Garvey as an "undesirable alien."

Owen gradually grew disillusioned with socialism, and he resigned from *The Messenger* in 1923. Thereafter the newspaper continued under a new, more moderate leadership, later becoming an official publication of the Brotherhood of Sleeping Car Porters; it ceased publication in 1928. Owen relocated to Chicago in 1923. There, he worked as a managing editor of the *Chicago Bee*, a black newspaper loyal to the Republican Party, which Owen soon joined. Owen ran for the U.S. House of Representatives on the Republican ticket in 1928. During World War II, he published an important pamphlet, *Negroes and the War* (1942), on behalf of the War Department. He remained active in Republican politics for the remainder of his life. He died in Chicago in 1967.

Biography

Chandler Owen was born in Warrenton, North Carolina, 5 April 1889. He received a B.A. from Virginia Union University, Richmond, Virginia, 1913; he did further study at Columbia University and New York School of Philanthropy after 1913. He was editor, *Hotel Messenger*, 1917; editor, *The Messenger*, 1917–1928; and managing editor, *Chicago Bee*, after 1923. Owen was a candidate for the New York state assembly, 1920, and the U.S. House of Representatives, 1928. He died in Chicago, Illinois, 2 November 1967.

CHRISTOPHER CAPOZZOLA

See also Black Press; Garvey, Marcus; Journalists; Magazines and Journals; Messenger, The; Randolph, A. Philip; Universal Negro Improvement Association

Selected Works

Negroes and the War. 1942.
The Messenger: New Opinion of the New Negro. 1969. (Reprint ed.)

Further Reading

Anderson, Jervis. *A. Philip Randolph: A Biographical Portrait.* New York: Harcourt Brace Jovanovich, 1973.

Kornweibel, Theodore, Jr. *No Crystal Stair: Black Life and the Messenger, 1917–1928.* Westport, Conn.: Greenwood, 1975.

———. *Seeing Red: Federal Campaigns against Black Militancy, 1919–1925.* Bloomington: Indiana University Press, 1998.

Pfeffer, Paula. *A. Philip Randolph: Pioneer of the Civil Rights Movement.* Baton Rouge: Louisiana State University Press, 1990.

P

Pa Williams' Gal

Pa Williams' Gal (1923) is a play by Frank Wilson (1886–1956). Although Wilson is best remembered as a distinguished actor, he also had a career as a dramatist, which began while he was performing at the Lincoln Theater with the Anita Bush company (later the Lafayette Players). Between 1914 and 1923, Wilson produced several one-act plays for the company, but *Pa Williams' Gal* was his first full-length play, a three-act comedy-drama. It premiered at the Lafayette Theater on 10 September 1923. No extant script has been found, and plot synopses are few; however, the play revolved around the conflict between a father and daughter over whom the daughter would marry.

Theophilus Lewis reviewed *Pa Williams' Gal* for *The Messenger* (October 1923); he pronounced it "a rather dull comedy by F. H. Wilson and John J. Coincidence." According to Lewis, the play's saving grace was its "very good" dialogue and the performances by Richard B. Harrison as Pa Williams and Dolores Haskins as his daughter, with support from H. Lawrence Freeman, Morris McKenny, and Rosalie (Rose) McClendon. All were described as "grade A," with two exceptions: "Mr. Wilson, who plays the part of the lad with the heart of gold, appears to suffer from stage fright, and Marie Young seems to be in doubt whether she is portraying a character that is just fidgety or afflicted with St. Vitus' dance." But Lewis ended his review with a note of encouragement: "Here's hoping that the theme of Mr. Wilson's next play will be as good as the dialogue of this one" (846).

In the *Amersterdam News* two separate columns, one with the byline of the critic Romeo Doherty, were devoted to Wilson and *Pa Williams' Gal* on 5 September 1923, before the play opened. The unsigned column urged Harlem to support Wilson's efforts: "We understand that 'Pa Williams' Gal' has nothing sensational or spectacular about it, but just a simple little story from life—a play without preachment or propaganda. That should carry a strong appeal to our people, whose support we crave in behalf of one of the most worthy young men of color seeking name and fame on the stage today." Doherty, in response to a statement that Wilson had made concerning his preference for writing for a black audience, urged him to "think as an *American* and not simply as a colored man," if he wanted to produce the "great American drama."

Lewis returned to the subject of *Pa Williams' Gal* in *The Messenger* of November 1923, noting its value despite its flaws:

> If I were a committee of one, authorized to award a prize for the year's most valuable contribution to the Negro Theatre, I would reach over "Runnin Wild" and the venture of the Ethiopian Art Theatre and pin the blue ribbon on F. H. Wilson's "Pa Williams' Gal." I say this without any desire to change my opinion of the play. . . . "Pa Williams' Gal" misses the poignancy of life and for that reason is not first-rate work . . . but it does capture a mite of the romance, reverence and humor of life and it entraps a great deal of the striving upward, snobbery and absurd posturing we see going on around us every day. That is enough to make it a respectable contribution to the nascent Negro drama. . . . "Runnin Wild" and the Ethiopian Art Theatre give only acting. Now the Negro Theatre is a national theatre, just beginning a

struggle for independence.... Drama is the very bones and nerves of a national theatre; acting is only the greasepaint on its cheeks. (923–924)

FREDA SCOTT GILES

See also Amsterdam News; Anita Bush Theater Company; Harrison, Richard; Lafayette Theater; Lewis, Theophilus; Lincoln Theater; McClendon, Rose; Messenger, The; Wilson, Frank

Further Reading

Kellner, Bruce, ed. *The Harlem Renaissance: A Historical Dictionary for the Era*. Westport, Conn.: Greenwood Press, 1984.

Monroe, John Gilbert. "A Record of the Black Theatre in New York City: 1920–1929." Ph.D. diss., University of Texas at Austin, 1980.

Peterson, Bernard L. *Early Black American Playwrights and Dramatic Writers: A Biographical Directory and Catalog of Plays, Films, and Broadcasting Scripts*. New York: Greenwood, 1990.

Pace, Harry H.

By the onset of the Harlem Renaissance, Harry Pace had already established himself as a successful banker, insurance administrator, and lyricist. Pace and William Christopher Handy became partners in 1907, in Memphis, as songwriters and publishers. In 1912, Pace moved to Atlanta to become the secretary of Standard Life Insurance, leaving much of the day-to-day operation to Handy. By 1920, business had grown so much that Pace left Atlanta to join Handy in New York at the new headquarters. With Pace as president and Handy as secretary and treasurer, the company found great success with the sale of Handy's "Saint Louis Blues," which quickly became one of the most popular songs of the day. Yet the success was bittersweet, as Pace was upset that white owners of record companies bought black songs and recorded them with white rather than black artists.

In March 1921, Pace left Handy on amicable terms to set up the Pace Phonographic Corporation, with a $30,000 investment. The company would record and distribute records on the Black Swan label. Pace surrounded himself with extremely talented and successful individuals such as Fletcher Henderson (recording manager and pianist), William Grant Still (music director), and Ethel Waters (recording artist); his board of directors included his college professor and mentor W. E. B. Du Bois, the businessman John E. Nail, Dr. Matthew V. Boutte, and Mrs. Viola Bibb. The company recorded blues, jazz, art songs, spirituals, operatic arias, and instrumental pieces and advertised its product as "the only genuine colored record—others are only passing for colored." Business was excellent until the end of 1923, when Pace filed for bankruptcy as a result of the emerging popularity of radio, which was detrimental to the record industry and particularly to the small independent labels. Pace sold the Black Swan catalog to Paramount records in March 1924. According to the Chicago *Defender*, Pace's entrepreneurial savvy had "forced white recording companies to do three things: to recognize the vast Negro market for recordings, to release 'race catalogues,' and to advertise in Black newspapers."

Pace returned to a successful career in insurance. In 1925, he organized Northeastern Life Insurance Company in Newark, New Jersey; and in 1929, he merged Northeastern with Supreme Life Casualty of Columbus, Ohio, and Liberty Life Insurance of Chicago (one of the largest and more successful black firms) to form the new Supreme Liberty Life Insurance. Pace served as president and chief executive officer until his death in 1943.

During the renaissance Pace was an extremely vocal opponent of Marcus Garvey and Garvey's "back to Africa" movement. As a "committee of eight," Pace, Robert S. Abbott (publisher of the Chicago *Defender*), John E. Nail, and five other distinguished black leaders wrote a letter to the U.S. attorney general, Harry M. Daugherty, protesting against the numerous delays in Garvey's trial for mail fraud in 1922.

In addition to Pace's display of corporate leadership, he was a profound and influential author during this period, often commenting on blacks in insurance and the economy.

Biography

Harry Herbert Pace was born on 6 January 1884, in Covington, Georgia. He studied at Atlanta University in Georgia, receiving a B.A. (as valedictorian) in 1903; and graduated from Chicago (Illinois) Law School with a J.D. (cum laude) in 1933. Pace taught at Haines

Institute in Augusta, Georgia, 1903–1904; and was a professor of Latin and Greek at Lincoln Institute, Jefferson City, Missouri, 1906–1907. In Memphis, Tennessee, Pace managed *Moon Illustrated Weekly*, 1905–1906; was a cashier at Solvent Savings and Trust Bank, 1907–1912; and was a cofounder of Pace-Handy Music Company, 1907–1920. In Atlanta, Georgia, he was a secretary at Standard Life Insurance, 1912–1920. In New York City, Pace was president of Pace-Handy Music Company, 1920–1921; and president of Pace Phonograph Corporation, 1921–1924. In Newark, New Jersey, Pace was a cofounder and executive of the Northeastern Life Insurance Company, 1925–1929. In Chicago, he was president and chief executive officer of Supreme Liberty Life Insurance, 1929–1943. He was also a member of the National Negro Insurance Association: He was its president, 1928–1929; statistician, 1929–1930; and general counsel, 1934–1938. As a member of the Elks, he was its grand secretary, 1908; and grand exalted ruler, 1911–1913. Pace was elected to the Order of Lincoln (an honorary law school fraternity) in 1933. In 1935, he was appointed assistant counsel of the Illinois Commerce Commission and also elected a member of the diocesan council of the Protestant Episcopal Church (Chicago). He was a member of the national board of directors of the National Association for the Advancement of Colored People (NAACP) and the Chicago board of the National Urban League, and president of the Citizens Civic and Economic Welfare Council (Chicago). Pace died in Chicago on 26 July 1943.

EMMETT PRICE

See also Abbott, Robert Sengstacke; Black Swan Phonograph Company; Garvey, Marcus; Handy, W. C.; Henderson, Fletcher; Musicians; Nail, John E.; Pace Phonographic Corporation; Still, William Grant; Waters, Ethel

Selected Works

"The Attitude of Life Insurance Companies Toward Negroes." *Southern Workman*, January 1928; *Chicago Defender*, 4 May 1935.
"The Business of Insurance." *Messenger*, March 1927.
"The Possibilities of Negro Insurance." *Opportunity*, September 1930.
"Premium Income and Jobs." *Amsterdam News*, 1 October 1930.
Beginning Again. 1934. (Inspirational essays.)

Further Reading

Allen, Walter C. *Hendersonia: The Music of Fletcher Henderson and His Musicians: A Bio-Discography*. Highland Park, N.J., 1973.
Arthur, Desmond. "Pace, Harry H." In *The Harlem Renaissance: A Historical Dictionary of the Era*, ed. Bruce Kellner. Westport, Conn.: Greenwood, 1984.
Handy, William Christopher. *Father of the Blues: An Autobiography*, ed. Arna Bontemps. New York: Macmillan, 1951.
Ingham, John N., and Lynne B. Feldman. *African-American Business Leaders: A Biographical Dictionary*. Westport, Conn.: Greenwood, 1994.
Ottley, Roi, and William J. Weatherby, eds. *The Negro in New York: An Informal Social History, 1626–1940*. New York: Praeger, 1967.
Southern, Eileen. "Pace, Harry." In *The Greenwood Encyclopedia of Black Music: Biographical Dictionary of Afro-American and African Musicians*. Westport, Conn.: Greenwood, 1982.
Thygesen, Helge, Mark Beressford, and Russ Shor. *Black Swan: The Record Label of the Harlem Renaissance*. Nottingham: VJM, 1996.

Pace Phonographic Corporation

Harry Pace, a music publisher and musician, began his own music production and recording company in 1921 in Harlem; it was called Pace Phonographic Corporation. Pace decided that his label would be owned by black stockholders, run by black employees, and serve the black musical community. A unit of Pace Phonographic was Black Swan Records, named after Elizabeth Taylor Greenfield, a nineteenth-century concert singer known as the "black swan." Black Swan soon began releasing Pace's recordings.

Shortly after beginning his company, Pace hired the bandleader Fletcher Henderson, a rising star, to work for Black Swan Records as its recording director. Henderson worked closely with William Grant Still, who was hired as a music arranger and music director for Black Swan. In May 1921, Black Swan released its first record. The blues singer Ethel Waters was an important factor in the company's early success. Her song "Down Home Blues" was Black Swan's first hit and led to the formation of the Black Swan Troubadours, a musical group conducted by Henderson and featuring Waters; they later toured throughout the South promoting Black Swan.

In 1922, Pace bought the Olympic Disc Record Corporation in order to sell Black Swan's recordings—which were being created by both black and white artists—to both black and white communities. But when Pace decided to include white artists, many disappointed blacks protested against his acquisition of Olympic.

In 1923, the Pace Phonographic Corporation and Black Swan Records went bankrupt. Evidently, this was largely because Pace did not have a sufficient financial reserve to avoid being taken over by one of the larger recording companies, such as Paramount, which were owned and run by whites. By 1924, Paramount removed Harry Pace from the musical recording business when it bought out the Black Swan catalog of recordings.

ANNE ROTHFELD

See also Black Swan Phonograph Company; Henderson, Fletcher; Pace, Harry H.; Still, William Grant; Waters, Ethel

Further Reading

"Black Swan Records." (Africana Web site.)
Gioia, Ted. *The History of Jazz.* New York: Oxford University Press, 1997.
Kellner, Bruce, ed. *The Harlem Renaissance: A Historical Dictionary for the Era.* New York: Methuen, 1984.

Padmore, George

Malcolm Ivan Meredith Nurse, known to history as George Padmore, stands as one of the most influential figures in pan-Africanism and, paradoxically, as one of the most obscure. He was born in Trinidad—his birth date has been variously given as 1901, 1902, and 1904—and grew up in Port of Spain. He apparently came to his anti-imperialism early in life: His closest boyhood friend was C. L. R. James, another towering figure in the history of black radicalism.

Nurse completed secondary school in Trinidad and, after a hiatus of several years, continued his studies in the United States. Between 1924 and 1928, he studied at Columbia, Fisk, and Howard University Law School, but he devoted most of his energy to politics. He joined the Communist Party in about 1927, adopting Padmore, the name of a cousin, as a nom de guerre. With Richard B. Moore, another Caribbean radical, he launched a party newspaper in Harlem, *The Negro Champion*. (In an apt irony, the budding journalist supplemented his income by working as a janitor at the Times Building.)

Padmore's career as a communist was brief but eventful. Enrolling at a moment of intense internal debate over the "Negro question," he initially rose rapidly in the party ranks. In 1929, he moved to the Soviet Union, where he became head of the Profintern's new Negro Bureau, as well as a member of the Moscow City Soviet. (Unlike Langston Hughes, W. E. B. Du Bois, Claude McKay, and other African Americans feted by the Soviet Union, Padmore traveled without an American passport or reentry visa, and so was prevented from ever returning to the United States.) He traveled widely on party business, including at least one trip to Africa, but his primary base was Hamburg, Germany, where he oversaw the newly established International Trades Union Congress of Negro Workers (ITUC-NW) and edited the union's monthly organ, *The Negro Worker*.

Padmore's chief contribution to the Harlem Renaissance came through the agency of Nancy Cunard. Cunard probably first learned of Padmore through his book *The Life and Struggles of Negro Toilers*, published in 1931; they met in Paris a year later. Although utterly different in background and temperament, the frugal West Indian revolutionary and the avant-garde white heiress were united by their zeal for racial justice, as well as by loyalty to the Communist Party. By Cunard's account, Padmore was one of the two most important influences on her massive anthology, *The Negro* (1934), contributing four essays and a wealth of advice and contacts.

By the time *The Negro* appeared in 1934, Padmore had experienced a dramatic reversal of fortune. The accession of the Nazis in Germany led to the banning of the Communist Party and the wholesale arrest of party activists; Padmore spent several months in jail. At the same time, the Comintern, anxious to cultivate better relations with the Western powers as security against Hitler, ordered the suspension of all agitation against European imperialism. The ITUC-NW was disbanded. Padmore, unable to abide what he regarded as a rank betrayal of colonial peoples, immediately resigned his party offices. The party responded by formally expelling him and launching a campaign of vilification, in which he was branded as a racialist and petit bourgeois nationalist.

Padmore spent the ensuing decades in London. Although he had close relations with the leadership of the Independent Labour Party, he never again joined a movement led by whites; people of color must be responsible for their own liberation, he insisted. He remained a prolific writer, producing another half-dozen books, from *How Britain Rules Africa*, an anti-colonial primer published in 1936, to *Pan-Africanism or Communism: The Coming Struggle for Africa*, published in 1956, in which he made the case for a nonaligned Pan-African movement. He also founded the International African Service Bureau, intended as a kind of nerve center for a developing global anticolonial movement. The cluttered kitchen of his apartment on Cranleigh Street became a virtual seminar room for a generation of African nationalist leaders, including Kwame Nkrumah, the first prime minister of independent Ghana; and Jomo Kenyatta, Nkrumah's Kenyan counterpart.

If Padmore is remembered at all today, it is usually in relationship to Nkrumah. The two met in mid-1945, when Nkrumah arrived in London from the United States, bearing a letter of introduction from C. L. R. James. A few months later, they jointly convened the Fifth Pan-African Congress in Manchester. (It was a measure of both men's historical sensitivity that they bestowed the chairmanship of the meeting on W. E. B. Du Bois, who had built the congress a generation before.) Claims that Padmore orchestrated Nkrumah's rise to power are clearly exaggerated, but he was a formative influence on the future leader. One of Nkrumah's first acts after the coming of independence in 1957 was to invite Padmore to Ghana to serve as a special adviser on African affairs.

Padmore spent his last two years in Ghana. In September 1959, he flew to London to seek treatment for a diseased liver, the result of an earlier bout of hepatitis. He died a few days later. At Nkrumah's request, Padmore's ashes were returned to Ghana and interred at Christiansborg castle, a former slave fort that had become the seat of the new government. In 1992, they were reinterred on the grounds of the George Padmore Research Library, a research center in Accra devoted to Africa's struggle for independence.

Biography

Malcolm Ivan Meredith Nurse, also known as George Padmore, was born c. 1902 in Tacarigua, Trinidad. He studied at St. Mary's College of the Immaculate Conception, Port of Spain, Trinidad; Columbia University, New York City; Fisk University, Nashville, Tennessee; and Howard University Law School, Washington, D.C. Padmore joined the Communist Party c. 1927 and founded a party newspaper, *The Negro Champion*, based in Harlem. Padmore traveled to the Soviet Union in 1929, served on the Moscow City Soviet, and headed the Negro Bureau of the Red International of Labor Unions (Profintern). He moved to Hamburg, Germany, in 1930 to oversee the International Trades Union Congress of Negro Workers (ITUC-NW) and edit its monthly organ, *The Negro Worker*. Padmore collaborated with Nancy Cunard on *The Negro: An Anthology*. Padmore resigned from the Communist Party in 1934 and moved to London, where he founded the International Africa Services Bureau. He moved to Accra, Ghana, in 1957 to serve as special adviser on African affairs to Prime Minister Kwame Nkrumah. Padmore died in London on 23 September 1959.

JAMES CAMPBELL

See also Cunard, Nancy; Moore, Richard B.; Negro: An Anthology; Pan-African Congresses; Pan-Africanism

Selected Works

The Life and Struggles of Negro Toilers. 1931.
How Britain Rules Africa. 1936.
Africa and World Peace. 1937.
How Russia Transformed Her Colonial Empire: A Challenge to the Imperial Powers. 1946.
Africa: Britain's Third Empire. 1949.
The Gold Coast Revolution: The Struggle of an African People from Slavery to Freedom. 1953.
Pan-Africanism or Communism: The Coming Struggle for Africa. 1956.

Further Reading

Cunard, Nancy. *The Negro: An Anthology*. London: Ballantyne, 1934.

Hooker, James R. *Black Revolutionary: George Padmore's Path from Communism to Pan-Africanism*. London: Pall Mall, 1967.

James, C. L. R. *Nkrumah and the Ghana Revolution*. Westport, Conn.: Lawrence Hill, 1977.

———. "Notes on the Life of George Padmore." In *The C.L.R. James Reader*, ed. Anna Grimshaw. Oxford: Blackwell, 1992.

James, Winston. *Holding Aloft the Banner of Ethiopia: Caribbean Radicalism in Early Twentieth-Century America.* New York: Verso, 1998.

Palms

Published in Guadalajara, Mexico, *Palms* was a poetry magazine edited by Idella Purnell. *Palms* provided an outlet for both new and established poets. The magazine published poetry by several well-known writers of the Harlem Renaissance and is noted for a special issue of African American poets, edited by Countee Cullen, in 1926.

Idella Purnell was born in Guadalajara and raised there by her father, an American dentist. She attended high school and college in the United States, graduating from the University of California at Berkeley. She returned to Guadalajara to live with her father after graduation, and decided to publish a literary magazine as an outlet for her creativity. At Berkeley, Purnell took a class with the acclaimed poet Witter Bynner, who served as an associate and contributing editor of *Palms*. Bynner mentored Purnell in the publication and encouraged well-known poets to submit work to it.

The first number of *Palms* was published in the spring of 1923. In her inaugural editorial statement, Purnell emphasized that poetry submitted to the magazine would be judged on merit without regard to the reputation of the authors or the school or form of poetry submitted. In subsequent numbers, poems were published without the authors' names. A note explained that authors' names and works would be listed in the following issue. Issues were published six times per year.

In addition to publishing established poets such as Robinson Jeffers, Mark Van Doren, and Louis Untermeyer, Purnell published works by undergraduates, scholars, journalists, businessmen, and housewives in *Palms*. The first number announced two regular awards that would be offered in association with the magazine: a readers' choice prize for best poem published during the year and an annual prize, sponsored by Witter Bynner and the Poetry Society of America, for the best poem or group of poems by an undergraduate.

Countee Cullen won second place in the Bynner competition in 1923 and first place in 1925. He won the *Palms* readers' choice award for "Ballad of the Brown Girl" in 1924 and for "Wisdom Cometh with the Years" in 1925. Both Witter Bynner and Idella Purnell admired Cullen's poetry, and in the January 1926 issue of *Palms* (Volume 3, Number 4), Purnell announced that Cullen would edit a "Negro Poets' Number of the magazine." In addition to the announcement, this issue included two poems by Langston Hughes and a positive review of Cullen's book *Color*.

Cullen's thirty-two-page "Negro poets" issue of *Palms* appeared in October 1926 (Volume 4, Number 1). The issue featured seventeen African American authors including Cullen, Arna Bontemps, Albert Rice, Clarissa Scott, Georgia Douglas Johnson, William Stanley Braithwaite, Waring Cuney, Anne Spencer, Lewis Alexander, Jessie Redmon Fauset, W. E. B. Du Bois, Richard Bruce Nugent, Gwendolyn Bennett, Helene Johnson, and Langston Hughes. Walter White wrote "The Negro Renaissance," an introductory essay on the development of Negro poetry, and Alain Locke contributed a positive review of Langston Hughes's *The Weary Blues*. This special issue was a great success and sold out within a month after publication. Like the "Harlem number" of *Survey Graphic* in March 1925, the "Negro poets" number of *Palms* increased the exposure of black writers during the Harlem Renaissance by putting their work before readers of traditionally white magazines.

Although the circulation of *Palms* never surpassed 2,000, and the magazine never turned a profit, poets and critics respected it. Idella Purnell dealt with political and social upheaval in Mexico as well as the effects of the stock market crash of 1929. She edited and published the magazine from 1923 through 1930. She sold it in 1930, and further issues were published from 1936 until the final issue of March–April 1940.

HEATHER MARTIN

See also Color; Cullen, Countee; Hughes, Langston; Magazines and Journals; White, Walter; *other specific writers*

Further Reading

Johnson, Abby Arthur, and Ronald Maberry Johnson. *Propaganda and Aesthetics: The Literary Politics of Afro-American Magazines in the Twentieth Century.* Amherst: University of Massachusetts Press, 1979.

Potter, Vilma. "Idella Purnell's Palms and Godfather Witter Bynner." *American Periodicals*, 4, 1999.

Shucard, Alan R. *Countee Cullen*. Boston, Mass.: Twayne, 1984.

Wintz, Cary D. *Black Culture and the Harlem Renaissance*. Houston, Tex.: Rice University Press, 1988.

Pan-African Congresses

During the early twentieth century, a series of conferences were held on an irregular basis as Afro-American, Afro-Caribbean, and African intellectuals convened to discuss matters of common concern and racial solidarity. The first of these events, which helped conceptualize the term "pan-Africanism," took place in London in July 1900, but it was not included in the numbering sequence of subsequent events that became known as the first through fifth Pan-African Congresses. Thus, the first Pan-African Congress took place in London on 19–21 February 1919; the second occurred between 28 August and 5 September 1921, with sessions held in London, Paris, and Brussels; the third was held in 1923 with sessions in London (7–8 November) and Lisbon (25 November); the fourth took place on 21–24 August 1927 in New York City; and the fifth took place on 15–21 October 1945, in Manchester, England. These gatherings reflect a geopolitical manifestation of many political and cultural ideologies that characterized the Harlem Renaissance.

Henry Sylvester Williams (1869–1911), a Trinidadian lawyer practicing in London, was the driving force behind the initial pan-African conference that was held in London in 1900. In 1897, Williams had established a group among the West Indians living in England that he called the African League, and this organization provided an impetus for the conference in London. Delegates of color from the British empire, the United States, and non-British colonial Africa were invited to gather to discuss how joint action defined by racial solidarity might bring greater freedom to the people of Africa. Bishop Alexander Walters (1858–1917) of the African Methodist Episcopal Church in the United States chaired the plenary session of the London conference.

W. E. B. Du Bois (1868–1963) was the leader of the U.S. delegation attending the meeting in London in 1900. Even though he had not yet become a true convert to pan-Africanism, Du Bois was selected to chair the "Address to the Nations of the World" Committee. It was in this role that he drafted a manifesto stating: "The problem of the twentieth century is the problem

of the color line" (Sundquist 1996, 100). He would later repeat the idea as a running theme in *The Souls of Black Folk* (1903).

Following the deaths of Williams and Walters, Du Bois became the effective leader of the incipient pan-African cause, and he decided to reenergize the movement by holding more regular meetings to consider the state of affairs in Africa and determine what course of action persons of color should take to advance the cause of self-rule there. The series of congresses that followed—all of which were specifically organized under the umbrella of pan-Africanism— are the sequentially numbered events of 1919, 1921, 1923, 1927, and 1945.

Du Bois organized the First Pan-African Congress, which was held in February 1919, to coincide with the postwar diplomatic conference in Paris that negotiated the Treaty of Versailles. The organizers of the congress believed that the rhetoric of national self-determination, especially that previously articulated by Woodrow Wilson in his Fourteen Points, might move the western European nations to consider a policy of decolonization in Africa. Because African colonial troops had supported the victorious Allied cause during World War I (1914–1918), the advocates of pan-Africanism believed that their call for home rule was justifiable as a means of equitable compensation for services rendered.

Du Bois had managed to obtain permission from the French government to hold the event in Paris through the intercession of Blaise Diagne, a member of the French chamber of deputies from Senegal. In addition to the French support, the governments of Belgium and Portugal officially recognized the event and sent representatives, but the United States and Great Britain did not sanction the meeting. In the end, fifty-seven delegates from fifteen nations attended the conference.

The Second Pan-African Congress (1921) is generally recognized as being the most radical of the gatherings. This event concluded on 29 August 1921, with the promulgation of a document titled "Declaration to the World" but more commonly known as the "London manifesto." The delegates charged that

> England, with all her Pax Britannica, her courts of justice, established commerce, and a certain apparent recognition of Native laws and customs, has nevertheless systematically fostered ignorance among the Natives, has enslaved them, and is still enslaving them, has usually declined even to try to train black

and brown men in real self-government, to recognise civilised black folk as civilised, or to grant to coloured colonies those rights of self government which it freely gives to white men. (Sundquist, 642–643)

Attendance waned at both the Third Pan-African Congress (1923) and the Fourth Pan-African Congress (1927), leading, in part, to the hiatus in further meetings until the end of World War II in 1945. Plans to hold a congress in the West Indies in 1925 were tabled for lack of interest. Nonetheless, delegates attending the meetings in 1923 and 1927 continued their call for decolonization and home rule in Africa, and also extended their concerns to include alarm at the rise of vigilantism and lynching within the United States. Delegates also tried to persuade the League of Nations to pursue the goals of the pan-Africanist movement.

The Fifth Pan-African Congress (1945) in Manchester, England, would prove to be the most consequential of these events. Ninety delegates attended, including twenty-six from Africa who would come to represent a "who's who" of postindependence African leadership. The "Manchester manifesto" that emerged from this meeting represented a passing of the torch of leadership from those pan-Africanists outside Africa to a young generation of pan-Africanist intellectuals within Africa. African delegates, including Kwame Nkrumah and Jomo Kenyatta, agreed that the promise of decolonization and home rule in Africa would arise only when African leaders internalized the pan-African struggle and effectively ended the colonial domination of Africa by external powers.

JUNIUS P. RODRIGUEZ

See also Du Bois, W. E. B.; Pan-Africanism

Further Reading

Adi, Hakim, Marika Sherwood, and George Padmore. *The 1945 Manchester Pan-African Congress Revisited.* London: New Beacon, 1995.

Allen, Marie Bouknight. "W. E. B. Du Bois and the Pan-African Congresses, 1919–1927." Master's thesis, University of South Carolina, 1974.

Mathurin, Owen Charles. *Henry Sylvester Williams and the Origins of the Pan-African Movement, 1869–1911.* Westport, Conn.: Greenwood, 1976.

Owugah, Lemuel. "The Manchester Pan-African Congress: A Turning Point in the Pan-African Movement." Master's thesis, San Jose State College, 1971.

Padmore, George, and W. E. B. Du Bois. *Colonial and Coloured Unity: A Programme of Action—History of the Pan-African Congress.* Manchester: Pan-African Federation, 1945.

Pobi-Asamani, Kwadwo O. *W. E. B. Du Bois: His Contribution to Pan Africanism.* San Bernadino, Calif.: Borgo, 1994.

Sundquist, Eric J., ed. *The Oxford W. E. B. Du Bois Reader.* New York: Oxford University Press, 1996.

Pan-Africanism

The ideology of pan-Africanism—one of the most significant intellectual trends of the Harlem Renaissance era—was a complex belief system that sought to unify persons of color to aspire to a calling beyond their own parochial interests. Pan-Africanists were expected to be color-conscious citizens of the world who would racially self-actualize their own experience and simultaneously deliver Africa from the hands of its colonial oppressors.

Intellectual antecedents of twentieth-century pan-Africanism can be found in the notions of black nationalism that were first articulated in the nineteenth century by leaders such as Martin R. Delany and Alexander Crummell. A strand of this self-reliant ideology would permeate the rhetoric of subsequent twentieth-century leaders such as Marcus Garvey and Malcolm X. Elements of the self-help philosophy remain popular among present-day pan-Africanists.

The essential doctrine of pan-Africanism was built on the premise that people of color shared a unique cultural and historical experience, regardless of their geographic circumstances, which bound them as kinfolk to the peoples of Africa. In such a worldview, the horrors of four centuries of transatlantic slavery, the resultant diaspora, and the subsequent yoke of colonialism that had been foisted on Africa by the hand of western Europeans were sufficient cause to unify peoples of color into a force that would work for social justice. Chief among the goals of pan-Africanists was the decolonization of Africa and the establishment of home rule—the basic idea that Africa should belong to the Africans.

Many of the strategies and tactics used by pan-Africanists borrowed heavily from the successful methods applied by abolitionists on both sides of the Atlantic to bring an end to slavery during the nineteenth century. Adopting a policy of moral suasion that was punctuated by the twin means of education and agitation, the pan-Africanists, much like their earlier abolitionist brethren, sought to fight evil with ideas. Yet unlike the abolitionist crusade, which had biracial support throughout its long history, the pan-Africanist movement was exclusively black. Additionally, the pan-Africanists found little support for their efforts from national governments that often considered their motives suspect.

Many of the ideological origins of the concept of pan-Africanism are found in the West Indies. The phrase was first articulated by Henry Sylvester Williams (1869–1911), a Trinidadian lawyer who had studied in Canada and was practicing in London. In 1897, Williams established an organization, which he called the African League, among his fellow West Indians living in England. Williams and the African League would be the driving force behind the initial pan-African conference that was held in London in July 1900.

In addition to Williams's involvement, a literary movement known as *négritude* that had developed among writers in the French West Indies also supported the ideals of pan-Africanism. Writers such as Aimé Césaire, Léon Damas, and Léopold Senghor began to produce literary works with a decidedly anticolonial sensibility. These authors criticized Europeans for their plunder of Africa's resources and their stifling control of African peoples. The authors also wrote with a sense of pride that celebrated African cultures and peoples for glorious traditions and history.

During the twentieth century the work of two individuals became synonymous with the cause of pan-Africanism. The Trinidadian author George Padmore became known to many as the "father of pan-Africanism," and in the United States W. E. B. Du Bois became the leading advocate of the pan-African crusade. Du Bois became the chief organizer of a series of five Pan-African Congresses that were held between 1919 and 1945. Padmore and Du Bois shared both nationalist and an internationalist visions of the political and cultural transformations pan-Africanism might generate, and as a result, both men became increasingly attracted to the doctrines of socialism and communism. Padmore and Du Bois would both spend their final years living in Ghana once that west African nation received its independence during the era of decolonization.

The issue of pan-Africanism became rather complicated in the United States during the Harlem Renaissance. Two different movements, each germinated from the same ideological seed of black nationalism and pan-Africanism, competed for the minds and hearts of African Americans. Each would develop its own constituency, and for a time, the two movements seemed to operate mutually exclusively.

Marcus Garvey organized the Universal Negro Improvement Association (UNIA) in 1914 and began a campaign promoting self-help for blacks and advocating racial pride. Garvey's message appealed to the black working masses whose population swelled in America's urban industrial centers as a result of the great migration. Garvey's later support of a "back to Africa" scheme attracted fewer adherents, but his strident rhetoric emphasized the cultural distinctiveness of African Americans as a nation within a nation. Du Bois's message of pan-Africanism was more appealing to middle-class intellectuals. In his view the primary objectives of the pan-African movement included the cultural regeneration of African Americans in their adopted land and an associated, concerted effort by racially conscious African Americans to become the social vanguard that would bring freedom and home rule to their colonized brethren in Africa.

The allure of Garveyism faded in the 1920s after its leader was convicted of mail fraud, imprisoned, and deported, but these events did not generate many converts to Du Bois's message of pan-Africanism. Even for those African Americans who were willing to accept an ideology of color-consciousness and advocacy, the continent of Africa was still a distant, dimly perceived place that had little real connection to their world. Pan-Africanists may have been genuinely sincere in their desired goals, but the practical dimension of how they would achieve their objectives lacked clarity. When the Fifth Pan-African Congress was held in Manchester, England, in 1945, a new generation of African-born pan-African leaders came to realize that the success or failure of their movement would rest on the sense of urgency and purpose that they brought to the cause. This cadre of pan-Africanists, including notable leaders Kwame Nkrumah and Jomo Kenyatta, would become the agents of change who delivered independence and home rule to much of Africa.

Junius P. Rodriguez

See also Césaire, Aimé; Damas, Léon; Du Bois, W. E. B.; Garvey, Marcus; Negritude; Padmore, George;

Pan-African Congresses; Senghor, Léopold; Universal Negro Improvement Association

Further Reading

Allen, Marie Bouknight. "W. E. B. Du Bois and the Pan-African Congresses, 1919–1927." Master's thesis, University of South Carolina, 1974.

Mathurin, Owen Charles. *Henry Sylvester Williams and the Origins of the Pan-African Movement, 1869–1911.* Westport, Conn.: Greenwood, 1976.

Owugah, Lemuel. "The Manchester Pan-African Congress: A Turning Point in the Pan-African Movement." Master's thesis, San Jose State College, 1971.

Padmore, George, and W. E. B. Du Bois. *Colonial and Coloured Unity: A Programme of Action—History of the Pan-African Congress.* Manchester: Pan-African Federation, 1945.

Pobi-Asamani, Kwadwo O. *W. E. B. Du Bois: His Contribution to Pan Africanism.* San Bernadino, Calif.: Borgo, 1994.

Party Politics

"I know the negroes better than they know themselves. You couldn't drive them out of the Republican Party with a sledgehammer." With this comment, Lemuel Eli Quigg, a Republican leader in New York, became an even more effective tool than the one to which he referred. A group of black politicians, led by James Carr and Edward "Chief" Lee, had approached Quigg, in late 1897, because they felt that blacks deserved more patronage—jobs—as a reward for their profound loyalty to the Republican Party. Not satisfied with Quigg's response, the black group then met with Richard Croker, leader of Tammany Hall, the Democratic political machine in Manhattan. The group left the meeting with Croker with the understanding that they would be rewarded commensurately with the number of black votes they delivered to the Democrats.

In January 1898, Carr, Lee and others formed the first black Democratic Party organization in the country, United Colored Democracy, a segregated unit of Tammany, responsible for all the black wards in the city. Croker was sufficiently satisfied with their efforts that Carr, a graduate of Rutgers and Columbia Law, was appointed to a position in the corporation counsel's office.

Lee, who was reportedly illiterate, received an appointment in the sheriff's office.

In 1905, Theodore Roosevelt appointed Charles William Anderson—a native of Oxford, Ohio, who was a supporter of Booker T. Washington and was active in the New York Republican Party—to be collector of Internal Revenue for the Second District of New York, which included the Wall Street district. T. Thomas Fortune wrote in *New York Age*, "No other president has given an appointment of that high character in the domestic service in the North to an Afro-American." Anderson served in that position until he was removed by Woodrow Wilson in 1915. In 1923, President Warren G. Harding appointed Anderson to the equivalent post in the Third District.

Between 1920 and 1930, the black population of Harlem increased by 150 percent, while the total population decreased by 4 percent. The increase was largely a result of in-migration. Between 1930 and 1940, the black population of Harlem increased by 41 percent, while the total population increased by 8 percent. In this case, natural increase was at least as important as in-migration.

The "assembly district," from which delegates were elected to the state legislature, was the basic unit of political organization in New York. During the Harlem Renaissance, "black Harlem" was divided, evenly, between two assembly districts—the Nineteenth, with a sizable Jewish population, and the Twenty-first, populated by a large Irish American community. Not until 1920 did blacks make up 50 percent of the population of any assembly district. By 1930, blacks had come to represent 70 percent of the population in each district, but "population" did not translate directly into political power. For the early decades of the twentieth century, the Afro-American community in Harlem had a choice, in national politics, between a Democratic Party seemingly dominated by plantation culture and by the Ku Klux Klan, and a Republican Party that took blacks for granted while following a "lily-white" southern strategy. At the local level, however, black people in Harlem benefited from lively two-party politics.

Although he was a card-carrying member of New York Local No. 1 of the Socialist Party, W. E. B. Du Bois considered the election of 1912 so important that black support for Eugene V. Debs, the Socialist presidential candidate, would be a waste. For Du Bois, the four years of the Taft administration had been disastrous. For the first time since the Civil War, the Republic Party platform of 1912 was silent on the Fourteenth and

Fifteenth amendments. For a few weeks, in *The Crisis*, Du Bois explored the possibility of supporting Theodore Roosevelt's Progressive or Bull Moose Party. But at the convention of the Progressive Party in Chicago, Roosevelt was more interested in gaining the support of white southerners than of African Americans. The convention denied seats to most black delegates and ignored a "civil rights" platform plank written by Du Bois and introduced by Joel Spingarn.

Despite mixed messages from the Democratic candidate, Woodrow Wilson, Du Bois and others convinced themselves that a Wilson administration would play fair with African Americans, and this was communicated to the black community in the pages of *The Crisis*. Some 100,000 African Americans voted Democratic in the presidential election of 1912, and lived to regret it.

In the first two decades of the twentieth century, party politics in Harlem consisted of a few self-appointed leaders delivering black votes to the Democratic and Republican parties in exchange for patronage appointments. About 1914, John M. Royall founded the United Civic League. Royall was very successful in the real estate and insurance businesses and, following the example of Philip Payton, participated in opening Harlem's real estate market to blacks. When he and a group of associates were denied a banking charter, Royall came to the conclusion that for economic power to develop, it had to be supported by political power.

The objective of the United Civic League was to make the transition from "appointive representation" to "elective representation"—from receiving patronage to being in a position to hand it out. The first documented black candidate for political office in New York was John M. Royall, in 1913; he was an unsuccessful candidate for the board of aldermen. Although in 1912 Royall had supported Theodore Roosevelt and the Progressive Party, most of the individuals identified with the United Civic League, including Fred R. Moore, the editor of *New York Age*, were Republicans. It was not until 1917 that a black man, Edward Austin Johnson, was nominated for public office by a regular district political organization. Johnson, nominated by the United Civic League, was the successful Republican candidate from Harlem's Nineteenth Assembly District, defeating, among others, A. Philip Randolph, who was running on the Socialist ticket. Johnson had been active in Republican politics in his native North Carolina and had been a professor of law and a dean at Shaw University in Raleigh. African Americans in North Carolina were disenfranchised in 1900 and pushed out of the Republican Party in 1902. Johnson moved to New York, in 1907, as part of the prewar migration of the "talented tenth."

A year after Johnson's election from the Nineteenth District, John C. Hawkins, an African American, was elected as a Republican to the state assembly from the Twenty-first District. It appears that Harlemites, like most Americans in the 1920s, became disillusioned with politics. Enjoying the relative prosperity of the war era but angry at the treatment of black soldiers during and after the war, black people in Harlem experimented with socialism, communism, black nationalism, and variations on Islam. At the very moment when the "Jazz Age" met the "New Negro" to form the Harlem Renaissance, politics in Harlem descended into corruption, venality, and gangsterism.

Walter (1989), writing in the voice of J. Raymond Jones, the first black "Tammany boss," explains that

> indigenous northern Blacks had, for the most part, become disenchanted with politics by World War I. The situation worsened when large numbers of southern Blacks, who were even more disillusioned by the political process, came north. "Why should I vote," I remember them asking. "What has politics done for me?" they would ask in righteous indignation as they slammed the door in my face. The answer lay in what politics *could* do, but by this time most New York City Blacks had developed a near-contemptuous attitude toward politicians.

As a West Indian, Jones could not understand that, for southern blacks, politics was a dangerous business.

Writing in 1940, the political scientist Ralph Bunche found that in the days before black folk moved to Harlem, black politics was divided along class lines. The "better element," led by their preachers, were Republicans. The "sporting house" crowd, led by saloon keepers, hotel proprietors, and such, were often Democrats. Black support for the Republican Party is usually explained as loyalty to the party of Abraham Lincoln and post–Civil War emancipation. But in New York, the story began in 1799, when emancipation was a local issue. At the end of the eighteenth century, the Federalists were the party of New York's elite, including the leadership of the Manumission Society, who succeeded in passing a law calling for the gradual emancipation of enslaved New Yorkers.

By the early twentieth century, the political culture of the Federalists had passed down to the present-day Republicans. The opposition party, which evolved into the present-day Democrats, was the party of small tradesmen, mechanics, and workmen. These "Democrats" opposed the emancipation of the slaves, in part because they feared competition from freed black laborers who would have historical and sentimental ties to elite Federalists. Three hundred black votes provided the balance of power, in favor of the Federalists, in the election of 1813 in New York. As a consequence, the "Democrats" pushed a bill through the state legislature in 1821 that largely disenfranchised New York's black voters. The African American franchise was not restored until the Fifteenth Amendment to the U.S. Constitution was ratified, in 1870.

After he was charged with mail fraud by the federal government, Marcus Garvey encouraged his followers to take an interest in national politics. According to Ottley and Weatherby (1967):

> He encouraged his West Indian followers to become naturalized, so that they could vote. He supported Coolidge for President, and Tammany Hall locally; he backed a white Democrat, Royal H. Weller, for Congress, against a Negro Republican, Dr. E. P. Roberts [sic]. Alfred E. Smith and Mayor John F. Hylan spoke at Liberty Hall during the fall campaign of 1924.

When Weller came up for reelection in 1924, Republicans again nominated Dr. *Charles* Roberts to oppose him. The National Association for the Advancement of Colored People (NAACP) rejected Roberts on the ground that he was a "reactionary," and Weller was reelected.

The "Tammany boss" J. Raymond Jones, a native of the U.S. Virgin Islands, had arrived in Harlem in 1917. In 1920, Jones joined Marcus Garvey's Universal Negro Improvement Association (UNIA) and began a long association with Ulysses Simpson Poston, who was in charge of most of the UNIA's business ventures other than the Black Star Line. The decline of the UNIA coincided with the decision by Tammany Hall to drop the two-term mayor "Honest John" Francis Hylan from the mayoral ticket. The man appointed by Tammany to replace Hylan was a state senator and songwriter, James J. "Jimmy" Walker.

When he was reelected in 1921, Hylan received three-fourths of the black vote. To hold on to his job, in 1925, Hylan organized his campaign around the issue of retaining the five-cent subway fare. Ulysses Poston and his protégé J. Raymond Jones formed the Hylan Five-Cent Fare Club of Harlem. Thus began the political career of the young West Indian immigrant who would rise to the leadership of Tammany in 1963. Hylan won Harlem but lost the primary to Walker. Through his connections to the Hylan campaign, Jones was hired as a "redcap" (porter) at Pennsylvania Station, and he and his acquaintances from the UNIA became the nucleus of a group of young, largely West Indian "new Democrats," who would work in politics in Harlem in opposition to the largely "indigenous" United Colored Democracy.

The black migration toward the Democratic Party was accelerated by the election of Jimmy Walker. During his campaign for mayor in 1925, in a speech in Harlem, Walker said: "I won't do a thing for Negroes. Nor will I do anything for Jews or Irishmen. But as mayor of this great city, I will work for the people." According to Claude McKay (1940):

> Negroes in Harlem regarded that stand as an expression of an equalitarian principle which Negro leaders seemed proud to hear. As a consequence of that speech, along with other considerations shown them, a large number of Negroes went Democratic and remained Democrats ever since.

During Walker's administration, a new building was constructed for the 369th Infantry, Harlem's much-decorated National Guard unit. Fred Moore, editor of *New York Age* and a Republican leader who cooperated with Walker, took much of the credit for this building and for a new police station built on 135th Street. Bunche (1973) reports that virtually every officer of the 369th held a federal, state, or city appointment, although most of these officers were Republicans. During Walker's administration, the number of blacks on the city payrolls increased from 247 to 2,275.

In 1925, during the Walker administration, five black physicians were appointed, for the first time, to the regular staff of Harlem General Hospital, and a training school for black nurses was created there. In 1930, the Walker administration reorganized the hospital, removing all racial barriers. By 1932, there were seventy black interns and physicians working there.

Despite misgivings, Walter White of the NAACP encouraged African Americans to vote for Al Smith, former Democratic governor of New York, in the presidential election of 1928. Smith, who had close ties to

Tammany Hall, had campaigned vigorously in Harlem when running for state office, but in his campaign for the presidency, he seemed concerned about alienating potential southern support. He received 28 percent of the vote in Harlem in 1928.

In 1930, Governor Franklin D. Roosevelt of New York and the state legislature created four new judgeships for Manhattan, two of them in Harlem. The assumption in the legislature was that the two judges in Harlem would be Republicans. Aware of the trend away from the Republican Party, Jones and the "new Democrats" decided to cooperate with the United Colored Democracy to elect black Democrats instead. James S. Watson, a West Indian, the candidate of the "new Democrats"; and Charles Toney, a law partner of the United Colored Democracy's leader Ferdinand Q. Morton, were elected. This cooperation with the United Colored Democracy strengthened the "new Democrats" and enhanced their sense of themselves as the future of Harlem politics.

In 1928, the Republican candidate for president received 66 percent of the black vote in New York. In 1932, the Republican received only 46 percent.

In 1915, the year Booker T. Washington died, Ferdinand Q. Morton, who had been educated at Harvard, assumed leadership of the United Colored Democracy. In 1919, Charles F. Murphy, who succeeded Richard Croker as boss of Tammany, appointed Morton as assistant district attorney. Morton reigned over black Democratic politics in New York until the liberal Republican Fiorello La Guardia was elected mayor in 1933. With no access to patronage under La Guardia's American Labor Party administration, the United Colored Democracy went out of business. Morton accepted La Guardia's offer of a position on the Civil Service Commission in exchange for breaking his ties with Tammany and the Democratic Party. Liberated from Morton's dictatorship, the Democrats of Harlem took control of the local political organizations away from the old white bosses, who in turn had been contolled by Tammany. The Nineteenth Assembly District fell in 1935 and the Twenty-first in 1939.

ROBERT HINTON

See also Crisis, The; Du Bois, W. E. B.; Fifteenth Infantry; Garvey, Marcus; Harlem General Hospital; Moore, Frederick Randolph; Morton, Ferdinand Q.; New York Age; Politics and Politicians; Spingarn, Joel; United Colored Democracy; Universal Negro Improvement Association

Further Reading

Bunche, Ralph J. *The Political Status of the Negro in the Age of FDR.* Chicago, Ill.: NT University of Chicago Press, 1973.

Greenberg, Cheryl Lynn. *"Or Does It Explode?" In Black Harlem in the Great Depression.* New York: Oxford University Press, 1991.

Hamilton, Charles V. *Adam Clayton Powell, Jr.: The Political Biography of an American Dilemma.* New York: Atheneum, 1991.

Lewis, David Levering. *W. E. B. Du Bois: Biography of a Race, 1868–1919.* New York: Holt, 1993.

McKay, Claude. *Harlem: Negro Metropolis.* New York: Dutton, 1940.

Moon, Harvey. *Balance of Power: The Negro Vote.* New York: Doubleday, 1948.

Morsell, John Albert. "The Political Behavior of Negroes in New York City." Ph.D. diss., Columbia University, 1950.

Osofsky, Gilbert. *Harlem: The Making of a Ghetto—Negro New York, 1890–1930.* Chicago: Ivan R. Dee, 1996. (Originally published 1963.)

Ottley, Roi, and William J. Weatherby, eds. *The Negro in New York: An Informal Social History, 1626–1940.* New York: Praeger, 1967.

Sherman, Richard B. *The Republican Party and Black America from McKinley to Hoover, 1896–1933.* Chattottesville: University Press of Virginia, 1973.

Walter, John C. *The Harlem Fox: J. Raymond Jones and Tammany, 1920–1970.* Albany: State University of New York (SUNY) Press, 1989.

Weiss, Nancy J. *Farewell to the Party of Lincoln: Black Politics in the Age of FDR.* Princeton: Princeton University Press, 1983.

Passing

"Passing," often associated with "masquerade," occurs when an individual assumes an identity different from what his culture understands to be his or her "real," biologically determined identity. For instance, in "gender passing," a woman may assume a male identity and live the sociocultural role of a man, as the jazz musician Billy (Dorothy) Tipton did. Dorothy Tipton began passing as a man when she entered the jazz scene in the 1930s; she married several times, adopted a child, and lived publicly as a man for the last fifty-four years of her life. As this example suggests, passing challenges the idea that identity markers such as gender and race are innate biological categories;

it indicates, rather, that physical appearance is unreliable and that performance is an important aspect of identity. In other words, passing suggests that categories such as gender and race are ideological, culture-specific constructions.

Although gender passing was a known phenomenon during the Harlem Renaissance, the term "passing" was more often used in the context of race. In the United States, racial classifications are traditionally made by assigning significance to specific phenotypical characteristics (such as skin color, hair texture, and facial features). Also important is an individual's racial heritage (the legal racial classification of his or her progenitors). Racial passing can occur when a person who is legally classified as a member of a particular race does not exhibit the physical characteristics typically associated with it. For instance, in the United States a person with an African American parent or grandparent, or even a single African American great-grandparent, was historically legally classified as "black" under the notorious "one drop rule." However, as a result of "interracial" procreation (what white supremacist pseudoscientists called "miscegenation" or "amalgamation"), legally black people can be physically white. That is, even though a person may be legally, psychologically, or socially African American, he or she may also have "white" skin and, say, blond hair and green eyes. Because the American racial system is largely based on visual clues, such a person will not be recognized as black and may function within the culture as "white" as long as his or her African American heritage is publically unknown. Similarly, legally white people could be mistaken for, or live by choice as, African Americans. However, given the legal and socioeconomic implications for African Americans under slavery and then under Jim Crow and segregation, most recorded racial passing has been from black to white. For example, before the Civil War, notices about escaped slaves testify that some African Americans took advantage of their light skin and "white" features to free themselves by passing as white. During Reconstruction, "redemption," and the rise and heyday of Jim Crow, some light-skinned African Americans passed in order to gain socioeconomic advantages that white cultural practices and laws prohibited them from attaining as blacks. The reasons that might motivate an individual to pass are innumerable, and because passing by its very nature obscures legal racial identity, it is impossible to know how many African Americans "crossed the color line."

As scholars and "ex-passers" have been quick to note, however, passing could come with a high price.

Many blacks passed as white only during their work hours, but for others, passing meant ending all communication with black relatives and friends. Furthermore, passers were often haunted by the threat of exposure and suffered under a burden of necessary silence when encountering a black family member or friend. Additionally, to avoid suspicion, passers often had to remain silent on racial issues, especially when they were involved in conversations that elicited or encouraged expressions of white supremacy or racism. Such reticence sometimes led to feelings of remorse for the loss of their black community or guilt over "abandoning their race." Still, passing was at some level satisfying because it remained a way to fool whites and to expose the myths of biologically based racial inequality.

The sacrifice, denial, tension, and subversiveness surrounding passing made excellent material for authors. Although some novels about passing were written to support ideas of innate biologically based racial inequality, most such novels debunked biological theories. Incorporating passing into a plot gave an author a way to expose the illusion of separate, biologically distinct, unequal races that "mix" through "amalgamation." Some authors represented passing as righteous for and advantageous to a character who had been raised as white and had little or no connection to blacks; these authors scoffed at the "one-drop rule" that defined such a person as black. Other authors, though, represented passing as an act of betrayal to "the race," regardless of how remote a character's connection to black people might be. Given the prominence of racial uplift as an ideology at the turn of the twentieth century, it is not surprising that many authors rejected passing as a way to form one's identity. Such an author would emphasize that to be "successful," people—even light-skinned people—who were legally black had a responsibility to cast their lot with African Americans and apply their own abilities to improve the condition of all.

By the 1920s, passing was a well-established literary theme, entwined with the socioeconomic and political discussions of the day. Several black authors (some of whom were being supported by white patrons) were influenced by W. E. B. Du Bois's concept of the "talented tenth" and Alain Locke's concept of the "New Negro" and accordingly took up the idea of passing in their narratives and treated it in various ways to reflect those concepts. In their works, passing may be used to protest against the idea of innate biological inequality, to claim a positive black identity, to consider how identity and race are entangled (and try to disentangle them), to assert the responsibility of African Americans to "the race," to expose the effects of white racism on African Americans, or to reject "race" as a significant marker of identity—or to achieve any combination of these purposes. These authors included Langston Hughes, James Weldon Johnson, Jessie Redmon Fauset, Nella Larsen, George S. Schuyler, Jean Toomer, and Walter White.

Although passing to some extent reinforces the ideological categories of race and gender by invoking boundaries that passers "transgress," passing has historically suggested that categories of identity such as gender and race are a matter of performance or social construction. By representing gender and race as performed rather than biologically determined, passing illustrates how people subjugated by and within rigid sociopolitical systems of racial and gender classification could and did manipulate those systems.

JULIE CARY NERAD

See also Fauset, Jessie Redmon; Hughes, Langston; Johnson, James Weldon; Larsen, Nella; Passing: Novel; Schuyler, George S.; Toomer, Jean; White, Walter

Further Reading

Bennett, Juda. *The Passing Figure: Racial Confusion in Modern American Literature.* New York: Peter Lang, 1996.

Browder, Laura. *Slippery Characters: Ethnic Impersonators and American Identities.* Chapel Hill and London: University of North Carolina Press, 2000.

Butler, Judith. "Passing, Queering: Nella Larsen's Psychoanalytic Challenge." In *Bodies That Matter: On the Discursive Limits of Sex.* New York and London: Routledge, 1993.

Fabi, M. Giulia. *Passing and the Rise of the African American Novel.* Urbana and Chicago: University of Illinois Press, 2001.

Ginsberg, Elaine K., ed. *Passing and the Fictions of Identity.* Durham, N.C., and London: Duke University Press, 1996.

Gubar, Susan. *Race Changes: White Skin, Black Face in American Culture.* New York and Oxford: Oxford University Press, 1997.

Middlebrook, Diane Wood. *Suits Me: The Double Life of Billy Tipton.* Boston, Mass., and New York: Houghton Mifflin, 1998.

Sánchez, Maria Carla, and Linda Schlossberg, eds. *Passing: Identity and Interpretation in Sexuality, Race, and Religion.* New York and London: New York University Press, 2001.

Sollors, Werner. *Neither Black nor White Yet Both: Thematic Explorations of Interracial Literature.* New York: Oxford University Press, 1997.

Wald, Gayle. *Crossing the Line: Racial Passing in Twentieth-Century U.S. Literature and Culture.* Durham, N.C., and London: Duke University Press, 2000.

Passing: Novel

Nella Larsen's novel *Passing* (1929) addresses a dominant theme of African American fiction in the 1920s: the experience of light-skinned blacks who crossed the color line and "passed" for white. Larsen explores, in unusual depth, the psyche of her mixed-race female protagonist—in contrast to male writers of the time, who tended to reduce such a character to an exotic, primitive stereotype. Larsen's setting also offers a complex picture of Harlem during the Jazz Age, as a place where the black and white elite gathered for charity dances, teas, and cocktail parties.

Passing presents a series of encounters between two middle-class, light-skinned African American women, who are often seen as doubles: Irene Redfield, who occasionally passes for white but claims loyalty to her dark-skinned husband and children; and her childhood friend, Clare Kendry, who has permanently crossed the color line and married Jack Bellew, a wealthy white man who is unaware of his wife's racial identity. Clare attempts to return to her racial roots by entering Irene's social circle, but at the same time she wants to keep her identity a secret from her racist husband. *Passing* is both a statement on African American "double consciousness"—a phrase coined by W. E. B. Du Bois to describe the duality of black identity—and an important commentary on the social construction of race.

Although *Passing* was highly praised by reviewers for its exploration of the psychology of racial passing, it faded into obscurity—along with its author, whose writing career effectively ended when she was accused of plagiarizing a short story in 1930. Like Larsen's only other novel, *Quicksand* (1928), *Passing* was rediscovered in the 1970s and was recognized, in particular, for its treatment of female sexuality. McDowell (1986) suggests that the novel "passes" because the narrative of racial passing disguises an equally powerful subtext: the sexual attraction between the two women. Thus *Passing* addresses not only racial identity but also gender and sexual identity, shedding light on the lesbian and gay subculture of the Harlem Renaissance.

Passing ends with the death of Clare: Her husband has discovered her identity and has intruded on a party she is attending with the Redfields; immediately afterward, she falls from the roof of an apartment building in Harlem. For this reason, *Passing* has also been read as a version of the "tragic mulatto" theme, which was popular in nineteenth-century African American literature. The "tragic mulatto" is a mixed-race character, usually a beautiful woman, who comes to an untimely end. Some black writers used this convention to appeal to white readers, who would presumably be able to identify with a nearly white protagonist, and Wall (1995) believes that Larsen adopted the theme for this reason.

However, Larsen's unexpected and perplexing denouement has led to a "problem of interpretation" (Tate 1980). *Passing* is complex and ambiguous in part because the third-person narrator, Irene, is unreliable. One unresolved ambiguity is Clare's death, which can be read as an accident, suicide, or murder—either by the enraged Bellew or by Irene, who suspects Clare of having an affair with her husband, Brian. *Passing* has been criticized for this unsatisfactory ending; it has also been criticized for its focus on a narrow stratum of black life, the middle class. Still, *Passing* is a significant work at least partly because of its ambiguity, which reflects the ambiguous identity of the characters. Moreover, it offers a broader picture of the Harlem Renaissance in terms of intersections of race, class, gender, and sexuality. It endures as one of the most remarkable depictions of black women's experience during this time.

LORI HARRISON-KAHAN

See also Larsen, Nella; Passing; Quicksand

Further Reading

Davis, Thadious. *Nella Larsen, Novelist of the Harlem Renaissance*. Baton Rouge: Louisiana State University Press, 1994.

DuCille, Ann. *The Coupling Convention: Sex, Text, and Tradition in Black Women's Fiction*. New York: Oxford University Press, 1993.

McDowell, Deborah. "Introduction." In Nella Larsen, *Quicksand and Passing*. New Brunswick, N.J.: Rutgers University Press, 1986.

Tate, Claudia. "Nella Larsen's *Passing*: A Problem of Interpretation." *Black American Literature Forum*, 14(4), Winter 1980.

Wall, Cheryl. *Women of the Harlem Renaissance*. Bloomington: Indiana University Press, 1995.

Washington, Mary Helen. "The Mulatta Trap: Nella Larsen's Women of the 1920s." In *Invented Lives: Narratives of Black Women, 1860–1960*. Garden City, N.Y.: Anchor, 1987.

Patterson, Louise Thompson

The educator, political activist, cultural critic, and social worker Louise Thompson Patterson (1901–1999) was a link between the literati of the Harlem Renaissance and the left-wing politics of the Popular Front.

Patterson spent her childhood following her mother (a domestic worker) and stepfather (a chef) as they moved through a succession of predominantly white towns in the Pacific Northwest. Confronted with racism, isolation, and economic discrimination, she and her mother, who were both light-complexioned, occasionally passed for white or Mexican. The family settled in Oakland, California, in 1919, and Patterson began attending the University of California at Berkeley. There she heard a lecture by W. E. B. Du Bois that so stirred her that she was "for the first time in my life, proud to be black" (Lewis 2000, 103). In 1925, she accepted a teaching position at State College in Pine Bluff, Arkansas, but discovered that her students were barely able to read and that she was expected to teach them Spanish among other subjects. It was less than a year before she took a post teaching business administration at Hampton Institute in Virginia, which was then arguably America's premier black institution of higher education. But students complained that Hampton's white principal had treated them with contempt ever since Virginia had passed the Massenburg Bill, which required blacks and whites to be separated in public halls in the state; that he had appointed known members of the Ku Klux Klan to the faculty; and that even teachers from the North had referred to students as "heathens." When the students went on strike in 1927 in protest against Hampton's repressive paternalism, Patterson wrote to Du Bois at *The Crisis* asking him to support them. He promptly published her letter, and she was pressured by the administration to resign.

In June 1928, Patterson came to New York City to accept an Urban League Fellowship to study at the New York School of Social Work. In New York she befriended the painter Aaron Douglas and his wife, Alta.

By the end of August 1928 she had married the writer Wallace Thurman; the marriage failed within six months, however, as a result of Thurman's homosexuality, chronic alcoholism, and depression. Patterson intended to get a divorce in Nevada and then in Mexico but did not succeed, and they remained married, though estranged, until his death in 1934.

At Hampton, Patterson had met Langston Hughes, who was then touring the country giving readings of his poetry. In 1929, as she was completing her degree and was looking for employment, Hughes recommended her as a secretary to his patron, Charlotte Osgood Mason, an affluent and influential white philanthropist. Mason added Patterson to her payroll, which included Hughes, Zora Neale Hurston, Aaron Douglas, Claude McKay, Alain Locke, Richmond Barthé, and Hall Johnson. For the year that Patterson was employed by Mason, she worked as Hughes' stenographer, helping him with his revision of *Not Without Laughter* (1929), and with the drafts of his and Zora Neale Hurston's play *Mule Bone*. But Patterson soon began to chafe at Mason's stifling patronage and racism: "I might comment on the beauty of a flower arrangement in her apartment, and she would be greatly pleased. 'I knew you would like them, you *would* like red,'" Patterson later recalled (quoted in Huggins 1971, p. 130).

Patterson next took a job as assistant to the director of New York's Congregational Educational Society (CES), a liberal organization interested in problems of race relations and labor. Under its auspices she traveled throughout the South, conducting seminars onboard a Pullman car, and she attended the American Interracial Seminar in Mexico in 1930; she also edited CES's newsletter. Her experiences with CES, the Great Depression, the Scottsboro case, and the growing strength of the American Communist Party all contributed to her political radicalization. In 1932, with the help of the artist Augusta Savage, she founded Vanguard, a left-wing group that operated out of her apartment in Harlem and sponsored theater performances, dances, concerts, and discussions on Marxist theory. The group soon metamorphosed into the Harlem branch of the Friends of the Soviet Union (FOSU), and Patterson's work with the organization caught the attention of James W. Ford, the leading black American communist of the day. Ford had just returned from the Soviet Union, and on behalf of the Meschrabpom film company was recruiting a group of black actors and actresses to make a movie in the Soviet Union that would document the history of race

relations in America. Patterson was appointed principal organizer of the group, and in June 1932 she traveled to Moscow as a member of the *Black and White* film project. Although the movie was never made, Patterson returned to New York with a renewed commitment to communism as a way for African Americans to challenge racism in the United States. She said in an interview:

> Russia was the only place where I was able to forget entirely that I was a Negro.... [The Russians] were shocked and unable to understand that we were not allowed equal accommodations with whites here in America.... Russia today is the only country in the world that's really fit to live in. I'd live there any time in preference to America. ("Prefers Russia" 1932)

In 1933, Patterson left the CES and joined the National Committee for the Defense of Political Prisoners (NCDPP) as its assistant national secretary. In May 1933, she participated in a march on Washington, D.C., in which more than 3,000 demonstrators demanded the release of the Scottsboro boys, and she was among the group from the Scottsboro Action Committee with whom President Franklin Roosevelt refused to meet.

In 1934, Patterson began a fifteen-year tenure with the International Workers Order (IWO). To bridge the divide between African American popular culture and the Communist Party's Popular Front, she organized cultural and political events on behalf of the party; she also persuaded the IWO to publish a pamphlet of Langston Hughes's radical poetry (*A New Song*, 1937). In 1938, when Hughes wanted to found a theater that would put on radical black "people's" plays, Patterson again appealed to the IWO, and the Harlem Suitcase Theater was born. Its first play, Hughes's *Don't You Want to Be Free? A Poetry Play: From Slavery through the Blues to Now—and Then Some!—with Singing, Music, and Dancing*, was derived from Patterson's selections from his radical poems. (In 1942, Hughes would dedicate his poetry collection *Shakespeare in Harlem* to Patterson.)

In 1940, she married the lawyer William Lorenzo Patterson, executive secretary of International Labor Defense, which had defended the Scottsboro boys. She then moved to Chicago, where she organized fund-raisers for his Abraham Lincoln School, an experimental black college whose curriculum was heavily influenced by socialist theory. Louise Patterson's other activities included traveling to Spain during its civil war as part of a relief effort for the Spanish

Republicans (1936); becoming a founder of the Civil Rights Congess (1946); organizing a national tour of black communities by Paul Robeson (1949); serving as secretary of a committee formed by Langston Hughes to present a gift of African American art to Ghana (1959); and helping to form Sojourners for Truth and Justice in the 1950s.

Louise Thompson Patterson died in New York in 1999. Her papers are at Emory University in Atlanta.

Biography

Louise Alone Thompson Patterson was born on 9 September 1901, in Chicago, Illinois. She received a B.S. from the University of California at Berkeley in 1923 and an M.A. from the New York School of Social Work in 1929. She taught at State College in Pine Bluff, Arkansas, 1925–1926, and at the Hampton Institute, Virginia, 1926–1928. She was a stenographer to Langston Hughes and Zora Neale Hurston in 1930; assistant to the director, Department of Social Relations, Congregational Education Society, 1930–1932; founder, Friends of the Soviet Union, Harlem Branch, 1932; corresponding secretary, Cooperating Committee for Production of a Soviet Film on Negro Life, 1932–1933; assistant national secretary, National Committee for the Defense of Political Prisoners, 1933; and an organizer, national recording secretary, secretary of the English Section, and vice president, International Workers Order, 1934–1948. She was a sponsor of the Harlem Suitcase Theater, 1938; and a founder of the Civil Rights Congress in 1946, and its black woman's auxiliary, Sojourners for Truth and Justice. In 1957, she was secretary, Afro-American Committee for Gifts of Art and Literature to Ghana. She also contributed articles to *The Crisis, Philadelphia Tribune*, and *Freedomways*. She received an award from the Urban League Fellowship in 1928. She died in New York City on 27 August 1999.

CLAIRE NEE NELSON

See also Black and White; Communist Party; Douglas, Aaron; Du Bois, W. E. B.; Mason, Charlotte Osgood; Scottsboro; Thurman, Wallace; *other specific individuals*

Selected Works

"The Hampton Strike." *Crisis*, 34, December 1927.
"The Soviet Film." *Crisis*, 40, February 1933.

"Southern Terror." *Crisis*, 41, November 1934.
"Frederick Douglass and Women's Rights." *Philadelphia Tribune*, 5 September 1940, p. 4.
"With Langston Hughes in the U.S.S.R." *Freedomways*, 8, Spring 1968.

Further Reading

Berry, Faith. *Langston Hughes: Before and beyond Harlem*. Westport, Conn.: Lawrence Hill, 1983.

Huggins, Nathan Irvin. *Harlem Renaissance*. London: Oxford University Press, 1971.

Hughes, Langston. *Not without Laughter*. New York: Knopf, 1930.

———. *Shakespeare in Harlem*. New York: Knopf, 1942.

Jennings, La Vinia. "Louise Thompson." In *Notable Black American Women*, ed. Jessie Carney Smith. Detroit, Mich.: Gale Research, 1992.

Kelley, Robin D. G. "Patterson, Louise Thompson." In *Black Women in America*, Vol. 2., ed. Darlene Clark Hine. Brooklyn, N.Y.: Carlson, 1993.

Kellner, Bruce. "Thompson [Patterson], Louise." In *The Harlem Renaissance: A Historical Dictionary for the Era*. Westport, Conn.: Greenwood, 1984.

Lewis, David Levering. *When Harlem Was in Vogue*. New York: Penguin, 1997.

———. *W. E. B. Du Bois: The Fight for Equality and the American Century, 1919–1963*. New York: Holt, 2000.

Nadasen, Pam. "Thompson, Louise." In *Encyclopedia of African-American Culture and History*, Vol. 5, ed. Jack Salzman, David Lionel Smith, and Cornel West. New York: Macmillan Library Reference, 1996.

"Prefers Russia Now to Living in America." *New York Amsterdam News*, 23 November 1932, p. 5.

Rampersad, Arnold. *The Life of Langston Hughes*, Vol. 1, *1902–1941*. New York: Oxford University Press, 1986.

Payton, Philip A.

Philip A. Payton Jr., often considered the "father of colored Harlem," was a black entrepreneur and founder of the Afro-American Realty Company of New York City, which Booker T. Washington once called "one of the most interesting and . . . most remarkable business enterprises" undertaken by African Americans. Payton's pioneering endeavors to integrate the housing market in uptown Manhattan eventually made it possible for tens of thousands of blacks to move to Harlem from lower Manhattan, the southern United States, the Caribbean, and Africa.

Payton was born in Massachusetts in 1876 and came to New York City in 1899. He worked as a barber until February 1900, when he found a job as a porter in a real estate agency—an experience that made him interested in pursuing real estate as a career. In October 1900, he and a business partner opened a real estate office in downtown Manhattan. That venture failed, as did some subsequent attempts by Payton to gain a foothold in real estate speculation, but then his business situation improved greatly as he began to secure more rental properties and began concentrating on properties in and around Harlem.

During the late nineteenth century, Harlem had been a wealthy white suburb, but by the start of the twentieth century, Eighth Avenue and Lenox Avenue subway lines provided quick, affordable transportation to Harlem; landlords and real estate speculators invested heavily in the area; and a building spree took place in the expectation that middle-class New Yorkers would move there from downtown. However, there was an economic crisis in 1904–1905, and the uptown housing market faltered and subsequently collapsed. Payton became successsful when he promised numerous white landlords that he could fill their vacant houses and apartments with black tenants. Although the white residents were not entirely happy about this situation, they did consider African American tenants cleaner and more suitable than European immigrants. Moreover, the African Americans were willing to pay the exorbitant rents demanded by Harlem's landlords because many black New Yorkers had been displaced from their neighborhoods downtown by construction projects and race riots and were attracted to the spacious, upscale housing available in Harlem.

Within two years, though, white property owners became alarmed by the influx of blacks into uptown Manhattan, especially when it flowed well beyond 135th Street east of Eighth Avenue. White realtors and landlords therefore formed the Hudson Realty Company, intending to purchase all property that housed black tenants and then evict them. On 15 June 1904, Payton, James C. Thomas, and nine other business associates reacted by forming the Afro-American Realty Company as an all-black real estate development corporation that would buy property and lease it to blacks who wanted to live in Harlem. (Payton said that this idea had been inspired when he attended a meeting of the National Negro Business League in Richmond, Virginia, in 1902.) Afro-American Realty advertised heavily in the black press, in order to gain the support of the local black community against white real estate speculators.

From the outset, Afro-American Realty had problems. For one thing, although it had a lucrative period in 1904–1905, it always suffered from a lack of the capital needed to compete effectively in New York's housing market. Second, although Payton was clearly the driving force behind the company, he refused to take the post of president and general manager until 1906, after the corporation had already been damaged by divided leadership and internal reorganizations that had led to bitterness and uncertainty. Third, even under Payton's tenure as its head, the firm was harmed by bad publicity (for rent gouging), lawsuits (for shady business practices), and mounting debt (resulting from Payton's penchant for risky business decisions). Furthermore, "Phil Payton spent money faster than he made it" (Lewis 1989). Afro-American Realty folded in 1908, and Nail and Parker, a real estate company composed of former associates of Payton's, replaced it.

Payton continued to operate with modest success in Harlem as a realtor and businessman until his death in 1917.

Biography

Philip A. Payton Jr. was born on 27 February 1876, in Westfield, Massachusetts; his parents were Annie M. and Philip A. Payton Sr. His father trained him and his two brothers as barbers, and he studied at Livingstone College in Salisbury, North Carolina, in 1893 (but he did not complete his college education, largely because of a football injury that laid him up for nearly a year). Payton moved to New York City in April 1899. He married Maggie P. Lee on 28 June 1900. He opened a real estate office in New York in October 1900. Payton was the founder of the Afro-American Realty Company (1904–1908) and its president and general manager (1906–1908). Payton died on 29 August 1917, in New York City.

J. M. FLOYD-THOMAS

See also Afro-American Realty Company; Nail, John E.; National Negro Business League

Further Reading

Johnson, James Weldon. *Black Manhattan*. New York: Arno, 1968, pp. 147–149. (Originally published 1930.)

Lewis, David Levering. *When Harlem Was in Vogue*. New York: Oxford University Press, 1989, pp. 25–27.

Osofsky, Gilbert. *Harlem: The Making of a Ghetto, 1890–1930*. New York: Harper and Row, 1963, pp. 92–104.

Washington, Booker T. *The Negro in Business*. Boston, Mass.: Hertel, Jenkins, 1907, pp. 197–205.

Perry, Lincoln

See Stepin Fetchit

Peterkin, Julia Mood

Julia Mood Peterkin was the daughter of a prominent physician in South Carolina. Her mother died shortly after Julia's birth, so she was raised by an African American nursemaid, Lavinia "Maum Vinner" or "Mauma" Berry, from whom she learned Gullah patois, customs, and folklore. Recording the culture and lives of the Gullah became the primary focus and distinction of Peterkin's literary career.

Peterkin found herself as manager of a 500-person sharecropper plantation when her husband became ill. As a respite, she began taking piano lessons from Henry Bellaman, who, struck by her storytelling ability and her familiarity with the Gullah culture, encouraged her to write. He introduced her to Carl Sandburg, who persuaded her to send her work to H. L. Mencken. Mencken began publishing Peterkin's stories in *Smart Set* and the *Reviewer*. These first sketches and stories were collected as *Green Thursday* (1924); both Sandburg and W. E. B. Du Bois publicly praised the volume.

Peterkin followed *Green Thursday* with three novels: *Black April* (1927), *Scarlet Sister Mary* (1928), and *Bright Skin* (1932). In a review of *Black April* for *Opportunity*, Sterling Brown praised Peterkin for setting a model of new realism by using the vernacular and focusing on the indigenous, and proclaimed her a worthy model for black writers. Rather than depicting relations between blacks and whites, Peterkin keeps her focus within the African American community.

However, she was sometimes criticized for her emphasis on the "folk" aspects of Gullah culture, an emphasis that might lead her to romanticize and "exoticize" her subjects.

Scarlet Sister Mary received a Pulitzer Prize in 1929, and Verdelle praises the novel's "lyric beauty" and "keen sense of concept" (1998, vii). The protagonist of *Scarlet Sister Mary* maintains her expansive spirit in the face of poverty, desertion by her husband, and her community's condemnation of her because she bears nine children out of wedlock. Starkly realistic, as are all of Peterkin's works, this novel is notable for its sympathy for and details of the lives of fieldworkers. Her novels and stories often center on folk beliefs and religion, but typically remain skeptical as to how positive a force they exert. *Scarlet Sister Mary* was dramatized in 1930 by Daniel Reed; the stage version was performed by a white cast with Ethel Barrymore in the lead, wearing blackface.

Black April and *Scarlet Sister Mary* were extremely popular choices at the branch of the New York Public Library most frequented by residents of Harlem, and the novels sold well across the North. *Bright Skin* has a mulatto heroine, a change in focus that proved less successful. An effort with the photographer Doris Ulmann, *Roll, Jordan, Roll* (1933), met with little interest.

Peterkin visited New York and met many notable Harlemites, including Langston Hughes, with whom she reportedly had several vibrant discussions. However, in 1932, on a tour of the South, Hughes was turned away from Peterkin's house by an unidentified white man; it is not clear whether Peterkin condoned this action. When Hughes was raising money for the defendants in the Scottsboro case, Peterkin at first did not answer his requests, but eventually she donated items for auction.

After 1936, Peterkin wrote little, devoting herself to caring for her grandson after his mother's suicide. She died in obscurity in 1961. Feminist criticism brought new attention to her depictions of the lives of Gullah women, particularly in *Scarlet Sister Mary* and in her short stories. This attention culminated in the late 1990s with reprint editions of most of her works by the University of Georgia Press and a full-length study by Susan Millar Williams in 1997.

Biography

Julia Mood Peterkin was born in 1880 on a plantation in Laurens County, South Carolina. She attended

Converse College in Spartansburg, South Carolina, receiving a B.A. in 1896 and an M.A. in 1897. Peterkin taught at a rural school in Fort Motte, South Carolina, in 1898. She married William Peterkin in 1903 and was responsible for the management of his plantation, Lang Syne. They had one son. She received an honorary doctorate from Converse College in 1927 and a Pulitzer Prize in 1929. She died in 1961 in South Carolina.

KATHRYN WEST

See also Brown, Sterling; Hughes, Langston; Mencken, H. L.; Scottsboro

Selected Works

Green Thursday. 1924. (Reprint, 1998.)
Black April. 1927. (Reprint, 1998.)
Scarlet Sister Mary. 1928. (Reprint, 1998.)
Bright Skin. 1932. (Reprint, 1998.)
Roll, Jordan, Roll. 1933.
Plantation Christmas. 1934. (Reprint, 1987.)
Collected Short Stories of Julia Peterkin, ed. Frank Durham. 1970.

Further Reading

Blain, Virginia, Isobel Grundy, and Patricia Clements, eds. *The Feminist Companion to Literature in English: Women Writers from the Middle Ages to the Present.* New Haven, Conn.: Yale University Press, 1990.

Hutchinson, George. *The Harlem Renaissance in Black and White.* Cambridge, Mass.: Belknap Press of Harvard University Press, 1995.

Lewis, David Levering. *When Harlem Was in Vogue.* New York: Oxford University Press, 1979.

Verdelle, A. J. "Foreword." In *Scarlet Sister Mary.* Athens: University of Georgia Press, 1998. (Reprint.)

Weaks, Mary Louise, and Carolyn Perry, eds. *Southern Women's Writing: Colonial to Contemporary.* Gainesville: University Press of Florida, 1995.

Williams, Susan Millar. *"A Devil and a Good Woman, Too": The Lives of Julia Peterkin.* Athens: University of Georgia Press, 1997.

Peterson, Dorothy Randolph

Langston Hughes once said of Dorothy Randolph Peterson (1897–1978) that she was "a charming colored girl who had grown up mostly in Puerto Rico, and who moved with such poise among colorful celebrities that I thought when I first met her she was a white girl of the grande monde, slightly sun-tanned."

Peterson, a teacher, was well known for her literary salons, which she held first in her family home, encouraged by her father, and later in her own apartment. She was also known for her connection to Jean Toomer. In the 1920s Peterson discovered the teachings of George Ivanovich Gurdjieff through Toomer, who was one of his converts. Gurdjieff's philosophy included Eastern thought, Russian philosophy, and long hours of "inner observation and silent concentration" to achieve cosmic consciousness. Toomer came to Harlem to share Gurdjieff's teachings, and some acquaintances thought that Peterson had become smitten with him. However, Toomer married someone else (a white woman), and Langston Hughes summed up the relationship with Peterson as follows: "The one Afro-American woman Toomer was once thought to care about [was] a sad-eyed, beautiful teacher of Spanish and aspiring actress named Dorothy Peterson, whose love for Jean Toomer was legend among their Harlem friends."

Peterson was in various ways very much engaged in the artistic scene in Harlem. During the time when she was involved with Toomer, she managed to finish a novel she had been working on, although it was never published. Also, she was one of the first patrons of the journal *Fire!!—A Quarterly Devoted to the Younger Negro Artists*, launched by Wallace Thurman. In addition, she and Regina Anderson cofounded the Negro Experimental Theater in 1929, in the basement of the 135th Street branch of the New York Public Library, and she was also associated with the Harlem Suitcase Theater. During a leave of absence from teaching, she made a notable stage appearance as Cain's girlfriend in an all-black production of Marc Connelly's *Green Pastures.*

Peterson was dedicated to preserving black arts and culture. In the 1940s she founded the James Weldon Johnson Memorial Collection of Negro Arts and Letters at Yale University and assisted Carl Van Vechten with the preservation of the work of many Puerto Rican Negroes. She also created, at Wadleigh High School in Harlem, the Jerome Bowers Peterson Collection of Photographs of Celebrated Negroes. J. B. Peterson—her father—died in 1943, and Van Vechten provided the photos for this memorial collection.

Late in her life Peterson converted to Catholicism and became extremely conservative, refusing to discuss the Harlem Renaissance and referring to it as a "frivolous, silly time" in her youth.

Biography

Dorothy Randolph Peterson was born on 21 June 1897, to Jerome Bowers Peterson, one of the founders of the publication that became *New York Age*, and Cornelia S. White, the daughter of Phillip A. White, the first black member of the board of education in Brooklyn. In 1904, J. B. Peterson was appointed the U.S. consul to Puerto Cabello, Venezuela, for two years; later he was deputy collector of the Internal Revenue Service in San Juan, Puerto Rico; thus Dorothy began her multilingualism overseas at a very young age. Her mother volunteered with several charities in New York, serving on various boards and councils throughout her life. Peterson's brother, Jerome "Sidney" Peterson, was a medical doctor who was also active in the literary and cultural scene in Harlem. Dorothy Randolph Peterson graduated from Puerto Rico University and studied French at New York University. She taught Spanish at a public high school in Brooklyn; she also taught at Wadleigh High School for Girls in Harlem and briefly worked at the Harlem branch of the New York Public Library. In the late 1950s, seeking a warm climate to relieve her arthritis, she went to live in Spain; eventually she returned to the United States and moved to the Lathrop Nursing Home in Northampton, Massachusetts. She died on 4 November 1978, at age eighty-one.

VERONDA J. PITCHFORD

See also Anderson, Regina M.; Fire!!; Green Pastures, The; Hughes, Langston; Negro Experimental Theater; 135th Street Libary; Toomer, Jean; Van Vechten, Carl

Further Reading

Berry, Faith. *Langston Hughes: Before and beyond Harlem.* Westport, Conn.: Lawrence Hill, 1983.

Davis, Thadious. *Nella Larsen, Novelist of the Harlem Renaissance: A Woman's Life Unveiled.* Baton Rouge: Louisiana State University Press, 1994.

Kellner, Bruce, ed. *The Harlem Renaissance, a Historical Dictionary for the Era.* Westport, Conn.: Greenwood, 1984.

Lewis, David Levering. *When Harlem Was in Vogue.* New York: Oxford University Press, 1981.

Smith, Jessie Carney. *Notable Black American Women.* Detroit, Mich.: Gale Research, 1992.

Philanthropy and Philanthropic Organizations

Philanthropy for black Americans reached the peak of its influence during the era of the Harlem Renaissance. Although historians have thoroughly examined earlier philanthropic ventures, including the educational crusade associated with Reconstruction and the "industrial philanthropy" championed by Booker T. Washington and his patrons, gifts from northern whites to black religious, cultural, and educational activities were more extensive in the 1920s and 1930s than ever before. During this time, key philanthropic leaders directed financial aid not only to black schools, but also to carefully selected artists and scholars. Recipients of aid from foundations included a virtual who's who of the Harlem Renaissance: James Weldon Johnson, Arna Bontemps, Langston Hughes, Claude McKay, Zora Neale Hurston, and Aaron Douglas, among many others.

The most important philanthropic foundations of the period were the General Education Board, funded by the Rockefellers, and the Julius Rosenwald Fund, supported by the chief executive and primary shareholder in Sears, Roebuck, and Company. Religious philanthropies, such as the American Missionary Association (Congregationalist) and the American Church Institute for Negroes (Episcopalian), also continued to make significant donations to black education, but they tended to accept the policies and assumptions of the secular foundations.

Although scholars have vigorously debated the ultimate impact of northern philanthropic activity for Negroes, the basic facts are clear enough. On the one hand, the philanthropists—or more precisely their agents and spokesmen—tolerated many contemporary injustices by placing their confidence in gradual change or the "slow processes of evolution." On the other hand, private giving greatly strengthened selected black colleges and universities, successfully promoted public support for black primary and secondary education, and helped create and sustain a small educational and artistic elite. "Our work is education, not agitation," the philanthropists affirmed, confident that indirect and "nonpolitical" methods would eventually change American race relations.

Critics of philanthropy have argued that the activities of private givers, especially the programs of the major foundations, had quite the opposite result, prolonging the life "of the system that so effectively subordinated African Americans" (J. Anderson 1988). Some scholars assert not only that northern philanthropy strengthened white control over southern blacks, but also that this consequence was deliberately planned, rather than unintended or incidental. Other scholars reject the idea that the foundations were active accomplices in "some sort of conspiracy with the white supremacy movement." The evidence, they argue, does not support the claim that northern philanthropy was aiming at a "new slavery" for southern Negroes.

Judging from their internal correspondence and private working papers, the managers of northern philanthropies were, in fact, genuine reformers, although not entirely free from racial prejudice. They considered the South backward and believed southern racism and black ignorance threatened national stability. Whatever the limitations of their worldview, these outsiders undeniably wished to modify race relations in ways that would be unacceptable to most white southerners, as well as many people in the North. Their commitment to significant reform cannot be explained away as crude self-interest. Although they did not challenge segregation, neither did the philanthropists seek to develop a permanent caste education for African Americans. They did not have a master plan, as some researchers have claimed, to restrict black higher education, which, in any case, expanded rapidly after 1920. Nor did they use their power to minimize black contributions to American culture.

Background

From the beginning, northern philanthropists interested in the "Negro problem" gave more money for schools than to anything else. In the first half-century after the Civil War, northern philanthropy for blacks was primarily religiously motivated and distributed through Protestant denominations seeking to use education to "elevate the freedmen." Far from "melting away" after Reconstruction, as several scholars have assumed, this sort of private giving reached new highs in the early twentieth century. As McPherson (1975) found, the major missionary societies (Congregational, Methodist, Presbyterian, and Baptist) spent four times as much on black education in 1906 as they had in 1876.

The work of the missionary societies was at first supplemented and then ultimately overshadowed by secular foundations. The Peabody Fund (established 1867) and the Slater Fund (created in 1881) promoted southern education as "a patriotic duty that could not well be shirked without disaster," in the words of the millionaire merchant John F. Slater. This more secular motivation for educational philanthropy reached fuller elaboration, under more complex organization, in the early twentieth century. The establishment of the General Education Board (GEB) in 1902 marked a new phase in foundation philanthropy. Endowed with $33 million in gifts from the Rockefellers during its first decade of operation, GEB was committed to an ideal of scientific and efficiently organized philanthropy that was significantly different from the goals and organization of earlier donors. Rejecting "sentimental" giving that responded to mere symptoms, these new philanthropists believed that they could eliminate the root causes of social problems through research and the careful application of insights.

Thanks to its focused goals, immense resources, and energetic officers—men who were both creative and well connected with business and political leaders in the North and South—GEB quickly became more influential and visible than any other philanthropic group supporting black education. Other foundations, such as the Southern Education Board (established 1901), Jeanes Fund (founded 1907), Phelps-Stokes Fund (established 1911), and Julius Rosenwald Fund (organized in 1917), worked closely with GEB, imitating its organization, responding to its initiatives, and sharing trustees in what has been called an "interlocking directorate of calculating altruism."

Although the gifts of missionary societies and individual donors to black schools at first outstripped GEB's contributions to black education, GEB acquired immense prestige, enabling its planners and theorists to set the philanthropic agenda. In 1910, for example, the primary missionary societies and donors to Hampton Institute and Tuskegee Institute contributed about $2 million to black education—compared with less than $90,000 from GEB. Yet when GEB's officers called a conference on Negro education in 1915, they did not even invite the leaders of missionary philanthropy. By the 1920s, as GEB's spending for black education dramatically increased, its support of particular schools or programs had become a kind of imprimatur, a warrant of worthiness for other givers interested in black education.

Instead of challenging the new philanthropy, missionary philanthropists gradually adopted the key positions of GEB and other foundation philanthropists—including the idea that private education for Negroes should be replaced wherever possible by public schools, supported by taxation and controlled by white voters. One of the oldest missionary societies, the American Missionary Association (AMA), moved from supporting forty secondary schools in the early twentieth century to maintaining only one in 1950. Reflecting on the results of this policy, the head of AMA recognized that every decision to turn over one of its schools to the public school authorities had been received by black parents and students as a "death sentence." The policy would never have been adopted if AMA's leaders had based their policy on the counsel of "principals, teachers, parents, and patrons" in the South.

Students of northern philanthropy have often emphasized the power of the great foundations. Rich and influential as the northern philanthropic agencies were, however, they did not enjoy unlimited freedom. As Sealander (1997) has observed, it is possible to exaggerate the power of philanthropy both for good or ill. Foundation initiatives did not automatically become government policy, nor could philanthropists be sure that a program would be eliminated if they withdrew their support.

Early Opposition

Foundation philanthropy was highly sensitive to southern white criticism of its activities. As early as 1903, Booker T. Washington protested to Wallace Buttrick, a key officer in GEB: "We have already gone as far as decency permits in our attempt to avoid stirring up southern feeling." But during the early twentieth century, in an atmosphere of deteriorating race relations, even the mildest program of reform met with intense opposition from many white southerners, who suspected that the reformers intended to elevate blacks at their expense. White extremists denounced both Washington and his northern friends, accusing the promoters of black schools of failing to prepare African Americans for their subordinate place in a segregated society and "training the negroes to the vain hope of social equality with whites."

This opposition created an indelible impression on the foundation executives. "The Board was aware

from the start," wrote Raymond B. Fosdick, an officer of GEB and author of an official history of it, "of the dangers inherent in a Northern institution working in the highly charged emotional atmosphere of a biracial South. . . . A single misstep could be disastrous" (1962). Fear of opposition from southern whites played an important role in the structuring of northern philanthropy for the South. This is especially true of GEB's decision in 1911 to endorse the "policy of cooperating with the white people of the South in promoting Negro education," thus making the stimulation of government spending on public education the first priority of its programs for black education—with aid for private and denominational schools a distinctly secondary emphasis. Other foundation initiatives suggested a similar strategy of countering opposition by avoiding direct confrontation as much as possible. For example, GEB's program of appointing state supervisors of Negro rural schools minimized opposition by making these supervisors subordinate to the state superintendent of public instruction, by recommending no blacks for these positions, and by simply not making an appointment where significant opposition existed. In other cases, GEB attempted to forestall criticism by using indirect funding and euphemisms such as "county training school" in place of "high school."

Perhaps most important of all, opposition by southern whites helped shape the decision by GEB, the Southern Education Board, and other philanthropic agencies to promote the development of a comprehensive educational system for whites, rather than focusing primarily on blacks as the abolitionists and neoabolitionists of the missionary societies had done. The secular philanthropists assumed that southern whites would not tolerate large-scale aid to blacks until whites had an adequate educational system. Although GEB began as an outgrowth of John D. Rockefeller Jr.'s vision of a "Negro Education Board," in the end only 19 percent of GEB's gifts went to black education.

From the start, the foundation philanthropists were much less concerned about black leaders' criticism of their activities. They expected black leaders to be disappointed with the pace of progress and were prepared to be "greatly misunderstood" by "our colored friends" as they cautiously sought to awaken southern whites to their responsibilities. Calculating that their scientific philanthropy would "take years and perhaps even successive generations" to achieve appropriate results, the philanthropists (with few exceptions) did not share the sense of crisis felt by most

African American educators, nor did they see a need for urgent, even desperate action. Instead, they feared provocation, overextension, and unwise spending.

After 1920: A Surge in Spending

By the 1920s, foundation philanthropy was directed, for all practical purposes, by foundation staffs rather than by the original donors. Many of these philanthropic bureaucrats were primarily interested in black educators' experiments for their relevance to the overall progressive educational agenda, including the elimination of "dead languages," the introduction of "practical" vocational training, and reformation of the curriculum to promote "life adjustment." As Abraham Flexner of GEB put it, "The effort of those who think they are progressive in education is to modify the existing curriculum . . . very much in the direction of what is . . . proposed in the South as especially fitting for colored children." Educational innovation was easier to carry out in weak and underfunded black schools than in more secure white schools.

The philanthropists' early commitment to the "Hampton-Tuskegee idea" faded even before the death of Booker T. Washington. As the foundations intensified their support for black education in the late 1920s, black collegiate education increased dramatically, and small private industrial schools modeled on Tuskegee largely disappeared. Hampton and Tuskegee evolved into little more than cautious imitations of the standard American college. By the 1930, Washington's philosophy and network of influence were no longer preeminent in black educational philanthropy.

Foundations supported black causes at an unprecedented rate after 1920. For example, in an eight-year period (1924–1931) GEB appropriated nearly $25 million for black education, or about three times the total spending of the previous two decades. The bulk of the increased aid went to private colleges and secondary schools, not public institutions. (This striking burst of philanthropy represented nearly 40 percent of GEB's entire effort for black education from 1902 to 1960.) Although the Great Depression wrought havoc with philanthropic endowments, GEB appropriated another $15 million in the decade after 1931.

The spending surge was less an attempt to initiate progress than a response to the real advances that had already occurred in the first three decades of the twentieth century. The philanthropists could plausibly claim that much of their original program had succeeded by 1930. The notion that blacks could be essentially excluded from education, a politically viable idea in 1902, had been thoroughly discredited. In every southern state, the makers of public policy accepted the idea that white taxpayers had some obligation to Negro schools, and these institutions were no longer seen as a special project of northern missionaries. Black education had dramatically expanded, although dominant whites still often treated black schools with high-handed inequity. Between 1900 and 1930 black literacy jumped from 50 percent to 80 percent, the proportion of black children in school reached nearly 90 percent, and, for the first time, black public high schools became common. The number of African American college students increased at a spectacular rate, rising from a mere 1,600 c. 1914 to eight times as many twelve years later. Thus by almost every measurement, including the number (and proportion) of black children in school, literacy rates, educational expenditure, and the quality of buildings and equipment, the school system for black southerners was markedly better thirty years after Robert Ogden of the Southern Education Board launched his crusade for southern education.

This educational progress continued even during the desperate Depression years, with blacks achieving parity with whites in one important category. For the first time, almost all black children attended elementary school. By the end of the decade, southern Negro children age five to fourteen went to school in the same proportions as white children in the same age group. Ninety percent or more of older potential black elementary students (age ten to fourteen) were in school in nine southern or border states, with percentages of blacks exceeding those of whites in Texas, Tennessee, Arkansas, and Kentucky. Across the South, even in states where Negrophobic demagoguery flourished, spending for black schools increased sharply in the 1930s. Measuring progress from a pathetically low baseline, Mississippi's per pupil expenditure for black education nearly doubled between 1910 and 1935, and South Carolina tripled its support (in constant dollars) for black learning. Other states, including North Carolina, Tennessee, Virginia, Florida, and Texas, offered more substantial support to black education. In some cases the gap between white and black had narrowed by the 1930s. In North Carolina, for instance, the state spent $32.92 per black pupil in 1935, about 64 percent of the expenditure for a white student.

There were other signs of real change during the 1930s. Black high school enrollment jumped by nearly

60 percent in sixteen southern and border states in the six academic years between 1933–1934 and 1939–1940, with dramatic, above-average increases in such improbable places as Alabama (88 percent) and Florida (105 percent). Even more striking progress can be seen in higher education. Many schools that were "colleges" in name only in 1900 had realized the hopes of their founders by the 1930s. Public higher education, virtually unknown in 1900, was rapidly growing in significance. The number of Negro college students nearly tripled during the 1930s.

Long a major focus of foundation activity, teacher training took on new urgency in the face of the rapid expansion of segregated education. Quite simply, soaring enrollments and increased public support of black education dramatically increased the demand for teachers, which, in turn, helped push philanthropic spending to new highs in the 1920s and 1930s.

New Directions

Northern philanthropies not only spent more money in the era of the Harlem Renaissance, but they also spent money for new purposes. For the first time, the foundations funded fellowships for individual academics and professionals, instead of focusing exclusively on institution-building. Another departure was the decision in 1929 to begin aiding artists and writers, as well as professors and administrators. The Great Depression led to two other innovations: (1) emergency operating expenses for selected schools (from GEB), and (2) greater cooperation between the foundations and an activist federal government.

Beginning in 1924, GEB provided fellowships for selected black college teachers and administrators to secure graduate education in the North. Individual grants were modest, but the long-term impact was dramatic. As Fosdick observed in 1962, "Hardly a college president, dean, or ranking faculty member escaped the distinction of being a Board fellow at some time in his career." The Rosenwald Fund created a similar program in 1928. Among the scholars who received such fellowships in the 1930s were W. E. B. Du Bois, St. Clair Drake, John Hope Franklin, Abram Harris, Percy Julian, Ralph Bunche, and Frank Snowden.

In the fellowship initiatives, as in other programs, the major foundations carefully coordinated their activities. From the earliest years of the twentieth century, foundation philanthropists had sought to create a "clearinghouse" for gifts to black education, believing that indiscriminate donations, based on limited information, led to unwise spending and even to waste. By the 1930s the goal of a clearinghouse had been achieved, at least in some critical areas. The Rosenwald Fund and GEB were able to agree on broad lines of educational policy. Edwin Embree, a veteran of the Rockefeller Foundation and president of the Rosenwald Fund from 1928 to 1948, used the language of political coalition. Speaking of the carefully selected projects to be supported by the Rosenwald Fund, he stated: "I think . . . we should work out these projects in consultation with the General Education Board. While our two boards may not always cooperate in the same enterprise, each should know what the other is doing and contemplating and thus represent a *united front*." In addition, the two foundations agreed "that neither Board would grant a scholarship to a person who had been refused by the other board without consultation with that board." Such collaboration reverberated throughout the world of segregated southern education, as church leaders, accreditation associations, state departments of education, and individual donors took cues from the actions of the large foundations, especially GEB.

Under Embree's leadership the Rosenwald Fund took the lead in promoting "the Negro in the arts" by offering fellowships to "creative workers." He had been encouraged in this experiment by James Weldon Johnson, who was a prolific writer and editor, a leader in the National Association for the Advancement of Colored People (NAACP), and a significant figure in the Harlem Renaissance. Johnson saw cultural subsidies as crucial to the long-term objectives of the fund. "Artistic effort and creative achievement among Negroes are just beginning," he declared, "and so it is not so much a matter of the needs and opportunities of the present moment as it is the fostering and development of the potential powers of the Negro in the five, ten, fifteen, or twenty years to come."

Embree and his associates believed that "achievement in the arts" would gain recognition "for the individual concerned and for the Negro race as whole." They also expected black artistic accomplishments to "counteract" unfavorable impressions created by the "migration of large numbers of Negroes into Northern cities."

The fellowships, like other gifts from the foundations, were motivated by a distinctive philosophy that focused on stimulating new gifts from other sources. Both Rosenwald and the Rockefellers sought to address current problems through their benefactions, with no desire to create perpetual organizations. Both foundations were prepared to spend principal as well as income, and by the late 1930s began looking to their own termination. The Rosenwald Fund went out of existence in 1948, and GEB, although technically continuing until 1960, had in fact spent most of its capital by the early 1950s. (As early as 1937, Fosdick had spoken of GEB as "in liquidation," its life "running to its close.") "To anyone imbued with the ancient ideal [of almsgiving]," Embree observed, "ours will seem strange philanthropy. Our aim is to give as little as possible for as short a time as possible."

This way of giving is well illustrated in the most famous philanthropy of the time—the Rosenwald program to support the building of Negro public schools. In roughly two decades before the program was phased out in the early 1930s, the Rosenwald Fund was able to promote the construction of some 5,300 school buildings. Although these schoolhouses cost roughly $28 million, the fund contributed little more than $4 million of the total cost, requiring matching gifts from public funds and community donations for each new building. At the height of the program's success, moreover, Embree began phasing it out, beginning in 1930 with a decision to stop supporting the construction of one-teacher rural schools.

In the area of higher education, the foundations, especially GEB, had long been interested in promoting a few strong schools and eliminating "unnecessary duplication." In the era of the Harlem Renaissance, this commitment took the form of creating four "university centers" in Atlanta, New Orleans, Nashville, and Washington, D.C. Using both their prestige and the promise of money, the foundations were able to accomplish a great deal. Meharry Medical School was relocated and reorganized, beginning in 1928. The following year GEB set in motion the sweeping Atlanta "affiliation plan"–a plan that was not completed until 1950 and entailed a new library, an endowment campaign, and the relocation of Atlanta University, Morris Brown College, Clark University, and four theological seminaries. The foundations prompted the creation of a single, unified university in New Orleans (Dillard University) in 1935 and encouraged the expansion of professional education at the District of Columbia's semipublic Howard University.

The foundations did not have the luxury of making only long-term plans. GEB—its farsighted visions interrupted by the drastic deflation of the Great Depression—chose to become involved in philanthropic rescue work as well. For the first time, GEB gave money directly to the current expenses of selected black colleges, rather than restricting gifts to long-term projects such as endowment, buildings, and faculty development. Between 1931 and 1935 twenty-seven black colleges received urgent emergency grants totaling $400,000. Never an uncritical observer of the foundations, W. E. B. Du Bois spoke truer than he knew when he declared that, despite its early mistakes, "the General Education Board in later years has been the salvation of education among Negroes." GEB also rescued the Rosenwald Fund, providing it with "advances" and even some outright gifts when the fund's income from its stock holdings ceased in the spring of 1932. The Carnegie Corporation also helped the Rosenwald Fund, paying for some library appropriations out of its own funds.

Also as a result of the upheaval of the Depression, philanthropies became more closely allied with the federal government, sometimes in ways that were difficult to detect in their direct appropriations or programs. Unlike most of the capitalists whose wealth sustained the foundations, foundation executives admired Franklin D. Roosevelt, and in Washington during the New Deal they often found sympathetic officials and a respectful hearing for their ideas. Roosevelt's famous "black cabinet" was a significant example of this collaboration, since the idea of "racial advisers" in key departments began with Embree, who first persuaded Interior Secretary Harold Ickes to accept the idea and then put forward the name of a former Rosenwald Fellow (Clark Foreman) to fill the first such position. A Rosenwald trustee, Will W. Alexander, then used his influence as head of the Farm Security Administration to help in securing the appointment of several members of the "black cabinet."

In the eyes of many African Americans during the Harlem Renaissance era, foundation aid was a mixed blessing, a gift that elicited ambivalent responses. Grants from these well-intentioned philanthropists were at the same time liberating and constraining. For a harried scholar such as Du Bois or Howard University's noted biology researcher E. E. Just, intermittent help and abrupt refusals and arbitrary postponements provoked both despair and intense gratitude, making possible certain real achievements while frustrating other visions. The foundations sought to create leaders and sustain institutions. To the degree that they succeeded, they also fed new demands for autonomy, more intense expectations of change.

For researchers, the extensive and well-organized papers of the General Education Board at the Rockefeller Archive Center are the indispensable starting point. See also the papers of the Rosenwald Fund (Fisk University) and Julius Rosenwald (University of Chicago).

ERIC ANDERSON

See also Higher Education; Historically Black Colleges and Universities; Howard University; Johnson, James Weldon; Rosenwald Fellowships; *specific recipients*

Further Reading

Anderson, Eric, and Alfred A. Moss, Jr. *Dangerous Donations: Northern Philanthropy and Southern Black Education, 1902–1930.* 1999.

Anderson, James D. *The Education of Blacks in the South, 1860–1935.* 1988.

Beilke, Jayne R. "To Render Better Service: The Role of the Julius Rosenwald Fund Fellowship Program in the Development of Graduate and Professional Educational Opportunities for African-Americans." Ph.D. diss., Indiana University, 1994.

Embree, Edwin R., and Julia Waxman. *Investment in People: The Story of the Julius Rosenwald Fund.* 1949.

Fosdick, Raymond B. *Adventure in Giving: The Story of the General Education Board.* 1962.

McPherson, James M. *The Abolitionist Legacy: From Reconstruction to the NAACP.* 1975.

Sealander, Judith. *Private Wealth, Public Life: Foundation Philanthropy and the Reshaping of American Social Policy from the Progressive Era to the New Deal.* 1997.

Pickens, William

William Pickens overcame childhood poverty, graduated from Yale University, taught college, and worked as a college administrator before moving to New York in 1920. During the Harlem Renaissance, he was a prominent orator, author, and civil rights activist.

Pickens was one of the most popular public speakers of the renaissance. In fact, according to Avery (1989), Pickens was the leading African American orator from 1915, when Booker T. Washington died, until Martin Luther King, Jr., gained influence in the 1950s. Pickens's talent as an orator was first noticed during his undergraduate days at Talladega College, and after graduating from Yale he received a lucrative offer to tour America and Europe for three years as a lecturer. He declined that offer and spent the next sixteen years as a college educator and administrator, but during his tenure as dean at Morgan State College he was Zora Neale Hurston's oratorical coach. Hurston, who met Pickens when she attended Morgan's high school division, wrote about his influence in her autobiography, *Dust Tracks on a Road.* During Pickens's more than fifty years as an orator, he was often a featured speaker for the National Association for the Advancement of Colored People (NAACP) and for other organizations. He won praise from many of his contemporaries, including Langston Hughes, A. Philip Randolph, George Schuyler, Walter White, and Roy Wilkins.

However, Pickens reached his largest audience as a contributing editor and syndicated columnist for the Associated Negro Press, the largest black news syndicate in the United States. By the late 1920s, Pickens's weekly articles appeared in more than 100 African American newspapers. *The New Negro: His Political, Civil, and Mental Status and Related Essays* (1916), a compilation of Pickens's pieces focusing on the right of African Americans to full citizenship, was one of the first books to introduce concepts related to the "New Negro," such as self-definition and self-expression, that fueled the Harlem Renaissance.

Pickens's *Bursting Bonds* (1923), an expanded edition of *The Heir of Slaves* (1911), was the first autobiography by a literary figure of the Harlem Renaissance. It illustrates some of the ideas in his collection of essays, documenting his life before he came to Harlem—a time when he battled adversity and racism and used education as his pathway to prominence. *Bursting Bonds* is a pioneering narrative, but it has been eclipsed by the autobiographies of Hughes and Hurston and has been mainly ignored by modern-day readers and scholars.

Pickens was also one of black America's most important civic leaders during the Harlem Renaissance. As an assistant field secretary and later field secretary of the NAACP, he had direct contact with the African American masses, enlisted members, and established new branches. Pickens facilitated communication between headquarters and the branches, generated funds, investigated lynchings, collected evidence of racial discrimination, and lobbied the U.S. Congress. As a result of his lobbying at the beginning of World War I, an African American officers' training facility was established at Fort Des Moines, Iowa. Pickens remained an important civil rights leader until 1945.

Biography

William Pickens was born 15 January 1881, in Anderson County, South Carolina. He studied at a grammar school in Argenta, Arkansas; high school in Little Rock, Arkansas; Talladega College, Alabama (1899–1902); and Yale University (A.B., 1904). He was a professor of languages, Talladega College (1904–1914); president, Alabama Colored State Teachers' Association (1911–1914); chair of the department of Greek and sociology, Wiley University, Marshall, Texas (1914–1915); dean, Morgan State College (later Morgan State University), Baltimore, Maryland (1915–1918); and vice president, Morgan State (1918–1920). Pickens was a member of the Niagara Movement, 1905; a member of the Committee of 100 for the National Association for the Advancement of Colored People (NAACP), 1910; assistant field secretary, NAACP, 1920–1921; and field secretary, NAACP, 1921–1942. He was a lecturer at adult education centers for the Federal Forum Project, 1937; a contributing editor and syndicated columnist of the Associated Negro Press, 1919–1940; and director of the International Section of Treasury Department Savings Bonds, 1941–1950. His honors included membership in Phi Beta Kappa; a Litt.D. from Selma University, Alabama, 1915; and an LL.D. from Wiley College, Marshall, Texas, 1918. Pickens died on board the S.S. *Mauritania*, near Kingston, Jamaica, and was buried at sea on 6 April 1954.

LINDA M. CARTER

See also Associated Negro Press; Hughes, Langston; Hurston, Zora Neale; National Association for the Advancement of Colored People; Randolph, A. Philip; Schuyler, George S.; White, Walter

Selected Works

The Heir of Slaves. 1911. (Enlarged ed., *Bursting Bonds*, 1923.)
The New Negro: His Political, Civil, and Mental Status and Related Essays. 1916.
The Vengeance of the Gods and Three Other Stories of the Real American Color Line. 1922.
Bursting Bonds. 1923 (Enlarged ed. of *The Heir of Slaves*; reprint, 1991, intro. William L. Andrews.)
American Aesop: Negro and Other Humor. 1926.

Further Reading

Andrews, William L. "William Pickens." In *The Oxford Companion to African American Literature*, ed. William L. Andrews, Frances Smith Foster, and Trudier Harris. New York: Oxford University Press, 1997.
Avery, Sheldon. *Up From Washington: William Pickens and the Negro Struggle for Equality, 1900–1954*. Newark: University of Delaware Press, 1989.
Barton, Rebecca Chalmers. *Witnesses for Freedom: Negro Americans in Autobiography*. New York: Harper, 1948.
Carter, Linda M. "William Pickens." In *Notable Black American Men*, ed. Jessie Carney Smith. Detroit, Mich.: Gale Research, 1999.
Hurston, Zora Neale. *Dust Tracks on a Road*. New York: HarperPerennial, 1991. (Originally published 1942.)
Logan, Rayford W., and Michael R. Winston, eds. *Dictionary of American Negro Biography*. New York: Norton, 1982.

Pigfoot Mary

See Dean, Lillian Harris

Pittsburgh Courier

The *Pittsburgh Courier*, established in 1907, was a primary vehicle for spreading the gospel of the Harlem Renaissance throughout the nation. The paper began regular publication in 1910, and Robert Lee Vann—a lawyer born in North Carolina in 1879 and educated at Wilberforce University and the University of Pittsburgh School of Law—became its editor. Under Vann's leadership, the paper, which focused on sports and other news of interest to a wide range of readers, reached a maximum circulation of nearly 200,000. The *Courier* vied with the *Chicago Defender* to be ranked as the nation's leading black newspaper.

Vann, who was a follower of Booker T. Washington, often focused on local issues of economic advancement. One column, for instance, provided business advice. In contrast to A. Philip Randolph's *Messenger* and W. E. B. Du Bois's *Crisis*, and even regional papers such as Roscoe Dunjee's *Oklahoma City Black Dispatch* and the *Baltimore Afro-American*, the *Courier* had a moderate tone. It looked inward to development of the black community, rather than to great campaigns like the crusade against lynching.

The *Courier*'s emphasis on sports and sensational issues that were of interest to less militant readers distinguished it from the other leading vehicles of the renaissance. That may have contributed to its appeal. It also allowed the *Courier* to reach different readers from those of other newspapers and periodicals. In 1920, Vann started a monthly magazine, *The Competitor*. It lasted for nearly two years and then folded because it was losing money. Like the *Courier, The Competitor* was moderate in tone.

Despite Vann's relatively conservative stance, on occasion the *Courier* took aggressive positions. From 1912 onward, it repeatedly urged readers to vote—and pointed out the harm they might suffer if they failed to develop political power. Like other leading black journals, the *Courier* emphasized the hypocrisy of Americans whose rhetoric during World War I was of freedom, but who denied blacks equal rights in the United States and even in the armed forces. The *Courier* was famous for its campaign against the radio show *Amos 'n' Andy* in the early 1930s. At other times, its articles brought news of particular interest to black readers. For example, in the early 1930s it ran articles written by Marcus Garvey, who was then living in exile in Jamaica.

Sometimes it seemed that Vann steered the *Courier's* coverage in the direction that would help increase its circulation. For example, he supported A. Philip Randolph's Brotherhood of Sleeping Car Porters, a position that won him converts among porters who were essential in carrying the *Courier* to other cities. The *Courier* advocated other causes, such as limitation of discrimination in housing, public health, and education. In those instances, Vann's stance was influenced by his emphasis on self-help for African Americans.

In areas like sports, the *Courier* sought to break down barriers to achievement. Vann's coverage of Joe Louis's boxing career helped bring Louis to prominence and may possibly have "created" Louis. At the least, Vann brought attention to Louis and encouraged the development of his talents. Somewhat later, the *Courier* supported the integration of baseball and gave extensive coverage to Jackie Robinson.

Vann had a rocky relationship with W. E. B. Du Bois. In 1926, Vann ran an article accusing the National Association for the Advancement of Colored People (NAACP) of mismanagement of finances. The article singled out for attention Du Bois's expenditure of $5,000 on a study of education. Such aggressive journalism—perhaps a result of Vann's overly sensitive ego—caused a lengthy battle between the NAACP's periodical *The Crisis* and the *Courier*, which was settled in 1930 when Vann printed a retraction. Following his resignation as editor of *The Crisis*, Du Bois used the *Courier* as a vehicle for publishing his essays, just as Marcus Garvey used the paper to disseminate his ideas. The *Courier* also published other leaders of the renaissance. Zora Neale Hurston served as a correspondent, and Walter White and James Weldon Johnson contributed to the *Courier*. Its own correspondents were important leaders of the renaissance as well. For example, the historian Joel Rogers wrote a column on black history, focusing on the contributions of ancient Africa to Western civilization, and George S. Schuyler, called by some the "black H. L. Mencken," wrote editorials in the 1920s.

At times Vann entered into political conflicts. Although he was initially a strong supporter of the Republican party, Vann shifted his support to the Democrats shortly before Franklin D. Roosevelt's election in 1932. In "Patriot and the Partisan," an address to a Democratic audience in Cleveland in September 1932, Vann reported that blacks were "turning the picture of Lincoln to the wall." This address was widely reprinted and was critical in turning black support to the Democratic Party. President Roosevelt rewarded Vann by naming him special assistant to the U.S. attorney general. Vann had been optimistic about the possibilities for reform in this position, but he found that the attorney general had little interest in his counsel. In 1935, he returned to Pittsburgh and two key stories—Joe Louis and Italy's invasion of Ethiopia—which the *Courier* used to boost its circulation to a quarter million.

Vann served as editor and publisher until his death in October 1940. The managing editor, Ira Lewis, then took over. Lewis's editorials were often more strident than Vann's had been. During World War II, Lewis supervised the "double V" campaign, urging victory on two fronts: over the Axis powers abroad and over racism at home. It began in February 1942—three months after the United States entered the war—when a worker in Wichita, Kansas, wrote a letter to the *Courier* asking for victory at home and abroad. The campaign quickly spread to other leading black papers. Although the *Courier* had largely escaped criticism for radicalism under Vann's leadership, there were increasing fears that the FBI might try to censor black papers, including the *Courier*, which had an estimated circulation of about 200,000 at the time—the largest of any black newspaper in the country—and was becoming increasingly vocal in support of equal rights.

Following the war, the circulation of the *Courier* peaked at approximately 350,000 in 1948. Circulation declined to about 100,000 by the mid-1960s, when the paper was sold to the publisher of the *Chicago Defender*. As of this writing the *Courier* was still published, under the name *New Pittsburgh Courier*, a fact that testifies to the continued vitality of one of the twentieth century's important newspapers.

ALFRED BROPHY

See also Amos 'n' Andy, Baltimore Afro-American; Black Press; Brotherhood of Sleeping Car Porters; Crisis, The; Du Bois, W. E. B.; Garvey, Marcus; Hurston, Zora Neale; Johnson, James Weldon; Journalists; Messenger, The; Rogers, Joel Augustus; Schuyler, George S.; Vann, Robert L.; White, Walter

Further Reading

Brewer, James H. "Robert Lee Vann, Democrat or Republican: An Exponent of Loose Leaf Politics." *Negro History Bulletin*, 21, 1958, pp. 100–103.

Buni, Andrew. *Robert L. Vann of the Pittsburgh Courier: Politics and Black Journalism.* Pittsburgh, Pa.: University of Pittsburgh Press, 1974.

Hogan, Lawrence D. *Black National News Service: The Associate Negro Press and Claude Barnett, 1919–1945.* Rutherford, N.J.: Fairleigh Dickinson University Press, 1984.

Jordan, William G. *Black Newspapers and America's War for Democracy, 1914–1920.* Chapel Hill: University of North Carolina Press, 2001.

Lewis, David Levering. *W. E. B. Du Bois: The Fight for Equality and the American Century, 1919–1963.* New York: Holt, 2000.

Washburn, Patrick S. *A Question of Sedition: The Federal Government's Investigation of the Black Press during World War II.* New York: Oxford University Press, 1986.

Poetry: Dialect

American dialect poetry is a written genre that attempts to represent the rhythms, accents, and idioms of the speech and singing of people of a certain ethnicity, race, region, class, or even—as in the case of children's dialect—age. It is important to distinguish dialect poetry written in Creole French, Pennsylvania Dutch, or Gullah from dialect poetry meant to be suggestive of the different ways in which people in America speak English. The former was typically written by and for speakers and students of the language. The latter, by contrast, was generally not written by poets who actually spoke this way. In addition, it was meant to be understood by all English speakers. As a result, the poetry is more of a figurative, rather than literal, dialect. As a literary genre, it quickly became beholden to its own literary conventions rather than to actual spoken language variations. Examples of dialectal literary conventions include the use of quasi-phonetic spellings of words, misspelled words that look different from standard English (even if one would not pronounce them any differently), elisions and contractions, idioms, and irregular syntax.

Beginnings

During the late nineteenth century, dialect poetry had reached its heyday. Poets wrote in approximations of various dialects including Yankee, Hoosier (Indiana), German-American "broken" English, Irish-American dialect, Chinese-English pidgin, and Negro dialect. Negro dialect poetry, initially written by white poets, became the most popular. At the turn of the twentieth century the Negro, as he or she would be again during the Harlem Renaissance, was in vogue.

Dialect Poetry and the Harlem Renaissance

James Weldon Johnson began his career writing dialect poems, some of which are included in his first volume of poetry, *Fifty Years and Other Poems* (1917). With his brother J. Rosamond Johnson he set some of this dialect to music intended for the New York stage. However, he eventually felt limited by dialect, and he wrote in his preface to *The Book of American Negro Poetry* (1922) what at the time many black writers and critics considered the definitive statement on dialect poetry. Although he praises the nineteenth-century African American writer Paul Laurence Dunbar for perfecting the dialect poem, he also notes the limitations of the genre. Dialect, he famously wrote, has "but two full stops, humor and pathos" (xl). In order to express a range of emotions, poets would have to break free of the literary conventions of the past and invent a new form, one that would "express the racial spirit by symbols from within rather than by symbols from without, such as the mere mutilation of English spelling and pronunciation" (xli). (Johnson does not mention that in 1872 an African American woman poet, Frances Harper, had broken with convention in her collection of dialect folk poetry, *Sketches of Southern Life*.) Johnson is careful to specify that dialect itself is not inherently offensive. Rather, he says, it has become hopelessly associated in readers' minds with offensive stereotypes, with representations of the Negro as either happy and lazy or pathetically down and out. Some subsequent discussions of dialect poetry by writers and critics of the Harlem Renaissance more or less repeat Johnson's argument. And given the negative associations that dialect had acquired, some "New Negro" poets understandably tended to avoid it; to them, Negro dialect carried the taint of slavery and minstrelsy.

Claude McKay, while he was still in Jamaica, published two collections of poetry written in Jamaican dialect (*Songs of Jamaica* and *Constab Ballads*, both 1912). Ironically, although Johnson liked these poems so much that he did not think McKay would ever be able to write anything else as "touching and charming" (xliv), McKay never wrote another poem in dialect. Perhaps he felt that the language of the "old Negro" did not fit with his newfound militancy. Perhaps he agreed with Countee Cullen, who wrote that "the Negro poet would be foolish indeed to turn to dialect" (1927, xiv).

Foolishly or not, however, a handful of writers did continue to experiment with dialect poetry. These included Jean Toomer, Langston Hughes, and Sterling Brown. For these poets, as noted above, the challenge was to break with traditional conventions. The result was some of the most original poetry to come out of the Harlem Renaissance. (In his anthology Johnson also includes dialect poetry by John W. Holloway. He says in his preface that Holloway "more than any Negro poet writing in the dialect to-day, summons to his work the lilt, the spontaneity and charm of which Dunbar was the supreme master." However, little else is known of this poet.)

Jean Toomer's *Cane* (1923), a combination of poetry, short stories, and a play, includes poetry written in Negro dialect. Toomer, however, manipulated language so well that no one accused him of resurrecting the minstrel tradition. One of his contributions to dialect was to form contractions without replacing the missing vowels or syllables with an apostrophe. These words were visually cleaner, and they also made the old dialect of the nineteenth century seem new and different. Toomer, though, did not continue to write in this style.

Langston Hughes, in his first volume of verse, *The Weary Blues* (1926), captures the sounds of African American life by incorporating techniques from African American music. The stanzas of his poems use a blues form—the first line is repeated and then followed by a different line that rhymes with the first two. Hughes does not often replace *th* with *d*, a practice common in nineteenth-century Negro dialect. Instead, he alters spellings so that when the words are pronounced, vowel sounds predominate. The result is a more open, fluid sound. Although Hughes's poetry was popular, Redding concluded that the dialect form limited the range of potential expression (1939, 116). Interestingly, according to Redding, the concept of dialect became so offensive to African Americans that by the 1940s Langston Hughes had stopped reading his folksier poems to black audiences (1991, 145).

Johnson did not completely give up on dialect poetry. The verses in *God's Trombones: Seven Negro Sermons in Verse* (1927) are not, as Johnson points out in his preface, strictly dialect, but Johnson does consider them a continuation of the dialect tradition. He notes in his preface to this work that they are his attempt to create "a form that will express the racial spirit by symbols from within." Using "a fusion of Negro idioms with Bible English," he sought to re-create the feel of an African American sermon.

Of all the poets of the Harlem Renaissance who wrote in dialect, Sterling Brown was often considered the most successful. Although many of his dialect poems were published in magazines during the 1920s, his first collection, *Southern Road*, was not published until 1932. Locke (1935) considered this volume the beginning of a new era. It forced a reevaluation of the potential of literary conventions and of traditions that had been assumed to be outmoded. Gates describes Brown, triumphantly, as a "self-styled 'Old Negro'" (1989, 234). Although Locke preferred to call Brown's verses folk, rather than dialect, poetry, that was merely a matter of semantics. The important point was that Brown used dialect to express feelings that had never before expressed in poetry with dialect. His poems are often angry, bitter, and defiant. They describe lynchings, chain gangs, alcoholism, and the perils of city life. They are a long way from the traditional two stops.

VALARIE J. MOSES

See also Authors: 5—Poets; Brown, Sterling; Dunbar, Paul Laurence; God's Trombones; Hughes, Langston; Johnson, James Weldon; Johnson, John Rosamond; Literature: 7—Poetry; McKay, Claude; Toomer, Jean; Weary Blues, The

Further Reading

Brown, Sterling. *The Southern Road*. New York: Harcourt Brace, 1932.

Cullen, Countee. "Foreword." In *Caroling Dusk: An Anthology of Verse by Negro Poets*. New York: Harper and Row, 1927.

Gates, Henry Louis, Jr. *Figures in Black: Words, Signs, and the "Racial" Self*. New York: Oxford University Press, 1989.

Hughes, Langston. *The Collected Poems of Langston Hughes*, ed. Arnold Rampersad and David Roessel. New York: Vintage, 1995.

Johnson, James Weldon. "Preface." In *The Book of American Negro Poetry*. New York: Harcourt, Brace, 1922.

———. *Complete Poems*, ed. Sondra Kathryn Wilson. New York: Penguin, 2000.

Jones, Gavin. *Strange Talk*. Berkeley and Los Angeles: University of California Press, 1999.

Locke, Alain. "Sterling Brown: The New Negro Folk-Poet." In *Voices from the Harlem Renaissance*, ed. Nathan Irvin Huggins. New York: Oxford University Press, 1976. (Originally published 1935.)

McKay, Claude. *The Dialect Poetry of Claude McKay: Two Volumes in One*. Freeport, N.Y.: Books for Libraries, 1972.

Redding, J. Saunders. *To Make a Poet Black*. Chapel Hill: University of North Carolina Press, 1939.

———. "The Negro Author: His Publisher, His Public, His Purse." In *Scholars of Conscience*, ed. Faith Berry. Lexington: University of Kentucky Press, 1991.

Toomer, Jean. *Cane*. New York: Liveright, 1975. (Originally published 1923.)

Politics and Politicians

Politics and the role of politicians in Harlem during the 1920s represented a unique anomaly and contradiction involving power, interpersonal discord, and black race consciousness with local irrelevance, national portent, and international significance. In nearly every political realm in which blacks were engaged, white people played an important role. In local political affairs, the interaction between white bosses and ward heelers and fledgling black politicians depended largely on the sense of selfishness versus altruism of the white leader. White people involved in black issues of national portent, however, tended to be overwhelmingly altruistic, supported efforts by

blacks to sustain the organization, and made black leadership independent of and aloof from whites who would dominate for the sole purpose of holding power. Contrasts between blacks involved in local politics and organizations of national and international significance would prove interesting.

This marked a time when several fledgling protest organizations surfaced. The Equal Rights League, the African Blood Brotherhood (ABB), the Friends of Negro Freedom, and of course the Universal Negro Improvement Association (UNIA) endeavored to find ways to ameliorate the condition of Americans with African ancestry. Products of the migrant influx from the West Indies and the South, these organizations proved to be mutually contentious and inclined to compete for followers and the available meager resources necessary to carry forth liberating programs. With local, national, and international goals in mind, the organizations might appear as fanciful escapism to skeptics. But to those involved, notwithstanding the naïveté of the leadership and difficulty in achieving concrete results, the organizations signified hope.

Blacks who voted in Harlem found themselves unable effectively to exercise power because of the inexperience of their leaders. According to Clark (1965), the pejorative psychology of the ghetto pervaded the minds of black politicians, who showed evidence of helplessness and dependence on the white power elite. Lacking a strong economic base because of the penury of constituents and devoid of social influence because of omnipresent racism, the black politico had limited jurisdiction and became satisfied with meager rewards. Black politicians in Harlem during the 1920s revealed the components of a dependent, downtrodden leadership cadre working energetically to acquire positions in minor offices.

In New York City politics, Charles W. Anderson became the first politician of major significance. He was born in Oxford, Ohio, in 1866, and migrated to New York City at age twenty to make his fortune. As a resident of Manhattan, he joined the Republican Party, stumped for it in black wards, and in 1890 became president of the Young Men's Colored Republican Club of New York County. He rose from being the private secretary of New York's state treasurer to chief clerk in the state treasury, supervisor of accounts for the New York racing commission, and collector of Internal Revenue for the Second New York District. Anderson became the leader of black Republicans from the 1890s through the 1920s.

Despite his northern birth, Anderson proved a strong, if not ruthless, supporter of Booker T. Washington. He boasted of being an unwavering loyalist to Washington and gleefully undercut, when possible, anyone who opposed the wizard of Tuskegee. Though vicious in his treatment of black opponents, Anderson fashioned himself to be a true "race man" who relished finding patronage jobs for African Americans. Anderson certainly played the role of a black political hack perfectly; influential white friends enabled him to retain power long after Washington's death.

Anderson certainly profited from the influx of blacks into the city and their concentration in Harlem. Throughout the 1920s he became a member of the mayor's committee on receptions for distinguished guests and attended every major function the city produced. When the Republican boss Samuel S. Koenig appointed him collector of Internal Revenue in 1923, Anderson reached his apogee of power. Throughout his political career, to his credit, Anderson worked to achieve political opportunities for Harlem's black population and contributed to the "political wakening of Negro New York" (Osofsky 1965). In the words of James Weldon Johnson, Charles Anderson was "the very ablest Negro politician."

Despite Anderson's early foray into politics, black Harlemites remained on the periphery of political activity. Unfortunately for ambitious black politicians, Harlem's black constituents had been conveniently divided into two separate assembly districts: the Nineteenth and Twenty-first. Gerrymandered into larger white voting districts, black Harlemites remained subjected to the capriciousness of white political bosses from the Democratic and Republican parties. Nevertheless, competition between Republicans and Democrats covetous of the black vote provided African Americans with sufficient political leverage to act somewhat independently to acquire largess. Thus, when Edward A. Johnson became the first black from New York City elected to state office as late as 1917, black Harlemites reached a significant milestone. A portion of black Harlem, the Nineteenth Assembly District, would be represented in the state assembly.

Johnson had been born in Raleigh, North Carolina, in 1860 and had gained experience as a lawyer and as a professor of law and dean at Shaw University. When blacks were systematically excluded from voting during the early twentieth century and evidence of heightened racism appeared in North Carolina, Johnson moved to New York in 1907. The steady increase of Harlem's black population enabled Johnson to renew his legal practice and acquire property. As an assemblyman Johnson proved to be an able legislator for Harlem; he drafted and helped pass civil rights laws in the state of New York.

As the black influx into Harlem continued, blacks increased their political visibility. In 1918, John C. Hawkins won a seat in the state legislature to represent the Twenty-first Assembly District, and the following year Charles H. Roberts became the first black alderman elected in New York. By 1922 the first Democratic Party Club for blacks formed under the auspices of J. Raymond Jones and his West Indian friends who had an affiliation with the UNIA.

In 1923, Ferdinand Q. Morton, who had moved to Harlem from Mississippi, became politically prominent. He was a graduate of Phillips Exeter and Harvard, and he acquired leadership through a fledgling political club known as the United Colored Democracy. Savvy white politicians realized that Morton's education made him a formidable contender for political office and understood that his ambition must be satiated. Democratic leaders endeavored to appease Morton by offering him the position of magistrate. Morton declined the appointment but gained a seat on the Civil Service Commission. There, he established a reputation as "aggressive, egotistic, intellectual, and dedicated; stubborn and outspoken yet an organization man." Although Morton did not gain popularity with the rank and file of his political district, he did prove effective, efficient, and fair.

It would be presumptuous to assume that the elections and appointments of blacks to responsible positions were signs of racial advancement. People like the "Bookerite" Charles Anderson played a "gatekeeping" role for the Republicans, as did Ferdinand Morton for the Democrats. These men helped the white power structure retain power in Harlem as the number of black constituents and expectations increased dramatically. However, organizations like the UNIA and the cultural flowering and pride derived from the Harlem Renaissance undermined the legitimacy of the gatekeepers and provided black constituents with newfound strength to support and eventually elect true "race men" to authoritative positions.

During the 1920s black politicians in Harlem could claim responsibility for constructing playgrounds and parks and making other recreational facilities available for the poor. They could also be credited with having blacks hired as firefighters and policemen, and for placing African Americans in supervisory roles in municipal hospitals, the boards of education and health, city courts, and public agencies. But the gains of black New Yorkers paled in comparison with the successes achieved by black politicians in Chicago. Black politicians in Harlem achieved limited results for several reasons. First, they were unable to wrest power from white leaders, who exercised control through segregated Republican and Democratic clubs that dispensed largess and patronage to constituents. Second, the political fortunes of blacks depended entirely on the whims of white politicos. A beneficent, altruistic ward heeler or boss would make provisions to assist black constituents, whereas one who was indifferent or hostile to the black community offered little of consequence. Third, competition for power among black politicos undermined prospects for progress in black Harlem. Intraracial conflict invariably proved more debilitating than constructive in the 1920s. Fourth, leading black politicians like Charles Anderson and Ferdinand Morton shielded white bosses from demanding blacks who expected greater consideration and attention from political representatives. Finally, and with a bizarre twist, large numbers of blacks voting in Harlem contributed to a disproportionate result. Tammany Hall Democrats controlled city politics. When few blacks voted in an election, leaders of the "Colored Democracy"—the Democratic Party Club founded in 1922—rallied black Democrats and kept the membership intact. But when a substantial number of black Harlemites voted, ambitious black politicians competed for power and minimized or diffused the power of each leader.

The number of blacks appointed to responsible positions remained meager throughout the decade. In 1921, the attorney James C. Thomas became the first black selected to be an assistant U.S. district attorney, and John C. Hawkins (mentioned previously) was designated to serve as the associate counsel of the U.S. Shipping Board. Other minor appointments blacks acquired included positions in the U.S. Post Office and the Internal Revenue Service. Nevertheless, few African Americans could claim that black residents in Harlem achieved adequate representation from members of their own race.

By the late 1920s black leaders in Harlem demonstrated a nascent independence and proceeded to seek power for themselves. Encouraged by the success of black Chicago success in electing Oscar De Priest to a seat in the U.S. House of Representatives, Harlemites sought greater political influence and augmented the number of blacks running for public office. In 1929, Francis E. Rivers defeated the Republican machine boss Abraham Grenthal, to acquire a powerful seat in the state assembly. In the same election year Fred R. Moore, editor of *New York Age*, won a second term as a member of the board of aldermen. There were signs of further political advancement by blacks when a veteran of the Spanish American War and World War I, Lieutenant Colonel Charles W. Filmore, became the first black to head an assembly district and four blacks were elected to offices in the state assembly and on the board of aldermen. Although these successes represented black political ascendancy in Harlem, the Democrats who dominated New York City's politics still refused to nominate an African American for a seat in the U.S. Congress. Therefore, no black politician represented Harlem in Congress until after districts were redrawn in 1944.

Although many prominent residents made Harlem a center for artistic expression, others perceived Harlem as a useful laboratory for developing means to help the black working class. Radical thinkers envisioned Harlem as fertile ground to advance their cause, and none demonstrated more energy, daring, and commitment to use blacks than members of the Communist Party of the United States (CPUSA). Just as other fledgling organizations tested their political acumen in Harlem, so too did members of the Communist Party. In fact, the Communist Party's endeavors to court favor among African Americans far exceeded the efforts made by Democrats and Republicans. The communists aggressively looked for black leaders who would bring the black proletariat into the party.

Before becoming communists, many black leftists had connections with the Socialist Party. The socialists, however, failed to entice blacks to join their party because of their reluctance to recognize that the plight of black workers was attributed to both class and race oppression. Two of the most prominent blacks of Harlem who would leave the Socialist Party were A. Philip Randolph and Chandler Owen. As early as November 1917, Randolph and Owen's radicalism became evident when they founded their magazine, *The Messenger*. Their statements against the United States' participation in World War I placed them at odds with the federal government and led to their incarceration. Undaunted by accusations of sedition, the pair continued using *The Messenger* as a voice demanding rights for the black laboring class. In 1922, Randolph, an American nationalist at heart, split from his fellow socialists in Harlem, believing that doctrines for reform could not be shaped in Russia through the Communist International. After Owen left New York for Chicago, Randolph would devote time to organizing the Brotherhood of Sleeping Car Porters and staving off communist attempts to infiltrate his new union.

Like Randolph and Owen, Otto Huiswood, Richard B. Moore, and Cyril Briggs left the Socialist Party but embraced communism. As immigrants from the Caribbean, these three had less allegiance to or concerns about the welfare of African Americans than in the philosophical arguments and principles inherent in communist ideology. Therefore, West Indian radicals would have reason to be more accepting of an international doctrine that espoused concern for workers throughout the world than of a focus entirely on issues specific to African Americans.

Even before the Sixth Congress International in Moscow in July 1928—the meeting that spoke directly to the "resolution of the Negro question"—communist influence in Harlem had become evident. Some members of the Communist Party decided to infiltrate the Socialist Party, establish black organizations like the African Blood Brotherhood, "and carry on agitation among Negro workers" to forge a union with all class-conscious laborers. Recognizing that the Socialist Party viewed blacks as a deterrent to the labor movement and that their leaders had ignored the especial oppression which African Americans experienced, the communists developed a unique strategy to win adherents. They believed that blacks, as the most exploited labor force in the United States, could be used to spearhead the Communist Party cause. Thus, to enlist the support of African Americans, the communists decided to focus on acquiring black disciples. First, they decided to look for leadership from blacks living in the industrial North. Next, party leaders founded recruitment cells in Harlem and other black enclaves in the United States to infiltrate black organizations, proselytize on behalf of communism, and increase the membership of CPUSA.

The communists initially became fixated on Harlem as a base of operations because of the successes demonstrated by Garvey and his UNIA. Garvey appealed to "grassroots" Negroes, people identified by communist ideologues as members of the proletariat. The CPUSA hierarchy, moreover, recognized that Garvey attacked African American leaders—the black bourgeoisie—and was meeting with considerable success, as evidenced by the soaring membership of UNIA and by the thousands of dollars raised for its various enterprises. Furthermore, the initial successes of Garveyism demonstrated to communist leaders that blacks abhorred the treatment they received from nondemocratic forces in America and that blacks, if given proper direction and focus, could be organized into a fervent and effective phalanx to fight oppression. Garvey also enabled the communists to realize that northern blacks were politically astute, and that recent southern migrants willing to test their newly acquired freedom could be enticed to join active, progressive organizations.

But while Harlem contained the greatest safe haven for advancing the communist ideology, excluding the "Deep South," CPUSA also met its greatest black adversaries in Harlem. Mutual antipathy developed between the communists on one hand and the NAACP, National Urban League (NUL), and Brotherhood of Sleeping Car Porters on the other. The communists took an overtly hostile attitude toward all moderate black organizations because of conservative black middle-class gradualism in addressing problems and rectifying wrongs. Leaders of CPUSA became incensed when the NAACP national committee of 1926 refused to endorse a trade union proposal introduced by the leftist black delegate James W. Ford. The communists also had cause for disenchantment with the NUL. Because the NUL depended on cooperation with corporate America, most leaders in the organization also opposed the union movement and the use of strikes. Automatically, the communists were at odds with black leaders of these organizations—the nonrevolutionary black bourgeoisie.

Despite modest gains made by local politicians, the most gifted black politicians who lived in Harlem belonged to organizations that addressed issues of national and international import. Even unsuccessful policies conceived and nurtured there—like the NAACP's inability to gain the passage of a congressional antilynching bill—naturally had far greater significance than the miniscule gains that local black Democrats or Republicans achieved through elections and appointments.

While Washington, D.C., served as the hub of national politics in the United States, the political center of the African American community and blacks worldwide was in Harlem. Politics and the role of politicians in Harlem during the 1920s represented a unique blend involving power, heightened interpersonal challenges, freedom from oppression, and black race consciousness. As the myriad of issues posed by

Harlem's "race men" were sown in New York, their concerns germinated and flowered in black communities throughout the nation and extended, through the Pan-African Congresses, to reach the entire world. For example, the Pan-African Congresses held in 1919, 1921, and 1923 had been assembled by the visionary W. E. B. Du Bois. Attendees from French and English African colonies, the West Indies, and Europe participated with Harlemites such as Du Bois, Walter White, and Jessie Redmon Fauset of the NAACP. In addition, topics specifically related to activities in Harlem carried international significance. On the eve of the Second Pan-African Congress in 1919, Liberia expressed concern that Garvey's movement could jeopardize governments in Africa. Similar concerns were raised by Blaise Diagne of France, who presided over the Pan-African Congress in Brussels in 1921. Diagne voiced his distaste for Garveyism and the pejorative connotations Garvey's "back to Africa" movement had for black francophones who, like their bourgeois African American counterparts, wanted assimilation into rather than separation from their peers in white society. Moreover, as Harlemites trekked to foreign countries to share information and provide counsel regarding pan-Africanism, distinguished visitors like F. E. M. Hercules of Trinidad and Dr. J. Edmeston Barnes of Barbados ventured to Harlem for consultation.

In the realm of politics, ideas, programs, policies, and objectives external to the borders of Harlem became far more important than Harlem itself. This world of national and international politics pertaining to racial and cultural issues unique to individuals of African ancestry evolved from within the depths of multifaceted Harlem politics.

The political climate in the United States, exemplified by the scores of race riots in 1919, placed blacks in an extremely uncomfortable, precarious situation. For race-conscious blacks, the salvation of the race was at stake. Therefore, the political infighting within Harlem characterized by vicious personal attacks may be perceived more as acts of desperation than deliberate attempts to destroy political opponents. The initial and most persistent issue that sullied the political climate in Harlem involved those who sought to integrate African Americans into mainstream America versus advocates of voluntary separation of blacks from whites. Counted among the political combatants demanding assimilation were W. E. B. Du Bois, the most prominent member of the NAACP, and A. Philip Randolph, head of the Brotherhood of Sleeping Car Porters. Their nemesis, Marcus Garvey, founder and president of the UNIA, strongly advocated racial separation and went so far as to enlist the support of the racist Ku Klux Klan.

Harlem would provide the proper milieu for opposing ideologies to wage a unique war for black amelioration. The struggle appeared reminiscent of the earlier quarrels between Du Bois and Booker T. Washington about the best means for procuring black success in a hostile United States. After Washington's death in 1915—one year before Garvey's move from Jamaica to New York City—Du Bois's integrationist views prevailed. But after Du Bois recommended that blacks "close ranks" in support of the United States' participation in World War I and black soldiers were received with hostility on returning from the war in France, Du Bois's logic was scrutinized, questioned, and attacked. Randolph and Owen excoriated Du Bois in *The Messenger*. Garvey also chastised Du Bois, claiming that Du Bois was old and controlled by white capitalists on the NAACP's board of directors. Du Bois had initially praised Garvey for his commitment to uplifting blacks by encouraging them to join the UNIA and invest in a commercial venture known as the Black Star Line; however, when Garvey endorsed voluntary black segregation, Du Bois broke with him. Joining Du Bois in the fray were members of the NAACP's central office hierarchy—Walter White and James Weldon Johnson—who fought incessantly to integrate blacks into the larger society. To those at the NAACP, Garvey's endorsement of segregation seemed heretical, even insane.

Given the circumstances people of African ancestry experienced in America, Garvey presented a logical ideological position. Thousands of frustrated black people despaired, sincerely believing that Negro people could never attain acceptance or equality in America. These people found solace in the black nationalist message that Garvey delivered: "Up, you mighty race"; "One God, one aim, one destiny"; "Back to Africa." Such appeals to pride and unity captivated disenchanted blacks near and far, bringing acclaim to Garvey and his UNIA. Countering the hostility of white racists, Garvey assumed the mantle of a black race radical that soothed the ego of a dispirited race.

However, the dissension between Garvey and the black establishment in Harlem digressed into name-calling that involved skin color. Because many of those who opposed Garvey, such as Du Bois and Walter White, were mulattos, Garvey perceived the attacks on him as being primarily determined by color. Therefore, Garvey applied what may be referred to as

981

"pigmentocracy" to explain why certain African Americans opposed him and the UNIA. He also made disparaging references to the light skin of his opponents, based on the distinction between blacks and mulattos in his native Jamaica. From his newspaper *Negro World*, published out of his headquarters at 120–140 West 138th Street, Garvey called Du Bois a "half-breed" who had ingratiated himself with white folks. Garvey derisively referred to other opponents as octoroons, quadroons, and "race defamers" because they used hair straightener and face bleach. Garvey's attacks went beyond individuals. He lashed out against the the NAACP and called those who opposed him "good old darkies," "Uncle Tom Negroes," and "wicked maligners." He also threatened his opponents with bodily harm if any one of them physically attacked proponents of the UNIA. Many African Americans in Harlem and elsewhere resented this characterization of an intraracial divide based on color and excoriated Garvey for his impertinence and for delving into this hidden and sensitive issue.

Name-calling began in earnest where the most insulting, derogatory terms were used by Garvey's opponents to demean and discredit him. "Garveyphobes" said that the UNIA stood for "Ugliest Negroes in America" and referred to Garvey as being squat, black, and fat, with "protruding jaws, . . . heavy jowls, small bright pig-like eyes and rather bull-dog like face." Du Bois wrote that Garvey was a living embodiment of black caricatures reminiscent of a sable vaudevillian, and declared him to be the "most dangerous enemy of the Negro race in America." Du Bois despised Garvey for pitting the privileged and exploited, educated and ignorant, rich and poor, and light and dark people of African ancestry against each other.

Though hardly inclined to join forces with Du Bois, A. Philip Randolph also attacked Garvey, for his own personal reasons. Randolph perceived Garvey as a threat to his efforts to ameliorate the condition of working-class Americans. Randolph believed that Garvey introduced class divisions and exploited class differences to enhance his position as the spokesperson for the black poor and dispossessed. Garvey's UNIA proved eminently successful in capturing the hearts and minds of the black masses—to a far greater extent than Randolph. Garvey's *Negro World* had a broader circulation than *The Messenger*. Sensing a profound challenge to his role as a leader of the black proletariat, Randolph saw a potential diminution of his role as a spokesman for the masses unless Garvey was controlled or eliminated.

Philosophical differences between the two men concerning the role of race in mobilizing workers also caused problems. Randolph endorsed a collectivization of black and white workers under the single banner of socialism. Garvey, conversely, believed that African Americans should operate independently of whites—a position that undercut the idealistic Randolph, who hoped to mitigate interracial differences by developing an economic bond to unify the races.

Ironically, differences between Garvey and his opponents occasionally transcended class, origin, or color. The UNIA appealed to middle- and working-class blacks as well as to native-born and Caribbean blacks. Some among the disgruntled bourgeoisie—frustrated by their inability to find work commensurate with their ability—were attracted by the opportunities of separatism. Meanwhile, the black masses derived gratification from the positive racial appeal Garvey presented. Moreover, it seems unlikely that mulattos who desired to enter the portals of Liberty Hall (Garvey's headquarters) would have been turned away. Therefore, another important factor—the sheer embarrassment of Garvey's persona—may be deemed responsible for the strident call for Garvey's removal. The ostentation and arrogance that Garvey projected, combined with what the mulatto bourgeoisie would consider physical homeliness, undermined the measured, demure pride that established blacks chose to display. It is hardly surprising, therefore, that Randolph thought Garvey a threat to the well-being of African Americans and called him "A Supreme Negro Jamaican Jackass." Chandler Owen—Randolph's fellow Socialist and close friend—also expressed his dislike of Garvey, calling him an ignoramus and a fool.

As early as 1920 native-born African Americans formed an organization called the Friends of Negro Freedom (chaired by Randolph) and initiated a "Garvey must go" campaign. While Randolph, Owen, and others believed, like Garvey, in racial pride, they adamantly opposed his penchant for baiting white liberals and calling for racial segregation. They also abhorred Garvey because of his contribution to the split between African Americans and West Indians.

Another sector of the black community at odds with Garvey evolved from an unexpected source—his fellow West Indians. Richard B. Moore, along with Wilfred Adolphus Domingo, Cyril Briggs, and other members of the African Blood Brotherhood (ABB) found considerable fault with Garvey; in fact, Domingo and Briggs agitated to have Garvey deported. The issue here involved opposing factions:

the UNIA espoused black nationalism while ABB endorsed communism.

Although some might contend that Harlem established a reputation as the most contentious black community in the world, others might add that it was also the most politically enlightened.

Some problems involving Garvey and other factions within Harlem had roots in dissension between native-born African Americans and newcomers from the West Indies. Restrictions on immigration limited the Europeans and Asians who could enter the United States, but these restrictions did not apply to people from the Caribbean, and so numerous West Indians came—particularly to New York. These migrants came from many different islands, including Jamaica, Barbados, Bermuda, the Bahamas, Saint Kitts, Nevis, and Montserrat. Although the immigrants represented different nationalities, the bonds established between neophytes in an alien nation created greater camaraderie among the newcomers than between them and American blacks. West Indians identified more with class divisions than with racial divisions; in this regard, they differed from African Americans who first and foremost felt the pain of racism. African Americans, in turn, resented the newcomers, who appeared to place radical class politics before the politics of race, and failed to join African Americans in the fight against racial discrimination.

Native-born blacks also resented the aggressiveness of the West Indians. Unlike other immigrant populations, first-generation West Indians abhorred menial labor. As soon as possible these enterprising people started businesses and turned a haughty mien toward less ambitious African Americans. A disproportionate number of small businesses in Harlem were owned by immigrants, including the *Amsterdam News*; this newspaper of black Harlem was owned by the West Indian P. M. H. Savory. Correspondingly, local black Harlemites resented the success of the black Caribbeans. Unfortunately, the lack of cohesion between native and immigrant peoples divided Harlem and limited the successes each group required for sustenance and escape from racial restrictions that limited social, economic, and political development.

Considering the stimulation evident in Harlem, which extolled "negritude" and supported organizations with racial amelioration in mind, it seems ironic that few direct correlations existed between the work and activity of national organizations and those specific to Harlem. The mediocre gains of Harlem's black politicians during the 1920s serve as a reminder that significant differences existed between politics at the local level and politics at the national level. Local issues involving patronage and reciprocity were petty and narrow in scope, occasionally rising to the state but seldom to the national level. Within the two black assembly districts of Harlem, local politicians like Charles Anderson and Ferdinand Morton would spend far more time following the dictates of ward bosses, maintaining the loyalty of the constituency, courting the favor of magistrates, and performing other duties that could ensure their own reelection or appointment to coveted positions or offices. Not even the many activities in Harlem that evoked race consciousness nationally caused local black Democrats or Republicans to deviate from mundane interests. The politicians appreciated the significant differences between the immediate local needs of constituents and concerns voiced at a national level that could have ramifications for the entire race.

Ironically, at the international center of black culture, local politics, local politicians, and local issues appeared irrelevant. Although people involved with the politics of the era lived and worked in proximity, Harlemites of long standing seemed passive as compared with the dynamism of black people who migrated into the city during the early decades of the twentieth century. Long-established blacks and energetic newcomers acted in isolation from each other. Blacks of Harlem made their most noteworthy political gains after the decade of the "Roaring Twenties" had passed.

H. VISCOUNT NELSON

See also African Blood Brotherhood; Anderson, Charles W. Briggs, Cyril; Communist Party; De Priest, Oscar; Ford, James William; Messenger, The; Moore, Frederick Randoph; Moore, Richard B.; Morton, Ferdinand Q.; New York Age; Owen, Chandler; Pan-African Congresses; Party Politics; Race Men; Randolph, A. Philip; United Colored Democracy; Universal Negro Improvement Association; Washington, Booker T.; *other specific individuals*

Further Reading

Anderson, Jarvis. *This Was Harlem: A Cultural Portrait, 1900–1950*. New York: Farrar, Straus and Giroux, 1981.

Clarke, John Henrik, ed. *Marcus Garvey and the Vision of Africa*. New York: Vintage, 1974.

Clark, Kenneth B. *Dark Ghetto: Dilemmas of Social Power*. New York: Harper and Row, 1965.

Cronon, E. David. *Black Moses: The Story of Marcus Garvey.* Madison: University of Wisconsin Press, 1969.

Dodson, Howard, Christopher Moore, and Roberta Yancy. *The Black New Yorkers.* Schomburg Illustrated Chronology. New York: Wiley, 2000.

Foner, Philip S., and Herbert Shapiro, eds. *American Communism and Black Americans: A Documentary History, 1930–1934.* Philadelphia, Pa.: Temple University Press, 1991.

Green, Charles, and Basil Wilson. *The Struggle for Black Empowerment in New York City: Beyond the Politics of Pigmentation.* New York: Praeger, 1989.

Lewinson, Edwin R. *Black Politics in New York City.* New York: Twayne, 1974.

Lewis, David Levering. *W. E. B. Du Bois: The Fight for Equality and the American Century, 1919–1963.* New York: Holt, 2000.

Nelson, H. Viscount "Berky." *The Rise and Fall of Modern Black Leadership: Chronicle of a Twentieth Century Tragedy.* New York: University Press of America, 2003.

Osofsky, Gilbert. *Harlem: The Making of a Ghetto—Negro New York, 1890–1930.* New York: Harper and Row, 1965.

Pfeffer, Paula F. *A. Philip Randolph, Pioneer of the Civil Rights Movement.* Baton Rouge: Louisiana State University Press, 1990.

Record, Wilson. *The Negro and the Communist Party.* New York: Atheneum, 1971.

Porgy and Bess

The opera *Porgy and Bess* began with DuBose Heyward's novel *Porgy* (1925), which was widely read and well reviewed. One reader was the composer George Gershwin, who, riveted, stayed up late on a summer night in 1926 and finished it in one sitting. He promptly dashed off a letter to Heyward, proposing that they collaborate on a musical version of the story. However, the project was postponed because of Gershwin's busy schedule, and meanwhile—in 1927—the Theater Guild in New York City presented a stage version by Heyward and his wife, Dorothy, on Broadway. The play was a hit, running for nearly two years in New York, on tour around the United States, and in London. The singer Al Jolson, best known for performing in blackface makeup, proposed a musical version of *Porgy* to Heyward and the Theater Guild, but the project fell through when his collaborators—the composers Jerome Kern and Oscar Hammerstein II—abandoned it.

Eventually, in 1933, when his schedule allowed, Gershwin, along with his brother Ira (who cowrote the lyrics and libretto), began a long-distance collaboration with Heyward, between South Carolina and New York City. The press eagerly anticipated this pairing of a successful southern novelist and his racial subject with one of the country's most popular composers.

Porgy and Bess, directed by Rouben Mamoulian (who had also directed *Porgy*) and produced by the Theater Guild, opened on 10 October 1935. The reviews were generally positive (although many music critics complained that it was not the "folk opera" Gershwin intended), and *Porgy and Bess* ran for 124 performances on Broadway. However, because of the large cast and the orchestra, the running costs were so high that the production lost money. After the New York run, the Theater Guild sent the show out on tour in an effort to recoup costs. It traveled to Philadelphia, Pittsburgh, Chicago, Detroit, and Washington, D.C. In July 1937, George Gershwin died of a brain tumor at age thirty-nine. *Porgy and Bess* was his last major work.

Porgy and Bess is set in "Catfish Row," a fictional African American neighborhood in Charleston, South Carolina. It tells the story of Porgy, a crippled beggar, and his love for Bess, a drug-addicted prostitute. The opera begins with a dice game, a drunken dispute, and a murder. Bess takes shelter with Porgy after her murderous boyfriend, Crown, flees. Redeemed by Porgy's love, she shares his home and slowly becomes part of the community of Catfish Row. But when she encounters Crown during a picnic on a nearby island, she succumbs to his sexual advances. She returns to the forgiving Porgy and confesses that Crown will be

Stage set of Porgy and Bess, 1935. (Photofest.)

returning to get her soon. The fishermen of Catfish Row set out early one morning a few weeks later, and a hurricane develops. Crown returns from the island, having miraculously survived the storm, and Porgy kills him. The police take Porgy to identify Crown's body, and Sportin' Life, a worldly drug-dealing outsider, induces Bess to accompany him to New York City by convincing her that Porgy will be locked up forever. The opera ends when Porgy returns and, learning of Bess's departure, sets out to follow her.

In creating the story and music of *Porgy and Bess*, Heyward and Gershwin—like many other artists of the Harlem Renaissance era—drew on African American folk culture. This impulse to marry "authentic" folk sources with high culture was also exemplified in formal concerts of African American spirituals; during the 1920s, singers like Roland Hayes, Paul Robeson, and Jules Bledsoe gained renown and drew large audiences to such recitals in the United States and Europe. In its promotional materials, the Theater Guild emphasized that Charleston was the origin and setting of *Porgy and Bess*, and most white commentators readily described the opera as a true depiction of African American life in the South. Some African American critics, though, were more skeptical with regard to the topical and musical authenticity of this work. The composer Hall Johnson described *Porgy and Bess* as "not a Negro opera by Gershwin, but Gershwin's idea of what a Negro opera should be." Nevertheless, *Porgy and Bess* provided an unprecedented opportunity for African American opera singers, since in the 1930s America's major opera companies refused to hire black singers. The original production starred Todd Duncan, a voice teacher at Howard University, as Porgy and Anne Brown, a graduate of Juilliard, as Bess. The cast also included Ruby Elzy, John Bubbles (half of the vaudeville team Buck and Bubbles), Abbie Mitchell, Georgette Harvey, Edward Matthews, Warren Coleman, J. Rosamond Johnson, and a fifty-five-member chorus.

Despite a consensus that *Porgy and Bess* had been a disappointment in 1935 (having received somewhat mixed reviews and having incurred financial losses), it went on to become a permanent fixture in the twentieth-century American cultural landscape. In 1941, Cheryl Crawford reassembled most of the original cast and streamlined the piece by drastically cutting its recitative; her version toured the United States and Canada for more than two years. In 1952, Blevins Davis and Robert Breen developed a production that toured the United States, Europe, Latin America, and North Africa for four years, generating enormous publicity; this production was sponsored overseas by the U.S. government, which considered *Porgy and Bess* an excellent vehicle for propaganda during the cold war. In 1959, a movie version of *Porgy and Bess*, made in Hollywood, featured the major African American film stars of the day: Sidney Poitier, Dorothy Dandridge, Sammy Davis Jr., and Pearl Bailey. African Americans' criticism of the opera mounted, particularly because many considered it an inappropriate representative of American culture for international audiences. Still, a reviewer writing in 1964 could be forgiven for his estimate that revivals of *Porgy and Bess* were taking the stage "every twenty minutes or so." In 1976, the Houston Grand Opera restored much of the music that had been cut from the opera over the years and marketed its *Porgy and Bess* as a return to Gershwin's original operatic version. Touring nationally, this production drew sell-out crowds, critical praise, and the Tony Award for best revival of a musical (1977). In 1985, fifty years after its debut, the Metropolitan Opera produced *Porgy and Bess* for the first time; it continues to be performed regularly by opera companies in the United States and around the world. A staggering number of jazz, popular, and classical recordings of songs from *Porgy and Bess* have appeared since the late 1930s. These recordings, by artists as diverse as Bing Crosby, Miles Davis, Willie Nelson, and Kiri Te Kanawa, ensure that many more people are familiar with its music than have ever seen *Porgy and Bess*.

ELLEN NOONAN

See also Bubbles, John; Gershwin, George; Heyward, DuBose; Johnson, Hall; Johnson, John Rosamond; Mitchell, Abbie; Porgy: Novel; Porgy: Play

Further Reading

Alpert, Hollis. *The Life and Times of Porgy and Bess: The Story of an American Classic*. New York: Knopf, 1990.

Hutchisson, James M. *DuBose Heyward: A Charleston Gentleman and the World of Porgy and Bess*. Jackson: University Press of Mississippi, 2000.

Porgy: Novel

The novel *Porgy* (1925), by the white Charlestonian DuBose Heyward, was the first major southern novel to portray African Americans in an honest, straightforward way, rather than hew to the nineteenth-century stereotypes of shiftless darkies or faithful servitors. The novel caused a sensation in the South, where many readers reacted negatively to Heyward's progressive views, and was uniformly applauded in the North, especially by intellectual circles in Harlem, where Heyward was seen as a leading light in the literary depiction of African Americans.

The novel tells the story of a crippled black beggar, Porgy, and his great love, Bess. It is set in Charleston in the first decade of the twentieth century, in a tenement neighborhood called Catfish Row. Bess is a "weak" woman who is victimized first by the brutal Crown (who kills a companion named Robbins in a dispute over a crap game and then goes into hiding), then by Sportin' Life, a trickster figure who represents the "city" Negro. He seduces Bess with cocaine, or "happy dust." In Crown's absence, Porgy courts Bess, they join together in a common-law union, and they informally adopt a baby girl. Porgy then protects Bess when Crown reappears, eventually killing him. Porgy goes to jail briefly and returns to find Bess gone off to Savannah with Sportin' Life, there presumably to fall into a life of drugs and prostitution. He takes off after her in his ramshackle cart, pulled by a goat.

Heyward based the novel on a newspaper report he had read, about one Sammy Smalls, a goat-cart beggar of King Street in peninsular Charleston, and Smalls's alleged shooting of a local woman, Maggie Barnes. The crime was never proved, but Smalls took off down the street in his goat cart when the police pursued him, giving Heyward the idea for a central tragicomic event in the novel—and for two central traits of the inhabitants of Catfish Row: their ingrained distrust of the white world, and the insularity of their own community.

Porgy was perhaps the most famous of a string of novels written by white authors at the time that showed the modernist interest in cultural primitivism; examples include Sherwood Anderson's *Dark Laughter* and Carl Van Vechten's *Nigger Heaven*. However, *Porgy* was more sympathetic than these novels, and it endeared Heyward to many writers of the Harlem Renaissance and propelled him on a course that was to make him famous. The novel was successfully dramatized for the stage in 1927 as *Porgy: A Play*, cowritten by Heyward and his wife, Dorothy (who was a playwright). Later, it was transformed into the opera *Porgy and Bess* with music and libretto by George and Ira Gershwin—America's first native folk opera.

JAMES HUTCHISSON

See also Anderson, Sherwood; Dark Laughter; Gershwin, George; Heyward, DuBose; Nigger Heaven; Porgy and Bess; Porgy: Play; Van Vechten, Carl

Further Reading

Alpert, Hollis. *The Life and Times of Porgy and Bess*. New York: Knopf, 198s9.

Durham, Frank. *DuBose Heyward: The Man Who Wrote "Porgy."* Columbia: University of South Carolina Press, 1954.

Hutchisson, James M. *DuBose Heyward: A Charleston Gentleman and the World of Porgy and Bess*. Jackson: University Press of Mississippi, 2000.

Slavick, William. *DuBose Heyward*. Boston, Mass.: Twayne, 1981.

Porgy: Play

In 1925, DuBose Heyward, a white former insurance broker from Charleston, South Carolina, published a novel titled *Porgy*. Before then, he had established himself as a regional poet and a proponent of southern literature, but *Porgy* brought him to the attention of the New York literary world, where critics (both black and white) praised his depiction of southern black life. One reader in New York was the composer George Gershwin, who in 1926 proposed to Heyward that they collaborate on a musical version. Eventually, this collaboration did produce the opera *Porgy and Bess*, which opened in 1935.

However, before the opera *Porgy and Bess* was created, Heyward and his playwright wife, Dorothy Kuhns Heyward, adapted *Porgy* into a play. This play, also called *Porgy*, was presented by the Theater Guild, a noncommercial theatrical company in Greenwich Village in New York City. The production was directed by Rouben Mamoulian and had sets by Cleon Throckmorton. *Porgy* had its debut on 10 October 1927; ran on Broadway for 217 performances; then toured small-, medium-, and large-sized cities around the country; had a run in London; and then returned to play Broadway and tour the United States again. It ultimately had nearly two years of continuous production, generating enormous publicity and unprecedented visibility for its African American cast. That cast included Rose McClendon, Frank Wilson, Percy Verwayne, Evelyn

Ellis, Georgette Harvey, Jack Carter, the writers Dorothy West and Wallace Thurman in background roles, and thirty-nine other black actors. Many of the performers had long experience in African American theaters but were making their Broadway debuts in *Porgy*.

In Heyward's novel *Porgy*, the title character is a beggar with crippled legs, Bess is a drug-addicted prostitute, and together they experience transforming love and, finally, heartbreak. The novel also details the lives and customs of the poor black fishermen, stevedores, domestic workers, and their families who inhabit Catfish Row, a decaying grand mansion in Charleston. The central characters, in addition to Porgy and Bess, include Crown, a hot-tempered stevedore who is Bess's lover; Maria, a protective maternal figure who is the proprietor of a cookshop; Serena, a deeply religious woman; Robbins, Serena's husband, who is killed by Crown; and Peter, a grandfatherly friend to Porgy. The time seems to be an ill-defined "golden age" in the late nineteenth or very early twentieth century; the novel's main events include a dice game that ends in murder, a "saucer burial" at which residents collect money to bury their dead, a funeral, a church picnic, a raging hurricane that leaves one baby an orphan, the manipulations of a drug-dealing outsider, encounters between various residents and the white police that result in jail terms, and a final murder. The novel ends when Porgy, after being jailed for five days, returns to Catfish Row to discover that Bess is gone, lured by alcohol to accompany a group of stevedores to Savannah.

Although the play remained largely faithful to the novel, the Heywards made a few changes that significantly diminished the novel's indications of desperation and racial injustice. The play moves out of the novel's "golden age" and into the present, and the action never leaves Catfish Row—Porgy's begging on the streets of Charleston and several scenes in the jail occur offstage. In the novel, Bess is a pitiful character, and there is little room for doubt that she sells her body for drugs. In the play, by contrast, Bess is worldly and flirtatious, more glamorous than desperate. Sportin' Life, a marginal figure in the novel, becomes a prominent character in the play. His unmistakably "New York" presence contrasts with the rest of Catfish Row; and at the play's conclusion, Bess leaves with him for New York, rather than leaving for Savannah with the stevedores. Whereas the novel ends with Porgy's despair that Bess has left him, the play concludes with Porgy gamely deciding to follow her,

and setting off in his goat-drawn cart "Up Nort'—past de Custom House." This change in the plot evoked the migration of African Americans to northern cities, which was peaking in New York City and elsewhere at the time the play was produced. Yet the migration is presented disapprovingly, because Sportin' Life is clearly a malevolent figure and Porgy's journey seems quixotic, given his physical disability and naïveté about the wider world.

As one of the first Broadway dramas with an all-black cast, *Porgy* had a crucial part in establishing the critical and commercial viability of African American performers in serious roles on Broadway. During the 1920s, roles for blacks in musical revues and the occasional drama on Broadway were still rare; and shows with predominantly African American casts might reframe but still reinforce familiar stereotypes of African American characters: southern rural simplicity, superstition, religious devotion, comic urban high style, and, above all, a reflexive musicality suitable to every occasion.

The Theater Guild and the Heywards used stage directions, program notes, and publicity to bolster the idea that *Porgy* was an authentic depiction of southern black life. White commentators assumed that Heyward, as a southerner, had firsthand knowledge of his subjects, and they took *Porgy* more or less as a documentary. One critic said, for instance: "One forgot that this was a mere theater, just 'off Broadway.' It was Charleston. It was Catfish Row. It was the colored quarter, seen intimately, graphically, photographically." In contrast, African American critics, though they too praised *Porgy*, emphasized the professionalism and talent of the cast and considered the production simply the first step in the creation of vibrant African American theater on Broadway.

Porgy was a critical and popular success as a play in the 1920s, but it would be largely supplanted by the opera *Porgy and Bess* (although anthologies of American drama regularly included the play until the 1980s). *Porgy* remains a contradictory illustration of the Harlem Renaissance era, when African American intellectuals viewed artistic accomplishment as a potent form of racial uplift. *Porgy* broke new ground for African Americans in professional theater, but the way it was produced and received remained, in many significant ways, rooted in the kind of stereotypes the intellectuals of the Harlem Renaissance were attempting to combat.

ELLEN NOONAN

See also Ellis, Evelyn; Heyward, DuBose; Gershwin, George; McClendon, Rose; Porgy and Bess; Porgy: Novel; Thurman, Wallace; West, Dorothy; Wilson, Frank

Further Reading

Alpert, Hollis, *The Life and Times of Porgy and Bess: The Story of an American Classic.* New York: Knopf, 1990.

Durham, Frank. *DuBose Heyward: The Man Who Wrote Porgy.* Columbia: University of South Carolina Press, 1954.

Hutchisson, James M. *DuBose Heyward: A Charleston Gentleman and the World of Porgy and Bess.* Jackson: University Press of Mississippi, 2000.

Slavick, William H. *DuBose Heyward.* Boston, Mass.: Twayne, 1981.

Porter, James Amos

As an important artist, art teacher, and art historian, James Amos Porter possessed a rare combination of gifts. As an African American, he created, inspired, and illuminated many of the most significant works of African American art during the Harlem Renaissance and into the 1960s.

During his college studies in the 1920s, Porter came to recognize that the contributions of African American artists had gone largely unremarked and unrecorded by the academic community. As an art instructor and art historian, he focused his research on these forgotten artists, carefully documenting the work of black potters, architects, painters, and weavers. The result was a series of pioneering scholarly articles, exhibition reviews, and presentations to the College Art Association. Porter hoped that increased knowledge about African American contributions to the arts would encourage more African Americans to study art, or at least to take pride in what others had created. In 1943, Porter published his full-length study *Modern Negro Art*. Largely because of this volume, which was the first serious study of African American art and is still considered an important reference work in the field, Porter is known today as the "father of African American art history."

Porter's own drawing and painting attracted attention during the 1920s and 1930s. His paintings were selected for several important exhibitions by the

James A. Porter, c. 1930s. (© Corbis.)

Harmon Foundation, the Smithsonian Institution, and the American Watercolor Society. Reportedly, Porter was frequently annoyed by the surprise critics expressed that a black artist could produce wonderful work. Porter's early works were often emotionally powerful portraits of his own inner circle, including *Sarah* (1928), for which he won his first award. His most famous painting from the period is an oil on canvas, *Woman Holding a Jug* (1932–1933), depicting a young African American woman. Later works showed the influence of Porter's travels in Africa, Haiti, and Cuba, both in their subjects and in their increasing expressionism.

Biography

James Amos Porter was born in Baltimore, Maryland, on 22 December 1905. He was educated at Howard University, Washington, D.C., receiving a B.S. in 1927; the Institute of Art and Archeology, University of Paris, receiving a Certificat de Présence in 1935; and

New York University, earning an M.A. in art history in 1937. He served as instructor at Howard University from 1927 to 1970 and was chair of the art department and director of Howard University Gallery of Art from 1953 to 1970. His awards included an honorable mention, Harmon Foundation Exhibition, 1929; Arthur Schomburg Portrait Prize, Harmon Foundation, 1933; and Distinguished Achievement in Art Education, National Gallery of Art, 1966. His memberships included International Congress on African Art and Culture, American Federation of Arts, and Symposium on Art and Public Education. Porter died in Washington, D.C., on 28 February 1970.

CYNTHIA BILY

See also Art Criticism and the Harlem Renaissance; Artists; Harmon Foundation; Visual Arts

Selected Works

Modern Negro Art. 1943. (Reprint, 1969.)
Robert S. Duncanson, Midwestern Romantic-Realist. 1951.
Ten Afro-American Artists of the Nineteenth Century. 1967.

Individual Exhibitions

1965: "James A. Porter, Retrospective Exhibition." Howard University Gallery of Art, Washington, D.C.
1992: "James A. Porter, Artist and Art Historian: The Memory of the Legacy." Howard University Gallery of Art, Washington, D.C.

Selected Group Exhibitions

1929: Harmon Foundation exhibition.
1929: Smithsonian Institution, Washington, D.C.
1932: American Watercolor Society.
1933: Harmon Foundation exhibition.
1940: American Negro Exhibition, Chicago.

Further Reading

Bearden, Romare, and Harry Henderson. *A History of African-American Artists from 1792 to the Present.* New York: Pantheon, 1993.
Driskell, David, et al. *Harlem Renaissance Art of Black America.* New York: Abrams, 1987.
Featherstone, Starmanda Bullock. *James A. Porter, Artist and Art Historian: The Memory and the Legacy.* Washington, D.C.: Howard University Gallery of Art, 1992. (Exhibition catalog.)
Jacobsen, Robert R. *Contemporary Authors*, Vol. 155, ed. Terrie M. Rooney. Detroit, Mich.: Gale, 1997.
Mabunda, L. Mpho, and Shirelle Phelps, eds. *Contemporary Black Biography: Profiles from the International Black Community*, Vol. 11. Detroit, Mich.: Gale, 1996.
Perry, Regenia A. *Free within Ourselves: African-American Artists in the Collection of the National Museum of American Art.* San Francisco, Calif.: Pomegranate, 1992.

Powell, Adam Clayton Sr.

Adam Clayton Powell Sr. was one of the most renowned African American ministers of his time. His parents, Anthony Powell (a mulatto) and Sally Dunning Powell (an African–Cherokee Indian), were sharecroppers and former slaves. Because his father had been killed during the Civil War, Powell was raised by his mother and stepfather.

On 1 October 1871, Powell began his formal education. Although Powell was very poor, he possessed determination and drive. He is said to have walked five miles daily, without shoes, to a log schoolhouse. His wardrobe was limited to a shirt and a pair of trousers. Powell studied under the tutelage of Jake Bowles, a white teacher who became his best friend. Powell was considered a very promising student; therefore, Bowles worked diligently with him. Demonstrating his capabilities for learning at a young age, Powell learned the English (i.e., Roman) alphabet, which was totally unfamiliar to him, in one day. After a few months, he memorized some of his books. Once Powell learned to read, he continued reading throughout his life.

Powell's stepfather had a tremendous effect on his life, especially his ministerial career. In 1872, Powell's stepfather introduced him to the Bible by giving him a copy of the Gospel According to St. John. He read this book no fewer than twenty times before he turned ten. Powell's stepfather supplied him with reading materials whenever he could. These materials included fragments of paper and a subscription to a weekly Washington paper.

Seeking employment on the tobacco farms, Powell and his family moved to West Virginia in 1875. Despite the hardships that Powell encountered in West Virginia, something positive came out of his stay there. When Powell was thirteen, he befriended a young girl, Mattie Fletcher Shaffer. She was seven years younger than Powell, and he often helped her across a hazardous bridge, especially during the winter, on their way to school. A very special friendship developed between them. Subsequently, she would become his wife.

Life in West Virginia also had its negative influences. During his adolescence, Powell became associated with people who were engaged in unlawful activities. In fact, Powell is said to have always had a pistol, some brass knuckles, and hard liquor in his possession. He even shot a man who was attempting to take something from the farm. Powell got into a great deal of trouble and became a juvenile delinquent.

Concerned for his own safety, Powell decided to relocate to Rendville, Ohio, in 1884. There, however, he found himself in a city where gambling was rampant. In addition to his other vices, Powell was soon possessed by gambling. He gambled all of his wages obtained from a job in the coal mines, borrowed money in order to gamble, and on one occasion even gambled away his overcoat.

On a Sunday morning in March 1885, Powell happened to go inside a Baptist church where Rev. D. B. Houston, the pastor, was conducting revival services. Powell experienced a moment of epiphany and was converted to Christianity; in 1888, he would enter the ministry. He enrolled in Wayland Seminary and College in Washington, D.C, and completed his studies within four years. Subsequently, he returned to West Virginia and married Mattie Shaffer in 1889; their marriage did not end until she died in 1945.

Powell's first pastorate was in 1892 at the Ebenezer Church in Philadelphia. Shortly, Powell and his wife moved to New Haven, Connecticut, in 1893. Several events occurred while Powell was in Connecticut: He became pastor of Immanuel Baptist Church, matriculated at Yale University, and became secretary of the Baptist Ministers' Conference, and he and his wife had two children, Blanche Fletcher (b. 1898) and Adam Clayton Powell Jr. (b. 1908), who would become New York's first black Congressman in 1945.

On 31 December 1908, Powell, a stately man who stood 6 feet 3 inches and weighed 190 pounds, became pastor of the Abyssinian Baptist Church, at West Fortieth Street in Manhattan, New York. This church had just celebrated its hundredth anniversary, but it was located in a red-light district; and Powell was interested in moving to where the people were so that the church could meet their needs. He eventually persuaded the

congregation to buy land in Harlem—at West 138th Street, between Lenox and Seventh avenues—and build a new church, which was completed in 1923.

During the early 1920s, in the aftermath of World War I, employment and housing were major concerns. Thousands of blacks were leaving the South and heading north looking for jobs; many blacks were seeking housing in Harlem. Whites were moving out of Harlem because of the decline in real estate value, and blacks were moving in. This migration gave rise to a cultural renaissance—a period of creativity for blacks—and Powell was in an ideal position to make many significant contributions to the movement.

As pastor of the Abyssinian Baptist Church, Powell played several major roles in establishing Harlem's culture: (1) He built Harlem's first community recreation center. (2) He was instrumental in establishing a social-religious education program, which could help eradicate many of the social ills. In addition to Bible classes, there were literacy classes, business classes, and sex education classes, to name a few. (3) He was responsible for spearheading the building of a home for the elderly on Saint Nicholas Avenue. (4) Powell was an advocate

Adam Clayton Powell Sr., c. 1928. (Photographs and Prints Division, Schomburg Center for Research in Black Culture, New York Public Library, Astor, Lenox, and Tilden Foundations.)

for the poor, and he stressed the need for better jobs. (5) During the Depression, Powell provided soup kitchens for the poor. (6) He emphasized racial justice. (7) Abyssinian became the largest black Protestant church in the United States, with a membership of approximately 14,000, before Powell's retirement in 1937.

When Powell retired, he was succeeded by his son, Adam Clayton Powell Jr. Even after his retirement, the elder Powell continued to fight for civil rights and equal opportunities for blacks. On his death, he was recognized as a remarkable minister and leader.

Biography

Adam Clayton Powell Sr. was born on 5 May 1865, in Soak Creek, Franklin County, Virginia. He studied at Rendville Academy in Perry, Ohio; and Wayland Seminary and College, Washington D.C., receiving a B.A. in 1892. He was a special student at Yale University Divinity School in 1895–1896. Powell was pastor of Ebenezer Baptist Church, Philadelphia, Pennsylvania, 1892–1893; Immanuel Baptist Church, New Haven, Connecticut, 1893–1908; and Abyssinian Baptist Church, New York City, 1908–1937. He was also an editorial writer for the *Christian Review,* a vice president of the National Association for the Advancement of Colored People (NAACP), and a founder of the National Urban League. His awards included an honorary D.D. from Virginia Union University in 1904, the Harmon Foundation Award in 1929, and being designated pastor emeritus from 1937 to 1953. Powell died in New York City on 12 June 1953.

NILA M. BOWDEN

See also Abyssinian Baptist Church; Harlem: Negro Metropolis

Selected Works

Against the Tide. 1938.
Palestine and Saints in Caesar's Household. 1939.
Picketing Hell. 1942.
Riots and Ruins. 1945.

Further Reading

Anderson, Jervis. *This Was Harlem: A Cultural Portrait, 1900–1950.* New York: Farrar, Straus and Giroux, 1983.

Hamilton, Charles V. *Adam Clayton Powell, Jr.* New York: Macmillian, 1991.
Haskins, James. *Adam Clayton Powell: Portrait of a Marching Black.* New York: Dial, 1974.
Haygood, Wil. *King of the Cats.* New York: Houghton Mifflin, 1993.
Powell, Adam Clayton, Jr. *Adam by Adam: The Autobiography of Adam Clayton Powell, Jr.* New York: Dial, 1971.
Powell, Adam Clayton, Sr. *Against the Tide: An Autobiography.* New York: Richard R. Smith, 1938.
———. *Riots and Ruins.* New York: Richard R. Smith, 1945.

Prather, IDA

See Cox, Ida Prather

Preer, Evelyn

The actress and singer Evelyn Preer was born in Mississippi in 1896 and was raised in Chicago, where she began her acting career c. 1916. During the early part of her career, she was active primarily in film. She worked extensively with the pioneering director Oscar Micheaux and starred in eight of his silent films: *The Homesteader* (1917), *Within Our Gates* (1919), *The Brute* (1920), *Deceit* (1921), *The Gunsaulus Mystery* (1922), *Birthright* (1924), *The Conjure Woman* (1926), and *The Spider's Web* (also 1926).

In the 1920s Preer reigned as the preeminent African American stage actress and was described as "an actress of rare ability, and intelligence" (*New York Age,* 1925). She joined the famous Lafayette Players of Harlem during their run in Chicago in 1920 and would remain a key member of this important theatrical company for the remainder of her life. She was especially active in their tours of the southern states in the mid-1920s. The Lafayette Players were by far the most esteemed of Harlem's theatrical organizations, and Preer, as their leading lady, was featured in many important theater productions of the 1920s. In 1923, these players performed a triple bill on Broadway: Oscar Wilde's *Salome;* Shakespeare's *Comedy of Errors;* and a new one-act comedy, Willis Richardson's *The Chip Woman's Fortune.* Preer's other notable appearances with the Lafayette Players included *Scandals, Why Wives Go Wrong, The Good Bad Girl,* and *The Warning.*

Her numerous additional stage credits of this period included *Anna Christie, Desire Under the Elms, Madame X, Bought and Paid For, Branded, Rain*, and *Over the Hill to the Poorhouse*. In the mid-1920s Preer appeared with increasing frequency on Broadway, finding success in such high-profile productions as *Lulu Belle* (1926) and *Porgy* (1927). She also appeared in musical comedies, such as Flournoy Miller and Aubrey Lyles' show *Rang Tang* in 1927.

In 1926–1927, Preer made more than a dozen jazz and pop recordings, working with such renowned jazz musicians as Duke Ellington, Clarence Williams, and Tom Morris; she also worked with leading white musicians, such as Red Nichols. Preer had a fine singing voice of the musical theater type, and these records constitute some of her best surviving work.

A final phase of Preer's career found her working in Hollywood. She went there in 1928, initially to appear in a stage production of *Rain* with fellow members of the Lafayette Players. While there, she appeared in all-black films, including two shorts in 1929: *Music Hath Harms* and *The Melancholy Dame*. These were based on the racially stereoptyped stories of Octavus Roy Cohen, and their director, Al Christie, was less skilled and less ambitious than Micheaux. Although Preer was only in her mid-thirties, she was increasingly cast in matronly roles and character parts during the late 1920s. While in Hollywood she also worked in mainstream white films. The last, and most notable, of these was *Blonde Venus* (1932), a vehicle for Marlene Dietrich. Preer died in Los Angeles in 1932.

Biography

Evelyn Preer was born on 26 July 1896, in Vicksburg, Mississippi, and was raised in Chicago, where she began her acting career c. 1916. She starred in eight of Oscar Micheaux's films (1917–1926) and was also a leading stage actress (1920s). She joined the Lafayette Players in 1920. As a singer, Preer made jazz and pop recordings (1926–1927). She went to Hollywood in 1928 and appeared in all-black films and some mainstream white films. In 1932, she and her husband, the actor Edward Thompson, had their only child, a daughter. Evelyn Preer died on 18 November 1932, in Los Angeles, at age thirty-six.

ELLIOTT S. HURWITT

See also Cohen, Octavus Roy; Ellington, Duke; Lafayette Theater; Lulu Belle; Lyles, Aubrey; Madame X; Micheaux, Oscar; Miller, Flournoy; Porgy: Play; Richardson, Willis; Williams, Clarence

Further Reading

Calvin, Floyd. "Evelyn Preer Ranks First as an Actress." *Pittsburgh Courier*, 16 April 1927.

Hammond, Percy. "The Theaters." *New York Tribune*, 8 May 1923.

New York Age, 17 October 1925.

Peterson, Bernard. *Profiles of African American Stage Performers and Theatre People, 1816–1960*. Westport, Conn.: Greenwood, 2001.

Thompson, Sister Francesca. "Evelyn Preer." In *Black Women in America*, ed. Darlene Clark Hine. Brooklyn, N.Y.: Carlson, 1993, Vol. 2, pp. 938–939.

Pridgett, Gertrude Malissa Nix

See Rainey, Gertrude "Ma"

Primitivism

In art, literature, music, dance, and theater, primitivism denotes the adoption of motifs, subjects, and styles associated with primordial, elementary, fertile, or preindustrial qualities. Throughout the history of art, objects from various cultures have inspired primitivist exploration, including sculptures from Africa, Asia, ancient America, and Oceania, as well as paintings and drawings by children, the mentally ill, or "outsiders." Primitivism marks the borrowing of forms and artistic expressions from other cultures as a means of renewal of and rebellion against "exhausted" values of mainstream Western civilization. It functions as a cultural corrective, in which the incorporation of primitivist forms and subjects signals renewal and return to some mythic, prehistoric origin of culture.

In the context of the Harlem Renaissance, primitivism signifies a constellation of interconnected ideas, styles, and cultural histories. A multilayered and often contradictory phenomenon, primitivism changes with the movement's shifting cultural paradigms and inflected perspectives. Like their European and white American counterparts, black American artists and writers perpetuated flawed constructions of a primitive Africa. Yet in addition to this well-aired predicament of primitivism, black artists' actual African ancestry added layers of meaning. Though generating equally flawed constructions of Africa as a site of otherness, primitivism provided black Americans with an arena in which to probe relationships between blackness and modernity. It fostered the assertion of African American identities in response to the rapid transformation of modern life.

Artists of the Harlem Renaissance were following in the wake of earlier primitivist movements, which had gravitated toward artifacts from Africa and the Pacific Islands. This occurred most notably in early twentieth-century European modernism when artists such as Pablo Picasso, Georges Braque, and Maurice Vlaminck turned to African sculpture as a source of artistic inspiration. Its atypical subjects and unfamiliar compositions gave African art the allure of primitive otherness. Artists' study of works from exotic locales resulted in the incorporation of new formal strategies in modernist art. This process of appropriation was fueled by long-standing European myths of African art as unmediated, instinctive, and uncensored—properties that corresponded with artists' desire to break away from traditional concepts of creative expression.

The problems with modernist approaches to primitivism have been widely addressed. Primitivism failed to address non-European artifacts in their respective cultural environments. Stripped of contextual information about their original use in rituals or everyday activities, African and Oceanic sculptures surfaced in European and American collections around the turn of the twentieth century. African art frequently lacked documentation about its provenance, or rather the circumstances of its looting during the colonial enterprise. Thus African sculptures were lumped together in collections according to formal similarities. Disregard for the aesthetic and social origins of African sculptures allowed Picasso and other modernists to embrace these artworks on a purely formal level. Pursuing stylistic affinities between the primitive and the modern, these artists left a far-reaching legacy that reduced the aesthetic and cultural complexities of African art to purely formal matters for much of the twentieth century.

Alain Locke's advocacy of a "New Negro" identity in the arts made primitivism a central tenet in Harlem Renaissance culture. Locke encouraged artists to recognize and incorporate an imaginary African heritage, which he positioned at the center of a new black cultural identity. Observing the influence of African art on European modernism, Locke proposed that it should have an even deeper impact on black Americans, whom he viewed as sharing an intrinsic, racial link with the "motherland." Following Locke's call for an authentic expression of their African cultural heritage, African American artists and writers modeled their approach to Africa in the same primitivist fashion as European artists. Yet African Americans were—historically and culturally—just as far removed from the original settings of African art as their white American counterparts were. Accordingly, the works of black American artists replicated the same shortcomings as the works of European modernists, for they viewed, and thus defined, African art in purely formalist ways.

Primitivism in African American art and literature gained additional momentum through Locke's backing of a white patronage system. The Harmon Foundation and philanthropists supported African Americans' pursuit of seemingly authentic black artistic expressions. Yet instead of encouraging African Americans to transcend aesthetic limitations, patronage restricted black artists to racialized themes based on flawed constructions of Africanness. The paradox of primitivism in the Harlem Renaissance becomes evident in the fact that the most conscious endeavors to embrace African-based identities returned to long-standing stereotypes. Thus the primitivist impulse in the Harlem Renaissance actually hindered the very development of cultural self-determination that it sought to encourage.

Primitivism affected all areas of culture in the Harlem Renaissance: literature, art, music, dance, and theater. Novels and poems by Claude McKay, Zora Neale Hurston, Nella Larsen, and others affirmed African origins or presented the continent as a lost paradise at a time when blacks continued to experience racial discrimination and economic hardships. Primitivist constructions of Africa provided solace in an alienated, industrialized world. Correspondingly, representations of African masks and sculptures abound in the visual imagery of the Harlem Renaissance. Aaron Douglas created his signature primitivist style by incorporating African motifs and embracing an extremely flat style. Similarly, William H. Johnson's paintings combined ordinary life, religious customs, and folk art traditions into a unique primitivist style. Palmer Hayden's primitivist appropriations and exaggerations of racial stereotypes accounted for the provocative nature of his works. Other artists who embraced primitivism include Richmond Barthé, Miguel Covarrubias, Malvin Gray Johnson, Lois Mailou Jones, and Horace Pippin, to mention only some of the better-known figures. Similarly, the employment of primitivist modes of expression translated into major stage successes for figures like Paul Robeson and Josephine Baker. The phenomenon extended to music halls and nightclubs such as the legendary Cotton Club, where primitivist decorations suggested black sensuality in exotic African settings. Primitivist experimentation during the Harlem Renaissance lasted until changing economic and political conditions yielded to social realist styles in the arts during the 1930s. Despite its contradictions and setbacks, primitivism constituted a vital aspect of renaissance culture, for it allowed artists to participate in ongoing modernist discourses. Positioning themselves in a network of cultural and historical relationships between the United States, Europe, and Africa, black artists and writers laid claim to the interconnections of the black diaspora and modern consciousness. And while much of the reality of a historically existing Africa may have eluded the primitivism of the Harlem Renaissance, the movement provided fresh perspectives for African Americans in search of their cultural identity.

JÜRGEN HEINRICHS

See also Baker, Josephine; Barthé, Richmond; Cotton Club; Covarrubias, Miguel; Douglas, Aaron; Harmon Foundation; Hayden, Palmer C.; Hurston, Zora Neale; Johnson, Malvin Gray; Johnson, William H.; Jones, Lois Mailou; Larsen, Nella; Locke, Alain; McKay, Claude; Robeson, Paul

Further Reading

Hiller, Susan, ed. *The Myth of Primitivism: Perspectives on Art*. London and New York: Routledge, 1991.

Kirschke, Amy H. "Oh Africa! The Influence of African Art during the Harlem Renaissance." In *Temples for Tomorrow: Looking Back at the Harlem Renaissance*, ed. Geneviève Fabre and Michel Feith. Bloomington: Indiana University Press, 2001, pp. 73–83.

Kraut, Anthea. "Re-Scripting Origins: Zora Neale Hurston's Staging of Black Vernacular Dance." In *EmBODYing Liberation: The Black Body in American Dance*, ed. Dorothea Fischer-Hornung and Alison D. Goeller. Münster, Germany: LIT, 2001, pp. 59–77.

Marx, Edward. "Forgotten Jungle Songs: Primitivist Strategies of the Harlem Renaissance." *Langston Hughes Review*, 14(1–2), Spring–Fall 1996, pp. 79–93.

McCabe, Tracy. "The Multifaceted Politics of Primitivism in Harlem Renaissance Writing." *Soundings: An Interdisciplinary Journal*, 80(4), Winter 1997, pp. 475–497.

Mudimbe-Boyi, Elisabeth. "Harlem Renaissance and Africa: An Ambiguous Adventure." In *The Surreptitious Speech: Presence Africaine and the Politics of Otherness, 1947–1987*, ed. V. Y. Mudimbe. Chicago, Ill.: University of Chicago Press, 1992, pp. 174–184.

Powell, Richard J., and David A. Bailey. *Rhapsodies in Black: Art of the Harlem Renaissance*. London and Berkeley: Hayward Gallery and University of California Press, 1997.

Stewart, Jeffrey C. "Black Modernism and White Patronage." *International Review of African American Art*, 11(3), 1994, pp. 43–55.

Professional Sports and Black Athletes

The 1920s are often referred to as the "golden decade" of American sports. But whereas white athletes like Babe Ruth, Jack Dempsey, and Red Grange thrilled the nation, most black athletes found themselves on the outside looking in, barred from equal participation by economic constraint, social custom, or simply racial prejudice. As tennis legend Arthur Ashe notes:

Black athletes were shut out of major league baseball, eased out of professional football, not allowed to join a fledgling professional basketball league, barred from Forest Hills in tennis, and unlawfully kept out of contention for the heavyweight boxing crown. Most sobering of all was the complete disappearance of the black turf jockey from a sport he dominated a mere twenty years before. (1993, 3)

Female athletes were doubly constrained, struggling to overcome not only racial antipathy but also cultural proscriptions against women's participation in competitive sports. As a result, many of the most talented black athletes of this period never received much recognition.

Nonetheless, black athletes were a significant presence during the Harlem Renaissance. They were extremely popular in the black press, and sports events were highlights of the black social calendar. Moreover, black athletes who did compete against whites helped disprove theories of racial superiority, smoothing the way for the eventual integration of most professional sports after World War II. The principal sports in which black athletes found success during the 1920s and early 1930s were boxing, baseball, basketball, football, and track.

Boxing

At the time of the Harlem Renaissance, boxing was one of the few professional sports that were not officially segregated; thus of all the major sports, it provided the greatest visibility for black athletes.

The most famous black boxer of the era was John Arthur "Jack" Johnson. He was born in Galveston, Texas, where he was known as "Lil' Arthur," and he became a dominant—and controversial—fighter. Johnson, who was physically imposing (more than 6 feet tall and weighing 200 pounds), became the first black heavyweight champion by defeating a Canadian, Tommy Burns, before 25,000 spectators in Australia in 1908. Burns had inherited the championship from Jim Jeffries, who had retired in 1905 rather than defend the title against a black challenger. In 1910, however, Jeffries—known as the "great white hope"—returned to the ring to face Johnson in Reno, Nevada. Johnson, who was wearing an American flag as a belt (the date was the Fourth of July), knocked Jeffries out in the fifteenth round. After the fight, rioting by angry whites around the country left thirteen blacks dead and hundreds wounded.

Johnson's notoriety, both before and after his fight with Jeffries, stemmed partly from his relationships with white women, three of whom he married. In 1912, Johnson (then still the champion) was convicted of transporting a white woman across state lines for immoral purposes. Rather than serve time in prison, he escaped to France via Canada. In 1915, he lost his title to a white challenger, Jess Willard, in Havana, Cuba, under suspicious circumstances: Johnson was accused of losing the fight for $30,000. He remained in exile for several more years before returning to the United States in 1920 to serve eight months of his original sentence.

After Willard lost to Jack Dempsey in 1919, white heavyweight champions again refused to face black fighters. No black contended for the title until Joe Louis in 1937. Evidently, the athlete who was most hurt by this situation was Harry Wills, the top heavyweight contender of the 1920s. There were, however, black champions in other weight classes, including the Senegalese light-heavyweight Louis "Battling Siki" Phal (1922); the middleweight Theodore "Tiger" Flowers, the "Georgia deacon" (1926); the bantamweight "Panama Al" Brown (1929); the welterweight Cecil Lewis "Young Jack" Thompson (1930); Eligio Sardinas, "Kid Chocolate" (junior lightweight, 1931; featherweight, 1932); and William "Gorilla" Jones, who shared the middleweight title in 1932–1933. One of the best-known fighters of the era never to win a title was Sam Langford (the "Boston tar baby"), who won 224 fights and lost only 23 from 1902 to 1923. Still, Johnson's dramatic career kindled black pride throughout the Harlem Renaissance, as evidenced by the opening lines of Sterling Brown's poem "Strange Legacies" (1932): "One thing you left with us, Jack Johnson./One thing before they got you./You used to stand there like a man,/Taking punishment/With a golden, spacious grin."

Baseball

Although there were more than sixty black ballplayers in white leagues before 1900, by the mid-1880s blacks had been squeezed out of professional baseball by an unofficial agreement, and the so-called national pastime would not reintegrate until well after the Harlem Renaissance. Instead, from 1900 to the 1940s, black professionals played almost exclusively in segregated leagues, occasionally appearing in exhibition games against white opponents on the barnstorming circuit. (Blacks and whites did oppose each other with perhaps surprising regularity in amateur and semiprofessional leagues, particularly in the Midwest. In 1925, for example, the all-black Wichita Monrovians defeated a local Ku Klux Klan team, 10–8, before an interracial crowd. But in the major leagues, segregation was the rule.) Despite the economic difficulties that beset black leagues, which typically turned a profit only on opening day and on Sunday—the only day of the week when most working blacks could attend games— black baseball remained vitally important to African American communities throughout the period.

The primary force behind organized black baseball was Andrew "Rube" Foster. After being a star pitcher in the early years of the century, in 1911 Foster formed his own team, the Chicago American Giants, and "won a reputation as a managerial genius equal to his friend, John McGraw" (Tygiel 2000, 116). In 1920, in order to keep control of black baseball away from white owners and booking agents, Foster created the National Association of Colored Professional Baseball Clubs, better known as the Negro National League

(NNL). The motto of the NNL was "We are the ship, all else the sea" (Ashe 1993, 27). Foster urged black fans, "It is your league. Nurse it! Help it! Keep it!"—though his long-term goal was to prepare black players for the eventual integration of major league baseball (Tygiel, 116). More leagues followed, including the Eastern Colored League (ECL), run by a powerful white booking agent, Nat Strong. In 1924, the champions of the two top leagues met in the first black World Series, won by the Kansas City Monarchs (NNL) over the Hilldale club (ECL). Another new circuit, the Negro Southern League—in which the legendary pitcher Satchel Paige launched his professional career—began in 1926.

Despite the emergence of so many leagues, scheduling games was difficult, because few black teams owned stadiums. The black teams were instead at the mercy of white agents like Strong, who controlled most of the ball fields on the East Coast. (Foster was accused of seeking similar monopolistic control in the Midwest.) By the early 1930s, the effects of the Depression, along with Foster's departure from the sport (owing to illness), nearly ended the black leagues entirely; and in 1932, there was no black major league for the first time since 1920. The leagues revived in 1933 under the leadership of Cumberland Posey, owner of the Homestead Grays (a top independent team from Pennsylvania that had not joined any league until 1929), and W. A. "Gus" Greenlee, owner of the Pittsburgh Crawfords. One of the most successful innovations of the 1930s was an annual black all-star East–West game, first played in 1933 before 22,000 fans. By the mid-1930s, these East–West games, featuring such stars as Paige, the star batter Josh Gibson, and James "Cool Papa" Bell (noted for his speed), were major events, outdrawing the black World Series and even receiving coverage in white metropolitan dailies.

Basketball

Blacks first participated in basketball in the late 1890s and early 1900s at black Young Men's Christian Associations (YMCAs), in the Ivy League, and in city club "fives" in the Northeast. The game soon became professionalized, but the real boost in its prominence came in 1923, when the black coach Robert L. "Bob" Douglas, who had immigrated to the United States from the West Indies in 1902, turned his Brooklyn Spartan Five (formerly the Spartan Braves) into the New York Renaissance, or Rens, the most successful all-black team of the era. At first the Rens played most of their games on Sunday nights at their home court, the black-owned

Renaissance Casino at 135th Street and Seventh Avenue, where each contest was followed by a dance. (In those days, the dance was in fact the real draw.) After two strong seasons, including a record of sixty-seven wins and only twelve losses in 1924–1925, the Rens began barnstorming against local and regional teams, including top white teams like the Original Celtics and the Philadelphia Sphas (South Philadelphia Hebrew Association). The Rens were barred from the first professional league, which started in 1925–1926, but they continued to maintain an independent schedule. The Original Celtics, perhaps in protest over the Rens' exclusion, had also refused to join the new league and remained the Rens' top opponent even after the founding of the Harlem Globetrotters in 1927. The Rens thrived even during the Depression, winning their first world professional championship in 1932 and remaining the top black team until they were overtaken by the Globetrotters in 1940.

Football, Track, and Other Sports

Football was one of the few sports open to blacks in the 1920s, although the gradual drawing of the color line eliminated African Americans from the professional ranks by 1933. After the formation of the American Professional Football Association (APFA) in 1919, the first successful black professionals came largely from white colleges, where many had been named to Walter Camp's influential All-American teams. These included Frederick Douglas "Fritz" Pollard (back) from Brown University; Jaye "Inky" Williams (end), also from Brown; Paul Robeson (end) from Rutgers; and Fred "Duke" Slater (tackle) from Iowa. A total of thirteen blacks played in the APFA and its successor, the National Football League (NFL), from 1920 to 1933, although by the late 1920s there were only one or two black players in the entire league. Two of the last black professionals were Ray Kemp, of the Pittsburgh Steelers, and Joe Lillard (the "Midnight Express"), a former star of four sports in Oregon, who was a back, quarterback, and kick returner for the Chicago Cardinals.

Although track and field was largely an amateur sport during the Harlem Renaissance, it generated some of the most significant athletic achievements by blacks. At the Olympics of 1924 in Paris, blacks took gold and silver medals in the long jump and a bronze medal in the men's 10,000 meters. In the Olympics of 1932 in Los Angeles, blacks dominated the sprint events: Thomas "Eddie" Tolan Jr. won gold medals in the 100- and 200-meter dash, and his teammate

Ralph Metcalfe won the silver and bronze medals. Edward Gordon of the University of Iowa also took a gold medal, for the high jump. Four years later, at the Olympics of 1936 in Berlin, Jesse Owens's unprecedented four gold medals would make a mockery of the Nazis' white supremacist propaganda.

In smaller numbers, and with less public fanfare, some black athletes also participated in such lower-profile professional sports as tennis and golf, both of which were firmly segregated.

Women Athletes

Opportunities for black female athletes during the 1920s and 1930s were severely limited, in part because of widespread suspicion that intense athletic competition was unfeminine. In 1923, for example, the influential National Conference on Athletics and Physical Education for Women and Girls recommended eliminating women's intercollegiate schedules in favor of intramural sports and "play days." Despite such barriers, black female athletes excelled in several sports during the Harlem Renaissance. They were important particularly in track: By the late 1930s, the Tuskegee women's team dominated events such as the AAU Nationals. Also, two black women were stars on the segregated women's tennis tour: Isadore Channels (who won four national titles between 1922 and 1926) and Ora Washington (who won eight titles from 1929 to 1937).

WILLIAM GLEASON

See also Harlem Globetrotters; Johnson, John Arthur; Renaissance Casino

Further Reading

Ashe, Arthur R., Jr. *A Hard Road to Glory: A History of the African-American Athlete, 1619–1918*. New York: Warner, 1988a.

———. *A Hard Road to Glory: A History of the African-American Athlete, 1919–1945*, Vol. 2. New York: Warner, 1988b. (See also rev. ed., New York: Amistad, 1993.)

Chalk, Ocania. *Pioneers of Black Sport*. New York: Dodd, Mead, 1975.

Gilmore, Al-Tony. *Bad Nigger! The National Impact of Jack Johnson*. Port Washington, N.Y.: Kennikat, 1975.

Henderson, Edwin B. *The Black Athlete: Emergence and Arrival*. Cornwells Heights, Pa.: Publisher's Agency, 1976.

Pendleton, Jason. "Jim Crow Strikes Out: Interracial Baseball in Wichita, Kansas, 1920–1935." In *Baseball*
History From Outside the Lines: A Reader, ed. John E. Dreifort. Lincoln: University of Nebraska Press, 2001.

Peterson, Robert. *Only the Ball Was White: A History of Legendary Black Players and All-Black Professional Teams*. Englewood Cliffs, N.J.: Prentice-Hall, 1970. (Reprint, New York: Gramercy, 1999.)

Rayl, Susan. "African American Ownership: Bob Douglas and the Rens." In *Basketball Jones*, ed. Todd Boyd and Kenneth L. Shropshire. New York and London: New York University Press, 2000.

Rogosin, Donn. *Invisible Men: Life in Baseball's Negro Leagues*. New York: Atheneum, 1983.

Tygiel, Jules. *Past Time: Baseball as History*. Oxford and New York: Oxford University Press, 2000.

Prophet, Nancy Elizabeth

One of the leading sculptors of the New Negro movement in the 1920s and 1930s, Nancy Elizabeth Prophet produced remarkable figures, busts, and heads representative of emotional states of mind.

After Prophet graduated in 1918 from the Rhode Island College School of Design, she made portraits occasionally in Providence, then went to Paris for more opportunities and to escape a difficult marriage. There she studied with Victor Segoffin at the École des Beaux Arts, completing at least two busts in 1923, one of which was included in a salon the following year. In 1924, Prophet made and sold batik and created her first life-size statue, *Volonté*, which she subsequently smashed because she found it mediocre.

In June 1926, lonely, frustrated, and nearly penniless, Prophet moved to a tiny atelier in Montparnasse, where she would live for the next seven years. Her first work there was *Poverty* (or *Prayer*), a life-size plaster female nude in *contrapposto*, with a snake curling about her ankles. Her other untitled figures and busts from the time are reminiscent of the work of Antoine Bourdelle, a student of Auguste Rodin: androgynous, with short or covered hair, drowsy eyes, enigmatic smiles, and slim bodies. Usually ethnically ambiguous, Prophet's works may reflect her ambivalence about her mixed African American and Naragansett-Pequot heritage.

Prophet occasionally used models but more often worked from her imagination, creating portraits of types (such as *Head of a Cossack* and *Reptile Woman*), rather than individuals. She sculptured in marble and wood, bronze, alabaster, granite, terra-cotta, plaster, and clay, and lightly painted some of her bas-relief carvings, such as *Facing the Light* (c. 1928–1931).

Prophet continually endured physical and emotional discomfort, and her titles—such as *Bitter Laughter*, *Discontent*, and *Silence*—seem to reflect her self-imposed, isolated condition abroad. Yet in other pieces, like *Peace*, *Confidence*, *Poise*, and *Le pèlerin*, Prophet may have expressed her ambition to maintain what she called the "abstract qualities" of poise and courage.

Prophet produced a striking series of black heads, including *Head of a Negro*, *Buste d'homme*, *Buste ébône*, and *Negro Head* (also called *Head of Roland Hayes*), in the 1920s. Her best-known work is *Congolais* (c. 1931), a cherry-wood head of a Masai warrior. It is unclear why she called her depiction of an East African a person from the Congo region or central Africa.

Buoyed by written support from W. E. B. Du Bois and Countee Cullen, Prophet often shipped sculpture to New York, Massachusetts, and Rhode Island for exhibitions, at which she won prizes. She also earned acclaim from the French press and exhibited her work at the Salon d'Automne and the Société des Artistes Français in Paris.

After her return to the United States, Prophet taught art at Spelman College in Atlanta for ten years, then moved back to Providence, where she worked for a few years at a commercial ceramics factory in the late 1940s and early 1950s. She converted to Roman Catholicism in 1951 and died childless, in obscurity in 1960. She is remembered as a sculptor of exceptional talent. Collections of her work are at the Black Heritage Society of Rhode Island, Providence; Rhode Island School of Design; and Whitney Museum of American Art, New York.

Biography

Nancy Elizabeth Prophet was born in Warwick, Rhode Island, on 19 March 1890. She received a diploma in drawing and painting in 1918 from the Rhode Island School of Design and studied at École des Beaux Arts, Paris. She married Francis Ford in 1915; they separated in 1932. She was an art instructor at Spelman College in Atlanta, Georgia, from 1934 to 1944. She also worked at a ceramics factory in Rhode Island from 1940 to 1950 and as a domestic after 1944. Her awards include the Harmon Prize for Best Sculpture, Harmon Foundation (1929); and the Richard Greenough Prize, Art Association of Newport (1932). Prophet died in December 1960.

THERESA LEININGER-MILLER

See also Artists; Cullen, Countee; Du Bois, W. E. B.

Selected Exhibitions

1924, 1925: Salon d'Automne, Paris.

1926: Boston Independent Exposition.

1927: Société des Artistes Français, Paris.

1928, 1932: Harmon Foundation, New York.

1929: Harmon Foundation, New York, Société des Artistes Français, Paris.

1930: Boston Independent Exposition, Société des Artistes Français, Paris.

1931, 1933: Whitney Sculpture Biennial, New York.

1934: Bannister Gallery, Rhode Island College, Providence.

1945: Providence Public Library. (Solo.)

1985: Bellevue Art Museum, Bellevue, Washington. (Traveling.)

Further Reading

"Anne [sic] Elizabeth Prophet Wins R. S. Greenough Prize." *New York Times*, 8(1), 9 July 1932.

"Art and Life." *Atlanta University Review of Race and Culture*. 1940.

"Beth Prophet Is Hailed in Paris as Real Artist." *Baltimore Afro-American*, 3 August 1929, p. 8.

"Can I Become a Sculptor? The Story of Elizabeth Prophet." *Crisis*, October, 1932, p. 315.

Cullen, Countee. "Elizabeth Prophet: Sculptress." *Opportunity*, July 1930, pp. 204–205.

Kirschenbaum, Blossom S. "Nancy Elizabeth Prophet, Sculptor," *Sage*, 4, Spring, 1987, pp. 45–52.

Leininger, Theresa. "Nancy Elizabeth Prophet." In *Notable Black American Women*, ed. Jessie Carney Smith. Detroit, Mich.: Gale Research, 1992.

Leininger-Miller, Theresa. "The Artistic Career of a Near Expatriate: Nancy Elizabeth Prophet, 1922–1934." In *New Negro Artists in Paris: African American Painters and Sculptors in the City of Light, 1922–1934*. New Brunswick, N.J.: Rutgers University Press, 2001.

Provincetown Players

The Provincetown Players, founded in 1915, became a major force in experimental American drama. During the 1920s, this theater company also became controversial by staging plays about blacks by white playwrights.

Inspired by Maurice Brown's Chicago Little Theater, four former midwesterners—George (Jig) Cram Cook, Susan Glaspell, Hutchins Hapgood, and Neith

Boyce—sought to create a theater devoted to presenting American writers without the glitter and expense of large Broadway productions. Joined by three Greenwich Village artists and bohemians—John Reed, Louise Bryant, and Mabel Dodge—they moved to Provincetown, Massachusetts, for the summer and formed a theater company after their work had been rejected by theaters in New York. In 1915, their first production, *Constancy*, a slight piece about the group's love affairs, was performed at Hutchins Hapgood's house in Provincetown and then on a wharf lent to the players by Mary Vorse O'Brien. In the fall, the group migrated back to Greenwich Village, where a permanent home was created on MacDougal Street near Washington Square. In 1916, Eugene O'Neill, then unknown, joined them in Provincetown.

The Provincetown Players were one of a number of white theater companies to produce plays about black Americans during the Harlem Renaissance. In 1917, Ridgely Torrence's *Three Plays for a Negro Theater*, produced by the Hapgood Players and Provincetown's set designer Robert Edmond Jones, marked the first time that black actors, rather than white actors in blackface, were hired for dramatic roles on Broadway. Two early one-act plays by Eugene O'Neill for the Provincetown Players, *Thirst* (1916) and *The Moon of the Caribbees* (1918), starred white actors in blackface; but in *The Dreamy Kid* (1919), his director, Ida Rauh, hired black actors instead. This one-act tragedy about Mammy Saunders, a dying grandmother awaiting her grandson Dreamy, who is wanted by the police, did not receive much attention, but it gave O'Neill the confidence to hire Charles Gilpin for his first full-length major production, *The Emperor Jones* (1920).

Gilpin, the first leading black actor on Broadway, woke up a star the morning after his debut, according to James Weldon Johnson. Although *The Emperor Jones* was a hit among white audiences, it sparked controversy among blacks, who objected to Brutus Jones's criminal past. For his powerful and memorable role, Gilpin received the Drama League Award in 1920; however, the Drama League withdrew Gilpin's invitation to the otherwise all-white dinner because that too had caused a controversy. O'Neill and the play's director, Kenneth MacGowan, leaked the problem to the press and encouraged sympathetic actors to decline their own invitations. This protest worked, and Gilpin was again invited.

Gilpin discerned a subtle racism at work in O'Neill's play. Brutus Jones, an opportunist and colonist, is the self-styled emperor of an island in the West Indies. Having escaped from America after killing a prison guard, he embezzles from the native people and convinces them that only a silver bullet can kill him. But Smithers (a cockney trader) and Lem (the chief of the tribe) undo the emperor. Jones escapes into the jungle to the underbeat of primitivistic tom-toms and his own encroaching paranoia. In O'Neill's most innovative device, there is a flashback to Jones's own past and the collective unconscious of black life in America—as a slave at auction, on a slave ship, and finally as a witch doctor in Africa. However, Jones is so distressed by his experience that he kills himself with his last bullet.

Gilpin expressed his displeasure with elements of the play, particularly O'Neill's continued use of the word "nigger," which Gilpin changed to "black baby." O'Neill was furious that Gilpin dared to change the text; moreover, Gilpin had problems with alcohol. O'Neill fired him after the first full run of the play and hired Paul Robeson for the revival of 1924 and the film of 1934.

In 1922–1923, the Provincetown Players shut down in order to reassess their mission in American theater. Many original members, such as John Reed and Jig Cook, had left or become disillusioned with the group. O'Neill, its main playwright, also grew tired of its direction. A year later it reopened as the Provincetown Playhouse, even more committed to experimental theater, under the direction of O'Neill, Kenneth MacGowan, and Robert Edmond Jones. Its offerings in the first year included August Strindberg's *Ghost Sonata* and O'Neill's racially provocative *All God's Chillun Got Wings* (1923).

O'Neill's play, which starred Paul Robeson, depicted an interracial marriage between Jim Harris, a law student preparing for the bar exam; and his white wife, Ella Downy, who goes insane because of her stress over the marriage. In this play about internalized racism, Jim wants to please Ella so much that he says he will become her "slave"; but Ella cannot fully love her black husband and thwarts his efforts at self-improvement.

Adam Clayton Powell Sr., pastor of the Abyssinian Baptist Church in Harlem, thought that the production would play on people's fear of interracial marriage. The Ku Klux Klan threatened O'Neill, and the mayor of New York tried to close down the production before it opened. All this publicity made O'Neill and Robeson a topic of debate and actually made the play more popular. In *Opportunity*, Robeson defended his roles in O'Neill's plays: "I honestly believe that perhaps never will I portray a nobler type than 'Jim Harris' or a more heroically tragic figure than 'Brutus Jones, Emperor,' not exceeding 'Othello.'" But Robeson also looked forward: "I am sure that there will come Negro playwrights of great power and I trust I shall have some part in interpreting that most interesting and much needed addition to the drama of America."

In 1926, the Provincetown Playhouse produced Paul Green's tragedy *In Abraham's Bosom*, a version of the "tragic mulatto" theme, which won the Pulitzer Prize. Huggins (1971) has written that it "came as close to dramatic realism as anything in the decade" but remained a flawed depiction of black life.

The Provincetown Playhouse ignited controversy among African American intellectuals and artists who objected to the depiction of blacks by white playwrights and deplored the dearth of drama by black playwrights. W. E. B. Du Bois, editor of *The Crisis*, wrote that plays "must be written by Negro authors who understand from birth and continual association just what it means to be a Negro today." In *The New Negro*, Montgomery Gregory, organizer and director of the Howard Players, called for a "National Negro theatre . . . that will merit the respect and admiration of America. Such an institution must come from the Negro himself, as he alone can truly express the soul of his people."

The Provincetown Playhouse disbanded in 1926 as O'Neill found greater fame. Though a functioning organization for only nine years, the Provincetown Playhouse changed American drama and encouraged the development of black theater in America.

MARY CHINERY

See also Emperor Jones, The; Gilpin, Charles; Green, Paul; O'Neill, Eugene; Powell, Adam Clayton Sr.; Robeson, Paul; Three Plays for a Negro Theater

Further Reading

Abramson, Doris E. *Negro Playwrights in the American Theatre, 1925–1959*. New York: Columbia University Press, 1969.

Bigsby, C. W. E. *A Critical Introduction to Twentieth-Century American Drama*, Vol. 1, *1900–1940*. Cambridge: Cambridge University Press.

Egan, Leona Rust. *Provincetown as a Stage: Provincetown, the Provincetown Players, and the Discovery of Eugene O'Neill*. Orleans, Mass.: Parnassus, 1994.

Huggins, Nathan Irvin. *Harlem Renaissance*. New York: Oxford University Press, 1971.

Hutchinson, George. *The Harlem Renaissance in Black and White*. Cambridge, Mass.: Belknap–Harvard University Press, 1995.

Johnson, James Weldon. *Black Manhattan*. New York: Knopf, 1930.

Krasden, David. "Whose Role Is It Anyway? Charles Gilpin and the Harlem Renaissance." *African-African Review*, 29(3), 1995.

Locke, Alain. *The New Negro: An Interpretation*. New York: Albert and Charles Boni, 1925.

Robeson, Paul. "Reflections on O'Neill's Plays." *Opportunity*, 2, 1924. p. 369.

Publishers and Publishing Houses

A major factor in the blossoming of African American literature in the 1920s and 1930s was a historic transformation of the publishing industry, including the emergence of a new group of publishing houses that showed greater interest than their predecessors in African American culture and authorship. Before World War I, American publishers were generally conservative to moderate "Christian gentlemen" of decidedly Anglo-American tastes and prejudices. Even if they were "sympathetic to the Negro," their conception of African Americans owed much to plantation-school traditions and minstrel stereotypes conveyed by the likes of Octavus Roy Cohen and Irvin Cobb. By the same token, the established publishers before World War I resisted political radicalism, feminism, and new treatments of human sexuality in fiction as well as nonfiction. They generally deplored literary naturalism and modernism, tendencies often described as decadent and "un-American," and they failed to respond to demographic changes—especially immigration and internal migration—that produced burgeoning new audiences. Old-line publishers feared the "alien" peoples crowding the cities, filling public libraries, and reading newspapers in exotic languages.

However, little magazines and theaters just before World War I had begun proving that audiences existed for new types of fiction, poetry, and drama, including works that approached African American culture seriously as an important and unappreciated aspect of the national scene. New theories of cultural pluralism and of culture as such challenged the "melting-pot" ideology and the glorification of "100 percent Americanism" in the age of the Ku Klux Klan, while new nationally based organizations like the National Association for the Advancement of Colored People (NAACP) brought civil rights activism into civic institutions based in New York with which new young publishers often became affiliated. Magazines espousing left-liberal and radical agendas had begun featuring the work of black authors as well as attacking lynching and racist imperialism. Thus a network of institutions gradually developed in which black authors and activists saw new opportunities.

Publishers of a more cosmopolitan bent than their predecessors wanted to detach American literature from its dependence on the English tradition; they both found and built an audience for Russian fiction, Irish drama, and other previously exotic literatures. Such interests transferred to African American literature as authors and critics saw in African American culture an analogue to the peasant cultures of Europe and Asia. Moreover, most of the new young publishers were Jewish and had little allegiance to the old ways of doing things in a publishing industry that had kept them in subordinate roles. In contrast, the old-line publishers—the vast majority of publishing houses of the period—showed absolutely no interest in African American literature, which they tended to class with cultural degeneracy (as they conceived it) being foisted on the public by neurotic decadents centered in Greenwich Village.

The new publishers had new attitudes in every phase of the business, from stylistic and ideological preferences to cultural and geographical range, marketing techniques, and typography and jacket design. Chief among the new firms in the 1920s were Alfred A. Knopf, Harcourt and Brace, Boni and Liveright, and Viking, joined later by a variety of houses representing a broader spectrum, from traditional houses like Harpers to radicals like International Publishers and the black-directed press based at Howard University, Associates in Negro Folk Education.

The most important black publisher of the Negro renaissance, William Stanley Braithwaite, was a poet, critic, and anthologist based in Boston and committed to late-romantic forms for the most part, somewhat isolated from the mainstream of black literary development after World War I. His publishing activity developed in part from his work as an anthologist of contemporary "magazine" poetry beginning in 1913, a role in which he had exerted some influence over the American literary scene, drawing attention to Edwin Arlington Robinson, Robert Frost, Bliss Carman, James Weldon Johnson, and others. Early in their poetic careers, black poets including Johnson, Claude McKay, and Countee Cullen particularly sought his advice and benefited from his encouragement. However, of these three only Johnson published a book

with him, *Fifty Years and Other Poems* (1917). Braithwaite's relationship with Georgia Douglas Johnson, on the other hand, was more long-standing, and Braithwaite was responsible for the appearance of each of her books with the presses over which he sequentially served as editor-in-chief: Cornhill, B. J. Brimmer, and H. Vinal.

Braithwaite encouraged African American poets and published their work, but he did not consider poetry by black writers to form a tradition separate from that of American poets in the English tradition more generally, and his critical tastes remained essentially late-romantic, much like those of Countee Cullen, who regarded him as a sort of mentor. Most books produced by his presses were written by white authors, usually based in New England, and long forgotten today. Moreover, Braithwaite never listed African American poets among those he considered the most important of his time.

Cornhill, Brimmer, and Vinal were essentially short-lived vanity presses. Authors were expected to subsidize the publication of their own books and work up lists of friends and associates to be solicited directly for sales in advance of publication, while Braithwaite puffed their work in his anthologies. As a contributing editor to *The Crisis* in its early years, Braithwaite influenced the magazine's publication of poetry, and in 1918–1919 Cornhill published volumes of poetry by several authors featured in the magazine's early issues: Joseph S. Cotter's *The Band of Gideon, and Other Lyrics*; Maud Cuney-Hare's *The Message of the Trees*; Georgia Douglas Johnson's *The Heart of a Woman and Other Poems* (1918); and Charles Bertram Johnson's *Songs of My People*. Angelina Weld Grimké's play *Rachel*, first produced by the NAACP drama committee in Washington in 1916, was also a Cornhill title. Leaving Cornhill during a restructuring of the company, Braithwaite helped found a new house, B. J. Brimmer, which brought out Georgia Douglas Johnson's *Bronze* (1922); and when that firm folded, he helped form another with the backing of a white friend, H. Vinal, which published Johnson's third book, *An Autumn Love Cycle* (1928). However, generational changes in American writing that explicitly reacted against the regional, aesthetic, and ideological positions with which he was affiliated left Braithwaite in a position of marginal importance to the direction of African American poetry while new firms based in New York brought out the books quickly identified with the "New Negro" movement and with black modernism.

The most important of these new firms, in terms of the quality of black writing it published, was that of Alfred A. Knopf. His entrance into the publishing industry was partly shaped by his mentor at Columbia University, Joel Spingarn, a president of the NAACP. Frustrated by the publishers he worked for after graduation, Knopf wanted to help steer American writing, particularly fiction, in new directions; and after opening his own house in 1915, he began publishing translated Russian fiction and American "modernist" authors including Carl Van Vechten, who by the mid-1920s had close connections with many African American authors or would-be authors. His most intimate friend, H. L. Mencken, edited the magazine *American Mercury* out of the Knopf offices and had a broad following among black readers and writers at the time. Knopf's wife, Blanche, essentially the second executive, also had much to do with the quality of the firm's list, particularly in African American literature.

In 1924, Knopf published Walter White's first novel, which prompted a meeting between White and the critic and novelist Carl Van Vechten that would have major consequences, as White introduced Van Vechten to a broad swath of the black intelligentsia in greater New York. The Knopfs developed a strong relationship with James Weldon Johnson (whose *Autobiography of an Ex-Colored Man* they republished in 1927) that also made them attractive to black authors. By way of White, Van Vechten, and Johnson, Knopf—by now one of New York's most esteemed publishers—soon had recruited Langston Hughes, Nella Larsen, and Rudolph Fisher. As this list suggests, Knopf was interested in a broad range of African American writing (although, for the most part, it sold poorly in its own day), and his firm's standards have stood the test of time. Titles included *The Fire in the Flint* (1924), *Flight* (1926), *The Weary Blues* (1926), *Fine Clothes to the Jew* (1927), *Not without Laughter* (1930), *The Ways of White Folks* (1934), *The Autobiography of an Ex-Colored Man* (1927; originally 1912), *Black Manhattan* (1930), *The Walls of Jericho* (1928), *Quicksand* (1928), and *Passing* (1929). But Knopf's influence derived as well from his list of titles by white authors, including works in fields such as anthropology and history, that had a great impact on black writing of the 1920s and 1930s.

One of Knopf's major competitors early on was the firm of Boni and Liveright, founded in 1917 and closely associated with the "rebellion" centered in Greenwich Village. Like Knopf, this house (owned initially by Albert and Charles Boni along with Horace Liveright) played an important role in bringing continental European literature to the attention of American writers, and its Modern Library series reprinted titles that were key to transatlantic "modernism." Boni and Liveright, however, was also closely affiliated with political and cultural radicalism. American authors identified with the imprint included Jack Reed, Eugene O'Neill, Sherwood Anderson, and Waldo Frank. Frank became Jean Toomer's closest comrade and literary confidant during the writing of *Cane* (1923), Boni and Liveright's first title by an African American author. Jessie Redmon Fauset's first two novels also came out from this house, as did Eric Walrond's *Tropic Death* (1926), some of which had been based on a trip the firm funded to Panama.

By this time, Horace Liveright had taken control of the company and the Bonis had gone their own way. They were also interested in black writing, however, and they commissioned *The New Negro* (1925) from Alain Locke, as well as *Blues—An Anthology* (1926) from W. C. Handy. In 1926, they offered a $1,000 prize for the best novel by an African American, but they never awarded it because the judges' committee found no worthy recipient. (Nella Larsen held back and sent her novel to Knopf instead because of gossip that the Bonis would accept almost anything, and she did not want to be "the best of a bad lot.") A. and C. Boni folded at the onset of the Depression; and Horace Liveright—as a result of risky publishing, gambling on stocks, and bad business decisions—was forced out of his firm at about the same time. Nonetheless, the two houses had helped open the doors of American publishing to new styles of black writing that, if they brought in little money, managed to win considerable critical attention and remain central to the canon of modern African American writing.

A firm that played a role second only to Knopf in the literary blossoming of the 1920s was Harcourt, Brace, which was founded in 1919 by a couple of disgruntled employees of the more traditional and "puritan" firm of Henry Holt, urged on by the budding author Sinclair Lewis (an important contact for black authors in the mid- and late 1920s). From the beginning, Harcourt, Brace was closely identified with the native literary "rebellion"—authors like Lewis and Carl Sandburg, whom Harcourt brought with him from Holt. Shortly after founding the firm, Alfred Harcourt and Donald Brace brought Joel Spingarn in as their adviser on literature and then as partner and vice president. By then president of the NAACP, Spingarn connected the firm directly with the New Negro movement, and one of the first books it published was

W. E. B. Du Bois's *Darkwater* (1920). Another was Carl Sandburg's *The Chicago Race Riots, July 1919* (1920). Much like his student Alfred Knopf, Spingarn (formerly a professor of comparative literature) felt that American literature needed the stimulation of models from outside England and so founded the firm's European Library in 1920, parallel to Boni and Liveright's Modern Library. The desire to bring a more cosmopolitan spirit to American letters coincided with the firm's connections with "New Negro" concerns. It brought out titles by Du Bois, James Weldon Johnson, Claude McKay, Sterling Brown, and Arna Bontemps, as well as M. T. Pritchard and Mary White Ovington's *Upward Path: A Reader for Colored Children* and the textbook *Readings from Negro Authors for Schools and Colleges* (1931).

As the new magazines and publishing houses began printing creative work by and about African Americans, older houses and journals began taking notice. Harper Brothers, more than a century old and one of the most venerable firms in New York, had been losing authors to the new firms when it decided it needed an overhaul and brought in a new book editor, Eugene Saxton, who happened to be friendly with Walter White. White soon started steering black authors to Harper, and its first list under the new leadership included Countee Cullen's first book of poetry, *Color* (1925). Cullen was particularly eager to have the Harper imprint on his work because of the long-standing prestige of the firm, and Harper's remained his publisher through the 1930s, bringing out several of his volumes in editions lavishly illustrated by a white artist he had chosen, Charles Cullen. McKay also came to Harper's after Harcourt, Brace; he published all of his fiction with Harper's as well as his autobiography. Harper's picked up Richard Wright as he emerged at the end of the Depression with *Uncle Tom's Children* (1940).

Viking Press was founded by two men, Harold K. Guinzburg and George S. Oppenheimer, who had been working for Knopf when they decided to strike out on their own in 1925. They were interested in African American literature from the beginning and had friendly ties to New Negro authors like Walter White and James Weldon Johnson. The house of Benjamin W. Huebsch, highly respected for its progressive list and the risks it had taken on "exotic" modern literatures, merged into Viking soon after the firm's founding, and helped burnish its image as a forward-looking house interested in new voices, often from "marginalized" groups. White began trying to interest black

writers in them, while Johnson began publishing with the firm immediately. His *Book of American Negro Spirituals* (1925), published with a great deal of fanfare to kick off the firm's first season, became a best-seller, and he stayed with the house after that. Nella Larsen very nearly moved from Knopf to Viking with her manuscript for *Passing* but was talked out of it by her friend Carl Van Vechten, one of Knopf's authors. As was true of Larsen, by the time Viking had gathered wind in the late 1920s, most black authors of that decade had made connections with their publishers, and although Johnson continued to work with Viking through the 1930s, the firm picked up no others. However, by then a growing number of publishing houses had begun publishing work by black authors.

Contrary to much commentary on the Harlem Renaissance, publishers did not lose interest in African American writing after the stock market crash. Not a single firm that survived into the 1930s gave up on its black authors, although for the most part the firms only lost money on these authors. Considerably more books of creative writing by African Americans came out in the 1930s than in the 1920s (and from more presses), even though book publishing as a whole shrank substantially. Moreover, important anthologies, textbooks, and critical studies also appeared in the 1930s, helping institutionalize the study of African American literature. In the 1930s, Lippincott, Covici-Friede, Macmillan, International Publishers, Doubleday Doran, and Stokes all published black writing for the first time. Zora Neale Hurston had never written a novel before an editor at Lippincott read a short story by her in 1933 and asked if she might have a novel in the works. She immediately moved to Florida to help get her creative juices flowing and produced *Jonah's Gourd Vine* (1934), which was accepted four months after she had started it.

Black writers, of course, were not always free of editorial interference, nor was that interference always bad. Knopf asked Nella Larsen to expand her first book, the manuscript of which was exceedingly short for a novel. Even she recognized it was too "thin" and expanded later sections of the novel, apparently, adding about a third of what we now know as *Quicksand*. Arna Bontemps's *God Sends Sunday* (1931) is considerably revised from the original novel he had written, as he was forced to reshape what had been a kind of quasi-autobiographical tale of a sensitive boy to focus more on elements fitting popular interest in the black "sporting life." Editors at Harper Brothers upset Claude McKay by editing some of the dialogue in *Banjo* (1929), which in part showcases the richness of black vernacular speech. Because the book was already in proofs when he discovered the changes, he had to pay for restoring the original wording. A later novel manuscript by McKay entitled "Savage Loving" that featured homosexuality, among other things, was never published. At the time Harpers had been losing money on McKay hand over fist, although the firm would subsequently publish his autobiography.

Overall, although extensive evidence of editorial meddling by white publishers has yet to be demonstrated, publishing houses of the 1920s and 1930s, as in all eras, could not survive independent of market demand, and the demand for black authors' creative writing was never very large. It seems, moreover, to have been confined primarily to greater New York. Even Nella Larsen's *Passing*, which was partly set in Chicago and which Knopf marketed heavily to bookstores there and elsewhere, sold only about 3,500 copies, almost all of them in New York. Claude McKay's *Home to Harlem* (1928) and James Weldon Johnson's *Book of American Negro Spirituals* were the only "best-sellers" in the Harlem Renaissance. McKay's many black critics, probably rightly, believed that his novel succeeded commercially because it suited popular tastes for "exotic" material of lower-class black life. *Cane*, although a critical succès d'estime, sold only 500 copies. Even at the 135th Street Branch of the New York Public Library, the intellectual crossroads of black Harlem, white authors' books about blacks were usually in higher demand than black authors' books on that subject, according to reports in the local black newspapers.

In addition to Hurston, several writers associated with the 1920s did not publish their first novels until the 1930s—Langston Hughes, George Schuyler, and Countee Cullen, for example—and others joined the ranks, such as William Attaway, George Wylie Henderson, Arna Bontemps, E. Waters Turpin, and Richard Wright. Clearly, the publishers of the 1920s had demonstrated that an audience and a cultural need existed for African American writing, even if market demand was slight. Nor, after looking carefully at the titles published by the various houses, is it easy to support the common conception that publishers were interested only in the "primitive and exotic" with regard to African American literature. Publishers open to black writing in the Harlem Renaissance represented a tiny minority of those then in business, and for the most part they had personal, cultural, or even political connections with the New Negro movement. They were generally new houses looking for new forms of American literature and seeking to help foment cultural change. Their interest in African American writing connected with many other aspects of their visions and strategies, which helped transform the publishing industry in the United States.

GEORGE HUTCHINSON

See also Specific houses and individuals; specific writers and works

Further Reading

Dardis, Tom. *Firebrand: The Life of Horace Liveright*. New York: Random House, 1995.

Dzwonkoski, Peter. *Dictionary of Literary Biography*, Vol. 46, *American Literary Publishing Houses, 1900–1980: Trade and Paperback*. Detroit, Mich.: Bruccoli Clark, 1986.

Exman, Eugene. *The House of Harper: One Hundred and Fifty Years of Publishing*. New York: Harper and Row, 1967.

Gilmer, Walker. *Horace Liveright: Publisher of the Twenties*. New York: David Lewis, 1970.

Gross, Gerald, ed. *Publishers on Publishing*. New York: Bowker–Grosset and Dunlap, 1961.

Harcourt, Alfred. *Some Experiences*. Riverside, Conn.: Privately printed, 1951.

Hutchinson, George. *The Harlem Renaissance in Black and White*. Cambridge, Mass.: Harvard University Press, 1995.

Knopf, Alfred. *Portrait of a Publisher, 1915–1965*, 2 vols. New York: Typophiles, 1965.

Lehmann-Haupt, Christopher. *The Book in America: A History of the Making and Selling of Books*, rev. ed. New York: Bowker, 1951.

Tebbel, John W. *A History of Book Publishing in the United States*, Vol. 3. New York: Bowker, 1972.

Waldron, Edward E. *Walter White and the Harlem Renaissance*. Port Washington, N.Y.: Kennikat, 1978.

Wintz, Cary D. *Black Culture and the Harlem Renaissance*. Houston, Tex.: Rice University Press, 1988.

Q

Quicksand

Nella Larsen's novel *Quicksand* (1928) was praised by W. E. B. Du Bois as "the best piece of fiction that Negro America has produced since . . . Charles Chesnutt" (1928), and it immediately secured Larsen's reputation among the literati of Harlem. In the year of its publication, *Quicksand* won a Harmon Foundation Bronze Award, placing second to Claude McKay's *Home to Harlem* in a vote that split the judges. The critical reception of *Quicksand* was mixed, although generally positive: It was lauded for its complex psychological portrait of the protagonist, Helga Crane. In an era when James Weldon Johnson cautioned that black writers could not afford to expose the foibles of the race, *Quicksand* was advertised by its publishers as "wholly free from the curse of propaganda," and Larsen won accolades for her portrayal of a flawed woman who fails in seeking self-realization and community. Interestingly, although not necessarily correctly, the reviewer for the *New York Times* (8 April 1928) thought that Helga Crane was a woman whose "essential tragedy has little to do with . . . being a Negro."

The novel opens at Naxos, a school (resembling the actual Tuskegee Institute) where Helga Crane is a teacher. Helga, the daughter of a Danish American woman and an African American man, is constantly at odds with her surroundings and, seeking solace, spends much of the novel in motion. After clashing with the administration at Naxos, including her fiancé, James Vayle, she leaves for Chicago, where she asks her white uncle, Peter, for money but is rebuffed. Eventually, she finds work as a companion for a woman who is traveling to New York. In New York, Helga is supported by Anne Grey, a wealthy Harlemite widow. Yet "it didn't last for long, this happiness of Helga Crane." When a check arrives from Uncle Peter, Helga visits her mother's family in Copenhagen, a place with "no Negroes, no prejudice, no problems." In Copenhagen, Helga wears colorful dresses and delights in a newfound sensuality. Initially taken with a portraitist, Axel Olsen, who paints her image and proposes marriage, Helga is shocked by his rendering of her as a "disgusting sensual creature." She returns to Harlem, where her "deliberate lure"—such as her exotic clothing—makes her popular, but again she attracts unwanted attention. After a transgressive moment with Anne Gray's new husband, Helga wanders the rainy streets and then collapses in a storefront church. She is swept up into the congregation, experiences a conversion, and then marries Rev. Mr. Pleasant Green and moves to rural Alabama with him. The novel ends with Helga sinking into a static life of childbearing and helpless confinement.

The dark ending of *Quicksand* continues to raise debate. Some scholars argue that Helga's passivity is inconsistent with a character who for most of the novel challenges her limitations. Others view the ending as the appropriate modernist conclusion to Helga's quest. Davis (1994, 243) notes that as a writer, Larsen was intrigued by "the mixedness of things"; and this work is characterized by suspensions and tensions that destablilize traditional notions of social "place." Through Helga, Larsen revises the stereotype of the tragic mulatto, satirizes the "talented tenth," creates a heroine dissatisfied by marriage and domesticity, and suggests the inseparability of class, race, and gender.

REBECCA MEACHAM

See also Chesnutt, Charles Waddell; Home to Harlem; Johnson, James Weldon; Larsen, Nella; Literature: 4—Fiction; McKay, Claude

Further Reading

Carby, Hazel. *Reconstructing Womanhood.* New York: Oxford University Press, 1987.

Davis, Thadious. "Nella Larsen (1891–1964)." In *The Gender of Modernism: A Critical Anthology.* Bloomington and Indianapolis: Indiana University Press, 1990.

———. *Nella Larsen, Novelist of the Harlem Renaissance.* Baton Rouge and London: Louisiana State University Press, 1994.

Du Bois, W. E. B. "The Browsing Reader: Two Novels." *Crisis,* 35. June 1928. (Review.)

"Helga Crane"; "Nella Larsen"; "Quicksand." In *The Concise Oxford Companion to African American Literature,* ed. William L. Andrews, Frances Smith Foster, and Trudier Harris. Oxford and New York: Oxford University Press, 2001.

Larson, Charles R. *Invisible Darkness: Jean Toomer and Nella Larsen.* Iowa City: University of Iowa Press, 1993.

McDowell, Deborah E. "Introduction." In *Quicksand and Passing.* New Brunswick, N.J.: Rutgers University Press, 1986, 1993.

McLendon, Jacquelyn Y. "Social Nightmare in Quicksand." In *The Politics of Color in the Fiction of Jesse Fauset and Nella Larsen.* Charlottesville and London: University Press of Virginia, 1995.

Miller, Ericka M. *The Other Reconstruction: Where Violence and Womanhood Meet in the Writings of Wells-Barnett, Grimké, and Larsen.* New York and London: Garland, 2000.

Wall, Cheryl. *Women of the Harlem Renaissance.* Bloomington: Indiana University Press, 1995.

Race Films

From the inception of the motion picture industry, stereotyped black characters were endemic, a holdover from the tradition of minstrelsy. Thus images of buffoonish, simpleminded, superstitious African Americans were presented to American moviegoers of all races and ethnic groups. Even before the public outcry by African Americans against D. W. Griffith's *Birth of a Nation* (1915), black newspaper columnists had waged campaigns against the stereotyping of African Americans in films. When white filmmakers continued to portray African Americans as simpletons providing comic relief or as sexual predators bent on ravaging white virgins, a number of African Americans responded by producing their own films, which featured black actors in major roles or, more generally, had all-black casts. These productions were called race movies or race films. Most race films were intended for black audiences. Many African American filmmakers did realize that, theoretically, profits, both financial and social, were to be made by reaching the white market; but in reality, race films were often rejected by white audiences, who wanted the presentation of African Americans onscreen to stay within the bounds of the current racial ideology.

Race movies originated around 1913 and were produced until the start of World War II. During this period, the production of these movies went through highs and lows, peaking in 1921 but struggling in the late 1920s and the early 1930s, when the Depression caused economic hardships and a new, cash-intensive technology—talkies—developed.

Reacting against the disturbing depictions of African Americans by white filmmakers in *Nigger in the Woodpile* (1904), *How Rastus Got His Turkey* (1910), *C-H-I-C-K-E-N Spells Chicken* (1910), and other such movies, William Foster (who wrote under the name Juli Jones Jr.) worked to produce films with all-black casts, starting in 1913. Actually, Foster's financial backing came from whites, and his films, such as *The Railroad Porter* (1913), followed the same formula and sometimes fell into the same racial stereotypes as their counterparts by white producers. Nevertheless, his Foster Photoplay Company began a tradition of films made by African Americans and supported by African American audiences. At about the same time as Foster, Peter P. Jones, a photographer in Chicago, also began making films for African American audiences, one rather problematically entitled *The Troubles of Sambo and Dinah* (1914).

From 1915 to 1920, more than thirty black film corporations were founded, some with financial backing from whites; they included the Dunbar Film Company, Florentine Film Manufacturing Company, Norman Studios, Heart of America Film Corporation, Allmon-Hudlin Film Company, and Unique Film Company. Most of them lasted only a few years; in fact, nearly 25 percent of all companies founded to produce race movies made no films whatsoever before folding, and none of them except Oscar Micheaux's various corporations survived the Depression and the transition to sound.

Despite the protests against it, Griffith's *Birth of a Nation* was a tremendous success, and African Americans sought a cinematic answer to this spectacle of white pride. Accordingly, Emmett J. Scott, secretary to Booker T. Washington, produced *The Birth of a Race* (1918). Scott's film was intended to celebrate African Americans, but financial mismanagement and corruption burdened the production, and the final product proved to have no relation whatsoever to his original vision. It was instead a jumble of scenes depicting biblical narratives and extolling universal brotherhood, and it was panned by both the black and white press.

In 1916–1917, Noble Johnson, who was an established bit actor for Universal Studios, and his brother George P. Johnson established the Lincoln Motion Picture Company, the first film company in the United States to be owned and financed by blacks. The Johnsons wanted to produce movies that would put African Americans in situations reflecting everyday life; they refused to highlight gambling, drunkenness, or stereotyped black characters. Noble Johnson was the president of Lincoln and also produced and starred in its first three films: *The Realization of a Negro's Ambition* (1916), *The Trooper of Troop K* (1917), and *The Law of Nature* (1918). George Johnson managed Lincoln's marketing and distribution from his home in Omaha, Nebraska. He had some useful connections, and he developed for the first time a network of black artists, theater owners, and newspaper writers through which to distribute and market African American films. His marketing tactics would become standard procedure for advertising and distributing race movies throughout the 1920s, because white theaters and their networks generally refused to carry black films. Lincoln's films were a great success among black audiences, so much so, in fact, that Universal demanded Noble Johnson's resignation from Lincoln, to avoid a conflict of interest. To ensure his future career with Universal, Johnson reluctantly agreed; after his departure, Clarence Brooks acted as Lincoln's president until 1923, when Lincoln folded. In all, Lincoln produced seven films; and the Johnson brothers' venture, which lasted longer than any other African American film company of the time, proved that a market existed for films with black casts—and that African Americans in film need not be relegated to the roles of comedians, buffoons, ne'er-do-wells, drunkards, mammies, sexual monsters, or Uncle Toms.

In 1918, Lincoln approached the African American novelist and South Dakotan homesteader Oscar Micheaux about obtaining film rights to his second book, *The Homesteader* (which he had published himself). After considerable negotiations, Lincoln dropped its attempt because Micheaux had insisted on coming to Los Angeles and personally directing the proposed film. However, during the course of his correspondence with the Johnsons, Micheaux had gathered a great deal of information about filmmaking, and he then proceeded to make the movie himself. Micheaux's film, *The Homesteader* (1919), was the first feature-length American movie with an all-black cast, and Micheaux went on to become the best-known and most prolific director of race movies. During his career he produced more than forty films, as well as seven novels. Micheaux's films were often controversial, depicting interracial love, inequality between blacks due to skin tone, and white racism from the perspective of African Americans. Micheaux's most controversial film, *Within Our Gates* (1920), presented the hanging and burning of a sharecropper and his wife, falsely accused of murder, the random beating (and inferred lynching) of a sycophantic black tattletale by bored whites, and the attempted rape of a black woman by a white man (a reversal of the stereotype of black men as sexual predators). Micheaux's films were in some respects problematic, celebrating lighter-skinned heroes and heroines and focusing on bourgeois ideals, but they proved enormously successful with black audiences. In 1928, Micheaux declared voluntary bankruptcy, probably because of the advent of sound films, which were much more expensive to make than silent films; but he formed other corporations and continued to produce films (some of these were "presented" by A. Burton Russell, his wife). A few years later Micheaux found a financial backer—Frank Schiffman, the owner of the Apollo Theater in Harlem—and produced his first talkie, *The Exile* (1931). *The Exile*, like *The Homesteader* and Micheaux's later film *The Betrayal* (1948), was about interracial romance on the western frontier, which is also the theme of three of his novels.

By the 1930s, when talkies had become standard in movie houses, race movies had fallen on hard times. In 1929, Fox released *Hallelujah!* and MGM released *Hearts in Dixie*, both with all-black casts; thus Hollywood, with its greater technological expertise and financial resources, had invaded the territory of independent filmmakers like Micheaux and tapped into the black market. Many of the Hollywood films reinstated stereotypes that earlier black directors had tried hard to dispel; nevertheless, the advent of talkies brought a new era of race films that had all-black casts but were financed by white backers (Astor Pictures, Herald Pictures, and Million Dollar Pictures, for example) or were actually produced by white studios. Micheaux continued to make films throughout the 1930s, though he lost much of his audience to splashier and technically superior Hollywood productions.

During the 1930s and early 1940s, race films broadened their scope to include gangster films such as *Underworld* (1936) and *Manhattan* (1937), westerns such as *Harlem on the Prairie* and *Bronze Buckaroo* (both 1938), and films with musical entertainment such as *The Duke Is Tops* (1938) and *Tall, Tan, and Terrific* (1946). Gradually, the kinds of race films that had been produced by the Johnsons or Micheaux lost their appeal to black audiences, who preferred more spectacular Hollywood productions. In fact, Micheaux's *God's Stepchildren* (1938) was considered heavy-handed and was criticized for depicting racist mulattos and for intimating that most African Americans preferred gambling to thinking (a theme that also appears in other films by Micheaux).

Throughout the 1930s, a wider range of roles for African Americans became available in Hollywood. However, certain subjects, such as miscegenation and the acquisition of significant political or social power, were still taboo. In Hollywood films, racial conflict was generally resolved on the personal, not the structural, level, so as to sidestep racial politics. Thus the distinction between race movies, whether financed by blacks or whites, and mainstream Hollywood films began to erode. At the height of the production of race movies in 1921, there had been some 300 black theaters, and by 1939 there were more than 400, some as far south as Alabama and as far west as Colorado and California. But by 1944, this number dropped to about 175. This decrease occurred partly because white theaters were opening up portions of their facilities, such as balconies or separate sections, to black audiences. Another fact was the institution of the "midnight ramble" in white theaters—this was a midnight showing of a film aimed at black audiences. Also, by the late 1940s, there had been some expansion of black roles in white films, and segregation was generally decreasing; as a result, African Americans frequented white theaters and saw mixed-race films more often, and there was less need for black-owned theaters, which white patrons had rarely frequented. In the period after World War II, race movies such as those made by the Johnsons and Micheaux no longer held the loyalty of black audiences; their place had been taken by Hollywood, and their ideology of racial uplift and self-definition had given way to Hollywood scenarios that were designed simply for profitability.

Still, black filmmakers did occasionally draw on African American fiction. Two of Paul Laurence Dunbar's stories were made into films: *The Scapegoat* (1917) and *Sport of the Gods* (1921). James Weldon Johnson's poem "Go Down Death" inspired Spencer Williams's film of the same title in 1944. Oscar Micheaux secured the rights to two of Charles Waddell Chesnutt's works: *The House Behind the Cedars*, which he filmed in 1926 and then remade in sound as *Veiled Aristocrats* in 1932, and *The Conjure Woman*, which he produced in 1926.

Most writers associated with the Harlem Renaissance did not become much involved with film, probably because of the intrusiveness of white corporate backers for films with all-black casts in the 1930s and 1940s. Langston Hughes did try to break into Hollywood as a writer, but he found that scenarios involving black actors remained stereotypical. Hughes collaborated with the actor Clarence Muse on the screenplay for a somewhat reactionary film, *Way Down South* (1939), and was also involved with the Meschrabpom Film Company in the Soviet Union in the early 1930s. That company's first film, *Black and White*, was to deal with racial issues in Birmingham, Alabama, but Soviet leader Joseph Stalin shut down the company before any filming began.

The black press—newspapers and magazines—did involve itself with film criticism from the inception of cinema. In the 1920s, critics in publications such as *Half-Century Magazine*, *New York Age*, the Baltimore *Afro-American*, and the *Chicago Defender* all looked to race movies as a hopeful sign of African Americans' participation in this new art and entertainment medium. By the 1930s, after almost two decades of black film production and with a trend toward white control of the market, black intellectuals and writers such as Sterling Brown, Alain Locke, James Weldon Johnson, and Zora Neale Hurston took the race films of Hollywood to task. But in various publications, these writers did not maintain a unified position. For instance, Hurston criticized black leaders for accepting Warner Brothers' simplistic vision of a black heaven in *The Green Pastures* (1938); but Brown and Locke said that *Hearts in Dixie* (1929) was "the truest picturization of Negro life to date" (quoted in Everett 2001, 190). Many writers of the Harlem Renaissance gave critical analyses of race movies and of cinema in general, even if they were not involved in creating films.

In conclusion, the appearance and growth of race movies in the 1910s and 1920s coincided with a growth of African American arts and culture generally, in metropolitan centers around the United States. Race movies were not necessarily directly associated with the Harlem Renaissance, but they were a significant part of the context of the renaissance and expanded the terms of this African American cultural moment.

DAN MOOS

See also Birth of a Nation, The; Birth of a Race, The; Black and White; Brooks, Clarence; Brown, Sterling; Chesnutt, Charles Waddell; Dunbar, Paul Laurence; Film; Film: Black Filmmakers; Green Pastures, The; Hallelujah; Hearts in Dixie; Hughes, Langston; Hurston, Zora Neale; Johnson, James Weldon; Johnson, Noble; Locke, Alain; Micheaux, Oscar; Muse, Clarence

Further Reading

Bogle, Donald. *Toms, Coons, Mulattoes, Mammies, and Bucks: An Interpretive History of Blacks in American Films.* New York: Viking, 1973.

Bowser, Pearl, Jane Gaines, and Charlie Musser, eds. *Oscar Micheaux and His Circle: African-American Filmmaking and Race Cinema in the Silent Era.* Bloomington: Indiana University Press, 2001.

Bowser, Pearl, and Louise Spence. *Writing Himself into History: Oscar Micheaux, His Silent Films, and His Audiences.* New Brunswick, N.J.: Rutgers University Press, 2000.

Cripps, Thomas. *Black Film as Genre.* Bloomington: Indiana University Press, 1978.

———. *Slow Fade to Black: The Negro in American Film, 1900–1942*, 2nd ed. New York: Oxford University Press, 1993.

Everett, Anna. *Returning the Gaze: A Genealogy of Black Film Criticism, 1909–1949.* Durham, N.C.: Duke University Press, 2001.

Gaines, Jane M. *Fire and Desire: Mixed-Race Movies in the Silent Era.* Chicago, Ill.: University of Chicago Press, 2001.

Green, J. Ronald. *Straight Lick: The Cinema of Oscar Micheaux.* Bloomington: Indiana University Press, 2000.

hooks, bell. "Micheaux: Celebrating Blackness." In *Black Looks: Race and Representation.* Boston, Mass.: South End, 1992.

Leab, Daniel J. *From Sambo to Superspade: The Black Experience in Motion Pictures.* Boston, Mass.: Houghton Mifflin, 1975.

Regester, Charlene. "The Misreading and Rereading of African American Filmmaker Oscar Micheaux: A Critical Review of Micheaux Scholarship." *Film History*, 7, 1995, pp. 426–449.

———. "Black Films, White Censors: Oscar Micheaux Confronts Censorship in New York, Virginia, and Chicago." In *Movie Censorship and American Culture*, ed. Francis G. Couvares. Washington, D.C.: Smithsonian Institution Press, 1996.

Reid, Mark. *Redefining Black Film.* Berkeley: University of California Press, 1993.

Richards, Larry. *African American Films Through 1959: A Comprehensive Illustrated Filmography.* Jefferson, N.C.: McFarland, 1998.

Sampson, Henry T. *Blacks in Black and White: A Source Book on Black Films*, 2nd ed. Metuchen, N.J.: Scarecrow, 1995.

Race Men

Harlem had the overwhelming number of those African Americans who would be considered "race men"—those with the sense of cultural pride and élan eager to move blacks forward to achieve a positive destiny. Black migrants from the Deep South, the border states, New England, other regions of the United States, and the West Indies moved to New York City during the first and second decades of the twentieth century to realize the "American dream"; and ambitious men instilled with a sense of purpose, blessed with organizational skills, covetous of followers, and imbued with ideologies that required expression ventured to Harlem during the 1920s. The combination of Harlem as a locale, the influx of black émigrés, and the longtime residents of New York led to a combustion that forever changed the cultural, political, and social norms of America.

The ideologies of Harlem's race men were as varied as the men themselves, and the organizations they created or represented. Staid, traditional black leaders—race men who espoused integration—could be found within the National Association for the Advancement of Colored People (NAACP) and the National Urban League. Black professional and undergraduate fraternal organizations had members residing in Harlem who were eager to use their talent to agitate and create opportunities for blacks in an integrated America; these organizations included Sigma Pi Phi (to which W. E. B. Du Bois belonged), Alpha Phi Alpha (Countee Cullen), Omega Phi Psi (Langston Hughes), and Sigma Pi Phi (James Weldon Johnson and A. Philip Randolph). At the opposite end of the spectrum were the cultural nationalists. The most outspoken race men in this group had, largely, migrated from the West Indies to Harlem. In the charged atmosphere of Harlem, the West Indians joined disgruntled native blacks who deplored racism in the United States and did not want to consort with white people. Invoking an aggressive pride in the black race, the African Blood Brotherhood and the followers of Marcus Garvey proved most emblematic of those who embraced black racial pride to the exclusion of whites.

Between the extremist positions of race men who advocated integration and those who advocated separation were numerous leaders, including radical unionists like Chandler Owen and A. Philip Randolph; religious leaders, represented by Adam Clayton Powell Sr.; social workers, represented by Eugene Kinckle Jones of the Urban League; and many writers who became cultural icons and whose work evoked "negritude," a term often associated with the race men of the Harlem Renaissance.

Perhaps the first group of race men who perceived Harlem as a "black mecca" were leaders in the NAACP. Du Bois, the first great "race man" to become prominent, ventured to New York in 1909. He became the only black charter member of the NAACP, and the founder and editor of its magazine *The Crisis: A Record of the Darker Races*. By 1920, Du Bois had been living in Harlem for more than a decade, and *The Crisis*, published at 70 Fifth Avenue, provided readers with African American news, features peculiar to the race, and cultural musings that appealed to racial pride. Throughout the 1920s, Du Bois personified the integrationist race man. Erudite, proud, immaculate in demeanor and appearance, and with a distinctive Vandyke beard, he sought to mingle with white people, provided that he was treated and respected as an equal.

When Booker T. Washington, who was considered an accommodationist, died in November 1915, Du Bois's views on prideful integration came to prevail among native-born African Americans. *The Crisis* had an unprecedentedly large circulation during the 1920s and presented the goals and objectives—democracy, justice, progress—dear to integrationist-minded African Americans. As a civil rights militant rather than a social or political revolutionary, Du Bois was in the vanguard of those who demanded full citizenship and equal rights in the United States.

James Weldon Johnson was also an integrationist race man. A native of Jacksonville, Florida, he flirted with living in New York at the turn of the century and then moved to Harlem permanently in the summer of 1914 to escape southern racism and seek his fortune as

a writer. By 1916, Johnson received endorsements to become a field secretary for the NAACP, and on 1 October 1920, he became its first African American executive director.

During his tenure as executive director, Johnson sought federal antilynching legislation, actively soliciting everyone in Congress who was likely to support an antilynching bill. The House of Representatives did pass the Dyer antilynching bill; although this bill failed in the Senate, Johnson received high praise for his efforts. Johnson, like Du Bois, was also a man of letters. He prepared an anthology of Negro poetry in 1921 that culminated in a forty-two page essay—"The Creative Genius of the Negro"—and a book eventually entitled *The Book of American Negro Poetry*. In 1925, Johnson and his brother John Rosamond Johnson published *The Book of American Negro Spirituals*. James Weldon Johnson was also the author of *God's Trombones* (1927), a collection of seven sermons in verse. Poet extraordinaire, civil rights activist, lyricist, and host to dignitaries at his home in Harlem, James Weldon Johnson epitomized the true race man.

Walter White of the NAACP also contributed to the literature of the era. White was blond and blue-eyed but identified himself as black and worked ardently on behalf of African Americans. In 1918, he settled in Harlem to become an assistant secretary of the NAACP. In 1924, he published *The Fire in the Flint*, a novel that depicted racial violence in the South and debunked the myth of white supremacy. White's book influenced critics and the general public with its realistic portrayal of life in a small town in Georgia where an aspiring Negro family tries to survive in the face of white southerners' hatred. White's methods of gathering information for this novel suggest his dedication as a race man. Passing as a white, he mingled with racist crowds and gathered pertinent and accurate facts that he also used in sequels to *The Fire in the Flint*: the novel *Flight* (1926) and the authoritative study *Rope and Faggot: A Biography of Judge Lynch* (1929).

However, White made his greatest contribution to the African American cause primarily after succeeding James Weldon Johnson as executive secretary of the NAACP. He was devoted to achieving full integration, and a better life, for his race. During the era when Harlem was the mecca for the "New Negro," White worked with James Weldon Johnson to attack lynching and integrate the African American into American life. White became responsible for the introduction of black physicians to Harlem General Hospital; he traveled throughout the nation to protect and defend black victims of racial discrimination (such as Ossian Sweet in Detroit, Michigan); and he encouraged the Supreme Court to begin its attack against the "white primary" in the case of *Nixon v. Herndon* (1927).

A. Philip Randolph, a man with similar intentions of helping working people, but with a far more aggressive approach, could be called a "radical" integrationist. Randolph was born in Florida in 1889 and spent his formative years in Jacksonville before moving to New York City in 1911. While attending evening school at the City College of New York, Randolph met Chandler Owen, a graduate student at Columbia University. Randolph and Owen shared a political and economic ideology, forged a union based on socialism, and created—along with the managing editor, George Schuyler—*The Messenger*, a magazine that espoused a radical philosophy: denigrating American capitalism, speaking on behalf of silent black laboring men and women, and excoriating anyone who upheld the white power structure. Randolph and Owen's attack on the established black leadership naturally incurred the wrath of the black bourgeoisie and contributed to conflicts among the proponents of integration.

When Owen left New York for Chicago in 1923, the ever pragmatic Randolph changed his tactics and broadened his appeal by making himself available to lead a black union. As early as 1919, *The Messenger* served as the official mouthpiece of the eventually moribund National Brotherhood Workers of America, a group designed to organize all black unions under a single banner. Therefore, when Randolph organized and founded the Brotherhood of Sleeping Car Porters (BSCP), he had considerable familiarity with the problems of collectivizing black labor. During his tenure in Harlem, Randolph became recognized as an untiring advocate for black people's rights and as a consummate street orator. As the first black union representative, Randolph faced tremendous odds fighting for recognition from an entrenched and obdurate Pullman Company. Nevertheless, from his headquarters in Harlem, he used every means at his disposal to maintain the existence of the BSCP.

Ironically, the most radical race men came from colonial island nations in the Caribbean. These men had migrated to the United States for the sake of freedom, and they chafed at the discrimination they found there. In Harlem—where they were in no danger of being attacked by a southern lynch mob—these black émigrés spoke out against racism. They identified fully with the plight of their brethren in the United States but considered African Americans too accepting of racism and too timid in response to racial slights; the West Indians balked at conformity and demanded, in the most militant terms, to be treated as equals.

Arguably, Marcus Garvey was the most prominent and most contentious of the black West Indians who contributed to the Harlem Renaissance. Garvey moved from Jamaica to New York in 1916 and established the Universal Negro Improvement Association, with the mottoes "One God! One aim! One destiny!" and "Up, you mighty race!" His headquarters in Harlem were at 114 West 138th Street, in a cavernous expanse that became known as Liberty Hall. Garvey intended to forge a movement that would let the lowly, disadvantaged members of the race rise to become proud and self-sufficient.

In 1920, Garvey called for a black international convention, hoping to attract delegates from every state of the Union, Central and South America, the West Indies, and Africa. The convention opened on 1 August in Madison Square Garden. In addition to delegates from the United States, there were blacks from twenty-five other countries. To keep the UNIA prominent in the minds of the delegates and the people of Harlem, Garvey presented a parade with enough pomp and circumstance to rival the ceremonies of European royalty. But Garvey and his UNIA proved to be far more than simply ostentatious: The UNIA drafted a "Declaration of the Rights of the Negro Peoples of the World," and Garvey was a devout race man who protested against the wrongs committed by whites toward blacks throughout the world. Moreover, Garvey's pronouncements on self-sufficiency were far more than rhetoric. He believed that black people should be independent of white economic dominance or largesse; accordingly, he sold stock to blacks throughout the nation and bought three ocean-going vessels to make up the Black Star Line—the *Shadyside, Kanawha*, and *Yarmouth*—thus keeping his disciples mindful of the success they could attain as supporters of the UNIA.

Garvey's newspaper, *Negro World*, which was based in Harlem, ranged between ten and sixteen pages in length and sold an estimated 2 million copies each week to black subscribers throughout the United States. *Negro World* presented Garvey's ideas about pride in black skin and Negroid features, characteristics to be lauded rather than ridiculed; he wanted to evoke a pride in blackness that would connect the entire black diaspora. Garvey's emphasis on African nationalism and his demands for respect for the Negro race won him followers in black Harlem and elsewhere.

Still, despite his flamboyance, energy, aggressiveness, and chauvinism, Garvey paled in comparison with some other race men of West Indian origin. Cyril Valentine Briggs founded the African Blood Brotherhood (ABB) between 1917 and 1918; during the 1920s, he and two fellow West Indians—Wilfred A. Domingo and Richard B. Moore—developed an organization that rivaled, and occasionally exceeded, the black nationalism espoused by Garvey. Although the origins of the ABB seem complex (it was a cross between nascent West Indian nationalism and the revolutionary rhetoric and fervor of Marxism), its objectives were clear. The ABB desired the liberation of Africa and of all people in the black diaspora.

Despite its radical orientation, the leaders of the ABB conveniently found allies through other entities and media. Briggs, Domingo, Moore, and the black communist Otto Huiswoud represented the ABB at the National Equal Rights League in 1923. Members of the ABB also expressed their views as professional street orators on soapboxes along the sidewalks of Harlem. In their original homes in the Caribbean—Jamaica, Barbados, Dutch Guiana, and Nevis—they had been under colonialism and had been unable to express their feelings; but now they orated, lectured, pamphleteered, and organized, providing a prelude for the militancy that would be evoked in the later civil rights movement. In the 1920s, the race men of the ABB contributed to making Harlem "the most militant community in the black world."

Arthur A. Schomburg, Harlem's most senior "race man," was born 24 January 1874 in San Juan, Puerto Rico. He migrated to the United States in 1891, settled in New York, and, for his own edification, collected books on topics related to black people. By 1920, his collection had grown significantly, comprising manuscripts, autographs, books, and prints. Although *The Crisis* made mention of Schomburg and his collection as early as 1922, his holdings did not become available to the public until after the Urban League purchased his collection in 1926 and created the Negro Division of the New York Public Library at 135th Street in Harlem, between Lenox and Seventh avenues.

In addition to his collection of Negro memorabilia, Schomburg's primary contribution to the Harlem scene was perhaps his ability to promote accord between African, West Indian, and African American intellectuals through the Negro Society for Historical Research.

Because he documented every significant "race" movement and promoted interest in black history and culture, his collection minimized hegemony or dominance and maximized mutual interests.

Schomburg also contributed to the literary tenor of Harlem. He provided Charles S. Johnson, the editor of *Opportunity* (the periodical of the National Urban League), with facts and details that enabled Johnson to speak forcefully and accurately about black history and culture. Johnson, in turn, published Schomburg's writings in *Opportunity*. Through *Opportunity*, Schomburg informed readers about black people of Spanish and West Indian ancestry who contributed to Harlem's breadth as the world center of information pertaining to Africa and the black diaspora. Schomburg certainly gained recognition through *Opportunity*, and through *The Crisis*, but his major literary contribution appeared in *Survey Graphic* in March 1925. This was "The Negro Digs Up His Past," a fourteen-page essay (later reprinted in Locke's anthology *The New Negro*) in which Schomburg provided the essential core of the New Negro movement—bringing forth knowledge of the past to remake the future.

Other race men served as cultural icons, giving credence and substance to the Harlem Renaissance. The poets Claude McKay (for example, in *Harlem Shadows*, 1922) and Countee Cullen (for example, in *Color*, 1925) established poetry as artful expression representative of the New Negro movement. McKay, a Jamaican immigrant, became famous in 1919 with his poem "If We Must Die," which endorsed "New Negro" militancy in response to race riots that had been erupting throughout urban America. Cullen—a native New Yorker (b. 1903), the adopted son of a Methodist Episcopal minister, a valedictorian of De Witt Clinton High School, a graduate of New York University, and (for a time) the son-in-law of Du Bois—wrote poetry that evoked pride in Africa and the black race. Cullen also contributed to the maturation of Langston Hughes, Harlem's most literary "race man." Hughes no doubt captured Harlem best and himself came to stand for it as the foremost center of black culture.

Hughes was born in Joplin, Missouri, in 1902; he led an itinerant life but eventually settled in New York after completing his education at Columbia University and Lincoln University in Pennsylvania. Hughes published poems in *The Crisis* that spoke glowingly of black history and culture; in 1921, for instance, he presented *The Crisis* with "The Negro Speaks of Rivers." In 1926, he published his first book of poems, *The*

Weary Blues, which earned him great acclaim. Between 1925 and 1929 Hughes won poetry prizes from *The Crisis* and *Opportunity* and published with Alfred A. Knopf. Hughes received recognition from prominent black intellectuals like Walter White, W. E. B. Du Bois, and Jessie Redmon Fauset; and from prominent whites such as Mary Ovington (a charter member of the NAACP) and the writer and literary critic Carl Van Vechten. Hughes effectively forced blacks and whites to recognize the significance of black language, and he publicized the contribution that those of African ancestry had made and were making to American society.

The actor Paul Robeson gave the Harlemite "race man" a visual, active dimension. Robeson was a native of Princeton, New Jersey, attended Rutgers University as an undergraduate, then attended law school at Columbia University (1919), but he found himself more intrigued by the effusion of black culture than by studying for the bar. He was strongly influenced at the time by the integrationist views of James Weldon Johnson and had a number of close friends who were white, but Robeson also displayed strong sentiments of racial pride that found expression through his artistry. Robeson began acting during a period when white literati were eager to establishing an artistic bridge with blacks, and he seized on this opportunity. He represented a cadre of black intellectuals who believed that individual artistic achievement rather than political pressure or polemics would mitigate racial tension and enable black Americans to attain the full rights of citizens. Robeson first became known as an actor in the play *Taboo*, then made a breakthrough playing two leading roles: Jim Harris in *All God's Chillun Got Wings* and Brutus Jones in *The Emperor Jones*, both in 1924. Robeson may be credited with extending the significance of Harlem's "race man" internationally. Soon after his successes on Broadway, he traveled to Europe and introduced the public there to the "negritude" developed in Harlem. People in London, in Paris, and on the French Riviera appreciated Robeson's charm and gained considerable insight from this "New Negro" about life in Harlem and the United States.

The adage "Behind every famous man is a woman" applies to the race men of Harlem. Jessie Redmon Fauset, for one, was a woman behind the scenes who enhanced the careers of some famous men of the Harlem Renaissance. Fauset was born in Camden County, New Jersey, in 1882 and was raised in Philadelphia; she graduated from Philadelphia High School for Girls and then from Cornell University (Phi Beta Kappa, 1905). In 1919, W. E. B. Du Bois invited Fauset to join him in New York and become the literary editor of *The Crisis*. In this capacity she encouraged Du Bois to include the arts and literature as a means of increasing the number of subscribers. Fauset was also a mentor to, or helped cultivate the talents of, such writers as Claude McKay, Jean Toomer, Arna Bontemps, Countee Cullen, and Langston Hughes.

Another woman who contributed immensely to the ambience that fostered the race men of Harlem was the socialite A'Lelia Walker (Lelia McWilliams). She was born in 1885 in Vicksburg, Mississippi; joined her mother, Madame. C. J. Walker, in the hairdressing business; and moved from St. Louis to Denver and eventually to New York in 1914. After her mother's death, A'Lelia Walker moved into a house at 108–110 West 136th Street in Harlem, where she fed and encouraged young black writers. By 1927, she had converted her home into a salon, called the "Dark Tower" (honoring Countee Cullen's work), where she exhibited paintings, held readings of poetry and prose, and entertained the black and white intelligentsia at extravagant parties.

H. VISCOUNT NELSON

See also African Blood Brotherhood; Black Star Line; Brotherhood of Sleeping Car Porters; Color; Crisis, The; Emperor Jones, The; Garveyism; Harlem Shadows; Messenger, The; National Association for the Advancement of Colored People; National Urban League; Negritude; Opportunity; Social-Fraternal Organizations; Survey Graphic; Universal Negro Improvement Association; Weary Blues, The; *specific individuals*

Further Reading

Berry, Faith. *Before and Beyond Harlem: A Biography of Langston Hughes*. New York: Wings, 1983.

Brown, Sterling. *Negro Poetry and Drama and the Negro in American Fiction*. New York: Atheneum, 1969.

Clarke, John Henrik, ed. *Marcus Garvey and the Vision of Africa*. New York: Vintage, 1974.

Cronon, E. David. *Black Moses: The Story of Marcus Garvey*. Madison: University of Wisconsin Press, 1995.

Duberman, Martin. *Paul Robeson: A Biography*. New York: New Press, 1989.

Harris, William H. *Keeping the Faith: A. Philip Randolph, Milton P. Webster, and the Brotherhood of Sleeping Car Porters, 1925–1937*. Chicago, Ill.: University of Illinois Press, 1991.

Hine, Darlene Clark, Elsa Barkley Brown, and Rosalyhn Terborg-Penn, eds. *Black Women in America: An Historical Encyclopedia*. Bloomington: Indiana University Press, 1993.

Johnson, James Weldon. *Along This Way*. New York: Viking, 1933.

———. *Black Manhattan*. New York: Atheneum, 1968.

Katz, William Loren. *Eyewitness: A Living Documentary of the African American Contribution to American History*. New York: Simon & Schuster, 1995.

Lewis, David Levering. *W. E. B. Du Bois: Biography of a Race, 1868–1919*. New York: Holt, 1993.

Lutz, Tom, and Susanna Ashton, eds. *These Colored United States: African American Essays From the 1920s*. New Brunswick, N.J.: Rutgers University Press, 1996, p. 192.

Nelson, H. Viscount "Berky." *The Rise and Fall of Modern Black Leadership: Chronicle of a Twentieth Century Tragedy*. New York: University Press of America, 2003.

Ottley, Roi, and William J. Weatherby, eds. *The Negro in New York*: New York: New York Public Library, 1967.

Rampersad, Arnold. *The Life of Langston Hughes*, Vol. 1, *1902–1941: I, Too, Sing America*. New York: Oxford University Press, 1986.

Ross, Lawrence C., Jr. *The Divine Nine: The History of African American Fraternities and Sororities*. New York: Kensington, 2000.

Sinette, Elinor Des Verney. *Arthur Alfonso Schomburg: Black Bibliophile and Collector—A Biography*. Detroit, Mich.: Wayne State University Press, 1989.

Weiss, Nancy J. *The National Urban League, 1910–1940*. New York: Oxford University Press, 1974.

White, Walter. *A Man Called White*. Bloomington: Indiana University Press, 1948.

Rachel

In *Rachel* (1916), a three-act drama by Angelina Weld Grimké, a young woman—Rachel Loving—who lives in the North and is bursting with the maternal instinct learns that her stepbrother and stepfather, an editor of a black newspaper, were lynched in the South ten years earlier. Her innocence thus abruptly ended, she concludes that it would be wrong for her to bring any children into the world: Having a baby would only provide another victim for colonialism and Jim Crow. But although Rachel rejects the traditional role of childbearing, she adopts a little boy and so fulfills her obligation to the next generation.

A year before *Rachel* was produced, segregation became the policy in the nation's capital, and the film *The Birth of a Nation* opened to great fanfare around the country. *Rachel* was produced as part of an effort to counteract the negative portrayal of African Americans in *The Birth of a Nation*. Grimké had hopes that the play, which she published as a book in 1920, might be produced on Broadway, but that never happened. The year after it was produced in Washington, D.C., by the National Association for the Advancement of Colored People (NAACP), the play was put on briefly in Boston and in New York. It then languished for a while; but in the 1960s, it was taken up as a cause célèbre by feminists who saw it as a pioneering example of black feminism.

The production of *Rachel* in Washington in 1916 was important for at least three reasons. First, everyone associated with it was African American, including the director, producer, playwright, and actors. This was something new in the legitimate theater, where positions of authority were almost invariably filled by whites even if some actors were African American. Second, as part of a strategy to offset the message of *The Birth of a Nation*—which exalted the Ku Klux Klan, apparently condoned lynching, and presented blacks as villains—*Rachel* portrayed ambitious and upright African Americans. Also, by stressing maternity and the impact of lynching on black families, *Rachel* sought to establish common concerns, and an alliance, with white women, who were engaged in their own campaign for social emancipation. Thus in both the subject and the production circumstances of *Rachel*, the idea of art as weapon in the political struggle is clearly evident. Third, the fact that this play was produced in Washington reminds us that the cultural activity of the Harlem Renaissance also occurred outside Harlem. Washington was in fact a very significant site of the renaissance, and resistance was a geographically diverse phenomenon. Grimké was one of many writers, including a number of women, who were living and working in Washington at the time; another playwright, Georgia Douglas Johnson, had a famous literary salon there, which Grimké attended.

BARBARA BREWSTER LEWIS

See also Authors: 4—Playwrights; Birth of a Nation, The; Grimké, Angelina Weld; Johnson, Georgia Douglas; Literature: 3—Drama

Further Reading

Harris, Trudier, ed. *Dictionary of Literary Biography: African-American Writers Before the Harlem Renaissance*, Vol. 50. Detroit, Mich.: Gale Research, 1986.

Herron, Carolivia. *Selected Works of Angelina Weld Grimké*. New York: Oxford University Press, 1991.

Hull, Gloria T. *Color, Sex, and Poetry: Three Women Writers of the Harlem Renaissance*. Bloomington: Indiana University Press, 1987.

Miller, Ericka M. *The Other Reconstruction: Where Violence and Motherhood Meet in the Writings of Ida B. Wells, Angelina Weld Grimké, and Nella Larsen*. New York: Garland, 2000.

Peterson, Bernard L., Jr. *Early Black American Playwrights and Dramatic Writers*. New York: Greenwood, 1990.

Wall, Cheryl A. *Women of the Harlem Renaissance*. Indianapolis: Indiana University Press, 1995.

Racial Iconography

The term "iconography"—from the Greek *eikon* (image) and *graphia* (writing)—refers to a group of widely recognized symbols or images associated with a particular discipline or era. Since the nineteenth century, the term has applied to the study of themes and motifs in the visual arts. Racial iconography denotes the representation of race in visual culture and the analysis of its vicissitudes and implications. During the Harlem Renaissance, the concepts of iconography and race dovetailed, owing to a rise in stereotypical imagery that dehumanized blacks. During the post-Reconstruction period and later, certain icons became ubiquitous, including the Sambo and the mammy (docile, childlike servants), the Jezebel (the sexualized black woman), and the black brute (a savage villain seen as menacing white women, for example in such films as D. W. Griffith's *Birth of a Nation*, 1915). These images symbolically revived former class relationships between slaves and slave masters, reinforced racial enmity, and allayed fears that the socioeconomic "superiority" of white Americans might be challenged by a free African American population.

The leaders of the Harlem Renaissance, such as the civil rights activist W. E. B. Du Bois and the philosopher Alain Locke, urged African American artists to counter racial stereotypes with positive self-images. Du Bois encouraged artists to create ennobling depictions that paid tribute to blacks as worthwhile subjects for artistic treatment and simultaneously proved the worthiness and talent of black artists. Locke, in his essay "The Legacy of the Ancestral Arts" (1925), called for a new "racially expressive art" rooted in African aesthetics. He pointed out that European art, once rendered pedestrian from overdependence on classical Greco-Roman models, had been revitalized at the turn of the twentieth century when Henri Matisse, Pablo Picasso, André Derain, and the German expressionists "discovered" African sculpture. No longer considered coarse and uninspired, African art had been rescued by the attentions of the European modernists and reevaluated as "cunningly sophisticated and masterful." Locke believed that if African art could cause so much excitement in the arena of European modernism, then surely it was not too much to expect that it would exert an equal, if not greater, influence on African American art.

Influential in the dissemination of Locke's ideas on racial iconography was the altruistic Harmon Foundation, which, beginning in 1926, offered awards to African American artists and sponsored exhibitions of their works. As a consultant to the foundation, Locke wrote articles to accompany its exhibition catalogs and publicity brochures and, in them, put forth his agenda. He stated in the essay for the catalog of 1931 that one of the most beneficial aspects of the successive Harmon shows was the mounting emphasis placed on "racial types" and characters in the artwork that was presented to the jurors and displayed in each annual exhibit. In what he referred to as the "downfall of classic models and Caucasian idols," he saw the early stages of African American art being supplanted by a mature period, and, with it, he perceived the dawning of a "truly racial school of art expression." Locke's assertions suggest that he sought two essential iconographic elements in "mature" African American art: a non-European aesthetic (in other words, the vigorous and austere abstraction of African sculpture) and "racial types" or black subjects.

The jurors and administrators for the Harmon Foundation were intent on selling the works they exhibited and therefore on attracting buyers (who were frequently white). Thus they often interpreted Locke's preference for "racial types" as a call for modified black truisms such as physical strength, a sense of rhythm, optimism and humor, simplicity, and aplomb—characteristics that were identified in a Harmon brochure of 1935 as fundamental to black art, and which, ironically, echoed some of the same stereotypes that Harlem Renaissance artists were being asked to dispel. The artist and historian James Amos Porter observed in his book *Modern Negro Art* (1943) that the Harmon shows promoted a myopic racial perspective that inhibited individual creativity by insisting on requisite subject matter and visual treatment. Porter believed that the Harmon rubric was disadvantageous in that it segregated black artists from the mainstream American art scene. For example, two leading lights of the Harmon shows—Albert Alexander Smith (1896–1940) and Palmer C. Hayden—created imagery that encapsulated the archetypes favored by the foundation and its Anglo-American supporters. Many of Smith's paintings and prints depicted blithe, ingenuous black characters in humble settings; and Hayden's motifs, at first seascapes and African sculptural still lifes, evolved into black genre scenes that bore a disturbing resemblance to popular stereotypes, replete with characters whose facial features were sometimes grotesquely exaggerated. Porter felt that Hayden's style was misguided if not altogether offensive and reminiscent of the ignoble billboards, which were once pervasive, advertising blackface minstrels. The artist, however, maintained that his intention was not to mock or to satirize, but rather to paint, in his own vernacular style, the life and people that he knew.

More resistant to the iconographic expectations of the Harmon Foundation and white patrons in general, other artists of the Harlem Renaissance, such as the sculptors Sargent Claude Johnson and Richmond Barthé, created elegant and restrained portrayals informed by African masks and physiognomy. The painter Aaron Douglas combined the African-inspired abstraction of cubism with expansive narratives that extolled black history and culture. William H. Johnson began his career painting outdoor views in a postimpressionist and expressionist vein, but he later shifted to black genre and religious scenes composed of figures derived from African sculptural forms. Archibald Motley Jr. painted sympathetic portraits of blacks as well as stylized tableaux of black pool halls, dance halls, and street scenes. Lois Mailou Jones alternated between rendering African masks, dignified African American portraits, and French impressionist landscapes. As this sampling suggests, the artists of the Harlem Renaissance walked a fine line between the representation of their own aesthetic visions and the portrayal of three distinct forms of racial iconography: the noble Du Boisian portrait, the African-inspired aesthetics of Locke, and the clichéd black innocence and exuberance that white patrons preferred.

LISA E. FARRINGTON

See also Barthé, Richmond; Douglas, Aaron; Du Bois, W. E. B.; Harmon Foundation; Harmon Traveling Exhibition; Hayden, Palmer C.; Johnson, Sargent Claude; Johnson, William H.; Jones, Lois Mailou; Locke, Alain; Motley, Archibald J. Jr.; Porter, James Amos

Further Reading

Dubin, S. "Symbolic Slavery: Black Representations in Pop Culture." *Social Problems*, 34(2), April 1987, pp. 122–140.

Du Bois, W. E. B. "The Immediate Program of the American Negro." *Crisis*, 9(6), April 1915.

Locke, Alain. *The New Negro: An Interpretation.* New York: Albert and Charles Boni, 1925.

Pieterse, Jan. *White on Black: Images of Blacks in Western Popular Culture.* New Haven, Conn.: Yale University Press, 1992.

Porter, James A. *Modern Negro Art.* New York: Dryden, 1943.

Reynolds, G. A. *Against the Odds: African-American Artists and the Harmon Foundation.* Newark, N.J.: Newark Museum, 1989.

Racial Stereotyping

A primary issue for the African American intelligentsia of the Harlem Renaissance, and for some whites who participated in the movement, was how best to counteract the negative or demeaning racial stereotypes of blacks that had proliferated since at least the mid-nineteenth century. Although not all whites had stereotyped ideas about blacks, and although not all blacks were free of such notions, most of the negative stereotypes of blacks that flourished at the beginning of the Harlem Renaissance were generally accepted as valid by white American culture; and African Americans as a group had struggled against these limiting and degrading images from their inception. Racial stereotypes appeared in a wide variety of media and discourses, including fiction, poetry, sermons, newspapers, consumer goods, advertisements, music, theater (especially minstrel shows), radio, and the new medium of film.

Many whites based such stereotypes on selective racial and racist pseudoscience of the day, constructing images of blacks to suit their own sociopolitical purposes and to justify first slavery and later segregation as necessary and legitimate institutions. By the time of the Harlem Renaissance, the figure of "Jumpin' Jim Crow," derived from minstrelsy, led the pack of popular antebellum "old Negro" stereotypes such as "Uncle Tom," "Sambo," "Zip Dandy," and "Mammy." Jim Crow, the happy-go-lucky "darky" whose primary purpose was to entertain whites, had the doubtful honor of being the namesake for a system of segregation that became entrenched during the 1890s and did not officially end until the 1960s. These "old Negro" figures were generally docile, ignorant, childlike, loyal to whites, and basically harmless, even if occasionally given to pretension, petty thievery, and lying. Such stereotypes helped white America maintain the socioeconomic status quo because they implied that African Americans needed white paternalism and, more important, were anything but equal to whites. Many whites ridiculed any attempt by blacks to assume a middle-class lifestyle or achieve an institutional education; falling back again on the terminology of racialist pseudoscience, they accused such African Americans of "aping whites" or straying dangerously outside their rightful sphere of domestic and manual labor. For instance, one stereotype—the "tragic mulatto"— was an interracial individual (often a woman) who suffered from having connections with the white world. As long as blacks stayed "in their place," so the logic went, the color line could exist unchallenged because it could be represented as maintaining the natural order of the races.

Not surprisingly, the writers and intellectuals of the Harlem Renaissance were intent on rejecting the "old Negro" image as they insisted on equal rights, both social and political. Furthermore, these stereotypes had to be rejected in order to combat the social tenet that blacks did not need (or could not retain) a formal liberal arts education. The "New Negro," who demanded the right to a formal education, was intelligent, talented, and motivated to effect social and political change. New Negroes held no romanticized notions of antebellum days and were not willing to entertain whites at the expense of human dignity and respect.

Two other, equally destructive stereotypes that black writers, artists, and intellectuals of the Harlem Renaissance faced were the "black beast" (the rapist) and the immoral, licentious black woman. These stereotypes, which implied that African Americans were incapable of restraining their sexual urges, existed in conjunction with the image of the passive, harmless "old Negro" (an incongruity that seemed to trouble no one). The notion of the "black beast" suggested that black men were a threat to white women and was used as a rationale for lynching and for rioting

directed against blacks (as in the "red summer" of 1919, but extending through the civil rights era). The image of the licentious black woman implied not only that black women were sexually unrestrained but also that they were sexually accessible; this stereotype presumably justified the sexual abuse that had taken place during slavery, and later it was used to justify disrespect for black women's sexual authority over their own bodies. The image of African Americans as sexually amoral and potentially violent, no less than the image of the "old Negro," played a crucial role in maintaining segregation, because it implied moral inequality. Ultimately, these stereotypes implied that social "intercourse" between blacks and whites would lead to violence and the downfall of white culture.

To combat these stereotypes, many leaders of the Harlem Renaissance, as well as much of the general black public, concentrated on presenting an image of middle-class social respectability and sexual morality. Although many blacks must have given little thought to actively refuting antiblack images, the stereotypes did have real consequences in the daily lives of other African Americans. In particular, the elite—W. E. B. Du Bois's "talented tenth"—felt impelled to distance themselves, and the mass of African Americans, from the entire range of negative stereotypes implying that blacks were appropriately content with second-class citizenship.

However, this resistance to and insistence on countering negative racial stereotypes led to a significant division among writers, artists, and intellectuals of the Harlem Renaissance. For some, the fear of promoting negative images of blacks led to a mandate against representing the folk culture or dialect of lower-class, "uneducated" African Americans. Langston Hughes, for instance, encountered resistance from black leaders when he insisted on incorporating dialect and jazz rhythms into his poetry. And Zora Neale Hurston was criticized for incorporating, in her fiction and her sociological studies, African Americans who had little to no formal education but were simply educated in the ways of black culture and the black community. Hurston's *Their Eyes Were Watching God* (1937) is now praised for capturing life in the all-black rural town of Eatonville, Florida, but at the time it was dismissed by some critics as lacking any redeeming sociological or artistic merit and criticized by others for promoting the negative stereotypes that the "talented tenth" were fighting against. The philosophical difference was great enough for Hurston and Wallace Thurman to refer to these intellectuals, half-playfully, as the "niggerati." Actually, folk characters such as those Hurston created differed vastly from the antiblack stereotypes created and promulgated by whites; the folk characters represented a full range of humanity rather than one-dimensional images of servile incompetence or savage sexuality.

The resistance to antiblack stereotypes during the Harlem Renaissance did not erase those images. However, the movement certainly offered a new image of educated, successful, complex African Americans that celebrated, without idealizing, black creativity, culture, and expression in the age of jazz and blues.

JULIE CARY NERAD

See also Hughes, Langston; Hurston, Zora Neale; Jim Crow; Niggerati; Racial Iconography; Riots: 2—Red Summer of 1919; Talented Tenth; Their Eyes Were Watching God; Thurman, Wallace

Further Reading

Cassuto, Leonard. *The InHuman Race: The Racial Grotesque in American Literature and Culture.* New York: Columbia University Press, 1997.

Geist, Christopher D., and Angela M. S. Nelson. "From the Plantation to Bel Air: A Brief History of Black Stereotypes." In *Popular Culture: An Introductory Text,* ed. Jack Nachbar and Kevin Lause. Bowling Green, Ohio: Popular, 1992.

Goings, Kenneth. *Mammy and Uncle Mose: Black Collectibles and American Stereotyping.* Bloomington: Indiana University Press, 1994.

Guber, Susan. *Race Changes: White Skin, Black Face in American Culture.* New York: Oxford University Press, 1997.

Lott, Eric. *Love and Theft: Blackface Minstrelsy and the American Working Class.* New York: Oxford University Press, 1995.

Racial Violence: Riots and Lynching

Racial violence in the form of riots and lynchings has occurred in the United States from at least the nineteenth century to the present, and such violence had a significant impact on the Harlem Renaissance. African American artists and race leaders played an active role in and were inspired by the antilynching crusade, for example, and themes of lynching and violence recur in a number of literary and other works produced in this period. Before discussing specific examples of riots and lynching during the Harlem Renaissance era, it is important to place these acts of violence within a historical context.

Following the end of slavery, there was a marked increase in lynchings, especially throughout the American South. Ida B. Wells Barnett, an African American who was an early leader of the antilynching movement, described lynching as a form of terror used by racist whites to maintain a caste system in the South. Her analysis of lynching suggests that whites used this form of violence to maintain control of all political, social, and economic institutions, so that African Americans would remain, at most, at the periphery of these institutions and more probably at the bottom of the American hierarchy. During Reconstruction and well into the era of the "New Negro"—a concept associated with the Harlem Renaissance—whites saw African Americans as a political, economic, and social threat. White vigilante groups such as the Ku Klux Klan relied on physical violence to prevent African Americans from challenging the status quo and demanding the rights associated with being American. A variety of methods were used to lynch African Americans in the postslavery era, including hanging, shooting, burning, maiming, tarring and feathering, and various combinations of these.

Any African American, regardless of age or gender, could fall victim to a lynch mob. Between 1880 and 1930, perhaps 3,344 African Americans were victims of lynch mobs in the United States (Madison 2001). By the end of the nineteenth century, most lynchings were occurring in southern states, and more often than not the victim was an African American man. African American women and children could also be victims of a lynch mob: They might be attacked because of their ties to an African American man who was suspected of a crime, especially if they were thought to be the man's accomplices, or women and children might be used as scapegoats when a mob could not find the man it wanted.

Wells Barnett (1969) identified three excuses given by whites for lynching African Americans. The first excuse was that blacks instigated race riots, and the only way to prevent riots was to lynch the accused instigators. This excuse was more common during slavery, when white plantation owners feared slave insurrections. The second excuse was that whites feared what might happen if blacks exercised their rights as free persons, especially their right to vote. Accordingly, many lynch mobs wanted to stifle African Americans' political voice, and a number of blacks were murdered for trying to vote. The third excuse was that "the Negroes had to be killed to avenge their assaults upon women"—that is, white women. In investigating 728 cases of lynching during Reconstruction, Wells Barnett found that one-third of the African Americans lynched had been accused of rape. (The rest had been accused of inciting violence, threatening whites, or being impudent in the presence of whites.) She and others note that this third excuse suggests mass hysteria on the part of some white Americans regarding black male sexuality—a reaction that seems directly related to the racist stereotype of the "black brute." Racism as a motive for lynching becomes even more apparent when one examines the disparity between the punishment of black men accused of raping white women and the lack of punishment of white men who raped black women.

In the years immediately leading up to the Harlem Renaissance, racial hatred was heightened as blacks migrated from the rural South to southern cities and to the urban North. Race riots as well as lynchings occurred around the United States following the "great migration" period, and whites justified both riots and lynchings by using the excuses identified earlier by Wells Barnett and others. A revival of the Ku Klux Klan in 1915 also contributed to the increased racial violence directed against African Americans, and for the first time the ideology and violent practices of the Klan shaped race relations not only in the South but in the North as well.

As African Americans returned from World War I, migrated to urban industrialized areas, and became actively involved in the racial uplift movement of the early twentieth century, they were seen as a threat to the economic security of whites. Following the war, many African Americans who had served in it assumed that they would therefore receive better treatment and even equal access to the freedoms associated with being an American. Instead of achieving acceptance and equality, however, African Americans found themselves the target of racial hatred and, furthermore, found that they had no legal recourse against racial violence—no way to obtain protection or to protect themselves.

During the "red summer" of 1919, racial violence increased, and African Americans refused to remain acquiescent. Hundreds of African Americans lost their lives as a result of the twenty-five race riots that occurred that summer. These riots resulted partly from racism rooted in slavery, but also—as mentioned above—from a perception on the part of many white Americans that African Americans were an economic threat. It should be noted that during this period African Americans were organizing and joining labor unions and demanding their rights as workers.

The riots and lynchings of the "red summer" took place across the United States in places such as Charleston, South Carolina; Washington, D.C.; Longview, Texas; Ellisville, Mississippi; Chicago, Illinois; Tulsa, Oklahoma; Omaha, Nebraska; and Helena, Arkansas. To justify the hate crimes committed against African Americans by white Americans, various reasons were offered, such as rape and attempts to organize black labor; in one instance, a race riot occurred because a black boy had drifted into the white section of Lake Michigan. (The boy was hit in the head by rocks thrown by a white man, and the riot broke out when both the black and the white communities learned what had happened.)

Riots and lynchings continued beyond the summer of 1919—in fact, well into the 1930s, covering the period of the Harlem Renaissance. The two best-known examples are a riot that occurred in the Greenwood district of Tulsa, Oklahoma, in 1921, and the lynching of two black men—Abe Smith and Tom Shipp—in Marion, Indiana, in 1930.

In Tulsa, on 1 June 1921, a mob of whites murdered a large number of blacks and destroyed what had become known as "Negro Wall Street of America (Madigan 2001). The mob used a traditional excuse—protecting the virtue of a white woman—to justify the violence. A few days earlier, a teenage black boy had been accused of assaulting a white girl. When rumors of the supposed assault reached the white community in Greenwood, many whites reacted with rage, hysteria, and racism, and an angry mob devastated the black community of Greenwood. Homes and businesses were destroyed; African American families were displaced; and many African American men, women, and children suffered psychological trauma. Many witnesses concluded that the American system of law and law enforcement was unwilling to protect the rights of African Americans.

In Marion, Indiana, on 7 August 1930, a white lynch mob dragged three black male teenagers from the Grant County Jail, intending to kill all three of them. The three young men—Tom Shipp, age nineteen; Abe Smith, age eighteen; and James Cameron, age sixteen—had been accused of raping an eighteen-year-old white woman named Mary Ball and of murdering

Claude Deeter, a twenty-four-year-old white man who was said to have been trying to protect her. Ball's father and a group of angry white men and women approached the sheriff; asked for the keys to the young black men's cells; then overpowered the sheriff, took the three young men out in front of the courthouse, and lynched Shipp and Smith. Cameron's life was spared, however, when Ball's father revealed to the crowd that the young men were innocent (Madison 2001).

The lynching of Shipp and Smith provides a case study in mob hysteria, and in the complicity of the media and the law enforcement system in the oppression and violent victimization of African Americans. A photograph was taken of Shipp and Smith hanging from a tree in front of the courthouse as white men, women, and children pointed and smiled at the bodies and at each other; this became one of the most famous documents in the history of mob violence directed against African Americans.

Although the excuses offered for rioting and lynching varied, all this violence was alike in at least one way: The white perpetrators went unpunished or virtually unpunished. African American leaders such as W. E. B. Du Bois, Walter White, and James Weldon Johnson brought lynching to public attention throughout the early part of the twentieth century. In 1922, for example, James Weldon Johnson, at the suggestion of Congressman L. C. Dyer of St. Louis, went to Washington, D.C., to lobby for the passage of the Dyer Antilynching Bill. The bill passed the House but failed in the Senate; however, the introduction of this bill in Congress increased awareness in American society about racial violence directed against African Americans (Shapiro 1988). As a result of this increased awareness, more Americans, white and black, joined in efforts against riots and lynching. At the beginning of the twenty-first century, racial violence had yet to be eradicated, but the United States as a society was beginning to confront the violence of the past.

DEIRDRE J. RAYNOR

See also Antilynching Crusade; Barnett, Ida B. Wells; Lynching; Racism; Riots: 1–4

Further Reading

Franklin, John Hope. *From Slavery to Freedom: A History of African Americans*, 8th ed. New York: McGraw-Hill, 2000.
Litwack, Leon. *Trouble in Mind: Black Southerners in the Age of Jim Crow*. New York: Random House, 1998.
Madigan, Tim. *Massacre, Destruction, and the Tulsa Race Riot of 1921*. New York: St. Martin's, 2001.
Madison, James. *A Lynching in the Heartland: Race and Memory in America*. New York: St. Martin's, 2001.
McMurry, Linda. *To Keep the Waters Troubled: The Life and Times of Ida B. Wells*. New York: Oxford University Press, 1998.
Shapiro, Herbert. *White Violence and Black Response From Reconstruction to Montgomery*. Amherst: University of Massachusetts Press, 1988.
Wells Barnett, Ida B. *On Lynchings: Southern Horrors, a Red Record, Mob Rule in New Orleans*. New York: Arno, 1969.
———. *Southern Horrors and Other Writings: The Anti-Lynching Campaign of Ida B. Wells, 1892–1900*, ed. and intro. Jacqueline Jones Royster. Boston, Mass.: Bedford, 1997.
Wilson, Sondra Kathryn. *In Search of Democracy: The NAACP Writings of James Weldon Johnson, Walter White, and Roy Wilkins (1920–1977)*. New York: Oxford University Press, 1999.

Racism

It is impossible to overstate the significance of racism in the history of the Harlem Renaissance. Racism shaped the renaissance from its moment of conception to its inevitable decline in the wake of the Great Depression. Indeed, the racist fears and fantasies of whites were the most significant force in the broader American context in which the renaissance was critiqued, consumed, and ultimately parodied and poorly copied.

By the middle of the 1910s, most of the gains made during the Reconstruction had been completely undone or otherwise diluted to the point of insignificance. As early as the 1870s, statewide initiatives in the Deep South had engendered a new series of social and political privileges for whites only, including vagrancy laws, intended to control the movement of the black population; and so-called grandfather clauses, aimed at restricting voting rights in statewide elections. A stunning series of decisions by the Supreme Court, concluding with *Plessy v. Ferguson*, had pronounced segregation laws to be legal under the United States Constitution. Irrational and unfounded fears of wandering "Negro rapists" encouraged the widespread lynching of black men in gruesome public spectacles known as "lynching bees."

It was in this context that African Americans, often together with white liberal progressives, began to lobby for an end to Jim Crow and, more immediately, for aggressive antilynching legislation. The two most enduring activist organizations to emerge were the National Association for the Advancement of Colored People (NAACP) and the National Urban League, both of which would play pivotal roles in funding, publicizing, and otherwise orchestrating the artistic and literary movement of the 1920s.

The NAACP and the Urban League drew strength and membership not just from that very small group of white liberals committed to racial reform, but also from the ascending masses of black Americans who, before, during, and after World War I, escaped the racism of "the nadir" in the South by following the railroad tracks northward—into major cities and away from those dark, rural places where Jim Crow seemed to be most deeply entrenched. This "great migration" would have no minor role in the renaissance, as the movement of black people into the cities of the North and South resulted in segregated neighborhoods almost exclusively populated by African Americans and, in some cases, Afro-Caribbean immigrants. Those new migrants competed with white people in cities for jobs and homes, with modest success. But the arrival of black people usually caused whites, fearing a range of social ills, to flee those same neighborhoods, plunging them into instability and decline, a racist phenomenon now known as "white flight."

Still, for the New Negro Renaissance, there was no more significant outcome of this complicated process than the transformation of Harlem from white enclave to black neighborhood over the 1910s and 1920s. Though it was racism that led the white residents of Harlem to flee, and racism that encouraged the white owners of property in Harlem to charge higher rents to black patrons, out of this abuse and mistreatment grew an urban community of tremendous cultural significance. The nearly spontaneous emergence of a black city-within-a-city in the urban North inspired Rudolph Fisher's literary creation, King Solomon Gillis, to flee North Carolina just two steps ahead of a lynching, and, once in Harlem, to set down his bags and marvel at it all—"Slowly, spreadingly, he grinned at what he saw: Negroes at every turn; up and down Lenox Avenue, up and down One Hundred and Thirty Fifth Street." Writers and activists imagined that from this cultural capital of black America, the supposedly natural aesthetic gifts of black folks could be harnessed to a social and political agenda of

world-shaking significance. "Harlem," Alain Locke wrote in 1925, "has the same role to play for the New Negro as Dublin has had for the New Ireland."

The Harlem Renaissance also grew out of the racist violence of the immediate postwar period, when, after the precious few legal successes of the 1910s, the NAACP and the Urban League—together with most black Americans—were stunned into a new direction. Cities like Chicago, home to new migrant communities from the South and returning black soldiers, exploded into rioting, leaving some African American communities in ruins or burning, leaving many people dead, scarring the sense of progress that had motivated the NAACP and the Urban League, and impelling a search for new avenues of racial advancement.

After this "red summer" of 1919, the NAACP and the Urban League were also driven to orchestrate the renaissance as a measured response to the largest mass movement of African peoples in the new world, organized under the rubric of Marcus Garvey's Universal Negro Improvement Association (UNIA). Under Garvey, the UNIA emphasized racial solidarity, dogged militancy in the face of racism, and self-help. Garvey was an Afro-Jamaican; as an "outsider" in Harlem, he was generally despised by the African American leadership class for his flamboyance, for his self-education, for his success in mobilizing millions of people in the United States, the Caribbean, and Africa, and even for his darker skin and West Indian origin. But Garvey's response to the "red summer" was so overwhelmingly powerful for so many that the NAACP and the Urban League were pushed to develop alternative strategies for public consumption even as some of the leaders of those two organizations worked behind the scenes to have Garvey indicted for mail fraud, imprisoned, and later expelled from the United States. The emphasis on arts and letters, which hit full stride at about the time Garvey was imprisoned, was one of these countermeasures.

In these confusing and multiple contexts, the leadership class of the renaissance elected to demonstrate the humanity of people of African descent through the careful production of high art, thought to be the bedrock of what was then called "civilization"— painting, poetry, literature, and sculpture. At the time, most Europeans and European Americans shared a belief that high art could be produced only by cultured men and women, who they generally assumed could be only white. Black Americans were thought to be capable only of imitation, not original, individually produced, sophisticated works. But the highest standards of culture were also thought to be universal and unchanging, making it possible, some in the NAACP and the Urban League thought, for the art and letters of black people to be more honestly and objectively judged on their merits: that is, on the skill and ability of the creative artist. As W. E. B. Du Bois put it, "until the art of the black folk compels recognition they will not be rated as human." James Weldon Johnson, in the introduction to his unprecedented collection *The Book of American Negro Poetry* (1922), hoped that this book would demonstrate "intellectual parity by the Negro through his production of literature and art."

For their part, white liberals, radicals, and publishers were also interested in black art, or at least were interested in literature and drama that focused on black people. H. L. Mencken, Vachel Lindsay, Carl Van Vechten, Sherwood Anderson, Waldo Frank, and Max Eastman, among others, supported the early efforts of younger black writers, if only because these artists represented the wellspring of new and different art. By the late spring of 1925, *Opportunity*—the magazine of the Urban League, edited by Charles S. Johnson—was offering literary prizes at an awards ceremony packed with white and black intellectuals. The Harmon Foundation and other white philanthropic institutions were supporting "New Negro" efforts in literature, poetry, painting, sculpture, and drama. A few wealthy white patrons supported a few individual black artists, as was the case for Langston Hughes, Zora Neale Hurston, and others. But this support and interest often came with strings attached; Sherwood Anderson's desire to "get inside the niggers and write about them," for instance, reflects a decidedly unhealthy fascination with black subjects.

More broadly, white audiences flocked to Broadway shows featuring black characters, or sometimes white actors in blackface, and ventured up to Harlem on urban safaris to seek out jazz clubs, rent parties, and gin joints. The 1920s may have been the first "modern" decade, but modernity brought with it different popular versions of Freudianism, with its emphasis on the therapeutic qualities of "primitive" cultures. To watch Josephine Baker dance, then, was to "enjoy" black culture as a representative of the unchanged past, as if black people were "nature" and white people were "modernity." Jazz, Langston Hughes summed up in his essay "The Negro Artist and the Racial Mountain," represented "the eternal tom-tom beating in the Negro soul—the tom-tom of revolt against weariness in a white world." All too many white people agreed, seeing in African Americans a kind of physicality and release that should be envied. Still, there were limits to this

fascination; many of the locations frequented by white visitors to Harlem were carefully segregated, to put a limit on the sort of social "mixing" that might take place.

The end result was that by the late 1920s Harlem increasingly became an occasional amusement park for white consumers, who were treated to a Jim Crow version of the place. Returning to an old haunt in Harlem after a few years away, Rudolph Fisher found himself "wondering if this was the right place—if, indeed, this was Harlem at all. . . . Except for the waiters and members of the orchestra, I was the only Negro in the place." "White people," Langston Hughes recalled,

> began to come to Harlem in droves. For several years they packed the expensive Cotton Club on Lenox Avenue. But I was never there, because the Cotton Club was a Jim Crow club for whites. . . . Harlem Negroes did not like the Cotton Club and never appreciated its Jim Crow policy in the very heart of their dark community. Nor did ordinary Negroes like the growing influx of whites toward Harlem after sundown, flooding the little cabarets and bars where formerly only colored people laughed and sang, and where now the strangers were given the best ringside tables to sit and stare at the Negro customers—like amusing animals in a zoo.

The long-term effects of this considerable white appetite for the most sensational representations of African American culture were detrimental to the primary mission of the renaissance that began, in the words of David Levering Lewis (1979), as a "cultural nationalism of the parlor." Mainstream publishers eagerly searched for the next Claude McKay, hoping to find an "authentic" black voice to give life to those white fantasies of black culture that emphasized criminality, sexual adventure, and playfulness. Few searched for the next Jessie Redmon Fauset, whose novels featured prim, intellectually sophisticated, literate upper-class African Americans. For those who hoped to break free of race altogether, like Jean Toomer, there was no audience at all, and certainly no interest from publishers. When Toomer proposed that his next novel after *Cane* would tackle more psychological subjects, and that he wished to no longer be identified as a "Negro" writer, his requests seem to have been cognitively unmanageable.

If the coercive stereotyping of the white consuming public warped the idealistic intentions of the Harlem Renaissance, it is also true that the original hope of literary production—that racism could be beaten back through the careful production of high art—was never realized. The same decade that produced Langston Hughes, Wallace Thurman, Zora Neale Hurston, and others was also the decade in which Jim Crow housing policies were implemented nationwide, in which pseudoscientific racism and eugenics surfaced in "mainstream" science, in which the Commonwealth of Virginia mandated its own "racial integrity" legislation that forbade marriage between whites and blacks, and in which sweeping federal legislation transformed immigration policy to allow the arrival of only the "best" white peoples from northern Europe.

MATTHEW PRATT GUTERL

See also Antilynching Crusade; Civil Rights and Law; Fisher, Rudolph; Garvey, Marcus; Great Migration; Great Migration and the Harlem Renaissance; National Association for the Advancement of Colored People; National Urban League; Racial Stereotypes; Riots: 2—Red Summer of 1919; Universal Negro Improvement Association; *specific individuals*

Further Reading

Huggins, Nathan Irvin. *Harlem Renaissance*. New York: Oxford University Press, 1971.

Lewis, David Levering. *When Harlem Was in Vogue*. New York: Knopf, 1979.

Rainey, Gertrude "Ma"

Gertrude "Ma" Rainey, known as the "mother of the blues," made her theater debut in 1900 in a talent show called the "Bunch of Blackberries." She took up minstrelsy in 1904 after marrying William "Pa" Rainey and quickly became the most popular "down-home" blues singer in both southern and northern cities.

After her introduction with the "Bunch of Blackberries," Rainey became famous for her tent shows, set up in small towns in the South. Tent shows traveled from city to city, usually by train; black shows with more than twenty-five performers sometimes bought their own railroad cars because they could not ride in the same cars as whites. Rainey performed with a number of traveling companies, most notably the Rabbit Foot Minstrels, whose tent was usually 80 by 11 feet with a stage made of boards across a folding frame. In these shows Rainey performed songs such as "Florida Blues" and "Walking the Dog" without a megaphone and could still be heard clearly outside her tent. According to Sterling Brown (1974), Rainey "wouldn't have to sing any words; she would moan and the audience would moan with her."

Rainey's minstrel performances, her tent shows, and later her recordings were a form of creative expression that affirmed black culture and also offered a way for black people, particularly black working-class women, to form a community and to contest bourgeois ideals of sexuality, gender, womanhood, domesticity, marriage, and dependence. For instance, in Rainey's performance of "Walking Blues," one can discern themes of emancipation, independence, and strength, for the woman in the song decides consciously—and very daringly for the time—to pursue the object of her desire by her manner of walking. Rainey's "Lost Wandering Blues" highlights the significance of travel and the individual's right to travel; whereas traveling is physical in "Walking Blues," here it is mainly emotional. Both compositions highlight issues of and experiences with freedom and personal and collective liberation and emancipation; and both, like many of Rainey's other compositions, establish a connection with the reality of black life in America. Rainey's blues, and the emergent blues in general, represented a new era in which black people's emotional needs and desires could be expressed and emphasized, after having been publicly suppressed during enslavement.

Roxane Orgill (2001) writes that Rainey was able to relate to "ordinary people," both as a personal gesture and as a style of performance, making her and her band instantly attractive to audiences. This quality of Rainey's blues—the relationship between performer and audience—also tended characterize blues as a whole, and it contributed to the growing influence of blues in popular culture, and thus to the rise of the black music and entertainment industry. However, record producers did not immediately recognize and appreciate Rainey's compositions and performances; although Rainey had been singing blues since 1902, it was not Rainey but Mamie Smith who, in 1920, made the first vocal blues recording by an African American. Possibly this was because Rainey was based in Chicago rather than in New York, where the major producers were; in any case, she was approached and signed by Paramount Records of Chicago in 1923. Rainey was then thirty-seven.

Rainey exemplified the blues singer as a vocalist—usually a woman—accompanied by instrumental ensembles of various sizes. Her popularity increased once she began to make recordings. Her first recording was "Bad Luck Blues," but her first recording to be

Ma Rainey. (AP/Wide World Photos.)

Rainey was among the greatest minstrel artists and blues singer and is often discussed along with other legendary figures such as Bessie Smith, Mamie Smith, Clara Smith, and Ida Cox. Another Smith—the historian C. E. Smith (1955, 1963)—has said of Rainey that she was "the voice of the South, singing of the South, to the South."

Biography

Gertrude "Ma" Rainey (Gertrude Pridgett) was born 26 April 1886 in Columbus, Georgia. Her theater debut was in 1900; she began singing blues in 1902. She entered the minstrel show business and married William "Pa" Rainey in 1904. She performed with the Smarter Set, the Florida Cotton Blossoms, Shufflin' Sam from Alabama, and the Rabbit Foot Minstrels and worked with managers such as C. W. Parks, Al Gaines, and Silas Green. Rainey toured with Tolliver's Circus and Musical Extravaganza from 1914 to 1916. In 1917, she toured and performed with her Georgia Smart Set in Badin, North Carolina. She moved from minstrelsy to being a national recording artist after winning a contract with Paramount in 1923. Rainey appeared in an advertisement in the *Chicago Defender* on 2 February 1924, after being signed by Paramount Records. She recorded eighteen songs for Paramount in 1924, including "Jelly Bean Blues" and "Countin' the Blues." In April 1924, she performed with her Wild Cats Jazz Band at Chicago's Grand Theater. Rainey began touring in a seven-person limousine and combined tent shows with performances on the Theater Owners' Booking Association (TOBA) circuit in 1926. She was praised in *The Paramount Book of Blues* as the "true mother of the blues" in 1927. In 1928, she recorded twenty titles for Paramount and once again worked with Thomas Dorsey. After 1928, Paramount ended their working relationship. Rainey died 22 December 1939. *Jazz Information* published the first known biography of Ma Rainey on 6 September 1940.

VALERIE F. KINLOCH

See also Blues; Blues: Women Performers; Cox, Ida Prather; Singers; Smith, Bessie; Smith, Clara; Smith, Mamie

Selected Compositions and Recordings

"Bad Luck Blues." (Lovie Austin.)
"Big Boy Blues." (Ma Rainey.)
"Blues, Oh Blues." (Ma Rainey.)

released was "Moonshine Blues." Other recordings included "Bo-Weevil Blues," "Weepin' Woman Blues," "Prove It on Me Blues," and "Cell Bound Blues." Most of her recordings were about love, losing a man, and being mistreated by men and expressed strong emotions such as rage. Her themes include violence, and even murder. In "Prove It on Me Blues," Rainey hints at her own sexual preferences: "They said I do it, ain't nobody caught me./Sure got to prove it on me./Went out last night with a crowd of my friends./They must've been women, 'cause I don't like no men."

In 1928, Paramount Records ended its relationship with Rainey, explaining that her material was no longer fashionable. There was also a general decline in black show business at the time, and in 1929, the stock market crashed. Rainey continued performing in southern minstrel shows until she retired in 1935. She bought a home in Columbus, Georgia, and joined a church where her brother was a deacon. She died of heart disease in 1939, at age fifty-three, and was buried quietly in Columbus. Her death certificate gives her occupation simply as "housekeeping."

"Bo-Weevil Blues." (Ma Rainey.)
"Broken-Hearted Blues." (Ma Rainey.)
"Cell Bound Blues." (Ma Rainey.)
"Daddy Good-Bye Blues." (Ma Rainey.)
"Deep Moaning Blues." (Ma Rainey.)
"Don't Fish in My Sea." (Bessie Smith and Ma Rainey.)
"Farewell Daddy Blues." (Ma Rainey.)
"Jelly Bean Blues." (Lena Arrant.)
"Lost Wandering Blues." (Ma Rainey.)
"Moonshine Blues." (Ma Rainey.)
"Prove It on Me Blues." (Ma Rainey.)
"Runaway Blues." (Ma Rainey.)
"Slave to the Blues." (Thomas Dorsey.)
"Soon This Morning." (Ma Rainey and Bessie Smith.)
"Southern Blues." (Ma Rainey.)
"Those Dogs of Mine." (Ma Rainey.)
"Walking Blues." (Ma Rainey and Lovie Austin.)
"Weeping Woman Blues." (Bessie Smith and Ma Rainey.)
"Ya Da Do." (Lovie Austin.)

Further Reading

Brown, Ken, and Albert McCarthy. "Mother of the Blues." *Jazz Music*, August 1943.

Brown, Sterling. *Southern Road*. Boston, Mass.: Beacon, 1974.

Collins, Patricia Hill. *Black Feminist Thought: Knowledge, Consciousness, and the Politics of Empowerment*. New York and London: Routledge, 1991.

Cone, James H. *The Spirituals and the Blues: An Interpretation*. New York: Seabury, 1972.

Davis, Angela. *Blues, Legacies, and Black Feminism: Gertrude "Ma" Rainey, Bessie Smith, and Billie Holiday*. New York: Vintage, 1998.

Fulbright, Thomas. "Ma Rainey and I." *Jazz Journal*, March 1956.

Lieb, Sandra. *Mother of the Blues: A Study of Ma Rainey*. Amherst: University of Massachusetts Press, 1981.

Nadal, Alan, ed. *May All Your Fences Have Gates: Essays on the Drama of August Wilson*. Iowa City: University of Iowa Press, 1994. (See Sandra Adell, "Speaking of Ma Rainey/Talking About the Blues.")

Orgill, Roxane. *Shout, Sister, Shout!: Ten Girl Singers Who Shaped a Century*. New York: Margaret K. McElderry, 2001.

Smith, Charles Edwards. "Ma Rainey and the Minstrels." *Record Changer*, June 1955.

————. "Ma Rainey." In *Notable American Women, 1807–1950*. Cambridge, Mass.: Radcliffe College, 1963.

Stewart-Baxter, Derrick. *Ma Rainey and the Classic Blues Singers*. New York: Stein and Day, 1970.

Wilson, August. *Ma Rainey's Black Bottom: A Play in Two Acts*. New York: New American Library, 1985.

Randolph, A. Philip

Asa (A.) Philip Randolph first made his mark as one of the "New Negro" radical leaders, became the best-known black labor leader in the United States as head of the Brotherhood of Sleeping Car Porters, and provided personal leadership and much of the strategy for the modern civil rights movement. Randolph's unique contribution to the rise of African Americans to full citizenship was his insistence that economic rights were necessary before civil rights could be fully effective.

Randolph was born in Florida, the son of a preacher and tailor. Education was an early and deep imperative instilled by his parents. He completed high school at Cookman Institute in Jacksonville but found he could get only manual jobs in the South. After several summers in New York, he moved there permanently in 1911, at age twenty-two. In Harlem, too, Randolph could get only menial work as an elevator operator, porter, and waiter. He was convinced very early on that black workers needed to join together to improve wages and working conditions.

Even before he moved to New York, while working as a waiter on the Fall River railroad line, Randolph had been fired for talking up the need for a union. In New York he made unsuccessful efforts to establish unions until 1925. A dream for Randolph in these early years in New York City was to become an actor. He took lessons and performed, and his oratorical style in later years would be much influenced by his Shakespearean apprenticeship. At the same time, Randolph was attracted by the vision and rhetoric of a radical union federation, the Industrial Workers of the World. He was also drawn to socialist leaders. By the time of his marriage to Lucille Greene in 1914, he was a committed socialist himself. A small intellectual black socialist group that owed much to the ideas of Hubert Harrison coalesced around Randolph in Harlem.

Randolph and his fast friend Chandler Owen became activists, soapbox orators, and, in November 1917, founders of *The Messenger*. In their words, it was "the only magazine of scientific radicalism in the world published by Negroes." The monthly magazine proved to be a lively forum espousing an alliance between black and white labor, the cause of unionism as central to the drive for social justice, socialism as the only way to secure it and eliminate racial intolerance, and the need for a new leadership for the black community.

Like all socialist ventures, *The Messenger* was hard hit by repercussions from the Bolshevik revolution in Russia. Just as the Socialist Party itself split, so did the editorial board of *The Messenger*. Several former close friends joined the new communist movement; others became black nationalists and separatists, among them Hubert Harrison and W. A. Domingo; but Randolph and Owen both remained socialists. At about this time *The Messenger* waged a vehement campaign against Marcus Garvey, with the slogan "Garvey must go!" Also at this time, Randolph developed a virulent, life-long anticommunism, as he blamed the communists for splitting black socialists.

With a declining readership, *The Messenger* needed to change in order to survive. It became second only to *The Crisis* and *Opportunity* in publishing the works of new young writers of the early Harlem Renaissance and in covering the cultural scene. *The Messenger*—which was the only one of the three magazines actually based in Harlem—published Langston Hughes, Countee Cullen, E. Franklin Frazier, Roy Wilkins, Jessie Redmon Fauset, Paul Robeson, Claude McKay, and Wallace Thurman.

By 1925, Randolph was the editor of a magazine perennially in the red, spending huge amounts of his time trying to raise money as the focus of the publication shifted. With a failing magazine and a string of unsuccessful organizational efforts behind him, Randolph at age thirty-six appeared to be going nowhere fast. That year, however, Randolph was approached by Pullman car porters to help establish a union. No black union had up to that time been established on a permanent basis. Though he himself was an integrationist, Randolph took up the task of organizing a segregated workforce, in the belief that blacks needed to have their own leadership, even as they participated in the broader labor movement. It was a principle from which he never waivered. Randolph became general organizer and president of the Brotherhood of Sleeping Car Porters (BSCP). Though he had never been a sleeping car porter, there were several good reasons for his role with the new organization. First, Randolph was well known in the black community. Second, he was a charismatic speaker. Third, after years of trying to organize black workers, he knew all about the problems involved. Fourth, he did not work

for the Pullman Palace Car Company, which had a near-monopoly in the industry as an employer, and therefore he could not be fired or otherwise intimidated. Even so, the task was daunting. The power of the company was immense. Moreover, porters were an elite group among black workers, so if any job action by the porters led to mass firings, there would be hordes of willing replacements only too eager to take their positions. The leadership of the black community, and the mass of the community itself, was very hostile to the whole idea of unions and believed that the Pullman Company was a friend to African Americans.

The success of the BSCP in its first few years was extremely heartening. By 1928, well over half the porters were members, meeting in secret despite strong efforts by the company to root out the union. An early attempt to gain a charter from the American Federation of Labor (AFL) failed, but its president, William Green, was sympathetic to the union. Randolph realized that without the full backing of the AFL, the BSCP's efforts were likely to fail.

An aborted strike in 1928 led to widespread disillusion with Randolph's leadership and to a precipitous decline in members. Only by dogged persistence and a remarkable group of regional leaders was the BSCP able to survive. As a wave of labor radicalism resulting from the Depression developed in 1933 and 1934, the BSCP was able to ride it and gain strength. New Deal legislation in those years also allowed the BSCP some legitimacy in its organizing efforts. By 1935, the BSCP had gained its international charter from the AFL, had achieved recognition as the bargaining agent for workers in its industry, and was in negotiations with the Pullman Company that led in 1937 to the first contract between the company and the union. It was a huge victory and one that propelled Randolph from a national figure of dogged determination and some renown into the leading black union leader, an icon to black workers nationwide. By then, the African American community had gone a long way toward embracing unions as a potentially liberating force for the community.

Randolph was never "just" a labor union leader. His vision was far broader. Inside the AFL, in 1935, Randolph forced the organization to investigate the racist exclusiveness of member unions and eloquently demanded serious consideration of the resulting report when the AFL's leadership tried to bury it. He fought for racial equality within the AFL until his retirement in 1968. As a race leader, Randolph cofounded the National Negro Congress and became its president from 1936 to 1940. He resigned in 1940, convinced that the organization had been subverted by communist influence.

Late in 1940 and into 1941, Randolph pressured the Roosevelt administration to insist on equal employment and wages in industries holding federal contracts for burgeoning production in preparation for World War II. His idea of a March on Washington movement took root in the black community and grew to a point where the government became truly apprehensive. When pressure and personal flattery failed to work on Randolph, President Franklin Roosevelt signed Executive Order 8802, setting up a Fair Employment Practices Commission (FEPC). Although it was temporary and far from everything demanded, it marked for the first time a public admission from the federal government that blacks suffered discrimination in employment and that it was the government's responsibility to provide a remedy. It was the first time that the nation had gone on record against racial discrimination in employment. The campaign made Randolph's name a household word. He became one of the most respected and best-known black leaders in America.

Randolph's tactics, both for the BSCP and for the March on Washington movement, were firmly based on his belief in the efficacy of nonviolent civil disobedience. At the time, he was called an "American Gandhi"; later, his tactics would be carried on into the modern civil rights movement Indeed, Randolph's civil rights activities were not divorced from his economic campaigns.

The 1940s and 1950s would be the apex of Randolph's influence. After the March on Washington movement, he founded the National Council for a Permanent FEPC, determined that the commission should not be jettisoned as soon as the war emergency was over. However, he refused a seat on the FEPC and declined to run for Congress. Although the campaign for a permanent FEPC failed, Randolph's next crusade, the Committee Against Jim Crow in Military Service and Training, produced a breakthrough. In 1948, badly needing the black vote, President Harry Truman bowed to Randolph's national nonviolent civil disobedience campaign to issue Executive Order 9981. The military went from the most segregated institution in American society to the most spectacular success story of integration.

In the AFL, Randolph, often alone, took the floor at annual conventions and privately to urge an end to racial barriers to union membership. In 1955, with the merger of the AFL and the Congress of Industrial Organizations (CIO), Randolph was elected a vice president of the new organization, despite the small size of his own union. He continued to urge full equality for black workers. While officially the AFL-CIO committed itself to full integration, its leadership did very little to push the issue. Frustrated, in 1959, Randolph urged the expulsion of any union that continued to insist on the color bar. In the convention that year, Randolph and George Meany, president of the AFL-CIO, clashed angrily. Meany acknowledged Randolph's role when he shouted, "Who the hell appointed you the guardian of all the Negroes in America?" Capitalizing on his new public title, Randolph organized the Negro American Labor Council (NALC) in November 1959 to plan a moral revolution, to eliminate discrimination, and "to secure the status of first class economic citizenship in the labor movement." Randolph remained its president from 1960 to 1966. In the early 1960s, the NALC was an effective part of the civil rights movement across a very broad area, concerned to make African Americans "first-class citizens" in every aspect of their lives.

Randolph was also deeply involved in the political struggle for civil rights. He helped promote Martin Luther King Jr. as a national figure through the Prayer Pilgrimage of 1957 and subsequently organized two Youth Marches for Integrated Schools in Washington, D.C., in 1958 and 1959. His protégé, Bayard Rustin, managed the details. It was Randolph—frustrated by a lack of progress—who had the idea for what became the culmination of the black campaign for civil rights, the March on Washington for Jobs and Freedom in 1963. This march, though far less militant than the original March on Washington movement of 1941, nevertheless brought together everyone, black or white, working in civil rights.

The following year, with his energy beginning to fail, and still mourning the death of his wife, Randolph established the A. Philip Randolph Institute to carry on his ideas and methods. Perhaps its grandest project was its Freedom Budget for All Americans, a kind of domestic Marshall Plan to end poverty through full employment. That same year, President Lyndon Johnson awarded Randolph the Presidential Medal of Freedom.

In his later years, as the civil rights movement fractured, Randolph—still in failing health and still maintaining the outlook of a lifetime—came under biting criticism, particularly in his support for the New York City teachers' unions in their struggle against the black community of New York in 1968, his support

Group portrait of members of the Brotherhood of Sleeping Car Porters taken at a national board meeting, c. 1925–1950. Left to right: C. L. Dellums, W. R. Daley, Bennie Smith, unidentified man, A. Philip Randolph, Thomas T. Patterson, Ashley L. Totten, Mr. Bradley. (Library of Congress.)

for the Democratic Party leadership, and what was considered favoring the interests of labor unions over those of the black community. Randolph retired in 1968. He died in 1979, at age ninety, in New York City.

More recently, A. Philip Randolph has been recognized as a direct link between the Harlem Renaissance and the civil rights movement. His talents never lay in organizational matters, in the day-to-day governance or management of anything. He was a voice articulating the hopes and aspirations of his community, a great speaker, agitator, and persuader. He inspired loyalty. In 1944, Edwin Embree (1968) concluded of Randolph: "Whatever the outcome of his present crusading, he is stating the goal of absolute justice and equality more drastically than any other colored leader. He has inspired the multitude with hopeful courage."

Biography

Asa Philip Randolph was born 15 April 1889 in Crescent City, Florida. He received a high school education at Cookman Institute in Jacksonville, Florida, and moved to Harlem in 1911. Randolph married Lucille Green in 1914. He worked as an elevator operator, porter, and railroad waiter and continued his education at City College and the Rand School of Social Sciences. From 1917 to 1928, he was coeditor of *The Messenger*. Randolph was the socialist candidate for New York

State comptroller in 1921. In 1925, he was a general organizer and president of the newly founded Brotherhood of Sleeping Car Porters, which in 1935 received an international charter from the American Federation of Labor. Randolph was named a member of the New York City Commission on Race following the Harlem race riot of 1935. He was president of the National Negro Congress from 1936 to 1940. In 1937, he negotiated the first contract with the Pullman Palace Car Company. He organized the March on Washington movement in 1941; this movement led to Executive Order 8802 and the Fair Employment Practices Commission. He was appointed to the New York Housing Authority in 1942. Randolph was a founder of Nonviolent Civil Disobedience Against Military Segregation in 1947. He was elected a vice president and executive council member of the AFL-CIO at its merger in 1955, the first black official at the highest level of the American labor movement. He was one of the leaders of the March on Washington for Jobs and Freedom in 1963 and a founder and the first president (1960–1961) of the Negro American Labor Council. Randolph retired from union activities in 1968. He died 16 May 1979 in New York City.

Stephen Burwood

See also Brotherhood of Sleeping Car Porters; Domingo, Wilfred Adolphus; Garvey, Marcus; Harrison, Hubert; Messenger, The; Owen, Chandler; *other specific individuals*

Further Reading

Anderson, Jervis. *A. Philip Randolph: A Biographical Portrait*. New York: Harcourt Brace Jovanovich, 1973.

Brazeal, Brailsford R. *The Brotherhood of Sleeping Car Porters: Its Origin and Development*. New York: Harper and Row, 1946.

Embree, Edwin R. *Thirteen against the Odds*. Port Washington, N.Y.: Kennikat, 1968.

Harris, William H. *Keeping the Faith: A. Philip Randolph, Milton P. Webster, and the Brotherhood of Sleeping Car Porters, 1925–1937*. Urbana: University of Illinois Press, 1977.

———. "A. Philip Randolph, Black Workers, and the Labor Movement." In *Labor Leaders in America*, ed. Melvyn Dubofsky and Warren Van Tine. Urbana: University of Illinois Press, 1987.

Kornweibel, Theodore, Jr. *No Crystal Stair: Black Life and the Messenger, 1917–1928*. Westport, Conn.: Greenwood, 1975.

Pfeffer, Paula F. *A. Philip Randolph, Pioneer of the Civil Rights Movement.* Baton Rouge: Louisiana State University Press, 1990.

Wright, Sara E. *A. Philip Randolph: Integration in the Workplace.* Englewood Cliffs, N.J.: Silver Burdett, 1990.

Razaf, Andy

Andy Razaf is considered the first full-time black lyricist of American popular song and black musical theater. During the 1920s and 1930s, he wrote lyrics to some of the era's most popular and memorable songs, including "Honeysuckle Rose" (1929), "Ain't Misbehavin'"(1929), and "(What Did I Do to Be So) Black and Blue?" (1929). This last song has come to be regarded as one of the first racial protest songs in American popular music. Its central role in Ralph Ellison's novel *Invisible Man* (1952), as a motif of the tragicomic irony of black experience, attests to the song's historical resonance and Razaf's pioneering significance as a politically conscious popular songster.

Razaf (whose original name was Andrea Menentania Razafinkeriefo) was born in Washington, D.C., to a nephew of Queen Ranavalona of Madagascar and a daughter of the famous black politician and American consul to Madagascar, John Louis Waller. Growing up, he absorbed his grandfather's anticolonialist attitudes and oratorical abilities, his singer aunt's love of music, and his mother's affinity for poetry. Though he excelled in school, he dropped out of high school while living in New York City and pursued songwriting and poetry. During the formative years of his career, the period after World War I, Tin Pan Alley was demanding patriotic themes and closing off opportunities to many black songwriters; but Razaf contributed protest verse to radical African American magazines like *The Messenger*, *Emancipator*, *The New Negro*, and *Crusader*. In 1921, with the successes of Mamie Smith's "Crazy Blues" and the jazz musical *Shuffle Along*, Razaf saw an opportunity for his songs, with their black themes, to gain a wider audience. He soon met and collaborated with the great stride pianist James P. Johnson and wrote several blues tunes while also contributing intermittently to Tin Pan Alley.

As a collaborator, Razaf came into his own, especially with the talented pianist Thomas "Fats" Waller. With music by Waller and Johnson, Razaf and Henry Creamer wrote the lyrics to the popular Broadway show *Keep Shufflin'* in 1928. In the same year, Razaf also had successes with "Honeysuckle Rose," in tandem with Waller, and the classic double entendre sung by Ethel Waters, "My Handy Man." He continued to write for Tin Pan Alley and the blues market while also creating lyrics to two more major musicals, *Hot Chocolates* (1929) and *Blackbirds* (1930). *Hot Chocolates* featured Waller and Razaf's hit "Ain't Misbehavin'," which has gone on to become one of the most celebrated standards in jazz history; and "Black and Blue," originally performed by Edith Wilson and made popular by Louis Armstrong. On *Blackbirds*, Razaf teamed with the great pianist-composer Eubie Blake to produce the hit "Memories of You."

For much of the 1930s, Razaf continued to write alone and collaborate with Waller, Blake, Paul Denniker, and others, enjoying success in theater and radio. Later, even though he had written the lyrics to the big band classics "Stompin' at the Savoy" (1936) and "In the Mood" (1939), Razaf was all but forgotten. But in 1978, five years after his death, his name was reinvoked in a Broadway musical celebrating Fats Waller, *Ain't Misbehavin'*.

Biography

Andrea Menentania Razafinkeriefo was born on 16 December 1895 in Washington, D.C. He sold a song to Shubert's *Passing Show* in 1917 and contributed poems and essays to *The New Negro*, *The Messenger*, *Emancipator*, and *Crusader* in 1918. He played baseball for the Cleveland Semi-Pro City League in 1920. He wrote and sold songs from 1921 to 1957 in New York and wrote for the *Herald-Dispatch*, Los Angeles, from 1953 to 1955. He was honored by the U.S. Treasury Department for songs "rendered in behalf" of the War Finances Program in 1944. Razaf was admitted to the Songwriters Hall of Fame in 1972. He died in North Hollywood, California, on 3 February 1973.

DAVE JUNKER

See also Armstrong, Louis; Blackbirds; Blake, Eubie; Hot Chocolates; Johnson, James P.; Musical Theater; Waller, Thomas "Fats"; Waters, Ethel; Wilson, Edith

Selected Songs

"Anybody Here Want to See My Cabbage." 1925.
"My Special Friend Is Back in Town." 1926.
"Louisiana." 1928.

"Dusky Stevedore." 1928.

"Willow Tree." 1928.

"Sweet Savannah Sue." 1929.

"Ain't Misbehavin'." 1929.

"(What Did I Do to Be So) Black and Blue." 1929.

"Honeysuckle Rose." 1929.

"My Fate Is in Your Hands." 1929.

"Zonky." 1929.

"Sposin'." 1929.

"I've Got a Feelin' I'm Falling." 1929.

"A Porter's Love Song to a Chambermaid." 1930.

"Memories of You." 1930.

"Stealin' Apples." 1932.

"Ain'tcha Glad?" 1933.

"Christopher Columbus (A Rhythm Cocktail)." 1936.

"Stompin' at the Savoy." 1936.

"The Joint Is Jumpin'." 1938.

"In the Mood." 1939.

"We Are Americans Too." 1941.

"I'm Gonna Move to the Outskirts of Town." 1941.

"Gee, Baby, Ain't I Good to You." 1944.

Musicals

Keep Shufflin'. 1928.

Hot Chocolates. 1929.

Kitchen Mechanic's Review. 1930.

Blackbirds. 1930.

Hot Harlem. 1932.

Harlem Hotcha. 1932.

Tan Manhattan. 1941.

Further Reading

Cayer, D. A. "Black and Blue and Black Again: Three Stages of Racial Imagery in Jazz Lyrics." *Journal of Jazz Studies*, 2, 1974, pp. 38–71.

Evans, Mark. "Andy Razaf, the Word Man of Broadway." *American Visions: The Magazine of Afro-American Culture*, October 1989.

Jasen, David A., and Gene Jones. *Spreadin' Rhythm Around: Black Popular Songwriters, 1880–1930*. New York: Schirmer, 1998.

Larkin, Colin, ed. *The Encyclopedia of Popular Music*. New York: Muze, 1992. (See also 3rd ed., 1998.)

Singer, Barry. *Black and Blue: The Life and Lyrics of Andy Razaf*. New York: Schirmer, 1992.

Sundquist, Eric J. *Cultural Contexts for Ralph Ellison's Invisible Man: A Bedford Documentary Companion*. Boston, Mass.: Bedford–St. Martin's, 1995.

Woll, Allen L. *Black Musical Theatre: From Coontown to Dreamgirls*. Baton Rouge: Louisiana State University Press, 1989.

Redding, J. Saunders

J. Saunders Redding (1906–1988) was an educator, writer, social commentator, historian, and literary critic. Throughout his career, he wrote about a number of writers of the Harlem Renaissance, including Sterling Brown, Rudolph Fisher, Zora Neale Hurston, Nella Larsen, George Schuyler, and Carl Van Vechten. Many of his literary judgments can be found in the weekly newspaper column he wrote for the *Afro-American* chain. This column consisted largely of book reviews and profiles of literary figures, but Redding also addressed a broad range of contemporary issues, such as the United States' foreign policy and being personally subjected to Jim Crow laws. By the end of his career, Redding had written more than 1,000 newspaper columns, but he remains best known for his debut book, *To Make a Poet Black* (1939), one of the first extensive critical works of African American literature from Phillis Wheatley to the Harlem Renaissance.

Redding came from a middle-class background: His mother was a schoolteacher and then a homemaker; his father was a postal worker. Both of his parents had graduated from Howard University and placed a great deal of importance on education. While still in his teens, Redding read W. E. B. Du Bois's *The Souls of Black Folk* (1903), a book for which he reserved his highest praise; its influence can be seen in his own variation on Du Bois's concept of double-consciousness. For Redding, the double-consciousness that results from being "both a Negro and an American" was a potential affirmation, rather than a crisis, of identity—an interpretation that acknowledges that identity is never monolithic (Du Bois 1903/1961, 17; Redding 1991, 193). Nonetheless, double-consciousness created problems for African American writers. According to Redding, these artists were often overwhelmed by a dual commitment to their race and to their art.

Redding considered himself a humanist, and in his case this meant that he was more concerned with what human beings shared than with what held them apart. He resisted separating African American literature from American literature, preferring instead an integrationist approach. Although he is famous for describing African American literature as a "literature either of purpose or necessity," he has also insisted that this description applied to all of American literature, at least until recently. Historically, he asserted, all American literature was less concerned with aesthetics and more concerned with "the practical aim of elevation and instruction" (1939, vii; 1991, 213). If he seems to have written more extensively about African American literature and history than any other, he did so in order to correct the exclusion of the African American experience from traditional scholarship.

In other ways, characterizing Redding's viewpoints proves to be no easy task. He has frequently been called a conservative, but such a label depends on the time period and one's outlook. In his first book, in 1939, he himself rejected what he called the conservatism of Booker T. Washington in favor of the liberalism of Du Bois. He criticized such writers as Angelina Weld Grimké and Leslie P. Hill, who, unlike the "New Negro" of the Harlem Renaissance, rejected black pride in favor of purportedly universal themes. Calling them bourgeois, shallow, and conservative, he pointed to Jean Toomer as their revolutionary antithesis (1939, 103–104, 128). He also found fault with Carl Van Vechten, Wallace Thurman, and Claude McKay for taking part in a "cult of primitivism." Citing portrayals of blacks as exotic and instinctive, he contended that the literature of primitivism encouraged the belief that all African Americans are essentially uncivilized (1991; see "The Negro Author: His Publisher, His Public, and His Purse"; "Absorption With Blackness Recalls Movement of 1920s"). In 1942, in an introduction to Redding's autobiographical work *No Day of Triumph*, Richard Wright praised the book and said that Redding was "the first middle-class Negro to break with the ideology of the 'Talented Tenth'"—a reference to W. E. B. Du Bois's term for an African American professional class that led the masses.

To others, however, Redding's liberalism started to sound conservative. To some degree, it was Redding's views that had shifted. By 1960, in a piece titled "The Negro Writer and His Relationship to His Roots," Redding was praising Toomer for having written about the particular experience of African Americans in a way that transcended superficial differences—an interpretation that sounds closer to that of the bourgeois conservatives he had earlier disdained. But the times themselves were also changing. Harold Cruse (1957–1958) argued that if African Americans wanted to preserve their culture and identity, they would have to resist the conservative call by the middle class for racial integration and assimilation. In 1959, Redding

responded to Cruse in an address at the First Conference of Negro Writers. He reasserted the need for full integration and disagreed with Cruse's contention that African American culture is distinct from American culture, prompting what some refer to as the "Cruse-Redding controversy" (Olaniyan 1992, 533–534).

In the 1970s, Redding became embroiled in a debate with Amiri Baraka. Baraka was part of the "black arts movement," which affirmed the existence of a uniquely black aesthetic, and he was a proponent of black studies at colleges and universities, arguing that successful integration was an unrealizable fantasy. Redding, however, denied the existence of a black aesthetic and maintained that its supporters were racial chauvinists perpetuating the idea of African Americans as inherently different. He opposed the development of black studies, reasoning that the discipline encompassed too much and that such categories should be created according to culture, not race (1970). In a rather belated published reply (1983), Baraka called Redding antiblack and bourgeois. Redding was now a part of the conservative middle class that he had, in his younger years, ridiculed.

In spite of his impatience with literary categorizations by race and with the cult of primitivism, Redding did not value supposedly "raceless" literature, that is, literature by African Americans in which the race of the characters is never made explicit. He celebrated the return to black folk life in Toomer's *Cane* and James Weldon Johnson's *God's Trombones*. He praised literature like Richard Wright's *Native Son*, a novel that depicts the lives of the urban poor. He also commended writers like Jessie Redmon Fauset who wrote about the black middle class. In these diverse representations of African American culture, Redding believed, readers would find facts about an essentially American culture as well as truths about the universal human condition. Like many writers and critics from the Harlem Renaissance, he trusted that "good" African American art and history, texts that insist on the common humanity of African Americans, would eventually destroy the color line.

Biography

James (Jay) Thomas Saunders Redding was born 13 October 1906 in Wilmington, Delaware. He attended Howard High School (1923); Lincoln University, Pennsylvania (1923–1924); Brown, Providence, Rhode Island (B.A., 1928; M.A., 1932); and Columbia University

(1932–1934). Redding taught at Morehouse College, 1928–1931; Louisville Municipal College, Kentucky, 1934–1936; Elizabeth City State Teachers College, North Carolina, 1938–1943; Hampton Institute, Virginia, 1943–1966; and George Washington University, 1968–1969. He was chairman of the English department, Southern University, Baton Rouge, Louisiana, 1936–1938; lecturer for the State Department, India, 1952; James Weldon Johnson Professor of Creative Writing, Hampton Institute, 1954–1963; and Ernest I. White Professor Emeritus of American Studies and Humane Letters, Cornell University, 1970–1975. Redding was a columnist for the Norfolk *Journal and Guide*, 1943, and for the *Afro-American* newspaper chain (based in Baltimore), 1944–1946. He was a book review editor for the *Afro-American* newspapers, 1946–1966, and drector of the Division of Publication and Research at the National Endowment for the Humanities, 1966–1970. Among his awards were a Rockefeller Foundation Fellowship, 1941; the North Carolina Historical Society's Mayflower Award for *No Day of Triumph*, 1944; Phi Beta Kappa, Brown University, 1943; and Guggenheim Fellowships in 1944 and 1959. Redding retired in 1975 and died in Ithaca, New York, on 2 March 1988.

VALARIE J. MOSES

See also Baltimore Afro-American; Brown, Sterling; Cane; Fauset, Jessie Redmon; Fisher, Rudolph; God's Trombones; Grimké, Angelina Weld; Hurston, Zora Neale; Johnson, James Weldon; Larsen, Nella; McKay, Claude; Schuyler, George S.; Thurman, Wallace; Toomer, Jean; Van Vechten, Carl; Wright, Richard

Selected Works

To Make a Poet Black. 1939.

No Day of Triumph, intro. Richard Wright. 1942.

"The Negro Writer and His Relationship to His Roots." In *The American Negro Writer and His Roots*. 1960.

Cavalcade: Negro American Writing From 1760 to the Present. 1971. (As coeditor, with Arthur P. Davis. See also rev. ed., *The New Cavalcade*, 2 vols., as coeditor with Arthur P. Davis and Joyce Ann Joyce. 1991 and 1992.)

"The Black Revolution in American Studies." *American Studies: An International Newsletter*, 1970. (Reprinted in *Sources for American Studies*, ed. Jefferson B. Kellogg and Robert H. Walker. Westport, Conn.: Greenwood, 1983.)

A Scholar's Conscience: Selected Writings of J. Saunders Redding, ed. Faith Berry. 1991. (Includes Redding's essay "W. E. B. Du Bois: A Mind Matched With Spirit.")

Further Reading

Baraka, Imamu Amir. "A Reply to Saunders Redding's 'The Black Revolution in American Studies.'" In *Sources for American Studies*, ed. Jefferson B. Kellogg and Robert H. Walker. Westport, Conn.: Greenwood, 1983.

Berry, Faith. "Saunders Redding as Literary Critic of Langston Hughes." *Langston Hughes Review*, 5(2), 1986.

Cruse, Harold. "An Afro-American's Cultural Views." *Presence Africaine*, 17, 1957–1958. (Reprinted in *Rebellion or Revolution?* New York: Morrow, 1968.)

Davis, Arthur P. *From the Dark Tower: Afro-American Writers, 1900–1960*. Washington, D.C.: Howard University Press, 1974.

Du Bois, W. E. B. *The Souls of Black Folk*, intro. J. Saunders Redding. New York: Fawcett, 1961. (Originally published 1903.)

Olaniyan, Tejumola. "African-American Critical Discourse and the Invention of Cultural Identities." *African American Review*, 26(4), 1992.

Savery, Pancho. "J. Saunders Redding." In *Dictionary of Literary Biography: Modern American Critics, 1920–1955*, Vol. 63, ed. Gregory S. Jay. Detroit, Mich.: Book Tower, 1988.

Wright, Richard. Introduction. In *No Day of Triumph*. London and New York: Harper, 1942.

Reiss, Winold

Winold Reiss was born in 1886 in Karlsruhe in southwestern Germany, the son of the respected Bavarian landscape painter Fritz Mahler Reiss. He studied under the direction of his father and attended the Kunstgewerbe Schule in Munich as a student of Franz von Stuck. The elder Reiss had trained at the Düsseldorf Academy, studying natural history, German landscape, and peasant portraiture, and handed these traditions down to his son. Von Stuck exposed him to two modern art movements—fauvism and cubism—and eventually encouraged him to enroll at the School of Applied Arts, where he would study commercial design and poster design under Julius Diez. Reiss painted folk groups in Sweden, the Netherlands, and Germany before his emigration to the United States in 1913. He probably became aware of cubism and African art at least by 1913, when he most likely saw an exhibition of Pablo Picasso's African-inspired cubist works in Munich. Von Stuck also introduced Reiss to Jugendstil ("youth style"), a German decorative arts movement that was rooted in French art nouveau. Reiss had worked as a designer in Munich and would apply this experience in New York, where he worked as an illustrator for magazines, books, and advertisements, using his training in commercial and poster art. Reiss was also no doubt familiar with the German folk art technique Scherenschnitt, a cutout technique that influenced his own simple black-and-white designs, often resembling cutouts or collages.

Reiss, along with other modernists in Munich, was attracted to ethnography. He was aware of the German expressionists' Blaue Reiter almanac (1912), which contained numerous photographs of the art of the Cameroons, Egypt, and Japan, as well as Bavarian and Russian folk art. Reiss therefore developed an interest in both ancient and modern art, and an awareness of contemporary experiments of modern artists.

Before becoming a premier artist in Harlem, Reiss spent a great deal of time traveling in the West, Canada, and Mexico, as well as in Central America, painting Indians and aspects of Native American life. He was particularly fascinated with the Blackfeet Indians, the Pueblo people, Mexicans, and African Americans. Reiss had always been interested in documenting various racial groups, "as a means to illuminate the distinctions and integrity of different ethnic groups." Reiss showed up in communities that were undergoing dramatic social changes, including the heirs of the Aztecs in Mexico in 1921 and the last survivors of the intertribal wars of the nineteenth century in Browning, Montana. Harlem provided such opportunities for unique documentation, a community that, according to Stewart (1989, 1990), Reiss "stumbled onto," finding a place "brimming with racial consciousness and a desire for dignified self-representation."

Reiss would have a profound effect on Aaron Douglas, the leading painter of the Harlem Renaissance. In 1925, Reiss was hired to create the cover for a special "Harlem issue" of the magazine Survey Graphic; Douglas, who was then a teacher in Kansas City, Missouri, saw this cover—a straightforward, realistic, dignified portrait of the singer Roland Hayes—and was deeply moved by it. Reiss showed Hayes looking off to the side thoughtfully and seriously and proudly displayed Hayes's African traits, including a full nose and lips. This was the "splendid portrait of a Black man by the famous German artist Fritz Winold Reiss" that Douglas referred to when discussing the impact Survey Graphic had on him. Douglas would study with Reiss for two years, on a scholarship, and would find encouragement to paint things African and explore a uniquely personal vein of artistic experience; a credo of Reiss's was the importance of using one's own life experiences and heritage as a source of inspiration for creating art. As Douglas's teacher, Reiss influenced Douglas not only regarding subject matter—Douglas's black heritage and Africanism—but also stylistically. Reiss's flat, modernist drawings in Survey Graphic, such as "Dawn in Harlem," showed a strong strain of cubism, Orphism, and precisionism. Douglas would use a very similar clear style in his works, including skyscrapers, smokestacks, and concentric circles, a motif he would take much further.

The "Harlem issue" of Survey Graphic also contained a brief discussion, probably written by Alain Locke, about the significance of Reiss's work. To Locke (presumably), Reiss's attention to American blacks was a particularly welcome development:

What [Paul] Gauguin and his followers have done for the Far East, and the work of Ufer and Blumenschein and the Taos school for the Pueblo and Indian, seems about to [be done] for the Negro and Africa: in short, painting, the most local of arts, in terms of its own limitations even, is achieving universality.

The drawings that surrounded this essay about Reiss consisted of a series of portraits with clear, straightforward facial features. All of Reiss's portraits are detailed in the face and hands, for which, in the originals, color pastel crayons are used. The clothing and bodies are not detailed but are almost sketchlike, in effect further emphasizing the sitters' sensitivity, seriousness, and dignity.

Reiss's work provided a source of pride and inspiration for black artists, who at this time often did not choose to paint black subject matter. For instance, his "Interpretations of Harlem Jazz" in Survey Graphic included a black dancer in a cabaret, dancing with a young woman, their faces accented only by thick overaccentuated lips, their bodies flat silhouettes. The piece has the stylized qualities of art deco and Egyptian art, with a touch of cubism (all of which would influence Douglas). An African mask, a bottle, and another dancer's leg appear in the background. All the black silhouette figures are accentuated by thick features, slightly slanted eyes (reminiscent of Dan sculpture of the Ivory Coast of Africa), thick lips, and black faces.

Reiss's involvement in the special Harlem issue of Survey Graphic and his position as Aaron Douglas's teacher established him as an important participant in the visual arts movement of the Harlem Renaissance.

Winold Reiss, *Steel Workers*, c. 1920. (Library of Congress.)

Biography

Winold Reiss was born 16 September 1886 in Karlsruhe, Germany. He studied with his father (the landscape painter Fritz Mahler Reiss) and at the Munich School of Applied Arts under Julius Diez. Reiss married Henrietta Luthy in 1912 and immigrated to the United States in 1913. In 1915, he lectured (on German posters) at the Art Students League in New York City; illustrated books and magazines; did murals; and began the Winold Reiss Art School. He traveled to Montana to draw Blackfeet Indians in1919, to Mexico in 1920, and to Germany and Sweden in 1922 (when he also published in *Century Magazine*). He provided cover art for *Opportunity* (the magazine of the National Urban League) in 1925, and for a special "Harlem issue" of *Survey Graphic*. His work appeared in *New York World*, *Chicago Evening Post*, and *The New Negro*. During the 1920s and 1930s, he had numerous individual and group exhibitions and published illustrations. In 1929, he designed the interior of the Tavern Club, Chicago. In 1930, he was in an annual group show at the Art

Institute of Chicago. In 1932, his work appeared in *Creative Art* and *Architectural Forum*. In 1935, he held the Winold Reiss summer school at Glacier Park, Montana. In 1936, he designed interiors of several restaurants in New York City and exhibited Indian portraits in several venues. In 1940, a reissue of *Blackfeet Indians: Pictures by Winold Reiss, Story by Frank Linderman*, appeared. During the 1940s, Reiss continued to design covers for *Survey Graphic* and to design restaurants; he had exhibits and continued to sketch Blackfeet Indians. In 1951, he illustrated *The Lewis and Clark Expedition* by Richard Neuberger and donated Harlem portraits to Fisk University. That year he also suffered a stroke. Reiss died 29 August 1953 in New York City.

AMY KIRSCHKE

See also Artists; Douglas, Aaron; Hayes, Roland; Locke, Alain; Survey Graphic; Visual Arts

Major Exhibitions

1920: E. F. Hanfstaengl Galleries. (Solo.)
1922: Memorial Art Gallery, Rochester, New York.
1925: 135th Street Branch, New York Public Library. (Solo.)
1928: Art Institute of Chicago. (Solo.)
1929, 1930: Annual Group Show, Art Institute of Chicago.
1931: Los Angeles Museum, Hill Collection. (Solo.)
1935: Brooklyn Museum. (Watercolors; group show.)
1936: Faulkner Memorial Art Gallery, Santa Barbara, Calif. (Solo.)
1947: Arizona State Museum. (Solo.)

Further Reading

Kirschke, Amy. *Aaron Douglas: Art, Race, and the Harlem Renaissance.* Jackson: University Press of Mississippi, 1995.

Stewart, Jeffrey. *To Color America: Portraits of Winold Reiss.* Washington, D.C.: Smithsonian Institution Press, 1989. (Note: This is the source for the above list of exhibitions.)

———. *Winold Reiss: An Illustrated Checklist of His Portraits.* Washington, D.C.: Smithsonian Institution Press, 1990.

Religion

No one disputes the significance of religion in general, and Christianity in particular, to African American

William H. Johnson (1901–1970), *Church on Lenox Avenue*, c.1939–1940. (© Smithsonian American Art Museum, Washington, D.C./Art Resource, N.Y.)

cultural and political history. As early as 1903, W. E. B. Du Bois described the church as the most important social institution in black life, seeing in it the clearest continuation of African cultural values and experience. If anything, the institutional power of the black church was enhanced during the Harlem Renaissance as the membership of northern churches swelled with southern migrants, creating some of the largest religious institutions in American history and propelling their leaders into positions of cultural leadership. At the same time, traditional religious institutions viewed the developments of the renaissance with some ambivalence. The diversification of social life in Harlem provided many avenues for social advancement. If the traditional churches were not moved off the center, they now competed with new religions, with new political and economic institutions, and with many new social diversions in the entertainment industry. Ironically, these many centers of social life threatened the church at the moment of its greatest strength. Similarly, the participants in the renaissance viewed the traditions of the church with some ambivalence. Countee Cullen described his tension between a "Christian upbringing" and a "pagan inclination." In a similarly divided manner, the intelligentsia of Harlem respected the historic significance of the churches, while feeling themselves part of a newer, more progressive, and more secular intellectual vanguard. In these respects, religion in Harlem participates in the larger dynamics of the place of religion within the discourses and practices of American modernism.

While the churches responded in various ways to the cultural and intellectual developments of the Harlem Renaissance, the context for that response was provided by the great migration. Shortly after Du Bois declared in *The Souls of Black Folk* that the black preacher was the archetype of black leadership, "a man at the center of a group of men," such leaders found themselves chasing after congregants who pulled up stakes for the promised land of the urban North. Indeed, by the full flowering of the renaissance in the 1920s, the vast majority of Harlemite ministers, even in traditional denominations, either had migrated from the South or were the children of migrants, a development that caused some discomfort among northern traditionalists. Northern churches grew exponentially as struggling congregations became juggernauts, seemingly overnight. Salem Methodist Episcopal, led by Countee Cullen's foster father, Frederick Asbury Cullen, grew from a small storefront mission church with three members to a 3,000-member congregation between 1902 and 1919. Crowded pews meant swelling coffers, and churches benefited from soaring property values as well. Following the immigrants to upper Manhattan, Abyssinian Baptist sold its building on Fifty-ninth Street and built one of the most imposing religious edifices in Manhattan to house its burgeoning congregation. Soon, more wealth and property were concentrated in the religious institutions of Harlem than in any other sector of African American society, so much so that how the churches used their money became a common point of criticism among other institutional leaders like Du Bois and James Weldon Johnson.

However, the great migration created much more than wealth and prestige. It also dramatically transformed the ministry and liturgy of many traditional churches. The generally conservative northern churches struggled to accommodate the more demonstrative worship styles of many southern immigrants. Cullen at Salem Methodist Episcopal, for instance, regularly invited George Wilson Becton, a flamboyant evangelist who appealed to the working classes, to share his pulpit.

Others incorporated spirituals and newly developing gospel music styles, sometimes at the expense of traditional members who could not tolerate the change. Nevertheless, many congregations did too little to make southern immigrants feel at home, and as a result innumerable storefront churches and cults sprang up to feed the spiritual needs of new arrivals. Some of these churches disappeared almost as quickly as they were organized. Others endured to become fixtures of African American religious life. The Pentecostal revivals begun on Azusa Street in Los Angeles burned fiercely across the continent in Harlem. Mother Horne's Mount Calvary Assembly Hall of the Pentecostal Faith of All Nations was a "storefront" operation that could seat up to 800 worshipers and gradually spread to several other cities. Other, less clearly Christian groups flourished as well. Perhaps most important of these, George Baker proclaimed himself Father Divine and built an interracial church on his amalgamation of Christianity and theosophy, emphasizing positive thinking, entrepreneurial self-help, and communal styles of living. The multitude of less familiar and more suspect religious movements lent some credence to the popular stereotype of Harlem as a site of religious chaos overrun with religious charlatans and fly-by-night messiahs.

This stereotype masks the many ways in which traditional and new religious movements met real social and psychic needs in Harlem. Religious groups of every stripe provided a space for social interaction and communal identity. Many religious groups sought to meet the material and political needs of their members. Father Divine is remembered less for his quirky theology than for the seemingly miraculous feasts that he provided for his followers. Many ministers in the traditional churches tended toward a version of the social gospel and sought to use their churches to serve the people of God on earth. Bishop Reverdy C. Ransom of the African Methodist Episcopal church and Adam Clayton Powell Sr. of Abyssinian Baptist both instituted a variety of ministries to the urban poor and advocated for public policies on their behalf. Even a relative theological conservative such as Frederick Asbury Cullen became president of the local chapter of the National Association for the Advancement of Colored People (NAACP); helped organize the Silent Parade of 1919; visited President Woodrow Wilson in the aftermath of the riots in Brownsville, Texas; and promoted various social ministries through his church and through the YMCA. Clearly, the religious scene in Harlem experienced the same kind of dynamism that was propelling achievement in the arts, so that we might say the Harlem Renaissance was a period not only of artistic and literary vitality but of religious vitality as well.

Direct relationships between the artistic and religious leaders are somewhat harder to trace. Langston Hughes's declaration that most of Harlem did not even realize that a renaissance had occurred seems borne out by the sermons and other writings of the religious figures of the day. Direct relationships that existed grew out of the traditional position of the black church as a social and cultural center. Adam Clayton Powell referred to Cullen and Hughes as evidence of black achievement, and Abyssinian Baptist was the site of the most famous wedding in Harlem during the 1920s, that of Countee Cullen and Yolande Du Bois, daughter of W. E. B. Du Bois. Frederick Cullen promoted his son's poetry, though his autobiography suggests he paid only the vaguest attention to the literary circles in which his son circulated. When religious figures did comment on Harlem's cultural scene, they were often most concerned with the debauchery they saw in the jazz clubs and speakeasies. Reverdy Ransom recognized the actors and musicians of New York as the sons and daughters of the church, but he was almost alone on this score and was denounced by some ministers for his efforts. Indeed, both Frederick Cullen and Adam Clayton Powell led crusades against the entertainment industry and against the bohemianism in which many of the literary figures of Harlem actively participated. In Powell's case, this crusade included specific attacks on the prevalence of homosexuality. The tension that could prevail on this score is symbolized by the minister who threatened to shut down a reading by Langston Hughes if Hughes did not stop reading blues poetry from the pulpit.

If the leaders of the churches could pay cursory attention to the literary world, the literary figures cannot be said to have given only cursory attention to the church. The literature of the period is awash with the representation of religion. Artists varied in their attitudes toward religion but can be roughly divided into three categories: those who sought, however tentatively, to embrace the traditions of black Christianity; those who rejected Christianity in favor of a more secular political activism; and those who looked to non-Christian traditions. While no particular artist held one of these positions to the absolute exclusion of any other, their prevalence suggests that attitudes toward religion in the artistic community were as dynamic as they were anywhere else in Harlem.

The best representative of the first attitude is Countee Cullen, who was adopted at age fifteen by Frederick Asbury Cullen, embraced his foster father's Methodism, and largely maintained his belief and practice throughout his life. While he admitted to tension between a Christian upbringing and a pagan inclination, a tension that animates his best poem, "Heritage," Cullen largely sought to quash his pagan longings in favor of the traditional sentiments of Christian orthodoxy. Cullen wondered in print why he had to write of blues instead of penning a hymn or a prayer. His magnum opus, "The Black Christ," has some suggestion of rebelliousness but finally endorses the traditions of Christian humility and long-suffering.

Figures like Langston Hughes and, at the tail end of the renaissance, Richard Wright had little use for such noble suffering. Although they both grew up in the church through the faith of their mothers, in adulthood they both moved toward a more overt political orientation that was openly critical of the church. Hughes's "Goodby Christ" satirically dismisses Christ as someone who has had his day in the past but now had to make room for the more politically engaged stance of the socialist worker. Wright similarly sees the Christianity of the past giving way before progressive political activism. Nevertheless, both writers try to imagine forms of Christianity that could mesh with their political activism. Indeed, Hughes spoke warmly of the ecstatic worship in the storefront churches, seeing in it something closer to the heart of the working class than the tight-laced traditions of the mainline churches. Such nuanced responses suggest that many African American writers were unwilling to abandon the church wholesale in the manner of European American writers like H. L. Mencken.

Among those who emphasized neither traditional Christianity nor political activism were Zora Neale Hurston and Jean Toomer. Toomer, in his trek into theosophy and the philosophy of the Russian mystic Gurdjieff, imagined a religious reality that transcended race. Despite Toomer's triumphant initiation of the renaissance with *Cane*, a book that succeeded in part because of its depiction of southern black religion, his decision to abandon a racial identity as a disciple of Gurdjieff also signaled the end of his literary participation in the renaissance. More common among African American artists was Zora Neale Hurston's attraction to African-derived religions such as vodun (voodoo). The child of a minister, Hurston remained involved imaginatively with Christianity throughout her life, as evidenced in novels such as *Jonah's Gourd Vine* and *Seraph on the Sewanee*. Nevertheless, the Christianity in such novels contributes as much to the characters' struggles as to their triumphs. More powerful in Hurston's estimation were the religions of the Caribbean, and the practices of various obeah men and women throughout the southern United States. Hurston described these practices in several books (most notably *Tell My Horse*) and even went through an initiation ritual in order to become a vodun priestess. These practices reflected Hurston's belief that, at the deepest level, "the Negro is not a Christian, really."

The tremendous diversity of literary responses to religion, as well as the religious ferment in Harlem generally, suggests that there is no monolithic relationship between black religion and black culture. Indeed, as scholars of black church history and sociology have been at pains to point out, it is impossible, except in the most abstract sense, to speak of something like "*the* black church." Rather, the diversity of religious practice in Harlem and the multiplicity of artistic responses to that diversity suggest the dynamism and vitality that characterized all aspects of cultural life during the Harlem Renaissance.

PETER KERRY POWERS

See also Abyssinian Baptist Church; Becton, George Wilson; Cane; Cullen, Countee; Cullen, Frederick Asbury; Cullen–Du Bois Wedding; Father Divine; Great Migration; Hughes, Langston; Hurston, Zora Neale; Powell, Adam Clayton Sr.; Religious Organizations; Toomer; Jean; Wright, Richard

Further Reading

Anderson, Jervis. *This Was Harlem*. New York: Farrar, Straus and Giroux, 1982.

Fauset, Arthur Huff. *Black Gods of the Metropolis: Negro Religious Cults of the Urban North*. Philadelphia: University of Pennsylvania Press, 1944, 1971.

Frazier, E. Franklin. *The Negro Church in America*. New York: Schocken, 1963.

Gregg, Robert. *Sparks From the Anvil of Oppression: Philadelphia's African Methodists and Southern Migrants, 1890–1940*. Philadelphia, Pa.: Temple University Press, 1993.

Hurston, Zora Neale. *The Sanctified Church: The Folklore Writing of Zora Neale Hurston*. Berkeley, Calif.: Turtle Island Foundation, 1981.

Sernett, Milton C. *Bound for the Promised Land: African American Religion and the Great Migration.* London and Durham, N.C.: Duke University Press, 1997.

———, ed. *African American Religious History: A Documentary Witness.* London and Durham, N.C.: Duke University Press, 1985. (See also 2nd ed, 1999.)

Religious Organizations

One dominant attitude toward religion in American cultural history has been suspicion of religious institutions, or, more broadly, suspicion of "organized religion." Ralph Waldo Emerson's dismissal of priestcraft and its attendant rituals, creeds, traditions, and offices sprang from his conviction that the machinery of religion interfered with, when it did not disable, an authentic experience of the divine. In this view of religion, the increasingly rationalized structures of churches and denominations are part and parcel of the bureaucratizing tendency of modernity, a tendency at some distance from more tender feelings for community or the dramatic desire for mystic transport associated with religious experience.

For African Americans of the early twentieth century, a different history and cultural impulse complicated this ideology concerning organized religious life. On the one hand, African American folklore is replete with jokes and stories about ineffective, naive, dishonest, or randy preachers on the make, narratives that participate in the tendency everywhere to put power and pretension in their place. Further, popular accounts of African American religion gave inordinate attention to the traditional shouting service or the frenzy of Pentecostal styles of worship. Such images of religion champion the virtues of "disorganization," or at least the virtues of religious experience organized only by the centering force of a preacher's charisma. W. E. B. Du Bois's emphasis on the preacher as a man "at the center of a group of men" in *The Souls of Black Folk* evokes a black religion driven by charismatic leadership and charismatic experience. Indeed, in this book a predominant theme of the chapter "Faith of the Fathers" is that contemporary bureaucratization into cold and unfeeling church structures is divorced from the authentic spirituality of African religious forefathers, an authenticity sustained as a residue in the spirituals and the frenzy of southern worship. Similarly, the story "Esther" in Jean Toomer's *Cane* portrays officially organized black Christianity as hand in glove with white power structures, whereas the folk prophet-preacher King Barlo can deliver the true word of African deliverance while caught up in a mystic trance.

On the other hand, this emphasis on mystical experiences and charismatic leadership obscures the degree to which organizational life as a whole and especially the life of religious organizations played a central role in both the development of individual identity and the shape of social and cultural life during the period of the Harlem Renaissance. Moreover, it obscures the ways in which "organized religion" proliferated during this period—in terms of new churches and denominations, new quasi-religious or parachurch organizations, and the newly complex and elaborate internal structures of urban churches undergoing the process of modernization.

Historians and sociologists have pointed out the important role that social organizations such as fraternal orders, churches, and labor unions played in the development of individual identity, local community, and broad-based political action. A person treated like a nobody during the day at work could be somebody at church in the evening or on Sunday, not only because of the emotional and psychological reassurance that visions of heavenly reward provided, but also because of the role an individual could play within the organizational life of the church. As Benjamin Mays and Joseph W. Nicholson described the typical congregants in an urban church of the 1920s, "Frequently their souls are crushed and their personalities disregarded. Often they do not feel 'at home' in the more sophisticated Negro group. But in the church on X street, she is Mrs. Johnson, the Church clerk; and he is Mr. Jones, the chairman of the Deacon Board" (Mays and Nicholson 1933). Though restricted in some respects, the religious organization provided a genuine space of freedom for the exercise of leadership, responsibility, and initiative. This was especially true for ministers. But in their autobiographies from the late nineteenth century to the Harlem Renaissance, ministers do not reflect much on their own charisma. For example, in *Against the Tide*, Adam Clayton Powell portrays his life and energies as subsumed by and committed to the development of religious life at Abyssinian Baptist in Harlem. Similarly, in *Barefoot Town to Jerusalem*, Frederick Asbury Cullen of Salem Methodist Episcopal marks success not so much by the attention that he personally receives as by the ways in which Salem grows and develops into an elaborate and powerful social organization under his leadership. In this way, religious organizations provided the necessary context out of which individual identity grew and individual power was exercised.

Ironically, once the floodgates of the great migration opened, this role of providing a sense of belonging and the opportunity for personal leadership and contribution helped destabilize the de facto religious hegemony exercised in northern cities by mainline denominations like the African Methodist Episcopal (AME) Church, the AME Zion Church, and the National Baptists. Southern migrants, used to smaller rural churches where they were known and knew others, sometimes felt alien and unappreciated in the larger urbanized churches of the North. More, denominations centered in the North practiced a less vibrant form of religious worship than the migrants had left behind. Facing cultural alienation even in the midst of a putative racial solidarity, many southerners chose to create new churches in their own image. These churches, and in some cases new religions, were the storefront churches, cults, and sects that have been the singular focus of most commentators on the religion of the period. Churches flowered overnight (or sprang up like weeds, depending on one's ideological point of view), and there sometimes seemed to be as many churches as people in Harlem during the 1920s. Indeed, it was not unusual for Harlemites to participate to various degrees in multiple churches at different times of the week or year, much as one might attend a different theater or nightclub to get a different show. By the 1930s, it was arguable that there were more churches per square mile in Harlem than anywhere else in the country, so many that Harlemites complained there were too many churches with too many preachers. This complaint perhaps reflects a concern that the endless multiplication of such organizations threatened to fracture the coherence of community life they might otherwise have been expected to secure.

Many of these churches did indeed seem to form primarily around the force and vision of a single personality, such as Father Divine's Peace Mission or the cult surrounding Daddy Grace. However, these also quickly developed relatively elaborate bureaucratic forms or branches of the religion in cities around the country, ultimately making the structure of the church as important as the founding personality. This tendency to elaborate structure through the process of mission and evangelism was also true of the spiritual churches and the more clearly Christian holiness or Sanctified churches. These churches, often accused of an overwhelmingly otherworldly focus in doctrine and practice, were this-worldly enough to develop significant denominational structures in response to the everyday demands of paying bills, finding places of worship, and providing for the spiritual needs of the congregation.

Another manifestation of the diversification of religious organization came in the form of otherwise secular institutions that adopted a religious ethos and used overtly religious rhetoric. To some degree, of course, the centrality of the church to African American cultural life meant that nearly every social organization in Harlem included some kind of religious flavoring. Fraternal orders such as the Masons explicitly drew on scripture in their organizational rituals, and members were often openly recognized as upstanding and important members of mainstream churches. Similarly, the black church in Harlem was sometimes referred to as "NAACP on its knees." This could not have been strictly true, since central figures of the National Association for the Advancement of Colored People such as James Weldon Johnson and Du Bois had traveled some intellectual distance from the churches of their childhood, and both chafed at the overwhelming influence of the church. Nevertheless, the aphorism does suggest the degree to which the religious and the secular interpenetrated one another in much of Harlem's social life. A. Philip Randolph, though an avowed atheist, conceived of the Brotherhood of Sleeping Car Porters in quasi-religious terms, depended on good relations with the church for the development of the union, and used frankly religious rhetoric in promoting the union's political ambitions. All of this suggests that the strict lines sometimes drawn between religious and secular organizations were permeable, more so in Harlem than in the dominant culture.

No organization reflected this interpenetration more than the most massive popular movement of 1920s, Marcus Garvey's Universal Negro Improvement Association (UNIA). Indeed, the UNIA exemplifies a quasi-religious movement that is read too simply as an extension of a demagogic personality. Though it would be impossible to understand the appeal of the UNIA without understanding the personal appeal of Garvey's vision and of Garvey himself, this vision was elaborated through a massive bureaucratic structure that attempted to give flesh to Garvey's vision of a pan-African religious, cultural, and political movement. Ironically, Garvey's ultimate downfall may have resulted less from his own corruption or from white conspiracies than from the inefficiencies of his organization and his inability to keep track of its far-flung enterprises and their tangled finances.

Besides underreading the organizational elements of Garvey's movement, scholars often dismiss or underestimate the religious shape of both Garvey's rhetoric and the structure of the organization as a whole. Nevertheless, Randall Burkett (1978) argues persuasively that Garvey needs to be understood as a thoroughgoing theological thinker who attempted to institutionalize a form of black civil religion. Early in the movement's history it was somewhat unclear whether or not the UNIA was on the road to becoming a religious denomination. Children of members were baptized both into the Christian religion and into membership in the association. Mass meetings were shaped around liturgies reminiscent of the high churches of the Christian faith. Even after the organization determined that it would not be a church, it maintained a hierarchy of chaplains intended to minister to the spiritual needs of the membership. Like its erstwhile rival, the NAACP, the UNIA depended extensively on sympathetic members of the Christian clergy for support, and not a few—such as Earl Little, the father of Malcolm X—managed to find a way to be both Christian ministers and UNIA organizers. Far from a peculiar institution based on the idiosyncrasies of its founder, and far from a purely secular political movement, in many respects the UNIA was characteristic of the unsettling energies and explosive growth that marked the new sects and religions in Harlem.

The unfamiliar makes the news, and this may account for the extensive attention given to new sects and cults in examinations of religions coming out of the great migration. Many had the flash and show to match anything appearing in the clubs and theaters on Lenox Avenue. Yet it is probably the case that the most enduring changes attendant on the migration took place within the institutional framework of the traditional churches. For one thing, faced with the unfamiliar demands of their new southern congregants for more exciting worship experiences, the mainline churches began integrating new forms of worship into their traditional liturgies, legitimizing cultural forms that the bourgeoisie initially considered vulgar and inappropriate. Gospel music, for instance, originated in the low-down churches but entered the cultural mainstream when mainline churches began incorporating it alongside traditional hymns, a process that eventually recast the traditional hymns themselves. Frederick Cullen welcomed the mass evangelist George Wilson Becton into the pulpit at Salem Methodist

Episcopal. Though Becton was never completely legitimated, Cullen's move at least symbolized a recognition on the part of the mainline that their southern congregants experienced the old-time religion best through fervent preaching that put more emphasis on getting congregants in touch with God emotionally than on explicating this or that point of doctrine.

To be sure, the religious establishment often cringed at the religious practices of the church general. Preachers wrote essays and conventions issued reports that lamented the state of the church, its otherworldliness, its anti-intellectualism, and its subpar clergy. And some churches did shrink from the unwashed masses of the South, deserving Du Bois's characterization of them as cold and unfeeling. Most traditional churches and denominations, however, at least sought to rise to the challenge in both program and rhetoric. In the process of rising, they changed the perception of their churches from houses devoted exclusively to holy worship into places where the doctrine and practice of the social gospel were given substantial flesh.

To some degree they had no choice. The apparently endless wave of migrants demanded some kind of change, some kind of attention, and the mainline churches were well aware that there were sirens enough willing to offer attention. Not only did the new religions threaten the religious hegemony of the mainline, the entertainments of the city and the developing intellectual class threatened to draw both the thinking and the unthinking away from the fold of the church, in some sense threatening the cultural hegemony of religion per se. Lacy Williams of Olivet Baptist in Pittsburgh, Pennsylvania, called frankly for new social, recreational, and community programs in the church as a way of counteracting the appeal of both new religious movements and the vices that city life readily offered. The AME hierarchy issued a denominational appeal for churches to use "multiplied forces and agencies, material and spiritual; with ceaseless vigilance and untiring activity" to counteract the vices of the city that threatened to attract the masses away from the church.

No doubt there is some significant self-interest in these calls for the church to find its mission in social service, but it is doubtful that programs as extensive and elaborate as those that developed could have been sustained for long simply through self-interest. The sheer number and variety of these programs testify to a significant change in the churches' self-understanding, whereby living the gospel meant providing for all the needs—this-worldly and otherworldly—of their congregants. In a report on the work of Baptist women to the National Baptist Convention, Nannie Burroughs remarked on the typical shortcomings of the church: Men in the pulpit were too little educated and gave too much attention to otherworldly concerns; the people spent their money on frivolity. Beyond complaint, the report issued a call for a broad range of programs: training programs to help the unemployed and underemployed; thrift clubs to teach the value of savings and investments; new investment in the Young Women's Christian Association. Burroughs's most interesting proposal was for the development of suffrage clubs as an extension of the educational mission of the church, on the belief that participation by females in the political process would help make "the world safe for Christianity." Another sign of the ascendancy of this kind of work was the election of Reverdy Ransom, a staunch if controversial advocate of the social gospel, to a bishopric in the AME Church.

Not every church heeded such denominational calls for greater social action. Many resisted ministers who wanted to move their churches in such directions. Indeed, denominational efforts to improve the status of the clergy continued to fall short. As late as 1933, Mays and Nicholson were reporting that the majority of ministers in black churches were poorly trained theologically and in general (though it is unclear whether ministers with multiple degrees necessarily did a better job in the vital work of making a congregant feel that he or she was at home in the church). Still, it seems clear that the most significant and powerful churches of the North in general and Harlem in particular responded to the needs of their new parishioners in ways that permanently changed the nature of African American religion. Under Williams, Olivet Baptist developed dozens of programs to serve its several thousand congregants. These included training programs like those described above, as well as kindergartens for child care and mothers' meetings for parental support. At Abyssinian Baptist Church in Harlem, Adam Clayton Powell developed not only a Home Relief Bureau that provided employment, but also programs in adult education, day care for children, and feeding programs for the hungry.

Ironically, the plethora of programs at the dominant churches and the bureaucracy necessary to run them may have contributed to a sense that the established churches were more like businesses than communities. The sheer numbers of people involved and the programs that had to be coordinated guaranteed that men like Powell, Cullen, and others were successful at least in part because they were organization men, good at shaping large numbers of people to a common purpose. They were unlikely, however, to know their congregants well, and many African Americans preferred the more intimate feel of the smaller churches, even when such churches were unable to offer them much in the way of social services. Nevertheless, the changes in the dominant churches meant that social action, like gospel music and emotionally fervent preaching, was legitimated as a part of the mainline. This change set the stage for the political and social action of the churches in the middle of the twentieth century.

If the churches moved in new directions to engage social and political life, engagement with the aesthetic concerns of the Harlem Renaissance, at least engagement with any kind of complexity or depth, seems much more ambiguous. As the central cultural institution of African American life, the church was inevitably involved in the life of the Harlem Renaissance. Abyssinian Baptist Church was the site of the most famous wedding of the period, that of Countee Cullen and Yolande Du Bois. Poets and writers of the period read regularly to large crowds in the sanctuaries of the tony churches of the period. Still, it seems clear that the artistic and intellectual movement was developing along a different trajectory from that of the religious organizations. The storefront churches by and large had no interest in high culture of the kind represented by Countee Cullen. Their preaching and singing were a poetry and drama of their own, as Langston Hughes recognized and tried to represent. The established churches welcomed poets to the degree that these poets represented African American achievement, but Langston Hughes had preachers prevent him from reading his blues poetry from the pulpit. Preachers regularly railed against the bohemianism that Hughes and some others embraced, and preachers of every type spoke against the overtly erotic sound of jazz and the morally degrading effect of the clubs where jazz could be heard. In this regard, with the possible exception of gospel music, the church insisted on a profoundly conservative aesthetic.

In their attention to religion, the writers and artists did not replicate the churches' benign neglect of the aesthetic developments in Harlem. If the churches did not particularly need Rudolph Fisher or Zora Neale Hurston, it seems clear that these writers and artists could not do without the church. Any artist taking up the experience of African Americans in the 1920s could not escape noticing that the crowded churches on Sunday morning matched the crowded clubs on

Saturday night. Every major writer of the period takes up African American religious life in some significant way: Toomer, for instance, represents southern religious life in *Cane*; Hurston portrays a preacher in *Jonah's Gourd Vine*; Cullen wrote a poem called "Black Christ." However, no major writer of the period other than Cullen participated regularly in the life of any religious organization. Even Hurston, who went through an initiation ritual to become a priestess of the vodun (voodoo) religion, was apparently a participant-observer (for the sake of her anthropological studies of the religion) as much as she was a devotee.

Hurston's example may suggest the degree to which the artists primarily approached religion out of aesthetic concerns, rather than out of a desire to give any full accounting of organized religious life. Overwhelmingly, depictions of religion focus on the storefront churches or on the rural South. Save for an extremely funny account of Hughes's meeting Adam Clayton Powell (whom Hughes gently ridicules by saying he looks like God and would thus be a good candidate for a role in *The Green Pastures*), there is scant attention given to the mainline churches, and almost no attention at all to the massive service programs and other forms of modernization that the churches undertook during the period. This may simply be a matter of aesthetics. The aesthetes of the Harlem Renaissance were fulfilling a role that artists have always filled: poking and prodding at the pretensions of official power. Further, and practically speaking, a down-home preacher at full throttle is more dramatic than the dusty paper pushing of bureaucratized religion. Finally, it may be that the narrow scope of the artistic concern with religion sprang from a realization, sometimes quite explicit, that the movers and shakers in the renaissance were positing themselves as institutional rivals to the mainline churches for positions of power and social leadership.

This was a battle that the renaissance writers and artists did not win in the 1920s, if winning is a matter of numbers. Still, this general picture of religious diversification on the one hand, and on the other the development of alternative forms of institutional life, suggests something about the Harlem Renaissance. If modernity is characterized in part by the rationalization of social life into separate spheres, with institutional and bureaucratic forms responsible for administering those different spheres, then life in Harlem clearly manifests a form of African American modernity and the renaissance a kind of modernism. This is evident both in the developments internal to religious organizations themselves and in the way those organizations connected to and were distinguished from the aesthetic and cultural institutions that nurtured the work of the renaissance.

PETER KERRY POWERS

See also Abyssinian Baptist Church; Becton, George Wilson; Cane; Cullen, Countee; Cullen, Frederick Asbury; Daddy Grace; Du Bois, W. E. B.; Father Divine; Garvey, Marcus; Great Migration; Hughes, Langston; Hurston, Zora Neale; Powell, Adam Clayton Sr.; Randolph, A. Philip; Religion; Toomer, Jean; Universal Negro Improvement Association

Further Reading

Burkett, Randall K. *Garveyism as a Religious Movement: The Institutionalization of a Black Civil Religion*. Metuchen, N.J., and London: Scarecrow American Theological Library Association, 1978.

Encyclopedia of African and African American Religions, ed. Stephen D. Glazier. New York: Routledge, 2001.

Fauset, Arthur Huff. *Black Gods of the Metropolis: Negro Religious Cults of the Urban North*. Philadelphia: University of Pennsylvania Press, 1944, 1971.

Frazier, E. Franklin. *The Negro Church in America*. New York: Schocken, 1963.

Gregg, Robert. *Sparks From the Anvil of Oppression: Philadelphia's African Methodists and Southern Migrants, 1890–1940*. Philadelphia, Pa.: Temple University Press, 1993.

Hurston, Zora Neale. *The Sanctified Church: The Folklore Writing of Zora Neale Hurston*. Berkeley, Calif.: Turtle Island Foundation, 1981.

Mays, Benjamin E., and Joseph W. Nicholson. *The Negro's Church*. New York: Institute of Social and Religious Research, 1933.

Sernett, Milton C. *Bound for the Promised Land: African American Religion and the Great Migration*. London and Durham, N.C.: Duke University Press, 1997.

———, ed. *African American Religious History: A Documentary Witness*. London and Durham, N.C.: Duke University Press, 1985. (See also 2nd ed., 1999.)

Renaissance Casino

The Renaissance Casino and Ballroom was an entertainment complex housed in a two-story redbrick building at 150 West 138th Street. From about 1915 until at least the mid-1960s, dances, balls, sporting events, and socials were held there. For many years, the Renaissance Casino was operated by a Harlemite entrepreneur, Robert "Smiling Bob" Douglas.

The two spacious floors of the Renaissance Casino were suitable for a wide variety of functions and events. Initially, the Renaissance was used exclusively for dances, but it eventually faced stiff competition from other popular ballrooms such as the Savoy. In the 1930s, it became a prime meeting place for the more respectable and dignified of Harlem's social clubs, charities, and unions. The Renaissance advertised such functions in electric lights over its doorway and split the receipts with its renters. For many years the upstairs space was home to the Harlem Rens, a superb basketball team active from about 1922 to 1949. The Rens' Sunday night games were a major social and sporting event in Harlem. Meetings of clubs and similar organizations were common in the 1920s, including some of the annual awards dinners held by the magazine *The Crisis*. Such events became increasingly important to the Renaissance Casino in the course of the 1930s. Among those who met there were the Brotherhood of Sleeping Car Porters (1936), the Harlem Dukes (1938), and the Dominican Benevolent Society (1939). Some of these affairs could be quite lavish. When the Business and Professional Men's Forum held its Annual Entertainment and Dance at the Renaissance Casino in May 1936, the entertainment included Bill "Bojangles" Robinson, the Small's Paradise Revue, the Ubangi Club Revue, the Dickie Wells Club, and a Spanish revue by the Teatro Campoamor.

For all its importance as a social hall and sports arena, the Renaissance Casino was even more important in the Harlem Renaissance as a venue for music, ranging from old-fashioned dance music to the hottest jazz. For much of the 1920s and 1930s, the house bandleader at the Renaissance was Vernon Andrade (1902–1966), a Panamanian bass and violin player who had moved to Harlem in the early 1920s. Andrade employed an oboist who was featured in waltzes and other polite dance music. Andrade's band also played "hot" jazz, featuring leading jazz musicians, including the trumpeter Louis Metcalf, George Washington (trombone), the reed man Happy Caldwell, Al Morgan (bass), and the drummer Zutty Singleton from New Orleans. The Andrade orchestra alternated with more famous bands that came in for one-night stands and short runs. These included the Fletcher Henderson Orchestra in September 1925, featuring Louis Armstrong on cornet. Elmer Snowden's band, with the fine young cornetist Rex Stewart, also appeared there during this period. Another illustrious band, featured regularly during 1928, included four of the great jazz soloists: the trumpeter Roy Eldridge, Dickie Wells (trombone), the clarinetist Cecil Scott, and Leon "Chu" Berry (tenor saxophone). From late 1942 to mid-1943, the Renaissance Casino was host to a big band led by the tenor saxophonist Al Sears, a former sideman for Andrade. The stellar rhythm section included the bassist Wellman Braud of New Orleans (a longtime member of Duke Ellington's band) and the drummer Christopher Columbus; the fine saxophone section included, aside from Sears himself, Budd Johnson, Jimmie Lunceford, and Edgar Hayes. Numerous other important swing bands performed at the Renaissance Casino during this period; it remained a popular venue for dances well into the 1960s.

ELLIOTT S. HURWITT

See also Armstrong, Louis; Brotherhood of Sleeping Car Porters; Crisis, The: Literary Prizes; Harlem: 3—Entertainment; Henderson, Fletcher; Professional Sports and Black Athletes; Robinson, Bill "Bojangles"; Savoy Ballroom; Small's Paradise

Further Reading

Charters, Samuel B., and Leonard Kunstadt. *Jazz: A History of the New York Scene*. New York: Da Capo, 1981. (Originally published 1962.)

Chilton, John. *Who's Who of Jazz: Storyville to Swing Street*. Philadelphia, Pa.: Chilton, 1972.

Driggs, Frank. *Jazz Odyssey*, Vol. 3, *The Sound of Harlem*. Columbia Special Products, C3L 33, c. 1965.

Driggs, Frank, and Harris Lewine. *Black Beauty, White Heat: A Pictorial History of Classic Jazz, 1920–1950*. New York: Morrow, 1982.

Programs and pamphlets files. Manuscripts Division, Schomburg Center for Research in Black Culture, New York Public Library.

Wallace, Thurman. *Negro Life in New York's Harlem: A Lively Picture of a Popular and Interesting Section*, ed. E. Haldeman-Julius. Little Blue Book 494. Girard, Kan.: Haldeman-Julius, 1928.

Revue Nègre, La

La Revue Nègre was an African American vaudeville show that opened in Paris at the Théâtre des Champs-Elysées on 2 October 1925, bringing the spirit of the

Harlem Renaissance to France and introducing the singer and dancer Josephine Baker to Parisian audiences. The idea for the *Revue Nègre* emerged when an American socialite, Caroline Dudley Reagan, approached André Daven, who was the codirector of the Théâtre des Champs-Élysées, about putting on a black revue in Paris that would be similar to popular African American theater productions such as *Shuffle Along, Runnin' Wild*, and *The Chocolate Dandies*. Daven agreed to the concept because he was having difficulties coming up with new ideas for shows, and African art and culture were already in vogue in Parisian entertainment circles at that time because of the success of a number of African art exhibits at French museums. Daven sent Reagan to New York to recruit the performers for the revue in the summer of 1925. She selected twenty-five people for the production, including Josephine Baker, the blues singer Maud de Forrest, the composer Spencer Williams, the bandleader-pianist Claude Hopkins, the dancer-choreographer Louis Douglas, the artist Miguel Covarrubias (as set designer), the saxophonist Joe Hayman, the trombone player Daniel Day, the tuba player Bass Hill, the drummer Percy Johnson, and the clarinet player Sidney Bechet. Rehearsals began in New York and continued onboard the *Berengaria* during the transatlantic voyage (15–22 September). After numerous revisions, rewrites, changes in costuming and choreography, and the creation of the show's posters by the artist Paul Colin, the *Revue Nègre* was ready for its premiere.

The *Revue Nègre* played to a full house, with such artists as Darius Milhaud and Jean Cocteau in attendance. It lasted less than an hour, serving as the second act of a two-act production. The show itself consisted of an orchestral introduction and nine theatrical sketches, including "Louisiana Camp Meeting," a scene with a peanut vendor that had a memorable clarinet solo by Sidney Bechet, and a levee scene called "Mississippi Steam Boat Race" that showcased the entire ensemble. At the high point of the steamboat scene, Josephine Baker pounced onto the stage on all fours while beating time with the palms of her hands to the tune "Boodle-am Shake," then started dancing the Charleston—bowing her legs, crossing her eyes, and emitting a high-pitched noise. However, the show-stopping number of the evening was the finale, "Charleston Cabaret." Set in a nightclub, this scene featured the groundbreaking *danse sauvage*, an African-inspired mating dance between Josephine Baker and the Caribbean dancer Joe Alex. According to the writer Janet Flanner:

Josephine made her entry entirely nude except for a pink flamingo feather between her limbs; she was being carried upside down and doing the splits on the shoulder of a black giant. Mid stage he paused and, with his long fingers holding her basket-wise around the waist, swung her in a slow cartwheel to the stage floor, where she stood, in a moment of complete silence. A scream of salutation spread through the theatre.

This display of unbridled sexuality and primitivism with an African theme created a sensation in Paris, and Baker immediately became the toast of the city. The production played to Parisian audiences for two months before embarking on a tour of Europe.

ERIN STAPLETON-CORCORAN

See also Baker, Josephine; Bechet, Sidney; Chocolate Dandies, The; Covarrubias, Miguel; Europe and the Harlem Renaissance: 4—Paris; Runnin' Wild; Shuffle Along

Further Reading

Colin, Paul. *Josephine Baker and La Revue Nègre: Paul Colin's Lithographs of le Tumulte Noir in Paris, 1927.* New York: Abrams, 1998.

Stovall, Tyler. *Paris Noir: African Americans in the City of Light.* Boston, Mass., and New York: Houghton Mifflin, 1996.

Richardson, Willis

Willis Richardson was the author of forty-six plays. He was most active during the Harlem Renaissance, though he spent most of his life in Washington, D.C. Only since the 1990s have Richardson's plays received much scholarly notice.

Richardson began his writing career in 1915, with a correspondence course called "Poetry and Versification"; but on seeing Angelina Weld Grimké's play *Rachel* (1916), he changed from poetry to drama. Richardson believed that plays written for African Americans should focus on problems within the black community. Whereas Grimké and other African American playwrights of the time focused on conflicts between blacks and whites, he began writing plays that concentrated on relationships between blacks.

The magazine *The Crisis* and its editor, W. E. B. Du Bois, were important in Richardson's career. Du Bois published Richardson's essay "The Hope of a Negro Drama" (1919), the first of six articles Richardson would write on African American theater. *The Crisis* published Richardson's plays *The Deacon's Awakening* (in November 1920) and *The Chip Woman's Fortune* (in 1922). Richardson also contributed plays to *The Brownies' Book*, a periodical issue by *The Crisis* for African American children: *The King's Dilemma* (December 1920), *The Gypsy's Finger-Ring* (March 1921), *The Children's Treasure* (June 1921), and *The Dragon's Tooth* (October 1921).

Richardson was the first African American to have a play produced on Broadway, when *The Chip Woman's Fortune*, a one-act folk drama, opened on 17 May 1923 at the Frazee Theater and played there for a week. Du Bois had made this possible by arranging for the Ethiopian Art Players, a group based in Chicago, to produce it. The group had written to Du Bois, asking if he knew of any plays written by African Americans; he had recommended *The Chip Woman's Fortune*, and it had opened in Chicago on 23 January 1923. Its first appearance in New York had been at the Lafayette Theater in Harlem on 7 May 1923. When it opened at the Frazee on 17 May, it was part of a triple bill with Shakespeare's *Comedy of Errors* and Oscar Wilde's *Salome*.

In 1925, Richardson placed first in the Krigwa Literary Contest, which was sponsored by *The Crisis*, for his play *The Broken Banjo*. He was unable to attend the awards ceremony in New York; but the next year, when he won first prize for *The Bootblack Lover*, he did go to New York. This occasion was the first time he and Du Bois actually met.

During the 1920s, Richardson's one-act plays were much in demand among African American "little theater" and community groups, school drama clubs, English departments, and churches throughout the country. In Washington, D.C., through his contacts at Howard University, Richardson began joining other artists and writers at the Saturday Nighters, an informal group that met at the home of the poet and playwright Georgia Douglas Johnson. Richardson was involved with this group from its formation in 1926 until it disbanded ten years later.

Carter G. Woodson, founder of Negro History Week and editor of Associated Publishers, a black publishing house in Washington, D.C., was also important to Richardson, who edited two collections of plays for him. The first collection, *Plays and Pageants From the Life of the Negro* (1930), included four of Richardson's plays, and Richardson also wrote the introduction. The second collection was *Negro History in Thirteen Plays* (1935).

During the 1940s, Richardson did less writing: The death of one of his daughters led to his adoption of her two children, and World War II seems to have changed the tastes of African American playgoers. In fact, from about 1945 until he died, he had only one publication—*The King's Dilemma*, a collection of his plays for children (1956)—and his attempts to have his later plays produced were unsuccessful.

Richardson realized the power of drama to reach African American audiences at a time when theater was largely controlled by whites and the "black experience" was presented mainly in musicals, and mainly as interpreted by whites. In Harlem and on Broadway, for example, such profitable shows as *Strut, Miss Lizzie* (1922), *The Chocolate Dandies* (1924), and *Lucky Sambo* (1925), with their song-and-dance routines, plantation settings, and characters pining for the old South, perpetuated damaging stereotypes of African Americans. Rather than attempt to conquer the white stage, Richardson presented his plays for and in the black community, creating vignettes of African American life and incorporating topics that spoke to this minority audience.

Du Bois, among others, was also concerned about the popularity of Broadway shows featuring black song-and-dance routines; specifically, he feared that they would kill the African American folk play, and so he organized "little theater" groups for African Americans through the auspices of *The Crisis*. These theater organizations were in effect laboratories for community-based productions, a venue Du Bois advocated. Some 470 African American little theater groups were founded between 1910 and 1930. Krigwa theater groups (originally Crigwa, an acronym for Crisis Guild of Writers and Artists) were formed in Harlem, Philadelphia, Baltimore, Washington, and other East Coast cities and were active from 1926 through 1935. Several of Richardson's plays were produced by Krigwa drama groups.

For more than one reason, Richard is distinctive among African American playwrights up to his own time. First, in his six critical essays, he commented explicitly on the educational nature and purpose of his plays. He and Du Bois agreed that the stage should be used to educate African American audiences and should do so by portraying aspects of their actual life. Second, Richardson's plays focus on issues within the black community, such as conflicts between African American landlords and tenants, parents and children, husbands and wives, and upper- and lower-class people. Some of his characters and situations are prototypes of those found in the work of later African American dramatists, such as Lorraine Hansberry, Amiri Baraka, and August Wilson.

Finally, three other plays by Richardson deserve mention. *Mortgaged* (1924) was presented at the theater at Howard University in Washington, D.C., the first work staged at Howard by an African American who was not matriculating there. In 1926, the Gilpin Players of Cleveland produced Richardson's play *Compromise*, the first play by an African American that this company had performed. In 1928, Richardson's play *The Broken Banjo* won the Edith Schwab Cup, an annual award given by Yale University to a promising new playwright.

Biography

Willis Richardson was born 5 November 1889 in Wilmington, North Carolina; because of race riots there in the late 1890s, his family moved to Washington, D.C., where he spent most of his life. After graduating from the M Street School in Washington (1910), he worked briefly at the Library of Congress. He was a clerk at the Bureau of Engraving and Printing from 1917 to 1954. Richardson twice won the award for best play in the literary contests held by *The Crisis* (1925 and 1926); he also won the Edith Schwab Cup at Yale for best new play (1928). He was a member of the Saturday Nighters, a literary group in Washington, D.C., and a founder of the Krigwa Players, also in Washington. He was recognized as "Outstanding Pioneer in Black Theater" by the Audience Development Committee (Audelco), New York City, 1977. Richardson died in Washington, D.C., 7 November 1977.

CHRISTINE RAUCHFUSS GRAY

See also Authors: 4—Playwrights; Brownies' Book, The; Crisis, The; Ethiopian Art Players; Grimké, Angelina Weld; Harlem Renaissance in the United States: 9—Washington, D.C.; Johnson, Georgia Douglas; Krigwa Players; Lafayette Theater; Literature: 3—Drama; Rachel

Selected Works

"The Hope of a Negro Drama." *Crisis*, 19, November 1919, pp. 338–339.

"The Negro and the Stage." *Opportunity*, 2, October 1924, p. 310.

"Propaganda in the Theatre." *The Messenger*, 6, November 1924, pp. 353–354.

"The Negro Audience." *Opportunity*, 3, April 1925, p. 123.

"Characters." *Opportunity*, 3, June 1925, p. 183.

"The Unpleasant Play." *Opportunity*, 3, September 1925, p. 282.

Plays and Pageants From the Life of the Negro. Washington, D.C.: Associated Publishers, 1930.

Negro History in Thirteen Plays. Washington, D.C., Associated Publishers, 1935. (As coeditor with May Miller.)

The King's Dilemma and Other Plays for Children: Episodes of Hope and Dream. New York, Exposition, 1956.

Further Reading

Gray, Christine Rauchfuss. *Willis Richardson: Forgotten Pioneer of African-American Drama*. Westport, Conn.: Greenwood, 1999.

Hamalian, Leo, and James V. Hatch, eds. *The Roots of African American Drama*. Detroit, Mich.: Wayne State University Press, 1991.

Locke, Alain, ed. *Plays of Negro Life: A Source-Book of Native American Drama*. New York: Negro University Press, 1968. (Originally published 1927.)

Sanders, Leslie Catherine. *The Development of Black Theater in America: From Shadows to Selves*. Baton Rouge: Louisiana State University Press, 1988.

Riots: 1—Overview, 1917–1921

East St. Louis, Illinois (1917); Houston, Texas (1917); Philadelphia, Pennsylvania (1918); Charleston, South Carolina (1919); Longview, Texas (1919); Washington, D.C. (1919); Chicago (1919); Omaha, Nebraska (1919); Knoxville, Tennessee (1919); Elaine, Arkansas (1919); Tulsa, Oklahoma (1921)—there were approximately twenty major riots from 1917 to 1921, and many other smaller episodes of organized attacks on black communities. In most instances, the riots involved white mobs (sometimes supported by the local authorities) attacking black communities.

The riots were sparked by labor unrest, when blacks served as strikebreakers; by social tension, when blacks began living or seeking recreation close to white neighborhoods; and by threatened lynchings. Although there were many proximate causes of the riots, they all drew from a common well: rising tension

Chicago race riots, 1919: an actual photo of a Negro being stoned to death by whites. (Brown Brothers.)

between blacks and whites. That tension rose because of the social upheaval caused by World War I. The war increased the economic power of blacks, increased their mobility, and gave new strength to calls for equal treatment. The United States' rhetoric of equality and freedom used in the world war led to calls in the black community for similar treatment at home. At the same time, blacks' political power was growing, as the U.S. Supreme Court forced northern and border states to recognize voting and other civil rights. Following several years of violence, the black and white communities throughout the nation reached accommodations and the violence decreased.

A key factor in most of the riots was an attempt to reestablish white supremacy, or to stop appeals to what was called "social equality." Within the black community, aspirations were rising in the years after 1910. The periodical literature of the renaissance, such as The Crisis and The Messenger, promoted the ideas that blacks should be able to live free from lynching, should be able to vote, should receive equal education, should be able to live free from ordinances imposing racial segregation, and should have an equal opportunity with whites to work. Such seemingly simple ideas were themselves radical, and whites viewed them as attempts at social equality. But these ideas had a powerful appeal in black communities,

which—throughout the nation—became increasingly insistent on receiving equal treatment. In May 1919, an editorial in The Crisis, entitled "Returning Soldiers," warned: "We return from fighting, We return fighting. . . . We saved [democracy] in France and by the Great Jehovah, we will save it in the United States of America, or know the reason why." Such thoughts circulated and were discussed widely in black communities and led, particularly among veterans of the war, to an increasingly militant stance.

As the self-image of blacks became stronger, and as their demands for equality became more insistent, some whites resisted and in fact took action to stop the demands. Actions by whites included efforts to deny blacks' voting rights, to pass municipal zoning ordinances to segregate housing, and in extreme cases to lynch individuals and even attack entire communities. There had been periodic attacks on communities, at least since the late 1890s, as whites engaged in "Negro drives" to run blacks out of towns and counties. And there had been other riots, such as one in Springfield, Illinois, in August 1908, in which white mobs invaded and burned black districts. But the riots became larger and more frequent beginning in 1917.

The first large-scale riots of the Progressive era took place in East St. Louis, Illinois, in May and July 1917. East St. Louis, like many cities, experienced a dramatic growth in population around the beginning of the world war. Perhaps 10,000 blacks migrated to East St. Louis between 1916 and 1918, where they competed with whites for unskilled jobs in the local manufacturing and packing plants. Racial tensions rose in 1916 after black workers took jobs during strikes at local manufacturing plants. Employers at those manufacturing plants and at packing plants began to recruit black workers from southern states, to counter all-white unions. President Woodrow Wilson, campaigning in East St. Louis in 1916, tightened the tension when he accused Republicans of "colonizing" blacks as voters in the city.

In late May 1917, following a meeting at city hall, where union members demanded action to limit black immigration, there were two days of rioting. The riot in May was sparked by a rumor, which circulated at the end of the city hall meeting, that a black man had shot a white clerk in the course of robbing a store. Throughout the evening white mobs attacked unarmed blacks on the streets. The next day, the Illinois militia disarmed blacks, but not whites. Thousands of unprotected blacks fled East St. Louis, but others smuggled weapons into the community, in preparation for further violence. By 1 June the riot was over; no one had died, but the stage was set for further violence. Throughout June, there was sporadic racial violence in East St. Louis.

The riot in July, which claimed the lives of at least thirty-nine blacks and nine whites (actually, perhaps seventy-five or more lives), was set in motion on the evening of 1 July, when a group of whites rode through the black section of East St. Louis, shooting into homes. Several black men armed to protect the community against attackers. Later that evening an unmarked police car, carrying a newspaper reporter, drove through the community, apparently to investigate the attack and the community's response. Mistakenly thinking that the car contained people who were about to attack them, several black men fired into the car, mortally wounding two detectives. The next morning, word of the confrontation spread, and whites began attacking blacks on the streets and then attacking the black neighborhood.

Throughout the morning of 2 July, the attacks on the black community grew. The local police refused to protect the community or to arrest white rioters; and although the state militia arrived in the afternoon of 2 July, the militiamen offered no more protection against white rioters. According to numerous accounts by white eyewitnesses, the police and state militia stood idly by as mobs chased, attacked, and killed black men and women. By the afternoon of 2 July, mobs were burning buildings in the black section of East St. Louis while the Illinois militia looked on but still failed to intervene. White men casually asked one another, "Have you got your n—er yet?" By the evening, much of the black section of East St. Louis had been destroyed by fire; perhaps 6,000 people had fled to St. Louis, and the riot was over. Property losses were estimated at approximately $400,000. Some victims and their families received compensation for their losses from the city in 1921, because a state statute allowed suits against a municipality where riots had occurred for failure to give protection from violence.

Politicians and reformers of the Progressive era sought to make scientific studies of the riots. Those studies provide important insight into the riots and also illuminate limitations to the understanding of riots. The first study was of the East St. Louis riot, made by a congressional investigating committee in the fall of 1917. The committee collected testimony from dozens of witnesses, mostly whites, in an attempt to determine the causes of the violence. The committee's report focused on racial tension, as exacerbated by conflict over scarce jobs. It also saw vice and corruption

as contributing to the problem and to the breakdown of respect for law. The report preserves important details about the origins of the riot but has to be read in light of the authors' concern with corruption and its effects on politics—a concern that led them to spend too much effort on peripheral issues. How, one is left wondering, did prostitution lead to the riot? The committee detailed the local prosecutor's lack of interest in prosecutions: He refused to even seek indictments from a grand jury against many police officers and rioters. At one point, ten police officers drew lots to decide which three of them would plead guilty to minor counts in exchange for dismissal of serious counts against the other seven. Eventually, though, nine whites and twelve blacks were sentenced to time in the state penitentiary for offenses stemming from the riot. Eleven of the blacks had been convicted of homicide in the death of the two detectives on the evening of 1 July. The conviction of Dr. Leroy Bundy, a prominent black dentist who had urged militant action in defense of the black community, attracted national attention and was eventually overturned by the supreme court of Illinois.

Whereas whites came to talk about the riot in East St. Louis as a result of crime in the black community, blacks began talking about it as a breakdown of law in the white community. East St. Louis marked the radicalization of the black community. Blacks were deciding to rely on self-help rather than on the authorities. In fact, they were concluding that the authorities often disarmed them and left them defenseless. This conclusion would be drawn again in other riots and would lead to divisions within the black community over the appropriate response to threats of lynching and riots.

Following East St. Louis, the next major riot was in Houston, Texas, on 23 August 1917. It began when more than 200 black soldiers sought the release of one of their officers who had been arrested by the white police in Houston. This officer had interfered with Houston policemen who were arresting a black woman and had then himself been arrested. The riot in Houston was different from the other riots of the era, because black soldiers took the offensive: They invaded the white section of Houston, killing fifteen whites, before they retreated to their base; two black soldiers also died. Afterward, nineteen soldiers were sentenced to hang for mutiny; sixty-three others were sentenced to military prison.

The next year, 1918, was relatively quiet. However, there was a deadly riot in Philadelphia, Pennsylvania, on 25–28 July 1918, in which three people—two whites and one black—were killed. It began when a black family moved into a white block.

At the conclusion of World War I in November 1918, race relations in the United States began to change dramatically. As black and white soldiers came home and as blacks drew on the rhetoric of freedom and democracy, there was a disjuncture between black people's aspirations and white people's expectations. That led to major riots during what became known as the "red summer" of 1919: in Washington in mid-July; in Chicago at the end of July; and in Elaine County, Arkansas, in October. There were also smaller riots in Charleston, South Carolina, in May; in Longview, Texas, in July; in Knoxville, Tennessee, in August; in Omaha, Nebraska, in September; and in some other cities.

The population of Washington, D.C., grew explosively in the months following the end of the war, as veterans returned from Europe. Perhaps as many as 120,000 veterans lived at least temporarily in Washington, which had a population of 400,000 during the war. One-quarter of Washington's population was black. Washingtonians found rampant inflation and an acute housing shortage; as a result, blacks began to move into previously white northwest Washington. At the same time, in the summer of 1919, there were numerous sensational newspaper stories about black men attacking white women. The riot in Washington started on 19 July with a rumor that a black man had assaulted (that is, raped) a white woman. Articles in the press, including the *Washington Post*, seemed to stir up feelings further by alluding to a growing mob sentiment and mentioning that sailors and soldiers were gathering to attack the black district. For four days, until 22 July, white former servicemen, along with some men in uniform, sporadically attacked blacks on streetcars and in the black district near the Capitol building. Military officials confined servicemen to their quarters, but they gave limited assistance to police officials in quelling rioting. Even more than in East St. Louis, black men responded to the attacks with force. The black community was becoming more aggressive in protecting itself and was responding in kind to random attacks on blacks. Blacks attacked and in some instances killed white bystanders, as well as white rioters and police officers. Approximately thirty-nine people were killed during this riot.

The riot in Chicago—perhaps the worst riot in terms of loss of property and one of the worst in terms of deaths—began a week later. Tension had been mounting in the city for months, as black immigration increased and as some affluent blacks began moving into predominantly white neighborhoods bordering the black neighborhood on Chicago's South Side. What set off the riot was the drowning of a black youth, Eugene Williams, on 27 July. He had been swimming in Lake Michigan and had drifted over to a portion of the shore reserved for whites only. He was stoned as he approached shore and was unable to swim back to the black section. The police refused to arrest white youths who had thrown the stones, and angry blacks clashed with angry whites at the scene. From that afternoon until 2 August, rioting gripped the city. The riots were especially severe for the first two days; white mobs invaded the black section of south Chicago, burning many homes and killing at least twenty-three blacks. Fifteen whites were also killed. The violence was worse in the "contested territory" between the central business district known as the Loop and the black section on the South Side. Some blacks lived in predominantly white neighborhoods in that contested territory, and blacks frequently traveled through the area on the way to work. In addition, a few whites who worked in the black section were killed, as were a few blacks who worked in the central business district. Some of the whites killed in the black section were not participating in the riot; they were hapless victims of random violence, just as many black victims were. The police (and after the fourth day, the state militia) were more evenhanded in Chicago than they had been in East St. Louis. Law enforcement officers attempted to protect blacks against mob violence that they witnessed. In 1921, the Chicago City Council paid more than $100,000 to the families of riot victims.

A blue-ribbon commission of social scientists, businessmen, and politicians investigated the Chicago riot of 1919. The 600-page report of the Chicago Commission on Race Relations, published in 1921, was called *The Negro in Chicago*. It remains one of the most comprehensive studies of race relations ever published. Like the congressional committee that investigated East St. Louis, the Chicago Commission focused on corruption. The commission discussed the factors leading up to the riot: migration, close proximity of black and white neighborhoods, racial intolerance. In its memorable first paragraph, the commission said: "Many white Americans, while technically recognizing Negroes as citizens, cannot bring themselves to feel that they should participate in government as freely as other citizens."

The commission identified a lack of faith in law enforcement as contributing to the violence. In one case, for instance, hundreds of blacks converged on an apartment building where a white person was rumored to have shot a black boy. The police searched the building but failed to find the shooter. Then someone in the crowd surrounding the building threw a brick at a police officer, and the police opened fire, killing four members of the crowd. The commission used this incident to demonstrate that lack of faith in the police led to further tension, and ultimately to violence. It also suggested that there was reason for the lack of faith and that law enforcement may have used excessive force when dealing with blacks. The commission explored ways to reduce racial tension, including increasing job opportunities, increasing the quality of housing, and improving the police. Many of the recommendations may now appear naive, and many present-day commentators think that the commission was too lenient in assigning blame on whites for the riot.

The riots of 1919 concluded with a massacre in Phillips County, Arkansas, in October. This incident (like the rioting in East St. Louis) stemmed from both labor conflict and a mistaken killing of a police officer. Leaders of a tenant farmers' union, the Progressive Farmers and Householders Union of America, composed of several hundred black workers, met in a church in a rural area outside the town of Helena, Arkansas, on the evening of 30 September. The union members were attempting to increase the price they would receive for cotton they grew and then harvested. Several police detectives were spotted near the church. The reasons they were there are unclear: Perhaps they were there to spy on the union meeting; perhaps their car had broken down. In any case, shooting broke out, and one detective was killed and the other wounded. As news of the shooting spread the next day, it was interpreted as a "Negro uprising." Whites from all over the area, along with 500 state militiamen, came to Phillips County to put down the uprising. Some blacks were chased into the cane fields and indiscriminately shot. Others who had been disarmed (or were unarmed) were also shot; scores of blacks were taken to jail. The best estimate of the death toll among blacks is 50 to 100.

Some of the blacks who were arrested were tortured into confessing their role in the "uprising," and six were sentenced to death, apparently after having been framed. The National Association for the Advancement of Colored People (NAACP) began a nationwide campaign to raise money for the defense of those who had been arrested and to publicize the unfair trials, which were described as legalized lynching. Justice Oliver Wendell Holmes eventually overturned their convictions in 1923, in *Moore v. Dempsey*, saying that "counsel, jury, and judge were swept to the fatal end by an irresistible wave of public passion."

The riot in Tulsa, Oklahoma, of 31 May and 1 June 1921 was not only the last of the major riots but probably also the worst. It also involved the most aggressive action by the black community to protect itself. The other riots had begun because black youths had stumbled into white territory, or because black strikebreakers had been attacked, or because blacks had supposedly committed crimes in white neighborhoods. By contrast, the riot in Tulsa began when blacks deliberately went into white space for a confrontation. Black veterans crossed the railroad tracks from Greenwood (the black community) into white Tulsa, where a young black man was jailed at the courthouse on an accusation of attempted rape. The well-armed veterans were following advice that had appeared in a newspaper, the *Tulsa Star*, "to march in a body and to take life if necessary to uphold the law." They refused to be disarmed at the courthouse, and at about ten o'clock at night fighting began between them and a white lynch mob that had also assembled at the courthouse. The next morning at dawn, a well-armed mob, composed of police deputies, worked in conjunction with local units of the National Guard to systematically disarm every resident of Greenwood who could be found. Shortly after Greenwood's residents had been arrested, deputies and some members of the mob looted and then burned Greenwood. By the time units of the National Guard arrived from Oklahoma City and restored order (around noon on 1 June), more than thirty blocks had been destroyed. The riot in Tulsa marked the destruction of the Greenwood community; it also marked the end of the riots of the World War I era.

Grimshaw (1959, 1969), following the lead of the study of the Chicago riot, *The Negro in Chicago*, hypothesizes that northern riots were often precipitated by conflicts over "secular" issues like housing and jobs and had a background of rising social tension, whereas southern riots tended to be precipitated by allegations of attacks on white women. On closer inspection, however, there are many similarities between riots, wherever they occurred. In many instances, the black community, particularly after East St. Louis, armed to protect itself. In each instance, there were reports that the black community had demanded social and political equality, and there was almost always talk afterward about vice in the black communities and the breakdown of the strict line separating black and white communities. The common denominators appear to be fear of the black community and the desire to put that community back in its place.

There were also some important patterns in the white community. In most riots, sensational newspapers inflamed white people's passions—for instance, by reporting that blacks were encroaching on white communities or that blacks had assaulted whites. Also, in most instances the authorities were to protect black communities against attack; in some cases the authorities disarmed blacks even before any rioting began. In other instances, authorities disarmed the black community after violence broke out. The similarities are so striking that one is tempted to characterize the mob violence so prevalent at the time as part of a larger cultural pattern. Communities seem to have copied previous riots. There was a national pattern of lynching and riots, designed to subordinate black communities. And while lynchings have in recent years received more attention, the riots (and associated "Negro drives") were probably more important in the attempts to reestablish white control. Hundreds died in the riots, and thousands were left homeless. The economic and social effects of riots touched a greater percentage of the black communities than did lynchings. Moreover, in the aftermath of the riot of 1921 in Tulsa, although lynchings continued, the rate was never so high as before the riot, and whites had become accustomed to at least a somewhat improved status for blacks.

ALFRED BROPHY

See also Crisis, The; Riots: 2—Red Summer of 1919; Riots: 3—Tulsa, 1921

Further Reading

Brophy, Alfred L. *Reconstructing the Dreamland: The Tulsa Race Riot of 1921—Race, Reparations, Reconciliation.* New York: Oxford University Press, 2002.

Chicago Commission on Race Relations. *The Negro in Chicago: A Study of Race Relations and a Race Riot in 1919.* Chicago, Ill.: University of Chicago Press, 1922.

Cortner, Richard C. *A Mob Intent on Death: The NAACP and the Arkansas Riot Cases.* Middleton, Conn.: Wesleyan University Press, 1988.

Grimshaw, Allen Day. "A Study in Social Violence: Urban Race Riots in the United States." Ph.D. diss., University of Pennsylvania, 1959.

———. *Racial Violence in the United States.* Chicago, Ill.: Aldine, 1969.

Grossman, James R. *Land of Hope: Chciago, Black Southerners, and the Great Migration.* Chicago, Ill.: University of Chicago Press, 1989.

Haynes, Robert V. *A Night of Violence: The Houston Riot of 1917.* Baton Rouge: Louisiana State University Press, 1976.

Jordan, William G. *Black Newspapers and America's War for Democracy, 1914–1920.* Chapel Hill: University of North Carolina Press, 2001.

Murray, Robert K. *Red Scare: A Study in National Hysteria, 1919–1920.* Minneapolis: University of Minnesota Press, 1955.

Rudwick, Elliott M. *Race Riot at East St. Louis, July 2, 1917.* Carbondale: Southern Illinois University Press, 1964.

Sandberg, Carl. *The Chicago Race Riots, July 1919.* New York: Harcourt, Brace, and Howe, 1919.

Senechal, Roberta. *The Sociogenesis of a Race Riot: Springfield, Illinois, in 1908.* Urbana: University of Illinois Press, 1990.

Stockley, Grif. *Blood in Their Eyes: The Elaine Race Massacres of 1919.* Fayetteville: University of Arkansas Press, 2001.

Tuttle, William M., Jr. *Race Riot: Chicago in the Red Summer of 1919.* Champaign: University of Illinois Press, 1996.

U.S. House of Representatives. *Report of the Special Committee Authorized by Congress to Investigate the East St. Louis Riots.* Sixty-fifth Congress, Second Session, Document 1231, 15 July 1918.

Williams, Lee E. *Anatomy of Four Race Riots: Racial Conflict in Knoxville, Elaine (Arkansas), Tulsa, and Chicago, 1919–1921.* Hattiesburg: University Press of Mississippi, 1972.

———. *Post-War Riots in America, 1919 and 1946: How the Pressures of War Exacerbated American Urban Tensions to the Breaking Point.* Lewiston, N.Y.: Mellen, 1991.

Riots: 2—Red Summer of 1919

The summer and winter months of 1919 were marked by numerous incidents of racial violence that exploded across the American landscape, visibly exposing the hostility of much of white America toward African Americans. Throughout the nation, from large metropolitan areas such as Chicago and Washington, D.C., to rural communities such as Elaine, Arkansas, and Longview, Texas, African Americans faced attacks from white mobs. Although this frenzy of mob violence was most apparent in the summer of 1919, attacks on blacks and black communities continued, and this era of white mob violence would include the Tulsa riot of 1921.

During these attacks on their communities, some blacks fought back, although in almost every case they were outnumbered, and they often faced not only white vigilantes but the police or state militias. In a number of places, including Longview, Texas, Chicago, and Washington, D.C., the blacks—many of them veterans—who resisted killed and injured whites who were attacking their neighborhoods. In most places, though, injuries and deaths among blacks far outnumbered those among whites.

These riots were often sparked by specific incidents in which blacks had violated unwritten rules about race and status. However, the root cause of most of the riots was the vast social dislocation caused by World War I. Black veterans had returned in uniform with a new sense of self-confidence that made them less inclined to accept the humiliations of segregation and white supremacy. Meanwhile, during the war the North had witnessed changes in population as more then 325,000 blacks moved out of the South. This migration threatened white hegemony in the North and created labor shortages in parts of the South. The waves of unrest created by population shifts, by the stress of war, and by white people's fears spilled over into mob violence in the summer of 1919 and beyond.

Thus the origins of the racial violence characterizing the "red summer" of 1919 can be traced to social, economic, and political conditions in the early twentieth century, most importantly at the time of World War I. The threatened loss of liberty and democracy signaled by the continually changing political alliances of various European nation-states forced people across the globe to put aside their differences and unite in a common cause: the preservation of freedom. In the United States, men and women who joined the labor force or enlisted in the armed forces symbolized this united front. African Americans made a contribution to this nationalistic goal, as exemplified by the formation and participation of the all-black 369th Infantry Regiment in France. For a brief period, the racial divide that troubled the United States was at least partially bridged or disregarded. The realities of World War I functioned as a call to action for all Americans, regardless of skin color, to uphold the ideas of democracy

and to combat any transgressions against liberty and freedom.

However, this new sense of racial harmony lasted for only a brief period. Segregation and discrimination in the military had led to great resentment among most black soldiers; and many whites had been shocked and deeply disturbed by the positive treatment blacks received in France. When the war ended, an atmosphere of fear and suspicion developed, as concerns over imminent revolution, racial and religious intolerance, and the sheer threat of anarchy haunted the minds of Americans. Those in power began to feel that the nation was being saturated by Bolsheviks and other dissident elements. The fear of communism intensified, and the rhetoric of hate pushed the nation deeper into bigotry.

There were in fact a few bombing incidents and other acts of subversion by the left wing; moreover, the national economy soured after the war. War contracts abruptly ended, causing hundreds of factories and industries to close or reorganize their infrastructure in order to adapt to the new peacetime climate. These changes resulted in a period of severe labor strife as millions of the unemployed—native whites, blacks, and the rising immigrant class—competed for a limited number of jobs. America's economic outlook became increasingly bleak and uncertain in 1919, as labor strikes became commonplace. The mounting uncertainty led to outward expressions of hostility toward blacks, immigrants, and anyone else who was perceived as a threat to the status quo.

Rampant suspicion, antiradicalism, and xenophobia developed into what became known as the "red scare" of 1919. Initially, African Americans were in general uninformed about or unaffected by this development. The "red scare" was at first perceived as a concern only for white Americans, as the political elite focused on suppressing socialists, communists, Wobblies (members of the Industrial Workers of the World, IWW), and various labor radicals. However, postwar tensions soon affected blacks when unemployed whites in the North turned their attention to recent "immigrants" from the South, and southern whites sought to reassert racial supremacy over blacks who had demanded greater equality during the war. Part of this new violence was a reaction against black veterans. Not since the Civil War had most white Americans seen blacks in uniform, proudly claiming equal status with whites. Black veterans, praised for their heroism and valor in the war effort abroad, faced discrimination and segregation at home. Many refused to accept this status. Their experiences in Europe had showed them that integration with and respect from whites were possible. Moreover, as veterans they felt that they had earned equality. Their attempts to gain equal treatment led to violence by whites.

At the same time, the rapid influx of African Americans into large northern cities in search of improved living and working conditions further destabilized the color line. Known as the "great migration," this large-scale movement of African Americans was driven primarily by economic factors. Between 1915 and 1916, the South experienced economic disaster as a result of torrential rains in some places, prolonged droughts in others, and the devastating effects of the boll weevil. With the southern economy suffering, white southerners often resorted to lynchings and other forms of violence to express their rage and anger over the current conditions. This situation, in turn, propelled African Americans to leave the South for better opportunities and a life free of racial strife.

Although the North held the promise of freedom and opportunity, the aftermath of World War I and the postwar situation quickly shattered African Americans' hopes for a better life. Eventually African Americans became ensnarled in the frenzy of the "red scare," becoming objects against whom white Americans vented their frustration. Anxious whites feared an impending loss of jobs and, most important, feared a loss of social status; accordingly, they were determined to maintain a segregated society. In their minds, the growing presence of African Americans in what had been white spaces represented the black man's quest for social equality. African Americans wanted to better their lives socially, economically, and politically, and many white Americans resented these aspirations. African Americans—by their very nature, skin color, and culture—threatened white people's sensibilities and, in particular, threatened the color line that had been so carefully and so rigidly maintained. African Americans, however, felt entitled to enjoy the rewards and opportunities associated with being an American, especially after their contributions to the war effort. The two races had different concepts of equality; and as doubts about the economic future plunged the nation into chaos, the racial climate, combined with feelings of anxiety and disorder as a result of the war, created an atmosphere in which hostility would inevitably be expressed.

Unsurprisingly, then, racial hostility intensified in 1919. Shootings, lynchings, beatings, and other acts of violence and terror occurred in rapid succession.

For instance, eleven men were burned at the stake, and the number of lynchings rose dramatically each month. The "red summer" of 1919 had begun. There were numerous incidents of racial violence during the "red summer." Some of the more noteworthy were the following.

On 10 May 1919, in Charleston, South Carolina, rumors spread about a racial incident involving a naval officer and a black man. Mobs of angry white servicemen and veterans, of whom many were armed and all seemed to be inspired by the rhetoric of hate, invaded one of Charleston's predominantly black neighborhoods. Eventually, this mob was out of control, and the city police called the naval command for help in subduing the rioters. To a certain extent, order was restored, but not before two black men had been killed and countless others had been beaten or otherwise wounded and injured.

In June 1919, John Hartfield was lynched in Ellisville, Mississippi. Hartfield, an alleged rapist, became the target of an angry white mob and was severely wounded. At first, his life was spared through the good graces of a doctor in the neighborhood, but then the inflammatory rhetoric of local newspapers took effect. White citizens felt that their cause was justified; moreover, some officials believed that mob violence could never be quenched unless justice was done—in this case, "justice" meant Hartfield's death. Hartfield was hanged, burned, and eventually shot by members of a crowd of 3,000 rioters.

A particularly ominous event occurred in Longview, Texas, a few weeks after the incident in Charleston. In Longview, racial tension had begun to intensify as a result of economic concerns. Specifically, whites had been unsettled by the activities of the National Negro Business League, an organization originally founded by Booker T. Washington to promote economic productivity for African Americans. The league had encouraged black farmers to negotiate business deals directly with their market buyers in nearby Galveston, Texas; as a result, black business owners were able to sell their products at lower prices than whites could offer. The incident began when the naked, mutilated body of Lemuel Walters was found and black residents, headed by members of the league, demanded an investigation. It soon became apparent that the local police force was not actively pursuing the investigation; furthermore, black residents expressed concern that evidence in the case would be destroyed. Mistrust between the races intensified. Then a black newspaper, the *Chicago Defender*, published an article alleging that

Walters had been killed by a mob because of his love for a white woman, that the police in Longview had refused to investigate the murder, and that the police had actually encouraged the mob violence against Walters. In reaction, a group of irate white men confronted S. L. Jones, a local agent for the *Defender*, and accused him of having written the article; Jones denied the allegation but was nevertheless severely beaten. He sought the aid of a local physician, C. P. Davis; he and Davis were then personally threatened, but they refused to leave Longview, and they thus became a target of impending racial violence. On the night of 10 July, tension between these two men and the white townspeople worsened, and several black citizens helped Jones and Davis prepare an assault against an approaching mob. Davis started a shootout in which four men were killed and others were wounded. Whites retaliated by burning black residents' homes and murdering Davis's father-in-law. Davis and Jones managed to escape, and martial law was eventually imposed. By then, however, many blacks and whites had died.

Another significant incident occurred in Washington, D.C. During the summer of 1919, there had been accounts of sexual assaults by black men against white women, and although some of these claims proved to be false, tension amounting to hysteria developed. As in other incidents, white citizens were egged on by the inflammatory rhetoric of local newspapers. In this case, the situation exploded during a night when a group of white servicemen roamed the streets, attacking any black person in sight. The local police force was unable or unwilling to control this group of marauders, and violence continued for three days. The well-known African American scholar Carter G. Woodson is said to have witnessed this outbreak of violence and indeed to have barely escaped with his life. African Americans then formulated plans to retaliate. They acquired weapons from people in nearby Baltimore and asked biracial soldiers to infiltrate white mobs and gangs as spies, to learn about plans for further attacks. However, the secretary of war, Newton Baker, asked the infantry to patrol the city's streets; and bad weather, in the form of torrential rains, soon discouraged any additional acts of violence. Still, before the violence ended, six people had died and hundreds more had been seriously injured.

Yet another episode of violence and insurrection took place in Chicago. It started at Lake Michigan, where whites threw rocks at a young black man, Eugene Williams, who was swimming too close to a customarily "white" beach. Williams attempted to swim back to the "black" beach but was drowned. Evidence later suggested that he had not been hit by the rocks, although his fear of being hit may have been a factor in his drowning. In any event, this incident resulted in a full-scale riot in Chicago. The rumor soon spread that a white youth had drowned after being assaulted by rock-throwing black youths; another rumor was that a local police officer had denied assistance to Williams. The truth became distorted beyond recognition; misinformation and hatred took hold, blacks and whites stormed the beach, gunfire broke out, and a race war began. Gangs of angry whites roamed the streets of Chicago's South Side, attacking blacks at random. The city's newspapers published racially biased and provocative articles depicting African Americans as undesirable and unfit to participate in society. The riot in Chicago lasted for perhaps thirteen days and led to the deaths of fifteen whites and twenty-three blacks. Also, according to the records, 537 people were injured, about two-thirds of them black and one-third white. Probably many more were actually injured but were not taken to hospitals and so were not included in the count. More than 1,000 black families were left homeless. In Chicago, as in Washington, the police did not handle the turmoil effectively.

These episodes of racial strife, and many others, crippled relations between whites and African Americans. Furthermore, the conflicting interests of labor and capital exacerbated hostility between the races. White Americans seemed determined to eradicate the presence of African Americans at any cost, and there was renewed interest in the radical hate group known as the Ku Klux Klan. Despite the countless deaths, the antiblack rhetoric, and the destruction of property, however, the incidents of the "red summer" provided one glimmer of hope: a reaffirmation of African Americans' sense of racial pride, as illustrated by the emergence of a new identity, the "New Negro."

Although the concept of the New Negro had existed years earlier, the events of 1919 created more interest in it. Generally, the term "New Negro" referred to middle-class African American men and women who were in a position to acquire their share of America's promised democracy and equal rights and to promote a new image of the race. The expression of racial pride was a focal point of the concept of the New Negro. After the events of 1919, the image of the lazy, shuffling, inferior African American would be cast aside and replaced by a new image of African Americans as proud, resolute, and dignified. Alain Locke's *The New Negro* (1925) served as a written manifesto of this new image. Armed with a new sense of self-expression and self-definition, the New Negro was prepared to demand equality, aggressively, at all costs.

Therefore, the months of conflict in 1919 strengthened African Americans' resolve to acquire a better life. The "red summer" fostered a growing feeling of outrage and militancy toward the oppressor. For example, a leading periodical of the Harlem Renaissance movement, *The Messenger*, published a series of articles praising its own readers for fighting back against acts of violence. *The Messenger* and other periodicals also saw the New Negro as someone who would not stand by idly and allow further degradation to occur. These publications developed a language of empowerment.

The New Negro, as a concept, implied and contributed to a positive self-image of the race. It also suggested that African Americans would need to use new methods in their quest for equality and democracy: "The German Hun is beaten, but the world is made no safer for Democracy. Humanity has been defended, but lifted no higher. Democracy never will be safe in America until these occurrences are made impossible either by the proper execution of the law or with double-barrel shot guns" (quoted in Lewis 1997). After the "red summer" of 1919, the New Negro would no longer serve as a scapegoat or victim.

In literature, perhaps the most poignant expression of African Americans' resolve to confront race relations defiantly was Claude McKay's important poem "If We Must Die" (1919), which was inspired by the events of the "red summer." This sonnet, published in McKay's collection *Harlem Shadows* (1922), pleads for the dignity of the oppressed: "If we must die, let it not be like hogs/Hunted and penned in an inglorious spot. . . ./If we must die, O let us nobly die/So that our precious blood may not be shed/In vain. . . ." McKay expressed an oppressed people's moral outrage and desire for dignity; he was hailed as a revolutionary poet, and his literary works became the voice of those who were victimized by the events of the "red summer." Other poems by McKay also capture these events. For example, "The Lynching" (1919) depicts the mentality of mob violence: "The ghastly body swaying in the sun/The women thronged to look. . . ." And "America" (1921) reflects the ambivalence many African Americans felt toward their nation, a land that promoted freedom and democracy but despised them as a race: "Although she feeds me bread of bitterness,/And sinks into my throat her tiger's tooth,/Stealing my breath of life,

I will confess/I love this cultured hell that tests my youth!" McKay's harsh, vivid imagery depicts life along the color line. Later generations would in their turn use poems such as "If We Must Die" as an international anthem of protest for all the world's oppressed and disenfranchised. In a speech during World War II, British prime minister Winston Churchill quoted "If We Must Die," though without attributing it to McKay; and in the early 1970s, after an uprising in the state prison at Attica, New York, a copy of this poem was found in the possession of one of the insurgent inmates.

LARNELL DUNKLEY JR.

See also Chicago Defender; Fifteenth Infantry; Great Migration; Harlem Shadows; McKay, Claude; Messenger, The; National Negro Business League; New Negro; Racial Violence: Riots and Lynching; Riots: 3—Tulsa, 1921; Woodson, Carter G.; World War I

Further Reading

Franklin, John Hope, and Alfred Moss. *From Slavery to Freedom: A History of African Americans*, 8th ed. New York: McGraw-Hill, 2000.

Huggins, Nathan Irvin. *Harlem Renaissance*. New York: Oxford University Press, 1971.

Lewis, David Levering. *When Harlem Was in Vogue*. New York: Penguin, 1997.

McKay, Claude. *Selected Poems*. New York: Dover, 1999.

Osofsky, Gilbert. *Harlem: The Making of a Ghetto—Negro New York, 1890–1930*, 2nd ed. New York: Harper, 1971.

Tuttle, William M., Jr. *Race Riot: Chicago in the Red Summer of 1919*. New York: Atheneum, 1972.

Watson, Steven. *The Harlem Renaissance: Hub of African-American Culture, 1920–1930*. New York: Pantheon, 1995.

Wintz, Cary D. *Black Culture and the Harlem Renaissance*. College Station: Texas A&M University Press, 1988.

Riots: 3—Tulsa, 1921

On 31 May 1921, the *Tulsa Tribune* carried a front-page story, "Nab Negro for Attacking White Girl in Elevator." The article was about an alleged attempted rape of Sarah Page by nineteen-year-old Dick Rowland (whom the newspaper identified as "Diamond Dick"). By late afternoon, there was talk of lynching, and Tulsa's black citizens were becoming alarmed. There was good reason to fear that Rowland would be lynched. Less than a year before, a white man had been taken out of the jail and lynched in the presence of police officers who did nothing to stop the killing.

Earlier, in 1920, when a black man was lynched in Oklahoma City, A. J. Smitherman had said in an editorial in his weekly paper, the *Tulsa Star*, that "any set of citizens had a legal right—it was their duty—to arm themselves and march in a body to the jail . . . and to take life if need be to uphold the law and protect the prisoner." Now groups of veterans met throughout the evening at the offices of the *Tulsa Star*, debating their next moves. Around seven o'clock that evening, black veterans of World War I appeared at the courthouse and offered their services to protect Rowland. They received assurances that Rowland was safe and were told by a black deputy sheriff that they were just stirring up racial trouble and that they should go home, which they did.

By ten o'clock that night, when a white mob had assembled and had not been dispersed, several dozen black veterans—who were carrying weapons—appeared at the courthouse. Their leader was someone named Mann, who had reportedly come back from the war in France "with exaggerated ideas about equality and thinking he can whip the world." When one of the men refused to relinquish his gun to law enforcement officers, shooting started and a riot began. As soon as the shooting began, members of the white mob broke into stores to get guns and ammunition. At about the same time, the police department began deputizing men to assist in what they saw as a "Negro uprising." After the riot, some whites testified that they were told to "get a gun, and get busy and try to get a nigger." The black veterans quickly headed north, across the railroad tracks that separated black and white Tulsa.

Local units of the National Guard began working with the police department to put down the "uprising." Dozens of cars patrolled along the border of the black community, Greenwood, and talk could be heard everywhere of driving into "Little Africa," as Greenwood was often called. Within Greenwood, veterans put on their uniforms and their helmets and got out their rifles.

Before dawn on 1 June, the National Guard, working in conjunction with the police and their deputies, began disarming and arresting black men along the outskirts of Greenwood. Beginning around dawn, the arrests became more widespread. Everyone in Greenwood was disarmed and arrested. Most of those arrested surrendered peacefully, but there were a few pitched battles, and some who refused to give up their guns were killed.

After the arrests were made, the mobs looted Greenwood. One white observer later testified that some rioters took phonograph players out of houses, starting playing them, and continued looting; then the rioters began to burn the houses. One photograph of the riot was labeled "running the Negro out of Tulsa," which is what the deputized mob was doing. Civilization broke down completely that day. There was cold-blooded killing of unarmed men and women; a man was dragged behind a car; there are even stories that airplanes shot at people on the ground.

The arrests were completed by about ten o'clock in the morning, and the burning and looting ended shortly afterward, as units of the National Guard arrived from Oklahoma City and enforced the martial law declared by the governor. The riot claimed perhaps as many as 150 lives and destroyed thirty-five blocks in Greenwood. Over the next several days, residents of Greenwood were released from custody, as their white employers came and vouched for them. Those residents who stayed on in Greenwood lived in tents, often for months, until they rebuilt their homes.

This riot, like others in the wake of World War I, had resulted from the rising aspirations of blacks and their refusal to defer to whites as the whites demanded. The grand jury investigating the riot attributed it to agitation for social equality and to radical literature circulating in Greenwood. The great periodicals of the Harlem Renaissance, such as *The Crisis*, the *Chicago Defender*, and *The* (Indianapolis) *Freeman*, were accused of disseminating radical ideas. Many commentators suggested that W. E. B. Du Bois, who had visited Tulsa a few months before, had stirred up "race trouble." The grand ideas of the renaissance were making their way out to the territories and were having important consequences.

After the riot, the city attempted to prevent rebuilding by rezoning the burned area for industrial uses. That rezoning was struck down as an interference with property rights; nevertheless, many residents of Greenwood left for such places as Chicago, St. Louis, Kansas City, Los Angeles, and Boston. Insurance companies refused to honor fire insurance policies, citing "riot exclusion" clauses, and the city was immune from lawsuits. Despite initial promises of assistance for rebuilding, the remaining residents of Greenwood received little help.

A. J. Smitherman, who was under indictment for inciting the riot, fled to Boston, where he wrote editorials promoting the cause of the riot victims in Tulsa. Smitherman also wrote a long poem to tell the story of the riot and to celebrate Tulsa's veterans for ensuring that the rule of law, not a lynch mob, would prevail. He concluded: "Nobly they had stopped a lynching,/Taught a lesson for all time. . . ./Though they fought the sacrificial/Fight with banners flying high,/Yet the thing of more importance/Is the way they fought—and why!"

ALFRED BROPHY

See also Riots: 1—Overview, 1917–1921

Further Reading

Brophy, Alfred L. *Reconstructing the Dreamland: The Tulsa Race Riot of 1921—Race, Reparations, Reconciliation.* New York: Oxford University Press, 2002.
Ellsworth, Scott. *Death in a Promised Land: The Tulsa Race Riot of 1921.* Baton Rouge: Louisiana State University Press, 1982.

Riots: 4—Harlem Riot, 1935

On 19–20 March 1935, 500 policemen patrolled central Harlem, where roving bands of black men and women smashed 626 windows and looted stores before order was restored. After initially being dispersed by the police into side streets during the late afternoon of 19 March, crowds soon returned to resume the assault on white stores on 125th Street. Harlemites attacked and looted stores between 120th and 138th streets and Fifth and Saint Nicholas avenues, hurling missiles down from roofs and windows onto the police. By the time the riot ended, more than 200 Harlemites had been injured or arrested, and seven policemen had been injured. The image of renaissance Harlem as a cultural magnet for white downtowners seeking the primitive under the guise of modernity—the image of the 1920s—was shattered with the plate glass; in the 1930s, Harlem appeared angrier. Alain Locke, in a postmortem article about the renaissance, noted that this riot, more than any other single event, had changed the public image of Harlem as a bright, superficial world of nightclubs, cabaret tours, and arty magazines.

The riot had been triggered by an erroneous rumor that a sixteen-year-old Puerto Rican, Lino Rivera, accused of stealing a knife from the Kress Store on West 125th Street, had been beaten to death by store officials and the police. In the history of American urban racial violence, it was unique: It was a riot against property and for commodities, and it stemmed from the economic deprivation wrought by the Great Depression. Before 1935, racial rioting usually involved (1) invasion by whites of black residential areas, sometimes provoking retaliation or self-defense; (2) pitched battles between black and white civilians in an area contiguous to both communities; or (3) attacks on blacks caught in white downtown areas. These elements had been present to varying degrees in earlier riots, such as those in Atlanta, Georgia (1906); Washington, D.C. (1919); Tulsa, Oklahoma (1921); and East St. Louis, Illinois (1917)—and in many of the twenty-six race riots of the "red summer" of 1919, including the largest, in Chicago. But these ingredients were not present in the Harlem riot of 1935, and this suggests the difficulty of classifying it as simply another race riot. What happened in Harlem—the activity of white and black communist agitators against police and white merchants during the rioting, and the attacks on white people's property instead of on the whites themselves—reveals undertones of an interracial class revolt against discrimination and unemployment within a more generalized racial rebellion by Harlemites.

Still, the riot in Harlem had some similarity to traditional urban racial disorders. In previous riots, one factor in the onset was smaller-scale violence related to various earlier grievances; this was also true in Harlem. For more than a decade, black newspapers like *New York Age* and the *New York Amsterdam News* had carried articles about white police brutality and use of excessive force in Harlem. In 1933, the police had attempted to stop the sale of copies of the *Liberator* (a black leftist publication) at a street meeting held by the communist-sponsored International Labor Defense; the reason given was that a front-page story exposing a white policeman's brutal attack on a black girl would have led to a race riot. The *New York Daily News* observed in an editorial: "There has been more street rioting in New York City in the first three months of Mayor [Fiorello] La Guardia's administration than in any similar period of time that we can remember."

The most significant clash before 1935, however, occurred on 17 March 1934 at a rally sponsored by the International Labor Defense to support the Scottsboro boys. Five thousand black and white demonstrators at

126th Street and Lenox Avenue became involved in a physical confrontation with the police, who used tear gas to break up the rally; at one point, a police car was driven onto the sidewalk and into the crowd. Several policemen and demonstrators were injured, and various organizations charged the police with brutality. The police claimed to have been reacting to violence by the demonstrators, who had hurled rocks, trash can covers, grapefruit, and so on; the police also denied that they had beaten a girl and a man at the rally and that they had drawn their revolvers on the crowd. A report by the chief inspector recommended disciplinary action against two policemen for using excessive force, and against an acting sergeant "for failing to exercise proper supervision" (a failure that resulted in the use of tear gas). However, the police commissioner, in a letter to Mayor La Guardia, disagreed with that report, and the commissioner's department later exonerated the two police officers. For many Harlemites, this incident at the rally increased their bitterness against the police and demonstrated the hopelessness of relying on internal discipline in the police department. Still, the incident did not provoke retaliatory violence from blacks and did not develop into a major riot. The people of Harlem may well have viewed the conflict as a confrontation between black and white communists on the one hand and the police on the other, rather than as a general community confrontation. It is worth noting, though, that the willingness of the Communist Party to stand up for blacks helped the party to organize in Harlem and contributed to its increasingly favorable image among some Harlemites who were not communists.

Another, more encompassing issue, then, was needed to make Harlem erupt. During the Great Depression, the most immediate issue, amounting to a crisis, was the extraordinarily high unemployment rate and the resulting struggle for food, clothing, and shelter. Meanwhile, white merchants and chain stores on 125th Street refused to employ black clerical and sales personnel; in the 1920s, this policy had caused resentment, but now, in the 1930s, it became the master symbol of white arrogance in the face of black deprivation. The initial impetus for a campaign to obtain jobs in white stores came from Sufi Abdul Hamid, who had led such a campaign in Chicago. In 1933, Hamid began aggressive picketing and boycotting of stores above 125th Street. Also, parishioners at Saint Martin's Episcopal Church, led by Rev. John H. Johnson, formed the Citizens' League for Fair Play, which became an umbrella organization for many groups in

Harlem, both working class and bourgeois, agitating for clerical jobs on 125th Street. Groups of varying ideologies, from black nationalism to integrationism to communism, at one time or another took part in the boycott or organized their own boycotts. To the middle class, the boycott was an opportunity to enter white-collar employment; to black nationalists, it was a prelude to taking over all the jobs and businesses of Harlem and ending "economic colonialism" there. To the Communist Party, initially, the campaign was a threat to their goal of solidarity between black and white workers—a ruse by which the black petit bourgeois intended to gain strength. But once the communists saw how popular the campaign was, they changed their tactics and began their own boycott and picketing.

The jobs campaign—and Harlem—appeared to achieve a victory in late July 1934, when Blumstein's department store agreed to hire thirty-five black saleswomen by September. However, Sufi Abdul Hamid's Negro Industrial and Clerical Alliance considered thirty-five an insufficient number and continued picketing; Arthur Reid and Ira Kemp of the Citizens' League then formed their own organization and continued picketing because Blumstein's gave the jobs to lighter-skinned rather than darker-skinned women. The courts began to prohibit picketing, merchants began to discriminate once again in hiring, and some stores fired the black workers who had been hired during the jobs campaign.

Ironically, one reason given by the courts for forbidding picketing was that it might lead to racial violence. For instance, Justice Samuel Rosenman of the state supreme court, who issued an order restraining back organizations from picketing the A. S. Beck shoe store in Harlem, said that a fear of race rioting had influenced his decision. Actually, the restraining order increased the chances of racial violence by precluding at least one peaceful alternative and adding to Harlemites' frustration.

The climate, then, was conducive to rioting; the false rumor of Lino Rivera's death merely provided the occasion. Many Harlemites were entirely prepared to believe the rumor, on the basis of their own experience with the police and with white merchants; and the way the incident unfolded did nothing to dispel the story. Rivera—who was not beaten—later stated that store employees threatened to take him down to the basement and beat him, although the store manager denied making this threat. The policemen took the youth through the basement to the rear entrance and released him there, to avoid the excited spectators;

this action led one black woman in the store to cry out that the boy was being taken to the basement to be beaten up. The coincidental appearance of an ambulance and a hearse appeared to support her idea, and to support the community's fear that Rivera had been killed. Accounts of what the police did at this critical juncture are contradictory. One policeman testified before the Mayor's Commission on Conditions in Harlem, which was charged with investigating the riot, that a committee of women was formed among the shoppers to search the basement, but the commission was never able to find these women. The police and the store managers testified that they had told the crowd gathered in the store that the boy was alive and unharmed. Others, however, testified that the police made no effort to inform the spectators, the boy's condition being none of the onlookers' business. It is possible that both the police and the spectators were testifying accurately, because the actual composition of the crowd and the police personnel changed over the course of the episode; in any case, the Harlemites evidently gave little credence to what the police said.

At five-thirty that afternoon, the crowd had become so agitated that the store was closed, but no violent confrontations had yet developed, either between blacks and whites or between Harlemites and the police. At this point, some white and black leftists sought to give direction to the crowd's anger; their idea was to form an interracial alliance to protest not only against the treatment of Rivera but more generally against social and economic conditions in Harlem. A white member of the Nurses and Hospital League, an organization fighting for black hospital workers, was pushed off a ladder on 125th Street by the police, who had long been antagonistic toward interracial gatherings and cooperation. A white member of the New York Students' League, an organization sympathetic to civil rights, was dragged off a lamppost on 125th Street, beaten, and arrested for attempting to address the crowd. At approximately the same time, a number of black residents of the Salvation Army's facility on 124th Street began throwing stones, breaking windows in the rear of the Kress store. The smashing of windows and subsequent looting of white stores along 125th Street gathered momentum as the evening wore on, with the crowds spreading to Seventh and Lenox avenues.

The leftist speakers were not the cause of the rioting, but they did try to channel the anger of the crowd toward white merchants and political leaders. In particular, the distribution of leaflets by the Young Communist League and Young Liberators has led some authorities to claim that the communists were responsible for the rioting. Actually, the leaflets did not appear on the streets before seven-thirty in the evening, after the rioting had begun. Still, these leaflets may have influenced the crowds to attack property rather than people. A circular issued by a leftist Harlem youth organization, the Young Liberators, claimed that Rivera had been beaten nearly to death; such circulars called for black and white workers to unite and also called for the arrest of the Kress store managers "responsible for the lynch attack."

Leaflets of the Young Communist League appeared on the streets after those of the Young Liberators. The league's wording stressed even more the need for interracial working-class solidarity and warned that any conflicts between black and white workers would benefit the capitalist "bosses." James Ford, the black leader of the Harlem section of the Communist Party, indicated that his organization and the Young Liberators rejected rioting as a legitimate vehicle for social change, but he was probably more disturbed by the possibility that rioting could lead to fighting between black and white workers (as in previous race riots) and thus destroy the party's program of working-class unity. Ford's issuance of a leaflet to defuse potential interracial clashes resembles his action during the Chicago race riot of 1919 when he and two fellow communists—William Z. Foster and Earl Browder—distributed leaflets to prevent the spread of racial rioting into the stockyards. To achieve a similar end in Harlem, the party distributed 15,000 copies of the *Daily Worker* and thousands of copies of the Young Communist League's leaflet. There were in fact no clashes between blacks and whites, but this cannot be attributed solely to the activities of the communists. In New York (unlike, say, Chicago or East St. Louis), there had been no significant clashes between striking white workers and black scab laborers before the riot; nor did Harlem have the high level of violence surrounding the integration of white residential areas, and whites tended to flee Harlem rather than engage in physical violence to maintain their dominance. Consequently, New York had a lower level of racial animus than many other cities.

After two nights of violence, the riot subsided. Then, public officials, community leaders, and the press all tried to explain the causes of such an outbreak in liberal New York. Two official explanations evolved for this riot, as for other urban race riots in the twentieth century. According to one explanation, the riot was attributable to the "riffraff"—irresponsible petty criminals and other social deviants. According to the second explanation, the riot was due to communists, anarchists, or socialists. On the second day of the riot, Mayor La Guardia released a statement expressing the "riffraff" theory: "The unfortunate occurrence of last night and early this morning was instigated and artificially stimulated by a few irresponsible individuals." He also sent into Harlem two patrol wagons loaded with circulars expressing this theory and saying that most Harlemites were decent, law-abiding citizens, not rioters. The mayor's assertion remained unsubstantiated. No polls were taken in Harlem after the riot of 1935 to ascertain people's attitudes (nor was any such poll taken after the riot of 1943); however, the impression formed by the mayor's investigatory commission was that "among all classes, there was a feeling that the outburst was justified and that it represented a protest against discrimination and privations resulting from unemployment." La Guardia does not seem to have considered massive unemployment and the racially discriminatory or indifferent policies of certain municipal departments as key causes of the riot.

William Dodge, the district attorney for Manhattan, expressed the second explanation, attributing the riot to "communist agitators"—a conspiracy of immigrant foreign communist provocateurs. As the attorney general of the United States, A. Mitchell Palmer, had done in 1919, Dodge said he would ask the commissioner of immigration to deport any alien rioters: "My purpose is to let the Communists know that they cannot come into this country and upset our laws." The Uptown Chamber of Commerce expressed similar sentiments.

However, most of the press did focus on economic conditions as the fundamental cause of the riot. The *New York Sun* said, for instance: "Seeing red is an official privilege, diversion, and avocation at the moment" in which "no disorder can occur without being attributed to those terror-inspiring Communists whose shadows darken the sky at noon-day. . . . Actually, the Communists are more likely to have been passengers on the ebullience of a volatile population than the authors of its effervescence." The liberal white press interpreted the riot to its readers as an explosion of an unemployed, ill-paid population who lived in poor, overcrowded, rent-inflated housing and had no adequate health care. (In Harlem, family income had declined 44 percent between 1929 and 1932, but the cost-of-living index for New York State had declined

only 17 percent. By September 1933, 43.2 percent of Harlem's families were on relief.)

African American community leaders and liberal whites also focused on problems that were common nationwide during the Depression and had simply been intensified in Harlem. Cecelia C. Saunders, executive director of the Harlem branch of the YWCA, mentioned "too much unemployment, too much poverty, too much idle time; . . . too small a proportion of Work Relief . . . ; too many people . . . on inadequate Home Relief." The leaders of the jobs campaign—Rev. William Lloyd Imes and Rev. John H. Johnson—saw the riot as retaliation against white merchants who refused to hire blacks.

The mayor's investigatory commission reached much the same conclusion: that the riot had been caused by severely depressed social and economic conditions, by rampant racial discrimination in the private sector, and by pervasive racial bias or indifference in city government. In fact, the commission ruled out criminality ("riffraff") and communist agitation as causes. (There was only one dissenter: Rev. William R. McCann, pastor of Saint Charles Borromeo Roman Catholic Church on West 141st Street, who thought the communists were responsible.) This conclusion was quite unusual—most such commissions established to investigate riots concluded, conservatively, that hoodlums and agitators were to blame.

The makeup of the commission in New York may have been a factor in this outcome. Unlike the other investigatory bodies, it had a majority of black Harlemite members (seven blacks to six whites). Its chairman was Dr. Charles H. Roberts of Harlem; its vice chairman was the white liberal publisher Oswald Garrison Villard; and its director of research was Dr. E. Franklin Frazier, a professor of sociology at Howard University. Interestingly, the commission did not include some of the more prominent and militant Harlem activists—such as Rev. Adam Clayton Powell Jr. and the socialist labor organizer Frank Crosswaith—and this omission had given rise to criticism and to fears of a whitewash. Yet the commission's final report was so critical of the city government that La Guardia asked for written rebuttals from city department heads and put off the official release of the report. The *Amsterdam News* in Harlem published a leaked copy of the report on 18 July 1936.

The riot of 1935 produced a slightly more responsive attitude in the La Guardia administration to community needs, though without altering the overall picture of black deprivation. In the year following the riot, certain appointments were made to defuse some of the criticism in the commission's report: the first black female public school principal; Dr. John West as director of the Central Harlem Health Center; Rev. John H. Johnson as a member of the advisory board for the Emergency Relief Bureau, and more blacks at the bureau itself; and five blacks as members of the medical board of Harlem General Hospital (instead of only one, as earlier). Also, La Guardia began to speak before black audiences, especially at religious conferences, promising Harlemites their fair share of appointments, school positions, playgrounds, and hospitals. However, three years after the riot, the income of the average black family was still insufficient to maintain a decent and healthful standard of living.

The riot of 1935 in Harlem represented a transition: The target of violence in riots was changing from black people (in the early twentieth century) to white property (in 1935) to white property and white people (in the 1960s, usually after some accusation of excessive police force). The fact that only property was attacked, and the dissemination of militant propaganda by black and white activists, made the riot of 1935 unique and led Claude McKay to deny that it was a riot at all—he preferred to describe it as an economic or class revolt. Still, throughout history the urban poor have often erupted in protest against their material destitution and powerlessness, and in this regard at least the riot in Harlem was traditional.

LARRY A. GREENE

See also Amsterdam News; Communist Party; Ford, James William; Frazier, E. Franklin; Hamid, Sufi Abdul; Liberator; Locke, Alain; McKay, Claude; Riots: 1—Overview, 1917–1921; Scottsboro; Villard, Oswald Garrison

Further Reading

Fogelson, Robert M., and Richard E. Rubenstein. *The Complete Report of Mayor La Guardia's Commission on the Harlem Riot of March 19, 1935*. New York: Arno and New York Times, 1969.

Greenberg, Cheryl Lynn. *Or Does It Explode: Black Harlem in the Great Depression*. New York: Oxford University Press, 1991.

Greene, Larry. "Harlem: The Depression Years—Leadership and Social Conditions." *Afro-Americans in New York Life and History*, 17, July 1993.

Naison, Mark. *Communists in Harlem During the Depression*. Urbana: University of Illinois Press, 1983.

Robeson, Paul

Paul Robeson (1898–1976), one of the twentieth century's greatest concert singers and actors, was a major contributor to the culture of Harlem from 1919 through 1929. From a tiny two-block enclave in 1900, black Harlem had grown by the end of 1919 into an African American mecca that nurtured a myriad of cultural treasures. The interaction of blacks from all parts of the United States, the West Indies, and distant Africa led to the growth of a highly race-conscious, sophisticated community.

Robeson arrived in the fall of 1919 from Rutgers College as America's foremost scholar-athlete, and by 1929 he would become one of the leading symbols of the Harlem Renaissance. He entered Columbia University Law School in early 1920, as an all-American football star and a member of Phi Beta Kappa, and with a reputation as an inspiring orator because of his memorable valedictory address to his graduating class at Rutgers College on 18 June 1919:

> May I not appeal to you . . . to join us in continuing to fight . . . until in all sections of this fair land there will be equal opportunities for all, and character shall be the standard of excellence; . . . [until] an injury to the meanest citizen is an insult to the whole Constitution; and until black and white shall clasp friendly hands in the consciousness of the fact that we are brethren and that God is the father of us all.

Some listeners said that this speech was the most eloquent message ever delivered at a Rutgers commencement.

Robeson found living quarters in central Harlem, at the hub of its cultural and social life. In great demand as a public speaker, he made many contacts among Harlem's elite and was soon welcomed into the exclusive group of intellectuals who set the cultural tone for the Harlem Renaissance. W. E. B. Du Bois and James Weldon Johnson, who was simultaneously the leader of the new black literary movement and the National Association for the Advancement of Colored People (NAACP), exerted the greatest influence on Robeson's thinking through their commitment to the idea that achievement of artistic recognition by blacks was the most effective means of advancing the cause of civil rights.

At Johnson's gatherings, Robeson cautiously entered the heated political debates. He was a good listener and a brief talker, and he asked penetrating questions without seeming to challenge. Even though he could not yet compete intellectually with the members of this formidable group, everyone was attentive when he sang. Sometimes J. Rosamond Johnson accompanied him; often, though, he sang a cappella.

It was during the summer of 1920 that Robeson made his first attempt at acting. A friend, Dora Cole Norman, revived a work by the white playwright Ridgely Torrence, *Simon the Cyrenean*, which had broken with theatrical stereotypes of black characters by telling the story of an African who carried Christ's cross to Golgotha. She persuaded Robeson to play the leading role. Kenneth McGowan and Robert Edmond Jones, two founders of the Provincetown Players, a successful experimental theater group in Greenwich Village and Massachusetts, saw Robeson's opening-night performance. After the show, they congratulated him and invited him to audition for them. But he went home, put the theater out of his mind, and returned to law school the next day as if nothing special had happened. He was much too busy studying law and developing his singing skills.

Moreover, Robeson needed to play professional football, to pay his expenses at Columbia Law School. When he and his friend Fritz Pollard were invited to join the Akron Pros during the season of 1920, at $500 or more a game, he accepted without hesitation. The Pros, led by Robeson and Pollard, won the championship and national fame; undefeated in thirteen games, they held all their opponents scoreless. Robeson, billed as the greatest defensive end in the history of football, consistently drew large crowds.

He did not return to the stage until April 1922, when he appeared as the main black character in a new play, *Taboo*. This play, the first work of Mary Hoyt Wiborg, a wealthy white socialite, opened its trial run in New York in late April at the Sam Harris Theater. Most critics gave it lukewarm or even cold reviews: They described it as "diffuse" and objected to its "obscure" plot. By contrast, Robeson's notices were generally favorable. He was given credit for a powerful stage presence and a magnificent speaking voice. Only the drama critic for the *New York Times*, Alexander Woollcott, dismissed Robeson's acting ability with the tart comment that he belonged almost anywhere but in the theater.

Robeson's next acting opportunity came his way purely by chance. Late one Saturday night in May 1922, he was standing on the corner of Seventh Avenue and 135th Street, talking to friends, when along came Harold Browning, who was the leader of a quartet called the Four Harmony Kings. They were singing in the black musical comedy *Shuffle Along*, which had become a hit on Broadway. Browning was bewailing the fact that the bass singer of the quartet had suddenly left for Chicago, and that unless another bass could be found by Monday, the Harmony Kings would have to drop out of the show.

Robeson, who had been restless ever since he finished his law exams, stepped up eagerly and said, "Brother, you're looking at your bass right here!" Out of sheer desperation, Browning took him home to try out a few notes. He was astonished to find that Robeson could sing three tones lower and many notes higher than the former bass, and that his voice was rich and beautiful. Robeson got the job and became one of the stars of the show.

This experience whetted his appetite for the legitimate theater, and in early 1923 he sought a meeting with Eugene O'Neill, who he felt might "possibly have Negro roles." The next month Robeson received a note from Kenneth McGowan, director of the Provincetown Players, inviting him to read for a leading part: Jim Harris in O'Neill's new play *All God's Chillun Got Wings*. This was the story of a tragic interracial marriage and was one of the first mainstream American plays to confront the issue of interracial marriage head-on. Robeson's audition almost hypnotized the audience of theater professionals. The part was his for the taking.

In late March, while waiting to make his debut with O'Neill's company, he took the opportunity to appear in a revival of *Roseanne* presented by the Lafayette Players. The all-black company, founded by Charles Gilpin, presented limited runs of the play for one week each at Harlem's Lafayette Theater and the Dunbar in Philadelphia. With the famous actress Rose McClendon in the title role, Paul played a wayward preacher who is rescued from his congregation by a strong woman.

On 1 April 1924, a review in the *Philadelphia Record* noted that "the players seem a good deal more interesting than the play itself. . . . Paul Robeson is a strapping man with a voice that rolls out of him like a vibrant tide. It would be extremely interesting to see what he could do with *Emperor Jones* or the frustrated young negro in *All God's Chillun Got Wings*."

Robeson focused on preparing for his role in *All God's Chillun Got Wings*. As matters developed, he would need all this concentration. The Provincetown Players decided to deflect attention from the controversy over the interracial theme by first reviving *The Emperor Jones* for a week, with Robeson playing the lead. Originally made famous by Charles Gilpin, this role was an ideal vehicle for Robeson because it offered both complexity and tragic possibilities—in short, a fully realized character.

Brutus Jones is a wily Pullman porter who becomes the self-proclaimed emperor of a small Caribbean island after having gotten into trouble in the United States and having escaped from prison by killing a brutal guard. Ultimately, Jones is the victim of his rebellious subjects, who inflict their revenge on him for his misrule. It required a tour de force to learn this role and the part of Jim in *All God's Chillun Got Wings* simultaneously.

The Emperor Jones opened on 6 May 1924, and the reviewers heaped praise on Robeson's performance. The critic for the *New York Herald Tribune* commented that the play was "vitalized by a Negro with power and a full measure of understanding." The *New York Telegram* reported that "Robeson held his audience enthralled. . . . He has a powerful voice that fairly booms, and it is resonant. . . . If [he] had the proper training he would become one of the greatest singers in the world."

When *All God's Chillun Got Wings* opened the following week—on 15 May 1924—not a single protester appeared, although there had been numerous threats that created a highly dramatic situation. Alexander Woollcott praised the "noble figure . . . superbly embodied and fully comprehended by Paul Robeson." Robert Welsh of the *New York Telegram and Evening Mail* wrote that the "difficult role" of the Negro husband was "played powerfully and with a convincing simplicity by Paul Robeson." And Heywood Broun commented in the *World* that Robeson brought "a genius to the piece," and wondered if he would play Othello someday.

In an interview with the *New York Herald Tribune* about his "possibilities," and in two articles for the black magazines *The Messenger* and *Opportunity*, where he discussed his own hopes and O'Neill's plays, Robeson set out his defense of O'Neill's black tragic heroes. He believed in Jim Harris and Brutus Jones in spite of the black stereotypes that still marred them, and he responded to the strong criticism leveled at

O'Neill's characterizations by much of the black press, by black nationalists, and by many black civil rights leaders:

> In *All God's Chillun* we have a play of great strength and beautiful spirit, mocking all petty prejudice, emphasizing the humanness, and, in Mr. O'Neill's words, "the oneness" of mankind. Any number of people have said to me: "I trust that now you will get a truly heroic and noble role, one portraying the finest type of Negro." I honestly believe that perhaps never will I portray a nobler type than "Jim Harris" or a more heroically tragic figure than "Brutus Jones, Emperor," not excepting "Othello."
>
> The reactions to these two plays among Negroes but point out one of the most serious drawbacks to the development of a true Negro dramatic literature. We are too self-conscious, too afraid of showing all phases of our life—especially those phases which are of greatest dramatic value. The great mass of our group discourage any member who has the courage to fight these petty prejudices. I am still being damned all over the place for playing in *All God's Chillun*. It annoys me very little when I realize that those who object most strenuously know mostly nothing of the play and in any event know little of the theater and have no right to judge a playwright of O'Neill's talents.

Robeson remained steadfast in his view that O'Neill's tragic hero was a transitional figure, a first step away from dehumanized caricature. His own ultimate goal was to portray black characters from a fully black perspective:

> One of the great measures of a people is its culture, its artistic stature. Above all things, we boast that the only true artistic contributions of America are Negro in origin. We boast of the culture of ancient Africa.
>
> I am sure that there will come Negro playwrights of great power, and I trust I shall have some part in interpreting that most interesting and much needed addition to the drama of America.

Later in 1924, Robeson appeared for the first time in a film by the black director Oscar Micheaux, the classic *Body and Soul*. Robeson performed the two leading male roles: a charming but evil preacher who is also a seducer, gambler, thief, and killer; and his twin, an upright young man who is a model of benevolence as he courts the heroine. Here was an interesting experiment for the fledgling actor. The fact that the film was silent deprived Robeson of his main asset, his speaking voice. Moreover, the film's low budget virtually precluded retakes, so for the most part he had to do everything right the first time. His later success as a film star throughout the 1930s was due in part to the experience he gained from working with Micheaux.

In March 1925, the distinguished accompanist-arranger Lawrence Brown had returned to the United States on receiving the news that his father was dying. After the funeral, he went to the flat of his friends the Sawyers at 188 West 135th Street, put his luggage down, and decided to take a walk. As he turned the corner, there was Paul Robeson, whom he had met briefly in Europe, standing by himself. If Brown had come at any other time, he would have missed Robeson. Brown recalled that by then, Robeson was the most popular man in Harlem. In response to Brown's greeting, Robeson asked Brown to accompany him in an impromptu concert of Negro spirituals he was singing at Carl Van Vechten's house that night. Brown agreed, and they were a great hit, Brown singing counterpoint tenor in several numbers. Van Vechten was so impressed that he organized a formal concert for them at the Greenwich Village Theater.

The reviews launched Paul Robeson's concert career. On 20 April 1925, the music critic of the *New York Times* wrote: "His Negro Spirituals . . . hold in them a world of religious experience; it is their cry from the depths, this universal humanism, that touches the heart. . . . Sung by one man, they voiced the sorrow and hopes of a people." At the end of Robeson's concert tour in 1925–1926, an article by Elizabeth Shepley Sergeant in the *New Republic* referred to Robeson as "a symbol . . . of the increasing important place of the American Negro on the American stage." Sergeant added: "Let us give thanks that we were not born too late to hear this Negro Chaliapin render the Spirituals reverently, with wildness and awe, like a trusting child of God."

By the end of 1926, Robeson had become a popular recording artist and radio personality. Thousands of people who listened to his spirituals at home found them intimate and compelling. From the concert stage, he firmly established the spiritual as an accepted art form. His entire program consisted of Lawrence Brown's authentic arrangements in the traditional folk style. In the first annual *Who's Who in Colored America*, Robeson was ranked twentieth among concert singers in the United States. He was also a record holder for the number of times his radio concerts were interrupted by applause from the studio audience.

Robeson continued to pursue a stage career. In 1926, he played the lead in *Black Boy*, a play based partly on the life of the black former heavyweight boxing champion Jack Johnson. His performance brought him excellent reviews and increasing fame. Brooks Atkinson, the critic for the *New York Times*, wrote on 7 October 1926, "From all this hugger-mugger Mr. Robeson's performance emerges as a fine-grained, resilient bit of characterization. His huge frame fits him well for the part of a prize fighter, and his full, deep voice has a sustaining beauty. . . . One suspects that he approaches the authors' conception of Black Boy more closely than does the play." However, no adequate dramatic vehicle was available to Robeson.

Then Jerome Kern, one of the greatest figures in American musical theater, composed the score for the hit musical *Show Boat* in 1926, and the famous Oscar Hammerstein II wrote the lyrics. The theme song "Ol' Man River" was dedicated to Paul Robeson, and Robeson's rendition of it captivated audiences around the world and became his signature piece.

Although Robeson was touring Europe in concert when *Show Boat* opened in New York in 1927, he starred in the London production in 1928. The show became a smash hit that would run for almost a year at the Drury Lane Theater, and all the reviews hailed Robeson's singing of "Ol' Man River" as the best part of the show. From then on, Paul Robeson singing "Ol' Man River" was an important fixture of American popular culture.

In late October 1929 Robeson, then age thirty-one, arrived in New York to begin a two-month national concert tour. His repertoire had been expanded beyond spirituals to include folk songs from many lands and selected classical compositions. On 5 and 10 November he became the first concert singer ever to sell out Carnegie Hall twice within a week. By the end of his tour, he was being compared to the great Russian bass Fyodor Chaliapin and had established himself as one of America's leading concert singers.

In the decade since his arrival on the scene in Harlem, he had enriched the culture of its renaissance as both performing artist and intellectual. The power to create beauty, which he realized he possessed, was, in his mind, the source of the grace he could offer.

Paul Robeson with gold football and Phi Beta Kappa key, c. 1929.
(Courtesy of Paul Robeson Jr.)

Truth, as a measure of right, was beauty's indispensable companion.

Robeson's preoccupation with beauty and truth stemmed in part from his close ideological kinship with W. E. B. Du Bois, who had eloquently expressed this theme in an essay published in *The Crisis* in October 1926. Du Bois called forth the vitality of the African American artistic tradition:

> We have within us as a race new stirrings; stirrings of the beginning of a new appreciation of joy, of a new desire to create, of a new will to be; as though in this morning of group life we had awakened from some sleep that at once dimly mourns the past and dreams a splendid future. . . . I am one who tells the truth and exposes evil, and seeks with beauty and for beauty to set the world right.

The black press referred to Robeson as the "king of Harlem," and when, one day in 1929, he appeared at Seventh Avenue near 135th Street, it took him half an hour to walk a block. In the eyes of most Harlemites, he had not only personified the beauty in their culture

but also invested it with power and dignity. In his own eyes, his proudest achievement was his initiation of a change in the popular culture from the neutered "Sambo" caricature of the black male to a virile image incorporating a full measure of heroism and nobility.

Arguably, Paul Robeson's greatest gift to the Harlem Renaissance was his full-throated challenge to the cultural foundations of American racism.

Biography

Paul Robeson, son of an escaped slave, gained national prominence at Rutgers College, where he was an all-American football player for two years, was elected to Phi Beta Kappa, and was the valedictorian of his graduating class. He completed Columbia University Law School in 1923 but chose instead to pursue a career in the performing arts. During the 1920s, Robeson established himself as the leading black stage actor, with roles in seven major theatrical productions, including two plays by Eugene O'Neill: *All God's Chillun Got Wings* and *The Emperor Jones*. Robeson's talent as a singer also brought him stardom in the nation's concert halls, where he introduced the Negro spiritual as an accepted art form. In 1924, he made his debut as a film actor in Oscar Micheaux's classic *Body and Soul*. From 1927 to 1938, Robeson was based in London and toured throughout Europe, becoming one of the world's leading performers in theater, on the concert stage, and in film. He also strove tirelessly to improve the conditions of his own people and of the less fortunate around the world. When Robeson returned home in 1939, at the start of World War II, his rendition of the patriotic song "Ballad for Americans" helped to unify America; at this time, he enthralled theatergoers in the title role of a record-breaking production of Shakespeare's *Othello* on Broadway. Having reached the pinnacle of success, he entered the struggle against racial segregation in the 1940s and helped lay the foundation for the civil rights movement of the 1960s. During the McCarthy era of the 1950s, every attempt was made to silence and discredit Robeson because of his political views and his dedication to civil rights. His consistent opposition to the cold war and his continued expression of goodwill toward the Soviet Union incurred relentless persecution by the U.S. government. In 1950, Robeson's passport was revoked, and his artistic career was abruptly halted. When Robeson's passport was revalidated by a decision of the U.S. Supreme Court in 1958, he embarked on a successful three-year tour of Europe and Australia. Illness ended Robeson's professional career in 1961, and he lived the remainder of his years in the United States among family and friends as a retired private citizen.

PAUL ROBESON JR.

See also Blacks in Theater; Du Bois, W. E. B.; Emperor Jones, The; Film: Actors; Gilpin, Charles; Johnson, James Weldon; Johnson, John Arthur; Johnson, John Rosamond; Lafayette Players; McClendon, Rose; Micheaux, Oscar; Music; O'Neill, Eugene; Provincetown Players; Show Boat; Shuffle Along; Singers; Theater; Van Vechten, Carl

Selected Works

Here I Stand. Boston, Mass.: Beacon, 1988.
"An Actor's Wanderings and Hopes." *Messenger,* January 1925. (See also *The Messenger Reader.* New York: Modern Library–Random House, 2000.)
"Reflections on O'Neill's Plays." *Opportunity,* December 1924. (See also *The Opportunity Reader.* New York: Modern Library–Random House, 1999.)

Further Reading

Duberman, Martin Bauml. *Paul Robeson.* New York: Knopf, 1988, chs. 1–7.
Robeson, Paul, Jr. *The Undiscovered Paul Robeson,* Vol. 1. New York: Wiley, 2001, chs. 1–8.
Stuckey, Sterling. *Slave Culture.* New York and Oxford: Oxford University Press, 1987, ch. 6. ("On Being African: Paul Robeson and the Ends of Nationalist Theory and Practice.")

Robinson, Bill "Bojangles"

Bill "Bojangles" Robinson was one of the most important American dancers of the twentieth century and one of the first black performers to gain critical acclaim and commercial fortune in the entertainment industry. His virtuosic stage appearances throughout the years of the Harlem Renaissance helped to create new images of African Americans onstage and thereby challenged racist theatrical representations lingering from the era of minstrelsy. Reflecting on Robinson's contributions to black culture, Marshall Stearns and Jean Stearns wrote, "To his own people Robinson became a modern day John Henry, who instead of driving steel, laid down iron taps" (1994). However, Robinson's legacy has been compromised by a series of films he appeared in throughout the 1930s that arguably undermined some of the many developments ushered in during the Harlem Renaissance.

"Bojangles," whose original name was Luther Robinson, was born to Maxwell Robinson and Maria Switching in 1878 and was raised in Richmond, Virginia, by his grandmother, a former slave. As a boy, Robinson earned small sums of money shining shoes and dancing in taverns and beer gardens. According to Robinson's biographers, he acquired the name "Bojangles" as a result of a childhood prank during his days on the streets of Richmond. In 1892, Robinson ran away to Washington, D.C., taking with him yet another name—that of his younger brother, Bill. Eventually, he appeared with Mayme Remington, a former burlesque dancer, in *The South Before the War.* In this black musical revue, Robinson appeared for fifty cents an evening as a "pick," or "pickaninny"— terms referring to black child actors. When he physically outgrew the role, Robinson moved back to Richmond and served in a regimental company in the U.S. Army.

By the turn of the century, Robinson was in New York City, dancing and singing at the Douglass Club, a late-night cabaret for New York's white elite. In 1905, he went on the Keith and Orpheum vaudeville circuit as the comedian George W. Cooper's sidekick. The pair performed in blackface, and their routines centered on racial and ethnic humor, which was a way to defuse the profound social discrimination they faced offstage. In order to protect himself from potential racial violence while on the road, Robinson actively sought acceptance into the National Vaudeville Artists' Association (NVA), which protected vaudevillians— but only white vaudevillians—from problems of housing and traveling. His petition was declined. Robinson decided to carry a concealed revolver on the road; this weapon, combined with his gambling and his quick temper, landed him in a number of encounters with the law. Robinson was arrested in 1908, charged with assault, and eventually found guilty. However, during a retrial, which took place in part because of the outstanding written affidavits that had been furnished by men in the entertainment industry, Robinson was acquitted. Jim Haskins and N. R. Mitgang (2000) suggest persuasively that Robinson was framed. Ironically, he was also a lifetime member of various police and fraternal associations, giving them large sums from his earnings and performing at their innumerable benefits, to maintain his relationships with civic and commercial leaders. Protecting the rights of black performers was one of Robinson's lifelong concerns. In 1936, he was one of the founding members of the Negro Actors Guild of America (NAG), a welfare and benevolent organization for mainly African American performers in New York City. He was named honorary president at its inception.

After the dissolution of his partnership with Cooper in 1908, Robinson, with the help of his agent Marty Forkins, carefully cultivated a public image that would enable him to pursue a solo career in white theaters. Forkins helped to project a positive image of Robinson, focusing on his rare ability to consume quarts of ice cream and sprint backward. In time, Robinson was a highly sought-after performer in the United States and Europe. With his solo performances, he not only earned up to $6,500 a week but also broke the "two-color" rule whereby no black performer could appear onstage alone. Soon thereafter, he would become one of the first black entertainers to refuse to perform in blackface, a racist theatrical practice left over from minstrelsy. These two significant breaks with theater tradition suggest that Robinson was aware of the political dimensions of theatrical representation, a connection that he would later be accused of disavowing.

In 1932, Robinson toured with a revue, *Hot From Harlem*, which in midtour changed its name to *Goin' to Town*. According to Haskins and Mitgang, as the Depression took hold, Harlem and its excessive theatrical forms lost their cachet in the vaudeville world. Although Robinson was rarely in New York for long periods of time (a fact that strained his marriage to Fannie S. Clay, the first of his three wives), he did move to Harlem, where he maintained a residence throughout his life as well as a lifetime association with the Hoofer Club and Cotton Club there. In 1933, he was named "mayor of Harlem," an honor that was immortalized in 1935 in a motion picture, *Hooray for Love* (RKO). In the same year, Robinson rescued Harlem's "tree of hope," an elm on Seventh Avenue and 131st Street that had become a symbol for aspiring black performers. When Robinson heard of its impending removal, he invoked the power of his unofficial office and successfully pleaded his case to Mayor Fiorello La Guardia.

Robinson's major breakthrough came when he was fifty and made his Broadway debut in the black musical *Blackbirds of 1928*. His performance in *Blackbirds*

not only received rave reviews but also firmly established the "Bojangles" style. Robinson's dancing throve on contradiction: His expressive face and humorous asides seemed to challenge the intensity and intricacy of his feet. Robinson brought tap dancing "up on the toes," moving away from previous styles of buck-and-wing dancing characterized by heavy-footed stomping and animated arms. His controlled style of dancing rarely used the torso and arms. Instead, he emphasized the clarity of tone and complex rhythms produced by his wooden heels and split-soled shoes. Langston Hughes once described Robinson's percussive dancing as "among the finest sounds in jazz music" (1957, 49). In 1940, Duke Ellington composed a short work, "Bojangles," inspired by the dancer's jazziness. While Robinson's performances appeared improvised, they were in fact highly choreographed and rehearsed. His most celebrated routine was a "stair dance," in which he tapped his way up and down a flight of stairs. He introduced this number in 1918 at the Palace Theater in New York. The stair dance became Robinson's signature routine; he would perform variations of it in subsequent stage and screen appearances. He is also credited with having introduced the "Suzie-Q" dance when, in 1936, he and Cab Calloway were headliners at the opening night of the new Cotton Club. Robinson claimed that his choreography and dance style were authentic. In fact, throughout his career he had taken credit for having taught a new generation of dancers, from Fred Astaire to the Nicholas Brothers. However, many artists have argued that Robinson borrowed or outright lifted steps from lesser-known performers.

During the Depression, Robinson, a man with no formal education, had a fortune estimated in the millions, which grew even greater once he moved from stage to screen. Although Robinson was cast in the all-black film *Harlem Is Heaven* (1933), it was his appearances in three films with the child star Shirley Temple that catapulted him into national prominence. Robinson and Temple were the first interracial couple to dance onscreen. The political import of this unprecedented pairing might have been more significant were it not for the fact that within each of these films, Robinson portrayed characters in subservient, if not menial, positions. For example, in *The Little Colonel* (1933), Robinson plays a domestic, and Temple is the granddaughter of a retired southern colonel; he dances to cheer her up. By portraying such thinly veiled minstrel characters, Robinson seemed to undercut the very developments in the representation of blacks for which he had helped open the door. Black audiences and critics suspected Robinson of pandering to white audiences for fame and fortune. Robinson expressed outrage at such notions. Reportedly, he went, with gun in hand, to the offices of Harlem's newspaper *New York* Age after reading a story that went so far as to call him an "Uncle Tom."

Robinson was later cast in leading roles. With the film *Stormy Weather* (1943), he had an opportunity to control, if not rehabilitate, his image. This film traces the life of a fictional legendary performer, Bill Williamson, played by Robinson. It opens with Williamson telling a group of black children about his rise to fame and fortune, a story that bears a striking resemblance to Robinson's own, minus the legal entanglements and the stints with Temple. The film's all-star cast includes Lena Horne (as Robinson's leading lady) and Cab Calloway.

Robinson died of heart failure in 1949; his funeral was held at the 369th Regiment Armory just outside Harlem, and although many blacks were ambivalent toward Robinson, it was attended by some 32,000 mourners. Ed Sullivan had arranged the funeral; Adam Clayton Powell Sr. gave the eulogy, which was broadcast on nationwide radio. Powell spoke against the notion that Robinson was an Uncle Tom and instead focused on Robinson's transcending of color lines.

Robinson's embattled legacy has been reflected in a broad range of performance tributes and dedications. In the year of his death, a group of tap dancers formed a fraternal organization in his honor. The Copacetics took their name from a term he had coined during his days in Richmond. On 7 November 1989, President George Bush signed a resolution establishing National Tap Dance Day in the United States on the anniversary of Robinson's birth. In 1996, the Broadway musical *Bring in 'Da Noise, Bring in 'Da Funk* offered a performance history of tap dancing. This work, conceived and directed by George Wolfe, focused on the influence of dancers such as Honi Cole, Chuck Green, and Buster Slyde rather than Robinson, who was in fact lampooned in one scene as "Uncle Huck-a-Buck." Uncle Huck-a-Buck appears onstage dressed in a smoking jacket and holding a martini, then disrobes to reveal a "pick" costume beneath. While dancing up and down a flight of stairs, he sings biting lines such as "Who the hell cares if I acts the fool, when I takes a swim in my swimming pool?" Uncle Huck-a-Buck is then joined by a character called Li'l Darlin, an animated doll resembling Shirley Temple. As they dance together, Li'l Darlin asks him, "Why do I make more money than you?" In 1990, the film

Bill Robinson, photographed by Carl Van Vechten, 1933. (Library of Congress.)

Bojangles (based on Haskins and Mitgang's biography) explored Robinson's achievements and the controversies surrounding his career. Robinson was played by another legendary tap dancer, Gregory Hines. This film makes little attempt to justify Robinson's professional choices or his criminal behavior, but it does suggest that Robinson had to navigate with care—in his personal and his professional life—through radically shifting social boundaries.

Biography

Bill "Bojangles" Robinson (Luther Robinson) was born in Richmond, Virginia, on 25 May 1878. He served in the U.S. Army, c. 1898–1900. Robinson performed in various clubs and cabarets in New York City, c. 1898–1902. He married Lena Chase in 1907. He toured on the Keith and Orpheum circuit from 1902 to 1914. He married Fannie Clay in 1922. Robinson was a performer on Broadway from 1928 to 1949 and a contract player with RKO Pictures from 1930 to 1934 and with Twentieth-Century-Fox from 1934 to 1938. He married Elaine Plaines in 1944. His awards and honors included being named honorary mayor of Harlem in 1933 and honorary president of the Negro Actors Guild in 1937. Robinson died in New York 25 November 1949.

PAUL SCOLIERI

See also Blackbirds; Calloway, Cabell "Cab"; Dance; Ellington, Duke; Hughes, Langston; New York Age

Stage Credits

South Before the War, c. 1892. (Traveling show, prod. Whallen and Martel.)

Blackbirds of 1928. 1928. (Revue, prod. Lew Leslie; Alahambra Theater, New York.)

Brown Buddies. 1930. (Revue, prod. Marty Forkins; Apollo Theater, Atlantic City; Liberty Theater, New York.)

The Hot Mikado. 1939. (Revue, prod. Mike Todd; Broadhurst Theater and World's Fair, New York.)

Film Credits

Dixiana. 1930. (Dir. Luther Reed; RKO.)

Harlem Is Heaven. 1933. (Prod. Jack and Dave Goldberg; Herald.)

The Little Colonel. 1935. (Dir. David Butler; Twentieth-Century-Fox.)

Stormy Weather. 1943. (Dir. Andrew Stone; Twentieth-Century-Fox.)

Further Reading

Fletcher, Tom. *One Hundred Years of the Negro in Show Business: The Tom Fletcher Story*. New York: Burdge, 1954.

Frank, Rusty E. *Tap!—The Greatest Tap Dance Stars and Their Stories*. New York: Morrow, 1990.

Haskins, Jim, and N. R. Mitgang. *Mr. Bojangles: The Biography of Bill Robinson*. New York: Welcome Rain, 2000.

Hughes, Langston. *Famous Negro Music Makers*. New York: Dodd, Mead, 1957.

Stearns, Marshall, and Jean Stearns. *Jazz Dance: The Story of American Vernacular Dance*. New York: Da Capo, 1994.

Rochester

See Anderson, Edmund Lincoln

Rockland Palace

See Manhattan Casino

Rogers, Joel Augustus

Joel Rogers was a historian, anthropologist, publisher, journalist, lecturer, novelist, and world traveler. He was born in Negril, Jamaica, to Samuel Rogers, a schoolteacher and Methodist minister, and Emily Johnstone. After failing to get a university scholarship, he served for four years in the British royal army. He emigrated to the United States in 1906, settling in New York City and later Chicago. For nine years he studied commercial art, supporting himself as a Pullman porter. But he was barred from a career in art because of anti-African prejudice, and he returned to New York City in 1921.

Rogers became a naturalized citizen in 1917, the same year in which he published the first of several major historical works, *From "Superman" to Man*. In the early 1920s, he began to write (including weekly historical columns) for many of the major African American newspapers of his day. They included *The Messenger*, *Chicago Defender*, *Pittsburgh Courier*, and *Amsterdam News* (he would write for the latter two until his death in 1966). He wrote regularly for two publications of Marcus Garvey's Universal Negro Improvement Association (UNIA): *Negro World* and *Daily Negro Times*. He also lectured to many local chapters of the UNIA. He wrote the novels *Blood Money* in 1923, *The Golden Door* in 1927, and *She Walks in Beauty* in 1963.

In 1925, Rogers went to Paris; this was his first trip to Europe. In 1927, he traveled to Germany; in 1928, to Egypt; and in 1930, to Paris and to Ethiopia, where he covered for the *Amsterdam News* the coronation of Ras Tafari, who became Emperor Haile Selassie. Rogers returned to Ethiopia in 1935–1936 to cover the Italian-Ethiopian war for the *Pittsburgh Courier*, becoming the first African American to serve as a war correspondent. While he retained his residence in Harlem, Rogers made Paris his international base of operations, traveling from there to do research in libraries, museums, churches, art galleries, and antiquarian bookstores in Europe and Africa. In 1930, Rogers addressed the International Congress of Anthropology, which was held in Paris and was opened by the president of France. He was a member of the Société d'Anthropologie in Paris, the American Geographical Society, the American Association for the Advancement of Science, and the Academy of Political Science. Because of Rogers's African heritage, his lack of an advanced degree, the nature of his research findings, and the persistence of entrenched white supremacist propaganda in the United States, American publishers rejected his work, forcing him to be his own publisher. His scholarship was viewed as controversial, and many of his conclusions were dismissed as erroneous, although after his death they were confirmed by scholars who did have university degrees.

In his lifetime Rogers devoted some fifty years to research and publication. He was one of the most prolific writers of his time; became fluent in German, French, Portuguese, and Spanish; and conducted exhaustive research in primary and secondary documents and historical artifacts in those languages in Africa, Europe, and the United States. His work combined history and anthropology, exploring the origins of the human race, the role of Africans in world history, and the genetic mixing of Africans and Europeans in the historical experience. He rejected the doctrine of African inferiority, and he sought to establish that success was not an exclusively European preserve and that enslavement was not an inherently African fate or condition.

Biography

Joel Augustus Rogers was born in Negril, Jamaica, 6 September 1880. He served for four years in the British royal army. He emigrated to the United States in 1906 and was naturalized in 1917. He published his first major historical work, *From "Superman" to Man*, in 1917. In the early 1920s, he wrote for African American newspapers including *The Messenger*, *Chicago Defender*, *Pittsburgh Courier*, *Amsterdam News*, *Negro World*, and *Daily Negro Times*. He traveled to Paris, 1925; Germany, 1927; Egypt, 1928; and Paris and Ethiopia, 1930. Also in 1930, he addressed the International Congress of Anthropology in Paris and covered the coronation of Emperor Haile Selassie of Ethiopia for the *Amsterdam News*. In 1935–1936, he covered the

Italian-Ethiopian war for the *Pittsburgh Courier*. He was a member of the Société d'Anthropologie in Paris, the American Geographical Society, the American Association for the Advancement of Science, and the Academy of Political Science. Rogers died in New York City, 26 March 1966.

AHATI N. N. TOURE

See also Amsterdam News; Chicago Defender; Messenger, The; Negro World; Pittsburgh Courier

Selected Works

From "Superman" to Man. 1917. (Reprints, 1924, 1941, 1968, 1972, 1990.)

As Nature Leads: An Informal Discussion of the Reason Why Negro and Caucasian Are Mixing in Spite of Opposition. 1919.

The Maroons of the West Indies and South America. 1921.

Blood Money. 1923.

The Golden Door. 1927.

The Real Facts About Ethiopia. 1932. (Reprint, 1982.)

100 Amazing Facts About the Negro. 1934. (Rev. eds., 1957, 1963, 1995.)

World's Greatest Men and Women of African Descent. 1935.

Sex and Race: Negro-Caucasian Mixing in All Ages and All Lands, Vols. 1–3. 1940–1944.

World's Great Men of Color, Vols. 1, 2. 1946–1947. (Rev. eds., 1972, 1996.)

Nature Knows No Color-Line: Research Into the Negro Ancestry in the White Race. 1952.

Africa's Gift to America: The Afro-American in the Making and Saving of the United States. 1959. (Rev. ed. 1961; reprint, 1997.)

She Walks in Beauty. 1963.

Further Reading

Clarke, John Henrik. "Africa and the American Negro Press." *Journal of Negro Education*, 30(1), Winter 1961.

"Historical News." *Journal of Negro History*, 51(3), July 1966.

Hutchinson, George. "Mediating 'Race' and 'Nation': The Cultural Politics of *The Messenger*." *African American Review*, 28(4), Winter 1994.

Logan, Rayford W., and Michael R. Winston, eds. *Dictionary of American Negro Biography*. New York: Norton, 1982.

Rogers, Helga M. "Biographical Sketch." In *100 Amazing Facts About the Negro With Complete Proof*. St. Petersburg, Fla.: Author, 1995.

Rogers, J. A. "How and Why This Book Was Written." In *World's Great Men of Color*, Vol. 1. New York: Macmillan, 1972.

Rooney, Terrie M., and Jennifer Gariepy, eds. *Contemporary Authors*, Vol. 153. Detroit, Mich.: Gale Research, 1997.

Salzman, Jack, David Lionel Smith, and Cornel West, eds. *Encyclopedia of African-American Culture and History*, Vol. 4. New York: Simon & Schuster Macmillan, 1996.

Thorpe, Earl E. *Black Historians: A Critique*. New York: Morrow, 1971.

Turner, W. Burghardt. "J. A. Rogers: Portrait of an Afro-American Historian." *Black Scholar*, 6(5), January–February 1975.

Roseland Ballroom

The Roseland Ballroom, a dance hall at Broadway and Fifty-first Street, was a thriving venue for jazz from the 1920s through the mid-1950s. Roseland opened in 1908. Following a hiatus during World War I and the great influenza pandemic of 1918–1919, it reopened, with great fanfare, in 1919. Like other midtown halls, Roseland catered exclusively to a white clientele for many years. It had a regular annual season beginning in September and ending in May. During the summer months, the leading resident bands would go off on tour, leaving Roseland to summer replacements.

Roseland offered ragtime and jazz for dancing beginning in 1919. Until the mid-1920s, its dance music was dominated by ensembles led by the white band-leader Sam Lanin. Some of these ensembles, such as Ladd's Black Aces, featured early jazz soloists such as the cornetist Phil Napoleon and the pianist Jimmie Durante. Another white band playing a combination of "sweet" and "hot" jazz at Roseland in this period was led by Mal Hallett. The first African American band to have a residency at Roseland was led by Armand J. Piron (1888–1943), a violinist, songwriter, and publisher from New Orleans; Piron opened at Roseland in 1924. The most important residency by a black jazz band at Roseland during the Harlem Renaissance was that of the Fletcher Henderson Orchestra. Henderson's band moved into Roseland on 8 September 1924 and played there regularly for the next fifteen years. During these years the band made numerous recordings featuring innovative arrangements by Don Redman, Benny Carter, and Henderson himself. The band's superb roster of soloists included Louis Armstrong from September 1924 to November 1925, Buster Bailey (clarinet) from 1924 to 1928, and Coleman Hawkins (tenor saxophone) off and on for over a decade.

By the autumn of 1926, Roseland was presenting a lavish mixture of dance music played by both black and white bands, sometimes pitting them against each other in direct competition. Lanin had departed, but there was a band led by his former sideman "Miff" Mole, a fine trombonist. The highly disciplined band of Jean Goldkette battled Fletcher Henderson's band one night during this season, and by all accounts vanquished it. Goldkette featured innovative arrangements by Bill Challis, and his band included Steve Brown (the finest bass player of the era) and the cornetist Bix Beiderbecke (considered the most exciting brass soloist to hit New York since Louis Armstrong). Another band at Roseland in the 1926–1927 season was led by the young Thomas "Fats" Waller, who was already a leading stride pianist in Harlem. In the autumn of 1928, another important big band, McKinney's Cotton Pickers, arrived, featuring the arrangements and reed work of Don Redman. A year later, the peerless drummer Chick Webb brought his orchestra to Roseland; although these musicians were usually in residence at the Savoy in Harlem, they returned to Roseland in the early 1930s. Roseland had good acoustics, and some bands actually chose to record there; among these were Glen Gray and his Casa Loma Orchestra in 1929. Even in the summer months the hall featured some of the best jazz orchestras in the country. In 1929, these included an excellent New Orleans combo led by the pianist Luis Russell. Throughout the 1930s numerous important big bands continued to play frequently at Roseland. Count Basie first opened there in December 1936; his band was enormously popular with dancers, and among its numbers of the period, one, "Roseland Shuffle," was a tribute to the ballroom. The orchestras of Ella Fitzgerald, Earl "Fatha" Hines, and Claude Hopkins were also featured at Roseland.

After World War II, Roseland became a center for Latin dancing in New York, bringing throngs to dance the newly fashionable cha-cha and mambo. In 1956, the original Roseland was demolished, and it was replaced by a facility nearby on Fifty-second Street (where it still is as of this writing). It continued to cater to Latin dancers, and also to disco dancers in the 1970s, but thereafter it increasingly presented rock and pop shows, often with little or no dancing or audience participation.

ELLIOTT S. HURWITT

See also Armstrong, Louis; Henderson, Fletcher; Savoy Ballroom; Waller, Thomas "Fats"

Further Reading

Charters, Samuel B., and Leonard Kunstadt. *Jazz: A History of the New York Scene*. New York: Da Capo, 1981. (Originally published 1962.)

Chilton, John. *Who's Who of Jazz: Storyville to Swing Street*. Philadelphia, Pa: Chilton, 1972.

Rosenwald Fellowships

Established in 1917 by the president of Sears, Roebuck and Company and incorporated in 1928, the Julius Rosenwald Fund concentrated on four philanthropic areas: education, race relations, health, and fellowships. In 1911, Julius Rosenwald, the son of German Jewish immigrants, met Booker T. Washington in Chicago and was favorably impressed with his self-help philosophy. Rosenwald was also affected by his subsequent trips to the South and his personal visits to the Tuskegee Institute. As a result, he decided to concentrate his philanthropic activities primarily on assisting African Americans.

The trustees of the Rosenwald Fund were initially concerned with building rural schools for blacks and helped in the construction of almost 5,000 public schoolhouses until the program ended in 1932. After investing much money in the creation of graduate-level university centers in Atlanta, Nashville, New Orleans, and Washington, D.C., the trustees felt that the development pace was slow and a scholarship fund was also vitally needed for the development of graduate training for African Americans. In 1928, the Rosenwald Fellowship program was established to financially assist American blacks (and later some white southerners) to pursue graduate and professional education at northern and western American universities (southern universities were deemed inadequate at the time) and also a few foreign institutions.

The original five-member fellowship committee consisted of Will Alexander, a white southerner who later served as the head of the Farm Security Administration

Mr. and Mrs. Julius Rosenwald, 1926. (Library of Congress.)

under Franklin D. Roosevelt; Charles S. Johnson, who became the first African American president of Fisk University; Henry Moe, who was born in Minnesota, was a Rhodes scholar, and later became the director of the John Simon Guggenheim Memorial Fellowship Program; and Edwin Rogers Embree, who was the president of the fund's board of trustees and was the grandson of a prominent abolitionist. These committee members helped shape the direction and philosophy of the fellowship program, which evidently became gradually more integrationist.

From 1928 through 1936, the fellowships mostly provided grants-in-aid for advanced training for nurses, social workers, and physicians. After 1932, the awards evolved from grants-in-aid to a more formal scholarship program. The fellowship awards were largely given to individuals with undergraduate or master's degrees in medicine or nursing, to those in vocational and industrial fields, and also to librarians and teachers in music and the fine arts. The awards, however, were not restricted to any specific subject field or activity. The fund recognized the importance of supporting black artists and writers and noted that "achievement in the arts gains recognition for the individual concerned and for the Negro race as a whole." After the economic downturn in the early 1930s, the trustees acknowledged the importance of concentrating their resources on individuals who might in the future "exert leadership in Negro life."

The fellowships were open to both men and women between the ages of twenty-four and thirty-five, although some older candidates were accepted. Competition was keen, and more than 800 applications were received in just one year. During the twenty-year fellowship program, the fund dispensed almost $2 million; a total of 1,537 fellowships were awarded, and 999 of the recipients were black. The Rosenwald Fund was nearly financially depleted by 1945 and officially ceased operations in 1948.

Some of the most distinguished African Americans of the twentieth century were recipients. They include the scientist and surgeon Charles R. Drew, the psychologist Kenneth Clark, the scholar W. E. B. Du Bois, the sociologist Clair St. Drake, the college president Horace Mann Bond, the chemist Percy L. Julian, and the United Nations official Ralph Bunche. The largest group of fellows was in literature and the fine and performing arts. These luminaries included Langston Hughes, Claude McKay, Countee Cullen, Arna Bontemps, Marian Anderson, Katherine Dunham, James Baldwin, Ralph Ellison, and Paul Robeson.

DONALD ALTSCHILLER

See also Johnson, Charles Spurgeon; Philanthropy and Philanthropic Organizations; *specific fellowship recipients*

Further Reading

Beilke, Jayne R. "The Changing Emphasis of the Rosenwald Fellowship Program, 1928–1948." *Journal of Negro Education*, 66(1), Winter 1997.

Embree, Edwin R., and Julia Waxman. *Investment in People: The Story of the Julius Rosenwald Fund*. New York: Harper, 1949.

Werner, Morris. *Julius Rosenwald: The Life of a Practical Humanitarian*. New York: Harper, 1939.

Runnin' Wild

Runnin' Wild is mostly remembered today as the show that started a worldwide craze for the Charleston, a

Runnin' Wild, dance number. (Billy Rose Theatre Collection, New York Public Library, New York City. © The New York Public Library/Art Resource, N.Y. Photo: White Studio, anonymous.)

dance indelibly associated with the flappers, the fashionable modern girls of the 1920s. *Runnin' Wild* was a direct successor to *Shuffle Along* and was one of the most successful black shows of the era.

Shuffle Along was still running successfully in 1923, but tension among the principals led the writers and comedians Flournoy Miller and Aubrey Lyles to break away and create their own new show. They were encouraged and financed by George White—famous for *The George White Scandals*—who was attracted by the idea of a "George White Black Scandals." The initial idea was to use the name *Shuffle Along* again, but Noble Sissle and Eubie Blake, the lyricist and composer, respectively, of *Shuffle Along*, blocked this attempt through the courts. The alternative title, *Runnin' Wild*, was taken from a song that was currently popular but was not actually featured in the show (much later, it would be performed memorably by Marilyn Monroe in the movie *Some Like It Hot*).

The fairly thin libretto, in two acts with five scenes, featured Miller and Lyles as their by now traditional "Jimtown" characters, Steve Jenkins and Sam Peck, from *Shuffle Along*. Jenkins and Peck have been forced to leave Jimtown because their insurance scam has been exposed. Their subsequent travels in search of food and warmth allow ample scope for their characteristic comedy routines, combining knockabout slapstick with clever wordplay. (For instance, Peck's financial misfortunes are due to "de ducks"—he "deducks" $10 for this and $10 for that.)

Added to the comedy was a dynamic dancing chorus and a rich selection of original tunes by the team of James P. Johnson (composer) and Cecil Mack (also known as R. C. McPherson, lyricist). Johnson was one of the great figures of jazz and stride piano playing. Mack was already a major figure in black music through his association with Bert Williams and George Walker, having written the lyrics for Aida Overton Walker's hit "That's Why They Call Me Shine." Also contributing musically was the legendary Will Marion Cook (orchestrations), with some assistance from the future dean of black classical composers, William Grant Still. The choreography was by Elida Webb, who later worked with Ziegfeld's Follies and the Cotton Club.

The cast included several stars poached from *Shuffle Along*, including the singers Adelaide Hall and Ina Duncan, the dancer Tommy Woods, and Mattie Wilkes, widow of the great Ernest Hogan. A very young Elisabeth Welch made her debut singing the Charleston song, titled "Charston" in the show. Other notable cast members included Revella Hughes and Katherine Yarborough. The show started with an out-of-town tryout at the Howard Theater in Washington, D.C., on 25 August 1923. It received enthusiastic reviews, and *Variety* reported that the audiences were three-quarters white.

Initially, the Charleston number did not attract much attention. "Old Fashioned Love" was the popular favorite. However, by the time the show reached New York via Boston, the exuberant dancing, with hand clapping and foot patting by the chorus, was making audiences sit up and take notice. The origins of the Charleston stretched back to the early days of slavery, and Maude Russell had danced it onstage the previous year in another show, *Liza*, to a different tune, but it had aroused little interest. This time, however, history was about to be made.

Runnin' Wild opened in New York at the Colonial Theater on 29 October 1923. It ran for a very profitable twenty-seven weeks and 213 performances. The mainstream critical response was highly favorable, though there were dissenting notes from some of the black intelligentsia, such as W. E. B. Du Bois, Alain Locke, Theophilus Lewis, and their white ally Carl Van Vechten. They felt there was still too much stereotyped material, such as the traditional scene of a Negro scared by a ghost, even though the critic for the *New York Times* detected less reliance on stereotypes than usual. Other black intellectuals like James Weldon Johnson and

Langston Hughes, who had an affinity with the emerging world of jazz, strongly endorsed the show.

After Broadway, *Runnin' Wild* continued to draw large audiences on the road. The major competition came from Lew Leslie and Florence Mills' show *Dixie to Broadway*; and from Sissle and Blake's ambitious but rather less successful response, *Chocolate Dandies*. Although *Runnin' Wild* had by far the longest Broadway run of the three, only *Dixie to Broadway* at the Broadhurst could claim to have been on Broadway proper. The Colonial, at Broadway and Sixty-second Street, was almost as far uptown from mainstream Broadway as *Shuffle Along* had been. On the other hand, *Runnin' Wild* and *Chocolate Dandies* not only had black casts but also had a libretto and music by black writers.

By August 1924, a full year after its debut in Washington, D.C., *Runnin' Wild* was still playing in Chicago, in opposition to *Dixie to Broadway*, both drawing full houses. It continued to play on the road and around New York for another two years, and a traveling company took it to London in 1928.

The success of *Runnin' Wild* was widely taken as evidence that the commercial niche opened up by *Shuffle Along* could still be successfully exploited. This encouraged a spate of black shows that continued throughout the 1920s with varying degrees of success. However, the relative failure of the more ambitious *Chocolate Dandies* suggested that commercial success was proportionate to the degree to which a formulaic approach was maintained. Van Vechten deplored this so vehemently that he wrote a "Prescription for the Negro Theatre," offering suggestions on how to break the mold and tap into what he considered the true genius of black talent.

In the overall context of the Harlem Renaissance, *Runnin' Wild* contributed to the image of happy-go-lucky blacks, with a talent for singing, dancing, and celebrating, that made Harlem a magnet for slumming whites. However, in a deeper sense, along with the other black shows of the period, it helped to develop a growing liaison between black entertainers and jazz musicians. Apart from composers like James P. Johnson, Eubie Blake, and Thomas "Fats" Waller, musicians such as Louis Armstrong, Duke Ellington, and Fletcher Henderson found a niche supporting the entertainers. This became the basis of a jazz-based popular culture that the United States would export to the world for decades to come. It has few more potent symbols than the Charleston.

BILL EGAN

See also Chocolate Dandies; Cook, Will Marion; Du Bois, W. E. B.; Hall, Adelaide; Hughes, Langston; Johnson, James P.; Johnson, James Weldon; Lewis, Theophilus; Liza; Locke, Alain; Lyles, Aubrey; Mack, Cecil; Miller, Flournoy; Musical Theater; Shuffle Along; Still, William Grant; Van Vechten, Carl

Further Reading

Bordman, Gerald. *American Musical Theatre: A Chronicle.* New York: Oxford University Press, 1978, p. 382.

Brown, Scott E. *James P. Johnson: A Case of Mistaken Identity.* Metuchen, N.J.: Scarecrow, 1986.

Graziano, John. "Black Musical Theater and the Harlem Renaissance Movement." In *Black Music in the Harlem Renaissance*, ed. Samuel A. Floyd Jr. Knoxville: University of Tennessee Press, 1993, ch. 6.

Johnson, James Weldon. *Black Manhattan*. New York: Knopf, 1939, ch. 16. (Reprint, New York: Da Capo, 1991.)

Southern, Eileen. *The Music of Black Americans: A History.* New York and London: Norton, 1971, p. 435. (See also 3rd ed., 1997.)

Van Vechten, Carl. "Prescription for the Negro Theatre." *Vanity Fair*, October 1925.

Woll, Allen. *Black Musical Theatre: From Coontown to Dreamgirls*. New York: Da Capo, 1991, ch. 6.

Saint Louis Blues

Saint Louis Blues (1929), a two-reel short written by William C. Handy and Kenneth W. Adams, was one of the first talking films with an all-black cast. It featured several influential actors and musicians of the Harlem Renaissance and contains the only existing footage of the singer Bessie Smith. The plot of the film, which Handy described as "a serious picture of Negro life," was loosely based on his popular hit song "Saint Louis Blues" (1914). Although the film was chiefly intended to showcase Smith's dazzling performance of the classic title song, *Saint Louis Blues* nevertheless represents a significant event in the history of African American cinema.

At Handy's recommendation, the film's white director, Dudley Murphy, cast as the female lead Bessie Smith, then thirty-five years old, who was a vaudeville blues singer and a recording star with Columbia. In 1925, she had recorded the definitive version of "Saint Louis Blues" at Columbia's studios in New York, accompanied by Louis Armstrong on cornet. The cast of the film also featured the dancer Jimmy Mordecai and the actress Isabel Washington. John Rosamond Johnson helped Handy arrange the choral music and conducted the forty-two-member Hall Johnson Choir that accompanied Smith in the picture. The stride pianist James P. Johnson and several former members of the Fletcher Henderson Orchestra performed onscreen in the film's jazz band.

Saint Louis Blues was produced by RCA Phototone and was shot on a small budget in June 1929 at Gramercy Studio in Astoria, Long Island. The seventeen-minute film was released later that year as a two-reel short to be shown before feature attractions, and it was screened in black theaters until 1932. *Variety*, in its review of *Saint Louis Blues*, described the film as "pungent with tenseness and action and replete with Aframerican local and other color."

The sparse plot, set in Memphis, centers on a long-suffering woman named Bessie (played by Smith), whose handsome, crap-shooting lover, Jimmy (Mordecai), physically abuses her and uses her for her money. Although Bessie supports him financially, Jimmy becomes romantically involved with another woman (Washington). A violent confrontation ensues in which Bessie attacks this woman after catching Jimmy and her together in the hotel room Bessie rents. Jimmy then batters and deserts Bessie despite her tearful pleadings. In the film's final scene, Bessie drowns her sorrows in bootleg liquor in a smoky saloon on Beale Street, and there, accompanied by the choir and jazz band, moans "Saint Louis Blues" for an appreciative crowd of patrons. Jimmy enters, embraces Bessie, and surreptitiously steals a roll of bills Bessie has tucked in her garter as they dance together. The film concludes with Bessie sinking into a deep depression after Jimmy abandons her permanently.

Since its release, *Saint Louis Blues* has met with mixed reviews by film historians and scholars of blues, although most have praised Smith's powerful screen presence and her electrifying performance of "Saint Louis Blues." Thomas Cripps (1977) considered the picture "the finest film of Negro life up to that time," but Donald Bogle (1973) asserted that the film

Scene from *Saint Louis Blues*, 1929. (Kisch/Photofest.)

"was marred by its white director's overstatement." Angela Davis (1998) has criticized the film not only because it "incorporates an overabundance of racist and sexist stereotypes," but also because it "flagrantly disregards the spirit of women's blues by leaving the victimized woman with no recourse." Despite such criticisms, *Saint Louis Blues* remains an important example of African American filmmaking and one that highlights the musical and acting talents of a number of prominent entertainers of the Harlem Renaissance.

PATRICK HUBER

See also Armstrong, Louis; Blues; Blues: Women Performers; Handy, W. C.; Henderson, Fletcher; Johnson, Hall; Johnson, James P.; Johnson, John Rosamond; Smith, Bessie; Washington, Isabel

Further Reading

Albertson, Chris. *Bessie*. New York: Stein & Day, 1972

Bogle, Donald. *Toms, Coons, Mulattoes, Mammies, and Bucks: An Interpretive History of Blacks in American Films*. New York: Viking, 1973.

Cripps, Thomas. *Slow Fade to Black: The Negro in American Film, 1900–1942*. New York: Oxford University Press, 1977.

Davis, Angela Y. *Blues Legacies and Black Feminism: Gertrude "Ma" Rainey, Bessie Smith, and Billie Holiday*. New York: Pantheon, 1998.

Handy, W. C. *Father of the Blues: An Autobiography*, ed. Arna Bontemps, foreword Abbe Niles. New York: Macmillan, 1941.

Saint Mark's Methodist Episcopal Church

Saint Mark's Methodist Episcopal Church was organized in June 1871 by Rev. William F. Butler. It was initially affiliated with the African Methodist Episcopal Zion (AMEZ) church, but Butler sought credentials through the Methodist Episcopal Church. He proposed the idea of a new church to Bishop Gilbert Haven of the Methodist Episcopal Church. This effort bridged the gap between black and white Methodist parishioners. There were a number of divisions within the Methodist faith that resulted in the formation of three African American denominations: African Methodist Episcopal (AME), AMEZ, and CME groups. White Methodists were divided into two groups: ME South and ME north. Saint Mark's is credited with having inaugurated one of the earliest Methodist churches for people of color.

Butler served as pastor for the newly formed church, which was originally located in Washington Hall on Broadway between Thirty-seventh and Thirty-eighth streets. Saint Mark's strove to meet the needs of African American Christians. In January 1873, a church was bought for $50,000, and the congregation of Saint Mark's moved into this permanent building, at 65 West Thirty-fifth Street between Fifth and Sixth avenues. During a period of expansion between 1873 and 1889, Saint Mark's had a number of ministers; in 1875, the leadership of William Butler ended, and in 1887 the congregation experienced another move.

In 1889, under the pastorate of Rev. Dr. Henry A. Monroe, Saint Mark's paid off its indebtedness and sought another church building. A building was found on Fifty-third Street and was obtained through an equitable exchange between Saint Mark's and the New York City Mission and Church Extension Society, leaving the church debt-free. In 1896, the church was incorporated under the direction of a board of trustees.

The twenty-six-year tenure of the eighth pastor, Rev. Dr. William H. Brooks, ushered in a period of significant change. Saint Mark's acquired additional properties: a church house, a parsonage, and a brick dwelling in New Rochelle, New York. Its investments in property provided seed capital that was used to expand the ministry. Eventually, all auxiliary church property was sold, netting a sum of $215,000. In November 1920, Saint Mark's bought a site on Edgecombe and Saint Nicholas avenues between 137th and 138th streets for $43,000. Also, Brooks contributed to the establishment of several other churches in Brooklyn, Manhattan, and Jamaica.

In 1923, Brooks retired from the full-time ministry and was succeeded by Rev. Dr. John W. Robinson. The cornerstone for the church at the new site was laid on 24 September 1924, during Robinson's pastorate. During the Depression, this new facility was a challenge for Saint Mark's, because it had required the congregation to carry a mortgage. However, the church remained and offered Harlem secular as well as religious leadership.

IDA JONES

See also Religion; Religious Organizations

Further Reading

Centennial Anniversary, 1871–1971 Saint Mark's United Methodist Church, New York City. New York, c. 1971.

Hagood, Lewis Marshall. *The Colored Man in the Methodist Episcopal Church.* Westport, Conn.: Negro Universities Press, 1970.

Hickman, Cynthia. *Harlem Churches.* New York: Dunbar, 2001.

Hodges, George W. *Touchstones of Methodism.* New York: Compact-Reflector, 1947.

Kellner, Bruce, ed. *The Harlem Renaissance: A Historical Dictionary for the Era.* New York: Methuen, 1984.

Lewis, David Levering. *When Harlem Was in Vogue.* New York, Penguin, 1997.

Lincoln, C. Eric, and Lawrence H. Maymiya, eds. *The Black Church in the African American Experience.* Durham, N.C.: Duke University Press, 1990.

Taylor, Clarence. *The Black Churches of Brooklyn.* New York: Columbia University Press, 1994.

Woodson, Carter G. *The History of the Negro Church.* Washington, D.C.: Associated Publishers, 1945.

Saint Philip's Protestant Episcopal Church

The roots of Saint Philip's go back as far as Trinity parish, which was formally organized in 1697; at that time, African Americans attended services at Trinity church. Around 1810, African Americans in Trinity parish had grown in number and often met separately in fellowship with one another. According to church records, the "colored" group grew so large that they found a room on Williams Street for their meetings, and then found a colored public school for

Saint Philip's Protestant Episcopal Church, 1920s. (Schomburg Center for Research in Black Culture, New York Public Library.)

that purpose. In 1812, Peter Williams served as lay reader for this growing congregation of African American Episcopalians. Williams, whose parents were slaves, became the first rector of Saint Philip's church.

Before being officially recognized by the Episcopal denomination in 1818, this group of African American Christians worshiped in facilities that they rented. There were then only forty parishes in New York State, nine of which were in New York City; Saint Philip's became the tenth parish in the city, and one of the first congregations to have a majority of African Americans. At this point a church historian noted that "our congregation is now in possession of the land. The next step is to build a church." Efforts to build were encouraged through donations and bequests from numerous sources, and a cornerstone was laid on 6 August 1818. By the end of the nineteenth century, Saint Philip's had experienced tremendous growth but also significant struggles; it had served as a barracks during the draft riots of 1863, as well as as a refuge for those seeking human and religious freedom.

There had been numerous ministerial appointments to Saint Philip's; however, the tenure of Rev. Hutchens Chew Bishop from roughly 1886 to 1923 was an especially remarkable period of growth and movement. Under his leadership, Saint Philip's acquired church property on 133rd and 134th streets in Harlem, and in 1910, he oversaw the construction of a new church and parish house. Bishop broadened the physical presence of Saint Philip's with the purchase of 207–219 West 133rd Street, as well as 117 West 137th Street. Through these properties, the church was able to offer the community camping and social services for children, housing for the elderly, and rental units. Moreover, the parish grew to more than 3,000 members. During this period of revitalization, Saint Philip's began to play an active role in Harlem not only as a church but as an institution.

As of this writing, Saint Philip's church was still an active congregation and was raising funds to restore and preserve its buildings and historical materials. The records of Saint Philip's are located in the manuscript division at the Schomburg Center.

IDA JONES

See also Religion; Religious Organizations; Schomburg, Arthur A.

Further Reading

The Anniversary Book of Saint Philip's Church, New York, 1943: Published in Connection With the 125th Anniversary of the Founding of the Parish. New York, 1943.

Hewitt, John H., Jr. *Protest and Progress: New York's First Black Episcopal Church Fights Racism.* New York: Garland, 2000.

Hickman, Cynthia. *Harlem Churches.* New York: Dunbar, 2001.

Lewis, David Levering. *When Harlem Was in Vogue.* New York, Penguin, 1997.

Lincoln, C. Eric, and Lawrence H. Maymiya, eds. *The Black Church in the African American Experience.* Durham, N.C.: Duke University Press, 1990.

Reaching Out: An Epic of the People of Saint Philip's Church. Tappan, N.Y.: Custombook, c. 1986.

Taylor, Clarence. *The Black Churches of Brooklyn.* New York: Columbia University Press, 1994.

Townsend, Craig Devine. *An Inexpedient Time: Race and Religion Among New York City Episcopalians, 1809–1853.* New York, 1998.

Woodson, Carter G. *The History of the Negro Church.* Washington, D.C.: Associated Publishers, 1945.

Salons

Most creative people need to share their work—to have others listen to it, critique it, and support it—and many creative artists found an audience in the literary salons of the Harlem Renaissance. Of course, not all the artists of the renaissance were actually in Harlem; many lived and worked elsewhere, particularly in Philadelphia, Chicago, Cleveland, Eatonville, Jamaica, and Washington, D.C.

A "salon" was not a fixed meeting place but a social event, usually held in someone's home. Its primary purpose was to provide a forum for introducing works in progress, presenting completed works, and exchanging ideas and criticism. African American artists and intellectuals came together to encourage each other, share and develop their work, and immerse themselves in black culture, philosophy, and politics. The only requirement for admission to a literary salon was talent, although it was definitely helpful to have a friend who knew the host or hostess.

A crucial element of the salon was the host or, more usually, the hostess. Although a few men did occasionally hold salons, a salon was typically organized by and held in the home of a creative woman. Thus African American hostesses were a lively part of the literary renaissance. They tended to be beautiful, well dressed, and gracious, but, more important, they provided a wonderful, exciting social incubator for the nurturing of writers, artists, politicians, and intellectuals. Although unlike in many ways, they had some common traits. For the most part, they were dynamic, socioeconomically middle to upper class, well educated, artistic in their own right, and generous. They provided elaborate food and drinks. Nearly all possessed a keen sense of humor, were socially outgoing, had a wonderful wit, and created a warm, welcoming climate. They opened their doors wide to friends, who usually brought more friends, often new artists who needed an introduction into literary society. The hallmarks of a salon were abundant laughter, great conversation, and wonderful times.

The hosts and hostesses of salons shared an ardent belief in the importance of the creative artist. They, and other participants in the salons, became champions of the younger artists. For many new artists the salons were responsible for the first publication of their works. If members of a salon did not personally promote an artist's work, they provided a network through which the artist could meet others who would be able to publish works, provide connections to publishers, and in general be of assistance. Each host or hostess enjoyed the friendship of the artists and was instrumental, to a certain extent, in shaping their work.

Hostesses, in particular, also provided a civilizing influence for a somewhat ideologically polarized group. During the renaissance, the direction art would take was challenged by almost every creative artist, and no attempt was made to formulate a common creed. But at a salon, all viewpoints and ideologies were accepted as having some validity, then analyzed and criticized. Although there was never a consensus, some agreement might be reached about style, goals, and artistic attitudes. Arnold Rampersad (in Locke 1970) has said that "something approaching a cultural revolution . . . was taking place among blacks in New York, as well as elsewhere in the United States and perhaps around the world." Revolutions do not occur in isolation; and in this regard, an atmosphere of safety usually pervaded the literary salons, so that participants felt free to discuss their work and their ideas without restraint, sharing their artistic concepts, their political ideology, and their personal convictions. The topics discussed were very diverse: socialism; folklore; vernacular traditions in African American literature; Jean Toomer's attempt to convert black intellectuals to the Gurdjieff system for the "harmonious development of man"; Zora Neale Hurston's refusal to be a member of the "sobbing school of Negrohood."

Georgia Douglas Johnson (1880–1966) was not only a significant and prolific African American writer but also the hostess of an important, intense, and enduring literary salon in her home at 1461 S Street NW, in Washington, D.C. Johnson published four volumes of poetry, a number of plays during the 1920s, short stories, and a weekly newspaper column, "Homely Philosophy." Several of her works have been lost—discarded after her death by family members who did not recognize their value—and these lost works include a book-length manuscript about her salon.

Johnson's weekly salons were important to her personally as well as for creative reasons. Johnson (who was a younger cousin of the writer Dorothy West) was a natural hostess, and her salon provided her with her own creative culture. She began occasionally opening her door to artists as early as 1920, and she and her husband, the attorney Henry Lincoln "Link" Johnson, enjoyed these social events. However, the weekly sessions began after his death in 1925: For more than ten years Georgia Johnson made her home available to the "Saturday Nighters"; the salons continued, infrequently, from 1935 until about 1942. The first public mention of Johnson's salon was made in October 1926 in Gwendolyn Bennett's column for *The Crisis* magazine. The regular attendees included Langston Hughes, Anne Spencer, Alain Locke, Jessie Redmon Fauset, Angelina Weld Grimké, William

Stanley Braithwaite, W. E. B. Du Bois, Alice Dunbar Nelson, Richard Bruce Nugent, Marieta Bonner, Lewis Alexander, May Miller, Willis Richardson, E. C. Williams, Gwendolyn Bennett, Clarissa Scott Delany, Zora Neale Hurston, and Jean Toomer (who is said to have begun the salons by asking Johnson to be the hostess for a weekly conversation among Washingtonian writers). It is also said that when Toomer read his "The First American" at Johnson's salon, someone present remarked, "You're white"; Toomer agreed and, in effect, left his life as an African American at that time. (Nevertheless, Toomer still attended black literary salons.)

Carrie Williams Clifford (1862–1934) also opened her home in Washington as a literary salon, though it was somewhat overshadowed by Johnson's. In a preface to her work *The Widening Light*, Clifford claimed that "the theme of the group here presented—the uplift of humanity—is the loftiest that can animate the heart and pen of man." Among those who gathered at Clifford's home for literary and political discussions were black intellectuals from Howard University and elsewhere in Washington who were vital in shaping the African American cultural and political heritage, like Mary Church Terrell, W. E. B. Du Bois, Alain Locke, Charles Chesnutt, and Georgia Johnson herself. Clifford was a political activist as well as a writer and helped organize the National Association for the Advancement of Colored People (NAACP) in 1910.

In Harlem, a notable salon, frequented by writers, artists, and intellectuals (including Toomer), was that of Ethel Ray Nance and her roommate Regina Anderson, a librarian, in 1924 and 1925. Anderson also helped to promote writing, by reviewing new books and preparing and distributing digests. A second salon in New York was held by Dorothy Peterson, a teacher, at her father's home. A third was held by Jessie Redmon Fauset, who was a novelist, a journalist, and the editor of the literary section of *The Crisis*; she opened her home on Sunday afternoons as a literary salon for Harlemite writers, artists, and intellectuals. The intellectual discussions at Fauset's salon were usually in French. Fauset was responsible for getting the work of many of the artists, including Langston Hughes, first published.

A'Lelia Walker, the beautiful, statuesque daughter of Madame C. J. Walker (1867–1919), held the most famous salon in New York. She had inherited her mother's wealth and businesses, and she opened her double town house at 108–110 West 136th Street in Harlem hundreds of times during the 1920s. She also held lavish parties at her cream-colored mansion on the Hudson, Villa Lewaro. Unlike the other hostesses, A'Lelia Walker was not herself a writer, had little interest in intellectual discussions, and rarely read books, although she had elegant bookcases filled with the writings of African Americans. She called her town house "Dark Tower" after Countee Cullen's column in *Opportunity*; and on the walls, poems by Cullen and Langston Hughes's "The Weary Blues" were letttered. Black and white patrons, artists, and publishers met regularly at Walker's town house, and a great deal of networking went on there, although some artists, like Richard Bruce Nugent, avoided this salon. Walker could be prankish regarding cultural stereotypes. Once, her white guests were served pigs' feet, chitterlings, and bathtub gin while the African Americans were served caviar, pheasant, and champagne.

Networking was also important at the salons of white patrons. Carl Van Vechten helped to organize the salon of Mabel Dodge Luhan, held in 1912–1914 at her apartment at 23 Fifth Avenue, in New York. She did not entirely share his love and acceptance of African American artists; but her salon was attended by a group of intellectuals from Greenwich Village, including Van Vechten himself, Max Eastman, John Reed, William English Walling, Sinclair Lewis, and H. L. Mencken, who assisted and promoted the work of African Americans. Luhan was possibly the person most out of place at her own salon. Van Vechten once brought the African American cast of J. Leuria Hill's *My Friend From Kentucky*, who sang "coon songs" and cakewalked, embarrassing and "shocking" Luhan. From then on, her guests tended to be people less offensive to her sensibilities, although they still seem to have been a diverse group: "ladies with bobbed hair and mannish cut garments," alongside men in evening dress and workmen's clothes.

Van Vechten became the most renowned white patron of the Harlem Renaissance. He was a music critic, photographer, and novelist, and his own work was critiqued by those who attended his salon-cum-soiree. For example, his novel *Nigger Heaven* (1926) was read in galley proofs by James Weldon Johnson and Walter White; Rudolph Fisher read it for "authenticity," and Langston Hughes wrote blues lyrics for later editions. Van Vechten's gatherings became legendary as huge all-night racially mixed drinking parties, but they included many of the same people, black and white, who attended more sober salons. Van Vechten, by promoting artists' work and by providing connections, was responsible for getting much of this work published and known. He was an unofficial "guide" to black Harlem and a close friend of many of the artists.

Many African Americans benefited from these salons. For example, Claude McKay, after having refused Van Vechten's offer of publication at Knopf, accepted the assistance of contacts he made at Luhan's salon. Through this salon, McKay also established an association with Max Eastman, Floyd Dell, and people at *Liberator*, the periodical in which he published his best-known poem, "If We Must Die." At one salon, Walter White was introduced to H. L. Mencken by James Weldon Johnson; eventually Mencken gave White's novel *The Fire in the Flint* to Knopf, which published it. Through these salons, White also came to know Heywood Broun, Claude McKay, Langston Hughes, Countee Cullen, Edna St. Vincent Millay, Sinclair Lewis, George Gershwin, Willa Cather, Alain Locke, and many other writers and artists. White reciprocated by taking Carl Van Vechten to NAACP events and elsewhere around Harlem, introducing him to African Americans.

There were essentially two types of salons: large, raucous groups of people who gathered to socialize but incidentally listened to and promoted the works of artists, and groups that met for the purpose of promoting creative art but had a raucous good time doing it. The adjective for each is "fun." Langston Hughes called these events "parties," and basically that is exactly what they were—parties that fostered and encouraged a special, serious, creative, fun-loving spirit among people who were good friends, shared good conversation, and encouraged each other in the name of a literary salon.

CARMALETTA M. WILLIAMS

See also Bennett, Gwendolyn; Johnson, Georgia Douglas; Knopf, Alfred A., Inc.; Liberator; Nance, Ethel Ray; Peterson, Dorothy Randolph; Van Vechten, Carl; Walker, A'Lelia; West, Dorothy; *other specific individuals*

Further Reading

Douglas, Ann. *Terrible Honesty: Mongrel Manhattan in the 1920s*. New York: Farrar, Straus & Giroux, 1995.

Huggins, Nathan. *Harlem Renaissance*. New York: Oxford University Press, 1970.

Hughes, Langston. *The Big Sea*. New York: Hill & Wang, 1993.

Hutchinson, George. *The Harlem Renaissance in Black and White*. Cambridge, Mass.: Harvard University Press, 1995.

Lewis, David Levering. *When Harlem Was in Vogue*. New York: Oxford University Press, 1979.

Locke, Alain. *The New Negro*, intro. Arnold Rampersad. New York: Atheneum, 1970.

Wall, Cheryl. *Women of the Harlem Renaissance*. Bloomington: Indiana University Press, 1995.

Watson, Steven. *Harlem Renaissance: Hub of African American Culture, 1920–1930*. New York: Pantheon, 1995.

Wintz, Cary. *Black Culture and the Harlem Renaissance*. Houston, Tex.: Rice University Press, 1988.

San Juan Hill, 1910–1915. (Brown Brothers.)

San Juan Hill

In the mid-nineteenth century, the black population of New York City began moving uptown, that is, northward in Manhattan. By the turn of the twentieth century, the bulk of the city's black population lived in the San Juan Hill district, which stretched between Sixtieth and Sixty-fourth streets (with a satellite community on its southern edge, extending down into Fifty-third Street), and bounded by Tenth and Eleventh avenues. This population grew with tremendous speed, partly or mostly because of an increasing migration of black people into the city, and soon became one of New York's most congested neighborhoods. One block alone housed upward of 5,000 residents.

At this point, San Juan Hill was less racially diverse than it had been in earlier decades. Although European immigrants and blacks lived in close proximity on adjacent blocks, individual tenement buildings and even entire streets tended to be racially homogeneous. The tension between blacks and their white immigrant neighbors made this area highly contentious. The open tracks of the New York Central Railroad—"which maimed black and white impartially"—offered a neutral ground between blacks in San Juan Hill and their "white enemies" to the west. The story is that San Juan Hill received its name not to honor the famous battle of the Spanish-American War but to satirize the constant clashes between its black and white residents.

Within the black population, different classes and ethnicities coexisted awkwardly. "Lewd women" lived alongside "neat, hard-working mothers," while "porters and longshoremen, night watchmen and government clerks" contrasted with men who "lounged on street corners in . . . dandified dress." Mary White Ovington, a white reformer who spent eight months in 1908 living in this notorious neighborhood, characterized the overcrowded tenements as "human hives, honeycombed with little rooms thick with human beings" (1909). The tiny apartments often opened into air shafts or narrow courtyards that admitted no fresh breezes, only the smell of the garbage down below. Many rooms had no windows at all.

As this district expanded, the number of neighborhood institutions serving the black community increased as well. Black churches followed their constituents to midtown. Saint Mark's Methodist Episcopal, Mount Olivet Baptist, and Saint Benedict the Moor all opened new buildings on West Fifty-third Street during the 1880s and 1890s. The rapid increase in the southern-born black population in this district contributed to the proliferation of storefront churches, often appealing to the specific needs and customs of city newcomers. The YMCA opened on West Fifty-third Street at the end of the nineteenth century as well. Many of the fraternal and benevolent societies, including the Grand United Order of Odd Fellows, the Colored Freemasons, and the Negro Elks, had locations in the neighborhood.

The artistic crowd also joined the march to San Juan Hill. The Marshall Hotel, with its headquarters on Fifty-third Street, became a center for black bohemia. Members of this elite cohort included Paul Laurence Dunbar, the jockey Isaac Murphy, James Weldon Johnson, Bert Williams, and George Walker. They added to the mix of this congested district, making San Juan Hill among the most vibrant and complex areas in Manhattan.

MARCY SACKS

1083

See also Black Bohemia; Dunbar, Paul Laurence; Johnson, James Weldon; Ovington, Mary White; Saint Mark's Methodist Episcopal Church; Williams, Egbert Austin "Bert"

Further Reading

Johnson, James Weldon. *Along This Way: The Autobiography of James Weldon Johnson*. New York: Viking, 1934.

Osofsky, Gilbert. Harlem: *The Making of a Ghetto—Negro New York, 1890–1930*. New York: Harper and Row, 1963.

Ovington, Mary White. *Half a Man: The Status of the Negro in New York*. New York: Longmans, Green, 1911.

———. "Vacation Days in San Juan Hill—A New York Negro Colony." *Southern Workman*, 38, November 1909, pp. 631–632.

———. *The Walls Came Tumbling Down*. New York: Ayer Company, 1947.

Scheiner, Seth M. "The New York City Negro and the Tenement, 1880–1910." *New York History*, 45, October 1964.

———. *Negro Mecca: A History of the Negro in New York City, 1865–1920*. New York: New York University Press, 1965.

Saturday Evening Quill

First published in June 1928 in Boston, the *Saturday Evening Quill* was a literary magazine edited by Eugene Gordon. The publication was a product of the Boston Quill Club, a literary salon of black intellectuals. The staff issued three numbers, published annually, before ceasing publication with the final issue of 1930.

Eugene Gordon, president of the Boston Quill Club, worked on the editorial staff of the *Boston Post*. He also contributed to the magazines *The Messenger* and *Opportunity*. In June 1928, in the inaugural number of the *Saturday Evening Quill*, Gordon explained that the main purpose of the publication was to serve as a literary outlet for the work of members of the club. The members paid for the production of the publication themselves and did not offer it for sale until the final number, published in 1930. The club published 300 copies of this third issue.

The *Saturday Evening Quill* featured stories, poems, plays, and essays. In the first number (June 1928), Roscoe Wright contributed an essay on the artificiality of "Negro" spirituals as performed by black concert singers. He maintained that the songs lost their spirituality when performed out of their natural environment. Wright also contributed four poems in addition to designing the cover and a monogram for the publication.

In addition to serving as editor, Eugene Gordon contributed work to the *Saturday Evening Quill*. The first number included two short stories by Gordon as well as a closing essay, "On Uncritical Criticism." In this essay, Gordon asserts that because black and white artists are American and receive the same training, it is ludicrous to think that black artists should be influenced by some innate connection to the African "jungle." This view contradicted the expectations of many whites regarding the primitive in black artists at that time.

Other contributors to the magazine included Alice Dunbar Nelson, Dorothy West, Waring Cuney, and Helene Johnson. West and Cuney were well known in Harlem and national literary circles, and both won prizes from *Opportunity* magazine for their work. Cuney contributed two poems—"Murder Blues" and "Old Man Death"—to the first number of the *Saturday Evening Quill*. Both poems use a blues rhythm to tell their stories. West's contribution to the third number was the short story "Funeral," about a girl's reaction to the funeral of her uncle. Edythe Mae Gordon, wife of the editor Eugene Gordon, contributed her first published work to the *Saturday Evening Quill* in 1928. The O. Henry Memorial Award Prize Committee honored her short story "Subversion" as one of the best short stories of the year.

In September 1928, in the magazine *The Crisis*, W. E. B. Du Bois praised the *Saturday Evening Quill* as the best of the literary magazines being produced by African American writers of the time. Du Bois considered the publication "well printed and readable" and commented that it "maintains a high mark of literary excellence." The *Saturday Evening Quill* also received praise from the *Amsterdam News*, *New York Age*, and *Commonweal*. Unlike *Fire!!*, *Harlem*, and other literary magazines of the Harlem Renaissance, the *Saturday Evening Quill* was a relatively conservative publication. Other literary publications of the period used black dialect and language considered offensive. Before the *Saturday Evening Quill* and other "little magazines" came on the scene, *The Crisis* and *Opportunity* provided the earliest literary publication outlets for blacks.

HEATHER MARTIN

See also Cuney, Waring; Fire!!; Harlem Renaissance in the United States: 1—Boston; Johnson, Helene; Nelson, Alice Dunbar; West, Dorothy

Further Reading

Burks, Mary Fair. *A Survey of Black Literary Magazines in the United States: 1859–1940.* New York: Author, 1979. (Dissertation.)

Du Bois, W. E. B. "The Browsing Reader." *Crisis,* 35, September 1928.

Johnson, Abby Ann Arthur, and Ronald M. Johnson. "Forgotten Pages: Black Literary Magazines in the 1920s." *Journal of American Studies,* 8(3), 1974.

———. *Propaganda and Aesthetics: The Literary Politics of Afro-American Magazines in the Twentieth Century.* Amherst: University of Massachusetts Press, 1979.

Roses, Lorraine Elena. Introduction. In *Selected Works of Edythe Mae Gordon.* New York: G. K. Hall; London: Prentice Hall International, 1996.

Savage, Augusta

Augusta Savage—an accomplished sculptor who was an important figure in the New Negro movement—was born in 1892 in Green Cove Springs, near Jacksonville, Florida. She was the seventh of fourteen children. Around 1907, her father, Rev. Edward Fells, a Methodist minister, moved the family to West Palm Beach, where she impressed her teachers with her artistic ability. While still at school, she earned pocket money by teaching sculpture to other students.

Savage married John T. Moore; but he soon died, leaving her with a young daughter. For the next few years, Savage made a small income from minor sculptures until she was commissioned to make a portrait of a local fair superintendent, George Graham Currie, who gave her a booth where she could sell her sculptures of animals. Currie recognized her talent and persuaded her to study in New York.

In 1921, Savage enrolled in art classes at Cooper Union. Unable to support herself in New York during the four years of the sculpture program, Savage was the first student awarded living expenses by the school. She soon became known for her portraits of black leaders. But in 1923, because of her race, she was rejected for an art study program sponsored by the French government at Fontainebleau. This incident became a cause célèbre: A number of well-known figures in the arts, scholars, and ministers protested in Savage's favor. As a result of the experience, Savage became engaged in problems confronting African American artists.

Savage's first major commission came from the Friends of the Harlem Library, for a portrait bust of W. E. B. Du Bois. Later she did a bust of Marcus Garvey, a powerful study of the dynamic black nationalist leader that conveys his forceful intellect and determined character. Savage then married Robert L. Poston, one of Garvey's assistants, who was a committed member of the New Negro movement. Poston died returning from Liberia, where he had worked to found a colony of former American slaves. At around the same time (1929–1930), Savage produced her famous *Gamin* (a bronze cast dated 1930). This shows a black boy, evidently quick-witted and full of impish charm. According to some sources, the subject was her nephew, Ellis Ford. *Gamin* led to a Rosenwald Fellowship that financed a period of study in Paris, where Savage met Henry Ossawa Tanner and Hale A. Woodruff.

In Paris, Savage entered the Académie de la Grande Chaumière and studied for a short time with the portraitist Charles Despiau. While she was in Europe, her work appeared in several exhibitions, although she was not interested in either the avant-garde or African art. She objected to Alain Locke's view that blacks should base their art on their African heritage.

In 1931, Savage returned to New York, impoverished by the Depression but determined to pursue her career and to encourage young black artists. Her main income came from portraits of black intellectuals, most notably the poet James Weldon Johnson. She worked for the Works Progress Administration (WPA) and helped several other artists, including Jacob Lawrence, find work there.

Savage spent a great deal of energy teaching and promoting black artists. In 1932, she opened the Savage Studio of Arts and Crafts, affiliated with the State University of New York (SUNY) and funded by a grant from the Carnegie Corporation. It was located in a basement at 163 West 143rd Street in Harlem. There she taught art to local children and led discussion groups on topics affecting black artists. From 1937 to 1942, the Savage Studio became the Harlem Community Art Center, which Savage directed until 1939. More than 1,500 black children were trained there in drawing, painting, printmaking, and sculpture. In 1934, Savage was elected the first African American member of the National Association of Women Painters and Sculptors.

One of Savage's most famous commissions came in 1937 from the World's Fair Board of Design, for a sculpture based on the theme "American Negro

Augusta Savage, shown in 1937 with two of her sculptures: *Susie Q* (left) and *Truckin'*. (© Bettmann/Corbis.)

Contribution to Music, Especially Song." She made a 16-foot-high plaster model inspired by James Weldon Johnson's poem and song "Lift Every Voice and Sing." It shows a group of singers forming the shape of a harp, and the work was also called *The Harp*. The folds of the singers' long robes resemble the harp strings, and a large, detached arm forms the base of the instrument. Kneeling at the front of the harp, a boy extends a bar of music. For lack of funds, the work was never cast. It was painted black for the exhibition and later destroyed.

Throughout her life, Savage was involved in a number of organizations dedicated to improving the status of black artists. Among these were the Harlem Artists' Guild and the Harlem Art Workshop (later part of the Schomburg Center for Research on Black Culture). The Harlem Artists' Guild evolved out of Savage's protests that the WPA did not award high-level jobs to qualified black artists. For a brief time in 1939, she ran an art gallery in Harlem, the Salon of Contemporary Negro Art, but it soon went out of business.

For a significant period of time, Savages's commitment to administration and political activism drained her energy away from her art. Also, she antagonized a number of people in positions of authority, and this too had an adverse effect on her career. In the 1940s, after a few unsuccessful exhibitions, Savage retired to a farm in upstate New York and produced almost no further work. Most of her works were never cast into bronze and, like *The Harp*, were eventually destroyed. Some are known only from photographs. The bust of W. E. B. Du Bois was stolen from the Harlem Library and (as of this writing) was never recovered.

Biography

Augusta Christine Savage was born in 1892 in Green Cove Springs, Florida. She began making sculptures in grade school. In 1921, she went to New York City and enrolled in the four-year sculpture program at Cooper Union. Her ability to reveal character in her portrait busts led to several commissions from leading members of the Harlem Renaissance. Much of her life was dedicated to the problems faced by black artists and to teaching. She was involved in founding and leading several organizations, such as schools and galleries, dedicated to helping blacks in the arts. Savage retired as a professional artist in the 1940s and moved to upstate New York. She died in 1962.

LAURIE ADAMS

See also Artists; Du Bois, W. E. B.; Garvey, Marcus; Johnson, James Weldon; Lawrence, Jacob; Rosenwald Fellowships; Tanner, Henry Ossawa; Woodruff, Hale; Works Progress Administration

Selected Works

Gamin. 1929.
Bust of W. E. B. Du Bois. (Lost.)
Head of Marcus Garvey. c.1930. (Collection of Amy Jacques Garvey.)
The Harp. (Destroyed.)
Bust of James Weldon Johnson. 1939. (Schomburg Center for Research in Black Culture, New York Public Library.)

Further Reading

Bearden, Romare, and Harry Henderson. *A History of African-American Artists from 1792 to the Present*. New York: Pantheon, 1993.

Leininger, Theresa. *Sculpting the New Negro: The Life and Art of Augusta Savage.* New Brunswick, N.J.: Rutgers Univesity Press, forthcoming.

Lewis, Samela. *African-American Art and Artists.* Berkeley: University of California Press, 1990.

Patton, Sharon F. *African-American Art.* New York: Oxford University Press, 1998.

Savoy Ballroom

On 12 March 1926, Moe Gale (owner) and Charlie Buchanan (manager) opened a dance hall space that occupied the second floor of an entire city block along Lenox Avenue between 140th and 141st streets. Designed to rival downtown ballrooms like the Roseland and the Arcadia, the Savoy boasted a marble staircase, a grand cut-glass chandelier, thick patterned carpets, and a soda fountain. It also boasted a 200-by-50-foot polished maple and mahogany dance floor that gained the club its reputation as the "home of happy feet" (in Harlem, simply "The Track"). The floor reputedly had to be replaced every three years to counter the wear and tear of the Lindy hop, the big apple, and other dances that developed there. The space could accommodate 4,000 people over the course of an evening—*Ebony* magazine estimated that 28 million feet had stomped there by 1946 (Anderson 1982, 307)—and housed two bandstands to allow for continuous music. On opening night, Leon Abbey's Savoy Bearcats and Fess Williams and His Royal Flush Orchestra alternated sets; in time, nearly every major jazz orchestra would play at the Savoy. The house bands alone included those of Claude Hopkins, Jimmie Lunceford, Chick Webb, Benny Carter, and Lucky Millinder.

The Savoy's entertainment was markedly participatory. The club featured dance contests, barn dances, and drag balls. If floor shows featured professional troupes like Whitey's Lindy Hoppers (1935–1941), the dancers were drawn from those, like Frankie Manning or Norma Miller, who first danced there socially. A 10-foot-square "Cats' Corner" to the right of the bandstand was reserved for the most competitive dancers (preserved by the occasional well-placed Charleston kick). A band's success at the Savoy depended on the customers who, literally, voted with their feet. Audience response also decided the celebrated battles of bands, such as the one Benny Goodman waged on 11 May 1937 with Chick Webb. (Webb's band had performed the debut of Edgar Sampson's "Stompin'

Band at the Savoy Ballroom, 1941. (Library of Congress.)

at the Savoy" in 1934, and their signature Savoy tempo made the band a house favorite.) The Savoy claimed that 25,000 fans tried to attend.

If the Savoy integrated performers and audiences, it was also remarkably integrated economically and racially. The white Goodman's organization (itself integrated) could square off against Webb's black orchestra; Charlie Barnet's band could be featured alongside those of Ella Fitzgerald and Erskine Hawkins. Although Gale paid well below union scale, the Savoy's radio network hookup was rarely offered to black bands elsewhere. Just down the block, the Cotton Club charged a $2.50 cover, featured Sunday "Celebrity Nights," and turned away black customers. The Savoy, in contrast, charged 50 cents (75 cents on weekends), sponsored a Thursday "Kitchen Mechanics Night" for domestic workers on their day off, and attracted a primarily black audience that might, nevertheless, be anywhere from 10 to 30 percent white. Indeed, when the police closed the Savoy for six months on vice charges in 1943—a year marred by nationwide race riots—many suspected that such social integration was the target. The Savoy would not close again until 1958, and in 1959, it would be torn down to make way for the Delano Village housing development.

RYAN JERVING

See also Cotton Club; Nightlife

Further Reading

Anderson, Jervis. *This Was Harlem: A Cultural Portrait, 1900–1950.* New York: Farrar, Straus and Giroux, 1982.

Burns, Ken, dir. *The True Welcome*. PBS Home Video, 2000. (Episode 4 of *Jazz*.)

Calloway, Cab, and Bryant Rollins. *Of Minnie the Moocher and Me*. New York: Crowell, 1976.

Crease, Robert P. "Divine Frivolity: Hollywood Representations of the Lindy Hop, 1937–1942." In *Representing Jazz*, ed. Krin Gabbard. London and Durham, N.C.: Duke University Press, 1995.

DeVeaux, Scott. *The Birth of Bebop: A Social and Musical History*. London and Berkeley: University of California Press, 1997.

Gold, Russell. Guilty of Syncopation, Joy, and Animation: The Closing of Harlem's Savoy Ballroom." In *Of, by, and for the People: Dancing on the Left in the 1930s*, ed. Lynn Garafola. Madison: University of Wisconsin Press, 1994.

Miller, Norma, with Evette Jensen. *Swingin' at the Savoy*. Philadelphia, Pa.: Temple University Press, 1996.

Ogren, Kathy J. *The Jazz Revolution: Twenties America and the Meaning of Jazz*. Oxford and New York: Oxford University Press, 1989.

Schomburg, Arthur A.

Arthur (Arturo) Alfonso Schomburg (1874–1938) gained a reputation as the "Sherlock Holmes" of black history during the Harlem Renaissance. His archival collection of rare books, manuscripts, and artifacts was a key resource for writers, researchers, and community activists of the period. A committed activist and researcher, both nationally and internationally, he made a number of major contributions to research on the African diaspora and to advocacy organizations. Schomburg was also a major figure in Puerto Rican and Cuban radicalism of the 1890s in New York City.

Schomburg's biographers have documented only a few facts about his birth, childhood, and family life. Schomburg was born 24 January 1874 in Cangrejos, a historically free black working-class neighborhood near the port of San Juan. Schomburg's mother, Maria Josefa Schomburg, bore him out of wedlock. He apparently never met his father. So far, researchers have not located records confirming Schomburg's own sometimes contradictory account of his family's transantillean history. He was married three times—in 1895 to Elizabeth Hatcher, in 1902 to Elizabeth Morrow Taylor, and in 1914 to Elizabeth Green—and had seven sons and one daughter.

There is also scant documentation about Schomburg's education. Information in his collected papers suggests that he may have attended the Instituto Civil de Segunda Enseñanza, the Instituto de Enseñanza Popular, or the Instituto de Párvulos, all in San Juan. While still a teenager, Schomburg also studied, perhaps formally, with the faculty at the College of Saint Thomas in the Virgin Islands. Shortly after his immigration to New York in 1891, he took night classes in English. He recounted his employment in a number of odd jobs during his first decade in the United States. He began working as a legal mail clerk for a Wall Street firm, Bankers Trust Company, in 1906 and remained with this firm until his retirement in 1929.

Schomburg's early introduction to Caribbean radicalism largely evolved within the workers' movement. The 1890s were a period of major social unrest and political upheaval in Puerto Rico and Cuba, and this led to a trickle of immigration to New York City when many Puerto Rican and Cuban activists went there as political exiles. After Schomburg arrived in New York in the early 1890s, he immediately became involved in political projects in the working-class expatriate community. In 1892, he cofounded and then became secretary of the Dos Antillas Club, a group informally linked to the Puerto Rican and Cuban sections of the Partido Revolucionario Cubano. Schomburg collaborated with a number of well-known revolutionaries of the period, including José Martí. His other acquaintances in New York City's Puerto Rican and Cuban political organizations included Ramón Emeterio Betances, Flor Baerga, Rafael Serra, Julio Henna, Sotero Figueroa, and Pachín Marín. In 1892, he also joined a Masonic lodge called El Sol de Cuba number 38, founded by Cuban and Puerto Rican migrants in the early 1880s. He helped the lodge prioritize the recruitment of new members from New York City's English-speaking black community. Around 1911 the lodge was renamed Prince Hall number 38 in honor of the founder of the first African American Masonic lodge. Although Schomburg was often active throughout his later life in a number of local and national organizations, including the National Urban League and the National Association for the Advancement of Colored People, his duties as a Mason clearly formed some of his primary lifelong commitments.

Schomburg published dozens of letters, articles, and bibliographies. His earliest articles were published in newspapers in New York; these articles included pieces he wrote for the Spanish-language

Arthur Alfonso Schomburg, c. 1900–1910. (Schomburg Center for Research in Black Culture, New York Public Library.)

periodical *Patria* under the pen name Guarionex. After 1900 he wrote and circulated a number of important essays and working papers, the originals of which are today archived as the Schomburg Papers at the Schomburg Center for Research in Black Culture. "The Negro Digs Up His Past," originally published in *Survey Graphic* in 1925, is considered Schomburg's most important essay. It was republished in Alain Locke's anthology *The New Negro*, also in 1925.

Schomburg's main contribution to American and black historical research is his work as a collector and archivist of books, papers, and art of the African diaspora. Although his biographers disagree about when precisely he began his collection and the extent of his travels, his correspondence suggests that he started his acquisitions project in earnest around the beginning of the twentieth century. He obtained most of his items by rummaging through used bookstores and sundry odd places in the United States, by following leads from other bibliophiles on private

holdings, and by petitioning his friends who traveled to Europe, Latin America, and the Caribbean to purchase for him specific books and documents whose whereabouts he had surmised through research. In 1911, he cofounded, with John Edward Bruce and others, the Negro Society for Historical Research, an international organization based in Harlem and dedicated both to recovering books and documents of the African diaspora and to educating the black community about the cultural and intellectual legacy of the diaspora. This organization welcomed autodidacts and other nontraditionally trained scholars, and sponsored a number of public lectures and exhibits in the 1910s and 1920s. Schomburg was elected in 1914 to the more erudite American Negro Academy and was its president from 1920 to 1929. In 1924, he chaired the Citizens Committee of Harlem's 135th Street Branch of the New York Public Library, which was dedicated to preserving and expanding the branch's black studies collection. This committee arranged for the Carnegie Corporation to purchase Schomburg's private collection and donate it to the library in 1926, as part of an effort to establish and maintain the library's Division of Negro Literature, History, and Prints. Schomburg's private collection included some 10,000 books, manuscripts, documents, works of art, prints, and other historical artifacts pertaining to the history of the African diaspora, and it became the cornerstone of the branch's permanent research collection, which is today the world's largest combined archives of the African diaspora.

Using part of the money he received for his private collection in 1926, Schomburg made a major research trip to Europe that same year. Schomburg received a pension from the Bankers Trust Company when he retired in 1929, and he stayed active as an archivist, curator, and collector during the 1930s. From 1930 to 1932 he held a temporary post at the Fisk University Library's Negro Collection, but otherwise his main professional activities of the 1930s centered on acquisitions and exhibits for the 135th Street branch in Harlem, where he worked pro bono as curator of the Division of Negro History, Literature, and Prints until his death on 10 June 1938.

Biography

Arthur (Arturo) Alfonso Schomburg was born 24 January 1874 in Cangrejos, Puerto Rico. He studied at parochial and public schools in San Juan from 1874 to 1891 and at the College of Saint Thomas, Virgin Islands, in 1891. He immigrated to New York City in 1891 and was initiated into El Sol de Cuba number 38 Masonic lodge in 1892. Schomburg was a messenger for a law firm (Pryor, Mellis, and Harris) from 1891 to 1896. He was a cofounder of the Dos Antillas Club in 1892, the Citizens Committee of the 135th Street branch of the New York Public Library, and the Negro Society for Historical Research in 1911. His first published article in Spanish was "Club Político Puertorriqueño las Dos Antillas" (*Patria*, 1892); his first published article in English was "Is Hayti Decadent?" (*Unique Advertiser*, 1904). From 1906 to 1929 he was a mail clerk supervisor at Bankers Trust Company. He had essays and letters published in *New Century, Negro World, New York Times, Papers of the American Negro Academy, The Crisis, Opportunity, African Times and Orient Review, Champion, AME Review, The New Negro, Survey Graphic, Light, Amsterdam News*, and other journals, books, and periodicals from 1902 to 1936. He was elected a member of the American Negro Academy in 1914. He received U.S. citizenship by imposition of colonial law in 1917. Schomburg was president of the American Negro Academy from 1920 to 1929. His private collection of books, documents, prints, and artifacts was purchased by the Carnegie Corporation in 1926. He made a research trip to Europe in 1926 and to Cuba in 1933. He was curator of Fisk University Library's Negro Collection from 1930 to 1932 and volunteer curator of the Division of Negro Literature, History, and Prints from 1929 to 1938. He was awarded the William E. Harmon Foundation medal in 1927. Schomburg died in New York City on 10 June 1938.

LISA SÁNCHEZ GONZÁLEZ

See also Bruce, John Edward; New Negro, The; 135th Street Library; Survey Graphic

Selected Works

"Economic Contribution by the Negro to America." N.d.
"Club Político Puertorriqueño las Dos Antillas." 1892.
"Is Hayti Decadent?" 1904.
"Plácido." 1909.
A Bibliographical Checklist of American Negro Poetry. 1916.
"The Negro Digs Up His Past." 1925. (Reprint, 1968.)
"West Indian Composers and Musicians." 1926.
"Creole/Criollo." 1927.
"In Quest of Juan de Pareja." 1927.
"Negroes in Sevilla." 1928.

"Unusual Books." 1930–1931.
"My Trip to Cuba in Quest of Negro Books." 1933.
"José Campeche." 1934.
Arturo Alfonso Schomburg: A Puerto Rican Quest for His Black Heritage, His Writings—Annotated with Appendices, ed. Flor Piñeiro de Rivera. 1989. (In Spanish, *Un puertorriqueño descubre el legado histórico del negro*.)

Further Reading

James, Winston. *Holding Aloft the Banner of Ethiopia: Caribbean Radicalism in Early Twentieth-Century America.* New York: Verso, 1998.

Ortiz, Victoria. "Arthur A. Schomburg: A Biographical Essay." In *The Legacy of Arthur A. Schomburg: A Celebration of the Past, a Vision for the Future.* New York: Schomburg Center for Research in Black Culture, New York Public Library, 1986. (Bilingual exhibit catalog, English-Spanish.)

Sánchez González, Lisa. *Boricua Literature: A Literary History of the Puerto Rican Diaspora.* New York: New York University Press, 2001.

Sinnette, Elinor Des Verney. *Arthur Alfonso Schomburg, Black Bibliophile and Collector: A Biography.* Detroit, Mich.: Wayne State University and New York Public Library, 1989.

Schuyler, George S.

George S. Schuyler was a prolific journalist, fiction writer, and political commentator, as well as one of the most controversial figures in African American history. Although he was a major contributor to the culture and legacy of the Harlem Renaissance, Schuyler nonetheless argued that neither "Negro art" nor the Harlem Renaissance as a definable movement ever truly existed.

Schuyler was born in 1895 to a family extremely proud of its apparently slaveless genealogy. He served in the army from 1912 to 1919 before moving to New York City. After enduring a period of homelessness and itinerant work, Schuyler joined the Socialist Party of America, through which he met A. Philip Randolph, later president of the Brotherhood of Sleeping Car Porters. In 1921, Randolph hired Schuyler to work at his magazine, *The Messenger*, which described itself as "the only magazine of scientific radicalism in the world published by Negroes." At *The Messenger*, with its socialist creed and well-cultivated iconoclasm, Schuyler developed the satirical style that would shape his novel *Black No More* and would inform much of his journalistic work. Schuyler later rejected socialism in favor of extreme conservatism (he was a staunch member of the John Birch Society), and his early membership in the Socialist Party and his position at the magazine were apparently not so much opportunities to advocate socialism as they were chances to gain invaluable experience as a journalist and editor. Nonetheless, Schuyler's articles and columns for *The Messenger* were mostly filled with rhetoric that would have done any socialist proud, even after the magazine had lost some of its radical fire well before Schuyler's name was added to the masthead. Regardless of his political views, though, Schuyler was first and foremost an unrepentant iconoclast who used his columns to comment on and frequently satirize everything and everyone, from W. E. B. Du Bois and the National Association for the Advancement of Colored People (NAACP) to Marcus Garvey and the Universal Negro Improvement Association (UNIA). In addition, any group or individual who supported any form of racism, whether actively or passively, felt the sting of Schuyler's barbs. Several months after Schuyler started writing his regular column for *The Messenger*, "Shafts and Darts: A Page of Calumny and Satire," he and its drama critic, Theophilus Lewis, drew up a topical philosophy for the column: "[Our] intention is . . . to slur, lampoon, damn and occasionally praise anybody or anything in the known universe, not excepting the President of the immortals."

Schuyler's work at *The Messenger* was hardly his sole outlet for satiric invective. Schuyler became a correspondent for the *Pittsburgh Courier* in 1924 and spent the early part of his forty-year career with the paper writing many columns similar to those in the magazine. After he was promoted to associate editor in 1926, Schuyler became an indispensable part of the *Courier*'s editorial staff, traveling around the nation to increase the paper's circulation and writing most of its editorials as well as the satirical column "Views and Reviews." Schuyler's controversial stances on contemporary issues soon earned him the nickname "the black H. L. Mencken." In addition, Schuyler wrote a handful of landmark columns for Mencken's *American Mercury* magazine and eventually became a great admirer and friend of Mencken.

Schuyler's most famous essay, "The Negro-Art Hokum," published in *The Nation* in 1926, argued against an essential African American artistic tradition.

This particular column was followed by Langston Hughes's "The Negro Artist and the Racial Mountain," which disagreed with Schuyler's argument at certain points. Both columns had a significant influence on the intellectual politics of the Harlem Renaissance. On matters of race, Schuyler was remarkably consistent in his inconsistency. He was inarguably antiracist in his general outlook and philosophy, but he repeatedly scoffed at the possibility of black cultural nationalism or a group identity as viable means for fighting racism. This opposition underscored much of Schuyler's work in the 1920s and 1930s. He delighted in lampooning anyone who supported any cause that resembled either racism or radicalism in his view, including Marcus Garvey and the UNIA, the NAACP, the African Blood Brotherhood, and the Ku Klux Klan. Simultaneously, however, Schuyler supported black economic cooperatives in Harlem and wrote predominantly in black publications for most of his career, with the focus almost always on "racial" issues.

Schuyler's literary reputation rests largely on his novel *Black No More: Being an Account of the Strange and Wonderful Workings of Science in the Land of the Free, A.D. 1933–1940* (1931), which stands as a double milestone in African American literature. It is simultaneously the first completely satirical novel written by an African American about African Americans and the first extended work of science fiction by an African American. It was also the crowning achievement of his journalistic work and enabled Schuyler to obtain a perspective on racial matters that he easily translated into crisp, deadly satirical jabbing. *Black No More* presented a world in which African Americans were able to turn white, thereby upsetting the American racial caste system. In the course of the plot, all the targets Schuyler excoriated in his essays received another lambasting.

Despite its pioneering achievements, *Black No More* remained, along with virtually all of Schuyler's early work, in relative obscurity for decades. Given Schuyler's iconoclasm, the common perception that he was an assimilationist trying to escape his "blackness," his sharp anticommunism, and his rancorous criticism of the civil rights movement, most critics of African American literature found it easy to dismiss his oeuvre. Not until the 1980s did interest in Schuyler grow, owing in part to increasing interest in the Harlem Renaissance in general and, arguably, to a wave of black neoconservatism in particular. Until Michael Peplow's biography of 1980, critical studies of Schuyler were confined almost exclusively to brief

George S. Schuyler, photographed by Carl Van Vechten, 1941.
(Library of Congress.)

His editorial positions included managing editor, *The Messenger*, 1923–1926; editorial writer, *Pittsburgh Courier*, 1924–1964; associate editor, *Pittsburgh Courier*, 1942–1964; business manager, *The Crisis*, 1937–1944; editor, *National News*, 1932; associate editor, *The African*, 1943–1945; and contributing editor, *Plain Talk*, 1946–1950. He also wrote for *American Mercury*, *American Opinion*, *Christian Herald*, *Cultural Freedom*, *Freeman*, *Harlem*, *Interracial Review*, *Inter-State Tattler*, *Manchester Union Leader*, *Modern Monthly*, *Modern Quarterly*, *The Nation*, *National News*, *Negro Book Club News*, *Negro Digest*, *New Masses*, *New South*, *New York Evening Post*, *Phylon*, *Spirit of Mission*, and *Transatlantic*. He was a member of the Socialist Party of America, 1921–1926; Friends of Negro Freedom, 1923–1928; Young Negroes' Cooperative League, beginning in 1930; Committee on Cultural Freedom, 1939–1954; Post World-War Council, 1945; American Writers Association, 1945; American Committee for Cultural Freedom, 1952–1954; John Birch Society, 1961–1977; Katanga Freedom Fighters, c. 1961–1964; New York State Conservative Political Association, 1961–1977; and North American Newspaper Alliance, 1965–1977. He was a candidate for the House of Representatives, Eighteenth District, New York, 1964, Conservative Party. Schuyler died 31 August 1977 in New York City.

DARRYL DICKSON-CARR

See also American Mercury; Harlem Renaissance: 1—Black Critics of; Hughes, Langston; Lewis, Theophilus; Literature: 5—Humor and Satire; Mencken, H. L.; Messenger, The; Pittsburgh Courier; Randolph, A. Philip

Selected Works

Rac(e)ing to the Right: Selected Essays of George S. Schuyler, ed. Jeffrey B. Leak. 2001.
Black and Conservative: The Autobiography of George S. Schuyler. 1966.
Black Empire, ed. Robert A. Hill and Kent Rasmussen. 1991.
Black No More: Being an Account of the Strange and Wonderful Workings of Science in the Land of the Free, A.D. 1933–1940. 1931. (Rev. ed., 1989.)
Ethiopian Stories, ed. Robert A. Hill. 1994.
"The Negro-Art Hokum." *The Nation*, 122(3180), 16 June 1926, pp. 662–663.
"Our Greatest Gift to America." In *Ebony and Topaz: A Collectanea*, ed. Charles S. Johnson. 1927, pp. 122–124.
Racial Intermarriage in the United States. 1929.

mentions in retrospectives on the literature of the Harlem Renaissance. Since then, however, many critical articles have appeared, and some of Schuyler's more obscure work has been reprinted, most notably his novel *Black Empire* (1991, originally serialized under the pseudonym Samuel I. Brooks from 1936 to 1938). Ultimately, Schuyler's significance is likely to rest on *Black No More* and his penchant for controversy.

Biography

George Samuel Schuyler was born 25 February 1895 in Providence, Rhode Island. He studied at public schools in Syracuse, New York. He enlisted in the United States Army, 1912–1915; was commissioned as a first lieutenant, 1917; and was discharged in 1919.

"The Reminiscences of George S. Schuyler." In *The Oral History Collection of Columbia University*, ed. Elizabeth B. Mason and Louis M. Starr, 1972.

Slaves Today: A Story of Liberia. 1931. (Reprint, 1969.)

Further Reading

Anderson, Jervis. *A. Philip Randolph: A Biographical Portrait.* New York: Harcourt Brace Jovanovich, 1973.

Buni, Andrew. *Robert L. Vann of the Pittsburgh Courier: Politics and Black Journalism.* Pittsburgh, Pa.: University of Pittsburgh Press, 1974.

Gruesser, John C. "Review of *Black Empire*, by George S. Schuyler, Edited by Robert A. Hill and R. Kent Rasmussen." *African American Review*, 27(4), 1993.

Hutchinson, George, *The Harlem Renaissance in Black and White.* Cambridge, Mass., and London: Belknap, 1995.

Kornweibel, Theodore, Jr. *No Crystal Stair: Black Life and the Messenger, 1917–1928.* Westport, Conn.: Greenwood, 1975.

Lawson, Benjamin S., "George S. Schuyler and the Fate of Early African-American Science Fiction." In *Impossibility Fiction: Alternativity, Extrapolation, Speculation*, ed. Derek Littlewood and Peter Stockwell. Amsterdam and Atlanta, Ga.: Rodopi, 1996, pp. 87–105.

Peplow, Michael W. "George S. Schuyler, Satirist: Rhetorical Devices in *Black No More.*a' *CLA Journal*, 28(2), December 1974, pp. 242–257.

———. *George S. Schuyler.* Twayne's United States Authors, 349. Boston, Mass.: Twayne, 1980.

Reed, Ishmael, and Steve Cannon. "George S. Schuyler, Writer." In *Shrovetide in Old New Orleans*, ed. Ishmael Reed. Garden City, N.Y.: Doubleday, 1978, pp. 195–218.

Tucker, Jeffrey. "'Can Science Succeed Where the Civil War Failed?': George S. Schuyler and Race." In *Race Consciousness: African American Studies for the New Century*, ed. Judith Jackson Fossett and Jeffrey A. Tucker. New York: New York University Press, 1997, pp. 136–152.

Scott, Emmett Jay

Emmett Jay Scott (1873–1957), as a "race man," anticipated the African American fervor and sense of pride that would characterize the Harlem Renaissance of the 1920s. In 1919 and 1920, respectively, he published books on the black soldier in World War I and on black migration. His daughter Clarissa Scott Delany was one of the budding poets of the Harlem Renaissance at the time of her death in 1927. Scott was not one to value art for art's sake or even, in an abstract sense, for the race's sake. Any of his undertakings in the realm of aesthetics were calculated to produce profits and promote specific interests of African Americans; an example is his campaign in 1916 and 1917 to produce the movie *The Birth of a Race* in response to the racism of D. W. Griffith's *Birth of a Nation*.

Scott launched his extraordinary, though largely unheralded, leadership in 1897 as private secretary and right-hand man to Booker T. Washington, the illustrious principal of Tuskegee and African American political boss. Scott was frequently said to be the "brains of the Tuskegee machine," because of his remarkable efficiency; his ability to anticipate Washington's thinking and act accordingly; and his work as a press agent, polemicist, and go-between in meetings with powerful whites and blacks to accomplish Washington's goals.

That Scott was prepared for such a role had much to do with his childhood and early career in Houston, Texas. He was born to Horace and Emma (Kyle) Scott and was the first of nine children of the family. Horace Scott had been born a slave in Virginia in 1850 and transported by his owner (who was also his father) to Texas in the early 1860s during the American Civil War. More than 182,000 slaveholders migrated to Texas, hoping to protect their property and perpetuate a slaveholding empire there. Scott's mother had been born and reared in the all-black community of Rosharon, Texas, and migrated to Houston after the Civil War to live with her brother. He introduced her to Horace Scott, and the two were married in the city in 1873. Horace Scott worked for the Houston and Central Railroad Company, and Emma Scott remained a housewife to raise the expanding family.

The Scotts were involved in efforts by the post–Civil War generation of African Americans to build a viable black community. Horace Scott, who lived in Houston's Fourth Ward, joined the Republican Party, armed himself to guarantee free political elections in Houston in 1873, and became a founding member of Trinity Methodist Episcopal Church, which ministered to blacks. Emma Scott notably enlisted the church's ministers to enroll Emmett in Wiley College, the first African American institution of higher education west of the Mississippi. At Wiley, Scott worked in the school's post office and central business office, gaining invaluable experience in economic management and governance. He was a precocious student and was recognized for his literary ability, but in 1889, he had to withdraw and go to work, to supplement the family income and help educate the younger Scott children. In the economically vibrant setting of downtown Houston, he was employed as a janitor—significantly—in the office of a newspaper, the *Houston Post*. His literacy, and the legibility of this handwriting, led to a promotion to addressing envelopes and a subsequent reportorial assignment to cover the commencement exercises at Prairie View College. In 1893—confident that he had the work ethos and skills necessary to begin his own newspaper company to cover events within and affecting black communities in Houston and statewide—Scott, along with two partners, organized the *Texas Freeman*. This is believed to be the first African American newspaper west of the Mississippi River.

Owing to his early activities on behalf of the Republican Party of Houston and his prescient essays in the *Texas Freeman* on politics and overall economic issues related to African Americans, Scott was hired by the state's ranking Republican political boss, Norris Wright Cuney of Galveston, an African American. Scott served Cuney well and loyally, as he would later serve Booker T. Washington. An important issue for blacks in Texas and throughout the nation was how to build better African American communities and capitalize on political and economic opportunities.

In Texas, Scott pressed for institutional and organizational growth and development in politics and economics. Blacks were urged to support the Republican Party and take advantage of economic, especially entrepreneurial, opportunities. For such advice—and for his newspaper essays underscoring this need—Scott became known as "Get-Together Scott." For a time, he found an ally and mentor in Cuney, who was preoccupied with African Americans' rights under the Fourteenth and Fifteenth amendments and was consequently known among whites as a "civil rights nigger." But Cuney was soon deposed, in 1896, and then died, in 1897. (Cuney had refused to support William McKinley's bid for the presidential nomination and had then been outmaneuvered and eventually toppled by McKinley's allies in Texas at the national convention of 1896.)

After Cuney's death, Scott focused on expanding his newspaper business in Houston and on supporting black leaders who shared his concern for community development in education, economics, and politics. His editorials had begun to extol the virtues of Booker T. Washington, in the aftermath of Washington's speech at the Atlanta Exposition in 1896, and Scott led an effort on the part of blacks in Houston to have Washington come there and address them. Washington's visit to and speech in Houston in 1897 resulted in his offer to Scott, whom he admired, to join the staff at Tuskegee as the principal's private secretary. Scott eventually accepted, but this was a difficult decision for him: He had recently married Eleanora Baker of Galveston, Texas; they were expecting a baby; and he was reluctant to pull up roots.

Arriving at Tuskegee in 1897, Scott quickly demonstrated remarkable skills in supporting Washington, who was seeking additional recognition and credibility as a leader, and in anticipating Washington's needs. Scott, as private secretary, handled Washington's mail with a sophistication and deftness rare for a young man. Scott's wisdom soon led to emissarial roles and concomitant responsibilities to sustain Washington as an African American leader; Scott was dispatched to meet with American presidents (notably Theodore Roosevelt and William H. Taft) and high-ranking businessmen (such as Andrew Carnegie and Julius Rosenwald). Scott also advised Washington about dealing with adversaries and foes such as W. E. B. Du Bois and William Monroe Trotter, to name two inveterate critics of Washington and of Washington's ideology for racial uplift and reform.

Scott relished most his role in the birth and nurturing of the National Negro Business League, which Washington founded in Boston in 1900 as a centerpiece of the program for economic uplift through the virtues of capitalism. Scott labored indefatigably, calling for annual meetings, identifying the ranking black entrepreneurs to be invited, and exploring means to promote black businesses.

After Washington died in 1915, Scott narrowly lost his bid to be Washington's successor at Tuskegee and in the African American community. Two years later, however, Scott became the highest-ranking African American government leader with his appointment as special adviser on Negro affairs to Secretary of War Newton D. Baker. In 1919—eager to escape from Tuskegee, where he was under the shadow of the new principal, Robert Russa Moton—Scott used this wartime appointment as the basis for new employment as secretary-treasurer and business manager of Howard University (founded 1867), which was considered the capstone of "Negro education." At Howard University, Scott used his ties to the Republican Party to obtain increased funding for the school and passage of the Enabling Act of 1926, which guaranteed Howard government funds for annual operating

Booker T. Washington, seated, and his private secretary Emmett Jay Scott, photographed by Frances Benjamin Johnston, 1906. (Library of Congress.)

expenses. Scott also led a successful campaign for Howard's first full-time elected African American president, Mordecai Johnson.

In the 1920s, black pride was manifested in such movements as the Harlem Renaissance; the Universal Negro Improvement Association (UNIA), led by the inimitable Jamaican Marcus Garvey; and remnants of Booker T. Washington's "Tuskegee machine," which was guided by Scott in political and economic activities such as supporting the Republican presidents Warren G. Harding, Calvin Coolidge, and Herbert Hoover. Scott also sought to expand African American business endeavors for both collective and personal economic uplift, reverting back to the promotion of activities of Booker T. Washington's time: black realtors, insurance firms, filmmakers, automobile producers, skin and hair care products, and the record industry. Notable in this regard were Scott's involvement in the making of the film *The Birth of a Race* and his efforts to establish an African American country club in Washington, D.C., where black businessmen could conduct negotiations in an agreeable and even opulent setting.

Scott remained a lifelong Republican. He served as the party's assistant publicity director from 1939 to 1942 in its efforts to restore blacks' historic allegiance and ties to it. In 1942, Scott rose to prominence as the director of the Sun Shipbuilding and Dry Dock Company's Yard Number 4, which built large maritime vessels for ocean transportation of supplies during World War II. This venture was an experiment in the use of black labor; the segregated black workforce numbered 12,000 at the height of production. Scott oversaw the yard's production of a transportation ship each month during the war.

Remaining loyal to the movement and ethos of Booker T. Washington, Scott sought at all times to involve himself in organizational and institutional efforts for reform and uplift. He served at varying times as secretary to the Southern Educational Fund, the Board of Indeterminate Sentence and Parole of the District of Columbia, and the Young Men's Christian Association.

Scott and his wife had five children. One of their daughters, Clarissa Scott, graduated from Wellesley College and achieved note as a promising poet during the Harlem Renaissance; their other two daughters, Evelyn and Lenore, were schoolteachers. Their elder son, Emmett Jr., became an architect; their younger son, Horace, became a physician. Scott's wife, Eleanora, died in 1939, and he himself died in 1957, both in Washington, D.C. His legacy was that of a Washingtonian, maintaining the Tuskegee approach to racial uplift throughout the twentieth century.

Biography

Emmett Jay Scott was born 13 February 1873 in Houston, Texas. He was educated in the public school system of Houston and at Wiley College, Marshall, Texas, from 1887 to 1889. Scott was founder and editor of *Texas Freeman*, 1893–1897. He was private secretary to Norris Wright Cuney, 1894–1897; private secretary to Booker T. Washington, 1897–1911; secretary of the National Negro Business League, 1900–1922; member of the American mission to Liberia, 1909; secretary of the International Conference on the Negro, 1912; and secretary of the Tuskegee Institute, 1912–1919. Scott was special assistant on Negro Affairs to Newton D. Baker, secretary of war, 1917–1919; and secretary-treasurer and business manager of Howard University, 1919–1938. He also was assistant publicity director of the Republican National Committee, 1939–1942; director of Yard Number 4 of the Sun Shipbuilding and Dry Dock Company, 1941–1945; and secretary of the Southern Educational Fund. Scott died in Washington, D.C., in 1957.

MACEO CRENSHAW DAILEY JR.

See also Birth of a Race, The; Delany, Clarissa Scott; Du Bois, W. E. B.; Moton, Robert Russa; National Negro Business League; Race Men; Trotter, William Monroe; Washington, Booker T.

Selected Works

Tuskegee and Its People. 1910.
Is Liberia Worth Saving? 1911.
Booker T. Washington: Building of a Civilization. 1916.
The American Negro in the War. 1919. (Rev. ed., *Scott's Official History of the American Negro in the World War.* 1969.)
Negro Migration During the War. 1920.

Further Reading

Booker T. Washington papers. Urbana: University of Illinois Press, 1872–1883, 13 vols.

Dailey, Maceo Crenshaw, Jr. "An Easy Alliance: Theodore Roosevelt and Emmett Jay Scott, 1900–1919." In *Theodore Roosevelt: Many Sided American*, ed. Natalie A. Naylor, Douglas Brinkley, and John Allen Gable. Interlaken, N.Y.: Heart of the Lakes, 1992.

———. "Neither 'Uncle Tom' nor 'Accommodationist': Booker T. Washington, Emmett Jay Scott, and Constructionalism." *Atlanta History: A Journal of Georgia and the South*, 38(4), 1995.

Harlan, Louis. *Booker T. Washington: The Making of a Black Leader, 1856–1901.* New York: Oxford University Press, 1972.

Scott, William Edouard

William Edouard Scott was one of the first African American artists to depict scenes of everyday African American life in his paintings, drawings, and prints. His determination to include African American subjects and themes in the early years of the twentieth century made him an important precursor to the Harlem Renaissance, when such interests and concerns became widespread among African American artists.

Scott was born in 1884 in Indianapolis. He studied at the Art Institute of Chicago before he went to Europe, where he lived from 1909 to 1914 except for occasional return visits to the United States. In France he studied with Henry Ossawa Tanner and at the Académie Julien and Académie Colarossi. While in Europe he exhibited his works at the Paris Salon and the Royal Academy of London. When he returned to the United States, he settled in Chicago, where he lived for most of the rest of his life.

Scott depicted a variety of fairly traditional subjects, including portraits, figures, and landscapes. His early works were impressionistic in style and subject matter. Scott was a very productive and popular portrait painter. He may have done more portraits than any other African American painter of the early twentieth century. His sitters were usually from the more affluent, educated black middle class. He also painted some historical portraits. Among these are paintings of Toussaint-Louverture and Booker T. Washington. Scott painted scenes of everyday life of rural African Americans in the South. During World War I, he traveled to France and sketched African American soldiers in action on the battlefields. His depictions of the rural South and African American soldiers were used as covers for the magazine *The Crisis*. In 1953, he painted portraits to commemorate the consecration of the first black bishops in the Roman Catholic Church.

Scott visited Haiti in 1931–1932, with a grant from the Rosenwald Foundation. During his relatively brief stay in Haiti, his style evolved considerably. His work became more personal, emotive, and expressive in the use of color and handling of paint. His brushwork became looser and his colors more intense. Essentially early-modernist principles became apparent in his paintings at this time. Scott produced 144 paintings and drawings in Haiti. Most of them were scenes of the everyday lives of Haitians. Among them are *Haitian Fisherman*, *Haitian Market*, *Turkey Vendor*, *Night Turtle Fishing*, and *When the Tide Is Out*. While he was in Haiti, an exhibit of his recent works was held in Port-au-Prince. The exhibit was promoted by the Haitian government, and twelve works were purchased by the president of Haiti. This exhibit was an enormous success for an artist of African descent at this time. In Haiti, Scott was also active in teaching art. He played a major role in invigorating Haitian art in the mid-twentieth century.

On returning to the United States, Scott became the most productive and popular African American muralist of his generation, although he had painted murals long before he went to Haiti. His first murals had been a series of twenty-four panels depicting biblical subjects for Indianapolis City Hospital in 1916. He painted a commemorative mural of Abraham Lincoln with his son for the Cook County Juvenile Courthouse in Illinois. He painted forty murals for churches in the Chicago area. He also painted many murals for field houses in Chicago's parks. In New York he painted murals for a YMCA in Harlem.

After several years of declining health, which included advanced diabetes and deteriorating vision, Scott died in 1964.

Biography

William Edouard Scott was born 11 March 1884, in Indianapolis. He was educated at Manual Training High School, Indianapolis; Art Institute of Chicago, 1904–1908; Académie Julien, Paris, 1912; and Académie Colarossi, Paris, 1913. He traveled to France, 1908–1915; and Haiti, 1931–1932. His awards and honors included first prize, Indiana State Fair, 1914; Frederick Manus Brand Prize, Art Institute of Chicago, twice; Harmon Foundation Gold Medal, 1927; Rosenwald Fellowship, 1931; Jesse Binga Prize, 1931; James McVeagh Prize, 1931; Municipal Art League Traveling Scholarship; and Legion of Honor, Government of Haiti. His memberships included the Art Institute of Chicago, Chicago Art League, and Hoosier Salon Alumni Association. Scott died 16 May 1964 in Chicago.

HERBERT R. HARTEL JR.

See also Crisis, The; Tanner, Henry Ossawa

Exhibitions

1912: Royal Academy, London.

1912, 1931: Salon d'Automne, Paris.

1928, 1931, 1933, 1934–1935: Harmon Foundation, New York.

1929, 1931: San Diego Fine Arts Society.

1931: Cincinnati Museum of Art; San Diego Museum of Art; Los Angeles County Museum of Art; Port-au-Prince. (Solo.)

1931, 1932: Art Institute of Chicago.

1931, 1935: Salon des Beaux Arts, Toquet, France.

1933: Smithsonian Institution, Washington, D.C.

1935: Findlay Galleries, Chicago; New Jersey State Museum, Trenton.

1936: Texas Centennial Exposition, Museum of Fine Arts, Dallas.

1940: American Negro Exhibition.

1941, 1945: South Side Community Art Center, Chicago.

1945: Howard University Gallery of Art, Washington, D.C.

Further Reading

Driscoll, David. *Two Centuries of Black American Art*. New York and Los Angeles, Calif.: Knopf and Los Angeles County Museum of Art, pp. 57, 90, 138.

Henderson, Harry, and Romare Bearden. *African-American Artists: From 1792 to the Present*. New York: Pantheon, 1993.

Lewis, Samella. *African-American Art and Artists*. Berkeley: University of California Press, 1990.

Patton, Sharon F. *African-American Art*. New York: Oxford University Press, 1998.

Powell, Richard J. *Black Art and Culture in the Twentieth Century*. New York: Thames & Hudson, 1997.

Reynolds, Gary. *Against the Odds: African-American Artists and the Harmon Foundation*. Newark, N.J.: Newark Museum, 1990.

"Scott, William Edouard." In *African-American Artists: A Bio-Bibliographical Dictionary*, ed. Theresa Dickason Cederholm. Boston, Mass.: Boston Public Library, 1973, pp. 249–250.

Taylor, William E., and Harriet G. Warkel. *Shared Heritage: Art by Four African-Americans*. Indianapolis, Ind.: Indianapolis Museum of Art and Indianapolis University Press, 1996.

Scottsboro

On 25 March 1931, nine young African American men were falsely accused of raping two white women on a train passing through northern Alabama. Eight of the nine were sentenced to die. Contemporary reactions to the fate of the Scottsboro boys, as they came to be known, suggest the complex interrelations of race, gender, and class-based oppression in America during the Jim Crow era and illuminate the significance of the Great Depression for the Harlem Renaissance.

The accused—all poor, all uneducated, and ranging in age from thirteen to nineteen—had been hitching rides on a freight train. After a fight between the youths and some white men, the train was stopped. Hastily deputized white men and a sizable mob

The Scottsboro boys. (Brown Brothers.)

quickly gathered to round up the blacks. Though only four of the youths had participated in the fight, all nine, along with one white man, were arrested for vagrancy. Two white women in overalls were also discovered illegally riding the train. Recently laid off from the cotton mills, the young, unemployed women were in search of jobs. One of them, Ruby Bates, claimed that she and her friend, Victoria Price, had been raped by the black men. Though evidence conflicts as to whether the women or a deputy first mentioned rape, the accusation protected Bates and Price against charges of vagrancy or violation of the Mann Act (crossing state lines for immoral purposes).

The nine accused rapists were immediately taken to Scottsboro, where a lynch mob had assembled outside the jail. Taking a stand against extralegal violence, the sheriff of Jackson County asked the governor to call in the National Guard. Twelve days after the arrests, the trials began. Despite conflicting testimony from the accused, the women, and other witnesses, and despite a lack of physical evidence, in four days the all-white juries had convicted eight of the defendants—convictions carrying a sentence of death. In 1932, the U.S. Supreme Court twice reversed guilty verdicts. The following year, Ruby Bates retracted her accusation of rape. Nevertheless, the last defendant, Haywood Patterson,

remained in prison until 1942, when he escaped. Clarence Norris, the last surviving Scottsboro boy, was pardoned in 1976 by Governor George Wallace.

The Struggle Over the Defense

As the case attracted worldwide attention, Scottsboro became a crucial measure of the influence of two groups: the reform-oriented National Association for the Advancement of Colored People (NAACP) and the revolutionary United States Communist Party (CPUSA). After the first trials, the International Labor Defense (ILD), the legal branch of the CPUSA, took over the defense. Declaring the case a "legal lynching," ILD representatives believed the murder of black men for the rape of white women to be one instrument in an arsenal of capitalist weaponry deployed against impoverished working-class Americans. In their view, the defendants, the plaintiffs, and those who believed the story were alike victims of "false consciousness"— ignorant, blighted by poverty, and easily manipulated by incendiary media portrayals of the youths as sexually uncontrollable beasts. Such portrayals, they argued, functioned to pit black and white workers against one another. In conjunction with its mass antilynching campaigns, the ILD hoped that demonstrating the boys' innocence would educate American workers of both races, paving the way for interracial labor solidarity and, eventually, the formation of a revolutionary American proletariat.

The NAACP, led by the anticommunist Walter White, initially stayed away from the case, fearing to be associated with either potential rapists or revolutionaries. The NAACP depended on the largely northern middle and upper classes for support, and its eventual fight for the defense was based on its commitment to eliminating race prejudice within the legal system of the United States. Both White and W. E. B. Du Bois claimed that the Communist Party had less interest in saving the defendants than in martyring them to the revolutionary cause. The communists, they argued, were taking advantage of Americans' increasingly precarious economic circumstances. However, as the trials dragged on and the CPUSA shifted its policy from domestic antiracism to the international fight against fascism, compromise became a necessity. By 1935, the ILD and the NAACP had joined with the American Civil Liberties Union (ACLU) to form the Scottsboro Defense Committee, which in 1937 brokered a plea to release four of the nine boys in exchange for a promised end to communist agitation about the case.

From the time of the arrests, protesters worldwide took up the call to "free the Scottsboro boys." In 1931, Harlem was the site of three significant protests, one of which turned violent. In 1933, 150,000 black and white protesters marched together through New York. In addition to marches and rallies, residents of Harlem signed mass petitions and sent hundreds of thousands of telegrams and letters to local, state, and national authorities. Harlem's involvement in these protests, sponsored by the ILD, signifies the extent to which the communists successfully radicalized significant numbers of African Americans during the Depression.

Literary Scottsboro

Divergent understandings of Scottsboro's meanings are illustrated in the poems, drama, and music of the Harlem Renaissance. Comparing representations of Scottsboro by Langston Hughes and Countee Cullen illustrates the tension between artists committed to Du Bois's notion of the "talented tenth" and those committed to writing for the common folk. Using the vernacular and familiar Christian iconography, Hughes's poem "Christ in Alabama" (1931) indicts the racism of organized religion as well as ironically recalling the historical and continuing rapes of black women by white men. In contrast, Cullen's "Scottsboro, Too, Is Worth Its Song" (1934) addresses poets, implying that race accounts for the conspicuous silence of those who he believes can effect change—black and white intellectuals and artists. Turning even further away from Alain Locke's belief in the leadership of the "enlightened minorities of both race groups" (1925/1997, 9), Hughes's increasing radicalism is manifest in his pamphlet "Scottsboro Limited" (1932). Focusing on the interrelations of racial and class oppression in America, the play in the pamphlet uses agitprop techniques to call for an end to capitalist exploitation. Together with the poems, the play *Scottsboro Limited* portrays the case in terms of the need for interracial solidarity among workers.

Other writers on Scottsboro include Sterling Brown, Robert Hayden, Theodore Dreiser, Kay Boyle, and Nancy Cunard. Dramas about Scottsboro include *Scottsboro Limited* and John Wexley's *They Shall Not Die*. Songs and ballads performed at protests and fund-raisers include L. E. Swift's "The Scottsboro Boys Shall Not Die" and Leadbelly's "The Scottsboro Boys."

SONDRA GUTTMAN

See also Brown, Sterling; Communist Party; Cullen, Countee; Cunard, Nancy; Dreiser, Theodore; Hayden, Robert; Hughes, Langston; National Association for the Advancement of Colored People; Talented Tenth; They Shall Not Die; White, Walter

Further Reading

Carter, Dan T. *Scottsboro: A Tragedy of the American South.* Baton Rouge: Louisiana University Press, 1969.

Frick, John W. "Staging Scottsboro: The Violence of Representation and Class-Race Negotiations in the 1930s." *New England Theatre Journal*, 6, 1995.

Goodman, James. *Stories of Scottsboro.* New York: Vintage, 1994.

Hughes, Langston. *The Political Plays of Langston Hughes: With Introduction and Analysis by Susan Duffy.* Carbondale and Edwardsville: Southern Illinois University Press, 2000.

Kelly, Robin D. G. *Hammer and Hoe: Alabama Communists During the Great Depression.* Chapel Hill: University of North Carolina Press, 1990.

Locke, Alain. "The New Negro." In *The New Negro: An Interpretation*, ed. Alain Locke. New York: Albert and Charles Boni, 1925. (Reprint, New York: Scribner, 1997.)

Maxwell, William J. *New Negro, Old Left: African American Writing and Communism Between the Wars.* New York: Columbia University Press, 1999.

Naison, Mark. *Communists in Harlem During the Depression.* New York: Grove, 1984.

Thurston, Michael. "Black Christ, Red Flag: Langston Hughes on Scottsboro." *College Literature*, 22(3), October 1995.

Second Harlem Renaissance

The second Harlem Renaissance (1930–1945) differed importantly from the first. With the Depression, economic conditions in New York had changed, with dramatic and disastrous effects on blacks in Harlem. Soaring unemployment, heightened discrimination, and political neglect all worked to transform Harlem's once glittering facade into an ever-expanding array of decaying tenements and lost opportunities. The "talented tenth," the old Harlemites of literary and cultural acclaim who had dominated the 1920s, retreated into their enclaves on Sugar Hill even as the great migration of southerners decreased to a small trickle. During the Depression Harlem became a world of vanished dreams.

Yet the infusion of funding through the New Deal, in the form of the federal arts, theater, and music programs, provided the impetus for a second Harlem Renaissance. If 125th Street, the Apollo Theater, and the Cotton Club had been the center of the first Harlem Renaissance, in the 1930s 135th Street became the cultural center for the second. In a stretch of two blocks, from just off Seventh Avenue eastward to Lenox, stood the Harlem YMCA, the Schomburg Collection of the Harlem Branch of the New York Public Library, and the offices of the National Association for the Advancement of Colored People (NAACP), the National Urban League, and the *Amsterdam News*. Four blocks to the South lay Harlem's legitimate theater, the Lafayette, home to the Harlem unit of the Federal Theater Project; and one block to the north, between Seventh and Lenox avenues, stood Harlem General Hospital. Harlem's largest church, Abyssinian Baptist, led by Rev. Adam Clayton Powell Jr., occupied a Tudor-Gothic building on 138th Street and had a congregation estimated at 13,000. Members of Harlem's artistic community gravitated to the corner of 135th Street and Seventh Avenue, where they might encounter James Weldon Johnson, Countee Cullen, Claude McKay, or the sculptor Augusta Savage, and the painters Aaron Douglas, Charles Alston, Romare Bearden, and Jacob Lawrence.

Bearden expressed well the paradoxical effect of the Great Depression on Harlem's artists. "The 'movement,'" he recalled, "was a positive, proud, and participatory realization of what it meant to be black—not on the soirée scale of the Harlem renaissance, *but on a mass scale.*" During the second Harlem Renaissance, New York's African American painters, sculptors, writers, musicians, actors, dancers, and poets expanded the meaning of modern African American culture. Through the support of the federal arts and theater projects, artists in Harlem affirmed their artistic independence and engaged in a political struggle for racial equality. Whereas writers had dominated the first Harlem Renaissance, visual artists led the second renaissance. Bearden, Savage, Alston, and Lawrence used the resources of Harlem and the New Deal to transform New York's racial and artistic dialogue.

The sculptor Augusta Savage emerged as a central figure in the creation of the second Harlem Renaissance. She was born in Florida and educated at Cooper Union; in the 1920s, she had worked as a laundress as she struggled to gain acceptance in the arts. In 1931, with support from the Carnegie Foundation, she opened her own studio school on 143rd Street. Savage's Harlem Community Arts Center, later funded by the Federal Arts Project, reached out to the community, offering workshops to more than 1,500 students, including the psychologist Kenneth B. Clark and the sculptor Gwendolyn Knight, between 1931 and 1936.

In 1935, seventy-five African American artists joined Savage to form the Harlem Artists Guild, which devoted itself to sharpening the focus of black artists on issues of racism, poverty, and unemployment. It had headquarters on 136th Street, and it found a supporter in the politically active abstract painter Stuart Davis, who approved of the guild's strategy of pressuring the Federal Arts Project (FAP) of the Works Progress Administration (WPA) to accept more black participants. As Alston remembered, "We formed it originally to create a pressure group to get more Black artists on the federal projects." While the FAP eventually hired 115 African American artists, supervisory positions remained virtually impossible to obtain.

Charles Alston became the first Harlem artist, and the first African American, appointed as a supervisor by the FAP, when he was chosen to direct the mural project at Harlem General Hospital. When the mural directed by Alston, *Mystery and Medicine* (1938–1939), was unveiled, a wave of criticism surged up. White officials at the hospital insisted that Alston alter the mural, which showed blacks and whites working together on an equal footing. In response, Alston mobilized the Harlem Artists Guild and with the support of Burgoyne Diller, the FAP's administrator for the mural division, forced the hospital to accept the work.

Alston, who had been educated at Columbia University, loved jazz and blues and often frequented the Schomburg Library, whose collection of African art tempered his training as a modernist. Despite his triumph in the controversy over the mural, Alston did not consider himself a political artist. "In those days it was Negro pride, now it's black and African," he recalled. Alston felt that, as a black artist, "you cannot but be concerned about how [art] affects your people."

Like Savage, Alston created a community art program, the Harlem Art Workshop, which he located at a renovated stable at 306 West 141st Street. Studio 306, or just "306," became the hub of the FAP in Harlem and the heart of the second Harlem Renaissance. Both Jacob Lawrence and Romare Bearden studied with Alston at 306; Alston lived in an apartment at the rear of the building, and Lawrence maintained a small studio there in the late 1930s. Buoyed by the financial and political support of the WPA, 306 brought Harlem's artists together. Alston, Lawrence, Bearden, Gwendolyn Wright, and Ralph Ellison worked and argued with Harlem's older artistic generation. As Lawrence remembered, 306 offered "a social and artistic atmosphere. I would hear talk about the various problems in their special fields of acting, theater, and so on. Bearden . . . was experimental and scholarly, very much involved and curious."

Bearden and Lawrence emerged as the dominant young painters of the second Harlem Renaissance. Lawrence's work tied Harlem's artistic revival directly to the second "great migration" of African Americans to New York. Set off by World War II, the second great migration brought hundreds of thousands of rural blacks from the South to the cities of the North. As New York broke out of the Depression and its economy boomed, the city lured blacks with promises of freedom and opportunity.

"People would come up to the centers," wrote Jacob Lawrence of his early apprenticeship at the Harlem Artists Guild. "People like Katherine Dunham, Countee Cullen, Langston Hughes. They may not have talked with me because I was too young, but I would hear their conversations with each other." Lawrence, whose southern-born mother migrated to New York with him in 1930, had first studied with Alston at 306 and then studied at the American Artists School downtown on Fourteenth Street. Between 1937 and 1938 Lawrence painted a forty-one canvas series on the life of Toussaint-Louverture, the first of his explorations of black history. "Having no Negro history makes the Negro people feel inferior to the rest of the world," he wrote.

In the early 1940s, Lawrence painted his masterpiece, the series called *The Migration of the Negro*. Working in a modern narrative style, Lawrence used the panels of this series to tell the stories of the African American migration northward during World War I. Perhaps prophetically, he chose to tell this story on the eve of the second great migration during World War II. Lawrence, as if following Bearden's injunction, focused on the epic journey of African American masses, satchels in hand, leaving the South for the "promised lands" of New York, St. Louis, and Chicago. Lawrence's work is painted in a collage-cubist vocabulary, crowding the subjects together as they press against each other and struggle to board the trains that will take them northward. Lawrence told his audience that African Americans left the South to escape racial violence and hatred, for fear of their lives. He showed his audience that the migrants encountered a new form of racism and a new kind of urban melancholy when they arrived.

Later Lawrence turned to African American life in New York. The *Harlem Series* combined elements of his earlier experimentalism with collage-like figures and bold graphic images. Lawrence painted wartime Harlem, moving his gaze from poverty and cheap bootleg whiskey to the newly rich middle class who dress to the nines as they prepare for a night on the town. As in the *Migration Series*, Lawrence continued to use the flattened perspective of modernism together with decorative patterns reminiscent of Henri Matisse. In the *Harlem Series*, Lawrence painted the social world that he and Bearden had come to know.

As young men, both Lawrence and Bearden often took off from 306 to gather at Joe's on 136th Street or at the Savoy Ballroom, whose manager admitted artists free of charge. At the Savoy, they listened and danced to the era's great jazz bands, black and white, from Benny Moten to Benny Goodman. Bearden and Alston formed what the *Amsterdam News* called the "dawn patrol," hitting all the after-hours spots like Mom Young's, where "for twenty-five cents you could get a beer that she made herself in a coffee can. . . . This was a place where the artists came, and the show people came after the show." Young's, like Alston's 306 or the Harlem Artists Guild and Savage's Harlem Community Art Center, gave Harlem during this second renaissance its own institutions, which replaced the white-owned patronage of the 1920s. Black pride combined with modernist artistic accomplishment and direct political engagement, rather than racial uplift, characterized the second Harlem Renaissance. From the Lafayette Theater, a few blocks South of 306, the actors Rex Ingram and Canada Lee often walked to join Ellison, Bearden, Lawrence, and Alston at 306. Alston's studio, remembered Bearden, "evoked the feeling in African American artists of belonging to a creative community." Nothing, he added, was more stimulating to the crowd at 306 than the WPA Negro Theater Project.

Established in 1935 in the wake of the Harlem riots of March 1935, the Negro Theater Project of the Federal Theater Project at the Lafayette Theater was directed by John Houseman, who, concerned that the Negro Theater Unit produce plays for and by black people, appointed African American deputies and gave regular employment to black actors like Jack Carter, Canada Lee, and Eric Burroughs. Houseman, together with Orson Welles, produced an extraordinary "voodoo" *Macbeth* in April 1936. They pulled out all the stops in this epochal production. Set in Haiti and featuring a troupe of African drummers, the new *Macbeth* transformed Birnam Wood into Napoleonic Haiti. Like Lawrence's series about Toussaint-Louverture, "voodoo" *Macbeth* re-created a critical chapter in black history.

The show played at the Lafayette for ten weeks and then on Broadway for another eight. The Federal Theater subsequently produced it nationally. Following this triumph, praised wildly by Brooks Atkinson in the *New York Times*, Houseman left the Negro Theater Unit and turned it over to his African American colleagues. Like the federally supported programs in the visual arts, the Negro Theater experiment belongs to the second Harlem Renaissance. There, African Americans in the 1930s assumed control of their artistic organizations and created art on their own terms, often addressing the racial inequities in American life but also confirming the value and richness of African American culture. Without the Lafayette Theater and the Harlem Artists Guild, the federal theater and arts projects in Harlem would have simply mirrored the segregation in American society. Augusta Savage's Harlem Community Art Center and Charles Alston's Studio 306 provided the means for Harlem's youth to become artists, writers, and actors. The Depression provided an unintended blessing. Supported by federal programs and mobilized by community needs, Harlem's artists used their isolation to form a new artistic community. Within the political and social context of the New Deal, the artists of Harlem's second renaissance worked alongside their white counterparts downtown as they broke through New York's de facto segregation.

New York's federal arts programs initiated a process that within a decade abolished Jim Crow in New York, a dream that many in the first Harlem Renaissance had embraced as well. Moreover, the second Harlem Renaissance linked Harlem's literary movement of the 1920s with the far more militant bebop jazz and civil rights revolutions of the late 1940s. Without the second Harlem Renaissance, it would become almost impossible to imagine the self-conscious independence and brilliance of Charlie Parker, Dizzy Gillespie, and Miles Davis.

PETER M. RUTKOFF
WILLIAM B. SCOTT

See also Abyssinian Baptist Church; Alston, Charles; Bearden, Romare; Cullen, Countee; Douglas, Aaron; Ellison, Ralph; Federal Programs; Harlem General Hospital; Johnson, James Weldon; Lafayette Theater; Lawrence, Jacob; Lee, Canada; McKay, Claude; Savage, Augusta; Savoy Ballroom; Works Progress Administration

Further Reading

Alston, Charles. Interviews, 1962 and 1968. Archives of American Art, Smithsonian Institution.
———. Papers. Archives of American Art, Smithsonian Institution.
Bearden, Romare, and Harry Henderson. *History of African-American Artists*. New York, 1993.
Schwartzman, Myron. *Romare Bearden, His Life and Art*. New York, 1990.
Scott, William B., and Peter M. Rutkoff. *New York Modern: The Arts and the City*. Baltimore, Md., 1999.
Wheat, Allen Harkens. *Jacob Lawrence, American Painter*. Seattle, Wash., 1986.

Senghor, Léopold

Léopold Sédar Senghor was both a poet and a statesman. His life in some ways parallels that of Langston Hughes—a child of the hinterland, raised largely by his mother and her family, and assured of a classical education by an ambitious, entrepreneurial father. Both struggled with poetic sensibility grafted onto Negro or African roots and identity.

Senghor's early years were spent among an extended matrilineal family and the griots of Joal, Thiés region, on the Atlantic coast South of Dakar. Although his family status freed him from sharing the labor of transhumant economic existence, he felt the poverty of the agricultural milieu and formed the ambition to become a teacher and priest. At age seven, he was transplanted from a Muslim and traditional setting to Catholic mission schools. His mother called him "Toubab," or white man, when he visited during holidays from Collège Libermann, a seminary in Dakar. Father Lalouze, director of the seminary, decided that, despite his academic excellence, Senghor lacked a religious vocation (1927). At a public secondary school (later Lycée van Vollnhoven), Senghor earned two French baccalaureates (1927 and 1928).

In 1928, he won a scholarship from the governor general of French West Africa for study in Paris and entered the Lycée Louis-le-Grand (where he became a close friend of his classmate Georges Pompidou). He studied at the École Normale Supérieure and then the Sorbonne (1931–1935) and did fieldwork on indigenous Senegalese languages under Paul Rivet (director of the Museum of Man) and Lilias Homburger. He also frequented the salon of the Nardal sisters from Martinique and discovered the American writers W. E. B. Du Bois, Langston Hughes, Jean Toomer, and Claude McKay. McKay's *Banjo,* translated into French by the fall of 1931, became a major influence; and Senghor translated the works of Hughes, Countee Cullen, and other writers of the Harlem Renaissance. With the West Indian Aimé Césaire and the Guianan Léon Damas, he developed an ideology of pride in African culture and helped found the Association of West African Students and the journal *L'Étudiant Noir* (*Black Student*), in which the term *négritude* (negritude) first appeared. Ethnological studies by Maurice Delafosse and Leo Frobenius underscored the significance of African contributions to world culture, which Senghor incorporated into his philosophical writings and poetry. He wrote a thesis, "Exoticism in Baudelaire," and obtained the equivalent of a Ph.D. in French grammar. He was appointed professor of literature and grammar at two lycées; during World War II, he served in the army and was a prisoner of war. He became a professor of African languages and civilization at the École Nationale de la France d'Outre-Mer (National Overseas School of France; later the Institute des Hautes Études d'Outre-Mer). He was also selected as one of the first two delegates to the French assembly from Senegal. He was immediately placed in charge of ensuring that the new constitution would be written in the purest French, entering on a career that involved many international cultural and scientific organizations.

Senghor's first published poems appeared in a review, *Volontés* (*Offerings*): "In Memoriam" and "To the Senegalese *Tirailleurs* Who Died for France" (1939). Following the appearance of his first book of poetry in 1945, *Chants d'ombre* (*Songs of Shadow*), he helped a fellow Senegalese, Alioune Diope, found the review *Présence Africaine* (1947). Other volumes of poetry included *Hosties noires* (*Black Hosts*) and *Anthologie de la nouvelle poésie nègre et malgache* (*An Anthology of the New Black and Madagascan Poetry*), for which Jean-Paul Sartre wrote an introduction entitled "Orphée noire" ("Black Orpheus"). Sartre's interpretation of negritude as a manifestation of existentialism enhanced Senghor's reputation. Senghor's own poetry is rich in African subject matter and allusion; most poems specify types of drums or musical instruments—sometimes jazz ensembles—that should accompany their reading.

In 1950–1951, Senghor was a delegate to the Fifth Session of the United Nations General Assembly; in 1952, he was secretary of state for scientific research and a founder of what became the University of Dakar. He was mayor of Thiés in 1955–1956, published *Ethiopiques* (poetry) and married Colette Hubert of Normandy in 1956, and became leader of a new political party in Senegal and adviser to Charles de Gaulle in 1957–1958. Cautiously urging effective self-determination for Senegal and other colonial entities, Senghor helped to dismantle colonial rule. In 1960, he was instrumental in persuading de Gaulle to endorse formation of the Mali Federation and shortly after was elected president of the newly formed republic of Senegal (5 September 1960). In 1961, on a visit to the United States, he arranged for Langston Hughes to be invited to a dinner at the White House so that they could meet.

During twenty years as president (reelected at intervals), Senghor published poetry (notably *Nocturnes* in 1961) and essays (*Liberté*, Vols. 1–4, 1964–1969) and received countless honors, among them the Apollinaire Prize for poetry (1974), honorary degrees from several universities, and election to the Academy of Moral and Political Science of the Institute of France (1969).

Senghor's broad worldview included African traditions of his birthplace, his Catholic education, his concentration on New Negro writing in the 1920s and 1930s, and his involvement in new trends of ethnology and religion through academic advisers and Teilhard de Chardin, to whom he dedicated a compilation of essays (*Liberté*, Vol. 5, 1993). Senghor attributed some of his inspiration explicitly to the international leadership of the Harlem Renaissance and to renaissance principles, especially respect for the civilizations of Africa and the influence of the African diaspora, the common heritage of blacks everywhere, and the need to ameliorate problems of the working classes.

Critics of "negritude" like Wole Soyinka (1999), who accused Senghor of yielding to his youthful ambition to become a priest and teacher, focus on conservative aspects of the concept; but Senghor's approach to political involvement was unquestionably inspired by internalized African values and "New Negro" ideas. Senghor's videotaped address to a three-day celebration by UNESCO of his ninetieth birthday confirmed his lifelong identification with a tradition of prophetic admonition and a plea for cultural *métissage* (blending) and for integrated humanism based on the cross-fertilization of values among the cultures of Africa and its diaspora, of Asiatic peoples, and of Europeans and their dispersed cultures. Senghor is sometimes compared to Martin Luther King Jr. with regard to religious fervor and activism; such comparisons must have pleased Senghor, who admired King and who consistently preached universal tolerance throughout a long and distinguished career.

Biography

Léopold Sédar Senghor was born in Ndjitor, Senegal, 14 August 1906 (father Serer, mother Mandinke or Peul-Fulani). He was educated at Catholic mission schools in Joal and N'Gasobil; Collège Libermann, Dakar; Lycée Louis-le-Grand, École Normale Supérieure (Licence des Lettres, 1931); and the Sorbonne (Diplôme d'Études Supérieures, 1932), studying linguistics with Ferdinand Brunot and Charles Bruneau. Senghor promulgated the concept of "negritude" with Aimé Césaire and Léon Damas, inspired partly by writers of the Harlem Renaissance. Senghor was the first African to earn the Agrégé de l'Université (1935). He was a professor of literature and grammar, Lycée Descartes, Tours (1935–1938) and Lycée Marcelin-Berthelet near Paris (1938–1940, 1942–1944). During World War II, he was an infantryman, a prisoner of war, and a member of the Resistance. In 1945, his first book of poetry, *Songs of the Shadow*, was published, and he was chosen as the first delegate to the French Constituent Assembly from Senegal. He married Ginette Eboué in 1946; they divorced in 1955. He married Colette Hubert in 1956; they had a son, Philippe Maquilen. Senghor was an adviser to Charles de Gaulle. He was president of the Mali Federation, then was elected president of the new republic of Senegal in 1960; he resigned in 1980. He was a gold medalist and member of the French Academy and received numerous prizes, awards, and honorary degrees in the United States, France, and Europe. The French University of Alexandria, Egypt, was named for him. He died in Normandy 20 December 2001.

NAN SUMNER-MACK

See also Césaire, Aimé; Damas, Léon; Negritude

Selected Works

Anthologie de la nouvelle poésie nègre et malgache (*An Anthology of the New Black and Madagascan Poetry*). Paris: Presses Universitaires de France, 1969.
Ce que je crois: Négritude, francité, et civilisation de l'universel (*What I Believe*). Paris: B. Grasset, 1988.
Chants d'ombre (*Songs of Shadow*). Paris: Éditions du Seuil, 1945.
The Collected Poetry, trans. Melvin Dixon. Charlottesville: University Press of Virginia, 1998.
Ethiopiques. Paris: Éditions du Seuil, 1956.
Hosties noires. Paris: Éditions du Seuil, 1948.
Liberté I: Négritude et humanism. Paris: Éditions du Seuil, 1964.
Liberté V: Le dialogue des cultures. Paris: Éditions du Seuil, 1993.
Nocturnes, trans. John Reed and Olive Wake, intro. Paulette J. Trout. New York: Third Press, 1971.
On African Socialism, trans. and intro. Mercer Cook. New York: Praeger, 1964.

Further Reading

Ba, Sylvia Washington. *The Concept of Negritude in the Poetry of Léopold Sédar Senghor*. Princeton, N.J.: Princeton University Press, 1973.
Guibert, Armand. *Léopold Sédar Senghor: l'homme et l'oeuvre*. Paris: Présence Africaine, 1962.
Hymans, Jacques Louis. *Léopold Sédar Senghor: An Intellectual Biography*. Edinburgh: University Press, 1971.
Kesteloot, Lilyan. *Les écrivains noirs de langue française: naissance d'une littérature*. Bruxelles: Université Libre de Bruxelles, Institute de Sociologie, 1971. (See also English version: *Black Writers in French: A Literary History of Negritude*, trans. Ellen Conroy Kennedy. Philadelphia, Pa.: Temple University Press, 1974.)
Markovitz, Irving Leonard. *Léopold Sédar Senghor and the Politics of Negritude*. New York: Atheneum, 1969.
McKay, Claude. *Banjo: A Story Without a Plot*. New York and London: Harper, 1929.
Mezu, Sebastian Okechukwu. *Léopold Sédar Senghor et la défense et illustration de la civilisation noire*. Paris: M. Didier, 1968.
Milcent, Ernest, and Monique Sordet. *Léopold Sédar Senghor et la naissance de l'Afrique moderne*. Paris: Éditions Seghers, 1969.
Sartre, Jean-Paul. "Orphée noir." In *Anthologie de la nouvelle poésie nègre et malgache*. Paris: Présence

Africaine, 1948. (See also English version: *Black Orpheus*, trans. S. W. Allen. Paris: Présence Africaine, 1963.)

Soyinka, Wole. *The Burden of Memory, the Muse of Forgiveness*. New York and Oxford: Oxford University Press, 1999.

Vaillant, Janet A. *Black, French, and African*. Cambridge, Mass.: Harvard University Press, 1990.

Servant in the House, The

The Servant in the House (1907), a play by Charles Rann Kennedy (1871–1950), reflects the author's Christian idealism and the "social gospel" movement. Kennedy was an ardent advocate of Christian principles and used his plays to explore their religious and sociological implications. The resulting works were not always effective as drama, although Thomas Dickinson observed of *Servant in the House*: "The American stage has not elsewhere seen as perfect an example of adaptation of dramatic format to didactic purpose" (1967, 180).

The Servant in the House opened on 23 March 1908 at the Savoy Theater, New York, produced by Henry Miller. It ran for eighty performances, closed on 1 June 1908, then started touring. Its English premiere was on 25 October 1909 at the Adelphi in London. It was revived four times in New York: in 1918, 1921, 1925, and 1926; and it was part of the repertoire of the Lafayette Theater in Harlem.

This play, in five acts, concerns Rev. William Smythe, his wife, and their niece Mary; they are anxiously awaiting the arrival of two bishops, who they hope will help with the funding needed repairs to their dilapidated church. One, the rich and worldly bishop of Lancashire, is Smythe's brother-in-law; the other, the bishop of Benares, is Smythe's brother. Another brother—Robert, Mary's father—is also visiting, but he is not entirely welcome: He is a common laborer, and because of his own experiences with suffering, he is rather antagonistic to the church. The bishop of Lancashire and Robert arrive, with a humble servant called Manson, but there is no sign of the bishop of Benares. As they are wondering about his absence, Manson guides them to reflect on their lives, reviews past mistakes and suffering, and brings the family members to a reconciliation. He then reveals himself as Smythe's brother.

Charles Rann Kennedy came from a family of classical scholars. He married a famous actress, Edith Wynne Matthison, and became an American citizen in

1917. His career as a playwright reached its height before World War I, though after the war he continued to create plays and worked with students at Bennett College. *The Servant in the House* was made into a film in 1918; it was directed by Hugh Ryan (Jack) Conway and had its premiere in July 1920 at the Strand Theater in Washington, D.C.

Amy Lee

See also Harlem: 3—Entertainment; Lafayette Theater

Further Reading

Bordman, Gerald. *American Theatre: A Chronicle of Comedy and Drama, 1869–1914*. New York: Oxford University Press, 1994.

Dickinson, Thomas H. *Playwrights of the New American Theatre*. Freeport, N.Y.: Books for Libraries, 1967.

Loney, Glenn. *Twentieth-Century Theatre*, Vol. 1. New York: Facts on File, 1983.

Meserve, Walter J. *An Outline History of American Drama*. New York: Feedback Theatrebooks and Prospero, 1994.

Munden, Kenneth W., ed. *The American Film Institute Catalog of Motion Pictures Produced in the United States*, Vol. 1, *Feature Films, 1911–1920*. New York: Bowker, 1971.

"Servant in the House." *Internet Broadway Database*. (Web site.)

Seven Arts

Seven Arts was a pacifist political and literary magazine, founded by a poet and former social worker, James Oppenheim, in 1916. Oppenheim asked the writers Waldo Frank and Van Wyck Brooks to be associate editors, and they were soon joined by the radical Floyd Dell and other figures of the "lost generation." Oppenheim also obtained the sponsorship of a patron, Annette Kittredge Rankine. *Seven Arts* was a groundbreaking venture: Unlike any other American writing at the time, it presented a courageous, almost brazen mix of poetry, fiction, and drama. It promoted art as a regenerative social force and covered topics of interest to New York's intellectuals, such as cultural criticism, pacifism, and psychoanalysis.

Seven Arts published Claude McKay's first poem, "The Harlem Dancer," under the pseudonym Eli Edwards in 1917, making him the first black American to appear in a white avant-garde literary magazine.

This early work was the first substantial poem by a black writer in print since Paul Laurence Dunbar's dialect pieces at the turn of the twentieth century. "The Harlem Dancer" and the Silent Protest Parade of the same year—1917—may also mark the beginning of the movement that came to be known as the Harlem Renaissance.

Though it was published for only one year, *Seven Arts* had a significant impact on the New Negro movement. Because books were too expensive to reach a broad readership, the movement depended on periodicals, including but not exclusively those of the black community, to facilitate a conversation between writers and readers. *Seven Arts*, one of the most dynamic publications of the "lost generation," helped to launch Sherwood Anderson (a businessman turned writer) and introduced the French avant-garde to the United States. It also provided a forum for the pacifist cultural critic Randolph Bourne. It published one of the first manifestos proclaiming the imminent conquest of art and humanism over materialism.

When the editors of *Seven Arts* opposed the United States' participation in World War I, Rankine withdrew her financial support; as a result, the journal collapsed after one year in print. It merged with the literary journal *The Dial*, which was published until 1929.

KATHLEEN COLLINS

See also Anderson, Sherwood; Dunbar, Paul Laurence; Frank, Waldo; Lynching: Silent Protest Parade; Magazines and Journals; McKay, Claude

Further Reading

Kellner, Bruce, ed. *The Harlem Renaissance: A Historical Dictionary for the Era.* New York: Methuen, 1984.

Lewis, David Levering. *When Harlem Was in Vogue.* New York: Penguin, 1987.

Oppenheim, James. "The Story of the Seven Arts." *American Mercury*, 20, 1930.

Watson, Steven. *The Harlem Renaissance, Hub of African-American Culture, 1920–1930.* New York: Pantheon, 1995.

Shipp, Jesse A.

Jesse A. Shipp (1859–1934) was a producer, director, playwright, librettist, and performer in musical and dramatic theater. He was a pioneer in black musical comedy and contributed to the dismantling of holdovers from the minstrel tradition. As a chief librettist and director of Bert Williams and George Walker's shows, he was also one of the earliest blacks to direct a musical on Broadway and indeed may have been the first.

Shipp began his career touring with the Sam P. Jacks Revue in 1879; in the 1880s, he performed in beer gardens and variety halls. He toured with the Beethoven Quartet and later worked with the integrated Eureka Minstrels, a troupe of African Americans and white Englishmen. After the Eureka Minstrels broke up, many of the African Americans, including Shipp, continued to work together as the Georgia Minstrels. Shipp then joined another integrated troupe, Primrose and West's Forty Whites and Thirty Blacks, but eventually he left minstrelsy for musicals. The first musical in which he performed was *The Octoroons* (1895); the second was *Oriental American* (1896).

Beginning in 1899, Shipp cowrote (mainly with Alex C. Rogers), directed, and performed in most of Williams and Walker's musicals, including *The Policy Players*, 1899; *The Sons of Ham*, in which he played Old Ham, 1900–1902; *In Dahomey*, in which he played Hustling Charlie, 1902–1905; *Abyssinia*, in which he played the Tegulet, a chief justice, 1906–1907; *Bandana Land*, 1907; and *Mr. Lode of Koal*, 1909. The highly successful Williams and Walker Company also produced plays at the Shaftesbury Theater in London.

In 1910, Shipp headed the Jesse A. Shipp Stock Company at the Grand Theater in Chicago. He wrote, produced, and directed *A Night in New York's China Town* for that group, and it had a notable production at the Pekin Theater in Chicago. He also produced *The Lime Kiln Club* with this stock company, in 1911; in the same year, he produced *Dr. Herb's Prescription* and toured with a vaudeville act, the Tennessee Ten. He played Barabbas in the Hapgood Players' production of *Simon the Cyrenian* in 1917–1918. Shipp wrote a number of shows that were produced at the Lafayette Theater between 1919 and 1925.

In October 1922, the Peter P. Jones Photoplay Company announced the formation of the Seminole Film Producing Company; its first production, *Shadows and Sunshine*, was based on an original story by Shipp and starred the renowned black actress Bessie Coleman. Shipp also wrote for Whitney and Tutt's *North Ain't South*, 1923; and for James P. Johnson's and Cecil Mack's *Moochin' Along*, 1925. He was also one of several collaborators on *Darktown Affairs* in 1929; it reached Broadway in 1930 under the title *Change Your Luck*. In addition, Shipp wrote vaudeville acts for several groups, including the Down Home Ten, the Dixie School Days' Company, and the Mills Sisters.

In 1930, Shipp played Abraham in the original Broadway production of *The Green Pastures*; he also directed *Kilpatrick's Old Time Minstrels*, a retrospective tribute to minstrelsy that played in a theater in downtown New York.

Biography

Jesse A. Shipp was born in 1859 in Cincinnati, Ohio. He toured with Sam P. Jacks Revue in 1879, and with the Beethoven Quartet, the Eureka Minstrels troupe, the Georgia Minstrels, and Primrose and West's Forty Whites and Thirty Blacks. He performed in *The Octoroons* in 1895, *Oriental American* in 1896, *The Policy Players* in 1899, *The Sons of Ham* in 1900–1902, *In Dahomey* in 1902–1905, *Abyssinia* in 1906–1907, *Bandana Land* in 1907, *Simon the Cyrenian* in 1917–1918, and *The Green Pastures* in 1930. Shipp was a member of the Frogs Theater Group and headed the Jesse A. Shipp Stock Company. He died in Richmond Hill, Queens, New York, on 1 May 1934.

CARMEN PHELPS

See also Green Pastures, The; Johnson, James P.; Lafayette Theater; Mack, Cecil; Williams, Egbert Austin "Bert"

Selected Works

A Night in New York's China Town. 1910.
Dr. Herb's Prescription, or It Happened in a Dream. 1910.
Shadows and Sunshine. 1922.
North Ain't South. 1923.
Moochin' Along. 1925.
Change Your Luck. 1929.
Kilpatrick's Old Time Minstrels. 1930.

Further Reading

Johnson, James Weldon. *Black Manhattan*. New York: Da Capo, 1930.
Mapp, Edward. *Directory of Blacks in the Performing Arts*. Metuchen, N.J.: Scarecrow, 1978.
Peterson, Bernard. *The African-American Theatre Directory, 1816–1960*. Westport, Conn.: Greenwood, 1997.
———. *Profiles of African American Stage Performers and Theatre People, 1816–1960*. Westport, Conn.: Greenwood, 2001.
Sampson, Henry T. *Blacks in Black and White: A Source Book on Black Films*. Lanham, Md.: Scarecrow, 1995.
Spradling, Mary Mace, ed. *In Black and White: A Guide to Magazine Articles, Newspaper Articles, and Books Concerning More Than 15,000 Black Individuals and Groups*, 3rd ed., 2 vols. and supplement. Detroit, Mich.: Gale Research, 1980, 1985.

Show Boat

The hugely successful musical *Show Boat* opened at the Ziegfeld Theater in New York City on 27 December 1927. It was based on Edna Ferber's Novel *Show Boat* (1926); the lyrics and libretto were by Oscar Hammerstein II, the score was by Jerome Kern, and the director was Zeke Colvan. *Show Boat* was the first musical to break away from stereotypical portrayals of African Americans as comical, even farcical, characters; instead, it focused on social issues faced by African Americans living in the South. It is considered a masterpiece of American musical theater, fully integrating memorable music, a complex story line, invigorating choreography, and vivid characterizations; and it prompted all other composers and producers of musicals to rethink the genre. Several of the songs from *Show Boat* became standards, including "Ol' Man River," which is reminiscent of spirituals; "Can't Help Lovin' Dat Man," which is inspired by blues; and the love ballads "Make Believe" and "Why Do I Love You?"

Show Boat is a sprawling epic in two acts that follows the lives of three generations of performers and crew from the mid-1890s to the late 1920s. Cap'n Andy Hawks and his wife, Parthy, run the *Cotton Blossom*, a showboat on the Mississippi River. Other characters include the Hawks's daughter Magnolia; their maid, Queenie, and her stevedore husband, Joe; the actress Julie La Verne and the actor Steve Baker, Julie's husband; and the vaudevillians Frank Schultz and Ellie May Chipley. The musical opens with the showboat docking at Natchez, where it is welcomed by townspeople and dockworkers singing "Cotton Blossom." After the crowd leaves, a devilish riverboat gambler named Gaylord Ravenal meets Magnolia, and their mutual attraction is made obvious in their duet "Make Believe."

Later Magnolia asks Joe what he thinks of Gaylord, but Joe tells her to ask the river—the Mississippi—for advice "bout dem boys." Joe then breaks into the song "Ol' Man River," the signature piece of the show. In the original production, he was accompanied by the famous Jubilee Singers as a group of black bargemen.

The next scene finds Julie, Magnolia, and Queenie in the kitchen of the *Cotton Blossom*, where Julie sings "Can't Help Lovin' Dat Man" after the three of them discuss the difficulties of relationships. Shortly thereafter Julie is discovered by the local authorities to be breaking laws against miscegenation because she is of mixed blood and her husband is white. Julie and Steve leave the ship, accompanied by "Mis'ry's Comin' Aroun'" sung by a black chorus. Magnolia and Gaylord—who conveniently needs to leave Natchez because of gambling debts—are recruited to take Julie's and Steve's places in the showboat company, and during their first performance together on the *Cotton Blossom* they express their love in the duet "You Are Love." Shortly thereafter they marry, and the curtain falls on the first act.

The second act opens in 1893, on the Midway Plaisance at the World's Columbia Exposition in Chicago, where Magnolia, Andy, and Parthy are waiting for Gaylord, who is late. He soon appears with news of a financial windfall from a successful wager, and he and Magnolia sing the romantic duet "Why Do I Love You?" This is soon followed by a lively and visually stunning African village song and dance, "In Dahomey." In the next scene, the year is 1904. Gaylord and Magnolia have left the showboat and moved to Chicago; there, his gambling intensifies, and he ultimately deserts her. Magnolia finds a job at the Trocadero Music Hall, where Julie—who has herself been abandoned some time ago by her husband, Steve—is the star. Julie brings down the house with her rendition of the song "Bill" but then generously gives her starring role to Magnolia. Magnolia becomes an instant hit with her rendition of the popular ballad "After the Ball" and goes on to a successful career as a performer. The final scenes are set in the year 1927. Magnolia has returned to the *Cotton Blossom*; her daughter, Kim, has become a star on Broadway; and Gaylord returns for a reconciliation. The curtain falls after Joe's reprise of "Ol' Man River."

Show Boat ran for nearly two years in New York, playing 575 performances and grossing about $50,000 a week. The original cast included Edna May Oliver (Parthy), Charles Winninger (Andy), Norma Terris (Magnolia), Howard Marsh (Gaylord), Eva Puck (Ellie), Sammy White (Frank), Helen Morgan (Julie),

Charles Ellis (Steve), Jules Bledsoe (Joe), and Tess Gardella (Queenie). From 6 May 1929 through March 1930 the production toured the United States, and in 1932, the original cast returned to New York for an additional 180 performances. During the Broadway run of *Show Boat* there were also a number of productions abroad. These included a production at the Drury Lane Theater in London in 1928 and productions in Australia and Paris in 1929. For the production in London, Paul Robeson was cast as Joe; he had been intended to take this part in the original New York production. A revival opened at the Ziegfeld Theater on 5 January 1946 and ran for 418 performances.

Show Boat was adapted for the screen three times—by Universal Pictures in 1929 and 1936 (with Irene Dunne in one of the leads) and by MGM in 1951 (with Ava Gardner and Howard Keel). On 8 April 1954, *Show Boat* entered the opera repertoire, when it was performed by the New York City Opera.

Show Boat was revived on Broadway by Hal Prince in 1994, with great success: The production was nominated for ten Tony awards in 1995 and won in five categories—best revival, best featured actress, best director, best costume designer, and best choreographer.

Erin Stapleton-Corcoran

See also Bledsoe, Jules; Musical Theater; Robeson, Paul

Further Reading

Bordman, Gerald Martin. *Jerome Kern: His Life and Music*. New York: Oxford University Press, 1980.

Engel, Lehman. *The American Musical Theater*. New York: Collier, 1975.

Ferber, Edna: *Show Boat*. New York: Doubleday, 1926.

Kislan, Richard. *The Musical: A Look at the American Musical Theater*. New York: Applause, 1995.

Krueger, Miles. *Show Boat: The Story of a Classic American Musical*. New York: Oxford University Press, 1977.

Peterson, Bernard L., Jr. *A Century of Musicals in Black and White: An Encyclopedia of Musical Stage Works by, About, or Involving African Americans*. Westport, Conn.: Greenwood, 1993.

Shuffle Along

The musical *Shuffle Along* (1921) had a book by Flournoy Miller and Aubrey Lyles and music by Eubie

Blake (composer) and Noble Sissle (lyricist). It opened at the Sixty-Third Street Music Hall in New York on 23 May 1921.

Looking back on the 1920s in his autobiography *The Big Sea* (1940/1993), Langston Hughes suggested that the Harlem Renaissance effectively began with the opening of *Shuffle Along*. He called it "a honey of a show" and remembered it as "funny, rollicking and gay, with a dozen danceable, singable tunes" (such as "I'm Just Wild About Harry" and "Baltimore Buzz"); but what made it most noteworthy for him was the outstanding array of African Americans who had brought it to the stage. In addition to Miller, Lyles, Blake, and Sissle, there were the performers Josephine Baker, Caterina Jarboro, Florence Mills, and Trixie Smith onstage; the musicians included the noted choir director Hall Johnson and the composer William Grant Still as oboist. *Shuffle Along* was a monumental success; it ran for 504 performances on Broadway and then spent two more years on the road as a touring show. As James Weldon Johnson recalled in *Black Manhattan* (1930/1991), this show "made the Sixty-Third Street Theater one of the best-known houses in town and made it necessary for the Traffic Department to declare Sixty-Third Street a one-way thoroughfare."

Actually, though, *Shuffle Along* had emerged from humble beginnings. It was first conceived when Sissle and Blake—the Dixie Duo, established stars of the vaudeville circuit—agreed to perform in a benefit show of the National Association for the Advancement of Colored People at the Paul Laurence Dunbar Theater in Philadelphia. Sharing the bill with them, as a comic team, were Miller and Lyles, two alumni of Fisk University who were also veteran vaudevillians. The two pairs were impressed by each other's performance; later, when they met again in New York, Miller and Lyles expressed an interest in reviving a play called *The Mayor of Dixie*, a farce they had staged in Chicago in 1907. It had a simple plot (Miller and Lyles played schemers and cheats who become rivals in a mayoral election and both lose), and Miller thought that it could be brought to Broadway inexpensively. Sissle and Blake, who had already tried to sell songs on Broadway, were eager to collaborate. The show went into production early in 1921; the meager plot was fleshed out with catchy song-and-dance numbers, and there were limited runs at the Dunbar in Philadelphia and the Howard Theater in Washington, D.C. *Shuffle Along* was financed mainly by its four creators, from their earnings in vaudeville, and it

arrived in New York in May $18,000 in debt. But although it was apparently a financial risk, although there were no big names on the marquee, and although the theater was somewhat run-down, enthusiasm spread like wildfire after the premiere. *Shuffle Along* went on to gross more than $8 million.

As the first successful play written and produced by African Americans on Broadway since Bert Williams's *Mr. Lode of Koal* closed in 1909, *Shuffle Along* cleared a path for numerous black musical productions throughout the 1920s. These included *Chocolate Dandies* (1924, music by Eubie Blake and Spencer Williams), *My Magnolia* (1926), *Keep Shuffling* (1928, featuring music by Thomas "Fats" Waller), and *Hot Chocolates* (1929, which introduced the standard "Black and Blue" by Fats Waller and Andy Razaf, made popular as a recording by Louis Armstrong). *Shuffle Along* certainly established the black American musical as a marketable commodity in New York: As early as 1922, the white singer Gilda Gray was performing a number in the Ziegfeld Follies called "It's Getting Dark on Old Broadway"; the lyrics joked uneasily, "Real dark-town entertainers hold the stage/You must black up to be the latest rage."

Shuffle Along has always been regarded as significant for having given exposure to its African American performers and for having opened the door to other all-black shows, but relatively recently scholars have also considered the importance of its content to the social concerns of the Harlem Renaissance. For example, Eileen Southern (1997) argues that *Shuffle Along* brought uniquely African American expressivity to the development of American musical theater, through its use of jazz and black folk dances like the buck-and-wing. Jacqui Malone (1996) suggests that the sixteen-woman chorus line in *Shuffle Along* may have been its most notable innovation; these dancers performed folk steps and also popularized an assortment of contemporary jazz dance steps: slow-motion acrobatics, tap, and legomania. As Eubie Blake himself remembered decades later (Huggins 1976), *Shuffle Along* changed the way chorus lines performed onstage—they now danced with a verve that had been lacking in earlier white reviews like the Ziegfeld Follies, in which the chorus line was a mostly static group intended only to showcase the women's beauty. John Graziano (1990) argues that *Shuffle Along* should be considered in relation to the "racial advancement" project of intellectuals such as W. E. B. Du Bois and James Weldon Johnson, who sought to improve the social status of African Americans through excellence in the arts. *Shuffle Along* did not represent the "high" art championed by the intelligentsia, but Graziano suggests that its financial success and its idiomatic use of elements from blues and jazz contributed to the widespread recognition of black creativity that these intellectuals were trying to facilitate.

Shuffle Along also worked against stereotypes from nineteenth-century minstrelsy that had persisted in, and dominated, black theatrical projects in the early twentieth century. Ann Douglas (1995) argues that *Shuffle Along* was a self-conscious parody of blackface minstrel traditions, a "free-form mock homage." Its songs about Dixie, its slapstick violence, its occasional exaggerated black dialect, and its hackneyed plot all appeared rooted in minstrel conventions. But the show unsettled the stability of those practices through juxtaposition, by situating them in combination with modern African American dance and innovative jazz. According to Douglas, *Shuffle Along*, with its sophisticated parody and its financial triumph, occurring after a decade when there had been no black musical theater on Broadway, "spelled the decline of white blackface," which had been the predominant representation of African American life on the Broadway stage in the interim.

MICHAEL BORSHUK

See also Baker, Josephine, Blake, Eubie; Chocolate Dandies; Hot Chocolates; Johnson, Hall; Lyles, Aubrey; Miller, Flournoy; Mills, Florence; Musical Theater; Sissle, Noble; Smith, Trixie; Still, William Grant

Further Reading

Douglas, Ann. *Terrible Honesty: Mongrel Manhattan in the 1920s.* New York: Farrar, Straus and Giroux, 1995.

Graziano, John. "Black Musical Theater and the Harlem Renaissance Movement." In *Black Music in the Harlem Renaissance: A Collection of Essays*, ed. Samuel A. Floyd Jr. New York: Greenwood, 1990.

Hughes, Langston. *The Big Sea*, intro. Arnold Rampersad. New York: Hill & Wang, 1993. (Originally published 1940.)

Huggins, Nathan Irvin. "Interview with Eubie Blake, 16 October 1973." In *Voices From the Harlem Renaissance*, ed. Nathan Irvin Huggins. New York and Oxford: Oxford University Press, 1976, pp. 336–340.

Johnson, James Weldon. *Black Manhattan*, intro. Sondra Kathryn Wilson. New York: Da Capo, 1991. (Originally published 1930.)

Malone, Jacqui. *Steppin' on the Blues: The Visible Rhythms of African American Dance.* Urbana and Chicago: University of Illinois Press, 1996.

Rose, Al. *Eubie Blake.* New York: Schirmer, 1979.

Southern, Eileen. *The Music of Black Americans: A History*, 3rd ed. New York and London: Norton, 1997.

Singers

The Harlem Renaissance created significant opportunities for African American singers. They performed in venues that were previously not available to them, such as Broadway theaters, and they introduced new genres, such as blues, to their audiences. Their success in the 1920s, however, did not materialize overnight; it had been preceded by almost half a century of achievements. During the last decades of the nineteenth century, African American vocalists made great strides in public performances. They appeared in classical concerts, vaudeville, variety shows, and musicals. The Hyers sisters, Anna Madah (1853–1930s) and Emma Louise (1855– c. 1899), led a company in the 1870s and 1880s that performed operatic excerpts as well as sentimental songs in evening-long entertainments. Their shows toured the country from coast to coast with great success. In the 1890s, various entrepreneurs produced entertainments that combined popular song, operetta, and opera excerpts. Vocalists generally could be classified into one of two categories: those who sang popular songs of the period and those who sang operatic excerpts. The most important operatic singers of the period were Marie Selika (Williams, 1849–1937), Flora Batson (1864–1906), and Sissieretta Jones (1868–1933, known nationally and internationally as "Black Patti"). These three women followed in the footsteps of the Hyers sisters, studying and singing arias by Verdi, Donizetti, and Bellini, as well as lighter pieces by Offenbach, Jacobowski, and Arditi, and joining with members of their companies to sing ensemble pieces, such as the quartet "Bella figlia dell'amore" from Giuseppi Verdi's *Rigoletto*. Jones's career from 1892 through 1896 was one of the most important indicators of the progress of African American performers in the United States: Her engagements were managed by a well-known talent agent, James Pond, whose portfolio of artists included Mark Twain and John Greenleaf Whittier. Pond was able to negotiate a higher salary for her than any other black performer had yet received. Her appeal to both

Roland Hayes, c. 1920s. (Schomburg Center for Research in Black Culture, New York Public Library.)

Marian Anderson. (Brown Brothers.)

black and white audiences made it clear that a high level of talent was emerging from the African American community. By the turn of the twentieth century, a number of African American entertainers who sang vernacular songs were also achieving recognition and acclaim from white, as well as black, audiences. Among the most important women singers were Belle Davis, Ada Overton Walker (1880–1914), Abbie Mitchell (1884–1960), and Stella Wiley (b. c. 1870s). The most important male singers included Ernest Hogan (1865–1909), Robert "Bob" Cole (1868–1911), George Walker (1872–1911), John Rosamond Johnson (1873–1954), and, preeminently, the renowned Egbert Austin "Bert" Williams (1874–1922). Williams recorded eighty songs for two companies—Victor and Columbia—over a twenty-year period, more than any other African American performer of the time. As with many of his contemporaries, Williams's repertoire mostly consisted of comic narrative songs that focused on the protagonist's bad luck with money, women, and landlords, as well as topics that were particularly directed to African American audiences. Williams' signature song, "Nobody," told of his bad

luck in a number of situations in which no one offered to help him. "He's a Cousin of Mine" took up the infidelity of a young woman: "You're gwine to get somethin' what you don't expect," the infidelity of a husband. In 1910, Williams was hired by Florenz Ziegfeld to appear in the Follies. His performances, as the only African American in casts that over the years included distinguished performers such as Leon Errol, Fanny Brice, Eddie Cantor, and W. C. Fields, were significant in the same way that "Black Patti"'s appearances on otherwise white programs were in the early 1890s.

Vaudeville provided expanded opportunities for African Americans to be seen by a wide variety of audiences. During the first decade of the twentieth century, Bob Cole and John Rosamond Johnson played the major vaudeville circuits; their salary was said to be $750 per week. Other performers included the composer, comedian, and singer Irving Jones (c. 1874–1932), who appeared in an act with his brother and wife, Ada Walker, after her husband, George, was incapacitated by syphilis; and Florence Mills, who was featured with her sisters. Concert singers did not fare as well; most of their concerts, as had been the case during the

Ethel Waters. (Library of Congress.)

nineteenth century, were given at black churches, usually in conjunction with local talent. Yet several persevered in spite of the difficulties. Harry Thacker Burleigh (1866–1949) gave recitals of art songs for almost two decades after his graduation in 1896 from the National Conservatory of Music. His repertoire included German lieder, English and American songs, and, after 1910, arrangements of spirituals. Roland Hayes (1887–1976) began singing while still a student at Fisk University. He joined the Fisk Jubilee Singers before giving solo recitals. From 1916 to 1919, Hayes organized his own recital tours. He sang in cities from coast to coast and appeared with many prestigious African American groups in New York City, Washington, D.C., Chicago, and elsewhere. His career attracted little notice from mainstream audiences until he returned from Europe in 1923 after a triumphant three years of concertizing, which included a command performance before George V of England. Rachel Walker (1873–1940s) based her career in Europe from 1900 to 1915, when she returned to the United States. After a few additional years of concertizing, she settled in Cleveland, where she gave voice lessons. In 1914, Marian Anderson (1897–1993), a

teenager from Philadelphia, began her professional career singing with James Reese Europe's Clef Club orchestra. In 1922, she gave a debut recital at Town Hall, and the following year she sang another. In 1925, she won a singing competition that offered her the opportunity to sing with the Philharmonic Society at Lewisohn Stadium on the campus of the City College of New York. Her appearance there resulted in critical acclaim, unlike the reviews she had received in response to her concerts at Town Hall. During the next four years, Anderson appeared in many concerts. In 1929, she departed for Europe for further study.

Whereas "Black Patti" and other singers of her generation had been able to perform with established opera companies only after great difficulty, during the Harlem Renaissance there were more opportunities for African American women to sing in complete staged performances, particularly in Europe. They were usually cast in exotic roles so that audiences would not be concerned with the issue of "miscasting." Thus Lillian Evanti (1890–1967) was heard in Nice and Paris, where she sang the title role in Léo Delibes's *Lakme*; Florence Cole Talbert (1890s–1961) sang the title role in Verdi's *Aida* in Cosenza, Italy, in 1927; and Caterina Jarboro (1903–1986) appeared in Milan in 1930 and with the Chicago Opera Company in 1934 in the same role. African American men faced more resistance to roles in opera, so most of them turned to solo concerts or appeared as soloists in oratorios. William Richardson (1869–1930s), for example, was known in the Boston area as a fine soloist in oratorio; he toured throughout the United States and the West Indies, giving solo recitals of art songs, from his formal debut in Jordan Hall in 1919 to his death. Similarly, the tenor George Garner (1890–1971) toured with his wife during the late 1920s and 1930s after studying for several years in London with the well-known singer and conductor George Henschel (1850–1934).

A number of African American singers appeared both in concert venues and in musical theater productions. Abbie Mitchell (1884–1960) began her career in 1898 in Paul Laurence Dunbar and Will Marion Cook's *Clorindy, or the Origin of the Cake Walk*. During the first decade of the twentieth century, she appeared in leading roles with Williams and Walker's company. During the late 1910s, she continued to sing parlor songs, ragtime numbers, and early jazz pieces from the popular repertoire. In 1921, however, she began lessons once again, studying classical song in Paris with the famous tenor Jean de Reszke (1850–1935), while performing vernacular songs with her Full

Harmonic Quartet. After her studies were completed, Mitchell then gave concerts of art songs in Europe and the United States. Her singing career ended with her portrayal of Clara in George and Ira Gershwin's *Porgy and Bess* in 1935. The mezzo-soprano Minto Cato (1900–1979) appeared in revues and in the musicals *Keep Shufflin'* (1928), *Hot Chocolates* (1929), and Lew Leslie's *Blackbirds of 1930*. During the 1930s, she was heard in several operatic roles, including Amneris in Verdi's *Aida* at the New York Hippodrome. Taylor Gordon (1893–1971) began his career in vaudeville in 1919; he toured on the Keith-Albee circuit for two years. He then joined with John Rosamond Johnson to sing concerts of spirituals. In 1925, he returned to vaudeville as a member of the Inimitable Five. Later in his career, he appeared in musicals on Broadway. The baritone Jules Bledsoe (1898–943) had moved to New York City in 1919 to study medicine at Columbia University. While in school, he began to take voice lessons. By 1924, when he made his solo debut at Aeolian Hall, Bledsoe had decided to change careers. In 1926, he made his stage debut in an opera by Frank Harling (1887–1958), *Deep River*. The following year, he created the role of Joe in Jerome Kern's *Show Boat*, in which he later toured Europe. Bledsoe was chosen to sing the title role for the European production of Louis Gruenberg's opera *The Emperor Jones*, based on Eugene O'Neill's play; he was the first African American to undertake the role, which he sang in New York also. In the 1930s, he sang several other operatic roles, including Amonasro in *Aida* and the title role in *Boris Godunov* in Europe. He also appeared in the London production of *Blackbirds of 1936*. The most prominent African American singer to have major musical careers both as a concert artist and in musical theater (and to act in dramatic plays and on film) was Paul Robeson (1898–1976). He had been singing since childhood, and one of his first professional engagements was as a member of the chorus in Sissle and Blake's *Shuffle Along* (1921), the first black musical to be seen on Broadway in more than a decade. After appearances in several shows in Harlem, Robeson made his solo debut in 1925 at the Greenwich Village Theater, singing an entire program of spirituals. His success with the program enabled him to tour with it to countries all over the world for several decades and to record many of the spirituals. In 1928, Robeson was chosen to play the role of Joe for the first London production of *Show Boat*. In 1936, he also appeared in a film version of the musical. At the very end of the Harlem Renaissance, a young singer, Todd Duncan

(1903–1998), was recognized as a major talent when he created the role of Porgy in Gershwin's *Porgy and Bess*. His costar, Ann Brown (b. 1915), achieved fame as well for her portrayal of Bess. Both went on to major careers.

For many African American singers, the 1920s were the decade of the musical. The profusion of shows during the years of the Harlem Renaissance—on Broadway, in road companies, and in Harlem's speakeasies—provided continuous employment for black singers and dancers. After a hiatus of eleven years, black musical theater returned to Broadway with *Shuffle Along*, a farcical book musical that ran for more than two years and generated three road companies. Its great success with audiences and the critics gave many young singers their first exposure on Broadway, and it ushered in a cascade of shows, both book musicals and revues, that constituted a significant percentage of musical theater productions in New York City until the Great Depression. These shows provided showcases for a large number of talented performers, several of whom achieved stardom. While some performers, such as Inez Clough (c. 1870s–1933), Georgette Harvey (1883–1952), and Florence Mills (1895–1927), had careers that dated back to the beginning of the century, most of the singers who achieved prominence were just beginning their careers at the start of the renaissance. Clough had first performed in John W. Isham's shows *The Octoroons* and *Oriental America* during the late 1890s. She then joined Williams and Walker's company, appearing in three of their shows. During the renaissance, she appeared in *Shuffle Along* and *The Chocolate Dandies* (1924). Harvey's career began in 1905 when she joined the cast of *Rufus Rastus*, a musical starring Ernest Hogan. She then formed a female quartet that toured Europe for several years, finally disbanding in Russia. Harvey stayed in Saint Petersburg until the revolution, then went to the Far East, where she remained until 1921. On her return to New York, she appeared in the musicals *Strut Miss Lizzie* (1922) and *Runnin' Wild* (1923) and several other shows. In 1935, she appeared in *Porgy and Bess*, and at the end of her long life she appeared in Kurt Weill's *Lost in the Stars* (1949). Mills started her career as a "pickaninny" (a child performer in vaudeville) when she was four years old. In her teens, she and her sisters formed a trio that played the vaudeville circuits. In 1916, she became one of the Panama Trio, with Ada "Bricktop" Smith and Cora Green. After creating a sensation as Gertrude Saunders's replacement in *Shuffle Along*,

Mills was managed by the Broadway producer Lew Leslie, who starred her in his *Plantation Revue* (1922), *From Dover to Dixie* (1923), *Dixie to Broadway* (1924), and *Blackbirds of 1926*. She was scheduled to star in *Blackbirds of 1928* but died suddenly of appendicitis. Cora Green (c. 1890s–c. 1940s), who sang with Mills in the Panama Trio, was a contralto. She appeared in many shows during the 1920s, including *Put and Take* (1921), *Strut Miss Lizzie*, and (with Mills) *Dixie to Broadway*. In the 1930s and 1940s, Green also appeared in several movies by the black filmmaker Oscar Micheaux. Eva Taylor (1896–1977) began her career at the age of three as a pickaninny in Josephine Gassmann's troupe. As a teenager, she was seen on Broadway in a number of musicals. After her marriage to Clarence Williams around 1920, she sang with his instrumental group and also appeared in a number of musicals, including *Shuffle Along*, her husband's musical *Bottomland* (1927), *Keep Shufflin'*, and *Queen o' Hearts* (1928). Taylor recorded extensively, sometimes using pseudonyms. In her teens, Gertrude Saunders (1890s–1940s) joined Billy King's Chicago troupe. After developing her skills for a few years, she moved to New York and auditioned for *Shuffle Along*, in which she played Ruth Little, a friend of the ingenue. Saunders created a sensation at every performance with her rendition of "I'm Craving for That Kind of Love," which can be heard on a recording she made in 1921. She left the show to star in a revue by Hurtig and Seamon, which was a flop. She then played the vaudeville circuits until she was chosen to star in Maceo Pinkard's musical *Liza* (1924). She appeared in several other shows and in a race film, *Big Timers* (1945). Another contemporary, Alberta Hunter (1895–1984), began her career in Chicago when she was fifteen. In 1923, she starred in Eddie Hunter's musical *How Come?*, and in 1927, she appeared with Robeson in the London production of *Show Boat*. Ethel Waters (c. 1896–1977) also began her professional career during her teens. After a major recording career with Black Swan, Waters appeared in several Broadway shows, including *Africana* (1927), Lew Leslie's *Blackbirds of 1930*, and *Rhapsody in Black* (1931). She also appeared in *On With the Show* (1929), a film in which she sang "Am I Blue?" and "Birmingham Bertha." The career of Edith Wilson (1896–1981) was similar to that of Waters and Hunter: She started performing professionally while still a teenager; began recording in 1921; and appeared in *Put and Take* (1921), *From Dover to Dixie*, *Chocolate Kiddies* (1925), *Blackbirds of 1926*, and Connie's *Hot Chocolate Revue* (1929). Valaida Snow (c. 1900–1956) was seen in Sissle and Blake's *The Chocolate Dandies* (1924) and *Rhapsody in Black* (1931). Adelaide Hall (c. 1901–1993) began her career as a member of the chorus of *Shuffle Along*. Her extraordinary talent propelled her into starring roles in *Runnin' Wild*, *Chocolate Kiddies*, *Blackbirds of 1928* (in which she replaced Florence Mills), and *Brown Buddies* (1930). She also recorded with Duke Ellington's band. Blanche Calloway (1902–1978), the older sister of Cab Calloway, was first seen in one of the road companies of *Shuffle Along*. She then joined James P. Johnson's musical revue *Plantation Days*, with which she toured until 1927. Thereafter she became a nightclub entertainer and toured during the early 1930s with her band, the Joy Boys. One of the most important performers to achieve stardom after beginning as a chorus member in *Shuffle Along* was Josephine Baker (1906–1975). Her antics in that show called attention to her and led to her being cast in Sissle and Blake's next show, *The Chocolate Dandies*. After appearing at the Plantation Club in 1925, she left for Paris to appear in *La Revue Nègre*, which was originally planned as a vehicle for Ethel Waters. Baker's Parisian debut, in which she was entirely nude except for a feather or two at strategic places, made her a star overnight. Most of the remainder of her career was centered in Paris, with an occasional trip to the United States. Rosa Henderson (1896–1968) was one of the few singers whose careers were centered in Harlem. She performed at the three major uptown theaters—the Lincoln, the Lafayette, and the Alhambra—in musicals such as *The Harlem Rounders* (1927), *Blackouts of 1929*, and *Blackberries Revue* (1930). She was also a prominent recording artist of blues from 1923, when her first recording was released, to 1931.

Although female black singers dominated musical theater during the Harlem Renaissance, several male entertainers achieved prominence as well. They were multitalented as writers, composers, lyricists, and producers, and they also sang, danced, and acted. Salem Tutt Whitney (1869–1934) was first noticed in the 1910s, when he and his younger brother, J. Homer Tutt (b. 1870s), established a company, the Smarter Set, that produced their original musicals, the most important of which were *George Washington Bullion Abroad* (1915), *Darkest Americans* (1918), and *Children of the Sun* (1919); the company toured the country with various shows until 1923. Though they were primarily creative artists, Whitney and his brother starred in all their shows. *Bamboula* (1921) was seen in Harlem, and their show *Oh, Joy* (1922), though not a great success, was seen briefly on Broadway. Whitney also toured the vaudeville circuits as a song-and-dance man during the 1920s. In 1930, he joined the cast of *The Green Pastures*, where he played the role of Noah until shortly before his death. Noble Sissle (1889–1975) and Eubie Blake (1883–1983), like Tutt and Whitney, initially intended to work as a songwriting team, but they soon were seen in vaudeville and later appeared in the musicals they wrote. Sissle and Blake met in Baltimore in 1915; their first song, "It's All Your Fault," which was picked up by Sophie Tucker, became a hit and established them as successful songwriters. In 1916, they became part of the inner circle of James Reese Europe (1881–1919), who had founded the Clef Club in 1910. After his death, they appeared in vaudeville in 1919 and 1920. A meeting with the comedians Flournoy Miller and Aubrey Lyles led to the collaboration that produced *Shuffle Along*, for which Sissle and Blake wrote all the music. Although Sissle appeared in the role of Tom Sharper in the show, Blake was seen only in the penultimate scene, when he and Sissle interrupted the plot to present some of their songs, as if they were appearing in vaudeville. They were dressed in tails, with Blake at the piano, and the scene was called "A Few Minutes With Sissle and Blake." At the end of their musical set, the show resumed. In 1923, they wrote the words and music for a white show, *Elsie*, and in 1924, they teamed up with Miller and Lyles once more to produce *The Chocolate Dandies*. Through 1926, they were headliners on the vaudeville circuits again, in the United States and in England and France. While they were performing in London, they wrote the score for the producer Charles Cochran's *Revue of 1926*. When their European tour ended, Blake chose to return to the United States. Sissle decided to remain in Europe, thereby dissolving the partnership. Both continued to perform, although Blake's reputation rested more on his accomplishments as a composer. Another composer-performer was Shelton Brooks (1886–1975). His first fame was as a songwriter, as three of his early songs—"Some of These Days" (1910), "I Wonder Where My Easy Rider's Gone" (1913), and "Darktown Strutters' Ball" (1917)—quickly became standards. During the late 1910s, Brooks played the vaudeville circuit as a singer-pianist. He then joined with Florence Mills in Lew Leslie's *Plantation Revue*, *Dixie to Broadway*, and *Blackbirds of 1926*. He also produced and performed in *Nifties of 1928*. Cabell "Cab" Calloway (1907–1994) is now known primarily as a bandleader, but his early career was as a singer in musicals. In 1927, he joined the cast of *Plantation Days*, a revue in which his sister, Blanche,

was appearing. In 1929, he formed his own band, but a year later he dissolved it and joined the road company of *Hot Chocolates*. When that show closed, he replaced Ellington at the Cotton Club, where he appeared as a singer-bandleader-composer. One of the first songs he wrote, "Minnie the Moocher," became the theme song of his band and his signature piece. Thomas "Fats" Waller (1904–1943) is also known as a pianist-composer. Waller composed songs for two shows in Harlem—*Tan Town Topics* (1926) and *Junior Blackbirds* (1927)—and the Broadway shows *Keep Shufflin'* and Connie's *Hot Chocolates*. As a soloist, he sang many of his own songs as well as those by other composers, and he recorded extensively after 1926; in 1930, he was featured on a radio program, *Paramount on Parade*, broadcast on New York's WABC. The singer-dancer John Sublett (1902–1986), known as John Bubbles, of the team Buck and Bubbles, started with his partner in vaudeville in the late 1910s. In addition to their vaudeville appearances, they were seen in two musicals during the renaissance: *Ziegfeld Follies of 1921* and *Blackbirds of 1930*. In 1931, they appeared at the Palladium in London for two weeks, and in 1935, Sublett created the role of Sportin' Life in *Porgy and Bess*.

During the Harlem Renaissance, many movie houses included a vaudeville show as part of the entertainment. First-rank performers were able to join the Keith-Albee circuit or one of the other national booking services, which guaranteed them continuous employment. When black entertainers were not able to join one of the white circuits, they could join the Theater Owners' Booking Association (TOBA), which provided the same services as its white counterparts. It was founded during the 1910s by Sherman H. Dudley (1873–1940), who was a former minstrel and a member of the Smart Set. During the 1920s, TOBA was able to provide continuous employment for many black entertainers. Although it was not totally competitive with its white counterparts, a number of entertainers were able, after several years of touring, to tighten their acts and move on to one of the better-paying white agencies. In addition to those vaudeville performers already mentioned, the following singers should be noted. J. Turner Layton (1894–1948) was a songwriter who, with the lyricist Henry Creamer (1879–1930), contributed numerous songs to several book musicals and revues, including *Strut Miss Lizzie*. In 1923, Layton joined with Clarence "Tandy" Johnstone (c. 1890s–1953) in a vaudeville act, which they took to the Empire Theater in Paris in 1924. From Paris, they journeyed to London, where they settled for the remainder of the decade. Layton and Johnstone were favorites with the British public; they played most of London's largest vaudeville venues and gave command performances for the royal family. They recorded frequently in the 1920s and were heard on BBC radio in the 1930s. Layton and Johnstone disbanded their act in 1935. Layton remained in London as a popular solo performer. Another popular team, Jody Edwards (1895–1967) and Susie Hawthorne (c. 1896–1963), toured as Butterbeans and Susie. Their vaudeville act was first seen in 1914, several years before they were married on the stage of the Standard Theater, a black-owned auditorium in Philadelphia. As members of the TOBA circuit, they performed in many revues during the 1920s. They formed their own company toward the end of the 1920s and produced their own shows, including *Laughing Lightning* (1929), *Ease on Down* (1930), and *Harlem Bound* (1932). They recorded frequently during the last half of the decade and appeared with Clarence Williams, Bessie Smith, and Ethel Waters, among others. The early career of Ada "Bricktop" Smith (1895–1984) included singing as one of the three Panama Girls. She continued as a solo act in the early 1920s. In 1924, she went to Europe to sing in several Parisian cafés; two years later, she opened her own club, Chez Bricktop, which she operated until the start of World War II. Smith performed frequently at her club and also imported other African American talent to appear there. One important artist who got her start at Bricktop's, and appeared there frequently, was the British singer Mabel Mercer (1900–c. 1990s). Mercer lived in Paris during the Harlem Renaissance and toured in most of Europe until her emigration to the United States in 1938. Hattie McDaniel (1895–1952) is best-known for her Oscar-winning performance in *Gone With the Wind*. Earlier in her career, though, she had great success as a vaudeville entertainer; she was sometimes billed as the "colored Sophie Tucker." During the 1920s and early 1930s, McDaniel sang in musical revues, was heard on the radio, and appeared in a film version of *Show Boat* (1936).

The origin of blues is shrouded in the mists of musical history. References to the genre are known as early as the mid-nineteenth century. Undoubtedly, blues songs were transmitted by itinerant singers who could not notate them. By the 1910s, blues existed in two forms: folk and, for want of a better term, commercial. Folk blues, which maintained a simple musical style that incorporated a repeated text and a tag line, were performed by bluesmen, who generally accompanied themselves on a guitar or banjo. Commercial

blues, which achieved prominence through the early compositions of W. C. Handy (1873–1958), such as "Memphis Blues" and "Saint Louis Blues," were patterned on the popular song forms of the period. Commercial blues were usually performed by a small group of jazz musicians and were heard in vaudeville and as solo and ensemble songs in virtually every musical on Broadway after 1918. Because folk blues songs did not lend themselves to extravagant production numbers, performers of this style are not as well known as those who sang the commercial songs. A typical folk blues singer was Charley Patton (1887–1934), who sang and played guitar as a teenager in the Mississippi Delta region. Although his reputation was established in the early 1920s, his first recording dates from 1929. He continued to record until his death. Although commercial blues were performed during the second decade of the twentieth century, it was not until Mamie Smith recorded "Crazy Blues" that the genre was established as part of mainstream popular music. Gertrude "Ma" Rainey (1886–1939) sang blues in variety shows and vaudeville as early as 1902. By 1904, she and her husband were touring the South with their vaudeville act. She appeared as a solo act as well, accompanied by jug bands and jazz ensembles. From 1923 on, she recorded frequently. Mamie Smith (1883–1946) began her professional career in vaudeville. She was a member of the Smart Set company around 1910. By 1913, she was seen in cabaret shows. Smith included blues numbers in her act, and blues became her central focus after the commercial success of her early blues recordings, which in addition to "Crazy Blues" included "You Can't Keep a Good Man Down" and "It's Right Here for You." All three songs were by Perry Bradford (1893–1970), who had recommended Smith to Okeh Records when Sophie Tucker was unavailable. During the 1920s, Mamie Smith toured in the United States, appearing in cabarets and in vaudeville with her Jazz Hounds. As a teenager, Bessie Smith (1894–1937) toured with black minstrel shows. During the 1910s, she met "Ma" Rainey, who became a major influence on Smith's singing style. Smith appeared in vaudeville during the 1920s, usually accompanied by jazz musicians. Her many recordings between 1923 and 1933 were made with leading black jazz musicians, including Fletcher Henderson, James P. Johnson, and Clarence Williams. She also toured with her own band, the Midnight Stoppers, and made a two-reel film, *Saint Louis Blues*, in 1929. Clara Smith (1894–1935), who was not related to either of the other Smiths, was active as a blues singer during the 1920s, when she was billed as the "queen of moaners." As with the blues singers discussed above, Clara Smith was a frequent recording artist, and she can be heard in duet with Bessie Smith on two disks. Three other singers who regularly recorded blues were Ida Cox (1896–1967), Beulah "Sippi" Wallace (1898–1986), and Bertha "Chippie" Hill (1905–1950). During the 1910s, Cox toured with several traveling shows. In the 1920s, her recorded performances were accompanied by Fletcher Henderson, among others. Cox produced her own traveling shows in the late 1920s and 1930s. Wallace performed with tent shows during World War I; in 1923, she settled in Chicago, where for the next seven years she recorded blues. Hill's career began when she was a teenager singing in Harlem's nightclubs and cafés. She toured with Ma Rainey in the early 1920s and, like Wallace, settled in Chicago in the early 1920s. Her first recording appeared in 1925; her many recordings during the remainder of the decade were accompanied by jazz groups, including Louis Armstrong and his band.

While jazz is primarily an instrumental form of music, some numbers include vocals. Louis Armstrong (1901–1971) is known primarily as a trumpeter, although singing was always one of his talents. Armstrong appeared in several shows, most notably *Hot Chocolates* and *Hot Chocolates of 1932*. James "Jimmy" Rushing (1903–1972) was a singer-pianist whose career started in nightclubs in and around the Los Angeles. In 1925 and 1928, he appeared with Walter Page's Blue Devils; from 1929 to 1935, he appeared in Benny Moten's band.

Female vocalists have also appeared with jazz bands from time to time. During the 1920s, Duke Ellington recorded with Alberta Prime, Florence Bristol, and Alberta Jones. Helen Humes (1909–1981) began her professional career as a nightclub singer. After her first jazz recording appeared in 1927, she sang in hotels and clubs. She recorded many jazz vocals in the following years.

The Harlem Renaissance was a watershed for African American musicians in general, and for vocalists specifically. Although classically trained singers were making some headway in being accepted by their white colleagues, the most important venue for singers was black musical theater, which underwent a dramatic resurgence at the start of the renaissance. Although some of the shows had short runs, a few of them attracted critical attention and propelled their performers into stardom. *Shuffle Along* was certainly the most important of the musicals that played a

crucial role in inspiring the revival. Broadway shows, combined with the interest of white audiences in the various clubs and theaters in Harlem, generated an increased public interest, which continued through the 1930s. Many singers appeared in a variety of venues: in musicals, on Broadway, in Harlem, and on the road; in vaudeville, through both the white and black booking organizations; in the late-night clubs and speakeasies in New York, Chicago, and many other American cities and in various large cities in England, France, Germany, and Russia; on radio and in movies. While it is known that blues are an old genre, the public craze for the commercial form did not coalesce until 1920, when the first blues recordings were sold. For the remainder of the decade, a number of female singers were recorded singing blues, usually accompanied by a small jazz band. By the end of the renaissance, blues were accepted as an important component of American popular music, as most composers of songs included blue notes and blues progressions. As the Harlem Renaissance progressed, jazz became an increasingly important genre. Although vocalists were not of prime importance to the development of early jazz, several singers were recorded with jazz groups, setting the stage for the emergence of singers, such as Billie Holiday and Ella Fitzgerald, during the 1930s. Much of the multifaceted artistic activity that occurred during the Harlem Renaissance in the 1920s was abruptly halted by the onset of the Great Depression. Some activity in a few musical venues continued during the early 1930s, but by the mid-1930s a confluence of factors reduced the opportunities for African American singers to provide their varied contributions to the musical arts in America.

John Graziano

See also Black Swan Phonograph Company; Blackbirds; Blues: Women Performers; Clef Club; Chocolate Dandies; Emperor Jones, The; Hot Chocolates; Liza; Micheaux, Oscar; Music; Musical Theater; Porgy and Bess; Runnin' Wild; Saint Louis Blues; Show Boat; Shuffle Along; Theater Owners' Booking Association; *specific singers and musicians*

Further Reading

Jasen, David, and Gene Jones. *Spreadin' Rhythm Around: Black Popular Songwriters, 1880–1930.* New York: Schirmer 1998.

Sampson, Henry T. *Blacks in Blackface: A Source Book on Early Black Musical Shows*. Metuchen, N.J.: Scarecrow, 1980.

Southern, Eileen. *Biographical Dictionary of Afro-American and African Musicians*. Westport, Conn.: Greenwood, 1982.

———. *The Music of Black Americans: A History*, 3rd ed. New York: Norton, 1997.

Tucker, Mark. *Ellington: The Early Years*. Urbana: University of Illinois Press, 1991.

Woll, Allen. *Black Musical Theatre: From Coontown to Dreamgirls*. Baton Rouge: Louisiana State University Press, 1989.

Sissle, Noble

Noble Lee Sissle was a singer, lyricist, and bandleader. By 1915, he had considerable performing experience, beginning in high school glee clubs, then touring with the Edward Morris Male Quartet and Hann's Jubilee Singers. He decided to enter show business after an encounter with James Reese Europe, founder of the Clef Club, while on tour. In 1915, while he was with Joe Porter's Serenaders in Baltimore, Sissle met the ragtime pianist and songwriter Eubie Blake; the two would form one of the most enduring and productive partnerships in show business, writing songs together over the coming decades.

In 1915–1916, Sissle was with Bob Young's Royal Poinciana Sextet in Baltimore, then in Palm Springs (Florida), and finally in New York. Sissle reintroduced himself to James Europe in 1916 and was soon appearing with Europe's popular dance orchestras in New York. He sang and played bandolin (a banjo-mandolin hybrid, now extinct) with the Europe Double Quintet, 1916–1917. He made his first recordings in 1917.

Also in 1917, Sissle enlisted in the American Expeditionary Force. He served with New York's 369th Regiment, the famous "Harlem Hellfighters," in World War I. The unit, including the band, saw heavy fighting in France and was decorated by the French government; Sissle rose to the rank of second lieutenant. The Hellfighters Band, led by James Europe, was acclaimed the finest American band of the war; Sissle served as a singer and drum major with it. In 1919, after the conclusion of the war, the Hellfighters Band returned to the United States and went on tour. During an engagement in Boston, Europe was murdered by a deranged band member; Sissle then briefly took over the direction of the band. Shortly before Europe's death, the band had made twenty-four sides for Pathé; Sissle sang on nine of these.

In 1919–1921, Sissle and Blake became popular as a duo act. In 1921, their show *Shuffle Along* took Broadway by storm, playing more than 600 performances in New York and on tour. The performers included the authors of the script—Flournoy Miller and Aubrey Lyles—as well as Sissle and Blake. Immortal songs from the show included "I'm Just Wild About Harry" and "Love Will Find a Way." Sissle and Blake collaborated on other shows, including *In Bamville* (originally titled *Chocolate Dandies*, 1924), but these were less successful. The first revival of *Shuffle Along* was produced in 1928.

During the 1920s, Sissle and Blake toured widely as a duo in vaudeville, achieving great acclaim both in the United States and in England. In 1923, Sissle made a very early short sound movie for De Forest Phonofilms. Sissle recorded in duo format with Blake (and occasionally others) every year from 1920 to 1928. An English tour with Blake in 1925 was an immense triumph. The pair split up in 1926, when Blake returned to the United States, while Sissle remained in England and then returned to New York separately.

In October 1927, Sissle returned to France with other black veterans for an American Legion convention; he laid a wreath at the statue of Joan of Arc on Rue Rivoli in Paris (commemorating his performances of the song "Jeanne d'Arc, la victoire est pour vous" during the war). In 1928, Sissle played at English music halls with the songwriter Harry Revel at the piano. In Paris, where he had a long residence at the club Les Ambassadeurs, he formed an African American expatriate band with musicians living in Montmartre, including the soprano saxophonist Sidney Bechet. In 1929–1931, Sissle toured Europe and the United Kingdom with a big band; eventually he brought it to New York. In 1931, he was in residence at the Park Central Hotel and began regular broadcasts on CBS radio. Sissle encountered financial difficulties during the Great Depression, filing for bankruptcy in 1929 and 1932; but he was an optimist by nature and always regrouped and started over. In the late 1930s, his orchestra featured the young Lena Horne as vocalist.

In the 1930s, Sissle and Blake teamed up again for performances, including revivals of *Shuffle Along* in 1933 and (most successfully) in 1945–1946, as a USO camp show to entertain the troops. A final revival in 1952 was a failure, largely because of "modernizing" touches added by others.

Noble Sissle, photographed by Carl Van Vechten. (Library of Congress.)

From the 1920s to the 1950s, Sissle was a successful as a bandleader, performing widely and recording for several labels. His big bands often included leading jazz musicians, such as Bechet, the clarinetist Buster Bailey, and the trumpeter Tommy Ladnier. Sissle recorded as a bandleader in 1921 and repeatedly between 1928 and 1937. He was in residence at Billy Rose's nightclub in New York, the Diamond Horseshoe, from 1938 to 1942.

Sissle was a leader in black entertainment organizations and founded the Negro Actors Guild. He helped organize "Oh, Sing a New Song"—a pageant of "the Negro experience in America"—performed at Soldiers' Field in Chicago in 1934. He took an active role in the Republican Party and performed at the first inaugural ball for President Dwight D. Eisenhower in 1953. Sissle was tireless in entertaining American troops in World War II and the Korean War and served on the board of directors of the USO. Although Sissle retired from active band-

leading in 1963, he sent a band out to entertain the troops in Vietnam in 1968; he was recorded with Blake by Columbia Records for an LP set, *The Eighty-Six Years of Eubie Blake*, in 1969.

Sissle received many honors in his later years. He was voted mayor of Harlem in 1950, following the death of Bill "Bojangles" Robinson; and in 1960, a portrait bust was erected in his honor at the 369th Regiment Armory in New York.

Sissle had a pleasant, somewhat thin tenor voice and an energetic but formal stage manner. Despite his obvious dignity, he enjoyed clowning onstage, which made him a great favorite in vaudeville. A highly moral, refined person, he had a personality that contrasted strongly with that of many of his fellow entertainers. His lyrics, while they lack the brilliance of those by his greatest contemporaries, such as Ira Gershwin and Andy Razaf, are charming and memorable. Several are still being sung more than eighty years after they were written.

There is a clippings file for Noble Sissle at the Schomburg Center for Research in Black Culture, New York Public Library.

Biography

Noble Lee Sissle was born 10 July 1889 in Indianapolis, Indiana. He was the son of Rev. George A. and Martha Scott Sissle, from a highly respected family. Sissle studied at DePauw University and Butler University, both in Indiana; he left the latter in 1915 without graduating. He began performing in high school glee clubs, then toured with the Edward Morris Male Quartet and Hann's Jubilee Singers. He and Eubie Blake, his longtime partner, met in 1915. Sissle performed with James Reese Europe's dance orchestras and other groups. He served in the 369th Regiment in World War I and was a member of its famous band, led by James Europe; after the war ended and James Europe died, Sissle briefly led this band. In 1919–1921, Sissle and Blake became popular as a duo act; in 1921, their hit musical *Shuffle Along* opened. Later they collaborated on other musicals, and in the 1920s they continued touring as a popular vaudeville duo. However, their partnership ended in 1926. Sissle was also a recording artist, performed at music halls in England, formed a band in Paris, and was a radio performer (CBS, beginning in 1931). He and Blake teamed up again for performances in the 1930s. Into the 1950s, Sissle was a successful bandleader. He was also a leader in black entertainment organizations. He retired from active bandleading in 1963. Sissle died 17 December 1975 in Tampa, Florida, age eighty-six.

ELLIOTT S. HURWITT

See also Bechet, Sidney; Blake, Eubie; Europe, James Reese; Fifteenth Infantry; Lyles; Aubrey; Miller, Flournoy; Musical Theater; Shuffle Along

Selected Songs

"Baltimore Buzz."
"If You've Never Been Vamped by a Brownskin."
"I'm Craving for That Kind of Love."
"I'm Just Wild About Harry."
"It's All Your Fault."
"Love Will Find a Way."
"You Were Meant for Me."

Further Reading

Badger, Reid. *A Life in Ragtime: A Biography of James Reese Europe*. New York: Oxford University Press, 1995.

Baltimore Afro-American, 1 October 1927; 11 February 1928.

Billboard, 18 May 1946.

Bolcom, William, and Robert Kimball. *Reminiscing With Sissle and Blake*. New York: Viking, 1973.

New York Age, 19 December 1925.

New York Amsterdam News, 27 December 1975.

New York Times, 18 December 1975.

Pittsburgh Courier, 20 December 1930.

Sissle, Noble. "Ragtime by U.S. Army Band Gets Everyone 'Over There.'" *St. Louis Post-Dispatch*, 10 June 1918. (Reprinted in various forms throughout the summer.)

———. "Memoirs of 'Jim' Europe." 1942. Library of Congress. (Unpublished manuscript, dated 1942, but parts probably written earlier.)

Small's Paradise

Small's Paradise, at 2294½ Seventh Avenue near 135th Street, was owned and operated by Edwin Smalls and was one of the premier nightspots in Harlem during the late 1920s. Smalls, a former elevator operator, was a descendant of Captain Robert Smalls, a former slave who became a captain in the Union navy and later a congressman from South Carolina. Small's Paradise (usually so spelled, with a misplaced apostrophe) was one of the most successful and best-known nightclubs in the history of Harlem, and the most prestigious club owned by an African American. Its reputation for first-class musical acts, elaborate floor shows, and dancing waiters attracted thousands of patrons who were eager to participate in the exciting nightlife of Harlem during the Roaring Twenties.

By the time he opened the Paradise in the autumn of 1925, Ed Smalls was already an experienced nightclub owner. Since 1917 he had been running a popular joint in Harlem called the Sugar Cane Club, which catered primarily to an African American clientele. But Small's Paradise was a much more elaborate venture, and one designed to attract not just local Harlemites but also moneyed white revelers from downtown. When the Paradise opened its doors on 26 October 1925, Smalls marked the occasion by throwing a spectacular gala. Nearly 1,500 guests jammed themselves into the brand-new basement club and danced to the tunes of Charlie Johnson's jazz band, which would serve as the house band for the next ten years. Of course, national Prohibition was in full force at the time, but patrons at Small's could either drink discreetly from their own bottle or flask of hooch, or else buy bootleg liquor from the waiters (at an exorbitant price).

In 1929, the entertainment magazine *Variety* listed eleven major nightclubs in Harlem that catered to a predominantly white crowd. The four most popular were Small's Paradise, the Cotton Club, Barron Wilkins's Exclusive Club, and Connie's Inn. The tremendous financial success of these clubs was due, in large part, to the fascination that many white people at the time felt for black culture. Huge numbers of white people swarmed into Harlem during the 1920s to experience the "exotic" or "primitive" African American nightlife. Many wealthy white curiosity seekers actually preferred some of the other big-name clubs—especially the Cotton Club and Connie's Inn—to Small's Paradise, because these other clubs were owned by whites and admitted only white patrons. While the entertainers and the waiters at these establishments were almost exclusively black, African American customers were firmly turned away unless they were true celebrities, such as the dancer Bill "Bojangles" Robinson. Small's Paradise, in contrast, appealed to whites who wanted to attend a club where African Americans made up a sizable portion of the audience. But despite the racially integrated nature of Small's Paradise, all its patrons were financially well-off; the high prices for both food and liquor were enough to force most working-class Harlemites to seek out a more affordable speakeasy. Although Small's was not as expensive as Connie's Inn, for example, an average tab at Small's was about $4 per person in 1929, when the average domestic laborer in Harlem earned between $6 and $12 a week.

One of the signature features of Small's Paradise was its dancing waiters, who would balance heavy trays full of bootleg liquor while dancing the Charleston, sometimes on roller skates, as they moved among the tables. Small's also carved out a niche for itself in the competitive nightclub business by staying open much later than most other clubs, including the aristocratic Cotton Club. After other cabarets closed down at three or four o'clock in the morning, black and white patrons alike would descend on Small's Paradise for one of its famous early-morning "breakfast dances." The floor show, complete with twenty-five or thirty dancers and showgirls and two dozen musicians, would go on at six o'clock in the morning, and the dancing might last until noon or even later. The entertainment at Small's was always first-rate, and some of the most famous musicians of the Harlem Renaissance played there, including Willie "the Lion" Smith and Duke Ellington. And in the early-morning hours, many of the finest musicians in Harlem who were engaged by other clubs met at Small's for impromptu jam sessions.

More than most nightclubs in Harlem, Small's Paradise figured prominently in the lives of many important artists and writers of the Harlem Renaissance, including Alain Locke, Harold Jackman, Countee Cullen, and Langston Hughes. Even William Faulkner is said to have attended a party at Small's during a visit to New York. One of the club's most loyal customers was Carl Van Vechten, the wealthy white writer who helped launch the careers of many famous figures of the renaissance. In fact, some critics claim that Van Vechten based his description of the Black Venus, a nightclub prominently featured in his controversial novel *Nigger Heaven*, on his experiences at Small's Paradise. After *Nigger Heaven* was published in 1926, the managers of Small's were so offended by its portrayal of Harlem that they permanently banned Van Vechten from his favorite watering hole, much to his dismay.

Small's Paradise holds the distinction of being the longest-operating nightclub in Harlem, witnessing the rise of not just jazz but rock and roll and even disco before it finally closed its doors in 1986. After

Ed Smalls sold the business, the Paradise changed hands a number of times. The late basketball star Wilt Chamberlain owned the club briefly in the 1960s, renamed it Big Wilt's Small's Paradise, and featured Ray Charles as his star performer. Although the doors have now closed on Small's Paradise, the frequent references to the club in newspapers, essays, autobiographies, and fiction from the 1920s testify to its enduring legacy as one of the most popular racially integrated nightclubs of the Harlem Renaissance.

KATHLEEN DROWNE

See also Cotton Club; Cullen, Countee; Ellington, Duke; Hughes, Langston; Jackman, Harold; Locke, Alain; *Nigger Heaven*; Nightclubs; Nightlife; Smith, Willie "the Lion"; Van Vechten, Carl

Further Reading

Anderson, Jervis. *This Was Harlem: A Cultural Portrait, 1900–1950*. New York: Farrar, Straus and Giroux, 1981.

Dance, Stanley. *The World of Duke Ellington*. New York: Da Capo, 1970.

Haskins, Jim. *The Cotton Club*. New York: Random House, 1977.

Hughes, Langston. *The Big Sea*. New York: Hill and Wang–Farrar, Straus and Giroux, 1997. (Originally published 1940.)

Lewis, David Levering. *When Harlem Was in Vogue*. Oxford and New York: Oxford University Press, 1979.

Schoener, Allon, ed. *Harlem on My Mind: Cultural Capital of Black America, 1900–1968*. New York: Random House, 1968.

Watson, Steven. *The Harlem Renaissance: Hub of African-American Culture, 1920–1930*. New York: Pantheon, 1995.

Williams, John A. "Harlem Nightclub." In *Harlem: A Community in Transition*, ed. John Henrik Clarke. New York: Citadel, 1964.

Smith, Ada

Ada Smith was called Bricktop because of her red hair; her full name was Ada Beatrice Queen Victoria Louisa Virginia Smith. She was born in 1894 in West Virginia; when she was about four or five, her father died, and her mother relocated the family to Chicago. Shortly after the family's relocation, Smith made her stage debut in a local production of *Uncle Tom's Cabin*. When Smith was about fourteen, she auditioned for and received a part in the chorus at the Pekin Theater (one of the first theaters in Chicago dedicated to black drama). Although her mother made her leave the chorus and return to school, one of Smith's greatest ambitions was to become a saloon performer, and by age sixteen she dropped out of school to pursue her dream, joining the chorus of Flournoy Miller and Aubrey Lyles's vaudeville comedy team. Just before her eighteenth birthday, Smith was given an opportunity to perform in the Roy Jones saloon in Chicago. During the next few years, she performed in various clubs, including the Cabaret de Champion, the Panama Club, and the Watts Country Club. While she was with a group called the Crosby Trio, she first met Barron Wilkins, who owned a café on Seventh Avenue in Harlem (and who is said to have given her the nickname Bricktop). In 1916, she, Florence Mills, and Cora Green formed the Panama Trio and toured as vaudevillians. By 1922, Smith was back in New York performing at Barron Wilkins's café. By this time, his café was catering to the rich and famous, so Smith was able to meet celebrities such as John Barrymore, Charles MacArthur, and Jack "Legs" Diamond.

In 1924, Smith moved to France to perform at the nightclub Le Grand Duc, and at this point her career began to soar. She met people like F. Scott Fitzgerald, Fred Astaire, Ernest Hemingway, Josephine Baker, Elsa Maxwell, Cole and Linda Porter, and Langston Hughes (who worked as a busboy at Le Grand Duc). In 1926, she opened her own club, called Chez Bricktop, which would remain open until war broke out in 1939 and Smith left Europe.

After Smith returned to Harlem, her life was vastly different. In France, there had been no segregation, but in the United States, she encountered racism everywhere. She found it difficult to get singing engagements in either white or black clubs, and she was never able to re-create the success she achieved in France. However, she continued to perform until 1964, when she announced her retirement. Throughout her entire career, Smith recorded only one song, "So Long Baby," with Cy Coleman.

Biography

Ada "Bricktop" Smith was born 14 August 1894 in Alderson, West Virginia. Around 1898 or 1899 her father died, and her mother relocated the family to Chicago, where Smith made her stage debut in a local production of *Uncle Tom's Cabin*. Around 1908 Smith auditioned for and received a part in the chorus at the Pekin Theater, although her mother made her leave it and return to school. By around 1910 she dropped out of school and joined the chorus of a vaudeville duo. She performed in various clubs and in 1916 formed the Panama Trio with Florence Mills and Cora Green. She appeared in Barron Wilkins's club in Harlem. In 1924, she went to Paris, where she opened her own club, Chez Bricktop, in 1926. At Chez Bricktop she met the saxophonist Peter Duconge; they were married in December 1929. She returned to the United States in 1939. Smith retired in 1964 and died in January 1984.

Teri Weil

See also Lyles, Aubrey; Miller, Flournoy; Mills, Florence; Singers

Further Reading

Duconge, Ada Smith, and James Haskins. *Bricktop*. New York: Atheneum, 1983.

Hine, Darlene Clark, ed. *Black Women in America: An Historical Encyclopedia*. Brooklyn, N.Y.: Carlson Publishing, 1993.

Jackson, Kenneth T., ed. *The Scribner Encyclopedia of American Lives*. New York: Scribner, 1998.

Kellner, Bruce, ed. *The Harlem Renaissance: A Historical Dictionary for the Era*. New York: Methuen, 1984.

Smith, Jessie Carney, ed. *Notable Black American Women*. Detroit, Mich.: Gale Research, 1992.

Southern, Eileen. *Biographical Dictionary of Afro-American and African Musicians*. Westport, Conn.: Greenwood, 1982.

Who Was Who in America, Vol. 8, *1982–1985*. Chicago, Ill.: Marquis Who's Who, 1985.

Smith, Bessie

One day in 1923, the "empress of the blues" walked into a recording studio with her piano player, Clarence Williams, and performed "'Tain't Nobody's Bizness If I Do" nine times and "Down-Hearted Blues" two times for Columbia Records' producer Frank Walker. The next day she returned to the studio and performed "Down-Hearted Blues" again. This time her voice was so powerful that Walker simply declared the audition "satisfactory." This was the beginning of the "empress's" highly successful recording career: Within six months after she signed with Columbia, her first recording sold 780,000 copies, and she eventually became the highest paid black entertainer of her time.

The "empress" was Bessie Smith. Born into poverty in 1894 in Tennessee, she grew up in what she described as a "little ramshackle cabin," and by age ten she had witnessed the failing health and subsequent death of her mother, her father, and a brother, leaving her older sister, Viola, responsible for caring for the other five children, including Bessie. For poor black southerners at the turn of the twentieth century, the prospect of success—educationally or financially, for example—appeared dim; but Bessie Smith would gradually emerge from her poverty-stricken, parentless situation. She performed song-and-dance routines on the streets, made her professional debut at the Ivory Theater in Chattanooga at age nine, and became a dancer with the Moses Stokes minstrel troupe at age eighteen.

Bessie Smith had not only a powerful voice but a powerful performance style and a formidable stage presence. People who knew her, including the noted photographer Carl Van Vechten and the clarinetist and saxophone player Mezz Mezzrow, offered descriptions such as "mesmerizing," "a beautiful face," and "a real woman." Smith was 5 feet 9 inches tall and weighed 200 pounds; and as a performer she exuded charm and queenly grace. Within a year after Smith had joined the Moses Stokes minstrels, her special quality and her natural talent as a singer were impelling audiences to throw money onto the stage when she performed such early favorites as "Weary Blues."

Around 1910, Smith performed on a southern circuit of segregated tent shows and black theaters with the well-known blues singer Gertrude "Ma" Rainey, who evidently gave Smith some guidance and teaching. These traveling shows included singers, jugglers, comedians, dancers, and wrestlers; and Smith eventually joined other such shows, including the Florida Cotton Pickers and then her own group, the Liberty Belles. Patterning herself after Rainey, the "mother of the blues," Smith became a popular entertainer in both southern and northern cities.

Eventually Smith joined the Theater Owners' Booking Association—the black vaudeville circuit—and she was soon performing more and more blues in as many as twenty different acts in various shows. In 1918, she was a featured performer at the Douglas Gilmor Theater in Baltimore, Maryland, sharing the bill with well-regarded acts such as Holmes and Edwards, the Crazy Man and the Maid, and Ralph Harris and Alda Fatima. One factor in her popularity was her ability to attract both white and black audiences, although her numerous recordings (more than 160 in all) were categorized as "race music."

Like Rainey, Smith sang of such themes as love and sexuality, emotional battles and mistreatment, independence and freedom, and self-respect, particularly in relation to black womanhood. In "Get It, Bring It, and Put It Right Here," for example, she says: "I've had a man for fifteen years, given him his room and his board./Once he was like a Cadillac, now he's like an old worn-out Ford. . . ./Oh, there'll be some changes from now on, according to my plan./He's got to get it, bring it, and put it right here . . . " Many of her compositions and performances have political implications, suggesting her public response to a patriarchal society and patriarchally structured relationships. She expressed the tension between black men and black women and boldly challenged anyone who attempted to assert authority over black women, by implication challenging the "roles" of dependence and independence in black people's lives. All this allowed Smith to connect with her audience, perhaps especially in such popular pieces as "Mistreatin' Daddy," "Money Blues," and "Hateful Blues." In "Mistreatin' Daddy," for instance, the singer is despondent after being abused by a man (". . . you mistreated me and drove me from your door") but also asserts her own freedom, independence, and sexuality: "If you see me setting on another daddy's knee/Don't bother me, I'm as mean as can be." In "Money Blues" a woman explicitly demands money and other material pleasures from her husband: "'Daddy, I need money now.'/All day long I hear that song/'Papa, it's your fault if I go wrong.'" Angela Davis (1998) argues that for her mostly working-class black audiences, Smith "made the blues into women's music and a site for the elaboration of a black cultural consciousness that did not ignore the dynamics of gender" (142).

The recording contract that Smith signed with Columbia after her "satisfactory" audition in 1923 was important for her and for the company. Her recordings were successful immediately and, as noted above, appealed to both whites and blacks. These numerous records averted a possible bankruptcy at Columbia, and her association with Columbia gave her a foothold that might otherwise have been hard to find. This was a time when black entertainers and performers had difficulty becoming a part of the commercialized world of established recording companies

Bessie Smith, photographed by Carl Van Vechten, 1936.
(Library of Congress.)

and producers. Smith's popularity gave her considerable status at Columbia, but some years earlier she had auditioned for and been turned down by at least two other companies. (One of them was Black Swan, which was owned by blacks and had W. E. B. Du Bois and John Nail on its board of directors, but rejected her anyway.) With the release of her first "race record" by Columbia, Smith began to see an increase in her performance fees as well as her recording fees.

Smith's appeal to a large number of white listeners was significant. Unlike Ma Rainey, who performed for almost exclusively black audiences, Smith proved that her music was captivating enough to imply a redefinition of racial lines and of listeners' interests. At the same time, though, Smith's music and performances helped to create a space in which the social conditions and daily realities of black people's life could be addressed, in the aftermath of slavery and in the context of Jim Crow. Davis (1998) writes: "For masses of black people during the decade of the twenties—for those who remained geographically rooted in traditional southern culture as well as for migrant populations in the North and Midwest—Smith was an articulator and shaper of African American identity

and consciousness" (142). The objection might be raised that although Smith's audiences were diverse, even interested white Americans could not easily ignore, break through, or erase the existing barriers of race, and that for this reason white people's exposure to blues might actually reinforce their sense of black people's inferiority. But Smith's powerfully emotional songs and presence directly connected to the experiences of working-class black people and made such experiences meaningful and significant even within a generally racist society.

Smith prospered as an entertainer, performer, and recording artist in the 1920s; her popularity was at its peak from 1923 to 1930. During the Depression, though, she met with hard times. In 1931, Columbia Records dropped Smith from its roster because sales of her records were falling. She continued to compose and perform, still focusing on themes that were familiar in her life, such as poverty, love, independence, and even alcoholism. She appeared in nightclubs and theaters in Philadelphia, New York, and some southern cities, maintaining her large following. But with the persistent economic depression and Smith's own personal depression, her career eventually declined. In 1933, during her final recording session, she sang "Down in the Dumps," a piece that reflected the end of a great career. In 1937, at age fifty-three, Smith was on the verge of establishing a second career when she died in an automobile accident in Mississippi.

Through her memorable voice and her serious subject matter, Smith made an important contribution to blues, to jazz, and to the Harlem Renaissance.

Biography

Bessie Smith was born in 1894 in Chattanooga, Tennessee. In 1912, she joined the Moses Stokes minstrel troupe as a dancer. She joined the Theater Owners' Booking Agency and in 1918 was featured at the Douglas Gilmor Theater in Baltimore, Maryland. Smith signed a recording contract with Columbia Records in 1923 and released four songs, including "Saint Louis Blues," "Down-Hearted Blues," and "Gimme a Pigfoot." That same year, she sold 780,000 records in six months and became the highest paid black entertainer of the time. Her recording fee increased from $150 to $200 in 1924. Smith adopted a six-year-old boy in 1926. She was dropped from Columbia Records in 1931. In 1933, she made a record with swing-band accompaniment. She sang "Down in the Dumps" during her last recording session, also in 1933. On the night of 26 September 1937, Smith was involved in an automobile accident and died.

VALERIE FELITA KINLOCH

See also Black Swan Phonograph Company; Blues; Blues: Women Performers; Rainey, Gertrude "Ma"; Saint Louis Blues; Singers; Theater Owners' Booking Association; Van Vechten, Carl; Williams, Clarence

Selected Compositions and Recordings

"After You've Gone." (T. Layton and H. Creamer.)
"Alexander's Ragtime Band." (Irving Berlin.)
"Baby Doll." (Bessie Smith.)
"Backwater Blues." (Bessie Smith.)
"Blue, Blue." (Bessie Smith.)
"Dirty No-Gooders Blues." (Bessie Smith.)
"Dixie Flyer Blues." (Bessie Smith.)
"Down-Hearted Blues." (Alberta Hunter and Lovie Austin.)
"Gimme a Pigfoot." (Wesley Wilson.)
"Golden Rule Rules." (Bessie Smith.)
"Hateful Blues." (E. Johnson.)
"He's Gone Blues." (Bessie Smith.)
"Hot Springs Blues." (Bessie Smith.)
"In the House Blues." (Bessie Smith.)
"It Makes My Love Come Down." (Bessie Smith.)
"Lonesome Desert Blues." (Bessie Smith.)
"Long Old Road." (Bessie Smith.)
"Lost Your Head Blues." (Bessie Smith.)
"Mistreatin' Daddy." (Porter Grainger and B. Ricketts.)
"Money Blues." (D. K. Leader and H. Eller.)
"Moonshine Blues." (Ma Rainey.)
"My Man Blues." (Bessie Smith.)
"Saint Louis Blues." (W. C. Handy.)
"Shipwreck Blues." (Bessie Smith.)
"'Tain't Nobody's Bizness If I Do." (Porter Grainger and E. Robbins.)

Further Reading

Ackerman, Paul. "Historic Bessie Smith Set Aimed at Youth Market." *Billboard*, 30 July 1970.

Albertson, Chris. *Bessie*. New York: Stein & Day, 1972.

Baker, Houston A., Jr. *Blues, Ideology, and Afro-American Literature*. Chicago, Ill.: University of Chicago Press, 1984.

"Bessie Smith Set Pattern for Today's Blues Singers." *Ebony*, August 1950.

"The Bessie Smith Story: 'Back Water Blues' One of Singer's Best." *Afro-American*, December 1951.

Brooks, Edward. *The Bessie Smith Companion*. New York: Da Capo, 1982.

Collins, Patricia Hill. *Black Feminist Thought: Knowledge, Consciousness, and the Politics of Empowerment*. New York and London: Routledge, 1991.

Cone, James H. *The Spirituals and the Blues: An Interpretation*. New York: Seabury, 1972.

Davis, Angela. *Blues, Legacies, and Black Feminism: Gertrude "Ma" Rainey, Bessie Smith, and Billie Holiday*. New York: Vintage, 1998.

"Death of Bessie Smith: Ballad for Twelve-Strings." *Voices*, Winter 1950.

"'Down Hearted Blues' Was Bessie's First Hit Record." *Afro-American*, December 1951.

Elwood, Philip. "A Re-Creation of Bessie Smith." *San Francisco Examiner*, April 1985.

Feinstein, Elaine. *Bessie Smith: Empress of the Blues*. New York: Penguin, 1985.

Giovanni, Nikki. "Only Bessie Could Equal Bessie Smith." *Encore*, June 1973.

Gleason, Ralph. *Celebrating the Duke and Louis, Bessie, Billie, Bird, Carmen, Miles, Dizzy, and Other Heroes*. New York: Delta, 1975.

Orgill, Roxane. *Shout, Sister, Shout!—Ten Girl Singers Who Shaped a Century*. New York: Margaret K. McElderry, 2001.

Terkel, Studs. "Bessie Smith: Empress of the Blues." In *Giants of Jazz*. New York: Crowell, 1975.

Smith, Clara

The singer Clara Smith was called "queen of the moaners." It is believed that she began her career around 1910, performing in southern vaudeville acts and tent shows. By 1918, Smith was a featured star on the Theater Owners' Booking Association circuit. She spent the next five years performing in cities such as Columbus (Georgia), New Orleans, Nashville, and St. Louis. In 1923, Smith relocated to Harlem, where she was placed under contract with Columbia Records.

In Harlem, Smith performed in and managed numerous revues. In 1924, the Clara Smith Theatrical Revue Club was born. The following year, Smith performed in two of her own shows, the *Clara Smith Revue* and the *Black Bottom Revue*. Over the next decade, Smith appeared in various revues, including the *Swanee Club Revue*, the *Ophelia Show from Baltimore*, *Dream Girls*, and *Candied Sweets*. She performed in such theaters as the Alhambra, the Lafayette, the Lincoln, the Ambassador, the Harlem Fifth Avenue, and the Opera House.

Through her recording, performing, and management of revues Clara Smith sang with some great figures in blues and jazz. For example, while she was under contract to Columbia, she and Bessie Smith recorded three songs together: "Far Away Blues," "I'm Going Back to My Used to Be," and "My Man Blues." Clara Smith and Bessie Smith were not related, although they were said to be great friends until an argument in 1925. Clara Smith reportedly recorded some 125 songs, accompanied by jazz musicians such as Fletcher Henderson, Louis Armstrong, James P. Johnson, Don Redman, Charlie Green, Porter Grainger, and Joe Smith (who was not a relative of hers).

Smith became known as the "queen of the moaners" because of the way she would begin a song—with a long emotional moan that gripped her listeners and drew them into the music. A striking example is her recording of "Awful Morning Blues."

To dramatize her performances, Smith drew on her experiences in vaudeville and musical revues. She used dress, facial expressions, tears, and her trademark mournful moans to convey the emotion behind a song. Smith was able to express sadness very effectively, but she was also a comedienne, as she demonstrated in her performance in the revue at Club Alabam.

Between 1925 and 1928, Smith made the recordings that are thought to be her best. At about this time, her music changed from "moaning blues" to a more highly charged, more explicit sound. She continued to perform in revues in Harlem's theaters until 1931, and around the country until 1934.

Biography

Clara Smith was born about 1894 or 1895 in Spartanburg, South Carolina. There is little or no information on her early childhood. She may have performed in vaudeville acts and tent shows about 1910; by 1918, she was featured on the Theater Owners' Booking Association circuit. She came to Harlem in 1923, contracted with Columbia Records, performed in and managed revues, and formed the Clara Smith Theatrical Revue Club. She married Charles Wesley in 1926. In February 1935, after returning home from an appearance in Detroit, Smith checked

into a hospital with chest pains; she died eleven days later.

TERI WEIL

See also Alhambra Theater; Armstrong, Louis; Blues: Women Performers; Henderson, Fletcher; Johnson, James P.; Lafayette Theater; Lincoln Theater; Singers; Smith, Bessie; Theater Owners' Booking Association

Further Reading

Clarke, Donald, ed. *The Penguin Encyclopedia of Popular Music*. New York: Viking, 1989.
Garraty, John A., and Mark C. Carnes, eds. *American National Biography*. New York: Oxford University Press, 1999.
Harris, Sheldon, ed. *Blues Who's Who: A Biographical Dictionary of Blues Singers*. New Rochelle, N.Y.: Arlington, 1979.
Harrison, Daphne. *Black Pearls: Blues Queens of the 1920s*. New Brunswick, N.J.: Rutgers University Press, 1988.
Kernfeld, Barry, ed. *The New Grove Dictionary of Jazz*. London: Macmillan, 1988.
Smith, Jesse Carney, ed. *Notable Black American Women*. Detroit, Mich.: Gale Research, 1992.
Southern, Eileen. *Biographical Dictionary of Afro-American and African Musicians*. Westport, Conn.: Greenwood, 1982.

Smith, Mamie

Mamie Smith was reputedly born in Cincinnati, Ohio, on 26 May 1883. Bitten early on by the performing bug, she was on the road with the Four Dancing Mitchells at around the age of ten. After touring with the Smart Set Company in 1912, Smith made New York City her home base beginning in 1913.

While she was performing in Harlem, she appeared in Perry Bradford's revue *Made in Harlem*, which ultimately led to Smith's first recordings, inaugurating the boom in blues recordings of the 1920s. Bradford had selected two songs from the revue—"That Thing Called Love" and "You Can't Keep a Good Man Down"—for Smith to record for Victor in 1920, but Victor rejected the idea of an African American recording the songs. Fred Hager at Okeh, too, hesitated to record Smith, but with Bradford's urgings bravely proceeded to record her rather than his first choice,

Sophie Tucker. The *Chicago Defender*, which had been pushing for recordings by "race" artists since 1916, helped make the record a success. Buoyed by its sales, Okeh recorded Smith again on 10 August 1920, producing the first vocal blues record by an African American, "Crazy Blues" backed with "It's Right Here for You (If You Don't Get It . . . 'Tain't No Fault of Mine"). These were two composed and sophisticated blues, based on folk blues of the type that had been performed informally around the South for twenty years or so, reflecting a stage and city orientation in their structure and performance. This record sold 75,000 copies in its first month of release and inaugurated the era of blues recordings by African Americans, including the blues craze of the 1920s, which was dominated by female blues artists up until 1926. As a result of this success, Smith, billed as "queen of the blues," revisited the recording studios many times, appearing in New York City and around the country in revues and stage shows performing her own brand of vaudeville blues and pop songs to highly appreciative audiences. Okeh Records, in fact, even proclaimed a "Mamie Smith Week" in the spring of 1922 in recognition of her popularity and record sales. Recording on occasion with accompanists such as Willie "the Lion" Smith, Coleman Hawkins, and Sidney Bechet, Smith established the genre of vaudeville blues that created a space for Gertrude "Ma" Rainey, Bessie Smith, Lucille Hegamin, Victoria Spivey, and, ultimately, male blues performers in the recording industry, and fashioned a sophisticated but sassy style for numerous female singers who performed in Harlem's cabarets in the 1920s to take up.

Following a European tour in 1936, Smith returned to the United States. She made five movies, which, though not enough to revive a flagging career, still demonstrated her ability and her popularity with African American audiences.

After approximately two years in Harlem Hospital, Smith died in 1946; she was buried in Frederick Douglass Memorial Park Cemetery in Staten Island, New York. Smith was a pioneer who helped gain recognition for African Americans in American popular culture through her spirited performances of vaudeville-style blues.

Biography

Mamie Smith was born 26 May 1883 in Cincinnati, Ohio (unconfirmed). She toured with the Four Dancing Mitchells in 1893. Smith worked as a chorus dancer with J. Homer Tutt and Salem Tutt-Whitney's Smart Set Company in 1912. She worked in clubs, cafés, and cabarets in New York City from 1913 to 1920, and in Perry Bradford's *Made in Harlem* at the Lincoln Theater. She recorded prolifically for Okeh Records from 1920 to 1923 and toured the country as a result of the success of her recordings. She recorded for Ajax (1924), Victor (1926), Okeh (1929, 1931), and Victor (1929). Smith appeared in the musical comedy *Follow Me* at the Lafayette Theater in 1923. She headlined in the revues *Struttin' Along*, *Syncopationland*, *Dixie*, *Syncopated*, *Frolicking Around*, *Sugar Cane*, *A Riot of Fun*, and *Sun Tan Frolics* during 1923–1929. She appeared in the film *Jailhouse Blues* in 1929 and continued to appear in musical revues in New York City. She toured with Fats Pichon in her *Yelping Hounds Revue* from 1932 to 1934 and toured Europe, appearing in theaters around 1936. Smith appeared in the films *Paradise in Harlem* (1939), *Mystery in Swing* (1940), *Murder on Lenox Avenue* (1941), and *Sunday Sinners* (1941), and the short *Because I Love You* (1943). She was the first African American to record vocal blues. Okeh Records proclaimed a "Mamie Smith Week" in 1922. Smith died in Staten Island, New York, c. September–November 1946.

STEVEN TRACY

See also Bechet, Sidney; Blues; Blues: Women Performers; Bradford, Perry; Hegamin, Lucille; Rainey, Gertrude "Ma"; Singers; Smith, Bessie; Smith, Willie "the Lion"; Spivey, Victoria

Selected Works

Mamie Smith: The Complete Recorded Works in Chronological Order, Vols. 1–4. Document Records, 1995.

Further Reading

Bradford, Perry. *Born With the Blues*. New York: Oak, 1965.

Charters, Samuel, and Leonard Kunstadt. *Jazz: A History of the New York Scene*. New York: Doubleday, 1962.

Dixon, Robert M. W., John Godrich, and Howard Rye. *Blues and Gospel Records, 1890–1943*, 4th ed. Oxford: Clarendon, 1997.

Harris, Sheldon. *Blues Who's Who*. New Rochelle, N.Y.: Arlington House, 1979.

Harrison, Daphne Duval. *Black Pearls*. New Brunswick, N.J.: Rutgers University Press, 1988.

Obrecht, Jas. "Mamie Smith: First Lady of the Blues." *Blues Revue*, 17, 1995.

Romanowski, Ken. Liner notes. *Mamie Smith: The Complete Recorded Works in Chronological Order*, Vols. 1–4. Vienna: Document Records, 1995.

Southern, Eileen. *Biographical Dictionary of Afro-American and African Musicians*. Westport, Conn.: Greenwood, 1982.

Stewart-Baxter, Derrick. *Ma Rainey and the Classic Blues Singers*. New York: Stein & Day, 1970.

Smith, Trixie

Trixie Smith was among the more successful singers who recorded during the 1920s, the heyday of "classic blues." She is often compared to the other "singing Smiths" of the era—Bessie, Mamie, and Clara—who were not related to her or each other. Trixie Smith emerged during the early period of a boom in "race records" that was set off by the success of Mamie Smith's "Crazy Blues" (1920). Like others who were part of that boom, Trixie Smith was from the South (Atlanta, in her case) and began her career as a vaudeville and minstrel entertainer who performed comedy, danced, acted, and sang in traveling shows. Unlike most other black entertainers of the era, though, she came from a middle-class background and was well educated; she attended Selma University in Alabama.

Attracted by the lure of show business and the North, Smith moved to New York at age twenty and worked in a number of cafés and theaters in Harlem and Philadelphia. Between 1916 and the early 1920s, she toured as a featured singer in shows and on the Theater Owners' Booking Association circuit with acts such as the popular comedy team Butterbeans and Susie (Edwards and Edwards).

Smith's career changed dramatically in 1922, when she competed in the highly publicized first blues contest, held at the Manhattan Casino. Billed as the "southern nightingale" and singing her own composition "Trixie's Blues," she won first prize. Shortly afterward she signed with Harry Pace's newly established Black Swan label and began a recording career that brought her success and fame. Smith's voice, though not as rough, powerful, or emotional as the voices of some better-known women who sang classic blues, was pleasing and convincing. She made four dozen recordings for Black Swan, Paramount, and Decca between 1922 and 1939. In her Down Home Syncopaters

and other recording groups, she was backed by some of the biggest names in jazz, including Louis Armstrong, James P. Johnson, and Fletcher Henderson. Most of Trixie Smith's recordings were made during a four-year period, 1922–1925; her sessions in 1925 featuring Armstrong are considered her best early work.

In 1926, Smith's recording career declined, but she continued to work throughout the 1920s in local shows and traveling revues, sometimes in nonsinging roles. Thus, whereas the careers of many classic blues singers faded before 1930, Smith continued to sing, act, and tour in shows. In 1931, she performed in a road show with the legendary star Mae West. She appeared in four films, including Oscar Micheaux's *Swing* (1938) and *God's Stepchildren* (1938). Her singing career was revived briefly during the late 1930s, when she performed in clubs in New York and—after an eleven-year absence from the studio—made what some people think are her best recordings. Backed by an all-star band that featured Sidney Bechet and Charlie Shavers, Smith recorded half a dozen songs, including remakes of her earlier releases "Trixie's Blues" and "Freight Train Blues," as well as her best-remembered song, "My Daddy Rocks Me." By 1940, her career waned again, and she faded into near obscurity, performing only occasionally until her death at age fifty-eight. Trixie Smith was considered one of the more versatile black performers of early recorded classic blues. Her vocal style was a successful blend of vaudeville and southern blues traditions. Compared with Bessie Smith and other legendary blues singers (who recorded more often and had more successful singing careers), Trixie Smith had a lighter sound, with less depth and conviction. Her later recordings have a laid-back, mellow quality more characteristic of popular singers of the swing era. Her twelve-bar blues songs and vaudeville-style pop songs have common themes—love, grief, travel, sexual mischief, and good times—conveyed with Smith's distinctive mood, which is dominated by a feeling of humor, joy, and optimism.

Biography

Trixie Smith—a blues singer, vaudeville entertainer, and actress (also known as Tessie Ames and Bessie Lee)—was born in 1885 in Atlanta, Georgia. She came from a middle-class background and attended Selma University in Alabama. She moved to New York at age twenty and worked in cafés and theaters in Harlem and Philadelphia. She toured with the

Theater Owners' Booking Association, 1916–early 1920s. She won a blues contest at the Manhattan Casino in 1922, then signed with the recording company Black Swan. When her successful recording career waned, she continued to perform in traveling shows and revues; she also appeared in films. Smith died of an illness on 21 September 1943 in New York City.

MICHAEL WHITE

See also Armstrong, Louis; Bechet, Sidney; Black Swan Phonograph Company; Blues; Blues: Women Performers; Henderson, Fletcher; Johnson, James P.; Manhattan Casino; Micheaux, Oscar; Smith, Bessie; Smith, Clara; Smith; Mamie; Singers

Selected Works

"Everybody Loves My Baby." 1924.
"Freight Train Blues." 1924, 1938.
"Messin' Around." 1926.
"My Daddy Rocks Me." 1938.
"Trixie's Blues." 1922, 1938.
"The World's Gone Jazz Crazy and So Am I." 1925.

Further Reading

Briggs, Keith. Liner notes. *Trixie Smith: Complete Recorded Works*, Vols. 1 and 2. Document Records (DOCD 5332 and 5333), 1995.

Charters, Samuel B., and Kunstadt, Leonard. *Jazz: A History of the New York Scene*. Garden City, N.Y.: Da Capo, 1981.

Harris, Sheldon. *Blues Who's Who: A Biographical Dictionary of Blues Singers*. New York: Da Capo, 1985.

Harrison, Daphne Duval. *Black Pearls: Blues Queens of the 1920s*. New Brunswick, N.J.: Rutgers University Press, 1988.

Stewart-Baxter, Derrick. *Ma Rainey and the Classic Blues Singers*. London: Vista Studio, 1970.

Yanow, Scott. "Trixie Smith." In *All Music Guide to the Blues*, 3rd ed. San Francisco, Calif.: Backbeat, 2003.

Smith, Willie "the Lion"

The pianist and composer Willie "the Lion" Smith is considered by many one of the fathers of Harlem stride piano, along with "Abba Labba," Eubie Blake, James P. Johnson, and Luckey Roberts. Smith's boldness, flamboyance, and braggadocio made him a legend around Harlem during the 1920s and 1930s and beyond. He was one of the more popular "ticklers" on the rent-party circuit and was a mentor to many other pianists, including James P. Johnson, Fats Waller, Joe Turner, Sam Ervis, Count Basie, and most notably Duke Ellington.

By his teen years Smith had established a reputation as an extraordinary ragtime pianist and was lauded for his exemplary use of the left hand, his ability to play in all keys, and his thorough approach to accompanying. Before 1914, he performed primarily in and around Newark, New Jersey, and was a mainstay at legendary venues such as Randolph's café (where he met his closest friend, James P. Johnson) and Buss's saloon.

In 1914, Smith left Newark for Atlantic City, New Jersey. A lover of excitement and the daring adventure of nightlife, Smith emerged in the red-light district of Atlantic City and established himself as a main attraction at Kelly's Café (replacing Eubie Blake, who was on his way to New York in 1915) and at Ralph (Rafe) Welloff's New World. Smith now wore fine suits, custom-made shoes, and a derby hat and carried a cigar and a cane.

In November 1916, Smith enlisted in the army, joining the Ninety-second Division, 153rd Negro Brigade, 350th Field Artillery Unit. For his proficiency as an A-1 gunner and for his courageous acts on the front line of battle, he was nicknamed "Willie the Lion." Smith also served as drum major and pianist for the 350th Field Artillery Marching Band, also known as the "Seventy Black Devils."

After his discharge in 1919, Smith settled in Harlem and became known as "the Lion." Even though he was a headliner at clubs such as Leroy's and the Catagonia Club (also known as Pod's and Jerry's) in Harlem and the Onyx on Fifty-second Street, he was much more sought-after for rent parties. As a member of the "big three" (along with Johnson and Fats Waller), Smith spent a great deal of time during the 1920s and 1930s performing at society parties and private social gatherings (often accompanied by Waller).

In 1920, Mamie Smith and Her Jazz Hounds, with Smith as the bandleader and pianist, made the first of numerous recordings catering to a new black audience; they were issued under the Okeh label and marketed as "race records." During the 1920s, Smith accompanied many vocalists, often in cabaret settings. In 1927,

Smith performed on Broadway as a cast member in Dana Burnet and George Abbott's *Four Walls*.

As a composer, Smith highlighted his unique use of the left hand and his love for ragtime. By the 1930s, Smith had also incorporated elements of impressionistic counterpoint. After a number of years recording as a sideman, "the Lion" recorded and toured extensively with his own group: Willie Smith and His Cubs.

Biography

William Henry Joseph Bonaparte Bertholoff Smith was born 25 November 1897 in Goshen, New York. He studied piano and organ as a child with his mother; attended Newark High School; and studied theory, counterpoint, and harmony with Hans Steinke in New York during the 1930s and 1940s. Smith served in the U.S. Army's Ninety-second Division, 153rd Negro Brigade, 350th Field Artillery Unit; he was a drum major for the 350th Field Artillery Marching Band, the "Seventy Black Devils." He was a member of the American Society of Composers, Authors, and Publishers (ASCAP). Smith died in New York City 18 April 1973.

EMMETT G. PRICE III

See also Blake, Eubie; Ellington, Duke; House-Rent Parties; Johnson, James P.; Smith, Mamie; Waller, Thomas "Fats"

Selected Compositions

"Keep Your Temper." 1925.
"Fingerbuster." 1934.
"Echo of Spring." 1935.
"Passionette." 1935.
"Rippling Waters." 1939.

Recordings

Mamie Smith and Her Jazz Hounds. "Crazy Blues" and "It's Right Here for You." Okeh 4169, August 1920.
Gulf Coast Seven. "Santa Claus Blues" and "Keep Your Temper." Columbia 14107D, November 1925.
Clarence Williams's Jug Band. "What If We Do." Philips LP 7521, June 1929.
Seven Gallon Jug Band. "Wipe It Off." Columbia W149690–2, December 1929.

Clarence Williams's Washboard Band. "Shim Sham Shimmy Dance" and "High Society." Columbia 2806, Philips LP 7521, July 1933.
Mezz Mezzrow and His Orchestra. "Apologies" and "Sendin' the Vipers." Victor 25019, Bluebird 10250, Label "X" LP 3015, May 1934.
———. "Old Fashioned Love" and "35th and Calumet." Victor 25202, Bluebird 10251, Label "X" LP 3015, May 1934.
Willie Smith and His Cubs. "There's Gonna Be the Devil to Pay" and "What Can I Do?" Decca 7073, April 1935.
———. "Streamline Gal" and "Harlem Joys." Decca 7074, April 1935.
———. "Breeze" and "Sittin' at the Table." Decca 7086, May 1935.
———. "Echo of Spring" and "Swing Brother Swing." Decca 7090, May 1935.

Further Reading

Brown, Scott E. *James P. Johnson: A Case of Mistaken Identity*. Metuchen, N.J.: Scarecrow and Institute of Jazz Studies, Rutgers University, 1986. (Originally published 1982.)
Dobbins, Bill. "Smith, Willie 'the Lion.'" In *The New Grove Dictionary of American Music*, ed. H. Wiley Hitchcock and Stanley Sadie. New York: Macmillan, 1986. (Originally published 1980.)
Feather, Leonard, and Ira Gitler. "Smith, Willie 'the Lion.'" In *The Biographical Encyclopedia of Jazz*. New York: Oxford University Press, 1999.
Smith, Willie "the Lion," with George Hoefer. *Music on My Mind: The Memoirs of an American Pianist*. New York: Da Capo, 1978. (Originally published 1964.)
Southern, Eileen. "Smith, William Henry Joseph Bonaparte Bertholoff ('Willie-the-Lion')." In *The Greenwood Encyclopedia of Black Music Biographical Dictionary of Afro-American and African Musicians*. Westport, Conn.: Greenwood, 1982.
Waller, Maurice, and Anthony Calabrese. *Fats Waller*. New York: Macmillan, 1977.

Snow, Valaida

Valaida Snow is a remarkable figure in the history of jazz. Her first instrument was the trumpet, but she also played saxophone, clarinet, violin, cello, accordion, banjo, mandolin, and harp; in addition, she was a conductor, an arranger, and a dancer. Her admirers included Louis Armstrong and Earl Hines. Hugues Panassié and Madeleine Gautier (1956) call her a "good singer and an astonishing trumpet player." Bobby Short (1971) remembers that Snow "traveled in an orchid-colored Mercedes-Benz, dressed in an orchid suit, her pet monkey rigged out in an orchid jacket and cap, with the chauffeur in orchid as well." She had a successful career in the United States, and her extended tours abroad created a sensation. Yet she only partially recovered from a traumatic experience during World War II, and today she is largely, and undeservedly, forgotten.

After performing in Atlantic City, New Jersey, and Philadelphia, Snow had an extended run at Barron Wilkins's cabaret in Harlem in 1922, and later she toured with Will Mastin and his trio. Snow made her debut on Broadway in 1924, as Manda in *Chocolate Dandies*. In 1926, she went to Shanghai with Jack Carter's octet (featuring the New Orleans clarinetist Albert Nicholas); and she toured Europe, Russia, and the Middle East in 1929–1931. She also began recording (with the Washboard Rhythm Kings, Earl Hines, Billy Mason, Noble Sissle, and others). Already well known in Europe, Snow became famous at home through Lew Leslie's production of Sissle and Eubie Blake's *Rhapsody in Black* (1931), in which, billed simply as "Valaida," she costarred (and feuded) with Ethel Waters. Snow performed the show's most popular song, "Till the Real Thing Comes Along." Another highlight for her was a dramatic entrance during which she played splitting high C's on a trumpet while perched atop a mammoth drum.

Other shows followed, including *Grand Terrace Revue* (1933) and *Blackbirds of 1934*. Snow claimed to have been in two Hollywood films—*Take It From Me* and *Irresistible You*—though no proof such films exists; she did, however, appear in two French films: *L'alibi* (1935), in which Sidney Bechet also appeared, and *Plieges* (1939). Snow played at the Apollo Theater before embarking on a five-year tour all over Europe in 1936. She arrived in England shortly after Louis Armstrong's first tour there; and although the unusual sight of this glamorous, beautiful woman playing a brass instrument may have initially been confusing, Snow soon became a star there as well. She was billed as "queen of the trumpet" and "little Louis"; a reviewer at the time noted her broad tone, sharp sense of swing, and "a most unfeminine vibrato" (Placksin, 1982). Her signature tune, which she also wrote, was "High Hat, Trumpet, and Rhythm."

In 1941, Snow was arrested in Sweden and deported; soon afterward she was detained in Nazi-occupied Copenhagen. The circumstances remain unclear, but she spent nearly two years under arrest by the Nazis, either at Wester-Faengle concentration camp or in a jail for prisoners of war. When she returned to the United States, she bore scars and weighed only sixty-eight pounds. Jack Carter financed a six-month rehabilitation for her at a sanitarium in New York. Later, she married her manager, Earle Edwards. (Snow had been married twice before: to a dancer who went by the stage name King Knappy Brown, and to the dancer Ananias Berry.)

Snow resumed her career, but with little success; in the 1950s, she was reduced to working at resorts in the Catskills in New York State. According to friends and associates, she had become virtually unrecognizable, both physically and emotionally. Snow died in New York on 30 May 1956.

Biography

Valaida (possibly originally Valyda) Snow was born in Chattanooga, Tennessee, on 2 June 1900, 1903, or 1905. When her father died, she moved to Washington, D.C., with her mother and two sisters, Lavaida and Alvaida. She was encouraged by her mother, a music teacher, who taught her to play the trumpet. Snow's first instrument remained the trumpet, although she also played saxophone, clarinet, violin, cello, accordion, banjo, mandolin, and harp. She performed in Philadelphia and Atlantic City c. 1920; performed at Barron Wilkins's cabaret in Harlem, 1922; toured with Will Mastin, 1923; made her Broadway debut in *Chocolate Dandies*, 1924; toured in Shanghai with Jack Carter's band, 1926; had a long engagement with Earl Hines's band at Chicago's Grand Terrace, 1929; toured Europe and Asia, 1929–1931; appeared in *Rhapsody in Black*, 1931; appeared in *Blackbirds of 1934*; recorded extensively for the Parlophone label (of England) in the 1930s; toured Europe, 1936–1941; was arrested and held in Nazi-occupied Denmark, 1941–1942; and returned to United States, 1942. Snow died in New York City in 1956.

GREGORY MILLER

See also Armstrong, Louis; Bechet, Sidney; Blackbirds; Chocolate Dandies; Leslie, Lew; Waters, Ethel

1131

Selected Works

"Imagination." 1935.
"High Hat, Trumpet, and Rhythm." 1936.
"Take Care of You for Me." 1936.

Recordings

Hot Snow: Queen of Trumpet and Song. DRG 8455 2CD.
Valaida Snow: 1933–1936. Classics Jazz 1158. (CD.)
Valaida Snow: 1937–1940. Classics Jazz 1122. (CD.)

Further Reading

Charles, Mario A. "The Age of a Jazz Woman: Valaida Snow, 1900–1956." *Journal of Negro History,* 80(4), 1995.

Dahl, Linda. *Stormy Weather: The Music and Lives of a Century of Jazzwomen.* New York: Pantheon, 1984. (See also New York: Limelight Editions, 1996.)

Dance, Stanley. *The World of Earl Hines.* New York: Scribner, 1977.

Kimball, Robert, and William Bolcom. *Reminiscing With Sissle and Blake.* New York: Viking, 1973.

Panassié, Hugues, and Madeleine Gautier. *Guide to Jazz,* trans. Desmond Flower. Boston, Mass.: Houghton Mifflin, 1956; Cambridge, Mass.: Riverside, 1956.

Placksin, Sally. *American Women in Jazz: 1900 to the Present—Their Words, Lives, and Music.* New York: Seaview, 1982.

Reed, Bill. *Hot From Harlem: Profiles in Classic African-American Entertainment.* Los Angeles, Calif.: Cellar Door, 1998.

Short, Bobby. *Black and White Baby.* New York: Dodd, Mead, 1971.

Wideman, John Edgar. "Valaida." In *Fever: Twelve* Stories. New York: Holt, 1989. (See also New York: Penguin, 1990.)

Social-Fraternal Organizations

Although creative writers and artists rarely played a prominent role in the life of social clubs, benevolent societies, and fraternal lodges, such organizations helped create the vibrant environment in which the Harlem Renaissance flourished. In her play *The Starter* (1927), Eulalie Spence (1894–1981) depicted a resident of Harlem as a young man of promise: He paid "dues in a club, two Societies and a Lodge."

Migration to big cities made possible the creation of a rich fabric of African American voluntary associations. White racism restricted African Americans to organizations that they created for themselves, sites for community, dignity, and pride. Unlike the black churches, black social organizations were mostly for men or for women only. Often they were connected, with male societies recognizing female auxiliaries.

Diverse and overlapping, social organizations are difficult to categorize. Despite their central function of providing an opportunity for social intercourse, many of them were more than simply social organizations. The most numerous are best called clubs, often local and brief-lived and without much formal structure. Club members might play cards, discuss books, perform music, raise money for charity, function as church auxiliaries, organize picnics, or serve innumerable other purposes. Although black social organizations existed to provide occasions for sociability, they could be enlisted to support political agitation. Many women's civic clubs were affiliated with the National Association of Colored Women's Clubs and its New York division, the Empire State Federation of Women's Clubs.

Members of the African American elite often preferred clubs with restricted memberships to more heterogeneous organizations. Clubs provided opportunities to develop a network of professional connections. Some prestigious clubs were small enough to meet at the homes of members. Large societies, such as the Savoy Ballroom "400," founded in 1927 and noted for its elaborate initiation ceremonies, could not be as choosy about their members. History often remembers no more than the names of many clubs, such as the Wall Street Boys Association, organized around 1925. The Gay Northeasterners, for young women, which began in 1930, survives as simply the Northeasterners.

The most exclusive and prestigious society in the black community was the first Greek-letter fraternity organized by African Americans, Sigma Pi Phi, founded in 1904 and often called the Boulé after an ancient Athenian governing body. Sigma Pi Phi was not a college fraternity. It provided fellowship for African American men who already held college degrees and were established in the professions or business. This fraternity's sixth boulé was Zeta Boulé in New York City, organized in 1912 at the office of *The Crisis,* with its editor W. E. B. Du Bois as a charter member.

In practice, through their postcollege activities, African American undergraduate fraternities and sororities also functioned as clubs for the privileged elite, both people who had joined during their student days and a few co-opted men and women. For instance, Alpha Phi Alpha, organized in 1906, claimed Du Bois as a member; and Phi Beta Sigma, organized in 1914, claimed James Weldon Johnson and Alain Locke .

Other organizations—generally called benevolent societies—brought together large numbers of blacks who had migrated to New York City from a particular southern state or West Indian island, together with their children. Along with social and cultural functions, such societies provided insurance for burial and in times of illness. Typically they were male societies, with female auxiliaries, and had as leaders business entrepreneurs and professionals or their wives. For instance, the Sons and Daughters of Virginia and the prosperous United Sons and Daughters of Georgia were organized in 1920; and the Greneda Mutual Association was organized in 1926.

As early as the 1880s, reacting to the influx of migrants, the Society of the Sons of New York admitted into full membership only applicants who had been born in New York, some of whom had Dutch names that underscored the long residence of their families. Although it was a relatively elite organization, in Harlem this meant a membership that included headwaiters as well as professionals. Its clubhouse was located on West Fifty-third Street. Women organized a parallel Society of the Daughters of New York. The Sons of New York held an annual ball in April.

For the most part, fraternal lodges were affiliated with national or regional organizations. Characterized by quasi-Masonic rituals and regalia, they too existed largely to promote sociability. The journalist George S. Schuyler regarded black fraternal societies as evidence that African Americans were not a distinct people. He pointed out that, like whites, "Aframericans" joined "the Elks, Masons, and Knights of Pythias" (*Nation*, 16 June 1926). In fact, all fraternal societies were racially segregated, and some black societies, like the True Reformers (based in Virginia), did not share their name with a white counterpart. When there was a parallel white organization, it sometimes sued to prohibit the African American society from using a similar name.

Fraternal societies were showier than clubs and benevolent societies. They were societies with secrets, such as rituals and distinctive handshakes and passwords, but membership in them was not secret. Lodge brothers loved to parade in costume before an admiring audience. In his autobiography, *The Big Sea*, Langston Hughes (1940/1976) said that "on Sunday afternoons in the spring when the lodges have their turnouts, it is good to stand on the curb and hear the bands play and see the women pass in their white regalia with swinging purple capes, preceded by the brothers in uniform, with long swords at their sides and feathered helmets, or else in high hats, spats, and cutaway coats." He added that "once I saw such a lodge parade with an all-string band leading the procession, violins and mandolins and banjos and guitars playing in the street." The celebrated photographer James Van Der Zee left a visual record of Harlem's colorful fraternal regalia and banners.

The Elks, a relatively new organization, constituted Harlem's largest fraternal society. The male Elks sponsored a women's auxiliary, the Daughters of the Improved Benevolent Protective Order of Elks of the World. The *New York Times* (24 August 1927) reported that during a national convention held in Harlem, 30,000 male and female Elks, attired in costumes and encouraged by twenty-five bands, paraded before 100,000 onlookers. According to Jervis Anderson (1981), the marchers "cakewalked and Charlestoned . . . to tunes like 'Me and My Shadow' and 'Ain't She Sweet.'" On a showery afternoon, the "grand exalted ruler" reviewed the procession from a grandstand at Seventh Avenue and 145th Street. When 1,034 delegates representing 565 lodges met at Mother Zion AMEZ Church, at 140 West 137th Street, African Americans from around the country acquired firsthand knowledge of Harlem.

Harlem had several prosperous local Elks lodges, including the Imperial lodge and the heavily Caribbean Henry Lincoln Johnson lodge. The largest local organization, with 2,000 members, was the Manhattan lodge, whose impressive headquarters at 266 West 139th Street included club rooms, an assembly hall, and offices. Its orchestra and band played at parks and schools in Harlem.

Another Elks affiliate, Monarch lodge, founded in 1907, owned a hall located at 245 137th Street, where concerts and dances were held. Members could relax at a first-floor bar. The lodge helped members find jobs and housing, organized boat rides and parties, and sponsored a marching band. It also raised money for a variety of purposes, from education to politics. One of Harlem's best-known residents, Casper Holstein, headed the Monarch lodge at the time of the Harlem Renaissance. He made a fortune in the numbers racket, won popularity as a philanthropist, and attracted considerable attention when he was kidnapped and held for ransom. In 1929, he unsuccessfully vied for the first office in the national Elks organization. His opponents used his foreign birth against him (Holstein came from the Virgin Islands, which the United States had only recently purchased from Denmark).

Other than the Elks, the leading fraternal societies were the Prince Hall Masons, the Odd Fellows, and the Knights of Pythias, each of them supported by a female auxiliary. In 1916, the Masons built a large temple in Harlem. Blacks from the Caribbean dominated the Ancient Order of Shepherds, the Mechanics, and the Free Gardeners. Membership in fraternal societies often overlapped from one organization to another and frequently was brief. Reflecting the economic realities of the African American community, most members were working class or lower middle class. After World War I, fraternal societies generally lost membership, but this varied. In fact, some new black societies were founded: for instance, the Grand United Order of Toussaint-Louverture in 1921 and the Lebanon Foresters in 1923.

Arguably, fraternal societies as a whole reached their institutional peak in the 1920s even if their membership already was in decline. For instance, in New York City, the white Masons erected a seventeen-story building in 1926; the white Pythians built a massive temple in the same year; the Knights of Columbus erected a fifteen-story building in 1927; and the white Elks erected a thirteen-story building in 1928.

Prominent men of Harlem often belonged to fraternal societies. For instance, a biographical sketch, published in 1927, of a physician born in Jamaica proudly reported that he was a thirty-second-degree Mason, a past exalted ruler of an Elks lodge, and a member of the Knights of Pythias, the Independent Order of Saint Luke, and the Ancient Order of Foresters. Membership in the Freemasons carried special prestige. It was the fraternal society that members of the black elite were most likely to join. Du Bois, for example, was a Mason. The book collector Arthur A. Schomburg spent much of his time in carrying out his duties as grand secretary of the Grand Lodge of New York, Prince Hall Masons, from 1918 to 1926. Out of frustration with petty internal disputes, he quit the Masons in the 1930s, but he had been an active member for more than four decades. Schomburg also was the first treasurer of the Loyal Sons of Africa, founded by John Edward Bruce. For some black intellectuals, no doubt, membership in a fraternal society was only nominal, but for others it entailed weekly lodge meetings.

Often relying on ministers and politicians to provide leadership, black fraternal societies were integrated into the larger African American community. Most fraternal societies offered some kind of mutual insurance, and the founders of many African American commercial insurance companies learned their craft in the lodges. In *Black Manhattan*, James Weldon Johnson complained that burial insurance bulked too large in the work of fraternal societies: "Very often the amount of money spent for burying the dead is out of proportion to that in caring for the living." In his autobiography, Langston Hughes (1940/1976) poignantly remembered that on weekdays lodge funerals took place at night to allow working people to participate: "Sometimes at ten or eleven at night, you hear a funeral march filling the air on Seventh Avenue."

Other organizations borrowed the rhetoric and symbols of fraternalism: trade unions like the Brotherhood of Sleeping Car Porters and Maids, founded in 1925; black nationalist organizations such as the Universal Negro Improvement Association, whose leader, Marcus Garvey, was a Mason; and radical organizations such as the multiracial, communist-tinged International Workers Order (IWO). The Harlem Suitcase Theatre (1937) staged plays at an IWO hall, and Louise Thompson Patterson worked for this leftist organization.

Scholars of the African American experience have been ambivalent about black fraternal societies. Did they merely imitate white organizations, or did they draw on West African cooperative traditions? Did they foster self-reliance and mutual aid, or did they surrender to the bourgeois values of the white community? Were they embarrassingly noisy and tawdry, riven with petty quarrels and personal ambition, or should blacks be proud of their heritage of fraternal societies? As a result of such uncertainties, neglect has been widespread. A paper prepared for the Works Progress Administration by Baxter Leach, "Fraternal Orders in Harlem" (1939), was never published. Among relatively recent books, the study by Irma Watkins-Owens (1996) stands out for its attention to fraternal societies.

Scholarly interest may be awakening. From 28 March to 1 July 2003, the black studies program of City College of New York (CCNY) and the Institute for Research on the African Diaspora in the Americas and the Caribbean sponsored an exhibit that documented the history of one of Harlem's Elk lodges, Monarch lodge, from 1907 to 1997. The exhibit focused on the rhetoric of the African American Elks, expressed in language, rites, and regalia. A professor at CCNY, Venus Green, who served as chief curator, opened the exhibit with a presentation about rescuing from a dumpster nearly a hundred boxes of archival materials of the Monarch lodge, including photographs, posters, uniforms, and banners.

DAVID M. FAHEY

See also Brotherhood of Sleeping Car Porters; Bruce, John Edward; Du Bois, W. E. B.; Holstein, Casper; Johnson, James Weldon; Locke, Alain; Patterson, Louise Thompson; Schomburg, Arthur A.; Schuyler, George S.; Universal Negro Improvement Association; Van Der Zee, James

Further Reading

Anderson, Jervis. *This Was Harlem: A Cultural Portrait, 1900–1950.* New York: Farrar, Straus and Giroux, 1981.

Diasporic Rites, Rhetoric, and Regalia: Language and Representation in the Benevolent and Protective Order of Elks, Harlem, U.S.A., 1907–1997: An Exhibit. New York: City College, Cohen Library, 2003. (Brochure by Venus Green and Emilyn Brown.)

Hughes, Langston. *The Big Sea: An Autobiography,* foreword Amiri Baraka. New York: Thunder's Mouth, 1976. (Originally published 1940.)

Johnson, James Weldon. *Black Manhattan.* New York: Knopf, 1930.

Osofsky, Gilbert. *Harlem: The Making of a Ghetto—Negro New York, 1880–1930.* New York: Harper & Row, 1963.

Schneiner, Seth M. *Negro Mecca: A History of the Negro in New York City, 1865–1920.* New York: New York University Press, 1965.

Schoener, Allon, ed. *Harlem on My Mind: Cultural Capital of Black America, 1900–1968.* New York: Delta, 1979.

Sinnette, Elinor Des Verney. *Arthur Alfonso Schomburg: Black Bibliophile and Collector.* Detroit, Mich.: New York Public Library and Wayne State University Press, 1989.

Skocpol, Theda, and Jennifer Oser. "Organization Despite Adversity: The Origins and Development of African American Fraternal Associations." *Social Science History,* 28(3), Fall 2004.

Watkins-Owens, Irma. *Blood Relations: Caribbean Immigrants and the Harlem Community, 1900–1930.* Bloomington: Indiana University Press, 1996.

Wesley, Charles H. *History of Sigma Pi Phi: First of the Negro-American Greek-Letter Fraternities.* Washington, D.C.: Association for the Study of Negro Life and History, 1969.

Wilder, Craig Steven. *In the Company of Black Men: The African Influence on African American Culture in New York City.* New York: New York University Press, 2001.

———. "New York City: Civic, Literary, and Mutual Aid Associations." In *Organizing Black America: An Encyclopedia of African American Associations,* ed. Nina Mjagkij. New York: Garland, 2001.

Spencer, Anne

Nearly thirty of Anne Spencer's poems can be found in influential anthologies of the Harlem Renaissance, but she never published her own volume. Greatly influenced by the nineteenth-century romantics, she wrote about nature, simplicity, freedom, immortality, life and death, chaos and peace, love, and transcendent beauty, using conventional forms like the sonnet and lyric. At first appearance, her work deviates from the themes of social protest and modernity and the jazz and blues aesthetics characterizing much of the literature of the Harlem Renaissance; as a result, she has been overlooked or misunderstood in discussions of the era. Similarly, she has invited backward glances to such writers of the "American renaissance" as Ralph Waldo Emerson and particularly Emily Dickinson, whom she resembles in her metaphysical themes and enigmatic voice, as well as in having written a large body of works that she never published. Yet her poems—such as "Before the Feast at Shushan" (1920), her first publication; "White Things" (1923); "Lady, Lady" (1925); "Letter to My Sister" (1927); and "Grapes: Still-Life" (1929)—also raise themes of women's liberation and racial equality, or they experiment with modernist styles and forms.

Spencer grew up "in the home of a middle-class Black family . . . in a primarily white community" (Honey 1989), and she was of black, white, and Native American ancestry. Her formal schooling exposed her to students from Virginia's black elite, and her home became a center of intellectual discussions and social activism for African American educators, writers, entertainers, and political figures. Her residence in Lynchburg, Virginia, at 1313 Pierce Street, doubled as a literary salon where her guests included luminaries such as W. E. B. Du Bois, Langston Hughes, Paul Robeson, and Sterling Brown. Those who attended Spencer's salon found her elegance and intellect a welcome respite from the humiliations of segregated conveyances, restaurants, and hotels endured by blacks of all social strata as they traveled through the South during the era of Jim Crow. Her mentor James Weldon Johnson introduced her to critics like H. L. Mencken and assisted her in publishing in the leading "race magazines"—*The Crisis, Survey Graphic,* and *Opportunity*—as well as in the books that defined the era: Alain Locke's *The New Negro* (1925), Countee Cullen's *Caroling Dusk* (1927), and Johnson's own *Book of American Negro Poetry* (1922), among others.

Spencer combined artistic seclusion with the iconoclasm and public daring of a pioneer in civil rights. On the one hand, she could retreat to write and meditate in her garden cottage, Edankraal, enjoying a privileged introspection and isolation that most southern married women could not experience, regardless of race and class. On the other hand, she generally was in the thick of civil rights activities when writing or not. She avoided and publicly objected to segregated transportation and public services, helped found the Lynchburg branch of the National Association for the Advancement of Colored People (NAACP), and fought to secure state funding for a library in the all-black city high school, which she subsequently supported by serving as its librarian.

Subsequent generations value her poetry because its formal, classical, and pastoral elements remind us of how widely approaches and attitudes ranged among artists of the Harlem Renaissance. Her work also stands as a reminder of the cultural richness that we lose and social history that we skew by centering the Harlem Renaissance in New York, Chicago, and all other points North of the Mason-Dixon line.

Biography

Anne Spencer was born 6 February 1882 in Henry County, Virginia. She graduated from a private school—Virginia Seminary in Lynchburg—in 1899. She was a teacher (second grade) from 1899 to 1901. She married Edward Spencer (a postal worker and businessman) on 15 May 1901. She taught at Virginia Seminary in 1911. Spencer published major poetry during 1920–1931. She was a cofounder of the Lynchburg NAACP in 1918. She was a librarian at

Dunbar High School from 1924 to 1946. Spencer died in Lynchburg, Virginia, on 27 July 1975.

BARBARA McCASKILL

See also Authors: 5—Poets; Brown, Sterling; Crisis, The; Cullen, Countee; Du Bois, W. E. B.; Hughes, Langston; Johnson, James Weldon; Literature: 7—Poetry; Locke, Alain; Mencken, H. L.; New Negro, The; Opportunity; Robeson, Paul; Salons; Survey Graphic

Selected Works

"Before the Feast of Shushan." *Crisis,* February 1920.
"White Things." *Crisis,* March 1923.
"Lady, Lady." *Survey Graphic,* March 1925.
"Grapes: Still-Life." *Crisis,* April 1929.
The Book of American Negro Poetry, ed. James Weldon Johnson. 1922.
The New Negro, ed. Alain Locke. 1925.
Ebony and Topaz, ed. Charles S. Johnson. 1927.
Caroling Dusk: An Anthology of Verse by Negro Poets, ed. Countee Cullen. 1927.

Further Reading

Bryan, T. J. "Women Poets of the Harlem Renaissance." In *Gender, Culture, and the Arts: Women, the Arts, and Society,* ed. Ronald Dotterer and Susan Bowers. Selinsgrove, Pa.: Susquehanna University Press, 1993.
Ford, Charita M. "Flowering a Feminist Garden: The Writings and Poetry of Anne Spencer." *Sage,* 5, 1988.
Greene, J. Lee. *Time's Unfading Garden: Anne Spencer's Life and Poetry.* Baton Rouge: Louisiana State University Press, 1977.
Honey, Maureen. *Shadowed Dreams: Women's Poetry of the Harlem Renaissance.* New Brunswick, N.J.: Rutgers University Press, 1989.
Wall, Cheryl A. "Poets and Versifiers, Singers and Signifiers: Women in the Harlem Renaissance." In *Women, the Arts, and the 1920s in Paris and New York,* ed. Kenneth W. Wheeler and Virginia Lee Lussier. New Brunswick, N.J.: Transaction, 1982.

Spingarn, Arthur

Arthur Spingarn was born in New York City in 1878 to Sarah Barnett Spingarn and Elias Spingarn, a

Arthur Spingarn. (Library of Congress.)

prominent tobacco merchant of Austrian Jewish heritage. His family included his older brother Joel Elias Spingarn, another leading civil rights activist. Spingarn earned an A.B. from Columbia in 1897, an A.M. in 1899, and a law degree from the same institution in 1900. He served as a captain in the U.S. Army Sanitary Corps from 1917 to 1919; during the war, he married Marion Mayer, a social worker, on 27 January 1918. They had no children.

Spingarn's early experience as a lawyer convinced him of the need to address racial prejudice through his work. He joined the National Association for the Advancement of Colored People (NAACP) in 1911, soon after its founding. From 1911 to 1940, he was a vice president of the organization and chairman of the NAACP's National Legal Committee. In the latter role, Spingarn played a crucial part in the development of the NAACP's efforts to achieve civil rights by working through the legal system. He guided the NAACP's contribution of an amicus brief in *Guinn v. United States* (1915), which challenged the use of

"grandfather clauses" to protect poor whites from being disenfranchised by laws aimed against black voters; it was the organization's first victory in the courts. Spingarn also spearheaded another early victory for the NAACP in *Buchanan v. Warley* (1917), which overturned an ordinance in Louisville, Kentucky, that required residential segregation by race. Throughout the 1920s, Spingarn helped increase the visibility of the NAACP. In 1925, Spingarn brought Clarence Darrow, the most prominent lawyer of the times, into the NAACP's fold. After Ossian Sweet, an African American doctor in Detroit, moved into a white neighborhood in 1925, mob violence by whites led to another man's death; the authorities in turn charged Sweet with murder. Spingarn and Darrow helped clear Sweet of all charges.

Spingarn and the NAACP also challenged the exclusion of African Americans from voting booths. In 1923, the legislature of Texas passed a law restricting participation in Democratic Party primaries to whites only, effectively disenfranchising black voters in the overwhelmingly Democratic state. Spingarn scored another victory in *Nixon v. Herndon* (1927), arguing in the U.S. Supreme Court in support of Dr. L. A. Nixon's challenge to the Texas law. When white Texans continued to maneuver around court rulings, Spingarn argued another successful challenge in *Nixon v. Condon* (1932). Spingarn also played an important role in the NAACP's effort in 1930 to block the nomination of John J. Parker, an avowed racist, to the U.S. Supreme Court.

Spingarn also participated in the rich cultural life of the Harlem Renaissance. In 1913, Spingarn and his wife, Amy, began amassing what would become an unparalleled collection of rare books and manuscripts on African and African American topics. The collection was later donated to Howard University. Spingarn contributed annual bibliographies on black books to the NAACP's publication *The Crisis*, and worked closely with W. E. B. Du Bois while Du Bois was its editor. As Du Bois became more explicitly Marxist in the 1930s, Spingarn split with him. Du Bois resigned as the editor of *The Crisis* in June 1934.

In 1940, the NAACP's National Legal Committee became an independent organization, the NAACP Legal Defense and Educational Fund. Spingarn served as president of the group from 1940 to 1957. During these years, the litigation arm of the civil rights struggle achieved numerous victories against segregation, most notably in *Brown v. Board of Education* (1954). From 1940 to 1966, Spingarn also served as president of the NAACP itself. His gradualist approach to social change and his faith in the legal system made enemies among more strident activists; others objected to the fact that one of the nation's leading organizations for black civil rights was led by a white man. While sympathetic to radicals, Spingarn rejected their separatism. As the civil rights movement became increasingly militant in the mid-1960s, Spingarn came under increasing attack. Hurt by the criticism, Spingarn resigned in 1966 at age eighty-seven. He died in New York City in 1971.

History has judged Arthur Spingarn a moderate, but this interpretation does not reveal the moral passion that informed Spingarn's legal crusade in the early twentieth century, when courts were systematically hostile to African Americans.

Biography

Arthur Barnett Spingarn was born in New York City on 28 March 1878. He received degrees from Columbia University (A.B., 1897; A.M., 1899; LL.B., 1900), Howard University (LL.D., 1941), and Long Island University (L.H.D., 1966). He was admitted to the New York bar in 1900 and had a private legal practice, 1900–1969. In the National Association for the Advancement of Colored People, he was vice president, 1911–1940; chairman, NAACP National Legal Committee, 1911–1940; and president, NAACP Legal Defense and Educational Fund, 1940–1957. Spingarn died in New York City on 1 December 1971.

CHRISTOPHER CAPOZZOLA

See also Civil Rights and Law; Crisis, The; Du Bois, W. E. B.; National Association for the Advancement of Colored People; Spingarn, Joel

Further Reading

Goings, Kenneth W. *The NAACP Comes of Age: The Defeat of Judge John J. Parker*. Bloomington: Indiana University Press, 1990.

Kellogg, Charles Flint. *NAACP: A History of the National Association for the Advancement of Colored People*. Baltimore, Md.: Johns Hopkins University Press, 1973.

Ross, Barbara Joyce. *J. E. Spingarn and the Rise of the NAACP, 1911–1939*. New York: Atheneum, 1972.

Spingarn, Arthur. *Laws Relating to Sex Morality in New York City*. 1915. (Rev. ed., 1926.)

Tushnet, Mark V. *The NAACP's Legal Strategy Against Segregated Education, 1925–1950*. Chapel Hill: University of North Carolina Press, 1987.

Spingarn, Joel

Despite the relative oblivion into which his name has fallen, Joel Spingarn's influence on African American life in the first half of the twentieth century is notable. His acquaintances and colleagues included many of the most noteworthy individuals associated with the achievements of the Harlem Renaissance. Trained as a literary scholar of the Italian Renaissance, Spingarn was also very much a man of his own times. He frequently claimed that personal dignity was measured by the extent to which one was willing to perform one's responsibilities toward society at large. After a relatively brief but influential career as a scholar of comparative literature at Columbia University (1899–1911), Spingarn turned his focus during the 1910s and 1920s toward social activism, largely through his involvement with the National Association for the Advancement of Colored People (NAACP). His service is still commemorated through that organization's annual presentation of the Spingarn Medal, an award he instituted in 1914 to recognize outstanding achievement by Americans of African descent.

In addition to his work with the NAACP, he acted privately as a patron and informal adviser to a number of artists (such as Claude McKay, whose work Spingarn helped to publish as early as 1917). Along with a number of notable black and white figures (for example, Ida B. Wells Barnett, W. E. B. Du Bois, and Oswald Garrison Villard), Spingarn helped to found the NAACP in 1909. His most active period of participation in the group would not begin until the next year, though, when he joined its New York Vigilance Committee, adding his considerable political clout (he ran for Congress unsuccessfully in 1908) and social clout to legal actions undertaken on behalf of African Americans. After his dismissal from Columbia University in 1911, Spingarn intensified his involvement with the NAACP. By 1913, he was making national speaking tours in which he spoke of the "new abolitionism" and condemned the gradualism and assimilationism espoused by Booker T. Washington.

Spingarn established a close relationship with Du Bois during this period, and their collaboration would prove invaluable for the direction of the fledgling

Joel Elias Spingarn, c. 1910–1920. (Library of Congress.)

NAACP. In 1910, Spingarn had contacted Du Bois seeking advice on how to operate the Heart of Hope Club, an organization Spingarn had created to provide food and leisure activities for the poor African Americans of Amenia, New York, the small town near Spingarn's estate, Troutbeck. The two quickly became close friends, although their relationship was marked by lengthy periods of intense ideological disagreement. Du Bois was an influential ally for Spingarn in the organization and greatly aided Spingarn's rise to the post of chairman of the NAACP's board of directors in 1913. In August 1916, Spingarn was host to the historic Amenia Conference, which Du Bois said was intended to unify African Americans and their allies. Among the attendees at this conference were James Weldon Johnson, William Pickens, and Mary Burnett Talbert, all of whom would play important roles in the Harlem Renaissance.

Spingarn volunteered for military service in 1917 and combined his service with social activism, urging African Americans to support the war effort whole-heartedly as he fervently lobbied the War Department for the institution of a training facility for African American officers. Spingarn's concession that this facility would most likely have to be segregated was unpopular with many of his colleagues in the NAACP, who recalled his denunciations of Washington's strategy of integration by accommodation. A number of African American publications openly questioned Spingarn's motives and even went so far as to accuse him of being a white saboteur who was perpetuating racism from within the NAACP by pretending to be a friend—an argument that some scholars have perpetuated. As the larger movement of African American cultural empowerment gained momentum in the early 1920s, African American leaders such as Du Bois, Johnson, and Alain Locke gained favor within the NAACP over white "fellow travelers" such as Spingarn. Nevertheless, Spingarn remained an active participant in the organization for most of his remaining life, serving as both its treasurer and its president.

The mid-1920s and early 1930s were a period of extensive publication for Spingarn, whether as an editor, an author, or a publisher. He had helped to found the publishing firm Harcourt Brace in 1919 and became editor of its "European Library" series during the 1920s. At Du Bois's request, Spingarn participated along with Jessie Redmon Fauset, Countee Cullen, Langston Hughes, Charles Waddell Chesnutt, and nearly twenty others in a symposium called "The Negro in Art: How Shall He Be Portrayed?" that was published over the course of several months in *The Crisis* in 1926 and 1927. Spingarn took a view corresponding fairly closely with Du Bois's idea that artistic depictions of African Americans—whether by white or black writers—were inherently politicized. However, his critics associated him with the more incendiary ideas of other white contributors to the series, such as Carl Van Vechten and Vachel Lindsay; and so Spingarn was criticized as lacking understanding of and sympathy with the cause of African American uplift.

In 1924, suffering from recurrent chronic exhaustion, Spingarn went on inactive status at Harcourt and returned home to Troutbeck. He spent the remainder of his life engaged in a somewhat more subdued blend of his previous pursuits. He published two series of what he called the "Troutbeck Leaflets," which ranged from Du Bois's summary of the Amenia conference of 1916 to a collection of twelve poems written by Spingarn's wife, Amy. He gave six well-received lectures on a variety of literary and social topics at the New School for Social Research in New York in 1931. He addressed the NAACP's national convention in 1932 and then was host to a second Amenia conference in 1933; the attendees at this conference included such social and intellectual luminaries as Du Bois, Johnson, Ralph Bunche, Charles Houston, Juanita Jackson, Walter White, and Roy Wilkins. Almost all of Spingarn's published work subsequent to 1932 dealt with his horticultural interest in the clematis vine, a subject on which he is still considered the foremost American authority. In 1939, he accepted a teaching post at Atlanta University, but he died before he could make the trip.

Biography

Joel Elias Spingarn was born in New York City on 17 May 1875. He attended public schools in New York; Collegiate Institute of New York City, 1893; City College of New York, 1893; Columbia University, A.B., 1895; Harvard University, 1895–1896; and again Columbia, Ph.D., 1899. He was an assistant professor of comparative literature at Columbia, 1899–1904; associate professor, 1904–1909; professor, 1909–1911; and chair of the division of modern languages and literature, 1910–1911. He was the owner and publisher of the *Amenia* (New York) *Times* from 1911 to 1926. Spingarn was a cofounder of the National Association for the Advancement of Colored People, 1909; chairman of its board of directors, 1913–1919; founder of the Spingarn Medal, 1914; treasurer, 1919–1930; and president, 1930–1939. He was host to the Amenia conferences in 1916 and 1933. He was a cofounder of Harcourt Brace in 1919 and its literary editor from 1919 to 1932. Spingarn died in Amenia, New York, on 26 July 1939.

DEREK MAUS

See also Amenia Conference, 1916; Amenia Conference, 1933; Crisis: The Negro in Art—How Shall He Be Portrayed? A Symposium; Du Bois, W. E. B.; Harcourt Brace; McKay, Claude; National Association for the Advancement of Colored People; Publishers and Publishing Houses; Spingarn, Arthur; Spingarn Medal

Selected Works

A History of Literary Criticism in the Renaissance. 1899. (See also rev. augmented ed., 1908; reprinted with new introduction, 1963.)
The New Hesperides. 1901. (Reprinted, with additions, as *The New Hesperides and Other Poems.* 1911.)

Critical Essays of the Seventeenth Century, 3 vols. 1908–1909. (As editor; reprint, 1957.)
The New Criticism. 1911.
A Note on Dramatic Criticism. 1913.
Creative Criticism: Essays on the Unity of Genius and Taste. 1917. (Rev. and enlarged as *Creative Criticism and Other Essays.* 1931. Reprints, 1964, 1979.)
Scholarship and Criticism in the United States. 1922.
Poems. 1924.
The Troutbeck Leaflets. 1924–1932. (As series editor.)

Further Reading

Babbitt, Irving, "The Modern Spirit and Dr. Spingarn." *Journal of Philosophy, Psychology, and the Scientific Method,* 11, 9 April 1914.
Du Bois, W. E. B. *Dusk of Dawn.* New York: Harcourt Brace, 1940.
Mencken, H. L. "Criticism of Criticism of Criticism." In *Prejudices.* First Series. New York: Knopf, 1919.
Mumford, Lewis. "Scholar and Gentleman." *Saturday Review of Literature,* 20, August 1939.
Ross, B. Joyce. *J. E. Spingarn and the Rise of the NAACP, 1911–1939.* New York: Atheneum, 1972.
Van Deusen, Marshall. *J. E. Spingarn.* New York: Twayne, 1971.

Spingarn Medal

The Spingarn Medal was created in 1914 by Joel Spingarn, the newly elected chairman of the board of directors of the National Association for the Advancement of Colored People (NAACP). It was to be given annually in recognition of the "highest or noblest achievement by an American Negro during the preceding year." This medal was the first and most important of the many prizes for African Americans established during the Harlem Renaissance. As of this writing, it had been awarded by the NAACP every year since 1915 except 1938.

The plan for the award was first announced in June 1914 in *The Crisis,* which featured on its cover a drawing of the medal's obverse—a female figure wearing classical draperies and a blindfold, holding aloft the scales of justice in one hand and leaning on a sword with the other, flanked by the words "For Merit." Behind this figure shone the rays of a brightly rising sun. According to *The Crisis,* candidates from "any field of elevated or honorable human endeavor" were eligible for the award, "whether that field be intellectual, spiritual, physical, scientific, commercial, educational or any other" (June 1914, 88). Spingarn promised to furnish $100 per year for the cost of producing each gold medal. To ensure that the award would survive his death, Spingarn bequeathed $20,000 to the NAACP in his will to endow the prize, with the further provision that it would be administered by the president of either Howard University or Fisk University if the NAACP itself ceased to exist.

The first medal was awarded in March 1915 to Professor Ernest Everett Just of Howard University Medical School for distinguished research in physiology and biology. Indeed, the first several medals bore out the promise made by *The Crisis* that the selection committee would consider nominees from a wide range of fields. The second winner, recognized for his service to Liberia, was Major Charles Young, the ranking black officer in the U.S. Army. (He would soon be promoted to lieutenant colonel.) The third winner was the musician, singer, and composer Harry Thacker Burleigh. As the aesthetic dimension of the Harlem Renaissance became prominent, artists began to dominate the list of winners. After Burleigh's prize in 1917, five of the next eleven medals went to writers, actors, singers, and poets, including William Stanley Braithwaite (1918), Charles Gilpin (1921), Roland Hayes (1924), James Weldon Johnson (1925), and Charles Waddell Chesnutt (1928). Other honorees from the 1920s include a former president of the NAACP, Archibald Grimké (1919); W. E. B. Du Bois (1920); Mary Burnett Talbert (1922); the agricultural scientist George Washington Carver (1923); Carter G. Woodson (1926); Anthony Overton, president of the Victory Life Insurance Company (1927); and Mordecai W. Johnson, the first black president of Howard University (1929). Winners from the early 1930s include H. A. Hunt, president of Georgia's Fort Valley Industrial School (1930); Richard Harrison (1931); Robert Russa Moton (1932); Max Yergan of the YMCA, who was an activist in Africa (1933); W. T. B. Williams, dean of the college at Tuskegee Institute (1934); and Mary McLeod Bethune (1935). Three early winners—Grimké, Carver, and Overton—had been born in slavery; one winner, Harrison, was the son of fugitive slaves. Until the singer Marian Anderson received the Spingarn Medal in 1939, only two of the first twenty-three recipients had been women.

From its inception, the medal was regarded as an important marker of black achievement in white America and thus a potentially useful tool for improving race relations. In describing Ernest Just's qualifications for the award, for example, *The Crisis* declared: "This is the sort of man that this Association, this race and this country delight to honor" (April 1915, 284). Writing to his wife, Amy, in November 1916 from the University of North Carolina (where he had a speaking engagement), Spingarn succinctly summarized the medal's larger purpose: "I realize that the problem is to convince the white man that the Negro really has capacity for higher things. The Spingarn medal is a trifle, but the Spingarn medal idea is the main thing." In October 1923, in a letter to Spingarn, the newly honored medalist Carver agreed:

> The larger view as to the medal's value, to my mind, supersedes everything else and is giving a kind of education that nothing else will give. It is certainly having its effects right in our own little town. The white people seem to be even more anxious to see this medal than my own people. I must confess again that I do not feel worthy of such a distinction. However, I shall endeavor, with all that is within me and as fast as the great Creator gives me light, to at least make my friends have no regret that it came this way.

The medal was not without controversy. When Chesnutt received the award in 1928 not for his achievements of the preceding year but instead for "his pioneer work as literary artist depicting the life and struggle of Americans of Negro descent," the Cleveland *Gazette* wondered why the award had taken so long to bestow, noting that Chesnutt had last published a book in 1905. Other commentators were less enthusiastic about Chesnutt's selection, complaining that candidates who were better qualified—and more relevant to the time—had been overlooked. This public grumbling led Du Bois, the editor of *The Crisis*, to defend the selection of Chesnutt vigorously in the issue of August 1928, insisting that it was not simply Chesnutt's "pioneer work" as a writer but also his direct influence on the present "renaissance of American Negro literature" that had earned him the award. "Perhaps no single man could be picked out who is more worthy to be called the Dean of the young black artists who are writing today," Du Bois asserted (1928, 176).

In later years several other people prominent during the Harlem Renaissance would also receive medals, including Walter White (1937), A. Philip Randolph (1942), Paul Robeson (1945), and, near the end of his long career, Langston Hughes (1960).

WILLIAM GLEASON

See also Crisis, The; Du Bois, W. E. B.; National Association for the Advancement of Colored People; Spingarn, Joel; *specific medal recipients*

Further Reading

Carver, George Washington. Letter to Joel Elias Spingarn, 8 October 1923. Joel E. Spingarn Papers, New York Public Library, New York.

Douglas, Melvin I. *Black Winners: A History of Spingarn Medalists, 1915–1983*. Brooklyn, N.Y.: Gaus, 1984.

Du Bois, W. E. B. "The Fourteenth Spingarn Medal." *Crisis*, 35, August 1928, p. 176.

Johnson, James Weldon. *Black Manhattan*. New York: Knopf, 1930.

Lewis, David Levering. *When Harlem Was in Vogue*. New York: Knopf, 1981.

Spingarn, Joel Elias. Letter to Amy Spingarn, 25 November 1916. Joel E. Spingarn Papers, New York Public Library, New York.

"The Spingarn Medal." *Crisis*, 8, June 1914, p. 88.

"The Spingarn Medal." *Crisis*, 9, April 1915, p. 284. (Editorial.)

Spirituals

Spirituals are religious folk songs created by Negro slaves during the eighteenth and nineteenth centuries. They used these songs to record the history of the slave experience and to express their religious beliefs, their emotions, and their attitude toward slavery. Spirituals were part of the education and religious worship of both slaves and freedmen.

As a song form, spirituals shared many characteristics of African music: the oral transmission of history, descriptions of family and community life, expressions of religious beliefs, communal participation, the call-and-response form, and the use of movement and rhythmic percussion in performance. Spirituals may be classified into three different styles: (1) slow with long sustained melodies, (2) rhythmic up-tempo shouts, and (3) call and response performed by a leader with chorus. The origins of the songs may be traced back as early as the late 1700s along the Atlantic coast and in the southern regions. The earliest formal record of spirituals was Allen, Garrison, and Ware's collection *Slave Songs of the United States*, in 1867.

Spirituals were often created and performed by slaves during camp-meeting revivals or secret religious services held at night in the woods. These secret meetings, described as the "brush harbor meetings," laid the foundation not only for the African American church but also for the use of singing, shouting, and other forms of religious expression within African American culture. The brush harbor meetings gave slaves an opportunity to describe openly the experiences and hardships they may have endured during the day. Their response to these experiences was expressed in song.

The primary sources of the texts were the Bible and secular experiences. Although slaves were discouraged from reading the Bible—and in some situations were forbidden to read it—many did learn to read and interpret this source. Slaves identified strongly with the trials and tribulations as well as the victories of the Hebrew slaves, and with the Hebrews' faith in God. They also expressed a strong faith and belief in Jesus as their savior. In addition to the literal meanings, spirituals conveyed "coded" messages or hidden meanings through the use of metaphors. The hidden meanings in spirituals were perhaps the most important means of communication for the Underground Railroad. For example, the metaphor for the North or freedom was "heaven," the slave master was "Satan," and slaves were the "Hebrew children." Moses was identified with both the biblical figure and people such as Nat Turner and Harriet Tubman. Tubman and other "engineers" were often called "Moses." The song "Steal Away" was said to have been created by Turner to communicate plans for a revolt and later used by Tubman to signal to the slaves the time for escape. The spirituals "Deep River" and "Swing Low, Sweet Chariot" were used to signal plans for escape. One of the most famous songs of the Underground Railroad was "Follow the Drinking Gourd," which detailed finding the road to escape by following the North Star or the Big Dipper.

Spirituals as folk music began to diminish in popularity during the years following emancipation, but they were revived by the Fisk Jubilee Singers in formal concerts in 1871. At the beginning of the twentieth century, spirituals began to emerge in a more formalized version through the choral and solo arrangements of Nathaniel Dett, Harry Thacker Burleigh, and Hall Johnson. In 1925–1926, James Weldon Johnson and John Rosamond Johnson produced a two-volume collection of Negro spirituals. During the Harlem Renaissance, spirituals became an important source of cultural pride and struggle, expressed in poetry and other literature by Langston Hughes, James Weldon

Johnson, and W. E. B. Du Bois. Spirituals also began to gain popularity in formal concerts through performances by Roland Hayes, Paul Robeson, and Marian Anderson in the United States and Europe. They were also used as material for theater, as in *The Green Pastures*, for which Hall Johnson did the musical arrangements and directed the choir.

In recent times spirituals have sustained their popularity through public performances by college and high school choirs and professional choruses, using contemporary arrangements by composers such as Moses Hogan, Roland Carter, William Dawson, and Jester Hairston. They have also maintained their presence in the African American church; and they are recognized as the basis for or an element in many other styles of music, including gospel, jazz, and blues. They are a staple of the American tradition and a universal language of hope.

BRENDA ELLIS

See also Anderson, Marian; Burleigh, Harry Thacker; Dett, Nathaniel; Green Pastures, The; Hayes, Roland; Johnson, Hall; Johnson, James Weldon; Johnson, John Rosamond; Music; Musicians; Robeson, Paul; Singers

Further Reading

Allen, William Francis, Lucy Garrison, and Charles Ware. *Slave Songs of the United States: The Classic 1867 Anthology*. New York: Dover, 1995.

Epstein, Dena J. *Sinful Tunes and Spirituals: Black Folk Music to the Civil War*. Champaign: University of Illinois Press, 1981.

Fisher, Miles Mark. *Negro Slave Songs in the United States*. New York: Carol, 1990.

Johnson, James Weldon, and J. Rosamond Johnson. *The Books of American Negro Spirituals*. New York: Viking, 1942.

Southern, Eileen. *The Music of Black Americans: A History*. New York: Norton, 1971.

Work, John W. *American Negro Songs and Spirituals*. New York: Crown, 1988.

Spivey, Victoria

Though she may not have been as famous or talented as Bessie Smith or Gertrude "Ma" Rainey, Victoria Spivey is considered one the most significant and enduring of the classic women blues singers of the 1920s. She is noteworthy for her prolific output as a songwriter; her southern, folk-influenced "moaning" vocal style; and her direct and honest treatment of sordid and frightening subjects. Many of her songs offer instructive parallels to many of Langston Hughes's early "blues poems," which were criticized by some members of the black elite for their depiction of "lowdown" black life.

Spivey was born in Houston, Texas, in 1906. She grew up on church hymns, her family's string band music, and the music of the bordellos, honky-tonks, and picnics where she began her career playing piano. Here she met and shared the stage with other Texas blues musicians, including the legendary singer and guitarist Blind Lemon Jefferson. Encouraged by her idol, the blues singer Ida Prather Cox, Spivey soon left the Houston area to work as a songwriter for the St. Louis Music Company. She made a name for herself in 1926 with "Black Snake Blues," which she wrote and recorded for the Okeh label. Other notable records from the Harlem Renaissance period included several with the guitarist Lonnie Johnson. "No. 12, Let Me Roam" (1927) stands as a shining example of a traveling blues in which Spivey's country-blues vocals distinguish her from more refined classic blues women who sang with an urban sensibility. Like her peers, however, she recorded many playful double-entendre songs, such as "Organ Grinder Blues" (1928). These songs, which were typical fare for women who performed classic blues, usually veiled taboo sexual themes by using suggestive imagery and amusing metaphors.

Spivey's contribution to the challenge blues presented to social propriety also took more serious forms. "Blood Hound Blues" (1929), for example, illustrates Angela Davis's claim (1998) that early "blues women" created a discourse of feminist self-definition and empowerment by singing about the reality of male violence and their reactions to it. In this song, the narrator tells matter-of-factly of being a victim of domestic abuse ("He kicked me and blacked my eyes") and of taking action against it ("I poisoned my man"). Other stark and seedy topics Spivey sang about candidly could be found in "Dope Head Blues" (1927), considered the first blues song to address the reality of cocaine abuse.

Although the market for blues fell off dramatically for most women artists during the Depression, Spivey stayed active, touring with bands and variety shows, even forming a stage act with her husband, the dancer Billy Adams. She played a minor role in the all-black musical *Hallelujah* in 1929 and continued to record throughout the 1930s for RCA Victor, Vocallion, and Decca. She also moved for a short time to Chicago, where she performed variously with "Georgia" Tom Dorsey, Memphis Minnie, and Washboard Sam.

Aside from a brief period during the 1950s, when her only musical activity was as a church organist, Spivey stayed committed to blues. In the early 1960s, she was rediscovered by the folk and blues revivals, and was inspired to return to the stage and start up her own record label, Spivey Records, in 1962.

Biography

Victoria Regina Spivey was born 15 October 1906 in Houston, Texas. She performed in Houston (1918–1925) and recorded for Okeh (1926–1929), RCA Victor (1929–1930), Vocallion (1931, 1936–1937), Decca (1936), and Spivey (1962). She performed in *Hallelujah* (1929), *Tan Town Topics* (1933), and the revue *Hellzapoppin* (1934). She worked as a church organist in Brooklyn, New York, in the 1940s. She founded Spivey Records in 1962. Spivey died in New York on 3 October 1976.

DAVE JUNKER

See also Blues: Women Performers; Cox, Ida Prather; Hallelujah

Selected Works

"Black Snake Blues." 1926.
"Arkansas Road Blues." 1927.
"T. B. Blues." 1927.
"Dope Head Blues." 1927.
"Blood Thirsty Blues." 1927.
"Nightmare Blues." 1927.
"Murder in the First Degree." 1927.
"Organ Grinder Blues." 1928.
"Furniture Man Blues." 1928.
"Blood Hound Blues." 1929.
Victoria Spivey: Complete Recorded Works, 1926–1941, Vols. 1–5.

Further Reading

Davis, Angela. *Blues Legacies and Black Feminism: Gertrude "Ma" Rainey, Bessie Smith, and Billie Holiday.* New York: Pantheon, 1998.

Harrison, Daphne Duval. "Blues Was Her Business: Victoria Spivey." In *Black Pearls*. New Brunswick, N.J.: Rutgers University Press, 1987.

Hughes, Langston, "Shadow of the Blues." In *The Best of Simple*. New York: Hill & Wang, 1961.

———. *The Collected Poems of Langston Hughes*, ed. Arnold Rampersad. New York: Knopf, 1994

Oliver, Paul. *Conversations With the Blues*. London: Cassell, 1965.

Santelli, Robert. *The Big Book of Blues: A Biographical Encyclopedia*. New York: Penguin, 1993.

Stewart-Baxter, Derrick. "Wild Women Get the Blues: Ida Cox and Victoria Spivey." In *Ma Rainey and the Classic Blues Singers*. New York: Stein & Day, 1970.

Stevedore

Stevedore (1934) is a play by two white intellectuals: Paul Peters and George Sklar. It opened on 18 April 1934 at the Civic Repertory Theater in New York and ran for 111 performances; it was revived on 1 October the same year, running for another 64 performances. It had a racially mixed cast that included Canada Lee, Abbie Mitchell, and Edna Thomas; and it also drew racially mixed audiences. On 6 May 1935, *Stevedore* opened at the Embassy Theater in London.

This play belonged to a then fashionable genre, protest drama, that focused on liberal causes such as social, economic, and racial problems. In the South, such plays might focus specifically on conflicts between whites and blacks. *Stevedore*, however, included Marxist ideas and took up the theme of anticapitalism, linking racial prejudice to economics and social class.

The main character in *Stevedore*, Lonnie Thompson, is an outspoken black dockworker who is falsely accused of raping a white woman. Apparently, this accusation is a punishment for his attempts to unionize other black dockworkers. Thompson is defended by a white union organizer who sees capitalists as the real enemy of the people. Together, they work for cooperation between black and white workers to fight against capitalistic exploitation.

Stevedore can be seen as representative of a new generation of protest plays in which the theme of conflict between blacks and whites has deeper implications. Whereas earlier protest plays tended to center on revealing prejudice against the black race in a white society, newer playwrights responded to changes in economic conditions by examining not just racism but also the class conflict, to which it was in many ways seen as related. As a result of new initiatives in industry, African Americans had a better chance to join the workforce, but this development also opened up new possibilities for social, economic, and class conflicts between and within the black and white communities. Accordingly, dramas might focus not just on how African Americans were exploited but also on how white communities needed to deal with the effects of a more fluid class structure—effects such as increased mixing with blacks in daily life.

AMY LEE

See also Lee, Canada; Mitchell, Abbie; Thomas, Edna Lewis

Further Reading

Dickinson, Thomas H. *Playwrights of the New American Theatre*. Freeport, N.Y.: Books for Libraries, 1967.

Kellner, Bruce, ed. *The Harlem Renaissance: A Historical Dictionary for the Era*. New York: Methuen, 1984

Loney, Glenn. *Twentieth-Century Theatre*, Vol. 1. New York: Facts on File, 1983.

Meserve, Walter J. *An Outline History of American Drama*. New York: Feedback Theatrebooks and Prospero, 1994.

"Stevedore." *Internet Broadway Database*. (Web site.)

Still, William Grant

By far the most prominent composer of concert music of the Harlem Renaissance, William Grant Still (1895–1978) was also important for his contributions as a commercial musician, especially for his innovations as an arranger for early radio.

A major early influence on Still's career was his exposure as a teenager to Victor Red Seal opera recordings. In 1911, after graduating from M. W. Gibbs High School, one of the few black high schools in the South with a college preparatory program, he enrolled in Wilberforce University, where he was musically active although there was no music curriculum. He attended for four years but left before receiving his degree. After spending some time as a freelance musician in Ohio—in Dayton, Columbus, and Cleveland— Still went to work as a performer and arranger for W. C. Handy in Memphis in the summer of 1916. This

is where he learned the Delta blues tradition on which Handy drew so successfully. Having received a small inheritance, he left Handy after a few months and enrolled at Oberlin, where he had wanted to study from the first. He interrupted his studies there to volunteer for the navy after the United States entered World War I, serving as a busboy on a ship for a year. He returned to Oberlin briefly in 1919 but left again to rejoin Handy, who by then had relocated permanently in New York City.

In New York from 1919 to 1934, Still began by performing in and writing arrangements for black theater orchestras, starting with Noble Sissle and Eubie Blake's landmark musical *Shuffle Along* (1921). (Blake later wrote that George Gershwin had heard Still improvise the tune that became "I Got Rhythm" on his oboe before one of the performances.) *Shuffle Along* played for more than a year before moving to Boston; there, Still studied composition with the director of the New England Conservatory, George Whitefield Chadwick. Returning to New York, he became recording director for Harry H. Pace's Black Swan Recording Company. At this time, he began two years of composition study with Edgard Varèse, then the most prominent of the white avant-garde "ultramodern" composers. Still's double life as both a working commercial musician and a composer of concert music can be followed fairly clearly from this point on. After Black Swan folded, he played and conducted at the Plantation Club and elsewhere, sometimes on tour, until he was able to support himself and his family through his arrangements. (Still had played oboe, cello, and violin but preferred to arrange and compose.) Among the people for whom he made arrangements during his career were Will Vodery, Eubie Blake, Sophie Tucker, Earl Carroll, Willard Robison, Donald Voorhees (with whom he worked for several years), and Paul Whiteman (for whom he made radio arrangements during 1929–1930). His arrangements for radio, especially those for *Willard Robison's Deep River Hour* (1931–1932), were considered particularly effective and innovative. (For a time Still also conducted Robison's radio orchestra, becoming the first black man to conduct an all-white commercial orchestra.) Later, after moving to Los Angeles in 1934, he worked for a time at Columbia Pictures and Twentieth-Century-Fox.

In his concert music, which included symphonies, ballets, shorter symphonic works, and operas, Still sought a fusion of the African American experience and the European-based traditions of opera and

William Grant Still, c. 1930–1950. (Library of Congress.)

concert music. Evidence of this can be found in most of his scores, although it is not always apparent to the ear and was sometimes missed by white and black critics. (Harold Bruce Forsythe is the main exception.) At first, Still was welcomed by white critics as one of the promising young modernist composers of the 1920s; but in the 1940s, his concert music was sometimes criticized for being too "commercial." Critics who were part of the "black power" movement of the 1960s either ignored his work or objected that it was not sufficiently "black." Nevertheless, Still had a substantial audience for more than three decades. In the 1930s and 1940s, his symphonic works were performed frequently by major symphonies in New York, Philadelphia, Cincinnati, and Rochester, making him one of the most successful American composers of his time.

Works that were performed in the 1920s in concerts of new music include *From the Land of Dreams*, *From the Black Belt*, *From the Journal of a Wanderer*, *Levee Land*, and *Africa* (a major symphonic work that is entirely unknown to modern audiences). The *Afro-American Symphony* (1931, premiered in Rochester), his most famous work and the first of five symphonies, is based on a blues theme, a new departure at the time. He chose the blues style as his source, Still wrote, because blues pieces "unlike Spirituals, do not exhibit the influence of Caucasian music." His ballets include *Sahdji* (produced in Rochester in 1930 and revived there several times); *La Guiablesse* (produced in Chicago, 1936); and *Lenox Avenue* (1937), which was commissioned by the CBS radio symphony, then converted to a ballet. *Song of a City* was commissioned as background music, playing continuously at the Perisphere at the New York World's Fair in 1939. Still's major protest piece, *And They Lynched Him on a Tree* (a setting of a poem by Katherine Garrison Chapin), was premiered by the New York Philharmonic at Lewisohn Stadium in 1940. As of this writing, most of these works and a number of others were available on compact discs.

Still aspired to compose operas from the first, but he had few opportunities until he received a Guggenheim fellowship in 1934, enabling him to give up most of his arranging work and move to Los Angeles, where he eventually composed eight. His first opera, *Blue Steel* (1935, libretto by Harold Bruce Forsythe), never produced, is set in the bayou country of Louisiana. When Langston Hughes approached him with a scenario based on a play about the revolution in Haiti, Still jumped at the opportunity. Although the opera was completed by 1941, getting a production took eight more years. *Troubled Island* became the first opera by an American composer to be produced by the New York City Opera Company and the first by an African American composer and writer to be produced by a major opera company. The production, in 1949, turned out to be the high point of Still's career. He continued to compose operas, most on American themes, even though productions were slow in coming: *A Southern Interlude*, *Highway One USA*, *Bayou Legend*, *Costaso*, *Mota*, *The Pillar*, and *Minette Fontaine*.

Still lived in poverty in his later years, embracing anticommunism and writing for amateur and school groups who remained interested in his music. Relatively recently, there has been a strong revival of interest in his music.

Biography

William Grant Still was born 11 May 1895 and raised in a racially mixed middle-class neighborhood in Little Rock, Arkansas. He graduated from M. W. Gibbs High School and then studied at Wilberforce

University but left before receiving his degree. He married Grace Bundy in 1915. In 1916, he went to work as a performer and arranger for W. C. Handy; he worked for the Pace and Handy music publishing company in Memphis and then in New York City. He served in the navy during World War I. In 1921, he played oboe in the orchestra of the hit musical *Shuffle Along* on Broadway and on tour. In 1923, he studied at the New England Conservatory in Boston; he also studied in New York City with Edgard Varèse, and he became a recording director for Black Swan. In the late 1920s, Still received grants and awards and created jazz arrangements for Artie Shaw. He is also noted for composing European-style classical music. His Symphony No. 1, the *Afro-American Symphony*, was first performed in 1931 by the Rochester Philharmonic Orchestra. He moved to Los Angeles in 1934, working for Columbia Pictures and Twentieth-Century-Fox. Still died 3 December 1978 in Los Angeles.

CATHERINE PARSONS SMITH

See also Black Swan Phonograph Company; Handy, W. C.; Hughes, Langston; Music; Musicians; Shuffle Along

Further Reading

Smith, Catherine Parsons. *William Grant Still: A Study in Contradictions.* Berkeley: University of California Press, 2000.

Still, Judith Anne, Michael J. Dabrishus, and Carolyn L. Quin. *William Grant Still: A Biobibliography.* Westport, Conn.: Greenwood, 1996.

Stribling, Thomas Sigismund

Thomas Sigismund Stribling (1881–1965), who began his literary career writing light adventure fiction, became a major influence in the development of social realism in the southern novel in the 1920s and 1930s. With the publication of *Birthright* (1922), a realistic novel about the Negro from a black man's point of view, Stribling provided a great liberating impetus not only for southern writers but also for black writers of the Harlem Renaissance, like Jessie Redmon Fauset, who felt compelled to write sincerely and realistically about the problems of black people. Deeply influencing the literary awakening known as the southern renaissance, Stribling was also frequently called a "white novelist of the Harlem Renaissance."

Using sociojournalistic methods, Stribling brought a fresh breath to southern fiction, which was dominated by a quite conservative and sentimental rendering of the region. The local colorists and historical romancers were favoring the southern white viewpoint in their works and avoiding all the negative aspects of race relations like bigotry, prejudice, oppression, and laws against miscegenation. This "genteel tradition" received a harsh blow from Stribling's realistic and bitter depiction of the South as a declining region of poverty and endless defeat. Being a bold social critic, Stribling offered a new image of the South as repudiating spiritual and humanistic values in favor of materialism.

In his novels set in the provincial South, Stribling presents a hostile image in the manner of critical realism. *Teeftallow* (1926), published the year after the Scopes trial, attacks southern fundamentalism, and it became a great popular and critical success. Its sequel, *Bright Metal* (1928), fits into the "revolt from the village" trend, which took on momentum nationwide with the publication of Sinclair Lewis's *Main Street* (1920). *The Forge* (1931), the Pulitzer Prize–winning *The Store* (1932), and *Unfinished Cathedral* (1934) make up Stribling's "trilogy of the South," his most noteworthy literary production. Set in Florence, Alabama, the trilogy traces the history of the Vaiden family from the beginning of the Civil War through the 1920s. With this trilogy, Stribling became the only writer of the 1920s and 1930s who anticipated William Faulkner's panoramic vision of the history of the South.

Although Stribling achieved widespread popularity and received a Pulitzer Prize, he never won very high critical acclaim. Robert Penn Warren, who gave Stribling a low assessment, dismissed his work as propagandist art. The "agrarian new critics" found his fiction inartistic. Indeed, Stribling was not a writer who gave priority to aesthetic considerations. A fiction writer with sociological inclinations, he was a critical realist who believed that literature had to serve a broad political purpose. For Stribling, propaganda and art were not mutually exclusive forms, and "propagandist art" was a worthy vehicle to incite necessary social reform. He defended propagandistic literature and the merits of realistic writing with a serious social purpose as opposed to aesthetic perfection.

In the 1920s and 1930s, Stribling was one of the most popular and prolific southern writers who attacked provincial mentality and its materialistic basis and deconstructed the myth of the South, thus paving the way for other writers to depict the problems of the region realistically.

Biography

Thomas Sigismund (T. S.) Stribling was born in Clifton, Tennessee, on 4 March 1881. He graduated from Florence Normal School in 1903 and from the University of Alabama School of Law in 1905. He was an editor, *Clifton News*, 1900; clerk and short-story writer, *Taylor-Trotwood Magazine*, 1907–1908; and reporter, *Chattanooga News*, 1917. Stribling traveled extensively in Cuba, Europe, and South America, 1908–1916; Canada, 1919; Venezuela, 1921; West Indies, 1934; and Mexico, 1943. He taught and lectured at several universities, including Columbia University from 1936 to 1940 and the University of Colorado in 1936. Stribling was awarded the Pulitzer Prize in letters for "The Store" in 1933; he received an honorary doctor of literature degree from Oglethorpe University, Atlanta, in 1936. He died in Florence on 8 July 1965. His autobiography, *Laughing Stock*, was published posthumously, 1982.

ASLI TEKINAY

See also Birthright

Selected Works

The Cruise of the Dry Dock. 1917.
Birthright. 1922. (See also new ed., ed. Edward J. Piacentino, 1987.)
East Is East. 1922.
Fombombo. 1923.
Red Sand. 1924.
Teeftallow. 1926.
Bright Metal. 1928.
Clues of the Caribees. 1929. (Collection of five mystery stories.)
Strange Moon. 1929.
Backwater. 1930.
The Forge. 1931.
The Store. 1932.
Unfinished Cathedral. 1934.
The Sound Wagon. 1935.
These Bars of Flesh. 1938.
Laughing Stock, ed. Randy K. Cross and John T. McMillan. 1982. (Autobiography.)

Further Reading

Becker, George J. "T. S. Stribling: Pattern in Black and White." *American Quarterly*, 4, Fall 1952.
Eckley, Wilton E. *T. S. Stribling*. Boston, Mass.: Twayne, 1975.
Hilfer, Anthony Channell. *The Revolt from the Village, 1915–1930*. Chapel Hill: University of North Carolina Press, 1969.
Hobson, Fred. *Tell About the South: The Southern Rage to Explain*. Baton Rouge: Louisiana State University Press, 1983.
Piacentino, Edward J. *T. S. Stribling: Pioneer Realist in Modern Southern Literature*. New York and London: University Press of America, 1988.
Rocks, James E. "T. S. Stribling's Burden of Southern History: The Vaiden Trilogy." *Southern Humanities Review*, 6, Summer 1972.
Warren, Robert Penn. "T. S. Stribling: A Paragraph in the History of Critical Realism." *American Review*, 2, February 1934.

Strivers' Row

Strivers' Row—a name that suggests black Americans' striving to achieve—actually comprises four rows of private homes and three apartment buildings on 138th and 139th streets between Seventh and Eighth avenues (now known as Adam Clayton Powell and Frederick Douglass boulevards). The brownstones, built between 1889 and 1891, were designed by several architects, including James Brown Lord, Bruce Price, Clarence S. Luce, and Stanford White. These homes were first known as the King Model Houses, after their developer, David King Jr., who built Stanford White's Madison Square Garden and the base of the Statue of Liberty. Although architectural styles vary from block to block, each residence features a courtyard, a driveway, and iron gates that open to a rear alley. The town houses contained as many as fourteen rooms and two bathrooms—with modern plumbing that was a luxury at the turn of the twentieth century—and were appointed with elegant woodwork, French doors, Corinthian columns, tiled fireplaces, and oak staircases.

Like most property in Harlem in the early 1900s, the King Model Houses were originally owned by wealthy whites. However, with the financial panic of 1893 and a bust in speculative housing in 1904, the

Equitable Life Assurance Company took title to the houses. In 1919, the company made the buildings available to black buyers in a transaction handled by John Nail of the Afro-American Realty Company, which was based in Harlem. Advertised in the black press as "the finest group of Negro residences in the country," the brownstones sold within eleven months; and according to James Weldon Johnson, in 1925 they fetched $2,000 to $5,000 apiece, for an aggregate price of $2 million.

During the Harlem Renaissance, the tree-lined streets of Strivers' Row provided a quiet enclave for blacks of social prominence. Many residents were esteemed musicians, such as the composer Fletcher Henderson, the pianist Eubie Blake, the songwriter Noble Sissle, and W. C. Handy, "the father of the blues." The singer and actress Ethel Waters, who in the late 1920s was said to be the highest paid black entertainer in the world, lived only a few streets away from the heavyweight boxer Harry Wills. Stars like Josephine Baker often visited. The neighborhood was also home to upscale professionals, like Louis T. Wright, the director of Harlem General Hospital, and Vertner Tandy, the first commissioned African American architect in New York State. Doctors and dentists had offices in suites just below street level.

Numerous writers of the Harlem Renaissance used Strivers' Row as a setting. In Nella Larsen's *Quicksand* (1928), for example, the protagonist initially admires another character's brownstone on 139th Street, with its large cream-colored rooms; and in Jessie Redmon Fauset's *Plum Bun* (1928), dark-skinned Virginia has a spacious flat in Strivers' Row, while her light-skinned sister, Angela, "passes" in cramped Greenwich Village. In 1939, the neighborhood set the scene for Abram Hill's "On Strivers' Row," a satire featuring the Van Strivens and their brownstone, lavishly decorated despite the "Room to Rent" sign tucked in the French door.

In 1967, the neighborhood was officially designated the Saint Nicholas Historic District. It still evokes images of upward mobility and creativity: In 2001, the publishing company Random House launched a "Strivers' Row" imprint specifically for emerging black writers.

REBECCA MEACHAM

See also Afro-American Realty Company; Baker, Josephine; Blake, Eubie; Fauset, Jessie Redmon; Handy, W. C.; Harlem: 5—Neighborhoods; Henderson, Fletcher; Johnson, James Weldon; Larsen, Nella; Nail, John E.; Quicksand; Sissle, Noble; Waters, Ethel; Wright, Louis T.

Further Reading

Anderson, Jervis. *This Was Harlem: A Cultural Portrait, 1900–1950*. New York: Farrar, Straus and Giroux, 1982.

Dodson, Howard, Christopher Moore, and Roberta Yancy. *The Black New Yorkers: The Schomburg Illustrated Chronology*. New York: Wiley, 2000.

Dolkart, Andrew S, and Gretchen S. Sorin. *Touring Historic Harlem: Four Walks in Northern Manhattan*. New York: New York Landmarks Conservancy, 1997.

Douglas, Ann. *Terrible Honesty: Mongrel Manhattan in the 1920s*. New York: Farrar, Straus and Giroux, 1995.

Harris, M. A. *A Negro History Tour of Manhattan*. New York: Greenwood, 1968.

Johnson, James Weldon. *Black Manhattan*. New York: Knopf, 1930. (See also New York: Arno and New York Times, 1968.)

Lewis, David Levering. *When Harlem Was in Vogue*, New York: Knopf, 1981. (See also New York and Oxford: Oxford University Press, 1989.)

Osofsky, Gilbert. *Harlem: The Making of a Ghetto—Negro New York, 1890–1930*. New York: Harper & Row, 1963. (See also 2nd ed., 1971; Chicago, Ill: Ivan R. Dee, 1996.)

Ottley, Roi, and William J. Weatherby. *The Negro in New York: An Informal Social History, 1626–1940*. New York: Praeger, 1967, 1969.

Schoener, Allon, ed. *Harlem on My Mind: Cultural Capital of Black America, 1900–1968*. New York: Random House, 1968, 1969. (See also New York: New Press–Norton, 1995.)

Stylus

Stylus was a literary magazine published from 1916 to 1941 by the Stylus Literary Society of Howard University under the supervision of faculty members such as Alain Locke, T. Montgomery Gregory, Benjamin Brawley, and Sterling Brown. The student members of the literary society were a small, select group, said to be the best, brightest, and most promising scholars on the campus. The honorary members of the society included the "most representative Negro men and women of letters" in the United States: William Braithwaite, W. E. B. Du Bois, Charles Waddell

Chesnutt, Alice Dunbar Nelson, James Weldon Johnson, Arthur Schomburg, and John Edward Bruce. The literary society that gave rise to the periodical was founded by students at Howard University "to encourage original literary expression" there, and to serve as an "organization where the forms of literary composition could be studied and practiced under more favorable conditions than the classroom could offer." Both the society itself and the periodical were also intended to give emerging student writers an opportunity to publish their work.

The students and the faculty advisers as well contributed to *Stylus*, and its published issues illustrate an array of literary forms and stylistic techniques. A total of ten issues were published—in 1916, 1917, 1921, 1929, 1934, 1935, 1936, 1937, 1938, and 1941. After the issue of 1917, *Stylus* suspended publication because of World War I, but publication was resumed with the issue of 1921. As of the present writing, libraries such as those at Howard University, the Schomburg Center, and the Wisconsin State Historical Center hold a small number of issues in their collections.

The issue of May 1921 was of particular importance, especially because it marked the beginning of the career of Zora Neale Hurston, who was a student member of the literary society. This issue included her poem "Oh Night" and her first short story set in Eatonville, "John Redding Goes to Sea." This story was in effect her ticket to New York; it resulted in an invitation from Charles Spurgeon Johnson to come there and further develop her craft, at a time when the literary Harlem Renaissance was flourishing.

PEARLIE PETERS

See also Braithwaite, William Stanley; Brawley, Benjamin; Brown, Sterling; Bruce, John Edward; Chesnutt, Charles Waddell; Du Bois, W. E. B.; Hurston, Zora Neale; Johnson, Charles Spurgeon; Johnson, James Weldon; Locke, Alain; Magazines and Journals; Nelson, Alice Dunbar; Schomburg, Arthur A.

Further Reading

Bontemps, Arna. *The Harlem Renaissance Remembered*. New York: Dodd Mead, 1972.

"Foreword to Our Readers." *Stylus*, 1(1), June 1916, pp. 3–4. (Washington, D.C.: Howard University.)

Hemenway, Robert. *Zora Neale Hurston: A Literary Biography*. Chicago: University of Illinois Press, 1977.

Hurston, Zora Neale. *Dust Tracks on a Road*. New York: Lippincott, 1942.

Johnson, Abby, and Ronald M. Johnson. "Forgotten Pages." *Journal of American Studies*, 8(3), 1974, pp. 363–382.

Kellner, Bruce. *The Harlem Renaissance: A Historical Dictionary for the Era*. New York: Methuen, 1984.

Lewis, David Levering. *The Portable Harlem Renaissance*. New York: Penguin, 1994.

Locke, Alain. *The New Negro*. New York: Boni, 1925.

Logan, Rayford. *Howard University: The First Hundred Years, 1867–1967*. New York: New York University Press, 1969.

Roses, Lorraine, and Ruth E. Randolph. *Harlem's Glory*. Cambridge, Mass.: Harvard University Press, 1996.

Sublett, John

See Bubbles, John

Sugar Hill

Sugar Hill in Harlem is generally considered to extend northward from 145th Street to 155th Street, and from Amsterdam Avenue on the west to Edgecombe Avenue on the east. It has long had connotations of the finer life for African Americans, along with an older and smaller neighborhood, Strivers' Row. Both areas were populated by the rich and near-rich, although there were also middle-class and working-class residents. However, whereas most of those who lived in Strivers' Row bought their homes, most of the inhabitants of Sugar Hill rented apartments, at a very high price. These apartments had large rooms and spectacular views of the valley of Harlem, the Harlem River, and the Polo Grounds.

The Harlem Renaissance was a factor in the rental market; it increased the appeal of Sugar Hill (and also of Strivers' Row), and some landlords took advantage of the glamour surrounding the renaissance to charge outrageous rents. Many middle- and lower-class tenants had to struggle to pay these rents; as a result, rent parties and boarders were not unusual in Sugar Hill. But other residents of Sugar Hill could easily afford their apartments. Some of them had criminal associations that allowed for an expensive lifestyle; others, though, were simply respectable African Americans who lived like upper-class whites of the time.

Evidently, Sugar Hill began as an outgrowth of Strivers' Row, which consisted of only two blocks—138th and 139th streets between Seventh and Eighth avenues—and did not offer enough space for the increasing numbers of well-to-do blacks. By the late 1920s, an area that had once been part of Washington Heights was gradually becoming Sugar Hill. This new upscale neighborhood would eventually become home to black celebrities such as Cab Calloway, Paul Robeson, and A'Lelia Walker and would have an influence on the Harlem Renaissance because the writers, musicians, athletes, civic and political leaders, and others who came to live in Sugar Hill sponsored and participated in talks, soirees, and literary gatherings there.

Two particular buildings are often mentioned in discussions of Sugar Hill. One is a fourteen-story apartment house at 409 Edgecombe Avenue that was both the tallest and the most exclusive building in Sugar Hill. During the 1930s and 1940s, its tenants included W. E. B. Du Bois, Thurgood Marshall, and Walter White. The second is the Roger Morris Apartments at 555 Edgecombe Avenue, which featured hardwood floors, uniformed elevator operators and doormen, and bright canopies.

There were, of course, other desirable and exclusive residential areas—and numerous cultural attractions—elsewhere in Harlem. Still, a special myth clung to both Sugar Hill and Strivers' Row, suggesting that during the renaissance these two places represented Harlem's best.

Lou-Ann Crouther

See also Calloway, Cabell "Cab"; Harlem: 5—Neighborhoods; House-Rent Parties; Robeson, Paul; Strivers' Row; Walker, A'Lelia; White, Walter

Further Reading

Anderson, Jervis, *This Was Harlem: A Cultural Portrait, 1900–1950*. New York: Farrar, Straus and Giroux, 1982.

Bloom, Jennifer Kingso. "Looking to a Name to Revive the Allure of Sugar Hill." *New York Times*, 5 February 1995, p. CY6.

Chappell, Kevin. "Can Harlem Bring Back the Black Mecca Era?" *Ebony*, 56(10), 2001.

Johnson, James Weldon. *Black Manhattan*. New York: Arno and New York Times, 1968.

Lewis, David Levering. *When Harlem Was in Vogue*. Toronto: Random House of Canada; New York: Knopf, 1981.

McKay, Claude. *Harlem: Negro Metropolis*. New York: Dutton, 1940.

Ottley, Roi. *New World a-Coming*. New York: Arno Press and New York Times, 1969.

Ottley, Roi, and William J. Weatherby. *The Negro in New York: An Informal Social History*. New York: New York Public Library and Oceana, 1967.

Schoener, Allon, ed. *Harlem on My Mind: Cultural Capital of Black America*. New York: Random House, 1968.

Whitaker, Charles. "Cultural Revival Empowers and Transforms." *Ebony*, 56(10), 2001.

———. "New Money, New Economic Development Create New Mood." *Ebony*, 56(10), 2001.

Survey Graphic

One of the defining publications of the Harlem Renaissance was a special issue of the magazine *Survey Graphic* devoted to "Harlem: Mecca of the New Negro." This special issue, which was edited by Alain Locke and included contributions from many of the most significant participants in the Harlem Renaissance, is a key example of African Americans' efforts to create and distribute images of themselves, in the hope that providing readers with information about African Americans might help undermine racism.

Survey Graphic was a monthly magazine edited by Paul U. Kellogg. Along with *Survey Midmonthly*, it was published by Survey Associates, a social work organization that defined itself as promoting "social exploration." *Survey Graphic*, so named because it included a great deal of visual material, often ran special issues that introduced its mostly white readers to groups of people from around the world, and it took particular interest in cultural nationalist movements. In the early 1920s, for example, it ran special issues on such developments in Ireland, Mexico, and Russia.

The catalyst for the special issue on Harlem was the Civic Club dinner organized by Charles Spurgeon Johnson in March 1924. Kellogg was one of the invited guests, and he was impressed by the African American writers who read their work and by comments from other speakers. The next day, he wrote to a friend, describing his plans for a special issue on African Americans that would emphasize their contributions to American society and culture. The issue was published in March 1925, and it was quite successful. The circulation of *Survey Graphic* in 1924 was about 21,000, but the first printing of the "Harlem issue" was increased to 30,000 copies. Its popularity was immediate, and a second printing of 12,000 copies was arranged, with 3,000 of those distributed to African American students and organizations. Even before the special issue appeared, the Boni brothers" publishing company asked about reprinting its contents as a book. Locke added many more essays, a good deal more fiction, and more poetry and visual arts to turn the magazine into *The New Negro*.

The special issue of *Survey Graphic* opened with two essays by Locke in which he defined the New Negro movement, asserted its connection to developments in American culture, and linked it to cultural nationalist movements in other countries. These and other issues Locke raised here—particularly the growing race consciousness of African Americans, the importance of African Americans' literary and artistic accomplishments, and the need to battle racism and segregation—became recurring themes of the Harlem Renaissance.

The remaining texts, contributed by some of the most important participants in the Harlem Renaissance, were grouped into three sections. The first section included a number of texts that described Harlem and its residents; the second focused on African Americans' accomplishments in literature, music, and the visual arts; and the third offered essays about various aspects of race relations. The essayists were Locke, James Weldon Johnson, Charles S. Johnson, W. A. Domingo, J. A. Rogers, Albert Barnes, Arthur Schomburg, Melville Herskovits, Konrad Bercovici, Walter White, Kelly Miller, Eunice Roberta Hunton, Elise Johnson McDougald, Winthrop D. Lane, and George Haynes. W. E. B. Du Bois, Countee Cullen, Anne Spencer, Angelina Weld Grimké, Claude McKay, Jean Toomer, Langston Hughes, and Rudolph Fisher contributed short stories and poems.

Some of the essays are illustrated with photographs of streets, homes, and churches in Harlem, but the most significant visual texts are two series of portraits by the Bavarian artist Winold Reiss: "Harlem Types" and "Four Portraits of Negro Women." These proved to be one of the most controversial aspects of the issue. These portraits, along with others by Reiss, were shown in an exhibit at the Harlem Branch of the New York Public Library which opened the same month that the issue was published. Some viewers saw them as unflattering depictions of African Americans. This criticism led Locke to write an essay for *Opportunity* magazine, "To Certain of Our Phillistines [sic]," in which he defended the depiction of African Americans in the portraits. He also defended the fact that they were by a white artist, arguing that Reiss, as a European, was free of the racism shown by so many white Americans. The place of these portraits in the special issue of *Survey Graphic*, then, sparked debate about what texts should show about African Americans and about who should be creating them.

Other texts in the special issue raise a number of additional questions that received attention during the Harlem Renaissance. For example, part of the point of the publication was to offer positive images of African Americans, but Hunton described Harlem as a ghetto, and Lane focused on the corruption in the area. These essays prompted discussion of whether writers should create what Du Bois would later call propaganda, or if they should show both the positive and the negative aspects of African Americans' lives. Significantly, Locke included neither of these essays in *The New Negro*. And, though he included three of Reiss's four portraits of black women in the book, he replaced Reiss's "Harlem Types" with portraits of African American intellectuals. *The New Negro*, then, offered a more optimistic depiction of Harlem than had been presented in *Survey Graphic*, and its portraits drew attention to elite African Americans rather than the folk.

Despite the popularity of the "Harlem issue" of *Survey Graphic* in the 1920s and its role as the precursor of Locke's anthology, the issue has received only limited attention from contemporary scholars. Part of the problem may be that few copies of the original issue remain. In 1981, though, it was republished by Black Classic Press, and a hypermedia version was later prepared at the University of Virginia's Electronic Text Center. It also has been reprinted as part of *The Emergence of the Harlem Renaissance*, edited by Cary Wintz (1996). The issue is mentioned by a number of scholars of the Harlem Renaissance, mostly with reference to its connection to *The New Negro*; but given its significance as an early definition of the movement and an announcement of key themes of the renaissance, the special issue of *Survey Graphic* deserves much more extended analyses.

ANNE CARROLL

See also Civic Club Dinner, 1924; Kellogg, Paul U.; Locke, Alain; New Negro, The; Reiss, Winold; *other specific contributors*

Further Reading

Carroll, Anne. "The *Survey Graphic*'s Harlem Issue: Defining the New Negro as American." In *Word, Image, and the New Negro: Representation and Identity in the Harlem Renaissance*. Bloomington: Indiana University Press, 2004.

Chambers, Clarke A. *Paul U. Kellogg and the Survey: Voices for Welfare and Social Justice*. Minneapolis: University of Minnesota Press, 1971.

Hutchinson, George. *The Harlem Renaissance in Black and White*. Cambridge, Mass., and London: Belknap–Harvard University Press, 1995. (See also paperback, 1997.)

Lewis, David Levering. *When Harlem Was in Vogue*. New York: Knopf, 1979. (See also paperback, New York and Oxford: Oxford University Press, 1989.)

Locke, Alain. "To Certain of Our Phillistines [sic]." *Opportunity*, May 1925, pp. 155–156.

Long, Richard A. "The Genesis of Locke's *The New Negro*." *Black World*, 25(4), 1976.

Stewart, Jeffrey C. *To Color America: Portraits by Winold Reiss*. Washington, D.C.: Smithsonian Institution Press for National Portrait Gallery, 1989.

Wintz, Cary D., ed. *The Emergence of the Harlem Renaissance*. New York and London: Garland, 1996.

T

Taboo

Taboo (1922) by Mary Hoyt Wiborg, a white woman, was written and produced during a period when several other plays focusing on the life of African Americans were being written. Black characters and themes relevant to African Americans were also being widely addressed in American music, poetry, and dance during the early 1920s.

The plot of *Taboo* centers on the character of a black slave who falls asleep on a plantation and in his dreams returns to his homeland of Africa. The dream becomes the setting and context in which black Americans/native superstitions and myths, purportedly rooted in Africa, are explored. As the main character falls asleep, he sings the black spiritual "Go Down Moses." During one performance, this song elicited such a strong response from the audience that the director of the play, Augustin Duncan, encouraged audience members to request more songs for the cast to sing.

The play opened on 4 April 1922 at the Sam H. Harris Theater in New York. Paul Robeson had been asked to take the leading role, after Duncan saw him in an amateur performance at the Harlem YWCA; *Taboo* marked Robeson's first professional appearance as an actor. He played opposite the English actress Margaret Wycherly.

Taboo closed after only three days, evidently because its plot was weak; the critic Alexander Woollcott remarked that Robeson belonged anywhere except on the stage. Although it was not a success in Broadway, *Taboo* was performed on tour in England, where Robeson appeared with the famous English actress Mrs. Patrick Campbell.

AMY LEE

See also Robeson, Paul

Further Reading

Baraka, Amiri. "Paul Robeson and the Theatre." *Black Renaissance*, 2(1), Fall–Winter 1998, pp. 12–34.
Dickinson, Thomas H. *Playwrights of the New American Theatre*. Freeport, N.Y.: Books for Libraries, 1967.
Loney, Glenn. *Twentieth-Century Theatre*, Vol. 1. New York: Facts on File, 1983.

Talbert, Mary Burnett

Mary Burnett Talbert is known primarily for her work as the chairman of the Dyer Anti-Lynching Bill Committee and for her role as the vice president of the National Association for the Advancement of Colored People (NAACP). Talbert contributed to the development of the Harlem Renaissance in several ways, however. A club leader, civil rights activist, educator, and lecturer, Talbert was an expert organizer for a wide variety of racial causes throughout her life. She was born and educated in Oberlin, Ohio; she graduated from Oberlin College in 1886 with honors, after only three years. In 1887, Talbert became the first woman in the state to hold the position of assistant principal, the highest position to which any woman had acceded. One year later, she became principal of the Union High School of Little Rock, Arkansas, before moving to her permanent home in Buffalo, New York. From there, Talbert became the founder and president of the Christian Culture Congress; a member of the Phillis Wheatley Club; and the founder of the Empire State Federation of Colored Women, an organization active in prison reform, in 1911. In this organization, she served as the second president from 1912 to 1916. Talbert also led a successful campaign to redeem and restore the Frederick Douglass Home in Washington, D.C., as a memorial and center for black history, and as part of the national centennial celebration of Douglass's birth.

She was a national organizer for the National Association of Colored Women (NACW) in 1913, and by 1914 she was its vice president. By 1916, its members elected her president, and she served in this capacity for two terms, from 1916 to 1920. Talbert also helped to organize branches and increase circulation for the newsletter of the NAACP. While raising funds for the United War Work Campaign, Talbert conveyed the NAACP's message throughout the South. Following her presidency of the NACW, she became a fieldworker for the NAACP, yet she continued to lead local campaigns—for example, raising $5,000 for a church-affiliated home for black working girls. She went to Europe during World War I to serve as a Red Cross war and canteen worker for black troops in France. Following the war, Talbert attended the Pan-African Congress in Paris and the International Congress of Women in Zurich, Switzerland. These international experiences led her to join the newly formed International Council of Women of the Darker Races of the World in 1921.

As the director of the Anti-Lynching Crusaders, a national network of black women working to raise money—and to raise consciousness about lynching and the need for a federal antilynching bill—she also worked with Congressman Leonidas Carstarphen Dyer, the sponsor of the federal bill, when she was president of the NACW. Her ad hoc group of black women built on fund-raising networks established during World War I and became official in 1922 as the Anti-Lynching Crusaders. She continued in a leadership role within the NAACP as a member of the board of directors and as vice president; she was the first woman to receive the NAACP's Spingarn Medal, for her years of dedicated service.

Biography

Mary Burnett Talbert was born on 17 September 1866 in Oberlin, Ohio. She studied in public schools in Oberlin, Ohio, and graduated from Oberlin College in 1886. She served as principal of Union High School of Little Rock, Arkansas, in 1891, the year she married William A. Talbert. She was a charter member of the Phillis Wheatley Club, 1899; founder and president of the Christian Culture Congress, 1911; president of the Empire State Federation of Colored Women, 1912–1916; national organizer, president, and vice president for the National Association of Colored Women, 1913–1920; organizer, International Council of Women of the Darker Races of the World, 1921; director of the Anti-Lynching Crusaders; and board member and vice president of the NAACP, 1918–1923. She was an elected delegate to the quinquennial conference of the International Council of Women in 1920. Talbert was awarded the NAACP's Spingarn Medal in 1922 and appointed to the League of Nations Committee on International Relations. She died at age fifty-seven of coronary thrombosis in Buffalo, New York, on 8 October 1923, after a lengthy illness.

CARMEN PHELPS

See also Antilynching Crusade; National Association for the Advancement of Colored People; Pan-African Congresses; Spingarn Medal

Further Reading

Johnson, James Weldon. *Black Manhattan*. New York: Da Capo, 1930.

Kellner, Bruce, ed. *The Harlem Renaissance: A Historical Dictionary for the Era*. Westport, Conn.: Greenwood, 1984.

Logan, Rayford W., and Michael Winston, eds. *Dictionary of American Negro Biography*. New York: Norton, 1982.

Salem, Dorothy C. *African American Women: A Biographical Dictionary*. New York: Garland, 1993.

Talented Tenth

The "talented tenth"—that is, the upper 10 percent of African American society—was hailed by some as the model to which all other African Americans should aspire. The concept was first promoted by W. E. B.

Du Bois as part of his program of racial uplift in *The Negro Problem* (1903); he emphasized the necessity for higher education for a black elite who would, as a result of its knowledge and character, provide leadership for the race. According to Du Bois, "It is, ever was and ever will be from the top downward that culture filters. The Talented Tenth rises and pulls all that are worthy of saving up to their vantage ground." Du Bois, like many other black intellectuals of the time, feared that an overemphasis on industrial and vocational training would permanently relegate the majority of African Americans to second-class citizenship. In many respects, Du Bois's program of civic and cultural uplift challenged Booker T. Washington's program of economic freedom, which Washington had proposed in 1895 in his "Atlanta compromise." Washington believed that material prosperity should take priority over political and cultural progress. Du Bois, on the other hand, felt that, in order to for blacks to achieve full political and civil status as American citizens, it was important to educate "the best and most capable" of black youth, who would become "leaders of thought and missionaries of culture among their people" by setting the ideals of the community where they live, directing its thoughts, and heading its social movements. Through the introduction of the "college-bred Negro" into African American communities across the United States, Du Bois hoped that "the Best of this race . . . may guide the Mass away from the contamination and death of the Worst."

Du Bois's program of social uplift was also culturally conditioned, espousing the formula that art should be earnest, beautiful, and above all didactic. For Du Bois, art was essentially a tool for race-building that could solve the problem of the color line, because he believed that the "great mission of the Negro to America and the modern world is the development of Art and the appreciation of the Beautiful" (Rampersad 1976).

Thus, Du Bois actively promoted the works of artists that conformed to the ideal of the talented tenth: Novels such as Jessie Redmon Fauset's *There Is Confusion* and *Plum Bun* and the poetry of Countee Cullen were considered paragons of this approach. Fauset's works, in particular, represented the lifestyle of the talented tenth to outside readers, both black and white, for her characters were educated, urbane, and Republican, and often aspired to be lawyers, dentists, and doctors. Like the society she mirrored, black characters in Fauset's work often entertained in their own homes; attended prestigious universities such as Fisk, Howard, or Atlanta; joined Negro Greek-letter fraternities and sororities; made formal debuts; and aspired to live in the most fashionable areas of major urban centers such as New York, Boston, and Philadelphia. Cullen came to epitomize the precocious flowering of the talented tenth, and with his charm, manners, and impeccable attire was invariably described as "a perfect gentleman" (Watson 1995).

Many of the photographic portraits of James Van Der Zee sought to give a visual record of the members of the talented tenth, who, with their beauty, pride, and dignity, offered an impressive example of this "new" Negro (McGhee 1969).

Other black intellectuals seconded Du Bois's social theories, although not without some misgivings. Carter G. Woodson believed, like Du Bois, that "the educational system of a country is worthless" unless it revolutionizes the social order. "Men of scholarship, and prophetic insight, must show us the right way and lead us into light which is shining brighter and brighter" (1918/1994). However, Woodson was concerned about the mass migration of educated blacks from the Southern states to northern cities, a movement that left an entire region of the country without its supposed leaders.

Alain Locke shared Du Bois's belief in the natural aristocracy of the educated elite and hoped that the talented tenth would become cultural role models and ultimately win from whites fair judgment of the race. Locke was less enthusiastic about Du Bois's use of art as propaganda for race-building, however; instead, he envisioned Harlem more as a cultural phenomenon that embraced all aspects of black culture and less as a political center embroiled in the "arid fields of controversy and debate" (1925/1992).

Ironically, this class-bound approach to art, which was supposed to inspire and uplift the masses, often had the opposite effect, creating hostility and resentment between the talented tenth and those they would enlighten. This schism is most visible between two warring camps: the NAACP's magazine, *The Crisis*, which was edited by Du Bois and touted the virtues of authors who came from the talented tenth, such as Fauset and Cullen; and Wallace Thurman's *Fire!!*, which embraced the vices of "Niggeratti Manor" and the folk idiom. "Talented tenthers" were often accused of elitism, and those less fortunate frequently used pejorative terms such as "dicty" (nouveau riche, haughty) and "lampblack whites" (blacks who aspire to white ways) to express their anger and resentment at what they saw increasingly as a black aristocracy that merely mimicked white European culture. Even Du Bois himself came to reformulate his ideas about the success of the talented tenth, feeling that the black aristocracy had been seduced by its economic advantages and had turned its back on the masses: "My faith hitherto had been in what I once denominated the 'Talented Tenth.' I now realize that the ability within a people does not automatically work for its highest salvation. . . . Naturally, out of the mass of the working classes, who know life in its bitter struggle, will continually rise the real, unselfish and clearsighted leadership" (1952).

Contemporary theorists have continued to debate Du Bois's concept of racial uplift. David Du Bois believes that "little more is passed on to our youth today of W. E. B. Du Bois than the elitist concept of black leadership" and that this idea exists today in the "most unlikely places," such as in marginalized militant groups (1993). Joy James and Lewis Gordon reject Du Bois's reformulated concept of working-class black leadership, and instead find it prominent "in the literature of cultural studies, critical race theory, feminisms, black postmodernism, and Afrocentrism" (1997). For James and Gordon, the leadership capacity of such writing "excises Du Bois's democratic radicalism and his conviction that those with the least to lose, and therefore the most to gain, are most likely to provide exemplary leadership in liberation struggles."

RANDALL SHAWN WILHELM

See also Crisis, The; Cullen, Countee; Du Bois, W. E. B.; Fauset, Jessie Redmon; Fire!!; Locke, Alain; Thurman, Wallace; Woodson, Carter G.

Further Reading

Du Bois, David. "Understanding the Legacy of W. E. B. Du Bois." *Emerge*, October 1993, p. 65.

Du Bois, W. E. B. *In Battle for Peace: The Story of My Eighty-Third Birthday*. New York: Masses and Mainstream, 1952.

———. "The Talented Tenth." In *The Negro Problem*. New York: AMS, 1970. (Originally published 1903.)

Gaines, Kevin K. *Uplifting the Race: Black Leadership, Politics, and Culture in the Twentieth Century*. Chapel Hill: University of North Carolina Press, 1996.

James, Joy, and Gordon, Lewis. *Transcending the Talented Tenth: Black Leaders and American Intellectuals*. New York: Routledge, 1997.

Locke, Alan. "The New Negro." In *The New Negro: Voices of the Harlem Renaissance*, ed. Alain Locke. New York: Macmillan, 1992. (Originally published 1925.)

McGhee, Reginald. *The World of James Van Der Zee: A Visual Record of the Black Race*. New York: Grove, 1969.

Rampersad, Arnold. *The Art and Imagination of W. E. B. Du Bois*. Cambridge, Mass.: Harvard University Press, 1976.

Watson, Steven. *Harlem Renaissance: Hub of African American Culture, 1920–1930*. New York: Pantheon, 1995.

Woodson, Carter G. "The Migration of the Talented Tenth." In *The Portable Harlem Renaissance Reader*, ed. David Levering Lewis. New York: Viking, 1994. (Originally published 1918.)

Tannenbaum, Frank

Frank Tannenbaum was a labor leader, a social and political activist, an economist and criminologist, a specialist in race relations and prison reform, and a professor of Latin American history. He was born in Austria in 1893, immigrated to the United States in 1905, and died in New York in 1969. As a young man, Tannenbaum became involved in one of the radical political groups that operated on the fringes of the bohemian movement centered in Greenwich Village. He associated with Emma Goldman and became active in the International Workers of the World (IWW). In early 1914, he assumed leadership of a mob of unemployed workers who began marching on churches in lower Manhattan demanding food and shelter. After about ten days of relatively peaceful confrontations, his demonstrators clashed violently with the police, and Tannenbaum was arrested and sentenced to one year in prison.

After prison, with the help of warden Thomas Mott Osborne, Tannenbaum entered Columbia University, where he distinguished himself as an honor student and was a member of the Phi Beta Kappa honor society. After graduation in 1921, he worked for a time as a correspondent for *Survey* magazine in Mexico, then served a tour in the U.S. Army during which he was stationed in the South. During his military service he became interested in race and its impact on the South, and he began a study that resulted in two books on the African American experience. After leaving the army, he earned his Ph.D. in economics at the Brookings Institution with a dissertation on land reform in Mexico. He then spent several years in Mexico, conducting research on rural education and serving as an adviser to President Lázaro Cárdenas. In 1932, he returned to the United States to teach criminology at Cornell. He also helped devise the legislation that established the Farm Security Administration, and in 1935 he joined the faculty at Columbia, ultimately becoming professor of Latin American history.

Tannenbaum's connection to the Harlem Renaissance centered on his groundbreaking study of race and racial violence in the South. This study, begun during his military service, resulted in his first book, *Darker Phases of the South*, published in 1924. Tannenbaum examined several aspects of southern life in his effort to uncover the explanation for the region's economic plight and its racial violence. He especially focused on the horrors and brutality endured by blacks in the southern penal system—the prisons, and especially the prison camps and the chain gangs—and the racial violence of the Ku Klux Klan. Avoiding emotionalism, he presented a starkly detailed description of the dehumanizing system of violence, which, he argued, affected both the victim and the perpetrator. Tannenbaum did more than expose the worst abuses of racism. He also described the oppressed condition of white workers ensnared in the legalized peonage of the mill towns, company-owned towns in which all aspects of the workers' lives were controlled by their employers. It was this lack of hope and joy, shared by farm tenant and mill-town worker, that led to lynchings and that provided members for the Klan. Racial violence, he suggested, was a temporary escape from the dull monotony of daily life for these oppressed whites; it also addressed the "underlying current of apprehension that the South will be outstripped in population by the colored as against the white. It is fear of losing grip upon the world, of losing caste, of losing control" (Tannenbaum 1924). Tannenbaum believed that the migration of blacks out of the South, and their replacement by European immigrants and labor conflict, might ultimately resolve racial conflict in the region and in the nation.

Tannenberg's image of the South was compatible with that presented by Walter White in his study of racial violence, and with the work of other black novelists and poets. Tannenbaum's descriptions helped define the racial views of white liberals during the 1920s and 1930s. His work supported that of W. E. B. Du Bois and the National Association for the Advancement of Colored People (NAACP) in their antilynching crusade of the 1920s. Two decades later, Tannenbaum's views on racial issues, especially on the oppressive role of monotony in southern life, as well as his suggestion that the racial problem in the South might be solved if white southerners were distracted by labor problems and overrun with foreign immigrants, were cited by Gunnar Myrdal in his pathbreaking study *An American Dilemma*.

Tannenbaum returned to the study of race in 1947 with *Slave and Citizen: The Negro in the Americas*. This was a pioneering study of comparative slavery by a white American scholar. He argued that greater intermarriage and the protective role of the Catholic Church lessened the impact of race in Latin America. Although more recent scholarship has challenged Tannenbaum's argument, his comparative approach inspired other historical studies of race and slavery, such as those by Stanley Elkins, Eugene Genovese, and Herbert Klein.

Tannenbaum retired from Columbia in 1965, best known for his work in Latin American history and the theory of criminology. His writings on race and slavery, surpassed by later scholarship, are much less known.

Biography

Frank Tannenbaum was born in Austria in 1893 and immigrated to the United States in 1905. He became active in the International Workers of the World and spent a year in prison in around 1914 after clashing with the police during a labor demonstration. After his release, he attended Columbia University, graduating in 1921; later he earned a Ph.D. in economics at the Brookings Institution. He served in the U.S. Army and was stationed in the South. He published *Darker Phases of the South* in 1924. He taught criminology at Cornell (1932) and Latin American history at Columbia (1935). He published *Slave and Citizen: The Negro in the Americas* in 1947. Tannenbaum retired from Columbia in 1965 and died in New York in 1969.

CARY D. WINTZ

See also Antilynching Crusade; White, Walter

Further Reading

Goldman, Emma. *Living My Life*, Vol. 2. New York: Knopf, 1931.

Horsley, Carter B. "Dr. Frank Tannenbaum, 76, Dies; Organized Columbia Seminars." *New York Times*, 2 June 1969, p. 45.

Stansell, Christine. *American Moderns: Bohemian New York and the Creation of a New Century*. New York: Holt, 2000.

Tannenbaum, Frank. *Darker Phases of the South*. New York: Putnam, 1924.

———. *Slave and Citizen: The Negro in the Americas*. New York: Knopf, 1947.

Tanner, Henry Ossawa

Henry Ossawa Tanner was a pioneering African American artist and one of the most successful in the pre–Harlem Renaissance Period. He served as an inspiration and model to many artists who followed him. Tanner began sketching at age thirteen, when a painter in Philadelphia's Fairmount Park inspired him to draw images of animals at nearby zoos. Tanner began formal training in visual art in December 1879, when he enrolled as the only African American student at the Pennsylvania Academy of the Fine Arts in Philadelphia. For the next six years he studied landscape and seascape naturalism under the Anglo-American painters Thomas Eakins and Thomas Hovenden. During this period he also exhibited his work at the academy and in other sections of Philadelphia. After spending a couple of years renting a studio in Philadelphia to practice the craft, in January 1889 Tanner moved to Atlanta, Georgia, to set up a gallery of professional photography. Lack of business forced him to abort this venture and, a year later, to secure a job teaching at Atlanta's Clark University.

Throughout these student years and his early career, Tanner had been making oil paintings of three subjects: seascapes, including *Seascape, Seascape-Jetty*, and *Ship in a Storm* (c. 1876–1879); landscapes, such as *Sand Dunes at Sunset, Atlantic City* (c. 1886), and *Mountain Landscape, Highlands, North Carolina* (*Cumberland Foothills*, c. 1889); and animals, such as *"Pomp" at the Zoo* (c. 1880) and *Lion Licking Its Paw* (*After Dinner*, 1886). In December 1890, he exhibited many of these paintings at the headquarters of the board of education of the African Methodist Episcopal (AME) Church in Cincinnati, Ohio. The money he earned from this exhibition funded his travel a month later to Europe, where he sought to intensify his academic study of the visual arts. During his time abroad, Tanner underwent a crucial maturation in his approach to painting.

Initially, Tanner intended to study in Rome. After sojourning in Liverpool and London and then in the distinctive comforts of Paris, however, he decided to remain in Paris and to enroll in the Académie Julien. While studying under the French masters Jean-Joseph Benjamin-Constant and Jean-Paul Laurens, he soon discovered the Salon—that is, the Salon de la Société des Artistes Français. He proposed his artwork for the Salon's annual spring exhibition of the best and brightest painters of Europe and the United States, but the Salon rejected this artwork because of its nonnormative style. Indeed, Tanner's remnant predisposition toward naturalism and his current attraction to contemporary American "genre" realism proved incompatible with the predominant French "impressionist," "synthetist," or "symbolic" style of art, which concentrated more on colorful and moody abstractions of the human emotions, psyche, and spirit. In the early to mid-1890s, Tanner oscillated between these two kinds of painting. His genre paintings comprised *The Bagpipe Lesson* (1892–1893), *The Banjo Lesson* (1893), *The Thankful Poor* (1894), and *The Young Sabot Maker* (1895); his *Bois d'Amour* (1891) and *Aix-en-Provence* (1894) suggest that he had experimented, however briefly, with French avant-garde styles.

After a bout with typhoid fever, Tanner returned to Philadelphia and accepted an invitation to speak at the Congress on Africa at the World's Columbian Exposition, held in Chicago on 14–21 August 1893. His lecture, "The Negro in American Art," affirmed the competitiveness of African Americans with Anglo-Americans in the visual and fine arts. Lasting until October 1894, Tanner's sojourn in the United States marked his increased participation in and affection for African American communities. In 1894, he attended an AME conference in Tallahassee, Florida, as well as a commencement ceremony at Hampton Institute in Virginia. The black press and even African American leaders revered him. Booker T. Washington lauded Tanner in his autobiography, *Up From Slavery* (1901), and W. E. B. Du Bois two decades later heaped comparable praise onto him in *The Gifts of Black Folk* (1924).

Coincidentally, the mid-1890s marked Tanner's momentary and explicit artistic interest in African American genres. While *The Banjo Lesson* and *The Thankful Poor*, for example, seem to use tropes from minstrelsy (the banjo in *The Banjo Lesson*, religiosity in *The Thankful Poor*, the signs of socioeconomic poverty in both paintings), they still show the transmission of knowledge from an older to a younger generation as a form of emotional and intellectual uplift. This theme of uplift also informs his other genre paintings of the period, *The Bagpipe Lesson* and *The Young Sabot Maker*. Fame accompanied the exhibition of this genre work. In May 1894, the Salon had accepted one of these paintings, *The Banjo Lesson*, but hung it so high on the wall that it went virtually unnoticed. Still, the acceptance boosted Tanner's self-confidence, which had already been soaring one month earlier when he had exhibited fifteen of his latest paintings with a former mentor at the Pennsylvania Academy, Thomas Hovenden. Fortunately for Tanner, never again would the Salon marginalize his paintings. The Salon would not only select but also give prominence to a painting from him for each of the next twenty years, until 1914.

In the 1890s, Tanner's confrontation with the politics of identity, race, and nation influenced his personal, artistic, and professional motives. The historical tendency of writers in American media and intellectual societies to address Tanner's African ancestry frustrated him. By contrast, Parisian media less frequently discussed his racial identity and, he felt, concentrated more appropriately on the aesthetic qualities of his paintings. He moved to France in 1895.

In the expatriate period of Tanner's career, *Daniel in the Lions' Den* (1895) captured his new thematic approach to painting. Although it was not his first painting of a religious subject—for that we must consider *Waiting for the Lord* (1882)—*Daniel in the Lions' Den* represented Tanner's decisive turn toward the Bible, especially the New Testament, for stories of humanity. Tanner, according to an acquaintance, W. S. Scarborough, in 1902, was aware of the religious symbolism of Daniel for the African American community, an idea undoubtedly passed on by his father, a prominent bishop of the AME Church, who regularly preached and wrote on the subject. Tanner's humanism and his own religious experiences consistently complicated the racial identification of humanity in his biblical paintings, however. Human representation in *Daniel in the Lions' Den* and the various versions of *Flight Into Egypt* (1899, 1916, 1923), for example, lacks racial specificity. The physiognomic and phenotypical traits of racial identity are at best ambiguous in these illustrations. *The Resurrection of Lazarus* (1896) more clearly contrasts the skin tones of the onlookers and Jesus Christ, but here, too, Tanner is emphasizing multiracial heterogeneity, not racial homogeneity. Tanner's subsequent biblical paintings similarly refrain from consigning humanity to one racial typology and try instead to convey a universalism that accommodates the histories and interests of all types of people.

Tanner's biblical paintings were widely acclaimed for their aesthetic merit and thematic nobility. Among them, his acknowledged masterpieces include *The Annunciation*, which Tanner completed and the Pennsylvania Museum and School of Art purchased in 1899; *Nicodemus*

Henry Ossawa Tanner (1859–1937), *Self-Portrait*, c. 1910; pencil and Conté crayon on paper, 8½ by 8⅜ inches.
(© Smithsonian American Art Museum, Washington, D.C./Art Resource, N.Y.)

Visiting Jesus, created the following year and awarded the American Lippincott Prize; *Daniel in the Lions' Den*, which won silver medals at the Pan-American Exposition in Buffalo, New York, in May 1901, and three years later at the Louisiana Purchase Exposition in St. Louis; and *Two Disciples at the Tomb* (1906), which won the Chicago Art Institute's Harris Prize in summer 1906 for being "the most impressive and distinguished work of art of the season."

By 1908, Tanner also had earned the right to hold solo exhibits of his own paintings. Numbering between fifteen and thirty at a time, these exhibits took place at prestigious galleries mostly in the United States: New York's American Art Galleries in 1908, Chicago's Thurber Art Galleries in 1911 and 1913, New York's Knoedler's Gallery in 1913, Boston's Vose Galleries in 1921, the Association of Fine Arts (Des Moines) in 1922, and New York's Grand Central Art Galleries in 1924. During these decades—the 1890s and the early twentieth century—Tanner achieved other professional milestones. Most notably, in 1905 the Pennsylvania Academy selected him to judge its annual exhibitions. Three years later, the National Academy of Design elected him an associate member. In 1914, he became a member of the American Negro Academy in Washington, D.C. During World War I he served in the American Red Cross in France. It was

1161

not until near the end of his life that he received the recognition routinely given to his white peers. Finally, in 1927 the National Academy of Design designated him a full academician, and the European chapter of the American Artists Professional League inducted him as a member in 1930.

Despite these successes, however, Tanner could not escape the implications of his race. His frustration with this issue spilled over in his often-cited letter of 1914 to the Anglo-American poet, novelist, and journalist Eunice Tietjens. Tanner assailed an article she had sent him in which she stereotyped paintings by whites as "clean" and "objective" and paintings by blacks as "mystical" and "subjective"—qualities that she thought he would appreciate in association with his work. He was also bothered by certain African American intellectuals and critics who expressed dismay with his shift to biblical images at the expense of progressively nuanced, sophisticated, and uplifting images of the African diaspora.

In spite of such negative commentary, Tanner remained prolific. By the end of his life, Tanner had produced more than one hundred major paintings and innumerable sketches. Only when his wife died after twenty-six years of marriage did Tanner's productivity decline. A little less than one month from his seventy-eighth birthday, Henry Ossawa Tanner died in Paris.

Biography

Henry Ossawa Tanner was born on 21 June 1859 in Pittsburgh, Pennsylvania, to Sarah (Miller) Tanner and Benjamin Tucker Tanner. His formal training in visual art began in December 1879 at the Pennsylvania Academy of the Fine Arts, Philadelphia. He enrolled in the Académie Julien in 1891 and returned to Philadelphia in August 1893. Tanner married Jessie Macauley Olssen 14 December 1899; they had a son, Jesse Ossawa Tanner, on 25 September 1903. Tanner's *The Annunciation* (1899) was purchased by the Pennsylvania Museum and School of Art in 1899. *Nicodemus Visiting Jesus* (1900) was awarded the American Lippincott Prize in 1900. *Daniel in the Lions' Den* (1895) won a silver medal at the Pan-American Exposition in Buffalo, New York (1901), and a silver medal at the Louisiana Purchase Exposition in St. Louis (1904). *Two Disciples at the Tomb* (1906) won the Chicago Art Institute's Harris Prize in 1906. Tanner was a judge for the Pennsylvania Academy in 1905; an associate member of the National Academy of Design

in 1908; a member of the American Negro Academy in Washington, D.C., in 1914; a full academician in the National Academy of Design in 1927; and a member of the European chapter of the American Artists Professional League in 1930. He served in the American Red Cross during World War I. Henry Ossawa Tanner died 25 May 1937 in Paris.

GENE JARRETT

See also Artists; Europe and the Harlem Renaissance: 4—Paris

Selected Paintings

Aix-en-Provence. 1894.
The Annunciation. 1899.
The Bagpipe Lesson. 1892–1893.
The Banjo Lesson. 1893.
Bois d'Amour. 1891.
Daniel in the Lions' Den. 1895.
Flight Into Egypt. 1899, 1916, 1923.
Lion Licking Its Paw (After Dinner). 1886.
Mountain Landscape, Highlands, North Carolina (Cumberland Foothills). c. 1889.
Nicodemus Visiting Jesus. 1900.
"Pomp" at the Zoo. c. 1880.
Sand Dunes at Sunset, Atlantic City. c. 1886.
The Resurrection of Lazarus. 1896.
Seascape, Seascape-Jetty, Ship in a Storm. c. 1876–1879.
The Thankful Poor. 1894.
Two Disciples at the Tomb. 1906.
Waiting for the Lord. 1882.
The Young Sabot Maker. 1895.

Further Reading

Boime, Albert. "Henry Ossawa Tanner's Subversion of Genre." *Art Bulletin*, 75(3), September 1993, pp. 415–442.

Harper, Jennifer J. "The Early Religious Paintings of Henry Ossawa Tanner: A Study of the Influences of Church, Family, and Era." *American Art*, 6(4), Fall 1992, pp. 69–85.

Locke, Alain. "Henry Ossawa Tanner, 1859–1937." In *Memorial Exhibition of Paintings by Henry O. Tanner*. Philadelphia, Pa.: n.p., 1945.

———. "The Legacy of the Ancestral Arts." In *The New Negro*, ed. Alain Locke. New York: Simon and Schuster, 1997, pp. 254–267. (Originally published 1925.)

—. *Henry Ossawa Tanner: Catalogue.* Philadelphia, Pa., and New York: Philadelphia Museum of Art and Rizzoli International, 1991. (1st trade ed.)

Matthews, Marcia M. *Henry Ossawa Tanner: American Artist.* Chicago, Ill.: University of Chicago Press, 1969, pp. xi–xiv.

Tenderloin

New York City's infamous Tenderloin district was a key location of nineteenth-century African American settlement. The neighborhood was also noted for vice and corruption. A city policeman, Alexander "Clubber" Williams, is said to have given the area its curious name. When speaking with a newspaper reporter after being transferred to the district (already known as "Satan's Circus") in 1876, Williams reportedly stated, "All my life I have never had anything but chuck steak. Now I'm gonna get me some tenderloin." Numerous saloons, brothels, gambling joints, and dance halls led to calls for neighborhood reform.

Elsroad (1995) identifies the Tenderloin as being bounded to the North by Forty-second Street, to the east by Fifth Avenue, to the South by Twenty-fourth Street, and to the west by Seventh Avenue. By 1860 many of the city's black residents lived on the west side of Manhattan between Tenth and Thirtieth streets, and gradually relocated north. New York's nonwhite population moved into the neighborhood from the diverse Five Points district, east of today's Foley Square in downtown Manhattan. By 1890, New York City's African American community lived primarily between Twentieth and Fifty-third Streets.

Changes in infrastructure and new opportunities spurred perpetual migration to Harlem, away from the Tenderloin. In 1873, New York City annexed Harlem, and new elevated rail service was announced. Slow waves of real estate speculation inflated market values and led to commercial and residential construction. Companies like Philip A. Payton's Afro-American Realty offered housing units to interested renters during an era when housing covenants kept blacks out of many apartment buildings throughout the city. Neighborhood stability and safety also stimulated the move to Harlem. On 15 August 1900, turbulent race rioting had erupted in the Tenderloin when hundreds of angry white New Yorkers, attending a wake for a slain police officer, Robert Thorpe, created havoc in the streets. Small gangs attacked black residents. Thorpe had been fatally stabbed by an African American,

Arthur Harris, allegedly for having made unwelcome advances to Harris's wife, May Enoch, at the corner of Forty-first Street and Eighth Avenue. Scores of white policemen are reported to have taken part in the riots, doing virtually nothing to restrain the perpetrators. Houses were sacked and burned, and places that employed blacks were raided.

Residents of the Tenderloin were further displaced during the construction of Pennsylvania Station (1906–1910), increasing the intensity of the migration to Harlem. Business, religious, educational, and cultural institutions followed. The United Colored Democracy moved uptown in 1915, and T. Thomas Fortune's newspaper *New York Age* profiled Harlem as a vibrant, progressive neighborhood during the first decade of the twentieth century. The National Urban League conservatively estimated the black population in New York City to be 183,428 in 1923. Two-thirds of that population resided in Harlem, demonstrating how the migration from the Tenderloin had altered New York.

The former Tenderloin district now includes the site of the Empire State Building, the garment district, and Herald Square. The area is no longer known as the Tenderloin.

R. Jake Sudderth

See also Afro-American Realty Company; New York Age; United Colored Democracy

Further Reading

Elsroad, Linda. "Tenderloin." In *The Encyclopedia of New York City*, ed. Kenneth T. Jackson. New Haven, Conn.: Yale University Press, 1995.

Johnson, James Weldon. *Along This Way: The Autobiography of James Weldon Johnson.* New York: Viking, 1961.

Lewis, David Levering. *When Harlem Was in Vogue.* New York: Oxford University Press, 1989.

Locke, Alain, ed. *The New Negro: An Interpretation.* New York: Albert and Charles Boni, 1925.

McKay, Claude. *Harlem: Negro Metropolis.* New York: Harcourt Brace Jovanovich, 1968.

Meier, August. *Negro Thought in America, 1880–1915.* Ann Arbor: University of Michigan Press, 1966.

Osofsky, Gilbert. *Harlem: The Making of a Ghetto—Negro New York, 1890–1930.* New York: Harper and Row, 1966.

Scheiner, Seth M. *Negro Mecca: A History of the Negro in New York City, 1865–1920.* New York: New York University Press, 1965.

Theater

Theater in the United States during the Harlem Renaissance was marked by an incredible self-conscious effort to define a black aesthetic in light of contemporaneous political, social, and economic issues. Heated debates abounded about the definition of black theater. Styles emerged only to become devastating stereotypes. Segregation maintained divisiveness in Harlem's theater scene. Still, African American theater artists attempted to cast off the old stereotypes of the minstrel tradition in order to create a more serious and accurate portrayal of black life. There were many different types of artists, audiences, tastes, issues, and implications. A movement swept across not just the area around 125th Street in Manhattan but major cities all over the country. The major issues concerning theater during this time include musical comedies, serious drama, folk drama, the debate over art versus propaganda, the Negro "little theater" movement, and theater in higher education.

Langston Hughes claimed that the black renaissance began with theater: the black musicals *Shuffle Along* and *Runnin' Wild*, jazz rhythms, and the Charleston. In theaters during the Harlem Renaissance, audience members saw Louis Armstrong, Josephine Baker, Butterbeans and Susie, Duke Ellington, Roland Hayes, Jackie Mabley, Rose McClendon, Florence Mills, Ma Rainey, Paul Robeson, Bessie Smith, Fats Waller, Ethel Waters, and many others. White New Yorkers came to

James Van Der Zee (1886–1983), *Dress Rehearsal I*, 1928, sepia tone print, 8 by 9¾ inches. (Collection Fred Jones Jr., Museum of Art, University of Oklahoma, Norman; Gift of the Richard and Ellen Sandor Family. Collection in honor of Molly Shi Boren, 1999.)

Harlem for the music and the shows, and black New Yorkers capitalized on the opportunity.

According to Alain Locke and James Weldon Johnson, the nation was poised to reevaluate African Americans, and nothing would do more to change attitudes and raise the status of African Americans than the proof of intellectual parity with Caucasians in literature and art. In other words, culture was the key. *The New Negro*, a book-length anthology of essays and creative writing edited by Alain Locke, highlights some of the major issues of the day regarding the arts. Although Locke's omissions (e.g., blues, Marcus Garvey, and radical socialism) are problematic, what he does include are important representations. Locke and others believed that it was through the arts that African Americans would progress socially and politically. Locke argued for fewer rhetorical and overtly race-conscious motives in creating the art of the Harlem Renaissance. Only then, according to Locke, would African American artists be able to speak as individuals and not as representatives of the entire race.

African Americans made significant contributions to the American musical. Singers, writers, and dancers in black musical comedy were influenced by variety acts, minstrelsy, black vaudeville, jubilee singers, dance contests, traveling road shows, cabaret acts at clubs like the Cotton Club and Connie's Inn, and social dancing and music of southern "jook" joints and northern clubs like the Savoy. In these venues, artists shook off the vestiges of minstrelsy and variety, combined the jazz beat and frenetic dance steps with a skeletal plot to create a show, and created less stereotypical black characters. Musical theater helped boost the careers of Louis Armstrong, Josephine Baker, Eubie Blake, Aubrey Lyles, Flournoy Miller, Florence Mills, Noble Sissle, Fats Waller, Bert Williams, Ethel Waters, and many more.

The Cotton Club was a Jim Crow club "for gangsters and monied whites," according to Langston Hughes. Black Harlemites tended to resent the influx of whites into Harlem at night, drawn by cabarets such as the Cotton Club. Tension often existed over the issue of to whom the shows catered, a white audience or a black audience. "Nigger heaven" existed so that black patrons could watch Broadway shows from a segregated balcony. Although black audiences could not go downtown and sit among white audience members in Broadway theaters, the shows that came out of Harlem's cabarets and moved to Broadway did much to combat segregation in the theater. When the shows became commercial successes downtown, the spirit of theater in the Harlem Renaissance changed. It became a matter of pleasing the tourist. Stages became bigger, and routines became flashier.

In 1898, Bob Cole, one of the major contributors to black musical theater, issued the "Colored Actors' Declaration of Independence of 1898." This was a call to black performers to write and produce shows for a black audience. Cole's ideas were later taken up by W. E. B Du Bois, who called for an African American theater "by us, for us, near us, and about us." Also in 1898, Bob Cole and his partners Billy Johnson and Stella Wiley presented *A Trip to Coontown*, the first musical written, directed, and performed by black artists.

In 1899, two brothers, John Rosamond Johnson and James Weldon Johnson, moved to New York from Florida with a letter of introduction and the dream of presenting an original operetta on Broadway. They talked to a few producers and finally met Oscar Hammerstein, who opened doors for them and introduced them to many leading figures in musical theater, both black and white. Although "coon songs" (degrading minstrel songs) were the rage, the Johnson brothers refused to write them and composed instead songs that avoided popular stereotypes and sought to elevate the image of African Americans. Their songs grew in popularity, and their achievements helped promote the argument that black artists were equal to white artists. Although white critics complained that the brothers and their collaborator, Bob Cole, were too imitative of white works and should stick to minstrelsy, the Johnson brothers succeeded in challenging assumptions about African Americans in the theater.

Bert Williams, Ada Overton Walker, and George Walker were also important figures in early black musical theater. George and Ada Overton Walker helped increase the popularity of the cakewalk in Harlem, and the comedy team of Bert Williams and George Walker was very popular. These three people also worked to legitimize the role of the black performer. They made moves that we might tend to think of as unfortunate but might actually be recognized as small steps forward. For example, they billed themselves as "real coons" (as opposed to the grotesque and devastating images created by white minstrels). Although we would object to the use of the term "coon," we should applaud the trio for attempting to add dignity to the roles afforded them. The light-skinned, highly trained Bert Williams had to black-up, stoop over, speak with a minstrel accent, and become the slow dim-witted straight man to George Walker's dandy.

Williams was the first black man to star with whites in a large-scale vaudeville sketch, the first to star in the Ziegfeld Follies, and the first to join Actors' Equity. Although classically trained, Williams worked in blackface throughout his entire career, because his producers and fans would accept nothing else.

As far back as 1903, Williams, Walker, and Walker began exploring back-to-Africa themes with *In Dahomey*, the first all-black show to play a major Broadway theater.

Although black musical comedies were in decline for a number of years in the 1910s, they soared in popularity again in the 1920s. The epitome of the genre was *Shuffle Along,* a show created in 1921 about a corrupt mayoral race in the Southern city of Jimtown. The show was a move away from melodramatic sentimentality, but it retained some of the vestiges of the minstrel and vaudeville stages. *Shuffle Along* was an unexpected success that paved the way for many black musicals during the 1920s. It was the model for subsequent black musical theater. Other important shows of this time include *The Chocolate Dandies*, *Hot Chocolates*, *Blackbirds* (with several revivals), *Dixie to Broadway*, *Keep Shufflin'*, *Clorindy*, and *Runnin' Wild*.

With the stock market crash in 1929 and the growing popularity of talkies, many people thought black musical theater would not last, but the genre remained vibrant for a long time. More black musicals and revues appeared in the early 1930s than at any time in the 1920s. This was mostly because they were relatively cheap to produce; certainly, they were cheaper than white shows. Eventually, however, the Depression hit black theaters as well. *Porgy and Bess* marked the end of an era. It is, ironically, remembered by some as one of the best black musicals of the early twentieth century, even though George Gershwin ran the show and whites did all the offstage work. Many black critics found it inauthentic, and many white critics decried the idea of a black folk opera.

Although black musical comedies were an important part of the Harlem Renaissance, many theater people thought they needed to expand from the limited opportunities available to black performers. In June 1925, in an article in *Opportunity*, Willis Richardson, the first serious black writer to have his work performed on Broadway, stated, "One of the first questions every person who is seriously interested in the drama asks is why melodrama, musical comedies and mere shows so far outnumber what [George Bernard] Shaw calls higher dramas."

According to Montgomery T. Gregory, a professor at Howard University, although "serious Negro drama" was in its infancy, it was the field in which black performers had to succeed in order to win real recognition for their contributions to American drama. He considered the ideal national Negro theater one in which the black playwright, musician, actor, dancer, and artist collaborated to create a drama that would earn the respect and admiration of the United States. This must come from African Americans themselves, Gregory argued; only then would the nation get authentic stories. The rhetoric of authenticity was vital. For too long blacks had been inauthentically represented by whites. In April 1924, an article in *Opportunity* stated: "Up to eight or nine years ago it is doubtful if in the entire range of the American drama there was to be found a single authentic Negro character." Buffoonery, parody, and the grotesque prevailed. Interestingly, the question of whether it is ever possible to represent a race authentically was never debated. Rather, it was assumed that, if given the opportunity, black playwrights and serious performers would do a better job at creating serious authentic works about black life than white artists. Paul Robeson claimed, "I do feel there is a great future on the serious dramatic stage. Directions and training will do much to guide any natural ability one may possess." So, while black musical comedies flourished, other efforts were in place. The hope for serious portrayals of black characters in what was deemed "higher" art was more than just a desire for better roles. It was inextricably linked to the desire for all African Americans at this time to be taken seriously and admired. It indicated an elevation to the respectable, honorable echelons of society. It helped disprove the myth of black inferiority. Gregory claimed that "until we are willing to have not the exceptional but the average life of the Negro honestly and impartially reproduced in fiction and drama, we might as well wallow in crude and vulgar variety shows or in sickening melodramas where the black man is of course the shining example of all the virtues. Truth is Beauty. Let us have more of it!"

One battle that needed to be fought was against the myth of natural propensity. Proponents of this myth argued that blacks had a natural ability for singing and dancing in the jazz style of the musical comedies, while whites were better at serious drama. Value judgments about the worth of the types of theater surfaced, and a hierarchy from "high" down to "low" developed in which black musical comedies were on a low rung and serious dramas on a high one. As an example of this myth of natural propensity, James Reese Europe's band had won over French, Belgian, and British audiences, who were fascinated by the "talking" trumpet. French musicians could not repeat the sound, so they inspected the instrument for a hidden valve or chamber. When they could not find one, they concluded that the ability was a black anomaly. This theme resurfaces throughout the era as the notion that blacks' achievements in the arts were due not to skill, training, or talent but rather to some natural racial tendencies. This essentialist argument resulted in the simultaneous creation of a black aesthetic and a system that limited black performers to the genre of musical comedy. Reviewers in black newspapers also fell into the rhetorical trap of racial natural proclivity. One review of a young vaudevillian claimed, "Part of [his success] was training, but most of it was the natural expression of his racial instinct for rhythm, music and gesture. His play, or his acting, was so natural that it was hard to distinguish between them." The review goes on to describe the backstage scene: "Even off stage they [the performers] are minstrels, fun-making actors. A white minstrel off stage would have sat upon a trunk, and glumly cursed the heat." Rowena Woodham Jelliffe discussed the black performer's assets in 1928 and claimed that they were "a peculiar quality of motorness," an "extraordinary body expressiveness," a "sense of rhythm, manifest in his movement and his diction alike, and his never failing vitality."

By April 1923, the All American Theater Association, a national integrated organization, articulated a desire to support black contributions to serious drama, believing that African Americans had as much to contribute to the genre as to musical comedy. They vowed to help organize and support theater for black artists in Chicago's South Side, with hopes of national expansion and to bring more well-known novelists, poets, dramatists, and artists before audiences in Chicago.

Dismissing notions that they were being too "ambitious," black actors, writers, and critics set out to uplift black theater. One strategy used to promote the development of high-quality, authentic portrayals of black life surfaced in the form of contests sponsored by black periodicals. Du Bois, who had founded and became editor of the NAACP's magazine *The Crisis* with Jessie Redmon Faucet, initiated a drama committee in the NAACP to provide a method of using the stage to effect social change. He launched a literary contest, cosponsored by *Opportunity* magazine, that awarded cash prizes and ceremonies for the best writers of short stories, essays, poetry, and one-act plays.

Charles S. Johnson (editor of *Opportunity*) stated that the importance of *The Crisis* and *Opportunity* was that they provided an outlet for young black artists and scholars who were denied a forum elsewhere. They also provided recognition and monetary compensation, both of which contributed to the belief in the endeavor as worthwhile. *Opportunity* was more interested in arts and culture than *The Crisis*, whose focus was more sociopolitical. *Opportunity*'s contests and dinners were very successful; although there were only three such contests, they were very influential in defining the era. Writers contributing to the magazine found publishers, and the larger mainstream press started paying attention. Although playwriting was an important component in these contests, the efforts rarely resulted in major productions. The success of these efforts, in terms of playwriting, was called into question in 1927 when the editors of *Opportunity* lamented the fact that the contributions to the drama part of the contests lagged behind the other genres in quality. They thought the majority of contributions were limited to low comedy and propaganda. They perceived a belief, on the part of playwrights, that audiences wanted to see only stereotypes and not authentic characters. Black playwrights, according to the editors, were just beginning to see the possibilities. The entries that did win the contests tended to reject the stereotypes. In 1930, Randolph Edmonds echoed these sentiments when he claimed that the slow progress in drama was puzzling, especially when compared with poetry, music, the novel, and essays. He went so far as to claim that "the so-called 'Negro Renaissance' has been almost a total failure in so far as the development of the drama is concerned."

Followers of Marcus Garvey also advocated variety and dignity in the portrayal of African Americans onstage. The United Negro Improvement Association (UNIA) had a dramatic club and was interested in plays that educated, entertained, and promoted morality and racial equality. UNIA called for black actors to reject demeaning roles.

The prevailing belief was that serious black drama must develop from the folk tradition of African American life. According to Gregory, "the highest cultural achievements have emanated from below— from the folkways of society." Professor Frederick H. Koch began an experiment in North Dakota and North Carolina in which his students wrote one-act plays based on the lives of black people in their respective parts of the country. The efforts to document black life in North Carolina resulted in the Carolina Players.

Most of the winning plays in the magazine contests, as well as other attempts to write serious black drama, depicted black folk life. Also known as "native dramas," these folk plays about the black experience are less well known than the black musical comedies but are no less important. Most of these plays were written by middle-class blacks (usually women), the folk themselves, and white playwrights.

Lorraine Hansberry, whose classic play *A Raisin in the Sun* premiered in 1959, is generally recognized as the first major black female playwright. Black women were writing plays long before that time, however, and black women are responsible for many of the early folk plays available. Interestingly, many women won the play contests. Black men often wrote about life in Harlem and other major cities, but black women embraced more diverse subject matter and wrote about both rural and urban life, although plays about rural life prevailed. The main characters in these dramas were usually women in decision-making roles. White characters were absent, partially because of the typical domestic setting, but the effect of racism was a dominant theme. The plays were both dramas and comedies and succeeded in presenting a more realistic and wider spectrum of the black experience than did the plays written by whites about blacks. Many of the folk plays were written from a female perspective. Lynching was an important common theme in these folk plays; other themes included the untrustworthiness of whites, hope in Christianity for salvation, and faith in the legal system. Most of these plays were set in the homes of poor, rural, southern black matriarchs who spent their time cooking, cleaning, sewing, and praying. The patriarchs were either lynched or worked hard to support the family. Whites were not to be trusted, faith in God was tested, and everyone hoped for a better life.

Still other themes of folk plays included poverty, education, superstition, and miscegenation. *Plumes* by Georgia Douglas Johnson won first prize in *Opportunity*'s contest of 1927. In this play, a mother of a dying girl must choose between spending money for a white doctor whom she mistrusts and saving the money to pay for a funeral with plumes on the horses. *A Sunday Morning in the South*, also by Johnson, is about the lynching of an innocent, promising black man for associating with a white woman. *Aftermath* by Mary P. Burrill is about a boy who returns from World War I only to discover that, while he was fighting for his country, his father has been lynched. *They That Sit in Darkness*, also by Burrill, concerns the devastating effects of keeping poor black women ignorant about birth control. The only songs in these plays were spirituals, and most of the characters had nothing to dance about. They were good people who were unjustly suffering yet maintained their pride and respectability. Other important folk playwrights of the era include Marieta Bonner, Alice Dunbar Nelson, Shirley Graham, Angelina Weld Grimké, Langston Hughes, Zora Neale Hurston, May Miller, Willis Richardson, Jean Toomer, and Lucy White.

Kathy Perkins speculates that one reason why so many contest winners and so many playwrights working with Locke and Gregory were women was that women had no positions of leadership in society. Plays provided an opportunity for their voices to be heard.

Although many of these plays were collected and anthologized by Carter G. Woodson, black folk dramas as represented by the folk themselves are less well known today because they were less supported by the middle and upper classes, who focused more on mainstream models. Theophilus Lewis, drama critic for *The Messenger*, went so far as to accuse the black middle class of ignoring the actual folk while celebrating plays written about them by others. Pageants and what we would now call community theater did not even have the small resources of the "little theater" groups (see the following discussion). Many of the plays were passed down orally and physically, and there were seldom single authors to take all the credit for creating the pieces. For these reasons and others, we do not know much about this aspect of theater during the Harlem Renaissance, and it is a topic ripe for further study.

A number of white playwrights were interested in writing serious drama featuring black characters. Ridgely Torrence was praised for his plays *Granny Maumee*, *The Rider of Dreams*, and *Simon the Cyrenian*, all of which provided better roles for black performers. Paul Green, who wrote *The No 'Count Boy*, *Granny Boling*, and *White Dresses*, received both criticism and praise for his depictions of aspects of black folk life. *The Green Pastures* by Marc Connelly was one of the most successful black folk plays of the era.

The most famous white playwright of black drama was Eugene O'Neill. Like Harriet Beecher Stowe with *Uncle Tom's Cabin*, O'Neill introduced sympathetic black characters to white audiences who might never have seen or read other examples of serious black drama. Also like Stowe, O'Neill received mixed reviews from African Americans who saw his portrayal

of black characters as stereotypical and inauthentic. One reviewer feared that O'Neill would be unsuccessful because African Americans would consider his work too propagandistic and white Americans would see it as a personal attack. Paul Robeson defended O'Neill by saying that he had met and talked to O'Neill, and "if ever there was a broad, liberal-minded man, he is one. He has had Negro friends and appreciated them for their true worth. He would be the last to cast any slur on the colored people." Though many have debated this characterization, we can say that *All God's Chillun Got Wings* and *The Emperor Jones* brought serious black drama to larger audiences and were catalysts for the career of Robeson, one of the most important black performers of the time. Jim Harris, the protagonist in *All God's Chillun Got Wings*, was a particularly sympathetic and positive portrayal. Gregory thought *The Emperor Jones* would "tower as a beacon-light of inspiration." He thought it marked the "breakwater plunge of Negro drama into the main stream of American drama." Eric D. Walrond, writing about *All God's Chillun Got Wings*, claimed that "no better study of the relations of whites and colored people in the United States has ever been projected on the American stage."

In 1928, the writer Eulalie Spence discussed the fact that a number of black performers existed but not many dramatists. White writers, she claimed, were providing most of the material for serious black actors. Some black actors shunned plays by white playwrights, but most were grateful for the vehicles. Spence claimed that the drama was twenty to thirty years behind the novel and short story in subject matter. People were still hesitant to deal with a wider range of topics—and there was also the fact that playwriting was not as respected as other art forms, and many of the plays were not even written to be performed but just to be read. Spence advised against propagandistic drama because she thought that whites were cold and unresponsive and African Americans were hurt and humiliated. "We go to the theater for entertainment, not to have old fires and hates rekindled. . . . Let him [the black dramatist] portray the life of his people, their foibles, if he will and their sorrows and ambition and defeats."

The degree to which folk plays should promote an overtly political agenda was hotly contested. The major players in the debate were W. E. B. Du Bois, Alain Locke, and Montgomery T. Gregory, among others. Du Bois called for total control of black theater by blacks and saw theater as a powerful political tool in the larger societal struggle. He thought that theater could serve the cause if plays were written as propaganda illustrating the ills of society and provided didactic solutions to race relations. This theater would be a means for communicating messages to the masses. The primary goal of this theater was to effect social change. In October 1926, in *The Crisis*, Du Bois stated that "all art is propaganda, and ever must be . . . for gaining the right of black folk to love and enjoy."

Locke and Gregory argued that the function of art was not propaganda and argued for the aesthetic enrichment of the community and individual. Locke thought that art used for propaganda assumed the inferiority of the group even while crying out against it. Rather, Locke said, art should be a means of self-expression, self-contained and therefore unsuitable as propaganda. He argued that folk plays should depict the black experience without focusing on oppression by laying blame and calling for change. The main goal was to entertain and educate without offending. Locke wanted drama "with no objective but to express beautifully and colorfully race folk life." Plays with "more of the emotional depth of pity and terror" would prove the worthiness of the race without being heavy-handed.

In an article in *Opportunity* in October 1924, the playwright Willis Richardson discussed the importance of theater as an educational tool. He claimed that the theater had the attention of more reasoning adults than any other institution besides the church. The intelligent patrons of the theater went precisely to be interested and have their ideas challenged. Lamenting the limits of the fool character, Richardson embraced the possibilities of the legitimate stage. He argued that black actors were just as capable as white actors and that audiences should demand the same quality of performance.

In an article in July 1928, reviewer Rowena Woodham Jelliffe claimed that "sociological considerations should be secondary. Nor should the theatre be considered a medium of propaganda. Undue concern about putting the best racial foot foremost should be forgot." These sentiments were part of her call to "escape the bonds of race consciousness."

One consequence of the attitude that drama should be used to promote the image of positive and authentic black folk life was the belief that no negative portrayals of black characters should exist. *The Emperor Jones* received this criticism because the main character was a craps-shooter and an escaped convict. Willis Richardson talked about an audience member at a production of his play *The Chip Woman's Fortune* who corrected the grammar of the performers and seemed scandalized when an actor took off his shoes. In 1925, Richardson stated: "Playwrights who have depicted unpleasant Negro characters, have gotten very little encouragement from the Negro group. In fact, they have been frowned upon."

An interesting twist in the debate over serious drama versus musical comedy occurred when Max Reinhardt, a prominent German director, exalted black musical comedy in 1924 for its potential to be a great example of modernism, expressionism, and uniquely American drama. In an interview with Charles S. Johnson and Alain Locke, Reinhardt expressed his interest in the genre, much to their initial chagrin. He claimed that musical comedies "are highly original in spite of obvious triteness and artistic in spite of superficial crudeness. To me they reveal new possibilities of technique in drama, and if I should ever try to do anything American, I should build it on these things." Johnson and Locke had hoped to discuss the possibilities of Negro art drama (that is, serious drama). Reading their expressions of dislike, Reinhardt further explained that he meant the genre not as it existed then but for what it would become. Pantomime, he thought, was at the root of dramatic expression, and black performers had that art as their "forte," their "special genius." Though they were relegated to trite comedy, Reinhardt saw masterful technique in "the voices, the expressive control of the whole body, the spontaneity of motion, the rhythm, the bright emotional color." Whether or not Reinhardt's words proved prophetic of an American or African American expressionism is debatable; however, his concluding remarks illustrate a major tenet of the ethos of the Harlem Renaissance: "Be original . . . develop the folk idiom."

The Negro "little theater" movement developed during this time to produce legitimate theater for black artists. In the autumn of 1920, six men and women formed a dramatic social club devoted to "high art" drama. This group became known as the Gilpin Players, after the famous actor Charles Gilpin. Their mission was to use the medium to present the important contributions of the race. Their first performance was in 1921, and by 1928 they had produced sixty-one plays. One of the main challenges the Gilpin Players faced was resisting the urge to cater to the audiences' initial desire for base comedy.

In 1923, Raymond O'Neill founded the Ethiopian Art Theater in Chicago, worked with the All American

Theater Association, developed awards for plays based on black life, and made his way to Broadway. He focused on adaptations of Oscar Wilde's *Salomé* and Shakespeare's *The Comedy of Errors* but was most successful with his production of Willis Richardson's *The Chip Woman's Fortune*. In a review of *Salomé*, Esther Fulks Scott quotes a wealthy patroness as saying, "This performance, so full of gifts of joy, humor and dramatic ability which the actors give and show to their audience should entirely banish all prejudice from the mind of anyone seeing it." Evelyn Preer, who played the title character, Laura Bowman, who played Herodias, and Sidney Kirkpatrick, who played Herod, all expressed their desire to help the race through their talents as serious dramatic performers. Bowman went so far as to assert that the "race problem" might be solved through artistic and cultural avenues.

To further encourage the development of drama written by blacks, Du Bois organized the Krigwa Players in 1926. Krigwa (originally Crigwa) was an acronym for the Crisis Guild of Writers and Artists. The company did not last long, but Du Bois was able to encourage the formation of other small theaters throughout the country.

More than a dozen theater groups existed during the Harlem Renaissance. Companies like the Lafayette Players and Lincoln Players performed works of quality regardless of race. Companies like the Rose McClendon Players and the Pioneer Drama Group wanted to show that blacks and whites were equal. Companies like Krigwa and the Negro People's Theater performed "respectable" black drama.

Theater was also significant in higher education at the time. Black colleges developed theater departments with the goals of creating original race plays. While Du Bois and Krigwa were promoting race or propaganda plays, Gregory, Locke, Marie Moore-Forrest, and others were promoting folk plays at Howard University in Washington, D.C. Gregory brought national attention to the Howard Players when he organized the Department of Dramatic Arts for the purpose of establishing the first National Negro Theater in the United States. It provided professional training in acting, playwriting, and production. Before this endeavor, practically no institution provided professional theatrical training for blacks, especially in playwriting. The African Grove Theater of the early nineteenth century was long defunct. Gregory's philosophy was that, in order for Negro drama to survive, it had to be exposed to the larger society. The institutions of higher education provided a valuable means to achieve that exposure.

Some thought the Harlem Renaissance would mean the end of oppression and that art would solve the "race problem." In reality, at least in terms of theater, it was a time of struggle and progress for a few.

Nadine George-Graves

See also Authors: 4—Playwrights; Blacks in Theater; Bonner, Marieta; Community Theater; Du Bois, W. E. B.; Gilpin, Charles; Grimké, Angelina Weld; Hurston, Zora Neale; Krigwa Players; Literature: 3—Drama; Little Theater Tournament; Locke, Alain; Musical Theater; Richardson, Willis; Shuffle Along; United Negro Improvement Association; Williams, Egbert Austin "Bert"; Woodson, Carter G.; *other specific individuals; specific theater groups; specific works*

Further Reading

Haskins, James. *Black Theater in America*. New York: Crowell, 1982.

Hatch, James V., ed. *Black Theater, U.S.A.: Forty-Five Plays by Black Americans, 1847–1974*. New York: Free Press, 1974.

Krasner, David. *A Beautiful Pageant: African American Theatre, Drama, and Performance in the Harlem Renaissance 1910–1927*. New York: Palgrave Macmillan, 2002.

Mitchell, Loften. *Black Drama: The Story of the American Negro in the Theater*. New York: Hawthorn, 1967.

———, ed. *Voices of the Black Theater*. Clifton, N.J.: White, 1975.

Peterson, Bernard L., Jr. *The African American Theatre Directory, 1816–1960: A Comprehensive Guide to Early Black Theatre Organizations, Companies, Theatres, and Performing Groups*. Westport, Conn.: Greenwood, 1997.

Woll, Allen. *Black Musical Theatre: From Coontown to Dreamgirls*. Baton Rouge: Louisiana State University Press, 1989. (Reprint, New York: Da Capo, 1991.)

Theater Owners' Booking Association

The Theater Owners' Booking Association (TOBA)—also known as the Toby Circuit or Toby Time—was founded "in order to correct the deplorable conditions then prevalent in the world of black theatre" (Burdex). It was a network of predominantly white-owned theaters in black areas of towns in the South and the Midwest, from Galveston to Jacksonville and from

Cleveland to Kansas City, where black entertainers performed before exclusively black audiences. Although some theaters did attempt to integrate some shows with a limited number of white attendees in the balcony, most of these efforts were undermined by local authorities. With black audiences, however, performers were able to broaden their material. Although many still wore blackface, the emphasis of their performances transcended the one-dimensional representations of black buffoonery that had been characteristic of minstrel shows. Now, jokes about racial injustice—which would have been taboo in other arenas—could dominate the show, depending on the demeanor of the audience during any given performance.

Because segregation made touring with white vaudeville companies impossible for most black entertainers, TOBA was one of the few ways for blacks to enter the profession. For entertainers working in an industry where only top stars considered their career prospects secure, TOBA allowed black artists to plan weeks in advance. Performers typically traveled in touring companies of approximately thirty-five members, performing two or three forty-five-minute shows per night. Because comedy was usually the most important part of the show, the shows with the best comics were generally the most successful.

The TOBA circuit was grueling, and the various difficulties performers faced led many to quip that TOBA actually stood for "Tough on Black Artists" or "Tough on Black Asses." There was always the possibility that a gig might be canceled less than a week in advance. Additionally, TOBA houses were usually small, having small stages, few props, and house bands with whom company members were usually unfamiliar. Adding to these difficulties was the fact that TOBA audiences were extremely demanding, not being afraid to boo performers offstage. Moreover, entertainers were forced to place themselves at the mercy of racist local authorities as they traveled to the next town after a show, potentially violating local curfew laws that applied only to blacks. As most performers had to provide their own transportation from town to town, most of their earnings were often spent before they were received, just to keep the show on the road. As a result of these conditions, many entertainers failed to last very long on the circuit, giving up on their dreams of stardom and opting for jobs that provided more security.

While comedy was the principal focus of TOBA, many limitations governed what black performers could and could not do onstage. Many white club owners were unabashed racists, so performers could not present overtly political material. Furthermore, while a few black comedians did adopt a monologue approach, most avoided this type of performance, which might be seen as a declaration of equality and might thus lead white bookers to shun an artist. Performers generally avoided making direct eye contact with the audience and would never just walk out onto the stage and begin a routine; instead, the comedians would come onstage talking to each other in such a way that the audience members felt empowered, as if they were listening in on a private conversation. Black performers' second-class status was reflected in this type of performance, even after white performers such as Jack Benny and Milton Berle adopted the monologue approach. In short, the bulk of comedy that appeared on stage was situational, such as Dewey "Pigmeat" Markham's routine "Here Come de Judge" (which was resurrected years later when Sammy Davis Jr. performed it on *Rowan and Martin's Laugh-In*) and the staged marital squabbles of two husband-and-wife teams: Stringbeans and Sweetie May, and Butterbeans and Susie.

Many of the performers on the TOBA circuit have never received proper credit for much of the material they may have originated. This is because the comedy routines were (and still are) more famous than their writers. (For example, Davis had to tell the producers of *Laugh-In* that "Here Come de Judge" was Markham's material, so that Markham could collect royalties.) Because jokes cannot be copyrighted, much of the best material from these shows has been pirated, with those who made routines famous receiving credit for them, regardless of who actually wrote them.

With skit comedy dominating most shows and with only so many performers in each troupe, band members, singers, and dancers would often perform roles as needed. For example, legendary film stars such as Eddie "Rochester" Anderson, Stepin Fetchit, and Bill "Bojangles" Robinson (who was perhaps most famous for dancing with Shirley Temple) all danced with TOBA before becoming recognizable as comedians in film, on radio, and on television. Other TOBA-affiliated artists included Count Basie, Jackie "Moms" Mabley, Bessie Smith, and Ethel Waters.

TOBA played a vital role in shaping African American comedy (as well as American comedy in general, as is evidenced by white performers such as Milton Berle pirating jokes from black comics at the Apollo), but it has not received its fair share of coverage in academic or nonacademic media. Although Burdex has developed an excellent annotated bibliography of the coverage of TOBA in the *Pittsburgh Courier* and the *Chicago Defender* from 1921 to 1930, most information about TOBA remains anecdotal. Except for the work of Hill (1996), Stearns and Stearns (1966, 1968), and Watkins (1999), there has been little rigorous cultural criticism. Nor have critics been able to come to a consensus regarding TOBA's history. For example, Watkins says that TOBA was founded in 1907 by F. A. Barrasso, an Italian businessman in Memphis; Hill says that TOBA was actually founded two years later by Barrasso's brother, A. Barrasso, because F. A. Barasso had been so financially successful as a proprietor of black theaters. In contrast, Burdex says that TOBA was founded in 1921, when a feud with the Southern Consolidated circuit ended with TOBA's absorbing it. The one point critics have agreed on is that TOBA was a casualty of the Great Depression; in its wake, the Apollo Theater emerged as the most desirable place for black entertainers to perform.

MICHAEL MIKLOS

See also Apollo Theater; Armstrong, Louis; Baker, Josephine; Ellington, Duke; Fetchit, Stepin; Hayes, Roland; Johnson, James Weldon; Locke, Alain; McClendon, Rose; Mills, Florence; Rainey, Ma; Robinson, Bill "Bojangles"; Smith, Bessie; Waller, Thomas "Fats"; Waters, Ethel; Williams, Egbert Austin "Bert"

Further Reading

Burdex, Monica, "The Theater Owners' Booking Association (TOBA): An Annotated Bibliographical Listing from the *Chicago Defender* and the *Pittsburgh Courier* Weekly Newspapers, 1921–1931." (TOBA Web site.)

Foxx, Redd, and Norma Miller. *The Redd Foxx Encyclopedia of Black Humor.* Pasadena: Ward Ritchie, 1977.

Haskins, James. *Black Theater in America.* New York: Crowell, 1982.

Hill, Anthony D. "Improving Conditions on the TOBA Black Vaudeville Circuit." In *Pages from the Harlem Renaissance: A Chronicle of Performance.* New York: Peter Lang, 1996, p. 65.

Kellner, Bruce, ed. *The Harlem Renaissance: A Historical Dictionary for the Era.* Westport, Conn.: Greenwood, 1984.

Stearns, Marshall, and Jean Stearns. "Frontiers of Humor: American Vernacular Dance." *Southern Folklore Quarterly*, 30, 1966.

———. *Jazz Dance: The Story of American Vernacular Dance.* New York: Macmillan, 1968.

Watkins, Mel. "The Theatre Owners Booking Association and the Apollo Theatre: Changing the Joke and Slipping the Yoke." In *On the Real Side: A History of African American Literature from Slavery to Chris Rock.* New York, 1999.

Their Eyes Were Watching God

Zora Neale Hurston wrote her novel *Their Eyes Were Watching God* (1937) while completing anthropological research in Haiti. The novel follows a circular pattern, opening with the protagonist Janie's return to Eatonville after the end of her adventures.

Janie tells the story of her upbringing by her grandmother, Nanny. Nanny raises Janie when her mother is unable to do so after being raped by the local schoolteacher. Nanny dreams of bettering Janie's life, so she has Janie marry, at age sixteen, the elderly Logan Killicks, who owns sixty acres of land. After Nanny's death, Janie becomes restless and leaves Logan for Joe Starks, a Georgian who is heading to Florida. Joe dreams of a town populated by and run by black people. He builds up the town, buying 200 acres of land, opening a store and post office, buying a street lamp for the town, and becoming mayor. Joe's dream of making Janie into a lady—the mayor's wife—isolates her from the community. Joe makes her work in the store and then routinely ridicules her in public. After twenty years, Joe becomes increasingly ill, and Janie uses his illness as an opportunity to publicly challenge his domination over her. This challenge to his authority leads to his death, giving Janie an opportunity to rediscover her childhood self. Janie then meets the incarnation of her dreams in Tea Cake, a blues musician. Janie thinks "he could be a bee to a blossom—a pear tree blossom in the spring. He seemed to be crushing scent out of the world with his footsteps." Janie marries Tea Cake and accompanies him to the Florida Everglades. Their idyllic life comes to a violent end with a hurricane—the Everglades are flooded, and Tea Cake is bitten by a rabid dog. In his delirium, Tea Cake threatens Janie, and she shoots him in order to survive.

In a very influential review in *New Masses*, Richard Wright (1937) criticized *Their Eyes Were Watching God* for having "no theme, no message, no thought." The novel was out of print until a revival of interest in Hurston began in the late 1970s. In 1977, Robert Hemenway wrote *Zora Neale Hurston: A Literary Biography*, the first serious treatment of her life and work. Alice Walker wrote the essays "Looking for Zora" and "Zora Neale Hurston: A Cautionary Tale and a Partisan View" and edited the *Hurston Reader*. Since her rediscovery, Hurston has become a canonical figure in American literature, widely taught in undergraduate courses across disciplines throughout the country.

Since the initial celebration of Hurston's work, a number of questions have arisen about the novel's heroine and its style of narration. Some recent critical essays on *Their Eyes Were Watching God* focus on voice. An especially influential examination of the novel has been Gates's discussion (1988) of free indirect discourse, which strives to account for shifts between an omniscient narrator and Janie's voice, and the merging of the two at different times in the novel. The narrator's voice becomes indistinguishable from the character's voice in the following passage: "The spirit of the marriage left the bedroom and took to living in the parlor. It was there to shake hands whenever company came to visit, but it never went back inside the bedroom again." Awkward (1988) has questions about whether Janie achieves a voice and, if so, whether that voice is based on visual rather than auditory signs. He traces his doubts to the language describing the pear tree: "It had called her to come and gaze on a mystery. . . . It was like a flute song forgotten in another existence and remembered again. . . . This singing she heard had nothing to do with her ears. The rose of the world was breathing out smell." He also questions the desirability of Janie's relationship with Tea Cake, a relationship involving physical abuse.

Critics have raised a variety of questions about the novel, questions that attest to its continued importance and interpretive richness. Carby's discussions (1988, 1990) of the folk in the novel have fueled debates about Hurston's essentialist and ahistorical approach to black culture. Carby asserts that Hurston provides images of unchanging black people who exist without any relationship to historical events. Her work on blues women has also encouraged a number of articles about the importance of blues in Hurston's work. For example, Wall (1995) has a chapter on Hurston's "traveling blues." Hill (1996) situates Hurston's fiction relative to her drama, which is rarely examined. In this regard, Hill is part of a growing group of critics who have examined Hurston's other writings, which include ethnographies, short stories, essays, and dramas, as well as her own reviews and criticism. Lamothe (2000) brings Hurston's anthropological work to bear on the novel by examining Hurston's use of vodou (voodoo)

imagery in the latter. Lamothe interprets the gate in terms of the deity Legba, who is the keeper of the crossroads. Janie "searched as much of the world as she could from the top of the front steps and then went on down to the front gate and leaned over to gaze up and down the road. Looking, waiting, breathing short with impatience. Waiting for the world to be made." Lowe (1994) examines Hurston's comedy. In contrast to Wright, who described Hurston's humor as "the minstrel technique that makes the 'white folks' laugh," Lowe describes it as both cosmic and comic. Such comedy addresses questions of ethnic humor, which has traditionally been confused with ethnic stereotypes.

KIMBERLY J. BANKS

See also Hurston, Zora Neale; Wright, Richard

Further Reading

Awkward, Michael. "'The Inaudible Voice of It All': Silence, Voice, and Action in *Their Eyes Were Watching God*." In *Black Feminist Criticism and Critical Theory*, ed. Joe Weixlmann and Houston Baker Jr. Greenwood, Fla.: Penkevill, 1988.

Batker, Carol. "'Love Me Like I Like to Be': The Sexual Politics of Hurston's *Their Eyes Were Watching God*, the Classic Blues, and the Black Women's Club Movement." *African American Review*, 32(2), 1998, pp. 199–213.

Carby, Hazel. "'It Jus Be's Dat Way Sometime': The Sexual Politics of Women's Blues." In *Gender and Discourse: The Power of Talk*, ed. Alexandra Dundas Todd and Sue Fisher. Norwood, N.J.: Ablex, 1988.

———. "The Politics of Fiction, Anthropology, and the Folk: Zora Neale Hurston." In *New Essays on Their Eyes Were Watching God*, ed. Michael Awkward. New York: Cambridge University Press, 1990.

Gates, Henry Louis, Jr. *The Signifying Monkey: A Theory of African-American Literary Criticism*. New York: Oxford University Press, 1988.

Gates, Henry Louis, Jr., and K. Anthony Appiah, eds. *Zora Neale Hurston: Critical Perspectives Past and Present*. New York: Amistad, 1993.

Hemenway, Robert E. *Zora Neale Hurston: A Literary Biography*. Chicago: University of Illinois Press, 1977.

Hill, Lynda Marion. *Social Rituals and the Verbal Art of Zora Neale Hurston*. Washington, D.C.: Howard University Press, 1996.

Lamothe, Daphne. "Vodou Imagery, African American Tradition, and Cultural Transformation in Zora Neale

Hurston's Their Eyes Were Watching God." In *Zora Neale Hurston's Their Eyes Were Watching God: A Casebook*. New York: Oxford University Press, 2000.

Lowe, John. *Jump at the Sun: Zora Neale Hurston's Cosmic Comedy*. Chicago: University of Illinois Press, 1994.

Walker, Alice. *In Search of Our Mothers' Gardens*. New York: Harcourt Brace Jovanovich, 1984.

Wall, Cheryl. *Women of the Harlem Renaissance*. Bloomington: Indiana University Press, 1995.

Wright, Richard. "Review of *Their Eyes Were Watching God*." *New Masses*, 5 October 1937.

There Is Confusion

Jessie Redmon Fauset's *There Is Confusion* (1924) holds the honor of being the first novel published during the Harlem Renaissance. In his review for *Opportunity*, Montgomery T. Gregory mistakenly heralded it as the first novel by a "Negro" woman, comparing Fauset to Phillis Wheatley, whose poetry was the first volume of creative literature published by a black American. Although mistaken, the comparison proved apt in that, like Wheatley's work, Fauset's novel has for many years been dismissed or deplored by black critics and ignored by whites, largely owing to its perceived formal and thematic inability to stand as a representative "black" text.

There Is Confusion interweaves the narratives of three primary characters: Joanna Marshall, who is determined above all else to be a "great" dancer, despite—and, indeed, because of—the overwhelming racial discrimination she faces; Peter Bye, whose inherited "shiftlessness" is countered by a desire to fulfill his beloved Joanna's expectation that he become a "famous" surgeon; and Maggie Ellersley, who supports herself and her mother through her cosmetology business, while longing to marry into the middle-class lifestyle and status the others enjoy. Fauset contextualizes their stories with a generous genealogical background and a vast supporting cast. The novel traces the impact of race, class, and gender oppression on its characters. Ultimately, Joanna sacrifices her struggling stage career for the joys of marriage to Dr. Bye (who eventually is successful), and Maggie discovers, after divorcing one husband and surviving a second, that she is a businesswoman capable of providing financial security and decency for herself.

Initial praise from critics like Gregory and Alain Locke (who called it the "novel that the Negro intelligentsia have been clamoring for") centered on Fauset's portrayal of ambitious, educated, middle-class blacks, which was greeted as a welcome change from the negative stereotypes that appeared in the white literature of the day. *There Is Confusion* emerged and remained in the shadow of work by younger writers seen as more modern and aesthetically successful, however; as representations of "blackness" (as opposed to emphasis on the commonalities between African Americans and whites) were increasingly valued, Fauset's writing became marginalized. African American literary critics of the mid-twentieth century (predominantly black men, e.g., Bone, Brown, and Gayle) dismissed and even ridiculed *There Is Confusion*, calling Fauset's work "sophomoric, trivial, and dull" and Fauset herself a "sentimental . . . apologist" for the "Negro middle class." Only in the latter part of the century did the novel begun to receive serious critical attention, primarily as a result of black feminist scholarship by critics like McDowell (1985) and Wall (1995), who have reevaluated Fauset's writing in terms of its critique of oppressive gender norms in conjunction with racism.

Most critics, sympathetic or not, have found the form and structure of the novel problematic. From suggestions that its title too aptly describes its sprawling narrative, to arguments that its marriage plot is unfortunately conventional and necessitates a forced, unrealistic ending, *There Is Confusion* is typically deemed a flawed novel reflecting Fauset's limited abilities, her ideological baggage, or the social standards constraining her as a single black woman. Relatively recent criticism (e.g., by Kuenz, McCoy, and Miller), however, has begun to challenge this assessment, arguing that Fauset's sometimes grating stylistic choices are deliberate; they are a compelling means of representing the dilemmas facing her black heroines.

EVIE SHOCKLEY

See also Civic Club Dinner, 1924; Fauset, Jessie Redmon; Literary Criticism and the Harlem Renaissance; Literature: 4—Fiction; Liveright, Horace

Further Reading

Bone, Robert. *The Negro Novel in America*. New Haven, Conn.: Yale University Press, 1958. (See also rev. ed., 1965.)

Brown, Sterling. *The Negro in American Fiction*. New York: Atheneum, 1969. (Originally published 1937. Excerpted in *Remembering the Harlem Renaissance*, ed. Cary D. Wintz. New York: Garland, 1996.)

Davis, Thadious M. Foreword. In *There Is Confusion*, by Jessie Redmon Fauset. Boston, Mass.: Northeastern University Press, 1989.

Du Bois, W. E. B., and Alain Locke. "The Younger Literary Movement." *Crisis*, 27, February 1924. (Reprinted in *The Emergence of the Harlem Renaissance*, ed. Cary D. Wintz. New York: Garland, 1996.)

Kuenz, Jane. "The Face of America: Performing Race and Nation in Jessie Fauset's *There Is Confusion*." *Yale Journal of Criticism*, 12(1), 1999.

Levison, Susan. "Performance and the 'Strange Place' of Jessie Redmon Fauset's *There Is Confusion*." *Modern Fiction Studies*, 46(4), 2000.

Lewis, David Levering. *When Harlem Was in Vogue*. New York: Penguin, 1997.

McCoy, Beth A. "'Is This Really What You Wanted Me to Be?': The Daughter's Disintegration in Jessie Redmon Fauset's *There Is Confusion*." *Modern Fiction Studies*, 40(1), 1994.

McDowell, Deborah E. "The Neglected Dimension of Jessie Redmon Fauset." In *Conjuring: Black Women, Fiction, and Literary Tradition*, ed. Marjorie Pryse and Hortense J. Spillers. Bloomington: Indiana University Press, 1985.

Miller, Nina. "Femininity, Publicity, and the Class Division of Cultural Labor: Jessie Redmon Fauset's *There Is Confusion*." *African American Review*, 30(2), 1996.

Sylvander, Carolyn Wedin. *Jessie Redmond Fauset, Black American Writer*. Troy, N.Y.: Whitston, 1981.

Wall, Cheryl A. *Women of the Harlem Renaissance*. Bloomington: Indiana University Press, 1995.

They Shall Not Die

In 1934, the Theatre Guild, a distinguished professional organization, produced *They Shall Not Die*, a play by John Wexley that dramatized a particularly notorious example of American racism known as the Scottsboro case. *They Shall Not Die* opened in New York on 21 February 1934 at the Royale Theater at 242 West Forty-fifth Street and ran for sixty-two performances. The cast on opening night included Claude Rains, Ruth Gordon, Tom Ewell, and Dean Jagger. Philip Moeller directed the production, and Lee Simonson, a major influence in American theatrical design, created the sets.

Wexley's play expressed the outrage that many American citizens felt as a result of the trials of the nine African American youths, who became known as the Scottsboro boys and whose plight attracted international attention during the early 1930s. The nine, who were riding a freight train near Scottsboro, Alabama, were arrested for vagrancy and disorderly conduct. Later, two white women who also had been riding the train accused them of rape. Despite overwhelming evidence to the contrary, and after only four days of trials, an all-white jury in Alabama convicted all nine of the Scottsboro boys and sentenced eight of them to death. The Supreme Court overturned the convictions in 1932, and a series of new trials began; these too drew national attention, largely through the efforts of the International Labor Defense, an organization that came to the aid of the accused youths and publicized the case. Petitions were sent to President Franklin D. Roosevelt, and demonstrations took place in more than twenty-five countries, often involving protests aimed at American embassies. Many prominent individuals protested against the trials and convictions, including Albert Einstein, Maxim Gorky, Sinclair Lewis, Thomas Mann, Edna St. Vincent Millay, George Bernard Shaw, and Virginia Woolf. A "Scottsboro parade" took place in Harlem, and there was a "Free the Scottsboro Boys" march on Washington, D.C. Langston Hughes composed a one-act verse play, "Scottsboro Limited"; Countee Cullen wrote the poem "Scottsboro, Too, Is Worth Its Song"; and John Wexley wrote the play *They Shall Not Die*.

In Wexley's play, the setting is a fictitious town called Cooksville in an unnamed southern state; the defense attorney for the youths, a New Yorker named Nathan G. Rubin (played by Claude Rains), makes a final impassioned speech on their behalf: "We're only beginning . . . and if I do nothing else in my life, I'll make the fair name of this state stink to high heaven with its lynch justice. . . . These boys, they shall not die!"(Wexley 1934, 191). The actual trials continued throughout the 1930s, and although the all-white juries never acquitted the defendants, all of them eventually gained their freedom: four because the charges were dropped, four because of early paroles, and one because of a successful escape. The last of the "Scottsboro boys" did not leave prison until 1950, however.

Wexley's career as a playwright and screenwriter focused on political and social concerns. His play *The Last Mile*, produced in 1930, was released as a film in 1932 and remade in 1959. In 1931, he wrote and directed the play *Steel*. Wexley worked with Anatole Litvak on a number of screenplays for socially aware film noir productions, including *City for Conquest* (1938), starring James Cagney; *Confessions of a Nazi Spy* (1939); and *The Long Night* (1947), which starred Henry Fonda as a steelworker who is a veteran of World War II. Wexley also wrote or cowrote *Angels with Dirty Faces* (1938) and, with Bertolt Brecht, the screenplay for Fritz Lang's *Hangmen Also Die!* (1942). He worked primarily as a screenwriter during World War II and after the war worked on documentaries and other projects until he was blacklisted during the McCarthy era. In 1955, Wexley published *The Judgment of Julius and Ethel Rosenberg*, an early account of the famous espionage trial, in which he maintained that the FBI had framed the Rosenbergs.

MARTHA AVALEEN EGAN

See also Scottsboro

Further Reading

Buhle, Paul, and Dave Wagner. *Radical Hollywood: The Untold Story behind America's Favorite Movies.* New York: New Press, 2002.

Carter, Dan T. *Scottsboro: A Tragedy of the American South.* New York: Oxford University Press, 1972.

Priestly, J. B. *The Wonderful of the Theatre.* New York: Doubleday, 1969.

Wexley, John. *They Shall Not Die.* New York: Knopf, 1934.

———. *The Judgment of Julius and Ethel Rosenberg.* New York: Cameron and Kahn, 1955.

Thomas, Edna Lewis

Edna Lewis Thomas made her stage debut in 1920 in a cameo role for a charity benefit at a theater in Brooklyn, the Putnam, affiliated with the Lafayette Players, the leading stock company during the Harlem Renaissance. Before being persuaded to appear at the Putnam, she had no intention of being an actress. She was a socialite and a good friend of A'Lelia Walker, whose lavish lifestyle she coveted.

In Boston, where she had grown up, Thomas had married a much older, very wealthy businessman. After she was widowed, she married again. She and her second husband, Lloyd Thomas, were drawn to Harlem and its cultural and social excitement. What began as a theatrical lark soon became a dedicated pursuit. In 1921, she performed at the Lafayette

Theater in *Turn to the Right*. In her role in a jazz version of *A Comedy of Errors* produced by the Ethiopian Art Theater in 1923, Thomas charmed the critic Percy Hammond, a hard man to please. In 1926, she appeared on Broadway in David Belasco's *Lulu Belle*, about a black prostitute—a role played by Lenore Ulric in blackface. Even during the Harlem Renaissance, Thomas, as an African American actress, rarely had featured roles on Broadway.

Thomas met the critic Carl Van Vechten, with whom she and her husband maintained a lifelong friendship, and Olivia Wyndham, an Englishwoman who was a distant relative of Oscar Wilde. Wyndham moved in with the Thomases, and it is believed that the three maintained a ménage à trois for the rest of their lives. Thomas worked with some regularity during the 1930s, appearing in *Ol' Man Satan* in 1932, in *Run Little Children* in 1933, and in *Stevedore* in 1934. In 1936, Thomas was cast as Lady Macbeth in the production of *Voodoo Macbeth*, which Orson Welles, then twenty years old, had set in Haiti on the recommendation of his wife. It was a daring production. Percy Hammond, the same critic who had been captivated by Thomas thirteen years earlier, dismissed *Voodoo Macbeth* as "deluxe boondoggling," but this did not keep audiences from coming.

After its debut in Harlem, which was sold out for ten weeks, the show moved downtown to the Adelphi and then went on national tour to a number of venues associated with the Federal Theater Project. Just before the Federal Theater was shut down, Thomas performed again with the Harlem Unit in 1938 in *Androcles and the Lion*, by George Bernard Shaw. In the 1940s, she performed on Broadway several times. She appeared with Helen Hayes in *Harriet* in 1943, in *Strange Fruit* by Lillian Smith in 1945, and in Tennessee Williams's *A Streetcar Named Desire* in 1947, as the Mexican woman, a role she repeated for subsequent revivals and in the film version in 1956.

Biography

Edna Lewis Thomas was born in 1886 in Lawrenceville, Virginia, and grew up in Boston, where she studied in public schools. Thomas acted on the New York stage for several decades and was part of the original cast of *A Streetcar Named Desire*. She died in New York City on 22 July 1974.

BARBARA BREWSTER LEWIS

See also Ethiopian Art Players; Lafayette Players; Lulu Belle; Stevedore; Van Vechten, Carl; Walker, A'Lelia

Further Reading

Gill, Glenda E. "Edna Thomas: The Grand Dame." In *White Grease Paint: A Study of the Federal Theatre, 1935–1939*. New York: Peter Lang, 1988.

Hine, Darlene Clark. *Black Women in America: An Historical Encyclopedia*, Vol. 2. Brooklyn, N.Y.: Carlson, 1993.

Houseman, John. *Unfinished Business: A Memoir*. London: Chatto and Windus, 1986.

Smith, Jessie Carney, ed. *Notable Black American Women*. Detroit, Mich.: Gale Research, 1992.

Thompson, Sister M. Francesca. "The Lafayette Players, 1917–1932." In *The Theater of Black Americans*, ed. Errol Hill. Englewood Cliffs, N.J.: Prentice-Hall, 1980.

Thompson, Louise

See Patterson, Louise Thompson

Three Plays for a Negro Theater

Three Plays for a Negro Theater (1917) are works by Frederick Ridgely Torrence (1875–1950). Torrence had established his literary reputation as a poet and journal editor before turning his attention to drama. As a member of the "Judson circle," led by William Vaughn Moody, Torrence first attempted two verse plays—*El Dorado* and *Abelard and Heloise*—which were published but not produced. Spurred on by the success of Moody's prose drama *The Great Divide*, Torrence turned to folk stories and a heightened prose style with which to create "poetic drama in prose" (Clum 1972, 105). He also looked into his own childhood in Xenia, Ohio, a city where a number of white southerners and African Americans had migrated before the Civil War. Xenia had been an important stop on the Underground Railroad, and Wilberforce University, a historically black institution, was located there. Torrence's mother had come from a slaveholding southern family; his father, a farmer, retained several trusted black employees; and Torrence had gone to a high school and church that admitted some African Americans. In addition to these influences on his

Ridgely Torrence, 1933. (Library of Congress.)

playwriting, Torrence had been greatly impressed by performances given in the United States by Ireland's Abbey Theater and especially by the plays of John Millington Synge.

Granny Maumee, the first of Torrence's Negro plays, written in 1914, is often compared to Synge's *Riders to the Sea*. The setting is a cabin occupied by Granny Maumee and her great-granddaughter, Pearl. Granny has waited fifty years for a male heir to avenge the lynching of her son, accused of a crime he did not commit and burned alive in a bonfire; Granny herself was blinded and badly burned when she tried to reach for him through the flames. Pearl's sister, Sapphie, has recently given birth to a son, whom she is bringing for a visit. When Granny holds the child, her sight returns briefly. To her shock, the child is nearly white. Not only must she bear this tainting of her pure African blood, of which she is proud, but she learns that the father of the child is the grandson of the man who lit her son's bonfire. Granny resorts to voodoo incantation to avenge herself, determined that father and child should die. Before she can carry out her plan, she has a vision in which her son, Sam, counsels her to forgive. Determined to make her peace with God, she dies.

Granny Maumee, with a white cast, was produced for one performance by the Stage Society, a group that mounted small productions in New York's theaters on Sundays (when the theaters were ordinarily dark); these presentations were attended primarily by theater professionals. The play was well received, and it was considered by other producers, including the actress-manager Minnie Maddern Fiske, but it was not produced until the socialite Emilie Hapgood provided backing. She hired Robert Edmond Jones, a purveyor of the "new stagecraft," not only to design the production but also to take on his first professional assignment as a director. To accompany the folk tragedy of Granny Maumee, Torrence added two more one-act plays: a folk comedy, *The Rider of Dreams*; and a pageant play, *Simon the Cyrenian*. Unlike the other two plays, which were written in dialect, *Simon the Cyrenian* was written in verse.

In *The Rider of Dreams*, Madison Sparrow and his wife, Lucy, are polar opposites. While Lucy labors assiduously to save money to purchase a home, Madison strums his guitar and simply dreams of prosperity. Duped by a white con man, Madison loses the family's savings. Their landlord, however, has observed the swindle, recovers the money, and accepts it as payment in full for their rented house. Madison, shaken, tries to return to his dreams.

Simon the Cyrenian, which is based on the accounts in the gospels, presents Christ's final hours before the crucifixion from the viewpoint of Simon, a black African. Simon is depicted as a rebel who plots to save Christ and violently attack the Romans. He finds an unlikely ally in Procula, the wife of Pilate, who fears the consequences of the crucifixion. Hearing the voice of Jesus, Simon realizes that Christ is the answer and that the crucifixion is of great moment and purpose. Not only does he help Christ bear the cross, but he also is crowned with thorns and vows to bear the pain until Christ "comes into his own."

Three Plays for a Negro Theater opened with an African American cast at the Garden Theater in Madison Square, on the fringes of Broadway, on 5 April 1917. Much was made of Jones's and Torrence's efforts to assemble the cast, many of whom were veterans of the Lafayette Players. A "singing orchestra" under the direction of J. Rosamond Johnson provided musical interludes between the plays. *The Rider of Dreams* was performed first, then *Granny Maumee*, then *Simon the Cyrenean*. Opal Cooper's performance as Madison and Inez Clough's as Procula led the critic George Jean Nathan to place them on his lists of the ten best actors and actresses of the year. Critical response was universally enthusiastic. Robert Benchley stated in his review in the *New York Tribune* that he may have witnessed "the beginnings of a new movement on the American stage . . . the first stirrings of a really distinctive American drama" (Clum, 109). Black critics were equally enthusiastic. Years later, in *Black Manhattan*, James Weldon Johnson reprinted the show's program and declared that "April 5, 1917 is the date of the most important single event in the entire history of the Negro in the American theatre; for it marks the beginning of a new era" (1930/1977, 175). Torrence had drawn characters, not caricatures, and the African American actors were given an opportunity to be taken seriously as a performing artists. Torrence was credited by W. E. B. Du Bois and others as the harbinger of the theater to come, a new theater that would reflect not the old minstrel images but the "New Negro."

Fate intervened, however. The day after opening night, the United States formally entered World War I, and the nation became focused on the ensuing crisis. Hapgood tried to keep the show alive by moving it to the Garrick Theater, which was closer to the center of the theater district, on 16 April, but *Three Plays for a Negro Theater* closed there after one week.

Later, Macmillan published *Three Plays for a Negro Theater*; and Alain Locke and Montgomery Gregory included *Granny Maumee*, *The Rider of Dreams*, and another play by Torrence, *The Danse Calinda*, in their landmark anthology *Plays of Negro Life*.

FREDA SCOTT GILES

See also Clough, Inez; Johnson, James Weldon; Johnson, John Rosamond; Lafayette Players; Locke, Alain

Further Reading

Anderson, Jervis. *This Was Harlem: 1900–1950*. New York: Farrar Straus and Giroux, 1982.

Archer, Leonard C. *Black Images in the American Theatre*. Brooklyn, N.Y.: Pageant-Poseidon, 1973.

Bontemps, Arna. *The Harlem Renaissance Remembered*. New York: Dodd, Mead, 1972.

Clum, John M. *Ridgely Torrence*. New York: Twayne, 1972.

Curtis, Susan. *The First Black Actors on the Great White Way*. Columbia: University of Missouri Press, 1998.

Huggins, Nathan Irvin. *Harlem Renaissance*. New York: Oxford University Press, 1971.

Isaacs, Edith J. R. *The Negro in American Theatre*. New York: Theatre Arts, 1947.

Johnson, James Weldon. *Black Manhattan*. New York: Atheneum, 1977. (Originally published 1930.)

Kellner, Bruce, ed. *The Harlem Renaissance: A Historical Dictionary for the Era*. Westport, Conn.: Greenwood, 1984.

Locke, Alain, and Montgomery Gregory, eds. *Plays of Negro Life*. Westport, Conn.: Negro Universities Press, 1970. (Originally published 1927.)

Mitchell, Loften. *Black Drama: The Story of the American Negro in the Theatre*. New York: Hawthorn, 1967.

Torrence, Ridgely. *Granny Maumee, The Rider of Dreams, Simon the Cyrenian: Plays for a Negro Theatre*. New York: Macmillan, 1917.

Thurman, Wallace

The career of Wallace Thurman, enfant terrible of the Harlem Renaissance, is symbolic of the movement in that it developed speedily and turbulently only to fade away quickly. After trying out medical studies at the University of Utah, Thurman studied journalism at the University of Southern California–Los Angeles in 1922. He never completed his studies in Los Angeles; instead, he undertook what was to develop into a rather short, yet intense and singular literary career.

Thurman described his adolescence as filled with literature in every form, from juvenile books to Ralph Waldo Emerson, Shakespeare, Plato, Hardy, and Freud. He worked his way through literature without any scholarly guidance.

Thurman's career in journalism started in Los Angeles in 1923 when he became an associate editor of the black newspaper *Pacific Defender*. In order to supplement his income, he also worked in the post office, where, in 1924, he first came into contact with the Harlem Renaissance by way of meeting Arna Bontemps. Bontemps published a piece in *The Crisis* in 1924 and left for Harlem. Thurman decided to create his own black literary movement on the West Coast by founding the magazine *The Outlet*, of which six issues were published. As a result of financial difficulties (a recurrent theme in Thurman's life), Thurman left Los Angeles, reaching Harlem in 1925.

Again, Thurman engaged in journalism, first working for the theater critic Theophilus Lewis, a job that did not prove financially profitable but did earn him Lewis's long-lasting friendship. In late 1925, Thurman joined the left-wing magazine *The Messenger*, and in 1926, he became circulation manager at *The World Tomorrow*. Thurman's literary activities during his first year in Harlem are various and indicate his extraordinary status as an African American literary figure: He served as a literary critic; opened up the pages of the publications he worked for to young writers of the Harlem Renaissance; and published poetry, short fiction, and satirical essays in *Opportunity*.

Together with a friend, the artist and writer Richard Bruce Nugent, Thurman moved into a residence at 267 West 136th Street, which became the central meeting point for Harlem's black bohemia. Thurman set out to shock the Harlem Renaissance establishment, represented by such figures as W. E. B. Du Bois and Alain Locke, through his extravagant lifestyle. His life involved sexual transgressions in the form of interracial and intraracial alliances in both heterosexual and homosexual contexts. For example, Thurman lived for a time with a white Canadian friend, Jan Harald Stefansson, with whom he was also sexually involved.

Thurman furthermore sought to be provocative through his literary ventures. He organized the most transgressive literary collaboration of the renaissance, the short-lived journal *Fire!!* (1926). The magazine failed, only a few copies having been sold (later, the remaining copies were accidentally burned), and Thurman was left deeply in debt; yet he continued his literary activities as well as his bohemian lifestyle.

Thurman published articles in major periodicals such as *The New Republic*; wrote reviews; wrote his first novel, *The Blacker the Berry* (1929); joined (for a brief period) the cast of the play *Porgy*; produced a guide to contemporary Harlem, *Negro Life in New York's Harlem* (1928); and wrote a play, *Harlem* (1929), a reworking of the short story "Cordelia the Crude," which he had contributed to *Fire!!*. Thurman collaborated with a white writer, his friend William Jordan Rapp, on the play. He also collaborated with Rapp on the play *Jeremiah the Magnificent* (1935), which was based on the life of Marcus Garvey. Thurman and another white writer, Abraham L. Furman, wrote *The Interne* (1932), set in a hospital. The play *Harlem*, dealing with the struggles of an African American southern family in New York City and involving love, gambling, and murder, was controversial but successful and was even staged on Broadway.

Despite his prominent position within the Harlem Renaissance and his significant literary output, Thurman became increasingly dissatisfied; and he experienced a severe setback when his third attempt at creating a literary magazine, *Harlem: A Forum of Negro Life* (1928), survived for only one issue. Disillusioned with his own work and with the way the movement was developing, and furthermore physically damaged as a result of his personal excesses, Thurman apparently attempted to introduce stability in his life by marrying Louise Thompson. The wedding took place before the premiere of *Harlem*, but the marriage quickly failed. Acrimonious divorce proceedings, including attempts at blackmail, followed, but there was never a legal divorce.

Thurman opted to escape from Harlem, leaving for Salt Lake City and the West Coast shortly after the publication of *The Blacker the Berry* in February 1929. This novel has as a theme the folk saying "The blacker the berry, the sweeter the juice"—a theme it treats with bitter irony. Emma Lou, the protagonist, is subjected to discrimination and rejection because of her dark skin. Significantly, Thurman set himself apart from other writers of the Harlem Renaissance by focusing not on the issue of racism but on the far more controversial subject of intraracial color prejudice: that is, the practice among African Americans of assigning status according to the relative lightness or darkness of a person's skin. Critics have frequently held that Thurman's fiction contains strong autobiographical elements; discrimination and social ranking based on color, a reality within the African American community, formed part of Thurman's own experience, as he was relatively dark skinned.

Thurman's second novel, *Infants of the Spring* (1932), also has an autobiographical strain. Though it was not published until 1932, this book was apparently near completion in early 1930. *Infants of the Spring* is a satiric account of the Harlem Renaissance, invoking real figures associated with the movement. Thurman's own stand-in, thinly disguised, is the protagonist Raymond Taylor, who throughout the novel reflects on issues of race and art. Friendship and love are two other major themes. The most famous section of the novel is a scene at a literary salon where all the great figures of the renaissance are gathered. They have a heated discussion about race, art, and the direction the movement is to take, ending in shouting matches and chaos. *Infants of the Spring* appeared on the market after the renaissance had passed its height, and at a time of economic depression, and it never received much critical attention.

Thurman continued his literary work, focusing on the world beyond the black artistic milieu. As indicated in his correspondence, he worked on plays and stories, and from 1932 on he also held two jobs: as "ghost editor" for the magazine *True Story* and as editor-in-chief of a publishing company, Macaulay. He was the only African American employed in such a position at a white publishing company. Meanwhile, though, his dependence on alcohol increased.

In 1934, Thurman signed with Foy Productions in Hollywood, creating two stories for the screenplays of *Tomorrow's Children*, a movie about sterilization, and *High School Girl*, which centered on abortion and teenage pregnancy. In mid-1934, Thurman returned to New York City with new plans for literary ventures, but these were not realized. He died after a six-month stay in the "incurables' ward" of City Hospital.

Thurman never quite lived up to his artistic promise, and success often escaped him. Nevertheless, he shaped the Harlem Renaissance from within, proving himself a valuable contributor to, and critic of, the movement. He remains an outstanding figure of the Harlem Renaissance who managed to cross the barriers normally limiting African American writers and artists by working as a writer, editor, and critic not only in a black professional environment but also in the white-dominated publishing and entertainment industry.

Biography

Wallace Henry Thurman was born on 16 August 1902 in Salt Lake City, Utah. He attended West Salt Lake High School, 1914–1919; did premedical studies at the University of Utah, 1920; and attended the School of Journalism, University of Southern California—Los Angeles, 1922–1923. He was associate editor at the black Los Angeles newspaper the *Pacific Defender*, 1923; editor of *The Outlet*, 1924; reporter and writer for *The Looking Glass*, 1925; an editor at *The Messenger*, 1925–1926; editor of *Fire!!*, 1926; circulation manager at *The World Tomorrow*; 1926; editor of *Harlem: A Forum of Negro Life*, 1928; ghost editor and writer for *True Story*, 1932; and editor-in-chief of the Macaulay Company, 1932. Thurman died on 22 December 1934 in City Hospital, Welfare Island, New York.

A. B. CHRISTA SCHWARTZ

See also Black Bohemia; Bontemps, Arna; Douglas, Aaron; Du Bois, W. E. B.; Fire!!; Harlem: A Forum of

Negro Life; Homosexuality; Hurston, Zora Neale; Infants of the Spring; Lewis, Theophilus; Locke, Alain; Macaulay; Messenger, The; Nugent, Richard Bruce; Porgy: Play

Selected Works

The Blacker the Berry. New York: Macaulay, 1929.

The Collected Writings of Wallace Thurman: A Harlem Renaissance Reader, ed. Amritjit Singh and Daniel M. Scott III. New Brunswick, N.J.: Rutgers University Press, 2003.

Infants of the Spring. New York: Macaulay, 1932.

The Interne. New York: Macaulay, 1932. (With Abraham L. Furman.)

Negro Life in New York's Harlem: A Lively Picture of a Popular and Interesting Section. Girard, Kan.: Haldeman-Julius, 1928.

Further Reading

Henderson, Mae Gwendolyn. "Portrait of Wallace Thurman." In *The Harlem Renaissance Remembered: Essays Edited with a Memoir*, ed. Arna Bontemps. New York: Dodd, Mead, 1972.

Hicks, Granville. "The New Negro: An Interview with Wallace Thurman." *Churchman*, 30 April 1927.

Klotmann, Phyllis. "The Black Writer in Hollywood, Circa 1930: The Case of Wallace Thurman." In *Black American Cinema*, ed. Manthia Diawara. London: Routledge, 1993.

Notten, Eleonore van. *Wallace Thurman's Harlem Renaissance*. Amsterdam and Atlanta, Ga.: Rodopi, 1994.

Nugent, Richard Bruce. "Gentleman Jigger." In *Gay Rebel of the Harlem Renaissance: Selections from the Work of Richard Bruce Nugent*, ed. Thomas H. Wirth. Durham, N.C.: Duke University Press, 2002. (Excerpt, n.d.)

Silberman, Seth Clark. "Looking for Richard Bruce Nugent and Wallace Henry Thurman: Reclaiming Black Male Same-Sexualities in the New Negro Movement." *In Process*, 1, 1996.

Singh, Amritjit. "Foreword to the 1992 Edition." In *Infants of the Spring* by Wallace Thurman. Boston, Mass.: Northeastern University Press, 1992.

———. Introduction. In *The Collected Writings of Wallace Thurman: A Harlem Renaissance Reader*, ed. Amritjit Singh and Daniel M. Scott III. New Brunswick, N.J.: Rutgers University Press, 2003.

West, Dorothy. "Elephant's Dance." In *The Richer the Poorer: Stories, Sketches, Reminiscences*. New York: Doubleday, 1995. (Originally published 1970.)

Tolson, Melvin B.

Melvin B. Tolson was an African American poet, newspaper columnist, and university teacher of literature and drama. His reputation rests largely on two controversial books of poetry: *Libretto for the Republic of Liberia* (1953) and *Harlem Gallery* (1965). Tolson's career as a poet approached success only toward the end of his life, and it is only in recent years that he has been granted critical appreciation as a major literary figure.

Although Tolson is not usually placed in the Harlem Renaissance, as it is generally understood, he consistently and enthusiastically associated himself with it in his writings and public lectures. Tolson often spoke of his personal familiarity with the writers that he referred to as the Harlem group. He is known for his long poem about Harlem in the 1920s, *Harlem Gallery*, Book 1, *The Curator*; this poem is often invoked as a cosmopolitan literary work that captures the revolutionary spirit of the movement. Tolson's idea of what he wanted to write about Harlem evolved over the course of thirty years, and *Harlem Gallery* is but the first of a planned five-volume epic history of black Americans. That his historic poem began with the Harlem poems demonstrates the centrality of Harlem in Tolson's thought.

Tolson, a native Oklahoman who lived in Texas, was in New York during 1931 and 1932 while attending graduate courses in literature at Columbia University. While doing research for his master's thesis, "The Harlem Group of Negro Writers," Tolson interviewed several of the writers who lived in New York at the time, and he also read all the available books and articles covering the twenty-year period of the Harlem Renaissance. For Tolson, the movement began in 1917, and he continued to revise his thesis as late as 1937. Although Tolson's thesis on the Harlem writers was the earliest effort by an African American to study the Harlem Renaissance, his study was overlooked by nearly every subsequent inquiry into this literary movement. This is surprising, given that Tolson's research and methodology were based on written sources and his findings were in line with the subsequent studies of the Harlem Renaissance that began to appear thirty years after his thesis. As a critic, Tolson was ahead of his time in several ways. With a grasp of the complexity of the artistic production of the Harlem group, he observed that in Countee Cullen's classicism and conservatism and Langston Hughes's experimentalism and radicalism are to be found the "antipodes of the Harlem Renaissance." Even though he limited his discussion to African American writers, he placed Harlemite writing within a culturally pluralistic framework that related black writing to what was happening in the national culture.

Tolson stated that his aims were to give the social background to the literary development of the New Negro, to apply modern criticism to the lives and works of the leading contemporary writers, and to interpret the attitudes and stylistic methods discovered in the Harlem Renaissance. Tolson's 139-page thesis is the first listing of the major Harlemite writers, or canon; it includes Cullen, Hughes, W. E. B. Du Bois, Jessie Redmon Fauset, Rudolph Fisher, Claude McKay, George Schuyler, Eric Walrond, and Walter White. Tolson's evaluation of major writers differs from the canon arrived at in the subsequent seventy years, which elevates Zora Neale Hurston, Nella Larsen, and Jean Toomer over any of Tolson's choices. Tolson's thesis also provided two initial chapters that located the Harlem movement historically and socially.

Tolson's relatively brief stay in Harlem was in many ways the formative experience of his life. Tolson had taken a year of leave from his teaching duties at Wiley College in Marshall, Texas, and after completing his coursework he returned to the classroom. Tolson did not hand in his thesis until 1940, though he had a nearly complete draft in 1932.

While in Harlem he conceived an ambition to write an epic poem about Harlem, and this led him to write *A Gallery of Harlem Portraits*, a 340-page manuscript of 200 verse portraits, patterned after Edgar Lee Masters's *Spoon River Anthology*. He completed this work in 1935. Although the setting was the 1920s, the poems were heavily influenced by leftist politics and were written in the proletarian mode of Depression-era social realism. Because of the radical political positions expressed in *Harlem Portraits*, Tolson was unable to publish this manuscript.

Nevertheless, the early epic laid the groundwork for *Harlem Gallery*, the high-modernist long poem for which Tolson has been receiving increased critical attention since Bérubé's study (1992) of the critical reception of Tolson and Thomas Pynchon. The renewed interest in *Harlem Gallery* resulted in a new edition: *"Harlem Gallery" and Other Poems* (1999), edited by Raymond Nelson. Although Tolson adopted the modernist literary style, he continued to affirm his adherence to Marxism.

Harlem Gallery, a sequence in the high-modernist style, is a narrative composed of twenty-four densely allusive Pindaric odes, each titled after a letter of the Greek alphabet. This work has often been compared to T. S. Eliot's *The Waste Land* and Stephen Crane's *The Bridge*. However, it is also noted for its faithfulness to Harlem as a milieu; for example, Russell (1980) examines the poem's depiction of Harlem in the 1920s. The subject of much of *Harlem Gallery* is race, although this theme is interwoven with questions about art. The setting is Harlem, chiefly a nightclub and an art gallery, and much of the poem is given to abstract sociological and philosophical questions as they are debated by the poem's two main characters: the curator, the director of the Harlem Gallery; and Dr. Obi Nkomo, an art critic. As an indication of the paradoxes that characterize the poem, the curator is an octoroon (a person with ancestry that is one-eighth black) and brags that he is able to pass for white, while Nkomo is a dark-skinned African. When these two men debate, it is in language that is so allusive and ironic as to give little idea of the positions they are advocating. At times the poem descends from its difficult style and presents passages, in the jazz poetry of Hideho Heights, that celebrate Louis Armstrong and John Henry, and the imagist poems of the composer Mister Starks.

Biography

Melvin Beaunorus Tolson was born on 6 February 1898 (the date is disputed) in Moberly, Missouri. He attended public high school in Kansas City, Missouri; Fisk University, Nashville, Tennessee, 1919; Lincoln University, Oxford, Pennsylvania, B.A., 1923; and Columbia University, New York City, M.A., 1940. He taught at Wiley College, Marshall, Texas, 1924–1947; and Langston University, Langston, Oklahoma, 1947–1965. His awards included first place, National Poetry Contest, American Negro Exposition, Chicago, Illinois, 1939; Omega Psi Phi award for creative literature, 1945; Bess Hokim Award, *Poetry* magazine, 1951; doctor of letters, Lincoln University, 1954; Bread Loaf Fellow, 1954; Avalon Chair in Humanities, Tuskegee Institute, 1965; doctor of humane letters, Lincoln University, 1965; and Poetry Award, American

Academy of Arts and Letters, 1966. Tolson died in Langston, Oklahoma, on 29 August 1966.

JON WOODSON

See also Literature: 7—Poetry; Modernism

Selected Works

Caviar and Cabbage: Selected Columns by Melvin B. Tolson, ed. Robert M. Farnsworth. 1982.
A Gallery of Harlem Portraits, ed. Robert M. Farnsworth. 1979.
Harlem Gallery, Book 1, *The Curator*. 1965.
The Harlem Group of Negro Writers, ed. Edward J. Mullen. 2001.
Libretto for the Republic of Liberia. 1953.
Rendezvous with America. 1944.

Further Reading

Bérubé, Michael. *Marginal Forces/Cultural Centers: Tolson, Pynchon, and the Politics of the Canon*. Ithaca, N.Y.: Cornell University Press, 1992.
Farnsworth, Robert M. *Melvin B. Tolson, 1898–1966: Plain Talk and Poetic Prophecy*. Columbia: University of Missouri Press, 1984.
Flasch, Joy. *Melvin B. Tolson*. New York: Twayne, 1972.
Russell, Mariann. *Melvin B. Tolson's "Harlem Gallery": A Literary Analysis*. Columbia: University of Missouri Press, 1980.

Toomer, Jean

Jean Toomer was a poet, dramatist, novelist, essayist, philosopher, and teacher. He was the author of several books, including *Cane* (1923), and was a bridge between two distinct but contemporaneous groups of American writers. The first group consists of authors such as Sterling Brown, Langston Hughes, Zora Neale Hurston, and Nella Larsen, whose writings define the scope of the New Negro movement, or Harlem Renaissance. The second group consists of such writers as Sherwood Anderson, Waldo Frank, and Gorham Munson, who dominated the literary scene of Greenwich Village and whose writings are characterized by experimentalism and political liberalism. Toomer was a comrade-in-letters to Frank

and Munson, and a distant but influential figure to Hughes and Hurston, who admired the achievement of *Cane*, the three-part collection of sketches, poetry, and drama that established a standard for writers of the New Negro movement and that conveyed the profound search for meaning at the core of American modernism.

In 1918, Toomer completed "Bona and Paul," the first of several stories in *Cane*. Although he had no firm prospects, his career as a writer was slowly taking on direction and significance. In 1920, during a sojourn in Greenwich Village, where he established friendships with Frank and Munson, he assumed the name Jean Toomer (having been born Nathan Pinchback Toomer). In search of a means to solidify his emerging identity as a writer, Toomer adopted the new name shortly after his immersion in the literary life of Greenwich Village and after reading Romain Rolland's *Jean Christophe* (1904), in whose protagonist Toomer had glimpsed his own potentiality as an artist.

Toomer's acceptance in the summer of 1921 of a two-month appointment as acting principle at the Sparta Agricultural and Industrial Institute in Georgia provided him with experiences that forged a new identity in art. Visiting the South for the first time, Toomer was captivated by the landscape of Georgia; its complex history of displacement, slavery, and segregation; and the impact of African Americans on the development of southern culture. Enthralled by the beauty of African American vernacular culture, Toomer also detected its dissolution in the historic migration of African Americans from the South to the North, and also in the enlarging reach of industrialization.

Returning to Washington, Toomer began writing the masterpiece which he would later reject but on which his reputation as a writer remains secure. By December 1921, he had written "Kabnis," the drama that makes up the third section of *Cane*. One year later he had completed the experimental work that is a record of his discovery of his southern heritage, an homage to a folk culture that he believed was evanescent, and an exploration of the forces that he believed were the reason for the spiritual fragmenting of his generation. With the assistance of Frank, who wrote the foreword to the first edition, Toomer's first and most important book was published in the spring of 1923 by Horace Liveright. Although it was praised by reviewers, *Cane* sold fewer than 500 copies, casting a shadow across Toomer's otherwise triumphant literary debut.

After *Cane*, Toomer did not return to the setting and culture that had inspired the only book of fiction he published during his lifetime. While the search for wholeness remained a central theme in Toomer's large but uneven canon, African American life was never again the subject. His later writings bear the influence Georgei I. Gurdjieff, a Russian mystic and psychologist whose theories of human development Toomer accepted and promoted as gospel. Beginning in the year of *Cane's* publication and continuing with few interruptions until his death, Toomer's commitment to Gurdjieff's theories had disastrous consequences for his writings. In his unpublished writings, Toomer created situations that were little more than propaganda for Gurdjieff's theories. In these works, one discovers protagonists who bear resemblances to Toomer himself and who function as guides to characters possessing only a vague awareness of their spiritual potentiality. This regrettable mixture of cant and vanity explains Toomer's obscurity after 1923. While Toomer continued to write until a few years before his death, he never again produced a work comparable in power and influence to *Cane*.

Of racially mixed heritage, Toomer defined himself not as an African American but simply as an American. Toomer's lifelong effort to transcend what he regarded as the narrow divisions of race is fully explored in *Essentials* (1931) and the epic *The Blue Meridian* (1936). Toomer's position on race is the principal reason for the absence of racial themes in the writings produced during and after his discovery of Gurdjieff, as well as for his conscious disassociation from *Cane* and from the writers and artists of the Harlem Renaissance.

Biography

Jean Toomer (Nathan Pinchback Toomer) was the only child of Nina Pinchback and Nathan Toomer. He was born on 29 March 1894 in Washington, D.C. Five years later, his mother divorced his father and returned to the home of her parents, Nina Hethorn Pinchback and P. B. S. Pinchback, who had been a lieutenant governor of Louisiana during Reconstruction. After Nina Pinchback's death in 1909, the Pinchbacks assumed full responsibility for the rearing of their grandson. Toomer was encouraged in his literary pursuits by his grandmother, to whom *Cane* is dedicated, and by his uncle Bismark Pinchback. He was educated in the segregated public schools of Washington and graduated from Paul Laurence Dunbar High School in 1914. Between 1914 and 1919 he explored a spectrum of intellectual interests and enrolled at the University of

Wisconsin, the American College of Physical Training in Chicago, the University of Chicago, and New York University; he returned to Washington in 1919 without a degree, however. In 1921, he was acting principle at the Sparta Agricultural and Industrial Institute in Georgia. *Cane* was published in 1923. Toomer became an adherent of the mystic Georgei I. Gurdjieff at about this time; the association had an adverse effect on his writing. Toomer died on 30 March 1967.

RUDOLPH P. BYRD

See also Anderson, Sherwood; Brown, Sterling; Cane; Frank, Waldo; Hughes, Langston; Hurston, Zora Neale; Larsen, Nella

Selected Works

Cane, ed. Darwin T. Turner. New York: Norton, 1988.

The Collected Poems of Jean Toomer, ed. Robert B. Jones and Margery Latimer Toomer. Chapel Hill: University of North Carolina Press, 1988.

Essentials, ed. Rudolph P. Byrd. Athens, Ga.: Hillstreet, 1999.

The Wayward and the Seeking: A Collection of Writings by Jean Toomer, ed. Darwin T. Turner. Washington, D.C.: Howard University Press, 1980.

Further Reading

Baker, Houston A. *Modernism and the Harlem Renaissance*. Chicago, Ill.: University of Chicago Press, 1984.

Byrd, Rudolph P. *Jean Toomer's Years With Gurdjieff: Portrait of an Artist*. Athens: University of Georgia Press, 1990.

Davis, Charles T. "Jean Toomer and the South: Region and Race as Elements Within a Literary Imagination." In *Black Is the Color of the Cosmos*. New Haven, Conn.: Yale University Press, 1989.

Fabre, Geneviève, and Michel Fabre. *Jean Toomer and the Harlem Renaissance*. New Brunswick, N.J.: Rutgers University Press, 2001.

Jones, Robert B. *Jean Toomer and the Prison-House of Thought: A Phenomenology of the Spirit*. Amherst: University of Massachusetts Press, 1993.

Kerman, Cynthia Earl, and Richard Eldridge. *The Lives of Jean Toomer: A Hunger for Wholeness*. Baton Rouge: Louisiana State University Press, 1987.

Larson, Charles R. *Invisible Darkness: Jean Toomer and Nella Larsen*. Iowa City: University of Iowa Press, 1993.

McKay, Nellie Y. *Jean Toomer, Artist*. Chapel Hill: University of North Carolina Press, 1984.

O'Daniel, Therman B., ed. *Jean Toomer: A Critical Evaluation*. Washington, D.C.: Howard University Press, 1988.

Rusch, Frederick L., ed. *A Jean Toomer Reader: Selected Unpublished Writings*. New York: Oxford University Press, 1993.

Scruggs, Charles, and Lee Vandemarr. *Jean Toomer and the Terror of American History*. Philadelphia: University of Pennsylvania Press, 1998.

Turner, Darwin T. *In a Minor Chord: Three Afro-American Writers and Their Search for Identity*. Carbondale: Southern Illinois University Press, 1971.

Woodson, Jon. *To Make a New Race: Gurdjieff, Toomer, and the Harlem Renaissance*. Jackson: University of Mississippi Press, 1999.

Tree of Hope

The "Tree of Hope" was a large elm outside the Lafayette Theater at 132nd Street and Seventh Avenue, in the heart of Harlem's club and theater district. The tree became a gathering place for unemployed black entertainers, and it acquired a reputation for bringing work—and good luck in general—to those who rubbed or kissed its bark. Performers of Harlem could often be found socializing and practicing their acts under the tree. Agents and club owners often passed by the tree on their way to entertainment venues, stopping to talk with the entertainers and often bearing news of available or forthcoming jobs and opportunities.

It is unclear whether the tree was cut down in the 1930s to make way for a redevelopment project on Seventh Avenue, or was destroyed in 1941 when an automobile crashed into it. According to one legend, Bill "Bojangles" Robinson, known as the unofficial mayor of Harlem, paid to have it moved rather than see it destroyed. Local people were said to have been distraught at the tree's demise and to have pulled off pieces of bark as keepsakes and good-luck charms.

The Apollo Theater obtained part of the stump. It was placed beside the stage at the Apollo, where performers continued the tradition of rubbing it for good luck before going onstage. The "Tree of Hope" also returned to the Lafayette Theater; part of the stump was placed at the stage entrance. Robinson also managed to create a memorial to the tree. A plaque at 132nd and Seventh Avenue in Harlem, where the tree once stood, reads: "The Original Tree of Hope Beloved by Citizens of Harlem. You Asked for a Tree of Hope, So Here 'Tis and Best Wishes—Bill Robinson."

VERONDA J. PITCHFORD

See also Apollo Theater; Lafayette Theater; Robinson, Bill "Bojangles"

Further Reading

Kellner, Bruce, ed. *The Harlem Renaissance: A Historical Dictionary for the Era*. Westport, Conn.: Greenwood, 1984.

Lewis, David Levering. *When Harlem Was in Vogue*. New York: Oxford University Press, 1981.

Tri-Arts Club

The Tri-Arts Club was part of the "little theater" movement; the three arts referred to in its name are acting, playwriting, and musical performance. In 1923, the Tri-Arts Club presented three one-act plays at the Harlem branch of the Young Women's Christian Association (YWCA) on West 132nd Street.

During the Harlem Renaissance, African American theater lagged behind the other arts in popularity and in its significance to black culture. There were at least three reasons for this. First, little or no African American tradition of theater had developed by the turn of the twentieth century, and between 1910 and 1930 only about a dozen major theater groups were formed. Second, black actors and dramatists needed work, and they could not commit themselves to serious drama, which simply did not attract paying audiences. Third, theater required the collaboration of many people and involved substantial production costs.

Like most other theater groups of Harlem at this time, the Tri-Arts Club sponsored light plays. In so doing, it offended Theophilus Lewis, who was then the only regular African American drama critic. In February 1924, Lewis lamented in his column in *The Messenger* that the group might have devoted its efforts to subject matter more relevant to African American life. He hoped that the "little theater" movement would serve as precursor to, and a component of, a national black theater. To Lewis's disappointment, Tri-Arts instead staged three one-act plays: *The Lady of the Hairpins*, a Japanese drama; *The Criminal*, by Leroy N. Jorgeson; and *The Wooing of Frazee*, by Frederick Hogan.

If these works were light, however, they were also notable for having been organized, written, produced, and managed by blacks in an effort to combat the negative image of African Americans that still persisted from traditional minstrelsy. The casts included Ruppert Marks, Lillian Mattison, Marie Santos, Arthur Taylor, and John Watson. Details of these productions have been lost to time, but it is possible that a woman wrote *The Lady of the Hairpins*. The little theater movement, significantly, provided opportunities for new women playwrights, who commonly addressed issues of gender in their work.

In relying on the Harlem YWCA as its production facility, the Tri-Arts Club followed a common practice of the little theater movement. Theater groups in this movement lacked the money to create their own production facilities, and so they used venues that were seeking African American audiences for other purposes. The YWCA, for instance, wanted to recruit women members, and it used entertaining events, discussion groups, lectures, light calisthenics, and cooking classes as a draw. The stage for the plays would have been a small one, probably in the basement, with an accompanying minimalist set. Chairs would be set up to accommodate a small audience of fewer than 200 people.

The Tri-Arts Club sponsored no more dramatic productions, and evidently no references to this organization can be found after 1923.

CARYN E. NEUMANN

See also Lewis, Theophilus; Messenger, The

Further Reading

Bontemps, Arna. *The Harlem Renaissance Remembered.* New York: Dodd, Mead, 1972.

McKay, Nellie. "Black Theater and Drama in the 1920s: Years of Growing Pains." *Massachusetts Review,* Winter 1987, pp. 615–626.

Tropic Death

Tropic Death (1926) is a collection of short stories by Eric Walrond. It was published eight years after Walrond arrived in New York from the West Indies, and it contributed to a sense of pan-Africanism among foreign-born blacks in the United States.

Tropic Death, often regarded as a literary counterpart and rival to Jean Toomer's *Cane* (1923), contains ten short stories, many of which are broken into various parts as well as being written in varieties of speech. The stories—set in the West Indies, particularly Barbados, Panama, and British Guiana—contain autobiographical elements. They offer insight into black life and the harsh realities associated with these colonized islands and the people who inhabit them, including family struggles and poverty.

Tropic Death was highly influential throughout the Harlem Renaissance. Walrond was especially interested in encouraging and supporting blacks without using the propaganda that was so common at the time. As a black author, he believed it was important for him to write works that did not focus on the "race problem." Rather, he felt that social protest could be ingrained in objective fiction; therefore, his work presented social and cultural dimensions of black life from a black perspective, in order to preserve the richness of that life.

Walrond uses imagery in *Tropic Death* to paint pictures of all aspects of black life, including unfavorable aspects. The themes and ideas in *Tropic Death* are conveyed through the beauty and evil of the earth, through folk traditions and hymns, and through the presence of obeah as revealed in the many lives and stories introduced in each narrative. Some of the themes in Walrond's work were considered controversial during the Harlem Renaissance, and some blacks were outraged that he exposed the harsh conditions of life in the West Indies. His themes include the desire of blacks to rise in society, the desire of blacks and mulattoes for "whiteness," the oppression inflicted by white racism, and the class conflict and adjustments entailed by colonialism and industrialization introduced from the West. In *Tropic Death*, Walrond used private lives to make specific statements about society; the stories provide an outlook on cultural diversity and the ability or inability of diverse cultures to coexist.

The story "The Yellow One," which focuses on racial discord and racial and gender anxiety, takes place aboard a migrant ship filled with passengers of varied cultures and races. "The Palm Porch" is about a mulatto mother who seeks wealth and power and ultimately is upset when her light-skinned daughters marry black men. "Subjection" comes closest to being protest literature: In this story, a white marine searches for and brutally kills a black worker who has spoken out against the marine's violence toward a fellow worker.

Tropic Death was not Walrond's initial connection to the Harlem Renaissance; he was a member of the editorial staff of Marcus Garvey's *Negro World* in the early 1920s. It was *Tropic Death* that bolstered his reputation as a significant author of Caribbean fiction, however, because of his skill in presenting the vivid reality of peasant life in the West Indies and the ability of his work to speak to all humanity

LISA A. CZERNIECKI

See also Cane; Negro World; Walrond, Eric

Further Reading

Parascandola, Louis J. *Winds Can Wake the Dead: An Eric Walrond Reader*. Detroit, Mich.: Wayne State University Press, 1998.

Ramchand, Kenneth. "The Writer Who Ran Away." *Savacou: A Journal of the Caribbean*, 2, 1970, pp. 67–75.

Wade, Carl A. "African-American Aesthetics and the Short Fiction of Eric Walrond: Tropic Death and the Harlem Renaissance." *CLA Journal*, 42(4), 1999, pp. 403–429.

Trotter, William Monroe

William Monroe Trotter, a pioneering publisher and activist, was one of the most important figures in the struggle for African American civil rights in the early twentieth century, and an influential predecessor of some of the most strident writers and activists of the Harlem Renaissance.

Trotter was raised in Boston, in that city's abolitionist tradition, and he absorbed a passion for racial equality from his father, James Monroe Trotter, a noted political organizer and scholar of African American music. Trotter graduated with honors from Harvard College in 1895 and earned a graduate degree a year later. He entered the real estate profession, setting up his own business as an insurance agent and mortgage negotiator in 1899, the same year that he married Geraldine Louise Pindell. The Trotters were active in the social and political life of Boston's black elite: Trotter helped found the Boston Literary and Historical Association in March 1901 and the Massachusetts Racial Protective Association (MRPA) later that year; both groups were intended as challenges to the accommodationism of Booker T. Washington.

Trotter soon abandoned real estate for publishing. In November 1901, together with Geraldine Trotter and two fellow members of MRPA, George W. Forbes and William H. Scott, Trotter began publication of the *Boston Guardian*, a weekly paper that sought "to voice intelligently the needs and aspirations of the colored American." Within a year, it had achieved a circulation of 2,500. In every issue, Trotter took on the ideas of his archenemy Booker T. Washington, insisting that political rights and access to a complete academic education were key elements of advancement for blacks. The two faced off on 30 July 1903, when Trotter and a group of associates interrupted a speech by Washington at the Columbus Avenue AME Zion Church in Boston; the meeting degenerated in chaos and near-violence, and Trotter was arrested. Outraged by the episode, Washington saw to it that Trotter was prosecuted to the full extent of the law, but Trotter's sentence of thirty days in prison had the unintended effect of making him a hero to members of the black community discontented with Washington's views. Washington would later secretly finance three weekly papers in Boston in the 1900s to challenge Trotter's influence.

Trotter founded numerous political organizations, although his notoriously difficult personality and his lack of interest in mass political mobilization meant that none of these groups ever achieved popularity at the grassroots level. For a brief period, he worked closely with W. E. B. Du Bois; their collaboration led to the formation in July 1905 of the Niagara movement, which pushed for equal political and educational rights. Trotter headed up the group's committee on the press and public opinion, and he and Du Bois drafted its founding "Declaration of Principles." Trotter soon split with Du Bois, however, resigning from the Niagara movement in 1907; without the *Boston Guardian* as its mouthpiece, the group quickly folded, and most of its members joined the National Association for the Advancement of Colored People (NAACP). Although Trotter attended the NAACP's opening convention in May 1909, he refused to join, on the grounds that the organization was too moderate and was dominated by its white leadership. Instead, he poured his energies into his own group, the Negro-American Political League, later renamed the National Equal Rights League (NERL). Founded in April 1908, NERL was conceived as "an organization of the colored people and for the colored people and led by the colored people," a direct challenge to the NAACP.

Trotter's agenda included the defense of black people's civil rights and resistance to the emerging

1187

segregation and disenfranchisement of the era. Trotter never wavered in his militancy: When he met with President Woodrow Wilson in November 1914 to protest the segregation of the federal government, Trotter was summarily ejected from Wilson's office after uttering some harsh words and shaking a finger at the president. In 1915, Trotter led protests against the racist film *Birth of a Nation*; he and ten others were arrested when the film was screened at the Tremont Theater in Boston. Trotter frequently courted arrest in order to get publicity, long before such an approach was adopted by the postwar civil rights movement.

During World War I, Trotter came under federal surveillance because of his strident demands for civil rights and his cooperation with the radical activist Hubert H. Harrison's Liberty League. He refused to attend a government-sponsored conference of black editors, choosing instead to organize the National Liberty Congress in Washington in June 1918. After the war, Trotter hoped to represent NERL at the Versailles Peace Conference to urge the adoption of a provision outlawing racial discrimination. Certain that the Wilson administration would deny him a passport, Trotter traveled to France as a cook on a transatlantic ship. He arrived after Du Bois's Pan-African Congress had ended; although Trotter made some connections with the Japanese delegation, he had almost no influence on events at Versailles. He later testified against the treaty in the U.S. Congress.

In the 1920s, the emergence of a new generation of political activists emboldened by the war and the expansion of the black press combined to displace Trotter from the national spotlight. He had also lost the editorial and emotional support of his wife, who died in an influenza epidemic of 1918. The circulation of the *Guardian* declined noticeably, and more and more of Trotter's own personal funds were needed in order to publish it. He did continue his activism, speaking out in his paper against the philosophies of Marcus Garvey, and meeting with President Calvin Coolidge in 1926 to protest segregation in the federal government. He engaged in some protest activities in Boston. In 1921, when *The Birth of a Nation* was again released in Massachusetts, Trotter collaborated with the NAACP and the Knights of Columbus, a Catholic fraternal order, in efforts that led to the adoption of stringent legal censorship of motion pictures in the state. He also challenged the segregation of Harvard's dormitories and successfully fought for the integration of city hospital staffs.

In April 1934, almost bankrupt, Trotter either jumped or fell to his death from the roof of his apartment building in Boston. His sister Maude Trotter Steward continued publication of the *Boston Guardian* until her death in 1957.

Biography

William Monroe Trotter was born in Chillicothe, Ohio, on 7 April 1872. He attended Hyde Park Grammar School and Hyde Park High School, Boston, Massachusetts; and Harvard College (A.B., 1895; A.M., 1896). He was an editor, *Boston Guardian*, 1901–1934. He was a founder, Boston Literary and Historical Association, 1901; Massachusetts Racial Protective Association, 1901; National Negro Suffrage League, 1903; Boston Suffrage League, 1903; New England Suffrage League, 1904; Niagara movement, 1905; and National Equal Rights League, 1908. Trotter died in Boston, Massachusetts, on 7 April 1934.

CHRISTOPHER CAPOZZOLA

See also Birth of a Nation, The; Du Bois, W. E. B.; Guardian, The; Harrison, Hubert; Niagara Movement; Washington, Booker T.

Further Reading

Du Bois, W. E. B. "William Monroe Trotter." *Crisis*, 41, May 1934, p. 134.

Fox, Stephen R. *The Guardian of Boston: William Monroe Trotter*. New York: Atheneum, 1970.

Puttkammer, Charles W., and Ruth Worthy. "William Monroe Trotter, 1872–1934." *Journal of Negro History*, 43, October 1958, 298–316.

Schneider, Mark R. *Boston Confronts Jim Crow, 1890–1920*. Boston, Mass.: Northeastern University Press, 1997.

Tucker, Earl "Snakehips"

Earl "Snakehips" (or "Snake Hips") Tucker was a charismatic dancer who set the standard for the "snakehips" dance. Although he was among the celebrities of the Harlem Renaissance, little is known of his family history or early biography. Illiterate, he apparently moved from Baltimore, Maryland, to New York City in the mid-1920s. He danced in New York nightclubs as an "eccentric" act, working solo at Connie's Inn and the Cotton Club. Tucker performed to Duke Ellington's composition "East St. Louis Toodle-Oo" (1926), and Ellington, with whom the dancer worked frequently, later composed "Snake Hips Dance" for him. His breakthrough performance in the Broadway revue *Blackbirds* in 1928 solidified his fame and influence. He also appeared at the Savoy Ballroom, the Roseland Ballroom, Small's Paradise, and the Stork Club.

So-called eccentric dancers emphasized extreme isolation of body parts in rhythmic motion to create mesmerizing dances. These dancers were unfamiliar to most audiences in the United States but reflected African-based dance practices seen in the Caribbean. Many audiences found Tucker's dance sexually explicit.

Tucker's stage act varied little in practice during his ten years of celebrity, and its five basic elements can be seen in the short film *Symphony in Black: A Rhapsody of Negro Life* (1935). He typically entered with a sliding step of the feet as his body cascaded, seemingly without the limitation of bones, in abrupt rhythmic accents. He performed the "snakehips" dance itself, moving his pelvis in wider and wider circles as his feet crossed each other, tracing small circles on the floor. He followed this physical exaggeration with a brief pantomime parody of the Charleston dance, and then a sliding "belly roll" segment in which he isolated segments of his torso with great rhythmic control, working upward from the knees, through the pelvis, and into the torso, chest, and shoulders as the feet slid in counterpoint. Tucker also performed a "tremble" segment, in which he held his body as a single unit but allowed a fast inner rhythm to emerge from his feet and vibrate his entire body. His standard costume emphasized his exaggerations: He wore a loose white silk blouse and tight black pants finished with a sequined waist sash and tassel. His performance persona was at once menacing and provocative.

Tucker has been described as "the first male headliner who did not tap." His influence was profound and far-reaching; and his expertise and charisma drew audiences to consider extravagant isolations of the torso and pelvis, an interest that trickled down to latter-day male dancers including Elvis Presley and Prince.

When Tucker suddenly became ill, Duke Ellington, who treated him like a musician in the Ellington orchestra, paid the hospital bills. Tucker died of unspecified "internal ailments" in 1937.

Biography

Earl "Snakehips" Tucker was born c. 1909 near Baltimore, Maryland. He moved to New York City in the mid-1920s and began performing at Connie's Inn and the Cotton Club, often with the Duke Ellington Orchestra. His Broadway debut was in *Blackbirds of 1928*. He remained a celebrity for a decade. Tucker died in New York City in 1937.

THOMAS DEFRANTZ

See also Blackbirds; Cotton Club; Dance; Ellington, Duke; Roseland Ballroom; Savoy Ballroom; Small's Paradise

Selected Works

"Rhythmania." (Cotton Club.)
Symphony in Black: Rhapsody of Negro Life. (Film short, 1935.)

Further Reading

Cunard, Nancy, ed. *Negro Anthology Made by Nancy Cunard 1931–1933.* London: Wishart, 1934, p. 46.
Stearns, Marshall, and Jean Stearns. *Jazz Dance: The Story of American Vernacular Dance.* New York: Schirmer, 1979, pp. 236–238. (Originally published 1964.)

Tuskegee Experiment

The Tuskegee syphilis experiment was a study conducted between 1932 and 1972 in which 399 African American men with syphilis were left untreated in order to study the course of the disease. The study, run in its later years by the Centers for Disease Control, also involved 201 men who did not have the disease; they were used as controls in order to have a group of men with similar backgrounds to compare against the infected men.

Women were not used, because it would have been more difficult to identify their date of initial infection, and it was important to the findings to use subjects who were in the tertiary stage (the last and most damaging phase of syphilis). In this phase, common complications include crust-covered ulcers on the skin, deterioration of the bones, and scar tissue forming in the heart or the stretching of its vessel walls, causing an aneurysm and possibly an aortic rupture, leading to sudden death. Doctors involved in the study found it convenient to use the term "bad blood" instead of explaining the meaning of "syphilis"; it was not uncommon for the terms to be used interchangeably. To those being tested, the term "bad blood" covered a diversity of ailments, including problems as simple as common headaches and body aches. At the end of the experiment, many did not understand that they had syphilis and were still under the impression that they were being treated.

An important study of syphilis had taken place in Macon County, Alabama, a year before the Tuskegee experiment began. The Julius Rosenwald Fund—a philanthropic organization that set forth as one of it primary goals the financial support of causes and organizations that would improve the conditions of African Americans—joined the U.S. Public Health Service (PHS) to carry out demonstrations of syphilis control in six locations, targeting rural southern areas with a large number of blacks. Among the six areas chosen was Macon County, Alabama, the home of Tuskegee Institute. Of the six areas tested, Macon County was found to have the highest rate of infection, 36 percent.

PHS hoped to continue the study, but state and local health officials seemed unable to contribute any substantial amount of money—and a defining rule of the Rosenwald Fund was that local organizations had to help carry out the programs. Expansion would be necessary if the demonstration continued, and the Rosenwald Fund could not, financially, undertake the task of curing and caring for an entire county. The standard process for treating syphilis in the 1930s took more than a year to administer to each patient and involved several drugs (including two arsenic compounds and mercury). In addition, the program would have had to expand to include other diseases. With regret, the Rosenwald Fund withdrew monetary support.

When the head of PHS, Dr. Taliaferro Clark, finished a report on the syphilis control demonstration, however, an idea occurred to him for a new study that would become "the longest non-therapeutic experiment on human beings in medical history" (Jones 1993, 91). Clark felt that the population of Macon County offered an exceptional opportunity to study the course of untreated syphilis. Only thirty-three of the 1,400 blacks involved in the demonstration had received any type of treatment for the disease, and

none of those thirty-three had received the standard full course of medication. No study using the scientific method had ever proved that syphilis affected blacks and whites differently. This belief—based only on doctors' observations—was discussed in medical literature; many physicians in the 1930s hypothesized that during the later stages of syphilis the cardiovascular system was more likely to be attacked in blacks and the neural system in whites. An important study on syphilis, the Oslo study, had been completed using white patients in 1929, but it was based on the case records of these patients. Clark felt he could improve the study design by being able to conduct live physical examinations. He appeared to have no ethical conflicts regarding the study; he used "phrases like 'unparalleled opportunity' and 'ready-made opportunity' in referring to the study. The phrases seemed to equate the absence of obstacles with a mandate. They were not the words of a man who entertained any ethical or moral qualms about what he was proposing" (Jones, 94).

When first conceived, the study was scheduled to last only about six months. Therefore, the ethical implications of not treating these patients seemed unimportant: Medication could be made available afterward. Eventually, as a concession to the state board of health of Alabama, Clark agreed to provide some medication to those who tested positive. It was expected, not unrealistically, that the patients would be cured; in any event, however, it was hoped that they would become noninfectious for some period of time.

Clark placed Dr. Raymond A. Vonderlehr in charge of the study. Vonderlehr's postgraduate work included an extensive study of cardiovascular syphilis, which was Clark's main interest with respect to the Tuskegee experiment. During the initial experiment, the men received an extensive physical examination, and on a separate visit most received a spinal tap. At the original end date of the study, Vonderlehr submitted his findings to the American Heart Association and was told that these findings were inconclusive. The Heart Association's panel believed there was no substantial proof that syphilis was the direct cause of the cardiovascular complications in the subjects. Vonderlehr disagreed and wanted to continue the study in order to find more support for his claim, but PHS was under a financial strain. It was unlikely the experiment would continue.

The Tuskegee experiment was kept alive by the retirement of Clark as the head of PHS. His successor was Vonderlehr, who—with a new, influential position—made sure that the study continued. He expanded the scope of the experiment. The patients would now be seen through to the time of their autopsy. Much more information about the effects of the disease on the body could then be obtained than were possible with a physical examination. The addition of 200 men as a control group would give a basis for comparison. The men received periodic examinations, placebo drugs, and promises that they were being treated for "bad blood." It is estimated that by 1969 between twenty-eight and one hundred men died as a direct result of complications from the disease.

By the end of the 1930s, the study moved forward and had a well-established bureaucracy. American health organizations traveled throughout the country targeting syphilis, but the men of the Tuskegee experiment were repeatedly prevented from receiving treatment. In the late 1940s, as penicillin became the standard treatment, PHS would still insist that the experiment was more important.

The story reached national attention on 25 July 1972, when it was reported by the Associated Press. A congressional panel was established, and the study was officially terminated in October. A lawsuit filed by the National Association for the Advancement of Colored People provided the survivors with a settlement of more than $9 million. In addition, the federal government would be responsible for providing free medical care and burial services to the remaining participants and their families. On 16 May 1997, President Bill Clinton publicly acknowledged the wrongdoing of the government with a formal apology.

EBONY Z. GIBSON

See also Harlem: 6—Public Health

Further Reading

Gamble, Vanessa. "Under the Shadow of Tuskegee: African-Americans and Health Care." *American Journal of Public Health*, 87(4), 1997.

Gray, Fred D. *The Tuskegee Syphilis Study: The Real Story and Beyond*. Montgomery, Ala.: Black Belt, 1998.

Johnson, Charles Spurgeon. *Shadow of the Plantation*. Chicago, Ill.: University of Chicago Press, 1934.

Jones, James H. *Bad Blood: The Tuskegee Syphilis Experiment*. New York: Free Press, 1993.

Parron, Thomas. *Shadow on the Land: Syphilis*. New York: Reynal and Hitchcock, 1937.

Reverby, Susan M., ed. *Tuskegee's Truths: Rethinking the Tuskegee Syphilis Study*. Chapel Hill: University of North Carolina Press, 2000.

Schick, Tom W. "Race, Class, and Medicine: 'Bad Blood' in Twentieth-Century America." *Journal of Ethnic Studies*, 10, Summer 1982.

267 House

From 1926 to 1928, 267 House at 267 West 136th Street, known as "Niggeratti Manor," was the residence of Richard Bruce Nugent and Wallace Thurman, famous members of Harlem's literati. Nugent and Thurman's room, where many parties and gatherings took place, became one of Harlem's bohemian centers. There, black men and women "in the life" (gay men, lesbians, bisexuals, and transgendered people) met, drank bathtub gin, listened to music, watched performances, and discussed black art.

Unlike Harlem's other bohemian centers, 267 produced a literary journal, *Fire!!—Devoted to Younger Negro Artists*, though it produced only one issue (November 1926). The idea for this journal arose when Nugent met Langston Hughes at one of Georgia Douglas Johnson's weekly literary salons in Washington, D.C.; however, most of the work for *Fire!!* was done at Niggeratti Manor. Thurman became its editor; at the Manor, he and Nugent tossed a coin to see who would write a story "about homosexuality" and who would write one "about prostitution"—their intention being to obtain free publicity by getting *Fire!!* banned in Boston. Their contributions represented their goal as bohemians, "the cradle of revolt against establishment arts" (Lewis 1979, 193). *Fire!!* was indeed scorching, and it made the Manor widely known, if reviled in genteel company and in print. As a result, the Manor became a magnet for kindred iconoclast spirits.

One of those spirits was the writer Zora Neale Hurston, whom many scholars give credit for helping name 267. "Thurman and Hurston also mocked themselves by calling 267 House 'Niggeratti Manor,' and all the younger artists called Thurman their 'leader'— the fullest embodiment of outrageous, amoral independence among them" (Lewis, 193). Long before the scholarly revival of the Harlem Renaissance, however, Nugent and Thurman were themselves interested in positioning their Manor and staking a claim for its bohemian, avant-garde art. They did so with Nugent's unpublished novella "Gentleman Jigger" (c. 1930) and Thurman's novel *Infants of the Spring* (1932). These similar histories of the Manor barely conceal the real people on whom the characters are modeled, with exaggerations and editorial comment.

"Gentleman Jigger" sidesteps the question of who coined the term "niggerati" but focuses on the Manor, "the meeting place for all Negroes who could even pretend to the greatness that was to be the Negro under the new order." The figures who appear include Nugent (as the character Jerome Stuartt) and Thurman (as the character Raymond "Rusty" Pellman), as well as five others involved in creating *Fire!!*: Gwendolyn Bennett, John Davis, Aaron Douglas, Langston Hughes, and Hurston. They "were the all-in-all to the entire Negro Art Movement. Night after night they met to plan the future, the cultural future of their Race, with the aid of much gin and a Victrola [a brand of phonograph]. And as Stuartt had foreseen, Rusty and he were the nucleus of all this wonderful movement." *Infants of the Spring*, however, removes Thurman from the nucleus, leaving just Paul Arbian (Nugent's character), the most bohemian habitué of the Manor. Arbian coins the term "Niggeratti Manor" and decorates the place with his erotic drawings. The Manor comes alive through Arbian, "his six foot body, graceful and magnetic, his dirty yellow face aglow with some inner incandescence, his short stubborn hair defiantly disarrayed, his open shirt collar forming a dirty and inadequate frame for his classically curved neck" (44).

The Manor offered radical freedom, and it even attracted—as described in "Gentleman Jigger"—"the older school of nincompoops and fogies" whom the "Niggeratti" aimed to usurp. Both this work and *Infants of the Spring* describe how a character called Dr. A. L. Parkes (based on Alain Locke) tries to coordinate a literary salon at 267 and preside over "the outstanding personalities in a new generation [who] are not, as were [their] predecessors, concerned with donning armor, and clashing swords with the enemy in the public square" (233–234). Parkes warns, however, that he is "somewhat fearful of the decadent strain" distracting artists from their work (234). After a silent pause, pandemonium erupts. The Manor's "outstanding personalities" clash over their different and sometimes glib opinions about the nature and purpose of black art. It is suggested that this lack of unity contributes to the demise of the Manor.

The real Niggeratti Manor officially ended when Nugent and Thurman moved to a rooming house at 128th Street between Lenox and Fifth avenues, where Thurman's friendship with Louise Thompson developed. Soon afterward, Thurman and Thompson were married. According to *Infants of the Spring*, the Manor's patron, Euphoria Blake, wants her indigent bohemians to leave so that she can transform 267 into a dormitory for "young bachelor women." Raymond Taylor (Thurman) moves in with Lucille (Thompson) after the denizens of the Manor have scattered. In "Gentleman Jigger," the demise of 267 is conveyed through Rusty's declining health. Stuartt lands a role as an extra in the New York debut of *Porgy* and then follows the production to London.

SETH CLARK SILBERMAN

See also Black Bohemia; Fire!!; Homosexuality; Hurston, Zora Neale; Infants of the Spring; Locke, Alain; Niggerati; Nugent, Richard Bruce; Patterson, Louise Thompson; Thurman, Wallace

Further Reading

Kalaidjian, Walter. *American Culture between the Wars: Revisionary Modernism and Postmodern Critique.* New York: Columbia University Press, 1993.

Kisseloff, Jeff. *You Must Remember This: An Oral History of Manhattan from the 1890s to World War II.* New York: Schocken, 1989.

Lewis, David Levering. *When Harlem Was in Vogue.* New York and Oxford: Oxford University Press, 1979.

Van Notten, Eleonore. *Wallace Thurman's Harlem Renaissance.* Amsterdam and Atlanta, Ga.: Rodopi, 1994.

United Colored Democracy

Although black populations in New York City requested political appointments during the 1880s and 1890s, their requests were often ignored or mocked by the Republican Party. During the latter years of the nineteenth century, members of the black community were given the lowest offices that white politicians could offer. They were given positions as assistant janitors, street cleaners, and common laborers, with titles such as "street inspector" or "detailed inspector of garbage." Osofsky (1960) verifies that black New Yorkers often sold their votes for minimal monetary sums on election day.

In 1898, two disgruntled black Republicans in New York, Edward E. Lee and James C. Carr, broke with the party and established the United Colored Democracy (UCD), the first black Democratic organization. Initially the community socially ostracized members of this new organization. For their political support of the New York Democratic County Committee at Tammany Hall, however, they were given greater political power than any blacks had experienced. Edward "Chief" Lee, an illiterate native of Virginia, was a bellman when he was named as the first Negro Democratic leader. Lee was appointed county sheriff for his political patronage and secured many jobs for blacks during his fifteen-year tenure as leader. Many blacks received more lucrative and impressive positions than Lee, however, probably because Lee was uneducated. Edwin Horne, grandfather of singer Lena Horne and secretary general of the United Colored Democracy, was named assistant inspector in the Combustible Division of the New York Fire Department.

Beginning in 1905, a black person was routinely named assistant district attorney.

White Democrats were organized through regional voting districts with individual leaders for each district, whereas UCD represented all black Democrats in the city. Black leadership was appointed, not elected, with black leaders represented by white leaders in the Tammany organization. Blacks were not integrated into the Democratic Party on the city or state level and were not able to organize at a grassroots level. UCD's leaders benefited greatly from this relationship, while few rank-and-file members received precinct- or district-level positions. Because UCD was so broadly spread, it was ineffective in serving the needs of blacks in Harlem and other areas where blacks lived. Black activists tried to secure additional positions for black nurses and doctors at Harlem General Hospital, which served most of the city's black citizens, in the 1920s. Unfortunately, the hospital was under white Tammany district control and did not lend its support to an increased black presence.

Although the Democratic affiliates firmly controlled most of the municipal patronage in the city, they faced strong patronage competition from the black Republican leader Charles Anderson on the state level. Anderson, who served as president of the Young Men's Colored Republican Club of New York County beginning in 1890, supplied state patronage for black Republicans in numerous positions. Beginning in 1915, Ferdinand Q. Morton served as UCD leader; he was successful in getting blacks positions on the state assembly and council of aldermen. He was an ambitious, excellent organizer and orator whose success surpassed that of Anderson. Morton was named an assistant district attorney from 1916 to 1921 and later was named municipal civil service commissioner in 1922 by Mayor John F. Hylan. When James "Jimmy" Walker later had a successful mayoral candidacy, he rewarded Morton by reappointing him as commissioner in 1927.

In addition to conflicts with black Republicans, UCD also had problems with Caribbean-born Democrats, who under the leadership of J. Raymond Jones sought municipal patronage from UCD. State corruption investigations and the Seabury corruption scandal led to the resignation of Mayor Jimmy Walker in 1932. Morton recognized the power shifting to Republicans. The newly elected mayor, Fiorello La Guardia, offered to reappoint Morton as commissioner if he changed political parties. Morton resigned his UCD leadership and his Democratic Party membership in 1935. To keep his position as commissioner, Morton joined the American Labor party.

Upon Morton's defection, local blacks gained control over Harlem's black Assembly District 19 and District 21. UCD lost all its power, and blacks were gradually included in the larger Democratic body.

KAREN COTTON MCDANIEL

See also Anderson, Charles W.; Morton, Ferdinand Q.; Party Politics; Politics and Politicians

Further Reading

Katznelson, Ira. *Black Men, White Cities: Race, Politics, and Migration in the United States, 1900–1830, and Britain, 1948–1968.* London: Oxford University Press, 1973.

McKay, Claude. *Harlem: Negro Metropolis.* New York: Dutton, 1940.

Mjagkij, Nina, ed. *Organizing Black America: An Encyclopedia of African American Associations.* New York: Garland, 2001.

Osofsky, Gilbert. *Harlem: The Making of a Ghetto—Negro New York, 1890–1930.* New York: Harper & Row, 1960.

Salzman, Jack, ed. *Encyclopedia of African American Culture and History,* Vol. 5. New York: Macmillan, 1996.

Universal Negro Improvement Association

The Universal Negro Improvement Association (UNIA) was the brainchild of the black nationalist leader Marcus Garvey. Garvey was born on 17 August 1887 in Saint

Parade through Harlem by the United Negro Improvement Association (UNIA) convention, 1920. (Schomburg Center for Research in Black Culture, New York Public Library.)

Ann's Bay, Jamaica. He learned early—after several failed attempts to organize black workers—about the subtle nature of racism within the English administrative and political system. Garvey traveled to several areas in Central and South America, where he studied the conditions of Africans. In 1912, he traveled to London; there he came across Booker T. Washington's autobiography *Up From Slavery.* This book transformed Garvey's life and gave him a vision for building a great African kingdom.

In the summer of 1914, he returned to Jamaica, where, on 20 July, he formed the Universal Negro Improvement and Conservation Association and African Communities League (UNIA). The organization was designed to unite all peoples of color and African heritage. Originally, UNIA worked as a fraternal and benevolent organization dedicated to racial uplift and industrial training for blacks. It followed Booker T. Washington's Tuskegee model. UNIA struggled in Jamaica but it blossomed when Garvey relocated to Harlem. By 1916, UNIA had headquarters in a small basement room in Harlem. Garvey was a tireless worker preaching racial uplift and self-help, and his efforts paid off as branches of UNIA began to spring up all over the country and several areas in the world.

By 1920U, NIA had spread to Canada, the Caribbean, Africa, and Central America. Garvey organized ordinary African Americans into a small army of loyal independent-minded citizens dedicated to his message of self-help and economic development. Garvey rallied these troops at large gatherings where he preached his positive message of racial uplift and black people's greatness. He gave his followers a sense of belonging, creating a number of entities that offered them an opportunity to lead and participate—a right unavailable in the larger society.

UNIA had an African League for young men. African American women had the Black Cross Nursing Corps and the Universal Motor Corps. UNIA also offered a juvenile division, a youth corps for young people who wanted to participate. UNIA had an official flag—red, black, and green. It also developed official poems, slogans, prayers, poetry, and songs to unite its followers.

On 17 August 1918, UNIA began publishing *Negro World*, its official newspaper, edited by Garvey. *Negro World* had a large circulation, reaching not only most major cities of the United States but the Caribbean, Canada, Europe, and Africa as well. In the early 1920s, the paper was made more accessible to its readers by including a women's section and by having French and Spanish editions. Several European countries banned the paper because of a fear of Garvey's call for black independence.

UNIA was supported by its philosophy of economic independence. The Negro Factories Corporation was created to finance black business enterprises. The idea was to create businesses that could support African American workers, produce black goods, sell to black customers, and supply black services. UNIA wanted to create a chain of black factories, retailers, services, and other businesses that could power an independent black economy, which could in turn support the black world. Garvey encouraged local branches of UNIA to own their own buildings and business enterprises. The branches owned such businesses as bakeries, millinery and hat factories, steam laundries, grocery stores, and haberdasheries.

The most celebrated enterprise of UNIA was the Black Star Line, a steamship company modeled after the White Star Line. It was opened on 23 June 1919 to promote commerce among African people worldwide. The company sold stock, allowing ordinary people to invest in the ambitious venture. The stock was sold through agents, rallies, advertisements in *Negro World*, and mailed circulars. UNIA purchased three ships: the *Frederick Douglass, Antonio Maceo,* and *Shadyside.*

As a business venture, the Black Star Line was a failure. UNIA was overcharged for the three ships, which all had major structural or engineering defects. Between 1919 and 1922, when the company finally went bankrupt, UNIA lost more than $1 million. Many people in the African American community chided UNIA for its extravagance in buying the ships and paying the administrators.

The business dealings of the Black Star Line presented an opportunity for the FBI under J. Edgar Hoover to investigate and undermine the organization. FBI agents intensified their ongoing investigation, started in 1919, into Garvey and the organization. In all, Hoover coordinated the efforts of seven governmental agencies investigating UNIA. Early in 1922, the federal government charged Garvey with fraud, when UNIA officials mailed out advertisements for the Black Star Line even though they knew the company was bankrupt.

UNIA received a critical blow when Garvey, its leader and founder, was convicted of fraud and sent to prison in 1925. Membership in the organization declined significantly during the period 1925–1927, when Garvey was imprisoned. The organization was rocked by internal squabbling and outside pressures as it struggled to survive despite Garvey's absence. In 1927, Garvey was released from prison and deported back to Jamaica, setting off a scramble for control of the organization. In 1929, Garvey reincorporated the organization in Kingston, Jamaica. This created two UNIAs: one in New York led by Fred Foote, and a rival organization in Kingston. In 1935, Garvey moved his organization to London, where it remained until his death in 1940. Eventually, James Stewart was elected the leader of the organization, which then had headquarters in Cleveland, Ohio. He relocated the headquarters to Monrovia, Liberia, where UNIA struggled to survive.

ABEL BARTLEY

See also Black Star Line; Garvey, Marcus; Negro World

Further Reading

Cronon, David. *Black Moses: The Story of Marcus Garvey and the Universal Negro Improvement Association.* Madison: University of Wisconsin Press, 1955.

Vincent, Theodore G. *Black Power and the Garvey Movement.* Berkeley, Calif.: Rampart, 1971.

Utopia Players

On Sunday, 26 May 1929, the Utopia Players, a theater group composed of students, were scheduled to perform *The Whole Town Is Talking* at the Elks Auditorium in Harlem. Although there is no evidence that the performance ever occurred, the Utopia Players reflect the synergy of artistic production, location, and communal support that underpinned the Harlem Renaissance and its theatrical branch, the "little theater" movement.

The Utopia Players were directed by Gladys McDonald, formerly a branch librarian for the 135th Street Public Library. The group's ability to organize and perform demonstrates the possibilities created during the Harlem Renaissance for young artists by other innovative young artists, as well as the importance of the artistic spaces created in public places like the 135th Street Library.

Most scholars agree that the little theater movement began in 1914, when an ambitious young woman named Anita Bush decided that she would found the theater company that eventually became the Lafayette Players. The financial success of the Lafayette Players encouraged the activities of many other troupes, including the Utopia Players. At their peak, the Lafayette Players often had larger crowds than the small theater spaces where they performed could accommodate. Nonetheless, critics began to call for plays performed about black people, decrying the Lafayette Players' performances of prominent Broadway hits.

In response to both the commercial success of the Lafayette Players and the ideological tension they generated, W. E. B. Du Bois and the magazine *The Crisis* founded the Krigwa Players in 1926. The Krigwa Players (originally Crigwa, an acronym for the Crisis Guild of Writers and Artists) had a performance space in the basement of the 135th Street Library, which was occupied by successive companies of players after the Krigwa group became inactive in 1930. For example, the Sekondi Players and the Harlem Experimental Theater used the library's basement lecture room (later renamed the Krigwa Playhouse). Artistic production at the 135th Street Brach Library was not limited, however, to the practice space and performances of these particular troupes. As a matter of fact, the consistent exposition of artistic material and speakers surely had an affect on Gladys McDonald, who would go on to become a student in the drama department of New York University and to found the Utopia Players.

As had happened with both the Lafayette Players and the Krigwa Players (although Du Bois participated in founding the Krigwa Players, Eulalie Spence was a primary force in the troupe's productions), a young woman decided to start the Utopia Players. This theater company included Helen Depogny, who worked in education; Milton Weston and Gladys Fowlkes, students at Columbia University; Helen Tynes and Joseph Jackson, students at the New York School of Social Work; Mildred Burch, a graduate of Boston University; Frances Jeffers; Mary Smith; Sedalia Ten Eyck; and others.

SOYICA S. DIGGS

See also Anita Bush Theater Company; Community Theater; Krigwa Players; Lafayette Players; Little Theater Tournament; 135th Street Library; Theater

Further Reading

Krasner, David. *A Beautiful Pageant: African American Theatre, Drama, and Performance in the Harlem Renaissance, 1910–1927.* New York: Palgrave Macmillan, 2002.

Monroe, John G. "A Record of the Black Theatre in New York City." Ph.D. diss., University of Texas at Austin, 1980.

———. "The Harlem Little Theatre Movement, 1920–1929." *Journal of American Culture*, 6(4), Winter 1983.

"Utopia Players under Gladys McDonald to Give Play on May 26." *New York Age*, 11 May 1929.

Van Der Zee, James

James Van Der Zee was the leading photographer of the Harlem Renaissance. His prints, negatives, and glass plates, numbering some 75,000, document the spirit of the movement and were designed to foster pride in being black in the United States between World War I and World War II. Van Der Zee's images combine social documentation and portraiture with an aesthetic sensibility influenced partly by the portraits of the old masters, partly by the soft focus of impressionism, and partly by the Victorian tableau. His photographs constitute a panorama of life in Harlem: marriage portraits, mothers and children, clergymen, members of fraternal orders (he himself was an Elk), politicians, entertainers, artists, athletes, schoolchildren, funerals, marches, political rallies, pool halls, social teas, barbershops, drugstores, and domestic interiors.

Van Der Zee was born on 29 June 1886, in the relatively affluent town of Lenox, Massachusetts, where his father was a sexton at Trinity Episcopalian Church. One of five children, he had two brothers and two sisters. His parents—who had worked in New York as maid and butler to the Union general Ulysses S. Grant—were both musical. Van Der Zee himself played the piano and violin, and musical instruments would later become a theme in his photography. At age fourteen, he bought his first camera and a darkroom kit from a mail-order house. Through high school, he took pictures of his family and friends in Lenox and taught himself how to develop them. Nearly all his mature photographs are black-and-white silver prints.

In 1906, at age twenty, Van Der Zee moved to New York City, where he worked as a waiter and elevator operator. He married Kate Brown and moved to Phoebus, Virginia, the following year, again working in a restaurant. They had two children, a boy who died at age two and a girl who died at fifteen. These losses probably contributed to the prominence of death and funerals in Van Der Zee's imagery. While in Virginia, Van Der Zee made a photograph of a blacksmith shop inspired, he said, by Henry Wadsworth Longfellow's "The Village Blacksmith." The rich dark background of the shop from which figures and objects seem to emerge in light is reminiscent of Caravaggio's tenebrism. The role of memory, which inspired this photograph, would also become a major theme in Van Der Zee's later pictures.

In 1908, the Van Der Zees returned to New York, where James taught piano and violin, and played in various orchestras. His first job in photography materialized in 1914, when he was hired as a darkroom assistant for the Gertz department store in Newark, New Jersey. His salary was $5 a week. By 1916 he had opened the Guarantee Photo Studio on 135th Street in Harlem.

He became quite successful as a portraitist, and in the early 1930s he opened the GGG Studio at 272 Lenox Avenue. His partner was his second wife, Gaynella Greenlee, whom he married after divorcing Kate Brown. In the 1940s and 1950s, Van Der Zee's income began to decline as the heyday of the Harlem Renaissance came to an end. At the same time, photography was becoming a popular hobby so that fewer people sought out professional portrait photographers—

instead, they began taking their own pictures of family and friends.

In 1960, Van Der Zee lost his house and studio, and by 1967 he was living in poverty. His fortunes did not recover until after 1967, when he met Reginald McGhee. McGhee was doing research to find images for an exhibit called "Harlem on My Mind," to be held in 1969 at the Metropolitan Museum in New York, and he had come across Van Der Zee's work. Van Der Zee had more pictures in the show than any other artist. This brought him renewed recognition, and he was once again in demand as a portrait photographer.

In his later career, he was assisted by his third wife, Donna Van Der Zee. This was a period in which Van Der Zee received a number of awards. In 1970, he became a Life Fellow at the Metropolitan, which acquired sixty-six of his pictures for its permanent collection. In 1971, he had his first retrospective at the Studio Museum in Harlem.

Between the two world wars, Van Der Zee responded to Alain Locke's advocacy of the "New Negro" by photographing the black middle and upper-middle class of Harlem. Although his photographs are documentary, they are also infused with the cultural aspirations of black America during the Harlem Renaissance. His portraits reflect a sense of pride in being black, affluent, and talented. His pictures of Harlem's streets show a bustling, vibrant neighborhood, and a black community proud of its heritage and optimistic about its future. In *Theresa Bar and Grill* (1933), Van Der Zee captures the lively ironwork patterns of the balcony and windows over the entrance. The entrance itself is decorated with lettering and enlivened by interior lights.

Van Der Zee was the official photographer for Marcus Garvey's Universal Negro Improvement Association (UNIA). In this capacity, he photographed the leaders of the movement, their rallies, parades, and funerals. One of his photographs, designed to reflect pride in the contemporary achievements of blacks, shows black Americans being awarded the French Croix de Guerre for military service. Van Der Zee's funeral photographs were collected and published in 1978 as the *Harlem Book of the Dead* (an allusion to the ancient Egyptian *Book of the Dead*, and therefore to black roots in Africa).

Van Der Zee's portraits of local people create the image of a comfortable black lifestyle. His subjects typically wear fashionable clothes, which he himself provided if they arrived to be photographed in less-than-impeccable dress. He might, for example, produce a fur stole to dress up a female sitter or a new jacket if the one worn by his male sitter was frayed or missing a button. He often arranged his sitters to resemble a tableau, creating a set piece of life in early-twentieth-century Harlem.

In 1929, he photographed a couple against a painted snowy street. Although warmly dressed (the woman is in a fur-trimmed coat and the man is in a suit and overcoat), the figures betray the fact that the snow is only a backdrop. Both hold, rather than wear, their gloves, so that their rings are visible; and rather than boots, they wear shiny leather shoes. In one of his most famous actual outdoor portraits, made in 1932, Van Der Zee shows a couple in raccoon coats and stylish hats. They are posed with a shiny new car on a Harlem street; the high polish of the chrome is repeated in the woman's patent-leather high-heeled shoes. The variations of texture visible in this photograph are generally characteristic of Van Der Zee's style.

When taking pictures in his studio, Van Der Zee used props (often musical instruments) and painted backdrops, improving the photographs in order to improve the image of Harlem. For the same purpose, he also retouched negatives and prints, even though he was a relatively straight photographer. In one portrait of a man smoking, for example, he scratched in a thin, swirling line of smoke emanating from the tip of the cigarette. In a group portrait of musicians, he scratched a musical staff and notes to look as if they were sounds emerging from the instruments.

Van Der Zee's pictures typically convey an atmospheric quality created by a soft-focus technique and diffused lighting. His tendency toward romanticism is evident when he blends negatives in order to evoke different periods of time, to make absent figures seem present, or to suggest an image envisioned by his sitters. He also had a penetrating psychological sense and was able to capture the essence of character.

In a photo of 1925, Van Der Zee reflects the theme of time by showing a family looking at a family photo album. He contrasts the relaxed, pleased expressions of the older generation with the subtle tension visible in the poses and expressions of the younger generation. In *Daydreams* (1925), he uses the technique of photomontage to reveal a woman's inner fantasy. She sits alone on a bench, surrounded by flowers; a beach scene with her absent lover is superimposed so that he seems to be embracing her. In *Memories* (1938), Van Der Zee uses the same technique to show both the passage of time and the fact that in our unconscious mind (the storehouse of memory) there is no time.

Here, a father and his three children are looking at a photo album. The family dog is seated beside them on the floor. The missing, deceased mother is made present by being superimposed in the background. Van Der Zee also uses photomontage to evoke the future in an undated wedding portrait. Here a bride and groom are seated by an elaborate fireplace. On the floor playing with a doll is the superimposed image of the daughter they hope to have. In his many pictures of soldiers going off to war, Van Der Zee suggests a more uncertain future, never knowing if the young men will survive to return.

In a photo of the funeral of Blanche Powell (daughter of Rev. Adam Clayton Powell Sr. of the Abyssinian Baptist Church), Van Der Zee records the scene from above. The pews are filled with mourners dressed in black, facing a white coffin surrounded by patterns of flowers. The choir members wear white robes and are illuminated from behind by imposing windows. At the upper right, Van Der Zee has blended a large, visionary image of the dead girl towering over the scene.

Of Van Der Zee's many pictures of children, one of the most insightful is *Portrait of Young Girl on the Telephone* (1926). The girl is dressed up, with a large bow in her hair that matches her white socks. She stands out from the soft-focus background, which emphasizes her own clarity and precisely rendered contours. She kneels on a chair, with her elbow resting on the back, in a decidedly adult pose. Her delight in being able to talk on the phone like an adult is evident in her radiant smile.

In addition to local members of the Harlem community, the documentation of UNIA, and images of families and soldiers going off to war, Van Der Zee made many portraits of well-known figures. These constitute a comprehensive record of black celebrities who were Van Der Zee's contemporaries. Among the entertainers he photographed are the dancer Bojangles (Bill Robinson), the jazz singer and pianist Hazel Scott, Eubie Blake, Bill Cosby, Ossie Davis, Ruby Dee, and Duke Ellington. The literary figures include the poets Countee Cullen and Langston Hughes, and the *salonière* A'Lelia Walker. Boxers include the fighters Joe Louis and Muhammad Ali; politicians include Marcus Garvey and Lester Walton, the U.S. ambassador to Liberia. Among the clergy, Van Der Zee photographed the Moorish Jew Rabbi Matthews, the evangelist Father Divine, and Daddy Grace of Grace Church (the United House of Prayer for All People), as well as Adam Clayton Powell Sr. In 1981, he photographed

James Van Der Zee, *Couple in Raccoon Coats*, photograph, 1932. (Copyright ©1996 by Donna Van Der Zee.)

the artist Romare Bearden, and in the following year the graffiti artist Jean-Michel Basquiat, who then painted a portrait of Van Der Zee.

In 1993, Van Der Zee was honored with a retrospective exhibition at the National Portrait Gallery. Today his pictures are in many private collections, and at the Schomburg Center for Research in Black Culture, the Harlem Studio Museum, and the Metropolitan Museum of Art.

Biography

James Van Der Zee was born on 29 June 1886, in Lenox, Massachusetts. He became the leading photographer of the Harlem Renaissance and was appointed the official photographer of the Universal Negro Improvement Association (UNIA) by Marcus Garvey. His major body of work documenting the Harlem Renaissance was made from 1918 to 1945. Although his career declined in the 1950s and 1960s, it revived after the exhibit "Harlem on My Mind" of 1969 at the Metropolitan Museum in New York. In addition to recording middle- and upper-middle-class life in Harlem, Van Der Zee is known for his insightful portraits of celebrities in the black community. At the age of ninety-seven, on 15 May 1983, Van Der Zee died in Washington, D.C., where he had gone to receive an honorary doctorate in humane letters from Howard University.

LAURIE ADAMS

See also Visual Arts; *specific sitters for portraits*

Further Reading

Billops, Camille, and Owen Dodson. *The Harlem Book of the Dead: Photographs by James Van Der Zee.* Dobbs Ferry, N.Y., 1975.

De Cock, Liliane, and Reginald McGhee, eds. *James Van Der Zee.* Dobbs Ferry, N.Y., 1973.

Schoener, Allon, ed. *Harlem on My Mind: Cultural Capital of Black America 1900–1968.* New York, 1968.

Studio Museum in Harlem. *Harlem Renaissance of Black America.* New York, 1987.

Willis-Braithwaite, Deborah. *Van Der Zee.* National Portrait Gallery, Smithsonian Institution, Washington, D.C. (22 October 1993–11 February 1994.)

Willis-Thomas, Deborah. *Black Photographers, 1840–1940.* New York and London, 1985.

Van Doren, Carl

Carl Van Doren became familiar with Harlem's literary circles through his friendships with African American writers during the early 1920s. Writer and editor Claude McKay introduced him to colleagues who promoted interaction among black and white authors. On the eve of McKay's departure for Russia in 1922, James Weldon Johnson gave a farewell party in his honor and invited prominent writers of both races, perhaps the first major gathering of the black and white literati of New York on a purely social level. Van Doren was treated to an evening of discussion with the black writers and editors W. E. B. Du Bois, Walter White, Jessie Redmon Fauset, Arthur Schomburg, and John Rosamond Johnson.

At the Civic Club dinner in New York City on 21 March 1924, Van Doren publicly acknowledged the importance and scope of Harlem's writers in an address titled "The Younger Generation of Negro Writers." Charles S. Johnson, editor of the Urban League's monthly magazine, *Opportunity*, had invited Van Doren to speak at this dinner, which was being held, at least nominally, to celebrate the publication of Jessie Fauset's novel *There Is Confusion*. Van Doren told his black listeners that they were uniquely qualified to bring to American literature the "color, music, gusto, the free expression of gay or desperate moods" it sorely needed. Van Doren further observed: "The Negroes of the country [now] are in a remarkable strategic position with reference to the new literary age which seems to be impending. . . . If the Negroes

are not in a position to contribute these items, I do not know what Americans are." Du Bois added legitimacy to Van Doren's comments by acknowledging that previous generations of African Americans had been denied an authentic literary voice. Van Doren was soon invited to judge writing contests sponsored by *Opportunity*, a widely read African American magazine. He judged its short-story contests in 1924–1925 and 1925–1926.

Van Doren viewed the Harlem Renaissance as a new era of American literary and artistic output, but not as a cultural revolution. In his autobiography *Three Worlds* (1936), he wrote, "The best American music had sprung from [black voices], which had gathered power until they flooded America. . . . I was not Negro, but I was American, and these ancient black voices were in some dim way a part of me too" (259). His view was shared by a small group of critics based in New York, including Henry A. Murray; Raymond Weaver, a professor at Columbia University; and Carl Van Vechten, who also championed a shift toward streetwise, secular mass arts in the literary renaissance of the 1920s.

Van Doren identified two representative examples of art as Harlem-style expression: the journalist H. L. Mencken's persistent commentary, and the play *The Emperor Jones*, starring the African American actor Charles Gilpin, which opened in New York's Greenwich Village in 1920. Van Doren was impressed with Mencken's rebellion against the strain of Puritanism in American literature and with Gilpin's ability to eradicate racial stereotypes, making Eugene O'Neill's powerful work come alive.

Van Doren lived his convictions about the importance of new literature. He declined an invitation to win election to the traditional, conservative National Institute of Arts and Letters in November 1924.

In addition to being an editor at two magazines—*The Nation* and *Century*—Van Doren also edited *The Cambridge History of American Literature* (1917–1921). His varied writings include *Many Minds* (1924), *The Ninth Wave* (1926), *Jonathan Swift* (1930), *American Literature: An Introduction* (1933), and a study of Sinclair Lewis (1933). He also wrote *Benjamin Franklin* (1938), which won a Pulitzer Prize; *The American Novel, 1789–1939* (1940); *Secret History of the American Revolution* (1941); and *The Great Rehearsal* (1948).

The Carl Van Doren Papers are available at the William L. Clements Library at the University of Michigan. The collection includes 147 items and covers the years 1938 to 1950. Much of the material is correspondence between Carl Van Doren and members of the Clements Library staff relating to his research in preparation for his *Secret History of the American Revolution*.

Biography

Carl Van Doren was born 10 September 1885 in Hope (Vermilion County), Illinois. He and his four younger brothers lived comfortably with his parents on a farm near town during his first fifteen years. The family moved to Urbana, Illinois, as Carl, the eldest, entered high school. Van Doren's father was a successful physician and landlord who amassed wealth rapidly. His studious mother was an avid reader who encouraged her children to excel in school. Van Doren graduated from the University of Illinois in 1907 and received his Ph.D. from Columbia University in 1911. He married Irita Bradford of Tallahassee, Florida, in August 1912 and began spending his summers in Cornwall, Connecticut, in Litchfield County. The couple had three daughters: Anne (1915), Margaret (1917), and Barbara (1920). Irita and Carl eventually divorced. Van Doren lectured at Columbia until 1916, when he resigned his primary position to become headmaster of the Brearley School in New York City, an elite secondary school for young women. He continued to teach one graduate class in American literature until 1930. After three years Van Doren left Brearley to become literary editor of *The Nation*. He eventually left his position at *The Nation* and became literary editor of *Century Magazine*. In the late 1930s Van Doren married Jean Wright. He died 18 July 1950 in Torrington, Connecticut.

R. JAKE SUDDERTH

See also Civic Club Dinner, 1924; Du Bois, W. E. B.; Fauset, Jessie Redmon; Johnson, John Rosamond; Nation, The; Opportunity Literary Contests; Schomburg, Arthur A.; White, Walter; *other specific individuals*

Further Reading

Chesnutt, Charles W. "The Negro in Art: How Shall He Be Portrayed?" *Crisis*, November 1926, pp. 28–29.
Douglas, Ann. *Terrible Honesty: Mongrel Manhattan in the 1920s*. New York: Farrar, Straus and Giroux, 1995.
Du Bois, Shirley Graham. *Paul Robeson, Citizen of the World*. Westport, Conn.: Negro Universities Press, 1971. (Foreword by Carl Van Doren. First published 1946.)
Van Doren, Carl. *Three Worlds*. New York: Harper, 1936.

Van Vechten, Carl

Carl Van Vechten—a music critic, novelist, photographer, and collector—was one of the most highly regarded figures who contributed to the Harlem Renaissance, and many of his activities were fundamental to making the movement possible. Because he was white, Van Vechten's contributions are a matter of contemporary debate, not with respect to how much they furthered the movement, but with regard to his motives in relation to such issues as primitivism, stereotyping, and exploitation.

Van Vechten's influence on the Harlem Renaissance came about in several ways. He made direct contributions of funds to cultural activities, such as *Fire!!*, the literary magazine that was briefly the organ of the younger, more experimental members of the Harlem Renaissance (it lasted for only a single issue). He wrote *Nigger Heaven* (1926), a novel that first attracted a white readership to works about blacks in Harlem. Because *Nigger Heaven* contributed greatly to the emergence of Harlem as the center of African American culture, its depiction of African Americans stimulated a discussion concerning the type of literature that blacks should create in response to Van Vechten's novel. Van Vechten saw to it that works of fiction by Rudolph Fisher, Nella Larsen, and Wallace Thurman were published, and he also helped the artist Aaron Douglas find outlets for his graphic designs. Van Vechten extensively archived materials that later composed five major library collections of African American cultural materials. His parties, which gathered accomplished artists, intellectuals, writers, and musicians without regard for race, allowed for important social contacts between blacks and whites. Finally, during his long career as a portrait photographer, he created an invaluable visual record of the personalities of the Harlem Renaissance.

In contrast to the rural provincialism that dominated Cedar Rapids, Iowa, where Carl Van Vechten was born in 1880, his parents were relatively sophisticated and well educated. His mother had been associated with the suffragist Lucy Stone at Kalamazoo College and was responsible for the library in Cedar Rapids. His father, who later went into the insurance business, was the cofounder of a school for black children in Piney Woods, Mississippi. Van Vechten grew up exposed to books and literary periodicals and at an early age developed a devotion to reading and writing. His family was also musical, and all the children played instruments, Carl being a pianist. Many theatrical companies passed through Cedar Rapids, and Van Vechten was exposed to plays and musical shows.

Van Vechten attended the University of Chicago, graduating in 1903. During the period of his college education, he was exposed to black entertainers of the ragtime era, becoming familiar with Bert Williams, Carrie Washington, and Carita Day. After graduating, he found employment at the *Chicago American* newspaper as a reporter and news photographer. In 1906 he relocated to New York, where he began to work as an assistant to the music critic at the *New York Times*. Moving on to other assignments as a correspondent in Paris for the *Times*, and drama critic for the *New York Press*, he worked as a journalist until 1914. Subsequently, he worked for a year as a freelance critic, contributing articles to several national publications, and he married actress Fania Marinoff in October 1914.

As early as 1917, Van Vechten had begun promoting African American novelists, poets, dancers, singers, and artists by publishing articles in mainstream publications, such as *Vanity Fair* magazine, in which he favorably mentioned blacks even though they were not necessarily connected to the subject at hand. Van Vechten is not generally associated with intellectual movements, yet he fits in well with the American cultural nationalism advocated by Van Wyck Brooks, which in its pluralism recognizes the contribution of blackness to American culture. Van Vechten's publication of articles on black music in *Seven Arts* connects him to the group of romantic nationalists that included Lewis Mumford and Randolph Bourne. The connection may be further evidenced in Van Vechten's efforts to publicize *Moby-Dick* and Herman Melville's later writings, writings that Van Vechten praised at a time when critical regard for those books was not as great as it is today.

Van Vechten published five volumes of his critical essays between 1916 and 1919. Because these books sold poorly, he turned to writing about cats and published *A Tiger in the House* (1920) and *Lord of the Housetops* (1921). Although he had published seven books to good reviews, Van Vechten had not made any money as a writer, and he turned to writing novels as a consequence. In his fiction, he adopted a comic mode that

expressed sophistication and absurdity, and these writings found a ready audience. His first novel, *Peter Whiffle*, a fictional biography, went through eight printings in 1922.

Van Vechten wrote six additional novels, concluding with *Parties* in 1930; although he is remembered now only for *Nigger Heaven* (1926), he was one of the most popular writers of the 1920s. Van Vechten was prompted to begin work on *Nigger Heaven* because he had read Walter White's novel *The Fire in the Flint* and had met White though their joint publisher, Alfred A. Knopf. Through Walter White, Van Vechten gained introductions to the black intelligentsia, and he soon became acquainted with every black person of note in New York. Van Vechten began to socialize with the prominent African Americans of Harlem, and he became a regular attendee at parties and celebrations. His enthusiasm for proselytizing African American culture through magazine articles in *Vanity Fair*, a prominent magazine of the period, soon gained him a reputation as an authority on Harlem, and in Europe it was believed that he was black. Van Vechten is often credited with popularizing Harlem as a playground for white people, and he did become a habitué of Harlem venues of every kind from upscale cabarets that catered to white clients to drag balls and rent parties. The list of prominent white figures whom he conducted on tours through Harlem is long and included Somerset Maugham and Edmund Wilson. Van Vechten also became active as a philanthropist, funding awards at *Opportunity* magazine for excellence in writing.

One of Van Vechten's most significant contributions to the Harlem Renaissance was his work on behalf of getting black writers into print. An admirer of James Weldon Johnson's documentary novel, *The Autobiography of an Ex-Colored Man* (1912), which had been out of print, Van Vechten made arrangements for Knopf to revive it. The novel was reprinted in 1927. Van Vechten's appreciation for Johnson's novel was reflected in the documentary characteristics of *Nigger Heaven*, which interjected propagandistic and documentary materials at various points in the narrative. He also prevailed on Knopf to publish Langston Hughes's book of poems *The Weary Blues* (1926), and he helped Hughes to place poems and articles in prominent periodicals such as the *New Republic* and *The Nation*. Van Vechten had met Hughes, the premier poet of the Harlem Renaissance, through Walter White in 1924, and they remained close friends for the rest of their lives. Through Van Vechten's efforts,

Knopf published Nella Larsen's novels *Quicksand* (1927) and *Passing* (1929), and Rudolph Fisher's novel *The Walls of Jericho* (1928).

It is chiefly through Van Vechten's famous parties in his chic apartment at 150 West Fifty-fifth Street that the Harlem Renaissance may be connected to the "roaring twenties." Just before the stock market crash in 1929, Van Vechten inherited $1 million from his sister-in-law, Fannie Van Vechten, further insulating him from economic necessity. Already well off from his novels, he was able to throw lavish parties that often went on all night. His parties were connected to a particular type of antiracist social engineering that he had invented and that he pursued along with the hostess Muriel Draper. According to Van Vechten's theory, he mixed the races at his parties to demonstrate that prejudice against blacks was a result of ignorance about them, for they were just people. By allowing whites and blacks of the intelligentsia to mingle socially, reasoned Van Vechten and Draper, eventually the realization that no serious difference existed between the races would percolate down to the common man through the efforts of intellectuals in positions of cultural power and through works of art that combated racial stereotypes. Eventually, it was thought, racism would simply dissolve. Van Vechten's guests included such notables as Salvador Dalí, Theodore Dreiser, George Gershwin, Fannie Hurst, Paul Robeson, Helena Rubenstein, Bessie Smith, and James Weldon Johnson, and they might include celebrities from across the entire globe. It was also through Van Vechten that African Americans were able to meet one another, as when Zora Neale Hurston was introduced to Ethel Waters at a dinner that included Sinclair Lewis and Anna May Wong among the guests.

Despite a regimen of continual drinking and carousing and with little sleep for months, Van Vechten wrote his most famous novel rapidly, completing three drafts during the winter of 1925–1926. *Nigger Heaven* became cause for a controversy from the moment of its publication, for its title, used by a white person, offended many blacks. He used the title because he felt that it carried the weight of his view of Harlem as a place that was at once a refuge from the South and an embodiment of the social conditions that remained uncorrected—at once symbolic, ironic, and tragic. On publication in August 1926, the novel sold 100,000 copies, bringing the author $68,000. In the following two years, the book went through two more printings and translations in nearly a dozen European languages. Through his novel, Van Vechten hoped to show that African Americans were just people and thereby help to eliminate the foundation for racism. The novel also revealed the social divisions that exist within the black society of Harlem, which showed blacks as individuals. Those black writers who approved of the novel, such as the reviewer Eric Walrond, saw it as expressive of a level of objectivity about African American life that they themselves were not equipped to equal; thus, for some, Van Vechten set the standard for a new type of literature. Those who disapproved of the novel saw it as a continuation of the derogatory depiction of African Americans that they hoped to overcome through the depiction of blacks as agents of uplift and social and professional attainment.

After his last book, *Sacred and Profaner Memories* (1932), Van Vechten began a new career as a photographer. He worked as a photographer for the next thirty-two years. He was resolved to document African American culture; however, he photographed a wide range of subjects from many fields of endeavor, such as the architect Philip Johnson, the novelist William Faulkner, and the dancer Martha Graham. Having begun to work in the area of photographic documentation, he began to establish collections so that the materials he was assembling would have permanent locations. These collections included the James Weldon Johnson Memorial Collection of Negro Arts and Letters at Yale University (1941), the George Gershwin Memorial Collection of Music and Musical Literature at Fisk University (1944), the Rose McClendon Memorial Collection of Photographs of Celebrated Negroes at Howard University (1946), and the Jerome Bowers Peterson Collection of Photographs by Carl Van Vechten of Celebrated Negroes at the University of New Mexico (1954). Following these original deposits, other collections have been established, so that the Library of Congress in Washington, D.C., has 1,395 photographs by Van Vechten, and there's a collection at the National Portrait Gallery.

Following James Weldon Johnson's death in 1938, Van Vechten worked with the Memorial Committee to establish a collection documenting Johnson's contributions in arts, literature, education, and public service at Yale University. Beginning in 1950, Van Vechten began the painstaking task of preparing his own papers for deposit in Yale University. The Johnson collection established by Van Vechten now includes the papers of Richard Wright and Jean Toomer, as well as significant holdings concerning other prominent African American writers. Van Vechten also saw to it

Miguel Covarrubias, *Caricature of Carl Van Vechten.* (Library of Congress.)

Selected Works

The Blind Bow-Boy. 1923.
Excavations. 1926.
Music and Bad Manners. 1916.
Nigger Heaven. 1926.
Parties. 1930.
Peter Whiffle: His Life and Works. 1922.
Sacred and Profane Memories. 1932.
The Tiger in the House. 1920.

Further Reading

Bernard, Emily, ed. *Remember Me to Harlem: The Letters of Langston Hughes and Carl Van Vechten, 1925–1964.* New York: Knopf, 2001.

Byrd, Rudolph P., ed. *Generations in Black and White: Photographs by Carl Van Vechten.* Athens: University of Georgia Press, 1993. (From the Weldon Johnson Memorial Collection.)

Davis, Keith. *The Passionate Observer: Photographs by Carl Van Vechten.* Albuquerque: University of New Mexico Press, 1993.

Kellner, Bruce. *A Bibliography of the Work of Carl Van Vechten.* Westport, Conn.: Greenwood Press, 1980.

———. *Carl Van Vechten and the Irreverent Decades.* Norman: University of Oklahoma Press, 1968.

———, ed. *Letters of Carl Van Vechten.* New Haven, Conn.: Yale University Press, 1987.

Lueders, Edward G. *Carl Van Vechten.* New York: Twayne, 1965.

Mauriber, Saul, comp. *Portraits, the Photography of Carl Van Vechten.* Indianapolis, Ind.: Bobbs-Merrill, 1978.

Van Vechten, Carl. *The Dance Photography of Carl Van Vechten,* intro. Paul Padgette. New York: Schirmer, 1981.

———. *Portraits by Carl Van Vechten: A Photographic Exhibition.* Nashville, Tenn.: Carl Van Vechten Gallery of Fine Arts, Fisk University, 1981.

that the papers of many of his associates, such as Muriel Draper, were preserved at Yale University.

Biography

Carl Van Vechten was born in Cedar Rapids, Iowa, in 1880. He attended the University of Chicago and received a Ph.D. in 1903. He was employed as a journalist by the newspaper *Chicago American* until 1906. He then moved to New York and wrote music criticism for the *New York Times* from 1906 to 1912, and then drama criticism for the *New York Press* from 1913 to 1914. He then worked as a freelance journalist, until becoming a successful novelist. He was awarded an honorary doctoral degree by Fisk University in 1955. Van Vechten died on 21 December 1964 in New York.

JON WOODSON

See also Nigger Heaven; Seven Arts; Vanity Fair; White Novelists and the Harlem Renaissance; White Patronage; *specific individuals*

Vanguard

Vanguard was a left-wing political club formed by the sculptor Augusta Savage and the activist Louise Thompson (Louise Thompson Patterson) in 1933. It served as an important link between intellectuals of the Harlem Renaissance and the Communist Party of the United States.

Savage, who was born and reared in Florida, emerged as one of the most respected artists in Harlem by the early 1930s. In 1929, she won the Julius Rosenwald Award for her sculpture *Gamin*. In 1932, she returned to Harlem after three years of studying and sculpturing in France. Louise Thompson, although not herself an artist, was a central figure in the Harlem Renaissance. Soon after her arrival in New York in 1928, she was briefly married to Wallace Thurman. She befriended several leading intellectuals of the renaissance, including Arna Bontemps, Aaron Douglas, Langston Hughes, Zora Neale Hurston, Jacob Lawrence, Alain Locke, and Richard Bruce Nugent.

Thompson and Savage, like many young intellectuals in Harlem, became interested in radical politics during the early 1930s, in part because of the devastating effects of the Depression. The success of the American communist movement in building mass support to free the Scottsboro boys (nine African American adolescents who, in 1931, were falsely accused of raping two white women on a freight train in Alabama and then sentenced to death) also drew black intellectuals to the left. A skilled organizer, Thompson joined the Communist Party in 1933, and she quickly emerged as one its leading national spokespersons.

As popular efforts to free the Scottsboro boys gained momentum, and as the New Deal was launched, Savage and Thompson founded Vanguard—an informal group—in 1933. The group's primary goal was to spread interest in radical politics in artistic circles. Savage held parties on Saturday evenings and political forums on Sunday afternoons at her apartment in Harlem. Visual artists such as Romare Bearden, Aaron Douglas, and other close friends of Savage and Thompson attended these events. The group debated continuing developments in the Scottsboro case and mass efforts to free Angelo Herndon, a charismatic nineteen-year-old African American communist who in 1932 was charged with inciting an insurrection for helping to organize an interracial hunger march in Atlanta. The group also discussed the racial implications of the National Industrial Recovery Act of 1933, an important early piece of New Deal legislation.

Vanguard not only created space for intense political debates about Marxism, the Soviet Union, racial politics, and the New Deal. The group also helped make left-wing politics fashionable in Harlem's artistic circles. These goals seemingly contradicted the communist leaders' desire that Vanguard would serve primarily to recruit Harlemite intellectuals into the party.

Because Vanguard reached only a small audience, however, the party leadership endorsed the organization.

Vanguard disbanded within a few years of its founding, but Louise Thompson and many of its members continued to associate closely with the left for years to come.

ERIK S. MCDUFFIE

See also Communist Party; Patterson, Louise Thompson; Savage, Augusta; Scottsboro

Further Reading

Augusta Savage and the Art Schools of Harlem. New York: Schomburg Center for Research in Black Culture, New York Public Library, 1988.

McDuffie, Erik S. "Long Journeys: Four Black Women and the Communist Party, USA, 1930–1956." Ph.D. diss., New York University, 2003.

Naison, Mark. *Communists in Harlem during the Depression.* New York: Grove, 1983.

Patterson, Louise. Interview with Ruth Prago, Oral History Project of the American Left, 16 November 1981. Tamiment Library, Bobst Library, New York University, tape 4.

Solomon, Mark. *The Cry Was Unity: Communists and African Americans, 1917–1936.* Jackson: University of Mississippi Press, 1998.

Vanity Fair

The magazine *Vanity Fair*, one of the most popular monthlies in America in the 1920s, was published by Condé Nast between 1913 and 1936. Under the editorship of Frank Crowninshield, it carried a range of material appealing to an upper-middle-class readership, humor by the great wits of the age (P. G. Wodehouse, Dorothy Parker, Robert Benchley), and considerable coverage of the arts, particularly theater. Until the mid-1920s, almost all of this concerned white, often European art and artists (Jean Cocteau, Erik Satie, Paul Manship, etc.). The first area of African American endeavor to gain significant coverage in *Vanity Fair* was musical theater. The spectacular success of the show *Shuffle Along* and the great popularity of the performer Florence Mills were noted with a brief article and a portrait in 1922. An article dealing with this milieu at length, by the popular culture critic Gilbert

Seldes, appeared later in the same year. A photo portrait of Florence Mills, as she appeared in the show *Dixie to Broadway*, occupied a full page of the magazine in February 1925.

Later in 1925, Carl Van Vechten joined the magazine (he had already written a few pieces for it during World War I). By 1925, he had become fascinated with African American music and culture, virtually his only subject by that time and his life's work. Van Vechten introduced *Vanity Fair*'s readers to the major new poets, such as Langston Hughes and Countee Cullen, in 1925–1926. He also wrote a series of important articles on black theater and singers of spirituals and art song. In some of these, he took provocative, perhaps presumptuous, liberties in attempting to steer concert singers like Roland Hayes toward what Van Vechten considered sufficiently "Negro" material. Most important, however, was his coverage of the leading "city" or vaudeville blues singers—Bessie Smith, Clara Smith, and Ethel Waters—who had recently become major singing stars on records. During the mid-1920s, *Vanity Fair* also carried numerous drawings of black entertainers, many by the Mexican caricaturist Miguel Covarrubias. The magazine also had photo spreads depicting white stars, such as Bessie Love and Ann Pennington, doing the current jazz dances of black origin such as the Charleston and the black bottom.

Vanity Fair was never particularly devoted to political or racial coverage. The magazine did carry some politically charged pieces, however, such as Sherwood Anderson's article "The South." This article was hardly delicate regarding the racial sensitivities of black southerners (or white ones for that matter), and it was frankly written from the perspective of an outsider. By the autumn of 1926, Van Vechten had again disappeared from the pages of *Vanity Fair*, whereupon coverage of African American life and culture at the magazine vanished almost entirely. There were occasional photos of famous black performers, and some additional caricatures by Covarrubias, but the intense focus shown in 1925–1926 was now over. In keeping with a greatly increased emphasis on movies, however, there was a full-page photo spread of King Vidor's film *Hallelujah*, the first full-length feature film with an all-black cast, in 1929.

In 1936, *Vanity Fair* merged with another magazine, *Vogue*. In 1983, it once again became an independent publication under the name *Vanity Fair*.

ELLIOTT S. HURWITT

See also Anderson, Sherwood; Hallelujah; Mills, Florence; Shuffle Along; Van Vechten, Carl

Further Reading from Vanity Fair

Anderson, Sherwood. "The South." September 1926.
Chotzinoff, Samuel. "Jazz: A Brief History." June 1923.
Collins, Joseph. "The Dance 'Mania.'" February 1926.
Cullen, Countee, and Carl Van Vechten. "The Poetry of Countee Cullen." June 1925.
Gabriel, Gilbert W. "From Cake-Walk to Spiritual." January 1926.
Hoffenstein, Samuel. "The Jazz Muse." May 1924.
McMullin, John. "The Fashions and Pleasures of New York." September 1922.
Seldes, Gilbert. "The Darktown Strutters on Broadway." November 1922.
Van Vechten, Carl. "The Folksongs of the American Negro." July 1925.
———. "The Black Blues." August 1925.
———. "Prescription for the Negro Theatre." October 1925.
———. "Negro 'Blues' Singers." March 1926.
Walrond, Eric. "Charleston, Hey! Hey!" April 1926.

Vann, Robert Lee

Newspaperman, lawyer, and politician, Robert Lee Vann built the Pittsburgh *Courier* into black America's most influential and widely read weekly paper.

Vann was born in Ahoskie, North Carolina, on 27 August 1879. His mother, Lucy Peoples, a former slave, worked as a cook and domestic worker; the identity of his father remains uncertain. In a curious echo of antebellum custom, the child received the surname of the white family for whom his mother worked.

Vann received a rudimentary elementary education in a dilapidated one-room schoolhouse, alongside sixty other black students. He spent the next six years working variously as a field hand, fisherman, cook, and janitor. He eventually accumulated the funds to enroll at Waters Training School, an academy run by the Baptists in nearby Winton, North Carolina, from which he graduated as valedictorian. After two years at Virginia Union University, he won a scholarship to the Western University of Pennsylvania (soon to be renamed the University of Pittsburgh). Although one of only a handful of black students, Vann flourished at the university, winning election as editor-in-chief of the school newspaper. On graduation, he enrolled in the university's law school, working as a night waiter on the Pittsburgh and Lake Erie Railroad to pay the tuition. He qualified as a lawyer in 1909.

Vann's early experiences imprinted themselves on his character. While notoriously opportunistic in his partisan affiliations, he remained a deeply conservative man, who believed that progress for blacks would come not through radical agitation but through individual enterprise, thrift, and hard work. A supporter of Booker T. Washington and Washington's successor at Tuskegee, Robert Russa Moton, Vann would fill the columns of his newspaper with tales of African Americans who had risen from penury to become successful businessmen.

Vann earned the lion's share of his income from his law practice, which survived until 1933, but it was as a journalist that he made his historical mark. In 1910, a group of businessmen in Pittsburgh chartered a weekly newspaper, the *Courier,* to serve the needs of Pittsburgh's burgeoning black community, whose existence the city's white newspapers scarcely acknowledged. Vann initially provided legal counsel and occasional copy, but by the end of the first year he had been promoted to editor, a position he would retain until his death thirty years later.

Vann's editorial leadership was characterized by innovation, a keen eye for talent, and a healthy dose of political opportunism, all in the interests of building readership. In 1925, for example, the typically pro-business *Courier* became the first African American newspaper to endorse the efforts by the socialist A. Philip Randolph to create the Brotherhood of Sleeping Car Porters. A year later, it became the first black newspaper to sponsor its own radio show, the *Pittsburgh Courier Hour*, which was broadcast weekly on New York's station WGBC.

Vann's most inspired decision, however, was to hire the controversial black satirist George Schuyler, who joined the staff in 1925. For an initial salary of $3 a week, Schuyler (who remained at the *Courier* for nearly forty years) contributed a weekly column—"Views and Reviews"—as well as all the paper's editorials. Schuyler also undertook a nine-month tour of the American South on the *Courier*'s behalf, the fruits of which appeared in *Aframerica Today*, a brilliant weekly series blending detailed sociological analysis with flights of coruscating wit. By the end of the tour,

the *Courier* boasted an unrivaled network of southern agents, as well as 10,000 new subscribers.

Over the course of the 1920s, the *Courier* blossomed into a genuinely national newspaper, with features for every taste—from Alice Dunbar Nelson's weekly column, "From the Woman's Point of View," to the premier sports section in black journalism, devoted almost exclusively to the exploits of black athletes. Vann himself wrote a weekly business column, while Walter White oversaw the influential book reviews section. (White's antilynching novel, *The Fire in the Flint*, was serialized in the paper in 1926.) The *Courier* even had its own African correspondent, Joel A. Rogers, whose articles on the Egyptian and Ethiopian origins of "Nordic civilization" contributed to African Americans' swelling interest in their ancestral continent.

Vann's forays into politics were less satisfying. As chairman of Pennsylvania's black Republicans, he placed the *Courier* at the service of Republican candidates in local, state, and federal elections, only to be snubbed when patronage was dispensed. In 1932, he stunned observers by endorsing Franklin D. Roosevelt and the Democrats; it was time, he declared in a famous editorial, for African Americans to turn "the picture of Lincoln to the wall." As a reward, he was appointed special assistant to the U.S. attorney general, but it proved a purely token position from which he resigned in frustration in 1935. In 1940, shortly before his death, he returned to the Republican fold, endorsing Wendell Wilkie.

Vann devoted his final years to the *Courier*. Prizing circulation over consistency, he welcomed columns from Marcus Garvey and W. E. B. Du Bois, both of whom the paper had pilloried in the 1920s. With the Italian invasion of Ethiopia, he dispatched Joel Rogers back to Africa as war correspondent; the issue featuring Rogers's interview with Emperor Haile Selassie sold an extra 25,000 copies. Vann scored perhaps his greatest coup when he secured exclusive access to the life story of a rising black prizefighter, Joe Louis. As Louis's fame swelled, so did the circulation of the *Courier*, cresting at a quarter million in 1937.

Biography

Robert Lee Vann was born on 27 August 1879. He studied at Waters Training School, Winton, North Carolina; Virginia Union University, Richmond, Virginia; Western University of Pennsylvania (University of

Pittsburgh), B.A., 1906; and University of Pittsburgh Law School, J.D., 1909. He had a private law practice from 1909 to 1933. Vann was editor and publisher of the *Pittsburgh Courier* from 1910 to 1940. He was special assistant to the attorney general, U.S. Department of Justice, in 1933–1935. Vann died on 24 October 1940 of cancer.

JAMES CAMPBELL

See also Abbott, Robert Sengstacke; Black Press; Chicago Defender; Journalists; Pittsburgh Courier; Rogers, Joel Augustus; Schuyler, George S.

Further Reading

Buni, Andrew. *Robert L. Vann of the Pittsburgh Courier: Politics and Black Journalism.* Pittsburgh, Pa.: University of Pittsburgh Press, 1974.

Schuyler, George S. *Fifty Years of Progress in Negro Journalism.* Pittsburgh, Pa.: Pittsburgh Courier, 1950.

———. *Black and Conservative: The Autobiography of George Schuyler.* New Rochelle, N.Y.: Arlington House, 1966.

Scott, Armistead Pride, and Clint C. Wilson III. *A History of the Black Press.* Washington, D.C.: Howard University Press, 1999.

Vaudeville

Developed in the 1880s by a white minstrel, Tony Pastor, vaudeville was offered as a "straight, clean variety show." By the 1890s, vaudeville was a family entertainment. It brought together touring acts and also featured sketches and short plays. Vaudeville remained a popular form until the 1930s. The demise of vaudeville is generally attributed to the popularity of film, but, in reality, much of what had been effective for African American performers in vaudeville was taken over for musical revues and musical theatre pieces such as *Shuffle Along* by Eubie Blake and Noble Sissle (1921).

The first African American minstrels probably existed as early as the 1850s, although it was not until after the Civil War that African American performers, including minstrels, were prevalent on the American popular stage. As was the case for white minstrelsy, multiple skills were demanded of African American minstrels and vaudevillians. The African American minstrel and vaudeville star Tom Fletcher recalled in his book *100 Years of the Negro in Show Business* (1954) that "in those days you were not hired or even considered in show business unless you could sing, dance, talk, tumble or play some instrument in a brass band." Despite the demanding requirements, African Americans clamored for the few paying spots available. In 1894, 2,000 African Americans applied for forty minstrelsy slots in a new troupe. Thomas Riis (1989) suggests that the oral culture elements of "exaggeration and [the] grotesque" integral in minstrelsy and vaudeville appealed to the African-based culture of African Americans. Minstrelsy and vaudeville offered, on a grand scale, opportunities for both trained and untrained musicians and performers.

African American minstrelsy blended into African American musical revues and vaudeville around 1890, and thus a mixed legacy developed. James Weldon Johnson reflected, in *Black Manhattan*:

> Minstrelsy was, on the whole, a caricature of Negro life, and it fixed a stage tradition which has not yet been entirely broken. . . . Nevertheless, these companies did provide stage training and theatrical experience for a large number of colored men. They provided an essential training and theatrical experience, which, at the time, could not have been acquired from any other source. Many of these men, as the vogue of minstrelsy waned, passed on into the second phase, or middle period, of the Negro on the theatrical stage in America; and it was mainly upon the training they had gained that this second phase rested. (1930, 93)

A glance at the names of the early African American musical performers and composers, those of Johnson's "second phase" (Bert Williams, George Walker, Will Marion Cook, J. Leubrie Hill, Paul Laurence Dunbar, Jesse Shipp, Bob Cole, J. Rosamond Johnson, and James Weldon Johnson himself) offers a sense of the creative potential fed by African American minstrelsy and nurtured in vaudeville.

Two important vaudeville circuits that booked African American performers were the Keith-Orpheum and Theater Owners' Booking Association (TOBA), nicknamed "Tough on Black Actors," "Tough on Black Asses," and "Toby." African American women began performing regularly on the minstrelsy and vaudeville circuits in the 1890s, with both men and women serving as musicians.

During this late stage of minstrelsy and early stage of vaudeville, several African American women performers ran their own companies. Among these, the best known were the Whitman sisters from Lawrence, Kansas (birthplace of the great vaudevillian George Walker), the daughters of a well-known minister. Despite Walker's efforts with their father, the Whitmans were not allowed to become professionals until they completed their schooling, which included five years at the New England Conservatory of Music. They first began working with their father on an evangelical tour, and then Essie and Mabel formed an act called the Danzette Sisters in 1899–1900. In 1900, the Whitman Sisters Novelty Company began as a group in the Augusta (Georgia) Grand Opera House. They were managed by their mother at that time; by 1904, Mabel took over the management of the group, and they changed their name to the Whitman Sisters New Orleans Troubadours. Their debut in New York was in 1906, with the encouragement of Will Marion Cook. They worked the Keith and Proctor, Poli and Fox, and TOBA circuits, as well as most theatrical houses.

They became truly successful by 1910, occasionally reconfiguring themselves so that several sisters could work independently. Known for their talent and beauty, "these bright, pretty mulatto girls . . . have wonderful voices. . . . The sisters play banjo and sing coon songs with a smack of the original flavor. Their costuming is elegant; their manner is graceful and their appearance striking in a degree as they are unusually handsome," wrote one reviewer in Alabama early in their careers. Oftentimes billed as a "coon" act, the Whitmans added two young male dancers—Willie Robinson and "Pops" Whitman (Alice's son)—in the 1920s, the latter being billed as a child prodigy. One of their acts, "Befoh de Wah," was reviewed in 1907; in it, the Whitmans seem to have parodied the plantation scenes so necessary to early African American minstrelsy.

Aida Overton Walker (also known as Ada Overton, 1880–1914) was one of the greatest performers who defined the dance of black vaudeville, the cakewalk. Walker began her career with the concert singer Sissieretta Jones, known as the "Black Patti," and her Troubadours. She met George Walker, her future husband, and his comedy partner Bert Williams when they all posed for a photograph for a trade-card sponsored by the American Tobacco Company in 1898. Interestingly, before Aida Overton became a partner of the pair, George Walker sometimes played the female in Williams and Walker's comic duets. Williams and Walker were pioneers in introducing ragtime to their vaudeville work, and Aida Overton helped them introduce the cakewalk, a dance reminiscent of slaves' mockery of white society that was then used by the white minstrels in their frenetic walkarounds. During her short lifetime, Aida Overton Walker became the principal delineator of the cakewalk, but she also was responsible for all the choreography of Williams and Walker's revues. Therefore, she contributed to the changeover from the coon show to African American musical revues, as dance was just as integral to the work of Williams and Walker as the music and the comedy.

Ultimately, black vaudeville is credited with being the incubator for two distinctly African American forms of popular entertainment: the musical revue (defined as an assemblage of musical numbers with a loose plot and usually featuring vaudeville routines) and black humor. The black musical revue *A Trip to Coontown* (1898) was developed by the vaudevillians Bob Cole and Billy Johnson. Then, Cole teamed up with J. Rosamond Johnson to write *A Shoo-Fly Regiment* (1905–1907) and *The Red Moon* (1908). Bert Williams and George Walker went from their vaudeville routine "Two Real Coons" to developing the musical revue *In Dahomey* (1902). Flournoy Miller and Aubrey Lyles formed their own vaudeville act in 1908, and in 1921 they teamed with Sissle and Blake to produce *Shuffle Along*, the first full-length black musical to appear on Broadway. Eubie Blake and Noble Sissle, ragtime pianist and singer-lyricist, had also formed their own vaudeville team, the "Dixie Duo."

As Watkins (1994) recounts, the lasting legacy of black vaudeville is its cultivation of black humor as a genre based in a distinct style. This style, according to Watkins, toned down the exaggerated and grotesque characterization of the black body by white minstrels into something more "cool" (164). Bert Williams, who died in 1919, carried over this style from the early heyday of black musical revues (1898–1910) to their revival in *Shuffle Along*. Williams developed a character, based on slowness and laggardness, that at first served as a contrast to George Walker's highly energized dandy character. He began to study pantomime after Walker became ill, and his comic genius depended less on verbal sparring with a partner. With the retirement of Walker from the stage in 1909 (he died in 1911), Williams further developed his characterizations based on two of his most famous songs, "Nobody" and "Jonah Man." Williams insightfully realized the source of his character's humor. He wrote in 1918:

> The character I try to portray is a shiftless darky to the fullest extent, his fun, his philosophy. Show this artless darky a book and he won't know what it is all about. He can't read. He cannot write. But ask him a

question and he'll answer it with a philosophy that's got something. (quoted in Watkins, 178)

Bert Williams was the only black performer in the Ziegfeld Follies from 1911 to 1919. He experienced racism from the cast and crew while he was associated with the Follies; of him, W. C. Fields remarked, "Bert Williams . . . is the funniest man I ever saw and the saddest man I ever knew."

Pioneered by Ernest Hogan, the low-comedy urban trickster was further developed in vaudeville by the team of Miller and Lyles. The trickster character had been a staple of minstrelsy, but Miller and Lyles gave the trickster a new, urban flair. They did not sing or dance, so their interplay was completely based on verbal dueling, resulting in what they called "mutilatin'" black language. Their most famous routine, recounted by Watkins, was "Indefinite Talk," based on two characters talking, and interrupting, each other.

The slow-witted, philosophizing character of Williams and the urban trickster of Miller and Lyles are perhaps the most lasting comedic legacy of black vaudeville. That legacy, coupled with the use of ragtime music in *Shuffle Along* and the introduction of the cakewalk, gave the Harlem Renaissance a smile, a dance, and something to laugh at that was less about imitation and more about the development of distinctly African American styles of performance.

ANNEMARIE BEAN

See also Cole, Bob; Cook, Will Marion; Dunbar, Paul Laurence; Johnson, John Rosamond; Lyles, Aubrey; Miller, Flournoy; Minstrelsy; Shipp, Jesse A.; Shuffle Along; Theater Owners' Booking Association; Williams, Egbert Austin "Bert"

Selected Works

Blake, Eubie. *Shuffle Along: Selections.* New World Records, 1976.

Williams, Bert. "Natural Born Gambler." In *Slapstick Encyclopedia*, Vol. 1, *In the Beginning: Film Comedy Pioneers.* Kino International Video, 1998.

———. *Nobody and Other Songs*, comp. and annot. Samuel B. Charters. Folkways Records, 1981.

Further Reading

Charters, Ann. *Nobody: The Story of Bert Williams.* Englewood Cliffs, N.J.: Da Capo, 1970.

Fletcher, Tom. *100 Years of the Negro in Show Business: The Tom Fletcher Story.* New York: Burdge, 1954.

George-Graves, Nadine. *The Royalty of Negro Vaudeville: The Whitman Sisters and the Negotiation of Race, Gender, and Class in African American Theatre, 1900–1940.* New York: Palgrave Macmillan, 2000.

Hughes, Langston, and Milton Meltzer. "Bert Williams"; "Just About Everything"; "TOBA." In *Black Magic: A Pictorial History of the African American in the Performing Arts*, foreword by Ossie Davis. Englewood Cliffs, N.J.: Da Capo, 1990.

Johnson, James Weldon. *Black Manhattan.* New York: Knopf, 1930, pp. 94–125.

Krasner, David. *Resistance, Parody, and Double Consciousness in African American Theatre, 1895–1910.* New York: St. Martin's, 1997.

"Pink's Morton Theatre, Black Vaudeville, and the TOBA." In *New Perspectives on Music: Essays in Honor of Eileen Southern*, ed. Josephine Wright with Samuel A. Floyd Jr. Warren, Mich.: Harmonie Park, 1992.

Riis, Thomas L. *Just before Jazz: Black Musical Theater in New York, 1890–1915.* Washington, D.C.: Smithsonian Institution Press, 1989.

Southern, Eileen. *The Music of Black Americans*, 3rd ed. New York: Norton, 1997.

Watkins, Mel. "Black Minstrelsy to Vaudeville" and "Vaudeville and Early-Twentieth Century Black Humor." In *On the Real Side: Laughing, Lying, and Signifying—The Underground Tradition of African-American Humor That Transformed American Culture, from Slavery to Richard Pryor.* New York: Touchstone, 1994, pp. 104–133, 138–180.

Viking Press

The Viking Press was founded in 1925 by Harold K. Guinzburg and George S. Oppenheimer, two optimistic men in their twenties. Within a few months they merged with B. W. Huebsch, giving the fledgling company an experienced editor and a much-needed backlist that included authors such as Sherwood Anderson, Mohandas Gandhi, James Joyce, and Elizabeth Madox Roberts. The publishers intended to limit the number of books they issued each season and to seek out high-quality authors who had been overlooked by other publishing houses. Viking grew to become one of the largest and most distinguished houses; as of the present writing, it is a division of the Penguin group.

In its first season, Viking published four books, including *The Book of American Negro Spirituals* (1925) by James Weldon Johnson and J. Rosamond Johnson. Although the house actively sought to recruit other African American writers of the era (including Walter White), Viking was a latecomer to the vogue for all things "Negro." Nearly all the major writers of the Harlem Renaissance had already developed relationships and contracts with other publishers before Guinzburg and Oppenheimer opened their firm. Viking published six of James Weldon Johnson's books, however, including most notably *God's Trombones: Seven Negro Sermons in Verse* (1927) and *Along This Way: The Autobiography of James Weldon Johnson* (1933).

ERIK BLEDSOE

See also Anderson, Sherwood; God's Trombones; Johnson, James Weldon; Johnson, John Rosamond; Publishers and Publishing Houses

Further Reading

Hutchinson, George. *The Harlem Renaissance in Black and White*. Cambridge, Mass.: Belknap Press of Harvard University Press, 1995.

Madison, Charles A. *Book Publishing in America*. New York: McGraw-Hill, 1966.

Tebbel, John. *Between Covers: The Rise and Transformation of Book Publishing in America*. New York and Oxford: Oxford University Press, 1987.

Villard, Oswald Garrison

The publisher and activist Oswald Garrison Villard was a leading figure in the politics and journalism of the Harlem Renaissance. He was born in 1872 to a wealthy American family then traveling in Germany; his grandfather was the famous abolitionist William Lloyd Garrison, and several other relatives were active in support of civil rights for African Americans. After studying at Harvard University, Villard embarked on a career in journalism with a brief stint in 1896–1897 as a reporter for the *Philadelphia Press.*

Villard achieved national prominence as editor and owner of the *New York Evening Post* and its weekly magazine supplement, *The Nation*. He had joined the *Evening Post*, then owned by his father, in 1897, and inherited control of the two publications following his father's death in 1900. Villard used the publications to speak out in support of liberal causes such as women's suffrage and pacifism. Villard maintained a passionate lifelong commitment to racial equality, and he played a key role in the founding of the National Association for the Advancement of Colored People (NAACP). Villard was one of many Americans outraged by a race riot that took place in August 1908 in Springfield, Illinois, the birthplace of Abraham Lincoln; the riot led to eight deaths and caused more than 2,000 people to flee the city. In early January 1919, the journalist William English Walling and the progressive social workers Mary White Ovington and Henry Moskowitz persuaded Villard to issue, on 12 February 1909 (the hundredth anniversary of Lincoln's birth), a call for a national conference on black civil rights. The founding document of what would become the NAACP, "The Call" was signed by sixty-five prominent social activists, among them only seven African Americans.

The National Negro Conference gathered leading progressive thinkers and activists in New York City in May 1909; out of the conference grew the Committee for the Advancement of the Negro Race and a smaller Committee of Forty on Permanent Organization. With Villard's financial backing and meeting space in the offices of the *New York Evening Post*, the organization hired its first full-time employee in February 1910. The NAACP was incorporated under its current name in June 1911, with Villard as chairman of the executive committee and later as chairman of the board of directors. Villard took charge of the NAACP's information-gathering division and used his journalistic savvy to get publicity for the group and its causes; he also brought writers from the *New York Evening Post* into the organization. Villard was among the first white editors to address the biased coverage of African Americans in the mainstream white press. He denounced the explicit racism in the lurid, sensational stories of tabloid journalism; his influence also led many papers to cease the practice of identifying African Americans by race in all newspaper articles. During this period, Villard also published *John Brown: A Biography Fifty Years After* (1910), a study of the radical white abolitionist leader.

Villard had initially supported Woodrow Wilson for the presidency in 1912, but he was bitterly disappointed by Wilson's moves to implement segregation in the federal bureaucracy in 1913. At a meeting between the two in May 1913, Villard proposed a government-sponsored National Race Commission, to be organized under the auspices of the NAACP; Wilson later rejected the idea. In 1915, Villard pushed for a commission to study the United States's occupation of Haiti. The Wilson administration again refused, and so the NAACP later sent its own representative, James Weldon Johnson, to conduct an investigation.

Throughout his tenure as board chairman, Villard insisted that the NAACP must remain moderate in tone: although he had broken privately with the accommodationist leader Booker T. Washington by 1910, he believed that the NAACP should not criticize Washington publicly, for fear of alienating moderate blacks or arousing antagonism from whites. This stance angered the more strident members of the NAACP, particularly Joel E. Spingarn and W. E. B. Du Bois. By 1913, Villard and Spingarn were no longer on speaking terms, following several public instances in which Villard criticized Spingarn. Villard clashed with Du Bois over the tone and content of *The Crisis*, the organization's magazine, edited by Du Bois. As an editor himself, Villard felt empowered to offer criticisms and suggestions; Du Bois insisted that *The Crisis* must remain independent of the board's control. Their battle prompted Villard's resignation as chairman of the board at the end of 1913; Joel Spingarn replaced him in January 1914.

Villard remained active in the organization over the course of the next few years. In August 1916, he participated in the Amenia Conference, held at Spingarn's farm in upstate New York, a conference designed to bring together supporters and critics of Booker T. Washington following Washington's death a year earlier. Villard, a pacifist, opposed the United States's entry into World War I and argued that the conscription of African American men for a war "to make the world safe for democracy" was an act of hypocrisy by a racist government. He is also credited as the force behind a silent parade in New York City on 28 July 1917, in which 8,000 African Americans marched down Fifth Avenue to protest against a recent race riot in East St. Louis, Illinois. He eventually supported the NAACP's efforts to obtain fair treatment for black soldiers, but he bitterly opposed Du Bois's efforts to obtain a military position during the war, and he even tried to use the episode to push Du Bois out of the leadership of the NAACP. Villard's pacifism also posed problems for his publications during World War I: He fought off an attempt by federal authorities to deny mailing privileges to *The Nation* in September 1918, but public criticism and declining circulation forced Villard to sell the *New York Evening Post* in 1918.

In 1919, thoroughly alienated from the organization that he had founded, Villard resigned from his position as treasurer of the NAACP. During the 1920s, he maintained only distant relations with the NAACP, but he continued his support for racial equality

Oswald Garrison Villard. (Brown Brothers.)

through his writings in *The Nation*. During this decade, the magazine emerged as a leading voice of liberal thought in national politics, and its weekly circulation rose to nearly 38,000. Villard spoke out against the resurgent Ku Klux Klan, against the U.S. occupation of Haiti, and in favor of federal antilynching legislation. He also provided financial support to several of the artists and writers of the Harlem Renaissance. He supported the New Deal policies of President Franklin Roosevelt; later, his pacifism led him to oppose the United States' intervention in the war in Europe, and he broke with *The Nation* over the issue, resigning from the magazine's editorial board in June 1940. A heart attack in 1944 curtailed his activities considerably; he died in New York City in 1949.

Biography

Oswald Garrison Villard was born in Wiesbaden, Germany, on 13 March 1872. He earned an A.B. from

Harvard College in 1893 and an A.M. from Harvard University in 1896. He was president of the Nation Press, 1900–1918; editor, *New York Evening Post*, 1900–1918; and owner and editor, *The Nation*, 1918–1932. He was a founder of the National Association for the Advancement of Colored People, 1909; chairman of the executive committee, 1911–1912; chairman of the board of directors, 1912–1913; and treasurer, 1911–1919. Villard died in New York City on 1 October 1949.

CHRISTOPHER CAPPOZZOLA

See also Amenia Conference, 1916; Du Bois, W. E. B.; Lynching: Silent Protest Parade; Nation, The; National Association for the Advancement of Colored People; Spingarn, Joel

Selected Works

The Disappearing Daily: Chapters in American Newspaper Evolution. 1944.
Fighting Years: Memoirs of a Liberal Editor. 1939.
Free Trade—Free World. 1947.
The German Phoenix: The Story of the Republic. 1933.
Germany Embattled: An American Interpretation. 1915.
Henry Villard: A True Fairy Tale. 1931.
John Brown, 1800–1859: A Biography Fifty Years After. 1910.
Our Military Chaos: The Truth about Defense. 1939.
Prophets True and False. 1928.
Some Newspapers and Newspaper-Men. 1923.
Within Germany. 1940.

Further Reading

Gronowicz, Anthony, ed. *Oswald Garrison Villard: The Dilemmas of the Absolute Pacifist in Two World Wars*. New York: Garland, 1983.
Humes, Dollena Joy. *Oswald Garrison Villard: Liberal of the 1920s*. Syracuse, N.Y.: Syracuse University Press, 1960.
Lewis, David Levering. *W. E. B. Du Bois: Biography of a Race, 1868–1919*. New York: Holt, 1993.
Wreszin, Michael. *Oswald Garrison Villard: Pacifist at War*. Bloomington: Indiana University Press, 1965.

Visual Arts

The visual arts of the Harlem Renaissance have long gone without the renown and attention given to the literature of the period. Indeed, the Harlem Renaissance is most often characterized as a specifically literary phenomenon fueled by racial demographic and cultural shifts from the American South to the North. In fact, the visual arts experienced a distinct and related renaissance beginning in the mid-1920s, inextricably tied to the era's writers and intellectuals, but also rooted in less-developed creative traditions and using an alternative set of inspirational sources. If writers such as Langston Hughes and Zora Neale Hurston were inventing a body of literature that valued black vernacular culture in reaction to a tradition from earlier black writers that had emphasized narratives of tragedy and uplift, then the painters, sculptors, and photographers of the Harlem Renaissance were reacting to a tradition that had been very nearly silent on the subject of black life, even from an earlier generation of black artists. If playwrights and poets of the renaissance mined working-class life for inspiration, visual artists were encouraged to look to African art forms.

The visual arts of the Harlem Renaissance—seen in the work of the painters Aaron Douglas, Palmer Hayden, and Hale Woodruff; the sculptors Meta Warrick Fuller and Augusta Savage; and the photographer James Van Der Zee, among others—represents the earliest moment when significant numbers of black artists turned to black life as legitimate subject matter. This fact distinguishes their achievements from those of their writer colleagues whose work followed and built on earlier race-based literary traditions. Moreover, many visual artists attempted to represent African American life through a prism of African-inspired European modernist art in seeking to define a racially identifiable style of art. The task with which these artists were charged was, therefore, a tremendous one: In a vacuum of "positive" black imagery, they were asked to invent a style that paid homage to a legendary ancestral past from Africa while also representing that which was new, modern, folk-based, urban, and above all honored black life. That some of these artists generated controversy, became disillusioned, were later criticized for mediocrity, were forgotten, or left the arts altogether is not surprising. What is surprising is the considerable success they enjoyed and the degree to which their work was embraced and supported. Their successes are an enduring index of how much their work was needed.

The iconic achievements of the visual artists of the Harlem Renaissance are best understood against the dearth of unstereotyped images of African Americans in the fine arts during the late nineteenth century and the early twentieth. Among the best-known black artists of the nineteenth century, the painters Henry Ossawa Tanner and Robert Duncanson both worked primarily with nonracial subjects. Duncanson is best known for his landscapes of the Ohio River and his fantasy landscapes painted in the 1850s and 1860s, a time when landscape paintings as visual metaphors for national identity and destiny dominated American art. Whereas Tanner's most famous paintings today are African American genre scenes of the 1890s like *The Thankful Poor* and *The Banjo Lesson*, during his lifetime he was admired for the lion's share of work that represented biblical themes or exotic landscapes. It seems that, during the nineteenth century, the most successful and prominent African American artists were those who eschewed racial subject matter in favor of what were considered more universal themes.

The work of the sculptor Meta Warrick Fuller evidences a change in that view by about 1915. Fuller's work reaches maturity relatively early in the century, between 1914 and 1920, but it is rightly considered a sort of harbinger of the aesthetic priorities that would be explicitly laid out as part of the "New Negro" movement in the mid-1920s. Fuller is one of the first African American artists to choose black subjects for much of her work. *Ethiopia Awakening* (1914), her signature piece, is an allegory of pan-Africanism that ties American slavery to African colonialism in a representation of a female figure emerging from a centuries-long slumber, newly aware of her history and strength. In what would become a recurrent source of inspiration for other artists of the Harlem Renaissance, *Ethiopia Awakening* draws inspiration from African art for its formal vocabulary. The black figure is wrapped from the waist down—an allusion to mummification—and wears a royal Egyptian headdress.

Fuller's background and career development also establish other commonalities with future artists of the Harlem Renaissance. She was from a middle-class family that supported her decision to pursue a career in the arts. She benefited from greater access to formal art training than many of her nineteenth-century predecessors had received; she trained at the Pennsylvania Museum School of Industrial Art (later the Philadelphia College of Art). Even more significantly, Fuller went to Paris, where she met the French sculptor Auguste Rodin while studying at the École des Beaux-Arts, gaining the European training considered a prerequisite for a serious career as an artist. The work of Meta Warrick Fuller represents a turning point in the history of African American art—a highly trained artist steeped in formal art historical tradition begins to see in her

own cultural background themes and subjects appropriate to representation in the visual arts. Ten years later, under the influence of many of the same cultural shapers that articulated the intellectual basis for the Harlem Renaissance as a literary movement, a new generation of black artists would also turn to African art and African American culture for creative inspiration.

To a great extent, the intellectual community that cultivated and supported the writers of the Harlem Renaissance did much the same for visual artists. The sociologist Charles Johnson, director of the National Urban League; the activist W. E. B. Du Bois; and the philosopher Alain Locke each nurtured the visual arts as an essential complement to the creative literary achievements of the period. Johnson is often considered a promoter chiefly of the literary arts, but it was Johnson who was directly responsible for bringing the painter Aaron Douglas, the artist most closely associated with the renaissance, to Harlem. And Johnson, as editor of the magazine *Opportunity*, was determined to include illustrations by black artists in its pages; those artists included Douglas, Richard Bruce Nugent, Albert A. Smith, and others. Additionally, in *Opportunity*, Johnson featured sculptures by Augusta Savage and Richmond Barthé in articles intended to highlight the achievements of visual artists. Du Bois, in his capacity as editor of *The Crisis*, the periodical of the National Association for the Advancement of Colored People (NAACP), also acted as a patron of the visual arts by commissioning illustrations from black artists. Du Bois would later confess, in the 1930s, that he was more interested than either Johnson or Locke in the uses of art as propaganda. His political interest in cultivating both the visual and the literary arts was described in a speech published in *The Crisis* in October 1926.

It was Locke more than either Du Bois or Johnson who nurtured the visual arts in particular as a vital component of the New Negro movement and who emphasized study of and creative inspiration from African arts. In March 1925, Locke was the editor of a special issue of the magazine *Survey Graphic*: "Harlem: Mecca of the New Negro." This issue formalized the movement's creative agenda and is often said to have given rise to the Harlem Renaissance. Though many essays, sociological studies, poems, and other literary contributions in the special issue were written by blacks, virtually all the illustrations were produced by the German artist Winold Reiss, a visual irony that cannot have been lost on the editor, Locke. Reiss was considered by many of the intelligentsia of the Harlem Renaissance to be sympathetic in his portrayals of

African American subjects, an artist who could depict black subjects without using stereotypes. But his wide popularity was also seen as evidence of a need for African American visual artists.

Later in 1925, in *The New Negro*—an expanded volume of essays developed out of the special issue of *Survey Graphic*—Locke wrote "The Legacy of the Ancestral Arts." In this essay, which was illustrated by photographs of African sculpture, Locke sets out a social agenda that would influence black artists for the next three decades or more. He exhorts black artists to seek inspiration in African art—drawing from that body of work not only formal innovation, in the way that European modern artists were, but cultural meaning and pride of heritage as well:

> But what the Negro artist of today has most to gain from the arts of the forefathers is . . . the lesson of a classical background, the lesson of discipline, of style, of technical control pushed to the limits of technical mastery. A more stylized art does not exist than the African. If after absorbing the new content of American life and experience, and after assimilating new patterns of art, the original artistic endowment can be sufficiently augmented to express itself with equal power in more complex patterns and substance, then the Negro may well become what some have predicted, the artist of American life. (256–258)

It is difficult to overstate the impact of Locke's thinking on this matter. Until well into the 1960s, black artists would struggle with the issue of incorporating elements of African art into their work.

Charles Johnson, W. E. B. Du Bois, and Alain Locke all recognized that the renaissance needed a visual "New Negro" to complement the literary concept that was being constructed through novels, poems, and popular journals. They recognized that a substantial gap existed in the representation of the "New Negro" that they were inventing, and that only through cultivating specific visual artists could this visual lack be addressed. To a great extent, they relied on the work of one artist to begin addressing that visual space: the painter Aaron Douglas.

In 1927, James Weldon Johnson published *God's Trombones: Seven Negro Sermons in Verse*, a volume of poetry inspired by the vernacular sermons of black preachers all over the South, illustrated by Aaron Douglas. Johnson was a respected writer, orator, and statesman in 1927, well into his fifties, with a lifetime of notable achievements behind him. Douglas, not yet

thirty, had recently completed his undergraduate training at the University of Kansas and was at the beginning of his career. He was best known as a magazine illustrator at the time, though one with a promising future. Douglas was already a regular contributor to both *Opportunity* and *The Crisis*. Nonetheless, Johnson, as the more established artist, was taking a chance on Douglas, and the chance paid off. In retrospect, Douglas's eight illustrations to *God's Trombones* can be viewed as the perfect embodiment of the visual arts of the Harlem Renaissance. The illustrations fused the era's aesthetic priorities that emphasized developing a racially identifiable and inspired style in the visual arts with literature that took black cultural phenomena as its subject. Douglas's work in *God's Trombones* represented a break from the tradition-bound artistic traditions of the late nineteenth century and the early twentieth, derived inspiration from African and Egyptian art, and provided the much-needed visual complement to the "New Negro" that was described and defined in literature.

In the illustrations for *God's Trombones*, Douglas's fully developed painting style is displayed, probably for the first time. Additionally, the illustrations make explicit the tie between visual arts and literature of the period. As part of the text, each black-and-white illustration appears facing the beginning of the one of James Weldon Johnson's poems. In terms of style, Douglas uses abstract silhouettes of human forms to represent figures, bodies depicted frontally and faces in profile, a convention often seen in ancient Egyptian painting. Pictorial space is flattened and geometrically subdivided in Douglas's paintings, a style that has been called "geometric symbolism." The emphasis on subdividing the image geometrically, abstracting human forms, and the hard-edged angularity of Douglas's style are a direct result of Locke's insistence that African American artists look to African art styles for inspiration; these African traditions emphasized figural abstraction with symbolic ends.

Beyond the interest in African-inspired aesthetics, Douglas demonstrated a willingness to manipulate art historical convention in this set of illustration. *Crucifixion* represents a clear break with the traditional Christian iconography that conventionally shows Christ nailed to the cross with mourners at his feet. Douglas's image is constructed around the two primary figures of Christ and Simon, the North African from Cyrene who was pressed into service to carry the cross up to Mount Calvary when the weight became too great for Christ to bear. Christ is a relatively small figure in the central portion of the lower half of the illustration. Despite his size, Christ is readily identified by the abstracted halo around his head, by his light hue, and in the highlighted geometric design overlaid on the illustration, concentric circles pierced by a cone suggestive of light. The second dominant figure, Simon, is the large, darker-valued figure, represented partially in shadow and partially in the cone of light, and straining under the weight of the cross. A Roman soldier is pressed against the picture plane in the foreground, and other members of the procession recede into a shallow background defined by progressively darker shades of gray and diminishing size. It is a complex composition in which figures are located, sized, and color-valued according to their importance within the context of the story. What is noteworthy is that Christ and Simon are equally important in Douglas's interpretation of the crucifixion. Simon is perceived as significant by virtue of his size and Christ by his location at the focal point of the geometric composition and by the light color value. By making Christ and Simon equally important, Douglas forces the viewer to reevaluate the story of the crucifixion and question the role of the relationship between the two dominant figures.

Douglas's primary focus in *Crucifixion* on the relationship between Simon and Christ may be interpreted as a metaphor for American society's treatment of African Americans. The moment of crucifixion is, for Christ, the moment of both his defeat and his triumph. He is the persecuted savior. Douglas chooses to represent a moment just before this triumph, however, when Christ passes the symbol of his burden and his victory to Simon, a black man. Douglas uses this image to proclaim African American contributions to western society, and specifically to American society. Simon's gesture, his assumption of the "weight of the world," represents the forgotten contributions of all black people. The crucifixion itself represents an established history and a civilization that refuses to acknowledge the value and merit of its own citizenry. That notion of unrecognized and unappreciated communal contribution appropriately dovetails with the cultural strategies of the "New Negro" movement in the emphasis on artistic achievement as a means to achieve societal enfranchisement.

In another illustration, *Prodigal Son*, Douglas constructs an urban genre scene, possibly from Harlem itself. He incorporates elements of contemporary African American culture in the interpretation of a biblical story. The composition centers on three figures—a man and two women, one on each side; again represented only as facially profiled silhouettes. All three appear within a cone-shaped ray of light emitted from a ceiling lamp and are dancing and drinking. At the top of the illustration is the silhouetted image of a band, or more specifically trombones, and a record. Pressing in from the sides in the foreground are oversized representations of vice: a dollar bill, cards, dice, and a gin bottle. In the postures of his figures, the symbols of vice, and the representation of a jazz band Douglas is referring to African American social life and culture in Harlem during the 1920s. He is transforming the Old Testament parable of fall and redemption into an African American genre scene. And in describing the scene, he uses specific elements of the urban culture that characterized Harlem.

Rent parties, held to raise rent money for the hosts, and nightclubs or cabarets were vital components of the social life of Harlemites in the 1920s. Both were popular because of the presence of jazz musicians, the availability of liquor (an important attraction during Prohibition), and gambling. Douglas's illustration may be a composite image of both types of event. The typical rent party, like the scene represented in *Prodigal Son*, was a jam-packed event, complete with food, liquor, and card playing. The compressed and congested space of Douglas's illustration, conveyed by the restricting cone of light and the intrusive symbols of vice, implies the crowded space of a rent party. The trombones at the upper edge of the illustration, however, suggest a larger, more permanent establishment: a nightclub.

Nightclubs featured the same types of entertainment as rent parties but on a grander scale. Both whites and blacks frequented nightclubs (though some, like the famous Cotton Club, were exclusive to whites), and all featured black entertainers. It was these clubs that would have featured a full band. The representation of trombones in the *Prodigal Son* is almost certainly a reference to nightclubs and their prominent role in Harlem's social life. The trombones also refer to the significance of music and jazz in African American culture generally, and in Harlem specifically. At the same time, they foreshadow the prodigal son's return to his family and to a moral, upright lifestyle by referring back to "God's trombones," the African American preachers whom James Weldon Johnson is celebrating.

Aaron Douglas's reputation as the "official" artist of the Harlem Renaissance was established by works like those he created for *God's Trombones*. He invented a graphic style that incorporated elements of African art traditions in describing the appealing and frequently ennobling aspects of African American culture. Like the work of the writers whom his illustrations support, he transforms what is commonplace in rapidly emerging black urban life, making that culture fit subject matter for high art. And while Douglas's achievements are significant, so too is the cultivation of his talent by important individuals and institutions.

By way of comparison, the pan-Africanist nationalist Marcus Garvey's United Negro Improvement Association (UNIA) operated as a sort of working-class alternative to the more academic and elite organizations of the Urban League and the NAACP. Garvey, through UNIA, emphasized economic independence for the African American community and eventually formed the Black Star shipping line and developed two periodical publications. Although UNIA was not particularly focused on advancing opportunities for black artists generally, it did contribute significantly to the success of the best-known African American photographer during the Harlem Renaissance era. James Van Der Zee was Marcus Garvey's personal photographer and the official photographer for UNIA and is probably the most famous African American artist to emerge during the Harlem Renaissance years. His photographs document an emerging and increasingly prosperous black middle class during the 1920s and into the 1930s. His *Couple with a Cadillac* (1932) reflects the material wealth and status that upwardly mobile Harlem residents sought. The exquisitely attractive couple sit in a polished new car, lavishly attired in fur coats. The figures are posed, but not in an overly formal way. It is an image intended to project the illusion of capturing the beautiful and prosperous in a moment of leisure.

Van Der Zee, like many photographers, taught himself his craft. He operated a series of photographic studios in Harlem for nearly fifty years, becoming the photographer of choice for many of the community's residents. Unlike many of his competitors, however, Van Der Zee honed his craft as an art form rather than treating the medium simply as livelihood. He experimented with special effects and retouching techniques long before such methods were commonplace, photographed subjects in or out of the studio in order to achieve a desired effect, and was generally committed to photography as image making rather than as a documentary record. In addition to his formal studio portraits, Van Der Zee recorded the life of Harlem as a community through photographs of important events, funerals, social organizations, and street scenes.

In addition to the support offered by African American organizations like UNIA, the Urban League, and the NAACP, the visual artists of the Harlem Renaissance received substantial patronage and educational support from white sponsors, especially through philanthropic organizations like the Harmon Foundation and the Barnes Foundation.

The physician Albert Barnes formed his philanthropic foundation in 1922 to "promote the advancement of education and the appreciation of the fine arts." It was based outside Philadelphia and operated in conjunction with its founder's assembly of a major collection of both modern European paintings (from artists like Picasso, Modigliani, and the Impressionists) and traditional African art. From the outset, Barnes was concerned with providing opportunities for arts education to African American artists and collectors. He was associated with Alain Locke and contributed an essay to a special issue of *Survey Graphic* entitled "Negro Art and America." The Barnes Foundation sponsored fellowships for African American artists to study its collection; one of these fellowships was awarded to Aaron Douglas. Notably, Alain Locke, himself a collector of African art, chose to illustrate his own essay "The Legacy of the Ancestral Arts" with works from the Barnes collection. Outside its educational mandates, the most significant contribution of the Barnes Foundation is the opportunity it provided for developing artists to view modernist paintings along with their African sources; no separation existed between the two types of work in the foundation's installations. Such a display would have underscored for new artists the African aesthetic vocabulary being manipulated in European modernist painting, elucidating new methods to achieve Alain Locke's prescribed African-inspired African American art.

Even more important than the Barnes Foundation, in terms of patronage, was the Harmon Foundation, formed by the philanthropist and real estate tycoon William E. Harmon in 1922. This foundation sponsored five juried exhibitions of work by African American artists between the years 1928 and 1933. During those years, the foundation also awarded cash prizes to artists whose work was shown in the exhibitions. These related programs represent one of the earliest efforts to organize and exhibit the work of African American artists, and to provide a reliable source of income for those artists. Many notable young painters and sculptors would first exhibit their work through the Harmon Foundation and would use the cash prizes to further their studies and begin long-term careers in the visual arts. They include the painters William H. Johnson, Lois Mailou Jones, Archibald Motley, and Hale Woodruff, as well as the sculptors Sargent Johnson and Richmond Barthé.

In 1926, the first recipient of a Harmon Foundation prize for achievement in fine arts was the painter Palmer Hayden, who had been trained more informally than either Fuller or Douglas. Hayden won the award for a seascape produced during a summer at the Commonwealth Art Colony in Boothbay, Maine. He was based in New York, however, and at the time he won the prize he was working as a janitor at the offices of the Harmon Foundation. Hayden used the prize money to travel to France to continue his studies; he lived there from 1927 to 1932. In 1933, after his return to the United States, Hayden won a second Harmon Foundation award for his most famous painting, *Fétiche et Fleurs*, a still life composed of a vase of flowers juxtaposed with a Fang reliquary head sculpture and Kuba textile, both traditional African art forms. Although Hayden did not undertake the same formalized art training as many artists of the Harlem Renaissance and did not make the same sort of literary connections, he was clearly aware of the emerging interest in African art both in the United States and abroad. As evidenced by *Fétiche et Fleurs*, he, too, was seeking ways to incorporate those artistic traditions into his own work. Hayden's work of the 1930s was more figurative; he turned to African American genre scenes, many of which were controversial because they played with stereotypical representations of black subjects. In fact, an early historian of African American art, James Porter, would later censure Hayden sharply for using stereotypical images. The changes in Hayden's work and the controversy around his shift to figurative styles suggest the degree to which black artists struggled to find appropriate and critically acceptable means of representing their own culture. Moreover, they demonstrate that critical responses could be complicated and unpredictable. Hayden, the African American artist who had been embraced by a white-dominated philanthropic institution, found himself condemned by a later black arts establishment for producing images that were undignified and not sufficiently positive.

The Harmon Foundation also supported the work of emerging sculptors, an important area for cultivation, given that sculptors did not have the audience for mass-produced graphic art that two-dimensional artists might rely on. Among the sculptors whose work was shown at the Harmon Foundation exhibitions was Augusta Savage, an artist who was connected to many of Harlem's cultural and political institutions and who was an insider in its arts community. Few of Savage's works survive; the work most often reproduced is a 9-inch bust of a boy, possibly the artist's nephew, entitled *Gamin*. The piece captures the aloof posturing and charm of boyhood. The subject is represented with his hat cocked to one side, a disaffected expression on the face. It is a sympathetic, ennobling, and truthful depiction of an African American boy. That Savage left the subject's identity in question by calling the piece *Gamin* pushes what is taken for an informal portrait into a scene from everyday life. The boy becomes a sort of stand-in for the many other boys like him in Harlem.

Augusta Savage arrived in Harlem in 1921; although she did not come from a privileged background, she managed to enroll in the sculpture program at Cooper Union, completing her four-year program in only three years. She was a contributing author for UNIA's publication *Black World* when she came to the attention of W. E. B. Du Bois, who arranged a scholarship for her to study abroad. Savage was unable to accept the scholarship, but her studies in France were later supported by the Urban League in combination with grants from the Julius Rosenwald Fund and the Carnegie Foundation. Savage associated with many other writers and artists of the Harlem Renaissance, including Aaron Douglas, Langston Hughes, Zora Neale Hurston, and Richard Bruce Nugent. In short, Savage was an artist of tremendous talent, supported by a considerable array of individuals and institutions. Although the vast majority of her work has been lost, her career encapsulates the spirit of possibility and community of support that existed for black artists associated with the Harlem Renaissance.

The opportunities that appeared so easily and abundantly for this first generation of racially focused African American visual artists were rapidly declining by the mid- to late 1930s and had all but evaporated by World War II. Their creative and critical successes would be tempered by later revisions of the initial critical acclaim. Aaron Douglas, after expanding his geometric symbolist style into mural paintings for the 135th Street branch of the New York Public Library in the 1930s, left New York to continue his career as a teacher at Fisk University in Nashville. He and Palmer Hayden were both later criticized for work that was seen as a caricature or pastiche of African art forms. James Van Der Zee would be forced to close his studio by 1960 after seeing a slow twenty-year decline in demand for his services due to the advent of personal cameras. In the 1940s, Augusta Savage retired to a farm in upstate New York; with the loss of most of her own work, her greatest legacy became largely the success of those to whom she was a mentor.

The Harlem Renaissance as manifested in highly motivated individuals and cultural institutions was, for a time, viewed as encouraging mediocrity rather than excellence in the arts. A subsequent generation of African American artists, notably Romare Bearden, would chafe at the subject matter prescribed and defined by Alain Locke and others in the "New Negro" movement. To a great extent, the achievements of the generation of "New Negro" visual artists must be understood as a product of networks of influence and social engineering on the part of a circle of black intellectuals and their white patrons. But those achievements also reflect a sort of daring spirit on the part of the artists who emerged from that period. In the face of histories of art and artists that had ignored them and been silent, the "New Negro" artists made their mark.

NICOLE GILPIN HOOD

See also Artists; Barnes, Albert C.; Barthé, Richmond; Bearden, Romare; Douglas, Aaron; Fuller, Meta Warrick; Garvey, Marcus; God's Trombones; Harmon Foundation; Hayden, Palmer C.; House-Rent Parties; Locke, Alain; Johnson, Charles Spurgeon; Nugent, Richard Bruce; Porter, James Amos; Reiss, Winold; Savage, Augusta; Survey Graphic; Tanner, Henry Ossawa; United Negro Improvement Association; Van Der Zee, James; Woodruff, Hale; *other specific artists*

Further Reading

Johnson, James Weldon. *God's Trombones: Seven Negro Sermons in Verse*. New York: Penguin, 1927. (Reprint, 1990.)

Leininger-Miller, Theresa. *New Negro Artists in Paris: African-American Painters and Sculptors in the City of Light, 1922–1934*. New Brunswick, N.J.: Rutgers University Press, 2001.

Locke, Alain. "The Legacy of the Ancestral Arts." In *The New Negro*. 1925.

Patton, Sharon F. *African-American Art*. New York: Oxford University Press, 1998.

Porter, James A. *Modern Negro Art*. New York: Dryden, 1943.

Reynolds, Gary A., and Wright, Beryl J. *Against the Odds: African-American Artists and the Harmon Foundation*. Newark, N.J.: Newark Museum, 1989.

Studio Museum in Harlem. *Harlem Renaissance: Art of Black America*. New York: Abrams, 1987.

Walker, A'Lelia

A'Lelia Walker—Lelia McWilliams or Walker, depending on the biographical source—was born on 6 June 1885 in Vicksburg, Mississippi, to Sarah Breedlove and Moses McWilliams. Sarah Breedlove claimed a unique space in African American social, cultural, and entrepreneurial history as the millionaire Madame C. J. Walker, the "empress" of hair-care products for blacks, particularly straightening chemicals and irons. A'Lelia Walker (she gave herself the name A'Lelia) attended Knoxville College in Tennessee. When she was thirty-five years old, with an adopted daughter, she found herself the sole heiress of her mother's enterprise and fortune; this success story presented certain social challenges in her life as a black American.

A'Lelia Walker was caught between two worlds. On the one hand, she was among the richest black women of her time. On the other hand, her wealth did not entirely disguise or compensate for the fact that she had emerged from a poor black rural background and had acquired at best a limited liberal arts education. Moreover, her extravagance and her "fast" life made her something of a social outcast, and she had none of the intellectual or artistic ambitions that were so highly valued during the Harlem Renaissance as the best means of social amelioration. Because of her wealth, she moved in exalted social circles, where she was perhaps regarded as an exotic entertainment. She is, then, an example of the social struggle experienced, in the early twentieth century, by African Americans caught between a disparaged past and the modernity of the future, which held out the promise of a black "American dream."

Walker was a social anomaly—upwardly mobile, but often snubbed and rejected by a black elite that was itself operating within a dominant white social class structure. She proceeded to carve out her own unique space, and fortunately for her she had enough money to be independent of the usual social mores. She was clever and innovative, and she was able to meet challenges by adapting various social styles presumably befitting a young, ambitious black heiress in the 1920s. The strategies she applied are suggested by the descriptions her contemporaries—such as Langston Hughes, Richard Bruce Nugent, and Carl VanVechten—offered of her: a "joy goddess," a "mahogany millionairess," a "patron of the arts," a "literary salon hostess," a "shrewd businesswoman," a "gorgeous dark Amazon," and "the de-kink heiress," to mention just a few.

Because of Walker's "transgressive" public behavior, her image in most people's minds was that of a party-throwing, sexually savvy, spoiled African queen. In fact, though, she had profound experience of ordinary life and considerable acumen as a businesswoman. She had been born into poverty, the child of a single mother (reportedly, her biological father had fallen victim to a lynch mob when she was two years old); she had lived in households that lacked windows, running water, and heat. By the age of twenty-three she was managing her mother's offices in Pittsburgh, Pennsylvania, and she participated consistently in the phenomenal growth of the hair-care business. When her mother died in 1919, A'Lelia Walker became the company president, and in that capacity she accomplished some important firsts in the history of black businesses. For example, in 1928 she constructed the Walker Building in Indianapolis,

A'Lelia Walker, photographed by R. E. Mercer, 1920s. (Schomburg Center for Research in Black Culture, New York Public Library.)

settings for her parties were sensuously, excitingly decadent, and she presented herself equally excitingly: turbaned, bejeweled, and elegantly booted. Her four marriages added to her scandalous mystique.

A'Lelia Walker died, in 1931, as extravagantly as she had lived—after consuming an entire lobster, a chocolate cake, and a bottle of champagne in the middle of the night. Through her financial power and her personal eccentricities, she had positioned herself at center stage and had become perhaps the most famous hostess of the Harlem Renaissance. In retrospect, this has been her most acknowledged contribution to black history.

Biography

A'Lelia Walker (Lelia McWilliams, or Walker) was born on 6 June 1885 in Vicksburg, Mississippi. She studied at Knoxville College in Knoxville, Tennessee. She was a manager in the hair-straightening enterprise of Madame C. J. Walker (her mother) and became an heiress in 1919. During the Harlem Renaissance, she was a patron of the arts and held a salon during the mid- to late 1920s. Walker died in 1931 in Long Branch, New Jersey.

LAURA ALEXANDRA HARRIS

See also Salons; Walker, Madame C. J.

Indiana; this was the first enterprise of its kind owned and managed by blacks. It contained a Walker College of Beauty Culture offering both barbershop and beauty salon services, a grocery store, a pharmacy, professional offices, and the Majestic Walker Theater.

Evidently, Walker felt most deeply about her patronage of African American arts; as a generous patron she became an intimate of a bohemian black avant-garde that was challenging the expectations of the black "old guard" and of dominant whites. For Walker, it would seem, throwing luxurious, elaborate parties that aroused gossip and scandal was a way of developing a modern persona, cultivating her reputation, and reigning supreme. Her guest lists always included a wide range of people, from European dignitaries to artistic deviants. The parties were held either at her splendid mansion, Villa Lewaro, or at her town house, which was on a smaller scale but was nonetheless very well appointed and renowned as the "Dark Tower"—it was named after a column by Countee Cullen column and a poem by Hughes. The

Further Reading

"A'Lelia Walker: The Harlem Renaissance Salon Lady." Eric Garber Papers. San Francisco (Calif.) Gay and Lesbian Archives.

Bundles, Perry A'Lelia. *On Her Own Ground: The Life and Times of Madame C. J. Walker*. New York: Scribner, 2001.

Hine, Darlene Clark. *Black Women in America: An Historical Encyclopedia*. Brooklyn, N.Y.: Carlson Publishing, 1993, pp. 1203–1205.

Hughes, Langston. *The Big Sea: An Autobiography*. New York: Hill and Wang, 1963.

Hull, Gloria T. *Color, Sex, and Poetry: Three Women Writers of the Harlem Renaissance*. Bloomington and Indianapolis: Indiana University Press, 1987.

Kellner, Bruce, ed. *Keep a-Inchin' Along: Selected Writings of Carl Van Vechten about Black Art and Letters*. Westport, Conn.: Greenwood, 1980.

———, ed. *The Harlem Renaissance: A Historical Dictionary for the Era*. Westport, Conn.: Greenwood, 1984.

Lewis, David Levering. *When Harlem Was in Vogue*. New York: Oxford University Press, 1989.

Nugent, Richard Bruce. "On the Dark Tower." Schomburg Collection, New York Public Library.

Watson, Steve, *The Harlem Renaissance: Hub of African-American Culture, 1920–1930*. New York: Pantheon, 1995.

Walker, Madame C. J.

Madame C. J. Walker was an early exemplar of the "New Negro," encouraging African Americans to take pride in their appearance and enhance their self-respect. She also embodied the new mood of militancy in the African American community after World War I, as well as the renewed race-consciousness and pride that was at the heart of the Harlem Renaissance. Through both her business enterprise and her philanthropy, she promoted equal rights, supported black education, and expanded the economic horizon for thousands of African Americans.

Sarah Breedlove McWilliams Walker, better known as Madame C. J. Walker, was the first self-made African American female millionaire. She made her fortune from her own line of cosmetic and hair-care products, starting with a homemade formula for softening hair. Madame C. J. Walker's "Wonderful Hair Grower" was intended for use with a heated iron comb that would enable African American women to create "long, styled hair" without resorting to the harsh techniques of pulling or ironing their hair widely used in the late nineteenth century. She did not approve of skin bleaching or hair straightening as such. Instead, she saw her products as enabling black women to enhance their appearance while affirming their self-worth and dignity. The use of the Walker System by the dancer Josephine Baker attracted the attention of a French firm, which produced a pomade called "Baker-Fix."

As a young widowed mother without much formal education, whose own parents had been slaves, Sarah McWilliams supported her daughter Lelia by working as a laundress and a domestic in St. Louis, Missouri. When she began to lose her hair, she devised both an ointment and a method for grooming hair and promoting hair growth. Her first tentative steps in business were to sell the "Walker System" by traveling around the black neighborhoods of St. Louis, knocking on doors. In 1905, she went to live with her widowed

sister-in-law in Denver, Colorado, and from there soon expanded her operations, traveling throughout the southern states and promoting her system to women at their homes, in clubs, and in churches. She hired and trained agents to sell her products and to do demonstrations on skin and hair care, while also developing the manufacturing side of her business. In 1908, Walker opened a second office in Pittsburgh; then, in 1910, she established the headquarters for her fast-growing enterprise in Indianapolis. Not only did she set up a manufacturing company, she also founded the Walker College of Hair Culture, employing some 3,000 people, in addition to the many thousands of sales agents throughout the country. Women beauticians purchased a franchise from Walker in which they used both the Walker products and the Walker system. In this way, Madame C. J. Walker facilitated business opportunities for thousands of black women throughout the United States, extending their work options at a time when the labor market was racially segregated and few occupations were open to women.

From the outset, Walker worked through existing institutions in African American communities in order to promote her business. Cosmetics and hair care were frowned on by the clergy, but Walker extolled the virtues of personal care and donated generously to Baptist and African Methodist Episcopal churches. Black women's clubs and colleges were additional venues for the promotion of her message about beauty care. She succeeded in setting up beauty parlors in some women's colleges while promoting industrial education for women. She was a major donor to Bethune-Cookman College, established by the prominent black activist Mary McLeod Bethune, and she funded scholarships for women at the Booker T. Washington's Tuskegee Institute in Alabama. Walker was an active member of the National Association of Colored Women, established in 1896, seeking to act as a bridge between the African American communities of workingwomen and clubwomen. While the political import of African American beauty culture may not have been obvious to contemporaries or even to later generations, Walker saw her work in the context of racial uplift. Physical appearance was central to issues about identity, economic mobility, and social acceptance in a racially segregated society. By encouraging self-esteem through the use of beauty products, Walker contributed to the enhancement of the status of black women, and, thereby, the status of all African Americans.

In 1916, at the instigation of her daughter, A'Lelia, Madame C. J. Walker moved to Harlem, where she

Madame C. J. Walker (at wheel of car), c. 1910. (Schomburg Center for Research in Black Culture, New York Public Library.)

bought two houses, at 108 and 110 West 136th Street, one as her home and the other as a salon and a college. She became increasingly active in African American politics and participated in the organizing committee for the Silent Protest Parade of July 1917. A few days later she was part of a delegation, along with James Weldon Johnson, to present President Woodrow Wilson with a petition seeking his support for antilynching legislation. Wilson declined to see the delegation personally and sent his secretary to meet them. In 1918, Walker was invited to address fund-raisers organized by the National Association for the Advancement of Colored People (NAACP) as part of the organization's antilynching campaign; also in 1918, she was honored by the National Association for Colored Women for her generous donation to the campaign to save the home of Frederick Douglass, a leading abolitionist. Walker was a member of the International League of Darker Peoples, founded in 1919. Her business was an international one, and she had made promotional tours to Jamaica, Cuba, Haiti, Costa Rica, and Panama. At her country mansion—Villa Lewaro in Irvington-on-Hudson, New York, designed by the black architect Vertner Woodson Tandy—Walker hosted gatherings of black leaders. Just before her death in 1919, she donated $5,000 to the NAACP's antilynching campaign, its largest donation to that date, and requested that Villa Lewaro be left to the organization after her daughter's death.

Biography

Sarah Breedlove McWilliams Walker was born on 23 December 1867 in Delta, Louisiana. She married Moses McWilliams in 1871 and had one daughter, A'Lelia, in 1885. She was widowed in 1887; she married Charles J. Walker in 1905. She was a laundress from 1887 to 1905 and an entrepreneur from 1905 to 1919. She was owner and president of Walker College of Hair Culture and the Walker Manufacturing Company, Indianapolis, Indiana, from 1910 to 1919. Walker was a activist for civil rights and human rights and a philanthropist. She died in New York City on 25 May 1919.

MAUREEN MONTGOMERY

See also Antilynching Crusade; Baker, Josephine; Bethune, Mary McLeod; Lynching: Silent Protest Parade; Walker, A'Lelia

Further Reading

Bundles, A'Leila Perry. "America's First Self-Made Woman Millionaire." *Radcliffe Quarterly*, 1987.

———. *Madam C. J. Walker, Entrepreneur.* New York: Chelsea House, 1991.

Hine, Darlene Clark, ed. *Black Women in America: An Historical Encyclopedia*, 2 vols. Brooklyn, N.Y.: Carlson, 1993.

James, Edward T., ed. *Notable American Women, 1607–1950: A Biographical Dictionary.* Cambridge, Mass.: Belknap Press of Harvard University Press, 1971.

Latham, Charles, Jr. "Madam C. J. Walker and Company." *Traces of Indiana and Midwestern History*, 1(3), 1989.

Low, W. Augustus, and Virgil A. Clift, eds. *Encyclopedia of Black America.* New York: McGraw-Hill, 1981.

Peiss, Kathy. *Hope in a Jar: The Making of America's Beauty Culture.* New York: Metropolitan–Holt, 1998.

Salem, Dorothy C., ed. *African American Women: A Biographical Dictionary.* New York: Garland, 1993.

Sicherman, Barbara, and Carol Hurd Green, eds. *Notable American Women: The Modern Period—A Biographical Dictionary.* Cambridge, Mass.: Belknap Press of Harvard University Press, 1980.

Walker, Margaret

Margaret Walker—a poet, author, essayist, lecturer, and educator—dedicated seven decades of her life to writing about the black experience in America, which she chronicled in poetry and prose, centering on such themes as time, racial equality, love, and freedom. In Walker's *This Is My Century* (1989), she credits her parents—Sigismund C. Walker, a Methodist minister, and Marion (Dozier) Walker, a music teacher who played ragtime—for inspiring her to write early in her life. Her mother also introduced her to the poetry of Paul Laurence Dunbar, John Greenleaf Whittier, and William Shakespeare. Between the ages of eleven and fourteen, she read the poetry of Langston Hughes and Countee Cullen, and she launched her writing career with her first poems while attending the Gilbert Academy in New Orleans. By the age of sixteen, she had met Hughes, who was a family friend and who became her literary mentor. He read her poetry, recognized her talent, suggested she strive for musicality in verse, and encouraged her parents and her teacher, Miss Fluke, to provide the necessary climate conducive for an aspiring writer outside the South. During her undergraduate studies at her father's alma mater, Northwestern University, she met the editor, scholar, and author W. E. B. Du Bois, who was influential in publishing her poetry in *The Crisis* in 1934. Her creative writing teacher, Edward Buell Hungerford, admitted her to the Northwestern chapter of the Poetry Society of America.

After graduating from Northwestern, Walker lived in Chicago for four years, working first as a social worker and later as a member of the Works Progress Administration (WPA), which allowed her to shape her writing craft. It was when she joined the South Side Writers' Group, initiated by the author Richard Wright, however, that her own poetic talent emerged. Between 1936 and 1939, Walker associated with such artists and scholars as the novelists Nelson Algren and Frank Yerby; the poets Arna Bontemps, Gwendolyn Brooks, and Frank Marshall Davis; the artists Katherine Dunham and Margaret Taylor Goss Burroughs; and the playwright Theodore Ward. Her most valuable literary experience was perhaps with Richard Wright, who, while sharing their work, broadened her vision of literature, in particular, as a vital part of political action. After he moved to New York in 1937, she continued to assist him with materials to compose *Native Son*. Two years later, her friendship and mentorship with Wright ended rather abruptly and painfully; she would write about this in her detailed biography of him (1988). Her tenure with the Federal Writers' Project also expired; Walker then entered the University of Iowa, where she completed her master's degree thesis with her first collection of poems, *For My People*, in 1942.

Walker's vision reached fruition in her award-winning collection of twenty-six poems. Through rhythmic verses and strong imagery, the work affirms the proud heritage and integrity of black Americans. For the most part, critics, reviewers, and peers praised her work. Some critics found fault with her use of lyrical sonnets, while others seemed impressed with the ballads and the long-line free verse punctuated with short lines. In her title poem, her best-known and most anthologized work, her form captures what Richard Barksdale calls "the source of the Black people's blues" and "it radiates the promise of our future" (Collier 1984).

While writing poetry, teaching when possible, and marrying and raising four children with her husband Firnist James Alexander (1943), Walker returned to the University of Iowa in 1962 to pursue a doctorate and to complete *Jubilee*, which she had begun at Northwestern. In 1965, she finished both the degree and her dissertation, which was published in 1966, becoming her second most popular work. Described as an "ambitious," "neo-slave narrative" that incorporates actual and historical events from slavery to Reconstruction, the novel chronicles the life of the daughter of a slave and a white plantation owner. When the novel was first published, it had a mixed reception, but over the years the novel has been given more favorable criticism, focusing specifically on Walker as an important historian, her characterization, and the use of music.

After she published her novel, Walker's creative energies flourished. She returned to writing poetry, and her next volume to receive high acclaim was *Prophets for a New Day* (1970). This slim volume, unlike *For My People*, reveals an even more expansive political consciousness and includes her civil rights poems influenced by the turmoil of the 1960s. Walker published *October Journey* (1973), followed by two books—*A Poetic Equation: Conversations between Nikki Giovanni and Margaret Walker* (1974); and a definitive biography, *Richard Wright: Daemonic Genius* (1988). A year later Walker published her last volume of poetry, *This Is My Century: New and Collected Poems* (1989), a culmination of her collective political vision. A few years before Walker died, she published, with editorial assistance from Maryemma Graham, *How I Wrote Jubilee and Other Essays on Life and Literature* (1990). Her final published work was *On Being Female, Black, and Free: Essays by Margaret Walker, 1932–1992* (1997).

Walker bridged the generations of the Harlem Renaissance of the 1920s and the black arts movement of the 1960s. She was one of the United States' foremost poetic historians for the African American race.

Biography

Margaret Abigail Walker was born on 7 July 1915 in Birmingham, Alabama. She completed her high school education at Gilbert Academy in New Orleans, Louisiana; attended New Orleans University (now Dillard University) for two years; then attended Northwestern University (B.A., English, 1935). She worked with the Works Progress Administration (WPA) from 1936 to 1939. She attended the University of Iowa (M.A., 1940; Ph.D., 1965). She taught at Livingstone College, 1941–1942; West Virginia State College, 1942–1943; Jackson State University, 1946–1979; and Northwestern University, as a visiting professor, spring quarter, 1968–1969. She was founder and director, Institute for the Study of History, Life, and Culture of Black People (now the Margaret Walker Alexander National Research Center), 1968–1979. She received a D.F.A., Denison University, 1974; and D.H.L., Morgan State University, 1976. She was professor emerita at Jackson State University, 1979–1998. Her awards included Yale Younger Poets Award, 1942; Rosenwald Fellowship, 1944; Ford Fellowship, 1953; University of Iowa Fellowship, 1963; Houghton Mifflin Fellowship, 1966; a Fulbright fellowship to Norway, 1971; Senior Fellowship from the National Endowment for the Humanities, 1972; the Living Legacy Award, the Lifetime Achievement Award of the College Language Association, 1992; the Lifetime Achievement Award for Excellence in the Arts, 1992; the White House Award for Distinguished Senior Citizen; and six honorary degrees. She was inducted into the African American Literary Hall of Fame in October 1998. Jackson, Mississippi, designated 12 July "Margaret Walker Day." Walker died in Chicago of breast cancer on 30 November 1998.

LORETTA G. WOODARD

See also Hughes, Langston; Literature: 7—Poetry; Wright, Richard; Yerby, Frank; *other specific individuals*

Selected Works

The Ballad of the Free. 1966.
For Farish Street Green. 1986.
For My People. 1942.
How I Wrote Jubilee and Other Essays on Life and Literature. 1990.
Jubilee. 1966.
October Journey. 1973.
On Being Female, Black, and Free: Essays by Margaret Walker, 1932–1992. 1997.
A Poetic Equation: Conversations between Nikki Giovanni and Margaret Walker. 1974.
Prophets for a New Day. 1970.
Richard Wright: Daemonic Genius. 1988.
This Is My Century: New and Collected Poems. 1989.

Further Reading

Barksdale, Richard K. "Margaret Walker: Folk Orature and Historical Prophecy." In *Black American Poets between Worlds, 1940–1960*, ed. R. Baxter Miller. Knoxville: University of Tennessee Press, 1986.

Bonetti, Kay. "Margaret Walker." In *Conversations with American Novelists: The Best Interviews from the Missouri Review and the American Audio Prose Library*, ed. Kay Bonetti et al. Columbia: University of Missouri Press, 1997.

Caton, Bill. "Margaret Walker Alexander." In *Fighting Words: Words on Writing from Twenty-one of the Heart of Dixie's Best Contemporary Authors*, ed. Bill Caton and Bert Hitchcock. Montgomery, Ala.: Black Belt, 1995.

Collier, Eugenia. "Fields Watered with Blood: Myth and Ritual in the Poetry of Margaret Walker." In *Black Women Writers (1950–1980): A Critical Evaluation*, ed. Mari Evans. Garden City, N.Y.: Anchor-Doubleday, 1984.

Davis, Arthur P. *From the Dark Tower: Afro-American Writers, 1900 to 1960*. Washington, D.C.: Howard University Press, 1974.

Debo, Annette. "Margaret Walker." In *Contemporary African American Novelists*, ed. Emmanuel S. Nelson. Westport, Conn.: Greenwood, 2000.

Freibert, Lucy M. "Southern Song: An Interview with Margaret Walker." *Frontiers: A Journal of Women Studies*, 9(3), 1987.

Graham, Maryemma. "The Fusion of Ideas: An Interview with Margaret Walker Alexander." *African American Review*, 27(2), Summer 1993.

Pettis, Joyce. "Margaret Walker: Black Woman Writer of the South." In *Southern Women Writers: The New Generation*, ed. Tonette Bond Inge. Tuscaloosa: University of Alabama Press, 1990.

Traylor, Eleanor. "Music as Theme: The Blues Mode in the Works of Margaret Walker." In *Black Women Writers (1950–1980): A Critical Evaluation*, ed. Mari Evans. New York: Doubleday, 1984.

Ward, Jerry W., Jr. "A Writer for Her People: An Interview With Dr. Margaret Walker Alexander." *Mississippi Quarterly*, 41(4), Fall 1988.

Waller, Thomas "Fats"

Although famous for his larger-than-life personality, onstage antics, risqué wit, and numerous popular song standards, Fats Waller was among the greatest jazz musicians and songwriters to emerge from Harlem. To many leaders of the Harlem Renaissance, jazz represented one of several African American idioms useful in classical forms, but it was not considered high art. Therefore, his important contributions to jazz and popular song of the era have rarely been noted alongside those of composers such as William Grant Still. Yet in connecting stride piano of the 1910s and 1920s (featuring vigorous and challenging left-hand technique) with the increasingly complex jazz styles of the 1920s, Waller influenced Count Basie, Duke Ellington, Fletcher Henderson, Art Tatum, and countless others. Moreover, Waller was the first jazz organist, and his songs, such as "Ain't Misbehavin'" and "Honeysuckle Rose," have become American classics.

Waller was born on 134th Street in Harlem to Edward and Adeline Waller. A religious family, the Wallers had been members of the Abyssinian Baptist Church before converting to the Pentecostal faith. After the conversion, Edward Waller became a street-corner preacher on Lenox Avenue, and young Thomas Waller accompanied the services by playing hymns on a portable reed organ. He began piano lessons at age six and played in his school band, but most of his early training was informal—imitating music he heard in church, theaters, and vaudeville houses during the 1910s. His first job in music came at age fifteen, accompanying movies at the Lincoln Theater on 135th Street, drawing crowds among local teenagers and eventually young musicians. His parents were upset at Fats's performing in the "devil's workshop" and rejected outright any forays into jazz. Edward Waller even took his son to see the concert pianist Ignacy Paderewski to encourage a more respectable musical career. Although Fats was quite impressed with Paderewski, the lure of Harlem's culture, nightlife, and music was too strong.

After his mother's death in 1920, Waller moved in with the pianist Russell Brooks, who introduced him to James P. Johnson, dean of Harlem stride "professors" and the idol of anyone aspiring to the craft. Johnson became Waller's mentor, teaching him stride technique, introducing him to fellow pianists such as Willie "the Lion" Smith, and helping him obtain a contract with the QRS piano roll company.

During the early 1920s, Waller began to gain a local reputation. With the help of Johnson and his own burgeoning skills, he became a regular performer on the "rent party" circuit. These socials not only helped tenants make rent payments, but they also served as tournaments for stride pianists, who were responsible for keeping dance music going all night. Rent parties featured "cutting contests," in which pianists would challenge each other, playing as many as 100 choruses of a solo piano piece. These events, more than formal lessons, served as the "school" for young pianists such as Waller.

This period also saw Waller emerge as a songwriter and recording artist. Through his association with Clarence Williams, he cut his first solo 78 rpm records in 1922, published his first songs in 1923, and served as a sideman for singers including Alberta Hunter. Throughout, he maintained his organ work at the Lincoln Theater, and he performed in vaudeville shows on tour and in New York, including the first featuring black performers at the Lafayette Theater in 1925. Recordings with several groups, including "Fats and His Buddies," put him in contact with a widening circle of elite jazz performers, and numerous Tin Pan Alley composers recognized his skill as a songwriter.

By the end of the decade, although Waller was regarded as the preeminent stride pianist by his peers and his music was enjoyed by many jazz fans, he had yet to sing on record or develop the buoyant stage presence that would earn him fame. Moreover, he was constantly in debt, and he was jailed twice for nonpayment of alimony. His fortunes began to change in 1928, when James P. Johnson recommended that Waller and his sporadic lyricist-collaborator Andy Razaf cowrite a new vehicle for the vaudeville team of Flournoy Miller and Aubrey Lyles (*Keep Shufflin'*, 1928). The popularity of *Keep Shufflin'* led to completion of another review (*Hot Chocolates*, 1929) introducing two of their biggest hits: "Ain't Misbehavin'," which helped propel the careers of Cab Calloway and Louis Armstrong, and "Black and Blue." The latter tune was originally commissioned as a comical look at conflicts between light- and dark-skinned blacks, but the songwriters saw no humor in the conflict and wrote a poignant statement on racism instead. The pair attempted to parlay their success into financial security, but they often sold compositions anonymously for quick money, a fate common to many black songwriters. This cost them large payoffs after the songs were recorded, and it has led to credible speculation that some works by Irving Berlin and the white songwriting team of Fields and McHugh were actually the work of Waller and Razaf.

After his manager and Razaf encouraged him to sing his own material, in 1931 Waller overcame his earlier shyness, and an exuberant, clowning, rakish stage personality emerged during the early 1930s. At the same time, a series of radio broadcasts from New York (WABC) and Cincinnati (WLW) and consistent touring gained him a widening audience, more attracted to his sly and mischievous wit than his musicianship. In 1934, a contract with Victor to record Waller's quintet "Fats Waller and His Rhythm," and his own CBS radio show, earned him fame and, for the first time, financial security. His traveling increased, including three tours of Europe and several trips to Hollywood after 1935 to make films. By World War II, his international renown was second only to that of Louis Armstrong among jazz musicians.

Fats Waller. (© Bettmann/Corbis.)

The rigorous schedule, including overseas performances for black soldiers during wartime, as well as a lifelong overindulgence in food and whiskey, had taken its toll on the 300-pound Waller, and his health began to fail in the early 1940s. While returning from a 1943 trip to California to film *Stormy Weather*, he died, probably of pneumonia, on a train near Kansas City, Missouri, at age thirty-nine.

Biography

Thomas Wright "Fats" Waller was born in New York City on 21 May 1904. He was educated at New York City public schools until age fourteen. He studied piano with James P. Johnson and (probably) Leopold Godowsky; and he studied composition (probably) with Carl Bohm (at Juilliard). He was the organist at the Lincoln Theater in New York(1919–1926), the Lafayette Theater in New York (1925–1927), and the Royal Grand Theater in Philadelphia (1928). His significant recording contracts included QRS (piano rolls, 1923); Okeh (1922–1924); Columbia (1931); Victor (1926–1930, 1934–1943). He performed during the 1920s and 1930s with Henry "Red" Allen, Una Mae Carlisle, Fletcher Henderson, Ted Lewis, McKinney's Cotton Pickers, the Mills Brothers, Don Redman, Erskine Tate, Jack Teagarden, and Clarence Williams; and he was accompanist for the singers Rosa Henderson, Alberta Hunter, Sara Martin, Hazel Meyers, and Maude Mills. Groups under his own name were Fats Waller and His Buddies (1927–1929) and Fats Waller and His Rhythm (1934–1943). Important songwriting collaborators were Andy Razaf, Clarence Williams, and Spencer Williams. Waller had radio broadcasts from Fox Terminal Theater (Newark, New Jersey) and WHN (New York), 1923; WOR (New York), 1928–1929; WABC "Paramount on Parade," 1930–1931; "Radio Roundup" 1931; WLW "Fats Waller's Rhythm Club" and "Moon River" (Cincinnati, Ohio), 1932; and CBS (New York) "Rhythm Club" and "Columbia Variety Hour," 1934. His significant engagements included performing as "Ali-Baba, the Egyptian Wonder" with the Ellington Orchestra at the Kentucky Club and New Amsterdam Theater, New York (1924); at Carnegie Hall, as pianist in James P. Johnson's *Yamekraw* (1928); his first solo jazz concert at Carnegie Hall (1942); and with the Les Hite Orchestra at the New Cotton Club, Los Angeles (1935). His European tours included Paris, with performances at Bricktop's (1932),

England, the continent, and Scandinavia (1938, 1939). Waller died near Kansas City, Missouri, on 15 December 1943.

WILLIAM J. NANCARROW

See also Calloway, Cabell "Cab"; Columbia Phonograph Company; Henderson, Fletcher; Hot Chocolates; House-Rent Parties; Hunter, Alberta; Jazz; Johnson, James P.; Lafayette Theater; Lincoln Theater; Musical Theater; Razaf, Andy; Smith, Willie "the Lion"; Williams, Clarence

Selected Songs and Compositions

"Ain't Misbehavin'." 1929. (With Andy Razaf.)
"Anybody Here Want to Try My Cabbage." 1924. (With Andy Razaf.)
"Fractious Fingering." 1938.
"Honeysuckle Rose." 1929. (With Andy Razaf.)
"Lenox Avenue Blues." 1927.
London Suite. 1939.
"My Feelin's Are Hurt." 1929.
"Squeeze Me." 1923. (With Andy Razaf.)
"Stealin' Apples." 1936. (With Andy Razaf.)
"Valentine Stomp." 1929.
"Viper's Drag." 1930.
"Whiteman Stomp." 1927.
"Wildcat Blues." 1923. (With Clarence Williams.)
"(What Did I Do to Be So) Black and Blue." 1929. (With Andy Razaf.)
"Your Feet's Too Big." 1939.

Musical Theater

Hot Chocolates (*Connie's Inn Hot Chocolates*). 1929. (With Andy Razaf and Harry Brooks.)
Junior Blackbirds. 1926.
Keep Shufflin'. 1928. (With Andy Razaf, James P. Johnson, Harry Creamer, and Clarence Todd.)
Load of Coal. 1929. (With Andy Razaf.)
Tan Town Topics. 1926. (With Spencer Williams.)

Films

Hooray for Love. 1935.
King of Burlesque. 1935.
Stormy Weather. 1943.

Further Reading

Balliett, Whitney. *Jelly Roll, Jabbo, and Fats: Nineteen Portraits in Jazz*. London: Oxford University Press, 1983.

Charters, Samuel, and Leonard Kunstadt. *Jazz: A History of the New York Scene*. Garden City, N.Y.: McGraw-Hill, 1962.

Kirkeby, W. T., ed. with Duncan P. Scheidt and Sinclair Traill. *Ain't Misbehavin': The Story of Fats Waller*. New York: Da Capo, 1975.

Machlin, Paul S. *Stride: The Music of Fats Waller*. Boston, Mass., and London: G. K. Hall, 1985.

Shipton, Alyn. *Fats Waller: His Life and Times*. New York: Universe, 1988.

Vance, Joel. *Fats Waller: His Life and Times*. Chicago, Ill.: Contemporary, 1977.

Waller, Maurice, and Anthony Calabrese. *Fats Waller*. New York, Schirmer, 1977.

Walls of Jericho, The

The Walls of Jericho (1928) is a novel by Rudolph Fisher. By 1928, Fisher was already a respected author of numerous short stories. Nevertheless, the publication of this seriocomic novel solidified his status as a writer of the Harlem Renaissance and revealed him to be an accomplished social satirist. The novel resulted from a wager by a friend that Fisher could not construct a novel that would successfully blend Harlem's "high" and "low" cultures. *The Walls of Jericho* succeeds masterfully in this regard and was well received by most reviewers, thanks precisely to its evenhanded portrayal of the full range of society in Harlem. Fisher's balanced treatment was a timely balm, too, for those critics who lamented the "primitivism" of Claude McKay's *Home to Harlem* (1928) and Carl Van Vechten's controversial *Nigger Heaven* (1926). Yet despite good reviews and the added respectability of being published by Alfred A. Knopf, the commercial success of the novel was undoubtedly hindered by its being branded a "light" work, as well its print run being limited to 5,000 copies without the benefit of major publicity.

The Walls of Jericho has two parallel intertwining plots. The first involves Joshua "Shine" Jones, a piano mover whose pride and comfortable pretense of indifference are threatened by his romance with Linda Young, a sensitive, intelligent woman with ambitions beyond her employment as a maid. Ultimately Linda succeeds in making Shine understand that the walls they each have erected around themselves serve only to prevent their being happy together. The second plot involves the lawyer Fred Merrit, an avowed hater of whites who, by virtue of his wealth and light skin, purchases a house in an all-white neighborhood strictly for the purpose of causing trouble. Trouble follows when Merrit's house is burned down; however, it turns out that the black owner of a pool hall who holds a grudge against Merrit is the culprit rather than the supposed white neighbors. Considered as a whole, the novel eschews propaganda while ambitiously tackling numerous serious racial issues, including class consciousness, color consciousness, racial uplift, inter- and intraracial relations, miscegenation, passing, white flight, white philanthropy, and the black urban experience—all the while still succeeding as a satire and comedy.

Critical reaction to the novel has been largely positive, with most attention focused on Fisher's deft handling of the white philanthropist Agatha Cramp and the balcony scenes at the General Improvement Association's costume ball. Singh (1976) claims that the work "stands alone among Harlem Renaissance novels as a high comedy"; Gloster (1948) lauds Fisher as "the first Negro author skilled in comic realism." Others cite Fisher's objective dual criticism of black and white cultures as one of the novel's chief strengths, while more recent treatments by de Jongh (1990) and Balshaw (2000) highlight the novel's value as a critique of the early black urban experience. Nevertheless, *The Walls of Jericho* has always proved of less interest to scholars than Fisher's short fiction, a condition likely to be furthered by the growing critical popularity of Fisher's landmark detective novel, *The Conjure Man Dies*.

CRAIG GABLE

See also Conjure Man Dies, The; Fisher, Rudolph; Home to Harlem; Nigger Heaven; McKay, Claude; Van Vechten, Carl

Further Reading

Balshaw, Maria. "Space, Race, and Identity." In *Looking for Harlem: Urban Aesthetics in African-American Literature*. London: Pluto, 2000.

Bremer, Sidney H. "Home in Harlem, New York: Lessons from the Harlem Renaissance." *PMLA*, 105(1), 1990.

Davis, Arthur P. "Rudolph Fisher." In *From the Dark Tower: Afro-American Writers, 1900 to 1960*. Washington, D.C.: Howard University Press, 1974.

Gayle, Addison, Jr. "The Outsider." In *The Way of the New World: The Black Novel in America*. Garden City, N.Y.: Anchor-Doubleday, 1975.

Gloster, Hugh M. "Fiction of the Negro Renascence." *Negro Voices in American Fiction*. Chapel Hill: University of North Carolina Press, 1948.

Huggins, Nathan Irvin. "Heart of Darkness." In *Harlem Renaissance*. New York: Oxford University Press, 1971.

McCluskey, John, Jr. "Introduction." In *The City of Refuge: The Collected Stories of Rudolph Fisher*. Columbia: University of Missouri Press, 1987.

Perry, Margaret. *Silence to the Drums: A Survey of the Literature of the Harlem Renaissance*. Westport, Conn.: Greenwood, 1976.

Singh, Amritjit. "The Dicties and the Shines: Class in Black America." In *The Novels of the Harlem Renaissance: Twelve Black Writers, 1923–1933*. University Park: Pennsylvania State University Press, 1976.

Tignor, Eleanor Q. "Rudolph Fisher: Harlem Novelist." *Langston Hughes Review*, 1(2), 1982.

Walrond, Eric

In 1918, Eric Walrond, a young, unknown West Indian journalist, arrived in New York. Less than a decade later, he was heralded as an influential essayist, editor, and short-story writer of the Harlem Renaissance.

Initially Walrond was disappointed in his efforts to further his writing career in the United States. Unable to gain employment with a newspaper, he held various jobs that did not tap into his experiences as a former reporter for the *Panama Star and Herald*. Walrond eventually resumed his career as a journalist with the *Brooklyn and Long Island Informer* as well as the *Weekly Review*, a publication of Marcus Garvey's Universal Negro Improvement Association (UNIA). Walrond's prize-winning sketch "A Senator's Memoirs," along with his appointments as assistant editor and then associate editor of UNIA's *Negro World*—a literary journal that counted among its contributors Zora Neale Hurston, Alain Locke, Claude McKay, Arthur Schomburg, and Walrond—marked his literary entrance into Harlem. Walrond's tenure with *Negro World* from 1921 to 1923 was significant for his career. *Negro World*, with its circulation of 200,000, provided greater exposure for Walrond's talents. While Walrond performed his editorial responsibilities at *Negro World*, his prose began appearing in other publications; he wrote articles, reviews, and short stories for more than thirty-seven national and international periodicals including *Current History, The New Republic, The Crisis, The Messenger, Forbes, Vanity Fair, Chicago Defender, New York Herald Tribune, Saturday Review of Literature, Lectures du Soir* (Paris), *Voilà* (Paris), *Ahora* (Madrid), *Spectator* (London), and *Black Man* (London). In "The New Negro Faces America" (1923), which may be Walrond's most important article, he boldly excoriates black leaders (Booker T. Washington, W. E. B. Du Bois, and Marcus Garvey) and offers characteristics of a new black identity. In addition, Walrond wrote about racism in the United States and abroad, migration (Caribbean men and women to the United States and blacks to the North), reactions of blacks in the United States to West Indians, pan-Africanism, racial pride, literature versus propaganda, and Harlem. Walrond also reviewed books by contemporaries including Countee Cullen, Jessie Redmon Fauset, Rudolph Fisher, Claude McKay, and Walter White, as well as art exhibits and theatrical productions.

Another periodical figured prominently in Walrond's career. *Opportunity*, the National Urban League's monthly magazine edited by Charles S. Johnson, awarded Walrond's short story "Voodoo's Revenge" third prize in 1925. That same year, Walrond became *Opportunity*'s business manager. According to Parascandola (1998), Walrond's two-year stint with *Opportunity* was important for at least three reasons: (1) He adeptly handled the magazine's finances, maintaining solvency; (2) he spearheaded a special issue in November 1926 that focused on the Caribbean and increased the journal's international appeal; and (3) he recommended other young writers of the Harlem Renaissance for publication in *Opportunity*.

Walrond's accomplishments at *Negro World* and *Opportunity* were impressive; however, *Tropic Death* (1926), a collection of ten short stories, was his greatest literary success. While a number of figures in the Harlem Renaissance advocated uplifting the black race by writing only about the elite, Walrond believed that less-than-flattering aspects of black life should also be depicted and that literary expression was more important than propaganda. Some members of the black literary establishment were less than pleased with *Tropic Death*'s grim Caribbean settings rampant with poverty, famine, and death as well as racism, but *Tropic Death* was recognized as a stellar achievement for Walrond and a major work of the Harlem Renaissance. Langston Hughes, W. E. B. Du Bois, Benjamin Brawley, and Sterling Brown, along with the anonymous authors of reviews in the *New York Times*

Book Review and *New York World*, commented favorably on *Tropic Death*. Decades later, *Tropic Death* is an infrequent recipient of critical attention, yet recent studies by Agatucci, Bogle, Berry, Parascandola, Wade, and others have acknowledged the book's literary merits. Walrond skillfully blended realistic, naturalistic, impressionistic, gothic, autobiographical, and avant-garde elements in his collection. *Tropic Death*, unlike most fiction of the Harlem Renaissance, did not use Harlem or other locations in the United States as its setting. Walrond's portrayal of Caribbean life added a new perspective to renaissance literature.

Walrond was held in high regard by his peers. He is immortalized in Wallace Thurman's satirical novel of the renaissance, *Infants of the Spring* (1932). Thurman, another young member of the Harlem Renaissance, praises his West Indian character Cedric Williams (Walrond) as one of the rare authors of the period with a message and a writing style. Indeed, after *Tropic Death* was published, expectations were high concerning Walrond's literary future. It was generally assumed that his writing career would continue to thrive long after the Harlem Renaissance ended.

Walrond's most productive years were concurrent with the Harlem Renaissance, however. In the late 1920s, Walrond began working on a book about the Panama Canal tentatively titled *The Big Ditch*, and he sent a letter to the Guggenheim Foundation in 1960 announcing his intent to finish the book. He never completed it, however. *Tropic Death* and *Black and Unknown Bards: A Collection of Negro Poetry* (1958), a book he compiled with Rosey E. Pool, are Walrond's only published full-length works. A perusal of Parascandola's bibliography of Walrond's published prose, the most comprehensive list to date, reveals that from the 1930s to 1954 he continued to write for periodicals (primarily European), including Marcus Garvey's publication in London, *Black Man*. Scant details are known about Walrond's life after he left Harlem. Walrond traveled to various Caribbean locations in 1928 as well as Paris, from 1929 to 1932; and he moved to England in 1932. His death in 1966 leaves two unanswered questions: Why did Walrond, a well-known writer of the Harlem Renaissance, live in relative obscurity during his later years? And why did he fail to produce additional major works after *Tropic Death*?

Although Eric Walrond remains a rather mysterious figure, his contemporaries and subsequent generations have corroborated his status as an innovative and influential participant in the Harlem Renaissance.

Biography

Eric Derwent Walrond was born 18 December 1898 in Georgetown, British Guiana (now known as Guyana). He studied at Saint Stephen's Boys' School in Black Rock, Barbados; public and private schools and with tutors in Colón in the Panama Canal Zone; City College (now known as City University of New York), 1922–1924; and Columbia University, 1924–1926. He was a clerk in the health department of the Canal Commission in Cristobal, Panama; reporter, *Panama Star and Herald*, 1916–1918; porter, janitor, secretary, and stenographer, New York, 1918–1921; co-owner, editor, and reporter, *Brooklyn and Long Island Informer*, New York, 1921–1923; associate editor, *Weekly Review*, New York; assistant editor, then associate editor, *Negro World*, New York, 1921–1923; business manager, *Opportunity*, New York, 1925–1927; contributing editor, *New Masses*, 1926–1930; and freelance writer. His awards included the Harmon Award in Literature, 1927; being named a Zona Gale scholar at the University of Wisconsin, 1928; and Guggenheim Award, 1928. Walrond died in London, England, in 1966.

LINDA M. CARTER

See also Infants of the Spring; Negro World; Opportunity; Tropic Death

Selected Works

Black and Unknown Bards: A Collection of Negro Poetry, 1958. (As comp., with Rosey E. Pool.)
"The New Negro Faces America." February 1923.
Tropic Death. 1926.
"Winds Can Wake Up the Dead": An Eric Walrond Reader, ed. Louis J. Parascandola. 1998.

Further Reading

Agatucci, Cora. "Eric Walrond." In *African American Authors, 1745–1945: A Bio-Bibliographical Critical Sourcebook*, ed. Emmanuel S. Nelson. Westport, Conn.: Greenwood, 2000.

Bassett, John E. "Reviews of *Tropic Death* by Eric D. Walrond." In *Harlem in Review: Critical Reactions to Black American Writers, 1917–1939*. Selinsgrove, Pa.: Susquehanna University Press, 1992.

Berry, Jay R. "Eric Walrond." In *Dictionary of Literary Biography*, Vol. 51, *Afro-American Writers from the Harlem Renaissance to 1940*, ed. Trudier Harris and Thadious M. Davis. Detroit, Mich.: Gale Research, 1987.

Bogle, Enid E. "Eric Walrond." In *Fifty Caribbean Writers: A Bio-Bibliographical Critical Sourcebook*, ed. Daryl Cumber Dance. Westport, Conn.: Greenwood, 1986.

Carter, Linda M. "Eric Walrond." In *Notable Black American Men*, ed. Jessie Carney Smith. Detroit, Mich.: Gale Research, 1999.

Lewis, David Levering. *When Harlem Was in Vogue*. New York: Oxford University Press, 1979.

Martin, Tony M. "The Defectors: Eric Walrond and Claude McKay." In *Literary Garveyism: Garvey, Black Arts, and the Harlem Renaissance*. Dover, Mass.: Majority, 1983.

Ramchand, Kenneth. "The Writer Who Ran Away: Eric Walrond and *Tropic Death*." *Savacou*, 2, September 1970.

Thurman, Wallace. *Infants of the Spring*. New York: Macaulay, 1932.

Wade, Carl A. "African-American Aesthetics and the Short Fiction of Eric Walrond: *Tropic Death* and the Harlem Renaissance." *CLA Journal*, 42(4), 1999.

Walton, Lester

Lester Walton was a journalist, diplomat, entrepreneur, and songwriter. His career in journalism began before he reached the age of twenty, first with the *St. Louis Globe Democrat* and then, from 1902, with the *St. Louis Star*. Walton worked primarily as a sports reporter. He also had ambitions as a songwriter and a publisher. In an effort to achieve these goals, he founded the Douglas Music Publishing Company with Richard D. Barrett. Four of their songs were registered for copyright in 1905. In 1903, Walton had written lyrics for several songs by Ernest Hogan, a leading black entertainer. These were purchased by Joseph Stern and Company, a major Tin Pan Alley concern. The connection with Hogan bore fruit in 1907, when Walton wrote lyrics to Hogan's successful show *The Oyster Man*. Walton continued to write songs, some of which he published himself, and he attempted to interest publishers in his work into the 1950s. His last effort in this area was the song "Jim Crow Has Got to Go!"

In 1908, Walton became the theater critic of *New York Age*, retaining this post until 1914. He reviewed the important black entertainers of the day, and his columns are a major firsthand source for contemporary opinion on Bert Williams, the Clef Club, and others. His stature within the theater community led to his gaining membership in "The Frogs," an association of top black entertainers of the day, including Williams and Walker, Cole and Johnson, and James Reese Europe.

As this second stint in journalism wound down, Walton became seriously involved in theater. In 1914, the firm of Walton and Morgenstern leased the Lafayette Theater and brought over the Anita Bush Company from the Lincoln Theater. Renamed the Lafayette Players Stock Company, they became the leading theater troupe of the Harlem Renaissance, and Walton remained associated with them until 1923. In 1915, he also produced a musical show, *Darkydom*. Despite a great array of talent (with lyrics by Henry Creamer and music by James Reese Europe and Will Marion Cook), the show was a costly failure. In 1921–1922, Walton worked for Black Swan Records as tour manager for their leading act, Ethel Waters's Black Swan Troubadours. Later, Walton was active in the Coordinating Council for Negro Performers.

In the 1920s, Walton returned to working primarily as a journalist. He wrote editorials and features for *New York World* from 1922 to 1931, possibly the first African American to gain such a high-profile position at a major white daily. He also wrote for *Literary Digest*, *Outlook*, and other major magazines. Walton had developed political consciousness early in his career, and he nted reform campaigns even in his entertainment columns. In 1913, he spearheaded a movement demanding that the word "Negro" always be printed with a capital "N." During the late 1920s and early 1930s, he rose through the ranks of the New York Democratic Party, serving on the National Democratic Campaign Committee (1924, 1928, 1932), and the New York Commission on Civil Rights.

In July 1935, President Franklin D. Roosevelt named Walton envoy extraordinary and minister plenipotentiary to Liberia. Walton served in this capacity until 1946. He assisted in the construction of the port of Monrovia, crucial to America's wartime operations in the eastern Atlantic. Walton worked for the restoration of territories seized by France, and he criticized Liberia's use of forced labor, corruption among high officials, and other abuses. After his term of diplomatic service, he returned to the United States, where he became active in business, politics, and charity. He served as arbitrator in a labor dispute between the Newspaper Guild and New York *Amsterdam News*, 1957–1959. Walton also worked with the Commission on Intergroup Relations during this period, focusing his efforts especially on fair housing practices.

Biography

Lester Aglar Walton was born on 20 April 1882, in St. Louis, Missouri. He had a career as a journalist, diplomat, entrepreneur, and songwriter. He married Gladys Moore, daughter of Frederick Randolph Moore, longtime publisher of *New York Age*. They had two daughters, Marjorie and Gladys. Walton's awards included honorary degrees from Lincoln University in 1927, Wilberforce University in 1945, and the University of Liberia in 1958. Walton died on 16 October 1965.

ELLIOTT S. HURWITT

See also Anita Bush Theater Company; Black Swan Phonograph Company; Lafayette Players; Lafayette Theater; Lincoln Theater; Moore, Frederick Randolph; New York Age

Further Reading

Badger, Reid. *A Life in Ragtime: A Biography of James Reese Europe*. New York: Oxford University Press, 1996.

Browning, Ivan Harold. "Londoners Honor Walton." *New York Age*, 12 October 1935.

Moon, Henry Lee. "New Minister to Liberia Knew First American Negro Diplomat." *New York Amsterdam News*, 24 August 1935.

New York Times, 17 October 1965. (Obituary.)

Smith, Eric Ledell. *Bert Williams: A Biography of the Pioneer Black Comedian*. New York: McFarland, 1992. (Lists Walton's columns for *New York Age*.)

Young, Artee F. "Lester Walton: Black Theatre Critic." Ph.D. Diss., University of Michigan, 1980.

Wanamaker Award

The Wanamaker Award—its full name is the John Wanamaker Masonic Humanitarian Medal—was created by the Grand Lodge of Pennsylvania at the December Quarterly Communication of 1993, under the leadership of Edward H. Fowler, who was grand master at that time. This award is presented to a male or female non-Mason who supports the ideals and philosophy of the Masonic fraternity. It is a prestigious award, and only five people have received it as of this writing. In 2001, the award was presented to Joseph V. Paterno, coach of the Pennsylvania State University football team, who was widely acclaimed as one of the greatest college football coaches.

John Wanamaker, after whom the award was named, was a well-known merchant. He was born in South Philadelphia, Pennsylvania, on 11 July 1838. His ancestors were early settlers, his father of German and Scotch ancestry and his mother of French Huguenot descent. At age thirteen, he worked as an errand boy for a publishing house. In 1856, he began a job in Barclay Lippincott's clothing store in Philadelphia, and later he became a salesman in Bennett's Town Hall on Market Street.

Gradual success in his career also brought health problems. In 1857, he took a long journey to the western United States to restore his health. He returned to become a paid secretary of the Young Men's Christian Association (YMCA)—its first paid officer in the country. His success in promoting the organization was so great that he was named national secretary by his supporters. In 1858, he founded the Bethany Sunday School. He backed temperance and Pennsylvania's "blue laws." Owing to his strong support for the Republican Party, however, he did not succeed in his bid for various political offices.

Wanamaker created a modest menswear business, Oak Hall, with his brother-in-law Nathan Brown in 1861. A year after Brown's death in 1868, Wanamaker opened John Wanamaker and Company, but he turned it over to his brothers in 1876 when he converted the old freight depot of the Pennsylvania Railroad into a huge store that contained a number of small specialty shops. The "Grand Depot," as it was known, initiated the department store phenomenon; later, after several expansions, it became one of the largest department stores in the United States.

Wanamaker's business success reflects a humanistic attitude in all his undertakings. The effective use of advertisements and a money-back guarantee brought customers to his stores, and he treated his employees like family members. In 1881, he set up an employees' mutual benefit association, with training classes for clerks, and continuation classes for boy and girls. This association later became the John Wanamaker Commercial Institute.

Apart from his mercantile activities, Wanamaker also devoted time to religious and patriotic work. In 1888, he raised funds to help in the election of Benjamin Harrison, and he was made a Postmaster General in 1889. During his term of office, he experimented with rural free delivery, advocated parcel post and postal savings, and made several other improvements to the system.

John Wanamaker was made a "Mason-at-sight" by the grand master William J. Kelly in March 1898, at age sixty-two. Two years later he was elected to become a member and a senior warden of the Friendship Lodge in Jenkintown, Pennsylvania, a rural community, and he served as worshipful master of the lodge the following year. Later he was appointed to serve the Grand Lodge as chairman of the library committee. At the end of his tenure as chairman, the library had collected more than 17,000 volumes, and more than 7,400 works of art and Masonic relics.

Wanamaker died after a long illness in December 1920.

AMY LEE

See also Social-Fraternal Organizations

Further Reading

Hutchison, George. *The Harlem Renaissance in Black and White*. Cambridge, Mass.: Belknap Press of Harvard University Press, 1995.
"John Wanamaker." In *Dictionary of American Biography*, Vol. 19, ed. Dumas Malone. New York: Scribner, 1956.
Lewis, David Levering, ed. *The Portable Harlem Renaissance Reader*. New York: Viking, 1994.

Ward, Aida

Aida Ward, a notable performer at the Cotton Club, was known for her humor as well as for her talent as a singer. She achieved some early notoriety when she embarrassed a young songwriter, Dorothy Fields, by substituting off-color lyrics in one of Fields's songs during a performance at the Cotton Club while Fields's parents were in the audience.

Ward emerged as a star in musical theater when she replaced the popular Florence Mills in the cast of the 1928 version of *Blackbirds*, following Mills's death. In the extended run of *Blackbirds* at the Liberty Theater downtown, Ward's costars were Adelaide Hall and Bill "Bojangles" Robinson. Ironically, the lyrics of Ward's hit song in *Blackbirds*, "I Can't Give You Anything but Love (Baby)," were by Dorothy Fields. Writing about the production in *Black Manhattan*, James Weldon Johnson attributed its success to the strength of the "whole company and the very excellent band," but he singled out two performers—Adelaide Hall and Aida Ward— as "very clever girls."

Blackbirds was an important boost to Ward's career. After she left the show she continued to perform at the Cotton Club and in other venues in Harlem. In 1932 she was associated with another hit song, "I've Got the World on a String," which she performed in the musical revue *Cotton Club Parade*.

In the mid-1930s, Ward's popularity earned her a starring role at Harlem's new Apollo Theater on 125th Street. She was one of the headliners in its opening-night program, "Jazz à la Carte," on 26 January 1934, along with Ralph Cooper, Benny Carter and his Orchestra, and sixteen dancers billed as the "Gorgeous Hot-Steppers." Ward continued to perform in Harlem and elsewhere in New York during the rest of her career, appearing onstage and, more frequently, on the radio.

As a performer, Ward contributed to the flowering of African American music and musical theater that was a major component of the Harlem Renaissance. Most of her acclaim came from her engagements at the Cotton Club, where she brought a bluesy jazz flavor to the works of songwriters like Dorothy Fields and Fields's partner Jimmy McHugh. Ward was accompanied by some of the best musicians of the period, including the bands of the great Duke Ellington and Cab Calloway.

Biography

Aida Ward was born on 11 February 1903 in Washington, D.C. She was one of the noted singers and performers during the Harlem Renaissance, best known for her appearances at Harlem's famous Cotton Club in the 1920s, her starring role in *Blackbirds of 1928*, and her headliner role at the Apollo Theater when it opened in 1934. She was also a featured performer on radio programs during the 1930s and 1940s. Ward died on 23 June 1984 in New York City.

Frank A. Salamone
Cary D. Wintz

See also Apollo Theater; Blackbirds; Cotton Club; Fields, Dorothy; Hall Adelaide; Robinson, Bill "Bojangles"

Further Reading

Anderson, Jervis. *This Was Harlem, 1900–1950*. New York: Farrar, Straus and Giroux, 1981.

Charters, Leonard, and Samuel. *Jazz: A History of the New York Scene*. Garden City, N.Y.: Doubleday, 1962.

DeLerma, Dominique-Rene. *Bibliography of Black Music*, 4 vols. Westport, Conn.: Greenwood, 1984.

Dennison, Sam. *Scandalize My Name: Black Imagery in American Popular Music*. New York: Garland, 1982.

Floyd, Samuel A. *Black Music in the United States: An Annotated Bibliography of Selected Reference and Research Materials*. Millwood, N.Y.: Kraus, 1983.

Locke, Alain. *The Negro and His Music*. New York: Knopf, 1936.

Southern, Eileen. *Biographical Dictionary of Afro-American and African Musicians*. Westport, Conn.: Greenwood, 1982.

Waring, Laura Wheeler

Laura Wheeler Waring was born in Hartford, Connecticut, in 1887. She was the daughter of Reverend Robert Wheeler, the college-educated pastor of the Talcott Street Congregational Church. Her father had created Connecticut's first black congregation, and his ties to the black community were impressive. Robert Wheeler's church had been built in 1826 and had housed fugitive slaves during the Civil War. It also served as a school for black children, where they were taught African history. Waring was raised in a home deeply committed to the black community, the black church, and the value of education. Her parents encouraged her early on to pursue her art, and they loved to watch her draw and paint, sometimes drawing with her.

Waring graduated from Hartford High School in 1906 and went on to study at the Pennsylvania Academy of the Fine Arts, where she would spend the next six years immersing herself in every aspect of studio art. She graduated in 1914 and received the Cresson Traveling Scholarship to study in Europe. Like many artists of the Harlem Renaissance, she sought in Paris an opportunity for the finest training and a free environment in which to improve her craft. She was also able to visit the finest galleries of Europe. This was the first of several trips Waring made to Europe. She returned to Paris in 1925 and stayed for eighteen months, studying painting with Boutet de Monvel and Prinet at the Académie de la Grand Chaumière, a private academy in the Montparnasse district with an excellent reputation and some of the finest teachers in Paris. She returned home when her funds were exhausted.

Because there were other children to support in her family, Waring had to work to help educate them. She taught at the Cheyney State Teachers College in Pennsylvania, where she became the director of the

Laura Wheeler Waring (1887–1948), *Anna Washington Derry*, 1927; oil on canvas, 20 by 16 inches. (© Smithsonian American Art Museum, Washington, D.C./Art Resource, N.Y. Gift of the Harmon Foundation.)

Biography

Laura Wheeler Waring was born in Hartford, Connecticut, in 1887. She graduated from Hartford High School in 1906 and the Pennsylvania Academy of the Fine Arts in 1914. She received a Cresson Traveling Scholarship. She attended Harvard University Summer School in 1918, Columbia University Summer School in 1920, and Académie de la Grande Chaumière, Paris, in 1924–1925. She received a first-place Harmon Foundation Medal in 1928. She was an instructor in the art department of Cheyney State Teachers College, Cheyney, Pennsylvania, from 1906 to 1925; and its director from 1925 to 1948. Waring died in 1948.

AMY KIRSCHKE

See also Artists; Crisis, The; Douglas, Aaron; Harmon Foundation

Major Exhibitions

Galerie du Luxembourg, Paris. 1929.
Howard University, Washington, D.C. 1940, 1949.
National Portrait Gallery, Smithsonian Institution, Washington, D.C. 1944, 1997.
Brooklyn Museum, New York, 1945.
Newark Museum, Newark, New Jersey, 1989.

Further Reading

Gips, Terry, ed. *Narratives of African American Art and Identity: The David C. Driskell Collection*, 1998.
Harmon Foundation Papers. Library of Congress, Boxes 43 and 45.

music and art departments. She had little time for her own work during the school year. In the summers she received training at Harvard and Columbia on how to teach drawing. In 1928, she was awarded the First Prize Medal from the Harmon Foundation.

Although Waring is known for her portraits, most notably those of Marian Anderson (1944) and W. E. B. Du Bois (n.d.), perhaps her greatest contribution to the Harlem Renaissance was as an illustrator for the magazine *The Crisis*, edited by Du Bois. She received numerous commissions to provide *Crisis* with both cover and interior illustrations. She created illustrations in black-and-white silhouette, delicate and detailed, flat and dramatic in their simplicity. She often contributed fantastic images of Africa, special covers for the annual Christmas issues, as well as a variety of other subjects. She was one of the most active illustrators of *The Crisis* during Du Bois's editorship, along with Albert Alex Smith and Aaron Douglas.

Waring remained at Cheyney State Teachers College until her death in 1948. Her work is included in numerous museums and private collections, including the National Gallery of Art in Washington, D.C.

Washington, Booker T.

Booker T. Washington prefigured many of the economic, cultural, and political themes of the "New Negroes" of the Harlem Renaissance. At the same time, he was a political foil for many people in the movement who detested his conciliatory rhetoric. Washington was born in West Virginia; was a former slave; imbibed the purported virtues of the Protestant ethic from General Samuel Chapman Armstrong during his years as a student at Hampton Institute; and founded Tuskegee Institute in 1881. Later, Tuskegee became a major center for technical and industrial training of blacks in the

United States and the central locus of Washington's famous (or infamous) Tuskegee political and patronage machine. On 18 September 1895, at the opening of the Atlanta Cotton States and International Exposition, Washington delivered a speech to a mixed audience that catapulted him into both national and international eminence as the leading black spokesman of his generation.

Washington's speech is often pejoratively referred to as the "Atlanta compromise" because it represented an accommodation regarding blacks' civil and political rights; at the same time, though, it was an aggressive assertion of the potency of self-reliance and a commitment to progress. African Americans, Washington argued, would eventually achieve equality, not by agitation for social equality, but by a "severe and constant" struggle in the marketplace. In keeping with his advocacy of technical and industrial training for blacks, in 1900 Washington founded the National Negro Business League in order to promote the business achievements of African Americans and to promulgate his economic and nationalist worldview.

In addition to significantly influencing the development and racial composition of Harlem, Washington and his "machine"—that is, Monroe Nathan Work and Robert Ezra Park in particular—contributed to a nuanced portrait of Africa and Africans that contrasted starkly with those of evolutionary anthropologists. Washington, who during the period before 1905 was influenced by nineteenth-century racist concepts of Africans, initially conceived of black people's African ancestors as barbarians. As he became more involved in African affairs and came under the influence of Work and Park, Washington modified his position to acknowledge the contribution of Africans to world civilization.

Work, who had become familiar with contributions and achievements of the so-called savages during his courses with William I. Thomas, a prominent member of the department of sociology and anthropology at the University of Chicago at the turn of the twentieth century, eventually published *A Bibliography of the Negro in Africa and America* (1928) in the midst of the Harlem Renaissance. Robert Ezra Park, along with Work, was a ghostwriter of the two-volume *Story of the Negro* (1909), a work that Harlan considers "significant for its consciousness of Africa" (1972, xxxviii).

Park, who held a German doctorate in sociology and who went on to establish himself as the leading sociologist of race relations in 1920s and 1930s, acknowledged his intellectual debt to Washington when he wrote: "I think I probably learned more about human nature and society, in the South under Booker

Washington than I had learned elsewhere in all my previous studies" (1950, vii). Like many patrons of and participants in the Harlem Renaissance, Park embraced a variant of racial romanticism and attributed the "race-consciousness" of the New Negro to a peculiar race temperament: he thought that black writing was "the natural expression of the Negro temperament under all the conditions of modern life" (294).

The artists and writers of the Harlem Renaissance tended to find fault with Washington's educational, political, and social policies, labeling them conservative. Although the disagreements between W. E. B. Du Bois and Washington were mainly superficial, the "New Negroes" nevertheless found Du Bois's ideas more appropriate for their temperament than those of Washington. They did, however, embrace his ideas in reference to black self-help, racial solidarity, and racial pride. Marcus Garvey, for example, was attracted to Washington's messages of self-help and racial independence, transforming those ideas into a radical political and economic nationalism.

Over the past thirty years, an intense dispute has arisen among literary critics, as well as among historians, over the issue of whether or not there is continuity between the "age of Washington" and the Harlem Renaissance. Historians such as Meier (1966) and literary critics such as Baker (1987) present the case for continuity. Baker, for example, argued that the Harlem Renaissance was a literary awakening during a continuous period between Washington's "Atlanta compromise" in 1895 and the publication of Richard Wright's autobiography, *Black Boy*, in 1945. Meier has argued, on the basis of his close examination of the relevant history, anthropology, and creative literature, that, as Alain Locke implied, "the roots of the New Negro, both as an artistic movement and as a racial outlook, were in the age of Washington" (259). For Huggins (1971) and Wall (1995), however, the Harlem Renaissance was a distinct period that bore little relationship to Washington's years of ascendancy. "To my mind," Wall has observed in reference to the proponents of continuity in general and Baker in particular, "Washington is at most a precursor of the Renaissance and one against which a number of authors write" (208–213).

Splitting the difference between those scholars who argue for continuity and those who argue discontinuity are Lewis (1981), Wintz (1988), and Hutchinson (1995). For Lewis, African American intellectuals, such as the sociologist and promoter of the "New Negroes" Charles S. Johnson, tended "to modify

1237

Booker T. Washington, c. 1890–1900. (Library of Congress.)

Suffice it to say, Washington's ideas about black self-reliance, racial pride, and interracial tolerance have been sufficiently potent to persist not only through the New Negro movement but to this day.

Biography

Booker Taliaferro Washington was born in the spring of 1856 (the year is disputed) in Hales' Ford, Virginia. He studied at the Hampton Institute from 1872 to 1875 and at Wayland Seminary, Washington, D.C., in 1879. Washington taught at Hampton Institute, 1879–1881; and at Tuskegee Institute, 1881–1889. He was principal, Tuskegee Institute, from 1881 to 1915. He founded the National Negro Business League in 1900. Washington died in Tuskegee, Alabama, on 13 November 1915.

VERNON J. WILLIAMS

See also Du Bois, W. E. B.; National Negro Business League; Scott, Emmett Jay; Work, Monroe Nathan

Selected Works

Frederick Douglass. 1907.
Future of the American Negro. 1899.
Selected Speeches of Booker T. Washington, ed. E. Washington. 1932.
The Story of the Negro: The Rise of the Race from Slavery, 2 vols. 1909.
Up from Slavery. 1901.

Further Reading

Baker, Houston. *Modernism and the Harlem Renaissance*. Chicago, Ill.: University of Chicago Press, 1987.

Harlan, Louis. "Introduction." *Booker T. Washington Papers*, Vol. 1, 1972.

Huggins, Nathan. *Harlem Renaissance*. New York: Oxford University Press, 1971.

Hutchinson, George. *The Harlem Renaissance in Black and White*. Cambridge, Mass.: Belknap Press of Harvard University Press, 1995.

Lewis, David Levering. *When Harlem Was in Vogue*. New York: Knopf, 1981.

Meier, August. *Negro Thought in America, 1880–1915*. Ann Arbor: University of Michigan Press, 1966.

Park, Robert. *Race and Culture*. New York: Free Press, 1950.

Wall, Cheryl. *Women of the Harlem Renaissance*. Bloomington: Indiana University Press, 1995.

Booker Washington to suit the tactics of the Talented Tenth" (49). Wintz has written: "While the accommodationist approach to racial problems associated with Washington was scorned by the new generation of black intellectuals, the New Negro accepted his doctrine of self-help and racial pride." More precisely, he concludes, "The 'New Negro' was never a simple or comfortable blend of ideologies; it was rather a dynamic ideology filled with internal conflicts and even contradictions whose fundamental questions remained unresolved" (47).

Finally, Hutchinson has argued that as early as 1928, Charles S. Johnson perceived continuity between Washington and the Harlem Renaissance:

The latter movement, Hutchinson surmises, would not have been possible . . . without Washington's success at precipitating a subjective transformation of a small but important segment of *white* American while simultaneously building up an educational, economic, and social foundation for black advancement. (179)

Wintz, Cary. *Black Culture and the Harlem Renaissance.* Houston, Tex.: Rice University Press, 1988.

Washington, Fredi

The actress Fredi Washington was a star onstage and in films, but her career never overcame society's focus on skin color. Her most memorable role was in the film *Imitation of Life* (1934), playing an uneasy, troubled, fair-skinned black woman, Peola Johnson, who decides to pass for white. This film, based on the novel by Fannie Hurst, brought Washington lasting fame but confined her to the narrow cinematic space of the racially adrift "tragic mulatto" figure. Washington, an assertive, self-identified black woman, found that neither Hollywood nor the black community knew how to handle her as an actor. Nevertheless, she earned respect and admiration for her work on the stage, in front of the camera, and as a crusader for racial justice.

Fredericka Carolyn Washington was born 23 December 1903 in Savannah, Georgia, the oldest girl in a family of five children. When her mother—who nicknamed her "Fredi"—died, the eleven-year old took care of her younger siblings. Following her father's remarriage, Washington, with her sister, Isabel, entered Saint Elizabeth's, a Catholic convent run by white nuns in Cornwell Heights, Pennsylvania. Washington later left the convent and moved to New York to live with her grandmother and aunt. There she finished high school and took additional courses in dramatic writing and languages. "I have had no formal training whatever in dramatics," Washington once wrote. However, her background and her natural talent impelled her toward the stage. While working as a bookkeeper at the Black Swan Record Company, she auditioned for a role in the musical that some historians say marked the beginning of the Harlem Renaissance: Eubie Blake, Noble Sissle, and Flournoy Miller's *Shuffle Along* (1922). She earned $35 a week as a chorus dancer, performing an "Apache dance specialty."

The decade of the Harlem Renaissance, the 1920s, was one of rising expectations for Fredi Washington. She established herself on stage and screen with a series of performances. In addition to her role in *Shuffle Along*, Washington danced at New York's Alabam' Club, where she earned $300 a week. She later formed a dance troupe and toured Europe with Charles Moore, her dance partner. In 1926, she obtained her first dramatic role, opposite Paul Robeson in *Black Boy*, a Broadway drama based on the life of the prizefighter Jack Johnson. Washington received positive reviews, although the reaction to the play itself was tepid. Her character, a light-skinned black woman trying to pass for white, led to her being typecast as the "tragic mulatto"—a role that she deepened, enlivened, but never escaped. Her first film appearance was as a dancer in *Black and Tan Fantasy* (1929), which was primarily a showcase for Duke Ellington's music. She also had roles in other musicals including *Sweet Chariot* (1930), based on the life of Marcus Garvey. An impressed talent scout advised her to pass for white, but she refused.

Fredi Washington reached the height of her film career in the 1930s. The eight films she made during this decade are essentially her complete film oeuvre. In 1933, she was again paired with Paul Robeson, in a film adaptation of Eugene O'Neill's play *The Emperor Jones*, about a railroad porter who becomes a Caribbean king. Washington played a prostitute. The studio insisted on reshooting a love scene between her and Robeson, fearing that audiences would mistake Washington for a white woman making love to a black man. She was forced to wear dark makeup for the remainder of the filming. The next year she starred in the film with which she is most identified, the controversial *Imitation of Life*. She again played a tragic mulatto—in this case, one who denies her mother and lives to regret her racial transgression. The film was a great commercial success and earned Washington critical praise, but her performance was perhaps too convincing: Some blacks suspected, erroneously, that the character's feelings about race were Washington's own feelings. Washington was forced to defend herself in personal appearances following the film's release. This film also generated criticism on other levels. Sterling Brown, a poet and professor at Howard University, gave the film a very bad review in the magazine *Opportunity*, saying that its portrayal of the female characters, especially the overly loyal mother, Delilah (played by Louise Beavers), was dishonest. He concluded that the defiant daughter, Peola (Washington's character), was more self-respecting and believable than the mealy mouthed, servile mother. Despite the success of *Imitation of Life*, Washington's career did not soar. By the end of the decade, it was taking another direction.

Convinced that black actors would not receive fair treatment in Hollywood until they had more artistic and financial clout, Washington became dedicated to improving conditions for black performers. In 1937, she was one of the founders of the Negro Actors Guild, and she served as its first executive secretary.

Fredi Washington. (Photofest.)

The guild's purpose was to educate black performers about their legal and professional rights, and to agitate on their behalf. From 1942 to 1947 she joined the staff of the newspaper *People Voice*, published in New York by her brother-in-law, Congressman Adam Clayton Powell Jr. She was a columnist and theater editor. She was also active in special events sponsored by the Urban League, and she served as administrative secretary for a Joint Committee of Actors Equity and Theater League that investigated hotel accommodations for black performers. Washington continued to act in theater. Her last screen role was in 1937, in *One Mile from Heaven*.

Biography

The actress Fredericka Carolyn Washington (Fredi Washington) was born on 23 December 1903 in Savannah, Georgia. She attended Saint Elizabeth's convent in Pennsylvania and public schools in New York City. Washington was married twice. Her first husband, Lawrence Brown, was a trombonist with the Duke Ellington Orchestra. They married in 1933 and divorced in 1951. In 1952, she married Dr. Hugh Anthony Bell,

a dentist in Stamford, Connecticut. She appeared in *Shuffle Along* in 1921, and in many other productions, as well as at clubs; her most memorable role was in the film *Imitation of Life* (1934). She was inducted into the Black Filmmakers Hall of Fame in 1975. Fredi Washington died on 28 June 1994 in Stamford.

AUDREY THOMAS McCLUSKEY

See also Beavers, Louise; Black Swan Phonograph Company; Brown, Sterling; Emperor Jones, The; Johnson, John Arthur; Robeson, Paul; Shuffle Along; Washington, Isabel

Broadway Theater

Sweet Chariot. 1930.
Run, Little Chillun. 1933.
Mamba's Daughters. 1939–40.
How Long Till Summer. 1949.

Films

The Emperor Jones. 1933.
Imitation of Life. 1934.
Mills Blue Rhythm Band. 1934.
Ouanga. 1936.
One Mile from Heaven. 1937.

Further Reading

Bogle, Donald. *Brown Sugar: Eighty Years of America's Black Female Superstars.* New York: Harmony, 1980.
———. *Blacks in American Films and Television.* New York: Garland, 1988.
Darden, Norma Jean, "O Sister! Fredi and Isabel Washington Relive 1930s Razzmatazz." *Essence*, 9, September 1978.
Null, Gary. *Black Hollywood: The Negro in Motion Pictures.* Secaucus, N.J.: Citadel, 1975.

Washington, Isabel

Isabel Washington was born in Georgia; her family moved to Washington, D.C., and then Harlem, while she was young. She was educated partly at a Catholic convent school. Her father, Robert T. Washington, was in charge of packing and shipping at Harry Pace's

Black Swan Records (1921–1924), and Isabel Washington did chores in the Black Swan office after school. The pianist Fletcher Henderson overheard her humming at her desk and felt she showed musical promise. They went into the studio around March 1923 and recorded two songs, "I Want To" by Willy M. Grant (a pseudonym for Black Swan's music director, the classical composer William Grant Still), and "That's Why I'm Loving You" by the team of Murray and White. The record was released as Black Swan 14141 in May 1923. A light "pop" record, it is stylistically related to show music of the kind heard in the musical *Shuffle Along*.

Isabel Washington's sister Fredi Washington began working in theater in the early 1920s, and Isabel, eager to follow, began hanging around theaters during her sister's rehearsals. She eventually broke into show business, becoming a chorus member, then star, of several shows, including *Harlem* (1929), *Bombolla* (1929), and *Singin' the Blues* (1931). She made a memorable appearance in the film *Saint Louis Blues* (1929), playing the "other woman" in a love triangle with characters played by Bessie Smith and the dancer Jimmy Mordecai. The only film made by Smith, it is a crucial document of the Harlem Renaissance.

Isabel Washington married the charismatic preacher Adam Clayton Powell Jr. in 1933; the wedding was a major event in Harlem. This marriage put an end to her career as an actress: Powell, who had overcome family objections to his marrying a showgirl, insisted that Isabel leave the stage. She made frequent appearances at church events and became Powell's constant companion in Harlem affairs. They organized boycotts of white-owned stores on 125th Street that refused to hire blacks, and they fought tirelessly for Harlem's residents. Over the next decade, Isabel Powell was among the best-known women in black America, often appearing in the front pages of the black press.

In 1944, Powell was elected to Congress, and he began commuting between Washington and his parish in Harlem. He and Washington then divorced, although she retained his name, which her son and grandson also bore. As Belle Powell, she became a fixture in Harlem. She found employment as a female barber—something of a novelty at the time—and remained active in the Democratic Party and in community affairs.

Biography

Isabel Washington (Isabelle Marion Marie Theodore Rosemarie Washington) was born on 23 May 1908 in Savannah, Georgia. She was the younger sister of the actress Fredi Washington and had three other siblings and half-siblings; she was a showgirl and was the first wife of Rev. Adam Clayton Powell Jr. The Powells had no children, but Isabel's son Preston, by a previous liaison, adopted the name Powell. In her later years Washington took particular delight in entertaining young children with storytelling. Her ninetieth birthday was celebrated with a gala dinner at the restaurant Chez Josephine; the guests included Congressman Charles Rangel (Adam Clayton Powell's successor in Congress) and Bobby Short, who sang "Happy Birthday" at the restaurant's piano. Washington—or Belle Powell—is still living in Harlem at the time of this writing, and maintains a summer home in Oak Bluffs on Martha's Vineyard.

ELLIOTT S. HURWITT

See also Black Swan Phonograph Company; Henderson, Fletcher; Saint Louis Blues; Still, William Grant; Washington, Fredi

Further Reading

Hurwitt, Elliott S. Interviews with Isabel Washington Powell, 29 March 1998–April 2002.

Kisseloff, Jeff. *You Must Remember This: An Oral History of Manhattan from the 1890s to World War II.* New York: Harcourt Brace Jovanovich, 1989.

Lewis, Barbara. "Isabelle Washington." In *Black Women in America: An Historical Encyclopedia*, Vol. 2, ed. Darlene Clark Hine. Brooklyn, N.Y: Carlson, 1993.

Waters, Ethel

Ethel Waters's career as a singer, stage performer, and actress coincided with dramatic changes in twentieth-century American popular entertainment. Waters emerged as one of the most popular stage performers during the Harlem Renaissance. Her career continued to flourish throughout the 1930s and was followed by featured appearances on stage and screen. In her later years, Waters made an occasional television appearance and toured with the Billy Graham Evangelical Association.

Waters got her first professional opportunity in 1917, when the black vaudeville team of Braxton and Nugent saw her perform in an amateur show in

Philadelphia and invited her to tour with them. Singing and dancing under the stage nickname "Sweet Mama Stringbean," Waters quickly became a favorite with audiences. What distinguished her from the other singers who also toured on the black vaudeville circuit was her low-key approach to singing the blues.

During the 1920s, Waters flourished as a recording artist and stage performer. In this decade, a prolific group of black female singers—including Waters, Alberta Hunter, Ma Rainey, Bessie Smith, Mamie Smith, and Sippie Wallace—cornered the market in black popular music. The classic blues singers brought a variety of styles and techniques to their performances. Improvisation, altered phrasing, and vocal dramatics consisting of groans, shouts, wails, and moans were common stylistic techniques. Waters differed from many of her contemporaries and established herself as a different kind of blues singer by using her smoother vocal tone, unique phrasing, and an exacting, if not theatrical, delivery to great effect. Although she could sing in the more dramatic fashion, she relied more on characterization, mimicry, parody, and crisp enunciation in place of vocal dramatics to sell a song.

It was an offer to appear in a stock show at the Lincoln Theater that brought Waters to Harlem. After she finished her engagement at the Lincoln Theater, she remained in Harlem and took a regular booking at Edmond's Cellar, a nightclub. Over time, Waters began drawing larger audiences. She also started experimenting with new material and broadened her repertoire to include the type of popular standards that were sung by white stage stars such as Fannie Brice. The careful articulation, opened vowels, and a speech-like delivery that she used in her blues worked well with this material. Waters herself was keenly aware that her singing was something different for both black and white audiences:

> I found that I could characterize and act out [popular ballads] just as I did with my blues. That I not only was able to please that brass knuckle crowd of regulars but began to draw the sporting men and downtown white people I credit to the fact that I had spunk and was also an enigma. (1950, 129–130)

In 1926, Carl Van Vechten, a white patron of the Harlem scene, wrote an article for the magazine *Vanity Fair* in which he skillfully described why he thought Ethel Waters stood out from her contemporaries: "She refines her comedy, refines her pathos, refines even her obscenities. . . . She never shouts. Her voice and her gestures are essentially Negro, but they have been thought out and restrained" (106). Waters' style was also appealing to African American audiences for many of the same reasons. James Weldon Johnson described Waters's performances in this way: "Miss Waters gets her audiences through an innate poise; through the quiet and subtlety of her personality. . . . She never overexerts her voice; she always creates a sense of reserved power that compels the listener" (1968, 240). In Johnson's opinion, Waters had indeed appeared to master a new way to communicate as a performer. She derived her presence not through an unrestrained voice but through a skillfully created interpretation and firm control of her material.

Mamie Smith's rendition of "Crazy Blues" (1920) showed recording companies that there was an untapped market in African American communities and set off a boom in the production of "race records." Other recording companies were anxious to capitalize on this new market. Black Swan Records, founded by Harry Pace, advertised itself as "the only company using racial artists in making high class records." Black Swan's mission was to bring a measure of sophistication and artistry to black music. It was in search of a blues singer who would fit its standards, and—after rejecting singers like Bessie Smith (who seemed to sound too gritty)—it turned to Waters. At this point, Waters had already made two recordings in 1921 for Cardinal Records, "New York Glide" and "The New Jump Steady Ball," and her voice and image matched up perfectly with Black Swan's ideals. Waters's first recordings for Pace were "Down Home Blues" and "Oh Daddy." The recordings enhanced her reputation and broadened her audience beyond the small vaudeville circuits. In the wake of this success, Pace arranged for Waters to tour with Black Swan's musical arranger, Fletcher Henderson.

By the time Waters finished her tours for Black Swan in July 1922, she was a well-established performer. The theater was the next logical step in her career. Waters continued attracting larger crowds to Edmond's Cellar and made featured appearances at places like the Lafayette Theater. Her growing popularity and success on records had caught the attention of theater producers, who were eager to cast her as a headliner in their shows. Waters appeared in such productions as *Oh Joy!* (1922) and *Africana* (1927); she also continued to do select engagements with Fletcher Henderson's Jazz Masters, and she performed as a headliner on the newly organized black theater circuit of the Theater Owners' Booking Association (TOBA).

Critics continued to be impressed by her performances, and they referred to her in laudatory terms as the black equivalent of some of the great white vaudeville stars of the time. One reviewer described her as the "ebony Nora Bayes," because she matched the famous vaudevillian's talents in gesture, poise, delivery, and facial work in dramatizing a song.

Waters's career reached another milestone in 1924 when she introduced the new song "Dinah" during a performance at Sam Salvin's Plantation Club. "Dinah" became an international hit and was also used as Waters's signature song in the production *Plantation Revue* (1925). The success that Waters had with "Dinah" enhanced her reputation and popularity and continued to bring her offers to star in black musical theatrical productions. Waters's first Broadway show, *Africana* (1927), opened at Daly's Sixty-Third Street Theater. It was a star vehicle for Waters because it was a compilation of all the shows that she had performed touring on the TOBA circuit. *Africana* was made up primarily of plantation scenes and swindles, standard features in many black revues. Waters was able to transcend this material, however, chiefly through her interpretation of the pieces she performed, such as the sentimental plantation song, "I'm Coming Virginia." Despite the plantation sentimentality, the stereotypes, and the lifestyle that the song promotes, Waters's recording of it is an artful and stately interpretation, with carefully cultivated words.

Although *Africana* had only a short run, it did manage to establish Waters as a star and as a performer who could carry a Broadway show on her own. On 19 September 1927, a few weeks after *Africana* closed, she made her debut as a headliner at the Palace on a bill that included Blossom Seeley, Jack Benny, and the Eddie Foy family.

In 1929, having made her mark in vaudeville, recordings, nightclubs, and revues, Waters appeared in Twentieth-Century-Fox's first all-talkie film musical, *On with the Show*. Waters was hired as a specialty act to play herself and perform two songs, "Am I Blue" and "Birmingham Bertha." Waters's artistic choices as a singer and entertainer broke through racial barriers and opened up a way for African American entertainers to perform and be perceived onstage. It was a model that popular entertainers would continue to follow for generations to come.

Waters's career continued to flourish throughout the 1930s. In 1931 she starred in *Rhapsody in Black*, and she continued to perform in other black popular shows and nightclubs. In 1933, Waters—accompanied by the Duke Ellington Orchestra—introduced Harold Arlen's torch song "Stormy Weather" at the Cotton Club in Harlem. This highly publicized and well-received appearance at the Cotton Club led to a featured role in Irving Berlin's musical revue *As Thousands Cheer* (1933). By 1935, Waters commanded star billing as a headliner in shows such as *At Home Abroad*; and she would end the decade with her dramatic debut on the legitimate stage in *Mamba's Daughters* (1939).

Waters made the biggest transitions of her career in the 1920s: from the sultry blues singer of suggestive lyrics to a more seasoned, sophisticated interpreter of popular song. She went from vaudeville and nightclubs, to recordings and the legitimate stage. In understanding what audiences expected of her, Waters presented herself as a performer who could master the demands and expectations of her own culture and the prerequisites for mass acceptance. Waters' sense of artistic freedom, creativity, and cultural savvy in developing her own performance style positioned her as one of musical theater's most popular performers throughout the 1920s and 1930s.

Ethel Waters, photographed by Carl Van Vechten, 1938.
(Library of Congress.)

The momentum Waters built up in her career during the Harlem Renaissance narrowed the divide between black and white styles and enabled her to achieve great success and popularity in the mainstream. Her performances onstage and on records represented a commingling of musical and theatrical styles of various genres, including elements of black cultural expression and the stylistic techniques of the American stage. She played a pivotal role in redefining black performance, while at the same time bringing a new level of complexity and sophistication to American popular performance styles. As a result, she was instrumental in creating new avenues for other artists, black and white, to follow.

Biography

Ethel Waters was born on 31 October 1896 in Chester, Pennsylvania. She was in *On With the Show* in Technicolor, Warner Brothers, in 1929; *As Thousands Cheer*, 1933; and *At Home Abroad*, 1935. Her first dramatic performance on Broadway was in *Mamba's Daughters*, 1939. She had a starring role in the Broadway production of *Cabin in the Sky*, 1940; and the film version of *Cabin in the Sky* (MGM), 1943. She earned an Academy Award Nomination as Best Supporting Actress for *Pinky*, 1949. Waters played Berenice in the original Broadway production of Carson McCullers's *The Member of the Wedding*, 1950; and starred in the film production of *The Member of the Wedding*. She starred in the television series *Beulah*, 1950–1951. Waters toured with the Billy Graham Evangelistic Association in the late 1950s. She died in Chattsworth, California, in September 1977.

DWANDALYN REECE

See also Black Swan Phonograph Company; Blues; Blues: Women Performers; Lafayette Theater; Lincoln Theater; Singers; *specific individuals*

Selected Discography

Cabin in the Sky: Le Hot Club de France Archive Series, 1992.

The Chronological Ethel Waters, 1923–1925. France: Classics Records, 1994.

The Chronological Ethel Waters, 1925–1926. France: Classics Records, 1992.

Ethel Waters: On Stage and Screen, 1925–1940. CBS Special Products.

Further Reading

Bogle, Donald. *Brown Sugar*. New York: Harmony, 1980.

———. *Toms, Coons, Mulattoes, Mammies and Bucks: An Interpretive History of Blacks in American Films*, 3rd ed. New York: Continuum, 1989.

Davis, Angela. *Blues Legacies and Black Feminisms: Gertrude "Ma" Rainey, Bessie Smith, Billie Holiday*. New York: Pantheon, 1988.

Douglas, Ann. *Terrible Honesty: Mongrel Manhattan in the 1920s*. New York: Noonday, 1995.

Giddins, Gary. "The Mother of Us All." In *Riding on a Blue Note*. New York and Oxford: Oxford University Press, 1981.

Harrison, Daphne Duval. *Black Pearls: Blues Queens of the 1920s*. New Brunswick, N.J.: Rutgers University Press, 1993.

Johnson, James Weldon. *Black Manhattan*, 2nd ed. New York: Arno and New York Times, 1968.

McCorkle, Susannah. "The Mother of Us All." *America Heritage*, February–March 1994, pp. 60–73.

Sampson, Henry T. *Blacks in Blackface: A Source Book on Early Black Musical Shows*. Metuchen, N.J., 1980.

Van Vechten, Carl. "Negro 'Blues' Singers." *Vanity Fair*, March 1926, pp. 67, 106, 108.

Waters, Ethel, with Charles Samuels. *His Eye Is on the Sparrow*. New York: Da Capo, 1950.

Woll, Allen. *Black Musical Theatre: From Coontown to Dreamgirls*. Baton Rouge: Louisiana State University Press, 1989.

Weary Blues, The

With *The Weary Blues* (1926), his first collection of poems, Langston Hughes immediately established himself as one of the signal voices of Harlem's literary renaissance, as well as one of the most innovative and important writers of his generation to emerge out of American literature as a whole. For Hughes, the book's publication by Alfred A. Knopf marked a coming-out of sorts. He had steadily ascended through the ranks of black literature, beginning with the inclusion of early work in W. E. B. Du Bois' series for juveniles, *The Brownies' Book*; continuing with the 1921 publication of "The Negro Speaks of Rivers" in *The Crisis*; and escalating in 1925 when he won a prize in *Opportunity*'s literary contest for what was to become the collection's title poem, "The Weary Blues." Early on, Hughes exhibited a talent for image and assonance, and an astute understanding of the development of modernist American literature. Hughes was well read in white antecedents like Walt Whitman, Amy Lowell, and Carl Sandburg, and he combined a respect for influence and tradition with a forward-looking sense of experiment. As a result, his early poems assert their place within America's broad literary heritage, even as they express African American experience in novel ways. For example, Lewis (1981) writes of Hughes's poem "The Negro Speaks of Rivers" that it is "Sandburgesque in its cadence," but "distilled" from Hughes's own specific sadness over America's insensitivity to the hardships of the black working class.

Hughes' sense of experimentation in this early poetry, though, was most recognizable in his commitment to modern African American music—jazz and "classic blues," the polished stylization of folk blues that attained mass popularity in the 1920s through recordings by artists like Ma Rainey and Bessie Smith. The most innovative lyric poems in *The Weary Blues* are those that try to capture the rhythmic play and improvisational thrust of the new black music, through either "nonsemantic" language or typographical play. In "Negro Dancers," for example, Hughes suggests the sound of music through the repetition of the syllable, "Da!"; in the "The Cat and the Saxophone (2 A.M.)"—whose title alludes to a Harlem nightclub—Hughes interrupts the flow of dialogue between two speakers with lyrics quoted in high-caps from Spenser Williams's jazz hit of 1924, "Everybody Loves My Baby." This suggests both Hughes's dedication to marking African American expressivity, a crucial component of the New Negro's political aesthetics, and his responsiveness to stylistic developments in modernist poetry. The multivocality of "The Cat and the Saxophone (2 A.M.)" seems irrefutably influenced by T. S. Eliot's *The Waste Land* (1921), but Hughes's poem moves beyond its stylistic antecedent by underscoring the importance of jazz and black vernacular expressivity to modernist aesthetics. While Hughes's experimentalism through jazz clearly seems, in retrospect, to have invigorated American poetics, however, the music poetry of *The Weary Blues* was not always received so favorably at the time of the book's release. For example, when Countee Cullen reviewed *The Weary Blues* for *Opportunity* in 1926, he was impressed by the more "conventional" lyrics and decried the "jazz poems as interlopers in the company of the truly beautiful poems in other sections of the book" (quoted in Dace 1997). With regard to "The Cat and the Saxophone (2 A.M.)," Cullen remarked, "I can't

say *This will never do*, but I feel that it ought never to have been done."

Later critics have defended Hughes's progressiveness in *The Weary Blues*, both aesthetically and socially. For instance, Hansell (1978) argues that Hughes's appeals to black music fostered the African American community and attempted to redress its historical struggles by giving them voice. Hansell emphasizes the social importance of the poet's focus on the vernacular; this emphasis corresponds with Hughes's own arguments in his famous essay, "The Negro Artist and the Racial Mountain" (1925), in which he says: "Jazz to me is one of the inherent expressions of Negro life in America . . . the tom-tom of revolt against weariness in a white world . . . the tom-tom of joy and laughter, of pain swallowed in a smile."

While *The Weary Blues* encompasses Hughes's aesthetic innovation and social awareness, the collection also displays the poet's responsiveness to, and ambivalence toward, the cult of primitivism that was so prevalent in Harlem during the 1920s. In *The Big Sea* (1940), Hughes recalled uneasily that "ordinary Negroes" did not like "the growing influx of whites toward Harlem after sundown, flooding the little cabarets and bars where formerly only colored people laughed and sang, and where now the strangers were given the best ringside tables to sit and stare at the Negro customers—like amusing animals in a zoo." This ambivalence over the economy of white voyeurism in Harlem manifests itself in a number of poems in *The Weary Blues*. For example, in "To Midnight Nan at Leroy's" Hughes accents this in the lines "Strut and wiggle,/Shameless gal" and suggests primitivist notions with an exaggerated refrain in dialect: "*Hear dat music . . ./Jungle night.*" While Hughes is ironic in his invocation of primitivist tenets, Chinitz (1997) argues that the poet does not dismiss primitivism altogether. As Chinitz argues, Hughes attempted to "rescue elements of primitivism that he continued to find meaningful—especially those pertaining to African American jazz." Similarly, Reini-Grandell (1992) suggests that Hughes's occasional turns to a primitivist ideology balanced criticism and recuperation, and they were intended to preserve jazz from being too easily dismissed by the Harlem intelligentsia as "low-rate." Although this conscious gesturing toward the problematic stereotypes that black intellectuals wished to avoid may appear reactionary in hindsight, it nevertheless suggests Hughes's conviction as a poet and his unwavering engagement with the paradoxes and potential controversies of American racial politics.

MICHAEL BORSHUK

See also Blues; Hughes, Langston

Further Reading

Chinitz, David. "Rejuvenation through Joy: Langston Hughes, Primitivism, and Jazz." *American Literary History*, 9(1), 1997, pp. 60–78.

Dace, Trish, ed. *Langston Hughes: The Contemporary Reviews*. Cambridge: Cambridge University Press, 1997.

Hansell, William H. "Black Music in the Poetry of Langston Hughes: Roots, Race, Release." *Obsidian*, 4(3), 1978, pp. 16–38.

Hughes, Langston. "The Negro Artist and the Racial Mountain." In *Voices from the Harlem Renaissance*, ed. Nathan Irvin Huggins. New York: Oxford University Press, 1976. (Originally published 1925.)

———. *The Big Sea*, intro. Arnold Rampersad. New York: Hill and Wang, 1993. (Originally published 1940.)

Lewis, David Levering. *When Harlem Was in Vogue*. New York: Oxford University Press, 1981.

Reini-Grandell, Lynette. "Langston Hughes's Invocation of the Blues and Jazz Tradition under the Double-Edged Sword of Primitivism." *West Virginia University Philological Papers*, 38, 1992, pp. 113–123.

Wells, Ida B.

See Barnett, Ida B. Wells

West, Dorothy

Dorothy West's work as a novelist and journalist played an important role in shaping the aesthetics and ideology of the Harlem Renaissance. Although West was one of the youngest writers of the era and was often regarded as the "little sister" of the Harlem Renaissance, she was behind two of the era's most important journals, *Challenge* and *New Challenge*. Her work with these two journals made a crucial intervention in the aesthetics of the period. Likewise, her first novel, *The Living Is Easy*, particularly in its complex depiction of the mother-daughter dyad, made a significant contribution to black women's writing.

West's literary talent was apparent at an early age. At the age of seven, she wrote her first short story, which was published by the *Boston Post*, as part of a contest for the best story of the week. A second short story, "The Typewriter," proved to be of signal importance to the West's career. "The Typewriter" won second place in a literary contest sponsored by *Opportunity* magazine, an honor that West shared with Zora Neale Hurston. In 1926, West moved to New York City to further her career. While in New York, West lived with her cousin, the poet Helene Johnson, and soon befriended the Renaissance luminaries Langston Hughes, Hurston, and Wallace Thurman.

Although West continued to write short stories, she worked briefly as an actress and had a small role in the 1927 production of *Porgy*, directed by Rouben Mamoulian. Notably, West got the role in the production by writing the Theatre Guild to ask for a position as a writer. Although she had no previous experience, she was hired as an extra in the production. West's weekly earnings of $17.50 helped sustain her in New York during the Depression era. In 1929, West accompanied the production to London, where the play was set to run for a year, after which the company planned to go to Paris. Audiences in London evidently did not understand the actors' speech, however, and the production returned to New York after only three months.

West's growing interest in acting did not end with *Porgy*, and in 1932 she and Langston Hughes traveled to Russia with a group of American actors. The group was scheduled to film a movie (called *Black and White*) about American race relations. The film was never completed, but she got a contract with another filmmaker and stayed in Russia for eleven more months.

When West returned to New York, she did so with a renewed commitment to writing. She quickly began work on a new project, and in 1934, with only $40, she founded and edited a new literary magazine, *Challenge*. This journal was dedicated to publishing fiction, without the propaganda characteristic of other journals of the era. It included pieces by Hughes, Hurston, and Countee Cullen, and operated until 1937. Later in 1937, West founded *New Challenge*, which dealt more explicitly with political issues. The inaugural issue of *New Challenge* was coedited by West, Richard Wright, and Marian Minus, and it heralded the emergence of the "Chicago renaissance," a period of cultural and political activity lead by African American writers from Chicago. The journal included pieces by Ralph Ellison and Waters Turpin, as well as Wright's groundbreaking manifesto, "A Blueprint for Negro Writing." Despite a promising beginning, financial difficulties and creative differences between West and Wright contributed to the journal's dissolution after only one issue. Importantly, West's tenure as editor of *Challenge* and *New Challenge* placed her in a rich tradition of black female editors, including Ida B. Wells and Pauline Hopkins.

After *New Challenge* folded, West worked for eighteen months as a welfare investigator in Harlem. West's experiences as an investigator most likely inspired her short story "Mammy," which depicts the trials faced by a Depression-era caseworker. The story appeared in *Opportunity* in October 1940. Later in 1940, West joined the Works Progress Administration (WPA) Federal Writers' Project; she worked for it until the program ended in the mid-1940s. While working for WPA, West also began writing short stories for the *New York Daily News*. She became a regular contributor and published more than twenty-five stories between 1940 and 1960.

In 1945, West settled on Martha's Vineyard, where she began work on her first novel, *The Living Is Easy*, which was published in 1948. The novel examines the conflicts in Boston's burgeoning black middle class. At the center of the novel is Cleo Judson, the manipulative protagonist, who seeks to control the lives and fortunes of her husband, daughter, and sisters. In many ways, the novel is autobiographical and reflects West's own upbringing as a part of Boston's black elite. Generally speaking, the novel received favorable reviews when it was released. It was reprinted by the Feminist Press in 1982, and it has since been praised for its stinging critique of Boston's black middle class as well as for its engrossing depiction of mother-daughter relationships.

While living on Martha's Vineyard, West continued to write short stories and articles. She became a weekly contributor to the *Martha's Vineyard Gazette*; her weekly column, "Oak Bluffs," covered activities of interest to local residents. West's second novel, *The Wedding*, was published in 1995. Like *The Living Is Easy*, *The Wedding* critiques the black middle class and examines issues of class and caste in an elite community. Interestingly, West began writing this novel in the late 1920s after she received a grant from the Mary Roberts Rinehart Foundation. She stopped working on the novel during the "black power" movement of the 1960s, however, for fear that the novel's middle-class

focus would be rejected by readers and critics. Three decades later, the novel received favorable reviews. West published a second collection of short stories and essays, *The Richer, the Poorer*, in 1995.

West remained on Martha's Vineyard until her death in 1998. As perhaps the last surviving member of the Harlem Renaissance, West occupied a special position in the African American literary tradition. Throughout her long career, West witnessed the changing landscape of African American literature, ranging from the Harlem Renaissance and protest eras to the black arts movement and black feminist cultural production. Thus, her impact on the Harlem Renaissance, as well as her impact on black women's writing, is receiving increased critical attention. Importantly, West's body of work provides a unique perspective on the creative tension at work during the Harlem Renaissance, as well as on the complexities inherent in the African American experience in New England.

Biography

Dorothy West was born on 2 June 1907 in Boston, Massachusetts. She received private lessons from Bessie Trotter and Grace Turner; attended the Farragut School, the Martin School, and the Girls Latin School; and studied journalism and philosophy at Columbia University. West acted in *Porgy* in 1927. In New York City she was founder and editor of *Challenge* and *New Challenge*; was a welfare investigator; and was a writer for the Works Progress Administration. She died at Martha's Vineyard, Massachusetts, on 16 August 1998.

MICHELLE TAYLOR

See also Black and White; Challenge; Cullen, Countee; Hughes, Langston; Hurston, Zora Neale; Johnson, Helene; New Challenge; Opportunity Literary Contests; Porgy: Play; Thurman, Wallace; Works Progress Administration; Wright, Richard

Selected Works

The Living Is Easy. 1948.
"Mammy." 1940.
The Richer, the Poorer. 1995.
"The Typewriter." 1927.
The Wedding. 1995.

Further Reading

Griffin, Farah. "Dorothy West." In *The Oxford Companion to African American Literature*, ed. William Andrews, Frances Smith Foster, and Trudier Harris. New York: Oxford University Press, 1997.

Johnson, Abby, and Ronald Johnson. *Propaganda and Aesthetics: The Literary Politics of Afro-American Magazines in the Twentieth Century*. Amherst: University of Massachusetts Press, 1979.

McDowell, Deborah. "Conversations with Dorothy West." In *The Harlem Renaissance Re-Examined*, ed. Victor A. Kramer. Troy, N.Y.: Whitston, 1997.

Rodgers, Lawrence. "Dorothy West's *The Living Is Easy* and the Ideal of Southern Folk Community." *African American Review*, Spring 1992.

Washington, Mary Helen. "I Sign My Mother's Name." In *"Mothering" the Mind: Twelve Studies of Writers and Their Silent Partners*, ed. Ruth Perry and Martine Watson Brownley. New York: Holmes and Meir, 1984.

White, Clarence Cameron

Clarence Cameron White was a renowned music educator, violinist, and composer. He was born on 10 August 1880 in Clarksville, Tennessee. His maternal grandfather was a member of the Oberlin-Wellington Rescue Company, an Underground Railroad action advocacy organization. His mother was an accomplished violinist and a member of Oberlin's graduating class of 1876; his father, James W. White, was a physician. Following the death of his father, he spent the early part of his life in Oberlin, Ohio, where he lived with his maternal grandparents. At age nine, White moved with his mother, Jennie Scott White, to Chattanooga, Tennessee, where she taught in the public school system. During that period, the young White became acquainted with his neighbors Anita Patti Brown and Roland Hayes, both of whom became accomplished vocalists. White's mother married William H. Conner and in 1890 the family relocated to Washington, D.C., after Conner accepted the position of medical examiner in the Government Pension Office. One year before their relocation, White began violin lessons with a violin given to him by his grandfather.

White continued his lessons in Washington under the tutelage of the violinists Will Marion Cook and Joseph Douglass. He also attended Howard University from 1894 to 1895. In 1896 White was admitted to the Oberlin Conservatory of Music. He remained at Oberlin until 1901, at which time he accepted a teaching position at the newly founded Washington Conservatory of Music (1903–1907). One of his earliest students was the poet Paul Laurence Dunbar. White continued his own musical education, receiving instruction from the celebrated African-British composer Samuel Coleridge-Taylor and the renowned Russian violinist Michael Zacherewitsch. He studied with Coleridge-Taylor in London during the summer of 1906 and returned to continue his studies from 1908 to 1911, at which time he received lessons from Zacherewitsch. White's extensive training led to his varied accomplishments not only as an instructor but also as an advocate for musicians, a performer, and a composer.

From 1912 to 1923, White, toured extensively, with his wife, Beatrice Warrick White, as his accompanist. In 1912, White had relocated his family to Boston, where he opened a studio. In 1916, White forwarded letters to various musicians with the intention of developing a National Association of Negro Music Teachers. This idea ultimately served as the foundation for the creation of the National Association of Negro Musicians. After a decade of touring, in 1924 White served as director of music at West Virginian State College, but he later left to study in Paris with Raoul Laparra, a French opera composer (1930–1932), on a Rosenwald fellowship. From 1932 to 1935, White served as chair of the music department at Hampton Institute in Virginia. In addition to teaching, White oversaw the production of various musical compositions.

White's works were reflective of African diasporic folk expressions and historical experiences. *Bandanna Sketches* (1919) was popularized when the noted violinist Fritz Kreisler recorded a piece from the work entitled "Nobody Knows the Trouble I See." Other works by White that won acclaim include *From the Cotton Fields* (violin, 1921), *Forty Negro Spirituals* (1927), *Dance Rhapsody* (orchestra, 1955), and *Elegy* (1955)—for which White won the "Tranquil Music" Benjamin Award.

Clarence Cameron White lived his final years in New York City with his second wife, Pura Belpré White. He died of cancer on 30 June 1960 in Sydenham Hospital in New York City.

Biography

Clarence Cameron White was born on 10 August 1880 in Clarksville, Tennessee. He studied at public schools in Washington, D.C.; Howard University, 1894–1895;

and Oberlin Conservatory of Music, 1896–1901. He had private instruction with Will Marion Cook, 1892; Joseph Douglass, c. 1892; Samuel Coleridge-Taylor, 1906, 1908–1911; Michael Zacharewitsch, 1908–1911; and Raoul Laparra, 1930–1932. He held positions as violin teacher; vice president, and registrar at Washington Conservatory of Music, 1903–1907; director of music at West Virginian State College, 1924–1930; and chair of the music department at Hampton Institute in Virginia, 1932–1935. White conceptualized the Nation Association of Negro Music Teachers, 1916, which later evolved into the National Association of Negro Musicians. His awards included am honorary master of arts degree from Atlanta University, 1928; an honorary doctorate of music form Wilberforce University, 1933; a Rosenwald Foundation award, 1930; a David Bispham award, 1932; a Harmon Foundation award, 1928; and a Benjamin Award for tranquil music, 1954. He was a member of the National Association of Negro Musicians; American Society of Composers, Authors, and Publishers (ASCAP); and Composers Guild; and he was an associate of the American Music Center. White died in New York City on 30 June 1960.

LELA J. SEWELL-WILLIAMS

See also Cook, Will Marion; Dunbar, Paul Laurence; Hayes, Roland; National Association of Negro Musicians; Rosenwald Fellowships

Selected Works

Bandanna Sketches. 1919.
Dance Rhapsody. 1955.
Elegy. 1954.
Forty Negro Spirituals. 1927.
From Cotton Fields. 1921.
Ouanga. 1932.
Symphony in D Minor. 1952.
Tambour. 1930.
Traditional Negro Spirituals. 1940.

Further Reading

Holt, Nora. "National Association of Negro Musicians: Chronological History of the NANM." *Music and Poetry*, July 1921, p. 15.
Logan, Rayford, and Michael R. Winston, eds. *Dictionary of American Negro Biography*. New York: Norton, 1982.
Salzaman, Jack, David L. Smith, and Cornel West, eds. *Encyclopedia of African-American Culture and History*, Vol. 5. New York: Simon & Schuster and Prentice Hall International, 1996.
Southern, Eileen. *Biographical Dictionary of Afro-American and African Musicians*. Westport, Conn.: Greenwood, 1982.

White Novelists and the Harlem Renaissance

White novelists served the goals of the Harlem Renaissance in several tangible ways, although their involvement brought complications and controversy, the legacy of which continues today. Among their positive contributions, these novelists helped bring the writing, themes, and concerns of the renaissance to white audiences nationwide; in several key instances, they facilitated the publication of black writers' work and promoted that work by providing forewords and prefaces addressed to white readers. White and black writers often guided and advised each other in fruitful and significant interracial exchanges that served the interests of both parties.

Increasingly more white writers embraced modernist ideology in the early twentieth century, shunning the technological developments and industrial spirit of the age as soulless and alienating. These modernists often looked to supposedly primitive peoples (Native Americans and African Americans in particular) as sources of spiritual and artistic renewal. They traveled through black communities to collect "authentic" material for their work, and they depicted black characters as "the perfect symbol of cultural innocence and regeneration" (Lewis 1981, 91).

Because white interaction in Harlem tended to be temporary, self-serving, and somewhat voyeuristic, however, whites who depicted black experience have been accused of perpetuating negative or reductive stereotypes. Brown notes "how obviously dangerous it is to rely upon literary artists when they advance themselves as sociologists and ethnologists" and argues that "the Negro has met with as great injustice in American literature as he has in American life" (1933, 179, 180). Novels by whites about black characters incited conflict because they undermined the goals of those activists who, like W. E. B. Du Bois, sought racial uplift through literature that illustrated

African Americans' best potential. Yet, as Hutchinson has pointed out:

> . . . many critics have rung charges on Du Bois's comment that the writing of the Harlem Renaissance was "written for the benefit of white people and at the behest of white readers," but have failed to notice that he himself heartily praised and encouraged some of the same white readers and authors whom some critics would now make prime examples of his point. (1995, 20–21)

Hutchinson's important observation illustrates the complicated dynamics at work here.

Several important contributions to the Harlem Renaissance came from writers affiliated with the "southern renaissance" movement at the University of North Carolina at Chapel Hill. In particular, T. S. Stribling's *Birthright* (1922) inspired Harlem's most important literary efforts. Stribling's novel attempted a realistic depiction of Negro characters by focusing on a Harvard-educated mulatto who struggles against racial oppression in the South. While its attention to an educated, sensitive black protagonist, the physician Peter Siner, does distinguish *Birthright* from earlier fiction by whites about blacks—*Uncle Tom's Cabin* (1852) is often cited in this context—the black critical response to *Birthright* set the tone for reactions to novels by whites about blacks throughout the renaissance. The novel failed so utterly in the opinion of Jessie Redmon Fauset that it propelled her and other black writers to action. She recalled, "We reasoned, 'Here is an audience waiting to hear the truth about us. Let us who are better qualified to present that truth than any white writer, try to do so'" (quoted in Lewis 1981, 123). As a result, Fauset's novel *There Is Confusion* (1924) and Walter White's *The Fire in the Flint* (1924) offered fictional responses to Stribling's work, and inspired other black writers to similar efforts. Not all black writers addressed their white counterparts in such adversarial terms, but a sense of competition—for commercial success, for authenticity, for critical acclaim—clearly animates the exchanges between the races.

Dorothy Scarborough, who was also affiliated with the southern renaissance, found her way to Negro themes through an interest in folklore that dated back to 1910, when she was in Texas. By 1916, she was living in New York and teaching at Columbia University and was, therefore, geographically close to Harlem. Scarborough's attention to poor, rural farm women appears in many of her novels, and her novel *In the Land of Cotton* (1923) has been included in at least one chronology of the Harlem Renaissance. Set in Waco, Texas, and deriving from her firsthand experiences among black and white sharecroppers and tenant farmers, the novel depicts the harsh demands of cotton farming. Scarborough herself was active in Harlem, having been invited to the Civic Club dinner held to honor Fauset's *There Is Confusion*; she was a judge for the *Opportunity* literary awards; and she later taught writing at Columbia, where one of her students was Dorothy West.

Another southerner, Julia Peterkin, focused on the Gullah natives of South Carolina in three of her novels, the best-selling *Black April* (1927), the Pulitzer Prize–winning *Scarlet Sister Mary* (1928), and *Bright Skin* (1932). Peterkin came to know black culture as the wife of a plantation manager in South Carolina and, although she was well aware of black society's diversity and range, her novels never depicted distinguished or educated characters; she preferred instead to romanticize the downtrodden. The essentially primitive and sensual nature of her characters can be best seen in the title character of *Scarlet Sister Mary*, a mother of nine children, eight of whom are illegitimate. (A commercial and critical success, *Scarlet Sister Mary* fared poorly when adapted for the stage, although it will be remembered for having featured Ethel Barrymore in blackface.) Harlem's opinion was divided about whether Peterkin's novels depicted its black folk characters sympathetically, and her own response to the symposium in *The Crisis* on "The Negro in Art" did little to assuage race-conscious critics. As Turner explains, "Julia Peterkin asserted that Irish and Jewish people were not offended by caricatures, so Negroes should not be. She used the occasion to praise the 'Black Negro Mammy' and to chastise Negroes for protesting against a proposal in Congress to erect a monument to the Mammy" (1997, 57). Many critics also cite *Roll, Jordan, Roll* (1933) as further evidence of Peterkin's racial myopia. This collection of photographs (for which she wrote the text) documents the lives of black workers on her plantation, and the whole endeavor, whether intentionally or not, celebrates the very plantation life through which the most degrading aspects of slavery are most clearly remembered.

DuBose Heyward, perhaps the best-known writer to emerge from the southern renaissance, also focused on the South Carolina Gullah. The popularity of his best-selling novel *Porgy* (1925) led Heyward and his wife Dorothy to collaborate on its dramatization (1927), which won the Pulitzer Prize; it led Heyward and George Gershwin to collaborate on the opera *Porgy and Bess* (1935). Like the folklorist Scarborough, Heyward immersed himself in the culture of Charleston's Catfish Row to learn its dialect, attitudes, and conventions. *Porgy*—the title is the name of a crippled and impoverished gambler—is peopled with drug addicts and criminals, and it repeatedly depicts these characters as driven by primitive urges beyond their control. Still, the novel's drama emerges from Porgy's struggle to find and maintain human dignity in the face of an overwhelmingly tragic fate. Following *Porgy*'s successful evolution, Heyward published *Mamba's Daughters* in 1929, and this, too, was dramatized in collaboration with his wife in 1939 (the play starred Ethel Waters). Far more diverse in its range of characters than *Porgy*, *Mamba's Daughters* chronicles black America's social, intellectual, and cultural multiformity.

Carl Van Vechten's *Nigger Heaven* (1926) stands as the representative example of commercial success. A runaway best-seller that sold out its initial run of 16,000 copies, the novel eventually ran through nine printings and appeared in several languages, thereby bringing to Harlem not only unprecedented attention but also a wide white reading audience's interest in its culture. Though the central plot focuses on a rather clichéd love triangle among three black residents of Harlem, the novel's opening and closing chapters offer seedy cabaret scenes that depict black life as alternately exotic, dangerous. and primitive. In one such tawdry scene, Van Vechten depicts two lovers: "Kiss me, Byron, she panted. I love you. You're so strong! I'm your slave, your own Nigger! Beat me! I'm yours to do with what you please!" Still, *Nigger Heaven* shows its central characters, the librarian Mary Love and her fiancé, the would-be writer Byron Kasson, in numerous conversations that amount to frankly pro-black propaganda interspersed with social criticism. The passage from which the title emerges best illustrates Van Vechten's didactic aspirations. In it, Byron rails against the segregationist logic that prohibits him and other educated blacks from reaching their full potential. "Nigger Heaven!" he complains,

> That's what Harlem is. We sit in our places in the gallery of this New York theatre and watch the white world sitting down below in the good seats in the orchestra. Occasionally they turn their faces up toward us, their hard, cruel faces, to laugh or sneer,

but they never beckon. It never seems to occur to them that Nigger Heaven is crowded, that there isn't another seat, that something has to be done.

Van Vechten was closely allied with numerous black writers, artists, musicians, and other Harlemites, and he encouraged his friend Alfred A. Knopf to publish works by Nella Larsen, Langston Hughes, and Rudolph Fisher, as well as to reissue James Weldon Johnson's *Autobiography of an Ex-Colored Man*, for which he wrote an introduction. Motivated by a genuine appreciation for and fascination with black culture, Van Vechten and his wife, the actress Fania Marinoff, held numerous interracial parties where they tried to promote racial integration through social celebration and cultural exchange. At the Van Vechtens', white writers and artists like H. L. Mencken, F. Scott Fitzgerald, Theodore Dreiser, and Sherwood Anderson mingled and socialized with blacks like Ethel Waters, Paul Robeson, Langston Hughes, and Nella Larsen.

While a great deal of the attention given to *Nigger Heaven* came from controversy over its title, Van Vechten was not the first white writer to broadcast the epithet: Clement Wood wrote a novel called *Nigger* (1923). While it, too, focused on black characters, Wood's fictional chronicle of several generations chronicled all manner of degradation as it traced one family's evolution from slavery onward. Indeed, Charles S. Johnson's review of the novel in *Opportunity* promoted it as a "step forward" in its ability to be "serious, honest, and tremendously impressive—a real tragedy" (in Hutchinson 1995, 198). A year after Wood's novel appeared, Van Vechten advised the British writer Ronald Firbank to retitle his novel *Sorrow in Sunlight* as *Prancing Nigger* for its New York reissue with Brentano's. Van Vechten also wrote the introduction to that edition. Although the former title was the novel's original, the latter continues to be the title under which the novel is reissued, even in England. *Prancing Nigger* focused on a family of West Indian blacks and the racial discrimination they faced in response to their social ambitions. Eric Walrond recommended the novel as "a work of haunting, compelling beauty" (in Hutchinson, 198). It was Firbank's most commercially successful novel, a fact which illustrates the appeal of black themes for ambitious white writers.

Sherwood Anderson also found financial success previously unknown to him by using black characters in *Dark Laughter* (1925). Anderson's novel celebrates its characters' capacity for primitive spirituality, and its essentialist celebration counterposes black identity to the sterile and soulless industrial age. Yet *Dark Laughter* seems to romanticize blackness as the central character, the white John Stockton, re-creates himself by assuming an identity as Bruce Dudley. As Dudley travels South in search of some meaningful connection to life, he hears a chorus of "dark laughter" that represents the spiritual essence he seeks. Like Van Vechten, Anderson was personally and socially involved in the lives of notable Harlemites, although for a much shorter time. And like Van Vechten, Anderson believed that black culture contained beauty and meaning that simply was not present among whites: "If some white artist could go among the negroes and live with them," he wrote, "much beautiful stuff might be got. The trouble is that no American white man could do it without self-consciousness. The best thing is to stand aside, listen and wait. If I can be impersonal in the presence of black laborers, watch the dance of their bodies, hear the song, I may learn something" (in Davis 1991, 410). After *Dark Laughter*, however, Anderson abandoned this "beautiful stuff."

Waldo Frank's novel *Holiday* (1923) represents his only fictional engagement with black culture; Frank's friendship with Jean Toomer served the novel well, because the two men traveled to Spartanburg, South Carolina, together as they researched their respective works (Toomer was writing *Cane* while Frank worked on *Holiday*). Indeed, with Toomer's assistance, the Jewish, dark-complexioned Frank passed as a black "professor" from the North while the two stayed in the black South. Frank drew on his friendship with Horace Liveright to encourage Boni and Liveright to publish Toomer's *Cane*, and Toomer himself encouraged the firm to advertise and promote the two books together. Frank's impressionistic novel depicts a horrific lynching by following the events of a single day in the fictional southern town of Nazareth. Rich in allegory, *Holiday* pays attention to how differently blacks and whites view John Cloud, its central character. "He is the color of dusk on the shadowed road he walks. White folk call him 'Lank.' They do not see how his height sings, they do not see how frail and hungry he is behind the pine. 'Big nigger' they see." Frank writes in rich, lyrical prose, and the novel examines the psychological, social, and cultural dimensions of lynching in the broadest possible terms. An innovative attempt to critically examine whiteness as a racial category, *Holiday* offers powerful and original insights about the psychological origins of mob action.

The literary output of the Harlem Renaissance (from both black and white novelists) waned following the stock market crash of 1929. Still, Fannie Hurst's *Imitation of Life* (1933) was published to commercial success and was subsequently adapted for two highly successful movie productions. Hurst had long been involved in Harlem and was a judge for the *Opportunity* literary awards in 1925, after which she hired Zora Neale Hurston as her secretary and traveling companion. Like other white novelists before her, Hurst undertook research of a sort when she and Hurston traveled by car through rural New York to Canada in 1931. Along the way, the two repeatedly encountered segregation and racism, although Hurston, obviously, suffered the more for it. *Imitation of Life* follows two widowed mothers: the nineteen-year-old white Bea Pullman and her housekeeper, the black Delilah Johnson, whose daughter, Peola, is light enough to pass for white. Bea builds a successful business by marketing not only Delilah's waffle recipe but also Delilah herself: Her jovial image becomes the trademark of B. Pullman and Company's products. Bea offers Peola comfort and care equal to that of her own daughter; she insists on paying Delilah handsomely and on sharing company stock with her. Nevertheless, Delilah's characterization fails to move beyond subservience and self-sacrifice; ultimately, she evokes the mammy.

Ironically, white authors seemed better able to capitalize on the commercial possibilities of novels about black folk than were black authors depicting their own experience. In an often-cited passage responding to the symposium in *The Crisis*—"The Negro in Art: How Shall He Be Portrayed?"—Carl Van Vechten captured the dilemma precisely: "Are Negro writers going to write about this exotic material while it is still fresh or will they continue to make a free gift of it to white authors who will exploit it until not a drop of vitality remains?" (quoted in Lewis 1981, 177). Many of the white writers who contributed to the symposium, such as Sherwood Anderson, DuBose Heyward, and Julia Peterkin, also answered its question by writing novels. The legacy of these novels continues to unfold. As Hutchinson argues, "while many of the participants in the Harlem Renaissance complained about white exploitation of the movement, they often did not agree on *which* whites were exploiters." In the end, virtually no black authors, except perhaps Claude McKay in *Home to Harlem*, were able to capitalize on their own popularity as subjects.

KATHLEEN PFEIFFER

See also Anderson, Sherwood; Birthright; Crisis: The Negro in Art—How Shall He Be Portrayed? A Symposium; Fauset, Jessie Redmon; Frank, Waldo; Heyward, DuBose; Hurst, Fannie; Nigger; Nigger Heaven; Peterkin, Julia Mood; Porgy; Porgy and Bess; Stribling, Thomas Sigismund; Van Vechten, Carl; *other specific individuals and works*

Further Reading

Braithwaite, William Stanley. "The Negro in American Literature." In *The Critics and the Harlem Renaissance*, ed. and intro. Cary D. Wintz. New York: Garland, 1996.

Brown, Sterling. "Negro Character as Seen by White Authors." *Journal of Negro Education*, 2, 1933.

Cooley, John. "White Writers and the Harlem Renaissance." In *The Harlem Renaissance: Revaluations*, ed. Amritjit Singh, William S. Shiver, and Stanley Brodwin. New York: Garland, 1989.

Davis, Thadious. "Race and Region." In *Columbia History of the American Novel*, ed. Emory Elliott et al. New York: Columbia University Press, 1991.

Douglass, Ann. *Terrible Honesty: Mongrel Manhattan in the 1920s*. New York: Noonday, 1995.

Hutchinson, George. *The Harlem Renaissance in Black and White*. Cambridge, Mass.: Belknap Press of Harvard University Press, 1995.

Kellner, Bruce. *Carl Van Vechten and the Irreverent Decades*. Norman: University of Oklahoma Press, 1968.

Lewis, David Levering. *When Harlem Was in Vogue*. New York: Oxford University Press, 1981.

Long, Richard. "The Outer Reaches: The White Writer and Blacks in the Twenties." In *Harlem Renaissance Re-Examined*, ed. Victor A. Kramer and Robert A. Russ. New York: Whitston, 1997.

Pfeiffer, Kathleen. "Introduction." In *Nigger Heaven*, by Carl Van Vechten. Urbana: University of Illinois Press, 2000.

———. Introduction. In *Holiday*, by Waldo Frank. Urbana: University of Illinois Press, 2004.

Russ, Robert A. "Chronology of the Harlem Renaissance." In *Harlem Renaissance Re-Examined*, ed. Victor A. Kramer and Robert A. Russ. New York: Whitston, 1997.

Singh, Amritjit. "Black-White Symbiosis: Another Look at the Literary History of the 1920s." In *Harlem Renaissance Re-Examined*, ed. Victor A. Kramer and Robert A. Russ. New York: Whitston, 1997.

Turner, Darwin T. "W. E. B. Du Bois and the Theory of a Black Aesthetic." In *Harlem Renaissance Re-Examined*, ed. Victor A. Kramer and Robert A. Russ. New York: Whitston, 1997.

White Patronage

"White patronage" refers to the complex, and at times artistically conflict-ridden or financially driven, symbiotic relationship between African American artists and wealthy white benefactors such as Carl Van Vechten, Charlotte Osgood Mason, the Spingarns, and others, who either were genuinely interested in promoting and showcasing African Americans' artistic accomplishments or were desirous of exploiting the black race as an example of the "primitive exotic." The impact of white patronage on the fledgling literary careers of Langston Hughes, Zora Neale Hurston, and other writers of the era, and even on the Harlem Renaissance itself, is, to varying degrees today, questionable and controversial. It is not clear if the Harlem Renaissance could have flourished without assistance from or access to white power and money. Nor is it always clear how much of the creative output of the era is truly a reflection of the black artist's needs and aspirations; W. E. B. Du Bois remarked that much of it was actually written for whites. African American writers, consequently, were torn between their need to write about their own experiences while negotiating the demands placed on them by philanthropic patrons who had their own agenda for the artistic future of the "New Negro" in modern society. Nevertheless, white patronage played a crucial role in the careers of many artists, and in the Harlem Renaissance itself. Without the presence and influence of white patronage, the Harlem Renaissance, as it is known today, may not have existed.

The intrigue, mystery, and exoticism surrounding the image of the "New Negro" quickly captured the imagination of many of Manhattan's leading white residents. These "Negrotarians," a term coined by Zora Neale Hurston that refers to white Americans who championed the cause of black racial uplift, began to flock to Harlem in droves. The "New Negro" was in vogue, and the "Negrotarians" opened their homes and their wallets to the newly discovered black artists of the era. Lavish parties and creative writing contests, such as the ones sponsored by the magazines *Opportunity* and *Crisis*, became all-important forums for white patrons to shower their black protégés with attention, financial opportunities, and, most important, access into the once-closed offices of major publishing houses.

The motives of white patrons were quite varied. Some patrons, such as Joel, Arthur, and Amy Spingarn, were earnestly devoted to the cause of racial uplift through their support of abolitionist causes and the founding of the National Association for the Advancement of Colored People (NAACP). In fact, the Spingarn Medal was awarded to well-known African American artists such as Langston Hughes, Walter White, and Paul Robeson as recognition for "the highest and noblest achievement of an American Negro." Some black critics and intellectuals, including W. E. B. Du Bois, took issue with the Spingarns' generosity, however, believing that a white presence was too strongly entrenched within black social, political, and artistic institutions. Nevertheless, the practical necessity of the Spingarns' involvement with racial causes could not be ignored, given the importance of the Spingarns' money and social status as a means of promoting current issues.

On the other hand, the motives of patrons such as Charlotte Osgood Mason, also known as "Godmother," illustrate the precarious nature of the patron-artist relationship. Mason is a prime example of a patron who had specific ideas about African American art, particularly as it pertained to primitivism or folk culture. She wanted these notions reflected in the art of her protégés, specifically the works of Aaron Douglas, Langston Hughes, Zora Neale Hurston, and Alain Locke. The end result was a controlling, confining relationship between Mason and the young African American artists, often shrouded in secrecy because "Godmother" insisted on anonymity while she financially supported artists. For example, in exchange for financial and materialistic support, "Godmother" controlled Hughes's life, dictating to him what books he could read or how he should write a literary work. Eventually, Hughes would find his relationship to his patron stifling, but he commented in several letters that his relationship with "Godmother," at least initially, was an exhilarating time.

Similarly, "Godmother" also subsidized Hurston's anthropological ventures; however, she stipulated that any artifacts Hurston collected would ultimately belong to Mason. Hurston, determined to present an accurate view of black folklore, manipulated the patron-artist relationship by secretly sharing her fieldwork with Hughes while presenting to Mason the persona of a loyal protégée who willingly obeyed her patron's wishes. Like Hughes, Hurston recognized Mason's important role as a financial supporter. She saw the necessity of maintaining this support if she hoped to pursue her career successfully.

Mason even controlled the actions of the black intellectual critic Alain Locke, who served as a middleman between the patron and the artists. In this instance, Locke received the financial support from "Godmother" necessary to fulfill his artistic vision realized in the publication of *The New Negro* (1925). In exchange, Locke relayed messages between Mason and her charges and occasionally monitored her protégés activities, especially if their loyalty to her was questionable.

Some black artists, such as Claude McKay, managed to avoid becoming too deeply entrenched in the patronage system. McKay's patrons, in particular Max and Crystal Eastman of *Liberator*, espoused leftist political views and were generally supportive of McKay's literary aspirations. Charlotte Osgood Mason also financially supported McKay. Despite these connections, McKay keenly observed that white patrons were "searching for a social and artistic significance in Negro art which they could not find in their own society." The actions of Charlotte Osgood Mason certainly illustrate this interest.

In Mason's view, as long as her charges veered away from artistic expressions of social protest and focused only on primitivism, they would always have her support. Unsurprisingly, Mason chronically severed her ties to "disloyal" artists. Once she did so, Mason made it clear to her former associates that they could never survive without her. At times, the price to pay for a patron-artist relationship was too costly on a personal and artistic level, for "this arrangement stigmatized Negro poetry and prose of the 1920s as being an artistic effort that was trying to be like something other than itself." (Huggins 1971).

The controversial impact of white patronage on the Harlem Renaissance is best illustrated through the contributions of Carl Van Vechten. Scholarship surrounding Van Vechten's contributions to the movement is divided, and some scholars have accused him of being a "literary voyeur who exploited his Harlem connections for profit" (Lewis 1997). His actual role as a patron, despite his seemingly good intentions, cannot be ignored; yet he epitomized the role of the patron as "teacher, guide, and judge" whose "search for authentic Negro voices was dictated by his own needs" (Huggins 1971).

Van Vechten was originally a music critic, and his preoccupation with black culture and arts preceded the advent of the Harlem Renaissance and soon consumed his time. As the first "Negrotarian," Van Vechten immediately found himself in the company of Harlem's literati, such as Countee Cullen, Zora Neale Hurston, and Wallace Thurman. He used his influence at *Vanity Fair* magazine and other publishing outlets to arrange for the first publication of literary works by Langston Hughes and Nella Larsen. Additionally, Van Vechten wrote several articles and reviews about African American music, literature, and culture.

As a permanent fixture of Harlem's nightclub scene, Van Vechten unabashedly shared his interest and passion in African American culture. His extravagant parties created a "melting pot" atmosphere for black artists and white patrons to freely engage in a discourse regarding the arts and politics of the times. In many ways, Van Vechten's role in the Harlem Renaissance helped bridge the racial divide and was instrumental in presenting the "New Negro" to the world.

However, Van Vechten's generosity also contributed to heated discussions regarding the presence of whites, and specifically patrons, in the Harlem community. Van Vechten's less-positive impact on the Harlem Renaissance is best seen in the publication of his novel *Nigger Heaven* (1926), a sensational account of Harlem's residents and nightlife. *Nigger Heaven* confirmed the critical belief held by many that Van Vechten's forays into African American culture were simply an excuse for him to exploit the black race for personal and financial gain. Ironically, the popularity of this novel heightened white readers' awareness of African American literature, firmly established Harlem as a cultural mecca, and aided in the influx of revenue to the neighborhood's clubs and speakeasies. Still, many readers could not move past the novel's offensive title or its depiction of Harlem's sordid nighttime activities. As a result, there was a split among black intellectuals and critics over the book's merit and Van Vechten's true intentions.

Some critics, for instance, see *Nigger Heaven* as Van Vechten's attempt to present Harlem society to a mainstream society presumably already curious about the "New Negro" vogue. The black novelist Wallace Thurman thought that *Nigger Heaven* had artistic merit, but W. E. B. Du Bois said he felt that he needed to take a bath after reading it. Van Vechten himself viewed his actions as sincere, because he wanted to present varieties of Harlem life. His novel can be seen as an expression of his deeply personal interest in African American people and their culture, despite its questionable title.

Despite the controversy surrounding *Nigger Heaven*, Van Vechten maintained his role as a leading patron of Harlem Renaissance artists. He sustained a lifelong friendship with Langston Hughes and persistently collected artifacts on black culture. Carl Van Vechten's popularity and influence undeniably shaped perceptions of the Harlem Renaissance and has facilitated society's access to the artistic achievements of the era.

Although the Spingarns, Charlotte Osgood Mason, and Carl Van Vechten were three of the most noteworthy patrons of the Harlem Renaissance, other white Americans generously contributed to the cause. These include William E. Harmon, Fannie Hurst, Robert C. Ogden, Dorothy Parker, and George Foster Peabody, to name just a few. A few patrons supported black artists in their belief that it was their "Christian duty to contribute to the training of Afro-Americans"; others pursued patronage as a means of "Christian charity and guilt, social manipulation, and politically eccentricity" (Lewis 1997). Some lavished money on African Americans' cultural interests solely as a means to acquire a profit.

Regardless of the reasons, the influence of white patronage clearly determined the widespread critical reception of the artists, then and now. The presence and financial connections of the "Negrotarians" created an opportunity for African Americans to pursue their artistic endeavors. This, in turn, fostered competition among black writers who sought recognition as premier artists who had the unwavering approval of mainstream society.

However, the quest for this recognition often came with a price, for in order to obtain a patron's approval black artists frequently had to compromise their artistic vision. This conflict is especially relevant because the "New Negro" was envisioned as a means to uplift the race through a positive self-promotion and recognition of the race and its accomplishments. As previously noted, one cannot help speculating about how much of the creative art of the renaissance might have been designed to appeal to the white mind.

Finally, the white patronage system illustrates how the nation's power structure forced writers of color to seek financial support from mainstream society. African Americans lacked access to the necessary political, social, and economic connections, but white patrons possessed, and in many cases willingly shared, these links. The relationship between white patrons and black artists, although not always amicable, was an essential union if the creative participants in the Harlem Renaissance hoped to achieve acknowledgment of their art.

LARNELL DUNKLEY JR.

See also Hurst, Fannie; Mason; Charlotte Osgood; Spingarn, Arthur; Spingarn, Joel; Spingarn Medal; Van Vechten, Carl

Further Reading

Bernard, Emily, ed. *Remember Me to Harlem: The Letters of Langston Hughes and Carl Van Vechten, 1925–1964.* New York: Knopf, 2001.

Coleman, Leon. "Carl Van Vechten Presents the New Negro." In *Harlem Renaissance Re-Examined*, ed. Victor A. Kramer and Robert A. Russ. Troy, N.Y.: Whitston, 1997.

Huggins, Nathan Irvin. *Harlem Renaissance.* New York: Oxford University Press, 1971.

Kaplan, Carla, ed. *Zora Neale Hurston: A Life in Letters.* New York: Doubleday, 2003.

Kellner, Bruce. "Refined Racism: White Patronage in the Harlem Renaissance." In *Harlem Renaissance Re-Examined*, ed. Victor A. Kramer and Robert A. Russ. Troy, N.Y.: Whitston, 1997.

Lewis, David Levering. *When Harlem Was in Vogue.* New York: Penguin, 1997.

Singh, Amritjit. "Black-White Symbiosis: Another Look at the Literary History of the 1920s." In *Harlem Renaissance Re-Examined*, ed. Victor A. Kramer and Robert A. Russ. Troy, N.Y.: Whitston, 1997.

Story, Ralph D. "Patronage and the Harlem Renaissance: You Get What You Pay For." *CLA Journal*, 32(3), 1989, pp. 284–295.

Watson, Steven. *The Harlem Renaissance: Hub of African-American Culture, 1920–1930.* New York: Pantheon, 1995.

Wintz, Cary D. *Black Culture and the Harlem Renaissance.* College Station: Texas A&M University Press, 1988.

White, Walter

Walter White's work for the National Association for the Advancement of Colored People (NAACP), his efforts on behalf of black writers, and his own literary production all attest to his importance as a central figure of the Harlem Renaissance. White also wrote dozens of articles and reports in newspapers, journals, and NAACP publications. Like the pages of journals such as *The Crisis*, where poems and lynching statistics could appear side by side, White's career demonstrates that the cultural productions of the Harlem Renaissance cannot be separated from the important political battles that were concurrently being fought.

When James Weldon Johnson invited White to move to New York and work for the NAACP, the organization employed only two officers and two clerical workers and did not know from month to month if their salaries could be paid. White, who began as assistant secretary in 1918 and became general secretary in 1931, deserves much of the credit for the success of the organization. White was directly involved in virtually every major initiative of the NAACP through the Harlem Renaissance. He traveled extensively, promoting the organization and attracting new members; fought numerous battles to allow blacks access to adequate schools and health care; petitioned against restrictive housing covenants; organized defense funds for both high- and low-profile black defendants; and lobbied lawmakers about topics ranging from voting rights to Supreme Court appointments to opportunities for black veterans. White particularly devoted his attention to publicizing the horrors of lynching and to attempting to have antilynching legislation approved by Congress. White was very light skinned and on several occasions "passed" in the South in order to obtain information about lynching directly from those involved. White's nonfiction study *Rope and Faggot: A Biography of Judge Lynch* was one of the first extended studies of the causes of lynching and one of few to directly address aspects of sexuality that earlier studies had avoided confronting. The book places lynching within the economic structures of the American South. It remains one of the most significant nonfiction works of the Harlem Renaissance.

White's first novel, *The Fire in the Flint*, also directly addresses lynching. The book tells of a successful and virtuous black doctor named Kenneth Harper who is ultimately killed by a lynch mob. The melodramatic book caused a stir, and the controversy concerning whether it was a fair or accurate portrait of the South led to much publicity and substantial sales. The novel is uncompromising in its portrayal of the dangers every black person faced in the South, but at times allows its political purpose to detract from the story itself. Many of the characters remain two-dimensional representatives of racist attitudes or cardinal virtues, and only the protagonist is truly individualized.

White's second novel, *Flight*, did not sell as well but is in many ways a superior literary achievement. *Flight* tells the story of Mimi Daquin, a Creole born in New Orleans to light-skinned parents; as a child she moves to Atlanta and has several experiences that lead her to develop racial awareness. Shortly after finishing high school, Mimi finds herself orphaned, unmarried, and pregnant. Outcast, she eventually passes for white, marries a blatantly racist husband, and at the end of the novel is contemplating a return to "her own people." *Flight* fits into a subgenre of "passing" novels published during the Harlem Renaissance and, like the novels of Jessie Redmon Fauset and Nella Larsen, explores the subtle interconnections between race and class that were most fruitfully examined through the creative writing of the period. *Flight* also explores the issues of prejudice based on skin color within the black community. Mimi feels at times ostracized by black society because she is "too light" and yet she is utterly unable to identify herself with the oppressive white society. Her experiences in the Atlanta riots had utterly convinced Mimi that she is black, regardless of how anyone might interpret her physical experience. In his autobiography, *A Man Called White*, written more than two decades after *Flight*, White recounts his own experiences of the Atlanta riots, which strikingly parallel those of his fictional heroine. White received a Guggenheim fellowship for a third novel exploring three generations of a black family, but because of his increasing responsibilities with NAACP the novel was never written. Suggs (1999) uncovered a partial manuscript for White's other unfinished novel, *Blackjack*, which is the story of a prizefighter and was clearly envisioned as a much more stylistically ambitious work than his earlier novels.

At some point, White seemed to realize that his genius did not lie in creative writing, but that he could continue to do much to further the careers of other talented black writers. White's role as a promoter of black writers was vigorous, but not uncontroversial. Indeed, Scruggs (1980) argues that White engaged in a battle with Alain Locke for control of the Harlem Renaissance. Both men were enthusiastic promoters of black writers, but they had differing attitudes toward which artists should be promoted and what constituted appropriate relationships with publishers and patrons. Scruggs characterizes White as ultimately self-serving and unforgiving of those who did not agree with him. White's letters show he did make several rather prescriptive suggestions to young writers but also that he was often more dedicated to helping them negotiate the complex world of New York publishing houses; others, like Locke, were often more concerned with artistic merit than with practical matters. White particularly promoted the poet Countee Cullen (White's letters make it clear that he considered Cullen superior to Langston Hughes); Claude McKay, for whom he raised money on more than one occasion; and the fiction writer Rudolph Fisher, whom White encouraged to move to New York. White's relationship with Hughes is instructive. White certainly was very encouraging of the young poet's early work but felt that Hughes's move into the blues idiom was restrictive and that Hughes should move back to the personal sketches taht he had written earlier. When Hughes disregarded White's advice, the relationship seemed to grow more distant. Still, White's frequent letters and his ability to gain numerous private audiences with publishers allowed him to aid the careers of many other writers, while perhaps promoting himself as well. Waldron refers to him as "an important

Walter White, c. 1920–1930. (Library of Congress.)

catalyst who helped make the Harlem Renaissance possible" (1973); White's contributions as writer, promoter, and activist are inextricably linked.

Biography

Walter White was born on 1 July 1893 in Atlanta, Georgia. He studied at Atlanta University (A.B., 1916). He was an office worker, Atlanta Life Insurance Company, 1916; assistant secretary to the National Association for the Advancement of Colored People (NAACP), 1918; and executive secretary of the NAACP, 1931. His awards included a Guggenheim Fellowship grant, 1926; Spingarn Medal from NAACP, 1937; Honorary doctorate of law, Howard University, 1939; Sir James Jeans Award from New London Junior College, 1943; honorary doctorate of law, Atlanta University, 1943; Haitian Order of Honor and Merit, 1950; and Star of Ethiopia, 1953. He died in New York City on 21 March 1955.

NEIL BROOKS

See also Antilynching Crusade; Cullen, Countee; Fire in the Flint, The; Hughes, Langston; Johnson, James Weldon; McKay, Claude; National Association for the Advancement of Colored People

Selected Works

The American Negro and His Problems. 1927.
The Fire in The Flint. 1924.
Flight. 1926.
A Man Called White: The Autobiography of Walter White. 1948.
The Negro's Contribution to American Culture. 1927.
Rope and Faggot: A Biography of Judge Lynch. 1929.

Further Reading

Brooks, Neil. "We Are Not Free! Free! Free!: *Flight* and the Unmapping of American Literary Studies." *CLA Journal*, 41(4), 1998, pp. 371–386.

Cannon, Poppy. *A Gentle Knight: My Husband, Walter White.* New York: Rinehart, 1956.

Cooney, Charles F. "Walter White and Sinclair Lewis: The History of a Literary Friendship." *Prospects*, 1, 1975, pp. 63–79.

Scruggs, Charles W. "Alain Locke and Walter White: Their Struggle for Control of the Harlem Renaissance." *Black American Literature Forum*, 14, 1980, pp. 91–99.

Suggs, Jon Christian. "'Blackjack': Walter White and Modernism in an Unknown Boxing Novel." *Michigan Quarterly Review*, 38(4), 1999, pp. 515–540.

Waldron, Edward E. "Walter White and the Harlem Renaissance: Letters from 1924–1927." *CLA Journal*, 16, 1973, pp. 438–457.

———. *Walter White and the Harlem Renaissance.* Port Washington, N.Y.: Kennikat, 1978.

Williams, Clarence

Because of his wide range of musical activities and collaborations with major early jazz instrumentalists, classic blues singers, and record companies, Clarence Williams ranks among the most important and influential musical figures of the jazz age. After moving to New Orleans in 1906, the largely self-taught pianist became active in the local jazz scene. Early attempts at songwriting led to Williams's decision to found a music publishing company in 1913 with the violinist A. J. Piron. The national success of Williams's composition "Brown Skin" prompted his move to Chicago in 1917.

When he saw the opportunities presented by the new "race record" market, Williams moved to New York in 1920. The next year, he married the popular vaudeville entertainer Eva Taylor, who remained his lifelong partner and musical associate. During the 1920s and early 1930s, Williams served in various capacities, including songwriter, pianist, publisher, bandleader, vocalist, vaudeville performer, record producer, talent scout, booking agent, promoter, and radio personality. He published some 1,500 songs, more than any other black publisher of the day. Williams is also credited with writing about 200 songs, many in collaboration with other songwriters, including Spencer Williams and Fats Waller. Although generally well respected, Williams was sometimes accused of claiming authorship of several songs written by others. It is impossible to determine to what degree he actually composed, cowrote, arranged, or refined much of the material with which he is credited, since it was common practice at the time for publishers and purchasers of songs to list themselves as full or part composers.

Williams became a leading figure in the "classic blues" boom of the 1920s, having written, published, and recorded hundreds of songs with popular, primarily female, blues artists. Between 1921 and 1941, Williams directed, played, or both on approximately 700 recordings, more than any black musician of the day except Fletcher Henderson. Every major record company of the time, including Okeh and Columbia, used his skills for finding talent and organizing recording sessions. Williams was partly responsible for the discovery and early success of the legendary singer Bessie Smith. He was the solo accompanist on her first recordings, including "Downhearted Blues," which became a hit in 1923. He also played on several of her best-remembered recordings, such as "Gulf Coast Blues." and "Nobody Knows You When You're Down and Out." He also organized small jazz bands to accompany Smith, Sarah Martin, Victoria Spivey, Eva Taylor, Sippie Wallace, and other popular blues singers on records.

Williams's recording bands made dozens of instrumental jazz classics under various names, including the Blue Five and the Washboard Five. These recordings often featured the most important musicians of the day, such as Louis Armstrong, Sidney Bechet, King Oliver, Don Redman, and Bubber Miley. Rather than explore the emerging big band style, Williams continued to experiment mainly within the smaller New Orleans ensemble jazz format, shifting instrumental roles and using more "down home" rhythmic instruments like washboards and jugs.

Although the technically demanding new Harlem stride piano style was beyond his rather modest abilities as a pianist, Williams recognized its commercial and artistic potential. He assisted in the success of leading stride pianists, like James P. Johnson, Willie "the Lion" Smith, and Fats Waller, by publishing, recording, and promoting their works. He published Johnson's notable stride piece "Carolina Shout."

After the popularity of "classic blues" and early jazz recordings diminished, along with the careers of many black artists, Williams continued to prosper into the 1930s by continuing to compose and publish songs, producing music instruction books, promoting stride pianists, and regularly performing on radio with his wife.

In 1943, Williams sold a large portion of his published song catalog to Decca records and retired from the music business. Often overlooked by historians, the quiet and unassuming Williams must ultimately be remembered for his outstanding contribution in the areas of recording, songwriting, and promotion of major black musical styles and artists of the Harlem Renaissance era.

Biography

Clarence Williams was born on 8 October 1893 (the date is disputed) in Plaquemine, Louisiana. He was a pianist, composer, band leader, music publisher, record producer, and promoter in early jazz, "classic blues," and vaudeville styles. Williams died on 6 November 1965 in Queens, New York City.

MICHAEL WHITE

See also Armstrong, Louis; Bechet, Sidney; Blues; Jazz; Johnson, James P.; Oliver, Joseph "King"; Smith, Bessie; Smith, Willie "the Lion"; Waller, Thomas "Fats"

Selected Songs

"Baby Won't You Please Come Home." 1919. (With Charles Warfield.)
"Everybody Loves My Baby." 1924. (With Spencer Williams and J. Palmer.)
"I Ain't Gonna Give Nobody None o' This Jelly Roll." 1919. (With Spencer Williams.)
"Right Key, but the Wrong Keyhole." 1923. (With Eddie Green.)
"Royal Garden Blues." 1919. (With Spencer Williams.)
"Squeeze Me." 1925. (With Thomas Waller.)
"Sugar Blues." 1919. (With Lucy Fletcher.)
"'Tain't Nobody's Business If I Do." 1920. (With P. Grainger, G. Prince, and E. Robbins.)

Selected Recordings

Clarence Williams 1921–1924; 1925–1926; 1926–1927; 1927; 1927–1928; 1928–1929. Classic Records 679, 695, 718, 736, 752, 810. (CDs.)

Further Reading

Charters, Samuel B., and Kunstadt, Leonard. *Jazz: A History of the New York Scene.* Garden City, N.Y.: Da Capo, 1981.
Chilton, John, and Sidney Bechet: *The Wizard of Jazz.* New York: Da Capo, 1996.
Jasen, David A., and Jones, Gene. *Spreadin' Rhythm Around: Black Popular Songwriters, 1880–1930.* New York: Schirmer, 1998.

Lord, Tom. *Clarence Williams*. Essex, England: Storyville, 1976.

Shaw, Arnold. *The Jazz Age: Popular Music in the 1920s*. New York: Oxford University Press, 1987.

Williams, Martin. *Jazz Masters of New Orleans*. New York: Da Capo, 1979.

Williams, Edward Christopher

Until the publication of his novel *When Washington Was in Vogue* in 2004, Edward Christopher Williams (1871–1929) was remembered chiefly as the first professionally trained African American librarian. In addition to being a librarian and novelist, he was a novelist, essayist, playwright, and professor of languages; and in the 1920s he participated in the literary and social life of black Washington, D.C.—a world he describes with great clarity and wit in his novel.

Williams was born in Cleveland, Ohio, in 1871 to a mixed-race couple. After attending public schools in Cleveland, he enrolled in Western Reserve University (now Case Western Reserve University), where he was inducted into Phi Beta Kappa. In 1892, he was valedictorian of his graduating class. In the same year, he accepted a position as first assistant librarian at Western Reserve. In 1894, Williams was promoted to head librarian of the university's Hatch Library, a position he held for eleven years. He left Cleveland temporarily in 1899–1900 in order to study at the New York State Library School in Albany. He married Ethel Chesnutt, the daughter of Charles W. Chesnutt, in 1902; they had one son, Charles.

In 1909, Williams moved to Washington, D.C., to become principal of the M Street School (now Paul Laurence Dunbar High School). In Washington, his literary life blossomed. Shortly after arriving, he joined the Mu-So-Lit club, a men's organization that often discussed literature, and in 1916 he helped form a drama committee for the local chapter of the National Association for the Advancement of Colored People (NAACP). In 1916, Williams became head librarian at Howard University, where he also taught classes in library science and foreign languages. In 1918, he helped form the Literary Lovers club. In Washington, Williams came into contact with a number of significant figures of the era, including Mary Burrill, Carrie Clifford, Angelina Weld Grimké, Zora Neale Hurston, Georgia Douglas Johnson, and Jean Toomer.

Williams produced a small but significant amount of written work in the 1920s. Three of his plays were performed at Howard: *The Exile* (1924), a two-act drama set in Renaissance Italy; *The Chasm* (1926), written in collaboration with Willis Richardson; and *The Sheriff's Children* (n.d.), an adaptation of Chesnutt's short story. Williams also contributed a number of anonymous pieces to little magazines affiliated with the Harlem Renaissance, some perhaps under the pseudonym "Bertuccio Dantino."

Williams's most important work, however, is his novel, *When Washington Was in Vogue*. Most likely the first African American epistolary novel, it originally ran serially and anonymously under the title *The Letters of Davy Carr: A True Story of Colored Vanity Fair* in A. Philip Randolph's magazine, *The Messenger*, from January 1925 through June 1926. The novel consists of a series of letters from Davy Carr, a fair-skinned veteran of World War I, to a friend in Harlem. In Washington to do research on the slave trade, Davy describes the world of the black bourgeoisie and eventually falls in love with Caroline Rhodes, who is younger, darker, and more socially adventurous.

Williams left Washington to pursue a Ph.D. in Library Science at Columbia University. While in New York, he succumbed to a sudden illness and died on December 1929.

Biography

Edward Christopher Williams was born in Cleveland, Ohio, in 1871. He graduated from Western Reserve University in 1892 and then became first assistant librarian at the university library. In 1894, Williams was promoted to head librarian, leaving Cleveland temporarily in 1899–1900 to study at the New York State Library School in Albany. He married Ethel Chesnutt, the daughter of Charles W. Chesnutt, in 1902. In 1909, Williams resigned his position and moved to Washington, D.C., where he became principal of the M Street School (later the Paul Laurence Dunbar High School); he joined Washington's Mu-So-Lit club that year. Williams was hired as head librarian and professor of languages at Howard University in 1916, and he also helped form a drama committee for the local NAACP. In 1918, he was involved in organizing the Literary Lovers club. Three of Williams's plays were performed at Howard in the 1920s: *The Exile* (1924), *The Chasm* (1926), and *The Sheriff's Children* (n.d.). In 1925–1926, his novel, *The Letters of Davy Carr:*

A True Story of Colored Vanity Fair (republished as *When Washington Was in Vogue*), ran in *The Messenger*. Williams moved to New York City in 1929 to pursue a Ph.D. in library science but died there shortly after his arrival.

ADAM MCKIBLE

See also Chesnutt, Charles Waddell; Harlem Renaissance in the United States: 9—Washington, D.C.; Messenger, The; Richardson, Willis

Further Reading

Josey, E. J. "Edward Christopher Williams: Librarian's Librarian." *Negro History Bulletin*, 33, 1970, pp. 70–77.

Porter, Dorothy B. "*Phylon* Profile, 14: Edward Christopher Williams." *Phylon*, 7, 1947, pp. 315–321.

Simmons, Christina. "'Modern Marriage' for African Americans, 1920–1940." *Canadian Review of American Studies*, 30(3), 2000, pp. 273–300.

Williams, Edward Christopher. *When Washington Was in Vogue*. 2004.

Williams, Egbert Austin "Bert"

Egbert Austin Williams was born 12 November 1875 in Antigua, British West Indies. His parents, Frederick and Julia Moncuer Williams, moved to Riverside, California, in 1885. There he attended public schools, with the hope of studying civil engineering at Stanford University. He began performing as a minstrel along the coastline to make money for tuition, but he did not raise the necessary funds and decided instead to focus on minstrelsy as a permanent career. He joined Lew Johnson's musical company in the spring of 1893, as a minstrel playing lumber camps for $12 a week and "cakes with an occasional chunk of pie."

The positive responses he received as a performer led Williams to craft a unique style by elaborating the so-called Negroisms in his dialects and movement. He was not a talented dancer, but he actually used this to his advantage, awkwardly tripping over his own feet and slouching. He wore a kinky wig, blackface, and black gloves, all of which helped conceal his actual heritage—he had a Danish grandfather. Williams developed a recitative (semi-recited) singing style and excellent comedic timing, which contributed to his success as a vaudevillian.

In the summer of 1893, Williams began performing at the San Francisco Museum for $7 a week in front of the curtain while sets were being changed for the next act. That autumn, Williams joined the Martin and Seig's Mastodon Minstrels of San Francisco. Sent to find an actor to play the end man for the lineup, he came upon George Walker from Lawrence, Kansas. In 1894, having become dissatisfied with the company, they formed their own team, Williams and Walker.

Williams and Walker's performance in John Isham's *The Octoroons* at the Pekin Theater in Chicago in 1895 before an unreceptive audience resulted in their being dropped from the bill. Throughout the first half of 1896, Williams became Walker's sidekick in their act, "Two Real Coons," which mocked white minstrels who wore blackface. By 14 September 1896, they found themselves in New York performing in Glen McDonough and Victor Herbert's musical farce *The Gold Bug*, which was well received.

By 1898 Williams and Walker were master cakewalkers and were performing in London, Boston, and San Francisco. In July 1898 they opened in Will Marion Cook and Paul Laurence Dunbar's operetta, *Clorindy, or the Origin of the Cakewalk*. Its failure brought them back to New York, where they changed agents and began to move from first-rate theaters to bookings in cheaper theaters that drew larger crowds and gave them greater recognition; in fact, they became known as the nation's major Negro performers.

Williams's marriage to Lottie (Cole) Thompson was kept a secret from all, including Walker, until it was announced before the opening of the *Sons of Ham* on tour. It was then, in 1900, that Williams wrote, "I'm a Jonah Man" with Alex Rogers, chronicling the hard times of an unlucky man. By 1901, Williams's recording career had begun; he had a five-year stint with Victor Records, and from 1906 to 1911 he produced seventeen titles with Columbia.

In 1903 the young Prince of Wales celebrated his birthday with Williams and the company of *In Dahomey*, an all-black musical playing on Broadway. *Theatre Magazine* recognized Bert Williams as a superior comedian, more talented than most contemporary white comedians. Williams made history when he joined the international Masons while in Europe, although his membership was never recognized in the United States.

In 1905, Williams' songwriting continued with "I'd Rather Have Nothin' All of the Time, Than Somethin' for a Little While" and "Nobody," which would become his signature song. In 1908 he opened in *Abyssinia* at the Majestic Theater.

Williams went solo in 1909, after sixteen years of performing with Walker. *Bandana Land* had to be revised for him and Ada Overton Walker (George Walker's wife). The absence of Walker proved a problem, though. After a year of performing in *Mr. Lode of Koal* (with lyrics and book by Alex Rogers and Jesse Shipp and music by John Rosamond Johnson), Williams gave up the company and joined the *Ziegfeld Follies*. After visiting a sanitarium and observing a mentally ill patient who was a former gambler, Williams developed another signature act, "The Poker Game." He performed this routine in his silent movie *A Natural Born Gambler*. Southern cinemas would not show a film with a black star, but the shorts (one-reel films) Williams made in 1914 with Biograph Film Studios were eventually shown as television specials in 1961 and 1963.

Williams starred in the Ziegfeld Follies until 1918, with Gene Buck, Will Rogers, Eddie Cantor, and W. C. Fields; but then he had a falling-out with Ziegfeld and left the revue. In 1919, he performed in *Broadway Brevities* at the Winter Garden theater. In August of that year, W. C. Fields petitioned the Actors' Equity Association to allow Williams to join the union. Bert Williams died in 1822.

Biography

Egbert Austin Williams was born 12 November 1875 in Antigua, West Indies. His vaudeville tours included Lew Johnson's Minstrels (1893); Martin and Seig's Mastodon Minstrels (1895); "The Real Coons" (1896); Keith Circuit (1897, 1914, 1919); Hyde's Comedians (1897); Koster and Bial's (1898); Procter's Theater (1900); and Midnight Frolics (1919). His stage credits included *The Octoroons* (1896); *The Gold Bug* (1896); *Clorindy, or the Origin of the Cakewalk* (1898); *A Lucky Coon* (1899); *The Policy Players* (1899); *Sons of Ham* (1900); *In Dahomey* (1902); *In Abyssinia* (1908); *Bandana Land* (1909); *Mr. Lode of Koal* (1909); *Ziegfeld Follies* (1909, 1910–1912, 1914–1917, 1919); *The Broadway Brevities* (1920); and *Under the Bamboo Tree* (formerly known as *The Pink Slip*, 1922). His songs (some with Alex Roger or George Walker) include "I Am a Jonah Man" (1903); "Nobody" (1905); "I Don't Like No Cheap Man!" (1897); "The Medicine Man" (1899); "The Fortune Telling Man" (1901); "When It's All Goin' Out, and Nothin' Comin' In" (1902); and "I'd Rather Have Nothin' All of the Time, Than Somethin' for a Little While" (1908). He made films for Biograph:

Darktown Jubilee (1914), *Fish* (1916); and *Natural Born Gambler* (1916). He was a member of the International Masons, the Promoters of High Art in Music and Literature (formerly known as Colored Actors Benevolent Association), The Frogs (he was chair of the art committee in 1908 and later president, in 1910), and the Actors' Equity Association. On 25 February 1922, Williams collapsed in Chicago during *Under the Bamboo Tree*, a production written for him, in which he starred and was the only black cast member. On Saturday 4 March 1922, he died at age forty-seven in his home in New York City.

Shirley Basfield Dunlap

See also Minstrelsy; Musical Theater

Further Reading

Andrews, William L., Frances Smith Foster, and Trudier Harris, eds. *The Oxford Companion to African American Literature*. New York: Oxford University Press, 1997.

Charters, Ann. *Nobody: The Story of Bert Williams*. London: Collier-Macmillan, 1970.

Hughes, Langston, and Milton Meltzer. *Black Magic: A Pictorial History of the Afro-American in the Performing Arts*. New York: Da Capo, 1990.

Isaacs, Edith J. R. *The Negro in American Theatre*. Maryland: McGrath, 1947.

Richards, Larry. *African American Films Through 1959: A Comprehensive Illustrated Filmography*. Jefferson, N.C.: McFarland, 1998.

Rowland, Mabel, ed. *Bert Williams: Son of Laughter*. New York: English Crafters, 1923.

Smith, Eric Ledell. *Bert Williams: A Biography of the Pioneer Black Comedian*. Jefferson, N.C.: McFarland, 1992.

Woll, Allen. *Black Musical Theatre: From Coontown to Dreamgirls*. Baton Rouge: Louisiana State University Press, 1989.

Wilson, Arthur "Dooley"

"You must remember this. . . ." Arthur "Dooley" Wilson is best known for his role as Sam in Michael Curtiz's film *Casablanca* (1942), which starred Humphrey Bogart and Ingrid Bergman. Wilson portrayed a pianist and singer, and his rendition of "As Time Goes By" in this role has helped *Casablanca* keep its hold on audiences. However, Wilson was also associated with, and contributed to, the Harlem Renaissance, primarily in the realms of music and theater.

Wilson was born in Texas in 1894, and he developed an affinity for African American entertainment through attending minstrels and other shows that toured East Texas. At age twelve, he began showcasing his own acting and musical talents as a minstrel in vaudeville shows. Wilson received the nickname "Dooley" from an Irish song that he performed as a (whiteface) minstrel. By age sixteen, Wilson had formed the first of several musical groups that he would lead for more than two decades: Primarily a drummer and singer, he played alto saxophone as well. Ultimately, he would perform in settings as famous as New York City's Clef Club and, for nearly the remainder of his life, Wilson would combine his explorations of music and acting in a number of different venues.

Bands with Wilson in front would tour England and the continent during the 1920s and the early 1930s, a period during which Europeans were as thirsty for jazz as the American public. Wilson's "Red Devils" also played in Casablanca (years later, it would be noted that Wilson was the only member of the cast of *Casablanca* who had ever actually been there). In the mid-1930s, Wilson returned to the United States and, although he did not forsake his musical career altogether, he once again pursued his interest in acting, a talent that had been showcased, albeit briefly, before his foray into jazz.

On 14 March 1908, Wilson had been featured in the musical *Two-Dollar Bill* at Robert Mann's Pekin Theater in Chicago. The Pekin, the first permanent black theater in the United States, was a springboard for a number of noted African American entertainers, including Wilson, Charles Gilpin, Flournoy Miller, and Aubrey Lyles. These and other talented showmen (and women) constituted the Pekin Stock Company, a group of resident actors, playwrights, musicians, and comedians.

Wilson was also a member of the Anita Bush Players, a critically important but short-lived acting troupe that opened at Harlem's famous Lincoln Theater on 15 November 1915, with *The Girl at the Fort*, and then made the transition to the more famous Lafayette Theater, where they opened on 27 December 1915. In 1916, the Anita Bush Players took their now better-known name: the Lafayette Players.

Years later, after his international travels as a jazz musician had ended and during the depths of the Great Depression, Wilson participated in the Roosevelt administration's Federal Theater Project, appearing

with screen giants such as Orson Welles. On 11 March 1936, at the Lafayette Theater, Wilson appeared in *The Conjure Man Dies*, a stage adaptation of Rudolph Fisher's novel. This production had shortcomings—in part because Fisher had died before he was able to revise the script for the stage—but the audiences consistently loved the performances. Four years later, Wilson portrayed Little Joe Jackson in a stage production of the immensely popular *Cabin in the Sky*. The critics in New York noted that remarkable performances by Wilson and Ethel Waters may have prevented the play from being just a parody of African American life and culture. Wilson would appear in one final Broadway production, *Bloomer Girl*, in 1944.

The heyday of the Harlem Renaissance had passed by the time Wilson began his film career with a part in *Keep Punching* (1939), a biography of the African American boxer Henry Armstrong. Over the following twelve years, Wilson appeared in nearly twenty films, the most notable of which was *Casablanca*. As was typical for African Americans in the 1930s and 1940s, most of Wilson's roles were minor supporting characters, and many of them fit the racially disparaging formulas of the era: waiter, butler, chauffeur, Pullman

"Dooley" Wilson in *Seven Days Ashore*, 1944. (Photofest.)

porter. A notable exception was his performance in *Stormy Weather* (1943), a film with an all-black cast that featured Bill "Bojangles" Robinson and Lena Horne. Wilson's last film appearance was in 1951, but he then appeared on the "small screen" as a major character in a popular television comedy, *Beulah*. Wilson died in 1953, shortly after his retirement.

In 2003, the Texas Film Hall of Fame honored Wilson, noting that its newest inductee had attempted to bring a level of dignity to African American acting in an age marked by consistent resistance to such attempts.

Biography

Arthur "Dooley" Wilson was born in Tyler, Texas, on 3 April 1894. At age twelve, he began his career as a minstrel and musician in vaudeville shows. He would later lead jazz groups that performed in venues as famous as the Clef Club; in the 1920s and early 1930s, his bands would make popular tours of Europe and North Africa. As an actor, Wilson performed in both Federal Theater productions and Broadway plays; he would become a member of famous acting troupes in Chicago and New York. His film career, which began in 1939 and lasted for a dozen years, was highlighted by his memorable performance as the pianist and singer Sam in *Casablanca*. Late in life, Wilson entered the world of television acting with a stint in a hit situation comedy, *Beulah*. He died on 30 May 1953, in Los Angeles, California.

C. C. HERBISON

See also Blacks in Theater; Bush, Anita; Clef Club; Conjure Man Dies, The; Film: Actors; Film: Black Filmmakers; Film: Blacks as Portrayed by White Filmmakers; Harlem Renaissance in the United States: 3—Chicago and the Midwest; Jazz; Lafayette Theater; Lincoln Theater; Muse, Clarence; Race Films; Theater

Further Reading

Bogle, Donald. *Toms, Coons, Mulattoes, Mammies, and Bucks: An Interpretive History of Blacks in American Films*, 4th ed. New York: Continuum, 2001.
Cripps, Thomas. *Slow Fade to Black: The Negro in American Film, 1900–1942*. New York: Oxford University Pres, 1993.
Peterson, Bernard L. *A Century of Musicals in Black and White: An Encyclopedia of Musical Works by, about, or Involving African Americans*. Westport, Conn.: Greenwood, 1992.
Sampson, Henry T. *The Ghost Walks: A Chronological History of Blacks in Show Business, 1865–1910*. Metuchen, N.J.: Scarecrow, 1988.
Watkins, Mel. *On the Real Side: A History of African American Comedy from Slavery to Chris Rock*. Chicago, Ill.: Lawrence Hill, 1994.
Woll, Allen. *Dictionary of the Black Theatre: Broadway, Off-Broadway, and Selected Harlem Theatre*. Westport, Conn.: Greenwood, 1983.

Wilson, Edith

Edith Wilson was a blues singer and entertainer. Beginning in about 1919, she performed in a trio with the pianist Danny Wilson and his sister Lena Wilson, also a singer. They appeared in small clubs in the Chicago area until 1921, when they relocated to Washington, D.C., performing there and in Atlantic City, New Jersey.

By mid-1921, Wilson was appearing in the Broadway revue *Put and Take*. For the next two decades she worked in numerous shows, mostly revues, particularly those produced by the prolific Lew Leslie. Her shows in the 1920s included Leslie's *Plantation Revue* (1922), *Creole Follies* (1924), and *Dixie to Broadway* (1924–1925). Two revues of this period paired her with great jazz musicians: She worked with Duke Ellington's Orchestra in *Jazzmania* (1927), and with Louis Armstrong and Fats Waller in *Hot Chocolates* (1929–1930).

Wilson's recording career began in 1921. Her first record was Perry Bradford's "Nervous Blues." Her sessions in September of that year, with a band that included Johnny Dunn on trumpet, were the first by a black blues singer on Columbia Records. She remained with Columbia through 1925, working with Fletcher Henderson and Don Redman, among others. Her final recordings for Columbia featured "Doc" Straine, her regular stage partner from 1924 to 1926. Wilson recorded for Brunswick with Bubber Miley and Wilbur de Paris in 1929, and she made several records for Victor in 1930. At this point, she took a long hiatus from recording.

Beginning with *From Dover Street to Dixie* (London, 1923, with Florence Mills), Wilson performed a great deal overseas. She undertook a long tour with Sam Wooding's Orchestra in the revue *Chocolate Kiddies* in 1925, traversing England, much of Europe, Russia, and finally South America. She appeared with Florence Mills again, in Lew Leslie's *Blackbirds of 1926* in London (1926) and Europe (1927). She toured again in Europe with Sam Wooding and his Chocolate Kiddies in *The Black Revue* in. 1928. She worked in theaters in Berlin and clubs in Paris until 1929.

Edith Wilson did extensive stage work in the 1930s, including the run of *Shuffle Along of 1932–1933*, *Blackbirds of 1933–1934*, and many other shows. She continued to perform frequently in Europe, appearing in Parisian nightclubs in 1931–1932, and in the London run of *Blackbirds of 1934*. Wilson also toured Europe with Sam Wooding's band in *Rhapsody in Black*, 1935. She sang with leading big bands in the mid-1930s, including those of Cab Calloway, Noble Sissle, Jimmie Lunceford, and Lucky Millinder.

In the 1940s, Wilson appeared in several Hollywood films, usually in nonsinging roles. The first of these was *I'm Still Alive* in 1940; her most notable film was the *To Have and Have Not* (a vehicle for Lauren Bacall and Humphrey Bogart) in 1944. She returned to Broadway in *Memphis Bound* (1945), a swing version of Gilbert and Sullivan's *H.M.S. Pinafore* that starred Bill "Bojangles" Robinson.

From the mid-1940s through the mid-1960s, Edith Wilson worked extensively in radio, often in non-singing roles. She played the Kingfish's wife in *Amos 'n' Andy* for many years beginning in the early 1940s. She signed a deal with the Quaker Oats company to play the character of Aunt Jemima on radio and in numerous personal appearances, many of them for charitable causes. She drew criticism from civil rights groups for these appearances, however, and Quaker Oats terminated her contract in 1965.

In the last five years of her life, Wilson enjoyed a career revival. She made a blues record for the Delmark label in 1976, backed by an old-timers' band led from the piano by Eurreal "Little Brother" Montgomery. She performed with Montgomery during the late 1970s, and also appeared with Eubie Blake. Her final appearances were made in 1980; these included the Bobby Short show *Blacks on Broadway*.

Edith Wilson was never a blues shouter in the mode of Bessie Smith, let alone a country blues singer. Rather, she was firmly in the cabaret blues category, along with such contemporaries as Ethel Waters and Alberta Hunter, and she was among the leading practitioners of this style for almost sixty years.

Biography

Edith Goodall Wilson was born on 6 September 1896 (some sources give 1906 as the year) in Louisville, Kentucky. She began singing in church, at talent contests, and at other local events, then worked at Louisville's Park Theater. In about 1919, she began performing in a trio with the pianist Danny Wilson (whom she married c. 1919) and his sister Lena Wilson. She was in the Broadway revue *Put and Take* in 1921; for the next twenty years she was in many shows and revues, particularly those produced by Lew Leslie. Also in 1921, she began a recording career. She toured extensively in Europe; in the 1930s, she sang with the leading big bands; in the 1940s, she appeared in films; she later performed on radio, notably in *Amos 'n' Andy*. Wilson died on 30 March 1981 in Chicago.

ELLIOTT S. HURWITT

See also Amos 'n' Andy; Armstrong, Louis; Blackbirds; Bradford, Perry; Blues: Women Performers; Calloway, Cabell "Cab"; Ellington, Duke; Henderson, Fletcher; Hot Chocolates; Leslie, Lew; Mills, Florence; Singers; Sissle, Noble; Waller, Thomas "Fats"

Further Reading

Dixon, Robert, Jon Godrich, and Howard Rye. *Blues and Gospel Records*, 4th ed. New York: Oxford University Press, 1997, pp. 1049–1050.

Harris, Sheldon. *Blues Who's Who*. 1979, pp. 580–582.

Harrison, Daphne Duval. *Black Pearls*. New Brunswick, N.J.: Rutgers University Press, 1988.

———. "Edith Goodall Wilson." In *American National Biography*, Vol. 23, ed. John A. Garraty and Mark C. Carnes. New York: Oxford University Press, 1999, pp. 563–564.

Wilson, Frank

Frank Wilson (1886–1956) was an actor and playwright. He was inspired to seek a career in theater when he saw Bert Williams and George Walker's *In Dahomey* in 1903. He gained his first recognition through organizing a vaudeville act, the Carolina Comedy Four, in 1908. In order to supplement his income, Wilson entered the postal service. From 1914 to 1917, he wrote, directed, and performed in dramatic and comedic sketches at the Lincoln Theater. In 1917, he began working as an actor with the Lafayette Players; he also studied in a theater course for black actors at the American Academy of Dramatic Arts. By the 1920s, Wilson had become prominent in Harlem's professional theater and "little theater." Among his plays, *Confidence*, *Pa Williams' Gal*, and *A Train North* were particularly popular, the last being optioned by the Ethiopian Art Theater.

Wilson worked with the Provincetown Playhouse in a supporting role in the original production of Eugene O'Neill's *All God's Chillun Got Wings* (1924) and in revivals of *The Dreamy Kid* and *The Emperor Jones* in 1925, winning the admiration of the downtown theater critics. When Jules Bledsoe was dropped from the cast of Paul Green's *In Abraham's Bosom* in 1926, Wilson took over the leading role. He was then cast in *Porgy* by DuBose and Dorothy Heyward in 1927.

In 1927, in the playwriting contest sponsored by *Opportunity*, Wilson took first prize for *Sugar Cain*, a melodrama; it was reprinted under the title *Sugar Cane* in *Plays of Negro Life*, edited by Alain Locke. In 1928, Wilson became one of only four African American nonmusical playwrights to have a commercial production on Broadway during the 1920s, with *Meek Mose*. Set in Mexia, Texas, the play tells the story of members of a black community and their leader, who suffer after being evicted from their property but prevail in the end, when oil is discovered in the swampland to which they have moved. The play was considered weak; it opened 6 February 1928 at the Princess Theater and closed on 3 March. The play was retitled *Brother Mose* and produced in 1934 by the Works Progress Administration. Wilson's *Walk Together Chillun* became the first legitimate production by the Federal Theater's Negro Unit at the Lafayette Theater in 1936.

In 1935, Wilson joined the cast of *The Green Pastures* in the role of Moses. Other major stage credits include *Watch on the Rhine* (1941), *Anna Lucasta* (1946–1947), and *The Big Knife* (1949). A featured role in *Take a Giant Step* (1953) was his last appearance on Broadway. His numerous film credits include *The Emperor Jones* (1933), *The Green Pastures* (1936), *Watch on the Rhine* (1943), and other Hollywood productions, as well as films by Oscar Micheaux. Wilson wrote the screenplays for *Paradise in Harlem* (1939), *Murder on Lenox Avenue* (1941), and *Sunday Sinners* (1941) for the producer Jack Goldberg. Although Wilson's acting career continued to flourish, his work as a playwright appears to have ended with the 1930s.

Biography

The playwright and actor Frank H. Wilson was born in Manhattan on 4 May 1886. Orphaned at the age of eight, he grew up in a "waifs' home." He put himself through high school, graduating at the age of fifteen. He organized a vaudeville act, the Carolina Comedy Four, in 1908. By 1911, Wilson had married Effie King, and became the father of Emmet Barrymore Wilson, as well as of two stepchildren. In 1914–1917, he was at the Lincoln Theater; in 1917, he began acting with the Lafayette Players; in the 1920s, he worked with the Provincetown Playhouse. Notable dramas in which he appeared include *The Emperor Jones*, *Porgy*, and *The Green Pastures*. In 1927, he won first prize in *Opportunity*'s playwriting contest. During the 1930s, he was associated with the Federal Theater Project; he also appeared in films and wrote screenplays. After a debilitating stroke, Wilson died in Queens, New York City, on 16 February 1956.

FREDA GILES

See also Emperor Jones, The; Ethiopian Art Players; Green Pastures, The; Green, Paul; Lafayette Players; Lincoln Theater; Micheaux, Oscar; Opportunity Literary Contests; Pa Williams' Gal; Porgy: Play; Williams, Egbert Austin "Bert"; Works Progress Administration

Further Reading

Abramson, Doris E. *Negro Playwrights in the American Theatre, 1925–1959*. New York: Columbia University Press, 1969.

Kellner, Bruce, ed. *The Harlem Renaissance: A Historical Dictionary for the Era*. Westport, Conn.: Greenwood, 1984.

Peterson, Bernard L. *Early Black American Playwrights and Dramatic Writers: A Biographical Dictionary and Catalog of Plays, Films, and Broadcasting Scripts*. Westport, Conn.: Greenwood, 1990.

Wise, Stephen Samuel

Rabbi Stephen Samuel Wise was an advocate of liberal religion and a leader in building Jewish-American support for African American civil rights in the early twentieth century. Born in Hungary, Wise emigrated with his family to the United States and was raised in New York City. He followed his father into the rabbinate;

after study at the College of the City of New York and Columbia University, he attained his first appointment as a rabbi in 1893. He married Louise Waterman in 1900 and moved that year to Portland, Oregon, where he served as rabbi of Temple Beth Israel and developed a national reputation for support of liberal social causes. He returned to New York in 1907 to found the Free Synagogue, devoted to social service and what Wise called "civic religion."

Wise's commitment to racial equality was part of his broader social vision. He signed "The Call" of February 1909 that led to the formation of the National Association for the Advancement of Colored People (NAACP) and served on its governing board, the Committee of Forty. Although he maintained a lifelong membership in the NAACP, he was not particularly active in the organization in later years. He wrote a personal letter to W. E. B. Du Bois protesting against the anti-Semitic passages in Du Bois's *The Souls of Black Folk* (1903); in a later edition, Du Bois removed the offending sections. Wise spoke at Atlanta University in 1910, at Du Bois's invitation. Wise also maintained close ties with Booker T. Washington; he delivered a passionate eulogy at the Free Synagogue after Washington's death in 1915.

Rabbi Stephen Samuel Wise, c. 1920–1940. (Library of Congress.)

Although Wise was never at home in a political party, he lent his support to the presidential candidacy of Woodrow Wilson in 1912. Like many other racial progressives, Wise was disappointed by Wilson's discriminatory policies and protested them widely. In 1915, the lynching of Leo Frank, a Jewish man accused of murder in Georgia, further convinced Wise that the concerns of all social minorities were related. Wise also protested the explicitly racist film *The Birth of a Nation* (1915); when the National Board of Censorship in Moving Pictures reversed its policy and approved the film's distribution, Wise led protests in the office of the mayor of New York.

In the 1920s, Wise continued to connect blacks' civil rights with the rights of other ethnic groups. At the Democratic national convention of 1924, Wise sought unsuccessfully for the adoption of a resolution condemning the Ku Klux Klan, then in resurgence and a powerful force in the Democratic Party. He spoke out against restrictions on immigration and denounced the religious and ethnic bigotry that surrounded the trial of the accused anarchists Sacco and Vanzetti and the presidential candidacy of Alfred E. Smith.

Wise's organizational home in the second half of his life was the American Jewish Congress, which he headed in its various forms between 1916 and his death. The group's prime concern was support for a Jewish homeland in the Middle East; at the Versailles Peace Conference after World War I, Wise testified on behalf of Zionist concerns. His leadership also put the American Jewish Congress on record in opposition to racism against African Americans; the organization's efforts for open university enrollments and against restrictive covenants intersected with similar drives by African American organizations.

In the 1930s, Wise and the American Jewish Congress did much to publicize the anti-Semitism of Adolf Hitler; beginning in 1942, when Wise learned the full extent of the Nazis' persecution of European Jews, he called for greater intervention by the Roosevelt administration. Through his leadership of the Jewish Institute of Religion, Wise also instilled his vision of liberal religion into a rising generation of rabbis, several of whom played key roles in the postwar civil rights movement. Wise died in New York City in 1949.

Biography

Stephen Samuel Wise was born in Erlau, Hungary, on 17 March 1874. He studied at College of the City of New York, 1887–1891; earned an A.B. at Columbia

College, 1892; and earned a Ph.D. at Columbia University, 1901. He was ordained in 1893. His rabbinates were Congregation B'nai Jeshurun, New York City, 1893–1900; Congregation Beth Israel, Portland, Oregon, 1900–1906; and Free Synagogue of New York, 1907–1949. He was the founder of Federation of American Zionists, 1897; and its secretary, 1898–1904. Wise was also a founder of the National Association for the Advancement of Colored People in 1909. He was a founder, American Jewish Congress, 1916; revived, 1920; vice president, 1921–1925; and president, 1925–1949. He was president, Zionist Organization of America, 1918–1920 and 1936–1938. Wise was a founder, Jewish Institute of Religion, 1922; and president, 1927–1948. He was an editor, *Opinion*, 1936–1949. He was a founder, World Jewish Congress, 1936; and president, 1936–1949. Wise died in New York City on 19 April 1949.

CHRISTOPHER CAPOZZOLA

See also Birth of a Nation, The; Du Bois, W. E. B.; National Association for the Advancement of Colored People; Washington, Booker T.

Selected Works

As I See It. 1944.

Beth Israel Pulpit: Sermons, 2 vols. 1905–1906.

Challenging Years: The Autobiography of Stephen Wise. 1949.

Child versus Parent. 1922.

Free Synagogue Pulpit: Sermons and Addresses, 10 vols. 1908–1932.

How to Face Life. 1917.

The Improvement of the Moral Qualities: An Ethical Treatise of the Eleventh Century by Solomon ibn Gabirol. 1901.

Personal Letters of Stephen S. Wise, ed. Justine Wise Polier and James Waterman Wise. 1956.

Stephen S. Wise: Servant of the People—Selected Letters, ed. Carl Hermann Voss. 1969.

Further Reading

Diner, Hasia R. *In the Almost Promised Land: American Jews and Blacks, 1915–1935*. Westport, Conn.: Greenwood, 1977; Baltimore, Md.: Johns Hopkins University Press, 1995.

Shapiro, Robert D. *A Reform Rabbi in the Progressive Era: The Early Career of Stephen S. Wise*. New York: Garland, 1988,

Urfosky, Melvin I. *A Voice That Spoke for Justice: The Life and Times of Stephen S. Wise*. Albany: State University of New York (SUNY) Press, 1982.

Within Our Gates

Within Our Gates (1920) is the earliest surviving film feature by an African American. It was the second film of the pioneer Oscar Micheaux. Two of his other films from the silent era also survive: *Symbol of the Unconquered* (1920) and *Body and Soul* (1925), which starred Paul Robeson. During a thirty-year career that began in the silent era and extended through the 1940s, Micheaux made more than forty films with black casts. As he did for most of his films, Micheaux wrote, directed, and produced *Within Our Gates* himself. Its star, Evelyn Preer, as Sylvia Landry, played one of the strong but conventional female roles that Micheaux favored. The film also starred Jack Chenault, Flo Clement, James D. Ruffin, and William Smith; it had numerous minor characters as well. *Jasper Landry's Will* (1923) is believed to be the sequel to *Within Our Gates*, but that film has not survived.

Within Our Gates was completed at the dawn of the Harlem Renaissance and only a few months after one of the bloodiest seasons of race rioting in America, later called the "red summer" of 1919. For that reason and because of Micheaux's unflinching depiction of white racists' violence against black people, the film was banned in some places and excised in others.

Some critics have called *Within Our Gates* a rebuttal of D.W. Griffith's hugely successful and influential race-baiting film, *The Birth of a Nation* (1915). Its purposeful exposé of the reality of the southern horror is an indictment of the entire system of white supremacy, however, not just a single representation of it. The film stripped away the anonymity provided by the hood-wearing nightriders by showing that racist violence against black people was a communal activity engaged in by ordinary white people.

Within Our Gates is the story of a woman, Sylvia Landry (played by Evelyn Preer), who wants to start a school for black children. Sylvia is the adopted daughter of the education-loving Landry family, who are despised by the white townsfolk after a black neighbor, seeking to please wealthy whites, tells them that Jasper Landry (played by William Starks), a sharecropper, "owns a mule," is "buying land," and is "eddicating" his children. A dispute occurs with the landowner when Jasper comes to settle his account after his his educated daughter, Sylvia, has made some bookkeeping corrections. When an irate white man who was also cheated by the landowner later kills the landowner, it is Jasper who is accused of the murder and brutally lynched, seemingly by consensus of all the white folks in town.

A potent theme in the film is Sylvia's susceptibility to sexual violence at the hands of a white man, which Micheaux presents as a corrective to the myth of white women being attacked by black male rapists. That charge, as the activist and journalist Ida B. Wells Barnett had argued in her antilynching pamphlets years earlier, was a subterfuge, but it nevertheless fueled the deadly work of white lynch mobs. With a plot twist that revealed Sylvia's would-be attacker to be her unknown white father, Micheaux uncovers the taboo subject of miscegenation and the myth of racial purity. Micheaux also documents the threat that many whites of that era and region read into black people's desire for education and property—a reading that could spark violent reactions.

The subtitle of the film, *A History of the Life of Blacks of the United States*, shows the director's concern with historical documentation. In fact, the original title of the film was *Circumstantial Evidence*; this was changed when it opened in Chicago and Detroit in January 1920. The graphic lynching scene caused censorship boards in several cities to ban the film, fearing an outbreak of race riots. Notably, the board of censors in Chicago excised several scenes. Micheaux, whose promotional abilities equaled his abilities as a filmmaker, used the resulting controversy to stir up interest in his film. As he accompanied the film to different cities, his advertisements in the local newspapers mention that "it took two solid months to get by the censor board" in Chicago. Another advertisement bearing his signature states: "Please Note! The Photoplay *Within Our Gates*, was passed by the Censor but, owing to a wave of agitation on the part of certain Race people (who had not even seen it), 1,200 feet was eliminated during its first engagement. The 1,200 feet have now been restored and the picture will positively be shown from now on as originally produced and released—no cutouts." With such shrewd tactics, Micheaux was able to reach his targeted black audience and overcome a negative press. The black press, specifically the nationally circulated *Chicago Defender*, helped energize an audience of blacks ready to see images that were

reflective of their realities and aspirations. In an editorial in the *Chicago Defender*, the film is praised as

> a favorable argument against southern mobocracy, peonage, and concubinage. The picture is a quivering tongue of fire, the burn of which will be felt in the far distant years. The spirit of *Within Our Gates* is the spirit of Douglass, Nat Turner, Scarborough, and Du Bois rolled into one, but telling the story of the wrongs of our people better than Douglass did in his speeches, [and] more dramatically transcendent than Du Bois in his *Souls of Black Folk*.

Critics and historians have built an important body of criticism of Micheaux's films—and of his literary works, which include eight novels—yet *Within Our Gates* remains one of the most scrutinized.

AUDREY THOMAS MCCLUSKEY

See also Barnett, Ida B. Wells; Birth of a Nation, The; Film: Black Filmmakers; Micheaux, Oscar; Preer, Evelyn; Riots: 2—Red Summer of 1919

Further Reading

Bowser, Pearl, Jane Gaines, and Charles Musser, eds. *Oscar Micheaux and His Circle*. Bloomington: Indiana University Press, 2001.

Bowser, Pearl, and Louise Spence. *Writing Himself Into History: Oscar Micheaux, His Silent Films, and His Audience*. New Brunswick, N.J.: Rutgers University Press, 2000.

Sampson, Henry T. *Blacks in Black and White: A Sourcebook on Black Films*. Metuchen, N.J.: Scarecrow, 1995.

Witmark, M., and Sons

M. Witmark and Sons was a music publishing company active from 1886 to 1929. It played a crucial role in the publishing of music by African Americans for several decades during two crucial periods in the development of American music, in the years around 1900 and 1920.

Witmark's publication of African American songs began early in its history. Among its earliest hits were three songs by Gussie Lord Davis (1863–1899), who made his reputation writing tearjerkers rather than stereotypical minstrel numbers. "Baby's Laughing in

Her Sleep," "Irene, Goodnight," and "Up Dar in De Sky" were all published by Witmark in 1892. Lesser successes written by Davis and published by Witmark included "Wedded at Last" (1894), "Honey, Don't You Shake Me" (1895), "The Bright Side of Life" (1896), and "The Night Father Sent Kate Away" (also 1896).

In 1896, Witmark also became heavily involved in the publication of ragtime songs, especially "coon songs," a genre that combined minstrel stereotypes with a rough, newly syncopated urban musical style. These songs, and their cover art, were among the most egregious exploitations of the African American image in the history of American culture. Nonetheless, black composers created this genre, and Witmark published some of the most popular examples, including "All Coons Look Alike to Me" by the comedian Ernest Hogan (1896), the progenitor of the form. Hogan's "The Congregation Will Please Keep Their Seats" was a smaller hit for the firm in 1900. Witmark also picked up republication rights for two blockbusters by Ben Harney, a light-skinned black passing for white: "Mr. Johnson, Turn Me Loose" and "You've Been a Good Old Wagon but You've Done Broke Down" (both 1896), as well as another hit by Harney, "The Cake-Walk in the Sky" (1899) and some of his lesser numbers.

In 1898, Witmark published the music from the successful show *Clorindy, or the Origin of the Cakewalk*. This musical—with lyrics by Paul Laurence Dunbar, the foremost black poet of the day; and music by Will Marion Cook (1869–1944), a leading musical talent of his generation—was a landmark in the history of American theater. *Clorindy* included three major hits, "Darktown Is Out Tonight, "Hottest Coon in Dixie," and "Who Dat Say Chicken in Dis Crowd." Other songs from the show included "Jump Back, Honey, Jump Back" and "Love in a Cottage Is Best." Witmark also published two instrumentals from the show, "Clorindy March and Two Step" and "Creole Dance."

Once the songs from *Clorindy* became hits, Cook decided he had made a poor publishing deal with Witmark. A hot-tempered genius, proud of his European training and high musical standards, Cook often quarreled with colleagues of both races. Accompanied by his white attorney, he appeared in the Witmark offices one day, without an appointment, demanding a favorable change in his contract. This gained him nothing; on the contrary, Witmark declined to have any further dealings with him.

Over the next two decades Witmark published only a few pieces by African Americans. These included "In

the Pyramids," cowritten by Cecil Mack for the show *Mrs. Black Is Back* (1904), and "I Think an Awful Lot of You," written by Joe Jordan for the show *The Shoo-Fly Regiment*. Witmark also published a classic song from the show *In Dahomey* in 1903: "I'm a Jonah Man" by Bert Williams and Alex Rogers. It was through the music for another important musical that Witmark made its great impact as a publisher during the Harlem Renaissance, however. The show was *Shuffle Along*, with a book by the comedians Aubrey Lyles and Flournoy Miller, and with songs by the ragtime pianist Eubie Blake and his lyricist, the singer and entertainer Noble Sissle. This show, which premiered in 1921, was the high-water mark of the African American musical, an immense success both in New York and on tour. Among the smash hits Witmark published were two of Blake's most famous compositions, "I'm Just Wild about Harry," and "Love Will Find a Way." Other songs from the show included "Bandanna Days," "Daddy Won't You Please Come Home," "Everything Reminds Me of You," "Gypsy Blues," "I'm Craving for That Kind of Love," "I'm Just Simply Full of Jazz," "In Honeysuckle Time," "Kentucky Sue," "My Vision Girl," "Oriental Blues," "Pickaninny Shoes," and the title song, "Shuffle Along." Witmark also published the instrumental "Baltimore Buzz," a hit in Blake's band recording.

The business relationship between Blake and the Witmark firm during the years 1919–1923 was quite close. The firm had published some of his collaborative work of the World War I era, such as "On Patrol in No-Man's Land" and "All of No-Man's Land Is Ours" (both 1919, cocomposed with James Reese Europe); and "Good Night, Angeline" (also 1919, cocomposed with Europe and Noble Sissle). Witmark also published the songs for another (unsuccessful) Sissle–Blake show, *Elsie*, in 1923. Songs from this show included "Baby Buntin'," "Elsie," "Everybody's Struttin' Now," "I Like to Walk with a Pal Like You," "Jazzing Thunder Storming Dance," "Jingle Step," "Love Chile," "My Crinoline Girl," "A Regular Guy," "Sand Flowers," "Two Hearts in Tune," and "With You." In addition to his songs, the firm published some of Blake's solo piano works, such as "Sounds of Africa."

During the Jazz Age, Witmark gradually stopped publishing work by African American composers. The firm was purchased by Warner Brothers in 1929—a desirable acquisition for a Hollywood studio, given the advent of sound films. By this time, Witmark's heyday as a publisher of African American talent was behind it.

ELLIOTT S. HURWITT

See also Blake, Eubie; Cook, Will Marion; Dunbar, Paul Laurence; Europe, James Reese; Mack, Cecil; Minstrelsy; Shuffle Along

Further Reading

Jasen, David. *Tin Pan Alley*. New York: Donald Fine, 1988.

Witmark, Isidore. *The House of Witmark: From Ragtime to Swingtime*. New York: Da Capo, 1976. (Originally published 1939.)

Woodruff, Hale

Hale Aspacio Woodruff, a leading painter of the first generation of the New Negro movement, was born in 1900 in Cairo, Illinois. His mother encouraged him to draw from an early age, so he copied newspaper cartoons and illustrations from the family Bible. He first worked as a cartoonist and graphic artist. Woodruff studied art at the Herron Art Institute in Indianapolis, where he was given a German book on African sculpture. This made a great impression on him, and he became one of the first black American artists influenced by African art. While studying in Paris on a Harmon Foundation award (1927–1931), he was also influenced by cubism and by Monet, Cézanne, and Picasso. During this period, Woodruff met Henry Ossawa Tanner, a leading American black artist in Paris.

On his return to the United States in 1931, Woodruff taught art at the Atlanta University Center. In the midst of the Depression, he adopted the artistic modes of regionalism and social realism, and he worked as an assistant to Diego Rivera in Mexico during the summer of 1936. At that time, he also saw works by Jos, Orozco, and David Siqueiros. In the watercolor entitled *Poor Man's Cotton* (1934), Woodruff combines social realism with a geometric quality and flattened space derived from cubism. He depicts cotton-workers as if they are dancing as they swing their hoes in a series of criss-crossing diagonals. And he punctuates their rhythmic movements with patterns of white cotton balls. A similar animation of space and form characterizes his graphic work.

Interested in black history, Woodruff participated in 1935 in an exhibition organized by the National Association for the Advancement of Colored People (NAACP) entitled "An Art Commentary on Lynching." He also organized an exhibition of work by black artists, held every year from 1942 to 1970, in Atlanta.

In 1943, Woodruff went to New York on a Rosenwald fellowship; in New York, he came into contact with the abstract expressionists and critic Clement Greenberg. He then turned to abstraction and, in 1950, painted *Afro Emblems*, which shows the influence of nonwestern art and the surrealism of Jackson Pollock.

Among Woodruff's best-known works are his murals. He collaborated with Wilmer Jennings on *The Negro in Modern American Life: Literature, Music, and Art* for the David T. Howard High School in Atlanta. *The Amistad Mutiny* is a mural in three panels (the mutiny, the trial and defense of the mutineers by John Quincy Adams, and the return to Sierra Leone) for the Talladega College Slavery Library in Alabama. *The Art of the Negro*, for the Trevor Arnett Library of Clark Atlanta University, is a series of six panels. Commissioned by the then president of Atlanta University, this work combines influences from African, pre-Columbian, Oceanic, and surrealist art. There is also a reclining figure in the style of Henry Moore. All the murals are characterized by exuberant, linear dynamics; bright colors; and spatial crowding.

Hale Woodruff (1900–1980), *Red Cross Nurse*, from the front cover of *Vogue* magazine, May 1918; color lithograph. (Bibliothèque des Arts Decoratifs, Paris, France/Bridgeman Art Library. Archives Charmet, CHT176050.)

Biography

Hale A. Woodruff was born in Cairo, Illinois, in 1900. He was attracted to art at an early age; his first jobs were as a cartoonist and graphic artist. He studied in Indianapolis and Paris before accepting a teaching post in Atlanta. After a summer working for Diego Rivera, he turned to murals, which occupied him for several years. Struck by the artistic possibilities of African sculpture, he was strongly influenced by the avant-garde, especially cubism and abstract expressionism. He combined an interest in African American themes with a thorough knowledge of mainstream developments in modernism. He taught at New York University until his retirement as a full professor in 1968; he died in 1968 at the age of eighty.

LAURIE ADAMS

See also Artists; Harmon Foundation; Rosenwald Fellowships; Tanner, Henry Ossawa

Selected Works

Afro Emblems. 1950. (National Museum of American Art, Washington, D.C.)

The Amistad Mutiny. 1939. (Mural in three panels, Talladega College, Slavery Library, Alabama.)

Art of the Negro. 1950–1951. (Mural in six panels, Clark–Atlanta University, Trevor Arnett Library, Atlanta, Georgia.)

The Card Players. 1930. (National Archives of American Art, Washington, D.C.)

Poor Man's Cotton. 1934. (Newark Museum, New Jersey.)

Further Reading

"Albert Murray: An Interview with Hale A. Woodruff." In *Hale A. Woodruff: Fifty Years of His Art.* Exhib. Cat. New York: Studio Museum in Harlem, 1979.

Bearden, Romare, and Harry Henderson. *A History of African-American Artists from 1792 to the Present.* New York: Pantheon Books, 1993.

Collins, Lizetta LeFalle, and Shifra M. Goldman. *The Spirit of Resistance: The African-American Modernists and the Mexican Muralist School.* New York: American Federation of Arts, 1996.

Lewis, Samela. *African-American Art and Artists.* Berkeley: University of California Press, 1990.

Patton, Sharon F. *African-American Art.* New York: Oxford University Press, 1998.

Prigoff, James, and Robin J. Dunitz. *Walls of Heritage, Walls of Pride.* San Francisco, Calif.: Pomegranate, n.d.

Studio Museum in Harlem. *Harlem Renaissance: Art of Black America.* New York: Abrams, 1987.

Taylor, William E., and Harriet G. Warkel. *A Shared Heritage: Art by Four African Americans.* Bloomington, Ind.: Indiana University Press, 1996.

Woodson, Carter G.

Born in 1875, the son of slave parents, the historian Carter G. Woodson grew up poor in rural Virginia. A thirst for education led him on a long journey of discovery, through high school (after working for several years in mines and railroads); to Berea College in Kentucky, where he graduated just one year before segregation barred all blacks; to the University of Chicago; and on to Harvard University, where he was the second black American to earn a Ph.D. in history (W. E. B. Du Bois was the first). Interspersed with his long and difficult path to the highest academic achievements were years spent teaching high school in Huntington, West Virginia; Washington, D.C.; and the Philippines. He was twice a school principal and went on to become dean at Howard University and West Virginia State College. At Howard, Woodson was also the first director of the graduate history program and presided over the establishment of the history department.

By 1915, Woodson reached the conclusion that blacks' enlightenment about history was fundamental to overcoming economic and political powerlessness and that the development of black history required organization. That year, Woodson and four associates founded the Association for the Study of Negro Life and History (ASNLH). The following January, Woodson edited the first edition of the *Journal of Negro History.* By 1920, he realized that he could not recover African American history for black Americans by being an academic administrator. Moreover, he was tired of being answerable to bureaucracy and bureaucrats. Black colleges and universities, he concluded, were not conducive to the development of black history. Their leaders tended to be white, finances tended to be in white hands, and thus black history that threatened to instill concepts of racial pride was considered controversial or dangerous, even by black bureaucrats.

In 1922, Woodson founded Associated Publishers to produce books and pamphlets on black history for an academic audience. The publishing house was also intended to provide materials for high school teachers and for children in elementary through high school, as little black history was taught even in segregated black schools. Denied access to the public through white publishers, and wishing to counter the racism of what was published about black people, Woodson and his associates investigated the black experience from colonial times through their own time. Woodson was interested in the black experience generally and also collected and published materials on Latin America, Africa, and the Caribbean. In addition, pioneering sociological studies were undertaken and published. Woodson's efforts thus predated, but also powerfully complemented, the cultural upsurge of the Harlem Renaissance.

To further extend his message of black pride, in 1926 Woodson established Negro History Week, which was a significant success. It was timed to coincide with the birthdays of Frederick Douglass and Abraham Lincoln; branches of the ASNLH across the country and other black groups held parades, dances, banquets, lecture series, and numerous other activities to celebrate the African American experience. Woodson provided increasingly sophisticated materials and suggestions for such groups extolling the African American achievement. By 1940, in *Dusk of Dawn*, W. E. B. Du Bois was ready to proclaim that Negro History Week was the greatest single achievement to arise from the artistic movement of the 1920s (the Harlem Renaissance). In 1976, the event was renamed Black History Month, a reflection of changed times and the success of African Americans in claiming for themselves more prominence in American society.

During the 1920s and early 1930s, Woodson hired a number of figures in the Harlem Renaissance to help in his work. From 1924 to 1925, Langston Hughes worked with Woodson on a study of free backs in the antebellum South. Similarly, Zora Neale Hurston was hired to collect black folklore and interview former slaves in Florida and Alabama. Her article "Cudjo's Own Story of the Last African Slaves" was published in 1927 by Woodson in *Journal of Negro History*. Woodson was also able to give funds to Alain Locke for a two-year study of African art.

The 1920s proved to be the peak of Woodson's scholarly output. He was not silenced by the effects of the Depression; however, whereas he had been extremely successful with white philanthropists in the 1920s, he found it increasingly difficult to obtain funding once the Depression arrived. He also chafed under

the philanthropists' instructions to affiliate with a black college or university. After 1935, Woodson lost all white funding for his work and became solely dependent on the black community. Although the volume of publishing by the ASNLH declined as a result, throughout the 1930s it became a clearinghouse for research assistance in black history to scholars and the general public. The change was to Woodson's liking and led to greater outreach to the mass of black Americans and to even more concentration on heightening community racial pride and cultural consciousness. To further this strategy, Woodson founded the *Negro History Bulletin* in 1937. Its wide appeal was testimony not only to the editorial trajectory but also to the vastly increased appeal of black history.

In his lifetime, Woodson was a controversial figure. To achieve his remarkable vision, Woodson was

Carter G. Woodson, c. 1911. (Photographs and Prints Division, Schomburg Center for Research in Black Culture, New York Public Library, Astor, Lenox, and Tilden Foundations.)

single-minded to a degree that often made others uncomfortable. He jealously guarded his control of ASNLH, *Journal of Negro History*, *Negro History Bulletin*, every research project, and the running of the office. Colleagues described him as a stern taskmaster, overbearing, acid-tongued, yet completely unpretentious. He devoted his life to black history, crossing the country as a speaker very much in demand for his dynamic presentations and charismatic delivery. His public service included research for the Chicago Commission on Race Relations (1920) and membership on advisory boards for various New Deal projects related to the black community. He was a founding member of the Washington, D.C., branch of the National Association for the Advancement of Colored People (NAACP), the nation's largest and most active; he was a strong supporter of Marcus Garvey's Universal Negro Improvement Association (UNIA) and of A. Philip Randolph; he was active in antilynching campaigns; he urged an economic boycott of white-owned businesses in black areas of Washington in 1915, long before the later "Don't buy where you can't work" campaigns; and he attacked the failure of black education and the leadership of the black community by its middle class. Like Du Bois, Woodson became more radical as he grew older. During the 1930s, he wrote regular columns in black newspapers urging black economic nationalism and black cultural nationalism.

After his death in 1950, Woodson was largely forgotten. It was only in the wake of the civil rights movement and the growth of black studies that his work has been more fully appreciated.

Biography

Carter Godwin Woodson was born on 19 December 1875 in New Canton, Virginia. He attended public schools in Buckingham County, Virginia; and Huntington, West Virginia. He then studied at Berea College, Kentucky (Litt.B., 1903); University of Chicago (B.A. and M.A., 1908); and Harvard University (Ph.D., 1912). He taught high school in Winona, West Virginia, 1898–1900; was principal, Douglass High School, Huntington, West Virginia, 1900–1903; was supervisor of schools in the Philippines, 1903–1907; taught at M Street (now Paul Laurence Dunbar) High School, Washington, D.C., 1909–1918; was principal, Armstrong Manual Training School, Washington, D.C., 1918–1919; was dean, school of liberal arts,

Howard University, 1919–1920; and was dean, West Virginia Collegiate Institute, 1920–1922. He established the Association for the Study of Negro Life and History (ASNLH) in September 1915 and published *Journal of Negro History* under the auspices of the ASNLH in January 1916 (first issue). Woodson was an editor, 1916–1950. He established Associated Publishers in 1922. He established Negro History Week in 1926 (renamed Black History Month in 1976). He founded *Negro History Bulletin* in 1937 and was an editor from 1937 to 1950. Woodson was awarded the Spingarn Medal in 1926 and doctor of laws, West Virginia State College, in 1941. He died 3 April 1950 in Washington, D.C.

STEPHEN BURWOOD

See also Association for the Study of Negro Life and History and Journal of Negro History; Black History and Historiography; Greene, Lorenzo; Hughes, Langston; Hurston, Zora Neale

Selected Works

The African Background Outlined: Or Handbook for the Study of the Negro. 1936.
African Heroes and Heroines. 1939.
African Myths, Together with Proverbs: A Supplementary Reader Composed of Folk Tales from Various Parts of Africa. 1928.
A Century of Negro Migration. 1918.
Education of the Negro Prior to 1861. 1915.
Free Negro Heads of Families in the United States in 1830. 1924.
Free Negro Owners of Slaves in the United States in 1830. 1924.
The Mind of the Negro as Reflected in Letters Written during the Crisis, 1800–1860. 1926.
The Mis-Education of the Negro. 1933.
The Negro as a Business Man. 1929. (As coauthor, with J. H. Harmon and Arnett G. Lindsay.)
The Negro in Our History. 1922. (See also 16th ed., 1987.)
Negro Makers of History. 1928.
Negro Orators and Their Orations. (As ed. 1925.)
The Negro Professional Man and the Community: With Special Emphasis on the Physician and the Lawyer. 1934.
The Negro Wage Earner. 1930. (As coauthor, with Lorenzo J. Greene.)
The Rural Negro. 1930.
The Story of the Negro Retold. 1935.
The Works of Francis J. Grimké. 4 vols. 1942.

Further Reading

Durden, Robert F. *Carter G. Woodson: Father of African-American History*. Springfield, N.J.: Enslow, 1998.

Goggin, Jacqueline A. *Carter G. Woodson: A Life in Black History*. Baton Rouge: Louisiana University Press, 1993.

———. "Woodson, Carter G." In *American National Biography*, ed. John A. Garraty and Mark C. Carnes. New York: Oxford University Press, 1999, pp. 819–821.

Greene, Lorenzo J. *Working with Carter G. Woodson, the Father of Black History: A Diary, 1928–1930*. Baton Rouge: Louisiana State University Press, 1989.

———. *Selling Black History for Carter G. Woodson: A Diary, 1930–1933*. Columbia: University of Missouri Press, 1996.

Haskins, James, and Kathleen Benson. *Carter G. Woodson: The Man Who Put "Black" into American History*. Brookfield, Conn.: Millbrook, 2000.

Hine, Darlene Clark. "Carter G. Woodson, White Philanthropy, and Negro Historiography." *History Teacher*, 19, 1986.

Martin, Tony. "Carter G. Woodson and Marcus Garvey." *Negro History Bulletin*, 40, November–December 1977.

McKissack, Patricia, and Frederick McKissack. *Carter Godwin Woodson: The Father of Black History*. Berkeley Heights, N.J.: Enslow, 2002.

Meier, August, and Elliott Rudwick. "Carter G. Woodson as Entrepreneur: Laying the Foundation of a Historical Specialty." In *Black History and the Historical Profession, 1915–1980*. Urbana: University of Illinois Press, 1986, pp. 1–72.

Scally, Sister M. Anthony. *Carter G. Woodson: A Bio-Bibliography*. Westport, Conn.: Greenwood, 1985.

Work, Monroe Nathan

A little-known social scientist of the Jim Crow era, Monroe Work pioneered the collection of bibliographical and statistical data on the black experience. Trained at the University of Chicago in the early twentieth century, Work, after a brief flirtation with W. E. B. Du Bois's Niagara movement (the precursor of the National Association for the advancement of Colored People, NAACP), joined the staff of Tuskegee University in 1908. He quickly established himself as an integral part of Booker T. Washington's "Tuskegee machine," providing important statistical information about various aspects of the black experience and serving as a researcher and ghostwriter for Washington. Work was a major contributor to Washington's two-volume history, *Story of the Negro* (1909), and established the department of records and research at Tuskegee. He also published the highly regarded *Tuskegee Lynching Report*, which eventually appeared in more than 2,000 papers, and inaugurated the wide-ranging *Negro Yearbook*, published annually through the 1940s. One of the most widely circulated sources of the period, *Negro Yearbook* served as a model for subsequent compilations.

By the 1920s, the wide circulation of *Negro Yearbook* led to the expansion of his work and much-deserved recognition. Not only did Tuskegee's department of records and research expand from a staff of two to six, but Work received grants from various organizations. In 1921, he received a Carnegie Corporation grant of $8,500 over five years to complete a bibliography on blacks in the United States. Additional support materialized for the project in 1926. At the annual Founder's Day celebration at Tuskegee, Anson Phelps, director of the Phelps-Stokes Foundation, examined the work and suggested that the bibliography be extended to cover Africa. The following year, with support from the Phelps-Stokes foundation, Work traveled to several European capitals to collect bibliographical information. His work netted an additional 1,100 references for the study. The final product, *A Bibliography of the Negro in Africa and America* (1928), included more than 17,000 references in seventy-four chapters and represented one of the most comprehensive bibliographies on the African experience to date. In 1929, Work received a $400 award from the Harmon Foundation for his efforts with *Negro Yearbook* and *Bibliography of the Negro*.

In addition to bibliographical and statistical studies, Work also participated in a number of other projects. For example, he initiated a National Health Initiative in 1922 to highlight African Americans' health concerns. This project was later taken over by the federal government, eventually becoming an annual initiative known as the National Negro Health movement. Given the vast statistical resources available to him, Work also served as a consultant to various groups such as the National Urban League, Social Science Research Council, and the Southern Sociological Society. He also worked closely with programs to improve the agricultural prospects of farmers in Savannah, Georgia. Some people also give credit to several meetings between Work and the historian Carter G. Woodson for the establishment of the Association for the Study of Negro Life and History in 1915.

Work's contributions to the social sciences were innumerable. Both the University of Chicago and Howard University awarded him honorary degrees. His *Negro Yearbook*, *Bibliography of the Negro*, and *Tuskegee Lynching Report* provided accurate and reliable information about African Americans in the Jim Crow era. Most important, his work at Tuskegee, long considered the site of accomodationist black thought, suggests the complexity of Booker T. Washington's legacy as well as the role of black institutions as centers for the promotion and application of social science techniques to the black experience.

Biography

Monroe Nathan Work was born in Iredell County, North Carolina, in 1866. He was educated in Arkansas City, Kansas; at Chicago Theological Seminary, Chicago, Illinois (B.D., 1898); and at the University of Chicago (A.B., 1902; M.A., 1903). He taught at Georgia State Industrial College in Savannah from 1903 to 1907. He was director of records and research, Tuskegee Institute, Alabama, 1908–1941. Work died in Tuskegee, Alabama, on 2 May 1945.

STEPHEN G. HALL

See also Association for the Study of Negro Life and History and Journal of Negro History; Niagara Movement; Washington, Booker T.; Woodson, Carter G.

Selected Works

A Bibliography of the Negro in Africa and America. 1928.
Industrial Work of Tuskegee Graduates and Former Students during the Year 1910. 1911.
The Negro Migration. 1924.
The Negro Yearbook. 1913–1934.
Population and Occupation Trends of the Negro, 1890–1930. 1933.
Secret Societies and Factors in the Social and Economic Life of the Negro. 1917.

Further Reading

Capeci, Dominic. "W. E. B. Du Bois's Southern Front: Georgia's 'Race Men' and the Niagara Movement, 1905." *Georgia Historical Quarterly*, 83, 1999, pp. 479–507.

McMurry, Linda O. *Recorder of the Black Experience: A Biography of Monroe Nathan Work*. Baton Rouge: Louisiana State University Press, 1985.
Tucker, Mark. "You Can't Argue With the Facts: Monroe Nathan Work as Information Officer, Editor, and Biographer." *Libraries and Culture*, 26, 1991, pp. 151–168.
Williams, Vernon. "Monroe N Work's Contribution to Booker T. Washington's Nationalist Legacy." *Western Journal of Black Studies*, 21, 1997, pp. 85–91.

Workers' Dreadnought

Edited by Sylvia Pankhurst, a radical suffragette and socialist, *Workers' Dreadnought* was a Communist Party and trade union newspaper based in London, England.

The publication's first incarnation was as *The Woman's Dreadnought*, a free weekly newspaper that Pankhurst started with the East London Federation of the Suffragettes (ELFS) in March 1914. The name "dreadnought" reflected the fearlessness required of women fighting for the vote. The paper advocated and reported on the struggle for women's suffrage and the plight of workingwomen in general. Pankhurst was editor, writer, proofreader, and fund-raiser. Women from the East End section of London also wrote for the publication. Its circulation reached 20,000 soon after it was published. In July 1917 the name of the paper was changed to *Workers' Dreadnought*, and it became an organ of the Communist Party British Section of the Third International (CP-BSTI).

The *Dreadnought*'s closest tie to the Harlem Renaissance was the poet and journalist Claude McKay, who contributed to the newspaper as a writer and editor. McKay traveled to England in 1919 at the invitation of a European couple who admired his work. He settled in London and frequented the International Socialist Club, a meeting place for socialists, communists, and many radical foreigners. Influenced by the people he met and the lectures he heard at the club, McKay delved into reading the work of Karl Marx.

McKay admired Sylvia Pankhurst, who had lectured at the International Socialist Club. Unlike most socialists and communists of the time, Pankhurst realized that the struggle for racial equality was as important as the class struggle. McKay was invited to work at *Workers' Dreadnought* in 1920. He contributed poetry, reviews, and articles to the publication. His topics included international communism, the race situation in the United States, British imperialism, and the use of socialism as a link between white and black workers. McKay also wrote articles about his experiences in London for African American newspapers such as *Negro World*.

At Pankhurst's direction, McKay covered the dock area in London and reviewed foreign-press stories for articles of interest to the *Dreadnought*'s readers. McKay often used pseudonyms for his work in the *Dreadnought*. He was cautious because police suspicions were aroused by Pankhurst's radical views and the paper's subject matter. This police scrutiny came to a head in 1920, after the paper published an English sailor's article criticizing the Royal Navy, voicing enlisted sailors' dissatisfaction with low pay, and supporting the working-class struggle. Police raided the *Dreadnought*'s offices, and McKay narrowly avoided arrest by denying any involvement with the paper. Pankhurst was arrested, charged with and tried for sedition, and sentenced to six months in jail.

The *Dreadnought*'s association with the Communist Party ended in 1921, and Pankhurst was expelled from the party because the paper was less focused on the Communist Party and trade unions and more concerned with literary criticism and poetry as well as theoretical writing. After this break with the Communist Party, Pankhurst received funding from former suffragette colleagues for the publication of the *Dreadnought*. The paper continued publication until 1924.

McKay's involvement with *Workers' Dreadnought* ended when he returned to the United States early in 1921. Although he traveled to Russia in 1922, he was disillusioned by the racism of the majority of communist and socialist groups in England. Pankhurst campaigned for British support in defeating fascist Italy's invasion of Ethiopia in 1935. She met the Ethiopian emperor Haile Selassie several times and interviewed him for her newspaper *New Times and Ethiopia News*. Pankhurst lived in Ethiopia until her death in 1960.

HEATHER MARTIN

See also Communist Party; McKay, Claude

Further Reading

Cooper, Wayne F. *Claude McKay: Rebel Sojourner in the Harlem Renaissance—A Biography*. Baton Rouge: Louisiana State University Press, 1987.

Cooper, Wayne F., and Robert C. Reinder. "A Black Briton Comes 'Home': Claude McKay in England, 1920." *Race*, 9, November 1970.

LeSeur, Geta. "Claude McKay's Marxism." In *The Harlem Renaissance: Revaluations*, ed. Amritjit Singh, William S. Shiver, and Stanley Brodwin. New York: Garland, 1989.

McKay, Claude. *A Long Way From Home*. New York: Arno, 1969.

Pankhurst, Richard, and E. Sylvia Pankhurst. *Sylvia Pankhurst, Artist and Crusader: An Intimate Portrait*. New York: Paddington, 1979.

Romero, Patricia W. *E. Sylvia Pankhurst: Portrait of a Radical*. New Haven, Conn.: Yale University Press, 1987.

Winslow, Barbara. *Sylvia Pankhurst: Sexual Politics and Political Activism*. New York: St. Martin's, 1996.

Works Progress Administration

The Works Progress Administration (WPA), an employment relief agency, began during the Great Depression in 1935 as part of Franklin Delano Roosevelt's New Deal and was formally ended in 1942 by presidential proclamation. WPA was headed by Harry Hopkins, a former social worker; its philosophy was to create jobs for the unemployed by supporting public works including the arts and cultural programs. Roosevelt maintained that employment, rather than direct financial relief, would lift people's spirits and ultimately do more for the country's overall good. WPA was the largest and most expensive of the New Deal agencies; it funded a variety of programs including malaria control; street construction; the destruction of slums; tree planting; and construction of schools, parks, bridges, and hospitals. It is, however, probably best known for Federal Project Number One, an organization made up of the Federal Arts Project, the Federal Theater Project, the Federal Music Project, the Federal Writers Project, and the Historical Records Survey.

The Federal Arts Project (FAP) encompassed a wide range of art forms including photography, sculpture, painting, architecture, set design, and graphic arts. Photographers (such as Sid Grossman, in his *Harlem* series) documented local life; graphic artists made posters for WPA offices, theater productions, art exhibits, and health and educational programs; sculptors created monuments for parks and other recreational facilities; and painters made murals in schools, hospitals, airports, and other public buildings. Other artists were employed as teachers in community centers, classrooms, art galleries, and newly created art centers. Several later famous artists, like Jacob Lawrence and Jackson Pollock, were sustained during the Depression by FAP.

Like FAP, the Federal Music Project (FMP) employed artists as music teachers in rural and urban areas, providing free music instruction, history, and appreciation to children and adults. Orchestras, bands, operas, and chamber music groups were organized in cities that before WPA had none. Other employees traveled the country recording examples of American folk music—spirituals, bluegrass, ballads—or cataloged the life, work, and performances of hundreds of composers for the Index of American Composers. Along with the index, FMP created the Composers Forum Laboratory, inviting composers to submit new pieces, which, if selected, would be rehearsed and performed. After a performance, the composer would invite comments and questions from the audience.

FMP sustained musicians who were suffering not only because of the Great Depression but also because of increased competition from radio. Likewise, the Federal Theater Project (FTP) sustained an art form that was under siege from the Depression, radio, and the rise of cinema. It used radio to introduce the public to new playwrights in *Federal Theater of the Air*, and it brought live theater, circuses, puppet shows, and dance performances to millions of people who would otherwise not have been able to afford them. In some cases, WPA theaters were built; in others. WPA workers formed traveling troupes. Additionally, FTP financed productions in Yiddish, French, German, Italian, and Spanish, as well as sixteen African American theater units. One of the more noteworthy productions by the African American theater in Harlem set an adaptation of Shakespeare's *Macbeth* in Haiti.

Like these other projects, the Federal Writers' Project (FWP) also employed soon-to-be successful artists including Arna Bontemps, Ralph Ellison, Robert Hayden, Langston Hughes, Zora Neale Hurston, Margaret Walker, and Richard Wright. Many of them worked on the American Guide Series, a series of guidebooks replete with collections of oral history, folklore, biographies, and essays about local life and ethnological history, as well as the more expected descriptions of historic and tourist sites. The 150-volume Life in America series chronicled the history of different ethnic groups in the United States. For the American Life History Interviews, employees collected the oral histories of former slaves, black and white farmers in the South, Jewish garment workers, and Chicago steel miners, among others. Other products of the Federal Writers' Project include collections of folklore from the bayou country, labor histories, and analyses of the influence of African arts and languages on American culture.

The Historical Records Survey was originally created under the auspices of the Federal Writers' Project, but in 1936 it became an independent part of the Federal One Project. Workers cataloged inventories of local government records—census returns, school records, and maps—as well as newspapers, church records, cemetery burials, and any manuscripts that could be of historical significance to the area. Their work initiated a flurry of microfilming across the country and has proved invaluable to historians as well as genealogists.

The Federal One projects supported and encouraged professional artists, funded the development of a national art rooted in local culture, and put art "within reach" of the public. Critics on the left, however, charged the organization with censorship (objectionable material was edited from guidebooks, and plays deemed inappropriate were banned). Critics on the right called the programs politically biased and accused them of "boondoggling"—wasting time or money on unnecessary projects. Toward the end of the 1930s, the House Committee to Investigate Un-American Activities went further, formally inquiring into the WPA's communist activity. In 1939, the House Appropriations Committee, objecting to governmental support of plays with radical messages, barred future use of WPA funds for the theater activities of the FTP. The other four appendages survived for a few more years, but the full-employment economy of World War II put a definitive end to the Works Progress Administration. Its legacy, however, continues to be felt in programs such as the National Endowment for the Arts.

VALARIE MOSES

See also Bontemps, Arna; Ellison, Ralph; Federal Programs; Federal Writers' Project; Hayden, Robert; Hughes, Langston; Hurston, Zora Neale; Lawrence, Jacob; New Deal; Walker, Margaret; Wright, Richard

Further Reading

Bloxom, Marguerite D. *Pickaxe and Pencil: References for the Study of the WPA*. Washington, D.C.: Library of Congress, 1982.

Bold, Christine. *The WPA Guides Mapping America*. Jackson: University Press of Mississippi, 1999.

Chafe, William H., ed. *The Achievement of American Liberalism: The New Deal and Its Legacies*. New York: Columbia University Press, 2003.

Flanagan, Hallie. *Arena*. New York: Duell, Sloan, and Pearce, 1940.

Gumbo Ya-Ya. Boston, Mass.: Houghton Mifflin, 1945.

Hobson, Archie. *Remembering America: A Sampler of the WPA American Guide Series*. New York: Columbia University Press, 1985.

Investigation and Study of the Works Progress Administration: Hearings before the Subcommittee of the Committee on Appropriations. Washington, D.C.: U.S. Government Printing Office, 1939–1940.

Leuchtenberg, William E. *Franklin D. Roosevelt and the New Deal*. New York: Harper and Row, 1963.

Mangione, Jerre. *The Dream and the Deal: The Federal Writers' Project, 1935–1943*. Boston, Mass.: Little, Brown, 1972.

McKinzie, Richard D. *The New Deal for Artists*. Princeton, N.J.: Princeton University Press, 1973.

O'Connor, Francis V., ed. *Art for the Millions: Essays from the 1930s by Artists and Administrators of the WPA Federal Arts Project*. Greenwich, Conn.: New York Graphic Society, 1973.

These Are Our Lives. Chapel Hill: University of North Carolina, 1939.

Weisberger, Bernard A., ed. *The WPA Guide to America: The Best of 1930s America as Seen by the Federal Writers' Project*. New York: Pantheon, 1985.

White, John Franklin. *Art in Action: American Art Centers and the New Deal*. Metuchen, N.J.: Scarecrow, 1987.

World War I

The involvement of the United States in World War I had an enormous impact on African Americans and on Harlem and influenced a number of developments in African American culture and the Harlem Renaissance. The war divided the African American community, especially the leadership. It certainly affected the lives and the men and women who went to war as well as those who remained behind, and it intensified issues of race and race relations and precipitated racial violence.

From the beginning, the war generated conflict among African Americans regarding their appropriate response to it. Most—including leaders like Robert

Moton, Emmett J. Scott, the National Association for the Advancement of Colored People (NAACP), and W. E. B. Du Bois—urged blacks to set aside their racial grievances and rally behind the flag. Du Bois enunciated this position most clearly in July 1918 in an essay in *The Crisis*: "Let us, while this war lasts, forget our special grievances and close our ranks shoulder to shoulder with our own white fellow citizens and the allied nations that are fighting for democracy." Other African Americans, especially those affiliated with the socialist left, disagreed, and argued that leaders who ignored racism and oppression in order to embrace patriotism and the war were betraying their race. One element of this group, the "new crowd Negroes," included young radicals like Hubert Harrison, Wilfred A. Domingo, A. Philip Randolph, and Chandler Owen. Writing in *The Messenger* (May–June 1919), Randolph asserted that Du Bois's "close ranks" essay would "rank in shame and reeking disgrace with the 'Atlanta Compromise' speech of Booker T. Washington."

Among the issues that concerned African Americans was the policy of the U.S. armed forces to assign black troops to segregated units, and to place these segregated units under white officers. The matter of segregated units was not seriously addressed, but early in the war the NAACP lobbied to provide training for African American officers. Joel Spingarn led the struggle, which resulted in the establishment of a segregated officers' training camp at Fort Des Moines, Iowa. Because the camp was segregated, this victory was bittersweet and generated opposition from many of the more militant black leaders; but the NAACP and Du Bois endorsed it as a necessary evil. More

Post School, Thirty-fifth Division, Commercy, Meuse, France, 7 February 1919. (Brown Brothers.)

significantly, in October 1917—in a move generally applauded in the black community—the secretary of war appointed Emmett J. Scott as special assistant and confidential adviser in matters affecting the interests of African American troops.

All together, 367,000 African Americans served in the U.S. armed forces during the war. Most served with the Army; African Americans were excluded from the Marines and were restricted to menial jobs in the Navy. Black troops faced discrimination during their military training. Most training facilities were in the South, and most southern communities did not welcome the presence of black trainees. Friction was widespread. The most serious incident occurred in Houston in August 1917: Violence erupted when black troops from the Twenty-fourth Infantry, inflamed by news of riots in East St. Louis and by ongoing discrimination in Houston, took up their weapons and marched on the city, killing nineteen people, including four black soldiers and four local police officers. In the aftermath of this episode, nineteen black soldiers were executed and ninety-one received prison sentences. Scores of less violent incidents occurred. One fairly typical example involved the Fifteenth New York Infantry (which became the 369th Infantry): In October 1917, members of this unit became involved in an altercation in Spartanburg, South Carolina. The incident began when Noble Sissle, the drum major of the infantry band, was humiliated and then assaulted in a downtown hotel. The bandmaster, Lieutenant James R. Europe, restored order; later that evening, however, the base commander barely averted an armed assault on the town like the one that had taken place in Houston. To prevent further violence, the unit was quickly shipped overseas.

In France, black troops faced a mixed reception. Mostly they were well received by the French—an experience that contrasted sharply with their experiences in the United States. Although some black troops saw combat, many others were frustrated by being assigned to work crews, construction crews, or stevedore battalions. Nevertheless, a number of African American units participated in combat, including the 369th, 370th, 371st, and 372nd U.S. infantry regiments. Perhaps the most notable was the 369th, called the "Hell Fighters" by the Germans. The French awarded the entire unit the Croix de Guerre for its action at Maison-en-Champagne, and 171 individuals received the Croix de Guerre and the Legion of Honor for exceptional gallantry in action.

In spite of their military record, African American troops could not escape controversy. Accusations circulated that African American troops in France were continually involved in rapes and attempted rapes, that the relative absence of discrimination in France threatened the social structure of the United States, and that the relationships African American men had enjoyed with Frenchwomen would lead to rape and violence in the United States. Another problem was the systematic removal of black officers from most black units, and the discrimination that black troops faced in terms of food, facilities, recreation, and entertainment. The problems facing black officers began as early as 1917, when Colonel Charles Young, the highest-ranking African American in the military, was removed from the service. As the war came to an end, many black officers were removed from their commands, and white officers began denigrating black troops as rapists and cowards.

In December 1918, Robert Moton traveled to France to investigate the charges against black troops and to assess the conditions that black soldiers faced in France. He found that the accusations of rape were seriously exaggerated and that the accusations of cowardice were untrue. Moton himself generated controversy, however, when he publicly urged blacks to behave well when they returned to the United States and, according to some reports, warned them that when they returned home they should not expect the freedom they had enjoyed in France. Du Bois also investigated the treatment of black troops in France in the months following the war; he presented his findings in The Crisis in May 1919. He reported on the allegations of misconduct made by white officers and white politicians and exposed the infamous "Secret Information Concerning Black American Troops," reportedly circulated in France by the American military command, warning that French people's attitude toward blacks was a threat to the American social order. Like Moton, Du Bois found the charges of rape among black troops greatly exaggerated. He pushed his investigation further, however, and documented biased reporting of black troops; he concluded that blacks were regularly subjected to racist white officers and noncommissioned officers, that they had been poorly led, and that they had frequently been sent into battle with inadequate equipment. Du Bois castigated Moton for not investigating the depth of discrimination in the American military in France, and he attacked Emmett J. Scott for largely ignoring these problems.

The reception of black troops on their return to the United States was also mixed. Most blacks were proud of their service and expected a hero's welcome. This certainly happened in New York, where the 369th paraded up Fifth Avenue to Harlem to the cheers of the throngs who lined the route. Homecoming celebrations such as this parade honored black soldiers and reinforced their accomplishment. However, such celebrations were often overshadowed by violence and racism. The "red summer" of 1919, with its race riots and lynchings, convinced many people that military service had changed nothing—that racial conditions were the same or had become even worse. If there was change, it was not in the greater acceptance of blacks by whites, but in the growing impatience and militancy among blacks, especially those who had served in France. This strengthened pride and determination to force change was embodied in the New Negro movement of the postwar years. It was expressed by the young radicals who had opposed the war, it was found in the nationalist movement established by Marcus Garvey, and it was enunciated most powerfully by the poet Claude McKay who responded to the mob violence of 1919 with the warning "If we must die . . . Like men we'll face the murderous, cowardly pack,/Pressed to the wall, dying, but fighting back!" Du Bois, too, dropped his "close ranks" philosophy; in May 1919, he wrote an essay for *The Crisis*— "Returning Soldiers"—in which he warned:

> *We return.*
>
> *We return from fighting.*
>
> *We return fighting.*
>
> Make way for Democracy! We saved it in France, and by the great Jehovah, we will save it in the United States of America, or know the reason why.

The war also had a significant social and cultural impact on African Americans. The "black migration" that had begun before the war accelerated as thousands of blacks left the rural South for jobs in urban industry. This movement continued through the 1920s, spreading the black population into the North, and to a lesser extent into the West, and urbanizing African Americans. The war, and especially the racial pride and black militancy that came out of the war, created an intellectual and cultural environment that gave rise to the Harlem Renaissance. Although few artists associated with the renaissance had served in the military during the war, and although the war produced no great African American war novel, there was a connection between the war and the art of the period. The black musicians who accompanied James Reese Europe and the 369th Infantry are credited with popularizing jazz in France. The musicians from other African American military bands also brought their music to the French and the British. The war also played a small part in several African American novels. Jake, the main character in Claude McKay's *Home to Harlem*, had volunteered for military service but deserted when he became frustrated with his assignment to a labor battalion in France; and the war altered the lives of Peter Bye and several other characters in Jessie Redmon Fauset's novel *There Is Confusion*.

Finally, the war helped internationalize African American consciousness, at least among political and intellectual leaders. Du Bois, Garvey, and others saw the war and the peace conference that followed as an opportunity to end colonialism in Africa; although this effort failed, it did revitalize the pan-African movement. The Bolshevik revolution also internationalized politics, especially among black radicals, and influenced McKay, Langston Hughes, Paul Robeson, and many other black writers and artists. Even for those less politically inclined, Europe especially, but Africa, the Caribbean, and Latin America as well, became part of the African American world.

Cary D. Wintz

See also Domingo, Wilfred Adolphus; Du Bois, W. E. B.; Europe, James Reese; Fauset, Jessie Redmon; Fifteenth Infantry; Garvey, Marcus; Great Migration; Harrison, Hubert; Home to Harlem; Hughes, Langston; McKay, Claude; Moton, Robert Russa; National Association for the Advancement of Colored People; New Negro Movement; Owen, Chandler; Pan-Africanism; Randolph, A. Philip; Riots: 2—Red Summer of 1919; Robeson, Paul; Scott, Emmett Jay; Sissle, Noble; Spingarn, Joel; There Is Confusion

Further Reading

Anderson, Jervis. *This Was Harlem: 1900–1950*. New York: Farrar Straus and Giroux, 1981. (See also Berkeley: University of California Press, 1972.)

Christian, Garna L. *Black Soldiers in Jim Crow Texas, 1899–1917*. College Station: Texas A&M University Press, 1995.

Franklin, John Hope, and Alfred Moss. *From Slavery to Freedom: A History of African Americans*, 8th ed. New York: McGraw-Hill, 2000.

Harris, Will. *The Hellfighters of Harlem: African-American Soldiers Who Fought for the Right to Fight for Their Country*. New York: Carroll and Graf, 2002.

James, Winston. *Holding Aloft the Banner of Ethiopia: Caribbean Radicalism in Early Twentieth Century America*. London: Verso, 1998.

Johnson, James Weldon. *Black Manhattan*. New York: Da Capo, 1991. (Originally published 1930.)

Jordan, William G. *Black Newspapers and America's War for Democracy, 1914–1920*. Chapel Hill: University of North Carolina Press, 2001.

Lewis, David Levering. *W. E. B. Du Bois: Biography of a Race, 1868–1919*. New York: Holt, 1993.

Wright, Louis T.

The physician, hospital administrator, and surgeon Louis Tompkins Wright was born in Georgia in 1891. His father—who died when Wright was four years old—was a doctor, a graduate of Meharry Medical School (1881), and may have inspired Wright's interest in medicine. Wright's stepfather, William Fletcher Penn, whom his mother married in 1899, was also a doctor; Penn nurtured Wright in academic pursuits and encouraged him to pursue medicine.

During his early education in Atlanta, Wright excelled in science, mathematics, and English. In 1911 he graduated from Clark University in Atlanta; in the autumn of 1911 he entered Harvard Medical School, from which he would graduate cum laude, fourth in his class, in 1915. He held an internship at the Freedmen's Hospital in Washington, D.C., from 1 July 1915 to 30 June 1916.

On 18 August 1918, he entered active duty with the U.S. Army as a first lieutenant in the Medical Reserve Corps. While serving in France, he was wounded in a gas attack; as a result, he was discharged from combat service and appointed an officer in charge of surgical wards at Field Hospital 366, Ninety-second Division. Wright also served as a member of the divisional blood transfusion team. He was promoted to captain on 11 November 1918. He received the Purple Heart and was discharged on 2 April 1919.

In 1919, he worked on the venereal diseases staff in New York City's department of health. Also in 1919, the board of Harlem General Hospital agreed to allow African Americans to serve as visiting surgeons and physicians. Wright was considered for such a position and four white physicians resigned in protest, even though his assignment was only as clinical assistant to the outpatient department. He was promoted to assistant adjutant visiting surgeon at Harlem General Hospital in June 1926, then to surgical director in August 1939. He was also the first African American police surgeon in New York City, a position he took in 1929.

Wright pursued professional excellence and interracial harmony through various means, such as working with the National Association for the Advancement of Colored People (NAACP) and establishing medical societies throughout New York's hospital community. In the New York medical community, Wright withdrew from the all-black North Harlem Medical society. He formed the Manhattan Medical Society in 1930.

Wright was the first African American doctor to be appointed to the staff of a hospital in New York City.

Louis T. Wright, c. 1930–1940. (Library of Congress.)

Over the course of his career, he published more than eighty papers. Some of his research methods broadened the medical community's understanding of the transmission of infectious diseases, racial bias medical testing, and bone-setting techniques.

Biography

Louis Tompkins Wright was born to Ceah Ketcham and Lulu Thompson Wright in La Grange, Georgia, on 23 July 1891. In 1911 he received a B.A. from Clark University, Atlanta, Georgia. In 1915, he graduated from Harvard Medical School. After an internship at Freedman's Hospital, Washington, D.C., he practiced with his stepfather, Dr. William F. Penn, in Atlanta. In 1917 Wright was commissioned as a first lieutenant in the Medical Physicians Reserve Corps of the U.S. Army and entered the training camp for medical officers at Fort Des Moines, Iowa; he actively served in the Army during World War I. In May 1918, he married Corinne M. Cooke; they had two children (Jane Cooke and Barbara Penn Wright). In May 1919, he began working in the state surgical clinic at Harlem General Hospital, the first African American to be appointed to a hospital staff in New York. In 1929, he was appointed surgeon of the police department of New York City. In 1930, he founded Manhattan Medical Society. From 1932 to 1939, he served as president of Crisis Publishing Company. He was elected a fellow of the American College of Surgeons, 1934; was chairman of the board of directors of the National Association for the Advancement of Colored People (NAACP), 1935–1952; founded Harlem Surgical Society, 1937; and received an honorary doctor of science degree from Clark University, 1938. He was certified by the American Board of Surgery, 1939; awarded the NAACP's Spingarn Medal, 1940; and elected a fellow of the New York Surgical Society, 1948. The Louis T. Wright Library of Harlem Hospital Dinner Testimonial was held in April 1952. Wright died of a heart attack on 8 October 1952, at age sixty-one.

IDA JONES

See also Harlem General Hospital; Spingarn Medal

Further Reading

Cobb, W. Montague. "Louis Tompkins Wright, 1891–1952." *Negro History Bulletin*, 16, May 1953, pp. 170, 178–180.

Contemporary Black Biography, Vol. 4. Detroit, Mich.: Gale Research, 1993.

"Dr. Wright Honored." *Crisis*, 59, June–July 1952, pp. 376–377.

Hayden, Robert C. *Mr. Harlem Hospital: Dr. Louis T. Wright—A Biography*. Littleton, Mass.: Tapestry, 2003.

Logan, Rayford W., and Michael R. Winston, eds. *Dictionary of American Negro Biography*. New York: Norton, 1982.

"Medical Family." *Ebony*, 6, January 1951, pp. 71–74.

"Miracle Drug." *Ebony*, 4, June 1949, pp. 13–17.

"NAACP Mourns Dr. Louis T. Wright." *Crisis*, 59, November 1952, pp. 548–550.

Ovington, Mary White. *Portraits of Color*. New York: Viking, 1927.

Smith, Jessie Carney, ed. *Notable Black American Men*. Farmington Hills, Mich.: Gale Research, 1999.

Wilkins, Roy. "Louis T. Wright: Fighters for Equality and Excellence." *Crisis*, 70, May 1963, pp. 261–269.

Who's Who among African Americans, 1996–1997, 9th ed. Detroit, Mich.: Gale Research, 1996.

Wright, Richard

Richard Wright rose from poverty on a plantation outside Natchez, Mississippi, to become one of the major writers of the twentieth century, one of the first internationally celebrated black American authors, and an early African American best-selling novelist. Wright's success, like his politics, offered a radical break with the past, and his work is often viewed as the fulcrum on which African American literature turned. According to Gates (1993), "If one had to identify the single most influential shaping force in modern Black literary history, one would probably have to point to Wright and the publication of *Native Son*."

Throughout his youth, Wright endured deprivation and racism. His father abandoned the family when Wright was five years old, and for the next ten years he was raised by a series of family members in various places in Mississippi and Arkansas. Eventually he graduated from high school, but with only a ninth-grade education.

Moving to Memphis in 1925, Wright supported himself through a series of menial jobs in which he regularly encountered the humiliation and hatred that characterized the racially divided South—experiences he would later write of in his autobiography, *Black Boy* (1945). By the time Wright moved to Chicago in 1928 and took a job with the postal service, he had developed a love of books and was ready to begin his career as a professional writer. He joined the John Reed Club in 1933 and became a member of the Communist Party; consequently, he published radical poetry in left-wing journals such as *Left Front*, *Anvil*, *Midland Left*, and Mike Gold's *New Masses*. Wright was increasingly influenced by Marxist ideology, and in his "Blueprint for Negro Writing" he emphasized the need for a more aggressive political literature that would directly address the debilitating effects of racism on the black psyche. Wright believed that Negro writers of the past had been merely "prim and decorous ambassadors who went a-begging to white America . . . dressed in the knee-pants of servility" ("Negro," 1937) and that contemporary black writers should use their "words as weapons" in the desperate struggle for racial equality. His first novel, *Lawd, Today!* (published posthumously), attempted to address these issues by combining elements of a bleak urban naturalism with experimental modernist structures that highlighted the Negro's fundamental position as an outsider in mainstream American society. Detailing the events of one day in the life of black postal workers, Wright developed ironic and penetrating contrasts between the indignities suffered by his struggling black protagonists and the patriotic aphorisms espoused by a society honoring Lincoln's birthday.

In 1937, Wright moved to Harlem, became involved with the New York Writers' Project, worked as editor of the communist newspaper *Daily Worker*, and continued to write short stories, essays, and poems. In 1938, Wright's first major work, *Uncle Tom's Children*, a collection of four novellas, appeared to much acclaim (a fifth story, the communist-inspired "Bright and Morning Star," was added in a subsequent edition). Set in the South, these stories dramatized the harsh, often violent, conditions blacks were forced to endure in a society pervaded by fear and suspicion. Despite his attempt to write a radical social document that would expose the brutal and debilitating effects of racism, however, Wright found that he had written such a lyrical work that "even bankers' daughters could read and weep and feel good about" it ("How Bigger Was Born," 1940).

His *Native Son* (1940) was a phenomenal success, and its sales were sustained by a white middle-class readership that kept it perennially in the Book-of-the-Month Club—a surprising outcome, considering the novel's excoriation of the injustices imposed on blacks through institutionalized white power structures. *Native Son* made Wright a celebrity status; and the sales of this book and his next—*Black Boy* (1945)—allowed

Wright to make a living by writing. In the character Bigger Thomas in *Native Son*, Wright also discovered new truths about social reality, for he came to realize the ubiquity of Bigger, that "there were literally millions of him, everywhere," whites as well as blacks ("How Bigger Was Born," 1940). This realization led to Wright's dissatisfaction with and ultimate rejection of Marxist ideology; he considered it overly dogmatic and said that it "had oversimplified the experience of those they sought to lead" and as a result "had missed the meaning of the lives of the masses" by conceiving of them in "too abstract a manner" (*Black Boy*).

Wright eventually rejected the United States as well; in 1947 he moved permanently to France. Under the influence of French existentialism, especially the works of Albert Camus, Wright explored further the conditions of human reality as a cosmic malaise. In works such as *The Outsider* (1953) and the posthumously published *Eight Men* (1961), Wright attempted to answer the existential question "What is man?" by reaffirming the conscientious act of moral idealism. As Cross Damon, the hero of *The Outsider*, puts it, "Existence was not perpetrated in malice or benevolence,

Richard Wright, photographed by Carl Van Vechten, 1939. (Library of Congress.)

but simply is, and the end of our thinking is that here we are and what can we make of it."

Wright's life as an expatriate led him to become "a citizen of the world" (Fabre 1993), In his last works, he not only moved away from Marxist ideology and the Marxists' concern with the proletariat, but he also adopted a more universal approach to the problems of identity and origins outside of the boundaries of race and nationality. Regardless of external circumstances, Wright's characters contain a vital spark of transcendent selfhood that, despite social and political oppression, offers to determined individuals a vision of hope and possibility. Thus Wright's work can be seen as the fruition of a radical militant literature that had its inception in works of the Harlem Renaissance such as Claude McKay's "If We Must Die." Brutal, brooding, and foreboding, Wright's work has been described (Gates 1993) as possessing "an artistry, penetration of thought, and sheer emotional power that places it into the front rank of American fiction."

Biography

Richard Nathaniel Wright was born 4 September 1908 near Natchez, Mississippi. He studied at schools in Natchez; Memphis, Tennessee; and West Helena, Arkansas. He graduated in Jackson, Mississippi, in 1925. That year he relocated to Memphis, where he worked at a series of menial jobs. In 1928, he moved to Chicago and worked for the postal service. Between 1930 and 1934, he began writing; joined the John Reed Club and the Communist Party; and published radical poetry in left-wing journals. Wright joined the editorial board of *Left Front* in 1934. He worked for the Federal Writers' Project, researching the history of blacks in Chicago, and participated in the Federal Theater Project, in 1935–1936. In 1937, Wright moved to Harlem, became editor of *Daily Worker*, and joined the New York Federal Writers' Project. He joined the editorial board of *New Masses* in 1938–1939. In Paris, he helped found the journal *Présence Africaine* in 1948. Wright played Bigger Thomas in a screen version of his book *Native Son* in 1949. He was involved with the Congress for Cultural Freedom in 1958. Wright was awarded a Guggenheim Fellowship in1939 and NAACP's Spingarn Medal in 1941. Richard Wright died in Paris on 28 November 1960.

RANDALL SHAWN WILHELM

See also Federal Writers' Project; Literature: 4—Fiction; New Masses, The; Springarn Medal

Selected Works

American Hunger. 1977.
Black Boy: A Record of Childhood and Youth. 1945.
Black Power: A Record of Reactions in a Land of Pathos. 1954.
Eight Men. 1961.
Lawd Today! 1963.
The Long Dream. 1958.
Native Son. 1940.
The Outsider. 1953.
Pagan Spain. 1957.
Savage Holiday. 1954.
Twelve Million Black Voices: A Folk History of the Negro in the United States. 1942.
Uncle Tom's Children: Four Novellas. 1938.
White Man, Listen! 1957.

Further Reading

Adell, Sandra. "Richard Wright's The Outsider and the Kierkegaardian Concept of Dread." *Comparative Literature Studies*, 28, Fall 1991, pp. 379–395.

Fabre, Michael. *The Unfinished Quest of Richard Wright*, trans. Isabel Barzun, 2nd ed. Urbana: University of Illinois Press, 1993.

Gates, Henry Louis, Jr., and K. A. Appiah, eds. *Richard Wright: Critical Perspectives Past and Present*. New York: Amistad, 1993.

Joyce, Joyce Ann. *Richard Wright's Art of Tragedy*. Iowa City: University of Iowa Press, 1986.

Kinnamon, Keneth, ed. *New Essays on Native Son*. Cambridge: Cambridge University Press, 1990.

Macksey, Richard, and Frank E. Moorer, eds. *Richard Wright: A Collection of Critical Essays*. Englewood Cliffs, N.J.: Prentice-Hall, 1984.

Miller, Eugene A. *Voice of a Native Son: The Poetics of Richard Wright*. Jackson: University of Mississippi Press, 1990.

Trotman, C. James. *Richard Wright: Myths and Realities*. New York: Garland, 1988.

Walker, Robbie-Jean. *Richard Wright, Demonic Genius: A Portrait of the Man, a Critical Look at His Work*. New York: Warner–Amistad, 1988.

Yerby, Frank

Few writers have received such a mixed response to their work as Frank Yerby. He became famous with his first novel, *The Foxes of Harrow* (1946), which sold 2 million copies and was widely compared to Margaret Mitchell's *Gone with the Wind* (1936); all together, his thirty-three novels sold more than 55 million copies. His novels were appreciated not only in the United States but also—and possibly more so—overseas; Yerby was particularly popular in Germany. Like many other black writers of the 1940s and 1950s, however, Yerby was sometimes criticized for ignoring the black experience in his novels; moreover, despite his reputation as a writer of historical fiction, and despite the fact that he helped deconstruct myths about the antebellum South, he was sometimes grouped with romance writers. Still, regardless of this criticism, and regardless of how the critics felt about the quality of his work, they all seemed to agree that Yerby's attention to historical detail was unmatched. Furthermore, he did sometimes depict the horrors of slavery and the appalling lives of slaves (even in *The Foxes of Harrow*, which he claimed to have written for the popular market, there is more than one attack on slavery as an institution), although on the whole his books containing such descriptions did not sell well.

Yerby was the son of Rufus G. Yerby and Whilemena Smythe Yerby. Yerby's father was an itinerant hotel doorman; it was his mother who was the primary caregiver for Yerby, his sister, and his two brothers. Yerby once remarked that, as a child, he would rather read than eat. He married Flora Helen Claire Williams on 1 March 1941 in New Orleans, Louisiana; they had four children (Jacques Loring, Nikki Ethlyn, Faune Ellena,

and Jan Keath) but were later divorced. In 1952, Yerby married Blanca Calle-Perez in Spain. Yerby taught for several years. During World War II, he contributed to the war effort by working at the Ford Motor Company in Detroit, Michigan, and at Cohen Fairchild Aircraft on Long Island. It was during this time that he wrote *The Foxes of Harrow*, his best-known work.

Typically, a novel by Yerby is set in an earlier historical period; has a strong hero; has a fast-paced plot filled with action, romantic intrigue, and violence; and includes a large cast of characters from diverse ethnic backgrounds. He often drew on his own experiences for inspiration. For example, while he was working for the Federal Writers' Project he joined a quasi-Islamic religious cult to obtain information about religious practices; years later, he wrote his acclaimed novel *The Dahomean* (1971). Some critics have described Yerby's characters as one-dimensional, but in general the only truly stock or stereotyped characters in Yerby's novels are the Caucasians.

Yerby includes some politically tinged themes, but he was not really a political writer. He once stated: "The novelist hasn't any right to inflict on the public his private ideas on politics, religion, or race. If he wants to preach, he should go on the pulpit." Yerby also felt strongly that writing—a craft he loved—should not become propaganda for any political cause. This philosophy may explain why he wrote escapist historical stories instead of chronicling the African American experience of his time. It cannot be denied, though, that Yerby was criticized for avoiding the civil rights movement, and that at times he insisted he was not black.

Because of the racism he experienced in the United States, Yerby became an expatriate in Madrid in 1955.

Frank Yerby. (Library of Congress.)

There, he led an apparently carefree life devoted to automobile racing and to frequenting beaches, but he also wrote the bulk of his work in Spain. In exile, Yerby continued to arouse controversy, partly because of his lifestyle and partly because of his work. Relatively recently, Yerby has gradually achieved more recognition as a literary figure—the first African American writer to produce a series of best-sellers—and he has come to be included in more and more books and articles about African American culture.

Yerby died of heart failure in Madrid, Spain, on 29 November 1991; as he was dying, he asked his wife to keep his death a secret for several weeks.

Biography

Frank Garvin Yerby was born on 5 September 1916 in Augusta, Georgia. He studied at Haines Institute in Augusta; Paine College (A.B. 1937); and Fisk University (M.A, 1938). He did postgraduate study at the University of Chicago. Yerby worked on the Federal Writers' Project of WPA. He taught at Florida Agricultural and Mechanical College, Tallahassee, Florida, from 1939 to 1940 and at Southern University, Baton

Rouge, Louisiana, from 1940 to 1941. During World War II he worked at Ford Motor Company in Detroit, Michigan, and at Cohen Fairchild Aircraft in Long Island. He received the O. Henry award for a first published short story for "Health Card" (1944). *The Foxes of Harrow* was made into a film, translated into twelve languages, and published in Britain, New Zealand, and Australia. *The Golden Hawk* (1948) also was made into a film. Yerby exiled himself in Madrid, Spain, in 1955 and died there on 29 November 1991.

ELLEN M. TSAGARIS

See also Federal Programs; Federal Writers' Project; Works Progress Administration

Selected Works

The Foxes of Harrow. 1946.
The Vixens. 1946.
Pride's Castle. 1949.
Floodtide. 1950.
A Woman Called Fancy. 1951.
The Saracen Blade. 1952.
The Devil's Laughter. 1953.
Fairoaks. 1957.
Griffin's Way. 1962.
Goat Song. 1967.
Speak Now. 1969.
An Odor of Sanctity. 1965.
The Dahomean. 1971.
The Girl from Storyville. 1972.
Tobias and the Angel. 1975.

Further Reading

Cowan, Tom, and Jack Maguire. *Timelines of African-American History.* New York: Berkley, 1994.

Fallon, Eileen. *Words of Love: A Complete Guide to Romance Fiction.* New York: Garland, 1984.

France-Nuriddin and Myrna Traylor-Herndon, eds. *African Americans: Voices of Triumph.* Richmond, Va.: Time-Life Books, 1994.

Hornsby, Alton, Jr. *Milestones in Twentieth- Century African-American History.* Detroit, Mich.: Visible Ink, 1993.

Ramsdell, Kristin. *Happily Ever After: A Guide to Reading Interests in Romance Fiction.* Littleton, Colo.: Libraries Unlimited, 1987.

Smith, Jessie Carney. *Black Firsts.* Detroit, Mich.: Visible Ink, 1994.

"Yerby, Frank (Garvin)." In *Current Biography Yearbook 1992.* New York: Wilson, 1992.

CONTRIBUTORS

Adams, Laurie Schneider
Ph.D. Program in Art History, The Graduate Center,
City University of New York

Alexander, Shawn
W. E. B. Du Bois Department of Afro-American Studies,
University of Massachusetts at Amherst

Allen, Danielle
Department of Classics and Political Science,
University of Chicago

Altschiller, Donald
Mugar Memorial Library, Boston University

Alvarado, Rocio Aranda
Jersey City Museum, New Jersey

Anderson, Eric
Department of History, Pacific Union College,
Angwin, California

Angel-Ajani, Asale
Gallatin School of Individualized Study, New York University

Ater, Renee
Department of Art History and Archaeology,
University of Maryland, College Park

Balshaw, Maria
Department of American and Canadian Studies,
University of Birmingham, England

Banks, Kimberly
Department of English, University of Missouri–Kansas City

Barnes, Sharon
Department of Interdisciplinary and Special Programs,
University of Toledo, Ohio

Bartley, Abel
Department of History, University of Akron, Ohio

Bates, Gerri
Morgan State University, Columbia, Maryland

Bean, Annemarie
Theatre Department, Williams College, Massachusetts

Bennett, Michael
English Department, Long Island University, Brooklyn Campus

Bernard, Patrick
Department of English, Franklin & Marshall College,
Pennsylvania

Bily, Cynthia
Department of English, Adrian College, Michigan

Blakely, Allison
African American Studies Center, Boston University

Bledsoe, Erik
East Tennessee State University, Johnson City

Boi, Paola
Dipt. di Filologie e Lett. Moderne,
Università degli Studi di Cagliari, Italy

Borshuk, Michael
Department of English, University of Alberta,
Edmonton, Canada

Boughn, Michael
Department of English, University of Toronto, Canada

Bowden, Nila
Department of English and Language Arts,
Morgan State University, Maryland

Contributors

Breda, Malcolm
Department of Music, Xavier University of Louisiana, New Orleans

Brooks, Marvie
Lloyd Sealy Library, John Jay College of Criminal Justice, New York

Brooks, Neil
Department of English, Huron University College, University of Western Ontario, Canada

Brophy, Alfred
School of Law, University of Alabama, Tuscaloosa

Brudvig, Jon
Social & Behavioral Sciences Division, University of Mary, North Dakota

Bucher, Christina G.
Department of English, Berry College, Georgia

Burwood, Stephen
State University of New York College at Geneseo

Byrd, Rudolph P.
Program of African American Studies, Emory University, Atlanta, Georgia

Calihman, Matthew
African and African American Studies, Washington University, St. Louis, Missouri

Calloway-Thomas, Carolyn
Department of Communication and Culture, Indiana University, Bloomington

Calo, Mary Ann
Department of Art and Art History, Colgate University, Hamilton, New York

Campbell, James T.
Department of Africana Studies, Brown University, Providence, Rhode Island

Capozzola, Christopher
Department of History, Massachusetts Institute of Technology, Cambridge

Cappucci, Paul
Department of English, Georgian Court College, Lakewood, New Jersey

Carlson, Brooke
Department of English, University of Southern California

Carreiro, Amy
Department of History, University of Tulsa, Oklahoma

Carroll, Anne
Department of English, Wichita State University, Kansas

Carter, Linda M.
Department of English and Language Arts, Morgan State University, Baltimore, Maryland

Cashman, John
Department of History, Boston College, Massachusetts

Cohen, Harvey
Department of History, University of Maryland, College Park

Cole-Leonard, Natasha
Department of English, Howard University, Washington, D.C.

Collins, Kathleen
Independent scholar, New York

Coste, Rosemarie
Department of English, Texas A&M University, College Station

Creary, Nicholas
Department of History, Marquette University, Milwaukee, Wisconsin

Criniti, Stephen
University of Cincinnati, Ohio

Crouther, Lou-Ann
Department of English, Western Kentucky University, Bowling Green

Crowder, Ralph
Department of Ethnic Studies, University of California, Riverside

Czarnecki, Kristin
Department of English, University of Cincinnati, Ohio

Czerniecki, Lisa
State University of New York College at Geneseo

Davis, Matthew
Department of English, University of Puget Sound, Tacoma, Washington

Davis, Rachel
Department of English, Florida State University, Tallahassee

DeFrantz, Thomas
Music and Theater Arts Section, Massachusetts Institute of Technology

De Gennaro, Mara
Department of English and Comparative Literature, Columbia University, New York

De Santis, Christopher
Department of English, Illinois State University, Normal

Dickson-Carr, Darryl
Department of English, Florida State University, Tallahassee

Diggs, Soyica
Department of English, Rutgers, The State University of New Jersey, New Brunswick

Downs, Jim
Department of History, Columbia University, New York

Drake, Kimberly
Department of English, Virginia Wesleyan College, Norfolk

Drowne, Kathleen
Writing Across the Curriculum Program, University of Missouri–Rolla

Dunkley, Larnell, Jr.
Department of English Language and Literature, Benedictine University, Lisle, Illinois

Dunlap, Shirley Basfield
Coordinator of Theatre Arts, Morgan State University, Baltimore, Maryland

Dworkin, Ira
Program in Afro-American Studies, University of Miami, Coral Gables, Florida

Eden, Brad
Department of Digital Projects, University of Nevada, Las Vegas Libraries

Egan, Bill
Independent researcher and writer, Canberra, Australia

Egan, Martha Avaleen
Independent scholar, Kingsport, Tennessee

Ellis, Brenda
Department of Music, Wright State University, Dayton, Ohio

Elmwood, Victoria
Indiana University, Bloomington

Estes-Hicks, Onita
Department of English Language Studies, State University of New York College at Old Westbury

Fahey, David M.
Department of History, Miami University, Oxford, Ohio

Farrar, Hayward "Woody"
Department of History, Virginia Tech, Blacksburg

Farrington, Lisa
Department of Critical Studies, Parsons School of Design/ New School University, New York

Fearnley, Andrew
Sidney Sussex College, University of Cambridge, England

Finkelman, Paul
School of Law, University of Tulsa, Oklahoma

Floyd-Thomas, J. M.
Department of History, Texas Christian University, Fort Worth

Francis, Terri
Program in Afro-American Studies, University of Miami, Coral Gables, Florida

Fullwood, Steven G.
Schomburg Center for Research in Black Culture, New York Public Library

Gable, Craig
Rudolph Fisher Newsletter, *Buffalo, New York*

Galm, John
College of Music, University of Colorado at Boulder

Garner, Thurmon
Emeritus, Department of Speech Communication, University of Georgia, Athens

George-Graves, Nadine
Department of Theatre, University of California, San Diego

Gibson, Ebony
Columbia University, New York

Giles, Freda Scott
Institute for African American Studies, University of Georgia, Athens, Georgia

Glasker, Wayne
Department of History, Rutgers, The State University of New Jersey, Camden

Glasrud, Bruce
Historian, writer, consultant, Seguin, Texas

Glassbrook, Daryn
Purdue University, West Lafayette, Indiana

Gleason, William
Department of English, Princeton University, New Jersey

Gray, Christine
Department of English, Community College of Baltimore County, Catonsville, Maryland

Graziano, John
City University of New York Graduate Center

Contributors

Greene, Larry A.
History Department, Seton Hall University, South Orange, New Jersey

Guterl, Matthew Pratt
African American & African Diaspora Studies, Indiana University, Bloomington

Guttman, Sondra
Department of English, Ithaca College, New York

Haas, Astrid
University of Münster, Germany

Hadley, Elizabeth Amelia
Department of Women's Studies, Hamilton College, Clinton, New York

Hall, Stephen
Department of History, Ohio State University, Columbus

Hanna, Judith Lynne
Department of Dance, University of Maryland, College Park

Hanson, Joyce
History Department, California State University, San Bernardino

Harker, Brian
School of Music, Brigham Young University, Provo, Utah

Harris, Glen Anthony
History Department, University of North Carolina at Wilmington

Harrison-Kahan, Lori
University of Pennsylvania, Philadelphia

Hartel, Herbert
Department of Art, Music & Philosophy, John Jay College of Criminal Justice, City University of New York

Heinrichs, Jürgen
Department of Art and Music, Seton Hall University, South Orange, New Jersey

Helbling, Mark
Department of American Studies, University of Hawaii at Manoa, Honolulu

Henry Boston, Genyne
Florida A & M University, Tallahassee

Herbison, C. C.
Department of African & African American Studies, University of Kansas, Lawrence

Hicks, Brian
Department of English, Vanderbilt University, Nashville, Tennessee

Hill, Claudia
Butler Library, Columbia University, New York

Hinton, Robert
The Africana Studies Program, New York University

Hood, Nicole
School of Art and Design, Georgia State University, Atlanta

Hood, Pamela
Philosophy Department, San Francisco State University, California

Howe, Andrew
Department of English, University of California, Riverside

Huber, Patrick
History and Political Science Department, University of Missouri–Rolla

Huot, Nikolas
Department of English, Georgia State University, Atlanta

Hurwitt, Elliott S.
Independent music scholar, New York

Hutchinson, George
Department of English, Indiana University, Bloomington

Hutchisson, James M.
Department of English, The Citadel, Charleston, South Carolina

Irving, Toni
Department of English, University of Notre Dame, Indiana

Jackson, Candice Love
Department of English, University of North Carolina at Chapel Hill

James, Winston
Department of History, Columbia University, New York

Jarrett, Gene
Department of English, University of Maryland, College Park

Jerving, Ryan
University Writing Program, George Washington University, Washington, D.C.

Johnson, Courtney
Department of English, University of California, Los Angeles

Johnson, Jeannine
Preceptor in Expository Writing, Harvard University, Cambridge, Massachusetts

Jones, Ida E.
Howard University, Washington, D.C.

Jones, Jacqueline
Department of English, Washington College, Chestertown, Maryland

Junker, Dave
University of Wisconsin–Madison

Kelley, James
Department of English, Mississippi State University–Meridian

Kilinski, April Conley
Department of English, University of Tennessee, Knoxville

Kinloch, Valerie
Teachers College, Columbia University, New York

Kirschke, Amy
Art and Art History Department, Vanderbilt University, Nashville, Tennessee

Kobrin, Joshua A.
Independent scholar, Washington, D.C.

Kornweibel, Theodore, Jr.
Department of Africana Studies, San Diego State University, California

Kotzin, Joshua
Department of English, Marist College, Poughkeepsie, New York

Lambert, Jasmin
Department of Theatre, Speech, and Dance, The College of William and Mary, Williamsburg, Virginia

Lamothe, Daphne
Department of English, Rutgers, The State University of New Jersey, New Brunswick

Landsberg, Alison
Department of History and Art History, George Mason University, Fairfax, Virginia

Lawrence, Amanda
Department of English, University of Tennessee, Knoxville

Lee, Amy
Department of English Language and Literature, Hong Kong Baptist University, Hong Kong

Leiker, James N.
History Department, Johnson County Community College, Overland Park, Kansas

Leininger-Miller, Theresa
School of Art, College of Design, Architecture, Art, and Planning, University of Cincinnati, Ohio

Levy, Heather
Brandeis University, Waltham, Massachusetts

Lewis, Barbara
Department of Theatre, University of Kentucky, Lexington

Little, Monroe
African American Studies Program, Indiana University–Purdue University, Indianapolis, Indiana

Lively, Janice Tuck
Department of English, University of Illinois at Chicago

Marino, John
Manager, Research and Cultural Affairs, National Italian American Foundation, Washington, D.C.

Martin, Anthony C.
Department of Africana Studies, Wellesley College, Wellesley, Massachusetts

Martin, Charles
Central Missouri State University, Warrensburg

Martin, George-McKinley
Art Division, District of Columbia Public Library, Washington, D.C.

Martin, Heather
Mervyn H. Sterne Library, University of Alabama at Birmingham

Maus, Derek
Department of English and Communication, State University of New York, Potsdam

Maxwell, William J.
Department of English, University of Illinois at Urbana–Champaign

McCaskill, Barbara
Department of English, University of Georgia, Athens

McCluskey, Audrey T.
African American and African Diaspora Studies, Indiana University, Bloomington

McDaniel, Karen C.
Paul G. Blazer Library, Kentucky State University, Frankfort

McDuffie, Erik S.
Afro-American Studies and Research Program, University of Illinois at Urbana–Champaign

McKible, Adam
Department of English, John Jay College of Criminal Justice, New York

McMillan, Felicia Piggott
Independent scholar, Winston-Salem, North Carolina

Meacham, Rebecca A.
English Department, University of Wisconsin–Green Bay

Contributors

Miklos, Michael
Department of English, University of Southern California

Miles, La'Tonya Rease
Department of English, University of California, Los Angeles

Miller, Eben
Department of History and Art History, George Mason University, Fairfax, Virginia

Miller, Gregory
Department of English, University of California, Davis

Miller, James A.
English Department, George Washington University, Washington, D.C.

Mills, Paul T., Sr.
Division of Sociology, District of Columbia Public Library

Mirro, Julya M.
Theatre Program Coordinator, Shaw University, Raleigh, North Carolina

Montgomery, Maureen
Department of American Studies, University of Canterbury, Private Bag, New Zealand

Montgomery, Maxine
Department of English, Florida State University, Tallahassee

Mooney, Amy
Department of Fine Arts, Washington State University, Pullman

Moos, Dan
Department of English, Rhode Island College, Providence

Moses, Valarie
Department of English Language and Literature, University of Michigan, Ann Arbor

Nancarrow, William J.
History Department, Boston College, Massachusetts

Nardi, Steven
Department of English, Princeton University, New Jersey

Nelson, Byron
Department of English, West Virginia University, Morgantown

Nelson, Claire Nee
Department of History, Yale University, New Haven, Connecticut

Nelson, H. Viscount
Center for Student Programming, University of California, Los Angeles

Nerad, Julie Cary
Department of English and Language Arts, Morgan State University, Baltimore, Maryland

Neumann, Caryn E.
Department of History, Ohio State University, Columbus

Nicholson, Stuart
Author and independent scholar, Newbury, England

Noonan, Ellen
American Social History Project/Center for Media and Learning, The Graduate Center, City University of New York

Nouryeh, Andrea J.
Department of Speech and Theatre, St. Lawrence University, Canton, New York

O'Hara, Catherine
School of Art & Design, University of Ulster, Belfast, Northern Ireland

Parascandola, Louis J.
Department of English, Long Island University, Brooklyn Campus

Perry, Jeffrey
Independent scholar and editor for Local 300, National Postal Mail Handlers Union, New York

Peters, Pearlie
English Department, Rider University, Lawrenceville, New Jersey

Pfeiffer, Kathleen
English Department, Oakland University, Rochester, Michigan

Phelps, Carmen
George Washington University, Washington, D.C.

Pitchford, Veronda
Chicago Multitype Library System, Chicago, Illinois

Pittas-Giroux, Justin
Department of English, College of Charleston, South Carolina

Powers, Peter Kerry
Department of English, Messiah College, Grantham, Pennsylvania

Price, Emmett G., III
Department of Music, Northeastern University, Boston, Massachusetts

Ragar, Cheryl
American Studies Program, University of Kansas, Lawrence

Raphael, Honora
Brooklyn College Library, New York

Raynor, Deirdre
Department of Interdisciplinary Arts and Sciences,
University of Washington, Tacoma

Reece, Dwandalyn R.
Senior Program Officer, National Endowment for the
Humanities, Washington, D.C.

Reibman, James
Lafayette College, Easton, Pennsylvania

Robeson, Paul, Jr.
Author and independent scholar, New York

Rossetti, Gina M.
Department of English and Foreign Languages, Saint Xavier
University, Chicago, Illinois

Rothfeld, Anne
History of Medicine Division, National Library of Medicine,
Bethesda, Maryland

Royster, Jacqueline J.
Department of English, Ohio State University, Columbus, Ohio

Ruotolo, Cristina
Department of Humanities, San Francisco State University,
California

Rutkoff, Peter
Department of History, Kenyon College, Gambier, Ohio

Saab, Joan
Department of Art and Art History, University of Rochester,
New York

Sacks, Marcy
Department of History, Albion College, Michigan

Salamone, Frank A.
Department of Sociology, Iona College, New Rochelle,
New York

Sanchez-Gonzalez, Lisa
Department of English, University of Connecticut, Storrs

Sandomirsky, L. Natalie
Lasell College, Newton, Massachusetts

Schwarz, A. B. Christa
Independent scholar, Berlin, Germany

Scifres Kuilan, Susie
Louisiana State University, Baton Rouge

Scolieri, Paul
Department of Dance, Barnard College, Columbia University,
New York

Scott, Daniel M., III
Department of English, Rhode Island College, Providence

Scott, William
Department of History, Kenyon College, Gambier, Ohio

Seiler, Cotton
Department of American Studies, Dickinson College,
Carlisle, Pennsylvania

Sewell-Williams, Lela
Moorland–Spingarn Research Center, Howard University,
Washington, D.C.

Sexton, Sharon
Independent scholar, Detroit, Michigan

Sharpley-Whiting, Tracy Denean
Department of Africana Studies, Hamilton College,
Clinton, New York

Shockley, Evelyn
Department of English, Wake Forest University,
Winston-Salem, North Carolina

Silberman, Seth Clark
Larry Kramer Initiative for Lesbian and Gay Studies, Yale
University, New Haven, Connecticut

Sims, Lowery Stokes
Director, Studio Museum in Harlem, New York

Singh, Amritjit
Department of English, Rhode Island College, Providence

Smalls, James
Department of Visual Arts, University of Maryland,
Baltimore County

Smallwood, Andrew
African American Studies, University of Houston, Texas

Smith, Catherine Parsons
University of Nevada, Reno (Emerita)

Smith, Katharine Capshaw
Department of English, Florida International University, Miami

Stapleton-Corcoran, Erin
University of Chicago, Illinois

Steed, Jason
English Department, Brigham Young University, Provo, Utah

Sudderth, R. Jake
Columbia University, New York

Sullivan, Michael
Independent scholar, Eugene, Oregon

Contributors

Sumner-Mack, Nan
John Carter Brown Library, Brown University, Providence, Rhode Island

Taylor, Michelle
African and African American Studies, University of Notre Dame, Indiana

Tekinay, Asli
Department of Western Languages and Literatures, Bogazici University, Istanbul, Turkey

Thaggert, Miriam
Department of English, University of Tennessee, Knoxville

Thomas, Lorenzo
Department of English, College of Humanities and Social Sciences, University of Houston–Downtown, Texas

Thompson, Mark
Department of English, University of Illinois at Urbana–Champaign

Toure, Ahati N. N.
African American Studies, University of Houston, Texas

Tracy, Steven
Department of Afro-American Studies, University of Massachusetts, Amherst

Traflet, Janice
Department of History, Columbia University, New York

Tsagaris, Ellen
Kaplan College, Davenport, Iowa

Tucker, Veta
Department of English, Grand Valley State University, Allendale, Michigan

Vogel, Shane
Department of Performance Studies, New York University

Washington, Roberta
Roberta Washington Architects, New York

Weil, Teri B.
Frederick Douglass Library, University of Maryland Eastern Shore, Princess Anne, Maryland

West, Kathryn
English Department, Bellarmine University, Louisville, Kentucky

White, Michael
Department of Languages, Xavier University of Louisiana, New Orleans

Wilhelm, Randall Shawn
Department of English, University of Tennessee, Knoxville

Williams, Carmaletta M.
Department of English, Johnson County Community College, Overland Park, Kansas

Williams, Erika R.
Wellesley College, Massachusetts

Williams, Regennia N.
Department of History, Cleveland State University, Ohio

Williams, Roland L., Jr.
English Department, Temple University, Philadelphia

Williams, Vernon J.
Department of History, Purdue University, West Lafayette, Indiana

Willoughby, David
Professor of Music, Emeritus, Eastern New Mexico University, Portales

Wilson, Melinda D.
Northwestern University, Evanston, Illinois

Wintz, Cary
Texas Southern University, Houston

Woll, Allen
Film Studies Program, Rutgers, The State University of New Jersey, Camden

Wolters, Raymond
Department of History, University of Delaware

Woodard, Loretta G.
Department of English, Marygrove College, Detroit, Michigan

Woods, Marianne
Department of Humanities and Fine Arts, University of Texas of the Permian Basin

Woodson, Jon
Department of English, Howard University, Washington, D.C.

Yon, Veronica Adams
Department of English, Florida A & M University, Tallahassee

Young-Minor, Ethel
Department of English, University of Mississippi, University

Zeitler, Michael
Department of English and Language Arts, Morgan State University, Baltimore, Maryland

Index

Index

41